BASIC ECONOMIC SYSTEMS

**GREAT DEBATE ONE:
THE MARXIAN CRITIQUE
OF CAPITALISM**

MACROECONOMICS   MICROECONOMICS

GREAT DEBATE TWO
THE ISSUE OF
MONETARISM

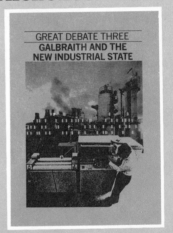

GREAT DEBATE THREE
GALBRAITH AND THE
NEW INDUSTRIAL STATE

CONTEMPORARY ECONOMIC PROBLEMS

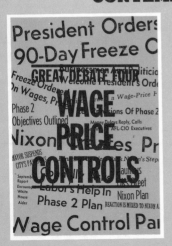

President Orders
90-Day Freeze
GREAT DEBATE FOUR
WAGE
PRICE
CONTROLS

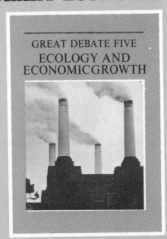

GREAT DEBATE FIVE
ECOLOGY AND
ECONOMICGROWTH

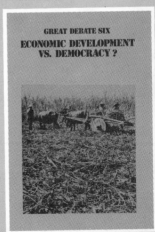

GREAT DEBATE SIX
ECONOMIC DEVELOPMENT
VS. DEMOCRACY ?

ECONOMICS
A TEXT WITH INCLUDED READINGS

ECONOMICS

A TEXT WITH INCLUDED READINGS

Richard T. Gill
Harvard University

**Goodyear
Publishing Company
Pacific Palisades
California**

ECONOMICS: A TEXT WITH INCLUDED READINGS
Richard T. Gill
© Copyright 1973 by
GOODYEAR PUBLISHING COMPANY, INC.
Pacific Palisades, California

Y-244X-4
ISBN: 0-87620-244-X
Library of Congress Catalog Card Number: 72-75589
Current printing (last digit):
10 9 8 7 6 5 4 3 2

Designed by Tom Lewis and Don McQuiston
Printed in the United States of America

Preface

This book is the product of two decades of thought about how to present the basics of economics to college students and other interested readers. Its fundamental premise is that economics is controversial, and never more so than at the present time. Controversy in itself would pose no special problem were it not for the fact that economics also has a detailed theoretical structure, the mastery of which is required even by those who sharply disagree. (Indeed, the structure lets opponents know *how* they disagree!) The problem of teaching and learning the fundamentals of economics is the problem of reconciling these contrary aspects of the field.

One way of tackling this problem is to employ a standard text and then to assign outside readings to give a balanced point of view. This was the approach I myself used for many years as the director of Economics I at Harvard. Its advantages are clear, but so are its disadvantages. The text, behaving rather like bad money under Gresham's Law, tended to drive the readings out of circulation. Learn the textbook, it was said, and you can forget the rest.

The readings also suffered from the disabilities that they were often written in different terminology from the text, were of widely unequal levels of difficulty, were in no way integrated with the rest of the course, and—depending on the libraries—were often inaccessible.

A major alternative approach—the one used here—is to include the readings within the text itself. The following volume contains over 500 pages of double-column text by the author, and nearly 300 pages of readings. As far as I know, this approach has never been tried in economics before.

The author is not the one to judge the success of his project. Clearly, there are negative aspects. If the readings weren't included, the text itself could be longer, more inclusive, more detailed. It would be foolish to pretend that, by including one thing, one need not exclude anything else. (After all, economics is sometimes defined as the science of choice.) All the author can state is what he *hoped* to achieve. The objectives were:

First, to convey, in the initial introduction to the field, that economics is not a technical discipline only, but that differences of opinion exist and are important. This is a matter of degree and emphasis. My objection to the standard approach is that while disagreements are *mentioned* in the text, they are then dropped while the author develops either the standard position, or his own special point of view. Whatever the faults of the present volume may be, I think it is fair to say that no one could read it and come away with the idea that economics is basically a settled, agreed-upon social science, with controversy limited to small details or to the ravings of a few cranks. The mechanism I have used in this connection is the *Great Debate*. There are six of these debates (Marxism, monetarism, the new industrial state, wage-price controls, ecology and growth, economic development and democracy) and, in each case, the debate is basic and the participants are outstanding economists past and present.

Second, to integrate the readings into the text so that the reader is prepared to handle them without overwhelming difficulties. This objective greatly influenced the selection of readings and the way they have been handled in the text. I should say that at one point I thought of attempting to adapt, or even re-write the articles (with permission, of course), but eventually decided against it. For one thing, I found a surprisingly deep inner resistance to tampering with the words of, say, Adam Smith or John Maynard Keynes. Instead, I have edited ruthlessly, trying to get around concepts that had not been previously introduced or that were expressed in different terminology from the text itself. Where this was impossible, I have tried in the surrounding text to make reasonably clear what the basic point of the readings is. In one case—monetarism—I have written a whole chapter, the main purpose of which is to serve as a guide to the issues involved in the conflicting readings.

Third, and finally, to use the readings to enrich the text. One of the great advantages of having the readings right in the text is that one can *use* them, i.e., employ them as materials for economic analysis. In one case, it may be the *Economic Report of the President* that one uses to show the applicability of economic concepts; in another case, it may be Malthus on population or Ricardo on trade; in still another case, it may be an economist's analysis of the implications of business conglomerates. The advantage, quite simply, is that instead of being tacked on as an afterthought, the readings have influenced the shape, scope, and approach of the text proper—and much to its benefit.

A few technical points

about the use of this book: Part One (Basic Economic Systems) should be studied first and Part Four (Contemporary Economic Problems) should be studied last, but Parts Two and Three (Macroeconomics and Microeconomics, respectively) can be studied in either order. Roughly speaking, a one-semester course could be either a macroeconomically oriented course (Part One and Part Two), or a microeconomically oriented course (Part One and Part Three). The ambitious might add a chapter or two from Part Four to these suggested course outlines, but Part Four is ideally studied after the student has had both macroeconomics and microeconomics.

The Great Debates are not rivetted to a particular logical point in the argument of the text, but are located in the chapters of the book that provide the essential background for them. One could, in theory, read through the whole book except for the Great Debates and then come back and read them all at the end. My own view is that this would be an unfortunate approach, but it does suggest that there is some flexibility as to when each debate may be studied.

As far as the readings in general are concerned, I have not rewritten the words of any author, but, as already mentioned, I have done substantial cutting and past-

ing together again. No reading in this book should be considered the equivalent of the original article. These are excerpts only, shaped for our particular purposes. This caution is important because in most cases, to prevent the articles from looking like the Morse code, I have left out the dots and dashes that customarily show omissions. When in doubt, always consult the original piece.

Except for the Great Debates, the other readings in the text should be read exactly where they are since they are either analyzed in the text, or assumed in later discussions. The only exceptions to this are the few readings in the appendices, all of which can be omitted.

A project of this size could not be accomplished without help from others. I owe a very great debt to my publisher, Al Goodyear, who was helpful from the inception of this book on, as he has been with most of my other books. In the course of preparing this text, I drew heavily on the two previous books I have done for Goodyear Publishing Company, *Economics and the Public Interest* and its companion, *Economics and the Private Interest*. Originally, we had thought we could accomplish our objectives by simply adding some readings to these already published works. As it turned out, a full scale revision was required, with hundreds of new pages added or changed. Throughout this process, Al Goodyear was a constant source of help and encouragement.

I am also grateful to Professor John E. Elliott of the University of Southern California, who has made numerous helpful suggestions and who has prepared the Student Involvement Manual for this book, to Professor James A. Phillips of Cypress College, who prepared the imaginative Study Guide, and to Professor Everett M. Kassalow of the University of Wisconsin, who has sent me useful comments on this book and on earlier books. My research could not have been completed without the help of Dr. Roger S. Nelson of the World Bank and Mrs. Myrtle G. Nelson of the Bureau of Labor Statistics. Gene Schwartz, Bob Hollander, Ann Harris, Sally Kostal, Tom Lewis, and Don McQuiston have similarly been invaluable in bringing this work to light.

In the background of all this is my debt to the literally thousands of students whose task it has been to listen to my lectures at Harvard over these past many years. They convinced me that there was a communications problem and that the communications problem could be solved.

More than anyone else, my wife deserves credit, not only for her extensive help in the preparation of the manuscript, but above all for her encouragement when above all encouragement was needed. It is one of the pleasures of writing books to be able to acknowledge debts as deep as these.

RICHARD T. GILL

Contents

Contents

Contents

ECONOMICS

A TEXT WITH INCLUDED READINGS

PART ONE
BASIC ECONOMIC SYSTEMS

1
The Economic Problem

We all know something about economics because we are everyday participants in the economic life of our society. "Getting and spending, we lay waste our powers," complained Wordsworth, and the complaint has decided relevance for a modern industrial economy. We do pass a great many of our waking hours "getting and spending." If we are clever, we even try to economize during the process. We try to economize on the things we buy; we try to economize on the time and effort we put into producing the products or services we are offering for sale.

In these respects, we are taking part in the economic system of the country, and we daily gain certain insights into how that system functions.

At other times, however, economics seems to be dealing with matters that are far removed from our personal knowledge and experience and, indeed, that seem far outside our personal control. The stock market rises or falls. Millions of people in Asia or Africa are suffering from malnutrition. The cost of living is going up. At such moments we feel we are being managed by external forces and we are inclined to say, as Mark Twain did about the weather: "Everybody talks about it, but nobody does anything about it." At such moments, the study of economics seems interesting, but also obscure and difficult.

ECONOMIC BREAKDOWNS— PAST AND PRESENT

The remarkable thing about a modern industrial economy is that it functions so smoothly. We become *aware* of this remarkable fact, however, mainly when the system breaks down. And let no one mistake the fact: economic systems do break down, and when they do, the costs and consequences are incalculable.

The following four examples show us some of the ways in which economic systems can malfunction. They will also help us understand the nature of the economic problem in a more general sense.

Example I: Wild Inflation in Germany

Prices rose in all European countries after World War I. In Britain and France, the price level rose 3 or 4 times compared to prewar. In Austria, the rise was much more rapid—about 14,000 times

3

the prewar level. Other countries suffered still more rapid inflation. In Hungary, prices rose 23,000 times their prewar level; in Poland, 2.5 million times; in Russia, 4 billion times.

But even these extraordinary increases pale beside those of Germany, where the forces of inflation went so wild that they virtually destroyed the fabric of society. Figure 1-1 shows what happened to the wholesale price level in Germany in the 1920s, but only up to a point. By 1922, the numbers would push the curve off the top of the page of this book and, indeed, up through the ceiling of any ordinary-sized room. By 1923, the curve would be out of sight in the clouds. In September 1923, German wholesale prices, in terms of marks, had risen 24 million times above the level of a decade earlier; two months later, the figure was close to a *trillion*!

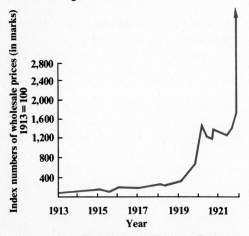

Figure 1-1. The German Hyperinflation of the 1920s.

This is an example of an inflation that got completely out of hand. By November 1923 in Germany, the index of wholesale prices that had stood at 100 in 1913 reached the level of 73 trillion!

Figures on a graph are one thing, human costs another—witness the following commentary:

Social Influences Of The Inflation

Constantino Bresciani-Turroni

The period of most acute and widespread poverty was 1923, that year in which the dollar exchange rate rose from 10,000 to 4,200 milliard paper marks! From personal observation it appears that the poverty of the German people was certainly not general, but it was limited to certain classes, in fact to those which had been most severely hit by the inflation. The poverty was revealed by many symptoms, some of which are measurable by statistics: the condition of children (underweight, spread of tuberculosis and rickets); lack of clothing; the lowered feeding standards (fall in the consumption of cereals, meat, butter, milk, eggs, etc., and the substitution of poorer foods, as, e.g., the substitution of rye for wheat, margarine and other inferior fats for butter, and all sorts of substitutes for coffee); the very poor condition of houses; the excessive work of women; the appearance of certain maladies formerly almost unknown in Germany, such as acne and scurvy; the rise in the number of suicides due to the lack of means of subsistence; deaths through malnutrition (which were very rare before the war); and the rise in the number of pauper funerals because relatives could not pay the expenses, although a decree by the Minister of the Interior permitted the substitution of pasteboard shells for wooden coffins, which were too dear!

The statistics of meat consumption

Excerpted from "Social Influences of the Inflation" from Constantino Bresciani-Turroni, The Economics of Inflation: A Study of Currency Depreciation in Post-War Germany (London: George Allen and Unwin, 1937). Reprinted by permission of the publisher.

reveal some curious details which throw an interesting light on social conditions in Germany in 1922 and 1923. While the consumption of the better quality meats (bullocks, calves, pigs, and sheep) declined, the consumption of horseflesh and, still more, of dogs increased: obvious proof, as Wirtschaft und Statistik wrote, of the increasing poverty of the German people. From the last quarter of 1921 to the last quarter of 1922 the number of pigs killed fell from 1,416,051 to 1,131,148, while the number of horses increased from 30,967 to 47,652. During 1923 the fall in the consumption of pork continued, and at the same time the conditions of some classes became so bad that they were eventually obliged to reduce their consumption of horse-flesh. But consumption of dog-flesh increased. Statistics show that 1,090 dogs were slaughtered in the third quarter of 1921; 3,678 in the third quarter of 1922, and 6,430 in the third quarter of 1923.

Another direct index of the worsening of the economic conditions of many classes was the increase in both open and clandestine prostitution. A typical symptom of the sad condition of the old middle classes was also given by the very great number of little shops which sold furniture, objets d'arts, jewellery, carpets, etc., belonging to very many families who, once well-to-do, were now living on the proceeds of the sale of their personal property.

Among the old middle classes, ruined by the inflation, extreme nationalist propaganda was started and made rapid headway, and among the workers communist ideas spread. The paper inflation, by reinforcing the economic position of those classes which formed the backbone of the "Right" parties, i.e., the great industrialists and the great financiers, encouraged the political reaction against democracy.

The great industrialists and landowners were enabled, by the profits obtained from the monetary depreciation, to finance generously the propaganda and the campaign against the Republic. It was carried on chiefly through the Press. The depreciation of the currency had created very serious difficulties for many papers, because of the enormous rise in the price of paper, of telegraph rates, and of the expense of maintaining their foreign correspondents, etc. Many papers were bought up by the controllers of the heavy industries. Besides this, they were astute enough to become masters of the most important news agencies which, by supplying news even to independent papers, were an effective instrument for influencing public opinion.

Large amounts of money were also used for the formation and maintenance of numerous national institutions of a military character which openly opposed the Republican-Liberal régime. Thus the currency inflation was responsible for the Liberal régime always showing a weak front to the new industrial and agrarian feudalism which was constantly threatening the basis of the new Republic.

Thus, the consequences of the German inflation were not only the hardships of the moment, but also a grave weakening of the political institutions of the nation. No wonder that it is often listed as a major contributing cause to the rise of Nazism!

Example II:
The Great Depression of the 1930s

An even greater economic catastrophe hit the Western world in the 1930s—the Great Depression, deeply familiar to anyone living in the United

States at that time. In the case of this country, the depression lasted basically from 1929 until our entry into the Second World War in 1941. In 1933, the worst year of the depression, there were 13 or 14 million Americans out of work—25 percent or more of our entire labor force. It has been estimated that over the whole of the period unemployment cost us the waste of 104 million man-years of labor.[1]

Again, personal observation often conveys an experience more forcefully than cold statistics. Following are some comments by the then-mayor of Youngstown, Ohio.

---

1. Lester V. Chandler, *America's Greatest Depression, 1929-1941* (New York: Harper & Row, 1970), p.6.

THE HUNGRY CITY
A Mayor's Experience With Unemployment
Joseph L. Heffernan

Throughout this period the distress of the people continued without abatement. The great industries had displaced thousands of men, and business conditions showed no signs of improving. Many of the unemployed who had had small reserves to fall back upon in the beginning had now exhausted their resources. One began to see destitute women walking the streets begging for food, and often small children trudged after them. In one week the chief of police reported to me that four women with nursing infants in their arms had sought shelter at police stations.

By the early summer of 1931, demands for relief had become so heavy that the

Excerpted from Joseph L. Heffernan, "The Hungry City: A Mayor's Experience with Unemployment," *The Atlantic Monthly*, May 1932, pp. 543–44, 546. Reprinted by permission of the publisher.

CULVER PICTURES

Life in the Great Depression. In the 1930s, with massive unemployment and few welfare services, many workers were reduced to near-beggary.

charity organizations were overwhelmed. Federal and state officials now admitted that they had sadly underestimated the gravity of the situation. By this time the city had come into possession of money from the first bonds that had been sold under the special bill passed by the legislature. We had planned a relief programme of our own to supplement that of the charities, with disbursements apportioned throughout the year. The head of the Community Chest pleaded with us, however, to take over immediately a number of his most urgent cases, and we could not refuse. Consequently we had to spend our money as rapidly as it came in, and the last half of the year was left to take care of itself, with the hope that other funds could be raised at that time.

In the autumn of 1931 a final blow laid the city of Youngstown prostrate. The atmosphere was poisoned with a new fever of apprehension, with rumors that began no one knew where and ended in panic. 'Have you heard?' everybody whispered excitedly. 'The banks . . . buzz, buzz, buzz . . . the banks!' People who were fortunate enough to have money deposited hurried to withdraw it. Day after day the drain continued, and the bankers had to stand by helplessly while their reserves melted away. Then three of the banks closed their doors, and fear ran riot.

At once concerted efforts were made to protect the other banks. Depositors were besought not to withdraw their savings and were urged to bring back what they had carried away to hide. Statements calling upon the people to have confidence were issued by everyone of supposed influence. The ministers joined the campaign with sermons on civic faith and hope. But confidence was shattered. Had not everybody in authority, from the President down, been making optimistic statements for two years, and had not subsequent events disproved all predictions? Could anybody be trusted to tell the truth? Did anybody really know? People stood on the street corners asking each other anxious questions. Never before had all the old landmarks of security been so shattered. Never had Youngstown suffered such a shock to the spirit which had made it one of the great industrial centres of the world. Nobody could now deny that America was in the throes of a panic.

Another winter was approaching. The numbers of the unemployed had increased, and suffering had grown acute. Many heads of families had not earned a penny in two years. There is a world of difference between mere poverty and pauperism. The honest poor will struggle for years to keep themselves above the pauper class. With quiet desperation they will bear hunger and mental anguish until every resource is exhausted. Then comes the ultimate struggle when, with heartache and an overwhelming sense of disgrace, they have to make the shamefaced journey to the door of public charity. This is the last straw. Their self-respect is destroyed; they undergo an insidious metamorphosis, and sink down to spiritless despondency.

This descent from respectability, frequent enough in the best of times, has been hastened immeasurably by two years of business paralysis, and the people who have been affected in this manner must be numbered in millions. This is what we have accomplished with our bread lines and soup kitchens. I know, because I have seen thousands of these defeated, discouraged, hopeless men and women, cringing and fawning as they come to ask for public aid. It is a spectacle of national degeneration. That is the fundamental tragedy for America. If every mill and factory in the land should begin to hum with prosperity to-morrow morning, the destructive effect of our haphazard relief measures would not work itself out of the nation's blood until the sons of our sons had expiated the sins of our neglect.

Even now there are signs of rebellion against a system so out of joint that it can only offer charity to honest men who want to work. Sometimes it takes the form of social agitation, but again it may show itself in a revolt that is absolute and final. Such an instance was reported in a Youngstown newspaper on the day I wrote these lines:

FATHER OF TEN DROWNS SELF

JUMPS FROM BRIDGE, STARTS TO SWIM GIVES UP, OUT OF WORK TWO YEARS

Out of work two years, Charles Wayne, aged fifty-seven, father of ten children, stood on the Spring Common bridge this morning, watching hundreds of other persons moving by on their way to work. Then he took off his coat, folded it carefully, and jumped into the swirling Mahoning River. Wayne was born in Youngstown and was employed by the Republic Iron and Steel Company for twenty-seven years as a hot mill worker.

"We were about to lose our home," sobbed Mrs. Wayne. "And the gas and electric companies had threatened to shut off the service."

Example III:
Famine Facing Upper Volta

Our first two examples have been historical. Our third example is both contemporary and ancient. The events described are happening today, but the causes are similar to those that have been operating throughout most of human history. For the incredible fact in the 1970s is that the majority of the world's population still lives in conditions that most of us would describe as extreme want. Upper Volta is a particularly poor country but its economic conditions do not differ that substantially from numerous other countries in Asia, Africa, and Latin America. These countries still face enormous hazards from natural disasters—witness the 1971 tidal wave and floods in East Bengal that took the lives of perhaps half a million people—and must struggle vigorously simply to achieve a margin above economic subsistence.

LOS ANGELES TIMES

Upper Volta Poised on Brink of Famine

Drought to Bring Disaster in 1972 for Subsistence Society of African Nation

---

OUAGADOUGOU, Upper Volta—This friendly, remarkably proud, but little-known country in West Africa is poised on the brink of famine.

It will come in the new year and it is inevitable, as is the disease and death that will strike down many of its children—and this in a country where already one in five babies dies and life expectancy at thirty-five years

From the *Los Angeles Times*, 28 November 1971, Sect. 1, p. 8, "Upper Volta Poised on Brink of Famine." Copyright, 1971, *London Observer*, reprinted with permission of Los Angeles Times/Washington Post News Service.

is one of the lowest in the world.

The famine is caused by too little rain. It should have fallen steadily from June to mid-October, the traditional rainy season, but the last rainfall was on Sept. 13. And when it did come it was in torrential downpours that burst the clay wells and washed them and the crops away.

Work Destroyed

These uncontrollable rainstorms also washed away most of the year's toil and the hopes of the farmers, their wives and their children, for they all work together in the

fields and live on what they produce. In a productive year a farmer with a working family of five can hope to earn about seventy dollars. This year many will earn no money at all, for the harvest will be pathetic and many of their animals will die of thirst. And as 95 percent of Upper Volta's 5.5 million people live this subsistence life on the land, a disastrous rainfall or drought for them is disaster for the whole country. As a voluntary worker said, "In a subsistence society you can only sit and wait—wait for God to do his thing, and if he doesn't . . . that's it."

And if ever there was a subsistence society, this is it. Only 29,000 Voltans have a paid job. The rest live in circles of mud-brick huts (known as "concessions"), often three generations together—for family loyalties are absolute on land that is hostile to human life. There are no services or machinery of any kind. Ninety percent cannot read or write.

Water a Problem

Their lives are dominated by the need and quest for water. Women, carrying their babies in slings on their backs, will set off from their circle of huts with a clay pot balanced on their heads, and with no apparent complaint and quiet dignity walk miles from their homes to the nearest well. Sometimes they do this two or three times a day. Like the men, their labors frequently are mocked by unforeseen calamities. A woman recently trudged, baby on her back, twelve miles for a bowl of water. She then turned and walked back. A mile from home a goat suddenly ran out from the scrub and so startled her that she dropped the bowl. Rather than face the family, she set off back the twelve miles to the well.

Even the country's name, Upper Volta, mocks the farmers, for it is named after the complex of three Volta rivers, two of them now dried up and the other now an unreliable contributor of water.

Of all the help the farmers of Upper Volta need to realize even the limited potential of this arid near-desert, most of all they need water. Rain they cannot cause or control,

but when it comes it must be kept, and where possible kept clean.

Need Well Program

Unfortunately, their inadequately constructed wells tumble in if the rain is lost. So a major need here is a massive well-building program. Concrete wells will save the time of the men so they can do more in the fields, and will reduce the hardship of the women and enable them to do more on the farm, and also devote more time to their children. Above all they will substantially reduce disease: many of the children are ill because the family is forced to drink, wash, clean clothes and water animals with whatever they can cart on their collective heads from a dirty waterhole or outsize puddle.

One time, two Americans, both about twenty-two years old, were making concrete at the foot of a well forty yards deep. They were sunburned, shiny with sweat, and surrounded by ten highly excited Africans—for they had "struck water." By the way they celebrated, it could have been oil.

This is part of a Peace Corps operation that (with some British help) has built 750 wells in the Upper Volta. You cannot help but be impressed by the enthusiasm and energy of these volunteers who have come from affluent American homes to live isolated and deprived lives for two years or more.

Upper Volta is possibly the poorest nation in the world—the gross national product per capita is only forty-eight dollars. If the hardship and the widespread

fatality that are part of this country's way of life were caused by a sudden disaster, there would probably be a world outcry. But because it is always there, it has created no stir at all. Even its famines are not news.

Unlike some places in the third world, affluence does not mock the country's hardship from even the smallest corners. Everyone is poor. One reason for the continued popularity of Sangoule Lamizana, who became president as a result of a coup backed by the people and the army in 1966, is that he has lived soberly himself, refusing the presidential palace, and has kept the economic margin between the country's educated elite and the majority reasonably narrow.

But what a dilemma the Voltan leaders face. No matter how resourceful they are, the country is hopelessly under-financed. Its total budget of $29 million would be unacceptable to any big city council in the United States. And the trouble with the hand-to-mouth economy is that investing in developing the country becomes impossible; the problem is always to keep it alive.

So there is no money for education (there are only thirty secondary schools), no money for health services, and—most important—no money to develop agriculture. The peasant farmer has to take all the risk. If he suffers even more hardship in order to save to use some modern tool or fertilizer and then the rains let him down, he has lost his money, his year's work, and his food for the following year.

| Some consequences of Upper Volta's poverty would be comic if their effects were not so frequently disastrous. For instance, whole projects have been ruined by the failure of a key man to perform his task, simply because he | ran out of gasoline and could not afford more. Some regional centers have only one telephone and the telephones in Ouagadougou, the capital with more than 100,000 people. close to the outside world at 6 p.m. | And all the time the land becomes drier, the soil becomes overused and eroded, and the farmer has to work harder to obtain less. That is in a good year. This year, with no rain, he has the famine to fear as well. |

Example IV: Poverty Amidst Affluence

But we do not really have to go abroad to find evidences of breakdowns in modern economic life. One of the curious facts about present-day economics is that the discovery of American affluence went hand in hand with the discovery of American poverty. Numerous writers have noticed that although our society in general is strikingly rich—on the average richer than any major society in the history of the world—nevertheless, there are important groups in our society where *relative* poverty is intense, and is also surprisingly difficult to remedy. Sometimes the poverty is regional, as in Appalachia, which over a decade ago attracted the late President Kennedy's great concern. Sometimes it is a by-product of our urban-industrial way of life, as in the problem of our "inner cities," whose deterioration is now a major social and economic threat. Sometimes, poverty is a problem of special groups in the society—the black, the chicano, the elderly, the uneducated, the physically or mentally handicapped.

One of the first social scientists to study the problem of American poverty was Michael Harrington, whose *The Other America*, published in the early sixties, helped cause a national reconsideration of this serious issue.

THE OTHER AMERICA

MICHAEL HARRINGTON

There is a familiar America. It is celebrated in speeches and advertised on television and in the magazines. It has the highest mass standard of living the world has ever known.

In the 1950s this America worried about itself, yet even its anxieties were products of abundance. There was introspection about Madison Avenue and tail fins; there was discussion of the emotional suffering taking place in the suburbs. In all this, there was an implicit assumption that the basic grinding economic problems had been solved in the United States. In this theory the nation's problems were no longer a matter of basic human needs, of food, shelter, and clothing. Now they were seen as qualitative, a question of learning to live decently amid luxury.

While this discussion was carried on, there existed another America. In it dwelt somewhere between 40 million and 50 million citizens of this land. They were poor. They still are.

To be sure, the other America is not impoverished in the same sense as those poor nations where millions cling to hunger as a defense against starvation. This country has escaped such extremes. That does not change the fact that tens of millions of Americans are, at this very moment, maimed in body and spirit, existing at levels beneath those necessary for human decency. If these people are not starving, they are hungry, and sometimes fat with hunger, for that is what cheap foods do. They are without adequate housing and education and medical care.

In New York City, for instance, there are some 300,000 "hard core" Public Assistance cases. These are the mentally ill, the aged, the sick, and their children. In good times and in bad, they are ever present, inhabiting the slums and housing projects. In a recession like that of 1958, their number is immediately increased by a hundred thousand or so people who live on the verge of economic helplessness. But this group is only the beginning, for, according to the New York State Interdepartmental Committee on Low Incomes, they represent less than one-fourth of those actually qualified for Public Assistance. In other words, there is a basic group of 1,200,000 who lack the "basic necessities" (food, shelter, minimal medical care) and who qualify for Public Assistance.

In the late fifties, 26 percent of the Public Assistance families in New York City lived in furnished rooms. Most of them will never work. There is another group living right next to them: the sweatshop operatives. In 1959 I. D. Robbins, president of the City Club of New York, testified before the State Commission on Governmental Operations that around 300,000 heads of families in New York City were making in the neighborhood of a dollar an hour (just a little better than $2,000 a year—if they received a year's work). He estimated that perhaps a fourth of the city budget—welfare, hospital, correction, fire, health, and school items—was attributable to "the enormous number of poor people living here."

In New York City, as one would expect, the minorities form an important part of the slum population. The Public Assistance recipients in the fifties included 31.3 percent whites, 40.0 percent Negroes, and 28.7 percent Puerto Ricans. New York, with an estimated two mil-

An Urban Slum. Poverty still exists in the affluent society, especially in our central cities, too often abandoned by the middle and upper economic classes.

lion Negroes and Puerto Ricans in the metropolitan area, would show minority participation in the slum culture more dramatically than most cities. Yet, the Northern migration of Negroes is affecting almost every city outside the South (and the poor white farmers, probably not too important a group in New York, are a major factor in many Midwestern and border-state cities).

Income is one index of the slum dweller; health is another. According to the New York City Health Department, there was a direct correlation in 1959 between slums and infant mortality rates. In the "worst district" that the Health Department found, central Harlem, the infant mortality rate was three times that of the best district and had increased by more than 5 percent since 1958.

The incomes are low; the housing is dilapidated; the health is bad. But now, it is important to trace the factors that intensify the pessimism and hopelessness that differentiate the new form of the slum from the old ethnic neighborhoods.

There is a wall around these slums that did not exist before: the suburbs. The President's Civil Rights Commission in 1959 reported that the suburban zoning laws keep out low-income housing and force the poor to remain in the decaying, central area of the cities. The very development of the metropolitan areas thus has the tendency to lock the door on the poor.

This becomes even more of a factor when one realizes how important color is in the new form of the old slums. There has never been a disability in American society to equal racial prejudice. It is the most effective single instrument for keeping people down that has ever been found. In this context, the decline of aspiration is partly a function of a sophisticated analysis of society: there *is* less opportunity than there was in the days of the huge ethnic slums. The people understand this even if they do not articulate it precisely.

To be sure, the older ethnic slums produced their share of violence and gangsterism. Yet their family patterns, their value systems, their very access to the outside world provided a strong counterforce to the degradation of environment. In the new form of the slum, these checks are not so strong, and the culture of poverty becomes all the more powerful for that fact.

Lastly, the inhabitants of the slums of the sixties are regularly the victims of a bureaucratically enforced rootlessness. The housing programs, and particularly the Urban Renewal activities of the mid- and late fifties, set off a migration within the cities. In 1959, for instance, the Mill Creek area of St. Louis was cleared as part of an urban renewal effort. In the place of a Negro slum there arose a middle-income housing development. Typically, the majority of those evicted were forced to find housing within the existing, and contracted, Negro ghetto. (In St. Louis 50 percent of the families displaced disappeared from sight of the authorities altogether; of those whose movements are known, only 14 percent found their way into low-cost projects.)

This constant movement makes it impossible for a community to develop in these slums. In 1958 a study in New York carried the poignant cry of an old resident in one of these transitional areas: "Nobody, not even an angel, can avoid trouble here! Too many people with no investment and no pride in the neighborhood! Too many just passing through! I feel sorriest for the kids—they've never known what a decent neighborhood is like!"

It should be clear that poverty of the sort described above, demoralizing as it is, does not represent a "breakdown" of our system comparable to the Great Depression. But it represents a deep flaw in that system, as does continuing unemployment, inflation, urban rot, air and water pollution, and numerous other ills.

Thus, even the most successful national economies have their flaws, and this causes us to wonder why such flaws should occur. Or—what comes to the same thing—it causes us to wonder how the modern economic system functions in the first place.

CHARACTER OF ECONOMIC PROBLEMS

If we were to try to link together the various problems we have been discussing, we should find, I believe, that they had certain common characteristics.

One such characteristic is that they usually have a *quantitative* side to them. If we look deeply enough at almost any economic problem we will sooner or later find some quantities—numbers—involved. We spoke of "getting and spending," and what we get and spend is, among other things, money; and money is measured numerically: so many dollars, so many marks, so many pesos. Furthermore, we typically get money by producing certain goods that we sell for certain prices. How much money we get depends on what quantities of goods we produce and how many dollars per unit the goods will sell for—both numbers.

Indeed, whenever we consider what we loosely think of as "economic" problems, we invariably seem to meet with these numbers. We may be concerned about the price level (a number); or the percentage of the labor force unemployed (a number); or the poverty level of income (a number, currently around $4,000 per year for a family of four); or the gross national product per capita in Upper Volta (currently, $48 per year); and so on. Some of these numbers are hard to come by. Some are even philosophically complicated. But there is hardly any major economic problem into which a number does not enter somewhere.

And this fact is important because it helps explain certain aspects of the approach of modern economists to their subject. This approach is slightly different from that of the historian or of many other students of society. It is more statistical, more mathematical, more like the approach one might find in the natural sciences. Economists actually like to think of their subject as a science; and if one takes a look at a typical professional economics journal of today, its pages covered with differential equations and matrix algebra, one might think that he had wandered into physics or biochemistry by mistake!

But if this quantitative side is the first common characteristic of economic problems, the second—their *institutional* side—is almost the reverse. Economic problems are not generally reducible to simple scientific formulae. They deal with society, they deal with people, they deal with institutions, history, culture, ideology. The field may be a science, but it is a social (not a natural) science. Behind the numbers, behind the hard facts of resources and technological capabilities, we ultimately come face to face with human beings and the psychology of their behavior, whether individual or collective. Since

this behavior is, in turn, conditioned by the past history of their society and its relationships to other societies, there is really no aspect of history, political science, or sociology that does not have some relevance to most major economic problems. Without knowing the history of twentieth-century wars, who could follow the movements of price levels in our century? Without knowing the differences of history and culture that separate the continents, who could explain why people eat well in Europe and North America and starve in Africa or Asia? Without knowing the whole complex sociology of urban-rural life in the country, who could explain what is happening to American cities in the 1970s? Suburbia, exurbia, megalopolis—how complex these terms are, and yet they clearly have deep economic implications which the economist must try to comprehend.

Furthermore, and largely in consequence of the above, there is a third and final characteristic of most economic problems: they are usually *controversial*. This, by the way, is not unfortunate. Indeed, most economists have been drawn to the field at one time or another because of its controversial side. Economic problems are full of zest and spice, and economic discussions are quite capable of turning friends into distant acquaintances and vice versa. The "Great Debates," appearing throughout this book, are testimony to the importance of controversy in this field.

Still, this aspect of our subject does demand a special kind of self-awareness when one is pursuing the analysis of an economic problem. We have to know whether what we are saying is true because we have carefully and objectively verified it or whether we are mainly expressing our own opinions—our own value judgments—that may conflict sharply with someone else's. Is my friend (or former friend) John wrong about the national debt because of logical error, empirical misinformation (he simply doesn't know the facts), or flaws in his moral character? Since John may also be asking the same questions about me, it is worthwhile to try to get the matter straight. Since economic problems characteristically weave these different threads together, it takes a particular effort of mental discipline to disentangle them.

SCARCITY AND
THE CIRCULAR FLOW

So much for general characteristics. Now let us probe a bit more deeply. Can we define the nature of economic problems in a more fundamental way?

The answer will vary somewhat from economist to economist, but a fairly central definition would go something like this:

Economic problems in general arise because of the fact that the means society has for satisfying the material wants of its citizens are limited relative to those wants. Human desires for material goods—for survival, for luxury, for ostentation, whatever—generally exceed the volume of goods that can be made available for satisfying these desires.

Another way of putting this is to say that there is, in most economic matters, a fundamental problem of *scarcity* involved. Our desires are relatively unlimited. Our resources are relatively limited. The tension between desire and means of satisfying that desire is a reflection of the degree of scarcity involved.

Now this way of looking at the matter brings out immediately some important points about most economic problems. For one thing, it helps explain why many people when they talk about economics sometimes say, "It's all a matter of supply and demand!" Actually, this is one of those interesting statements that are true in some interpretations and quite false in others. In the technical sense in which economists use the terms *supply* and *demand*,[2] the statement isn't true at all. In fact, there is relatively little in real-world economics that can be analyzed unqualifiedly in these terms. In the very general sense of our present discussion, however, the statement does have some validity. What it says is that there is this fundamentally two-sided nature of economic problems—human desires and scarce resources—and that economics is deeply concerned with the relationship of these two different sides.

This two-sided aspect of economic problems leads us fairly directly to a simple and rather general representation of economic life as shown in Figure 1-2. This representation may be called the *circular flow of economic life*. It shows the basic economic process as involving a relationship between human desires for goods—here located in the *Home*—and society's productive capacities—here symbolized by the *Factory*.

There are really two flows in this diagram: a money flow in the inner circle, and a goods-and-services flow in the outer. In money terms, what happens is that people at Home, wanting to buy goods, send money to the Factory to pay for these goods. The Factory, in turn, has to pay out money for labor and other productive services in order to be able to produce

2. See chapter 2, pp. 36–41, where the applicability of the technical terms *supply* and *demand* is discussed.

these goods. This money comes back to the Home, since consumers are also owners of labor and other productive services.

In goods-and-services terms, what happens is that the Factory takes the services of labor and other productive resources and combines these in such a way as to produce a stream of goods flowing out to the consumers in the Home. The goods-and-services flow goes clockwise in this diagram; the money flow counterclockwise. We could, of course, have shown it the other way around; whichever way we depicted it, however, the two flows would have had to be in *opposite* directions.

Now this diagram can be varied

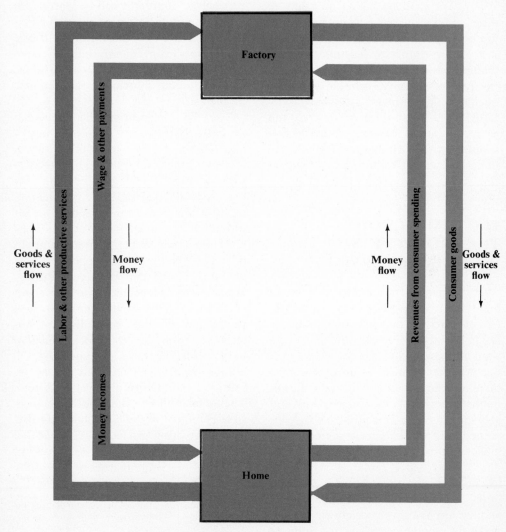

Figure 1-2. The Circular Flow of Economic Life.

in a number of ways to bring out different aspects of the economic problem. For example, in socialist societies many productive resources may be owned by the State and not by the Home. Or we might want to alter the diagram to show that many goods produced in the Factory go not to consumers directly but to building up productive capacity—that is, to expanding the Factory.

We shall be taking up many of these complications in later chapters of the book. For the moment we are using this picture simply to illustrate some of the implications of *scarcity* in economics. Because of scarcity, economics is frequently concerned with a two-sided relationship between human desires and scarce resources, between demand and supply, between Home and Factory. An important way of capturing this relationship vividly is through a circular flow diagram like Figure 1-2.

ECONOMIC CHOICE— THE PRODUCTION- POSSIBILITY CURVE

Another point that comes out quite clearly when we think about the notion of scarcity is that economic problems are frequently concerned with *choice*. We want all these various goods, but we cannot produce them all at once. We must therefore choose—either this or that, but not both. Scarcity forces choice on us, and a great many economic problems are concerned with the choices a society must make: what particular goods shall we produce? What scarce resources should we use in producing this or that good? And so on. Scarcity forces choice upon society, and the mechanisms a society employs to make its economic choices are quite as significant facts about that society as are

its political system or the way it organizes its family life. Indeed, as is obvious, these economic, political, and social matters are usually very much interrelated.

The choice problem can also be illustrated by means of a simple diagram. We should probably pause here to point out that economists often find graphs and diagrams useful in explaining their subject to others and in understanding it themselves. Indeed, it will be worthwhile lingering a moment on the graph in Figure 1-3. It not only illustrates the choice problem very conveniently, but also shows how we can use such graphs to organize and expand our thinking about economic problems.

The diagram is called a *production-possibility* curve or, sometimes, a *transformation curve.*[3] In order to draw it, let us imagine a very simple, hypothetical society that is capable of producing only two products: food and steel. The technologists in the society have given us the information contained in Table 1-1. They have told us what is the maximum amount of steel we can produce for each possible amount of food that we are producing. We begin by producing zero units of food; i.e., all our resources are going into steel production. We then begin diverting our resources from steel to food production, until finally, when we are producing 175 million bushels of food, there are no resources left, and steel production is zero. The table, in theory, describes all the possible combinations of food and steel that the society can produce—its *production possibilities*—when all its resources of land, labor, and machines are fully employed.

3. The word *transformation* is sometimes used because the diagram is designed to show how a society, using all its resources, can produce different combinations of goods—i.e., how it can transform (by different resource use) one good into another.

Table 1-1

When food production is (million bushels)	Then the maximum possible steel production is (thousand tons)
0	1,050
20	1,035
40	990
60	930
80	840
100	720
120	595
140	410
160	190
175	0

The figures from Table 1-1 have been displayed graphically in Figure 1-3. If we had a piece of graph paper, we could plot on it all the points shown in Table 1-1. Then if we joined them together in a smooth curve, we would have the diagram shown in Figure 1-3.

Now this diagram is nothing but

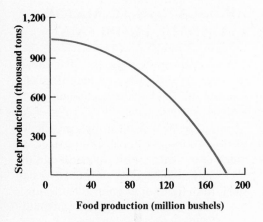

Figure 1-3. Production-Possibility or Transformation Curve.

This curve graphically presents the hypothetical data from the table above. It shows the characteristic bowed-out shape of the production-possibility curve.

a representation of the material presented in Table 1-1—i.e., basically it gives us no new information—but it does show us something that is not obviously read from the table: the *shape* of the production-possibility curve. We notice, in particular, that the curve is bowed out, or, technically, "concave to the origin"; it is not simply a straight line from the *x*-axis to the *y*-axis.

What does this bowed-out shape mean? And why is it a fairly characteristic shape for the production-possibility curve?

The *meaning* of the shape of the curve is fairly easy to see. It states that as we increase our production of one commodity it will be harder and harder to get still further units of that commodity. Harder in what sense? Harder in the sense that we will have to give up more units of the other commodity to add another unit of the first commodity. In other words, as we increase food production, we shall have to give up more and more units of steel to increase our food production by one unit.

The meaning of this last statement is illustrated in Figure 1-4. In the portion of the curve indicated by the roman numeral I, we are producing relatively little food and a great deal of steel. To increase food production by a given amount a is relatively easy—we have to give up only b_I steel to do so. Now contrast this with the situation in area II. Food production is much higher here. To increase food production by the same amount as before (a), we must now give up much more steel; i.e., b_{II} is much greater than b_I. And the same would, of course, be true if we were speaking of increasing steel production as opposed to increasing food production.

This, then, is what the shape of the curve *means*, but now we ask: *Why* does it have this particular shape? The

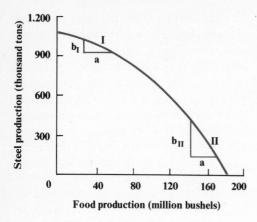

Figure 1-4.

The shape of the production-possibility curve illustrates this important generalization: as we produce more of one good, we must usually give up more of other commodities, to increase production of that good still further.

fundamental answer to this question derives from the fact that not all productive agents and resources—*factors of production* as economists usually call them—are equally well suited to the production of different commodities. If *all* commodities were the product of *one* factor of production—say, homogeneous labor—then there would be no need for the curve to bow out as it does. But this is obviously not so. In our particular case, steel production requires iron ore while food production requires fertile, cultivable soils. Now there is no reason to expect that the best farming land will also be the land containing the richest iron deposits—quite the contrary, in fact. What happens then as we keep increasing our food production?

In the beginning, when we are producing a great deal of steel and almost no food, we are using excellent cultivable soil in our search for whatever bit of iron ore it may

yield. By giving up just a bit of steel production, we release this rich land to the farmer and consequently gain a great deal of food production for a relatively small loss (b_1) of steel. As we keep increasing our food production, however, the situation changes. Now all the really good farming lands have been used. If we wish to increase food production any more, we must take over the land rich in iron ore but relatively poor for crops. This means that to get the same increase in food production we must make major sacrifices (to the amount of b_{11}) in our steel production.

Thus, it is empirically (though not universally or necessarily) true that it usually costs us more to produce more of a particular good, the more of it we have. The *opportunity cost*—the steel we have to give up to get more food—generally goes up as we proceed further and further in any one line of production.

APPLICATION TO MAJOR ECONOMIC PROBLEMS

We can now use this diagram to illustrate specifically and meaningfully some of the fundamental economic problems all societies face.

Figure 1-5 illustrates the choice problem that we have emphasized so much in our earlier discussion. Should the society locate itself at point *A* (lots of steel; little food) or at point *B* (little steel; lots of food) on its production-possibility curve? This is not the only kind of choice a society must make; but since economic problems tend to be interrelated, this choice is reflective of the solutions to many other choice problems as well.

How can or should this choice be made between *A* and *B*? Clearly, the

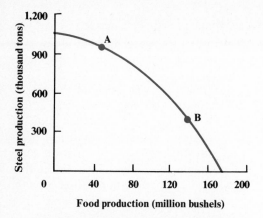

Figure 1-5. The Choice Problem.

Among the fundamental choices a society must make is the choice of the composition of its output (*A* or *B* or some other point). This choice will reflect not only the stage of development of the economy, but also its economic *system*. Is choice decentralized, centralized, mixed, or what?

choice the society will want to make will depend on a whole host of different factors. For example: if it has a very large population, then presumably it will need a fairly large production of food. If it is a very rich country, then it will presumably consume a higher proportion of industrial products (steel) as opposed to agricultural products (food). Even if it is a poor country, it may decide to sacrifice food production today, to make machines (steel), so that it can produce *both* more food and more steel in the future.

These are simply a few of the many considerations that will influence a society's choice between *A* and *B* on its production-possibility curve. *How* these factors influence that choice, moreover, is dependent upon a still further variable: the kind of economic *system* operating in that particular society. Does it have a traditional economy? A market economy? A planned or command economy? A mixed economy? The way in which these dif-

ferent possible economic *systems* work to influence economic choices will be a major concern for us in our remaining chapters of Part One.

Before carrying these matters further, however, let us use our diagram to illustrate two additional major economic problems. These two additional problems have received great attention among economists since the 1930s, and we will devote many later chapters to them.

The first of these two problems lies in the field of what we might call *short-run aggregative* economics. It asks: What factors determine the state of health of the economy as a whole in the short-run? One of the most important aspects of this question has to do with the employment problem. Are we utilizing all our available labor and other resources in production, or do we have men and factories standing idle and, consequently, a national income that is less than it might be? In terms of Figure 1-6, the two situations are contrasted at points *FE* (full-employment production) and *UE* (unemployment or undercapacity production). The production-possibility curve does not tell us where the society *will* be, but where, technologically, it *can* be. It will take us a good bit of analysis to show the forces that determine where the economy in the aggregate will, in fact, be located at any given moment of time.

The other problem that can be illustrated by our diagram is that of *long-run economic growth*. Here, as Figure 1-7 indicates, we are concerned with the shifting outward of the production-possibility curve over time. What these curves tell us is that in 1970 we were able to produce *both* more food and more steel than in 1960 and that, by 1975, we had hypothetically advanced still further.

Now this growth process—this

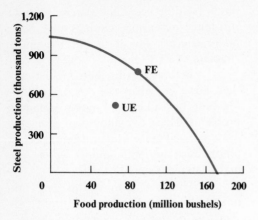

Figure 1-6. The Unemployment Problem.

Will total output be at its full employment potential level (on the production-possibility curve) or will it be at a point *inside* the curve, signifying unemployment? Note that at *UE* we can have more of both food and steel if we can only get our laborers and machinery back into full operation.

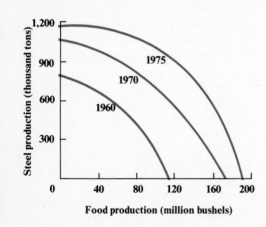

Figure 1-7. The Growth Problem.

A modern economy does not remain static but grows, as suggested by these outward shifts of the production-possibility curve.

shifting out of the production-possibility curve—does not happen automatically with the passage of time. Indeed, it is not too much of an exaggeration to say that

economic growth, in its modern sense, was really unknown to the world until the British industrial revolution of the late eighteenth and early nineteenth centuries. Even today there are vast areas of the world, especially in Asia and Africa, where this process has not yet fully taken root. In the advanced industrial countries, however, growth is now a characteristic feature of economic life. Through a continuing process that involves population growth, the accumulation of machines and other capital goods, and, above all, a constant attention to invention and innovation (new products, new discoveries, new technologies of production), these modern economies are shifting out their production possibilities at a rate unknown in the early history of mankind.

ARE OUR ECONOMIC PROBLEMS VIRTUALLY SOLVED?

The rapidity of modern growth has led some observers to wonder if we have not reached a stage where our basic economic problems have been solved, or at least will be solved in the not-too-distant future. People speak freely of the "affluent society." If affluence is the opposite of scarcity, and if scarcity is central to the economic problem, then perhaps that problem is now a thing of the past—or will be after just a few more decades of rapid modern growth.

This is a serious point, and we shall be coming back to it again later on. A few preliminary responses are in order, however:

In the first place, it is clear from what we have already said that this line of reasoning has little relevance for the majority of the world's population who live in the underdeveloped world. To speak of the "affluent society" in Upper Volta would be not only inappropriate but cruel. There are more hungry people in the world today than there were a century ago, because of the enormous growth of population in the poor countries of the world.

In the second place, there is evidence that the shoe still pinches in the United States, even among economic classes well above the poverty level. The concern about unemployment, the fear of inflation, the worries about taxes, pensions, old age, and health seem hardly less severe today than they were two decades ago. No one compares these problems with those of the Great Depression, but any politician will assure you that they do exist!

Finally—and this is a point that has become more and more apparent in the last few years—economic growth has costs as well as benefits. Some argue that by now the costs exceed the benefits by a substantial margin. Some would go so far as to argue that economic growth is taking us down the path to disaster, perhaps irreversibly. A listing of these costs, both direct and indirect, is like a catalog of the ills of modern industrial—or, perhaps better, *post*industrial—society. Growth has been held responsible for the population explosion, urban overcrowding and congestion, air and water pollution, the despoliation of our landscapes, the squandering of our resources, the alienation of the worker, of the young, of the old, and the creation of false values and a meaningless pattern of life.

These criticisms of modern industrial growth are all doubtless valid to some degree. Their net effect, however, is likely to *increase* rather than to decrease the importance of economics in the years ahead.

For what is being suggested by many critics of modern growth is that this growth has been purchased too cheaply, i.e., by a cavalier and profligate use of our natural and social environment. If we are to husband our resources more carefully, if we are to secure the comforts of an affluent society but *without* pollution and waste, and with a proper attention to the less fortunate members of society, then even modest economic growth may be very hard to come by. We may find, in short, that beneficial, socially desirable economic advance is very expensive.

Or to put it most simply: fundamental scarcity, the basis of all economic problems, seems likely to be with us for a very long time yet.

SUMMARY

We become aware of the workings of our economic system when there is some dramatic malfunction in one of its parts. Such malfunctions have occurred historically, as in the German hyperinflation of the 1920s or the worldwide Great Depression of the 1930s. However, deep economic problems still exist today, particularly in the underdeveloped countries of Asia, Africa, and Latin America, but also in the United States where poverty, unemployment, and inflation still pose serious difficulties.

The character of these various economic problems is similar in that (1) they usually involve a *quantitative* element—numbers appear in most economic problems; (2) they also involve an *institutional* element—they require a knowledge of the institutions, culture, and ideology of a particular society; and (3) they are often *controversial* problems—one must be careful to isolate value-judgments from questions of fact or logic.

More deeply, these various economic problems ultimately arise from the problem of *scarcity*—the fact that human desires for material goods and services generally exceed the volume of those goods and services the economy is capable of providing. The fact of scarcity suggests that many economic problems involve a two-sided relationship between human wants and a society's productive capabilities. The *circular flow* of economic life illustrates the process by which Home and Factory may be related in a simple economy.

The fact of scarcity also forces choice upon a society and the problems of choice are conveniently illustrated in a *production-possibility* or *transformation* curve. This curve enables us to show hypothetically how a society might choose between this or that different combination of goods.

The production-possibility diagram is also useful in allowing us to illustrate important aggregative problems such as (1) short-run unemployment and undercapacity production and (2) modern long-run economic growth.

QUESTIONS FOR DISCUSSION

1. List a few of the major economic problems facing the United States at the present time. What features of these problems lead you to characterize them as *economic* problems?

2. Economists of a century or two ago worried about the so-called *paradox of value:* water is very useful but cheap, while diamonds are much less useful but expensive. How does the fundamental role of scarcity in economic problems help you understand this paradox?

3. If there existed a *barter* economy (i.e., an economy in which goods and services are exchanged directly rather than for money), could economic life still be pictured in terms of a "circular flow"? Discuss.

4. Under what special circumstances might the production-possibility curve have a shape such as the following:

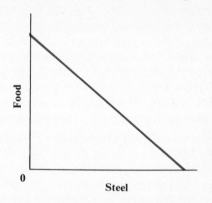

Could you imagine any circumstances in which it might have a shape such as this:

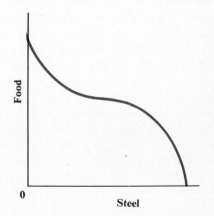

5. At the height of World War II, the United States was devoting some fifty percent of its total production to the war effort, yet private consumption, except for a few commodities, remained high. Use

the production-possibility analysis to illustrate how these facts might be reconciled.

SUGGESTED READING

Chandler, Lester V. *America's Greatest Depression, 1929–41.* New York: Harper & Row, 1970.

Heilbroner, Robert L. *The Making of Economic Society.* 2nd ed. Englewood Cliffs, N.J.: Prentice-Hall, 1968.

Mulcahy, Richard E. *Readings in Economics from Fortune.* 3rd ed. New York: Holt, Rinehart & Winston, 1967, chaps. 1–5, 16–17.

Shannon, David. *The Great Depression.* Englewood Cliffs, N.J.: Prentice-Hall, 1960.

Slesinger, Reuben E.; Perlman, Mark; and Isaacs, Asher, eds. *Contemporary Economics.* 2nd ed. Boston: Allyn & Bacon, 1967, pp. 1–51.

2
The Market Economy

The hard fact of scarcity can force many choices upon a society; and these choices, as we have indicated, will be deeply influenced by the kind of economic *system* operating in that society. In the next five chapters we shall be examining some of the different systems by which fundamental economic choices can be made. In this chapter, we shall focus on what economists sometimes call a *market economy*. We shall try to show how, through the operation of prices and markets, without any central planning or guidance, a society can solve its economic problems in a coherent way.

THE SPECIAL ASSUMPTIONS OF A MARKET ECONOMY

Since everyone brought up in the United States is familiar with the workings of prices and markets of various kinds, the subject of a market economy may seem one of the easier topics in economics.

However, this view is misleading for three reasons. The first is that the successful functioning of a market economy

is intrinsically complicated. Indeed, it is something of a social miracle. For the essence of such an economy is that nobody guides or even thinks about the economy as a whole. Everything is decentralized into the thousands and, indeed, millions of private, individual decisions being made by consumers, producers, and laborers, here, there, and everywhere. That such apparently haphazard means should produce anything like an orderly result is not something to be taken for granted—in fact, it should be regarded as rather astonishing.

The second reason for caution is that a pure market economy does not really exist in the modern world. Although we have all seen various markets—from the supermarket to the stock market—operating in the United States, it would be quite wrong to believe that this country makes all its crucial choices through the market mechanism. The government plays a considerable role in the present-day American economy, as, indeed, it does in all economies in the modern world. Furthermore, even in the private sector as we shall see later on, the roles of business and labor in real life are often quite different from those described by standard economic theory.

Finally, we should be aware that even from an historical point of view, a pure market economy is something of a rarity and that the conditions making it possible are of fairly recent origin. It is quite incorrect to view markets as the normal or "natural" way to organize economic life, an organization that has been modified by government intervention only in modern times. In recent centuries, the reverse is almost closer to the truth. The modern age was ushered into Europe under the auspices of mercantilist thought, which emphasized the need for detailed government regulation of every aspect of economic life. Mercantilist thought in its turn was derived in part from the highly regulated and tradition-bound approach of the medieval towns with their numerous local ordinances and guild restrictions. The self-regulating market is a concept dating from the eighteenth and nineteenth centuries only, a product in part of the English Industrial Revolution.

That this concept does involve quite special assumptions is a major theme of the writings of Karl Polanyi, whose *The Great Transformation* is a significant analysis of the historical origins and effects of the market economy. In the following reading, Polanyi makes these basic points: (1) a market economy was not characteristic in Europe under either feudalism or mercantilism; (2) the coming of such an economy required the assumptions (*a*) that economic life is separable from political and social life and (*b*) that labor, land, and money can be treated as commodities; and (3) that these are not normal but indeed "fictitious" assumptions. Although all economists will not agree with every detail of his analysis, most find Polanyi's work highly stimulating.

THE SELF-REGULATING MARKET

KARL POLANYI

A market economy is an economic system controlled, regulated, and directed by markets alone; order in the production and distribution of goods is entrusted to this self-regulating mechanism. An economy of this kind derives from the expectation that human beings behave in such a way as to achieve maximum money gains. Self-regulation implies that all production is for sale on the market and that all incomes derive from such sales. Accordingly, there are markets for all elements of industry, not only for goods (always including services) but also for labor, land, and money.

To realize fully what this means, let us return for a moment to the mercantile system and the national markets which it did so much to develop. Under feudalism and the gild system land and labor formed part of the social organization itself (money had yet hardly developed into a major element of industry). Land, the pivotal element in the feudal order, was the basis of the military, judicial, administrative, and political system; its status and function were determined by legal and customary rules. Whether its possession was transferable or not, and if so, to whom and under what restrictions; what the rights of property entailed; to what uses some types of land might be put—all these questions were removed from the organization of buying and selling, and subjected to an entirely different set of institutional regulations.

The same was true of the organization of labor. Under the gild system, as under every other economic system in previous history, the motives and circumstances of productive activities were embedded in the general organization of society. The relations of master, journeyman, and apprentice; the terms of the craft; the number of apprentices; the wages of the workers were all regulated by the custom and rule of the gild and the town. What the mercantile system did was merely to unify these conditions either through statute as in England, or through the "nationalization" of the gilds as in France. As to land, its feudal status was abolished only in so far as it was linked with provincial privileges; for the rest, land remained *extra commercium*, in England as in France. Up to the time of the Great Revolution of 1789, landed estate remained the source of social privilege in France, and even after that time in England Common Law on land was essentially medieval. Mercantilism, with all its tendency towards commercialization, never attacked the safeguards which protected these two basic elements of production—labor and land—from becoming the objects of commerce. In England the "nationalization" of labor legislation through the Statute of Artificers (1563) and the Poor Law (1601), removed labor from the danger zone, and the anti-enclosure policy of the Tudors and early Stuarts was one consistent protest against the principle of the gainful use of landed property.

That mercantilism, however emphatically it insisted on commercialization as a national policy, thought of markets in a way exactly contrary to market economy, is best shown by its vast extension of state intervention in industry. On this point there was no difference between mercantilists and feudalists, between crowned planners and vested interests, between centralizing bureaucrats and conservative particularists. They disagreed only on the methods of reg-

ulation: gilds, towns, and provinces appealed to the force of custom and tradition, while the new state authority favored statute and ordinance. But they were all equally averse to the idea of commercializing labor and land—the precondition of market economy. Craft gilds and feudal privileges were abolished in France only in 1790; in England the Statute of Artificers was repealed only in 1813-14, the Elizabethan Poor Law in 1834. Not before the last decade of the eighteenth century was, in either country, the establishment of a free labor market even discussed; and the idea of the self-regulation of economic life was utterly beyond the horizon of the age. The mercantilist was concerned with the development of the resources of the country, including full employment, through trade and commerce; the traditional organization of land and labor he took for granted. He was in this respect as far removed from modern concepts as he was in the realm of politics, where his belief in the absolute powers of an enlightened despot was tempered by no intimations of democracy. And just as the transition to a democratic system and representative politics involved a complete reversal of the trend of the age, the change from regulated to self-regulating markets at the end of the eighteenth century represented a complete transformation in the structure of society.

A self-regulating market demands nothing less than the institutional separation of society into an economic and political sphere. Such a dichotomy is, in effect, merely the restatement, from the point of view of society as a whole, of the existence of a self-regulating market. It might be argued that the separateness of the two spheres obtains in every type of society at all times. Such an inference, however, would be based on a fallacy. True, no society can exist without a system of some kind which ensures order in the production and distribution of goods. But that does not imply the existence of separate economic institutions; normally, the economic order is merely a function of the social, in which it is contained. Neither under tribal, nor feudal, nor mercantile conditions was there, as we have shown, a separate economic system in society. Nineteenth century society, in which economic activity was isolated and imputed to a distinctive economic motive, was, indeed, a singular departure.

Such an institutional pattern could not function unless society was somehow subordinated to its requirements. A market economy can exist only in a market society. We reached this conclusion on general grounds in our analysis of the market pattern. We can now specify the reasons for this assertion. A market economy must comprise all elements of industry, including labor, land, and money. But labor and land are no other than the human beings themselves of which every society consists and the natural surroundings in which it exists. To include them in the market mechanism means to subordinate the substance of society itself to the laws of the market.

The crucial point is this: labor, land, and money are essential elements of industry; they also must be organized in markets; in fact, these markets form an absolutely vital part of the economic system. But labor, land, and money are obviously *not* commodities. Labor is only another name for a human activity which goes with life itself, which in its turn is not produced for sale but for entirely different reasons, nor can that activity be detached from the rest of life, be stored or mobilized; land is only another name for nature, which is not produced by man; actual money, finally, is merely a token of purchasing power which, as a rule, is not produced at all, but comes into being through the mechanism of banking or state finance. None of them is produced for sale. The commodity description of labor, land, and money is entirely fictitious.

Nevertheless, it is with the help of this fiction that the actual markets for labor, land, and money are organized; they are being actually bought and sold on the market; their demand and supply are real magnitudes; and any measures or policies that would inhibit the formation of such markets would *ipso facto* endanger the self-regulation of the system. The commodity fiction, therefore, supplies a vital organizing principle in regard to the whole of society affecting almost all its institutions in the most varied way, namely the principle according to which no arrangement or behavior should be allowed to exist that might prevent the actual functioning of the market mechanism on the lines of the commodity fiction.

ADAM SMITH AND THE CLASSICAL ECONOMISTS

In *The Great Transformation* and other writings, Polanyi stressed the inhumanities and hardships that were attendant upon the historical birth of the market economy. The leading economists of that historical period were, however, of a rather different mind. In the eighteenth century, the notion was born that the price-and-market mechanism was a quite good way for a society to handle its basic economic problems—in fact, the *best* way. Around the 1750s and 1760s, a number of French economists (sometimes called *physiocrats*) began to stress the view that there was a natural harmony between the decisions individuals made privately and the general social welfare. *Physiocracy* means "rule of Nature." Private self-interest and the social welfare were seen not as in conflict but as in a fundamental union more or less as a matter of "natural law."

The most important development of this concept, however, came in Great Britain. Early British economists were interested in analyzing the implications of a market economy and in trying to demonstrate that if the government stayed in the background, the price-and-market mechanism could handle things quite satisfactorily. Since these early British economists did much to establish the field of economics as we know it today, it is worthwhile to say a word about them.

The key date is probably the year 1776. This year saw not only the beginning of the American Revolution—it saw also the publication of one of the most important economic treatises of all times: *The Wealth of Nations* by Adam Smith. Smith was quite a remarkable man, although his life was notably without incident. He never married. Except for a Grand Tour of the Continent—when, incidentally, he met some of the leading French physiocrats—he never traveled extensively. But he was a philosopher, a historian of science, and, above all, the greatest economist of his day. *The Wealth of Nations* is a spacious book that can be read for pleasure even now. It is filled with rolling eighteenth-century sentences but also with sharp phrases that catch whole pages of argumentation in a word or two. When Smith speaks of an "invisible hand" that brings private and social interest into harmony, he is not simply writing vividly; he is pinpointing an entire philosophy of economic life.

Smith is important not only because of his work, but because of the influence of that work on others. *The Wealth of Nations* became the rock on which a whole school of economists was founded. This school is usually called the *classical economists,* and it included, in the decades following Adam Smith, some of the most important writers in the history of the subject. There was Thomas Robert Malthus, the English parson whose ideas on population cast a pessimistic pall over nineteenth-century thought and greatly influenced the evolutionist Charles Darwin. There was

David Ricardo, who published his *Principles of Political Economy and Taxation* in 1817 after a highly successful career in business. Ricardo was one of a small number of economists who really have done well on the stock market. His work in economic theory was rigorous and systematic. Although not well known to the general public, he had an enormous impact on the development of technical economics.

Even in the middle of the nineteenth century, Smith's influence was still strong, and John Stuart Mill, who once had Ricardo for a tutor, is often regarded as a classical economist. Mill, of course, was a many-sided genius whose works in philosophy and political science easily match his very substantial contributions to economics.

Smith's message, however, carried beyond his fellow economists, to the world at large. And this message was, in essence, that except for certain unavoidable responsibilities,[1] the State ought to stay fairly well out of the economic sphere. Laissez-faire was the motto: leave the economy alone; have the State keep a hands-off policy. Or in terms of our discussion in this chapter, let the society solve its economic problems largely through the functioning of a market economy.

But what reasons did Smith offer in support of this view? In the first reading that follows—containing, incidentally, the famous "invisible hand" quotation—Smith is arguing against the policy of mercantilism and especially against the view

---

1. Smith acknowledged that the State had certain duties that would bring it actively into the economy: (1) national defense; (2) the administration of justice; and (3) the provision of certain socially necessary institutions—e.g., educational institutions—that private interests might neglect. Thus, neither he nor any of the classical economists advocated a truly *pure* market economy. The question was how much (or little) intervention was needed.

that it is nationally advantageous to re-strict imports from abroad. In the course of this argument, he brings out a number of principles that underlie the laissez-faire philosophy. The reader should note that Smith does *not* argue that private individuals are philanthropic or in any way devoted to promoting the public welfare. He is quite skeptical about those individuals who "affected to trade for the public good." The public benefits occur when the individual is seeking his own *self*-interest through the market mechanism. Why these benefits to society? Smith points out that the individual, in seeking his own advantage, will be more efficient; that he knows his own local situation much better than any statesman can; that in trying to produce the most value for himself he will be effectively producing the greatest value for society. By contrast, state interference with private markets tends to be hurtful—in the case of trade restrictions, forcing us to buy more expensively at home what we could get more cheaply from abroad.

Adam Smith (1723-1790). Often considered the founder of modern economics, Adam Smith influenced both economists and governments for many decades after he wrote. His central idea: that there is a basic harmony between private self-interest and social welfare and, consequently, that the State should (with some important exceptions) leave the economy to the workings of market competition.

Restraints upon Imports

ADAM SMITH

No regulation of commerce can increase the quantity of industry in any society beyond what its capital can maintain. It can only divert a part of it into a direction into which it might not otherwise have gone; and it is by no means certain that this artificial direction is likely to be more advantageous to the society than that into which it would have gone of its own accord.

Every individual is continually exerting himself to find out the most advantageous employment for whatever capital he can command. It is his own advantage, indeed, and not that of the society, which he has in view. But the study of his own advantage naturally, or rather necessarily leads him to prefer that employment which is most advantageous to the society.

First, every individual endeavours to employ his capital as near home as he can, and consequently as much as he can in the support of domestic industry; provided always that he can thereby obtain the ordinary, or not a great deal less than the ordinary profits.

* * *

Secondly, every individual who employs his capital in the support of domestic industry, necessarily endeavours so to direct that industry, that its produce may be of the greatest possible value.

The produce of industry is what it adds to the subject or materials upon which it is employed. In proportion as the value of this produce is great or small, so will likewise be the profits of the employer. But it is only for the sake of profit that any man employs a capital in the support of industry; and he will always, therefore, endeavour to employ it in the support of that industry of which the produce is likely to be of the greatest value, or to exchange

Excerpted from Adam Smith, "Restraints upon Imports" from *The Wealth of Nations* (New York: Modern Library, Random House, 1937), pp. 421–24. Reprinted by permission of Random House, Inc.

for the greatest quantity either of money or of other goods.

* * *

As every individual, therefore, endeavours as much as he can both to employ his capital in the support of domestic industry, and so to direct that industry that its produce may be of the greatest value; every individual necessarily labours to render the annual revenue of the society as great as he can. He generally, indeed, neither intends to promote the public interest, nor knows how much he is promoting it. By preferring the support of domestic to that of foreign industry, he intends only his own security; and by directing that industry in such a manner as its produce may be of the greatest value, he intends only his own gain, and he is in this, as in many other cases, led by an invisible hand to promote an end which was no part of his intention. Nor is it always the worse for the society that it was no part of it. By pursuing his own interest he frequently promotes that of the society more effectually than when he really intends to promote it. I have never known much good done by those who affected to trade for the public good. It is an affectation, indeed, not very common among merchants, and very few words need be employed in dissuading them from it.

What is the species of domestic industry which his capital can employ, and of which the produce is likely to be of the greatest value, every individual, it is evident, can, in his local situation, judge much better than any statesman or lawgiver can do for him. The statesman, who should attempt to direct private people in what manner they ought to employ their capitals, would not only load himself with a most unnecessary attention, but assume an authority which could safely be trusted, not only to no single person, but to no council or senate whatever, and which would nowhere be so dangerous as in the hands of a man who had folly and presumption enough to fancy himself fit to exercise it.

To give the monopoly of the home-market to the produce of domestic industry, in any particular art or manufacture, is in some measure to direct private people in what manner they ought to employ their capitals, and must, in almost all cases, be either a useless or a hurtful regulation. If the produce of domestic can be brought there as cheap as that of foreign industry, the regulation is evidently useless. If it cannot, it must generally be hurtful. It is the maxim of every prudent master of a family, never to attempt to make at home what it will cost him more to make than to buy. The taylor does not attempt to make his own shoes, but buys them of the shoemaker. The shoemaker does not attempt to make his own clothes, but employs a taylor. The farmer attempts to make neither the one nor the other, but employs those different artificers. All of them find it for their interest to employ their whole industry in a way in which they have some advantage over their neighbours, and to purchase with a part of its produce, or what is the same thing, with the price of a part of it, whatever else they have occasion for.

What is prudence in the conduct of every private family, can scarce be folly in that of a great kingdom. If a foreign country can supply us with a commodity cheaper than we ourselves can make it, better buy it of them with some part of the produce of our own industry, employed in a way in which we have some advantage. The general industry of the country, being always in proportion to the capital which employs it, will not thereby be diminished, no more than that of the above-mentioned artificers; but only left to find out the way in which it can be employed with the greatest advantage. It is certainly not employed to the greatest advantage, when it is thus directed towards an object which it can buy cheaper than it can make. The value of its annual produce is certainly more or less diminished, when it is thus turned away from producing commodities evidently of more value than the commodity which it is directed to produce. According to the supposition, that commodity could be purchased from foreign countries cheaper than it can be made at home. It could, therefore, have been purchased with a part only of the commodities, or, what is the same thing, with a part only of the price of the commodities, which the industry employed by an equal capital would have produced at home, had it been left to follow its natural course. The industry of the country, therefore, is thus turned away from a more, to a less advantageous employment, and the exchangeable value of its annual produce, instead of being increased, according to the intention of the lawgiver, must necessarily be diminished by every such regulation.

There was also another main line in Adam Smith's defense of private initiative and the market in addition to the "invisible hand" theme. This second line had to do with the growth of the economy over time. Smith believed that economic advance depended on the accumulation of capital,[2] and that the accumulation of capital depended on saving and "parsimony." The following reading brings out his view that private individuals, motivated by the desire to better their own conditions, would be far more likely to save and add to society's productive capital than would governments with their tendency to "extravagance" and "errors of administration."

---

2. Modern economists also believe that economic growth depends in part on the accumulation of capital, although modern notions of capital are somewhat different from those of Adam Smith. We tend to think of capital as machines, tools, equipment and so on. Smith tended to emphasize how labor was employed—whether "productively" (producing goods that could be stored up and saved) or "unproductively" (like household servants who worked but left nothing that could be accumulated). Smith also emphasized the *division of labor* as a major element in economic growth. Indeed, he thought capital accumulation would stimulate a continually greater division of labor over time. We shall be taking up a number of these points about economic growth later on. (See chapter 16.)

THE ACCUMULATION OF CAPITAL

ADAM SMITH

Capitals are increased by parsimony, and diminished by prodigality and misconduct.

Whatever a person saves from his revenue he adds to his capital, and either employs it himself in maintaining an additional number of productive hands, or enables some other person to do so, by lending it to him for an interest, that is, for a share of the profits. As the capital of an individual can be increased only by what he saves from his annual revenue or his annual gains, so the capital of a society, which is the same with that of all the individuals who compose it, can be increased only in the same manner.

Great nations are never impoverished by private, though they sometimes are by public prodigality and misconduct. The whole, or almost the whole public revenue, is in most countries employed in maintaining unproductive hands. Such are the people who compose a numerous and splendid court, a great ecclesiastical establishment, great fleets and armies, who in time of peace produce nothing, and in time of war acquire nothing which can compensate the expence of maintaining them, even while the war lasts. Such people, as they themselves produce nothing, are all maintained by the produce of other men's labour. When multiplied, therefore, to an unnecessary number, they may in a particular year consume so great a share of this produce,

as not to leave a sufficiency for maintaining the productive labourers, who should reproduce it next year. The next year's produce, therefore, will be less than that of the foregoing, and if the same disorder should continue, that of the third year will be still less than that of the second. Those unproductive hands, who should be maintained by a part only of the spare revenue of the people, may consume so great a share of their whole revenue, and therefore oblige so great a number to encroach upon their capitals, upon the funds destined for the maintenance of productive labour, that all the frugality and good conduct of individuals may not be able to compensate the waste and degradation of produce occasioned by this violent and forced encroachment.

This frugality and good conduct, however, is upon most occasions, it appears from experience, sufficient to compensate, not only the private prodigality and misconduct of individuals, but the public extravagance of government. The uniform, constant, and uninterrupted effort of every man to better his condition, the principle from which public and national, as well as private opulence is originally derived, is frequently powerful enough to maintain the natural progress of things toward improvement, in spite both of the extravagance of government, and of the greatest errors of administration. Like the unknown principle of animal life, it frequently restores health and vigour to the constitution, in spite, not only of the disease, but of the absurd prescriptions of the doctor.

Excerpted from Adam Smith, "The Accumulation of Capital," from The Wealth of Nations (New York: Modern Library, Random House, 1937), pp. 321, 325–26. Reprinted by permission of Random House, Inc.

Thus, Adam Smith combined a belief in the frugality and industry of private individuals with a conviction that the market would work in such a fashion that the profit-seeking self-interest of those same individuals would tend towards the public good. The corollary was: if the private sector can handle things so well, then the State need not intervene except for rather special and limited functions.

CHOICE THROUGH THE MARKET

Today we are aware of many qualifications to the "classical" view of the world, but we can also state their own arguments more precisely than they could, because we have developed certain analytic tools that were not at their disposal. Let us now approach this matter a bit more systematically.

The Problem

The tasks that a market economy must perform are numerous. For one thing, it must determine in one way or another how the income of society is distributed. One man earns $10,000 a year; another $2,000; another $75,000. Whether one applauds or objects to any particular arrangement, it is clear that every economic system must have *some* determinate way of distributing its goods and services among its members. Anything less would bring social chaos.

Similarly, every economic system must provide some determinate way of deciding how the goods and services of the society are to be produced. One might think that this question of how to produce potatoes or automobiles or table lamps is a purely technological—not an economic—question. But this is not so, for there are many different ways of producing any given product. All of these ways are feasible in a physical or engineering sense, but some may be better than others in an *economic* sense. Automation may be excellent for a society with a great deal of machinery and a shortage of labor, but it would hardly make sense for a society that is overflowing with unskilled labor and can barely afford the most rudimentary tools and ma-

chines. The question of how to produce different goods is vitally affected by the relative scarcities of the different factors of production. Thus, it falls squarely in the province of the economist; and like the question of the distribution of income, it is another problem for the market economy to solve.

Finally, there is the problem we have already spent some time on: what goods to produce? In terms of our earlier diagram (repeated here in Figure 2-1), shall we produce at point *A* (lots of steel; little food) or at point *B* (little steel; lots of food)? In the remainder of this chapter, we shall put particular emphasis on this aspect of the choice problem, for it will allow us to bring out quite clearly the essential features of the market economy in its overall operations.

Birds-Eye Solution—The Circular Flow

Now, in the very broadest sense, the way in which a market economy solves these various choice problems can be illus-

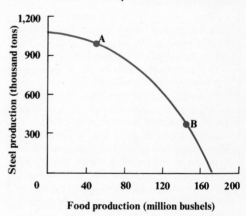

Figure 2-1. The Familiar Choice Problem.

In this chapter, we shall try to show how a decentralized market economy can make the choice between points *A* and *B* through the supply-and-demand mechanism.

trated by a circular flow diagram (Figure 2-2) similar to the one we used in chapter 1. We have made a few changes in this diagram to bring out the fact that we are now dealing specifically with a private market economy. Thus, instead of the very general term *Factory*, we have introduced the term *Private Business Firms*; similarly, we have replaced *Home* with *Private Households*.

The most interesting change, however, is that we have now inserted two new boxes on the right and left hand sides of the diagram, labelled respectively, *Product Markets* and *Factor Markets*. It is by the operation of these markets that our market economy will solve the various choice problems we have put to it. In the Product Market, the households face the business firms as buyers while the business

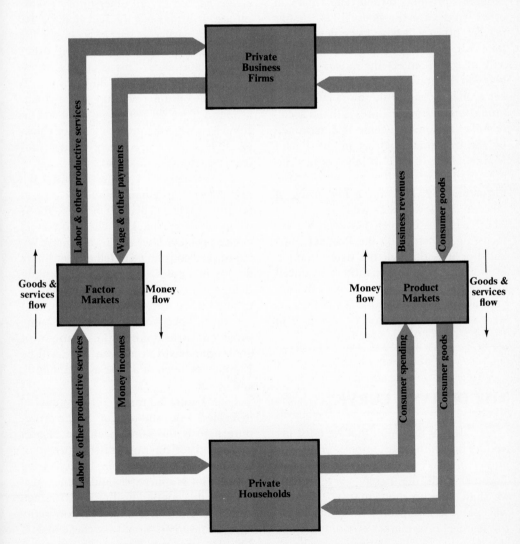

Figure 2-2. The Circular Flow of a Market Economy.

35

firms are the sellers. Prices will have to be determined for the various consumer goods brought to the market by industry. The quantities of these goods bought and sold will also have to be determined. In the Factor Market, the buying and selling relationship is reversed—the business firms are now the *buyers*. They are trying to buy the services of laborers and the other factors of production that are, in this economy, privately owned. The sellers, in other words, are the households. In this market, prices will have to be determined for labor, land, and capital; these prices will, of course, affect the *money incomes* going to the households. In a private market economy, one of the most interesting (and controversial) features is that a society's distribution of income is determined by the way prices get set in the Factor Market. A high price of labor is just another name for a high wage—which, also, unfortunately, goes for a low price of labor and low wages as well.

In this chapter, however, we are focussing primarily on the Product Market. For it is through the determination of the prices and the quantities produced and sold in this market that we can suggest how a market economy makes its steel versus food decision (*A* versus *B* in Figure 2-1).

THE DEMAND CURVE

It is at this point that we must introduce one of the most important and famous tools of economics, the *demand curve.* Together with the *supply curve,* which we shall take up momentarily, this tool will enable us to explain some of the essential features of a market economy. A demand curve may be defined as follows:

A demand curve is a hypothetical construction that tells us how many units of a particular commodity consumers would be willing to buy over a period of time at all possible prices, assuming that the prices of other commodities and the money incomes of the consumers are unchanged.

The last phrase in this definition is of some importance. It is usually called a *ceteris paribus* or "all other things equal" phrase. It brings out the fact that we are isolating a particular part of economic life for close inspection and holding other areas in abeyance. This is clearly necessary here. How can we tell how many units of steak a consumer will buy at one dollar a pound if we do not know what his income is or what the price of lamb or chicken is? Hence the need to proceed in this one-step-at-a-time fashion.

In Table 2-1 we have set out the raw data for a demand curve for a commodity: apples. (This will be our "food" when we come back to the food–steel choice problem later in this chapter.) We have asked consumers to tell us how many dozens of apples they would be willing to buy in a given month at prices ranging from $1.00 to 1¢ per dozen. Notice that we must specify the period of time involved: presumably the number of apples purchased at a given price will be 12 times as much in a year as in a month, and so on.

Figure 2-3 represents the material in Table 2-1 in a smooth curve. The procedure here is the same as in the case of our production-possibility curve of chapter 1. The points from Table 2-1 are charted on graph paper and then joined together in a continuous line (as if, in fact, we actually had information on how many apples consumers would purchase at 31¢, 32¢, 33¢, etc., per dozen.) This curve is

Table 2-1

At price	Consumers wish to buy per month
(per dozen apples)	(thousand dozens)
$1.00	20
.90	90
.80	150
.70	212
.60	278
.50	340
.40	402
.30	465
.20	530
.10	590
.01	650

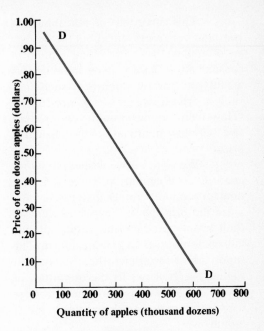

Figure 2-3.

DD represents the consumer demand curve for apples. It is drawn on the assumption that money incomes of consumers are constant and that prices of other commodities (e.g., oranges) are constant.

the consumer demand curve for apples.

Now you notice that the curve slopes downward from left to right. Why this particular shape? Actually, this is not too difficult to understand. At high prices for apples, the consumer will find that buying too many apples makes too big a dent in his budget; he will have to cut down his purchases. Furthermore, when apple prices are high, even the dedicated fruit lover will be tempted to substitute pears or peaches or oranges for apples. This, too, will mean fewer purchases. Thus, although we could imagine a few very curious exceptions if we wished to,[3] the customary shape of a consumer demand curve will be as we have drawn it: sloping downward toward the southeast.

Before leaving the demand curve, the reader should test his understanding of the concept by asking himself what will happen to our demand curve if some of the "other things equal" items happen to change. Suppose all consumers have a fifty percent rise in their money incomes? Suppose the price of bananas goes up? Suppose the price of oranges goes down? In each case, the answer is that the whole demand curve will *shift* its position. The reader should determine the direction of the shift and the reason it shifts in each case.

THE SUPPLY CURVE

The second tool we need for our analysis of the market economy is the *supply curve*.

3. A famous (among economists) exception to the rule of a downward-sloping demand curve is the so-called "Giffen paradox," named after a nineteenth-century British economist, Sir Robert Giffen. He noticed that when the price of potatoes goes up, very poor families may buy *more* potatoes. Why? Because the rise in the price of potatoes makes them poorer; and when they are poorer, they substitute potatoes for meat. This, however, is a very exceptional case and implies, among other things, that the commodity looms very large in the budgets of the consumers involved.

This curve tells us not about the consumers of apples, but about the *producers* of apples. Instead of going around to consumers and asking, "How many apples would you buy this month at such-and-such a price?" we now ask producers, "How many apples would you produce and sell this month at such-and-such a price?"

We could, if we wished, draw up another table similar to Table 2-1, this time for producers rather than consumers. Since the principle is clear, however, we shall simply produce the results of our information survey in graphical form. The supply curve for apples, then, is given in Figure 2-4. It shows us the quantities of apples that producers are willing to offer for sale at various prices over a given month.

Now in some respects the supply curve is a bit more complicated to grasp than the demand curve, or at least it seems so at first glance. Two problems arise: Under what assumptions can a determinate supply curve be drawn? What explains the upward (northeasterly) slope of the supply curve?

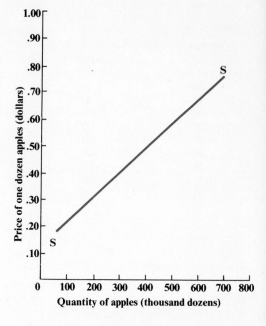

Figure 2-4.

SS represents the producers' supply curve for apples. It tells us that producers are willing to supply more apples only if the price of apples goes up. A lower price, conversely, will lead to a smaller quantity supplied.

ASSUMPTIONS BEHIND THE SUPPLY CURVE

One critical assumption is that apple producers take the prices of apples as given *by the market* and not as subject in any significant way to their personal control. They are price-takers, not price-setters. In technical economics terminology, they are *pure competitors*. We shall see in later chapters that *pure competition* is by no means the only form of real-life market structure, and this is one of the reasons our analysis of the market econ-

omy in the present chapter is necessarily only a beginning. By the term *pure competition*, we mean:

A market structure is purely competitive when the business firms comprising the industry in question are selling a homogeneous product and are so small in relation to the industry as a whole that they take the price of their product as given.

We shall be developing the implications of this definition in great detail (especially in Part Three); for the moment, however, it is important only that we understand that this kind of assumption is, in fact, being made when we draw our supply curve. And this can be seen simply by reflecting a moment on the question we asked each apple producer: "How many apples would you offer for sale at such-and-such a price per dozen?" He is being asked to respond to a *given price*. If this were not the case, the only *relevant* question we could ask him would be: "What price do you plan to *set* for apples this month?" But that is not the question we asked. Our question—the question underlying the supply curve—does build in the assumption of price-taking or pure competition.

The curve is based on other assumptions as well, and we should not be surprised to find that each supply curve (like each demand curve) has its *ceteris paribus* clause attached. In the case of the supply curve, the meaning of this clause seems a bit more complicated, however, for it is so obviously affected by considerations of *time*. It was the late nineteenth-century British economist Alfred Marshall who pointed out the great importance of the time period in speaking of producer behavior and the supply curve. In the very short run, when we allow virtually nothing to vary except the price of apples, the apple producer really has nothing to offer but his given stock of apples. The supply curve in this case might be practically nothing but a straight, vertical line—i.e., he would offer his given supply of apples at any price. In a somewhat longer run, he will have time to adjust production to different prices. When the price of apples goes up and stays up for a few months, he may hire more laborers to pick apples, to pack them, and to fill orders. In the still longer run, his adjustment may be more flexible yet. He may plant more trees, buy up more orchard land, acquire more farm machinery, and so on.

Thus, for any given supply curve, we must be careful to specify exactly what

time period we are thinking of and, consequently, what factors we are holding constant and what factors we are allowing to change.

SHAPE OF THE SUPPLY CURVE

Considerations of the time period are also important with respect to our second problem—explaining the upward (northeasterly) slope of the supply curve—for the shape of the supply curve will also be affected by what factors are being held constant and what time period is envisaged.

Now the main *general* reason that the supply curve goes in this northeasterly direction is that costs tend to rise as the production of any particular commodity is increased. This is most easy to see in short-run situations. Each farmer can expand production to some degree by adding more laborers, but basically he will have fixed quantities of land, apple trees, buildings, and other capital at his disposal. Thus, it will become increasingly difficult to increase apple production—i.e., eventually costs will start to go up.

Actually, what we are describing here is a version of another famous tool of the economist: the *law of diminishing returns*.

The law of diminishing returns *states that, in the production of any commodity, as we add more units of one factor of production (the "variable" factor) to a given quantity of other factors of production (the "fixed" factors), the addition to total product with each subsequent unit of the variable factor will eventually begin to diminish.*

To put it in terms of short-run apple production: as we hire more labor to increase apple production from a fixed amount of orchard land, we will find eventually that the added number of apples we get from each extra laborer begins to diminish. If the laborers come at a fixed wage, this means, in turn, that the *added cost* of getting apples will rise higher and higher the more apples we try to produce.[4]

What we have just said should help to explain why costs generally rise as a firm expands production in the short run. But how is this fact connected with the shape of the supply curve? The answer, essentially, is that if costs rise with output, business firms will be willing to expand output only at higher prices. If they did not get higher prices and still went ahead to expand output, they would find that the additional output cost them more than the revenues it brought in. It is only at the higher price that the expansion of output will prove to be profitable.

We have here an example of the workings of Adam Smith's principle of self-interest. The businessman will expand production at higher prices because it is in *his* interest to do so. When all businessmen in an industry behave this way, they will create an upward-sloping supply curve as shown in Figure 2-4.

These comments, of course, are about the short run. In the long run, the shape of the supply curve is somewhat more difficult to explain, though even in the long run the normal shape will still be upward-sloping in a northeasterly direction. The main difference will be that the rise in costs will be less steep. This, in turn, reflects the fact that, in the long run, there are many different ways of expanding output—buying more land,

planting more trees, purchasing new farm machinery and buildings. To put it generally: the long-run supply curve for a firm and industry will usually rise less steeply than the short-run supply curve for that same firm or industry.

THE "LAW" OF SUPPLY AND DEMAND

We have explained the general meaning and shape of both the demand and the supply curves. Now we are in a position to combine them. In Figure 2-5, we have put the demand curve for apples and the supply curve for apples in one diagram. With the aid of this diagram, we shall now be able to determine the equilib-

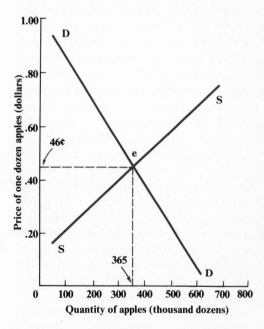

Figure 2-5.

Supply and demand are in equilibrium at point *e*, where the price of a dozen apples is 46¢ and the quantity bought and sold is 365 thousand dozens.

---

4. We shall return to the law of diminishing returns in chapter 6 and to its relation to the supply curve in Part Three, especially chapters 19 and 20.

rium market price of apples and the quantity of apples that will be bought and sold. This determination of the price and quantity of a particular product is what the so-called *law of supply and demand* is all about.

Needless to say, it seems likely that the key point will be where the two curves intersect. And, indeed, it is at this point that the equilibrium price and quantity are determined. In our diagram, the market price will be 46¢ a dozen and the equilibrium quantity produced will be 365 thousand dozens.

The deeper question is: Why is this intersection point significant? Why couldn't the price be somewhere else?

The answer to this, in essence, is that it is only at this particular price (46¢) that the quantity of apples consumers are demanding and the quantity of apples producers are willing to supply are exactly equal; i.e., supply = demand. At any other price, either the quantity supplied will be greater than the quantity demanded—in which case producers will be accumulating large quantities of unwanted and unsold apples; *or* the quantity demanded will be greater than the quantity supplied—in which case buyers will be clamoring for apples that producers simply do not have for sale. It is clear that neither of these alternatives could last long. If producers were accumulating unwanted apples, sooner or later they would decide to cut back on the production of apples. If, conversely, buyers kept asking for nonexistent apples, producers would sooner or later get the idea that it was time to raise prices and expand apple production.

It is only at this intersection point that these problems cannot arise. There is no accumulation of unsold apples; there are no queues of buyers trying to get apples that don't exist. We have then an equilibrium price—a price that will stay put unless some new fundamental change occurs—and this is the price at which supply and demand are equated.

CONSUMER SOVEREIGNTY— A SIMPLIFIED EXAMPLE

Our analysis so far has shown how the price and quantity of a particular commodity are determined in a market economy, all other things equal. This is an important step in understanding how such a decentralized, private economy can function.

Now, however, let us use these tools to go a step further. We want to show how a market economy makes some of those fundamental economic choices which all societies must face. One of those central choice problems, we recall, was whether to locate at point *A* (lots of steel; little food) or at point *B* (little steel; lots of food) on our production-possibility curve.

Now in a market economy, as Adam Smith understood, the essence of the process is that producers will find it in their own self-interest to produce what is socially desirable. In particular, they will adjust their production of different commodities so that they are in accord with consumer desires. This is what is meant by the concept of *consumer sovereignty*. If the economy is at point *A*, and consumers prefer to be at *B*, the market will operate to shift production in the desired direction.

With our newly acquired supply and demand curves, we can give a bit more definition to this process. Let us imagine that we are dealing with two commodities. Apples will be our food commodity; our steel commodity will be, say, washing machines.

Now let us imagine that, for whatever reason, there is a shift in consumer desires from washing machines to apples. The example is a bit farfetched, but the principle is clear enough: consumer preferences have changed. How is this reflected through the market in changed production of these two commodities?

The general nature of the answer is given in our two diagrams, Figure 2-6 (*a* and *b*). The increased demand for apples has resulted in an upward shift of the demand curve for apples. The decreased demand for washing machines has resulted in a downward shift in the demand curve for washing machines. The consequences of these shifts according to our diagrams are:

(1) a greater production of apples at a higher price,
(2) a lesser production of washing machines at a lower price.

Consumer preferences have shifted from washing machines to apples, and the result has been an increased production of apples and a decreased production of washing machines, and this without any planning or governmental intervention, but solely through the laws of supply and demand working in the marketplace.

Now this example is a first approximation, and it should be taken as suggestive rather than definitive. Actually, it wasn't until late in the nineteenth century, a hundred years after Adam Smith wrote, that economists began to pin down the full implications of a market economy. If we think about our circular flow diagrams of this chapter and chapter 1, we shall soon realize that it isn't possible to separate Product Markets (apples, washing machines, food, steel, etc.) from Factor

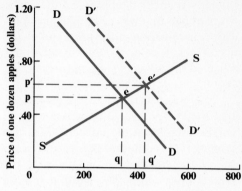

(a) **Quantity of apples (thousand dozens)**

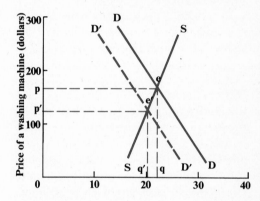

(b) **Quantity of washing machines (thousands)**

Figure 2-6.

These diagrams represent a simplified example of how consumer sovereignty operating through the supply-and-demand mechanism can alter the composition of output in a market economy. In particular, a shift in demand from washing machines to apples has led to an increased production of apples and a decreased production of washing machines. This new equilibrium would correspond to a new point on the society's production-possibility curve.

Markets (labor, orchard land, steel mines, machinery, etc.). What happens anywhere in the flow is likely to have effects elsewhere in the system. To put it another way: in order to follow through any significant change in an economy—even a shift in tastes involving apples and washing machines—we ultimately have to inspect the whole system at once.

Though we shall have to wait until later chapters to achieve this larger objective, our present analysis already tells us a great deal about the workings of a market economy. In particular, we have suggested some key links between the producers on the one hand and the consumers on the other. Why is it that in a pure market economy, producers produce the goods that consumers want? Answer: Because the market, working through the supply-and-demand apparatus, will make it profitable—in their self-interest—for them to do so.

THE MARKET AND THE PUBLIC INTEREST

The market economy, then, is a possible system. Is it also, as Adam Smith was inclined to believe, the *best* possible system?

The answer, as one might expect, is very complicated and subject to much disagreement among the experts. In a preliminary way, however, we can indicate at least two lines of argument that must affect all serious thinking about the subject.

The first line of argument really stems from the kind of analysis we have been presenting in this chapter. It emphasizes the essential viability of the market system. It says in effect: consider how beautifully the supply and demand apparatus works, how remarkable it is that, without governmental intervention or planning or forethought, all these thousands of individual decisions nevertheless do lead to such desirable social results.

This is in the full tradition of classical economic thought.

A second line of argument leads in quite a different direction. It stresses that there are important areas of economic life where competition and markets do not produce the results we want. To take one simple example: the analysis in this chapter has not even touched on the problem of unemployment. Essentially, in our washing machines and apples example we were assuming a full-employment economy. But we do know that unemployment can exist. Will the market economy be able to solve that problem? The critics would tend to be pessimistic. They would also be pessimistic about the way market economies deal with dozens of other problems: inflation, poverty, income distribution, pollution, and waste. They would point out that Adam Smith gravely underestimated the divergence between private and social interest.

History is partly on each side. We have already shown that the powerful Industrial Revolution of the early eighteenth and nineteenth centuries was born at a time when the market system was triumphing over earlier forms of economic organization. We shall also show in the next chapter how market elements keep intruding even in highly planned socialist economies. On the other hand, it is true historically and it is true today that a *pure* market economy has never been a reality. In one way or another, citizens of this and every country in the world have asked that governments step in to change this or that aspect of the functionings of a price-and-market mechanism. In the 1970s, such requests are by no means abating.

Thus, the crucial question, as far as the public interest is concerned, is not whether there should be *any* intervention—that question has really been settled by history—but what *degree* of intervention should be permitted. This question is not black and white, and it is definitely not easy.

AN EXAMPLE OF A MARKET

This chapter has dealt with rather large abstract issues. But markets can also exist on a very small scale. We therefore end the chapter with a reading on a market in Guatemala. The author, Sol Tax, brings out the fact that supply and demand can work in a daily, practical way; he also shows a number of important assumptions that underlie the notion of market competition.

PENNY CAPITALISM: A Guatemalan Indian Market

SOL TAX

The Indians of Panajachel, and the people among whom they live and with whom they do almost all of their business, are part of what may be characterized as *a money economy organized in single households as both consumption and production units, with a strongly developed market which tends to be perfectly competitive.*

In the market place, frequently the central plaza of the town, vendors spread their wares and buyers come to purchase them. Almost every town has its market day once or twice a week; the larger towns have them daily. The people who have produce to sell know where and when the markets are held, and they make their choice of markets in accordance with their particular circumstances. They know that if they go to a farther market, they will—other factors being equal—get better prices for

"Penny Capitalism: A Guatemalan Indian Market," by Sol Tax in *Smithsonian Institution Institute of Social Anthropology, Publication No. 16.* Reprinted by permission of the publisher. Excerpts from pp. 13–18.

their goods, which are worth more the farther from their source they are, but they may prefer to spend less time in travel and get a smaller price. Or the men may go to far markets with large quantities while the women go to sell in the local markets. Likewise, the purchasers of goods make a choice of markets according to what they want to buy and how much time they are willing to spend to get it more cheaply and closer to its source. Everybody in the region I have studied knows that Tecpán is the place to buy lime, that bananas are cheaper in Atitlán, that pitch pine and pigs are cheaper in Chichicastenango. If one wants a few ounces of lime for the weekly cooking of corn, he will not go to Tecpán for it. But if he wants a hundred pounds for the building of a house, it may pay him to take the journey. Nobody will normally take a day's trip to Chichicastenango for a few cents' worth of pitch pine, but if a person wants to buy a little pig or two for fattening, it will pay him to go there.

This basic knowledge about markets is known even to a child, and it is consistent-

ly acted upon when conditions permit.

People arrive at market at nine or ten in the morning and take their usual places, generally arranged so that vendors of the same product sit one next to the other. The vendor unloads his wares, arranges them on a mat or table in front of him, and waits for the customers. A prospective buyer comes up and looks over his tomatoes, for example, touching them at will. He asks how much they are. "Two cents a pound." The buyer offers a cent a pound and the merchant shakes his head. The buyer passes on, presumably to look for tomatoes elsewhere. He does not return. The same happens with several other prospective customers. The tomatoes are not selling at 2¢ a pound. Perhaps one of the buyers, when that price is mentioned, remarks that he is asking too much, that others are selling tomatoes for less. Even if this does not happen, the vendor after an hour may notice that he is selling no tomatoes at his price. Another customer comes. "How much are the tomatoes?" "Two cents." "One cent," says the buyer.

"No; my bottom price is 1½¢." The customer takes some at that price. The next customer perhaps counters the 2¢ proposal with an offer of 1½¢. "Take them," says the merchant.

Sometimes a merchant finds that he is the only one who happens to be selling tomatoes in this particular market this particular day. Seeing this, he perhaps asks 4¢ a pound. He soon finds, let us say, that despite his fortunate position, people prefer to do without than to pay more than 2¢ a pound. And eventually his price comes down to that. Or he may unluckily discover that everybody has the intention of selling tomatoes in this market this day; and our merchant who may have bought these tomatoes the day before in a market near the tomato-producing area for 1¢ a pound, may find himself unloading at half that price. Tomatoes are highly perishable, so the factor of chance is important. With respect to nonperishable items, however, there is still fluctuation in price with the supply and demand of the particular time and place, since if supply is short people will pay a little more to get what they want when they want it, while if supply is long a merchant will reduce his price at least to the point where the loss will be no greater than the value of the time spent in repeating a trip to market. Generally speaking, however, and particularly with respect to less perishable items, prices are established over longer periods of time in all of the market places together; hence there tends to

be a competitive market. The price itself of course varies with the product, the season, the distance of the market from the center of its production, and so on. Beyond such accidental factors as the toughness and business acumen of the merchant and upon his immediate financial and other circumstances (a sick child at home may cause a vendor who needs money quickly to accept a lower price and possibly depress the whole market), prices are fixed in accord with the usual ways of the market.

* * *

This rather impressionistic description suggests that the regional market—whether thought of in a general or abstract sense, or as the market place—may be characterized as perfectly competitive insofar as it tends to be (*a*) atomistic, (*b*) open, (*c*) free, and (*d*) based on "rational" behavior.

(*a*) It is atomistic, of course, in that the buyers and sellers are small (no one of them able significantly to affect the market) and act independently of one another. Characteristically, a number of small vendors of identical merchandise—standard bunches of onions, or peanuts sold by the pound, for examples—sit side by side in the market place, competing for the money of a large number of equally small and independent buyers who appear during the space of a few hours to purchase the same merchandise either for consumption or for resale. Likewise, an employer is able to choose among a number of potential workers, indepen-

dent of one another; and each worker characteristically has a choice of employers, none of whom is so large as to affect the wage rates substantially more than the others.

(*b*) It is open in that there is no barrier to new competitors entering or old ones leaving the market. I have never heard even a suggestion of an attitude that vendors or classes of vendors ought to be excluded from a market, much less any organized effort to do so.

(*c*) The market is relatively very free in that prices are set by the interplay of supply and demand with almost no authoritarian regulation. There is occasional interference with the price mechanism. Once during the period of this study the Government controlled the price, and to some degree the distribution, of corn when an extraordinarily short supply produced a crisis. The case emphasizes the rarity of such interference.

(*d*) Most economic behavior in the Indian economy of this region of Guatemala is generally highly "rational." The Indians may of course be wrong in their "estimates," but they weigh choices in accordance with the economic principle. Even gift exchange (in marriage, for example) and ceremonial disposition of goods and services are notoriously rationally oriented, with the cost carefully counted and often resulting from compromises of conflicting interests.

Even though the regional economy lacks firms, I find it hard to imagine a people more endowed with the spirit of business enterprise than the Indians (and Ladinos) that I know best. There is probably no Panajachel Indian over the age of ten who has not calculated a way to make money with his available resources. It is therefore | easy to go from descriptions of Panajachel to the writings of classical economists, for (as Adam Smith says): "Every individual is continually exerting himself to find out the most advantageous employment for whatever capital he can command." | The ethic of the community seems admirably suited to such an economy. There is frank admission that wealth is good. It is money that makes possible the fulfillment of recognized duties to the community and to one's family.

SUMMARY

A *market economy* is one in which the crucial economic decisions and choices are made in a decentralized fashion, by private individuals, operating through a price and market mechanism. Historically, the self-regulating market economy is a modern rather than an ancient invention, involving rather special assumptions such as the treatment of land and labor as commodities. This kind of economy—though never in a *pure* form—developed considerably at the time of the English Industrial Revolution. Most of the leading British economists of the day, especially Adam Smith, stressed the virtues of limiting government intervention in economic life so that the market, working through private self-interest, could bring benefits to society at large.

With modern analysis, we can give much sharper expression to Smith's views using such tools as *supply* and *demand curves*.

A demand curve for a product shows the quantities of the product that consumers are willing to buy over a given period of time at different prices. A supply curve shows the amounts of the commodity that producers are willing to sell over a given period of time at different prices. Both curves are drawn under certain important *ceteris paribus* or "other

things equal" assumptions. In the case of the supply curve, it is particularly important to notice the element of time, whether short run or long run, since, generally, costs will rise more steeply (and hence the supply curve will rise more steeply) in the short run than in the long run. The reason is that many of a firm's factors of production are fixed in the short run; thus, the *law of diminishing returns* comes into play.

Equilibrium price and quantity are determined in a market economy where supply and demand curves intersect. This is the so-called *law of supply and demand*, a law valid only under the special conditions of pure competition.

Using supply and demand curves, we can illustrate in a general way how consumer preferences are carried through the price system to affect the kinds of goods produced in the economy. If consumers want more apples and fewer washing machines in a market economy, supply and demand will work to produce this general result.

To prove that the market economy is a "possible" economy is one thing; to prove that it is the "best possible" economy is another. Economic analysis indicates points on both sides, as does historical experience. History does strongly suggest, however, that the issue is (and was) never one of a *pure* market economy, but rather one of what *degree* of government intervention should be allowed or encouraged.

QUESTIONS FOR DISCUSSION

1. In the thirteenth century St. Thomas Aquinas, the great Catholic philosopher, wrote: "To sell a thing for more than its worth or to buy it for less than its worth, is in itself unjust and unlawful." Would you consider this point of view to be consistent or inconsistent with the assumptions of a "market economy"? Why?

2. Adam Smith was aware that businessmen, given the chance, might meet together and conspire against the consumer. In view of this danger, can you see why the "invisible hand," if it works at all, will only do so in an economy with substantial competition?

3. The choice of methods of producing different commodities is not only a technological but also an economic question. Discuss.

4. What does the phrase "other things equal" mean when applied to the ordinary consumer demand curve?

5. Suppose that there is an invention that substantially lowers the costs of producing a certain commodity. What general effect would this invention have on the supply curve of that commodity? What would be the resulting effect on the equilibrium price and quantity produced of the commodity in question?

6. Discuss the role of the time period of adjustment in analyzing producers' responses to changes in market prices. Might consumer responses to different prices (as shown by the demand curve) also be affected by the length of the time period under consideration?

7. "When some people are very rich and others are very poor, the whole notion of 'consumer sovereignty' in a market economy is misleading and prejudicial." Discuss some of the issues raised by this statement.

SUGGESTED READING

Dorfman, Robert. *Prices and Markets.* Englewood Cliffs, N.J.: Prentice-Hall, 1967, chaps. 1–5.

Heilbroner, Robert L. *The Worldly Philosophers.* New York: Simon & Schuster, 1953, chap. 3.

Leftwich, Richard H. *The Price System and Resource Allocation.* 3rd ed. New York: Holt, Rinehart & Winston, 1966, chaps. 1–9, 13.

Marshall, Alfred. *Principles of Economics.* 8th ed. New York: Macmillan Co., 1948, Book V.

Samuelson, Paul A. *Readings in Economics.* 6th ed. New York: McGraw-Hill, 1970, readings 10, 11.

Smith, Adam. *The Wealth of Nations.* Modern Library Ed. New York: Random House, 1937.

3
Marx, The Command Economy, Socialism

In the last chapter, we said that a *pure* market economy was something of an abstraction, not to be encountered in its pristine form in the real world. Much the same can be said of its opposite: the *centrally planned economy* or the *command economy*, as it is sometimes called. Even in its closest approximation (the economy of the Soviet Union), important elements of a market system intrude—indeed with increasing frequency in recent years.

It is clear, however, that the study of central planning is of great importance to the serious student of modern economics. For the mechanism of economic planning is in wide use in the present-day world. Elements of this mechanism appear in our own economy. In Western Europe, even in countries where the basic system is privately organized, planning is often an explicit part of public policy. Great Britain's Labour Party has limited aspirations to socialism; France has developed an interesting mix of the public and private sectors through what she calls "indicative planning"; neutralist Yugoslavia, as we shall see in a moment, has experimented with "market socialism."

Furthermore, as everyone who follows the newspapers must be fully aware, there is a large fraction of the world's population who regard private enterprise and the market system with suspicion and, indeed, outright hostility. Communism in all its varieties puts a considerable emphasis on governmental action, centralization of decision, high-level planning of fundamental economic choices. By referring to some of these systems as *command economies*, we emphasize the fact that the decision-making process often goes not from individual consumers to individual producers but from central planning boards or commissions to enterprises that are either State-owned or highly regulated by the State.

Consumer sovereignty largely gives way to the collective preferences of the central planners. It is this fundamentally different approach to economic problems that we shall consider in this chapter.

THE MARXIAN CRITICISMS

In discussing the market economy, we went back to Adam Smith. In discussing the great planned economies of the modern world, we must go back to another early economist, the controversial Karl Marx (1818–1883). In most of these countries, Marx is regarded as the true founder of scientific economic thought.

Actually, if we go to Marx in the hope of finding a detailed blueprint of how a planned economy should work, we shall be largely disappointed. Marx gave comparatively little attention to this important problem. What he did do was two rather different things. First, he provided a massive critique of the working of the capitalistic market economy. (The Marxian Critique of Capitalism is the subject of our first Great Debate, pp. 55–77). Second, he provided a revolutionary ideology that has proved very vigorous historically in leading to the overthrow of established economic systems and the installation of highly centralized economies.

Karl Marx, the man, was an activist and revolutionary. He took part in the Communist League of 1848 and summoned his followers to action with ringing phrases in his *Communist Manifesto*. But he was also a scholar—intense, very well read, sometimes even pedantic. He was born in Germany, but he spent the latter part of his life in England working long hours each day in the British Museum in London. His major work, called *Capital,* is a vast document of literally thousands of pages, of which he was able to complete

only the first volume (1867) in his lifetime. The remaining volumes were published posthumously under the editorship of various of his followers, especially Friedrich Engels. Engels played a very important role in Marx's life, sustaining him spiritually and, at times, financially. The *Communist Manifesto* was actually a joint product of Marx and Engels, though Marx was the guiding light in the collaboration and clearly had the superior mind of the two.

Marx's first achievement was, as I have said, of a negative kind: to present a number of harsh criticisms of the capitalistic system. If he had perused the discussion of a market economy in our last chapter, he would have scoffed at its shortcomings as a description of historical reality. One objection he certainly would have made was that there was no reference at all to the different classes of society; in particular, that there was no reference to what Marx considered a fundamental feature of capitalism—the conflict between the capitalist class and the laboring class, between the owners of factories and machines and the dispossessed proletariat. For Marx, this *class conflict* was an absolutely central characteristic of capitalism and, indeed, he tended to view all past history as evidence of one kind of class conflict or another. To write about the beauties of supply and demand and how they reflected consumer preferences, but to ignore the struggle between the wealthy capitalists and the downtrodden laborers—this, in Marx's eyes, would be to shut out the fundamental facts of the real world.

Another objection he would have made was that we had failed to recognize the importance of *monopoly* elements in the price system. Our supply curve, we recall, was drawn on the assumption that producers were pure competitors or price-takers; i.e., each firm was too small to have any appreciable direct effect on the price of its product. As far as Marx was concerned, however, the result of free markets in the modern industrial and commercial world would almost certainly be that big, monopolizing firms would swallow up the small, individual producers. In his view, it was not the small firm but the giant industrial corporation that was characteristic of capitalism, particularly in its advanced stages. Indeed, he believed that these large firms would come to control not only the economies but to a great degree the governments of capitalistic countries. In such a world, the notion of producers responding meekly to the will and wishes of consumers would be a mockery.

Finally, he would have objected, as we ourselves recognized, that our description of a market economy took no account of the *unemployment* problem. For Marx, this would have meant living in a fairy-tale world. In his theoretical structure, unemployment was not an accidental but an intrinsic feature of a capitalist economy. One reason for this was that, in a capitalistic economy, productive capacity regularly tended to outrun consumption: there was a constant tendency to overproduction and economic crisis. Another reason for unemployment was that capitalists had to find some way to keep wages down. The way they chose, according to Marx, was to introduce machinery in place of labor whenever wages started to rise. This machinery displaced the laborers; consequently, there was serious general unemployment. If any laborer asked for a raise, his employer simply took him to the factory window and showed him the line of workers who had no jobs at all, a crude but effective method of settling wage disputes! In terms of our production-possibility curve, Marx would have said that a market economy charac-

CULVER PICTURES

Karl Marx (1818-1883). Marx emphasized the dominating role of economic factors in social and political life. He produced the most massive critique of capitalism ever written.

teristically operated at some point, *UE*, inside the production frontier (see Figure 1-6, p. 20). Indeed, Marx argued that this problem would get worse and worse as time went on. Capitalism would be subject to great crises and depressions. These crises would, in fact, do much to make the Communist revolution inevitable.

History has shown that most of these criticisms of a capitalistic market economy were seriously overstated. We would live in a fairy-tale world far more fanciful than the one that Marx condemned if we were to use Marxian analysis as a guide to what actually happens in countries where, as in the United States, heavy reliance is placed on the market mechanism. However, it would be just as misleading to think that there is no truth whatever in the Marxian criticisms. There

51

clearly are numerous inequities in the distribution of wealth, income, and power in a completely unregulated market economy. The large industrial corporation with considerable influence over its markets is a substantial feature of modern life. And as far as the displacement of labor by machines is concerned, what workingman in an advanced industrial economy has not wondered at some time or other whether his job may not give way to automation and the computer? The point is that Marx did have a number of significant specific insights into the workings of the capitalistic system. Where he went wrong was in missing the possibilities of improvement and evolutionary change that such systems have proved capable of carrying forward. Indeed, it may well be that the most serious flaws of capitalism are due not to its capitalistic but to its *industrial* character. The ecological and environmental costs of capitalism *or* socialism are drawing deep criticisms in both the West and the Soviet Union in the 1970s.

The second major aspect of Marx's thought that concerns us is his role as revolutionary. Marx was (and still is) the spiritual leader of communism, and his writings have served as inspiration for the revolutions that have created the major planned economies of the modern world.

Now in a sense, the most interesting and rather surprising point to be made in this connection is that the Marxist revolutions that have led to Communist governments have not been altogether in accord with Marx's own theory. Toward the end of his life, Marx once commented, "I am not a Marxist"; and, indeed, if he had seen some of the interpretations his doctrines have been subjected to since, he might have made the point even more emphatically. The problem is essentially this—Marx argued that the weaknesses in capitalism we have just been describing would cause the eventual collapse of the system after capitalistic evolution had run its full course. In theory, the revolution comes at, or toward, the end of the capitalist phase. In practice, the revolutions have not come in the advanced capitalistic countries but rather in poor, relatively backward countries that have scarcely had time to go through the capitalistic stage. Russia, in 1917, although she had made some economic progress by that time, was economically still far behind the advanced capitalistic countries of Western Europe and North America. The Chinese claim to be orthodox Marxists, yet they had their revolution in the 1940s before they could truly be said to have had any experience at all with modern industrial capitalism.

All this proves that Marx's theory was far from accurate in predicting when his own revolutions would occur. What happened, in effect, was that his doctrines were simply adjusted to the practical necessities of the situations at hand. In Russia, for example, there was Lenin, the great leader of the Revolution. Lenin had little time to worry about whether or not Russia was in the appropriate stage of development for the collapse of capitalism to occur. He was much more interested in the strategy of the Revolution itself. Another example is Stalin. Stalin was fully aware that Russia in the 1920s was not an economically advanced country. On the contrary, he emphasized her need to catch up with the advanced countries and therefore proceeded to sacrifice everything to rapid industrialization. With him, communism became not the stage that follows modern development, but rather an ideology for promoting forced-draft industrialization and growth.

And the reinterpretation goes on today. The post-Stalin leadership in Russia seems to have a somewhat more flexible view of economic organization than did its predecessors. The Chinese, however, seem to have embraced a particularly all-enveloping form of communism according to the precepts of Chairman Mao; to them, of course, the new breed of Russian leaders are crass revisionists.

Indeed, the main common bond we can find in all these manifestations of Marxism is a built-in predilection for a much higher degree of centralization and economic planning than in the major economies of the Western world. This takes us from the realm of ideology to the realm of economic organization and practice.

THE FUNCTIONING OF A COMMAND ECONOMY

A centralized command economy must face the same fundamental economic problems as a decentralized market economy. Let us first say a few words about the general functioning of such an economy. Then let us make some specific comments about the actual experience of planning in the Soviet Union.

In the command economy, it is not the market but the central government or some branch of the central government that makes the basic decisions concerning the society's production targets, its allocation of resources, its distribution of income, and its desired rate of growth. In the pure command economy, the State would normally possess ownership of all the means of production and most of the property in the economy. It would determine the incomes of different kinds of labor and the salaries of production managers, doctors, artists, and bureaucrats. It would determine the planned outputs of all the different productive enterprises in

the economy and the allocation of resources to each. In terms of our earlier examples, it would set, and attempt to secure fulfillment of, targets for food production and steel production, for the output of apples and the output of washing machines.

Now such a task, if carried through into every single corner of a modern economy, would be hopelessly complex and really beyond the capabilities of any group of planners, however sophisticated. Consequently, in most real-life command economies, at least some of these decisions are decentralized either to lower levels of authority or, in some cases, to what is a rough facsimile of a price-and-market mechanism. It is frequently the case that a command economy will direct its main planning energies to certain broad areas of the economy, or to certain particular targets that, for some reason, have special priority in the minds of the central planners.

Even when the task is limited in this fashion, it still involves a number of difficult and overlapping problems. These include problems of organization, coordination, efficiency, incentives, and basic goals.

(1) **Organization.** The first and most obvious requirement of a command economy is a bureaucratic organization that makes it possible for anything like effective planning to proceed. It is one thing to make decisions about what the pattern of economic activity in the society should be and another to see that these are carried out.

There must be, first, an organizational chain of command that makes it possible to transmit the decisions, targets, and directives of the central body down *through the system to the level of the actual production units in the economy. There must be, also, an organizational structure that permits information and data from the production units to rise up through the system to furnish the ultimate decision-makers with the knowledge required for any kind of intelligent planning. It should be clear that many countries do not possess, or could build up only very slowly, the massive administrative mechanism necessary to carry out these vital functions. Even under the best of circumstances, there is a tremendous burden of bureaucracy to carry in the command economy, which is at least partially avoided in a more decentralized system.*

(2) **Coordination.** It is not enough that targets and directives be quickly communicated through the system; they must also be economically consistent. There is a serious problem of coordination in any command economy, arising from the interdependent nature of the modern industrial economy.

The problem may be put in terms of what economists refer to as input-output analysis.[1] *The outputs of one industry in the economy can be thought of as inputs into some other industry in the economy. Machines are necessary to produce steel, but steel is necessary to produce machines. Actually, steel output will be used as inputs into literally hundreds of other industries in the economy: machines, tractors, automobiles, typewriters, building construction, and so on. And, indeed, a modern economy is an infinitely complex network of interdependence in which the production of one sector depends upon the inputs it can receive from a host of other sectors, while its own output will simultaneously be feeding back inputs into these and still other sectors. The point*

is that one cannot simply set a target for industry A and then, independently, *set targets for industries B, C, and D. One must be sure that there is sufficient production of A, so that the input requirements of B, C, and D are met, and vice versa. With the large number of industries involved and their intricate interconnections, the coordination problem facing a command economy is necessarily extremely complex.*

(3) **Efficiency.** Even consistency is not sufficient, however; for it is necessary or at least desirable that a command economy be *efficient*—that is, that it employ its scarce resources in such a way that it gets as much output as possible from them.

The subject of economic efficiency is a very large one that we shall be taking up in detail later on.[2] Suffice it to say here that a market economy is provided with some rough guidelines for efficient use of its resources, since the prices of the factors of production—land, labor, capital goods—will reflect their relative scarcities; hence it will be profitable for firms to economize on the use of particularly scarce (therefore expensive) productive factors. In a command economy, difficulties may arise in this area, particularly if there is an aversion to using anything that may look like "capitalistic" market pricing. Historically, indeed, this has been a fairly serious problem for many actual command or near-command economies.

(4) **Incentive.** In the command economy—as, indeed, in any economy— the workers, managers, and executives, not the central planners, produce the goods.

Continued on p. 78

---

1. For the standard reference on input-output analysis, see Wassily W. Leontief, *Structure of the American Economy, 1919–1939* (New York: Oxford University Press, 1951).

2. See chapters 17 and 22.

GREAT DEBATE ONE: THE MARXIAN CRITIQUE OF CAPITALISM

Without question one of the greatest debates among economists (and not economists alone) over the past century has been over the validity of Karl Marx's analysis of the evolution of capitalism. Was Marx right or was he wrong? Have his insights been helpful or basically misleading? Did he point to the future or simply to a blind alley?

The following group of articles brings out most of the important issues on which this debate has focussed. Each of these articles is written by an outstanding economist and, although these are all Western economists, the Marxian viewpoint is fully represented.

Where great men differ, each of us has no alternative but to come to his own individual conclusions. Hopefully the following pages will give the reader a useful framework for reaching an informed opinion about a matter that is still of considerable economic and political importance.

A. THE COMMUNIST MANIFESTO

The following reading is excerpted from one of the most famous documents in the Marxian literature, "The Communist Manifesto." This document was written jointly by Karl Marx and Friedrich Engels in 1848, though Engels in a later introduction points out that "the fundamental proposition which forms its nucleus belongs to Marx." Although no single writing of Marx could cover the full range of his thought, the following excerpts bring out a number of the most important points in the Marxian liturgy. The reader should notice these related themes: (1) the view that the

social and political conditions of a society are largely determined by its economic basis of production; (2) the view that history is a long story of class struggles; (3) the prediction that, under capitalism, economic classes will become more and more polarized into two contending groups—the bourgeoisie and the proletariat; (4) the related prediction that while small businessmen and others in the middle class will drop into the proletariat, the bigger capitalists will carry out production in large-scale factories, in effect getting bigger and bigger; (5) the view that there will be a strong tendency for the immiserization of the working-class proletarians over time; and (6) the analysis of capitalism in terms of internal contradictions, such as its tendency to overproduce and thus to need constantly expanding markets.

MANIFESTO OF THE COMMUNIST PARTY

KARL MARX

The history of all hitherto existing society is the history of class struggles.

Freeman and slave, patrician and plebeian, lord and serf, guild-master and journeyman, in a word, oppressor and oppressed, stood in constant opposition to one another, carried on uninterrupted, now hidden, now open fight, a fight that each time ended, either in a revolutionary re-constitution of society at large, or in the common ruin of the contending classes.

In the earlier epochs of history we find almost everywhere a complicated arrangement of society into

Excerpted from Karl Marx, "Manifesto of the Communist Party," reprinted in Capital and Other Writings of Karl Marx, edited by Max Eastman (New York: Modern Library, Random House, 1932), pp. 321–34.

various orders, a manifold gradation of social rank. In ancient Rome we have patricians, knights, plebeians, slaves; in the middle ages, feudal lords, vassals, guild-masters, journeymen, apprentices, serfs; in almost all of these classes, again, subordinate gradations.

The modern bourgeois society that has sprouted from the ruins of feudal society, has not done away with class antagonisms. It has but established new classes, new conditions of oppression, new forms of struggle in place of the old ones.

Our epoch, the epoch of the bourgeoisie, possesses, however, this distinctive feature; it has simplified the class antagonisms. Society as a whole is more and more splitting up into two great hostile camps, into two great classes directly facing each other: Bourgeoisie and Proletariat.

The bourgeoisie, historically, has played a most revolutionary part.

The bourgeoisie, wherever it has got the upper hand, has put an end to all feudal, patriarchal, idyllic relations. It has pitilessly torn asunder the motley feudal ties that bound man to his "natural superiors," and has left no other nexus between man and man than naked self-interest, than callous "cash payment." It has drowned the most heavenly ecstasies of religious fervor, of chivalrous enthusiasm, of Philistine sentimentalism, in the icy water of egotistical calculation. It has resolved personal worth into exchange value, and in place of the numberless indefeasible chartered freedoms, has set up that single, unconscionable freedom — Free Trade. In one word, for exploitation, veiled by religious and political illusions, it has substituted naked, shameless, direct, brutal exploitation.

The bourgeoisie cannot exist without constantly revolutionizing the instruments of production, and thereby the relations of production, and with them the whole relations of society. Conservation of the old modes of production in unaltered form was, on the contrary, the first condition of existence for all earlier industrial classes. Constant revolutionizing of production, uninterrupted disturbance of all social conditions, everlasting uncertainty and agitation distinguish the bourgeois epoch from all earlier ones. All fixed, fast frozen relations, with their train of ancient and venerable prejudices and opinions, are swept away, all new formed ones become antiquated before they can ossify. All that is solid melts into the air, all that is holy is profaned, and man is at last compelled to face with sober senses, his real conditions of life, and his relations with his kind.

The need of a constantly expanding market for its products chases the bourgeoisie over the whole surface of the globe. It must nestle everywhere, settle everywhere, establish connections everywhere.

The bourgeoisie has subjected the country to the rule of the towns. It has created enormous cities, has greatly increased the urban population as compared with the rural, and has thus rescued a considerable part of the population from the idiocy of rural life. Just as it has made the country dependent on the towns, so it has made barbarian and semibarbarian countries dependent on civilized ones, nations of peasants on nations of bourgeois, the East on the West.

The bourgeoisie keeps more and more doing away with the scattered state of the population, of the means of production, and of property. It has agglomerated population, centralized means of production, and has concentrated property in a few hands. The necessary consequence of this was political centralization. Independent, or but loosely connected provinces, with separate interests, laws, governments, and systems of taxation, became lumped together in one nation, with one government, one code of laws, one national class interest, one frontier, and one customs tariff.

The bourgeoisie, during its rule of scarce one hundred years, has created more massive and more colossal productive forces than have all preceding generations together. Subjection of Nature's forces to man, machinery, application of chemistry to industry and agriculture, steam-navigation, railways, electric telegraphs, clearing of whole continents for cultivation, canalization of rivers, whole populations conjured out of the ground—what earlier century had even a presentiment that such productive forces slumbered in the lap of social labor?

We see then: the means of production and of exchange on whose foundation the bourgeoisie built itself up, were generated in feudal society. At a certain stage in the development of these means of production and of exchange, the conditions under which feudal society produced and exchanged, the feudal organization of agriculture and manufacturing industry, in one word, the feudal relations of property became no longer compatible with the already developed productive forces; they became so many fetters. They had to burst asunder; they were burst asunder.

Into their places stepped free competition, accompanied by social and political constitution adapted to it, and by economical and political sway of the bourgeois class.

A similar movement is going on before our own eyes. Modern bourgeois society with its relations of production, of exchange and of property, a society that has conjured up such gigantic means of production and of exchange, is like the sorcerer, who is no longer able to control the powers of the nether world whom he has called up by his spells. For many a decade past, the history of industry and commerce is but the history of the revolt of modern productive forces against modern conditions of production, against the property relations that are the conditions for the existence of the bourgeoisie and of its rule. It is enough to mention the commercial crises that by their periodical return put on its trial, each time more threateningly, the existence of the entire bourgeois society. In these crises a great part not only of the existing products, but also of the previously created productive forces, are periodically destroyed. In these crises there breaks out an epidemic that, in all earlier epochs, would have seemed an absurdity—the epidemic of over-production. Society suddenly finds itself put back into a state of momentary barbarism; it appears as if a famine, a universal war of devastation, had cut off the supply of every means of subsistence; industry and commerce seem to be destroyed; and why? Because there is too much civilization, too much means of subsistence, too much industry, too much commerce. The productive forces at the disposal of society no longer tend to further the development of the conditions of the bourgeois property; on the contrary, they have become too powerful for these conditions by which they are fettered, and as soon as they overcome these fetters they bring disorder into the whole of bourgeois society, endanger the existence of bourgeois property. The conditions of bourgeois society are too narrow to comprise the wealth created by them. And how does the bourgeoisie get over these crises? On the one hand by enforced destruction of a mass of productive forces; on the other, by the conquest of new markets, and by the more thorough exploitation of the old ones. That is to say, by paving the way for more extensive and more destructive crises, and by diminishing the means whereby crises are prevented.

The weapons with which the bourgeoisie felled feudalism to the ground are now turned against the bourgeoisie itself.

But not only has the bourgeoisie forged the weapons that bring death to itself; it has also called into existence the men who are to wield those weapons—the modern working class—the proletarians.

Modern industry has converted the little workshop of the patriarchal master into the great factory of the industrial capitalist. Masses of laborers, crowded into factories, are organized like soldiers. As privates of the industrial army they are placed under the command of a perfect hierarchy of officers and sergeants. Not only are they the slaves of the bourgeois class and of the bourgeois state, they are daily and hourly enslaved by the machine, by the overlooker, and, above all, by the individual bourgeois manufacturer himself. The more openly this despotism proclaims gain to be its end and aim, the more petty, the more hateful, and the more embittering it is.

The lower strata of the middle class —the small tradespeople, shopkeepers and retired tradesmen generally, the handicraftsmen and peasants— all these sink gradually into the pro-letariat, partly because their diminutive capital does not suffice for the scale on which Modern Industry is carried on, and is swamped in the competition with the large capitalists, partly because their specialized skill is rendered worthless by new methods of production. Thus the proletariat is recruited from all classes of the population.

The proletariat goes through various stages of development. With its birth begins its struggle with the bourgeoisie. At first the contest is carried on by individual laborers, then by the workpeople of a factory, then by the operatives of one trade, in one locality, against the individual bourgeois who directly exploits them. They direct their attacks not against the bourgeois conditions of production, but against the instruments of production themselves; they destroy imported wares that compete with their labor, they smash to pieces machinery, they set factories ablaze, they seek to restore by force the vanished status of the workman of the Middle Ages.

At this stage the laborers still form an incoherent mass scattered over the whole country, and broken up by their mutual competition. If anywhere they unite to form more compact bodies, this is not yet the consequence of their own active union, but of the union of the bourgeoisie, which class, in order to attain its own political ends, is compelled to set the whole proletariat in motion, and is moreover yet, for a time, able to do so. At this stage, therefore, the proletarians do not fight their enemies, but the enemies of their enemies, the remnants of absolute monarchy, the landowners, the non-industrial bourgeois, the petty bourgeoisie. Thus the whole historical movement is concentrated in the hands of the bourgeoisie, every victory so obtained is a victory for the bourgeoisie.

But with the development of industry the proletariat not only increases in number; it becomes concentrated in greater masses, its strength grows and it feels that strength more. The various interests and conditions of life within the ranks of the proletariat are more and more equalized, in proportion as machinery obliterates all distinctions of labor, and nearly everywhere reduces wages to the same low level. The growing competition among the bourgeois, and the resulting commercial crisis, make the wages of the workers even more fluctuating. The unceasing improvement of machinery, ever more rapidly developing, makes their livelihood more and more precarious; the collisions between individual workmen and individual bourgeois take more and more the character of collisions between two classes. Thereupon the workers begin to form combinations (Trades' Unions) against the bourgeois; they club together in order to keep up the rate of wages; they found permanent associations in order to make provision beforehand for these occasional revolts. Here and there the contest breaks out into riots.

Further, as we have already seen, entire sections of the ruling classes are, by the advance of industry, precipitated into the proletariat, or are at least threatened in their conditions of existence. These also supply the proletariat with fresh elements of enlightenment and progress.

Finally, in times when the class-struggle nears the decisive hour, the process of dissolution going on within the ruling class—in fact, within the whole range of an old society—assumes such a violent, glaring character that a small section of the ruling class cuts itself adrift and joins the revolutionary class, the class that holds the future in its hands. Just as, therefore, at an earlier period, a section of the nobility went over to the bourgeoisie, so now a portion of the bourgeoisie goes over to the proletariat, and in particular, a portion of the bourgeois ideologists, who have raised themselves to the level of comprehending theoretically the historical movements as a whole.

Of all the classes that stand face to face with the bourgeoisie to-day the proletariat alone is a really revolutionary class. The other classes decay and finally disappear in the face of modern industry; the proletariat is its special and essential product.

Hitherto every form of society has been based, as we have already seen, on the antagonism of oppressing and oppressed classes. But in order to oppress a class, certain conditions must be assured to it under which it can, at least, continue its slavish existence. The serf, in the period of serfdom, raised himself to membership in the commune, just as the petty bourgeois, under the yoke of feudal absolutism, managed to develop into a bourgeois. The modern laborer, on the contrary, instead of rising with the progress of industry, sinks deeper and deeper below the conditions of existence of his own class. He becomes a pauper, and pauperism develops more rapidly than population and wealth. And here it becomes evident that the bourgeoisie is unfit any longer to be the ruling class in society, and to impose its conditions of existence upon society as an over-riding law. It is unfit to rule, because it is incompetent to assure an existence to its slave within his slavery, because it cannot help letting him sink into such a state that it has to feed him, instead of being fed by him. Society can no longer live under this bourgeoisie; in other words, its existence is no longer compatible with society.

The essential condition for the existence, and for the sway of the bourgeois class, is the formation and augmentation of capital; the condition for capital is wage labor. Wage labor rests exclusively on competition between the laborers. The advance of industry, whose involuntary promoter is the bourgeoisie, replaces the isolation of the laborers, due to competition, by their involuntary combination, due to association. The development of Modern Industry, therefore, cuts from under its feet the very foundation on which the bourgeoisie produces and appropriates products. What the bourgeoisie therefore produces, above all, are its own grave diggers. Its fall and the victory of the proletariat are equally inevitable.

B. MARX VERSUS ORTHODOX ECONOMISTS

Joan Robinson, the author of the following reading, has been an outstanding contributor to economic theory for four decades. A Cambridge University economist, she wrote the classic **Economics of Imperfect Competition** in 1933; her most recent book is **Freedom and Necessity: An Introduction to the Study of Society** (1970). Her **Essay on Marxian Economics** was published in 1942. In the excerpt below, her main theme is that, although Marx's analysis was imperfect, he nevertheless raised a set of problems that orthodox economics, following in the British classical tradition, had failed to cope with adequately. In the essay, she mentions the theory of "imperfect competition" (a theory to which she herself was a

major contributor) and this theory refers to the analysis of market structures that do not meet the test of **pure** competition: i.e., market structures where firms are either very large or in other ways influence the markets in which they sell their goods.

ESSAY ON MARXIAN ECONOMICS
JOAN ROBINSON

The fundamental differences between Marxian and traditional orthodox economics are, first, that the orthodox economists accept the capitalist system as part of the eternal order of Nature, while Marx regards it as a passing phase in the transition from the feudal economy of the past to the socialist economy of the future. And, second, that the orthodox economists argue in terms of a harmony of interests between the various sections of the community, while Marx conceives of economic life in terms of a conflict of interests between owners of property who do no work and workers who own no property. These two points of difference are not unconnected—for if the system is taken for granted and the shares of the various classes in the social product are determined by inexorable natural law, all interests unite in requiring an increase in the total to be divided. But if the possibility of changing the system is once admitted, those who hope to gain and those who fear to lose by the change are immediately ranged in opposite camps.

The orthodox economists, on the whole, identified themselves with the system and assumed the role of its

Excerpted from Joan Robinson, An Essay on Marxian Economics (London: Macmillan & Co., 1942), pp. 1–6, 115. Reprinted by permission of the author, St. Martin's Press, Inc., and Macmillan, London and Basingstoke.

apologists, while Marx set himself to understand the working of capitalism in order to hasten its overthrow. Marx was conscious of his purposes. The economists were in general unconscious. They wrote as they did because it seemed to them the only possible way to write, and they believed themselves to be endowed with scientific impartiality. Their preconceptions emerge rather in the problems which they chose to study and the assumptions on which they worked than in overt political doctrine.

Since they believed themselves to be in search of eternal principles they paid little attention to the special historical features of actual situations, and, in particular, they were apt to project the economics of a community of small equal proprietors into the analysis of advanced capitalism. Thus the orthodox conception of competition entails that each commodity in each market is supplied by a large number of producers, acting individualistically, bound together neither by open collusion nor by unconscious class loyalty; and entails that any individual is free to enter any line of activity he pleases. And the laws derived from such a society are applied to modern industry and finance.

Again, the orthodox conception of wages, which has its origin in the picture of a peasant farmer leaning on his hoe in the evening and deciding whether the extra product of another hour's work will repay the extra backache, is projected into the modern labour market, where the individual worker has no opportunity to decide anything except whether it is better to work or to starve.

The orthodox economists have been much preoccupied with elegant elaborations of minor problems, which distract the attention of their pupils from the uncongenial realities of the modern world, and the development of abstract argument has run far ahead of any possibility of empirical verification. Marx's intellectual tools are far cruder, but his sense of reality is far stronger, and his argument towers above their intricate constructions in rough and gloomy grandeur.

He sees the capitalist system as fulfilling a historic mission to draw out the productive power of combined and specialised labour. From its birthplace in Europe it stretches out tentacles over the world to find its nourishment. It forces the accumulation of capital, and develops productive technique, and by these means raises the wealth of mankind to heights undreamed of in the peasant, feudal or slave economies.

But the workers, who, under the compulsion of capitalism, produce the wealth, obtain no benefit from the increase in their productive power. All the benefit accrues to the class of capitalists, for the efficiency of large-scale enterprise breaks down the competition of the peasant and the craftsman, and reduces all who have not property enough to join the ranks of the capitalists to selling their labour for the mere means of existence. Any concession which the capitalist makes to the worker is the concession which the farmer makes to his beasts—to feed them better that they may work the more.

The struggle for life binds the workers together and sets them in opposition to the propertied class, while the concentration of capital in ever larger concerns, forced on by the development of technique, turns the capitalists towards the anti-social practices of monopoly.

But the condemnation of the system

does not only depend upon its moral repugnance, and the inevitability of its final overthrow does not only depend upon the determination of the workers to secure their rightful share in the product of their labour. The system contains contradictions within itself which must lead to its disruption. Marx sees the periodic crises of the trade cycle as symptoms of a deepseated and progressive malady in the vitals of the system.

Developments in economic analysis which have taken place since Marx's day enable us to detect three distinct strands of thought in Marx's treatment of crises. There is, first, the theory of the reserve army of unemployed labour, which shows how unemployment tends to fluctuate with the relationship between the stock of capital offering employment to labour and the supply of labour available to be employed. Second, there is the theory of the falling rate of profit, which shows how the capitalists' greed for accumulation stultifies itself by reducing the average rate of return on capital. And thirdly, there is the theory of the relationship of capitalgood to consumption-good industries, which shows the ever-growing productive power of society knocking against the limitation upon the power to consume which is set by the poverty of the workers.

In Marx's mind these three theories are not distinct, and are fused together in a single picture of the system, racked by its own inherent contradictions, generating the conditions for its own disintegration.

Meanwhile, the academic economists, without paying much attention to Marx, have been forced by the experiences of modern times to question much of the orthodox apologetic, and recent developments in academic theory have led them to a position which in some respects resembles the position of Marx far more closely than the position of their own intellectual forebears. The modern theory of imperfect competition, though formally quite different from Marx's theory of exploitation, has a close affinity with it. The modern theory of crises has many points of contact with the third line of argument, distinguished above, in Marx's treatment of the subject, and allows room for something resembling the first. Only the second line of argument — the falling rate of profit — appears confused and redundant.

In general, the nightmare quality of Marx's thought gives it, in this bedevilled age, an air of greater reality than the gentle complacency of the orthodox academics. Yet he, at the same time, is more encouraging than they, for he releases hope as well as terror from Pandora's box, while they preach only the gloomy doctrine that all is for the best in the best of all possible worlds.

But though Marx is more sympathetic, in many ways, to a modern mind, than the orthodox economists, there is no need to turn him, as many seek to do, into an inspired prophet. He regarded himself as a serious thinker, and it is as a serious thinker that I have endeavoured to treat him.

Marx, however imperfectly he worked out the details, set himself the task of discovering the law of motion of capitalism, and if there is any hope of progress in economics at all, it must be in using academic methods to solve the problems posed by Marx.

C. MARX WAS WRONG

In the late 1950s, Khrushchev challenged the West with a promise to "bury" us — economically speaking. This challenge drew a response from Adolf A. Berle, Jr., who points out below that Marx was in error in his predictions about the two contending classes—capitalists and labor —under capitalism and also in his view of the role of government in an advanced capitalistic society. (Marx had argued that such a government would be nothing but a tool of the ruling economic class.) Adolf A. Berle, Jr. has made many contributions to economics, perhaps his outstanding contribution being his collaboration with Gardner C. Means in the pathbreaking study, **The Modern Corporation and Private Property** (1934).

MARX WAS WRONG AND SO IS KHRUSHCHEV

ADOLF A. BERLE, JR.

"Your grandchildren will live under socialism," says Khrushchev to us. "We will bury you (capitalists)," he predicted to an American visitor in Moscow. Both comments capsule a major ingredient of Communist propaganda the world over: capitalism is doomed. It is self-destructive. Fate and history make communism the inevitably victorious system. Clever men had best get on the bandwagon now.

The line is not new. Westward-bound empire builders from Eurasia have always used it. Attila, Genghis Khan, Tamerlane, all urged their opponents to collapse gracefully because fate had written them off. But they did not base their claim on economics, or attempt a reasoned argument, as do present-day Communists.

But, in Moscow, doubts are arising.

From Adolf A. Berle, Jr., "Marx Was Wrong and So Is Khrushchev," New York Times Magazine, November 1, 1959. © 1959 by The New York Times Company. Reprinted by permission.

The American system, classified by Marxians as monopoly-capitalist and therefore due for death, gives surprisingly few signs of dying, or even of illness. Subtly, the Communist line is emphasizing a quite different note: "We can overtake and out-produce you; we can do everything you can faster and better."

One outspoken Soviet economist, Eugene Varga, ten years ago risked his career by predicting that the American system would not then destroy itself by a post-war economic crisis. After a period of disgrace, he was restored to favor. True, Karl Marx had asserted nearly a century earlier that capitalist industrial societies would create the conditions for their own self-destruction. But something had happened to delay the calculation, and careful Communist analysts knew it.

What had happened, certainly in the American case, was an evolution within the capitalist frame, knocking out the basis of Marx's prophecy and, incidentally, of the current Communist propaganda line. Briefly, the United States, without revolution, changed from a nineteenth-century "property system" to a social system. It did this in a way no Communist could have forecast, and it created what is, in essence, a different system; so different that one French scholar, Jacques Maritain, insists that it is a new and fluid system, still in the making, "which renders both capitalism and socialism things of the past."

Another scholar, Father Bruckberger, has recently written a book to prove it. It may not be an accident that both are French; the clearest estimates of America have come from France—witness Alexis de Tocqueville in the nineteenth century and

André Siegfried in the twentieth.

This American system has not yet received a distinctive name. It has been called "people's capitalism." A new book about to come out, by Dr. Paul Harbrecht, calls it "paraproprietal society" (a society beyond property). When Khrushchev and his associates talk about capitalism, they describe a system which perhaps did exist a century ago. But in America it stopped existing somewhere between 1920 and 1930. It is important both for the Soviet Union and for America to know this. Kremlin Communists are fighting a ghost, and their more sophisticated analysts know it. Americans are just coming to realize that they are operators of a system more advanced and, in its way, more revolutionary than the Marxian.

Predictions of a short life for capitalist society, as it functioned about 1900, had, I think, a reasonable basis at the time. Marx thought private ownership of factories, plants and industry inevitably would cause the rich to grow richer as their profits accumulated. Meanwhile the workers and the poor would stay at subsistence level. The small owner class, he insisted, would own and operate the government, the courts and all social organization. These would be used to defend the growing accumulations of this class. As the poor stayed poor (or grew poorer) markets for manufactured goods would not increase as fast as production—the masses would not have the buying power.

So, markets would have to be extended by military conquest and every capitalist state must become a built-in "imperialism," always seizing more territory to increase markets for its owner class. There would be recurrent crises of growing severity, as production outran markets and the going

got harder. Eventually an insuperable crisis would blow up the whole system. Then the Communist dictatorship of the proletariat representing the masses would take over. So ran the argument.

If we had looked at Europe in 1870— or at America from 1890 to 1900— circumstances would have lent color to the idea. At that time, individual owners of private capitalist enterprise were in fact accumulating, high, wide and handsome. In America we were having the "age of the moguls"— proprietor-tycoons piling up fabulous fortunes from the profits of railroads and mines, steel, copper and oil. In England, Charles Dickens had described the plight of the masses in "Bleak House" and "Oliver Twist." In the United States, Upton Sinclair and his friends were telling a similar story, American-style.

Marx was right in one respect: it could not (and in fact, did not) last. But he was completely wrong in his guess as to how it would change.

In the United States three new elements (among other less powerful factors) emerged and changed both the direction and structure of affairs, though none of them involved or contemplated blowing up the system.

The first development was the American corporation. This operated surprisingly. In one generation it replaced the individual or family-owners. In a second period, it displaced the tycoons and moguls, substituting professional management. It did not behave at all like a personal fortune-builder.

The second was the rise of American labor unions. These refused to try to seize the ownership position or take over government. Instead, they insisted only on representing workmen.

The third, and probably the most

important, was the position of the American democratic government. This simply declined to be owned and operated by and in the interest of the tycoon (or any other) class. It intervened from time to time to steer the economic system toward social goals. None of these possibilities had figured in Marx's calculation, and Russian commentators today find difficulty in explaining them.

First, the corporations. These organizations became and now are, the titular "owners" of American industry. But corporations are not individuals or families and do not behave like them. As productive organizations they can and do pile up huge aggregations of property. But simultaneously they must distribute much of their profit to a continuously growing proportion of the population of the United States. Corporations whose stock is listed on the New York Stock Exchange carry on at least three-fourths of all American industry; the 500 largest of them probably carry on about two-thirds of it. Were these 500 families, the results might have justified Marx's predictions and produced the foreseen catastrophe.

Actually, according to the New York Stock Exchange, they have about 12,500,000 direct stockholders. Even more important, a large and growing amount of their stock is held by institutions—notably pension trusts, mutual funds and, increasingly, life insurance companies. These in turn distribute the industrial profits. Probably 50,000,000 Americans who do not even know they derive income from stocks receive a share of these profits through the holdings of such institutions. This number will grow. Their proportionate take of industrial profits will also grow—both factors are expanding just now with consider-able rapidity.

Nor are the managers and groups controlling corporations owners. They are almost always salaried officials. They are becoming a kind of non-statist civil service. The corporate system at present is thus in effect operating to "socialize" American industry but without intervention of the political state. No Marxist could ever have thought up that possibility.

Then there is the phenomenon of the American labor movement. For practical purposes, organized labor became a substantial economic factor after World War I. It gained full recognition through the Wagner Act. It has now become a vast, permanent and powerful element in the American economic system.

But it refused to behave like its European ancestors. It did not wish to own and manage the plants. In fact, it has steadily declined to enter management. Instead, it aimed only to represent the workers and to get for them, through wages, pensions and fringe benefits, the largest practicable share of national income.

In the past thirty years it has succeeded in steadily raising the "real" wage of workers about three percent annually, or thirty percent in each decade—though workers do not receive this only in cash but also in shorter working hours, vacations and more leisure. The net result has been that American labor now has the highest workers' standard of living in the world. The workman himself lives, thinks and feels not as an oppressed proletarian seeking to be saved by revolution but as a member of the middle class to whose children any position is possible. It is, in fact, increasingly hard to find a "proletariat" in the United States except in a few isolated areas.

Still less has the labor movement followed European patterns in forming a political party or seeking to assume government; still less to overturn the existing system. It does get into politics very effectively to defend its own interests, dealing more or less impartially with both political parties. But it declines to become a Socialist party itself and shows no desire whatever to attempt creation of a "labor" government.

Finally, and certainly most important, the American Government most obstinately refused to be merely an expression of the "ownership class." According to Marx, such refusal could not happen—but it did. Surprisingly to European thought, many of the "ownership" group were outspoken in opposing that conception of government. President Theodore Roosevelt intervened violently against one ownership sector in the Mogul Age when he forced regulation of railroads and set a conservative party to control "malefactors of great wealth."

President Woodrow Wilson moved effectively against the financial ownership class, proclaiming the doctrines of the "New Freedom" and compelling passage of the Federal Reserve Act of 1913. With even more effect, he sponsored income and inheritance tax legislation about the same time.

In 1933, President Franklin Roosevelt and the New Deal undertook the larger task of hauling the whole system toward a socially directed commonwealth. Social Security legislation was one great instrument. Systematic direction of a larger share of national income toward farmers and agriculture was another. Development of public works and state-directed production when unemployment threatens was a third. Use of the credit system to assure housing, electricity and land reclamation was a fourth. And there were many more.

Thus, in mid-century, Americans are operating a so-called "capitalist system" in which all the elements dominant in the nineteenth century have changed. What is left of the old system is its form of organization and, in general, its separation from the political government.

That organization has achieved a per capita level of production beyond older dreams — so much so that equaling it is the present expressed dream of the Soviet Union and of Communist China. In terms of distribution it has done better than Communist systems because it had more to distribute. And its methods of distribution have been on the whole less arbitrary and infinitely less oppressive. The results have been more satisfactory to 175,000,000 Americans than those of Socialist distribution to the 210,000,000 citizens of the Soviet Union.

This American system is miles from being perfect. All kinds of things turn up in it that should not be there. All kinds of inequities have to be dealt with. Our methods for keeping production and distribution in balance are still unsystematic and crude; better means still need to be worked out. Steering an adequate amount of the national income into necessary noncommercial activities, notably education and the arts, remains a problem.

But, by comparative standards, our system is far out ahead. As a single example, during forty years of the Soviet system, Russia at all times has had more political prisoners in concentration camps behind barbed wire than the United States has ever had unemployed men—though Khrushchev is credited with having reduced the number materially in the past few years.

The vitality and rapid evolution of the American system—and it has not stopped growing and has not stopped evolving—has worried the Russian theoreticians. At the Twentieth Communist Congress in Moscow, a then favorite Communist doctrinaire, Dmitri Shepilov (later Foreign Minister), was put up as a principal speaker to explain true doctrine to the comrades. He did not ignore the fact that the United States and its system had evolved and was going great guns, but he had to prove nevertheless that "capitalism is doomed."

Taking account of the newer studies of the American system, he singled out for attention (along with John Foster Dulles) the work of Prof. J. Kenneth Galbraith of Harvard ("American Capitalism: The Concept of Countervailing Power") and a current book of mine. He made no attempt to meet the modern American facts. "It can't happen," he proclaimed. Socially directed capitalism, freed from the vices Marx had observed, must be like hot ice: it couldn't exist.

Sophisticated Communist scholars know better. A more serious explanation was attempted this summer, again by Eugene Varga, ablest of the Soviet economists. In the official "Problems of Peace and Socialism" last August, he published an article. He renewed the statement that "under capitalism crises of overproduction are inevitable," but he said we were now in a system of "state monopoly capitalism" and this system made it easier for "monopolies" to weather these crises.

Specifically, the state moved to support the "monopolies" (he means the big corporations) through Government orders, chiefly military, and thus assure a minimum of production even during crises. Further, we slowly inflated the currency, reducing real wages without direct wage cuts.

The fact that the corporations are not monopolies and neither control, nor are controlled by, the state, he ignored, and he omitted the fact that they now distribute profits as well as wages to a huge sector of the United States. Nor had he discovered that the real wage of the American workman steadily rises.

Still less, of course, had he noted that "Government orders" include nonmilitary items such as huge road systems, municipal improvements, housing, power, scientific development and other activities whose amount exceeds military expenditures. (If the armament burden were lifted tomorrow, that same machinery could be used with general approval from the American public to increase production and markets alike.) But he continues hopefully to assert that "the cyclic movement inherent in the capitalist mode of production will, we believe, resume its normal course with a world economic crisis occurring every six years or so."

Well, his reasoning does not take account of facts. It ignores the structural change in the property system achieved during the past fifty years, and the astonishing capacity of the American system to make new adaptations.

Its crises (there will be some) can be handled on a humane basis. They will be infinitely less dangerous than the recurrent bloody crises inescapable in the political power monopoly built into the Soviet dictatorship. The American system continues to evolve successfully, and is keeping right on.

D. MARX WAS RIGHT BUT SHOULD HAVE GONE FURTHER

　　Two highly influential American Marxist economists are Paul M. Sweezy and the late Paul A. Baran. In their analysis, Marx is credited with having foreseen the development of monopoly power under capitalism, but is not believed to have developed its full implications. Their writing, in the Marxist tradition, may be viewed as an attempt to extend the conclusions of the master. They point out, among other things, the all-pervasive nature of overproduction under monopoly capitalism and the irrationality of capitalist thought under modern conditions. When they use the term "surplus," they mean "the difference between total output and the socially necessary costs of producing total output." This is roughly the same thing as profits, broadly conceived.

MONOPOLY CAPITAL
PAUL A. BARAN
AND PAUL M. SWEEZY

Like the classical economists before him, Marx treated monopolies not as essential elements of capitalism but rather as remnants of the feudal and mercantilist past which had to be abstracted from in order to attain the clearest possible view of the basic structure and tendencies of capitalism. It is true that, unlike the classicists, Marx fully recognized the powerful trend toward the concentration and centralization of capital inherent in a competitive economy: his vision of the future of capitalism certainly included new and purely capitalist forms of monopoly. But he never attempted to investigate what would at the time have been a hypothetical system characterized by the prevalence of large-scale enterprise and monopoly. Partly the explanation is no doubt that the empirical material on which such an investigation would have had to be based was too scanty to permit reliable generalization. But perhaps even more important, Marx anticipated the overthrow of capitalism long before the unfolding of all its potentialities, well within the system's competitive phase.

Engels, in some of his own writings after Marx's death and in editorial additions to the second and third volumes of Capital which he prepared for the printer, commented on the rapid growth of monopolies during the 1880s and 1890s, but he did not try to incorporate monopoly into the body of Marxian economic theory. The first to do this was Rudolf Hilferding in his important work, Das Finanzkapital, published in 1910. But for all his emphasis on monopoly, Hilferding did not treat it as a qualitatively new element in the capitalist economy; rather he saw it as effecting essentially quantitative modifications of the basic Marxian laws of capitalism. Lenin, who was strongly influenced by Hilferding's analysis of the origins and diffusion of monopoly, based his theory of imperialism squarely on the predominance of monopoly in the developed capitalist countries. But neither he nor his followers pursued the matter into the fundamentals of Marxian economic theory. There, paradoxically enough, in what might have been thought the area most immediately involved, the growth of monopoly made the least impression.

Excerpted from Paul A. Baran and Paul M. Sweezy, Monopoly Capital, pp. 3–5, 108–11, 336–41. Copyright © 1966 by Paul M. Sweezy; reprinted by permission of Monthly Review Press.

MONOPOLY CAPITALISM IS SELF-CONTRADICTORY

Twist and turn as one will, there is no way to avoid the conclusion that monopoly capitalism is a self-contradictory system. It tends to generate ever more surplus, yet it fails to provide the consumption and investment outlets required for the absorption of a rising surplus and hence for the smooth working of the system. Since surplus which cannot be absorbed will not be produced, it follows that the normal state of the monopoly capitalist economy is stagnation. With a given stock of capital and a given cost and price structure, the system's operating rate cannot rise above the point at which the amount of surplus produced can find the necessary outlets. And this means chronic underutilization of available human and material resources. Or, to put the point in slightly different terms, the system must operate at a point low enough on its profitability schedule not to generate more surplus than can be absorbed. Since the profitability schedule is always moving upward, there is a corresponding downdrift of the "equilibrium" operating rate. Left to itself—that is to say, in the absence of counteracting forces which are no part of what may be called the "elementary logic" of the system—monopoly capitalism would sink deeper and deeper into a bog of chronic depression.

Counteracting forces do exist. If they did not, the system would indeed long since have fallen of its own weight. It therefore becomes a matter of the greatest importance to understand the nature and implications of these counteracting forces. Here we confine ourselves to a few preliminary remarks.

The self-contradictory character of monopoly capitalism—its chronic inability to absorb as much surplus as it is capable of producing—impresses itself on the ordinary citizen in a characteristic way. To him, the economic problem appears to be the very opposite of what the textbooks say it is: not how best to utilize scarce resources but how to dispose of the products of superabundant resources. And this holds regardless of his wealth or position in society. If he is a worker, the ubiquitous fact of unemployment teaches him that the supply of labor is always greater than the demand. If he is a farmer, he struggles to stay afloat in a sea of surpluses. If he is a businessman, his sales persistently fall short of what he could profitably produce. Always too much, never too little.

This condition of affairs is peculiar to monopoly capitalism. The very notion of "too much" would have been inconceivable to all pre-capitalist forms of society; and even in the competitive stage of capitalism, it described a temporary derangement, not a normal condition. In a rationally ordered socialist society, no matter how richly endowed it might be with natural resources and technology and human skills, "too much" could only be a welcome signal to shift attention to an area of "too little." Only under monopoly capitalism does "too much" appear as a pervasive problem affecting everyone at all times.

From this source stem a whole series of attitudes and interests of crucial importance for the character and functioning of monopoly capitalist society. On the one hand, there is a stubborn spirit of restrictionism which pervades the institutional structure. Union featherbedding and Henry Wallace's plowing under of little pigs are only the best publicized examples of practices which are all but universal in business and government: the most primitive reaction to an excess of supply is simply to cut back. During the 1930s, when "too much" took on the dimensions of a universal disaster, primitive restrictionism acquired, in the National Industrial Recovery Act and the National Recovery Administration, the dignity and sanction of official national policy.

But cutting back as a remedy for "too much," even if beneficial to particular groups or individuals, only aggravates the situation as a whole. A secondary and more sophisticated set of attitudes and policies therefore emerges, gropingly and slowly at first but with increasing purposefulness and momentum as monopoly capitalism develops. Their rationale derives from the simple fact that the obverse of "too much" on the supply side is "too little" on the demand side; instead of cutting back supply they aim at stimulating demand.

The stimulation of demand—the creation and expansion of markets—thus becomes to an ever greater degree the leitmotif of business and government policies under monopoly capitalism. But this statement, true as it is, can easily be misleading. There are many conceivable ways of stimulating demand. If a socialist society, for example, should find that through some planning error more consumer goods were being produced than could be sold, given the existing structure of prices and incomes, the simplest and most direct remedy would

clearly be to cut prices. This would reduce the amount of surplus at the disposal of the planning authorities and correspondingly raise the purchasing power of consumers. The threatened glut could be quickly and painlessly averted: everyone would be better off, no one worse off. Such a course of action is obviously not open to a monopoly capitalist society, in which the determination of prices is the jealously guarded prerogative of the giant corporations. Each makes its own decisions with a view to maximizing its own private profit. Except for short periods of all-out war, when inflationary pressures threaten the entire economic and social fabric, there is no agency charged with controlling prices. Moreover, every attempt to maintain or establish such an agency in peacetime has resulted either in ignominious failure (witness the fiasco of price control after the Second World War) or in the thinly disguised legalization of monopoly pricing practices in "regulated" industries. The plain fact is that the pricing process is controlled by the most powerful vested interests in monopoly capitalist society. To imagine that it could possibly be regulated in the public interest would be to imagine away the very characteristics of that society which make it what it is.

If stimulation of demand through price reduction is impossible within the framework of monopoly capitalism, this cannot be said of other possible methods. Take, for example, advertising and related forms of salesmanship. Every giant corporation is driven by the logic of its situation to devote more and more attention and resources to the sales effort. And monopoly capitalist society as a whole has every interest in promoting rather than restricting and controlling this method of creating new markets and expanding old ones.

Just as with price cutting and salesmanship, other forms of stimulating demand either are or are not compatible with the pattern of interests, the structure of power, the web of ideology that constitute the essence of monopoly capitalist society. Those which are compatible will be fostered and promoted; those which are incompatible will be ignored or inhibited. The question for monopoly capitalism is not whether to stimulate demand. It must, on pain of death.

THE IRRATIONAL SYSTEM

It is of the essence of capitalism that both goods and labor power are typically bought and sold on the market. In such a society relations among individuals are dominated by the principle of the exchange of equivalents, of quid pro quo, not only in economic matters but in all other aspects of life as well.

Not that the principle of equivalent exchange is or ever has been universally practiced in capitalist society. As Marx showed so convincingly in the closing chapters of the first volume of Capital, the primary accumulation of capital was effected through violence and plunder, and the same methods continue in daily use throughout capitalism's dependent colonies and semi-colonies. Nevertheless the ideological sway of quid pro quo became all but absolute. In their relations with each other and in what they teach those over whom they rule, capitalists are fully committed to the principle of quid pro quo, both as a guide to action and as a standard of morality.

This commitment reflected an important step forward in the development of the forces of production and in the evolution of human consciousness. Only on the basis of equivalent exchange was it possible to realize the more rational utilization of human and material resources which has been the central achievement of capitalism. At the same time, it must never be forgotten that the rationality of quid pro quo is specifically capitalist rationality which at a certain stage of development becomes incompatible with the underlying forces and relations of production. To ignore this and to treat quid pro quo as a universal maxim of rational conduct is in itself an aspect of bourgeois ideology, just as the radical-sounding assertion that under socialism exchange of equivalents can be immediately dispensed with betrays a utopian view of the nature of the economic problems faced by a socialist society.*

---

*Marx emphasized in his **Critique of the Gotha Program** that the principle of equivalent exchange must survive in a socialist society for a considerable period as a guide to the efficient allocation and utilization of human and material resources. By the same token, however, the evolution of socialism into communism requires an unremitting struggle **against** the principle, with a view to its ultimate replacement by the ideal "From each according to his ability, to each according to his need." In a fully developed communist society, in which social production would be organized as in one vast economic enterprise and in which scarcity would be largely overcome, equivalent exchange would no more serve as the organizing principle of economic activity than at the present time the removal of a chair from one's bedroom to one's sitting room requires charging the sitting room and crediting the bedroom with the value of the furniture. This is obviously not to imply that the communist society of the future can dispense with rational calculation; what it does indicate is that the nature of the rationality involved in economic calculation undergoes a profound change. And this change in turn is but one manifestation of a thoroughgoing transformation of human needs and of the relations among men in society.

But even during the life span of capitalism itself, quid pro quo breaks down as a rational principle of economic and social organization. The giant corporation withdraws from the sphere of the market large segments of economic activity and subjects them to scientifically designed administration. This change represents a continuous increase in the rationality of the parts of the system, but it is not accompanied by any rationalization of the whole. On the contrary, with commodities being priced not according to their costs of production but to yield the maximum possible profit, the principle of quid pro quo turns into the opposite of a promoter of rational economic organization and instead becomes a formula for maintaining scarcity in the midst of potential plenty. Human and material resources remain idle because there is in the market no quid to exchange against the quo of their potential output. And this is true even though the real cost of such output would be nil. In the most advanced capitalist country a large part of the population lives in abysmal poverty while in the underdeveloped countries hundreds of millions suffer from disease and starvation because there is no mechanism for effecting an exchange of what they could produce for what they so desperately need. Insistence on the inviolability of equivalent exchange when what is to be exchanged costs nothing, strict economizing of resources when a large proportion of them goes to waste — these are obviously the very denial of the rationality which the concept of value and the principle of quid pro quo originally expressed.

The obsolescence of such central categories of bourgeois thought is but one symptom of the profoundly contradictory nature of monopoly capitalism, of the ever sharpening conflict between the rapidly advancing rationalization of the actual processes of production and the undiminished elementality of the system as a whole. This conflict affects all aspects of society. While rationality has been conquering ever new areas of consciousness, the inability of bourgeois thought to comprehend the development of society as a whole has remained essentially unchanged, a faithful mirror of the continuing elementality and irrationality of the capitalist order itself.

Social reality is therefore conceived in outlived, topsy-turvy and fetishistic terms. Powerless to justify an irrational and inhuman social order and unable to answer the increasingly urgent questions which it poses, bourgeois ideology clings to concepts that are anachronistic and moribund. Its bankruptcy manifests itself not so much in the generation of new fetishes and half-truths as in the stubborn upholding of old fetishes and half-truths which now turn into blatant lies. And the more these old fetishes and half-truths lose whatever truth content they once possessed the more insistently they are hammered, like advertising slogans, into the popular consciousness.

The claim that the United States economy is a "free enterprise" system is a case in point. At no time was enterprise really free in the sense that anyone who wanted to could start a business of his own. Still the concept conveyed an important aspect of the truth by pointing up the difference between the relative freedom of competitive capitalism on the one hand and the restrictions imposed by the guild system and the mercantilist state on the other. Having long ago lost this limited claim to truthfulness and referring as it now does to the freedom of giant corporations to exercise undisturbed their vast monopoly powers, "free enterprise" has turned into a shibboleth devoid of all descriptive or explanatory validity.

Bourgeois ideology is no longer a world outlook, a Weltanschauung, which attempts to discern order in the existing chaos and to discover a meaning in life. It has turned into a sort of box of assorted tools and gimmicks for attaining the central goal of bourgeois policies. And this goal—which in its younger days the bourgeoisie defined in terms of material progress and individual freedom—is more and more explicitly limited to one thing only: preservation of the status quo, alias the "free world," with all its manifest evils, absurdities, and irrationalities.

It is of course impossible to advance a reasoned defense of this status quo, and indeed the effort is seldom made any more. Instead of taking the form of a demonstration of the rationality and desirability of monopoly capitalism, the defense increasingly focuses on the repudiation of socialism which is the only real alternative to monopoly capitalism, and on the denunciation of revolution which is the only possible means of achieving socialism. All striving for a better, more humane, more rational society is held to be unscientific, utopian, and subversive; by the same token the existing order of society is made to appear not only as the only possible one but as the only conceivable one.

The contradiction between the increasing rationality of society's methods of production and the organizations which embody them on the one hand and the undiminished elemen-tality and irrationality in the functioning and perception of the whole creates that ideological wasteland which is the hallmark of monopoly capitalism. But we must insist that this is not, as some apologists of the status quo would have us believe, "the end of ideology"; it is the displacement of the ideology of rising capitalism by the ideology of the general crisis and decline of the world capitalist order. That its main pillar is anti-Communism is neither accidental nor due to a transient conjunction of political forces, any more than is the fact that the main content of the political and economic policies of modern capitalism is armaments and Cold War. These policies can only be anti; there is nothing left for them to be pro.

E. CONFLICT YES, BUT NOT OF THE MARXIAN KIND

Former president of the University of California, Clark Kerr is also a distinguished economist specializing in labor and industrial relations problems. His view is that Marx was wrong in anticipating an intensification of class conflict under capitalism. What has happened instead is that conflict has become diffused over the whole society, and instead of being between those who do and those who don't own property, it is over the issue of who sets the rules and the life-style of the society.

CLASS CONFLICT AND CLASS COLLABORATION
CLARK KERR

As seen from a more modern viewpoint than that of Marx, the conflict over class has largely dissolved. Instead of six classes or five or two, there are said to be none at all in the Communist world—all men are equal and some are more equal than others; and, in the capitalist world, there are such infinite variations and gradations that it is better to speak of interest groups or status positions rather than class at all in the sense of a class set apart by its common attachment to grievances or to privileges or to a common ideology—all men are unqual and some are more unequal than others.

Morality attaches more to individual men than to classes, although there are now those who would urge a special moral position for the intellectuals. Evolution is leading towards an all-pervasive middle class—a middle class that expands its coverage so widely that it is no longer a class at all. There are few hard and fast lines in this middle group but, rather, many minor grades that shade off into one another; except that an 'under-class' may be clearly distinguished and is in some places more visible where it has a special racial composition, as in the United States. The under-class stands outside the embrace of the great productive 'middle' segment.

Conflict is not concentrated at one place and at one time—at the barricades that separate the proletariat and the bourgeoisie. Friction is spread around in the ball-bearing society that has evolved. Protest is fractionalized. It is not over property but over countless prices and rules. It is not against the capitalist alone, but also against the merchant and bureaucrat and politician. The evolu-

Excerpted from Clark Kerr, "Class Conflict and Class Collaboration" from Marshall, Marx and Modern Times: The Multi-Dimensional Society (London: Cambridge University Press, 1969), pp. 37–41, 122, 129–30. Reprinted by permission of the publisher.

tion of industrial society has helped this. There are fewer isolated masses in the lumber camp or textile town or mining village with common grievances against a single source of authority. The one-industry community is less frequent, and employer paternalism gradually passes away. Workers are concentrated into larger communities but these communities are so heterogeneous that the individual and the group are absorbed and contained and subdued. Conflict is everywhere and this saves it from being anywhere to a degree that causes revolution—it is too scattered over time and place.

Marx saw a process that went on stage by stage until its ultimate conclusion—but the process stopped at about the stage he saw and went little further. Workers coalesced into trade unions and in some capitalist countries into political parties, but the trade unions remained bread-and-butter trade unions and the political parties remained cooperating political parties, and neither became revolutionary instruments. In England, at the time of the General Strike, and in the United States, with the I.W.W.s, it looked for a time as though the process might go on as Marx saw it, but the process was arrested. The process of developing increasing group consciousness stopped at the stage of economic trade unions and participating political parties.

Relations of workers and employees became less violent, not more. Real wages rose. Trade unions developed power and influence in the work place—enough to get better rules and to settle grievances; and in individual industries—enough to be concerned with the profitability and growth of 'their' industry. As Bendix has noted, 'the willingness of entrepreneurial classes to compromise may increase along with the capitalist development*—not hold steady or decrease. Political parties with worker support came to rule governments. Marx never thought that the capitalists would yield so easily the authority he believed they had over the state—for this, to him, was 'suicide.' The state turned to welfare. The law was, to a degree, impartial and was not just a tool of the dominant class. Many buffers were created between contending parties. The 'new economics' of Cambridge replaced the old. Slichter once wrote of the crucial race between the engineer and the union leader, the one pushing greater productivity and the other higher money wages. A far more important race was between Cambridge economists and the great depressions, and Cambridge won.† The hard and intricate problem of counter-cyclical policy was solved.

Marx was wrong about the evolution of class in maturing capitalist nations. He expected revolution from the workers during an industrial crisis as the standard case. Communist revolutions have come instead more from the peasants and from war. Peasants to Marx represented 'barbarians' rather than civilized men. That they should have been important in Russia and particularly China and Cuba would have surprised him. Through foresight or by chance, however, he envisioned a war between Germany and Russia which 'will act as the midwife to the inevitable social revolution in Russia'. But Russia was not an advanced capitalist nation and thus

---

*Reinhard Bendix, **Work and Authority in Industry** (New York: John Wiley, 1956), p. 438.

† [Kerr is referring here to the work of John Maynard Keynes. See chapter 7.]

fell outside his central theory.

Communism has appealed less to the stage of late capitalism and more to early development than Marx had thought it would. It has had a special appeal to people undergoing the transition from a traditional to a modern society. It speaks to their sense of revulsion against the old dynastic elite or against foreign domination. It speaks to their sense of exploitation. It speaks to their increasing sense of misery as they face the psychological impact of the 'revolution of rising expectations'. Communism, also, has some answers to the problems of the transition—control by the state, a social plan, fast capital accumulation. It is less well adapted to the complexities of an advanced industrial society where many small decisions must be made, and where individuals and groups achieve a degree of independence. Thus, in a world marked by many countries in the early transitional stages into industrialization, Marxism has come to have substantial influence even though it has little appeal in more advanced societies.

THE NEW STRUGGLE

The old struggle was seen by Marx as being over the ownership of property since property determined power. The new struggle is directly over power, almost regardless of the ownership of property: power to set the rules, fix the rewards, influence the style of life. It takes place in modern industrial societies between the several forms of pluralism as against the monolithic society of Stalinism on the one extreme and anarchism without any central coercive authority at the other, and within and among the several forms of pluralism themselves. The old struggle pitted the workers under the banners of socialism against the capitalists with control of the state as the major prize. The new struggle pits the managed under the banners of freedom and participation against the managers with the control and the conduct of a myriad of organizations involved. Instead of trying to concentrate power in the state, the new effort is to fractionalize it everywhere—the old salvation is the new tyranny; and general revolution gives way to piece-meal evolution. Communism, not capitalism, now faces the greatest challenge, for power there is most centrally held—the old radicalism is the new conservatism.

The new problems of modern industrial society call for more flexibility, for more individuality. The new imperative is to 'humanize' the communities of work, adapt them to individual preferences. Rather than the unfolding of class relations or the perfecting of market mechanisms, the new force at work is further adaptation to individual preferences in many situations and for many reasons. The challenge once was to absorb and adjust to the factory, the worker and the capitalist; now it is to adjust to the more aggressive individual. Instead of socialism challenging the old capitalism, it is now anarchistic and individualistic and syndicalistic tendencies challenging the new communism and the new capitalistic pluralism. A new synthesis is in process.

Industrial pluralism has developed as the realistic alternative to both the monolithic and the atomistic society. Pluralism now struggles with some of the ultimate issues that go beyond class versus class and monopoly versus the market: (1) the role of the managed as against the managers, of the semi-managed as against the semi-managers, of the individual against the group; (2) the pressure of the ever newer technology to change the lives of men as against the desire of men to rule technology, to exercise their options in relation to it; (3) the interests of those inside the productive process as against those standing outside; and (4) the contrast between the imperfectibility of man and the hope for a more perfect society. No revolution, no alchemy of morality and knowledge can rid man of all his chains, can make all men into gentlemen; or so it seems one century later.

Continued from p. 54
Hence, there must be sufficient *incentive* established, monetary or otherwise, to assure a vigorous labor force and intelligent managerial direction.

This problem is not necessarily as insurmountable as it may have seemed to some critics in the past. Many of these critics were doubtless going on the assumption that any form of socialism would characteristically involve a fairly equal distribution of income, and consequently a denial of special rewards to those producers in the society who contributed most to the social product. However, there is nothing intrinsic in the nature of a command economy that requires an equal distribution of income and, in fact, most command economies have set up fairly elaborate bonuses and other incentives to spur managers and workers to the fulfillment or, if possible, overfulfillment of their production targets.

(5) **Basic Goals.** We have left to the last in this brief list what in some senses should have come first: the question of basic goals. If the central planners do not rely on the wishes and preferences of the consumers to set the basic economic targets for which they are aiming, what then do they rely on?

This is a complex question, for ultimately its answer depends on the particular political organization of the command economy and the psychology of its effective leaders. A rough generalization on the basis of historical experience would go something like this: In general, command economies, while not ignoring the preferences of consumers (including their preference for at least some choice in the goods they buy), have nevertheless usually set goals that were different from what might have been expected had the market mechanism had somewhat fuller

play. In particular, and probably because most of these economies tended to be somewhat economically backward at the outset, there has been a heavy emphasis on achieving economic growth at as rapid a rate as possible. The objective of catching up with the West has been paramount. If this has required sacrificing present standards of living to the demands of the future, then the sacrifice has been made, sometimes with a vengeance.

This last point can be illustrated by our familiar production-possibility curve. In Figure 3-1, we have drawn another such diagram, again with a choice between points *A* and *B*. This time, how-

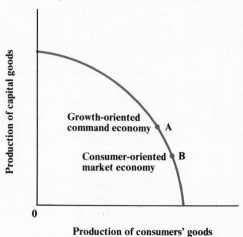

Production of consumers' goods

Figure 3-1.

In the determination of basic goals, most near-command economies in real life have put a heavy emphasis on investment and economic growth. They have moved in the direction of *A* (as opposed to *B*) on their production-possibility curve.

ever, we have placed "consumers' goods" on the *x*-axis and "capital goods" (or "producers' goods") on the *y*-axis. One of the choices all societies face is how much of their output to devote to immediate consumption and how much to *invest* in machines, tools, equipment, and plant—what we call *capital goods*—which will make possible a larger productive capacity in the future. What we have been saying then is that most command or near-command economies have tended to locate nearer to *A* than to *B*.

In saying this, however, we are speaking less of the intrinsic features of a command economy than of actual historical experience, especially that of the major exemplar of this general approach, the Soviet Union. Let us therefore now turn directly to the Soviet economy and make a few comments about its problems and accomplishments in the area of central planning.

THE SOVIET ECONOMY— PLANNING WITHOUT A FREE MARKET

The Soviet economy, as we would expect, is not a pure command economy in every way. It is perhaps the closest approximation to such an economy that exists, however, and its durability (since the 1917 Revolution) gives us an important opportunity to inspect both the strengths and weaknesses of this form of economic organization.

All the problems that we have mentioned in the previous section have troubled the Soviet government at one time or another. In the very early days of the Communist regime, for example, organizational problems proved temporarily insurmountable. With the dislocation of the economy following World War I and the Revolution, stringent economic controls had to be abandoned in the early 1920s and a return to prices, markets, and capitalistic incentives had to be permitted in substantial areas of the economy. This

was the period of the so-called New Economic Policy, a policy which, incidentally, was very successful in helping to restore the shattered Russian economy to its pre-World War I levels. Beginning in 1928, with the first Five-Year Plan, however, a near-command economy in most of the strategic sectors of the economy was established. Although this economy faced many difficulties, especially perhaps in the area of economic efficiency, and although, as we shall mention in a moment, modifications are now taking place, nevertheless the basic pattern of economic organization has remained fairly stable since 1928.

What conclusions, if any, can we draw from this experience? Has it been basically successful or unsuccessful? one clear conclusion we can draw is that a command-type economy is capable of very rapid economic growth. Since we will be taking up Soviet growth in another connection later (chapter 28), we will not develop this point here, but it is important for the reader to keep it in the back of his mind.

What we are concerned with now is primarily how the Russians were able to handle the problems of organization, coordination, incentives, and especially economic efficiency that we have mentioned earlier. It is not sufficient to say, "Well, her economy *did* grow!" because growth, however rapid, might have been better handled—i.e., been still more rapid, or involved less waste, fewer resources, less human suffering. Which, indeed, is what, on the whole, most Western commentators are inclined to say about the Soviet experience.

A balanced account of the matter, directly relevant to our concerns, is given by Z. M. Fallenbuchl in the following reading. Of particular note is Fallenbuchl's explanation of how the Soviet planners preserved *some* consumer choice while reserving most major productive decisions for themselves.

How does the Soviet economy function without a free market?

Z. M. FALLENBUCHL

I

In a free enterprise economy the basic economic problems of what to produce, how to produce and for whom to produce are decided through the operation of a market. In the Soviet-type economy these problems are solved through a combination of administrative commands and market forces which are allowed to operate within certain limits in respect of some economic activities.

Administrative commands can effectively be applied because the state and the party exercise an enormous degree of control over the economy. This control is based on the three main institutional features of the system.

There is, first of all, the totalitarian political power and the state monopoly of information and education which give the leaders a considerably greater freedom of decision than that which would ever be possible under political democracy, at least in peace time.

Another feature is the state ownership of the great majority of the means of production. The state sector is responsible for about 92 percent of the gross value of industrial output. The whole land is owned by the state and 16 percent of the total area under cultivation belongs to state farms while over 80 percent of the area is allocated to collective farms over which the state has complete control. In addition, the government has at its disposal nationalized banking and finance, transportation, the mo-

Excerpted from Z. M. Fallenbuchl, "How Does the Soviet Economy Function Without a Free Market?" *Queen's Quarterly* 70, no. 4 (Winter 1964): 559–74. Reprinted by permission of the author and publisher.

nopoly of international trade, domestic wholesale trade and over 90 percent of the retail outlets.

The third feature of the system is centralized planning with economic plans which are enacted as law and which are therefore backed by legal sanctions, supplemented by various kinds of administrative pressures and numerous economic and non-economic incentives.

This institutional framework enables the leaders to make some basic economic decisions in accordance with their own scales of preferences and to ignore, up to a certain point, the preferences of the consumers. It is impossible to understand the working of the Soviet economy without realizing that dictatorial objectives are the dominant force determining the direction of a great deal of economic activity.

However, not even the most autocratic leaders and the best planners can solve millions of detailed economic problems in a completely centralized way. Moreover, an excessive centralization and bureaucratization have serious drawbacks. The maintenance of an extensive bureaucratic machine is expensive, rigidity and inertia tend to develop and economic efficiency of the system declines. Hence the perennial dilemma of the Soviet economic organization: how to decentralize some economic activities without loosing the control over the economy and the possibility of central planning.

II

The communists have rejected the consumers' sovereignty but they have left consumers with some degree of free choice in the market for consumption goods. Contrary to the early communist dreams, the consumers receive their incomes not in the form of allocation of various consumption goods but in the money form. They are free to decide what they want to buy within the limits imposed by the existing quantities of commodities which have been produced in accordance with the planners' decisions.

Two problems are involved here. The first is the maintenance of an overall balance between the effective demand of the population, i.e., the sum of personal incomes which are likely to be spent on consumption and the aggregate supply of consumption goods available. Any discrepancy between the two can be eliminated by adjustments in the general price level which can easily be effected by changes in the rates of the sales tax, in the total wage bill or in the aggregate supply of consumption goods, if the authorities are prepared to do it.

The second problem is that of maintaining balances between demand for and supply of particular commodities. If there are discrepancies, then adjustments in relative prices, changes in the production plans and, in the case of some serious shortages, rationing can be introduced.

Although the consumers are free to choose among the produced consumption goods, they have only a very limited opportunity to influence the production pattern, which is mainly determined by the planners. The planners decide whether or not the consumers should have more textile or electrical appliances, for example.

How is it possible for the Soviet planners to leave the freedom of choice to consumers and, at the same time, to deny them the power to decide the pattern of production?

The answer can be found in the maintenance of a permanent state of full employment on the one hand and the ability to control inflation on the other. In all communist countries the leaders try to achieve the fastest possible economic growth by directing a huge proportion of resources to investment while, at the same time, they tend to increase "communal consumption" (education, health, social welfare, entertainment, public administration) and to maintain a high level of defence expenditures. As a result of this policy, there is a chronic shortage of producers' goods in relation to the amounts which are needed. The producers' goods industries have permanently more than sufficient demand for their output.

A relatively small proportion of resources is left for consumption and this relative shortage creates the sellers' market conditions. The existence of the sellers' market makes it easy to sell anything which has been produced and the planners do not have to fear any serious over-production of individual commodities. Although

cases of the overproduction of some particular commodities have occurred from time to time in the Soviet Union and other communist countries, so far these cases have been relatively insignificant under the conditions of general scarcity.

The policy of over-committing the resources eliminates the danger of insufficiency of aggregate demand and reduces the importance of overproduction of particular commodities, but it also has its disadvantages.

First of all, it implies a relatively low standard of living. It creates inconvenience for the consumers who are faced with various shortages, delays and difficulties. In addition to these there are also some serious dangers involved. The danger of inflation is always present. There have been periods of open inflation in the Soviet Union and other communist countries, but as the planners have some effective means to fight inflation, it is a suppressed inflation rather than an open inflation which is more typical for the Soviet-type economy.

The existence of suppressed inflation is, however, responsible for a number of inefficiencies. It leads to hoarding of machines and raw materials by state enterprises, to a deterioration in the quality of both consumption and producers' goods, to bottlenecks and interruptions in the productive process, and to the "take it or leave it" mentality in the distribution process.

III

The communists have rejected not only consumers' sovereignty but also the maximization of consumers' satisfaction (at least the present consumers' satisfaction) as guiding principles for the planners, and they have rejected maximization of profits as a guiding principle for productive enterprises.

Between 1928, when the planning era began, and 1964, there have been seven plans. Six of them were of five years duration and the most recent one covers the period of seven years. Four five-year plans were completed: the first (in four years), second, fourth and fifth. The third plan was interrupted by the Second World War and the sixth was abandoned in 1958 and replaced by the seven-year plan.

The method which is used in the preparation of the plans is the so-called "planning by material balances"—a crude input-output process expressed mainly in physical terms.

Because of the enormous practical difficulty of considering all interrelationships within the economy, the planners' approach has, until now, been to concentrate on certain key branches of material production which are selected by the Party leaders as the priority branches. The whole plan is built around output goals and investment projects in these key branches. The other branches of the economy are developed only to the extent which is required in order to achieve the main goals. This approach was recommended by Lenin who called it the principle of "decisive links." It simplifies planning and makes sure that the most important goals are achieved. Whenever their implementation requires more resources than have been planned for, the low-priority sectors are sacrificed. At the same time when plans were fulfilled, or even over-fulfilled in heavy industry, such branches of the economy as agriculture, housing and light industry were seldom able to fulfil their plans, although these plans were usually less ambitious than those for the high-priority branches of the economy.

The Soviet economy is often referred to as "a war economy" because of this concentration on a few major goals, breaking of successive bottlenecks, general scarcity and the mobilization of all efforts and resources irrespective of costs. Just as it happens during a war in any country, decisions of central authorities in respect of major goals and corresponding resources allocation are decisive throughout the whole economy.

This type of economic system is well adapted to achieve the selected goals but it cannot usually secure economic efficiency. In other words, it can solve the problem of "what to produce" in accordance with the planners' scale of preferences but it is not completely successful in solving the problem of "how to produce" the required product mix.

IV

As it is impossible for the central planning office to specify all details concerning the de-

sired assortment and methods of production, a certain number of decisions have to be left to the management of the productive enterprises.

The manager's first duty is to maximize gross value of output and also to fulfil other tasks specified by the plan, such as, for example, reduction of costs, increase in labour productivity and others. There is a whole system of material incentives, the purpose of which is to induce enterprises to conform to the plan.

Piece rates and bonuses are used to induce greater efforts by workers. For the achievement of planned tasks and, above all, for the fulfilment of output plans, managers receive bonuses which form a considerable proportion of their total incomes. In addition to material incentives there are a number of non-economic incentives and administrative pressures.

Evaluating the effects of the existing system of incentives, [Professor J.S.] Berliner [in his study of informal organization of the Soviet firm] concludes that it "has created a corps of managers dedicated to their work and responsive to the production demands made upon them" by the planners, but that at the same time certain features of the system are "directly responsible for motivating management to make a variety of decisions contrary to the intent and the interest of the state."

Together with excessively high targets and general full employment conditions, the system induces some undesirable changes in the product mix (for example, when the target is expressed in tons there is a tendency to produce a heavier product), the concealment of the real productive capacity of enterprises (to make the fulfillment of high targets easier), and the falsification of reports and the deterioration of quality.

The system, as it exists now, tends to encourage the largest possible output but it does not provide a sufficient inducement to ensure the most efficient ways of producing this output.

The system also induces waste of raw materials. When, for example, the enterprises producing a variety of products have their plan targets expressed in value terms, the incentive system works in such a way as to induce the use of more expensive materials as the cost, plus a fixed margin of planned profit, will add up to a higher price in this case and will automatically increase the value of production thus helping fulfil the plan.

The communist leaders are now aware of the problem and economists are discussing the ways in which the system could be made more efficient. At least some economists are sceptical whether any solution other than introduction of the principle of profitability will give the required results.

Although some serious mistakes have been made in the field of investment planning, the importance of the inefficiency of the system should not be overestimated. The Soviet economy has not been fully efficient but it works and it has been able to produce very high rates of growth. One can only speculate that with improved efficiency these rates would have been even greater.

V

The problem of "for whom the economy produces" is again solved mainly by leaders' decisions in accordance with what they believe is in the interest of the nation and partly by market forces, operating within certain limits.

The distribution of income among the members of the industrial labour force depends on the wage scale, which is sharply differentiated in accordance with a relative scarcity of a particular skill, the importance of an industry (the high priority industries have higher wage scales than the low priority industries) and the geographical area (higher wages are paid in remote areas).

In agriculture, workers employed by the state farms receive wages based on the same principle as industrial wages, while members of collective farms receive their remuneration in accordance with the nature of the work, which determines the allocation of the "trudodni" (work-days).

Although the general level of wages and the wage differentials are determined by the central authorities, a certain flexibility exists in practice.

Under the 1940 decrees unauthorized leaving of a job, as well as absenteeism or lateness were treated as criminal offences punishable by imprisonment, forced labour or fines. These decrees were not, however, applied in practice after 1953 and they were cancelled in 1956. At present the labour market is free in the sense that people can move to enterprises which offer higher wages. There is a penalty, however, if someone leaves his job and does not take another one within a month. Labour does not have the right to strike or to collective bargaining for wage increases.

The market forces operate in reality in a stronger way than it would appear on the basis of the study of existing regulations. In various ways managers are able to compete for better workers or scarce skills by offering higher wages than the official rates. This is often done by reclassifying upward a particular worker or by manipulation with bonuses and piece-work arrangements. There exists, therefore, a discrepancy between official and actual rates.

The labour market is, however, highly imperfect. There is usually only very limited knowledge of existing openings elsewhere. Geographical mobility is limited by housing shortages, the rigid system of housing allocation and by administrative restrictions imposed on moving to some areas. In addition, moving is complicated by the fact that usually more than one member of the family is working.

As a result of the imperfections of the market, workers with exactly the same skill have different wage rates in different industries, different geographical areas or even within the same industry and within the same area.

VI

Summarizing, we may say that the decisions of the central authorities determine, to a considerable extent, the solution of what? how? and for whom? These decisions are mainly enforced by direct controls, but market forces are also utilized in some areas to strengthen these orders or, sometimes, to replace them. In some cases market forces act, however, against the wish of the planners and create undesirable results.

On the whole the Soviet-type economy can solve the problem of "what to produce" rather well in the sense that it secures the priority of the production of producers' goods and high rates of growth. It makes possible the concentration of huge resources on some selected goals and, in general, the required composition of output is produced, although some distortions of the product mix of both consumption and producers' goods tend to occur.

The solution of the problem of "how to produce" seems to be much less satisfactory. The system involves considerable waste and inefficiency, some of which will, no doubt, be eliminated in the future with a further improvement in planning methods, decentralization of economic administration and introduction of a better system of material incentives.

The problem of "for whom the system produces" is solved well in the sense that the state can secure for investment, communal consumption, public admininstration and defence a very high proportion of national income. It does not seem to secure to labour, however, that part of the value of the total product which labour contributes and it does not always secure equal pay for equal skill and equal effort.

Fallenbuchl's article was written in the mid-1960s and since that time there is evidence that Soviet concern for a more efficient economic organization has increased. As her economy has matured, even her rapid rate of growth has become threatened by the kind of organizational difficulties we have been discussing.

An interesting consequence of this concern has been a willingness to experiment—still cautiously and incompletely—with what might heretofore have been considered capitalistic devices. A few years ago, several Soviet economists, especially E. G. Liberman, began to recommend the greater use of prices and markets and the criterion of profitability in the management of Soviet industry. In July 1965, two clothing factories in Gorki and Moscow adopted a version of the Liberman system and presently reported substantial increases in both output and profits. In 1966 and 1967 the system was further extended and, in the early 1970s, it appears likely that some of the reforms will be spread through the entire industrial sector.

Although the fate of the price mechanism in Russia cannot be fully foreseen, the above comments raise the interesting question as to how far an economy can go in introducing market elements into a system where the State owns the basic tools of production and wishes to influence important national objectives, as for example the distribution of income. To put it another way: Is it in fact possible to have *market socialism*?

MARKET SOCIALISM
IN THEORY

In theory, the answer is yes, as was shown by the Polish economist, Oskar Lange, in an important essay written in the 1930s.[3] Indeed, market socialism is often called *Lange-type socialism.*

Lange objected to many features of a private enterprise system—its inequitable distribution of income, its tendency to monopoly and unemployment, its failure to deal with cases where private and social interest do not coincide—but he was also, unlike some doctrinaire Marxists, fully aware of the efficiency of Adam Smith's "invisible hand." Decentralized decision-making through the market does get many tough economic jobs done. Lange knew this, and wanted to preserve as much of the market as he could.

What he worked out was a combination of command and market economies

3. Oskar Lange, "On the Economic Theory of Socialism," originally published in the *Review of Economic Studies* 4, nos. 1 and 2 (October 1936 and February 1937).

(or centralization and decentralization) along the following lines: the State will own the means of production of the society (land and capital), except that labor will continue to control its own labor services and will be free to offer these services on the market for wages. The wages of labor will not, however, constitute the full incomes of labor, since the State will be actively involved in subsidizing laborers in order to maintain a more equal (or otherwise more socially desirable) distribution of income. Consumers will be free to spend their incomes on consumer goods as they choose, but the State will largely determine the proportion of society's income devoted to the accumulation of capital. Business firms will produce and sell goods on the market, except that they will be instructed to behave as they would under conditions of pure competition. In effect, business managers are to *pretend* that they are in a market economy![4] Finally, supply and demand will be equated in the labor market, so that there will be no problem of mass unemployment.

A simplified circular flow diagram showing how such a system of market socialism might work is depicted in Figure 3-2. In the inner flow, we have the ordinary market for labor and consumers' goods, except that labor is receiving a subsidy from the State, in order to bring about a more desirable income distribution. In the outer flow, on the left side, the State is providing the firms of the economy with the services of the State-owned capital and land, to use in the production process. On the right side, the State determines the rate of capital accumulation for the economy by its orders of new capital goods from the producing firms.

Since there is an ordinary market only for consumers' goods and labor services, how are the "prices" of land and capital to be determined? Essentially, the process is this: The Central Planning Board sets certain prices for the factors of production. These are simply accounting prices, since they need not result in a flow of income between the State-owned firms and the State as factor owner. The managers of the firms, however, are instructed to use these prices just as they would use ordinary market prices in a private economy. If the price of a factor is originally set too high, this will be reflected in an excess supply of the factor; in the next period, an adjustment would be made by a trial-and-error lowering of the price. Conversely, the price would be adjusted upward if demand exceeded supply in the previous period. These trial-and-error adjustments of prices would be analogous to similar adjustments in a private market, and the final equilibrium—as in a market economy—would be where supply equaled demand.

The virtue of the Lange scheme and of its numerous variants was its demonstration of the possibility of combining the market and planning in a reasonably coherent way. But, as in the theory of the market economy, which also looks quite admirable in its ideal form, many difficult questions arise when we attempt to apply it to economic reality. Will income subsidies from the State affect the laborers' incentives to work? Will management be as efficient in the absence of opportunities for building up fortunes and amassing wealth? Should it be the State or the households or business firms who decide how much of a society's income should be devoted to capital accumulation?

In short, has anyone ever actually

---

4. In particular, they would be instructed to obey certain rules to guarantee efficient production. Such rules—for example, that the price of a product should equal the additional cost of producing a unit of that product—are developed (pp. 507–10).

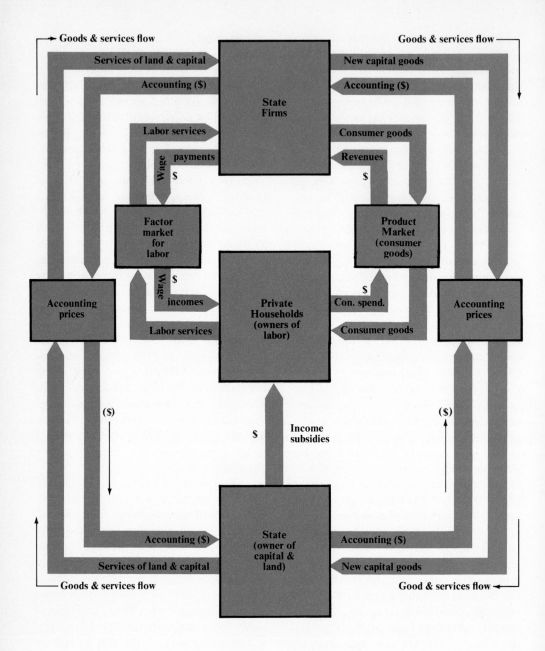

Figure 3-2. Simplified Circular Flow Under "Market Socialism."

**Under the Lange scheme, there would be an ordinary market for labor
services and consumer goods, but the State would own the capital
and land of the economy, would determine the rate of capital
accumulation, and would pay subsidies to households to bring
a "better" income distribution.**

tried to put market socialism into practice?

THE YUGOSLAV EXPERIMENT

The answer again is yes, although practice in economics never looks quite exactly like theory. Or, to put it another way, every example of economic practice has its own special features that are hard to disentangle from the general principles involved. Thus, it is often said that Yugoslavia is engaged in an experiment in market socialism, yet many elements in the Yugoslav economy are specific to her own situation.

Yugoslavia holds a particular interest for students of planning since she began her postwar development with highly centralized planning along the lines of the Soviet model, but then shifted to a decentralized socialism of the Lange variety. A relatively small country (population of 18.5 million at the time of the 1961 census), Yugoslavia was basically underdeveloped before World War II, and she emerged from the conflict with considerable damage to such productive capacity as she possessed.[5] In 1947, she embarked on a Five-Year Plan aimed at fostering rapid development and especially industrial development. Planning was detailed, weighted towards certain high-priority industries (electric power, steel, coal, etc.) and complicated by an elaborate bureaucratic structure at the federal and regional levels. Prices and wages were arbitrarily fixed, "profitability" was largely irrelevant at the enterprise level, and efficiency considerations generally took a back seat.

This highly centralized approach was modified and then abandoned at the end of the first Five-Year Plan in 1951. The political break with Stalin had already occurred in 1948. Moreover, although Soviet-style planning may have had its uses during the period of extreme economic difficulty immediately following the war, the defects of this approach soon became apparent. Plans drawn up for industrial enterprises were often unrealistic or inconsistent, necessary inputs were delivered late or not at all, consumer goods output fell far short of expectations, and agriculture "had a catalog of disasters all its own."[6]

Beginning in 1952, Yugoslavia embarked upon her distinctive program of market socialism. This program involves considerable public ownership of industrial enterprises and some central planning, but also a heavy emphasis on the market as a means of relating the individual enterprise to the economy as a whole and substantial worker participation in the actual management of the publicly owned enterprises. Briefly, there is private ownership in most of the agricultural sector (about 85 to 90 percent of arable land is in private hands) and in some small-scale trade outside of agriculture, but public ownership is dominant in the remainder of the Yugoslav economy. The publicly owned enterprises compete with each other in the marketplace; and their basic decisions about production techniques and output levels are guided by expected sales revenues in the market. Prices often vary according to supply and demand, although there have been periods of both increasing and decreasing price control since the dismantling of the cen-

---

5. Thus, in addition to a massive loss of human life (one person out of twelve of the population), Yugoslavia lost two-thirds of her prewar agricultural machinery and implements, forty percent of her factories, and most of her transport capacity. See F. E. Ian Hamilton, *Yugoslavia* (New York: Frederick A. Praeger, 1968), p. 93.

6. Thomas A. Marschak, "Centralized Versus Decentralized Resource Allocation: The Yugoslav 'Laboratory,'" *Quarterly Journal of Economics* 82, no. 4 (November 1968): 572.

tralized system in the early 1950s. As of 1967, price controls still applied to about half the industrial goods transactions in the Yugoslav economy.

Although publicly owned, industrial enterprises in Yugoslavia have the rather unique feature of being subject to management by Workers' Councils. The Workers' Council is elected by the workers of an enterprise through direct and secret ballot. This council, in turn, elects a Managing Board which, together with a Director, whose selection reflects both the workers' interests and those of the local government, is responsible for the management of the enterprise in question. Worker interest and participation are secured not only by this formal scheme but also by the fact that the incomes of the workers come from the net revenues or profits of the enterprise. The workers thus have a direct stake in the efficiency of the firm's operations, and they also have a say in determining what part of the firm's income shall be reinvested in the expansion of plant capacity.

Although planning of various kinds still exists in the Yugoslav economy, the trend in recent years has been toward even further decentralization. Until 1965, the central government had dominant control of funds available for the development of heavy industry, electricity, transport, and certain agricultural projects. Since that time, however, significant reforms have resulted in a decentralization of the banking system and hence of the availability of credit for investment purposes, and also in a relative increase in the funds available to individual enterprises and local governments as opposed to the central government. The net effect of this evolution has been that while in terms of ownership criteria the Yugoslav economy is largely socialist, in terms of the locus of decision-making authority it

has come more and more to resemble the market-style economies of the West.

How has this experiment worked? Has the peculiar Yugoslav "bridge between East and West"[7] been a success or a failure?

The evidences of the reasonable success of market socialism in Yugoslavia are several. The decentralization of the economy has undoubtedly limited bureaucratic waste and promoted efficiency in a number of ways. Worker influence in the management of industrial enterprises and their sharing in industrial profits have provided important incentives for labor and also a sense of participation in the life of the national economy. Agriculture, largely in private hands since 1953, has avoided the numerous pitfalls that seem everywhere to plague collectivized farming on the Soviet model.

As we might expect, however, there have also been numerous problems in the Yugoslav experience, and some of these at least appear to be connected with decentralization. For example, one of the advantages of centralized control of investment in a country like Yugoslavia, with very substantial regional differences in economic development, is that it permits special attention to be paid to improving conditions in the backward areas of the nation. One of the dangers of *decentralization* is that funds may flow more readily into the developed areas of the country and that regional imbalances will become more severe. Another danger—to which any market economy is subject—is the concentration of economic power in the hands of successful, large-scale enterprises. Socialist though she may be, Yugoslavia faces something of a monopoly problem! Although there is no evidence

7. George Macesich, *Yugoslavia: The Theory and Practice of Development Planning* (Charlottesville: The University Press of Virginia, 1964), p. vii.

to suggest that concentration of power in large enterprises is greater in Yugoslavia than in private market economies of comparable size, nevertheless the problem is potentially a serious one and may eventually require the attention of the central government.

Despite these and other difficulties,[8] two things do seem clear: one is that many observers of the Yugoslav scene, including some who believed in the necessity of centralized planning in the immediate postwar period, are convinced that the path of decentralization has brought far greater gains than losses in the period since 1952. And the second point—rather more impressive as evidence—is that other East European economies like Czechoslovakia, Hungary, and even, as we have seen, the Soviet Union have been tempted in the direction of greater decentralization. Had Yugoslavia's experiment been a failure, it is doubtful that quite such pressures for reform as are now stirring in Eastern Europe would have come into being.

SUMMARY

In analyzing the *centrally planned* or *command economy,* we naturally go back to Karl Marx, who gave the ideological backdrop for most of these economies in the modern world. Marx did not, however, provide a blueprint for economic planning; rather, he provided a detailed critique of capitalism—because of its class antagonisms between capital and labor, its monopolistic elements, and its inherent tendencies to depression and technological

unemployment—and he developed an ideology that (when flexibly interpreted) could serve the purposes of Communist revolutions.

In practice, the pure command economy must make difficult economic decisions that often require elaborate institutional arrangements in the modern industrial world. The areas in which problems are likely to occur are: (1) organization of an adequate planning bureaucracy; (2) coordination of economic targets in a consistent manner; (3) making production efficient in the economic sense; (4) securing proper incentives for workers and managers; and ultimately (5) setting proper goals for the economy when consumer sovereignty no longer provides the guidelines.

A near-approximation to the command economy has been the Soviet Union, whose economic experience over the past half century gives us our best case study of how the command mechanism works. Although the Soviet economy has demonstrated a high rate of growth (as we shall discuss later), her economy has shown many elements of inefficiency in the areas mentioned above. In recent years, Russia has, in fact, been experimenting with the introduction of certain market elements in her economic system. This raises the question of whether a mixture of centralization and decentralization along the lines of *market socialism* is a possible compromise approach.

Economic theory (as, for example, in the works of Oskar Lange) suggests that such a compromise is feasible, with the State owning the means of production and making certain decisions, but with many economic choices being left to the market. Practical experience in Yugoslavia in a specific version of market socialism (including, among other things, active Workers' Councils) tends to support the

---

8. Some of these difficulties—inflation and regional and technological unemployment—reflect not so much Yugoslavia's economic system as her economic *condition:* i.e., a substantially underdeveloped country trying to achieve (and actually achieving) a high rate of economic growth.

conclusion that such mixtures do work well, at least under certain circumstances.

QUESTIONS FOR DISCUSSION

1. Marx predicted an increasing class conflict between capitalists and the proletariat as the capitalistic system approached maturity. How well does this prediction stand up in the case of the United States, as judged by your general knowledge of American history? What economic factors may have moderated any tendency toward class conflict in this country?

2. Marxian economics, in a technical sense, is based on what is sometimes called the *labor theory of value*. This theory states that the prices of different commodities are proportional to the quantities of labor involved in producing those commodities. This theory is generally believed to be inadequate because it neglects the fact that there are different *qualities* of labor and also the fact that there are *other* factors of production besides labor (e.g., land and capital goods). Remembering your general supply-and-demand analysis from chapter 2, show how:

    (*a*) a country with a shortage of cultivable land might generally expect higher food prices than a country where land was abundant;

    (*b*) a sudden influx of highly skilled surgeons from abroad might lower the price of medical services.

3. In a pure command economy, what takes the place of a market economy's "consumer sovereignty"?

4. "The main problem with a command economy is that it has no way of providing incentives to its labor force and managers to work effectively and well." Discuss critically.

5. According to Fallenbuchl, the Soviet central planners have been able to allow some consumer choice while retaining control of many key production decisions. How has this been possible?

6. The Russian Revolution is often attributed in part to the fact that the Russian economy was relatively "backward" in the early twentieth century. Communism also has an appeal for a number of economically "backward" countries today. What factors do you imagine may have created this appeal for such countries? List what you would consider to be possible advantages and disadvantages of a highly centralized economic system for an economically backward nation.

7. Yugoslavia is a very different country from the United States in both size and stage of economic development. To what degree do you think her experience with market socialism is relevant to this country? (Incidentally, do you think that Workers' Councils are a solution to the problem of "alienation"?)

SUGGESTED READING

Bergson, Abram. *Planning and Productivity under Soviet Socialism.* New York: Columbia University Press, 1968.

Campbell, Robert W. *Soviet Economic Power.* 2nd ed. Boston: Houghton Mifflin Co., 1966.

Grossman, Gregory. *Economic Systems.* Englewood Cliffs, N.J.: Prentice-Hall, 1967.

Marx, Karl. *Capital.* 3 vols. Chicago: Charles Kerr & Co., 1906–1909.

Milenkovitch, Deborah. *Plan and Market in Yugoslav Economic Thought*. New Haven: Yale University Press, 1971.

Schumpeter, Joseph A. *Capitalism, Socialism and Democracy*. 3rd ed. New York: Harper & Row, 1950, part I.

Sherman, Howard J. *The Soviet Economy*. Boston: Little, Brown and Co., 1969.

Sweezy, Paul M. *The Theory of Capitalist Development*. New York: Oxford University Press, 1942.

4
The Mixed American Economy: Public Sector

It should be clear from our discussion of socialism in the last chapter that the pure form of command economy does not exist. In the Soviet Union, market elements have always played some role and have done so increasingly in recent years. Furthermore, there has been a growing interest in market socialism as the experience of Yugoslavia and other Eastern European economies suggests. Of course, we know that the pure market economy does not exist either. These are the extremes on a scale that runs from highly centralized planning at one end to highly decentralized private decision-making at the other. Every planned economy uses the market mechanism to some degree; every market economy involves certain areas of government intervention and control.

All of which is to say that the *mixed economy* is the characteristic form of economic organization in the modern industrial world. This is an economy in which both public and private decision-making have a significant effect on the direction and well-being of the society, where economic planning is often practiced by the large private as well as by the public enterprise, where, in general,

the interaction among government, business, and labor is constant and complex.

Of course, the proportions of the mix may vary considerably, and this is a matter of importance. Still, the old-fashioned view that put market economies on one side and planned economies on the other and said, "Choose one or the other, not both!" is simply inaccurate. Most modern countries *have* chosen both—but in different degrees.

Since this is the case, we shall devote the next two chapters to a study of the mixed economy. In this chapter we shall concentrate on the governmental or public part of the mix; in the next, on the private sector. We shall use the United States' economy as our example throughout this discussion, both because we are familiar with it and because of its enormous importance in the world economy generally.

GROWTH OF GOVERNMENT IN THE UNITED STATES

Let us begin by getting a few facts under our belts. It is often said that gov-

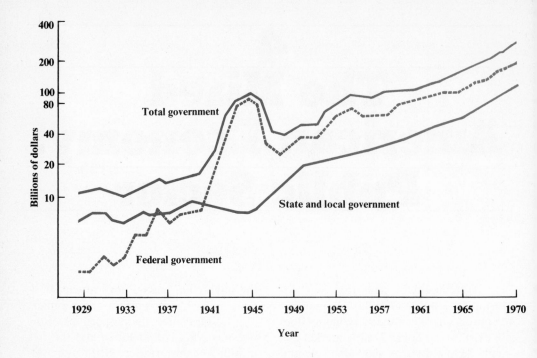

Figure 4-1. Total, Federal, and State and Local Government Expenditures.
Source: Economic Reports of the President, 1966, 1971.

ernmental activity has been growing rap-idly in this country in recent years. Has it? If so, how rapidly, and in what ways?

One way of estimating the growth of the public sector in the American econ-omy is to take all governmental expendi-tures—federal, state, and local—lump them together, and see how they have ex-panded over time. In Figure 4-1, the top line represents the sum of all govern-mental expenditures in the United States from 1929 to 1970. This chart is drawn on a semi-log scale, meaning that a straight line would represent a constant percentage increase. The strong upward drift of the curve makes it clear that the public sector has been expanding substan-tially in the United States—from about $10 billion total in 1929 to well over $300

billion at the present time.

To understand the extent of this expansion, however, it is necessary to in-spect these figures a bit more closely. In the first place, they are in "current dol-lars," meaning that they reflect the up-ward drift of prices over this period as well as the increase in real or physical purchases by government. Both consumer and wholesale prices have more than dou-bled between 1929 and 1970.

Second, we should notice that re-cent years have seen a particularly rapid expansion of state and local expenditures. People often have a tendency to think of government intervention in the economy only as "big government"—the federal government. But after a period of relative stagnation from 1929 until the end of

94

World War II, state and local expenditures have been expanding very rapidly, from less than $10 billion in 1946 to $119 billion in 1970. One of the reasons (though not the only reason) for this expansion is the large role state and local governments play in education: over one-third of all state and local expenditures go to schools and universities. An expansion of government of this sort is worth noticing, for it does not represent a new kind of government "interference" in the economy but is simply an expansion of an area long considered properly within the public sector.

A third point to make about these figures is that they include at least two fundamentally different kinds of governmental expenditures. In addition to ordinary government expenditures on goods and services[1] they also include *transfer payments*. The difference is important. In the case of an ordinary government expenditure, the government pays a clerk for his services in the Defense Department or buys a truck or other commodity from a private firm. The payment is for a good delivered or a service rendered. A *transfer payment*, however, involves neither a good delivered nor a service rendered. In a typical form it simply represents a transfer of purchasing power from a taxpayer to the recipient of the transfer payment. Social security payments are transfer payments. So also are payments for unemployment compensation. So also are some of the payments made to farmers under our various agricultural programs. In each case, the key fact is that the government does not produce goods itself or direct private production into certain channels by its orders for goods. The elderly couples on social security do not have to provide any services to the government, and they are free to spend their money in such ways as they see fit.

In our present discussion, the relevance of this distinction derives from two considerations: (1) although transfer payments necessarily involve a degree of government intervention in the economy, the degree is somewhat less than that of ordinary government expenditures, which represent a claim of the government on the nation's output of goods and services; (2) transfer payments have grown very rapidly in recent decades, increasing as a percentage of total governmental expenditures. Actually, this growth of transfer payments, as we shall see in a moment, does represent some important new functions of government in the American economy. But it also means that our figures on the expansion of government in Figure 4-1 may somewhat overstate the increasing impact of government on the economy during this period.

Finally, and perhaps most significantly, we should notice that while governmental activity has been growing over the past three or four decades, so also has the nation's economy as a whole. What we are interested in most directly is not governmental expenditures in isolation, but those expenditures in relation to the nation's total output of goods and services. Figure 4-2 represents the total of federal, state, and local expenditures expressed as a percentage of the U.S. gross national product.[2] Now this diagram makes it clear

---

1. Sometimes called *exhaustive expenditures* by economists. It should be noted that these exhaustive expenditures include both direct governmental production—i.e., services of policemen and teachers—and also government purchases of goods—typewriters, buildings, etc.—from the private sector.

2. Gross national product is a common measure of a country's total output of goods and services. We shall discuss its precise definition in detail in chapter 8, pp. 191–207. The reader should note that transfer payments, not representing an addition of goods and services output, would not be included in gross national product.

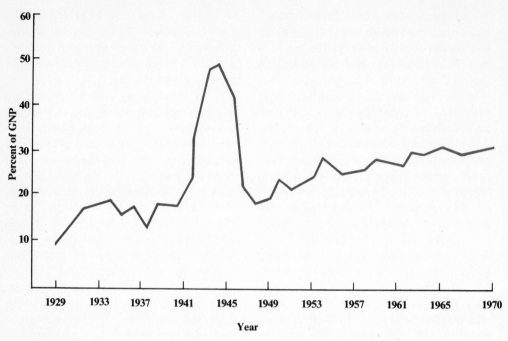

Figure 4-2. Total Government Expenditures as a Percentage of GNP, 1929-1970.

that in this all-important *relative* sense, the growth of government in the American economy is somewhat less dramatic than one might have expected. Indeed, the striking thing about the curve is not so much the growth of government in recent years—though the percentage has been increasing—but rather the extraordinary levels of expenditure reached during World War II. In 1943 and 1944, governmental expenditures were roughly *half* our total national output! There was a sharp cutback immediately after the war, then a gradual upward drift that has continued since that time. Overall, including transfer payments as well as ordinary expenditures, the general trend has definitely been upward—from fifteen to twenty percent of GNP in the 1930s to thirty percent or more of GNP at the present time—but it is less drastic in this relative sense than the absolute figures had suggested.

Of course, governmental expenditures are only *one* of a number of possible indicators of the role of the government in the economy as a whole. Actually, there are many functions of government that may affect the private sector very intimately and yet not show up in these particular numbers. For example: the Justice Department attempts to enforce various antitrust laws with respect to American business. In terms of national output percentages, the expenditure side of antitrust enforcement is trivial; but antitrust policy is a very important sphere in which the government is engaged in giving shape to the market economy. A similar situation exists with the many other regulatory functions of government, or with legislation such as the Wagner Act or the Taft-Hartley Act, affecting labor unions. Whether they are in the form of pure food and drug legislation or regulating airlines or requiring safety features on our automobiles, there are countless examples of government participation in the economy that do not show up in our expenditure graphs.

There is no way to quantify these manifold activities, although a rough generalization would be that they show very much the same picture that has emerged from our expenditure diagrams. That is to say: there has been a gradual expansion of these regulatory and other activities from the 1930s to the 1970s. As with expenditures, these other activities reached a great height in World War II when there were price and rent controls, rationing of goods, and a general mobilization of the economy for war. After the war, there was a relaxation of controls, and then, as with total governmental expenditures, there was a gradual, but still significant, increase from the prewar period. The wage-price controls instituted in 1971 and 1972 are the most dramatic example of this expansion to date.

CAUSES OF THE EXPANSION OF GOVERNMENT

Some of the forces behind the expansion of the public sector have been fairly clearly of an economic nature; others derive more from political, and especially international political, considerations. An important example of a factor that seems to stem largely from political causes is the great growth of defense expenditures in the American economy since the late 1930s. If one adds together our direct defense expenditures, veterans' benefits, our international programs, space research, and the interest payments and other costs of past wars, one has well over half of all federal government expendi-

tures in this country at the present time. Now it is probably true that economic factors are reflected in these programs to some degree—Marxists, of course, would claim that "imperialistic" wars stem largely from economic causes! It is certainly true that these large defense expenditures have a complex economic *impact*, as we shall be discussing in a moment. Still, it seems fair to say that the great pressures causing this part of federal expenditures to grow so rapidly lie in the international political sphere. If the Cold War in all its complicated ramifications were to end, this would certainly reduce many of the forces bolstering expansion in the federal budget.

Thus, the biggest single item of federal government expense is largely noneconomic in origin. Furthermore, it represents no new function of government. This last, as we have already noted, can also be said about most of our increasing expenditures on schools. A very great part of the modern expansion of government in America, therefore, has either resulted from noneconomic factors or has been in the traditional areas of governmental responsibility, or both. (Adam Smith, we recall, charged the State with the responsibility for defense and with certain duties with respect to public education.)

However, there has also been an expansion of government activity into relatively new areas of our common life, and for what are largely economic reasons. These are of particular interest to the student of economics. Through an increase in the role of the public sector, these activities attempt to correct deficiencies (or, more accurately, what the majority of Americans regard as deficiencies) in the workings of a market economy.

A listing of these new programs would be very long. But certain general areas of concern stand out. One is the broad area of *income distribution*.

Private market forces operate efficiently with respect to many economic problems, but they often leave certain groups in the society without adequate protection. Elderly people, the disadvantaged, the uneducated, minority groups, the ill or the infirm— such individuals or groups will ordinarily receive a very small share of the nation's total output, and yet their economic needs may be as great as, or often greater than, their more fortunate neighbors. A great many of the government's welfare programs, ranging from the initial social security enactments of the 1930s to Medicare and Medicaid in the 1970s, have been designed to meet these needs. Not all transfer payments go from rich to poor, but many do, under these new welfare programs, and they consequently represent a redistribution of national income in favor of the needy.

Another broad area of concern is unemployment or, more generally still, the problem of *stabilizing the economy* in the aggregate and promoting its growth.

*Ever since the 1930s, economists and, increasingly, public officials have recognized that an unregulated market mechanism does not ordinarily guarantee a full-employment economy. We shall be studying this problem in much more detail in Part Two of this book, showing some of the underlying forces that bring about general unemployment and price inflation in a modern industrial economy. Suffice it to say here that many governmental actions in the past thirty years have been designed to cope with this problem. Part of the Social Security Act of 1937 set up a system of unemployment compensation. More recently, the government has been using its formidable fiscal and monetary policies to stabilize the econ-*omy in the aggregate. The tax cut of 1964 was aimed primarily at reducing unemployment and speeding up economic growth. The stringent "tight money" policy of the Federal Reserve Board in 1966 was designed to combat inflation, as was the wage-price freeze of 1971. Even with active governmental intervention, these problems are not easy to handle, but it is now widely agreed that they do form an appropriate area for governmental concern and responsibility.*

A third general field for government action has been in *providing certain goods or services that are valuable to society as a whole,* but are not likely to be produced by private market forces, or at least not in sufficient quantities.

Some goods are naturally collective *as opposed to* private, *since it is difficult to withhold them from any citizen even if he doesn't pay for them (for example, defense, which shelters us all even if we do not pay a cent toward its cost).[3] But there are also many cases in which the marketplace will undervalue the actual social benefits to be derived from a particular act of production. A good example of this kind of problem is the construction of a dam. As a private party, I may build a dam on a river and find that a great many of the benefits of the dam go to other firms farther downstream. Now the dam may not be profitable for me to build, because although I must bear all the costs, I receive only part of the benefits. Yet if the government were to build the dam, the total benefits to society might be greater than the total costs. There are also important cases where there are significant social costs for which private*

3. For a fuller discussion of the distinction between *collective* and *private* goods, and also of the general issues treated in this paragraph, see Otto Eckstein, *Public Finance,* 2nd ed. (Englewood Cliffs, N.J.: Prentice-Hall, 1967), pp. 8–14.

parties are not charged—air pollution from private factories or private motorists is a notable example. Whenever there is a divergence between the private and social benefits or costs of an economic undertaking, there is a prima-facie case for governmental intervention.

We could list a number of other items that have influenced the expansion of the role of the American government in recent decades. Rather than going on, however, let us take three particular questions of government policy, trying to illustrate in this way the complexity of the interaction between the public and private sectors in our mixed economy.

LIMITED GOVERNMENT INTERVENTION— U.S. AGRICULTURE

American agriculture is a particularly good example of some of the paradoxes of a mixed economy. In some respects, the agricultural sector affords the closest approximation to a purely competitive market economy we have in this country. There are several million farm families, the average size of farming units

is quite small, and, in general, the conditions for "responding" to the impersonal market seem to be met. Furthermore, we often think of the American farmer as particularly individualistic and independent and determined to shape his own fate.

Yet for many decades the United States government has been active in this area of our economy. Until World War II, virtually all agricultural research was sponsored by the Department of Agriculture and other federal and state agencies.[4] Furthermore, the government has been involved in a whole series of price-support, acreage limitation, crop storage and loan, and international disposal programs that have crucially affected farm prices and farm incomes. Why have such programs come into being and what are their general effects?

The following selection from the *Economic Report of the President,* 1970, gives a useful summary of the problem and of the attempts made to solve it. It will also give us an opportunity to apply the basic supply and demand tools we developed in chapter 2.

---

4. In the past two decades, the leadership in agricultural research in the United States has passed to private parties and especially to the new "agribusiness corporations." This is an interesting reversal of what often seems the more usual trend from private to public enterprise.

THE ECONOMIC REPORT OF THE PRESIDENT, 1970
GOVERNMENT REGULATION OF AGRICULTURE

Government & Agriculture

Agriculture is another important sector of the economy where regulation has

Excerpted from the Council of Economic Advisers, *The Economic Report of the President,* 1970, pp. 104–7. Reprinted by permission.

been used in an attempt to make market performance more satisfactory.

Many of the problems of agriculture are the result of a steady increase in agricultural output per farmer, which has made farmers a continually dwindling minority, and of insufficient mobility, which has kept their average income below that of most other occupational

groups. As early as 1870, the number of farmers had dropped below the number of persons in other occupations. This trend has continued, and the proportion of the population gainfully employed in agriculture at the present time is only 5 percent. This is the usual transition in an advancing economy. Fewer and fewer people are required to produce the food and fiber for the rest of the population; or, stated another way, as the real income of consumers rises, an increasing proportion of income becomes available for other things than the basic necessities of life. Currently, about 16 percent of consumer income is spent on food.

Thus we get the familiar adjustment problem in the agricultural sector. Stimulated by the yield from public and private programs to develop and facilitate adoption of technological innovations, output grows more rapidly than consumer demand. Since the demand for farm products is relatively inelastic, increased supplies generally lead to markedly lower farm prices. As a result, farm incomes are depressed, and farmworkers and proprietors move to other occupations. But because there are impediments to this movement, per capita personal farm income does not catch up with the level in other sectors.

At the depth of the depression, per capita personal income of farm people was less than one-third that of the nonfarm population. In the middle fifties it was about 46 percent. Currently, the per capita personal income of farm people is about seventy percent of that of the rest of the population, but the narrowing of the income gap is due in large part to increasing Government payments to farmers, steady gains by farmers in adding to their income from nonfarm sources, and substantial declines in farm population. [See chart below.]

Government Intervention in Agricultural Markets

The depression of the 1930s led the Federal Government to intervene directly to support falling prices in

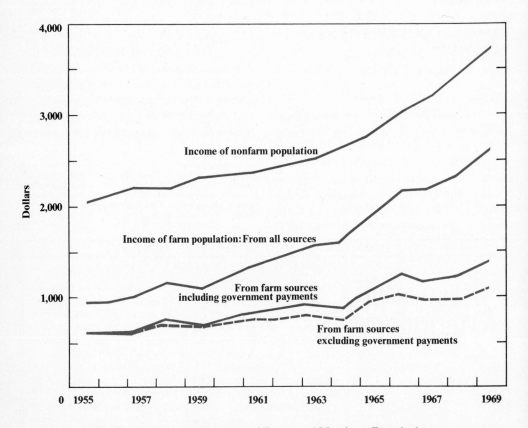

Per Capita Personal Income of Farm and Nonfarm Population.
Sources: Department of Agriculture, Department of Commerce, and Council of Economic Advisers.

agricultural markets with the objective of stabilizing farm income. Since that time, commodity programs that were originally adopted largely as emergency measures have varied only in emphasis from one decade to another. They have generally involved direct payments to farmers, production controls on output, price supports, and storage and marketing activities. All these programs have entailed substantial budgetary costs. Direct payments alone were about $3.75 billion in 1969, accounting for about 23 percent of realized net farm income.

Because most commodity programs have been related to output, their main benefits go to the larger commercial farms; for example, in 1968 the top 6 percent of the farms (those with sales of $40,000 or more) received nearly one-fifth of the Government payments and accounted for about one-third of the realized net farm income.

As another indirect form of regulation, Federal and State marketing orders and agreements are in effect for many perishable commodities such as milk, fresh fruit, and fresh vegetables. Milk marketing orders illustrate one method of market control. For each milk marketing order, minimum prices are established for the milk sold by dairy farmers. Using criteria provided by statute, the Secretary of Agriculture sets these prices; prices may be different for the same milk depending on its final use. Drinking or Class I milk carries a higher price than manufacturing or Class II milk.

The average or "blend" price is paid to all farmers.

In an attempt to reinforce price discrimination between the two classes of milk, the Food and Agriculture Act of 1965 provided for so-called Class I Base Plans in Federal milk markets. These plans, which are instituted at the request of dairy farmers, can be used to restrict production to the level of Class I requirements in an individual market. Under this plan, each producer receives a high price on his "base" (his share in the Class I market), rather than a "blend" price on all production. Milk produced in excess of the established base is then priced at the lower Class II level, thus discouraging the production of milk for manufacturing. When access to the Class I market with its higher prices is sharply restricted, title to a base may be very advantageous. The value of these bases subsequently becomes capitalized into production costs for new producers, who purchase them. And consumers of Class I milk must continue to pay substantially higher prices.

A Market-Oriented Agriculture Policy

Farm policies on field crops should give greater emphasis to market forces and thus reduce direct governmental participation in the marketplace. Specifically, three goals should be sought. First, prices should become more flexible so that they approximate equilibrium between supply and demand when averaged over a period of years. With this flexibility

farmers should be able to hold and even expand both domestic and foreign markets. Price supports should not interfere with normal commercial transactions, but should serve only as a price floor to prevent excessive fluctuations and to provide a basis for credit.

Second, production should not be controlled by limiting individual crop acreages; rather it should be guided by market prices. Because the Government cannot immediately withdraw the influence on production that it has exercised during its four decades of direct intervention, a gradual approach is needed by which greater freedom will be gained through restrictions on total land use only. Such a program would restore considerable freedom of choice to participating farmers, permitting each one to produce as much of any crop as he thinks will be most profitable up to the limits of his authorized cropland. Eventually, we may be able to discard even this control measure.

Third, direct income payments, properly applied, offer a more efficient way to support farm income than high price supports. The potential benefits of high prices are largely dissipated because they make additional purchases of inputs profitable. Direct income payments will be necessary for some time to compensate for inequities and to smooth the adjustment process. Reasonable limits on payments to individuals, however, would help prevent the undue enrichment of large operators at public expense.

We can make the analysis in the above report clearer by using some of the tools we have developed in earlier chapters. Notice that the report states that "the demand for farm products is relatively inelastic." This refers to certain properties of our familiar demand curve (chapter 2) under the general heading of *price-elasticity*. By this term we try to measure the responsiveness of the quantity of a commodity demanded or supplied (in our case, demanded) to changes in its price. More specifically:

Price-elasticity of demand is defined as the percentage change in the quantity of a commodity demanded divided by the percentage change in its price.

For example, if the quantity of apples demanded goes up by 10 percent when the price falls by 10 percent, we say that the price-elasticity of demand is 1. If the quantity demanded goes up 20 percent when the price falls by 10 percent, we say that the price-elasticity is 2 and that the demand curve is relatively *elastic* at that point. If the quantity goes up by only 5 percent under these circumstances, we say that the price-elasticity is .5 and that the demand curve is relatively *inelastic* at that point.

Another way of describing elasticity is in terms of the total sales revenues that come to an industry from selling their product. Thus, for example, if a demand curve is inelastic in the relevant region, a decrease in price would be associated with only a small increase in quantity demanded—hence, on balance, total sales revenues (price times quantity) would decrease with a decrease in price. Conversely, if demand is relatively elastic, total revenues would *in*crease with a decrease in price. The reader should be able to answer

the question of what happens to total revenues when there is a price decrease, and elasticity is precisely 1.

These concepts are illustrated in Figure 4-3 for the case of *inelastic* demand. At the original price (P_1) of 80¢ a dozen, farmers are able to sell 20 million dozen apples (Q_1) to consumers. Total revenues are .80 *times* 20 million ($P_1 \times Q_1$) or $16 million. At the lower price (P_2) of 40¢ a dozen, farmers are able to sell more apples ($Q_2 = 30$ million dozens), but since the percentage change in quantity is smaller than the percentage change in price, total revenues fall—i.e., to .40 *times* 30 million ($P_2 \times Q_2$) or $12 million. Because of inelastic demand, an increase in quantity and a decrease in price are associated with lower total income to these apple producers.

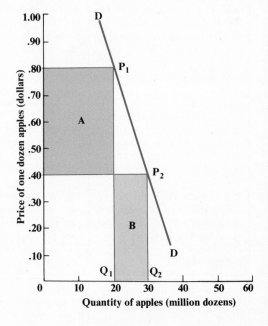

Figure 4-3.

When demand is *inelastic*, an increase in quantity and decrease in price will lead to lowered total revenue for apple producers.

The reader should note that a rough assessment of elasticity can be made by the use of various rectangles in Figure 4-3. When the price falls, the apple producers will lose revenue equal to the area of rectangle A and will gain revenue equal to the area of rectangle B. If area A is bigger than area B, demand is inelastic. If area A is smaller than area B, demand would be elastic. If area A and area B are exactly equal, elasticity equals 1. In this last case, of course, a rise or fall in price or quantity will, on balance, have no effect on the total sales revenues of the producers.

With Figure 4-3, we can now interpret the sentence in the report that reads: "Since the demand for farm products is relatively inelastic, increased supplies generally lead to markedly lower farm prices." Quite simply, as the production of farm products increases from Q_1 to Q_2, farm prices fall sharply from P_1 to P_2, and total farm incomes become depressed. This brief analysis should already make clear why one of the forms of government intervention in agriculture mentioned later in the report is "production controls on output." In effect, the government tries by regulation to raise farm income by reducing output from Q_2 back to Q_1. The reader should also now understand one of the cruelest paradoxes in economics—why it was that during the Great Depression of the 1930s, when millions were hungry, the government and the farmers were busily engaged in plowing under "excess" crops!

But there is more to the farm story than this. For the report also tells us what is happening over time as the supply and demand curves *shift outward.* There is also an elasticity concept involved here, but it is now the concept of *income-* (as opposed to *price-*) *elasticity:*

Income-elasticity of demand is defined as the percentage change in the quantity of a good demanded at a given price divided by the percentage change in consumer incomes.

In other words, if my income goes up 10 percent and my purchases of apples at, say, 80¢ a dozen go up 10 percent, then my income-elasticity of demand is 1. If my purchases of apples go up by *more* than 10 percent, my demand is relatively income-*elastic;* if *less* than 10 percent, it is relatively income-*inelastic.*

Now we already know from chapter 2 that consumers' incomes are among the givens (locked up in the *ceteris paribus* clause) behind a particular demand curve. Hence, when we talk about income-elasticity of demand, we are essentially talking about *shifts* in the demand curve. When we say that demand for farm products is relatively income-*in*elastic we are suggesting that these shifts outward will be relatively small as consumer incomes increase over time.

The analysis of the report can now be interpreted further by means of Figure 4-4. The analysis states that over time there has been a great increase in farm productivity and output, depicted in our diagram by the strong outward shift of the farm supply curve from SS to $S'S'$. At the same time, rising consumer incomes have not led to a proportionate increase in demand for agricultural products, with more of the higher incomes going for "other things than the basic necessities of life." In other words, demand has been income-inelastic with the result that the shift in the demand curve has been relatively small. The total effect is clear: the natural tendency over time will be for market prices to move from P_1 to P_2, a decline by no means compensated for (as far as the farmers are

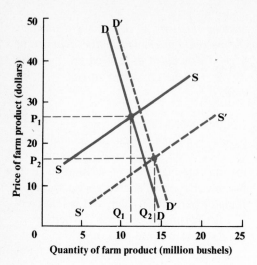

Figure 4-4.

Expansion of supply in American agriculture tends to outpace the expansion of demand over time.

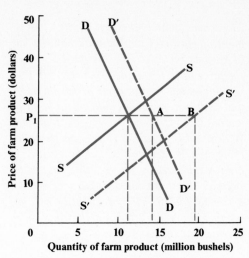

Figure 4-5. Government Price Support Program.

The government supports the price at P_1. When supply and demand curves shift, the government will have to purchase AB million bushels of the farm product, the excess of supply above demand at the publicly supported price.

concerned) by the smaller increase in quantity sold (from Q_1 to Q_2).

We can now also see in basic economic terms how a price support program in agriculture might work. Suppose, for example, that in order to raise farm incomes, the government offers to support a certain price (say, P_1 in Figure 4-5) by buying any excess of production above what consumers are willing to take off the market at that price. Now when the supply and demand curves shift over time, the quantity supplied at this price will far exceed the quantity demanded. The government will then buy up the difference (in Figure 4-5, amount AB) and then add the surplus to its stock of farm products in storage. Under such a program, the farmers incomes and revenues would not decline but rise over time.

The report ends by urging a greater market-orientation for agriculture in the future; but it acknowledges the need for continued direct payments to

farmers to "smooth the adjustment process." Since this process has already been going on for several decades, it seems likely that American agriculture will continue to be a "mixed" public-private sector of the economy for some time to come.

GOVERNMENT AND BUSINESS— THE MILITARY-INDUSTRIAL COMPLEX

If government participation in U.S. agriculture is of long standing, government participation in the defense of the nation clearly goes back to the first days of the republic. What is new in recent decades is the massive size of our defense establishment, its capacity for expansion over time, and its persistence even under circumstances when the nation is not engaged in all-out wars such as World War II.

Although radical critics of American society have done much to popularize the term *military-industrial complex,* the phrase was coined by President Dwight Eisenhower in his "Farewell to the Nation" in 1961. And concern has been expressed by relatively conservative econo-

mists such as Arthur F. Burns, who notes that the military-industrial complex "has not only been enlarging the scale of governmental operations and thereby complicating financial problems," but "has also been affecting profoundly the character of our society."[5]

5. Arthur F. Burns, "The Defense Sector: An Evaluation of Its Economic and Social Impact," in Seymour Melman, ed., *The War Economy of the United States* (New York: St. Martin's Press, 1971), p. 116.

THE MILITARY-INDUSTRIAL COMPLEX

DWIGHT D. EISENHOWER

A vital element in keeping the peace is our Military Establishment. Our arms must be mighty, ready for instant action, so that no potential aggressor may be tempted to risk his own destruction.

Our military organization today bears little relation to that known by any of my predecessors in peacetime, or indeed by the fighting men of World War II or Korea.

Until the latest of our world conflicts, the United States had no armaments industry. American makers of plowshares could, with time and as required, make swords as well. But now we can no longer risk emergency improvisation of national defense, we have been compelled to create a permanent armaments industry of vast proportions. Added to this, 3½ million men and women are directly engaged in the Defense Establishment. We annually spend on military security more than the net income of all United States corporations.

This conjunction of an immense Military Establishment and a large arms industry is new in the American experience. The total influence—economic, political, even spiritual—is felt in every city, every statehouse, every office of the Federal Government. We recognize the imperative need for this development. Yet we must not fail to comprehend its grave implications. Our toil, resources, and livelihood are all involved; so is the very structure of our society.

In the councils of government we must guard against the acquisition of unwarranted influence, whether sought or unsought, by the military industrial complex. The potential for the disastrous rise of misplaced power exists and will persist.

We must never let the weight of this combination endanger our liberties or democratic processes. We should take nothing for granted. Only an alert and knowledgeable citizenry can compel the proper meshing of the huge industrial and military machinery of defense with our peaceful methods and goals so that security and liberty may prosper together.

Excerpted from Dwight D. Eisenhower, "The Military-Industrial Complex," from President Eisenhower's Farewell to the Nation, *Department of State Bulletin,* February 6, 1961, pp. 180–81.

From the point of view of economic systems, the interesting thing about the military-industrial complex is its departure from the assumptions of either the market or the command economy. In terms of a market economy, we have first of all the fact that the buyer facing the

business firms in this area of the economy is not the private household but the State. If consumer sovereignty is exercised here it must be through the political process—i.e., by voting for those administrations that demonstrate views about defense spending similar to those of the public at large. Consumer sovereignty exercised in this fashion is, of course, rather more indirect than when individuals go out and buy (or not buy), and it is also severely limited in this area by the very fact that we are dealing with highly technical, sometimes emotional and often classified materials. The effectiveness of consumer choice under these circumstances must necessarily be rather small.

Second, there is a single buyer rather than the many thousands of buyers postulated in the competitive market economy. We have monopoly on the buying side, or what economists sometimes call *monopsony*.[6] American firms are unlikely to be called upon to build elaborate missile systems for the Russians if our Department of Defense turns them down.

Third, and related to the above, is the fact that the supply-and-demand apparatus can hardly be called upon to set prices and quantities under the circumstances we have described. In place of the market is the government contract, in which complex cost-accounting procedures and political policy mechanisms replace the old private risk-and-profit of a free enterprise economy.

On the other hand, the military-industrial complex does not signify that we are in a command economy either. The obvious fact is that, although defense expenditures are large, they still represent a relatively small fraction of our total gross national product. Moreover, whereas in the command economy, the Central Planners are sending directives to firms that are themselves organs of the State, in the military-industrial complex the firms that produce the goods and services are still private business firms that make profits,

are responsible to share-holders, reinvest part of their earnings, and so on.

Indeed, one of the most interesting features of this aspect of a mixed economy is that it becomes, in actual fact, rather difficult to distinguish the private from the public sector. Marxists might view this as an expected domination of the State by the capitalist industrialists. Conservatives might consider this an unfortunate intervention of the State into private affairs. In either event, as the following reading suggests, the tendency within the military-industrial complex is to an arrangement in which private and public units form one continuous management, rather than being opposed to each other, or qualitatively different. The mixture, in effect, becomes a compound.

Here is a brief analysis by a longtime student of these matters, Professor Seymour Melman of Columbia University:

FROM PRIVATE TO PENTAGON CAPITALISM

SEYMOUR MELMAN

The military-industrial firm and the effects of its operations have changed the internal economics of the firm and have altered key features of industrial capitalism as a whole. The extent of these effects is linked to the scale of military-serving industry.

Military industry in 1970 employed about 3 million persons on work directly traceable to the Department of Defense. In addition, 3.4 million men and women served in the

---

6. Literally, *monopoly* means "single seller" and *monopsony*, "single buyer." Of course, in real life we often have elements of monopoly or monopsony present rather than the pure thing. See pp. 610-11.

Excerpted from Seymour Melman, "From Private to Pentagon Capitalism," excerpted from *The War Economy of the U.S.* (New York: St. Martin's Press, 1971), pp. 1–3. Reprinted by permission of the publisher.

uniformed armed forces and about 1 million civilians were employed by the Department of Defense, mostly on military bases engaged in research, development, testing, prototype manufacture and supporting activities, and base maintenance. All told, about 22,000 enterprises have been linked to the Department of Defense as performers of contracted work.

The tacit assumption has been that the firms serving the Department of Defense are like other enterprises. What has proceeded almost unnoticed is that since 1945 there has been a twenty-five-year experience in which a new type of enterprise has been created that is basically different in many operating characteristics from the entrepreneurial firm of industrial capitalism. The combined effect of this network of enterprises has modified the economy as a whole because of the character and the size of military expenditures.

The autonomous capitalist firm has operated to extend the decision-power of its management, using cost minimization and profit accumulation as major instrumental measures. This extension has been characteristically measured in terms of percentage of a market, percent of capital investment, or change in the proportion of employees in a given industry. For this extension of decision-power, profitability has been calculated and accumulated as a vital source of fresh capital for investment. Thus, during the last half century, firms have become increasingly self-financed, relying increasingly on themselves for accumulation of capital for further investment. (Profit levels can vary substantially as a function of decisions by managements on allocating various fixed costs. Thereby the magnitude of profit in a given period is diminished as an autonomous indicator of management's operations.)

The character of the military-industrial firm is functionally defined by the way its management participates in decision-making. Managing includes decisions on what products to produce; how to accumulate capital; how to design and organize produc-

tion; the quantity of the product; the price to be charged; and the mode of distribution of the product. Together, these functions constitute management. The autonomy of the private firm rests on the fact that the final veto power over these decisions is in the hands of its own management. This central characteristic has been altered in the military-industrial firm.

From 1946 on, industrial firms were increasingly linked with military research institutes and with the Department of Defense in conformity with a policy regulation issued by the then Chief of Staff of the United States Army, General Dwight D. Eisenhower. Following that policy memorandum, the Pentagon arranged durable connections between nominally private firms, nominally private research laboratories (profit, university, and other nonprofit), and the military establishment. Through this period, the Department of Defense proceeded to act in ways that are characteristic of a large, monopolistic buyer—intervening in the internal affairs of the supplying firms to suit the convenience of the monopoly buyer.

Such activity by a monopoly buyer has been noted, for example, as characterizing the relations of large automotive firms to parts suppliers, or the relation of department stores or mail-order houses to suppliers of products, very often under brand names selected by the buyer. Following the Eisenhower policy that effectively founded the market network, which he later named the "military-industrial complex," the main elements of managerial decision-making within the Pentagon-serving private firm were increasingly subject to regulatory stipulations of the official *Armed Services Procurement Regulations.* (Since the monopolist buyer was also the Federal Government, there was the inevitable infusion of government-citizen relations into the buyer-seller pattern.)

After 1961, an organizational transformation was effected under the direction of Robert McNamara which changed the relation of the military-industrial firms to the

Department of Defense customer. Robert McNamara established, under the Office of the Secretary of Defense, a central administrative office, functionally similar to the type of unit that has operated in central-office-controlled, multi-division, major manufacturing firms.

With the establishment of this central office, whose nature and effects I detailed in *Pentagon Capitalism*, the relation of the military-industrial firms to the single customer shifted from one of, primarily, seller to buyer towards that of submanagement to top management. The Office of the Secretary of Defense, through its component institutions, took on the function of a top management formulating policy in relation to the nominally autonomous contracting firms. This relationship was enforced through a formal, nation-wide network of administrative offices, which supplemented the administrative organization that had previously existed and reported to the several armed services. The key element here was the concentration of control in new institutions, like the Defense Supply Agency set up by McNamara. The impact of the long-term regulatory process, plus the sharp change to formally centralized control in the new state management, induced a qualitative change in the character of military-industrial enterprise: Final decision-power over the main components of managerial control was vested in the new state management apparatus.

The military-industrial firm became a functionally dependent subdivision. Decisions on products were formally rendered by the top management in the Department of Defense. Only the most minor decisions on product characteristics were left to the individual firm. The government-based management provided capital, not only by making available land, buildings, or machinery, but also by guaranteeing loans obtained from private sources. The extension of the scope and intensity of the state management's control proceeded in every sort of decision-making: on how to produce, on quantity, price, and shipment. The net ef-

fect was to establish the state management as the holder of the final decision-power and also to limit the scope of the decision left to the managements of the defense contractors, the subdivisions of the state management.

Within industrial capitalism, subfirms frequently operate under central office control. In the military-industrial system, however, the central office is located in the executive branch of the Federal Government. It is unprecedented in size, and so is the number of submanagements. By 1968, the Department of Defense industrial system supplied $44 billions of goods and services. This exceeded the combined net sales (in billions) of General Motors ($22.8), General Electric ($8.4), U.S. Steel ($4.6), and DuPont ($3.4). Altogether, this constitutes a form of state capitalism operating under the Department of Defense—hence the designation "Pentagon Capitalism."

The military-industrial enterprise is not an industrial capitalist firm. It is not an autonomous entity, being under final control of the Pentagon's state management. Internally, it differs from the entrepreneurial business that is the model unit of industrial capitalism as illustrated by the role of profit and cost minimization.

Profit and loss statements are computed in military industry and a profit category is shown. However, this profit is not a reward for entrepreneurial risk-taking, the conventional justification for the profit accruing to the management or owners of the micro-economic unit of industrial capitalism. Risk of the ordinary sort is eliminated under conditions of assured (by contract) price and quantity of goods to be delivered to the Department of Defense. There may be residual "risk" of not getting further business, but that is another matter. Moreover, profits for a subunit can be readily regulated by the state management which is inclined to regard "profits" of its subunits as a cost to the top controllers.

Within the new military-industrial enterprise, the self-correcting mechanisms that characterize the private firm are altered, if not dissolved. When major managerial functions are poorly performed in the ordinary firm, it is the entrepreneurial obligation, then, to correct the malfunction. In the military-industrial firm, this may not be feasible insofar as final decision-making is in the hands of the state management. Thus unusually high costs, or problems in the design of the product, or problems in acquiring sufficient capital, are not, in a military-industrial enterprise, necessarily autonomously actionable problems for that management.

In the firm of private capitalism, high costs become important pressures for modification of industrial practice. For unduly high cost, as against the cost of alternative methods, can translate into competitive disadvantage and limited profits: hence, limited options for further capital investment; hence, limited options for further production decision-making by the management. Therefore, the manager of the classic industrial firm is moved to act to minimize costs. This is operative except in those circumstances where managements, either singly or in concert with others, restrict market competition and shift cost increases to price, while maintaining an acceptable profit margin for all. However, it is ordinarily understood that the latter practice is an alteration of the more characteristic cost-minimizing calculus of the private firm. In the military-industrial firm, cost increases or unusually high costs are dealt with mainly by raising price. The record shows that, on the average, the final price of major weapons systems has been about 3.2 times the initial estimate.

Finally, the conventional firm can move among markets when it finds that its products are not well accepted. No options of this sort exist for the military-industrial firm. For the Department of Defense is the market and the firm may not sell to anyone else except with permission of the Department of Defense—as, for example, to a politically allied foreign military establishment.

These modifications in the self-correct-

ing mechanisms of the classic business firm substantially alter the characteristics of that model entity, distinguishing the military-industrial firm and its controlling state management from the private and autonomous entrepreneurial enterprise.

INTERGOVERNMENTAL RELATIONS— REVENUE-SHARING

In the two previous examples, we have been considering the role of government in relation to the private sector of our mixed economy. In our third and final example of public sector activities, we shall now mention a problem of relations among branches of government *within* that sector. In the early 1970s, intergovernmental relations have become one of the most controversial matters in the American political-economic arena.

We have already spoken of the great expansion of governmental expenditures at the state and local levels. An important part of these increased expenditures has been in education as we know. In the first instance because of the postwar "baby boom," and continuing on because of the desire for increased education at all levels of our society, educational expenditures by state and local governments have increased ninefold in the past twenty years. But other expenses have also been increasing. In 1948, state and local governments were spending $2 billion on public welfare; twenty years later, the figure was over $12 billion. General expenses for health, hospitals, police, fire protection, and the dozens of other state and municipal services each citizen expects as a matter of natural right rose in total from $7 billion to $42 billion during this same period. In 1971, state and local governments were spending considerably more on nondefense expenditures than was the federal government.

Now while these *demands* on the state and local exchequers have been rising so dramatically, the ability to *meet* these demands has fared much less well. There are many reasons for this difficulty. The exodus of upper and middle income families from the central or "inner" cities is well known; at a time when the demand for public services has been increasing rapidly within the cities, the ability to finance such services has actually been declining. Another important factor, many observers feel, is that the federal government has more or less preempted the most efficient and (despite some flaws) most equitable means of raising tax revenues—namely, the progressive individual income tax. In fiscal 1968–69, for example, state and local governments raised only $9 billion from individual income taxes as compared to $31 billion from property taxes and $27 billion from sales taxes.

The problem of soaring requirements and limited sources of financing has led many economists and public officials to believe that some form of *revenue-sharing* from the federal to the state and local governments is the only possible solution. The idea was advanced in 1964 by Walter W. Heller, then chairman of President Kennedy's Council of Economic Advisors, and Joseph A. Pechman, a director of the Brookings Institution. It was advanced again in somewhat different form as official administration policy by President Nixon in 1971. President Nixon's plan would involve taking 1.3 percent of taxable personal income (about $5 billion) and distributing it more or less

without strings to the state and local governments; it would also reduce some of the restrictions on the state and local spending of the federal funds that are already flowing to lower levels of government under various existing programs.

Why the controversy? On the surface, this kind of proposal makes eminently good sense, considering what we have just said about demands and resources at the state and local levels. And, indeed, a number of mayors and governors do support the plan as the only way out of the current impasse.

At the same time, it should be clear that there are many possible grounds for objecting to this scheme. Revenue-sharing will disappoint expectations (1) if state and local governments prove to be less efficient (or more corrupt) than the federal government; (2) if the federal government takes this opportunity to reduce or not to expand sufficiently the *total* of federal resources flowing to the state and local governments—a simple substitution of one kind of aid for another is unlikely to be adequate; or (3) if the net effect is to place on smaller units of government responsibilities that ultimately should be handled by the society as a whole.

These and other issues are raised in the following article by Max Frankel, chief of the *New York Times* Washington Bureau. Since the article is rather critical of the Nixon plan, it should be remembered that the basic idea of revenue-sharing is fully bipartisan (Walter Heller advanced it under a Democratic administration), and that even critics of the 1971 plan would in many cases regard it as an improvement over the present highly unsatisfactory situation.

Revenue Sharing Is a Counter-revolution

MAX FRANKEL

The Revolution, if you haven't heard, is to be President Nixon's bloodless execution of the Federal monster by a technique called Revenue Sharing. Its promise is "cash and freedom" for the states and cities. Its slogan is "power to people." Its goal, a "new Federalism."

The governors, mayors and people need more money, right? Too much of their money now gets shipped off to Washington, right? Too many Congressmen and bureaucrats try to tell them how to run their affairs, right? Well, step right up and let us help yourselves: one pot for "general" revenue sharing—let's say twenty-five dollars a head to start, half to the states, half to the cities, no strings attached, no serious questions asked; a second pot for "special" revenue sharing, using moneys hitherto earmarked for definite projects—about fifty dollars a head, to be spent almost as freely, though with a little more guidance and accounting. Right? Right on!

Like all revolutionary doctrine, this is heady stuff. A good many governors and mayors are rushing headlong for this dole, duly reciting the selfless doctrines of the revolution—that revenue sharing

will not only rescue local government from financial collapse but also bring decision-making "closer to the people," eliminate waste and tyranny along the Potomac and generally breathe new life into our democracy.

The only trouble is that like all simplistic formulas, revenue sharing ignores a good many political facts of life. It dangles cash before some hard-pressed communities without really defining the object of such a costly "reform." Indeed, it proposes to commit an open-ended portion of our jointly owned treasure without achieving any significant reform. And it gives virtually no thought to the desired purposes of our Federal system, old or new.

The central flaw in the President's revenue-sharing scheme is that it would ignore this [Federal] system in the name of reforming it. It would begin to turn the Federal Government into little more than a tax collector and dispenser. It would leave the states and cities saddled with costs—welfare, for instance—that ought to be shared by the population as a whole. It would leave them free to tax their citizens in wildly unequal patterns. It would give them portions of the common national treasure with only negligible concern for their capacity to spend it effectively. A program that does not address the ways in which governments raise their revenues hardly deserves the name

revenue sharing. A program that does not relieve local governments of obligations they neither created nor sought should not be palmed off as burden sharing. The Nixon program is revolutionary only in the sense that it is antigovernment, hostile to the very idea that the Federal moneys and powers should be used to achieve desirable and necessary ends.

The President's judgment that the Federal edifice is buckling under the weight of a top-heavy steeple tends to ignore the fact that the rest of the American structure of government is in no condition to support anything. At the middle levels are the state and county administrations, mostly weak, outmoded or corrupt, even when they are not broke. At the lowest level, the foundation of local government can be described only as jerrybuilt.

There are more than 80,000 units of local government in the United States—21,000 of them juggling the affairs of the major metropolitan areas that house seventy percent of the population. That works out to an average of ninety-one governments for the typical metropolitan area, or forty-eight for each metropolitan county, including—besides the county government itself—twelve school districts, twelve municipalities, seven townships and sixteen special districts that run the water supply, treat the sewage or provide some other service.

Counties and school districts in this tangle exercise powers delegated to them by the states and therefore dovetail across the map in jigsaw pattern. All the other units of local government have sprung up in random and overlapping profusion.

To exercise "control" over these local governments, the citizen must pick his way through laundry-list ballots of nonentities. And controlled or not, local office holders can rarely find enough money or authority in their slender jurisdictions to fill even the most elementary needs of the citizens. Most of the thousands of local governments can neither attract nor afford the expertise and administrative skills that they so plainly lack.

There is little doubt that state and local governments, in the aggregate, need more money. Their expenses have increased more than twelvefold since World War II—to an estimated $132 billion—more than three times as fast as spending by the Federal Government or individual citizens. By 1975, presuming roughly the present range of obligations, the state and community budgets will total about $200 billion, and between $6 billion and $10 billion of that amount will be lacking.

Mr. Nixon argued that the Federal Government had "pre-empted and monopolized" the personal income tax as a source of revenue, leaving the states and cities to depend upon inferior and unfair taxes on property and sales. He noted, rightly

enough, that the Federal income tax was a far more equitable way of raising revenue and that some of the local levies were becoming an almost intolerable burden on many citizens, notably those least able to pay. But these were crocodile tears, shed for a system that the President treated as a state of nature, as if it were beyond the capacity of men and governments to change. Far from advocating local tax reform or making Federal aid contingent upon constructive change, he offered revenue sharing to the perpetrators of inequity. Instead of changing the deplored system, he proposed to underwrite it indefinitely.

Some of the most flagrant inequities in our national tax system result not from the Federal "surplus" and local "shortages" that allegedly trouble Mr. Nixon. They result from the disparities of wealth and need among the states, cities and communities, often within just a few miles of each other.

Throughout the country, groups of citizens have fled the central cities with their wealth, walled themselves off behind "local" governments and ordinances and left the inner cities and neighboring counties to cope with their growing problems and diminishing sources of revenue. Some of the local governments we hold so dear for being "close" to the people are in fact little more than fiscal sanctuaries erected to prevent genuine revenue sharing. For reasons of state and liberty, we may not be able to reorder things by telling people where they should

live and work. But we can certainly push their money around to spread the burdens and the wealth.

Even more disturbing is the evidence that many states and communities simply refuse to raise the revenues they so manifestly need for the services they crave and that the majority of local governments persist in rigging the taxes they collect so that they fall cruelly upon those least able to pay.

For all its imperfections, the Federal income tax stands as the most progressive levy yet devised to spread the burdens of government. It draws relatively more from the most fortunate and little or nothing from the unfortunate. No Federal edict prevents any state or locality from adopting an identical or similar tax system. They could even save themselves the collection costs and ride piggyback on the Federal tax structure by laying claim to any add-on percentage they wish, as they have been invited to do by the members of Congress most influential in these matters.

Some taxes on property and sales are obviously desirable at the lower levels to pay for facilities of direct benefit to local businessmen and residents. But as a principal source of general revenue for states and localities, which these taxes have become, they are viciously unfair. They produce such practical and theoretical absurdities as the requirement that a region's public education system be roughly commensurate with the market value of its real estate.

It is such unfair local taxes that have been rising the fastest and feeding the frustrations of taxpayers. The property tax has been a special favorite, largely, it is thought, because it can be adjusted and manipulated by administrative fiat, usually without legislative action.

Ten states, including New Jersey, Connecticut and Texas, have thus far refused to impose any income tax on their residents. Pennsylvania and Ohio are just getting around to thinking about one. Three other states tax only dividend income. Four large states, including Illinois and Michigan, tax only at a flat rate, to the obvious advantage of the wealthy. Of the remaining thirty-four states with nominally "progressive" income taxes, only seventeen bother to vary the rates on earnings beyond $10,000, and most of the other progressive scales don't go beyond $5,000. One consequence of this pattern of taxation is that citizens earning $15,000 or more, who pay 33 percent of all taxes collected by the Federal Government, pay only 8 percent of those collected by state and local governments.

The inequalities are horizontal as well as vertical. There is no precise way to compare the taxes paid in different parts of the country or the quality of services they buy. But there exist some estimates of the state and local tax burden borne by an average family of four with a gross income of $10,000 in the largest city of each state. That burden ranges from $1,121 in Baltimore to $387 in Charleston, W. Va. It is $816 in New York City; $610 in Hartford; $507 in Cleve-

land; $414 in Houston; and $398 in Seattle.

To bail out and subsidize such a tax system, as the President proposes, would not only reinforce the unfairness of it all. It would also pass up what may be a rare opportunity to use the power of the Federal dollar to coerce—or, if the ideologues prefer, to induce—real reform. For there exist dozens of formulas by which Federal aid could be used to promote local tax reform so that the burdens would fall more equally on all citizens.

Even a fair revenue system, however, would work unfairly unless we also arrange a logical and equitable distribution of governmental burdens.

Obviously, sending out checks to a million welfare recipients in New York City is a burden for City Hall. It is, in fact, a burden twice over, for those million people must also be provided with public services to which they contribute next to nothing in taxes. But why should this be the exclusive burden of other New Yorkers? We wouldn't dream of asking Alaska to bear a heavier share of the national defense budget because it happens to border on the Soviet Union. We don't expect St. Petersburg, Fla., to pay a larger share of Social Security taxes just because the elderly like to settle there. We don't ask Kansans to assume a bigger responsibility for subsidizing agriculture because the farmers are their neighbors. Yet we let Mississippi or Louisiana or Puerto Rico or Appalachia export its poorest citizens to New York or Chicago or Detroit and, if

they cannot earn their keep, throw much of the responsibility for their support on the states and cities in which the poor happen to congregate.

It is simply absurd to regard relief as a local responsibility. Just as veterans are helped from a sense of national obligation, so should the poor, and especially the poor descendents of slaves, be treated out of a sense of national duty. If they are deemed worthy of help they should not have to shop around for the counties and cities that offer more than others. And if they are deemed to be a common obligation, their support should not depend on local or state budgets.

Nor is welfare the only item on the agenda of intelligent Federalism. State laws requiring children to attend school and setting minimum standards for schools—even while the schools are administered "locally"—were among the earliest expressions of the doctrine that higher levels of government must protect the common interest in lower-level administration. Now the time has come for an even broader Federal standard and subsidy of education.

We have become a highly mobile country. A hundred communities may benefit from the schooling provided by one, and a hundred may suffer for the educational neglect of another. Yet many state governments have failed to assure at least minimum patterns of equal spending on education in their jurisdictions. And the Federal Government, now bearing only seven percent of the cost of public education, has not even begun the search for common minimal standards.

The Federal Government cannot and should not prescribe the *maximum* service that local citizens may wish to support. If some villagers want more traffic lights, they can organize to get them and pay the cost. Many local requirements are peculiar or particular and of little importance to higher levels of government. But we can and should work toward *minimum* standards of life throughout the nation.

The Federal Government has a right and duty to establish minimum standards of relief, education and health, as it does in setting minimum benefits under Social Securi-

ty. It has the right and duty to use its power and money to adjust for the spread of problems from one region to another, as it does in attacking air and water pollution. It has a right and duty to equalize the burdens on its citizens, as it does by taking relatively more tax money from wealthy communities and individuals and giving relatively more to poorer ones. It has a right and duty to induce and coerce the states to work toward the sharing of revenues and burdens within their jurisdictions, as well as without.

It would be refreshing if such ardent advocates of the needs and rights of the states as Mr. Nixon would occasionally speak to the obliga-

tions of the states and localities. For the failures of the Federal Government become quickly apparent to everyone, but the failures of local administration are never really rectified or even noticed until they become an oppressive burden on the country at large.

The President's "New American Revolution" would not only fail to remedy these shortcomings. It does not even recognize them. If we followed his advice, what is deceptively called revenue sharing would become a constant flow of money out of the Federal treasury that would not buy anything for the national interest. The new revolution is in fact a counterrevolution.

SUMMARY

The characteristic form of the modern economy is the *mixed economy* in which both government and the marketplace have important roles, though in different degrees in different countries.

In the United States, the public sector has grown substantially in the past three or four decades, though not so dramatically as is sometimes imagined. Total expenditures of governments at all levels have grown from about 20 percent of GNP in the 1930s to about 30 percent or more in the early 1970s. The growth in recent years has been particularly rapid in state and local expenditures, in governmental transfer payments, and in the very large federal expenditures in defense and defense-related areas.

Much of this expansion is due to political and other noneconomic forces,

and it represents no particularly new areas of government responsibility (e.g., defense, schools, etc.), but there has also been a growth of the role of government in the economy for economic reasons as well. These reasons involve concern for (1) welfare of the needy and income redistribution; (2) stabilization and growth of the economy in the aggregate; and (3) provision of collective goods and other goods where private and social benefits or costs diverge.

The complicated role of the public sector in a mixed economy can be illustrated by several examples from the modern American economy. American *agriculture* offers an example of a sector of the economy where many of the conditions of a market economy are fulfilled (many producers, much competition) and yet where the government has been highly active for many years in agricultural research and development and in many acreage restriction and price support programs.

Such programs can often be analyzed in terms of our basic supply-and-demand apparatus.

The *military-industrial complex* is an example of how complicated relations between government and business can be in a mixed economy. In a situation where there is a single buyer (the State) and the supply-and-demand apparatus cannot be applied in any ordinary sense and where, at the same time, the sellers are not units of the State (as in a command economy) but private profit-making firms, the distinctions between public and private sectors of the economy tend to become rather blurred.

Finally, the problem of *revenue-sharing* shows us that the complications of a mixed economy are not limited to the relations of government to business or agriculture—they occur in the relations among governments at different levels *within* the public sector. President Nixon's proposal in 1971 has met with a number of specific criticisms although most students of the matter believe that some form of federal financing of state and local activities is a clear necessity for the future.

QUESTIONS
FOR DISCUSSION

1. Although government expenditure figures give an important indication of the degree of government intervention in the economy, they are not the only measure of government activity. What are some other forms that public intervention may take? Give some specific examples from the experience of the United States or of other modern mixed economies.

2. What are transfer payments? Why have governmental transfer payments been growing rapidly in recent years?

3. Show how in the case of industrial air and water pollution there may be a significant divergence between private interest and the social welfare. Does this have any relation to arguments for or against public intervention in these areas?

4. Suppose that we have a farm product with a relatively inelastic demand curve and a perfectly inelastic vertical supply curve as follows:

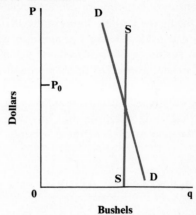

The government has two (politically feasible) alternatives:

(*a*) support the price at P_0 by buying up all the product that consumers will not buy at that price;

(*b*) guarantee the farmers the same total revenue as under the price support program, but do this by direct subsidy after the farmers have sold their entire crop to the public at the supply-and-demand-determined price.

Which program will cost the government more money?
Can you see any possible advantages to the more expensive program?

5. How do you think economic "risk" should be apportioned in the setting of a government defense contract? Should (*a*) the government bear it all; (*b*) the private

firm bear it all; or (c) each bear part of the risk? Consider the implications of your answer for the nature of the overall economic system in the present-day United States.

6. Write a rebuttal to the Frankel article, "Revenue Sharing is a Counterrevolution," under the title: "Revenue Sharing is a Genuine Revolution."

7. Considering the major economic problems facing the United States in the 1970s, do you consider it likely that there will be (a) further growth in federal government expenditures, (b) further growth in state and local expenditures, or (c) resurgence of private initiatives? Try to think of at least one example that might lead to expansion in each of these spheres.

SUGGESTED READING

Eckstein, Otto. *Public Finance,* 2nd ed. Englewood Cliffs, N.J.: Prentice-Hall, 1967, chaps. 1–3.

Hathaway, Dale E. *Government and Agriculture.* New York: Macmillan Co., 1963.

Levy, Michael, and DeTorres, Jean. *Federal Revenue-Sharing with the States: Problems and Promises.* Washington: National Industrial Conference Board, 1970.

Nieburg, H. L. "The Contract State." In *In the Name of Science,* H. L. Nieburg. Chicago: Quadrangle Books, 1970.

Phelps, Edmund S. *Private Wants and Public Needs.* New York: W. W. Norton & Co., 1964.

Shonfield, Andrew. *Modern Capitalism.* New York: Oxford University Press, 1965, chaps. 5–10, 13–14.

5

The Mixed American Economy: Private Sector

Despite the growth of government in the American economy, described in the last chapter, our mixed economy remains heavily oriented to the private side. If government expenditures amount to something over 30 percent of our gross national product, private expenditures amount to nearly 70 percent. Furthermore, many government expenditures are for the products of private industry, so that although government orders may determine the direction of certain areas of production, and although, as in the military-industrial complex, the distinction between government and industry becomes blurred, nevertheless the organization of production in the United States remains overwhelmingly in private hands. In this chapter, we shall look at some of the characteristic institutions of the private sector, attempting also to show some of the ways in which this and the public sector interact.

THE MIXED ECONOMY IN A SIMPLE CASE

A first approximation view of the private sector of the American economy can be given in terms of what we have earlier called a *pure market economy*. As a beginning, let us briefly reexamine our picture of the market economy and indicate the foundations it presupposes.

The main features of the market economy are that economic decisions are made individually and are brought to bear on the economy as a whole through a price system operating in terms of a supply-and-demand mechanism. In this economy, we thought of every individual commodity—apples or washing machines—as having a demand curve drawn on the basis of consumer preferences and also a supply curve derived from producers' responses to various possible market prices. The equilibrium price and quantity for each commodity were then determined where supply and demand curves intersected.

We also suggested that this same kind of mechanism could be applied to the factors of production. Thus, let us suppose that we are dealing not with a commodity—washing machines—but with a kind of labor—electricians. In Figure 5-1, we have drawn supply and demand curves for electricians. In the market economy, the price of electricians (which we would

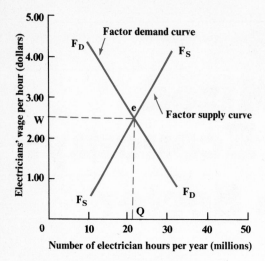

Figure 5-1. Supply and Demand for a Factor of Production.

In a market economy, we determine the price of the services of electricians (or welders or machinery) by supply and demand curves analogous to those determining prices of commodities. In the factor supply and demand curves, however, the business firms are the main demanders, and the suppliers are the owners of the factors of production (in the case of labor, the workingmen of the economy).

normally call their wage) and the number of electrician-hours employed would be determined by the intersection of these two curves.

Of course, we should not imagine that these supply and demand curves for the services of a factor of production are the same curves that we would draw for a commodity. When we were talking about washing machines, the demanders were the consumers who wanted to buy washing machines for their homes. When we are talking about electricians—or about welders or truck drivers or machine tools or blast furnaces—the demanders are typically not consumers but business firms that will produce the products that we

shall ultimately buy. The business firm, in other words, is characteristically a *supplier* of products to the consumer but a *demander* of the services of the factors of production.[1]

Now using this first approximation, we might picture a simplified mixed economy as in Figure 5-2. This is our familiar circular flow diagram except that we have drawn in suggestions of supply and demand curves in the Product and Factor Markets, and we have introduced the State as a provider of Public Goods and Services. This picture is simplified in many respects. For example, as we have shown it, the State provides public goods and services only to households and receives tax payments only from households. In the real world, as we know, business firms also receive public services and also pay taxes—corporate taxes, sales taxes, property taxes, and so on.

Our primary interest in this chapter, however, is with the private sector of the mixed economy and, in this connection, the main simplifying assumption we have made in Figure 5-2 is that the private sector can be treated as if it were a competitive market economy. Now this assumption would be completely satisfactory only if all firms in the economy were quite small, if they all responded to impersonal market conditions, if they had little direct power to influence the markets by their own actions—if, in short, they were *pure competitors* as defined in chapter 2.

Such a description is, however, inadequate to express both the variety of conditions in present-day American Product and Factor Markets and also the fact that there are many units in both markets—whether the giant modern corporation or the large modern labor union—

1. For the derivation of factor supply and demand curves, see chapter 21.

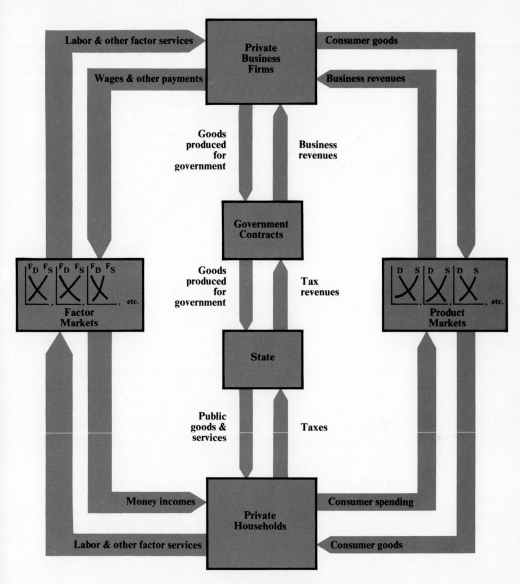

Figure 5-2. A Simplified Mixed Economy.

**This is a simplified view of a mixed economy in which all public
goods and services are provided to private households in
exchange for tax payments, and where the private sector meets
the assumptions of a competitive economy.**

that clearly have power to shape and
modify the market situations that they
face. This fact does *not* mean that the

study of purely competitive markets is a
waste of time. As we shall show in Part
Three of this book, the analysis of pure

competition is vital to the student of economics because: (1) it provides the only truly coherent picture of the workings of a market economy we have; (2) it gives us tools that can be usefully applied to the analysis of other market structures (including, incidentally, the economic activities of governments); and (3) it provides a possible criterion for the social or "welfare" evaluation of other forms of market organization.

We must not make the opposite mistake, however—i.e., to confuse this simplified picture of the world with a realistic description of business operations and labor organization in a modern industrial economy. In the remainder of this chapter (and again in chapters 24–26 and elsewhere throughout the book), therefore, we shall try to give full attention to the actual complexity of the private sector of our mixed economy.

THE MODERN CORPORATION

Perhaps the most striking feature of industrial organization in the United States is its enormous variety. There are over 11 million business enterprises in the United States today. These may have vastly different economic impacts (American Telephone & Telegraph as compared to the corner grocery store), and they may also differ in legal form:

(1) **Single proprietorship.** By number of firms (though not by economic impact), the overwhelming majority of American businesses are still single proprietorships where the individual businessman puts up his own capital and runs his own firm. This is the world of owner-employers that Adam Smith had in mind

when he developed his concept of the "invisible hand."

(2) **Partnership.** A much smaller number (around one million) business enterprises in America today are of the partnership variety. Here a group of people get together to pool their capital and to share the profits and financial obligations of an enterprise. Since each partner is liable to an unlimited degree for the debts of his partners, this form is not particularly widespread or significant in its impact.

(3) **Corporation.** In this form of business enterprise, the firm is a "legal person" that can own property, sell stocks, enter into contracts, etc. Furthermore, the corporation enjoys the privilege of limited liability. This is to say that the stockholders who own the corporation are *not* liable for the debts of the corporation beyond their original investment. By number of firms, the corporation is not much more common than the partnership—there are about 1.5 million corporations in the United States today (about one-sixth the number of single proprietorships)—but their economic impact is vast, as we shall see.

Because of the great size of some modern corporations, their activities are often characterized by what is termed a *divorce of ownership and control*. This concept was developed in the important study by Berle and Means, *The Modern Corporation and Private Property,* mentioned earlier (p. 64). When corporations are owned by many hundreds of thousands of stockholders and when, as in many cases, no individual stockholder holds more than a tiny fraction of the corporation's common stock, then the actual operation of the firm tends to fall into the hands of the management. The managers may be owners as well, but they need not be, and their ownership in such cases will represent only an insignificant proportion of the total ownership of the corporation, and often, as compared to their salaries, a very small fraction of their own personal financial interest in the firm. This fact has many possible implications. If a manager is primarily a salaried employee rather than an owner of the firm, will it necessarily be in his own self-interest to maximize the profits of the firm? In Adam Smith's owner-proprietor world, the self-interest of the operator of the firm could be identified with making profits for the firm. When the connection between ownership and control is severed, may not the management run the corporation with other objectives in mind? Indeed, is the manager in this case very much different from the socialist bureaucrat? The latter runs a state-owned firm for the benefit of "society"; the former runs a stockholder owned firm for the benefit of the society of stockholders. In neither case is the making of *personal* profits considered appropriate.[2]

The complexity of the organization of the modern corporation is matched by the variety of its sizes and forms. Many corporations are quite small and have as little impact as a typical single proprietorship or partnership. Perhaps half the corporations in the United States have assets of less than $100,000. At the other extreme, however, we have the giant modern corporation with assets and annual sales running into the billions of dollars. The economic scale of these giants is obviously a social fact of great importance.

The accompanying Table 5-1, from the *Fortune Magazine* annual list of the nation's largest corporations, is worth studying for a few moments. There are

many complications involved in gathering these numbers, but the general picture presented by the figures is quite clear. The largest American corporation by asset size (equipment, buildings, capital stock, etc.) in 1970 was American Telephone & Telegraph, which had nearly $50 billion of assets, or roughly $250 of assets for every man, woman, and child in the United States. AT&T was also the top employer, with over three-quarters of a million employees. General Motors had the largest annual sales of any American corporation, $18.8 billion in 1970. Actually, this figure is an understatement of GM's normal economic strength since 1970 was the year of the big GM strike. Its sales in the previous year, 1969, were $24.3 billion. In either case, its sales represented a total income much larger than that of many *nations* in the world.

Overall, in 1970, there were about 120 industrial corporations that had sales of $1 billion or over. And if these sums are not large enough to stagger the mind,

GRANT HEILMAN

2. We shall be returning to these issues again. See the reading by Edward Mason later in this chapter, pp. 129–32, and especially Great Debate Three: Galbraith and the New Industrial State, pp. 546–51.

AMERICA'S LARGEST CORPORATIONS, 1970   FORTUNE MAGAZINE

Table 5-1   THE 100 LARGEST INDUSTRIAL CORPORATIONS, 1970   (ranked by sales)

Rank '70 '69	Company	Headquarters	Sales ($000)	Assets ($000)	Employees
1 1	General Motors	Detroit	18,752,354	14,174,360	695,796
2 2	Standard Oil (N.J.)	New York	16,554,227	19,241,784	143,000
3 3	Ford Motor	Dearborn, Mich.	14,979,900	9,904,100	431,727
4 4	General Electric	New York	8,726,738	6,309,945	396,583
5 5	International Business Machines	Armonk, N.Y.	7,503,960	8,539,047	269,291
6 7	Mobil Oil	New York	7,260,522	7,921,049	75,600
7 6	Chrysler	Detroit	6,999,676	4,815,772	228,332
8 9	International Tel. & Tel.	New York	6,364,494	6,697,011	392,000
9 8	Texaco	New York	6,349,759	9,923,786	73,734
10 11	Western Electric	New York	5,856,160	3,743,623	215,380
11 10	Gulf Oil	Pittsburgh	5,396,182	8,672,298	61,300
12 12	U.S. Steel	New York	4,814,368	6,311,038	200,734
13 17	Westinghouse Electric	Pittsburgh	4,313,410	3,358,167	145,000
14 13	Standard Oil of California	San Francisco	4,187,762	6,593,551	44,610
15 14	Ling-Temco-Vought	Dallas	3,771,724	2,582,004	99,447
16 18	Standard Oil (Ind.)	Chicago	3,732,827	5,397,471	47,551
17 26	Boeing	Seattle	3,677,073	2,621,819	79,100
18 15	E.I. du Pont de Nemours	Wilmington, Del.	3,618,400	3,566,600	110,685
19 16	Shell Oil	New York	3,589,546	4,609,763	36,754
20 19	General Telephone & Electronics	New York	3,439,219	7,739,272	172,000
21 21	RCA	New York	3,291,888	2,936,125	127,000
22 20	Goodyear Tire & Rubber	Akron, Ohio	3,194,554	2,955,301	136,825
23 22	Swift	Chicago	3,076,378	825,482	38,900
24 24	Union Carbide	New York	3,026,326	3,563,795	102,144
25 28	Procter & Gamble	Cincinnati	2,978,750	1,854,990	44,225
26 25	Bethlehem Steel	Bethlehem, Pa.	2,935,408	3,331,206	130,000
27 27	Eastman Kodak	Rochester, N.Y.	2,784,643	3,042,793	110,700
28 32	Kraftco	New York	2,751,129	1,031,365	48,179
29 •	Greyhound	Chicago	2,739,962	1,201,685	67,227
30 29	Atlantic Richfield	New York	2,738,496	4,392,241	31,300
31 35	Continental Oil	New York	2,711,780	3,023,438	38,448
32 31	International Harvester	Chicago	2,711,535	2,217,571	101,920
33 41	Lockheed Aircraft	Burbank, Calif.	2,535,000	N.A.	84,579
34 34	Tenneco	Houston	2,524,740	4,343,793	60,000
35 30	North American Rockwell	El Segundo, Calif.	2,410,752	1,515,399	81,455

Fortune Magazine, America's Largest Corporations, 1970. Reprinted from the 1971 Fortune Directory by permission. Footnotes and some table columns do not appear here.

Rank '70 '69		Company	Headquarters	Sales ($000)	Assets ($000)	Employees
36	39	Litton Industries	Beverly Hills	2,404,327	1,934,012	118,300
37	36	United Aircraft	East Hartford, Conn.	2,348,945	1,546,375	68,481
38	37	Firestone Tire & Rubber	Akron, Ohio	2,334,717	2,097,074	105,203
39	38	Phillips Petroleum	Bartlesville, Okla.	2,273,100	3,056,977	32,208
40	44	Occidental Petroleum	Los Angeles	2,240,152	2,563,002	33,000
41	33	General Dynamics	New York	2,223,643	1,096,398	80,900
42	42	Caterpillar Tractor	Peoria, Ill.	2,127,800	1,813,600	64,040
43	45	Singer	New York	2,125,059	1,635,034	133,000
44	23	McDonnell Douglas	St. Louis	2,088,179	1,769,345	92,552
45	46	General Foods	White Plains, N.Y.	2,045,355	1,360,996	44,000
46	51	Continental Can	New York	2,036,509	1,534,961	72,025
47	43	Monsanto	St. Louis	1,971,632	2,144,664	62,940
48	47	Sun Oil	Philadelphia	1,941,906	2,766,722	28,365
49	75	Honeywell	Minneapolis	1,921,194	2,018,078	300,230
50	50	W. R. Grace	New York	1,917,559	1,575,168	61,656
51	49	Dow Chemical	Midland, Mich.	1,911,105	2,779,802	47,347
52	52	International Paper	New York	1,840,832	2,046,516	54,936
53	56	American Can	Greenwich, Conn.	1,838,146	1,473,895	54,000
54	54	Borden	New York	1,827,341	1,191,795	45,900
55	48	Rapid-American	New York	1,827,102	1,701,074	100,000
56	53	Burlington Industries	Greensboro, N. C.	1,821,539	1,401,733	87,000
57	58	Union Oil of California	Los Angeles	1,811,210	2,514,873	16,457
58	62	R. J. Reynolds Industries	Winston-Salem, N. C.	1,786,023	1,857,651	28,255
59	60	Sperry Rand	New York	1,755,443	1,413,529	97,565
60	71	Xerox	Stamford, Conn.	1,718,587	1,857,325	59,862
61	55	Boise Cascade	Boise, Idaho	1,716,860	2,267,475	47,889
62	65	Cities Service	New York	1,714,010	2,193,270	23,900
63	59	Minnesota Mining & Manufacturing	St. Paul	1,687,296	1,500,234	65,773
64	68	Consolidated Foods	Chicago	1,651,512	726,099	60,000
65	64	Gulf & Western Industries	New York	1,629,562	2,154,463	75,000
66	57	Textron	Providence	1,611,851	976,085	64,000
67	79	Coca-Cola	New York	1,606,401	1,005,777	30,443
68	61	TRW	Cleveland	1,585,188	1,074,103	80,996
69	63	Armco Steel	Middletown, Ohio	1,583,673	1,978,913	51,236
70	83	Beatrice Foods	Chicago	1,576,065	631,485	39,700
71	78	Ralston Purina	St. Louis	1,567,009	775,237	24,000
72	66	Uniroyal	New York	1,555,594	1,308,428	64,168
73	67	Aluminum Co. of America	Pittsburgh	1,522,418	2,628,192	48,307
74	80	American Brands	New York	1,447,569	1,985,202	49,000
75	72	Bendix	Southfield, Mich.	1,442,860	1,037,143	57,291

Rank '70 '69		Company	Headquarters	Sales ($000)	Assets ($000)	Employees
76	87	National Cash Register	Dayton, Ohio	1,420,576	1,644,600	98,000
77	82	American Standard	New York	1,417,846	1,247,151	70,300
78	74	Signal Companies	Los Angeles	1,412,187	1,322,690	29,800
79	101	Ashland Oil	Ashland, Ky.	1,407,166	999,880	21,500
80	85	Owens-Illinois	Toledo, Ohio	1,402,399	1,318,315	64,887
81	70	United Brands	New York	1,395,704	1,090,017	72,500
82	92	CPC International	Englewood Cliffs, N.J.	1,376,022	1,009,191	44,400
83	97	Standard Oil (Ohio)	Cleveland	1,374,404	1,747,269	20,800
84	69	Republic Steel	Cleveland	1,364,694	1,833,264	47,726
85	73	U.S. Plywood-Champion Papers	New York	1,355,994	1,191,794	39,847
86	77	FMC	San Jose, Calif.	1,330,494	1,031,760	47,438
87	94	American Home Products	New York	1,294,326	802,182	41,849
88	86	Raytheon	Lexington, Mass.	1,258,743	557,286	46,201
89	138	Warner-Lambert	Morris Plains, N.J.	1,256,597	1,006,765	55,500
90	95	Genesco	Nashville, Tenn.	1,250,675	587,569	68,000
91	81	Allied Chemical	New York	1,248,479	1,582,057	32,766
92	91	National Steel	Pittsburgh	1,248,363	1,567,616	30,547
93	89	Weyerhaeuser	Tacoma, Wash.	1,233,423	1,792,349	42,721
94	105	U. S. Industries	New York	1,231,506	848,521	43,300
95	104	Getty Oil	Los Angeles	1,221,170	1,946,303	13,190
96	84	Teledyne	Los Angeles	1,216,448	971,067	46,000
97	103	Colgate-Palmolive	New York	1,210,238	591,954	23,500
98	90	B. F. Goodrich	Akron, Ohio	1,204,754	1,303,991	48,858
99	98	Georgia-Pacific	Portland, Ore.	1,199,430	1,705,980	37,000
100	100	Whirlpool	Benton Harbor, Mich.	1,196,845	549,799	28,280

THE 10 LARGEST COMMERCIAL BANKS, 1970 (ranked by assets)

Bank '70 '69		Bank	Assets ($000)	Deposits ($000)	Loans ($000)	Employees
1	1	BankAmerica (San Francisco)	29,739,902	25,643,215	16,692,828	35,600
2	2	First National City Corp. (New York)	25,835,455	21,012,779	15,266,682	37,000
3	3	Chase Manhattan Corp. (New York)	24,525,703	21,227,395	13,928,999	25,154
4	4	Manufacturers Hanover Corp. (New York)	12,664,865	11,072,080	7,093,511	12,793
5	5	J.P. Morgan (New York)	12,112,419	9,576,337	5,902,351	8,142
6	6	Western Bancorporation (Los Angeles)	11,409,817	9,692,308	6,390,652	22,861
7	7	Chemical New York Corp.	10,979,483	8,981,478	6,178,568	12,523
8	8	Bankers Trust New York Corp.	9,930,646	8,575,155	5,157,995	13,194
9	9	Conill Corp. (Chicago)	8,863,550	7,154,144	4,442,524	8,207
10	11	Security Pacific National Bank (Los Angeles)	8,038,070	7,033,487	4,514,224	15,111

THE 10 LARGEST LIFE-INSURANCE COMPANIES, 1970 (ranked by assets)

Rank '70 '69	Company	Assets ($000)	Life Insurance in Force ($000)	Employees
1 1	Prudential (Newark)	29,134,352	156,775,266	58,500
2 2	Metropolitan (New York)	27,865,762	167,283,940	56,944
3 3	Equitable Life Assurance (New York)	14,371,372	76,909,206	22,576
4 4	New York Life	10,741,138	50,317,456	17,772
5 5	John Hancock Mutual (Boston)	10,048,444	60,896,318	23,140
6 6	Aetna (Hartford)	7,214,675	59,883,313	13,000
7 7	Northwestern Mutual (Milwaukee)	6,124,984	19,477,040	4,852
8 8	Connecticut General (Bloomfield)	5,065,289	36,064,588	6,935
9 9	Travelers (Hartford)	4,709,713	58,386,609	90,000
10 10	Massachusetts Mutual (Springfield)	4,287,684	19,614,214	6,981

THE 10 LARGEST RETAILING COMPANIES, 1970 (ranked by sales)

Rank '70 '69	Company	Sales ($000)	Assets ($000)	Employees
1 1	Sears, Roebuck (Chicago)	9,262,162	7,623,096	359,000
2 2	Great Atlantic & Pacific Tea (New York)	5,650,000	957,073	120,000
3 3	Safeway Stores (Oakland)	4,860,167	875,705	96,760
4 4	J.C. Penney (New York)	4,150,886	1,627,055	145,000
5 5	Kroger (Cincinnati)	3,735,774	767,777	83,817
6 6	Marcor (Chicago)	2,804,856	2,459,730	127,100
7 8	S.S. Kresge (Detroit)	2,595,155	926,227	80,500
8 7	F.W. Woolworth (New York)	2,527,965	1,436,297	225,275
9 9	Federated Department Stores (Cincinnati)	2,096,935	1,165,770	75,700
10 10	Food Fair Stores (Philadephia)	1,762,005	363,472	30,000

THE 10 LARGEST TRANSPORTATION COMPANIES, 1970 (ranked by operating revenues)

Rank '70 '69	Company	Operating Revenues ($000)	Assets ($000)	Employees
1 1	Penn Central (Philadelphia)	2,300,000	6,850,676	13,000
2 2	UAL (Chicago)	1,590,070	2,179,695	65,703
3 3	Southern Pacific (San Francisco)	1,272,289	3,066,260	41,604
4 4	Trans World Airlines (New York)	1,157,377	1,405,765	62,646
5 5	American Airlines (New York)	1,132,779	1,524,946	35,863
6 6	Pan American World Airways (New York)	1,125,702	1,838,592	39,279
7 7	Norfolk & Western Ry (Roanoke)	1,054,187	2,784,377	47,610
8 8	Burlington Northern (St. Paul)	1,018,980	2,926,155	50,462
9 9	Chesapeake & Ohio Ry (Cleveland)	1,009,707	2,717,841	49,529
10 10	Eastern Air Lines (New York)	971,050	1,128,559	31,500

THE 10 LARGEST UTILITIES, 1970 (ranked by assets)

Rank '70	'69	Company	Assets ($000)	Operating Revenues ($000)	Employees
1	1	American Tel. & Tel. (New York)	49,641,509	16,954,881	772,980
2	2	Consolidated Edison (New York)	4,448,918	1,128,480	23,726
3	3	Pacific Gas & Electric (San Francisco)	4,318,832	1,103,258	23,569
4	5	Commonwealth Edison (Chicago)	3,374,996	886,992	14,089
5	6	American Electric Power (New York)	3,241,888	665,667	14,489
6	4	Southern California Edison (Los Angeles)	3,226,881	720,661	12,299
7	7	Southern Company (Atlanta)	3,098,121	738,064	16,883
8	8	Public Service Electric & Gas (Newark)	2,639,395	741,252	14,833
9	11	General Public Utilities (New York)	2,134,115	416,789	10,229
10	13	Philadelphia Electric	2,091,915	504,371	10,424

consider the life-insurance industry. In 1970, the top 50 American life-insurance firms had life insurance in force to the value of $1.0 *trillion*! An appropriate sum, perhaps, since we now have a trillion dollar gross national product in the United States.

The leap from the world of Adam Smith to these corporate giants is clearly a large one!

CONCENTRATION IN AMERICAN INDUSTRY

Actually, the reference to our trillion dollar gross national product in the previous section is a useful one because, however dazzling the figures on the size of corporations may be, those figures—like similar ones about the size of governmental expenditures discussed in the preceding chapter—must be placed in the context of an economy that has itself grown enormously in modern times. A single factory might be a dominant factor in the economy of Upper Volta; a billion dollar corporation might be one of the smaller corporations in a particular in-

dustry in the United States.[3]

There are various ways of measuring the size of our large corporations in relationship to the context in which they operate. One simple way is to ask what proportion of total industrial sales or assets is accounted for by the largest 50, 100, 150 (etc.) firms. One estimate, for example, is that in 1962 the largest 282 nonfinancial corporations owned 44.6 percent of all nonfinancial corporate assets in the United States and that the largest 627 nonfinancial corporations owned 53.8 percent of all nonfinancial corporate assets.[4] One can also look at it from the bottom up, but still considering size from the point of view of the economy as a whole. Thus, in the same study referred to above, it was estimated that the 96 percent of the nonfinancial corpora-

3. For example, American Motors in 1970 was 110th on the *Fortune* list of industrial corporations, its sales being $1.1 billion. These sales were equal to only 3.5 percent of the sales of its three larger rivals, GM, Ford, and Chrysler. A clear case of a billion dollar corporation that hardly dominates its own industry. Incidentally—to stress the significance of context— American Motors sales in 1970 exceeded by a factor of three the "measured" national income of Upper Volta.

4. Joe S. Bain, *Industrial Organization*, 2nd ed. (New York: John Wiley & Sons, 1968), p.86.

tions in the economy that are small account for only one-sixth of total nonfinancial corporate assets. The 4 percent of large corporations own all the rest.

The trouble with such estimates is that they are so broad that it is difficult to know what to conclude from them. Should we stress the fact that 500 or 600 firms control so much, or rather the fact that, under many circumstances, there might be a great deal of competition among several hundred firms?

Consequently, economists usually go beyond the "largest 100" type of statistic to ask (1) what is happening in particular industries and (2) what is happening over time. With regard to specific industries, it is customary to speak of *concentration ratios*. These concentration ratios show how much of the sales of a particular industry are accounted for by the larger firms in the industry. Thus we might ask: What percentage of the sales of an industry are accounted for by the four largest firms, what percentage by the eight largest, and so on? Figure 5-3 shows a variety of concentration ratios for different industries, using the top four firms as the standard. The examples shown run from very high concentration ("100 percent") in aluminum to extremely low concentration in fur goods. In general, concentration tends to be highest in public utilities (including transportation) and manufacturing—these two sectors include the overwhelming majority of the giant nonfinancial corporations—and very low in the service industries, agriculture, and construction.

As far as trends are concerned, there is some disagreement as to whether concentration is increasing or staying roughly the same in the American economy, and some of this disagreement depends upon the period chosen for study. M. A. Adelman, professor of industrial

relations at MIT, notes that most studies suggest that concentration overall tended to decrease from the early 1930s to the late 1940s, then to return to the 1930s level and perhaps increase beyond it in the 1960s.[5] He adds:

The trend can be embellished, for polemical purposes, by measuring from low to high, i.e., comparing 1948 with 1968, rather than from high to high (or at least the earliest to the latest). It is a bit like comparing department store sales, August with December, to show that sales are doing fine. Extrapolate the 1948–1968 "trend" by twenty or fifty years, and there is as much to view with alarm as there was decades ago; only a spoilsport would ask what happened to those earlier predictions of an imminent monopolistic economy.[6]

A recent study (1969) by Nutter and Einhorn[7] has attempted to make an estimate of the amount of monopoly in the American economy in 1958 as compared to 1899. They divide industries in all sectors of the economy into three groups: (1) Effectively Monopolistic;[8] (2) Workably Competitive; and (3) Governmental or Governmentally Supervised. Their conclusion is that there is no clear evidence of an increase in the amount of monopoly in the economy over this period. In 1899, they found that 17.4 percent of national income was produced in effectively monopolistic industries, 76.1 percent

5. One (though not the only) reason for the increase in aggregate concentration in the 1960s was the conglomerate merger movement. See below, pp. 597–99.
6. M. A. Adelman, "The Two Faces of Economic Concentration," *The Public Interest*, Fall 1970, p. 123.

7. G. Warren Nutter and Henry Adler Einhorn, *Enterprise Monopoly in the United States* (New York: Columbia University Press, 1969).

8. "Effectively Monopolistic" industries are not limited to those in which there is literally a single seller of the product, but would include, for example, industries in which the four largest firms account for over 50 percent of the output of the industry.

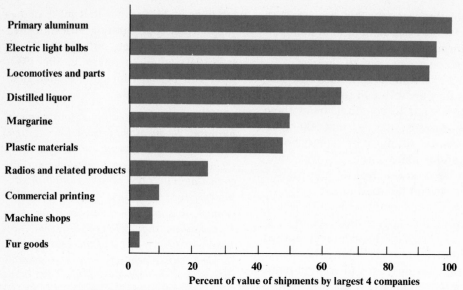

Figure 5-3. Concentration Ratios, Some U.S. Industries, 1954.

Source: *Concentration in American Industry,* Report of the Subcommittee on Antitrust and Monopoly, U.S. Senate Judiciary Committee, 85th Congress, 1st Session, Washington, 1957.

in workably competitive industries, and 6.5 percent in governmental industries. In 1958, depending upon the specific measures used, monopolistic industries had either increased by four percentage points or decreased by one percentage point relative to total nongovernmental production; because of the growth of government, monopolistic industries had by each measure declined relative to the economy as a whole. In the specific sector of manufacturing, they found a "remarkable stability in the extent of monopoly." Although, as the authors point out, these results must be used with great caution, most economists would probably agree that there is no very clear-cut evidence of increased concentration in the American economy, overall, in the past four or five decades. That there is a higher degree of concentration now than, say, at the beginning of our great industrialization surge in the early nineteenth century seems beyond doubt; but that this represents an irresistible trend towards ever-increasing monop-

olization of the private sector of the American economy is not borne out by experience.

BUREAUCRACIES— PRIVATE AND PUBLIC

Does this relative stability—or, at least, very slow rate of change—in the degree of concentration of American industry mean that the structure and organization of our business firms have been comparably stable over the past several decades? The answer is clearly no, for the growth in size of business corporations (even when they have not grown in relation to a rapidly expanding economy) is itself a significant fact and might be expected to have important consequences for the way in which these firms go about their business.

In particular, the "robber baron" of the nineteenth century has given way to the modern corporate bureaucracy. We no longer think of business firms in terms of particular individual leaders—who can name the presidents or chairmen of the boards of even half of the top ten industrial corporations on the *Fortune* list?—but in terms of committees, departments, memoranda, Xerox machines, and competent but faceless executives. We are in the world of the bureaucrat, a world strikingly similar whether it be in business, the university, the government, or, for that matter, the United Nations secretariat.

All of this raises deep questions about the meaning of "private" versus "public" sectors, perhaps even deeper than those raised by the military-industrial complex discussed in the last chapter. In the following reading, Edward S. Mason, former Harvard professor and dean of the Littauer School of Public Administration, a man who taught many of today's leading thinkers in the area of industrial organization, reflects on some dimensions of the questions we have just been discussing:

THE CORPORATION IN MODERN SOCIETY

EDWARD S. MASON

* * *

People who talk about a "managerial revolution" usually have in mind, on the one hand, the increasing importance of large corporations on the American scene and, on the other, changes in administrative techniques that have continually increased the size of the enterprise that can be effectively managed. Those who doubt the significance of this "revolution" point to figures on economic concentration, and indeed it is possible to show that, during

Excerpted by permission of the publishers from pp. 10–13, 15–19 of Edward S. Mason, ed., *The Corporation in Modern Society* (Cambridge, Mass.: Harvard University Press). Copyright, 1959, by the President and Fellows of Harvard College.

the last fifty years, there has been no significant increase, however measured, in the share of economic activity controlled by the largest corporations. The largest corporations have grown mightily, but so has the economy. This, in my view, does not dispose of the matter. In the first place, conclusions on the trend of concentration depend heavily on the date from which one measures the trend. If the date chosen is before the great merger movement of 1897–1903, it can be shown that concentration has, in fact, increased. In the second place, the phenomena we are concerned with are more a product of absolute size than of relative share. And about absolute size, however measured, there is no shadow of doubt. In the third place, there is probably a substantial lag between changes in the size of enterprises and changes in managerial techniques adapted to the new sizes. For these and other reasons, I conclude that, despite the lack of evidence of increased concentration during the last half century, there may well have occurred a profound change in the way industrial enterprises are managed. It goes without saying that in other broad sectors of the economy small-scale enterprise, managed in a traditional fashion, not only is holding its own but will continue to do so.

These changes in management are commonly grouped under the heading of bureaucracy. And bureaucracy, as the political scientists tell us, is characterized by a hierarchy of function and authority, professionalization of management, formal procedures for recruitment and promotion, and a proliferation of written rules, orders, and record keeping. All this is true of business administration in large corporations, but corporate bureaucracies also exhibit certain differences from typical government bureaucracies that are worth emphasizing. In the first place, corporate managements enjoy a much greater freedom from external influence than do the managements of government bureaucracies. As we have seen, management has pretty much escaped from ownership control, but though private ownership may no longer carry with it control, it does guarantee corporate management against most of the political, ministerial, and legislative interference that commonly besets public management. Perhaps in a corporate society this is becoming one of the primary contributions of private property. Needless to say, this independence of corporate management from any well-defined responsibility to anyone also carries with it the possibilities of abuse. . . .

In the second place, corporate managements have traditionally been considered to have as their single-minded objective, in contrast to most government bureaucracies, maximization of business profits. And traditionally the incentives connected with profit maximization have been thought to constitute an essential part of the justification of a private-enterprise system. Now managerial voices are raised to deny this exclusive preoccupation with profits and to assert that corporate managements are really concerned with equitable sharing of corporate gains among owners, workers, suppliers, and customers. If equity rather than profits is the corporate objective, one of the traditional distinctions between the private and public sectors disappears. If equity is the primary desideratum, it may well be asked why duly constituted public authority is not as good an instrument for dispensing equity as self-perpetuating corporate managements. . . .

Finally, since corporate managements work exclusively in the business area, which government bureaucracies ordinarily do not, it can be said that the possibility of monetary measurement in the former permits a closer adjustment of rewards to performance, and hence a closer observance of the causes of efficiency than is possible in the latter. This is true, and it is important, but the distinction is not between public and private efficiency but between the efficiency of operations susceptible to the measuring rod of money and the efficiency of those that are not. . . .

One of the leading characteristics of well-ordered bureaucracies both public and private—a characteristic justly extolled by the devotees of managerialism—is the increasing professionalization of management. This means, among other things, selection and promotion on the basis of merit rather than family connections or social status, the development of a "scientific" attitude towards the problems of the organization, and an expectation of reward in terms of relatively stable salary and professional prestige rather than in fluctuating profits. This professionalization of management has, of course, been characteristic of well-ordered public bureaucracies for a long time. It helps to explain why able young Indians, for example, have in general preferred to cast their lot with a civil service selecting and promoting on the basis of merit rather than with the highly nepotistic business firms of the subcontinent. But it is a relatively new phenomenon in American business and one of increasing importance.

The degree of freedom enjoyed by corporate managements, in contrast to their governmental counterparts, has affected personnel as well as other policies. And no one who has observed at first hand the red-tape inefficiencies of the United States Civil Service can fail to be aware of the superiority of corporate practice. This relative freedom from hampering restrictions on selection plus a high level of monetary rewards has brought the cream of American professional management into business corporations. No one doubts the superiority of American business management. Unwitting testimony, if testimony is needed, is supplied by the care with which Soviet planners examine American management practices.

* * *

The economies of Western Europe and, increasingly, that of the United States are frequently described as "mixed" economies. This phrase is commonly interpreted to indicate a situation in which the role of government as owner and regulator has become sufficiently large to cast doubt on the validity of "capitalist" and "free enterprise" as appropriate adjectives but not sufficiently large to justify the appellation "socialist." Government ownership and regulation are important ingredients, but they inadequately characterize the "mixture" of public and private that the rise of the large corporation has produced. The growth of the modern corporation has been accompanied by an increasing similarity of public and private business with respect to forms of organization, techniques of management, and the motivations and attitudes of managers. Government has sought increasingly to use the private corporation for the performance of what are essentially public functions. Private corporations in turn, particularly in their foreign operations, continually make decisions which impinge on the public—particularly foreign—policy of government. And government, in pursuit of its current objectives in underdeveloped areas, seeks to use techniques and talents that only the business corporation can provide. . . . Under these circumstances the classic arguments of the socialism-versus-free-enterprise debate seem a bit sterile, to say the least.

The increasing similarity of public and private enterprise has impressed both liberals and conservatives, though the conclusions drawn therefrom have tended to differ. In an early recognition of this trend, Keynes described it as a "tendency of big enterprise to socialize itself." A point is reached in the growth of big enterprises, he says, at which "the stockholders are almost entirely dissociated from the management, with the result that the direct personal interest of the latter in the making of great profit becomes quite secondary." American managerial spokesmen supplement this thought by emphasizing management's responsibility to workers, customers, suppliers, and others, though they would hardly describe living up to this responsibility—as Keynes probably would —as behaving like Civil Servants. These and similar considerations have led elements in the British Labour Party to the conclusion that the form of ownership of large enterprise is irrelevant. "The basic fact is the large corporation, facing fundamental similar problems, acts in fundamentally the same way, whether publicly or privately owned."

While large private corporations have been forced by their sheer size, power, and "visibility" to behave with a circumspection unknown to the untrammeled nineteenth century, government, on the other hand, has attempted to give its "business-like" activities a sphere of independence approaching that of the private corporation. Experience with the public corporation in the United States has, it is true, somewhat dampened an earlier enthusiasm for this type of organization. And even

Britain, which has sought much longer and harder than we for a workable compromise between independence and accountability in its publicly managed enterprises, has not yet found a satisfactory solution. Nevertheless, it remains true that managerial practices and attitudes in the public and private sectors of most Western economies tend to become more similar.

Private ownership in the United States, however, still confers an immunity from detailed government supervision that a public corporation does not enjoy. And government takes advantage of the independence and flexibility of the private corporation to contract out the performance of what are essentially public services. Private firms become official inspectors of aircraft; various types of military "operations analysis" are undertaken by Rand and other privately organized corporations, and substantially more than half of public research and development expenditures go to private rather than public organizations. In commenting on these phenomena, Don Price observes, "If the question (of public versus private) is seen in realistic terms, we shall have to devise some way of calculating whether a particular function can be performed best in the public interest as a completely governmental operation at the one extreme, or a completely private operation at the other extreme, or by some mixture of the nearly infinite possibilities of elements of ownership regulation and management that our variety of precedents suggests."

* * *

How really mixed—and perhaps mixed up—our economy is these days can be clearly seen by casting one's eye on United States policy and practices in the so-called underdeveloped areas of the world. Our announced policy is to give substantial assistance to the economic development of countries whose economies have long been stagnant. And our preferred means are the stimulation of private enterprise in the underdeveloped areas and the encouragement of United States private investment abroad. But in many of these areas, the opportunities for foreign private investment are negligible, and our grants and loans inevitably flow through local government channels. At the same time, in the provision of technical assistance we depend heavily on contracts with American private firms. And we actively encourage mixed enterprise, private and public and foreign and domestic, as a means of getting enterprise moving. The effort is sometimes described as an exercise in government-business cooperation in the promotion of foreign economic development, and perhaps that is as good a description as any. In any case, it is a good example of a mixed economy in motion.

This lack of a clear-cut separation of public and private authority and responsibility offends some people. And indeed, the eighteenth-century political philosophers and political economists provided for their epoch a much more satisfactory intellectual framework than any vouchsafed to us today. The fact seems to be that the rise of the large corporation and attending circumstances have confronted us with a long series of questions concerning rights and duties, privileges and immunities, responsibility and authority, that political and legal philosophy have not yet assimilated. What we need among other things is a twentieth-century Hobbes or Locke to bring some order into our thinking about the corporation and its role in society.

* * *

UNIONS AND THE AMERICAN LABOR MARKET

On the opposite side of the circular flow from the Product Markets are the Factor Markets. On this side of the flow are sold the services of the factors of production—labor, land, capital goods—that are then combined by business firms in production processes that ultimately lead to a stream of consumer and other goods.

Just as the existence of the large modern corporation affects the workings of the Product Markets, so also there are many institutions in the American economy that modify the pure "laws" of supply and demand in the markets for labor, land, and capital. Indeed, the existence of the large modern corporation also influences the Factor Markets since business firms are, of course, the buyers or "demanders" on the Factor Markets. One theory of the growth of labor unions, for example, is that they represent a *counter-vailing power* to the concentrated buying power of large business enterprises on the other side of the labor market.[9] The individual workman could hardly be expected to bargain with U.S. Steel or Standard Oil of New Jersey—unionization of the labor force was the only possible answer.

Even apart from the influence of large corporations and large unions, labor markets would probably not work as smoothly as we might, in theory, desire. There are all sorts of possible imperfections: laborers may not generally know about jobs in other localities or occupations; there may be significant discrimination against minority groups, and, if women's organizations are correct, against the female majority of the population; there may be general unemployment in the economy (according to Marxists, this permits employers to "exploit" all laborers); furthermore, in local areas, even fairly small firms may have a degree of monopsony buying power.

We shall come back to many of these problems later; for the moment, let us just say a few words about labor unions, which represent a particularly important institution in the largest of American Factor Markets—the labor market.

Figure 5-4 shows the growth of labor union membership in the United States in the course of the twentieth centu-

9. This approach was advanced in an early book by John Kenneth Galbraith, *American Capitalism: The Concept of Countervailing Power* (Boston: Houghton Mifflin Co., 1952).

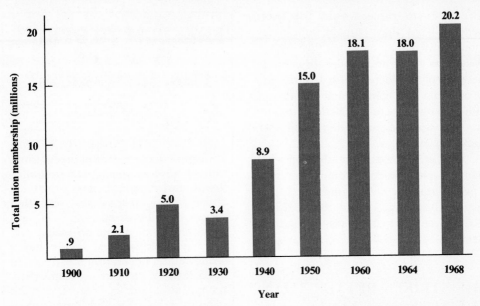

Figure 5-4. Labor Union Membership in the United States 1900-1968 (selected years).

ry. The trend has clearly been upward during this period although there have been notable ups and downs, and, in recent years, union membership has been relatively stagnant. With the increase in the number of white-collar, as opposed to blue-collar, workers in the American economy, labor unions actually face some difficult organizational problems in the years ahead.

Difficult problems, however, are nothing new to the American labor movement. In one sense, as the diagram shows, their progress has been fairly continuous. In 1886, the American Federation of Labor (AFL) was founded under the leadership of Samuel Gompers. In 1935, the Congress of Industrial Organizations (CIO) joined the fray under the leadership of the controversial John L. Lewis. In 1955, under George Meany, the two large organizations joined together into the massive present-day AFL-CIO. Organized labor now accounts for about 30 percent of

the nonagricultural labor force in the United States. In *another* sense, however, this progress has been pock-marked by problems and crises. This was especially true in the early days when American industry can hardly be said to have welcomed the new unions with open arms. Moreover, the attitude of the government was by no means friendly. The courts interpreted the Sherman Act of 1890 to restrict unions that were organizing in "restraint of trade"; and in the Danbury Hatters' case of 1908, the union was made to pay extensively for damages caused by a strike. It was not until 1914 that the Clayton Act stated explicitly that unions were not to be considered in "restraint of trade," and it was really not until the Wagner Act and other favorable legislation of the 1930s that the labor movement came strongly into its own.

Unions have an impact on many different aspects of the labor market. They have what we may think of as a primary objective—to raise wages for their members—but they bargain collectively about many more issues than this: seniority systems, hours and conditions of work, methods of production, job tenure, and so on. They are complicated institutions with their own meetings, elections, organizational structures, and often their own political views.

Let us present a reading on what many people consider the most dramatic aspect of union activities—the strike—and then analyze some of the complications of union efforts to raise wages for their members.

THE STRIKE—BETTER THAN THE ALTERNATIVES?

The strike would seem to represent the breakdown of labor markets in the most costly possible way. Neither unions nor management seem likely to gain from such economic warfare and society seems certain to lose. Many commentators, however, believe:

    (1) that the costs of strikes are vastly overrated by the general public and

    (2) that the alternatives to strikes are far more costly than sometimes imagined.

This is the point of view of the following reading. The reader should keep author Thomas Kennedy's arguments in mind because they clearly have a bearing not simply on the question of strikes but on the general question of wage-price controls.[10]

10. For this hotly contested issue of the 1970s, see Great Debate Four: Wage and Price Controls.

FREEDOM TO STRIKE IS IN THE PUBLIC INTEREST

Thomas Kennedy

HOW COSTLY ARE STRIKES?

Despite the fact that peaceful alternatives have replaced most organizational, jurisdictional, and grievance strikes, and despite the fact that strikes in utilities, oil refineries, and some chemical plants no longer create crises, strikes over new contract terms still do occur, and these can be quite costly to companies, employees, unions, suppliers, customers, and the general public. Also, of course, when the strike involves a critical material or service, the effect on the economy as a whole may be disastrous if the stoppage continues beyond a certain point.

Thus, while the strike performs a valuable function in our free collective bargaining system, it is legitimate to question whether the costs are too great in relation to the benefits. Might some alternative to the strike, such as compulsory arbitration, serve the interests of the parties and the public better? To answer this question, let us begin by examining the costs of strikes. We can next compare these with the costs of alternative procedures.

Because of the publicity which strikes get, it is easy for their extent and their impact on the economy to be overestimated. When one reads in the headlines that 147,000 GE employees have been on strike for over

Excerpted from Thomas Kennedy, "Freedom to Strike Is in the Public Interest," **Harvard Business Review,** July–August 1970, pp. 48, 52–57. © 1970 by the President and Fellows of Harvard College; all rights reserved.

three months, one is likely to be greatly impressed. But when one realizes that the GE strikers represent only 0.2 percent of the 71,000,000 non-agricultural employees in the country, one sees it in a different light (although for the company, its dealers, and its employees, the strike is still very significant).

It is estimated that there are approximately 300,000 labor agreements in the United States. On the average, about 120,000 of these agreements terminate each year. Thus, across the country during an average year, 120,000 management bargaining teams sit across the table from 120,000 union bargaining teams and try to work out agreements on new contract terms. The issues which they deal with are wages, benefits, hours, and other important working conditions. These are matters which are extremely vital to the companies, the unions, and the employees. Despite the difficulties of these issues, the parties are successful in 96 percent or more of the negotiations. Only 4 percent or less of the negotiations result in strikes, and in most cases these strikes are short-lived. The problem is that a peaceful settlement is seldom front-page news, whereas a strike may be good for a number of headlines.

The Bureau of Labor Statistics estimates that the amount of working time in the total economy which was lost directly as a result of strikes in 1969 was only 0.23 percent. Moreover, the general trend has been down. As illustrated in Exhibit A, from 1945 to 1949 the average time lost per year was 0.47 percent, compared with 0.26 percent from 1950 to 1959, and only 0.17 percent from 1960 to 1969. We have been losing far more time in coffee breaks than in strikes!

Industrywide Bargaining

The effect of a strike on the economy depends, among other things, on the nature of the product or service and the structure of the bargaining. In the steel industry, where the product is essential to many other industries and where the bargaining is practically industrywide, one might expect that a strike of any sizable duration would have drastic effects on the overall economy. Such studies as are available, however, indicate that such is not the case.

Following the 116-day steel strike in 1959, E. Robert Livernash of the Harvard Business School made an extensive study for the Department of Labor of the impact of that and earlier steel work stoppages on the economy. Livernash concluded that:

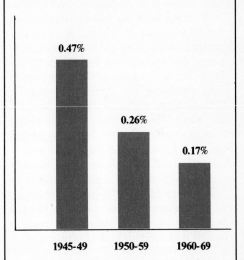

0.47%		
0.26%		
	0.17%	
1945-49	1950-59	1960-69

Exhibit A.

Working Time Lost in Strikes, as a Percent of Working Time in Total Economy.

Source: Data in Table 140, "Work Stoppages in the U.S., 1881-1967," in *Handbook of Labor Statistics 1969* (Washington, Bureau of Labor Statistics, 1970), pp. 352-353, plus data for 1968 and 1969 reported currently by the Bureau of Labor Statistics.

The actual adverse effects of steel strikes on the economy have not been of serious magnitude. A major reason why steel strikes have had so little measurable impact is that when a strike approaches a critical state, pressure upon the parties to settle becomes substantially irresistible. It is significant that the public interest has not been seriously harmed by strikes in steel, or by steel collective bargaining agreements, despite common public opinion to the contrary.

In January 1970 the Department of Labor published an extensive study of the effect on the economy of the 1963, 1965, and 1969 longshore strikes. The study concluded that, although the companies and workers involved suffered losses, as did some workers and owners in collateral industries, "the strike had no visible impact on the economy as a whole." Many companies, according to the report, prepared for the strikes by stepping up their business before the stoppages and catching up again afterwards. "There appears to be no evidence," the report stated, "of a permanent loss of export markets because of the strikes." In talking to newsmen when he released the longshore strikes study, Secretary of Labor George P. Shultze stated that "despite warnings of catastrophic economic effects during some major strikes such results are kind of difficult to find afterwards."

HIGH PRICE OF COMPULSION

It has often been proposed that strikes in the private sector be made illegal. The managements of the railroads and the maritime industry openly advocate compulsory arbitration as a desirable alternative to free collective bargaining. There is reason to believe that unions in industries where automation has reduced the strike power will also move to that position. Suppliers and customers hurt by a strike are likely to mutter, "It should be outlawed."

Unfortunately, it is not a matter of eliminating strikes by devices which have no costs. The various compulsory settlement methods also are expensive, and it may be that managements, unions, and the public would find such costs more onerous than the costs of strikes. We should be fully aware of these costs before abandoning the present free collective bargaining system in the private sector.

Specter of More Failures

The costliness of a strike to management and labor is in itself a strong incentive for them to reach agreement. What happens if that incentive is removed? There is reason to believe that the number of failures to reach agreement would increase greatly. This was our experience during World War II, when the strike was replaced with compulsory settlement by a government agency. It was also our experience in the late 1940s, when a number of states replaced free collective bargaining in public utilities with compulsory arbitration.

There are two reasons that the companies and unions find it more difficult to reach agreement when the possibility of the strike has been removed:

(1) The parties are not under so much pressure to work out a contract because, while the compulsory settlement may be less desirable than the contract that could have been negotiated, it does not carry a threat of immediate loss of production and wages.

(2) If the compulsory settlement authority — whether it be a government board, a court, or an arbitrator — has the right to decide on what it thinks is a fair settlement, then the company and the union may well hesitate to make a move toward a settlement, fearing that the other party will hold at its old

CLASSIFICATION OF TYPES OF STRIKES

□ A **political** strike, as the name implies, is one which is called in the hope of influencing government action. In France and Italy, where the unions tend to be affiliates of political parties, such strikes are common.

□ An **organizational** strike is used to force an employer to accept the union as the representative of his employees. By 1967, organizational strikes accounted for less than 1 percent of the number of workers involved in strikes.

□ A **jurisdictional** strike occurs when two or more unions each claim that certain work should be done by their members. For example, the carpenters, the electricians, and the sheet-metal workers might disagree with respect to whose members should do certain tasks involved in the installation of indirect lighting in a ceiling. If the management assigned the work to one of them, the other two would picket the building site and stop the construction. Since they were the victims of interunion disputes over which they had no control, both management and the public reacted strongly against this type of strike action. Consequently, Section 10(k) of the Taft-Hartley Act in 1947 accorded the NLRB the power to decide such disputes. Later the unions established their own settlement procedures, and these included arbitration.

As a result, jurisdictional strikes are no longer a very significant part of the overall strike picture. In 1967 they accounted for only 2.5 percent of the number of workers involved in strikes and less than 2 percent of the man-days lost because of strikes.

□ A **grievance** strike occurs when the employees stop production because of disagreement with management's handling of some day-to-day problems in the shop, such as promotion or discipline. In the early days of unions in this country, such strikes were frequent. Both unions and management came to realize, however, that the right to use the strike power every day could be very detrimental to both of them. As a result, the parties developed the labor contract, which is simply a kind of peace treaty.

It is estimated that there are approximately 300,000 labor contracts in effect in the United States, and that 94 percent of them provide there shall be no strikes or lockouts during the term of the contract; instead, grievances shall be subject to final and binding arbitration by an impartial person selected by the parties. Because not all contracts require arbitration, we still have some grievance strikes, especially in the construction, trucking, and coal-mining industries. Grievance strikes form only a small part of the total strike picture.

□ A **contract** strike occurs when the employees stop work because the union and the company are unable to reach an agreement regarding the terms of a new labor contract. While most labor agreements provide for arbitration of disputes which arise during their life, as indicated earlier, it is very unusual for the parties to agree to the arbitration of new contract terms. When the contract terminates, either side is free to use its economic power in the form of the strike or the lockout. In 1967, the majority of U.S. strikes were of this variety, and they accounted for more than 90 percent of the man-days lost as a result of all strikes.

position and that the board, court, or arbitrator will split the difference. If for example, the company is offering a \$.10-per-hour increase, and the union is asking for \$.16 per hour, why should the company move to \$.12 when there can be no strike anyhow and when the authority might then decide between \$.12 and \$.16 instead of between \$.10 and \$.16? For like reasons, the union hesitates to move down from \$.16 to \$.14. Thus, compulsory settlement interferes with the process of voluntary settlement.

In order to avoid the effect just described, the Nixon Administration now proposes that when strikes are threatened in the transportation industries, the President be permitted to order arbitration proceedings in which the arbitrator is required to decide only which of the two final offers of the parties is the more reasonable. It is believed that this method would remove one of the undesirable effects of the usual type of arbitration—that is, the hesitancy of the parties to improve their offers for fear that the arbitrator will split the difference. However, the new proposal has the disadvantage of forcing the arbitrator to choose between two proposals, both of which may seem unfair to him.

While the type of arbitration now proposed by the Administration would probably be less harmful than ordinary compulsory arbitration in terms of hampering efforts to reach a voluntary settlement, it would still have some such effect, for management and labor would not be prodded by fears of strike costs. I believe it is erroneous to expect that the number of disputes which would go to an arbitrator would be the same as the number of strikes which would occur without compulsory settlement. The removal of the strong incentive to settle would result in a great many more failures to reach agreement voluntarily. It would therefore be necessary to establish a sizable government bureaucracy to handle the increased volume of unsettled contract disputes.

More Federal Intervention

The size of the bureaucracy could be lessened by using private arbitrators (with the parties given an opportunity to choose the men they like) instead of a labor board or a labor court. However, the government would have to become involved when the parties were unable to agree on an arbitrator. Moreover, while the Federal Mediation and Conciliation Service has been free from political bias in placing arbitrators' names on its lists for selection by the parties in grievance arbitrations, there can be no guarantee that politics would not play a role in the selection process if the stakes were high enough—as they would be in the compulsory arbitration of new contract terms in the steel, coal, automobile, and other major industries.

If a board or labor court were used to settle disputes, it would have the possible advantage of being able to establish continuing policies. Nevertheless, appointment of at least some of the members would be made by the Administration. (A board could be tripartite, in which case some members would be appointed by labor and some by management.) One of the costs of compulsory settlement, therefore, would be to move management-labor disputes—to some degree at least—from the economic to the political arena.

Will Force Really Work?

Under the free collective bargaining system, the government has no problem of enforcement. For instance, while both the company and the employees suffered serious losses during the 14-week GE strike, once it was over both the management and the workers returned to their jobs voluntarily. This illustrates an important advantage of the present system which is often overlooked—that no use of force by the government is required. Moreover, since the agreement is one which the parties themselves have negotiated, the day-to-day operations under it are likely to be more cooperative. The company representatives sell it to management, and the union representatives sell it to the employees. Since the contract is the negotiators' own handiwork, they make a real effort to get it to work—a greater effort, I believe, than they would make if the agreement were the work of some authority appointed by the government.

This country's experience with legislation that has prohibited strikes on the part of public employees indicates that such legislation does not automatically put an end to the strikes. The Condon-Wadlin Act, which prohibited strikes by state and local government employees in New York State from 1947 to 1967, was violated often, but on only a few occasions were its penalties actually enforced. Since 1967 the Taylor Act, which also prohibits strikes by public employees in New York State, has been subject to numerous violations. Likewise, the illegality of strikes by federal employees has not prevented them from leaving the job.

What would happen, under compulsory settlement, if workers in the coal, steel, automobile, trucking, or some other major industry decided that they did not wish to accept the terms prescribed by the arbitrator or labor court and refused to work? How does a democratic government force 100,000 coal miners, 400,000 steel workers, 700,000 automobile workers, or 450,000 truckers to perform their tasks effectively when they elect not to do so? Perhaps it can be done—

but I suggest that this is a question which it is well not to have to answer. It is unwise to run the risk of placing government in a position where the government may reveal its impotence unless it is absolutely necessary to do so.

Threat to Capitalism

Finally, if government becomes involved in the determination of labor contract terms in order to avoid strikes, it may not be able to stop there. With our democratic political structure it would be impossible, I believe, to prevent compulsory settlement of wages for union members from leading to compulsory determination of all wages; that, in turn, would lead to government decisions concerning salaries, professional fees, and, finally, prices and profits.

So long as free collective bargaining is permitted, it forms an outer perimeter of defense against government regulation in other areas. If it falls, the possibility of more regulation in the other areas becomes much greater. It is worth noting that George Meany, the president of the AFL-CIO, stated several months ago that he would not be opposed to wage controls if similar controls were placed on salaries, prices, and profits. Meany's view of these relationships is one that many people might share.

CONCLUSION

How do the costs of the right to strike compare with the costs of the alternative, compulsory settlement? Taking strike costs first, my analysis indicates that:

It is easy to overemphasize the costs of strikes.

Much progress has already been made in replacing organizational strikes, jurisdictional strikes, and grievance strikes with peaceful alternatives.

Strikes—even the big industrywide ones—have a minimal effect on the economy.

Some strikes, such as those in public utilities, which once were very critical, are no longer so because of automation.

The number of man-days lost because of strikes is a very small part of the total (only 0.23 percent in 1969), and the trend has been definitely downward.

On the other hand, my analysis indicates that compulsory settlement involves major costs like these:

The elimination from collective bargaining of the strongest incentive to reach agreement which management and labor now have.

A great increase in the number of failures to reach agreement.

The development of a large government bureaucracy to adjudicate the larger number of unsettled disputes.

An increase in political aspects of collective bargaining.

The difficulty of enforcement of compulsory orders, with the attendant danger of divulging the impotence of government.

The likely development of other wage, salary, price, and profit controls by government.

I conclude that the right to strike is preferable to a compulsory settlement system. It does not follow that the government should never move to protect the public against strikes which create serious hardships, but it does follow that any move to prohibit the use of the strike in the private sector should be made cautiously and only to the extent which is clearly required. Any broad prohibition of strike freedom would prove to be very costly in itself and also lead to major government controls over other parts of the economy. Free collective bargaining, which includes the right to strike and the right to lockout, constitutes the outer defense of the private enterprise system.

UNION EFFECTS ON WAGES—A CAUTION

In 96 percent or more of labor negotiations, as Kennedy points out above, the result is not a strike but a new contract. One of the most important objectives of labor in the setting of this new contract will be to raise the level of wages. Let us briefly indicate how a union can cause a departure from the market-determined wage and then suggest why caution must be used in interpreting this piece of analysis.

Figure 5-5 shows the effect of a wage increase for electricians above the supply-and-demand determined price. W_1 is the wage that would obtain if there were no external intervention in the market. The union's objective is to raise the wage to W_2. If it succeeds—and if everything else remains unchanged (our familiar *ceteris paribus* clause)—then, when the wage rate is raised to W_2, business firms will cut their employment from E_1 to E_2. Actually, the measure of unemployment among electricians would be greater than the difference between those formerly employed and those now employed. The reason is that at the new and higher wage rate, more electricians' services would be offered than before. (This is what the supply curve tells us.) Consequently, the amount of unemployment is measured by the horizontal distance between the demand and supply curves at the new wage (W_2), or the distance AB.

Now it would seem from this analysis that the main impact of unions in this area of bargaining would be to raise the wage rates of their members and to curtail the employment of their members. And, indeed, the objective of securing a

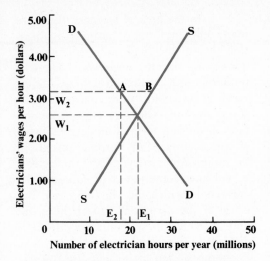

Figure 5-5. Effects of a Single Union on Wage Rates and Employment.

If one union in the economy succeeds in raising its wage (W_2) above the supply-and-demand determined wage (W_1), the consequences for those workers will be less employment but higher wages for those employed. One must not generalize this effect to the action of unions in the economy as a whole, however, since these curves are drawn on *ceteris paribus* assumptions that do not hold when all unions are acting together.

wage that is high relative to other income receivers in the economy is an important one for most unions.

We must not conclude that this effort will be successful *in the aggregate,* however. And this is where we must exercise some caution in interpreting our results. For we cannot say that when one union does something alone, the same results will be achieved for that union as when *all unions together* attempt a similar thing. The relevance of the *ceteris paribus* phrase is particularly important here. When *all* unions are attempting to achieve wage increases, then this clause is no longer appropriate for any one labor market—other things *are* changing. In partic-

ular, if all wages go up, this will have an effect on the demand for most products in the economy; and when the demand for products goes up, this, in turn, will have an effect on the demand for labor. We could, in fact, imagine a case where everything more or less canceled out: there were higher wages in general, higher prices in general (so that the higher wages would purchase the same number of goods in the economy as before), and no change in the employment of workers throughout the economy.

This might seem like an argument against unions, since it would mean that they hadn't achieved much for all their pains. On the other hand, it can also be used to combat an argument frequently used in the past against labor unions— namely, that they are responsible for mass unemployment in the economy.

What we have actually done in these last two paragraphs has been to move on from a particular part of the economy (washing machines, electricians, and so on) to a consideration of the economy in the aggregate. Thus, we are foreshadowing matters that we shall be taking up in some detail in Part Two of this book, beginning with chapter 7.

THE COMPLICATED MIXTURE— GOVERNMENT, BUSINESS, LABOR

We cannot end these two chapters on the mixed American economy without stressing one basic point. The point is that not only is the economy "mixed" in the overall sense that there is a public and private sector, each of some significance, but also in the sense that each sector is itself increasingly "mixed." This is clearly true of Factor Markets in the early 1970s, since the government has now become intimately involved in all major wage settlements via President Nixon's Pay Board as part of an overall system of wage-price controls.

But it is true of the public sector and corporate business sector as well. Indeed, it can be argued (and has been argued, as we know), that corporate executives and corporate objectives are not all that different from the executives and objectives apparent in the public bureaucracy, whether it be the Department of Defense or the Department of Agriculture. Furthermore, the life-styles of labor leaders are no longer that much different from those of business executives (except, as someone once suggested, that they are better dressed). The antagonistic clash between labor and management, like the predicted antagonistic clash between the public and private sectors (between socialism and free enterprise), has not materialized in the way that Marx, or, for that matter, anyone else, anticipated.

This blurring of the traditional categories is an important notion to have in mind as we move forward to a more in-depth analysis of the workings of a modern economy. It will help free us to look at economic realities with a fresh and imaginative point of view.

SUMMARY

Despite the growth of government in the American economy in recent decades, our economy remains heavily oriented towards the private sector. This private sector is, however, not quite what one would expect from a simple supply-and-demand analysis appropriate to a market economy.

In the area of business, there are many different forms of business organization such as the *single proprietorship,* the *partnership,* and the *corporation.* The corporation, with its limited liability, its divorce of ownership from control, and its sometimes massive size is perhaps the most significant form of modern industrial organization. Many corporations are in the billion dollar category, and these clearly will have some power to influence the markets in which they buy and sell. Because of the enormous size of the economy in which these giants operate, it is difficult to judge how powerful they are. Economists often try to measure *concentration ratios* (e.g., what percentage of shipments in an industry is accounted for by the four largest firms?) to determine the impact of firms relative to their particular industries. They also try to determine trends in concentration over time. Although the impact of large firms is certainly greater than it was, say, in the mid-nineteenth century, there is no clear-cut evidence of increasing concentration in the past several decades.

Even apart from concentration ratios, however, the simple bigness of the modern corporation probably has implications for the way in which it functions. Many observers have commented that public and private bureaucracies have increasingly come to share common features—the corporate manager and the public servant may not be so far apart as was once thought.

The Factor Markets of the American economy similarly function rather more complexly than simple supply-and-demand analysis might suggest. The labor union is a particularly important example of an institution that influences the functioning of our most important factor market. The effects of union action are not always what they seem. Strikes, for example, are probably much less costly to our society than is often imagined. Similarly, although one union may improve the position of its members relative to another's, it is not clear that, in the aggregate, labor unions can bring higher wages (i.e., in terms of real purchasing power) for all their members at once.

One general conclusion that emerges from a brief survey of the private sector of our economy is this: the American economy not only contains two sectors—public and private—but is in fact a thorough-going mixture of elements *within* each sector. There is very little black and white, but an astonishing range of greys.

QUESTIONS FOR DISCUSSION

1. Large modern corporations are clearly not *pure competitors* in the sense defined in chapter 2 (p. 38), but most businessmen would say that they definitely "compete" with each other and with foreign rivals, etc. What is your intuitive sense of what such "competing" involves? What forms of competition do you see most frequently in the present-day American economy?

2. John Kenneth Galbraith once said that when visitors from abroad come to study the efficiency of American industry, the firms they visit are the same ones most frequently visited by representatives of the Antitrust Division of the Justice Department. Why might this be?

3. How might the self-interest of a salaried manager differ from that of an owner-operator of a business firm? If you were the head of a large corporation (in

which you owned little or no stock), what motives do you think would guide your conduct?

4. "The existence of large, even giant, corporations means that American business does not respond to the dictates of the market, but rather manages the market for its own purposes. For this very reason 'consumer sovereignty' is largely a myth in the modern industrial world." Discuss.

5. Write an essay on the pros and cons of strikes as a means of settling labor disputes.

6. The distinguished American economist Thorstein Veblen (1857–1929) once called the struggle between business and labor a mere game "played between two contending interests for private gain." How might the leader of a modern labor union respond to such a criticism?

7. Why is it impossible to generalize from the effects of one union, acting alone, to the effects of all unions, acting simultaneously, on real wages and employment in the national economy?

8. Enumerate some of the ways in which the U.S. government attempts to protect the public interest in the face of the growth of big business and big labor. What do you consider to be the major difficulties in defining an effective policy in this area?

SUGGESTED READING

Adams, Walter, ed. *The Structure of American Industry*. 3rd ed. New York: Macmillan Co., 1961.

Caves, Richard. *American Industry: Structure, Conduct, Performance*. 2nd ed. Englewood Cliffs, N.J.: Prentice-Hall, 1967.

Galbraith, John K. *American Capitalism, the Concept of Countervailing Power.* Boston: Houghton Mifflin Co., 1952.

Phelps, Edmund S., ed. *Problems of the Modern Economy.* New York: W. W. Norton & Co., 1966, pp. 7–106.

Taft, Philip. *Organized Labor in American History.* New York: Harper & Row, 1964.

Trebing, Harry M., ed. *The Corporation in the American Economy.* Chicago: Quadrangle Books, 1970.

Weiss, Leonard W. *Case Studies in American Industry.* New York: John Wiley & Sons, 1967.

Wilcox, Clair. *Public Policies Toward Business.* Rev. ed. Homewood, Ill.: Richard D. Irwin, 1960.

6
The Underdeveloped Economy

In this chapter, the last in our discussion of basic economic systems, we move sharply from the affluent, industrial economy of the United States to the poor, *underdeveloped economy,* characteristic of much of Asia, Africa, and Latin America.

In discussing the underdeveloped economy, we are to some degree considering a set of economic conditions, rather than a kind of economic *system* (socialism, mixed economy, and so on). That is to say, the poor countries of the world at present operate under many different varieties of economic system, including specific national and local elements, some of which have no real analogue in the economically developed world. Still, the inclusion of this chapter in Part One is warranted on two grounds. First, there is the fact that the basic problems facing many of these countries are so overwhelming that they are likely to condition *any* economic system developed to meet them. And second, there is the fact (or at least the strong belief of most observers) that the characteristic underdeveloped country is likely to depart rather

substantially from the kind of economic system under which much of the Western world industrialized. In particular, it is widely believed that economic planning—specifically planning for growth—will loom larger in these countries than it did in many Western countries, certainly than it did in "early developers" like Britain and the United States when they were going through their industrial revolutions. In short, although there will still be variety, the economic systems of these countries are likely to show important similarities, if only because of the enormous problems they face.

MEANING OF ECONOMIC UNDERDEVELOPMENT

Many terms have been used to describe the underdeveloped economies of the world: e.g., "economically backward," "less developed," or "developing," to cite a few. The common element is simply *poverty,* the depth of which can be attested by any traveler who has seen the conditions in which many of these peoples live.

Poverty can also be confirmed by a great variety of statistical measures. One might look at figures on life expectancy, calories in the diet, number of teachers or doctors per head of population, steel output or electrical power output per capita, percentage of the population living in rural areas or working in the agricultural sector, number of automobiles, miles of road, movie theaters, household appliances, plumbing facilities, and so on. In each case, one would find a striking contrast between the material comforts of the industrialized world and the harsh facts of subsistence in their poorer neighbors.

Since economic "growth" is usually defined in terms of a rising output per capita, economists often use this index as a general measure of the degree of poverty or "underdevelopment" in any particular country. Actually, this measure is not a completely satisfactory one, for a number of reasons. One simple reason is that the necessary information often is lacking. Statistical collections in many poor countries are often either nonexistent or little better than not-so-educated guesswork. Another reason is that in many of these nations there is a great deal of production that never enters explicitly into the marketplace. A small village in India or in some African country may produce mainly for its own needs, with the result that only a small part of its total production would appear in formal statistics, even if we had them. There is also a fundamental difficulty involved in any attempt to make comparisons among societies that differ radically in their economic structure. If country A produces exactly the same goods as country B, and in the same proportions, but has ten times more of each good, then we can say fairly unequivocally that country A has ten times the total

output of country B. But if country A is a rich country and country B is a poor country, they will not in general be consuming the same goods and in the same proportions. Rice may be the most important product in country B, while in country A it may be automobiles, or washing machines, or vacuum cleaners. For that matter, what exactly would the significance of a vacuum cleaner be to country B if its villagers lived in huts with earthen floors? The point is that comparisons between countries with drastically different standards of living involve not only practical problems but also difficult philosophic problems. To a certain degree, these comparisons must be taken with a grain of salt.[1]

Still, the gap in levels of output per capita between the rich and the poor countries of the world is so great that even the very rough statistics we are able to gather tell a meaningful and dramatic story. Table 6-1 shows how great this gap is. A quarter of the world's population has an annual per capita output of below $100; another third of the world's population has a per capita output between $100 and $300. Even if we correct these figures upward (as we probably should), we still have the fact that perhaps half the people of the world live on a tenth of the income we are accustomed to enjoying in the present-day United States.

Such a huge gap did not exist two centuries ago or even one century ago. There were differences, of course. Some countries were richer than others, as has been the case throughout history. But the salient fact of the past 100 or 200 years

---

1. The same problems are also present when we try to measure the growth of a single country over very long periods of time. For a discussion of the meaning of a nation's output per capita and other "national income" concepts, see chapter 8. For the problems involved in measuring long-run growth, see chapter 16.

Table 6-1   ANNUAL PER CAPITA OUTPUT IN 1968*
(Converted to U.S. Dollars by Means of Foreign Exchange Rates)

Group A: Annual Per Capita Output of $0–$100

Africa			Asia and Middle East		Latin America
Angola	Ethiopia	Nigeria	Afghanistan	Muscat and Oman	Haiti
Botswana	Gambia	Rwanda	Bhutan	Nepal	
Burundi	Guinea	Somalia	Burma	Yemen	
Chad	Malawi	Tanzania	India		
Congo, Dem. Rep.	Mali	Uganda	Indonesia		
Dahomey	Mozambique	Upper Volta	Laos		
	Niger				

Group B: Annual Per Capita Output of $101–$300

Africa		Asia and Middle East	Latin America
Algeria	Senegal	Cambodia	Bolivia
Cameroon	Sierra Leone	Ceylon	Dominican Republic
Central African Republic	Southern Rhodesia	China (Mainland)	Ecuador
Ghana	Sudan	Iran	El Salvador
Kenya	Swaziland	Iraq	Guyana
Liberia	Togo	Jordan	Honduras
Madagascar	Tunisia	Korea (South)	Paraguay
Mauritania	United Arab Republic	Pakistan	Peru
Mauritius	Zambia	South Vietnam	
Morocco		Syria	
		Thailand	

Group C: Annual Per Capita Output of $301–$600

Africa	Europe	Asia and the Middle East	Latin America
Gabon	Bulgaria	China (Taiwan)	Brazil
Ivory Coast	Malta	Hong Kong	British Honduras
Reunion	Portugal	Korea (North)	Chile
	Yugoslavia	Lebanon	Colombia
		Malaysia	Costa Rica
Oceania		Philippines	Guatemala
Fiji		Saudi Arabia	Jamaica
		Turkey	Mexico
			Nicaragua
			Surinam

Group D: Annual Per Capita Output of $601–$1600

Africa	Asia and the Middle East	Europe	Latin America
Libya	Brunei	Austria	Argentina
South Africa	Cyprus	Greece	Neth. Antilles
	Israel	Hungary	Panama
	Japan	Ireland	Puerto Rico
	Singapore	Italy	Trinidad, Tobago
		Poland	Venezuela
		Rumania	
		Spain	

*Figures are for 1968 except when not available, in which case the most recent available year is used.

Table 6-1 *(continued)*

Group E: Annual Per Capita Output of $1061–$3000			
Europe		**North America**	**Oceania**
Belgium	Luxembourg	Canada	Australia
Denmark	Netherlands		New Zealand
East Germany	Norway		
Finland	Switzerland		
France	United Kingdom		
Iceland	U.S.S.R.		
	West Germany		

Group F: Annual Per Capita Output of Above $3000	
	Average Per Capita Output
Asia and the Middle East	
Kuwait†	$3738
Europe	
Sweden	$3315
North America	
United States	$4379

†Oil!

Sources: *United Nations Statistical Yearbook,* 1969, Frank Tachau, ed., *The Developing Nations: What Paths to Modernization* (New York: Dodd, Mead & Company, 1972).

is that the gap has been widening, not just absolutely, but in percentage terms, and not slowly but rapidly. The fundamental reason, of course, is that the nations of Europe and North America went through (and are continuing to go through) an industrial revolution during this period, while the poorer countries did not. Economically they stood still—in some cases, they may even have lost ground—while the advanced countries shot ahead at theretofore inconceivably rapid rates. Stagnation in one area of the world and rapid modern growth in the other brought about the great disparities in standards of living that are with us today.

HISTORICAL VERSUS MODERN DEVELOPMENT

The past twenty-five years have seen a sharp awakening, in both East and West, to the facts we have just been describing. Although the poor countries of the world are aware of some of the problems of industrialization, they want to have at least a fair share in the material progress that they have seen so bountifully distributed in the West.

Now to a certain degree the attempt to achieve this goal poses to the underdeveloped country of today the same problems faced by the economically advanced countries a century or two ago. One partial way of looking at the problem is to say that these countries are now trying to achieve the same kind of industrial revolution that Britain achieved in the late eighteenth century, the United States in the early nineteenth century, Russia and Japan in the late nineteenth century, and so on. To the degree that this is true, one can look to past history for clues to steps that these underdeveloped countries must undertake today.

This, however, is only a partial

and incomplete approach to the problem, because there are a number of important respects in which these countries face difficulties that are *different* from those of countries that achieved their industrial revolutions in the past. These differences, indeed, affect virtually every aspect of the development process, including, as we have already suggested, the form of economic system most appropriate for promoting rapid growth.

Let us spend the rest of this chapter taking up some of these differences with respect to the main factors behind economic development: (1) technological change; (2) capital accumulation; and (3) population growth.

TECHNOLOGICAL CHANGE IN POOR COUNTRIES

In chapter 1, when we were discussing how a country's production-possibility curve might shift outward over time, we suggested that technological change—the development of new products and new methods of production and distribution—would be an important element, perhaps the most important element, in the process. Interestingly, the one respect in which the modern underdeveloped country would appear to have a clear-cut advantage over its historical predecessors is in this area of technological change. Indeed, this constitutes the main single reason for some optimism about the ultimate prospects of the underdeveloped world.

The advantage derives from the fact that although these countries have been technologically stagnant during the past century, the world as a whole has not been. When England started her industrial revolution, she had to invent the steam engine, but for the underdeveloped

country of today, the steam engine already exists. So also does electricity, the railroad, the telephone, the airplane, and even atomic energy and electronic computers. During this period, there has been developed an enormous store of new technology that is potentially available even to the poorest and most backward countries. Instead of having to start from scratch, they have open to them all the major scientific achievements of the industrial world, and this gives them a running start, compared to the "early developers."

The possibilities that this opens up are suggested in Figure 6-1. We have added to a similar diagram from chapter 1 a production-possibility curve for an underdeveloped country. The diagram conveys the possibility that, using advanced Western technology, the underdeveloped country (though starting far down in the southwest corner) might in a few years leap upwards to join its more economically favored neighbors.

The advantage conferred by the availability of Western technology is, however, qualified by a number of important drawbacks.

(1) The advanced technology of the West is, in most cases, unsuited to the economic conditions prevalent in the less developed countries. Many of these countries are characterized by (*a*) an abundance of unskilled, semiliterate laborers and (*b*) a shortage of trained workers and managers, and also of machinery and other capital goods. The advanced technology of the West, however, requires both skilled labor and a great deal of machinery and other capital goods. The large-scale adoption of this technology in unmodified form would create enormous strains on an underdeveloped country and would also provide little employment for the vast

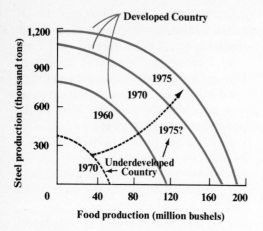

Figure 6-1. Rapid Technological Advance.

Can a poor country, using available western technology, leap forward in a few years to a much more developed state? There are, unfortunately, many difficulties in the way of such spectacular advances.

numbers of unskilled laborers in the economy. Consequently, modification of Western technology (to make it more suitable to conditions in the underdeveloped country) is highly desirable. But such modification is difficult and, in many cases, is tantamount to the development of "new" technology.

(2) Many less developed countries, particularly at an early stage of their efforts, do not have the productive capacity to produce the kinds of machinery, tools, and other equipment that the installation of Western technology requires. This means that they will often have to sustain large imports of industrial goods in the early stages of their development effort. But how are they to pay for these imports? In a country like India, where exports have been sluggish and where there has been a need to import not only capital goods but also food and raw materials, the problem of a balance of pay-

ments crisis may be a serious one, severely limiting the country's development potentialities.

(3) Not all Western technology is unequivocally helpful in promoting economic development. The clearest instance in this respect is public health and medical technology. As we shall see when we come to the problem of population growth, the importation of Western public health and medical technology has contributed to a sharp fall in the death rate in many underdeveloped countries. This is a desirable achievement in its own right, but it has contributed to the population explosion in these countries, which may pose grave obstacles to successful development.

These qualifications do not mean that the technological advantage of the modern underdeveloped country is completely nullified. It is still a major asset to have the storehouse of the industrial world to draw upon. Still, they make it clear that the advantage is somewhat less than might appear at first glance. Also, they make it clear that the effort simply to copy the latest and most advanced examples of Western technology may be an unwise and even foolhardy approach for many of these countries.

CAPITAL ACCUMULATION

Technological change is not the only factor making for an outward-shifting production-possibility curve. Another important element is the accumulation of capital goods. These goods include machines, tools, buildings, equipment, inventories of goods in stock, and any other *produced means of production* (in contrast, say, to natural resources that are not "produced" by man). Adam Smith, we recall, gave capital accumulation an important place in the growth process and attributed it largely to the frugality of private individuals, as opposed to the extravagance of governments. In the twentieth century, however, we have seen that governments often pursue capital accumulation more vigorously than private individuals— witness the fact that most command or near-command economies in modern times have tended to give a preference to capital goods relative to consumer goods (see pp. 78–79).

Two important generalizations can be made about capital accumulation in the modern underdeveloped country. The first is that this accumulation may be particularly important for such a country's growth, for reasons we have just been discussing under the heading of technological change. If, as we have suggested, Western technology uses a high proportion of capital relative to other factors of production, then the ability of a poor country to apply this technology will depend in great part on its capacity for capital accumulation. In other words, the technological potentiality can be converted into an actual advantage only via an expanded accumulation of capital.

The second point is that, although the need for more capital may be great in these countries, the problem of supplying it may be even greater than it was in times past. There are several reasons for this, an important one being that these countries are very poor, even poorer than many of the industrialized nations were a century or two ago when they were embarking on *their* course of development. As Adam Smith correctly pointed out, capital accumulation requires saving. The process in its essence involves the setting aside of some of today's income, saving it, and investing it in more machines, tools, etc. If output per capita is very low, people

may wish to consume all or nearly all of their very meager incomes. Indeed, some economists believe that there is a kind of vicious circle of poverty here:

Such a vicious circle will arise if saving depends upon output while output depends upon the rate of capital accumulation. Thus, in its simplest form, it would go: People are poor, therefore they do not save much. Since savings are small, capital accumulation will be slow. Since there is little capital accumulation, output will remain low. When output is low, people are poor. In other words, people remain poor because they are poor.

Other economists believe that these circles are not so vicious as might appear. They point out that historically even the poorest societies have been able to summon "surpluses" above consumption; for example, for waging wars. They also note that in many less developed countries there are extremely wealthy individuals—large landowners, merchants, the governing classes—who form a potential supply of savings and investment if the surplus can be tapped.

Still, no one would argue that general poverty is a condition that favors capital accumulation. Furthermore, there are other factors that may complicate the situation. The rapid development of communications in modern times has meant that poor nations are often keenly aware of the luxurious living standards present in the West. This increases their desire for growth, but it may also stimulate their desire for higher levels of consumption (and hence less saving and capital accumulation) in the immediate present. Also, the social structure of the underdeveloped country may not be favorable to the utilization of such economic surpluses as are potentially available. In the West, energetic private individuals developed the habit of frugality and thrift at an early stage, virtually as a matter of religious principle.[2] But the wealthy Latin-American landowner or the oil-rich potentate in the Middle East may prefer to live in luxury and ostentation and devote relatively little of the available surplus to growth-generating purposes.

All this is not to say that the modern underdeveloped country will not be able to summon the capital it so desperately needs. But it does mean that the effort to do so may impose a very great strain on the society and may possibly require a major reorganization of its structure.

The case of China is very interesting in this regard. After the end of the civil war in 1949, China took strong and immediate steps to raise her rate of capital accumulation. Although accurate figures are virtually impossible to come by, it would appear that gross investment,[3] which had been well below 10 percent of GNP in the 1930s, had risen to 19 percent by 1952 and to 25 percent or more in 1957. In 1958, moreover, China entered upon the period of her "Great Leap Forward." Through state action in industry (by 1957, over 96 percent of all industrial investment in China was undertaken by the government) and by collectivization of agriculture through the communes, which were to increase the available agricultural surplus, China made an effort to increase her total investment well above what was already an extremely high figure for such a relatively underdeveloped country.

These facts prove (1) that a poor country *can* raise its investment level substantially even in a very short period of time but also (2) that structural reorganizations of society of this magnitude can be very costly. There is little doubt that there was a general fall in the rate of investment in the early 1960s as China tried to recover from the extreme strains of the "Great Leap" period. Indeed, in the early 1960s, the economy was seriously depressed in both agricultural and industrial sectors. By 1970, China had recovered from this experience but she had also meanwhile gone through the strains of the "cultural revolution" (1966–69) and it seems fairly certain that her overall growth in the 1960s was slower than it had been in the 1950s.[4]

The point, then, is that although capital accumulation problems are not insurmountable in today's less developed country, they are very severe, owing to the combination of a large need and a relatively inadequate means of supplying that need. The great question—from the point of view of the public interest of the world as a whole—is whether this problem can be solved without steps that rend the fabric of society and cause great temporary hardships for the peoples involved.

THE POPULATION PROBLEM

We come now to the third of what we called the main factors in economic development: population growth. Because

---

2. Indeed, some economic historians have argued that it *was* a matter of religious principle. See, for example, the classic work: Max Weber, *The Protestant Ethic and the Spirit of Capitalism* (New York: Charles Scribner's Sons, 1952).

3. The term *gross investment* refers to the production of new capital goods, *including* those that simply *replace* old or obsolescent machines or buildings. See discussion p. 195.

4. In the case of the "cultural revolution," it can be argued that Chairman Mao was prepared to sacrifice high investment and high economic growth in order "to create a society radically different from those that now exist in the industrialized world." (Dwight H. Perkins, "The Economic Performance of China and Japan, 1842–1969," Harvard Institute of Economic Research, Cambridge, Mass., Discussion Paper Number 177, February 1971, p. 34). The highest possible rate of growth need not be the *only* objective, even in an extremely poor economy.

of its extreme importance for the underdeveloped countries (and for the world generally), we must spend a bit more time on this particular problem.

The problem in a nutshell is given in Figure 6-2. No one should attribute more accuracy to this diagram than it possesses—population statistics are historically unreliable and projections of curves into the future even more so. Still the basic situation is quite clear. There has been an enormous acceleration of world population growth in modern times. The period of doubling of world population—historically measured in centuries or millennia—is now thirty or forty years. Another thing is also quite clear—it can't go on this way. Increases at this rate would soon bring not only a "standing room only" world, but also an evidently impossible situation in which the physical weight of people would exceed the weight of the earth itself. Thus, these rates of population growth will stop; *how* they will stop is a matter of no small concern for anyone who has any feeling at all for the future of the human race.

THE MALTHUSIAN APPROACH

The analysis of this problem must begin with one of the British classical economists, Thomas Robert Malthus, who predicted population disaster for the world nearly two centuries ago. Malthus (1766–1834) was a wide-ranging thinker whose contributions to economics included, besides population theory, some very interesting speculations about the causes of depressions (what he called "universal gluts") that were taken up again in the 1930s. He can also be given some credit for being the *first* professional economist

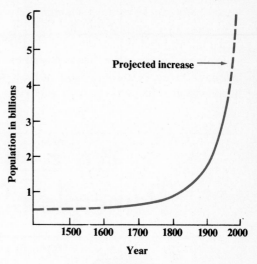

Figure 6-2.

The striking acceleration of population growth in modern times is made apparent in this curve. It should be noted that population figures for the world as a whole are only estimates, even today. For earlier centuries, they are very rough approximations.

because, although he was Reverend Malthus, he was also a professor of political economy in the East India College in Haileybury.

Malthus's views on population were presented to the world in *An Essay on the Principle of Population as It Affects the Future Improvement of Society,* the first edition of which was published in 1798. The immediate cause of his writing the *Essay* was a discussion with his father about the perfectibility of man and society. Young Malthus wished to show that such eighteenth-century optimists as William Godwin and the Marquis de Condorcet were far too hopeful in their philosophies. The effect of the *Essay* was dramatic, both immediately and in the long run. It went through six editions and had a direct impact on the views of contemporary economists (also influencing Charles Darwin's evolutionary theory, as we have mentioned before). The essayist Thomas Carlyle was so disturbed by his reading of it that he labeled economics the "dismal-science," a name that has persisted to this day. In the 1970s, it remains a basic starting place for any serious analysis of the problems of the underdeveloped economy.

Let us present Malthus's theory in his own words, and then, introducing some modern modifications, indicate its relevance for the present day.

An Essay on the Principle of Population

THOMAS ROBERT MALTHUS

The subject will, perhaps, be seen in a clearer light, if we endeavour to ascertain what would be the natural increase of population, if left to exert itself with perfect freedom; and what might be expected to be the rate of increase in the productions of the earth, under the most favourable circumstances of human industry.

In the northern states of America, where the means of subsistence have been more ample, the manners of the people more pure, and the checks to early marriages fewer, than in any of the modern states of Europe, the population has been found to double itself, for above a century and a half successively, in less than twenty-five years. Yet, even during these periods, in some of the towns, the deaths exceeded the births, a circumstance which clearly proves that, in those parts of the country which

Excerpted from Thomas Malthus, An Essay on the Principle of Population. 6th ed. (London, 1826), pp. 4–17.

supplied this deficiency, the increase must have been much more rapid than the general average.

In the back settlements, where the sole employment is agriculture, and vicious customs and unwholesome occupations are little known, the population has been found to double itself in fifteen years. Even this extraordinary rate of increase is probably short of the utmost power of population. Very severe labour is requisite to clear a fresh country; such situations are not in general considered as particularly healthy; and the inhabitants, probably, are occasionally subject to the incursions of the Indians, which may destroy some lives, or at any rate diminish the fruits of industry.

But, to be perfectly sure that we are far within the truth, we will take the slowest of these rates of increase. It may safely be pronounced, therefore, that population, when unchecked, goes on doubling itself every twenty-five years, or increases in a geometrical ratio.

The rate according to which the productions of the earth may be supposed to increase, it will not be so easy to determine. Of this, however, we may be perfectly certain, that the ratio of their increase in a limited territory must be of a totally different nature from the ratio of the increase of population. A thousand millions are just as easily doubled every twenty-five years by the power of population as a thousand. But the food to support the increase from the greater number will by no means be obtained with the same facility. Man is necessarily confined in room. When acre has been added to acre till all the fertile land is occupied, the yearly increase of food must depend upon the melioration of the land already in possession. This is a fund, which, from the nature of all soils, instead of increasing, must be gradually diminishing. But population, could it be supplied with food, would go on with unexhausted vigour.

Europe is by no means so fully peopled as it might be.

In Europe there is the fairest chance that human industry may receive its best direction. The science of agriculture has been much studied in England and Scotland; and there is still a great portion of uncultivated land in these countries. Let us consider at what rate the produce of this island might be supposed to increase under circumstances the most favourable to improvement.

If it be allowed that by the best possible policy, and great encouragements to agriculture, the average produce of the island could be doubled in the first twenty-five years, it will be allowing, probably, a greater increase than could with reason be expected.

In the next twenty-five years, it is impossible to suppose that the produce could be quadrupled. It would be contrary to all our knowledge of the properties of land. The improvement `of the barren parts would be a work of time and labour; and it must be evident to those who have the slightest acquaintance with agricultural subjects, that in proportion as cultivation extended, the additions that could yearly be made to the former average produce must be gradually and regularly diminishing. That we may be the better able to compare the increase of population and food, let us make a supposition, which, without pretending to accuracy, is clearly more favourable to the power of production in the earth, than any experience we have had of its qualities will warrant.

Let us suppose that the yearly additions which might be made to the former

Thomas Robert Malthus (1766-1834). Known for his pessimistic views on population, Malthus has had a modern revival as over-population has become a global problem.

average produce, instead of decreasing, which they certainly would do, were to remain the same; and that the produce of this island might be increased every twenty-five years, by a quantity equal to what it at present produces. The most enthusiastic speculator cannot suppose a greater increase than this. In a few centuries it would make every acre of land in the island like a garden.

If this supposition be applied to the whole earth, and if it be allowed that the subsistence for man which the earth affords might be increased every twenty-five years by a quantity equal to what it at present produces, this will be supposing a rate of increase much greater than we can imagine that any possible exertions of mankind could make it.

It may be fairly pronounced, therefore, that, considering the present average state of the earth, the means of subsistence, under circumstances the most favourable to human industry, could not possibly be made to increase faster than in an arithmetical ratio.

The necessary effects of these two different rates of increase, when brought together, will be very striking. Let us call the population of this island 11 millions; and suppose the present produce equal to the easy support of such a number. In the first twenty-five years the population would be 22 millions, and the food being also doubled, the means of subsistence would be equal to this increase. In the next twenty-five years, the population would be 44 millions, and the means of subsistence only equal to the support of 33 millions. In the next period the population would be 88 millions, and the means of subsistence just equal to the support of half that number. And, at the conclusion of the first century, the population would be 176 millions, and the means of subsistence only equal to the support of 55 millions, leaving a population of 121 millions totally unprovided for.

Taking the whole earth, instead of this island, emigration would of course be excluded; and, supposing the present population equal to a thousand millions, the human species would increase as the numbers, 1, 2, 4, 8, 16, 32, 64, 128, 256, and subsistence as 1, 2, 3, 4, 5, 6, 7, 8, 9. In two centuries the population would be to the means of subsistence as 256 to 9; in three centuries as 4096 to 13, and in two thousand years the difference would be almost incalculable.

In this supposition no limits whatever are placed to the produce of the earth. It may increase for ever and be greater than any assignable quantity; yet still the power of population being in every period so much superior, the increase of the human species can only be kept down to the level of the means of subsistence by the constant operation of the strong law of necessity, acting as a check upon the greater power.

OF THE GENERAL CHECKS TO POPULATION, AND THE MODE OF THEIR OPERATION.

The ultimate check to population appears then to be a want of food, arising necessarily from the different ratios according to which population and food increase. But this ultimate check is never the immediate check, except in cases of actual famine.

The immediate check may be stated to consist in all those customs, and all those diseases, which seem to be generated by a scarcity of the means of subsistence; and all those causes, independent of this scarcity, whether of a moral or physical nature, which tend prematurely to weaken and destroy the human frame.

These checks to population, which are constantly operating with more or less force in every society, and keep down the number to the level of the means of subsistence, may be classed under two general heads—the preventive, and the positive checks.

The preventive check, as far as it is voluntary, is peculiar to man, and arises from that distinctive superiority in his reasoning faculties, which enables him to calculate distant consequences. The checks to the indefinite increase of plants and irrational animals are all either positive, or, if preventive, involuntary. But man cannot look around him, and see the distress which frequently presses upon those who have large families; he cannot contemplate his present possessions or earnings, which he now nearly consumes himself, and calculate the amount of each share, when with very little addition they must be divided, perhaps, among seven or eight, without feeling a doubt whether, if he follow the bent of his inclinations, he may be able to support the offspring which he will probably bring into the world.

These considerations are calculated to prevent, and certainly do prevent, a great number of persons in all civilized nations from pursuing the dictate of nature in an early attachment to one woman.

If this restraint does not produce vice, it is undoubtedly the least evil that can arise from the principle of population. Considered as a restraint on a strong natural inclination, it must be allowed to produce a certain degree of temporary unhappiness; but evidently slight, compared with the evils which result from any of the other checks to population; and merely of the same nature as many other sacrifices of temporary to permanent gratification, which it is the business of a moral agent continually to make.

The positive checks to population are extremely various, and include every cause, whether arising from vice or misery, which in any degree contributes to shorten the natural duration of human life. Under this head, therefore, may be enumerated all unwholesome occupations, severe labour and exposure to the seasons, extreme poverty, bad nursing of children, great towns, excesses of all kinds, the whole train of common diseases and epidemics, wars, plague, and famine.

On examining these obstacles to the increase of population which I have classed under the heads of preventive and positive checks, it will appear that they are all resolvable into moral restraint, vice, and misery.

Of the preventive checks, the restraint from marriage which is not followed by irregular gratifications may properly be termed moral restraint.

Promiscuous intercourse, unnatural passions, violations of the marriage bed, and improper arts to conceal the consequences of irregular connexions, are preventive checks that clearly come under the head of vice.

Of the positive checks, those which appear to arise unavoidably from the laws of nature, may be called exclusively misery; and those which we obviously bring upon ourselves, such as wars, excesses, and many others which it would be in our power to avoid, are of a mixed nature. They are brought upon us by vice, and their consequences are misery.

The sum of all these preventive and positive checks, taken together, forms the immediate check to population; and it is evident that, in every country where the whole of the procreative power cannot be called into action, the preventive and the positive checks must vary inversely as each other; that is, in countries either naturally unhealthy, or subject to a great mortality, from whatever cause it may arise, the preventive check will prevail very little. In those countries, on the contrary, which are naturally healthy, and where the preventive check is found to prevail with considerable force, the positive check will prevail very little, or the mortality be very small.

In every country some of these checks are, with more or less force, in constant operation; yet, notwithstanding their general prevalence, there are few states in which there is not a constant effort in the population to increase beyond the means of subsistence. This constant effort as constantly tends to subject the lower classes of society to distress, and to prevent any great permanent melioration of their condition.

The concluding sentence of this reading makes clear the pessimism of the Malthusian position. Despite man's moral capacity for looking ahead and hence preventing population growth, the basic biological power is so great that Malthus is clearly doubtful that general distress can be avoided for the mass of humanity.

Most British economists of the early nineteenth century tended to accept this view, although not all of them put it in terms of Malthus's "arithmetical" and "geometrical" ratios. Many of them stated the principle in terms of a generalized version of the law of diminishing returns. This law, we recall, states that as we add more and more of a variable factor to a stock of fixed factors, the added product with each extra unit of variable factor will even-tually begin to diminish.[5] In this particular case, population—or, roughly, the labor force—is our variable factor; natural resources—the economist's "land"—are the fixed factors; and food is the product. Population growth is then seen as pressing against natural resources in the form of diminishing returns in the production of food and/or the other necessities of life.

Now the law of diminishing returns is not an *a priori* law, handed down from on high, and true in every conceivable circumstance. It is an empirical generalization, and could be wrong in any particular case. More significant, perhaps, is the fact that there can be other factors that *offset* the operations of this law. In-

---

5. See chapter 2, pp. 39–40.

deed, a fairly immediate and simple response to Malthusianism might be that his "principle" of population really holds only if there is no significant technological advance. If mankind can devise increasingly effective methods of producing food and other agricultural products, then, overall, natural resource limitations may not produce diminishing returns at all.

What Malthus and his followers would have said to this point is simply that such technological advance might help you temporarily but would certainly not in the long run. Think of it in terms of the supply and demand for labor. We might imagine the situation as in Figure 6-3. Suppose we started with a demand curve for labor such as D_1D_1, a labor force of L_1 and a wage rate of W_s—this is the *subsistence wage,* or the wage just sufficient to keep a given population alive with neither increase nor decrease.

Now suppose we have an invention that increases labor productivity and gives rise, as we may imagine, to a greater demand for labor; i.e., a shift to D_2D_2. What the Malthusians would say is this: in the *short* run, the wage would rise. Population and labor force are constant (L_1) for the moment. The increased demand would raise the wage to W_t; everybody would be better off. *But* this is temporary. Given the "constant effort in the population to increase beyond the means of subsistence," the labor force will now expand rapidly. In particular, it will expand all the way up to L_2. At L_2, the wage will be brought right back down again to W_s. And, indeed, this will clearly happen even if technological advance should manage to push the demand for labor way out to D_nD_n, or in fact as far out as can be imagined.

Temporary departures aside, the mass of mankind can never rise perma-

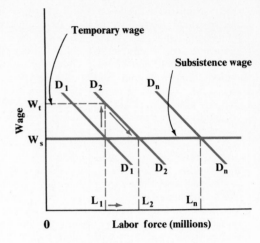

Figure 6-3. The Malthusian World.

Technological progress might push out the demand for labor (e.g., from D_1D_1 to D_2D_2) and raise the wage temporarily (from W_s to W_t), but, in the long run, population growth in the Malthusian world will bring the wage back down to the subsistence level once more.

nently above bare subsistence—this is the fundamental characteristic of the Malthusian world.

THE DIFFERENT EXPERIENCE OF DEVELOPED AND UNDERDEVELOPED ECONOMIES

Still, the Malthusian answer does not seem quite satisfactory, if only for the obvious historical reason that some countries are clearly not operating at economic subsistence, and indeed are apparently concerned with problems of "affluence." For this reason, we must divide off the population problems of the industrialized world from those facing the kind of economy we are studying in this chapter, the modern underdeveloped economy.

In the *developed* world, what happened historically was essentially two things. First of all, when the standard of living in these countries began to rise substantially above the subsistence level, population did *not* continue to expand at anything like its biologically maximum rate. The "preventive checks" proved to be far more active than Malthus would have thought.[6] People in the rich countries decided to have fewer children as a matter of choice, and it remains true today that birthrates are far higher in poor countries than in rich countries. This development slowed the rate of population growth considerably.

Second, the rate of technological advance and capital accumulation was far more rapid than Malthus had anticipated. It was not just that there were occasional outward shifts of the demand curve for labor; it was happening all the time and at a rate far exceeding the (slower than expected) rate of population increase.

For the rapidly advancing industrial countries, the flaw in the kind of logic suggested by Figure 6-3 was that the Malthusians *over*estimated how rapidly the labor force would grow from L_1 to L_2, and seriously *under*estimated how rapidly the DD curves would shift outward. Instead of the temporary wage sinking back to the subsistence level, there was always another big shift of the demand curve outward (owing to capital accumulation and technological change), and a new temporary wage, even *further* above W_s, was established. This kind of process could go on indefinitely, and in fact has been going on in these countries ever since the industrial revolution.

But this process did *not* take place in the underdeveloped economies. In these economies, the population problem has turned out in some respects to be even worse than Malthus anticipated. Many factors have played a role in this phenomenon, though the main single fact is that it has been possible to apply even in very poor countries many of the techniques of modern medicine, disease prevention, malaria control, public health, sanitation, and the like. This aspect of Western technological progress has been fairly easily transferable even to quite backward societies. The result has been very sharp declines in death rates in these countries. In some extreme cases, like Ceylon, the death rate fell to *one-third* its previous level in a matter of thirty-odd years. At the same time, birthrates have remained high—often twice the level of birthrates in the more developed countries.

Now this process is not exactly what Malthus had foreseen (he could hardly have anticipated the explosive advances in the medical sciences in the past century and a half), but the effects are similar to what he feared. Characteristic rates of population increase in today's underdeveloped economies are extremely high, ranging from 2 percent, to 2½ percent, to even 3 percent or above per year. These figures are much higher than those for the developed countries today and they are also higher than the rates of increase for most of the developed countries when *they* were beginning to industrialize.[7] A reasonable projection of future trends suggests that the share of the poor countries of Asia, Africa, and Latin America in world population will go up from 70 per-

---

6. For further discussion of why this was so, see pp. 400-401.

7. There were, of course, some advanced countries that had high rates of population growth in the nineteenth century (the United States was one), but these countries were in the so-called regions of recent settlement, where there was a superabundance of land and other natural resources. Population growth in this particular context may even have been advantageous.

cent to 80 percent over the next thirty years (Figure 6-4). There *is* a population explosion today and it is squarely located in the still poverty-stricken nations of the underdeveloped world.

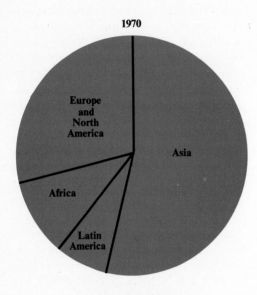

1970

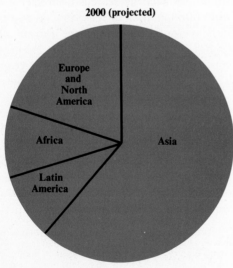

2000 (projected)

Figure 6-4. Percentage Distribution of World's Population.

CONSEQUENCES OF POPULATION GROWTH FOR THE UNDERDEVELOPED ECONOMY

The consequences of these very rapid rates of population growth are many. The general problem is that, with rapid population growth, a much higher rate of growth of output must be sustained if output per capita is to be raised at all significantly. With an annual 3 percent rate of growth of population, a country must maintain a 3 percent rate of growth of total output just to stay even. With a 4 percent growth rate, output per capita will rise only at roughly 1 percent per year. At such a rate of increase, a country that today has an output per capita of, say, $100 per year would still be well below $200 a year at the end of the twentieth century.

The problem is intensified, moreover, when we consider certain other aspects of population growth. For one thing, there is the structure of the population to consider. Countries with high birth rates will typically have a large proportion of children in their populations. Figure 6-5 contrasts the population structures of rapid-population-growth underdeveloped regions with those of slow-population-growth developed regions. A large proportion of children in the population means that there are more dependents and fewer productive workers in the society, creating a drain on the productive capabilities of the economy. Even more serious, perhaps, is the pressure that population growth creates in already densely populated areas.

Not all underdeveloped countries are overpopulated. There are regions in Africa, Latin America, and even in a few small countries in Asia that are relatively

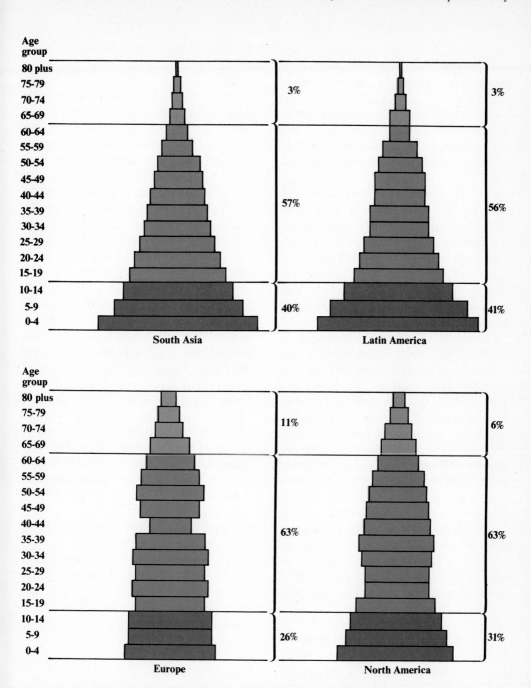

Figure 6-5. Age Structure of Population in Selected Regions.
(Width of bars indicates proportion of total population in age group.)
Source: Lester R. Brown, *Seeds of Change* (New York: Praeger, 1970), p. 125.

underpopulated. But the bulk of the world's poor live in countries where over-population is already a serious problem. (India with 550 million people and China with 800 million people comprise half or more of the underdeveloped world.) And in these countries additional numbers pose at least two extremely serious problems:

(1) **Pressure on the land in agriculture.** Population growth in these countries where land is already scarce means that the law of diminishing returns really does make further increases in agricultural output, and especially food supplies, very hard to come by. Some economists think that certain of these nations have already reached the stage of "absolutely diminishing returns"—i.e., where the further application of labor to the land brings no increase in agricultural output at all. If overcrowding on the land leads to less efficient methods of production, then food production might actually decrease as population increases. This does *not* mean that these countries will not be able to expand their food production in the future. The law of diminishing returns states what happens when only one element in the picture changes. But other elements may change, especially the technology of production, as we have noted before. The effects of overcrowding *do* mean, however, that favorable improvements will have to be that much stronger to offset the effects of rapid population growth.

(2) **The unemployment problem.** Perhaps even more serious is the unemployment problem to which rapid population growth in densely populated areas may give rise. There is no further room for employment in agriculture, because of the heavy rural overpopulation that already exists. On the other hand, the ability

of the industrial sector to employ more workers is seriously limited by the nature of the technology employed. We have already mentioned that modern technology makes great demands on capital goods and on skilled labor but relatively smaller demands on massive infusions of unskilled labor. But if the agricultural sector cannot take them and if the rate of expansion of the industrial sector is insufficient to take them, where will these increasing numbers of unskilled laborers find employment? To understand just how serious a problem this is, one has to have some idea of the magnitudes involved. India, for example, in the course of a fifteen-year period adds to her labor force about 70 million workers, or, roughly, the equivalent of the total labor force of the present-day United States. Moreover, India adds this extraordinary number of workers to an economy that is already suffering from serious unemployment. For example, at the end of India's second Five-Year Plan (1962), it was estimated that there were 9 million unemployed Indian workers and another 15 to 18 million partially unemployed or underemployed workers. The problem of finding jobs for such huge numbers of laborers is one of the great costs of rapid population growth in densely populated areas.

When we add together all the various difficulties that rapid population growth entails for these poor countries, when we remember, further, the problems of capital accumulation and the difficulties of adapting Western technology to the drastically different conditions of the modern underdeveloped country—when we put all this together, we may begin to understand why many economists feel that the poor countries today face much greater obstacles to successful development than did their historical predecessors.

REPORT OF THE
COMMISSION
ON INTERNATIONAL
DEVELOPMENT

Later in this book, we shall come back to the problems of the underdeveloped economy, hopefully to apply some of the tools of economic analysis developed in the course of the ensuing chapters.

For the moment, let us simply try to summarize where these economies stand now. In trying to do this, we are fortunate in having a report of the Commission on International Development, under the chairmanship of Lester B. Pearson of Canada. This report, published in 1969, is the work of a distinguished group of economists and statesmen whose mission was to "meet together, study the consequences of twenty years of development assistance, assess the results, clarify the errors and propose the policies which will work better in the future."

The following reading is excerpted from chapter 3 of this report in which the commission takes a large overview of the problems ahead for the underdeveloped economy in the 1970s.

THE PROBLEMS AHEAD
COMMISSION ON
INTERNATIONAL DEVELOPMENT

LESTER B. PEARSON, *Chairman*

Despite the achievements of the past two decades, we are still far from a situation

Excerpted from Lester B. Pearson, "The Problems Ahead," from *Partners in Development*, Commission on International Development, pp. 64, 66-73, 76-79. Published by permission of Praeger Publishers, Inc., New York and The Pall Mall Press, London.

in which the developing countries, relying solely on their own resources, can assure effective and early modernization of their economies. We are, at best, in midstream, with many obstacles and problems ahead. This chapter attempts to summarize some of the more important of these problems.

THE POLITICAL PROBLEM

The present form of the aspiration to development is relatively new. The drive toward modernization has inevitably created conflicts between guardians of tradition and those who seek change. The controversies take on different complexions in different parts of the world but underlying all is the demand for a more equitable sharing among individuals and nations of the benefits of progress. Pressures to this end put a premium on the adaptability of political and social structures. Resulting conflicts have been difficult but, on the whole, surprisingly manageable as political structures in developing countries have improved in flexibility and responsiveness.

The balance between social and political objectives and economic growth is always a delicate one and involves difficult choices. Sometimes, as a matter of national survival, economic growth must be subordinated to the maintenance or creation of national identity and national sovereignty. In other cases, the objective of rapid growth and equitable distribution of income appear in conflict. Stable development would seem to require a more equitable distribution of wealth and a greater degree of participation in political and economic life than has so far been characteristic of many developing countries. Without popular commitment and participation, the sacrifices that will be necessary for development will not be easily borne.

THE POPULATION DILEMMA

No other phenomenon casts a darker shadow over the prospects for international development than the staggering growth of population. It is evident that it is a major cause of the large discrepancy between rates of economic improvement in rich and poor countries. On the other hand, the likelihood of a rapid slowing down of population growth is not great, although some countries are in a far more favorable position than others in this respect.

Twenty years ago, it was not expected that population growth would become such a major problem in low-income countries. As late as 1951, a U.N. projection assumed that between 1950 and 1980 the populations of Africa and Asia would grow at an annual rate of 0.7–1.3 percent. The remarkable and largely unexpected success in reducing mortality brought a sharp change. The rate of population growth in developing countries increased steadily in the 1950s. By the mid-1960s, it settled down at an average level of 2.5 percent.

Mortality is continuing its decline, but over-all fertility rates are only now beginning to drop. While in a number of developing countries, fertility has been declining for some time, in others it is increasing as a result of improvement in health and medical services. Even if fertility should be considerably reduced in coming decades, the population of the less developed world will double before the end of this century.

All the burdens from large families and high growth rates are not borne by parents alone. When the population doubles in twenty-five years, the task of development and modernization is compounded. It may even be impossible to attain significant improvement in living conditions and independence of foreign aid. Some of the direct difficulties created by very rapid population growth are the following:

1. Expenditures for education, health, housing, water supply, and so forth increase sharply and create severe budgetary strains.

2. The quality of the next generation, on which the prospects for development crucially rest, is jeopardized. There is a strong inverse correlation between child health and family size. Rapid growth of the child population also delays educational improvement.

3. Considerable resources are devoted to the support of a large dependent population which would otherwise be available to raise living standards and increase capital formation.

4. Aid requirements are larger when population rises fast, and the possibility of future financial independence smaller than if fertility is declining.

5. The distribution of income is unequal, and population growth tends to make it more so by raising land values and rents while depressing wages. As ownership, too, is usually very unequally distributed, the bulk of the population may fail to participate in whatever improvement occurs.

6. Severe urban problems arise, partly from natural increase and partly from migration from the country into the cities. Urban populations tend to double in fifteen to eighteen years. Housing already presents almost insoluble problems in many developing countries.

Whether or not a deliberate policy on population should be adopted is a decision which each individual country itself must face. We are well aware of the controversial nature of the matter which, until very recently, placed family planning behind a wall of silence in the industrialized countries themselves. But it is clear that there can be no serious social and economic planning unless the ominous implications of uncontrolled population growth are understood and acted upon.

UNEMPLOYMENT AND URBANIZATION

The rapid growth of population adds to the already severe unemployment problem in developing countries. In many, if not most of them, unemployment is turning into a major social problem and obstacle to development. The failure to create meaningful employment is the most tragic failure of development. All indications are that unemployment and underutilization of human resources have increased in the 1960s, and that the problem will grow even more serious.

Although there is much evidence of the appalling magnitude of the unemployment problem, there is little specific information about it. The International Labor Organization is trying to muster the resources for a large employment survey in the developing countries, and this deserves all support. A great difficulty, especially in traditional societies, is that there is no hard and fast distinction between unemployment and underemployment. Underemployment describes a situation in which individual capacity to work is not fully engaged, as when highly trained personnel are forced to work at menial labor for lack of demand, or when agriculture does not begin to absorb the labor available. Although there are no firm estimates of underemployment, it is clear that recorded *un*employment in the developing countries understates the problem.

Both unemployment and underemployment are results of the failure to absorb the large increase of the labor force which has followed the acceleration of population growth. Population policies can greatly affect this problem but only in the long term. Those who will constitute the labor force over the next fifteen years are already born.

Progress must be made in solving the unemployment problem if social and political turmoil is not to arrest the development process. For it is in the volatile cities of the developing world that agricultural stagnation and industrial unemployment combine to produce their gravest consequences. Urban growth is almost universally twice as rapid as the growth of the population in general, and some of the largest cities have even higher rates of expansion. Rural stagnation stimulates a flow of migrants from the land, and urban death rates are often lower than those in the countryside while fertility generally remains high.

It must be asked whether urban trends can be left to be the by-product of other forces in society. If present trends continued, the largest city in India would have over 35 million inhabitants by the year 2000. Planning strategy in developing countries must emphasize the growth of small

and intermediate regional centers, to offer market, service and storage facilities, and light labor-intensive industries processing local materials. The construction of such new centers could offer a considerable measure of employment for unskilled labor.

AGRICULTURE

If the Green Revolution* signals a major breakthrough in food grain production, it also brings with it an array of new problems.

For one thing, continued heavy expenditures on agricultural research are necessary, as one seed variety is likely to last only for a few years and must be replaced by new varieties as new diseases evolve. Moreover, accelerated agricultural extension and massive investments in irrigation and fertilizer production are needed. Increasing production also raises the demand for better marketing and distribution facilities and for more farm credit. It will also be difficult to maintain a set of incentives for farmers which is adequate to elicit the necessary production, stimulate the continued adoption of new technology, and support diversification into other crops.

Increased tax revenue will be needed, but to tax agricultural income directly is difficult in most developing countries for the good reasons that most farmers are very poor, that such a tax would be politically explosive, and that the cost of collecting the tax might well exceed the yield. However, the new technology is raising some rural incomes sharply. If large increases in income are to arise in agriculture, some of the increased revenue must come from these incomes. Agricultural taxation and the general division of the fruits of increased agricultural productivity among urban consumers, rural producers, and landowners will present thorny policy issues which have grave political implications and will also affect future development.

Areas untouched by the Green Revolution, such as most of Africa and Latin

[*See our discussion of the Green Revolution, pp. 792–98.]

America, face a more difficult task in stimulating technological change in the countryside. Many of them still seriously neglect rural development. For all countries it is important to achieve new technical breakthroughs in crops other than foodgrains, especially in exportable ones, not only to increase the food supply but also to improve its quality.

Land reform and consolidation of fragmented holdings will be needed in many developing countries not only to accelerate technological change and stimulate production in the long run, but also to generate rural employment. History teaches us that land reform is seldom a tidy affair and is always time-consuming. However, most governments now have at their disposal the means to minimize the short-run disruptions and conflicts arising from a program of structural change in land ownership.

NUTRITION

Pervasive poverty and consequent low effective demand for food are among the causes of widespread hunger and nutritional deficiency, but fixed dietary habits also contribute to the nutritional deficiencies in many areas. The increases in foodgrain production which have been achieved by some of the less developed countries in the past few years are by no means the complete answer to the problem of providing adequate diets in the developing countries.

Malnutrition, which is a more serious scourge to mankind even than hunger, is to a larger extent a matter of ignorance and inappropriate food habits. Thus even when the commercial demand for food is met, this does not mean that nutritional needs are satisfied. In fact, nutritional deficiencies, especially in protein, are likely to persist for a long time to come. However, in order to raise general standards of health, the productivity of labor, and the general quality of life, improved nutrition is indispensable. It is especially important to child health.

Childhood malnutrition tends to retard both physical and mental development, often irreparably. In countries with a per capita income of less than $100 there are over 500 million children under the age of fifteen, and in the developing world as a whole this group represents over forty percent of the population. The physical and mental development of this generation is not only a matter of immediate humanitarian concern. It is also of central importance to the whole process of development. In only a few decades this generation will have taken the place of their elders.

INDUSTRY

During the last two decades, many developing countries favored industry while neglecting agriculture. Just as rural policy is now being reconsidered, so is industrial policy. Policy-makers have generally become aware that further advances in import substitution will be difficult. In many countries, import substitution has taken place almost regardless of price or quality, and many industries now find themselves with a highly distorted price structure which makes them noncompetitive in export markets.

Continued growth may require continued protection for new industries, but the point has been reached for many established industries where the system of protection should be restructured and absolute prohibitions turned into reasonable tariff protection. Infant industry support should be limited to activities showing promise of long-run competitiveness. There should be greater reliance on exchange rate policy to handle payment difficulties. Such liberalization, however, need not be sudden and traumatic, and in some cases it may take place within the context of gradual regional integration.

THE PRIVATE SECTOR

There are a great many impediments to the creation of a dynamic private sector. Some are institutional and others reflect ingrained attitudes. Too often the attitude of many of the less developed countries toward their domestic private sector remains negative, though it is improving in many cases. It is still unusual for them to regard private enterprise as a suitable instrument of economic growth, or to create conditions which actively favor the emergence of new firms, particularly the establishment of financial institutions to assure adequate credit for the private sector. This is regrettable since experience shows that a strong and vigorous private sector is an important element in the achievement of rapid growth. A strong domestic private sector also serves to attract direct investment from abroad which can greatly stimulate the development process.

RESEARCH AND DEVELOPMENT

For many reasons, research and development in low-income countries has been extremely limited. Based on uncertain data, it is estimated that expenditure for research and development in Latin America amounts to only some 0.2 percent of GNP, while in Asia such expenditures fall between 0.1 percent and 0.5 percent of GNP. In Africa, except for some programs sponsored by industrialized countries, public and private outlay for research and development is negligible. Comparable figures for the Soviet Union and the United States are 4.2 percent and 3.2 percent of GNP respectively, and for most European countries between 1 and 2 percent.

Many changes will be required for more effective use of research and development. This is particularly true in industry, where lack of information, shortage of managerial ability and, perhaps most often, overprotection, result in little incentive to improve products and reduce costs. The situation in agriculture is somewhat more encouraging because of progress in developing extension services which are of such importance in bringing the results of the research station to the farmer. It is clear, however, that innovation and dissemination of technical knowledge remain immense problems in both sectors.

EDUCATION

Impressive quantitative improvements in education should not be allowed to conceal the very serious problems of quality which plague the educational systems of so many developing countries.

Of one hundred children entering primary school in developing countries, no more than thirty finish. Indeed, in most African and Latin American countries, more than fifty percent of primary school pupils do not return to school after the second grade. Secondary schools are generally oriented toward academic study; vocational training represents less than 10 percent of total secondary enrollment. Moreover, only one of about ten graduates from academic courses actually enters a university. Few of the graduates from vocational schools become active in fields for which they have been trained. At universities, most students attend courses in law or political science, or in the traditional fields of engineering and only a small fraction ever graduate. Facilities are inadequate, textbooks are lacking or antiquated, teachers are poorly trained.

Education is a basic human right and the low-income societies need literate and active citizens as well as citizens with skills appropriate to the changing economic structure. Yet, their educational systems fail to provide a satisfactory general education or a level of skill in the labor force appropriate to the needs of the country.

In too many instances, children who finish primary school in rural areas seem rather *less* fit to become creative and constructive members of their own community than if they had never been to school. The measure of achievement is the ability to enter secondary school, which is again oriented toward academic study. Educational systems are not generally designed to produce intermediate skills or proficiencies that correspond to the needs of industry, agriculture, or government in the less developed countries. One special need is for post-secondary technological or professional institutions offering training related to the needs of the labor market.

THE EXTERNAL CONSTRAINT

Most of the serious issues which we have enumerated in this chapter depend for their solutions on the action taken by the developing countries themselves. But their policies must be pursued within an international framework over which they have little or no control.

The major external constraint may be summed up as the availabilty of foreign exchange. Foreign exchange is a crucial resource in development planning. All developing countries are forced to rely on imported equipment and, to a large extent, on imported raw materials and spare parts without which their own resources cannot be pressed into service. The developing countries face problems both in increasing their earnings of foreign exchange and in the increasing claims on available foreign exchange of rising debt payments and other essential commitments.

India's foreign exchange situation exemplifies these difficulties. India earns about $1.8 billion per year from exports, of which about $300 million is received in barter or inconvertible currencies. This leaves about $1.5 billion in convertible foreign exchange. Debt service obligations of all kinds are about $450 million, leaving some $1 billion for other purposes. This must finance the import of essential commodities and services which cannot be financed by aid (petroleum, long staple cotton, some food, and the freight costs on 480 food shipments), as well as raw materials and spare parts for export industries which have earned the right to use free foreign exchange and which must have access to the lowest-cost source of supply. It must also cover the needs of small-scale industry, special requirements in the agricultural sectors and the needs of public departments. This means that most of the imports of industrial raw materials, as well as vital machinery and equipment, fertilizer, and pesticides must be financed by aid. In case of a poor export year, India could not meet even the minimal import requirements which must be met with free foreign exchange. Even in a normal year, there is little flexibility to search for the lowest-cost supplier, to relax import restrictions, or to provide reserves against the risks of new policies. This scarcity of foreign exchange is, of course, partly a reflection of India's pre-1968 export performance and could be somewhat eased over time if that performance were improved. Nevertheless, this constraint has been and will continue to be a major obstacle to development.

Foreign exchange is available from three sources in addition to private investment: the country's own accumulated reserves, its export earnings, and aid.

The following paragraphs discuss prospects and problems for the developing countries in these areas, beginning with the critical shortage of reserves.

FOREIGN EXCHANGE RESERVES

After World War II and the Korean War boom, some developing countries were able to use their reserves to maintain high import levels, but they were soon depleted. Reserves of 15 percent in the above table are enough to finance no more than

FOREIGN EXCHANGE RESERVES AS A PERCENT OF IMPORTS

	1955–57 Average	1965–67 Average
Brazil	39.2	26.1
Colombia	22.8	15.8
Mexico	37.7	25.5
Morocco	39.4	15.7
Tunisia	43.7	13.6
U.A.R.	99.6	19.5
Ghana	123.1	36.4
Taiwan	94.2	56.9
Korea	127.8	42.1
Philippines	19.3	16.7
India	79.6	26.0
Pakistan	80.5	19.3
Turkey	53.8	19.6

Source: IMF.

two months' imports. This is barely enough for prudent financial management and makes reserves generally irrelevant to meet emergencies or to provide risk capital for new policies. For many developing countries an increase in reserves would be an important asset permitting greater policy flexibility and better allocation of resources.

Export Earnings

The importance of export earnings for the development of the poorer countries can hardly be overestimated. They are by far the most important source of foreign exchange. In recent years, they have been nearly four times as large as the flow of aid and private investment. But trade is also, in a deeper sense, an "engine of growth," especially for smaller countries which are particularly dependent on the international division of labor.

Import requirements in the developing countries grow at about the same rate as over-all production, or slightly faster. If the rate of economic growth is to be accelerated to at least 6 percent, which seems both feasible and necessary, imports have to grow at 7 to 8 percent a year while the investment ratios accelerate. If foreign aid requirements are not going to get out of hand, exports too will have to grow at this rate. Great instability in export earnings has proved disruptive to growth in the past, so growth of exports must not only be rapid but also steady.

There are three prerequisites to assure rapid growth in exports. World trade must continue to expand vigorously, sustained by steady growth in the industrialized world. Perhaps the greatest threat to international development is the risk that major industrial powers will constantly be faced with serious balance-of-payments problems which impair their possibilities of expansion.

Second, the growth of world trade must be accompanied by liberalization. This in its turn implies a willingness on the part of industrialized countries to make the structural adjustments which will enable them to absorb an increasing range of manufactures and semi-manufactures from developing countries.

Third, the less developed countries themselves must make great efforts to diversify their exports, to seize the opportunities of expanding world markets. The developing countries could, and should also reduce their dependence on imports from the industrialized countries and rely more on trade among themselves. At present, they take about seventy percent of their imports from developed countries and only twenty percent from one another.

The Debt Problem

The indebtedness of the developing countries imposes a large burden of debt service. There has already been a sequence of debt crises in the late 1950s and throughout the 1960s, and even a cursory inspection of the situation suggests that the debt servicing problems of the low-income countries will become even more serious in the years immediately ahead.

The external public debt of the developing countries rose by about 14 percent per annum in the 1960s. In June, 1968, the recorded debt stood at $47.5 billion. The reverse flow of debt service payments on official account amounted to $4.7 billion in 1967. In the last ten years, these payments have increased by as much as 17 percent per year.

In several countries (Brazil, Argentina, Uruguay, Mexico, Indonesia, India, Pakistan, U.A.R., Tunisia, and Yugoslavia), the ratio of public debt service to export earnings exceeds 15 percent.

Technical defaults on contractual obligations have not been common, but the repayment burdens have caused many debtor governments to deplete their reserves and suffer liquidity crises which have forced them to adopt stringent exchange controls. Most of these countries have sought and obtained a rearrangement of their debt. In some

OFFICIAL DEVELOPMENT ASSISTANCE (billions of dollars)								
1956	1961	1962	1963	1964	1965	1966	1967	1968
3.3	5.2	5.5	5.9	6.0	6.1	6.3	6.6	6.4

cases, a whole series of rescue operations have taken place in rapid succession.

The Crisis in Aid

Official development assistance increased rapidly between 1956 and 1961, increased very slowly through 1967, and began to decline in 1968. On the basis of aid commitments, a further decline can be expected in 1969.

The decline in official aid, its increased cost, and the growing complexity of the regulations by which it is provided come at a time when development expenditures in the low-income countries are rising rapidly. Despite major efforts at import substitution and export promotion, these accelerated development programs require additional external resources. The interests of both rich and poor require that developing countries advance at the most rapid feasible rate, but, in fact, many of them face the prospect of cutting back on their planned rates of growth because they must now assume significant reductions in aid.

It is precisely because the developing countries see their forward momentum threatened by bleak aid prospects that they feel a growing sense of frustration which tends to embitter relations between rich and poor. The developing countries feel that their problems are ignored and they see no sign of real commitment to help alleviate their tremendous problems of poverty, social change, and economic development.

The need goes deeper than a mere call for more aid. International development means a willingness to look to the total economic relationship between developing and industrialized countries.

The problems to be faced remain great, but they are now better understood. The achievements of the last ten years give hope that they can be solved. Equally, they underline the need for greater effort and more effective international cooperation.

SUMMARY

In this chapter, we have taken up the subject of the *underdeveloped economy*, focussing more on problems than on economic systems, although the tasks facing these economies are so great that they are all engaged in planning for economic growth to a certain degree.

The main economic characteristic of the underdeveloped country is its *poverty*. Although output per capita figures are somewhat suspect, the depth of poverty in these countries shows up clearly in any measure we might use. Their average family incomes are perhaps one-tenth or less of what we enjoy today in the United States. These countries are trying to achieve now what the economically advanced countries achieved a century or two ago—an industrial revolution that will put them on the path of modern economic growth—but the circumstances they face are quite different from those that faced the "early developers" of Europe and North America:

(1) **Technology.** The less developed countries have the entire storehouse of modern technology to draw upon. This is a clear advantage, but it is qualified by the fact that this technology is not well suited to conditions in these countries, that it may require costly imports from abroad, and that, in certain cases (notably public

health and medical technology) it may raise certain new problems (the population explosion).

(2) **Capital accumulation.** The need for capital goods in these countries is great, especially in view of the capital-intensive nature of much modern technology, but the ability to raise domestic savings and investment is limited by the general poverty of the countries, the desire for increased consumption now, and, in many cases, the absence of a social structure that promotes the productive use of economic "surpluses" that may exist.

(3) **Population growth.** Falling death rates (largely due to improved public health and medical technology) and very high birthrates have caused a population expansion that raises the specter of Malthusian problems for many underdeveloped countries. The rates of population growth in these countries are, on the average, much higher than they were in the economically advanced countries when they were setting out on the path of modern growth. The consequences are: the difficulty of raising total output fast enough to achieve increases in output per capita; the heavy burden of large numbers of dependent children on the productive workers of the society; and, especially in heavily populated regions, the problem of increasing agricultural output rapidly enough to feed the growing population and the difficulty of finding employment for these massive additions to the labor force.

The 1969 report of the Commission on International Development, surveying these and other problems of the modern underdeveloped countries, concludes that their problems are great but, with appropriate international cooperation, not insoluble.

QUESTIONS FOR DISCUSSION

1. Discuss the advantages and disadvantages for an underdeveloped country of borrowing the latest Western technological ideas and methods.

2. It is sometimes argued that the poor countries of today will be able to achieve modern growth only if they begin with rather drastic and rapid changes in their social and economic structures. This has given rise to what are sometimes called the "big push" theories of economic development. Do any of the factors discussed in this chapter seem to you to support such a view? What reasons might be offered for the hypothesis that slow, step-by-step growth is generally insufficient for today's underdeveloped countries?

3. "Population growth was not always a problem for the countries that developed economically in the nineteenth century, but it is public enemy number one for the less developed countries of today." Discuss.

4. Is the kind of unemployment or underemployment one finds in a country like India today the same as the kind of unemployment you might find in an industrial economy like that of the United States? What differences do you think there might be?

5. The Pearson Commission speaks of an "external constraint" facing poor countries trying to raise their living standards. What is meant by this term? What implications might this constraint have for the policies of economically developed countries?

SUGGESTED READING

Brown, Lester R. *Seeds of Change.* New York: Frederick A. Praeger, 1970.

Cochrane, Willard W. *The World Food Problem.* New York: Thomas Y. Crowell Co., 1969.

Hirschman, Albert O. *The Strategy of Economic Development.* New Haven: Yale University Press, 1958.

Lewis, W. Arthur. *Development Planning.* New York: Harper & Row, 1966.

Little, I. M. D., and Clifford, J. M. *International Aid.* Chicago: Aldine Publishing Co., 1966.

Nurkse, Ragnar. *Problems of Capital Formation in Underdeveloped Areas.* New York: Oxford University Press, 1953.

Pearson, Lester B. *Partners in Development: Report of the Commission on International Development.* New York: Frederick A. Praeger, 1969.

PART TWO
MACROECONOMICS: ANALYSIS AND PROBLEMS

Having discussed economic systems in a broad, overarching way in Part One, we must now dig more deeply into the problems which this survey has uncovered. This will require us to develop new tools of economic analysis and also to test out these tools in applications to important real-life economic situations.

In taking these further steps, we shall divide the field of economics into two related but nevertheless distinguishable subdivisions: 1) *Macroeconomics*, the study of the economy as a whole, or "in the aggregate," as it is sometimes put; and 2) *Microeconomics*, the study of the particular units (consumers, business firms, laborers, factor owners, etc.) that make up the economy and how their decisions and actions are interrelated.

These fields clearly are not wholly separable either in logic or practice. In Part Four of this book, we shall find that many of our most urgent contemporary economic problems require both microeconomic and macroeconomic tools.

Nevertheless, the division is a useful one, each of these fields having a certain history and logic of its own. In terms of the "circular flow of economic life," discussed frequently in Part One, we might say that while microeconomics analyses the component elements of the flow, macroeconomics is concerned with the overall dimensions of the flow. Thus, in microeconomics, we want to know how price and output and the employment of labor and other factors of production are determined for Industry A or Industry B. By contrast, in macroeconomics, we want to know what determines the price-level *in general*, and the levels of *national* output and employment. These problems in turn will involve us with other social "totals": total consumption, total business investment, the total money supply, and so on.

In Part Two, immediately following, we shall take up macroeconomics: in Part Two A, presenting the basic analysis, and in Part Two B, extending and applying this analysis to various economic problems.

Part Three will do the same thing for microeconomics; it can, if preferred, be studied before Part Two.

PART TWO A
THE BASICS OF NATIONAL INCOME DETERMINATION

7

Keynes and the New Economics

In 1947, the well-known American economist, Seymour Harris, edited a book called the *New Economics*. This book, in turn, was dedicated to an analysis and evaluation of an economist whose main work had been completed a decade earlier. The "new economics" referred to the theory contained in *The General Theory of Employment, Interest and Money* (1936), written by perhaps the most famous economist of the twentieth century, the late John Maynard Keynes.

Like Adam Smith and Karl Marx, Keynes was one of a half dozen economists whose work profoundly influenced large numbers of other economists and, indeed, the actions of statesmen and nations. Although the adjective "new" may seem a bit out of place for economics written so many years ago, the fact is that orthodoxies die hard. When President Nixon, in 1971, said, "I am now a Keynesian," it was a national news item. Conservative, and even middle-of-the-road public figures have, until quite recently, been distrustful of Keynesian thinking. Indeed, important scholars still are.[1]

From our point of view, the significance of Keynesian analysis is that it provided one of the major threads, and, from the theoretical point of view, *the* major thread, that leads to modern macroeconomic analysis. Much of our discussion in Part Two A will consist of explaining and developing the Keynesian contribution. Before going in this direction, however, let us be clearer in our minds about what sort of problems macroeconomics involves.

1. See p. 188.

177

PROBLEMS
OF THE ECONOMY
IN THE AGGREGATE

The first step is to alter somewhat the point of view we gain almost automatically from our daily participation in economic matters: a view of particular jobs, particular firms, and particular industries. We know that it is sometimes hard to find a job, or that some particular business firm may be having troubles; but now we ask: might the nation sometimes face conditions when businesses *in general* were failing, when people *in general* could not locate work? Actually, the question need not be put pessimistically. We could also ask: are there times when everyone has work, when labor is in great demand, when prices, profits, and wages are all high? The point, of course, is that these questions are about the performance of the economy as a whole.

Now if we look at the past in our own country or in other industrial countries, we can find many instances to prove that national economics do indeed suffer ups and downs in their general economic well-being. All of us know from our reading of American history of the great number of "panics" that have seized our country at one point or another. There were panics in the United States in 1819, 1837, 1857, 1893, 1907, 1914, 1920–1921, and, of course, the "great crash" in 1929. Various statistical measures of these ups and downs are also common. In Figures 7-1, 7-2, and 7-3, we present some diagrams of unemployment in the United States and the United Kingdom at various times in the past. These diagrams measure unemployment as a percentage of the labor force, and they indicate how variable this factor has been historically. The great leap in the unemployment percentage in the United States in the 1930s is a less picturesque but still telling way of

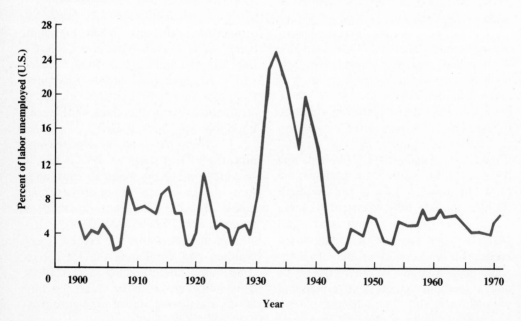

Figure 7-1. Unemployment in the United States (percent of the labor force, 1900-1971).

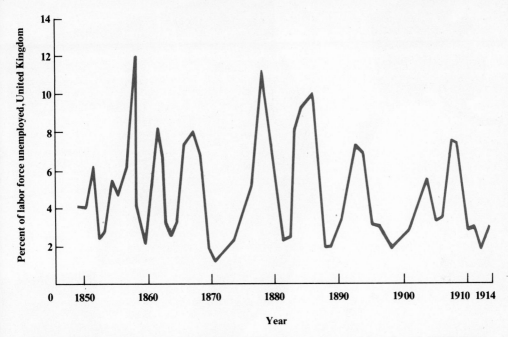

Figure 7-2. Unemployment in the United Kingdom (percent unemployed, 1850-1914).

describing the Great Depression, which we discussed in chapter 1. Figure 7-2 shows that the problem of unemployment in industrial societies goes back well before the twentieth century. Figure 7-3 indicates that unemployment is still a serious problem in the 1970s, particularly in certain states.

But economies can get out of gear in other ways besides unemployment. In the first chapter we also talked of the German hyperinflation of the 1920s, when the price level soared to the trillions. This was truly an exceptional incident, but no more exceptional than completely stable prices would be. Almost all industrial countries have had some experience with inflation in the twentieth century and, in many underdeveloped countries, rapid inflation is a week-to-week phenomenon. Figure 7-4 shows the general course of consumer prices in the United States from 1929 to the present.

We must remember that when we

talk about the price *level*, we are talking about something slightly different from the price of apples or the price of washing machines. When the price of apples alone goes up, our demand curve tells us that we will buy fewer apples because, among other reasons, it will be cheaper for us to satisfy our desire for fruit with peaches and pears. When we talk about the price *level* rising, however, we are referring to a rise not only in apple prices but in the prices of peaches and pears and washing machines as well.

Similarly, in the case of unemployment: if the wage of electricians goes down, people will turn toward other occupations, and fewer will offer their services as electricians. But suppose there is unemployment in all industries at once? What happens to the wage then? Where do people turn?

These are the heartland questions of macroeconomics. What determines the general level of employment? What deter-

Figure 7-3. United States Unemployment Rates by State, 1971.
Source: Department of Labor

mines the general level of national income?[2] What determines the overall level of prices? These are the problems of the economy in the aggregate.

2. The analysis of national income (or total production) that we shall consider in Part Two will be largely concerned with the short-run aspects of the problem, i.e., with the degree of utilization of a *given* labor force and productive capacity. In the short run (one or two years), this is a permissible assumption. In the long run, the labor force, the productive capacity, and the economy in general *grow*, and the problem changes. This problem of long-run economic growth will be taken up at the end of Part Two (chapter 16) and again in Part Four (especially chapter 28).

EARLY VIEWS

We have already indicated (Figure 7-2) that macroeconomic problems were around long before the 1930s. What then did earlier economists have to say about them? What kind of analysis did they offer?

Now the truth is that until fairly modern times the economics profession did not do very well in this particular de-

. Dakota
4.8

Minnesota
5.3

S. Dakota
3.5

Wisconsin
5.1

Michigan
8.2

Maine
7.7

Vermont
6.4

New Hampshire
4.9

Massachusetts
7.0

New York
5.7

Rhode Island
7.0

Connecticut
8.7

New Jersey
7.0

Delaware
5.0

Maryland
4.9

District of Columbia
2.9

W. Virginia
6.9

Nebraska
3.4

Iowa
4.1

Illinois
4.7

Indiana
5.7

Ohio
5.1

Pennsylvania
5.2

Virginia
3.6

Kansas
5.9

Missouri
5.4

Kentucky
5.8

N. Carolina
4.0

Oklahoma
4.9

Arkansas
5.4

Tennessee
4.7

S. Carolina
5.4

Mississippi
5.1

Alabama
5.3

Georgia
4.1

Texas
4.2

Louisiana
6.7

Florida
4.3

partment, especially when it came to the problem of unemployment. There are some exceptions, but, for the most part, prevailing economic theory in the nineteenth century tended either to ignore the problem—i.e., to proceed on the *assumption* of a full employment economy and then to go on to analyze other problems—or to argue that theoretically there could not be a general unemployment problem except in a temporary or "frictional" sense.

This argument was not simply a personal whim on the part of these early economists; rather, they had certain systematic reasons for believing that an unfettered market economy would automatically solve any short-run aggregative problems. Hence they could direct their attention to other areas, either to microeconomics or, in the case of the early classical economists, to population growth and food supplies, as discussed in chapter 6.

These systematic reasons are

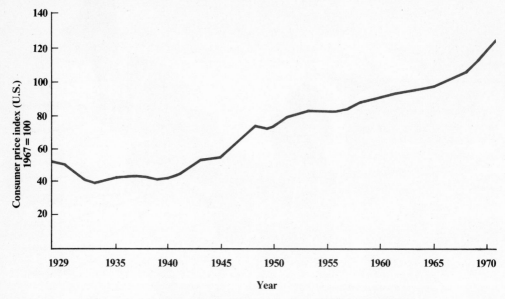

Figure 7-4. Inflation in the United States, 1929 through 1971.

The United States has experienced nothing like the German hyperinflation in the 1920s; nevertheless, like most countries, we have had a general rise in prices during the twentieth century.

sometimes summarized in what is called Say's law, after a French economist, Jean Baptiste Say (1767–1832). Say's writings were well known to the eminent British economists of the period such as David Ricardo and Thomas Robert Malthus, whom we have mentioned earlier. Ricardo fully subscribed to Say's law, though Malthus, as we shall see, had serious reservations about it.

Say's law states that, in the economy as a whole, supply creates its own demand. When we produce goods, according to this law, we create a demand for other goods; consequently, there can be no overproduction of goods in general. Since there can be no overproduction of goods in general, there can be no unemployment problem in general. To put it in different words: since there is always a market for the goods we produce, there is no overall limit on the number of jobs the society can sustain. If people are un-

employed, then it can be only because they make unreasonable wage demands or prefer leisure or are simply in transit between one job and another.

This is simply a statement of the law, not a defense. But Say and Ricardo, and in fact most nineteenth-century economists, also felt that they had a good defense for the law. The defense really had two parts. The first part consisted of relegating "money" to a minor role in the economy.

They said in effect: "Money is just a veil that covers the realities of economic life. Money is simply a medium of exchange. In order to understand what really goes on, let us look at potatoes, steel, wheat, shoes, and so on. Then we will not be deceived by mere monetary changes and we will reach the fundamental phenomena involved."

If the first step was to underplay the role of money, the second step was more positive.

They argued: *"Now look at this real, non-money economy. In this economy, when I put a laborer to work producing, say, more potatoes, I am increasing the supply of potatoes, but I am also increasing the demand for other goods. What will I use the potatoes for? Either I will consume them myself (my demand is increased), or I will offer them in exchange for some other commodity, say, clothing, and this will mean that the demand for clothing has increased. Either way, the added supply has created an added demand; thus, in general, supply creates its own demand. Hence, there can be no such thing as general overproduction or general unemployment. Q.E.D."*

These arguments are not nonsense. In fact, they are rather persuasive and, for most of a century, they did persuade most economists that aggregative economic problems could be set to one side.

Not all economists, however—Malthus worried about the problem and remained unconvinced. He saw the possibility that there might be a "universal glut" of commodities in the economy as a whole and that this might lead to widespread unemployment. He tried to argue the point with his friend, Ricardo; but Malthus's own arguments were far from airtight, and Ricardo won out on debating points fairly easily. Marx was another economist who remained unconvinced. As we have already seen, Marx made increasing unemployment an intrinsic part of his analysis of capitalism. This unemployment arose from the technological displacement of labor by machines, but Marx also spoke generally about an overall inadequacy of markets. The capitalistic system, he thought, might produce more goods than it was constituted to absorb. This could also contribute to crises and depressions.

Neither Malthus nor Marx, however, made much of a dent on this part of the main body of economic analysis, and it wasn't until the very end of the nineteenth century that really serious thought began to be given to these problems. Here special credit should be given to the Swedish economist Knut Wicksell (1851–1926), who anticipated many of the elements in the "revolution" in economic analysis that was soon to take place. The economists of Sweden were, indeed, generally in the vanguard of this particular development, although the great breakthrough must be attributed to the man we shall turn to now. It was his theory that really did the trick. That man was John Maynard Keynes.

KEYNESIAN ANALYSIS

Keynes (1883–1946), the man, was a most remarkable and versatile figure. He was at one time or another a businessman, teacher, college administrator, high government official, patron of the arts, and, of course, the foremost economist of his age. His wife was Lydia Lopokova, a prima ballerina, and she and Keynes were members of the famous Bloomsbury group that included renowned artists such as E. M. Forster and Virginia Woolf. Even in his academic work he was versatile. His first book was on the theory of probability. His economic writings included controversial comment on current issues—like his *Economic Consequences of the Peace,* which made such a stir after World War I—and also highly abstract theoretical works that are quite incomprehensible to the general public. His *General Theory of Employment, Interest and Money* is in the latter group. It has to be studied hard, and a background in technical economics is required if the reader is to make much headway with it.

During the next few chapters, we shall be developing much of the essence of the analysis from this book and also bringing in some modern modifications of that analysis. In the remainder of this

chapter, we shall simply suggest a few of the central features of Keynesian thought and comment about some of the controversy surrounding his work.[3]

What, then, in essence, was it that Keynes tried to do that sets his work off from that of most preceding economic theorists? Let us mention five charac-

---

3. For a somewhat more extensive discussion of Keynesian theory along the lines suggested here, see my *Evolution of Modern Economics* (Englewood Cliffs, N.J.: Prentice-Hall, 1967), chap. 6.

From the Preface to John Maynard Keynes'
General Theory of Employment, Interest and Money

This book is chiefly addressed to my fellow economists. I hope that it will be intelligible to others. But its main purpose is to deal with difficult questions of theory, and only in the second place with the applications of this theory to practice. For if orthodox economics is at fault, the error is to be found not in the superstructure, which has been erected with great care for logical consistency, but in a lack of clearness and of generality in the premises. Thus I cannot achieve my object of persuading economists to re-examine critically certain of their basic assumptions except by a highly abstract argument and also by much controversy. I wish there could have been less of the latter. But I have thought it important, not only to explain my own point of view, but also to show in what respects it departs from the prevailing theory. Those, who are strongly wedded to what I shall call "the classical theory," will fluctuate, I expect, between a belief that I am quite wrong and a belief that I am saying nothing new. It is for others to determine if either of these or the third alternative is right. My controversial passages are aimed at providing some material

for an answer; and I must ask forgiveness if, in the pursuit of sharp distinctions, my controversy is itself too keen. I myself held with conviction for many years the theories which I now attack, and I am not, I think, ignorant of their strong points.

The matters at issue are of an importance which cannot be exaggerated. But, if my explanations are right, it is my fellow economists, not the general public, whom I must first convince. At this stage of the argument the general public, though welcome at the debate, are only eavesdroppers at an attempt by an economist to bring to an issue the deep divergences of opinion between fellow economists which have for the time being almost destroyed the practical influence of economic theory, and will, until they are resolved, continue to do so.

The composition of this book has been for the author a long struggle of escape, and so must the reading of it be for most readers if the author's assault upon them is to be successful—a struggle of escape from habitual modes of thought and expression. The ideas which are here expressed so laboriously are extremely simple and should be obvious. The difficulty lies, not in the new ideas, but in escaping from the old ones, which ramify, for those brought up as most of us have been, into every corner of our minds.

Excerpted from the preface to *The General Theory of Employment, Interest and Money* by John Maynard Keynes. Reprinted by permission of Harcourt Brace Jovanovich, Inc.

BROWN BROTHERS

John Maynard Keynes (1883-1946). Keynes was the most influential Western economist in the first half of the twentieth century. He brought economic analysis, which in the late nineteenth century had often been far removed from real problems, to bear on matters of urgent public interest—especially the problem of depression. Keynes' work on the theory of national income determination, combined with increased sophistication in the collection of national income data, caused an intense new interest in *macroeconomics*. Since his theories led to an argument for increased government intervention in the economy, Keynes was sometimes attacked for being close to Marxism in his thinking. It is now widely recognized that Keynes provided a major *alternative* to Marx; indeed, his basic approach has been adopted in one form or another by virtually every nation in the world outside the Communist bloc.

teristics of his work and make a brief comment on each:

(1) Keynes put his emphasis very clearly on the kind of problems we have just been discussing, problems dealing with the *economy as a whole*. His work was fundamentally macroeconomic in approach, meaning that his key variables were total national output, the general level of employment, the price level, and the like. Insofar as most preceding economic theory had had a strong weighting towards microanalysis, this represented something of a break with the past.

(2) Keynes emphasized the key role of *aggregate demand* in determining the level of national income and employment in the economy as a whole. In chapter 2, when discussing a market economy, we spoke of supply and demand in particular industries. Keynes spoke of supply and demand in the aggregate. He felt that aggregate demand in a given economy might be high or low in relation to aggregate supply. In other words, he rejected the theory behind Say's law that suggested that supply invariably created its own demand in the economy as a whole.

(3) He believed that the economy might come to rest at a position of *unemployment equilibrium*; that is, a position where there would be no natural forces operating to restore full employment to the economy. Suppose, he said, that aggregate demand falls short of aggregate supply at the full-employment level. What will happen? According to Keynes, the shortage of demand would mean that businessmen in general would cut back on production and jobs. He believed this cutting back process would go on until an equilibrium of supply and demand had been achieved. But this equilibrium might involve a great deal of unemployment in the economy as a whole. Indeed, Keynes

felt that this analysis helped explain why such a phenomenon as the Great Depression, in full sway while he was writing, could occur in a modern industrial economy.

These last two points indicate that Keynes rejected not only the conclusions of Say's law but, necessarily, the argument that lay behind it. One of these arguments, as we know, was that it was permissible to relegate "money" to a minor role in the workings of an economy. And this brings us to a fourth characteristic of Keynesian analysis.

(4) Keynes tried to bring "money" back into economic analysis in a rather pivotal role. He attempted to perform a *synthesis of real and monetary analysis*.[4] More particularly, he argued that "money" was not simply a convenient medium of exchange. He called particular attention to a characteristic of money named *liquidity*. By *liquidity*, he meant "command over goods in general." If I have money, I can exchange it for goods or services or bonds or securities in any direction I choose. It is a perfectly generalized way of holding purchasing power. Now all commodities have some elements of liquidity. When I own a house, I can exchange it for some other goods if I so desire; however, I can never be quite sure what the house will sell for. Similarly, with securities (stocks and bonds): I can quickly turn them into money with which to buy other goods and services; still, it is never quite certain at what price I shall be able to sell them. They are nearly perfectly liquid, but not quite. In short, Keynes said that "money" had certain

---

4. We use the term *real* here, as is customary in economics, to refer to the goods and services (potatoes, automobiles, etc.) that underlie their customary representation in money terms. The role of money, or *monetary* phenomena, is a complex one both in measuring and in analyzing this "real" goods-and-services world, as we shall see in succeeding chapters.

special properties that gave it an important role in the functioning of the economy. By recognizing this role, he argued, one could explain the possibility of a discrepancy between aggregate demand and aggregate supply in the economy, and hence the possibility of general unemployment.

(5) Finally, Keynes argued that since a market economy could not guarantee full employment by its own devices, it might be necessary to have a somewhat greater degree of *government intervention* than had been thought desirable in the past. The government could remedy the problem directly, in the Keynesian view, by affecting aggregate demand by its own purchases of goods and services. On the other hand, it could also influence aggregate demand indirectly by lowering taxes (or raising them if the problem was too much demand) and thus stimulating private consumer and business demand. Still more indirectly, the government could affect the level of aggregate demand by altering the supply of money available to the economy. In general, however, the point was that since the market alone could not be counted on to do the job, the government might have to take a more active participating role.

This leads us directly to the more controversial aspect of Keynesian analysis: namely, the *degree* of government intervention thought necessary to make a mixed economy work.

CONTROVERSIES SURROUNDING KEYNESIAN THEORY

There are really two quite different kinds of controversy that surround the work of John Maynard Keynes. The

first is based on a failure to read or at least to understand what Keynes actually wrote and said. The second is based on differing judgments about the actual and important limitations of the Keynesian theory.

The most extreme form of the first type of criticism (fortunately heard less frequently these days) is the charge that Keynes was attacking the capitalistic system in more or less the same manner as Karl Marx had attacked it seventy-five years earlier. Actually, it is closer to the truth to say that Keynes provided the main alternative *to* Marxism. For the fact is that the approaches of these two economists to the capitalistic system were radically different. Marx argued that the diseases of capitalism were intrinsic, inevitable, and fatal; they could be removed only by the overthrow of the entire system. By contrast, Keynes argued that the basic features of the capitalistic system could be preserved and its problems eliminated by modifications of that system. The mixed economy—which we actually have in the United States and Western Europe—is the natural heir to Keynesian analysis; but it is anathema to the good Marxist. For if, through modification of the system, one can forestall serious problems from arising and can make the economy "work," then one has completely undercut the ground from the Marxist who believes that things *must* get worse and that "revolution" is the *only* cure.

No one would argue that the *General Theory* is a "conservative" book in the usual sense of the term; but it is not a "radical" book—certainly not in the Marxist sense—and, indeed, it does hope to "conserve" certain features of a private enterprise system. Keynes deeply prized individual liberty and also the economic efficiency of the market economy; he hoped that when one had solved the problem of depressions, these virtues might be preserved.

If this first line of criticism is of little interest to the serious student, the second line of criticism is quite a different matter. For the fact is that there *are* important limitations on the Keynesian analysis (it could hardly be otherwise, given the vast amount of economic research done in the past forty years) and, consequently, there are good grounds for debating both his arguments and his conclusions. A list of these limitations would be very long, but even a short list would include obviously important matters:

Keynesian theory is basically static; it is very much concerned with short-run problems, and it leaves to one side the whole matter of growth and changes in fundamental conditions.

Keynesian theory dwells in a purely competitive world where the real-life market structures of the modern corporation or labor union hardly figure at all.

Keynesian theory is based on rough "psychological" generalizations that are inadequate for the complexities of economic behavior revealed by subsequent research.

Keynesian theory does not recognize some of the complications and difficulties of applying governmental expenditure, tax, and monetary policies to the solution of unemployment, inflation, and other problems of the modern economy in the aggregate. Some have argued further that it does not give an adequate account of the powerful role of money in the economy.

It is apparent, just from this short list, that there is much ground for disagreement and debate even among serious students of Keynesian analysis.

Having said this, however, we should add that there are also some mat-

ters that really are not subject to much question among economists. For one thing, there is no doubt that Keynesian theory has had an enormous impact on the development of the subject of economics in the past three decades. Even his harshest critics have been stimulated enormously by the challenge to new research that his work provided. For another thing, it is clear that a majority of economists (including those aware of the limitations of this theory) accept his general contention that there are serious problems in keeping an economy at or near the full-employment level and that there are times when only government intervention (of one sort or another) will have sufficient impact to turn the trick.

Finally, there is the important fact that most governments in the Western world now tend to accept: (1) the fact that governmental actions do have a substantial effect on the health of the economy as a whole, and (2) a governmental responsibility for maintaining at least a reasonably close approximation to a full-employment economy.

Thus, despite its critics, the "new economics" is very much in business in the modern mixed economy. And it is essentially because of this economics and its modern additions that one can predict with a high degree of certainty that such a thing as the Great Depression of the 1930s could not happen again in the United States or in Western Europe. Considering the hardship and despair that that Depression caused, this is no small tribute to the legacy of the late Lord Keynes.

SUMMARY

We shall be concerned in Part Two with the economy in the aggregate. Our interest will focus on broad questions concerning the level of national income, the general level of employment and unemployment, and the overall level of prices.

The history of modern industrial economies makes it quite clear that there have been fluctuations in the levels of employment and prices in various countries over the past century or two. Early economists (with some exceptions such as Malthus and Marx) tended on the whole to set aggregative problems, and especially the unemployment problem, to one side. They were confident that they could rely on Say's law to guarantee no major problems. Say's law depicted a "moneyless" economy in which supply always created its own demand, thus preventing any problems of general overproduction or general unemployment.

In the twentieth century, many economists began to criticize this point of view, and the great theoretical breakthrough was made by John Maynard Keynes. Keynesian theory departed from its predecessors by (1) its heavy emphasis on macroeconomics, (2) its stress on the role of aggregate demand, (3) its acknowledgment of the possibility of underemployment equilibrium, (4) its synthesis of real and monetary analysis; and (5) its recognition of the important role of government in curing unemployment and other aggregative problems.

Keynesian theory has been subject to many valid criticisms and also to some not so valid (e.g., the false identification of Keynes and Marx). Despite the critics, however, there is general agreement about his impact on the development of economics as a field and about the influence his work has had on the actual policies of governments in the Western mixed economies. The "new economics," in one form or another, is widely accepted and utilized by modern nations to avoid such harrowing disasters as the Great Depression of the 1930s.

QUESTIONS FOR DISCUSSION

1. "The Great Depression of the 1930s made forever obsolete the view that an unregulated market economy could guarantee, save for a few minor frictions, full employment of the nation's labor force." Discuss.

2. What are the assumptions behind Say's law? Show how, given these assumptions, an economy would be able to find markets for an expansion of its total output caused, say, by a sudden immigration of labor from abroad.

3. What is meant by macroeconomics? By microeconomics?

4. We quoted Keynes (p. 184) from his *General Theory of Employment, Interest, and Money* as saying that the critics would fluctuate "between a belief that I am quite wrong and a belief that I am saying nothing new. It is for others to determine if either of these or the third alternative is right." What grounds might be offered today to support the third alternative?

5. Compare the views of John Maynard Keynes and Karl Marx on the problems facing capitalism and their prospective cures.

6. What evidence do you find today of the influence of Keynesian economics on actual governmental policies in the United States and in other modern industrial economies? Give as many specific examples as you can.

8
The
Concept of GNP

Having outlined the general area of macroeconomics, we shall now turn to a concept that is central to this field: the concept of *gross national product,* or GNP. The term GNP is widely used in our daily press, but the concept is somewhat complicated, and it is worth spending some time with it.

TOTAL OUTPUT
AND ITS FLUCTUATIONS

The basic idea behind the gross national product is simple enough. This is one of the important measures economists use when they try to estimate the total output of goods and services produced in the nation over a given period, say a year.

Furthermore, it is apparent that some such concept of total output is indispensable to the field of macroeconomics. For example, we have talked about the Great Depression of the 1930s, but mainly in terms of unemployment. We could just as readily have spoken about a fall in the nation's total output, its GNP, during that period. Indeed, we should generally expect that when there is heavy unemployment in an economy, its total output of goods and services would fall, or at least would not rise as rapidly as might otherwise be the case.

In Figure 8-1, we have charted the changes in the United States' GNP since 1910. Two things about this diagram should strike us immediately. The first is the pronounced upward trend in our GNP over this period of time—our annual total output of goods and services has increased some 5 or 6 times in sixty years. The second striking feature is the irregularity of the upward movement. The curve does not move upward continuously, but with spurts and pauses, with occasional downward movements followed by rapid accelerations, and so on.

Now the first feature of this diagram, the long-run growth of our total output, we shall postpone until later in Part Two and again in Part Four (see especially chapters 16, 28, and 31). There we will take up various factors, such as

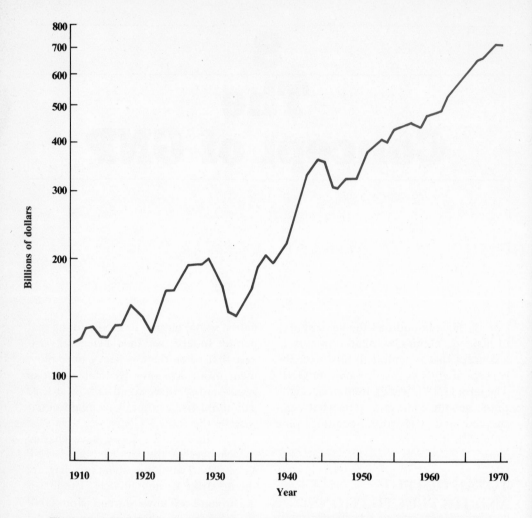

Figure 8-1. U.S. Gross National Product, 1910-1970 (in "constant" 1958 prices).

Growth and fluctuation of total output in the United States are brought out sharply in this diagram of sixty years.

population growth, capital accumulation, and technological change, that bring about long-run gains in a country's productive capacity. We shall also discuss the important *costs* of economic growth.

The second feature, however, is of central interest to us now. It tells us that there has been, in addition to long-run growth, a considerable *short-run fluctuation* in the level of GNP in our country. Another way to put this is to say that there

has been a changing gap between the total output our nation was actually producing in any given year and what it had the capacity for producing.

In Figure 8-2, we show the gap between actual and potential gross national product in the United States, as estimated for 1960-69 by the President's Council of Economic Advisers and for 1970-1971 by the author. This gap, when below the potential output line, reflects

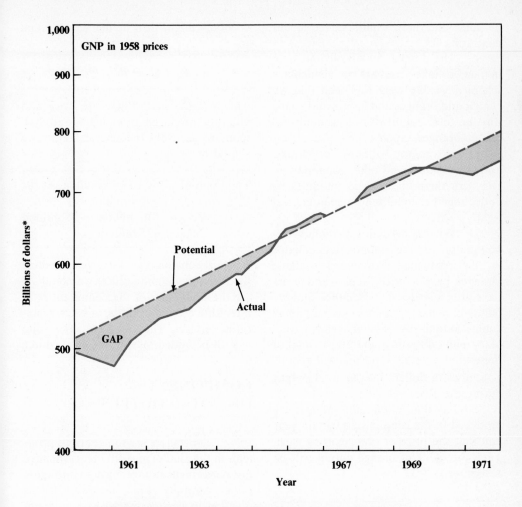

Figure 8-2. Gross National Product, Actual and Potential.
*Seasonally adjusted annual rates
Sources: Department of Commerce, Council of Economic Advisors, and the author.

underutilization of our productive capacity. Since potential output is defined by the Council as "the output in the economy would be producing when operating at a 3.8 percent unemployment rate," it is possible for actual output to exceed potential output when unemployment is very low. The gap is, in general, highly correlated with the rate of unemployment. Similarly, two questions are very closely related: What determines our level of GNP in the short run? What determines our level of employment in the short run?

MEASURING TOTAL OUTPUT

Having observed that GNP is an important concept, we now have to ask the more difficult question: is it a meaningful concept? What is this thing, "total output," and how would we go about measuring it?

The difficulty is an obvious one; in fact, it takes us back to elementary school days. We were told then that we cannot add oranges and apples and pears. But the total output of our economy includes oranges, apples, and pears, *plus* lathes, tractors, toy balloons, soft drinks, and several thousand other commodities. How can these different commodities be added together to form a single numerical total?

What is needed is a common denominator, and the common denominator in our particular economy is dollars. Oranges have a price; apples and pears have prices; so do tractors, lathes, and toy balloons. What we do is to give a money valuation to the production of each particular commodity, then add up the total of these money values, and this will give us a number in dollars for our total output during the given year.

Say that 600 million oranges are produced in the country in a certain year and that the price of oranges is 5¢ each. Then the value of orange output will be determined:

$$5¢ \times 600 \text{ million} = \$30 \text{ million}$$

We can then do the same thing for apples, pears, and lathes, and come up with money figures for each. We would then add these money figures together to form an estimate of aggregate output. To be specific: Suppose there is, in addition to oranges, only one other commodity in our economy: toy balloons. Toy balloon production is 50 million units a year at a price of 10¢ apiece.

Total output in this fictitious economy might then be defined as equal to

$$P_o \times Q_o + P_b \times Q_b$$

where P_o, Q_o and P_b, Q_b are price and quantity produced of oranges and balloons, respectively. In numerical terms, we should have:

$$
\begin{aligned}
\text{Total output} &= 5¢ \times 600 \text{ million} + 10¢ \\
&\quad \times 50 \text{ million} \\
&= \$30 \text{ million} + \$5 \text{ million} \\
&= \$35 \text{ million}
\end{aligned}
$$

It is fairly obvious that what we have done for these two commodities, we could do for the remainder of the commodities in a real-life economy: shirts, missiles, secretarial services. They all have prices and can all be added together in this fashion.

COMPONENTS OF TOTAL OUTPUT

Now there are some serious problems in the kind of measurements we have just performed, and we must go into these rather carefully. First, however, let us mention in passing the basic component parts into which the total output of the economy can be divided. The most common breakdown, and one we shall be referring to often in the future, is in terms of three main categories of goods and services:

(1) *Consumption.* There are first of all the goods bought by ordinary consumers like ourselves: clothing, food, automobiles, tennis racquets. These include consumer expenditures on services as well as commodities, and on durable as well as nondurable consumers' goods. The category of durable consumers' goods has grown very rapidly in recent decades as

we have expanded our purchases of automobiles, television sets, washing machines, and the like. In total, consumption expenditures in the United States currently average between 60 to 65 percent of our GNP.

(2) *Investment.* Part of the goods produced in the economy each year are funneled back into the productive process either to replace worn-out buildings, machines, and so on, or to add to our general stock of capital goods. Gross investment in our economy includes these replacement items and the net additions to our capital stock.[1] Investment expenditures in the United States may run in the neighborhood of 15 or 16 percent of GNP, though this percentage is subject to a fairly high degree of variability. The term *investment* in the sense we are now using it is, of course, different from the kind of investing we do when we buy a stock or a bond. It is better to regard the latter as *financial investment,* and to think of *investment* (unmodified) as indicating those goods devoted to building up the real productive capacity of the economy. The main categories of investment expenditure are fixed business investment (machinery, factories, etc.), residential construction (apartments and also private homes), and additions to inventories (stocks of products kept on hand to meet orders from other producers or consumers).

(3) *Government.* The third main category is governmental expenditures. If we exclude transfer payments—which, as we recall, do not represent governmental purchases of goods and services—then government expenditures currently run at something above 20 percent of GNP. We have already indicated (chapter 4) that a

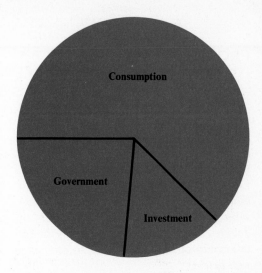

Figure 8-3. Major Components of United States' GNP.

These are average proportions of GNP. Remember that they change from year to year, investment being a particularly variable item.

great part of these government expenditures at the federal level are related in one way or another to defense. Educational expenditures are the most important single category at the state and local level. For our present purposes, the important point to note is that when the government buys goods and services, the destination it provides for the total output is exactly analogous to that provided by private investment or consumption purchases.

These then are the three main categories by which the total output of the society can be classified: consumption, private investment, and government expenditures.[2] We shall be mentioning each of these categories often in the pages that follow.

---

1. We shall come to the distinction between "gross investment" and "net investment" in a moment (p. 198.

2. A further category would be *net* exports of American goods abroad. We will mention this category again later; it is a very small category, however, perhaps 1 percent or so of GNP. See chapter 15.

PROBLEM
OF CONSTANT PRICES

But now it is time to return once again to the basic concept of total output. We said that our procedure of simply adding together the dollar values of different outputs involved a number of problems. Let us now mention three specific and major problems. The first is that of *constant prices;* the second is the problem of *double-counting;* the third concerns the relationship of measured GNP to *economic well-being.*

The first problem, the problem of what is happening to the price level in our economy as we try to measure total output is a complicated one. The difficulty arises when we try to compare total output or GNP in two different years. To return to our simplified world of oranges and toy balloons:

In our earlier example (p. 194), we determined that the total output of oranges and toy balloons in our economy was worth $35 million. Let us suppose this was for the year 1960. Suppose someone now comes along and tells us that the combined money-value of orange and toy balloon production in 1970 had risen to $70 million. The question is: what can we conclude from this fact? Can we conclude that both orange production and toy balloon production had doubled from 1960 to 1970? Or that if one product less than doubled in quantity, the other more than doubled? Or does the given information actually enable us to conclude nothing at all about the production of oranges and toy balloons in this period?

The correct answer, unfortunately, is the last. We can conclude nothing whatever about orange and toy balloon production in 1970 as compared to 1960 unless, and until, we know what has happened to the prices of these goods during that period. To take an obvious case: suppose the prices of both goods had *quadrupled* in this ten-year period. A rise in total output from $35 million to $70 million would, in this case, represent not an increase in real GNP, but a *halving* of GNP from 1960 to 1970. If, on the other hand, prices had remained absolutely constant, then it would be clear that real GNP was expanding; indeed, if prices are constant, then the changes in the money value of GNP would reflect changes in the real output value of GNP.

The problem thus becomes one of finding some rough equivalent to constant prices when prices are, in fact, changing all the time. The way economists do this is by taking prices for some given year and using these prices throughout the series of measurements of GNP in different years. Thus, you will notice that in the charts of United States' GNP (Figures 8-1 and 8-2), prices are described as "1958 prices." More generally, we should have to amend our formula for calculating total output to indicate a specific date for the prices involved. Using 1960 prices throughout, our comparison of the total output of oranges and toy balloons in 1960 and 1970 would look as follows:

(1) Total Output $(GNP)_{(1960)}$ =

$$P_{o(1960)} \times Q_{o(1960)} + P_{b(1960)} \times Q_{b(1960)}$$

(2) Total Output $(GNP)_{(1970)}$ =

$$P_{o(1960)} \times Q_{o(1970)} + P_{b(1960)} \times Q_{b(1970)}$$

In this way, by using 1960 prices throughout, the problem of fictitious changes in total output due to mere changes in the price level is removed, and the focus is put on changes in the actual outputs of the goods involved.

The reader should notice that the prices and quantities in equation (2) are differently dated; from what we have said, he should be able to explain this fact fully.[3]

PROBLEM OF DOUBLE-COUNTING

A second major problem arises in measuring GNP because many of the goods we produce in a given year are actually already included in the value of other goods being produced.

Suppose we are using all the oranges to produce frozen orange juice. Then we have:

Stage 1	Value of oranges produced (as sold by the grower)	$30 million
Stage 2	Value of canned orange juice (as sold by the canner)	$40 million
Stage 3	Value of canned orange juice (as bought by the consumer from the retailer)	$48 million

The double-counting problem arises here because the $48 million of final output produced includes the value of the

oranges and canned orange juice at the earlier stages of production. If we were to add them all together, we would get a fictitiously large total because of *double-counting*.

How does one avoid this problem, given the great number of different industries and different uses for their products in an economy like ours? One way (and the simplest conceptually) is to be careful to avoid all kinds of "intermediate" products when adding up GNP, and to concentrate wholly on "final" products in the various lines of production (i.e., to count only Stage 3 orange juice at $48 million and to exclude Stage 1 and Stage 2 orange products).

An equivalent, though more roundabout, way of achieving the same result is through what is known as the *value-added* method of calculating GNP. A firm's or an industry's *value added* to total output is the value of its sales minus its purchases of products from other firms or industries. If we assume for simplicity that the orange growers in our example purchased no inputs from other firms, then we could represent value added at each stage of orange production as follows:

Stage	Value of sales	minus	Purchases from other firms	equals	Value added
1	$30 million		$ 0		+ $30 million
2	$40 million		$30 million		+ $10 million
3	$48 million		$40 million		+ $ 8 million
Sum of *values added*				=	$48 million

The reader should notice that the sum of the values added equals the value of the final products ($48 million). He should

---

3. Before leaving the "constant prices" problem, it should at least be noted that when we are making comparisons of GNP over long periods of time, it is by no means easy to handle this problem. Prices are changing not only absolutely, but *relatively* (i.e., the price of oranges relative to the price of toy balloons), and when this happens, changes in "total output" do not have an unambiguous meaning. In general, using "earlier" prices will suggest a higher rate of growth than using "later" prices. This is sometimes called "the index-number problem."

prove to himself that this is not an accident but will necessarily be the case. The ultimate reason, of course, is that in both methods we have scrupulously avoided counting intermediate products.[4]

Before we leave the double-counting problem, however, we should remark on one aspect of measuring GNP where double-counting is in fact countenanced. The reader by now must have wondered why the "G" (Gross) is always prefixed to this measure of national production. The answer has to do with the way we evaluate the *investment* category mentioned earlier.

It should be clear that the proper way to evaluate the total output of machines, say, in a given year, would be to take the number of machines produced in that year and to subtract from it the number of machines that have become worn out, obsolete, and have been discarded during the year. Put it this way—we have been using machines throughout the year; when we produce a quantity of new machines, at least some of those machines are necessary to replace those that have become worn out through use; they do not all constitute a net addition to our stock of machines.

This is a problem that all businessmen are familiar with—the problem of depreciation and replacement. The difficulty, however, is that really accurate and meaningful depreciation figures are hard to come by, and even hard to define. Hence, economists and government statisticians often include *all* the machines produced in a given year without making the depreciation adjustment. This figure is called *gross*

investment. When gross investment is added to consumption and government expenditures, we call the total *gross* national product. If the depreciation of the country's capital stock is estimated and deducted, we would get *net* investment and, correspondingly, *net* national product (NNP).

PROBLEM OF ECONOMIC WELFARE

The distinction between "gross" and "net" that we have just drawn involves a consideration of the costs involved in producing a year's output in terms of the wear and tear on the society's capital stock. But what of other costs of producing that output—costs in terms of the depletion of our natural resources or in terms of adverse effects on the quality of our lives? Such questions involve the relationship between measured GNP and economic welfare.

This relationship is a very large matter that we shall be considering in detail later on.[5] The point to be made now is that this relationship is involved in the very definition of GNP. Since we have mentioned toy balloons, let us imagine a rather odd society in which one man's product is inflated balloons (he spends all day blowing up balloons and tying them) and another's is deflated balloons (he spends *his* day untying them and letting the air out). Common sense tells us that, however GNP is measured, there should be no addition to the total here, since from an economic welfare point of view we end up exactly where we started. But is this

---

4. In the early 1970s, there has been much discussion of a so-called "value-added tax." The reader should be able to understand from what we have just said that this is in many ways equivalent to a "sales tax" on the final values of commodities.

5. See the appendix to this chapter, which contains some reflections on this question by perhaps the world's outstanding authority on the measurement of national output, Simon Kuznets. Also see chapter 31.

farfetched example very different from, say, a society whose industrial activities pollute the air and whose GNP also includes the expenditures (on air conditioners, antipollution devices for automobiles, etc.) needed to restore the air more nearly to its original condition? Or consider this example of A. A. Berle, Jr.:

Cigarettes (to which I am addicted) satisfy a widespread want. They also, we are learning, engender a great deal of cancer. Now it is true that at some later time the service rendered in attempting to care for cancer (generated by cigarettes manufactured five years ago) will show up as "product"; so the work of attempted cure or caretaking will later appear as a positive product item. But that item will not be known until later. What we do know without benefit of figures is that against this year's output of tobacco products whose cash value is recorded we have also brought more cancer into being —an unrecorded "disproduct."[6]

The more one considers the relationship of measured GNP to society's welfare, the more complex it becomes. Is it appropriate to separate "economic welfare" from political or other social considerations? Whose judgment of welfare is to be considered decisive when opinions differ? If the pile of goods and services produced each year does not have any relationship to economic welfare, just what *does* it signify?

Some people feel, for example, that we have been accumulating far too many material goods during the past century. Such a person might be well within his rights in considering as additions to GNP during the next few years all the elaborate efforts and services of labor and machines that

would be required to dismantle and dispose of our material possessions and restore the "simple life." We are getting very close to our (perhaps not so farfetched) toy balloon example again!

In short, although it is easy enough to give a definition of "total output" with respect to some agreed upon method of eliminating double-counting, inflationary price increases, etc., it is by no means easy to determine what that final index means. Numerically measurable, GNP, in terms of economic welfare, remains somewhat shrouded in mystery.

PRODUCT AND INCOME CONCEPTS

The discussion so far, although mainly definitional, allows us to move fairly quickly into the heart of modern macroeconomic analysis. Much of this modern analysis proceeds from the recognition of a fact that we should be able to understand easily now, though it might have been obscure before. This fact is that there is a *basic equivalence between the national product or output of a society and the real national income of that society.* "Annual total output" is really another name for "annual total income." The latter, in turn, is the sum of all incomes earned in the production of this "total output": i.e., wages, profits, interest, and rents. These are basically two different ways of looking at the same thing.

The simplest way to convince ourselves on this point is to recall our value-added method of measuring GNP. At each stage of production, we subtracted from the value of the products a firm sells, the value that it has paid out to other firms for their products. Now the sum of these values added is our total "product," but it is also clearly our total "income."

6. A. A. Berle, Jr., "What GNP Doesn't Tell Us," *Saturday Review*, August 31, 1968.

For to what uses are these values added put? Since, by definition, they do not represent sales to other firms, they must represent either payments to the factors of production—wages to labor, rent on property, interest on borrowed funds—or profits to the firm. Indeed, profits can be thought of as being precisely the surplus of value added after payments are made to other factors of production. If we subtract all other incomes from our national product, we get profits as the residual, and profits, of course, are income. Hence the point is established: national product and national income are essentially equivalent concepts.

In present-day practice in the United States, we actually have a great number of related but still distinct "product" and "income" concepts for use in different connections. If we start with GNP and work downward, we get the following definitions:

Gross national product—Depreciation = Net national product

We have discussed this relationship earlier. "Depreciation" is sometimes replaced by the term "capital consumption allowances." NNP represents in a theoretical sense the basic *product* concept, all double-counting having been removed. In order to translate this into an *income* concept, we have to recognize that not all of the final values of commodities are reducible to factor incomes since these values include sales taxes and other *indirect business taxes*. When this deduction (and a number of much smaller deductions and additions) has been made, we get the national income concept:

Net national product—Indirect business taxes = National income

Although *national income*, so defined, is a basic income concept, it is not the same thing as the *personal income* paid out to the factor owners. There are two main reasons for this: (1) *Corporate income*—Corporations receive income, not all of which is paid out to individuals. Some of the income is retained by the firm (undistributed profits), some is paid to the government (corporate profit taxes), and some is set aside for contributions for social insurance; (2) *Government transfer payments*—Transfer payments, as we know (p. 95) are not a part of the product accounts but they do contribute to personal income. Thus, we have the following:

$$
\begin{aligned}
&\text{National Income} - \\
&\left\{
\begin{array}{c}
\text{Retained profits}^{\,7} \\
\text{Corporate profit taxes} \\
\text{Contribution for social insurance}
\end{array}
\right\} \\
&+ \text{ Transfer payments} \\
&= \text{ Personal Income}
\end{aligned}
$$

In terms of actually having money in our pockets, however, even personal income does not get us all the way. For, at this point, the government steps in and taxes us *directly* on our incomes; it is here that the personal income tax comes into play. Thus, we have finally:

Personal income—Personal taxes = Disposable personal income

In Table 8-1, we present figures for these various concepts for the United

7. There is another way of handling these deductions, which is equivalent to that used above. Instead of subtracting retained profits and corporate profit taxes, we could subtract the *whole* of corporate profits and then *add* the dividends that are paid out to corporate owners (stockholders) and that *are* a part of personal income. This equivalent method is shown in Table 8-1.

Table 8-1	U.S. NATIONAL INCOME ACCOUNTS, 1971 (in $ billions)		
Gross National Product			**1,046.8**
Less: Capital consumption allowances		95.2	
Net National Product			**951.6**
Plus: Subsidies less current surplus of government enterprises		.9	
Less: Indirect business tax and nontax liability		102.1	
Business transfer payments		4.3	
Statistical discrepancy		−4.7	
National Income			**850.8**
Less: Corporate profits and inventory valuation adjustment		80.7	
Contributions for social insurance		65.2	
Plus: Government transfer payments to persons		90.5	
Interest paid by government (net) and by consumers		31.9	
Dividends		25.5	
Business transfer payments		4.4	
Personal Income			**857.0**
Less: Personal tax and nontax payments		115.8	
Disposable Personal Income			**741.2**

States in 1971. We have also included some of the smaller deductions and additions beyond the major ones discussed above.

Incidentally, in the pages to come, we shall use the term *national income* in a less technical sense than in the above definition, as a symbol of the whole family of *total output* concepts. Where a more specific definition is called for, we shall note it explicitly in the course of the analysis.

NATIONAL INCOME AND THE CIRCULAR FLOW

Quite apart from definitions, the basic equivalence of income and output in the aggregate is not difficult to under-stand if we will reflect upon it for a moment. For what determines how much income you and I and our neighbors will have to share amongst ourselves? Ultimately, it has to be what all of us together have produced. Barring special cases where there is a net inflow of aid from abroad, there is simply no other source from which our collective incomes can emanate.

This equivalence is also illustrated by the diagram we have used in various forms in Part One—the *circular flow* diagram. In Figure 8-4, we show a very simple form of such a diagram for an economy producing and consuming $100 billion of output (or income) per year. In ordinary parlance, we might think of the "income flow" in this diagram as the inner arrow on the left-hand side and

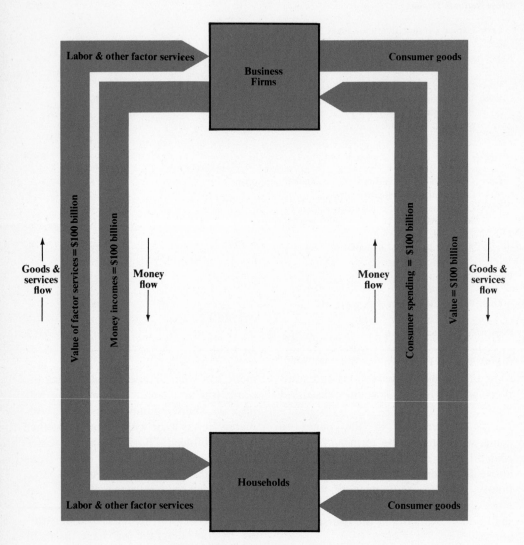

Figure 8-4. Circular Flow Diagram

In this simplified economy, there is no saving or investment. Problems of too much or too little aggregate demand do not arise.

the "output flow" as the outer arrow on the right-hand side: they are both equal to $100 billion. Since (in this hypothetical economy) there is no problem of capital consumption, corporate earnings, government taxes or transfer payments, etc., all the income and output concepts would amount to the same thing.

A circular flow diagram can also be used, however, to give us a first approximation view of how macroeconomic problems can arise. This begins to move us away from questions of definition to matters of actual economic behavior.

To illustrate what we mean, let us work with a slightly more complicated version of the circular flow, as shown in Figure 8-5. We may now imagine two changes occurring. Consumers have decided not to spend all their money incomes on consumers' goods, but to save $10 billion out of their annual income of $100 billion. In our primitive example, they have decided to do this by putting the money under their mattresses. Thus $10 billion goes under the mattress and $90 billion is left over to buy consumers' goods.

Business behavior has also changed. Businessmen have decided to build up their inventories of goods in stock by $10 billion. Thus, although they have produced $100 billion worth of consumers' goods as before, they now wish to invest $10 billion in added inventory and to sell $90 billion worth to the consumer. How did the businessmen get the money to make this $10 billion investment? Let's suppose they got it from a friendly banker. (Of course, they might also have got it from some of the consumers with their money under the mattresses. Or the consumers might have taken their money from under the mattresses and given it to the bankers who

then lent it out to the businessmen, etc. Clearly, all sorts of complications can quickly arise, but for the moment, we will concentrate on the bare essentials.)

Now notice that the flows in Figure 8-5 are still basically all right. That is to say, consumers come to the market wanting to buy $90 billion of goods and producers are there offering to sell $90 billion of goods. Thus not only is national income ($90 billion consumption and $10 billion saving) equal to national output ($90 billion consumers' goods and $10 billion inventory investment), but the aggregate demand for the goods the economy is producing is equal to the aggregate supply of goods the economy has produced.

But we can easily imagine a case in which this is not so. Let us suppose that households still wish to save $10 billion but that business firms do *not* wish to add $10 billion in inventories. They want to sell the whole $100 billion to consumers as consumer goods. The first question that may occur to us is: is this really possible? Can we have $100 billion going out in the income loop and only $90 billion coming back in the spending loop? The answer, essentially, is no, because incomes are created by customers buying the products of businesses. This, in a sense, is the whole point of the circular flow representation of economic life.

The second question becomes, then, how are the flows equated in the case we have described? One way this might happen is through inventory accumulation. Businessmen might find that they themselves were spending the missing $10 billion. They would do this by not selling $10 billion of the goods they had produced and thus automatically accumulating $10 billion of added inventories. This accumulation of added inventories would make the flows come out all right

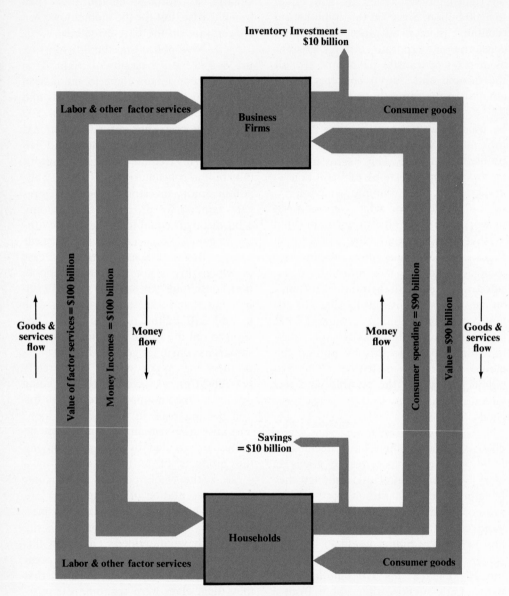

Figure 8-5. Circular Flow with Saving and Investment

If businessmen want to invest as much ($10 billion) as consumers want to save, everything works out fine. If not, serious macroeconomic problems can arise.

arithmetically, but it would hardly make sense *economically*. For, in contrast to our previous example, these added inventories are unwanted and unsought. What they tell the businessman is that he has produced more of his products than the market will bear. His natural reaction is to cut back output and employment until he finds himself producing just the amounts that his customers want.

The reader should recognize that what we have just done has been to describe what is nothing more nor less than a deficiency in aggregate demand. We recall from the last chapter that Lord Keynes attributed the major causes of depressions to precisely such deficiencies. What we have shown is that one reason why aggregate demand may be too low is that consumer spending may be too low (or, equivalently, consumer saving may be too high).

Still in this preliminary way, we might ask: can we also describe a situation where aggregate demand is too high? The answer is yes. Let us suppose this time that consumers want to spend all of their incomes on consumption goods (i.e., to save nothing). Let us suppose that at the same time businessmen, realizing that markets are good, want to divert part of the national product to investment, either in buildings and machinery or in added inventories. The consumers, then, want to spend the whole $100 billion on consumption goods. But businessmen want to spend some sum—say $20 billion—on investment.

Again, we ask: is this possible, and if it is possible in some mechanical way, is it economically possible? That is, what will the economic repercussions be?

The answer is that consumer and business behavior in this instance will create a situation in which "something has to give," and that the economic consequences of this behavior would normally be an *expansion* of national output and employment. Essentially, we have $120 billion of spending trying to buy $100 billion worth of goods. If we assume that prices are constant (actually, they would probably rise), the only way businessmen could meet the demand would be by selling off some of their inventories of goods in stock. Now this is a good thing from the point of view of the businessman—he has all these customers clamoring for his goods—but it is not something he will simply sit back and watch without doing anything. In particular, he will try to increase his employment and output to the point where he can not only meet consumer demands but also maintain (or add to) his stock of inventories. An excess of aggregate demand, then, will generally lead to a business expansion.

We have moved now from definitions into the very core of the modern theory of national income determination. We have seen that consumer decisions on consumption and saving may be crucial; we have also just seen how business investment decisions can influence the macroeconomic outcome. In short, we are now in a position to move ahead in a systematic way into this very important area of modern economics, and this will be our central task in the next chapter.

SUMMARY

In studying the modern economy in the aggregate and its short-run fluctuations, we need some measure of annual total output. *Gross national product* (GNP) is such a measure. Its major components are (1) consumption, (2) gross investment, and (3) government expenditures on goods and services.

The common denominator used to make possible the adding together of the various outputs in the economy is the price of each of these goods expressed in money terms. In performing this aggregation of outputs, however, three significant problems arise. The first is the problem of constant prices, or ruling out changes in GNP that derive simply from inflationary (or deflationary) changes in the price level and do not reflect changes in the real output value of GNP. To accomplish this end, prices in some one base year are used; e.g., "constant 1958 prices." The second problem is that of avoiding double-counting in adding up the outputs of different industries in the economy. This may be done by rigorously excluding intermediate products and concentrating on final goods and services only. Or, equivalently, it may be done by the *value-added* method of calculating national income. The third problem concerns the relationship of measured GNP to economic welfare. Particularly difficult to assess are the many economic costs that may accompany (and cancel part of) the production of a given level of GNP.

The value-added approach to measuring national income has the virtue of bringing out quite clearly the fundamental equivalence of national product and national income. In our society, our real income in the aggregate (wages, salaries, rents, etc.) is nothing but our total production in the aggregate. From this basic consideration a number of more specific measures are derived for national accounting purposes: gross national product, net national product, national income, personal income and disposable personal income.

This equivalence of product and income leads, in turn, to a circular flow representation of a modern economy. A money-income-and-spending flow, representing households as they sell their services (labor, land, etc.) to business firms and then buy the products of the business firms with their incomes, is matched by an opposite national-product-and-factor-services flow, showing the business getting the services of the factors of production and transforming these into useful commodities. With the circular flow diagram in mind, we can begin to understand how deficiencies or excesses of aggregate demand may make their presence felt in the modern economy. Thus, excessive consumer saving or deficient business investment might lead to a contraction of the flow, while too much investment and too little saving might lead to expansion. These matters will occupy our attention in detail in the next chapters.

QUESTIONS FOR DISCUSSION

1. Show the equivalence of the final-product and the value-added methods of measuring GNP.

2. Explain the basic relationships among the following terms: gross national product, net national product, national income, personal income, disposable personal income.

3. An increase in real GNP can be defined unambiguously only when the prices of all goods or the quantities of all goods change in the same proportions. If relative prices change and the relative quantities of goods produced change, then the change in GNP will be different depending upon what set of prices is used to make the measurement. This is known

as the *index number problem* (see footnote, p. 197).

In the following example, determine the percentage change in GNP from 1960 to 1970 as measured (*a*) in 1960 prices and (*b*) in 1970 prices:

	1960	
	Oranges	Toy balloons
Price	$.10	$.05
Quantity	1,000	2,000

	1970	
	Oranges	Toy balloons
Price	$.15	$.10
Quantity	3,000	2,500

Which measure—in 1960 prices or 1970 prices—gives the larger percentage change in total output? Can you see why this problem might pose some difficulties for measuring changes in GNP over long periods of time?

4. Distinguish *financial investment* from *investment* as a component of GNP. What is the difference between *gross investment* and *net investment?*

5. In a private economy, total output consists of consumption and investment while total real income consists of consumption and saving. Since total output and total income are equivalent, saving and investment must always be equal. However, *decisions* to invest and *decisions* to save are not the same. Is there any inconsistency in saying that saving must always equal investment but that decisions about saving and decisions about investment are often made by different people for different reasons? (Hint: Remember the supply and demand diagrams of chapter 2. The quantity of a good bought and the quantity of a good sold must always be equal. However, the decisions of buyers, reflected in the demand curve, are quite different from the decisions of sellers, reflected in the supply curve.)

6. Using the circular flow diagram as a guide, show how a decision of consumers to save more than businessmen want to invest can lead to a deficiency of aggregate demand. Show, conversely, how a decision of businessmen to invest more than consumers wish to save can lead to an excess of aggregate demand.

8
Appendix:
National Income and Welfare

Over the past several decades, the world's leading authority on the measurement of national income has been Simon Kuznets. Indeed, the empirical work done by Kuznets and his associates in the period before World War II is regarded by many economists as a foundation for modern macroeconomic analysis very nearly as significant as the theoretical contribution of Lord Keynes. Since the 1940s, Dr. Kuznets' work has branched out into many different fields and has been especially valuable in the study of growth in both developed and less developed economies. In recognition of his many contributions, he was awarded the Nobel Prize in Economics in 1971, the second American so honored.

The following reading, although published in 1946, is still relevant to a judgment of the relationship between measured national income and economic welfare.

National Income and Welfare

Simon Kuznets

Do estimates of national income measure the net contribution of economic activity to its primary goal—provision of goods to individuals—without errors of commission and omission? Do all commodities and services ordinarily included contribute to the satisfaction of consumers' wants, present or future? Are all the goods, i.e., all the sources of satisfying consumers' wants, made available in any year included in national income as estimated in this country today? We consider first the possible errors of commission, then those of omission.

Things desirable in the eyes of one individual may be matters of indifference to the group of which he is a member, or even considered deleterious by many; and things wanted by the majority may be frowned upon by the minority. In determining what are goods from the viewpoint of satisfying consumers' wants, we cannot assign both positive and negative signs to those wanted by some but deemed pernicious by others, then strike algebraic balances. Rather we must decide what, on the whole, are goods and should be included. In the statistical measurement of national income the question reduces itself to what commodities and services should be excluded because, by and large, they do not contribute to the goal of economic activity—satisfaction of consumers' wants. Specific examples may range from services, such as are rendered Mr. Smith by a professional gang of killers in disposing of his rival Mr. Jones, to commodities, such as harmful drugs or useless patent medicines.

If in such a classification needs and relevance to needs were defined in terms of an imagined application of scientific knowledge and broad principles of ethics, we would exclude from national income many commodities and services now included. Many foods and drugs are worthless by scientific standards of nutrition and medication;

Excerpted from Simon Kuznets, *National Income: A Summary of Findings,* National Bureau of Economic Research, Inc., New York, 1946, pp. 121–28. Reprinted by permission of the publisher.

many household appurtenances are irrelevant to any scientifically established needs for shelter and comfort; many service activities as well as commodities are desired for the sake of impressing foreigners or our fellow countrymen and could hardly measure up to ethical principles of behavior in relation to the rest of mankind. National income, as estimated here, is subject to errors of commission in that it includes commodities and services that are not goods, i.e., do not contribute to the satisfaction of needs, *if* the criteria are scientific standards and broad canons of ethics.

It would be instructive to estimate national income as the sum of products that are unequivocally sources of satisfying needs objectively determined from the viewpoint of mankind as a whole. The estimate could be described as a given nation's share in the world's current new supply of 'approved' goods. Such estimates would aid national groups in appraising their social activities in general and their economic performance in particular. But they would not be what national income estimates as customarily prepared are designed to be— measures of the contribution of the nation's economy to satisfying the wants society recognizes as legitimate.

We exclude all illegal commodities or services, e.g., hired murder and the manufacture and sale of illegal drugs, as far as we can with the · inadequate statistical data at hand. We include commodities and services not prohibited as long as they find a buyer (presumably they would not exist without

Simon Kuznets. By his research on the quantitative dimensions of national income, Kuznets did more than any other modern economist to provide an empirical foundation for the investigation of Keynesian-type questions. Winner of the Nobel prize, he has also conducted vast researches on the subject of economic growth.

one), though they may not be useful from any objective standpoint. In short, in the absence of society's explicit declaration to the contrary, the wants of the individual buyer are the criterion. Erratic test of legality may be (consider the prohibition years) and difficult of application to certain activities (consider a shady business deal that has not as yet been prosecuted in courts and may never be), but it is the only one at the disposal of a national income estimator unless he sets himself up as a social philosopher and decides to ignore the consensus of society as to what are not goods, i.e., not positive con-

tributions to the approved ends of economic activity.

There are of course numerous payments and transactions that do not represent a commodity produced or a service rendered: and whenever national income is estimated from payments (rather than from the value of commodities and services), such transfers also are omitted; e.g., gambling gains, net gains on sales of capital assets without any preceding input of resources to account for the gain, and gifts. All these transfers among individuals may greatly affect the eventual shares various members of society receive of the current net product;

but they do not directly determine its size, if it is defined as the net value of commodities and services produced during the year. The distinction between transfer payments and payments that are evidence of real production is scarcely so simple, but this is another of those problems we can no more than mention.

Judged in the light of all possible ways of satisfying consumers' wants, national income as customarily measured is subject to larger errors of omission than of commission. Errors of omission arise, first, from the deliberate restriction of national income to the net product of *economic* activity proper, and hence the deliberate exclusion of activities that may satisfy wants but are not economic. Even within the area of economic activities proper, especially if broadly defined, national income estimates omit some types of product. Finally, by definition, they neglect completely any consideration of such costs of economic activity as impinge directly upon consumers' satisfaction or the welfare of the community.

Life is full of activities that lead to the satisfaction of consumers' needs and hence their welfare, only some of which can be classified as economic. In extreme cases the distinction is easy. Taking a pleasant walk or playing a game of chess with a friend satisfies certain wants, but is not an economic activity; working in a factory or an office is. But what about the household services performed by the housewife and other members of the family? What about cultivating one's own vegetable garden?

It has become customary to base the distinction between economic and noneconomic activities on the closeness of ties with the market. Every pursuit whose products are either sold on the market or are largely directed toward it is treated as economic; no others are, though their yield in the way of satisfying wants may be substantial. This solution has a great advantage in that it segregates the sector of life concerned largely with economic activities, and in which measurement is feasible because the yardstick (no matter how it may have to be adjusted) is the market price. In a highly developed economy the disadvantages are reduced by the fact that the majority of the activities intended to produce goods for consumers are market-bound. Even so, the magnitudes omitted are far from minor. For example, the value of housewives' services are roughly estimated at some $23 billion in 1929, or more than one-fourth of national income. And in countries where the market is less developed than in the United States, the limitation of economic activities to those market-bound leads to a major undercount.

The national income estimator must choose between comprehensive definition—with the consequence that large sectors of the economy either cannot be measured on a continuous basis or cannot be included with more precisely measurable sectors because the errors are so enormous—and a narrower definition that confines economic activities to those market-bound—for which tolerably reliable estimates can be made. In current national income measurement in this country, the decision is usually in favor of the second alternative. And it finds support in the argument that the activities so segregated for measurement are the ones subject primarily to economic criteria and rationale; whereas those that are not directed at the market are much more a part of life in general. One may and does discharge a housekeeper for inefficiency in managing a household, but by itself this is rarely a ground for divorce.

However justified, this limitation results in omitting a substantial group of activities important in satisfying the needs and wants of the members of society. Moreover, some market-bound activities are omitted largely because they cannot be measured on a continuous basis—taking boarders or lodgers, spare-time jobs, and the like. In coverage, a continuous national income series is thus always on the short side even in terms of market-bound activities, which it tends to omit if they are casual and hence elusive of measurement.

The national income estimator cannot do much about such omissions, since scarcity or lack of data is inherent in the nature of the omitted areas. But in interpreting national income movements in terms of satisfying consumers' wants, the limitation of national income largely to noncasual market-bound activities must be stressed. In this country as in many others where the market is always being extended, the relative importance of the household as a source of consumer goods is declining. Many activities formerly performed by the housewife or other members of the family and not measured (baking, sewing, canning, etc.) have progressively been taken over by business enterprises and gone into market-bound activities; other household functions have vanished without leaving a direct substitute in business activity. Hence, national income totals tend to exaggerate the upward movement in the supply of goods to consumers, if such supply is comprehensively defined as coming from both market-bound and family activities. Likewise, a comparison of the national income of two countries at different stages of the commercialization of family production must take into account the differing importance of the market sphere in the total provision of goods to consumers. The omission of casual activities also imparts an upward bias to the secular trend of national income, since their importance relative to those covered diminishes as more people move to cities and engage in regular, full time, pursuits.

The effect on the interpretation of short term changes in national income is at least as great. During any expansion, whether associated with business cycles or with wars, people move from nonmarket to market areas and from occasional to full time jobs; and in the larger net product the proportion of measurable market-bound activities increases at the expense of nonmarket activities or occasional jobs. As many of us are all too aware, during recent years, when the pressure of war needs for the expansion of market-bound production was especially intense, the number of persons available for family household work decreased materially. *Total* net production, including production within the household, increased much less than production on farms, in factories, shops, and offices. During short term contractions, on the contrary, the shrinkage of the market sphere swells the number of persons available for services both within the household and for casual jobs. Being confined to noncasual market-bound activities, national income is thus a more cyclically sensitive index than a more comprehensive total that would include the large productive sector of the household as well as occasional jobs and pursuits. Variations in it therefore exaggerate short term changes in the more comprehensive total.

We come finally to what some may consider the gravest omission—the deliberate exclusion of the human cost of turning out the net product; i.e., such disadvantages as are concomitants of acquiring an income and cramp the recipients' (and others') style as a consumer. One example would be long working hours. If to turn out a net product of a given size requires a work week that leaves little time for leisure, the producers cannot derive much satisfaction as consumers, i.e., as individuals who have certain wants and preferences. Another example would be the strain some jobs impose. If by and large a task is disagreeable, exhausting, dull, monotonous, or nerve wracking, the cost to the producer as a consumer is higher than when the task is light, instructive, diversified, or amusing. The range of illustrations is wide—from these obvious ones to more tenuous allegations concerning the costs of unpleasant features of the business-urban civilization such as blatant advertising and the ruthless despoiling and defacing of the countryside.

National income is not intended to measure such costs. It gauges the net positive contribution to consumers' satisfaction in the form of commodities and services; the burden of work and discomfort are ignored. And it may well be questioned whether such costs are measurable; or if measurable, could be estimated in terms comparable to those in which net product is estimated. Nor is it easy to say whether the long term trends or short term fluctuations in these costs parallel those in net product or are in opposite directions. Some of these trends are clear. Working hours have been progressively shortened, and many of the heavier jobs, demanding stamina and endurance, are now performed by machinery. On the other hand, it is claimed that the monotony and dissatisfaction to the individual as an individual due to greater specialization and the repetition of a few motions have increased, and that so has the nervous tension. The balance of such claims and counterclaims cannot be struck.

The reason for calling attention to this aspect of economic activity, completely neglected in national income measurement, is its possible contribution toward understanding some of the longer term trends. It warns us against too easy an acceptance of the thesis that a high national income is the sole desideratum in theory or the dominant motive in fact in a nation's economy. The reduction in working hours, the decisions made by countries that discourage as rapid a growth of population and of national product as could be attained (consider immigration restrictions); the willingness of some business men to adopt a policy of live and let live when they might expect a greater net return from vigorous and aggressive competition; the emphasis some individuals put on the importance of other than economic incentives proper—are all indications that both in society at large and among the groups and individuals it comprises definite limits are set upon a maximum net product as measured in national income. Both recently and in the past a potentially larger net national product has been forfeited for the sake of mitigating some intangible costs of the type illustrated above. Though unable to measure them, we must recognize that their omission renders national income merely one element in the evaluation of the net welfare assignable to the nation's economic activity.

9
The Theory of National Income Determination

We have been setting the stage for the analysis we shall undertake now. It has to do with what economists usually call "the theory of national income determination," but a somewhat more vivid description might be: an analysis of the root causes of depressions and inflations in the modern industrial economy.

THE PROBLEM AND SOME CLUES

What we have done so far has been to state the problem and to provide a few clues to its solution.

The problem, briefly, is this: given the basic productive capacity of the nation, how can we determine where the actual level of GNP will be? We know historically that there have been gaps between actual and potential GNP in our own and in other industrial economies. What determines the size of these gaps?

To assist in the approach to this problem, we have developed a number of important clues to the nature of the solution.

We noticed that John Maynard Keynes, in his theorizing about these matters, placed great stress on the role of aggregate demand. *If aggregate demand fell short, Keynes argued, actual GNP would be below potential GNP and there would be substantial unemployment in the economy.*

We showed that national income and national product are basically two different views of the same object. This was illustrated by the familiar circular flow *approach to economic life. Businesses pay incomes to the owners of labor, land, etc., who then use these incomes to buy the goods and services that businesses have produced.*

We observed that the three main categories of GNP are: (1) consumption expenditures, (2) investment *expenditures, and* (3) government *expenditures.*

We showed how a deficiency in one of the spending categories (say, consumer spending) might lead through the circular flow to business troubles and thus to a contraction of output and employment. Such a deficiency in the spending flow, we said, was really what Keynes meant when he talked about inadequate aggregate demand. We also suggested how aggregate demand might be "too high," as it would be when businessmen want to invest more than consumers wish to save.

These clues give us the basic structure for analyzing the problem of national income determination. We must first determine the factors that influence the three main categories of spending: consumer spending, private business investment, and government expenditure. Then we must "add up" these expenditure items and see whether they will provide us with sufficient aggregate demand to sustain GNP at its full employment potential level. If they will not sustain full employment GNP, then we must ask: What *is* the level of national income that can be sustained? When we have answered these questions, our theory of national income determination will be basically complete.

We shall follow this suggested structure except for one point. In this chapter, we shall consider the theory of national income determination in a purely private economy—i.e., we shall assume that there are no government expenditures or taxes and that our only sources of aggregate demand are consumer spending and business investment spending. Having presented the theory in this simplified case, we shall introduce government once again in the following chapter.

This procedure, besides being easier to follow, also has the advantage that it enables us to show very clearly and explicitly what the impact of various government policies on the economy will be.

CONSUMPTION DEMAND

The level of national income that can be sustained in a private economy will be determined by the strength of (1) consumer demand for the various categories of consumption goods the nation can produce, and (2) business demand for goods to invest, i.e., to add to the stock of machines, buildings, inventories, and other capital goods in the economy. We shall consider these two components of aggregate demand in order.

What are the factors that influence consumption demand in a modern industrial economy? Can we generalize about them in any way?

Of course, the truth of the matter is that there are countless elements that may influence our demand for consumer goods to at least some degree. An advertising campaign may affect our buying habits and preferences. So may a medical report on the virtues or harmfulness of certain products. There may be consumer fads that sweep the nation, changes in ladies' fashions, new sports that interest either spectators or participants. In some societies, there may develop a general philosophy of "eat, drink, and be merry"— spend as much of your income on consumption today as possible! In other societies, there may be a puritanical and thrifty code: "a penny saved is a penny earned."

It is worth mentioning the great variety of factors influencing consumer demand because this makes it clear that if we single out any one factor as all-important, we are doing a certain injustice to the facts. Any generalization we get will be only in the nature of an approximation.

Still, even rough generalizations can be important—indeed, we seldom do much better than that in the social sciences—and many economists feel that such is the case in the area of consumer demand. The basic generalization, in this instance, states that consumer spending can be usefully related to consumer income. If you wish to know how much a family will spend on consumption, find out what their family income is. If you want to know how much the nation will spend on consumption in general, find out what the national income is. It is this *income-consumption* relationship that has played a pivotal role in the modern theory of national income determination.

The roots of this, as we would expect, were in Keynes' *General Theory*. In this book Keynes expressed his belief in a "psychological law" that as an individual's (or society's) income rises, that individual (or society) will spend part, but not the whole, of the increase in income on added consumption. Another way of putting this is to say that individuals or society will divide any increase in income into (1) added consumption and (2) added saving. Since saving is defined as that part of income that is not consumed, (1) + (2) will necessarily equal the given increase in income.

Today we can go somewhat further than this and suggest that, in the short run, saving will tend to increase absolutely and, to a lesser degree, as a percentage of national income as national income increases. A typical shape for the curve relating consumption to national income is shown in Figure 9-1. In this dia-

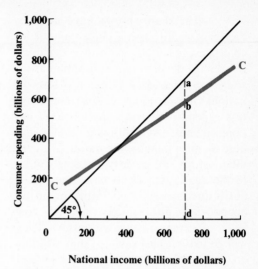

Figure 9-1. The Consumption Function.

This diagram shows a fairly typical consumption function. The line *CC* shows how much consumers will want to spend on goods and services at various levels of national income. The reader should understand that any line (e.g., *ad*) drawn from the 45° line to the horizontal axis will be equal to national income as measured at its point of intersection with the horizontal axis (in this case $700 billion). He should also understand that the distance *ab* will represent anticipated consumer saving.

gram, you will notice that we have drawn a 45° line from the origin. On this 45° line, vertical and horizontal distances from the axes are equal, meaning that the vertical distance is equal to national income. Since, in our simplified economy, consumption plus saving equals national income, we can calculate saving by measuring the distance between the consumption function and the 45° line.

What does the shape of this so-called *consumption function* mean? And on what kind of empirical evidence is it based?

The shape, as we have said, indicates a slightly rising percentage of income devoted to saving and a declining percentage devoted to consumption as income increases. At a rather low level of national income ($400 billion), consumption expenditures equal the whole of national income. At still lower levels—and here we must imagine the nation in a condition of general poverty—people would, in the aggregate, spend more than their entire incomes on consumption. In the economist's phraseology, at very low levels of income, people will *dissave*. They will go to their past savings; they will live on their capital assets, their homes and personal property, without replacing them; they will be consuming on the average more than they have actually produced that year. This is a pathological case (though not an unknown case, since there *was* net dissaving in the depths of the Great Depression in 1932 and 1933), and hence the more interesting part of the curve lies to the right of $400 billion. In this range, we can see that consumption is continually rising with income but that saving is increasing as a percentage of income.

The evidence for this general shape of the consumption function is both macro- and microeconomic in nature. In Figure 9-2, we have plotted out personal consumption expenditures in relationship to disposable personal income in the United States for each year from 1929 to 1970. The shape of the line we have fitted to this data is roughly what we should expect, although there are years that obviously need special explanation—for example, the years during World War II when voluntary saving was quite high even after large income taxes. Since the end of the war, savings have been a fairly constant fraction of personal disposable income.

Another quite different kind of information is provided by microeconomic studies of family spending at different income levels. Thus, we should expect that families with higher incomes will generally save more than families with lower incomes, not only absolutely, but also in percentage terms, and various studies have confirmed this general tendency. Thus, in 1950, a family with a disposable income of $4,000 a year probably saved little if anything on the average, while a family with $10,000 a year might save close to 20 percent of their larger income. In 1970, as everyone's incomes had risen, the percentages changed—at $4,000 a year, families were *dis*saving on the average; at $10,000, they were saving not 20 percent but closer to 10 percent—but the general relationship of higher percentage savings with higher levels of family income still remained valid.

It must be stressed that none of this evidence is absolutely conclusive. One problem that makes this whole area so difficult is that of distinguishing between long-run and short-run effects and causes. We do know that in the long run, a consumption function such as we have drawn in Figure 9-1 will shift upward. At a given level of income, as we have shown, families spent more in 1970 than in 1950, and they will presumably spend still more at that same level of income in 1980. Why? Because there were many new products in 1970 that hardly existed in 1950, and we can expect still more product changes in the 1970s. Even more significant, perhaps, is the fact that we are in a society in which everyone's family income (on the average) is rising. Insofar as our consumption expenditures reflect our relative position in the income distribution, then, if we stay at the same absolute level while other families around us are improving their positions, we may feel relatively

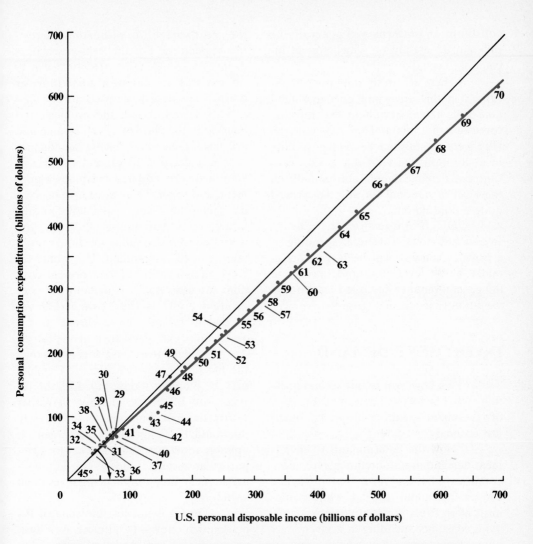

Figure 9-2. U.S. Consumption in Relation to Disposable Income, 1929-1970.

In this diagram, we have fitted a line to actual data on consumption in relation to income in the U.S. for each year, 1929-1970. In general, the data show the same pattern exemplified in our hypothetical consumption function, Figure 8-1.

poorer, and this may lower our willingness to cut consumption and save for the future.[1] To complicate matters still more, some economists, like Milton Friedman of the University of Chicago, have argued that our income is really of two sorts: "permanent income" and "transitory (or windfall gain or loss) income." Saving and

1. The dependence of our consumption habits on our relations to other consumers was stressed forcefully by Thorstein Veblen over seventy years ago. In his *Theory of the Leisure Class* (1899), Veblen emphasized the concept of "conspicuous consumption"—i.e., consumption to prove our superior status to our neighbors. More recently, another American economist, James S. Duesenberry added the notion that our consumption may be a function not of our absolute level of income but of our relative position in the income distribution of the society.

consumption patterns will generally be different depending on which sort of income we are talking about.

There are, in short, many complications in this area, and no one should take any statements about the income-consumption relationship as though they were established beyond possibility of doubt. Still, the view that makes consumption demand depend substantially on the level of national income has proved quite a durable one.

Our first question, then, is answered as follows: consumer spending in a private economy will be largely determined by the level of national income in the general manner described by the consumption function of Figure 9-1.[2]

INVESTMENT DEMAND

We now turn to our second question: What factors will determine the level of investment spending in our hypothetical economy?

Now the determinants of investment demand are, if anything, even more complicated than those that influence consumer demand. Indeed, while economists often stress the relative dependability of consumer spending at a given level of national income, they usually point out the great variability of business investment spending. For this reason, changes in investment spending are often seen to be pivotal in causing upswings or downswings in a modern economy.

To appreciate the problem, put yourself in the place of a businessman and ask what factors are likely to influence you in a decision to expand the size of your factory, to add new machines, equipment, and so on. There are a host of obvious factors that you would have to take into account at the outset. Basically, you would be trying to judge the future profitability of the investment. This would involve an assessment of your present position. Are sales good? Is demand for your product high? Is the extra machinery needed to produce more output? But it also requires an assessment of the future. Are sales likely to expand or contract over the life of the new machinery? Demand may be buoyant today, but does the future look bright or gloomy? In other words, the first thing one would have to do would be to formulate some general opinion about the future market for one's particular product. *Business expectations* are a crucial factor influencing investment spending.

But it is not just the state of the market that one has to estimate. As a businessman, you would also have to investigate whether there are new productive methods and processes available to you that will make the investment profitable in terms of reducing costs of production or producing an improved product. The kinds of plant, tools, and machinery we have in the economy today are vastly different from what they were fifty years ago, and this is a consequence of the fact that businessmen invest not only in more of the "old" machines, but also in replacing "old" machines with "new" machines.

2. This discussion of consumption and saving has been limited to household consumption and saving out of personal disposable income. In a fuller discussion, we should have to take into account the fact that business corporations also save and that their savings form an important source for business investment in the modern American economy. These corporate savings arise when businesses pay out less in dividends than their after-tax profits. These retained profits are part of national income but do not go to the consumers as personal income. The reader who wishes to follow through in this matter should consult the excellent treatment of the subject in Charles L. Schultze, *National Income Analysis*, 2nd ed. (Englewood Cliffs, N.J.: Prentice-Hall, 1967), especially chap. 3.

CHARLES PHELPS CUSHING

Joseph A. Schumpeter (1883-1950). Schumpeter, the Austrian born and later Harvard economist, emphasized the role of entrepreneurship and innovation in explaining business investment and economic growth.

Here we enter the whole area of *technological progress*. If there is an important new invention, for example, this may create a wide range of opportunities for profitable business investment. The great Austrian–American economist, Joseph A. Schumpeter (1883–1950) emphasized the pivotal role of new products and new productive methods as stimuli to business investment. He considered the introduction and absorption of innovational advances to be the mainspring of the major fluctuations of a modern economy. The judgment on whether investments in a new line of business or new productive process will work is not a mechanical one; it involves considerable uncertainty and, indeed, Schumpeter felt that those who took the lead in innovations had to have certain special qualities of character and leadership ability. Once these creative *entrepreneurs* had shown the way, other businessmen would follow in a swarm, introducing their new methods and business combinations. Schum-

peter found herein the whole secret of the business cycle:

The swarm-like appearance of new combinations easily and necessarily explains the fundamental features of periods of boom. It explains why increasing capital investment is the very first symptom of the coming boom, why industries producing means of production are the first to show supernormal stimulation, above all why the consumption of iron increases. It explains the appearance of new purchasing power in bulk, thereby the characteristic rise in prices during booms, which obviously no reference to increased need or increased costs alone can explain. Further, it explains the decline of unemployment and the rise of wages, the rise in the interest rate, the increase in freight, the increasing strain on bank balances and bank reserves, and . . . the release of secondary waves—the spread of prosperity over the whole economic system.[3]

Thus, technological progress in one area of the economy may lead to increased investment and expansion throughout the system as a whole.

There is still more to the matter of investment, however. Even if you were aware of the future state of demand and also the full range of technological possibilities open to you, you would not have solved the problem of whether or not to invest in a particular factory or piece of machinery. For you would now come up against the problem of financing the new investment. Does your firm have a great sum in the form of retained profits that can be used to purchase the added capital equipment? Or will you have to go to the

---

3. Joseph A. Schumpeter, *The Theory of Economic Development* (Cambridge: Harvard University Press, 1949), p. 230.

money markets to raise funds from the outside? In either case, the cost of borrowing money—the *interest rate*—will have to be a factor in your decision.[4] If interest rates are high, this will mean that you will have to pay more to borrow money and, consequently, that you will be more reluctant to undertake any vast expansion schemes. High interest rates are often associated with "tight money." It is difficult to get loans from the bank, and when one does get a loan, the interest charge is very stiff. In such circumstances, business investment is likely to be considerably curtailed.

In short, we have a whole series of factors that are likely to lead to more or less investment spending in the economy. Current demand for our product, pressure on our plant capacity, future expectations, technological progress, our profit position, the rate of interest—all these are factors that may significantly affect this second great component of aggregate demand, business investment expenditure.

We shall return to some of these factors later, especially when we come to our discussion of the economic effects of changes in the rate of interest (chapter 11).[5] For the moment, however, so that we can get on with our argument, let us simply assume that business investment spending has been determined. Let us suppose that all these various factors have done their work and that the net result

has been to give us a level of investment of, say, $100 billion. This is a short cut, but it will help us get the overall picture in the clearest possible terms.

Very well then. We have (1) a consumption-function (Figure 9-1) relating consumer spending to national income, and (2) a given $100 billion of investment demand. How then is the level of national income determined?

DETERMINATION OF THE LEVEL OF NATIONAL INCOME

The determination of the equilibrium level of national income takes place basically in the following way:

We add up the sum of planned consumer spending and planned business investment spending at each level of national income and determine whether this sum exceeds the level of national income or falls short of it. If there is an excess, it will mean that aggregate demand exceeds aggregate supply. In this case, forces will be set in motion to produce an expansion of national income. If, however, there is a deficiency, this will mean that aggregate demand is less than aggregate supply and this will bring about a fall in national income and, with it, of course, a fall in employment.

In short, the root cause of depressions, at least as far as our simplified economy is concerned, is a sum of consumption and investment spending that falls short of national income at the full-employment level.[6]

---

4. It might seem that the interest rate would affect our decision only if we had to borrow money from outside, say, take a bank loan, and not if we already had the funds ourselves. However, this is not so. If the machine promises us a return of 4 percent a year, and we can get 5 percent in a savings account, are we likely to purchase the machine? What will we do with our money?

5. We shall also consider investment in a microeconomic context in Part Three. There we shall show that, in a simple world, the interest rate is a means of adjusting the technological possibilities of capital accumulation to the society's preferences with respect to present versus future income. (See pp. 493–95).

6. In the remainder of this chapter, we shall speak mainly of the depression or unemployment problem. The opposite problem, inflation, will be taken up in a separate chapter (chapter 14), where we shall also consider the possibility—so important in the 1970s—that unemployment and inflation may coexist.

It is one thing to state the conclusion, another thing to demonstrate it in a convincing way. Actually, there are several approaches, all of which we have already suggested in our various clues along the way. One approach, for example, would be to return to our *circular flow* diagram of the last chapter and to show that consumers and businessmen will be content with what they are doing only when the sum of planned consumer spending and planned business investment in the spending flow is equal to the national product flow. In Figure 9-3, for example, we show an economy in which the sum of planned consumer spending and planned business investment spending is *less* than the national income of the economy, and hence we have an economy that is in macroeconomic *dis*equilibrium. This economy is due for a contraction of national output and employment.

Notice that we have used the term "planned" while talking about consumer and investment spending. Figure 9-3 makes clear why this is the case. In this particular example, *planned* investment is $100 billion, but *actual* investment is $150 billion. What has happened is that consumers have divided their national income of $900 billion into $150 billion of planned savings and $750 billion of planned consumption. Thus, the sum of planned consumption ($750 billion) and planned investment ($100 billion) is $850 billion. This is below the level of national income ($900 billion). Now the sum of *actual* consumption and investment must equal national income since there is no other place in a private economy for national product to go. The discrepancy is made up by unplanned, unwanted accumulation of $50 billion of added inventory. The consequence of actual investment exceeding planned investment is that businessmen will now want to cut back

on their total production and employment. This will lead to a fall in national income from $900 billion to, say, $870 billion or $790 billion.

To determine exactly how far national income would have to fall to bring about equilibrium, we would have to examine how savings and consumption spending responded to changes in national income. The circular flow approach is rather awkward for doing this, however, since it would require drawing a new diagram for each new level of income. An equivalent, but much clearer, approach is to build on the basis of our consumption function diagram (Figure 9-1).

In Figure 9-4, we have taken this earlier diagram and made two additions to it. The first addition is the vertical line *FE* drawn at the level of national income of $910 billion. This line tells us what national income (or product) would be if all the factors of production in the economy were fully employed. Actually, full-employment national income is not quite so definite a concept as this single line would suggest. The size of the labor force seeking jobs in the labor market is itself a function of economic conditions to some degree. Hence, we could, if we wished, think of *FE* not as a line but as a band of a certain width suggesting the range of possible full-employment outputs.

The second addition is the line $C + I$, which has been drawn above our C curve. The vertical distance between the two lines is $100 billion. This represents the amount of planned business investment that we are taking as determined by the host of factors influencing such investment. The vertical distance from the x-axis to the $C + I$ line at each level of national income represents the sum of investment and consumption demand at that level of national income.

How then will the equilibrium

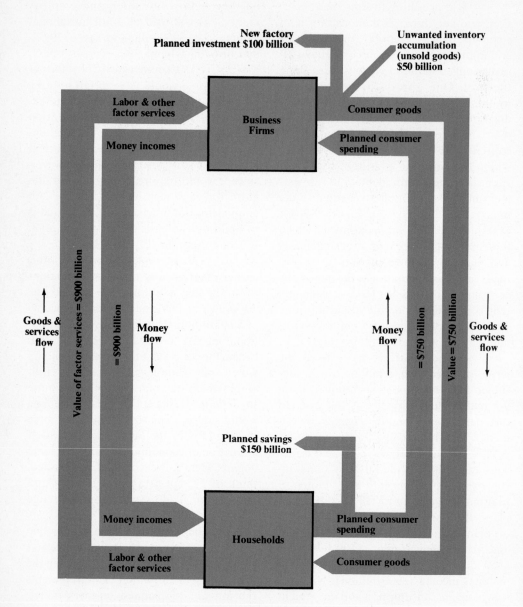

Figure 9-3. An Economy in Macroeconomic Disequilibrium.

In this economy, planned consumer savings exceed planned business investment. This would lead to an unwanted investment in inventory ($50 billion). But businessmen would not long put up with this situation. What would they do? Answer: Cut back on total production and employment.

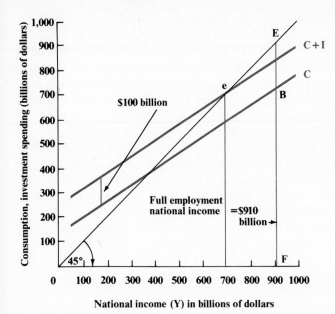

Figure 9-4. National Income Determination.

Equilibrium national income will be determined in this private economy at point *e*, where the *C+I* curve intersects the 45° line. The equilibrium level of national income in this example will be $700 billion.

level of national income be determined? To see the process involved, let us start out at the full-employment level, or at the national income of $910 billion. We now ask: what is the level of aggregate demand when the economy is fully employed? The answer can be read from the diagram. Consumption demand is equal to the distance *FB*, or $740 billion. Investment demand, of course, is $100 billion. The sum of the two therefore is $840 billion. This is $70 billion less than the value of full employment national income.

Now it does not take any very sophisticated analysis to show that this is an untenable situation. Businessmen are paying out into the income stream far more than consumers (through their consumption expenditures) and businessmen (through their own investment expenditures) are willing to pay back to them. The effects of this will be direct and compelling. If we assume that prices remain unchanged (they might actually start to fall somewhat under these circumstances),

businessmen in general will find that they are accumulating unwanted inventories of goods in stock. This is investment, but it is unplanned and unwanted investment. Furthermore it is a kind of investment that the businessman knows how to respond to directly: he will start cutting production and employment. This will be true of businessmen throughout the economy. There will be general cutbacks in national output and employment. Full-employment national income, in short, has proved unsustainable; employment and income will have to fall.

But how far? Where will the equilibrium level of national income in our economy be?

The answer is that equilibrium national income will be at the level determined by the intersection of the *C + I* line with the 45° line (point *e*). At this level of national income, aggregate demand will equal aggregate supply. Since the distance between the *C* curve and the 45° line equals the amount of their incomes consumers wish to save, this equilibrium level of national income is also one at which planned business investment and anticipated consumer savings are equal. In this instance, the amount businessmen want to invest and the amount consumers want to save are both equal to $100 billion.[7]

To prove that the point e has significance, we must show that levels of national income either higher or lower will not work. We must also show that higher levels will set in motion forces bringing national income *down*, whereas lower levels will set in motion forces bringing national income *up*.

Actually, we have already done half of this by showing the unsustainability of full-employment income and the way in which businessmen would react to unwanted inventories of their goods in stock. This logic can be applied to all points to the right of e in our diagram. In each case, there will be some accumulation of unwanted inventories and consequently a further reduction of production and employment.

Similarly, we can show that points to the left of e will not work either, though for an opposite reason. Here the sum of C + I exceeds the level of national income (Y). This fact would manifest itself to producers in the form of clamoring buyers who would be trying to purchase more of the firms' products than had been produced in the given period. If, again, we assume that prices remain unchanged (in this case they would have a tendency to rise), the consequence would be depleted inventories, empty store shelves, unfulfilled orders, and the like. The effect of this, in turn, would be to suggest to businessmen that they ought to expand production and employment. In short, at all levels of national income lower than e, we would have forces working for an expansion of national income.

Thus, at lower levels, national income will expand; at higher levels, national income will contract; at point e, aggregate demand will be just sufficient to match the output the economy is producing and thus there will be no forces effecting any change in the level of national income. Q.E.D.

At point e, do we have an equilibrium level of national income? Yes. No consumer, businessman or laborer can improve his situation by an indicated change in his pattern of actions. Do we have general contentment in the economy? Definitely no! Our equilibrium level of national income is short of full-employment income by $210 billion. Translated into employment figures, this amount means that our economy is suffering from massive unemployment. We are, indeed, precisely at the kind of "underemployment equilib-

---

7. Still another way of showing equilibrium national income is precisely by showing the interaction of the planned savings and investment schedules. This method is given in the following figure. The reader should test his understanding of this subject matter by (1) showing for himself exactly how the figure is derived from Figure 9-4, and (2) analyzing the process of national income (Y) determination (which we have done largely in terms of C + I = Y) in terms of savings and investment decisions (or I = S).

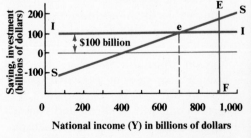

Determination of Equilibrium National Income by Saving and Investment Schedules.

rium" we mentioned in our discussion of Keynes. There are people who want work, but there are no jobs. There is, to use a phrase current in the 1930s, "poverty in the midst of plenty."

This, then, is the basic theory of national income determination in a purely private economy. Before one could apply such a theory to a real-life economy, he would have to develop it in a number of ways. First, one must bring in government expenditures and taxes; second, one must show the relationship of "money" and governmental monetary policy to this analysis, while also developing further the theory of investment demand; third, one must extend the analysis to cover closely related topics such as inflation and the macroeconomics of international trade. These topics are precisely those that we shall be taking up in the remaining chapters of Part Two.

The enumeration of what remains to be done is in itself a clear indication that the analysis of this chapter is only a first step along the way. It is, however, a major step. What we have done here is to equip ourselves with an important and flexible set of tools that can be used in many different connections. Whether the problem is inflation, the balance of payments, unemployment, or what have you, modern macroeconomic analysis essentially begins with the instruments we have provided in this chapter. Thus if careful attention is necessary here, that attention will have its reward in the numerous applications of the analysis we shall be able to make in the chapters ahead.

SUMMARY

In this chapter, we have presented the essentials of the theory of national income determination in a simplified private economy.

In such a private economy, the main components of aggregate demand will be consumer spending and business investment spending. Consumer spending is related to national income through the *consumption function.* This function tells us that consumers will consume more as their income increases, but that they will also save more. The evidence is that, in the short run, saving increases slightly as a percentage of income as income rises.

Investment spending is a function of many different factors including such important elements as business expectations, technological progress, the amount of profits available for investment purposes, and the cost of borrowing funds, or the rate of interest. Investment spending is, on the whole, a more variable and unpredictable factor than consumer spending. In our simplified analysis, we take a certain amount of planned investment as already determined by the workings of these various factors.

The equilibrium level of national income is determined at the level where aggregate supply equals aggregate demand or, equivalently, where the sum of planned consumption and investment spending equals national income (or output) or, equivalently still, where savings and investment decisions are equated. At levels of national income higher than this equilibrium level, forces will be set in motion to bring about a contraction in output and employment. At levels of national income below the equilibrium level, forces will be set in motion to bring about an expansion in output and employment. This equilibrium level is not necessarily a "full-employment" level and, indeed, is compatible with major mass unemployment in the economy.

Although simplified at this stage,

the present analysis is fundamental to modern thinking about macroeconomic problems and has a wide range of reference to everything from the monetary and fiscal policies of the government to the problems of inflation, employment, and trade.

QUESTIONS FOR DISCUSSION

1. State in your own words the basic theory of national income determination as you have understood it from this chapter.

2. Define the *consumption function*. What cautions should be kept in mind in employing this important tool?

3. In our analysis in this chapter, we have assumed that all saving is done by households and that all investing is done by businesses. In reality, however, households also invest (e.g., building homes) and businesses save (corporate saving now provides a substantial percentage of the funds for business investment in the United States). How might these facts modify the general analysis of national income determination as we have presented it?

4. In the pre-Keynesian era, it was sometimes argued that the main reason for unemployment in the economy was that labor was making unreasonable wage demands. If wages were lower, it was argued, employers would find that they could afford to hire more workers and the unemployment problem would be solved. Do you find this argument satisfactory? If not, why not? (Hint: Think back to the supply-and-demand curve for electricians of chapter 5. If electricians and all other workers accepted lower wages, would this be likely to affect the demand curves for electricians and for other workers? In what direction?)

5. If you were going to use the analysis of this chapter to help gain an understanding of the depression of the 1930s, what are some of the facts that you would look for in your research?

10
Fiscal Policy and the Multiplier

In chapter 9 we presented the basic tools of the modern theory of national income determination. In this chapter, we shall sharpen those tools and also apply them to an analysis of governmental expenditure and tax policies. Collectively, these policies are usually referred to as a nation's *fiscal policy*.

With the study of fiscal policy, we approach the heart of one of those areas of economics in which the public interest is very much at stake, and also in which controversy is rife. For the past three decades, a great debate has raged in this country about the effective use of fiscal policy. What we might call the classical view has been that the government ought simply to keep its own house in order and allow the rest of the economy to manage its affairs privately. In contrast, post-Keynesian economics has argued that government policy in a modern mixed economy should be guided at least in part by the objective of maintaining the overall health of the economy with respect to full employment, the price level, and economic growth.

The historian will record that the "new" economics, if it has not won an outright victory, has certainly made much headway during these decades. Economists still differ on the precise measures the government ought to use in implementing its goals, and there are still a few economists who adhere to something close to the classical position, but the great majority accepts the fact that the market itself does not guarantee the fulfillment of important macroeconomic objectives and, consequently, that the government must shoulder a share of the responsibility. More significantly, political leaders, both here and abroad, have generally come to the same overall conclusion.

All this does not mean that everyone must immediately become an enthusiastic partisan of "Keynesian economics"; it does mean, however, that everyone should keep an open mind in studying these matters, particularly when the analysis seems to conflict with the traditional, "common-sense" view.

INTRODUCING GOVERNMENTAL EXPENDITURES—G

In our discussion of a purely private economy in the last chapter, we dealt with only two components of aggregate demand: consumption, C, and investment, I. Now we shall introduce a third major element: government, G. To make the analysis as straightforward as possible, we shall deal separately with government expenditures and government taxation, and then combine them. In the course of this discussion, we shall introduce an important *general* tool of macroeconomic analysis: the *multiplier*.

We begin then with government expenditures. In a mixed economy, the government, along with households and private business investors, is purchasing goods and services. What will the effect of this government demand be?

The fundamental answer is that this demand will have precisely the same effect as any other demand. To the business firm producing, say, automobiles and trucks, it makes no essential difference whether the buyers are consumers, other business firms, or the United States government. In each case, the added demand means added sales and added profits.

Since this government demand is to be treated in the same general way as any other demand, we can represent it in our diagram by simply adding it on to our C + I curve, just as, earlier, we added investment spending to our consumption

function. Again, let us pull a number out of the hat. Suppose that in our hypothetical economy, government expenditures for goods and services are running at $50 billion a year. Neglecting the tax side, what will happen?

The answer is given in Figure 10-1, where $50 billion of G has been added vertically to the C + I curves. The consequence is that the equilibrium level of national income has been changed. Before, the equilibrium was at $700 billion; now it is where the C + I + G curve intersects the 45° line, or at $850 billion. As a result of governmental expenditures, this particular economy is much closer to full-employment national income than before.

In its most primitive and fundamental form, this is the justification for those who argue that the government ought to act to bring the economy as near as possible to the full-employment level.

But this is still a bit too primitive. We have not touched on taxation yet. Also, we have not explained exactly why the government expenditures have just this much impact and no less or no more. This second question, indeed, brings out a rather interesting feature of this whole analysis. One might have expected that a $50 billion addition of government expenditures would increase national income by the same amount, $50 billion. But, in fact, as our diagram shows, the equilibrium level of national income has gone up by a multiple of G—in our particular case by $150 billion.

Why this magnified effect? How can we determine whether an extra dollar of government expenditure will increase equilibrium national income by $1, $2, $5?

We reach here one of the most basic tools of modern analysis: the *multiplier*. Let us analyze this important concept.

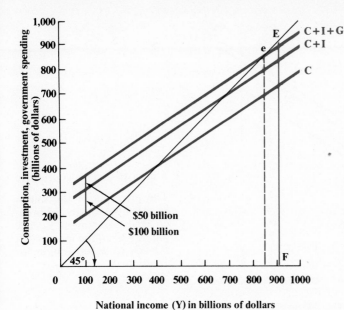

Figure 10-1. Adding Government Expenditures.

In this diagram, we add government expenditures of $50 billion and get an expansion of national income from $700 billion (without G) to $850 billion (with G). We have not, however, taken taxes into account at this point in the argument.

AN IMPORTANT GENERAL TOOL—THE MULTIPLIER

The *multiplier* tells us by how much an increase in spending will raise the equilibrium level of national income. If a $1 increase in spending leads to a $5 increase in equilibrium national income, the multiplier = 5; if the increase is $2, the multiplier = 2.

It is important to stress at the outset that the multiplier is a *general* tool applying to all categories of spending: consumption, investment, or government. So that there will be no mistake about this matter, let us first discuss the multiplier with respect to a change in investment demand, and then return to our example of government expenditures.

In Figure 10-2, we have gone back to a private economy again with the purpose this time of showing the effects of a change in investment demand on equilibrium national income. Investment demand was originally $100 billion. But now we imagine that some change has taken place (perhaps there has been an improvement in business confidence, owing to some international development, or perhaps there has been a new technological breakthrough, or perhaps the Federal Reserve System has lowered the interest rate), and planned investment spending has risen to $130 billion. The increase in investment is $30 billion, measured by the vertical distance between $C + I$ and $C + I'$. The effect of this change has been to raise equilibrium national income from $700 billion to $790 billion, or by $90 billion. A $30 billion increase in investment spending has brought about a $90 billion increase in national income. The *multiplier*, then, is 3.

Why 3? The geometrically-minded reader will see that the size of this number depends very much on

229

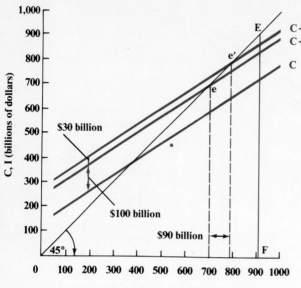

Figure 10-2. The Multiplier.

The principle of the multiplier is here illustrated in increased investment spending. A $30 billion increase in *I* leads to a $90 billion increase in *Y*.

National income (Y) in billions of dollars

how steep the consumption function (*C* curve) is. Indeed, everyone can see this in a general way. Imagine that the *C* curve in our diagram were perfectly horizontal, i.e., running parallel to the *x*-axis. In this case, a rise in investment of $30 billion would raise the intersection with the 45° line by $30 billion only and, consequently, would raise the national income level by only $30 billion. Here the multiplier = 1. If we imagined the *C* curve as very steep, however, we would get the opposite effect. Suppose the curve ran almost parallel to the 45° line; then one can see that even slight changes in investment spending would raise national income by great multiples.

Thus, we can see that the size of the multiplier in general depends on the steepness of the *C* curve. But we can be more precise than this. Let us first state our conclusion and then offer two different demonstrations of its validity.

The conclusion is that the multi-

plier (m) will in ordinary circumstances obey the following rule:

$$m = \frac{1}{1 - MPC}$$

where MPC refers to the *marginal propensity to consume* or, geometrically, the *slope* of the consumption function.

The meaning of this conclusion can be elaborated with reference to Figure 10-3 where we have blown up a small fragment of the CC curve. The marginal propensity to consume *is defined as that part of an extra dollar of income that consumers will wish to spend on consumption. In Figure 10-3, we give an example in which a $1 increase in income increases consumption demand by 67¢, roughly 2/3. The same result would be obtained if the numbers were not written in, but we simply measured distance BC and divided it by distance AC. This term BC/AC is the slope of the CC line,*

230

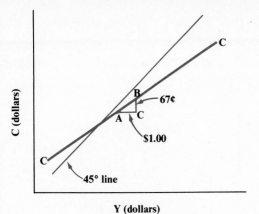

Figure 10-3. The Marginal Propensity to Consume.

The marginal propensity to consume (MPC) is equal to the slope of the consumption function or *BC/AC*. In this case, MPC = 67/100 or 2/3.

meaning that the marginal propensity to consume *is the slope of the consumption function. The multiplier in this example can be worked out as follows:*

$$m = \frac{1}{1-MPC} = \frac{1}{1-\dfrac{BC}{AC}} = \frac{1}{1-\dfrac{2}{3}} = 3$$

Another way of stating the same conclusion would be in terms of the *marginal propensity to save* (MPS). The MPS is defined as the part of an extra dollar of income that consumers wish to save. Since the extra dollar of income will be either saved or spent on consumption,

MPS = 1 − MPC (by definition)

This means that we could, if we wished, rewrite the multiplier very simply as:

$$m = \frac{1}{MPS}$$

What we have stated here (but

have yet not proved) is that the multiplier in our simplified private economy will be equal to the reciprocal of the marginal propensity to save, or, equivalently,

$$\frac{1}{1-MPC}$$

When we ask *why* this is so, we come to the matter of proof. Let us show in two different ways why the multiplier will follow this rule.

The first is a geometrical demonstration:

Figure 10-4 is simply Figure 10-2 with some additional notation. Say that we have an increase in investment of the amount b. *The diagram tells us that this leads to an increase in national income of the amount* a. *By definition, then, the multiplier is:*

$$(1) \qquad m = \frac{a}{b}$$

Our 45° line tells us that a = b + c; *hence equation (1) can be rewritten:*

$$(2) \qquad m = \frac{a}{a-c} = \frac{1}{1-\dfrac{c}{a}}$$

The marginal propensity to consume *(MPC), we know, is measured by the slope of the* C *curve, or,* MPC = BC/AC. *Since the investment curves are drawn parallel to the* C *curve, we can also say that* MPC = c/a. *Substituting for c/a in equation (2), we get:*

$$(3) \qquad m = \frac{1}{1-MPC}$$

And this was what we set out to show.

This geometrical demonstration is useful enough, but it gives us little insight into the economic logic of what is going on. The second demonstration, which we shall take up now, will make

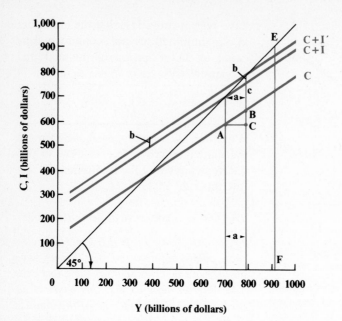

Figure 10-4.

this clearer. For it is based on observing what happens at each stage of the game as the increase in investment or other expenditure makes its way through the economy. The *economics* of what happens is essentially this: when businessmen decide to invest in a new factory, they buy products (iron, steel, machinery, etc.) from other people, thus creating *income* for these people. This is in the first stage. But now these people have more income than before, and *they* will want to spend more on consumption. So in the second stage, consumption spending increases. *But not by the whole amount of the increase in income.* That is to say, they will spend part, but also save part. In particular, the marginal propensity to consume tells us what fraction of this extra income they will want to spend. But then we go on to a third stage. The additional consumer spending (on food, shoes, etc.) creates more income for the producers of food, shoes, and other consumers' goods. This income, in turn, will also be spent in part

(determined by the MPC) on consumption. The process repeats itself indefinitely and, at each new stage, further income (though in increasingly smaller amounts) is added to national income.

Our second demonstration of the theory of the multiplier simply involves adding together all these successive rounds of additionally created income:

Let us suppose that there is a $100 increase in investment spending, and that the MPC = 2/3. The amount of income created at each stage will be as follows (to the nearest dollar):

Stage 1: $100 (the original added investment)
Stage 2: 2/3 ($100) = $67   (MPC × $100)
Stage 3: 2/3 ($67) = $44   [(MPC)^2 × $100]
Stage 4: 2/3 ($44) = $30   [(MPC)^3 × $100]
Stage 5: 2/3 ($30) = $20   [(MPC)^4 × $100]
      . . . .
Stage $n + 1$: (2/3)^n ($100) [(MPC)^n × $100]

The total of all these stages of added income will be the increase in the equilibrium *level of national income. If we use the term ΔY to signify the total increase in national income, then:*

(1) $\Delta Y = \$100 + \$67 + \$44 + \$30$
               $+ \$20 + \ldots$

or

(2) $\Delta Y = \$100 \, (1 + 2/3 + (2/3)^2$
               $+ (2/3)^3 + \ldots + (2/3)^n + \ldots)$

or, most generally, where ΔI is the added investment,

(3) $\Delta Y = \Delta I \, (1 + MPC + MPC^2$
               $+ MPC^3 + \ldots + MPC^n + \ldots)$

Since the multiplier is equal to $\Delta Y / \Delta I$, we get:

(4) $m = (1 + MPC + MPC^2 + MPC^3$
             $+ \ldots + MPC^n + \ldots)$

Knowing that MPC is less than 1, we can conclude from algebra that[1]

(5) $m = \dfrac{1}{1 - MPC}$

Which again is what we set out to prove.[2]

Both these demonstrations prove the same point about the multiplier, but the second is perhaps more vivid in bringing out the economic aspect of what is going on. We must always imagine the successive rounds of expenditures and in-

---

1. The general formula, where $|a| < 1$, is:

$$1 + a + a^2 + a^3 + \ldots + a^n + \ldots = \frac{1}{1-a}$$

2. We are dealing here with what is sometimes called the *instantaneous multiplier.* As every reader will recognize, it would normally take a considerable amount of time for all these successive stages of spending and income creation to occur. In more advanced treatments, the multiplier is often worked out over time in what is sometimes called *period analysis.*

comes created by any new act of spending. A businessman invests in an additional typewriter. This creates income for a seller of typewriters, who spends part of his increased income in buying a pair of shoes. This creates income for the producer of shoes, who now buys himself an umbrella. And on and on and on, the amounts getting smaller and smaller each time, as part of the added income leaks into added savings. Indeed, it will be precisely when savings in total have increased by the same amount as business investment that the process finally ends. This the reader can verify by looking at Figure 10-2 again. Notice that, at the new equilibrium level of national income, saving, like investment, has increased by $30 billion.

THE MULTIPLIER EFFECTS OF INCREASING G

With the multiplier concept in hand, we can now return to the mainstream of our argument, which was concerned with the effect of government expenditures on national income. Our original question was: why is it that the introduction of government expenditures of $50 billion (Figure 10-1) raised the equilibrium level of national income from $700 billion to $850 billion, or by $150 billion? The answer we can now give is that the multiplier is 3, and the reason it is 3 is that the marginal propensity to consume shown in Figure 10-1 is 2/3. (An exactly equivalent answer would be that the marginal propensity to save implied in Figure 10-1 is 1/3). This marginal propensity to consume can be determined by measuring the slope of the C curve in Figure 10-1.

Needless to say, the MPC need not always be 2/3. This is just what we assumed it to be in our hypothetical economy. What it is in any real-life modern economy at any particular period would, of course, have to be determined by careful empirical research.

The multiplier also allows us to say a further word about the effect of governmental expenditures. Suppose our economy is not yet at full employment and we wish to know by how much governmental expenditures would have to be increased (assuming no change in tax revenues) to bring us to the full-employment level. The needed change in G can easily be shown graphically. Figure 10-5 is our original Figure 10-1, except that we have added G' to represent the increased government expenditures necessary to bring us to full-employment national income.

What the multiplier tells us in this case is how much the increase in governmental expenditures will have to be in numerical terms. Before G' was added, equilibrium national income was $850 billion. We wish to raise national income to the full-employment level, which is $910 billion. The MPC in this figure, as before, is 2/3 and the multiplier is 3.

We can find our answer, then, simply by dividing the desired increase in national income, $60 billion, by 3. This gives us $20 billion, the amount by which we shall have to increase government expenditures if we wish to bring national income to the full-employment level.

GENERAL EFFECTS OF TAXATION—T

The preceding discussion has necessarily had an air of incompleteness. We have been discussing government expenditures without discussing government revenues. But we all know that the government taxes as well as spends. What can we say in a general way about the effects of tax policy on aggregate demand and equilibrium national income?

There are many different kinds of taxes, direct or indirect, taxes falling mainly on consumers or mainly on corporations, progressive or regressive taxes, taxes emanating from the federal, state, or local governments, and so on. In the United States, at the present time, the major sources of tax revenue are the following:

Individual income tax. This is the most important single tax and a tax with which most of us are familiar. It accounts for nearly half of all federal tax revenues, about one-sixth of state revenues, and a very small proportion of local revenues. Overall, it accounts for something over a third of tax revenues at all governmental levels. Because of its special importance, this tax will be discussed in a reading in the appendix to this chapter. The remaining two-thirds of governmental tax revenues are divided in varying proportions among the following main categories of taxes.

Payroll taxes. These are of importance at the federal level only, but they are a major source of federal revenue, running currently at between $40 and $50 billion a year. The main function of these taxes is to finance the large and growing federal social security program.

Corporation income taxes. Taxes are levied directly on corporations as well as on individuals. These taxes are collected by state governments as well as the federal government, although the latter is by far the larger collector. In 1970, corporate income taxes overall ran to about $38 billion in the United States.

Sales and excise taxes. This is by far the largest single category of revenue

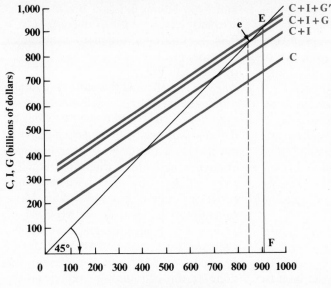

Figure 10-5.

In this diagram we have sufficiently raised government expenditures (*G*) to bring us to an equilibrium level of national income at full employment. (This assumes no change in tax revenues.)

at the state level, accounting for nearly half of state tax revenues; it is much smaller, though not insignificant (between 5 and 10 percent of tax revenues), at both the local and federal levels. These sales and excise taxes are important examples of *indirect taxes*. An indirect tax is one that is levied on goods and services, as opposed to direct taxes that fall "directly" on persons (e.g., the individual income tax). Thus, it can be said that while the U.S. federal government relies heavily on direct taxes, the states tend to rely much more on indirect taxes. In comparison to *other countries,* with a few exceptions, the United States depends more on income and other direct taxes in total and less on indirect taxes than do other national governments.

Property taxes: These are overwhelmingly the most important source of revenue at the local level today, accounting for about three-quarters of local governmental revenues. In fiscal 1969–1970, overall, property taxes in the United States accounted for $34 billion of revenue.

There are a number of other

taxes of lesser impact (for example, estate and gift taxes), but the above listing is enough to bring out the obvious point that the *way* in which taxes are raised will clearly have a significant impact on the avenues by which taxation influences aggregate demand and equilibrium national income. Thus, it may be argued that individual income taxes will tend to influence the rate of consumption most heavily, while business corporation taxes may affect retained earnings and hence business investment. The effects of a given number of dollars of taxation thus might be different both quantitatively and qualitatively depending upon which of these taxes was employed.[3]

In order to keep our overall argument clearly in mind, however, we must

3. Nor can these effects be directly deduced from the way in which the taxes appear to be levied, since tax burdens can be *shifted.* This is the large question of the *incidence* of taxation. It is very unclear, for example, whether the corporate income tax is largely borne by the corporations and their stockholders, or whether, as some have argued, it is almost entirely shifted to consumers or employees. For a discussion of these issues, see Joseph A. Pechman, *Federal Tax Policy,* rev. ed. (New York: W. W. Norton & Company, 1970), pp. 111–123.

simplify as much as possible. Let us suppose that the particular taxes that are levied fall entirely on the incomes of consumers. The government levies a tax of $30 billion on consumers in the economy. What effect will this have?

What we must do now is to reverse our field—or almost reverse it. G added demand, but T takes away income that might have added to demand. The effect of T, considered in isolation, then, is to reduce aggregate demand and hence to put a downward pressure on the economy.

The introduction of a $30 billion tax will lower equilibrium national income. Like government expenditures, taxation will have its effect magnified by the multiplier, but not in quite the same way. This is why we must "almost reverse" our field. There is a certain asymmetry in the effects of G and T. In particular, the multiplied downward effect of $1 of taxes is somewhat less than the multiplied upward effect of $1 of government expenditures.

To see why this is so, let us show how taxes affect the position of the consumption function in our case of a $30 billion levy. Figure 10-6 indicates, as we would expect, that the consumption schedule is shifted downward by the impact of taxes. At a national income of $600 billion, consumers now have at their disposal only the same amount of income that they previously had at a national income of $570 billion, the difference being the amount of the tax. Hence, their consumption demand at $600 billion will now be the same as it was previously at $570, or $513 billion. This is reflected graphically by moving horizontally to the right by the amount of T ($30 billion). (The reader should repeat this argument for other points on the consumption function; for example, the shift between $430 billion

and $400 billion national incomes.) The after-tax consumption function ($C'C'$), then, is simply the original consumption function, (CC) shifted horizontally to the right by $30 billion.

The effect of this shift on equilibrium national income is determined, however, not by rightward movements but by the *downward* shift of the schedule. It is the height of the $C + I + G$ line that ultimately determines where our equilibrium will be. Now this downward shift is not $30 billion, but $20 billion. More generally, it is equal to the MPC $\times$ T. This is easily seen in graphical terms, since the little triangles we have drawn at $600 and $430 billion represent the slope of the consumption function—the MPC—and if the horizontal side of the triangle is $30 billion, the vertical side must be $20 billion. The vertical side, of course, tells us how much the function has shifted downward.

To determine the effect of T on national income, we take this $20 billion and then multiply it by the same factor we used in the case of G; i.e., 3. The downward effect of $30 billion of T, therefore, will be $60 billion. This would be in contrast to the upward effect of an equal $30 billion of G, which would lead to a *$90 billion* increase in national income. We use the same factor (3) in each case, but we use a different starting point: $20 billion in the case of taxes, $30 billion in the case of an equivalent increase in government expenditures.

Why this asymmetry? The economic logic behind these differential effects can best be seen at the very first point of impact of G or T. When the government spends $1 to purchase some stationery for one of its offices, it has created in that very first step an added output (or income) of $1. This income then goes the rounds of consumption and saving, ac-

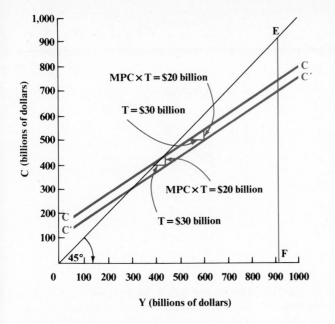

Figure 10-6. Effect of Taxes on Consumption.

A tax on consumers lowers the consumption function, but not by the full amount of the tax. If the MPC=2/3 and the tax is $30 billion, the CC curve will shift downwards by 2/3×$30 billion (=$20 billion).

cording to the multiplier principle. Now when the government taxes $1, it lowers consumption demand and income immediately, but not by the full $1. The consumer, had he not been taxed, would have *saved* part of this $1; in our case, he would have saved 33¢. This means that the initial impact of $1 taxes is to cut consumption demand not by $1 but by 67¢. And this explains why the total effect of a $30 billion tax increase in only 2/3 as great as an equivalent increase in government expenditures ($60 billion as opposed to $90 billion).[4]

---

4. When *G* and *T* are equal, we have a balanced budget in the government. The principle according to which national income will expand when there are equal increases of *G* and *T* is sometimes called the *balanced budget multiplier*. The size of this multiplier will depend very much on the kinds of taxes levied and expenditures undertaken. In our simplified case, however, the *balanced budget multiplier* will be 1. That is, an equal increase of *G* and *T* (in our case $30 billion) will lead to an increase of national income of $30 billion. This is essentially because the effects of *G* and *T* are the same, except that *G* has one extra round of impact—the very first—and in this first round the full amount of the government expenditures ($30 billion) is added to national income. Afterwards, the process cancels out as the effects of *G* and *T* match each other exactly.

G AND T COMBINED— DIFFERENT ROUTES TO MACROSTABILITY

We are now in a position to combine the effects of government expenditures and taxes and, even more important, to make some significant general comments about different kinds of fiscal policies.

Figure 10-7 represents a capsule summary of the points we have been making about the effects of government on the equilibrium level of national income. In Figure 10-7, (*a*) shows the purely private economy of the previous chapter; (*b*) introduces $30 billion of *G* without taxes; (*c*) includes $30 billion of *G* and $30 billion of *T*. This third picture shows us the effects of government when there is a balanced budget.

Now there are four main fiscal approaches an economy can use when it faces problems of unemployment and below potential national income. We can

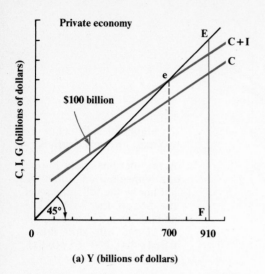

(a) Y (billions of dollars)

In (a), the problem is that, without government intervention, the private economy may not generate enough demand to produce full employment income.

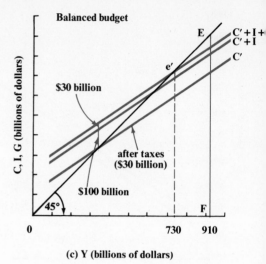

(c) Y (billions of dollars)

In (c), the same amount of *G*, *but now matched by equal taxes*, has raised national income by a lesser amount, $30 billion.

The fourth alternative—reducing taxes—can be assessed by comparing figures (b) and (c). If $30 billion in taxes from (c) are removed, then we get (b). This $30 billion tax reduction would raise national income from $730 to $790 billion, or $60 billion. (We use an MPC = 2/3, throughout.)

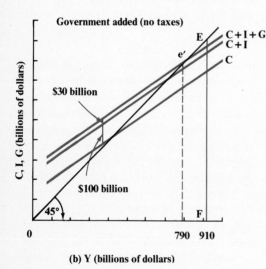

(b) Y (billions of dollars)

In (b), added *G* has increased national income by $90 billion.

Figure 10-7. Various Approaches to a Below-Capacity National Income

now state some of the advantages and disadvantages of these different approaches.

(1) *Laissez-faire or modified laissez-faire.* The most ancient approach is for the government to do nothing (always assuming, of course, some modest—or not-so-modest—role of government in defense, education, and the like). The disadvantages of this approach are quite obvious; and after the Great Depression of the 1930s, these disadvantages seem decisive to most economists. For the laissez-faire approach runs the risk of leaving the economy, as in Figure 10-7 (*a*), with substantial mass unemployment and unutilized productive capacity. The few economists who still support this view in anything like its pure form might argue either (*a*) that private recuperative forces are

much stronger than might be imagined and that, consequently, recoveries will proceed fairly quickly along natural lines; or (b) that unemployment is not too high a price to pay to avoid the encroachments of government on the private sector, or to fight inflationary price increases; or (c) that government policies, either because of political pressures or lack of information or bad timing, will not be as effective as pure theory supposes them and, indeed, may often make things worse, rather than better; or (d) that fiscal policy is basically ineffective, since it is the supply of money that crucially determines the health of the economy,[5] or, finally, (e) that no *discretionary* fiscal policy be used but that the job be left to the *automatic stabilizers* that already exist in the economy.

This last point, (e), explains why we called this first approach laissez-faire or *modified* laissez-faire. For some economists (though not many, even with this qualification) might say that although the government has a role to play in stabilizing the economy, it can fulfill this role without taking any direct or conscious action towards this end. The reason: so many government programs automatically achieve these stabilizing effects. When national income and employment go down, individual and corporate income tax receipts go down, unemployment compensation payments go up, farm subsidies go up, and so on. A recession automatically restores purchasing power to the private economy and hence moderates the fall in income and brings the economy closer to full employment than otherwise would have been the case.

The disadvantage of the modified laissez-faire approach is suggested by the word "closer" in the last sentence. For although there is no doubt that automatic stabilizers *help* in alleviating depressed conditions, there is no evidence that they can solve them completely, or even in great part.

(2) *Increase government expenditures.* The main macroeconomic advantage of an unmatched increase in government expenditures as a way of raising national income in a time of slump is that a dollar's worth of effort, so to speak, gives the maximum possible effect. In Fig 10-7(b), $30 billion of G alone raises national income by $90 billion. This is a greater impact than will result from any other policy. The disadvantages of this approach will be judged differently by different economists. The policy will ordinarily mean an expansion of the governmental national debt and will involve a greater impact of the government on the allocation of the resources of the economy. Some economists disapprove in varying degrees of both features. Other economists argue that the effects of an increased national debt may not be so harmful as generally supposed and that there are advantages in a greater public, as opposed to private, allocation of resources in an economy such as ours.

(3) *Reduce taxes.* This policy also increases the national debt (assuming that the government continues its spending unchanged); and it has the disadvantage that for a given increase in the debt, it has slightly less impact on national income than an equivalent expansion of government spending. This is because of the asymmetrical effect of T and G that we have already discussed. A reduction of taxes of $30 billion in our hypothetical economy will raise national income by $60 billion instead of by $90 billion. Another way of putting this is to say that the size of the increase in the national public debt necessary to raise national income to the full-employment level will be

5 For this last position, the position taken by some "monetarists," see p.304.

greater by this method than by the route of increased government spending. On the other hand, this method restores purchasing power to the private sector and therefore gives relatively greater private, as opposed to public, control over the allocation of resources in the economy.

(4) *Increase* G *and* T *equally.* The final basic method of using fiscal policy to cure macroeconomic ills in a depression is to expand government expenditures and taxes by the same amount. Such an expansion will lead to some expansion in the economy, although each step forward (increased government demand) is partially offset by a step backward (decreased private demand because of higher taxes). Figure 10-7(c) shows that a combined increase of $30 billion in both G and T will lead to an increase of $30 billion in national income. If we assume that the government has definitely been given the responsibility of maintaining full employment in the economy, then this approach maximizes the degree of public intervention in the economy. If the total required increase in national income is $180 billion, then the increase in governmental expenditures on this approach will have to be equal to that gap, or $180 billion. This would contrast with an increase in G unmatched by taxes, which would have to be only 1/3 of the gap, or $60 billion. Thus, a balanced budget approach involves, almost paradoxically, the highest level of governmental expenditure to achieve a given rise in national income. But then, of course, it involves no increase in the public debt.

These four approaches by no means exhaust all the steps the government might take (or not take) to deal with a problem of unemployment in the economy as a whole. There are any number of variants of tax and expenditure policies that could be used to reduce unemploy-

ment, or to achieve other objectives—say, a more equitable income distribution or a higher rate of growth—simultaneously. We must also consider the implications of increases or decreases in the national debt. These matters will be subjects for chapters later in this book.

There is one topic we must attend to now, however. This is the subject of *monetary policy.* For the government clearly can influence that national economy not only through the fiscal measures we have been discussing but also by measures designed to affect the supply of money and the interest rate in the economy. Indeed, quite apart from the issue of governmental policy, we have reached the point in our argument where we must show explicitly how "money" fits into the workings of the economy in the aggregate. When we do this, in the next chapter, we will have completed the basic structure of the theory of national income determination.

SUMMARY

In this chapter we have expanded our treatment of national income determination to include some of the effects of government tax and expenditure policy (*fiscal policy*) on the economy in the aggregate.

To make headway with this analysis, we introduced an important general tool of macroeconomics: the *multiplier.* The multiplier tells us by how much an increase in any kind of spending (consumption, investment, government) will raise the equilibrium level of national income. The size of the multiplier in a simplified economy is determined by the *marginal propensity to consume,* or the fraction of an extra dollar of income that consumers will spend on consumption. (The *marginal propensity to save*, by contrast, is the fraction of that extra dollar that consumers will be willing to save, or MPS = 1 — MPC.) The formula for the multiplier is:

$$m = \frac{1}{1-MPC}$$

or, alternatively,

$$m = \frac{1}{MPS}$$

The economic logic behind multiple expansions of national income as spending expands centers on the fact that each stage of spending creates further incomes that, in their turn, lead to further spending, further income creation, further spending, and so on. Each time, however, the amounts added to income are less because part of the income is leaked into extra savings.

With the multiplier concept, we were able to show more specifically what the effects of government expenditure and tax policies will be under certain simple circumstances. In general, the following conclusions were reached:

(1) An expansion of government expenditures (G) unmatched by an expansion of taxes would lead to a fully multiplied increase in national income.

(2) An increase of taxes (T) unmatched by G would lead to a multiplied decrease in national income, though the total effect would be somewhat less than under (1) because, in the first round, taxes cut down spending by less than the full amount of the tax. This, in turn, derives from the fact that part of the income taxed away would have been saved anyway.

(3) An equal increase of G and T will lead to some expansion of national income, but less than under an equivalent expansion of G or reduction of T taken singly. Under certain simplified conditions, an equal expansion of G and T would lead to an expansion of national income by the same amount (i.e., the multiplier in this case is 1).

In approaching the problem of underemployment, or below potential GNP, in an economy, the government may decide on many different courses; e.g., doing nothing, raising expenditures, cutting taxes, or raising both expenditures and taxes. The judgment about which policy is best to pursue in any given circumstance will be influenced by a host of considerations including confidence in the recuperative power of the private sector, desire to expand or contract the area of public intervention in the allocation of resources, one's views on the dangers of the public "national debt," one's faith in automatic stabilizers, and/or one's opinions as to the relative merits of fiscal versus monetary policy (to be discussed in chapter 11).

QUESTIONS FOR DISCUSSION

1. Imagine that there is a change in tastes resulting in an upward shift of the consumption function by $20 billion at each level of national income. Show how this could lead to an increase of $60 billion in national income if the MPC is 2/3. How much would the increase in national income be if the MPC were 4/5? 1/2? 9/10?

2. Our analysis in this chapter involved a number of simplifying assumptions. Some of the complications that may arise in reality are:

(a) The MPC falls as the level of national income rises.

(b) Investment is not a fixed amount but increases as the level of national income increases.

(c) Tax revenues of the federal government increase automatically (in the absence of any change in the tax structure) with any increase in national income.

In each case, explain why these complications may arise. Then show what the general effect of each complication would be on the graphs we have been using in this chapter. Finally, indicate the ways in which we would have to modify our multiplier analysis to take these effects into account.

3. *Discretionary fiscal policy* occurs when the government alters its tax and expenditure patterns to affect the overall stability of the economy. But we have said that there are also certain *automatic stabilizers* that work in the right direction even in the absence of any discretionary policy moves. The fact that federal income tax receipts automatically rise and fall with rises and falls in national income (see question 2c) is one such stabilizer. Name a number of other government programs that would be likely to have the effect of stabilizing the economy in this automatic way.

4. If the kind of government intervention discussed in this chapter leads to unfavorable effects on business confidence, then it could be at least partly self-defeating. In what ways do you think an active governmental fiscal policy might have an unfavorable impact on business confidence? Are there any ways in which the impact might be favorable? Is it your impression that the American business community is increasingly opposed to the "new economics"? Always was opposed to it and hasn't changed? Increasingly takes such governmental policies for granted?

10

Appendix:
Economics of the U.S. Federal
Individual Income Tax

The most important single tax in the United States, accounting for about 45 percent of federal tax revenues, is the U.S. individual income tax. The basic schedule of tax rates for the year 1971 is shown in Table 10-A. Let us make two brief comments about these rates and then present a short reading on the economic effects of this particular tax.

The first comment is to stress the fact that these rates apply to a category of "taxable income" and not to the whole of the money income received by an individual or a married couple. In order to go from an individual's entire income to his "taxable income," three basic steps are involved: (1) his gross income is *adjusted* by the exclusion of a number of categories of nontaxable income such as interest on state and local government bonds, unemployment compensation and social security transfer payments, half of the realized capital gains on certain assets, etc.; (2) from this adjusted gross income, the individual or couple is allowed to deduct certain expenditures either by a *standard deduction* (scheduled to rise to 15 percent by 1973, with a maximum of $2,000) or to *itemize* his deductions for certain medical expenses, charitable contributions, interest payments, etc.; and (3) he is also then allowed to deduct certain *personal exemptions* for himself, his spouse, his children, and other dependents (sched-

uled to rise to $750 each in 1973). It is only after these operations have been performed that the category of "taxable income" in Table 10-A is reached.

The second comment is related to the first in the sense that it stresses the difference between the actually effective tax rates individuals pay and what appears in the Tax Table. Because of the various provisions of the tax laws having to do with deductions, capital gains, income-splitting, and other special situations, the maximum actual tax rate for even the highest income classes is not the 70 percent shown on Table 10-A but 34 percent.[1] Thus, although many commentators still regard the individual income tax as one of our fairer taxes (compared, say, to indirect taxes, which tend to be regressive in their effects), it is still much less progressive in practice than it might seem to be in its theoretical structure.[2]

The following reading by one of the nation's outstanding tax authorities, Joseph A. Pechman, considers some of the economic aspects of the federal income tax, including its effects on macroeconomic stability.

---

1. Joseph A. Pechman, *Federal Tax Policy,* pp. 68–69.

2. Roughly speaking, the individual income tax tends to be most progressive—i.e., to take a higher percentage of higher incomes—in the range of incomes up to $100,000 or $200,000 a year. This effect seems largely to disappear with very high incomes.

Table 10A: 1971 TAX RATE SCHEDULES FOR U.S. INDIVIDUAL INCOME TAX

1 — Single Taxpayers

Taxable Income Over-	But not over-		Of excess over-
0	$500	14%	0
$500	$1,000	$70 + 15%	$500
$1,000	$1,500	$145 + 16%	$1,000
$1,500	$2,000	$225 + 17%	$1,500
$2,000	$4,000	$310 + 19%	$2,000
$4,000	$6,000	$690 + 21%	$4,000
$6,000	$8,000	$1,110 + 24%	$6,000
$8,000	$10,000	$1,590 + 25%	$8,000
$10,000	$12,000	$2,090 + 27%	$10,000
$12,000	$14,000	$2,630 + 29%	$12,000
$14,000	$16,000	$3,210 + 31%	$14,000
$16,000	$18,000	$3,830 + 34%	$16,000
$18,000	$20,000	$4,510 + 36%	$18,000
$20,000	$22,000	$5,230 + 38%	$20,000
$22,000	$26,000	$5,990 + 40%	$22,000
$26,000	$32,000	$7,590 + 45%	$26,000
$32,000	$38,000	$10,290 + 50%	$32,000
$38,000	$44,000	$13,290 + 55%	$38,000
$44,000	$50,000	$16,590 + 60%	$44,000
$50,000	$60,000	$20,190 + 62%	$50,000
$60,000	$70,000	$26,390 + 64%	$60,000
$70,000	$80,000	$32,790 + 66%	$70,000
$80,000	$90,000	$39,390 + 68%	$80,000
$90,000	$100,000	$46,190 + 69%	$90,000
$100,000	.....	$53,090 + 70%	$100,000

2 — Married Taxpayers (Separate Returns)

Taxable Income Over-	But not over-		Of excess over-
0	$500	14%	0
$500	$1,000	$70 + 15%	$500
$1,000	$1,500	$145 + 16%	$1,000
$1,500	$2,000	$225 + 17%	$1,500
$2,000	$4,000	$310 + 19%	$2,000
$4,000	$6,000	$690 + 22%	$4,000
$6,000	$8,000	$1,130 + 25%	$6,000
$8,000	$10,000	$1,630 + 28%	$8,000
$10,000	$12,000	$2,190 + 32%	$10,000
$12,000	$14,000	$2,830 + 36%	$12,000
$14,000	$16,000	$3,550 + 39%	$14,000
$16,000	$18,000	$4,330 + 42%	$16,000
$18,000	$20,000	$5,170 + 45%	$18,000
$20,000	$22,000	$6,070 + 48%	$20,000
$22,000	$26,000	$7,030 + 50%	$22,000
$26,000	$32,000	$9,030 + 53%	$26,000
$32,000	$38,000	$12,210 + 55%	$32,000
$38,000	$44,000	$15,510 + 58%	$38,000
$44,000	$50,000	$18,990 + 60%	$44,000
$50,000	$60,000	$22,590 + 62%	$50,000
$60,000	$70,000	$28,790 + 64%	$60,000
$70,000	$80,000	$35,190 + 66%	$70,000
$80,000	$90,000	$41,790 + 68%	$80,000
$90,000	$100,000	$48,590 + 69%	$90,000
$100,000	.....	$55,490 + 70%	$100,000

3 — Married Taxpayers (Joint Returns)

Taxable Income Over-	But not over-		Of excess over-
0	$1,000	14%	0
$1,000	$2,000	$140 + 15%	$1,000
$2,000	$3,000	$290 + 16%	$2,000
$3,000	$4,000	$450 + 17%	$3,000
$4,000	$8,000	$620 + 19%	$4,000
$8,000	$12,000	$1,380 + 22%	$8,000
$12,000	$16,000	$2,260 + 25%	$12,000
$16,000	$20,000	$3,260 + 28%	$16,000
$20,000	$24,000	$4,380 + 32%	$20,000
$24,000	$28,000	$5,660 + 36%	$24,000
$28,000	$32,000	$7,100 + 39%	$28,000
$32,000	$36,000	$8,660 + 42%	$32,000
$36,000	$40,000	$10,340 + 45%	$36,000
$40,000	$44,000	$12,140 + 48%	$40,000
$44,000	$52,000	$14,060 + 50%	$44,000
$52,000	$64,000	$18,060 + 53%	$52,000
$64,000	$76,000	$24,420 + 55%	$64,000
$76,000	$88,000	$31,020 + 58%	$76,000
$88,000	$100,000	$37,980 + 60%	$88,000
$100,000	$120,000	$45,180 + 62%	$100,000
$120,000	$140,000	$57,580 + 64%	$120,000
$140,000	$160,000	$70,380 + 66%	$140,000
$160,000	$180,000	$83,580 + 68%	$160,000
$180,000	$200,000	$97,180 + 69%	$180,000
$200,000	.....	$110,980 + 70%	$200,000

ECONOMIC EFFECTS OF THE INDIVIDUAL INCOME TAX

JOSEPH A. PECHMAN

Three issues are of particular importance in appraising the economic effects of the individual income tax: its role as a stabilizer of consumption expenditures, its effect on saving, and its impact on work and investment incentives.

ROLE AS STABILIZER

Stability of yield was once regarded as a major criterion of a good tax. Today there is general agreement that properly timed changes in tax yields can help increase demand during recessions and restrain the growth of demand during periods of expansion. The progressive individual income tax has the virtue that its yield automatically rises and falls more than in proportion to changes in personal income. Moreover, the system of paying taxes currently has greatly accelerated the reaction of income tax revenues to changes in income. An important by-product of current payment is that changes in tax rates have an almost immediate effect on the disposable income of most taxpayers. These features have made the personal income tax extremely useful for promoting economic stabilization and growth.

The automatic response of the individual income tax—its *built-in flexibility*—can be explained by the following example. Suppose a taxpayer with a wife and two children earns $10,000 a year when he is em-

Excerpted from Joseph A. Pechman, *Federal Tax Policy*, rev. ed. pp. 62–67, Brookings Institution. © 1971 by the Brookings Institution, Washington, D.C. Reprinted by permission of the publisher.

ployed and uses the standard deduction. His taxable income is $5,500 ($10,000 less $1,500 for the standard deduction and $3,000 for the personal exemptions), and the tax under 1973 rates and exemptions is $905. The following table shows what the effect on his taxable income and tax would be if his income dropped to $8,000:

Adjusted gross income	$10,000	$8,000
Less exemptions	3,000	3,000
Less standard deduction	1,500	1,200
Taxable income	5,500	3,800
Tax	905	586
Disposable income	9,095	7,414

Whereas adjusted gross income declined by only 20 percent, taxable income declined 31 percent (from $5,500 to $3,800), and the tax declined 35 percent.

Such examples are multiplied millions of times during a recession, while the opposite occurs during boom periods. Those with lower or higher incomes find that their tax is reduced or increased proportionately more than their income. As a result, disposable income is more stable than it would be in the absence of the tax. (In the above example, disposable income declined only $1,681 while income before tax declined $2,000.) Since disposable income is the major determinant of consumption, expenditures by consumers are also more stable than they would be in the absence of the tax.

Individual income tax rate changes are also used to restrain or stimulate the economy. The Revenue Act of 1964 reduced tax receipts by $11.4 billion, of which the individual income tax reduction accounted for $9.2 billion. The Vietnam war surtax, which was enacted in 1968 to reduce inflationary pressures, increased tax receipts by a total of $10.2 billion, including $6.8 billion of individual income tax. The tax cut was designed to raise the level of expenditures by consumers and businessmen and thus to stimulate a higher rate of economic growth. Consumer expenditures had already increased in anticipation of the tax cut when it went into effect for withholding purposes early in March 1964; in the succeeding year, they rose $28 billion. While the increase in consumption cannot be attributed wholly to the tax cut, this was undoubtedly the most important factor. However, the Vietnam war surtax did not have a major effect on spending, because monetary policy was relaxed prematurely and because expectations of inflation were more pervasive than had been anticipated. Those who believe that consumption is determined largely by what individuals regard as their "permanent" income argue that the surtax was not effective because it was a temporary tax change. Nevertheless, most people are persuaded that income tax changes can have a significant effect in helping to regulate the rate of growth of private demand, but that the effect is greater for permanent than for temporary changes.

Countercyclical changes in tax rates seem to be rare in most countries, partly because there are long delays in recognizing significant changes in economic conditions and partly because the legislative process is too slow. However, it should be possible to devise procedures for varying tax rates quickly in response to changes in the level of economic activity.

EFFECT ON SAVING AND CONSUMPTION

The individual income tax applies to the entire income of an individual whether it is spent or saved. Some have argued that the income tax is unfair to those who save because it applies both to the income that gives rise to the saving and to the income produced by the saving. But almost all economists now agree that, on equity grounds, this double taxation argument does not have much merit. At any particular point in time, an individual has the option to make a new decision to spend or save from the income that is left to him after tax. If he decides to save the income, he does not necessarily incur a new tax. It is only if the saving is invested in an income-producing asset that new income is generat-

ed, and this new income is subject to additional tax.

The individual income tax is often contrasted with a general consumption or expenditure tax, which is an alternative method of taxing individuals in accordance with "ability to pay." In the case of the income tax, the measure of ability to pay is income; in the case of the expenditure tax, the measure is consumption. The tax on consumption may also be levied at progressive rates (but the rates must be greater than 100 percent to equal the impact of the progressive income tax in the higher brackets).

Consumption taxes can be avoided simply by reducing one's consumption. This means that an expenditure tax encourages saving more than does an equal-yield income tax that is distributed in the same proportions by income classes. In practice, where the income tax is paid by the large mass of the people, much of the tax yield comes from income classes where there is little room in family budgets for increasing saving in response to tax incentives. As a consequence, the differential effect on total consumption and saving between an income tax and an equal-yield expenditure tax is likely to be small in this country.

Economics alone does not provide a basis for deciding whether the income tax is more or less "equitable" than an expenditure tax. The income tax reduces the gain made when an individual saves rather than consumes part of his income, while an expenditure tax makes future consumption relatively as attractive as present consumption. Under the income tax, the interest reward for saving and investing is reduced by the tax; under the expenditure tax, the net reward is always equal to the market rate of interest regardless of the tax rate.

While this subject has not been widely discussed in the United States, the continued heavy reliance on the income tax suggests that it is probably more acceptable on equity grounds than an expenditure tax. An expenditure tax was recommended by the Treasury during World War II, but it was rejected by the Congress primarily because of its novelty and complexity.

Graduated expenditure taxes are often proposed as a method of avoiding or correcting the defects of the income tax base, particularly in the top brackets, where the preferential treatment of capital gains, tax-exempt interest, depletion allowances, and other favorable provisions permit the accumulation of large fortunes with little or no payment of income tax. An expenditure tax would reach such incomes when they are spent without resort to regressive taxation. Despite this advantage, the expenditure tax has not been widely used. It is more difficult to administer and also raises more serious problems of compliance for the taxpayer. Although it is difficult to imagine total replacement of the income tax by an expenditure tax, the latter might be a useful supplement if and when it became necessary to discourage consumption. ...

WORK AND INVESTMENT INCENTIVES

The individual income tax affects economic incentives in two different directions. On the one hand, it reduces the financial rewards of greater effort and risk-taking and thus tends to discourage these activities. On the other hand, it may provide a greater incentive to obtain more income because it cuts down on the income left over for spending. There is no basis for deciding which effect is more important on an a priori basis.

Taxation is only one of many factors affecting work and investment incentives. This makes it extremely difficult to interpret the available statistical evidence or the results of direct interviews with taxpayers. The evidence suggests that income taxation does not significantly reduce the amount of labor supplied by workers and managers. Work habits are not easily changed, and there is little scope in a modern industrial society for most people to vary their hours of work or the intensity of their efforts in response to changes in tax rates. Nearly all people who are asked about income taxation grumble about it, but relatively few say that they work fewer hours or exert less than their best efforts to avoid tax.

As for risk-taking, the problem is much more complicated. In the first place, the tax rates on capital gains are much lower than those on ordinary incomes. Numerous studies have demonstrated that the opportunity to earn income in the form of capital gains stimulates investment and risk-taking. Second, taxpayers may offset business losses against ordinary income not only for the current year but also for three prior years and five succeeding years; capital losses may similarly be offset against capital gains, and half of these losses (up to $1,000 a year) may be offset against ordinary income for an indefinite period. Such offsets greatly diminish the consequences of loss by the investor. Third, much of the nation's investment is undertaken by large corporations. These firms are generally permitted to retain earnings after payment of tax at the corporation rate, which is more moderate than the rates applying to investors in the top personal income tax brackets. Finally, the law provides incentives to invest through generous depreciation allowances. In any case, experience suggests that the major stimulus to investment comes from a healthy and prosperous economy.

Much can be done to improve the structure of the income tax. But there is little basis for the assertions made from time to time that the income tax has had an adverse effect on the economy.

11
Money and
Monetary Policy

In the preceding four chapters, we have been setting out the basic structure of national income analysis and the relationship of this analysis to public policy. Our presentation so far has a basic limitation: it has omitted any explicit discussion of the role of "money" in the national economy. This omission of money in our analysis is a particularly serious one. Economists always have been concerned with this topic, and, indeed, it was in connection with speculations about the impact of "treasure" on the national economy that many of the first steps in the field were taken.[1] Furthermore, the development of the modern theory of national income determination is specifically related to certain developments in the theory of money. We mentioned when we were discussing the work of John Maynard Keynes that one of the main things he

did was to try to provide a synthesis of *real* and *monetary* analysis—attempting to show the impact of financial mechanisms and institutions on *real* things like output and employment. And, finally, we know from our reading of the newspapers that the management of our country's money supply is considered of vital importance to our overall economic health. *Monetary policy* is concerned with action designed to affect both the level of the interest rate and the size and availability of the money supply in the national economy. *Monetary policy* must be put next to *fiscal policy* (the government tax and expenditure programs we have just been discussing) as one of the main avenues by which the government can influence the overall level of employment, output, and prices in the nation.

Despite the importance of money and the long history of attempts to define its economic impact, however, it cannot be said that economists are agreed on the extent of that impact or even the avenues by which it is felt. The discussion to be presented in this chapter would be accepted in broad outline by most econo-

---

1. The so-called *mercantilist* writers of the sixteenth and seventeenth centuries, who antedated the classical school, devoted great attention to the problem of money—especially in the form of the precious metals. They also devoted great attention to problems of international trade, as we shall notice later on.

mists, but certainly not by all. The controversy over money and monetary policy—which has been described as the most highly contested issue in modern macroeconomics—will be taken up in chapter 13 and in Great Debate Two on Monetarism (pp. 305-33). So as not to interrupt the flow of the argument, we shall postpone qualifications to this chapter's analysis until then.

MONEY AND BANKS

Many different commodities have served as "money" in different cultures and times: paper, gold, other metals, cattle, shells, beads, etc. In an article written just after World War II, a British economist described the elaborate use of cigarettes as a currency in a prisoner of war camp.[2] Economists often distinguish a number of important functions that money serves: (1) a *measure of value* (prices are quoted in money); (2) a *medium of exchange* (money is acceptable for exchanges against all types of different commodities); and (3) a *store of value* (savings may be kept in the form of money for future purchases). In the POW camp, cigarettes served all these functions—prices, for example, were generally quoted in terms of cigarettes rather than in terms of particular commodities that might be bartered against each other. But cigarettes also suffered from some difficulties in serving as money. For one thing, like gold coins in the hands of a deceitful sovereign, they could be "clipped" or, more likely, "sweated by rolling them between the fingers so that tobacco fell out." More serious was the fact that they were

a very desirable commodity in their own right. When the Red Cross packages (the main source of the supply of cigarettes) failed to arrive, the smokers were likely to take over the nation's money supply:

Consequently our economy was repeatedly subject to deflation and to periods of monetary stringency. While the Red Cross issue of fifty or twenty-five cigarettes per man per week came in regularly, and while there were fair stocks held, the cigarette currency suited its purpose admirably. But when the issue was interrupted, stocks soon ran out, prices fell, trading declined in volume and became increasingly a matter of barter. This deflationary tendency was periodically offset by the sudden injection of new currency. Several hundred thousand cigarettes might arrive in the space of a fortnight. Prices soared, and then began to fall, slowly at first but with increasing rapidity as stocks ran out, until the next big delivery. Most of our economic troubles could be attributed to this fundamental instability.

The point of these comments about cigarettes is that, while almost any commodity *can* serve as money, not all commodities can serve money's functions equally well. In the old days, gold and other metals were valued as money because they had some useful value of their own, and were also durable and relatively easily divisible. In the American economy of today, although the dollar retains a vague (and recently changing) connection to gold, we no longer use gold as a medium of exchange within our domestic economy, nor for that matter is currency in the form of coins *or* bills the main source of our "money." For this, we have to go to our banking system. Important characteristics of the American money supply and how it is brought into being are described in the following reading from the Federal Reserve Bank of Chicago:

2. R. A. Radford, "The Economic Organization of a P.O.W. Camp," *Economica* vol. XII (1945), reprinted in Paul A. Samuelson, ed., *Readings in Economics*, 6th ed. (New York: McGraw-Hill, 1970), pp. 40-48.

MONEY AND ITS CREATION

FEDERAL RESERVE BANK OF CHICAGO

WHAT IS MONEY?

If money is viewed simply as a tool used to facilitate transactions, only those media that are readily accepted in exchange for goods, services and other assets need to be considered. Many things—from stones to cigarettes—have served this monetary function through the ages. Today, in the United States, there are only two kinds of money in use in significant amounts—currency (paper money and coins in the pockets and purses of the public) and demand deposits (checking accounts in commercial banks).

The amount of currency in use at any time depends solely on the public's preferences. Since currency and demand deposits are freely convertible into each other at the option of the holder, both are money to an equal degree. However, for specific transactions, one form may be more convenient than the other. When a depositor "cashes" a check, he reduces the amount of deposits and increases the amount of currency in circulation. Conversely, when more currency is in circulation than is needed, some is returned to the banks in exchange for deposits. Currency held in bank vaults is not a part of the money supply available for spending by the nonbank public.

While currency is used for a great variety of small transactions, most of the dollar volume of money payments in our economy is made by check.*

WHAT MAKES MONEY VALUABLE?

Neither paper currency nor deposits have value as a commodity. Intrinsically, a dollar bill is just a piece of paper. Deposits are merely book entries. Coins do have some intrinsic value as metal, but considerably less than their face amount.

What, then, makes these instruments—checks, paper money and coins—acceptable at face value in payment of all debts and for other monetary uses? Mainly, it is the confidence people have that they will be able to exchange such money for real goods and services whenever they choose to do so. This is partly a matter of law; currency has been designated "legal tender" by the Government. Paper currency is a liability of the Government, and demand deposits are liabilities of the commercial banks which stand ready to convert such deposits into currency or transfer their ownership at the request of depositors. Confidence in these forms of money seems also to be tied in some way to the fact that there are assets on the books of the Government and the banks equal to the amount of money outstanding, even though most of these assets themselves are no more than pieces of paper (such as customers' promissory notes) and it is well understood that money is not redeemable in them.

But the real source of money's value is neither its commodity content nor what people think stands behind it. Commodities or services are more or less valuable because there are more or less of them relative to the amounts people want. Money,

---

Excerpted from **Modern Money Mechanics: A Workbook of Deposits, Currency, and Bank Reserves**, Federal Reserve Bank of Chicago, September 1971, pp. 2-5. Reprinted by permission of the publisher.

---

*[Seventy-seven percent, or $176 billion, of the $228 billion total money supply at the end of 1971 was in the form of demand deposits.]

like anything else, derives its value from its scarcity in relation to its usefulness. Money's usefulness is its unique ability to command other goods and services and to permit a holder to be constantly ready to do so. How much is needed depends on the total volume of transactions in the economy at any given time and the amount of money individuals and businesses want to keep on hand to take care of unexpected or future transactions.

In order to keep the value of money stable, it is essential that the quantity be controlled. Money's value can be measured only in terms of what it will buy. Therefore, changes in its value vary inversely with the general level of prices. If the volume of money rises faster (assuming a constant rate of use) than the production of real goods and services grows under the limitations of time and physical facilities, prices will rise because there is more money per unit of goods. Such a development would reduce the value of money even though the monetary unit were backed by and redeemable in the soundest assets imaginable. But if, on the other hand, growth in the supply of money does not keep pace with the economy's current production, either prices will fall or, more likely, some resources and production facilities will be less than fully employed.

Just how large the stock of money needs to be in order to handle the work of the economy without exerting undue influence on the price level depends on how intensively the supply is being used. All demand deposits and currency are a part of somebody's spendable funds at any given time, moving from one owner to another as transactions take place. Some holders spend money quickly after they get it, making these dollars available for other uses. Others, however, hold dollars for longer periods.

Obviously, when dollars move into hands where they do little or no work more of them are needed to accomplish any given volume of transactions.

WHO IS RESPONSIBLE FOR THE CREATION OF MONEY?

Changes in the quantity of money may originate with actions of the Federal Reserve System (the central bank), the commercial banks or the public, but the major control rests with the central bank.

The actual process of money creation takes place in the commercial banks. As noted earlier, the demand liabilities of commercial banks are money. They are book entries which result from the crediting of deposits of currency and checks and the proceeds of loans and investments to customers' accounts. Banks can build up deposits by increasing loans and investments so long as they keep enough currency on hand to redeem whatever amounts the holders of deposits want to convert into currency.

This unique attribute of the banking business was discovered several centuries ago. At one time bankers were merely middlemen. They made a profit by accepting gold and coins brought to them for safekeeping and lending them to borrowers. But they soon found that the receipts they issued to depositors were being used as a means of payment. These receipts were acceptable as money since whoever held them could go to the banker and exchange them for metallic money.

Then, bankers discovered that they could make loans merely by giving borrowers their promises to pay (bank notes). In this way banks began to create money. More notes could be issued than the gold and coin on hand because only a portion of the notes outstanding would be presented for payment at any one time. Enough metallic money had to be kept on hand, of course, to redeem whatever volume of notes was presented for payment.

Deposits are the modern counterpart of bank notes. It was a small step from printing notes to making book entries to the credit of borrowers which could be spent by the use of checks.

WHAT LIMITS THE AMOUNT OF MONEY BANKS CAN CREATE?

If deposit money can be created so easily, what is to prevent banks from making too much, i.e., more than is needed to handle the volume of transactions resulting from optimum use of the nation's productive resources at stable prices? Like its predecessor, the modern bank must keep a considerable amount of currency (or balances with the central bank) on hand. It must be prepared to convert deposit money into currency for those depositors who request currency. It must make remittance on checks written by depositors and presented for payment by other banks (settle adverse clearings). Finally, a member bank* must maintain legal reserves equal to some prescribed percentage of deposits.

How do operating needs and legal requirements affect the amount of deposits that the commercial banking system can create? The public's demand for currency varies greatly, but generally follows a seasonal pattern which is quite predictable. The effects of these swings are usually offset by central bank action and are thus prevented from causing large temporary fluctuations in the quantity of money. Moreover, for all banks taken together, there is no net drain of funds

*For reasons of simplicity, all commercial banks are assumed to be members of the Federal Reserve System.

Although coins and currency are familiar forms of money, the most common form in the United States is demand deposits (our checking accounts).

through clearings. A check drawn on one bank will normally be deposited to the credit of another account in the same or another bank. The main factor, therefore, which limits the ability of the banking system to increase demand deposits by expanding loans and investments is the reserves that banks must hold against deposits.

Growth of deposits can continue only to the point where existing reserves are just sufficient to satisfy legal requirements. If reserves of 20 percent are required, for example, total deposits can expand only until they are five times as large as reserves. Ten million dollars of "excess" reserves, i.e., reserves in excess of the 20 percent requirement, could support up to $50 million of additional deposits. The lower the percentage requirement, the greater the expansion power of each reserve dollar. It is this "fractional-reserve system" that sets the potentials and the limits to money creation.

WHAT ARE BANK RESERVES?

Currency held in member bank vaults may be counted as legal reserves. The major part of member bank reserves, however, is in the form of deposits (reserve balances) at the Federal Reserve Banks. A bank can always obtain reserve balances by sending currency to the Reserve Bank and can obtain currency by drawing on its reserve balance. Because either can be used to support a much larger volume of ordinary bank deposits, currency and member bank reserve balances together are often referred to as "high-powered money."

For individual banks, reserve balances serve as clearing accounts. Member banks may increase their reserve balances by depositing checks, as well as currency. Banks may draw down these balances by writing checks on them or by authorizing a debit to them in payment for currency or remittance for customers' checks.

Despite the fact that reserve accounts are used as working balances, over every reserve period (one week for city banks and two weeks for country banks) each bank must maintain average reserve balances and vault cash which together are equal to the percentage of its deposit liabilities required by law.

WHERE DO BANK RESERVES COME FROM?

Changes in bank reserves reflect the net effect of a number of factors, but the essential point from the standpoint of money creation is that the reserves of commercial banks are, for the most part, liabilities of the Federal Reserve Banks and that their volume is largely determined by actions of the Federal Reserve System. Thus, the Reserve System, through its ability to vary both the total volume of reserves and the required ratio of reserves to deposit liabilities, influences the amount of bank assets and deposits. One of the major responsibilities of the Federal Reserve System is to provide a sufficient but not excessive amount of reserves to permit deposit expansion at a rate that will serve the needs of a growing economy while maintaining reasonable price stability. Such actions take into consideration, of course, any changes in the pace at which money is being used.

But a given increase in bank reserves does not necessarily cause an expansion in the money supply equal to the theoretical potential as determined by the legal ratio of reserves to demand deposits. What happens to the money supply will vary, depending upon the reaction of the commercial banks and the public. A number of leakages may occur. How many reserves will be drained into the public's currency holdings? To what extent will the increase in the reserve base remain unused as excess reserves? Which banks will gain the reserves? How much will be absorbed by time deposits against which, though they are not money, banks must also hold reserves?* The answers to these questions hold the explanation as to why deposit changes may be smaller than expected or may develop only with a considerable time lag.

---

*On some definitions, time deposits are also considered part of the "money supply." See p. 303.

THE ROLE OF MONEY— A SYNOPSIS

The above reading brings out a number of points that can guide us in trying to understand the complex role of money in our present-day economy. We now know that demand deposits in the commercial banks are a more important form of money than currency and that the central responsibility for regulating the money supply of the United States lies with the Federal Reserve System. It has also been suggested that expanding the quantity of money will tend to lead towards rising prices and more output and employment, while contracting the quantity of money may tend to lead to falling prices and national income.

But why? The best approach to this difficult matter is to sketch out the picture as a whole very quickly and then to come back and look at the details. Let us put the issue in this particular way:

How is the monetary policy of a government like that of the United States supposed in theory to affect the level of prices, output, and employment in the economy as a whole? By what chain of logic does government action affecting the money supply reach down into the economy and influence such important variables as the number of jobs available or the number of tons of steel produced or the cost-of-living index?

The chain of logic connecting these different variables can then be set out in four basic propositions. These are:

(1) An increase in the quantity of money, *cet. par.*, will generally cause a fall in the interest rate.

(2) A fall in the interest rate, *cet. par.*, will generally cause an expansion of business investment.

(3) An expansion of business investment, *cet. par.*, will generally cause an expansion of GNP and employment.

These first three points indicate that the basic direction of monetary policy in a depression or recession should be ex-

pansionary. According to these points, an expanded money supply will lead through changes in the interest rate and business investment to a higher level of GNP and employment in a previously depressed economy. A fourth point deals with the opposite problem of inflation—i.e., when there is not too little but too much aggregate demand.

(4) When the quantity of money is decreased, the opposite effects will generally occur; that is, a decrease in the money supply will cause a rise in the rate of interest, which will cause a fall in business investment, which, in turn, will cause a fall in GNP and employment or, if the problem is inflation, a reduction of inflationary pressures.

Since one would normally follow a contractionary monetary policy in an inflation and since the problem of inflation will be the subject of chapter 14 we shall concentrate for the moment solely on the first three points.

Each of these points represents one important link in the chain of logic connecting the money supply with national income and employment. As far as our understanding is concerned, these links are of very different degrees of difficulty, particularly in view of what we have already accomplished in earlier chapters. To make things as clear as possible, let us take up these links in the order of less to greater difficulty of understanding; this will mean proceding in the reverse order, beginning with point (3) and ending with point (1).

THE INVESTMENT-GNP LINK

The easiest link for us to understand is clearly that expressed in point (3):

An expansion of business investment, cet. par., *will generally cause an expansion of GNP and employment.*

This is nothing but our theory of national income determination again. Figure 11-1 is similar to diagrams we have used many times before, the difference being that we have put investment on the top, so that we could show more clearly the effects of an increase of investment. If investment goes up by whatever amount, national income will rise by a multiplied amount, the multiplier being determined in the simplest case by the formula:

$$m = \frac{1}{1 - MPC}$$

In this particular diagram, MPC = 2/3, and m = 3, the increase in investment is $25 billion and the resulting increase of equilibrium national income is $75 billion. This should be completely familiar to us from our previous work.

THE INTEREST RATE–INVESTMENT LINK

The next easiest link, though one we shall want to say a few words about, is that expressed in point (2):

A fall in the interest rate, cet. par., *will generally cause an expansion of business investment.*

Point (3) was about the *effects* of an increase in investment; this point is about the *causes* of an increase in investment. What is the logic behind the interest rate–investment link?

Actually, we have already discussed this matter briefly (chapter 9), but there are two further comments, one a clarification, the other a qualification, that we should add here.

The clarification has to do with ascertaining the *direction* in which changing interest rates move the level of investment. There is a potential possibility of misunderstanding here, largely because of the different ways we use the term "investment" in everyday discourse. Nowhere is it more important than now to remember our earlier distinction between "financial" investment (buying a stock or a bond) and ordinary business investment (building a new factory, adding to one's inventories of goods in stock, etc.). The reason for this special caution is that the effect of changes in the rate of interest will be very different—in fact, ordinarily in opposite directions—depending on which kind of investment one has in mind.

To make this point clear, let us consider "financial" investment first. Now from the point of view of the "financial investor" a high rate of interest is a good thing. The issue before him is not whether or not to build a factory, but whether or not to buy a bond. If the interest rate is high, this will not discourage him from buying the bond; on the contrary, it will ordinarily make him eager to do so. At 4 percent interest, he gets $4 a year by putting $100 into a bond. At 6 percent, he gets $6 a year from the same $100. In certain circumstances, this difference may induce him to buy an extra bond or two. The point is that for the "financial investor," the interest rate appears as a *payment* for the use of the money he has lent.

It is just the reverse when we come to investment in the ordinary sense in which we have been using the term—i.e., the actual adding of new productive capacity to our economy. For when we talk about this kind of investment we are approaching everything from the point of

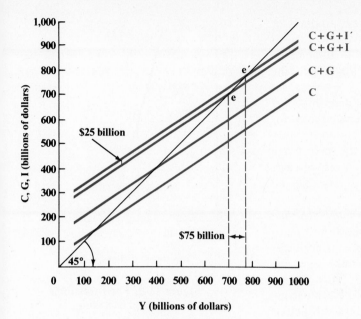

Figure 11-1. Effects of an Increase in Investment on National Income.

view not of the lender but of the borrower. The businessman wishes to borrow money to expand his productive capacity. To say that the interest rate has gone up is nothing but to say that the *costs* of borrowing have gone up. As a businessman, you wish, say, to invest in a new machine that costs $1,000. You go to the bank to finance this purchase with a loan. If the bank charges you 4 percent on the loan, then you have to pay out interest charges of $40 per year on the machine. If the rate is 6 percent, you have to pay out $60 a year. It may be the case that the machine will be just profitable to you at 4 percent, but not profitable at 6 percent, and decidedly unprofitable at 7 percent or 8 percent. A high interest rate then is not an encouragement but a definite *dis*couragement as far as ordinary business investment is concerned.

This clarification should make it apparent that the direction of changes in investment in this second sense will be in the opposite direction from changes in the rate of interest. A high interest rate will

tend to discourage investment. A low interest rate—meaning that the costs of borrowing are low—will tend to foster higher levels of investment. And this, in fact, is precisely what our point (2) states.

We now ask: how *great* an effect on investment will these changes in the interest rate have? And this leads us to a certain qualification that should be made in connection with point (2). For although the *direction* of this effect is now perfectly clear, it is much less certain how *large* that effect will be.

The problem, essentially, is that there are many different factors that influence business investment, and the interest rate is only one—in many circumstances not the most important one. We have mentioned some of these factors before: business expectations, technological progress, amount of retained profits, and, of course, the interest rate. If, say, business expectations are sufficiently pessimistic, then it may be that investment will stay small no matter how enticingly low the interest rate may be. Conversely, if there

257

are certain remarkable new products or processes available for investment, businessmen may be difficult to discourage, no matter what (within limits) are the costs of borrowing.

A technical way of describing this is to say that investment demand may, for wide ranges of different interest rates, be *interest-inelastic*; i.e., the percentage change in investment for a given percentage change in the interest rate may be quite small.[3]

An *investment demand schedule* displaying this feature is shown in Figure 11-2. The amount of investment businessmen are willing to undertake does increase with lower interest rates as we would expect; however, the percentage increase is rather slight. Thus, a substantial percentage reduction in the interest rate (from 5-1/2 to 4 percent) brings only a few billion dollars increase in investment.[4]

This does not mean that our point (2) is incorrect. It simply means that the strength of this link may not be great. If under particular circumstances a fall in the rate of interest produces only a modest increase in investment, then clearly this will limit the results we can hope for when we are trying to cure unemployment by interest rate changes.

The reader should notice that points (3) and (2) combined suggest that—other things equal—different levels of the interest rate will lead to different levels of national income. High interest rates will produce low levels of investment that, via the multiplier, will produce low

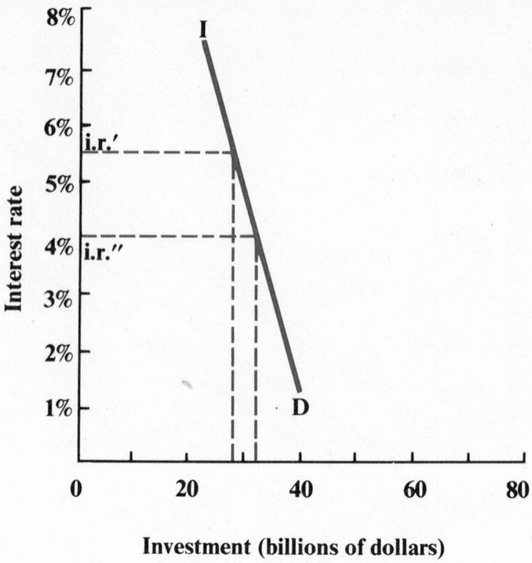

Figure 11-2. The Investment Demand Schedule.

levels of national income;[5] and conversely for low interest rates. However, this is only *half* the picture. For now we must turn to the crucial factor of the money supply itself.

MONEY SUPPLY–INTEREST RATE LINK

We are now ready to discuss point (1), the money supply–interest rate link. And here we shall have to linger a moment. For it is at this juncture that the role of money at last enters explicitly into our picture. Point (1) states:

An increase in the quantity of money, cet. par., will generally cause a fall in the interest rate.

If we can establish this point in a general way, then we shall have succeeded in building our logical chain from money, on

---

3. For a discussion of concepts of *elasticity*, see pp. 102–103.

4. The effect of interest changes will often be different depending upon the type of investment involved. Thus, while business spending on plant and equipment may be relatively insensitive to the interest rate, construction investment may be quite sensitive. See pp. 346–47.

5. This relationship is treated graphically in the appendix to this chapter. See pp. 270–74.

the one side, to national income, employment, and prices, on the other.

Now the way we shall analyze the effects of an increase in the quantity of money in the economy is by considering the manner in which such an increase might actually take place in the present-day American economy. We have earlier established that the responsible agency for managing the money supply in the United States is the *Federal Reserve System*. The Federal Reserve Banks were established in this country in 1913. They are ultimately responsible to Congress, and they usually work in cooperation with the president and the secretary of the treasury, although there have been times when there has been disagreement among these parties concerning what monetary policy should be followed. The Federal Reserve Board, or the *Fed*, as it is commonly called, is the institution through which an increase in our money supply would normally be initiated.

To understand the leverage that the Federal Reserve Board has over our money supply, we must recall two other points we mentioned before. The first point is that the most common form of money in this country is not cash or currency but *demand deposits. Demand deposits* are our checking accounts at the bank—they are payable by check "on demand." These deposits are as generally acceptable as hard cash for settling financial transactions in this country at the present time,[6] and are much more widely used than cash.

The second point to remember is that banks are legally required to hold certain *reserves* against their demand deposits. In 1970, city banks were required to have reserves equal to 17-1/2 percent of their demand deposits, and country banks had to have 13 percent. The need for some reserves is fairly obvious. Although deposits and withdrawals may often cancel out, nevertheless there are periods when particular banks face an excess of withdrawals or, indeed, when the banking system as a whole is faced with a run on the system. The required reserves of the commercial banks that are members of the Federal Reserve System are a defense against such occasional (but historically often serious) problems. What we must notice particularly, however, is the composition of these reserves. In the case of a member bank, the basic form of these reserves is not cash or currency (although most banks do, in fact, keep some "vault cash" on hand) but deposits of the member bank with the Federal Reserve Bank in its district. The Federal Reserve Bank serves as a bank's bank. The member bank makes deposits in the Federal Reserve Bank (just as you or I make deposits in the member bank), and these deposits then form the backbone of the bank's required reserves.

These two points—the importance of demand deposits as our typical form of money, and the nature of the required reserves held in the Federal Reserve Bank by the member banks—already bring us fairly close to the process by which the money supply in the United States may be expanded. Essentially, the Federal Reserve can bring about an expansion in the money supply either by making more reserves available to the commercial banks or by changing the legal reserve requirement. When either of these steps is taken, the commercial banks

---

6. It is true, of course, that if a stranger comes into town we may not accept his check. However, this is usually a case not of doubting the acceptability of demand deposits but of doubting whether the stranger actually has demand deposits in the bank to make his check good. When we are sure he does have the "money" in the bank, we will usually accept his check.

are then collectively able to expand the volume of demand deposits—money—in the economy.

The three main tools the Federal Reserve Board has for achieving this effect are: (1) simply lowering the legal reserve requirement from, say, 17-1/2 percent to 16-1/2 percent; (2) lowering the interest rate at which the member banks may borrow from the Federal Reserve Bank to replenish or augment their reserves (this particular interest rate is called the *discount rate*); and (3) by engaging in open-market purchases of government securities. This third method—"open-market operations" as it is often called—is a particularly important one, and also somewhat complicated to understand. Let us therefore follow it through in a step-by-step fashion. In this way, we shall be able to show (*a*) how the Federal Reserve can expand the money supply and (*b*) how the effect of this expansion will be to lower interest rates in the economy generally.

OPEN-MARKET OPERATIONS BY THE FED

Let us suppose that the Fed is interested in expanding the money supply, and it attempts to do this through open-market purchases of government securities. Let us suppose it buys a $100 government bond directly from one of the commercial banks in the system. The effect of this action will be to increase the reserves of the commercial banks in the system and, consequently, permit them to expand their loans to the public. As they expand their loans, the money supply in the economy will increase and the interest rate will fall.

To follow the process through, it is necessary to look at the balance sheets of the member bank in the system.

Our stripped-down examples on the next page represent the situation of the member bank *before* and *after* the Federal Reserve Bank has purchased the government bond. Three items are to be noticed before the purchase:

(1) The bank has $200 listed as deposits in the Federal Reserve Bank. These are the legally required reserves we have been speaking of. We are assuming that the legal reserve requirement in our hypothetical system is 20 percent of demand deposits.

(2) The second asset item represents loans, investments, and government bonds. Here the bank is engaged in lending out money or buying bonds or other securities in order to make money in the form of interest. These are the interest-earning assets of the bank, and they are, of course, an essential feature of the commercial banking system.

(3) On the liability side, we have $1,000 worth of demand deposits. In the real world, there are other forms of deposits as well, but we are concentrating on the fundamentals of the system only. These deposits are called liabilities because they are owed by the bank to its depositors. They are also the principal form of money in the American economy.[7]

This, as we have said, is the member bank's balance sheet *before* the Federal Reserve purchases a $100 government bond from the member bank. What

---

7. An actual bank balance sheet would, of course, be much more complicated than this. So also would the concept of "money." For example, banks carry not only demand deposits but also time deposits or savings deposits. One cannot write checks on these deposits, but they can be easily turned into cash.

SIMPLIFIED BALANCE SHEETS OF A MEMBER BANK

Before Open-Market Operation		After Federal Reserve Bank purchases $100 government bond	
Assets	Liabilities	Assets	Liabilities
$200 Reserves in the Federal Reserve Bank	$1,000 Demand deposits	$300 Reserves in the Federal Reserve Bank	$1,000 Demand deposits
$800 Loans, investments, bonds		$700 Loans, investments, bonds	

happens immediately *after* this purchase is shown in the balance sheet on the right. The loans, investments, etc., category has gone down by $100 through the sale of the bond. At the same time the Federal Reserve Bank has credited the member bank with an additional $100 in its reserves with that Federal Reserve Bank. This is the way in which the Federal Reserve Bank pays for the bond. The new totals are recorded: $300 in reserves; $700 in loans, investments, and bonds; $1,000 in demand deposits.

So far, we notice, there has been no change in the money supply. That is, we still have $1,000 in demand deposits. However, the stage has now been set for an expansion of the money supply, because this bank (and, consequently, member banks as a whole) now has $100 more in reserves. This means that this bank can now lend out money to businesses and individuals, because it has reserves in excess of its legal requirements. When it lends out money, it does so by creating demand deposits for those who are borrowing from it. But this is not all; the process goes beyond an additional $100 of demand deposits. And the reason is

that it is the *reserves* that have been increased by $100, and a $100 increase in reserves can ultimately sustain a fivefold (assuming a 20 percent reserve requirement) increase in demand deposits in the system as a whole. In other words, if the member banks are willing to lend out all their excess reserves, then ultimately the $100 open-market operation will lead to a $500 expansion in the money supply.

This process cannot be accomplished by one small bank alone. All it can do is to lend out the $100. But this $100 will then be deposited in some other bank, which will then find that *its* demand deposits and reserves have both been increased by $100. This second bank, in turn, will have excess reserves of $80 (it must keep $20 against its new demand deposits of $100) which it can then lend out. This, in turn, will create $80 of new reserves and demand deposits in still a third bank, which will find that *it* now has excess reserves of $64, and so on. The total of all these rounds of new demand deposits will be $500, which, with a 20 percent reserve requirement and $100 of new reserves, will be legally fine for everybody concerned.

MULTIPLE CREDIT CREATION

Still, the operation can seem a bit mysterious. It is rather like creating money out of thin air. In this, the process resembles the action of the national income multiplier of the last chapter. We increase consumer, government, or investment spending by $1 and get a $3 or $4 increase in national income. In the case of multiple credit creation, we get $1 more

---

THE PROCESS OF MULTIPLE CREDIT EXPANSION

After our original bank has loaned out its $100 in excess reserves, this $100 will be deposited in Bank A. If Bank A's original balance sheet was identical to our original bank's, the change will be reflected as follows:

1.

Bank A	Assets	Liabilities
(*Before* $100 is deposited)	$200 Reserves $800 Loans and investments	$1,000 Demand deposits

Bank A	Assets	Liabilities
(*After* $100 is deposited)	$300 Reserves $800 Loans and investments	$1,100 Demand deposits

Bank A now lends out $80 and its balance sheet becomes:

Assets	Liabilities
$220 Reserves $880 Loans and investments	$1,100 Demand deposits

Addition to money supply in first round = $100

---

2. The $80 loaned out by Bank A is now deposited in Bank B.

Bank B	Assets	Liabilities
(*Before* $80 deposit)	$200 Reserves $800 Loans and investments	$1,000 Demand deposits

Bank B	Assets	Liabilities
(*After* $80 deposit)	$280 Reserves $800 Loans and investments	$1,080 Demand deposits

Bank B now lends out $64 and its balance sheet becomes:

Assets	Liabilities
$216 Reserves $864 Loans and investments	$1,080 Demand deposits

Addition to money supply in second round = $80

---

3. **The $64 loaned out by Bank B is now deposited in Bank C.**

Bank C	Assets	Liabilities
(*Before* $64 deposit)	$200 Reserves $800 Loans and investments	$1,000 Demand deposits

Bank C	Assets	Liabilities
(*After* $64 deposit)	$264 Reserves $800 Loans and investments	$1,064 Demand deposits

Bank C now lends out $51.20 and its balance sheet becomes:

Assets	Liabilities
$212.80 Reserves $851.20 Loans and investments	$1,064 Demand deposits

Addition to money supply in third round = $64

In the next round, Bank D will be able to lend out 80 percent of $51.20 or $40.96; in the next round, Bank E will be able to lend out 80 percent of $40.96, or $32.77; and so on.

The *total* addition to the money supply (ΔM) when all the rounds are completed will be:

$$\Delta M = \$100 + \$80 + \$64 + \$51.20 + \$40.96 + \$32.77 + \dots$$

$$\Delta M = \$100 \ (1 + .80 + (.80)^2 + (.80)^3 + (.80)^4 + \dots + (.80)^n + \dots)$$

$$\Delta M = \$100 \ \left(\frac{1}{1 - .80} \right)$$

$$\Delta M = \$100 \ (5) = \$500$$

---

in reserves and $5 more in demand deposits, or money. Actually, in formal terms, the processes are very similar, the role of the MPS in the multiplier (remember that m = 1/MPS) being played in the case of credit expansion by the legal reserve requirement. Thus, assuming that all banks lend out all their funds up to the legal requirements, we would get, where ΔM equals the addition to the money supply, ΔR equals the new reserves, and LR, the legal reserve requirement:

$$\Delta M = (1/LR) \ \Delta R$$

The term, $1/LR$, can be thought of as the *money creation multiplier* or the *credit cre-*

ation multiplier. In this case, it would be 1/.20, or 5.

The best way of seeing all this, however, is to follow through the actual process, bank by bank, for a number of rounds. This is done in the group of balance sheets shown here.

If we consolidated all these balance sheets and looked at the process before, during, and after the expansion had taken place, it would look like the situation shown in the example on p. 264. The total reserves of the member banks have gone up from $2,000 to $2,100. As a consequence, and on the assumption that each bank at each stage of the game lends out any excess reserves that come its way,

---

CONSOLIDATED MEMBER BANK BALANCE SHEETS

If we assume that there are ten banks in the system, each with a balance sheet identical to those we have been describing, then we have:

1. **Consolidated balance sheet before Federal Reserve open-market operation:**

Assets	Liabilities
$2,000 Reserves in Federal Reserve Bank	$10,000 Demand deposits
$8,000 Loans and investments	

2. **Consolidated balance sheet immediately after Federal Reserve purchase of a $100 government bond:**

Assets	Liabilities
$2,100 Reserve in Federal Reserve Bank	$10,000 Demand deposits
$7,900 Loans and investments	

3. **Consolidated balance sheet after multiple expansion of credit has taken place:**

Assets	Liabilities
$2,100 Reserves in Federal Reserve Bank	$10,500 Demand deposits
$8,400 Loans and investments	

---

the demand deposits in the system have gone up from $10,000 to $10,500—i.e., for the Federal Reserve purchase of a $100 government bond, there has been a $500 expansion of the money supply.

Now at the same time that one is learning to understand this expansionary process, one is actually also learning to understand why an expansion of the money supply tends to bring the interest rate down—and this, of course, is the main point we are trying to demonstrate here.

To see this, all one needs to do is to visualize what is happening in the case of each of the banks in the system as it receives its share of excess reserves. Each bank, being a commercial institution, is now eager to make money by lending out this excess; there is a generally increased willingness on the part of lenders in the economy to lend. This is really analogous to the kind of supply-and-demand analysis for goods and services that we described in chapter 2. In this case the good is "loans" and the

"price" is the interest rate. There has been no change in the position of the borrowers (i.e., business investors) but there has been developed an increased willingness on the part of the banking system to supply more loans. The consequence, as we would expect, is that the price—i.e., the interest rate—will fall.

This is the essence of the process by which Federal Reserve open-market purchases of government securities can lead both to an expansion in the money supply and an easing of the terms on which banks are ready to lend to businesses, and especially a fall in the interest rate. (To test his understanding of the process, the reader should follow through the opposite policy, showing how Federal Reserve sales of government bonds to the member banks can lead to a contraction of reserves, multiplied contraction of demand deposits, or money, and a raising of the interest rate.) The banks find themselves with excess reserves. Whereas previously they would lend to businesses—or, for that matter, to home-builders or state and local governments—only at 6 percent interest, now they are willing to lend at 5-1/2 percent or 5 percent.

Thus, our point (1)—the link between the money supply and the rate of interest—has been demonstrated, and the chain connecting the money supply with the level of national income and employment is now complete.

A RECAPITULATION AND FURTHER DEVELOPMENT

Rather, the chain is "complete" subject to a number of additions and amendments. Let us first go over the whole process from beginning to end, and then make some further comments.

To recapitulate: The Federal Reserve Board finds the economy suffering from unemployment and below-potential national income. It can use *monetary policy* to combat this situation in many ways; e.g., changing the reserve requirement, lowering the discount rate, or engaging in open-market operations. Let us suppose it decides to combat the recession by open-market purchases of government securities. Let us suppose further that it purchases these securities directly from its member banks:

As a consequence of these open-market purchases, the member banks will find their reserves in excess of the legal requirements. They will be ready and eager to lend more to businesses. In this process of lending more, the money supply will be increased, and the banks will find themselves offering better terms—lower interest rates—to businessmen. Businessmen, in their turn, will find the lower interest rates attractive, an inducement to expand their investments. They will now be willing to undertake expansions of their plant and equipment and machinery that heretofore would not have *been profitable. The same also will be true of people who wish to borrow money to build homes, or of state and local governments who may need to float loans for new schools. In general, then, the lowered interest rates and the increased availability of money will cause an expansion of investment and other spending in the economy. This expansion of investment and other spending will, by virtue of the national income multiplier, lead to an expansion of national income and employment in the economy as a whole. Thus, monetary policy, like fiscal policy, is shown to be a tool by which the government can influence the level of spending and, consequently, the level of national income and employment in the economy.*

This, in capsule form, is the fundamental way by which the nation's monetary policy reaches down into the economy to affect the major economic aggregates of output, employment, and prices.

One factor we have not mentioned—though in all logic it should have been part of the chain that we have been attempting to construct—is sometimes called the *transactions demand for money.* One of the reasons we hold any of our wealth in the form of money (as opposed, say, to stocks or bonds or other assets) is quite simply that we need money to carry on the ordinary business of life. We need a certain amount of money to handle our normal day-to-day or month-to-month financial transactions. Now the *amount* of money we need for these transactions purposes will, on the whole, be determined by the amount of business we do or, for the national economy, by the level of national income in money terms. At a national income of $400 billion annually, we need considerably less transaction money than at a national income of, say, $1 trillion. The point is this: in our capsule summary we spoke of the end product of monetary policy as being a certain expansion of national income. What we did *not* do was to take account of the extra transaction demand for money that such an expansion brings. What this factor means, in essence, is that only *part* of the expanded money supply can, so to speak, go into financing a lower rate of interest; another part of it must be made available to finance the expanded transactions required by the increased national income.

Another matter we did not investigate fully was *how much* of an effect an expansion of the money supply might have in lowering the rate of interest. Some of that added money supply, as we have just said, may be needed to finance a higher level of transactions if national money income expands in response to Federal Reserve action. But what of the impact of the added money beyond this? We have already suggested that Federal Reserve action affecting bank reserves does not automatically bring about a fully multiplied expansion of the money supply. If interest rates are already low and business conditions look poor, then the member banks may not lend out all their excess reserves as assumed in our bank balance sheets above. They may decide to hold excess reserves, thus frustrating the multiple credit expansion that the Fed is attempting to promote. More generally, when interest rates are low, people in the economy as a whole may find that their desire to hold money as opposed to other assets is quite strong. For businesses and individuals want money not simply for the transaction purposes we have just mentioned, but also for what is sometimes called *liquidity* purposes. If you are holding a stock or a bond, its price may fall (say from $80 a share to $60 a share), and you will have sustained a monetary loss. In the case of money, the price of a dollar

remains forever a dollar. If interest rates are low (in which case the opportunity cost of holding money is low), you may decide to hold perfectly *liquid* money rather than take a risk that your stocks or bonds may fall in money value.[8] What this means is that even when the money supply is substantially increased, it may not have a very great effect on bringing down interest rates. As these rates get lower and lower, people may simply decide to hold all the additional money *as money*, for these liquidity reasons. After a certain point is reached, people may refuse to buy bonds and other securities, with the consequence that even if more money is pumped into the economy, it will not bring a lowered interest rate and hence will have little or no effect on business investment.

This last point not only suggests some potential weaknesses of monetary policy in curing a depression (Keynesians used to call this phenomenon the "liquidity trap"), but also leads us to a deeper understanding of the role of money in the economy in total. We might say that people want to hold wealth in the form of money for two main reasons: (1) *transactions* demand, and (2) *liquidity* or, sometimes, the *precautionary motive*. When the quantity of money in the economy is "too

---

8. A *liquid* asset is one readily turned into money. Since money *is* money, it is perfectly *liquid*. When interest rates are low, this is the same thing as saying that bond prices are high: $5 a year on a bond that sells for $200 is an interest rate of 2-1/2 percent; $5 a year on a bond that sells for $100 is 5 percent. When bond prices are high, people generally may fear that they are due for a fall. This is an important reason for preferring money to bonds when interest rates are low.

The reader should be clear that perfect liquidity does not imply a constant purchasing power. Although a dollar is always worth a dollar, it may be worth less in terms of real goods when there is a general inflation. Indeed, when prices in general are rising, the costs of holding perfectly liquid money are increased, since that money will be worth less (in real terms) in the future.

small" to sustain full employment income, we have the following situation in mind:

A high, full-employment national income will naturally create a great demand for the use of money for transactions purposes. This will leave only a small amount of the stock of money in the economy for liquidity or precautionary purposes. If the interest rate is low, people will feel that they want to exchange securities (say, bonds) for money to assuage their precautionary concerns. When everybody tries to sell their bonds, however, the price of bonds will fall, and this is equivalent to a rise in the interest rate. This rise in the interest rate, in turn, will cause some fall in investment and hence in national income. At equilibrium, when it is finally achieved, the fall in national income will have reduced the demand for money for transactions purposes and provided more for liquidity or precautionary purposes. The "cost" of a "too small" money supply, therefore, will be reduced national income and employment.[9]

With this general picture in mind, it can be said that we have completed the "basics of national income determination" that was the object of Part Two A of this book. There are many further points to be made and many applications of these basic tools that must be considered, and these are matters we will now turn to directly. The reader should recognize, however, that if he has mastered the materials in Part Two A he already has at his disposal a powerful theoretical apparatus that will enable him to achieve a deeper insight into the important mac-

roeconomic problems of our time. And this is no small achievement.

SUMMARY

In this chapter, we have brought the role of money explicitly into our analysis of national income, attempting to show how the monetary policy of the government may affect the levels of national income and employment in the economy.

The basic links in the logical chain connecting money with national income, employment, and prices are as follows:

(1) **An increase in the money supply will generally lower the interest rate.** The agency responsible for handling the money supply of the United States is the Federal Reserve Board. The Fed has various instruments available for increasing the money supply, including: changing the reserve requirements of its member banks; lowering the interest rate (*discount rate*) at which the member banks may borrow from the Federal Reserve Bank in their district; and making open-market purchases of government securities.

We followed through a Federal Reserve purchase of a government bond from one of its member banks. We showed that this purchase would (*a*) increase the reserves of the member banks; (*b*) lead to a multiple expansion of demand deposits in the economy; (*c*) bring about generally lowered interest rates and easier availability of credit to business investors. In understanding this process, it is necessary to remember that demand deposits are the most common form of money in the United States.

(2) **A fall in the interest rate will generally lead to an increase in business investment.** To understand this point, we

---

9. Just as the "cost" of a "too big" money supply would be inflationary pressures. See chapter 14. 342–43. For the graphically minded reader, the points covered in this brief paragraph in the text are discussed in terms of diagrams in the appendix to this chapter.

should recall that we are talking about "investment" in the sense of adding machinery and plant to the productive capacity of the economy (not "financial investment," i.e., buying a stock or a bond). To the businessman who is thinking of buying a new machine or expanding his factory, a low interest rate will mean lowered costs of borrowing money. Hence, it will generally encourage *investment*, in our sense of the word.

(3) **An increase in business investment will generally lead to an expansion of national income and employment.** This is simply our old friend the national income multiplier from earlier chapters.

(A *fourth* point relating decreases in the money supply to higher interest rates, lowered investment, and a contraction of aggregate demand was postponed until chapter 14, which deals with inflation.)

In evaluating this logical chain, one has to remember some important qualifications:

(*a*) A certain proportion of our money supply is used for *transactions* purposes. If national income expands, there will generally be an increased demand for money for transactions, with the consequence that not all of any given increase in the money supply will go into bringing lowered interest rates.

(*b*) A low interest rate may have fairly little impact on raising the level of investment if other factors affecting investment are strongly negative; e.g., the existence of excess capacity, pessimistic business expectations, and so on.

(*c*) If the banks are cautious about lending out their excess reserves and if there is a strong *liquidity* or *precautionary* demand for money in the economy as a whole, then the Fed may be largely frustrated in its efforts to bring interest rates down.

QUESTIONS FOR DISCUSSION

1. Define *money*. What are some other forms, besides money, in which people might hold their wealth? Rank the various assets you have listed according to their degree of liquidity.

2. What is meant by the phrase "a synthesis of real and monetary economics"? Is this synthesis achieved in the analysis presented in this chapter? If so, explain how.

3. Suppose an individual, having come to distrust the banking system, withdraws his $1,000 demand deposit from a commercial bank and buries the $1,000 in his backyard. Will this have any effect on the money supply of the economy? Follow through the steps involved.

4. It sometimes happens that the Treasury, unable to market government securities to the public on acceptable terms, sells them to the Federal Reserve System. The balance sheet of the Federal Reserve Bank is thereby altered as follows for a $1 million sale:

Stage I: The Treasury is credited with a $1 million deposit at the Federal Reserve Bank:

FEDERAL RESERVE BANK BALANCE SHEET

Assets

+ **$1 million government bonds**

Liabilities

+ **$1 million U.S. Treasury deposits**

Stage II: The Treasury spends the money, and the individuals who receive it deposit it in their commercial banks. The commercial banks thereby increase their reserves at the Federal Reserve Bank:

FEDERAL RESERVE BANK BALANCE SHEET

Assets

+ **$1 million government bonds**

Liabilities

+ **$1 million Member bank reserves**

What effect will this transaction be likely to have on the money supply of the country?

It has been said that this way of financing the federal debt is very much like "printing money." Do you agree?

Suppose the Treasury, instead of selling its bonds to the Federal Reserve System, sells them to private individuals who pay for them by check on their demand deposit accounts at their commercial banks. Will this have a similar or different effect on the money supply of the country? Explain.

5. Explain (*a*) the money supply-interest rate link; (*b*) the interest rate-investment link, (*c*) the investment–GNP link. Indicate the main weaknesses in these links if our objective happens to be to "cure" a depression by monetary policy.

11
Appendix:
Money and
National Income
Determination

In this appendix, we shall gather together a number of points we have made in chapter 11 and earlier chapters, showing graphically how money fits into our general analysis of national income determination.

We begin with the two different kinds of demand for money that we mentioned towards the end of chapter 11: (1) the *transactions* demand (depending mainly on the level of national money income) and (2) the *liquidity* or precautionary demand (depending mainly on the rate of interest). When national money income is high, the transactions demand for money will be high. When the rate of interest is high, the liquidity demand for money will be low. The reason is that, at high interest rates, people will prefer to hold their wealth in the form of interest-earning assets, rather than in the form of money. Also, we recall, a high interest rate on bonds implies a low price of bonds; hence, people may wish to hold bonds rather than money because they anticipate that the price of bonds may rise. The converse of these reasons will explain the opposite proposition, namely, that at low interest rates, the liquidity demand for money will be high.

These two demands for money are summed horizontally in Figure 1 for a given level of national income (Y_o).* Moving right from the vertical axis, we first have the transactions demand for money represented by a vertical line, indicating the fact that we are assuming a given level of national income (and hence of transactions). As we move further to the right, we add on the amounts of money that people wish to hold for liquidity purposes. These amounts will be greater and greater as the interest rate is lower and lower. The diagram, as drawn here, suggests the possibility of a "liquidity trap" at very low levels of the interest rate. That is to say, the curve becomes very nearly horizontal at low levels of the interest rate, meaning that even substantial additions to the money supply will not bring much further reduction in the interest rate.

In this diagram, if we assume that the Federal Reserve Banks have determined a given stock of money for the nation (M_0), then we can say that, *with the assumed level of national income, Y_0, the*

---

*The transactions demand for money will, of course, depend on the level of *money* national income, not *real* national income. In this appendix, however, we will assume that the price level is unchanged and, therefore, that changes in money income reflect changes in real income (i.e., income at constant prices). In this somewhat simplified world, we can say that the transactions demand for money will depend mainly on the level of real national income.

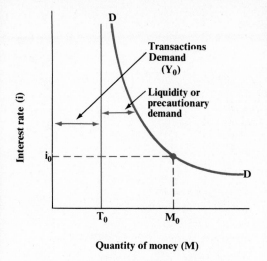

Figure 1. Demand for Money at a Given Level of National Income (Y_0).

Curve *DD* represents the demand for money in an economy at different interest rates, given a certain level of national income (Y_0). If the quantity of money in the economy is given (M_0), then the rate of interest compatible with this level of national income is i_0.

equilibrium rate of interest will be determined at i_0. Why an equilibrium rate? Because this is the rate of interest at which the amount of their wealth people are willing to hold in the form of money is exactly equal to the stock of money (as determined by the Fed) in existence. At a *higher* rate of interest, people want to hold (for both transactions *and* liquidity purposes) less money than was actually in existence. What would they then do? They would start trying to get rid of their money by buying securities, say, bonds. This attempt by everyone to buy bonds would raise the price of bonds, which, in turn, is equivalent to a *fall* in the interest rate. Hence, a higher interest rate than i_0 would lead to forces tending to bring the interest rate down. (The reader should show for himself that, by exactly analo-

gous logic, an interest rate *below* i_0 would set in motion forces tending to *raise* the interest rate.)

But we have just begun the story in Figure 1, because we are there assuming a given level of national income. However, it is the level of national income that we are precisely trying to determine.

To do this, we need to proceed further, the next step being to observe what happens to the demand for money at some different level of national income. In Figure 2, we have again a given level of national income but this time a higher level of national income ($Y_1 > Y_0$). The effect of this change is to push the transactions demand for money further out to the right. This, in turn, pushes the whole *DD* curve out to the right (to $D'D'$). The net result is that, for our given stock of money (M_0), the equilibrium rate of interest will be higher at the higher level of national income ($i_1 > i_0$).

This is an important point to note, because it suggests that we can use this logic to find a systematic relationship between the level of national income and the interest rate (always assuming a given stock of money). In particular, the higher the level of national income, the higher the equilibrium rate of interest will be. This relationship is depicted in Figure 3 in what economists usually call the *LM* curve (standing for liquidity–money). Notice that we have changed the quantity on the horizontal or *x*-axis. It is no longer the quantity of money, but the level of national income (Y). *LM* generally slopes upward from left to right, the basic reason being that a higher level of income raises the transactions demand for money and thus a higher interest rate is necessary to make people content to hold only the smaller amount of money left over for liquidity or precautionary purposes.

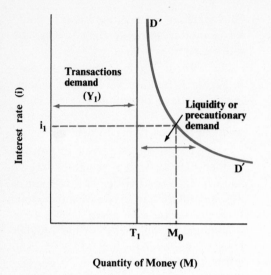

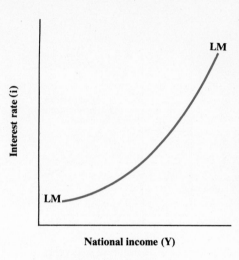

Figure 2. Demand for Money at a Higher Level of National Income (Y_1).

With a higher level of national income ($Y_1 > Y_0$), and the same quantity of money (M_0), the rate of interest will have to be higher ($i_1 > i_0$).

Figure 3. The *LM* (Liquidity-Money) Curve.

This curve shows that, for a given quantity of money (M_0), the equilibrium rate of interest will have to rise with national income. Notice that we now have national income (Y), not the money supply, measured on the horizontal axis.

We have now gone exactly *half* the way to the solution of our overall problem—which remains, as always, to determine the equilibrium level of national income. The second half, however, is much easier for us since we have already spelled it out verbally in chapter 11 (see pp. 255–58). There we stated that high interest rates would tend to go with low levels of national income, exactly the reverse of the *LM* relationship. Why was this? The logic was quite simply that a high interest rate would reduce investment and that a reduction in investment would, via the multiplier, cause a reduction in national income.

Of course, there is nothing contradictory between these two relationships. Indeed, if we did not have another relationship between national income and the interest rate beyond that shown in

Figure 3, we would be unable to determine the equilibrium level of national income. We would simply be able to say that, for this or that level of national income, we will have this or that interest rate.

Figure 4 pulls all this material together in one diagram. We have added what economists usually call an *IS* curve (investment–savings curve), which shows that the lower the level of the interest rate, the higher will be the equilibrium level of national income. The reason is, as we have stated, that lower interest rates will lead to high investment, which, via the multiplier (which guarantees us that planned investment and planned savings will be equated), will produce higher levels of national income.

In this diagram, we finally *do* determine the equilibrium level of national

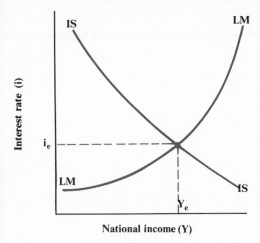

National income (Y)

**Figure 4. Overall
Equilibrium Achieved.**

Although subject to many qualifications, this is a very useful diagram for showing equilibrium where $I = S$ and also where the demand for money equals the given supply (M_0).

income. It is Y_e. We also determine the equilibrium rate of interest, i_e. At this overall equilibrium, planned investment and saving are equal, and also the amount of their wealth people want to hold in the form of money (for both transactions and liquidity purposes) is exactly equal to the assumed stock of money (M_0).

Now this diagram, properly understood, is remarkably helpful as an aid to coping with many of the different problems we have mentioned from time to time in this and preceding chapters. How, for example, would a change in the money supply—from M_0 to M_1—affect the equilibrium levels of national income and interest rate? The effect would be manifested through the LM curve. If, say, M_1 is greater than M_0, the general effect will be to push the LM curve to the right. You can see this by going back to Figure 1 and showing how an increase in the stock

of money will mean a lower equilibrium rate of interest for any given level of national income. Knowing that LM is shifted to the right, we can see that the general effect of the increase in the money supply will be a rise in the equilibrium level of national income and a fall in the equilibrium rate of interest.

The diagram can be used even more specifically than this, however. The reader should follow through the exercise below, which involves the analysis of both the shapes of these LM and IS curves and also shifts in these curves. If he works these problems out, he will hopefully agree that, despite a number of qualifications that we shall be taking up later on, these tools are really quite remarkable for organizing one's thoughts about the complexities of modern macroeconomics.

EXERCISE

Many economists believe that the following statements are wholly or partly true, and that they have a significant bearing on many macroeconomic issues. Your task is to show how to represent these statements in terms of the shapes and/or positions of the IS and LM curves:

(1) At very low levels of the interest rate, further increases in the quantity of money will not lead to any further reductions in the interest rate. (This is what we referred to in the text as the "liquidity trap.")

(2) Technological progress, if it stimulates businessmen to increase investment, may raise both the equilibrium level of national income and the equilibrium rate of interest.

(3) An increased desire to save (shift in the consumption function) can

lead to lower equilibrium levels of national income and interest rate.

(4) It is sometimes argued that while very high levels of interest rates may choke off investment, very low levels of interest rates may have little effect in increasing investment after a certain point. If true, how would this be reflected in our diagram?

(5) Suppose we live in an economy in which both points (1) and (4) above are true. It can be argued that in such an economy monetary policy may be effective in restraining an over-exuberant economy but that it will be of little use in curing a depression. (This is sometimes put in terms of the maxim: "you can pull on a string, but you can't push a string.") Explain your answer in terms of our diagrams.

PART TWO B
MACROECONOMICS: PROBLEMS AND APPLICATIONS

12
Fiscal Policy And The National Debt

In Part Two A, we presented the basics of national income determination in a roughly logical sequence, including as well the underlying theory of fiscal and monetary policy. Now, in Part Two B, we shall try to extend and apply this analysis to some of the problems facing a modern industrialized economy. In doing this, we necessarily touch on many issues on which economists differ among themselves. Whereas in the preceding chapters on macroeconomics we largely avoided controversy in order to present the argument in a reasonably uninterrupted way, we must now give full weight to these differences of opinion—some of which, indeed, are about the basic theory itself.

The topics under consideration—the national debt, monetarism, inflation, balance of payments problems, growth—are among the most fascinating in all of economics. At the end of Part Two B, the reader should have a sense (1) that economists do not have fully agreed upon answers to these problems, and yet (2) that modern economic analysis provides an indispensable starting point for approaching such issues—for the citizen quite as much as for the professional economist.

Let us begin with one of the most prickly of all economic issues—the matter of the public debt.

A DECLARATION OF POLICY

The accepted notion of most people in this country for a long time was that the national debt was quite simply a "bad thing." If you had asked the man in the street how he felt about the government, and especially the federal government, spending more than its tax revenues and thus adding to the national debt, he would likely have replied that it was certainly unwise and probably immoral. Yet in Part Two A, and especially in chapter 10, we spoke of "deficit financing" and increases in the public debt as though they were perfectly ordinary, and certainly not very alarming, features of a nation's fiscal policy.

This discrepancy in outlook is not simply an academic matter since the United States government has gone on record to state that it is a responsibility of the federal government to maintain the macroeconomic health and stability of the nation. This statement is contained in Section 2 of an important piece of legislation called the "Employment Act of 1946." Besides establishing the Council of Economic Advisers, requiring an annual Economic Report of the President, and setting up a Joint Committee (of the Senate and House) on the Economic Report, this act made law the following "Declaration of Policy":

The Congress hereby declares that it is the continuing policy and responsibility of the Federal Government to use all practicable means consistent with its need and obligations and other essential considerations of national policy, with the assistance and co-operation of industry, agriculture, labor, and State and local governments, to coordinate and utilize all its plans, functions, and resources for the purpose of creating and maintaining, in a manner calculated to foster and promote free competitive enterprise and the general welfare, conditions under which there will be afforded useful employment opportunities, including self-employment, for those able, willing and seeking to work, and to promote maximum employment, production, and purchasing power.

In the 1970s, this act seems innocuous enough, but in the 1940s it was a legislative landmark, and it represented the determination of the people of America that such a thing as the Great Depression would not be allowed to happen again.

But suppose that in promoting "maximum employment, production, and purchasing power," the federal government should be tempted to expand the national debt? Even in the 1970s Congress still has placed definite limits on the extent to which the federal government may go into debt, and a Republican administration, like Democratic administrations before it, has had to go to Congress for an extension of that limit upwards. In other words, can the national debt be thought of as a flexible item—a variable—in the operation of the nation's overall fiscal policy, or should it be considered a fixed constraint (this much debt and no more), or, even more narrowly, a burden to be reduced as quickly as possible?

DIFFERING VIEWS ON THE DEBT

Opposing views on this matter have affected national action on macroeconomic problems in the past, and, indeed, they still affect the policies of the federal government. Perhaps the best way to approach this issue is to suggest, through the words of their own spokesmen, three leading opinions about the public debt, and then to follow this with our own analysis.

View I: The Importance of a Balanced Budget

The traditional view, to which many political figures still pay tribute to this day, is that governmental budgets ought simply to be kept in balance. An often-quoted statement of this position is that of then Senator Harry Flood Byrd of Virginia in a speech in 1955 that was later recorded in the *Congressional Record*. The following is an excerpt from that speech:

The Importance of a Balanced Budget

Senator Harry F. Byrd

I am pleased to have this opportunity to speak on the subject: Is it important to balance the budget?

As I see it, balancing the budget without resorting to legerdemain or unsound bookkeeping methods is certainly in the category of our No. 1 problems.

Beginning with 1792, the first fiscal year of our Federal Government, and through 1916, Federal deficits were casual and usually paid off in succeeding years. In this 124-year period there were 43 deficit years and 81 surplus years. As late as July 1, 1914, the interest-bearing debt was less than $1 billion.

In Andrew Jackson's administration the public debt was paid off in toto, an achievement in which President Jackson expressed great pride.

It can be said for this first 124 years in the life of our Republic we were on a pay-as-you-go basis. In that

period I think it can be accurately said that we laid the foundation for our strength today as the greatest nation in all the world.

Then, in 1917, 1918, and 1919, World War I deficits aggregated $13 billion. Heavy current taxation in those years paid much of the war cost.

The next eleven years, from 1919 to 1931, were surplus years, and the war debt was reduced.

In 1932 Mr. Roosevelt came into office, and the most outstanding plank in his platform was to reduce Federal expenditures by 25 percent and to keep the budget in balance. He accused Mr. Hoover of "throwing discretion to the winds and indulging in an orgy of waste and extravagance." Mr. Hoover spent $4 billion in his last year, and the record shows that this spendthrift Hoover was the only President to leave office with fewer Federal employees than when he came in.

Mr. Roosevelt added more than $200 billion to the public debt during his administrations.

I took my oath as a Sena-

tor the same day Mr. Roosevelt took his as President—March 4, 1933. The first bill I voted on was the legislation recommended by President Roosevelt to redeem his economy pledge by reducing all expenditures 15 percent—a difference of 10 percent less than his original promise, it is true—but I thought this was a substantial redemption of a campaign pledge, as such things go, and I enthusiastically supported him.

The title of the bill was "A bill to preserve the credit of the United States Government." Our debt was then about $16 billion. This economy program was short-lived—about six months—and the spending then began to steadily and rapidly increase.

Mr. Roosevelt presented thirteen budgets and in every peacetime budget he promised a balance between income and outgo for the next year, but it turned out that next year never came. He was in the red all the way, and in every year of his administration a substantial deficit was added to the public debt.

Excerpted from "The Importance of a Balanced Budget," a speech by Senator Harry F. Byrd. Reprinted in *Congressional Record, 84th Cong., 1st sess., 1955, 101, pt. 4: 5693-95.*

There were eight Truman budgets. Three were in the black—those for fiscal years 1947, 1948, and 1951. Two resulted from war contract cancellations following the end of World War II and the third resulted from increased taxes for the Korean war before the war bills started coming due. Five Truman budgets were in the red.

Mr. Eisenhower has presented two budgets—both in the red but on a declining ratio. The Eisenhower deficit estimates for fiscal years 1955 and 1956 aggregate $7 billion as compared to the last Truman budget which alone contemplated a $9 billion deficit.

The cold facts are that for twenty-one years out of the last twenty-four years we have spent more than we have collected. In these twenty-four years we have balanced the budget in only three; and these were more by accident than by design.

We must recognize that we have abandoned the sound fiscal policies strictly adhered to by all political parties and all Presidents for considerably more than a century of our existence. It is true that during these twenty-one deficit years we were engaged in World War II for four years and in the Korean war for two years. Yet, in the years when the pay-as-you-go system prevailed we also had quite a few wars.

It is the quarter of a century of deficit spending which now makes balancing the budget so imperative. Young men and women, born in 1930, have lived in the red virtually all their lives. Our acceptance of deficit spend-

ing for so long a period has weakened public resistance to the evils of this practice. Bad habits are hard to change.

Will the deficits become permanent and continue to pile debt upon debt until real disaster comes? If we cannot balance the budget in this day of our greatest dollar income, when taxes are near their peak, and when we are at peace, I ask, when can we?

It is disturbing these days to hear some economists argue the budget should not be balanced and that we should not begin to pay on the debt because, they allege, it will adversely affect business conditions. Have we yielded so far to the blandishments of Federal subsidies and Government support that we have forgotten our Nation is great because of individual effort as contrasted to state paternalism?

EVILS OF DEFICIT SPENDING

Here are some of the evils of deficit spending:

The debt today is the debt incurred by this generation, but tomorrow it will be debt on our children and grandchildren, and it will be for them to pay, both the interest and the principal.

It is possible and in fact probable that before this astronomical debt is paid off, if it ever is, the interest charge will exceed the principal.

Protracted deficit spending means cheapening the dollar. Secretary Humphrey testified before the Finance Committee that the greatest single factor in cheapening the

American dollar has been deficit spending.

Since I have been in the Senate, interest alone on the Federal debt has cost the taxpayers of this country more than $75 billion. At present rates, on the Federal debt at its present level, interest on it in the next twenty years will cost taxpayers upwards of $150 billion.

Since 1940 the Federal Government has borrowed and spent a quarter of a trillion dollars more than we have collected in taxes.

Year by year, nearly in direct ratio to deficit spending, the purchasing value of the dollar has declined. Beginning with a 100-cent dollar in 1940, the value of the dollar had declined to 52 cents in 1954.

As proof of the fact that deficit spending is directly responsible for cheapening the dollar, let me mention that in 1942, when we spent $19 billion in excess of revenue, the dollar in that one year declined ten cents in value.

In 1943, another big deficit year, the dollar lost five cents more in value, and another nine cents in 1946. From 1940 through 1952, an era of heavy deficit spending the dollar lost forty-eight cents in value, or nearly four cents each year, and it is still slipping but in much lesser degree.

Some may regard these facts and figures lightly, but the loss of half the purchasing power of its money in thirteen years should be a serious warning to any nation.

Cheapened money is inflation. Inflation is a dangerous

game. It robs creditors, it steals pensions, wages, and fixed income. Once started, it is exceedingly difficult to control. This inflation has been partially checked but the value of the dollar dropped slightly again in the past year. It would not take much to start up this dangerous inflation again.

Public debt is not like private debt. If private debt is not paid off, it can be ended by liquidation, but if public debt is not paid off with taxes, liquidation takes the form of disastrous inflation or national repudiation. Ei-

ther is destructive of our form of government.

Today the interest on the Federal debt takes more than 10 percent of our total Federal tax revenue. Without the tremendous cost of this debt our annual tax bill could be reduced 10 percent across the board.

The interest charge would be greater if much of the debt was not short-termed with lower interest rates. Should this debt be long-termed at the 3¼ percent paid on recent thirty-year bonds, the interest would be nearly 15 percent of the Fed-

eral income. No business enterprise could survive such heavy interest out of its gross income.

I am an old-fashioned person who believes that a debt is a debt just as much in the atomic age as it was in the horse and buggy days.

A balanced budget could be in sight if (a) we do not increase spending, and (b) we do not reduce taxes. Assuming no further cut in taxes, only a 4 percent reduction in spending, in terms of the President's budget, would bring us to that highly desirable goal.

View II: We Owe the National Debt to Ourselves

A diametrically opposed view to that just presented is that the size of the national debt is really a matter of total irrelevance. There are few citizens—whether economists or laymen—who would take quite such an extreme position. Indeed, the author of the following excerpt, Abba Lerner, a distinguished economist, is well aware of the many complications of the debt issue. However, the tone of the following remarks is so different from the Byrd speech that it helps put the question of the debt in a dramatically different perspective. For, in the preceding analysis by the senator, there is the unmistakable implication that the national debt is a debt to someone else. Or, to put it in different words, there is no apparent awareness of the fact that as we are national "debtors," we are also national "creditors." For after all, we do in many instances hold government bonds and count them as part of our wealth. The full recognition of this fact is likely to lead to a much more sanguine view of the national debt than that suggested in View I.

THE NATIONAL DEBT
Do we owe it to Ourselves?

Abba Lerner

When an editor of a newspaper or a cartoonist runs out of ideas, he can always call attention to the "national debt." The cartoonist can show the citizen being crushed by an enormous burden. The editorial writer will express himself arithmetically. Since nobody knows what is meant by a million dollars, let alone two hundred and ninety billions of dollars, the arithmetic can be very impressive. For example, he might ask how long you thought it would take you to pay off the national debt if you were given a full-time job of repaying it at the rate of one dollar every second. Years? Maybe hundreds of years? Not so easy. To pay out two hundred and ninety billion dollars at one dollar per second for seven hours a day working 300 days a year would take about 40,000 years. And at the end of the

Excerpted from Abba Lerner, "The National Debt—Do We Owe It to Ourselves?" in *Everybody's Business* (East Lansing, Mich.: Michigan State University Press, 1961), pp. 104–14. Reprinted by permission of the publisher.

40,000 years would the national debt have disappeared? On the contrary, all this repayment would not even have begun to make a dent on the compounding of the debt into really astronomic trillions of trillions of dollars. It would take a *thousand* people each paying out a dollar a second just to pay off the interest so as to stop the debt from growing any bigger than the accumulated unpaid interest.

On Mondays, Wednesdays and Fridays the editorials frighten us with these unimaginably large numbers and tell us that the country is being destroyed by the tremendous national debt. But on Tuesdays, Thursdays and Saturdays the same editorial page will remind us that we are enjoying a higher standard of living and greater prosperity than ever before. If we remembered Monday's editorial on Tuesday we might wonder how we are able to manage so well in spite of the national debt and whether this could possibly be because we owe it only to ourselves.

Editorials dismiss the notion that we owe the national debt to ourselves as too ridiculous to deserve further analysis, and continue their arithmetical exercises. But when the scoffing and the arithmetic are over, the question still remains, "If we do not owe the national debt to ourselves, to whom *do* we owe it?" To this there is no answer. There *is nobody else* to whom we owe the debt. The national debt is a debt which the people in the United States owe, through the government, to the holders of the government bonds who, with some insignificant exceptions, happen to be the people in the U.S. No matter how funny it may seem to some, we don't owe it to Germany or Japan or Russia or any other country. We do, as a nation, owe the national debt to ourselves.

Our owing it to ourselves has important consequences. For every dollar which you and I as residents of the United States owe, through our government, to the owners of the national debt, there is a corresponding creditor who owns a United States debt certificate of one kind or another. When we

total the debt, it is our duty, if we do not want to mislead, to total the credit too. And if we count both, they cancel out.

While it is common for only the debit side of the national debt to be counted, I don't know of anybody who has counted only the credit side. But it could be said with equal logic, or rather illogic, that the United States is *richer* because among the things which Americans own are two hundred and ninety billions of national debt—in the form of first-class, gilt-edged securities guaranteed by the United States government. You can repeat the arithmetical exercises of the editorialist and see how long it would take to count this part of our *wealth*. This, of course, would be just as silly as doing the opposite. The United States is not any richer on account of the national debt than it is poorer because of it. Against the credit there is a debit, just as against the debit there is a credit.

Our conclusion is that we *do* owe the national debt to ourselves, that it is not a terrible danger to our society as imagined by those who think it is the same kind of thing as personal or inter-personal debt, and that there are some real problems, but that these problems are due to the existence and growth of *any* private claims to national wealth rather than of that part of private claims to wealth that are the counterpart of the national debt.

View III: A Balanced Budget but at Full Employment

An intermediate (though not necessarily correct) view, between the two suggested so far, is one that has attracted special attention in the early 1970s: balance the federal budget, argues this approach, but only as that budget would emerge in a *full employment economy*. In his *Economic Report* of February 1971, President Nixon clearly took this position:

We need to abide by a principle of budget policy which permits flexibility in the bud-

get and yet limits the inevitable tendency to waste and inflationary action. The useful and realistic principle of the full-employment budget is that, except in emergencies, expenditures should not exceed the revenues that the tax system would yield when the economy is operating at full employment.

This principle implies a criticism of the strict, year-by-year, balance-the-budget approach. It is based on the view that adherence to such a target when there is unemployment would mean effectively that the government was exercising an *inhibiting* effect on the expansion of the economy. Why? Because if the economy were at full employment, its tax revenues would automatically be higher than when the economy was producing at below its full-employment potential. Thus, for example, we know that the U.S. personal income tax automatically increases federal revenues when national income rises.[1] For a given level of federal spending, this increased tax revenue would imply a *full-employment surplus* in the federal budget. Thus, a balanced budget when the economy was suffering unemployment would imply that the effec-

tive policy with respect to full employment tended to be contractionary.

Although the full-employment balanced budget principle does depart considerably from the more narrow balanced budget view (and is consistent with the possibility of the national debt regularly increasing over time), it is still quite far from the notion implicit in View II that the public debt should be regarded primarily as a useful instrument in the operation of a flexible fiscal policy. For those who accept this flexible approach, the question remains: why limit yourself to the basically arbitrary principle of full-employment balance? Suppose that conditions in the economy are so depressed that the deficits implied by this principle are insufficient to cure a serious unemployment condition. Why should the government bind itself not to act in such grave circumstances?

That problems do arise with the full-employment balanced budget principle in practice is suggested by the report of President Nixon's Council of Economic Advisers in February 1972 (a year after the above declaration of policy). What is significant in the following statement is not so much that events have altered predictions, but that the administration considers "appropriate" the emergence of a full-employment *deficit* in 1972 despite the earlier policy declaration concerning full-employment balance.

---

1. This tendency of tax revenues to rise with every expansion of national income has been called *fiscal drag,* a term coined by Walter Heller, former Chairman of the Council of Economic Advisers.

FISCAL POLICY TO AUGUST 15

ECONOMIC REPORT OF THE PRESIDENT, 1971

The Administration's fiscal policy as reflected in the budget submitted in January 1971 was in gener-

Excerpted from "Fiscal Policy to August 15," in *The Annual Report of the Council of Economic Advisers* (Washington, D.C.: U.S. Government Printing Office, 1972), pp. 64–65.

al to keep expenditures from exceeding the revenues that would be yielded by the existing tax system under conditions of full employment. There were two reasons for the Administration's adoption of this principle. First, the conventional notion of balancing the actual budget more or less all the time had proved to be unworkable because either tax increases or expenditure cuts would be required whenever revenue was depressed by an economic slowdown, and this would be precisely the wrong time for a restrictive fiscal policy. In fact, this standard of fiscal policy had not been followed by an Administration for almost forty years. Second, some rule of policy that would confine expenditures within the limits of what the Government was willing to raise in taxes was necessary to enforce economy in Government. The principle that expenditures should not exceed full-employment revenues has the advantage that fiscal action likely to intensify the slowdown would be avoided while the discipline of the basic relationship between revenues and expenditures would be retained.

In conformity with this principle, the Administration's January 1971 budget called for the following relationship between expenditures and the revenues that would be collected at full employment:

[Billions of dollars]

	Outlays	Revenues at full employment	Excess of revenues
Fiscal 1971	212.8	214.2	1.4
Fiscal 1972	229.2	229.3	.1

The outcome for fiscal 1971 was close to these plans. Estimated full-employment revenues after the end of the fiscal year were only $0.1 billion below the January 1 estimates. Outlays were $1.4 billion, or about one-half of 1 percent, under the estimate. Instead of an excess of full-employment revenues of $1.4 billion there was an excess of $2.7 billion.

Developments in the first six months of 1971 more significantly changed the estimates of the full-employment budget for fiscal 1972. On the revenue side the postponement, from 1971 to 1972, of the increase in the base for Social Security contributions reduced estimated fiscal 1972 receipts by $2.6 billion. This was expected to be offset in part by an increase in the Social Security contribution rate to take effect January 1, 1972. The net effect of these and other smaller changes was to

reduce the estimated full-employment receipts by $1.9 billion. Estimated expenditures were raised by $4.7 billion. The largest item in this total was an increase of $1.4 billion of Social Security benefits above the budget. Other major items were an increase of $1 billion in the estimated payments for unemployment compensation because of the continued high rate of unemployment, and a possible increase of $0.8 billion in military pay as a result of congressional action.

Thus there was in prospect an excess of expenditures over full-employment revenues of $6.5 billion in fiscal 1972, compared to an excess of revenues of $2.7 billion in fiscal 1971.

This estimate for fiscal 1972 as it appeared in July depended heavily on action still to be taken by Congress. Although the estimate made some allowance for probable delays in the enactment of expenditure programs that had been proposed by the Administration, even longer delays were possible. And although the estimate also made some allowance for pending congressional proposals above the budget, not all of those possibilities were expected to materialize. Despite these uncertainties, it seemed highly probable in the summer of 1971 that there would be a significant shift from a full-employment surplus in fiscal 1971 to a full-employment deficit in fiscal 1972. The Administration considered this development appropriate in view of the sluggishness of the economy. At the same time the Administration was averse to making decisions that would add substantially to expenditure commitments for the future. Even within the limits of fiscal 1972, while more fiscal stimulus was desired, there was danger of excessive expansion in the prevailing inflationary atmosphere.

*   *   *

ARGUMENTS AND FACTS

Given the divergent viewpoints suggested by the readings above, we clearly must sort out the opposing arguments with some care. Let us do this now, first dispelling some alarmist notions, and then analyzing the actual costs and benefits of the public debt.

One common concern about the expansion of the national debt may be put this way:

The federal government is no different from any private individual. Everyone knows that a private individual cannot keep accumulating indebtedness all the time. Consequently, the federal government should (or must) reduce the size of the public debt.

Now this argument is, in part, a throwback to the view that Adam Smith expressed in his famous declaration: "What is prudence in the conduct of every private family can scarce be folly in that of a great Kingdom." And, indeed, this is part of the problem with it, because Smith's statement is clearly untrue in a number of important circumstances. To take a couple of obvious examples: it is clearly prudent for a private individual to refrain from printing money, but does this mean that it is folly for the national government to print money? It is prudent for a private individual not to take the law into his own hands, but are we then to conclude that it is folly for the state to maintain a police force and legal system? And so on. The point is that the actions of the state and the actions of private individuals are often regulated by different principles and that the argument by analogy from one to the other is filled with pitfalls.

In the particular case of the public debt, moreover, there is at least one feature that distinguishes it from the debt of private individuals. This is the feature brought out in the Abba Lerner reading. When I owe a debt to you, I owe it to an external party. The proper analogy in the case of the nation as a whole would be a debt owed to some foreign country, or an *external debt*. However, the public debt is not external but internal, and, indeed, we could imagine hypothetical circumstances in which the holders of government bonds and the payers of taxes were identical individuals, in which case it would be literally true that we owe the debt to ourselves.

But even if the analogy were completely correct, there is another major flaw in this particular argument. And this is the incorrect assumption that private parties—individuals or business firms—do not increase their indebtedness in the aggregate over time. Figure 12-1 shows what has been happening to the public debt of the federal, state, and local governments in recent decades, compared to the debt of individuals and private corporations. Although the federal debt was growing substantially relative to private indebtedness in the period from the 1930s to the end of World War II, the last twenty-five years have seen a complete reversal of form. Private debt has been growing much more rapidly in this period and, at the present time, it is almost three times as great in total as the whole public debt. Nor is this surprising. We all know that businesses regularly issue bonds to finance new ventures and expansions; in a growing economy, we should expect this kind of indebtedness to increase over time. This is also true of households. We do pay back each debt as it comes due; but in the meanwhile, we incur new debts. While we are buying a car on credit, we are also taking out a mortgage on a new house and buying a washing machine and dryer on the installment plan. As the population grows and the average real income per capita rises, we should naturally expect a continuing expansion in outstanding mortgage loans and consumer credit. And this is exactly what we do have.

These facts should bring home the danger of loose analogies between the government and private parties. For if we

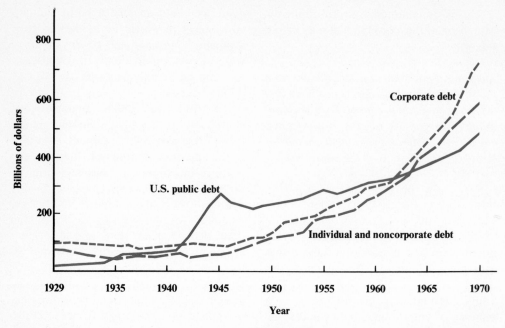

Figure 12-1.

were to take the analogy literally, then this would come perilously close to saying, "It's perfectly all right to expand the public debt indefinitely. After all, look at what consumers and businessmen are doing!" In short, this first argument is fallacious on two fundamental counts and would not be worth spending time on, except that it is heard so frequently in everyday discussion.

Much the same can be said for a second common worry about the public debt, which might be put this way:

All debts must ultimately be repaid, and so it is with the public debt. The U.S. federal debt is now between $300 and $400 billion. This sum is so enormous that any attempt to repay it will cause huge burdens on the economy. Under these circumstances, any further increases in the public debt will ultimately lead us to national bankruptcy.

Like the earlier argument, this one also involves at least two major problems. The first of these problems is the assumption (very evident in the Byrd speech) that all debts, including the federal debt, must in the aggregate be repaid. This assumption involves difficulties similar to those we have already noticed. In the case of private debt, each particular loan does get paid back (unless someone goes bankrupt) but, in the aggregate, private indebtedness increases over time, as indicated by Figure 12-1. Similarly, the government is regularly engaged in paying back its indebtedness to particular individuals as various government bonds come to maturity. But it then engages in issuing new bonds, with the result that although every individual can count on getting his money back at the proper time, the total of indebtedness can remain the same or increase for the government over time. In fact, it is inconceivable that the debt of the United States government ever will be repaid. It may be (and has been) reduced from time to time by surpluses in the federal budget, but the notion that we will ever get rid of the debt in total is ultimately fanciful. Nor is there any need to do so.

Moving away from these incomplete analogies between the private and public sectors, we run into another and more specific criticism of this alarmist argument. The real question of how "huge" the federal debt is cannot be decided by absolute figures in isolation. Is $300 billion or $400 billion "huge"? How can we say unless we indicate the standard that we are using for comparisons? There are different standards that one might choose, but a fairly obvious one is the size of the public debt (federal, state, and local government debt) in relation to the size of the economy as a whole, or roughly our annual GNP. Figure 12-2 shows this relationship in percentage terms over the past few decades. Notice that there has been a very substantial decline in the *relative* importance of the public debt since World War II. This is significant when people start worrying about national bankruptcy. If we managed to survive the great expansion of debt that took place during World War II, it seems highly unlikely that we are seriously threatened by anything that has happened since. This is particularly true if we are thinking of the *federal* debt, which has increased in absolute terms much more slowly than state and local government debt during the past two decades;[2] its decline relative to GNP has been even more rapid than suggested by Figure 12-2. This is simply to say that although the absolute debt has grown, the economy as a whole has grown much more rapidly, reducing the weight of the

2. Thus from 1950 to 1970, while state and local government debt was increasing by over *sixfold*, federal government debt was increasing only by about one-third. GNP during this same period more than tripled.

debt in relation to our capacity for sustaining it.

Still another common concern is this:

By increasing the public debt, we are putting the burdens of the present generation off onto the shoulders of the future generations. In Senator Byrd's words: "The debt today is the debt incurred by this generation, but tomorrow it will be debt on our children and grandchildren." In effect, we are saddling them with financial responsibilities that really ought to be borne by ourselves now.

This is a particularly interesting alarmist concern because it is always premised on the assumption that it would be a "bad thing" if today we were to put off any of our economic burdens to our children or to their children yet unborn. Yet would it be so unfair if we could manage it? After all, we do bequeath certain economic *assets* to our children's children. They have the whole stock of houses, buildings, factories, machinery, inventories of goods in stock—our national physical capital—that has been built up over the course of past generations and is simply handed over to them. Equally important, they have the enormous legacy of *intangible* capital: human knowledge, technological advances, skills, economic know-how. Would it then necessarily be inequitable if we handed on a few "burdens"?

Quite apart from this, however, there is the question whether we *could* manage the shifting of burdens implied in this statement of concern. Admittedly, there are some future burdens to the public debt—we shall come to these in a moment—but in the sense in which this worry is usually conceived, the possible shifting is very limited. We know from Figures 12-1 and 12-2 that our great mod-

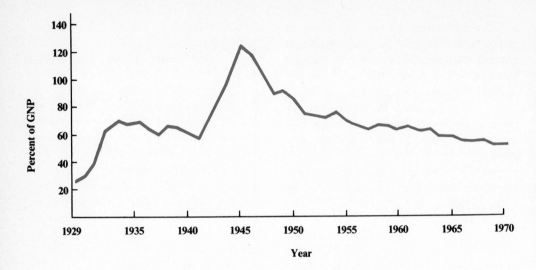

Figure 12-2. U.S. Public Debt as a Percentage of GNP.

ern increase in the national debt came during World War II. We ask, then: Does this mean that the fundamental burdens of fighting World War II were passed on to later generations? Are we in fact "paying for" the war now?

Had the war been financed by external debt to other countries, so that the resources to produce the tanks and planes and ships had come from abroad, and were it true in the 1970s that we were sending equivalent resources back to these foreign countries, then it would also be true that we were "paying for" the war now in an economic sense. But we did not borrow from abroad; consequently, the resources required had to be our own, and they had to be put up *then*, not now. We are certainly not producing tanks, planes, and ships for World War II at the present time. Subject to a qualification we shall mention presently, the resources had to be used and were in fact used in the 1940s. Imagine a full-employment economy operating on its transformation or produc-

tion-possibility curve.[3] If it wants to produce more of one commodity (armaments), it must give up some of the other commodity (private production). When a war effort of the magnitude of our own in the 1940s is involved—50 percent of our national income was given to defense purposes—then the basic costs must be sustained when they occur (by the current

---

3. See chapter 1, p. 17. Of course, it may be said that when we entered World War II, we were far from a full-employment economy. This, of course, is true, and it is further true that the economic sacrifices (not speaking, of course, of the tremendous human sacrifices involved) of the war in terms of actually "giving up things" were minimal. In a fundamental sense, we financed the war by taking up the tremendous slack in our economy—i.e., moving out to the production-possibility frontier—and also by pushing the curve outward. This, however, is not an argument against debt financing as opposed to the major alternative: total reliance on increased taxation. Indeed, it seems highly doubtful that without some debt financing we could have moved out so quickly to the production-possibility frontier. The huge burdens of taxation would have made mobilization on this scale very difficult. Hence while it is not right to say that the debt postponed the fundamental burdens of the war, it is fair to give debt financing some credit for easing the pains of the war effort at the time it occurred.

generation) and not in the future.

In sum, this source of alarm has little more fundamental foundation than the others we have discussed.

COSTS AND BENEFITS OF THE NATIONAL DEBT

Still, we must not go to the other extreme and assume that the size of the national debt is a complete irrelevance to our economic life. It clearly does involve certain burdens for the nation. It also may involve certain possible benefits. Without attempting to be all-inclusive, let us list a few features of the debt which may have real economic impact, primarily to get a sense of the scale of the problems involved.

Interest Charges on the National Debt

An important burden of the federal debt arises from the fact that we have to pay interest on it. Generally, as Senator Byrd's speech pointed out, these interest payments will have to be met by increased taxation, and taxes are not only personally unpleasant but may involve certain disincentive effects on effort and productivity in the economy.

This particular burden of the debt is somewhat offset by the fact that American citizens are (1) the taxpayers who finance the interest payments on the debt and (2) the bondholders who receive the interest payments. Even in the unlikely case that precisely the same individuals were involved, however, the net economic effect would still be some lessening of incentives, because the interest comes to us for doing nothing, but the taxes come out of our incomes produced by our hard efforts. If taxes rise high enough, then we may ask: why put in the extra hour or

two of effort if it will mostly go to the government anyway? The magnitude of this disincentive effect, however, must be judged in any given case by the magnitude of the interest charges in relation to our capacity to sustain them, or basically our GNP. Figure 12-3 shows that federal interest payments have declined somewhat as a percentage of GNP since the end of World War II. The relative constancy of this percentage since the 1950s reflects the twin facts that the federal debt has been declining as a percentage of GNP but that interest rates have been rising during this period. Since state and local government debt has also been rising substantially in these years, it should be clear that the interest burden of the total public debt is a real phenomenon.

It should be noted, however, that these interest payments are to some degree simply payments for benefits being currently received. A portion of government expenditure goes into what in the private sector we would call capital formation, as it does when highways, schools, dams, etc., are built by the federal, state, and local governments. Insofar as these capital projects are financed by increases in the public debt, they bring to us not only increased interest payments and taxes but also increased economic benefits.[4]

Postponing Burdens: The Problem of Investment

We mentioned in our discussion of World War II that there was a qualification to the basic truth that the costs of

---

4. Some countries in fact distinguish between the *current* expenditures of government (paying the mailman to deliver the mail) and *capital* expenditures (building a post office). Although one could argue that debt financing is especially appropriate for governmental capital expenditures, this in effect would imply a much too limited and inflexible role for a country's fiscal policy, which ultimately must be guided by the macroeconomic needs of the economy as a whole.

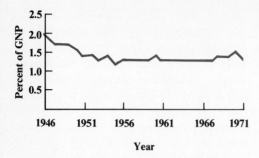

Figure 12-3. Interest Payments on the Federal Debt as a Percentage of GNP.

Interest payments on the federal debt have fallen slightly as a percentage of GNP in the post-war period, but they have been a relatively constant percentage since the 1950s because of the rise in interest rates.

the war were borne at the time of the war. This qualification arises from the fact that it is possible to postpone present burdens to the future to the degree that one "lives off" one's capital stock today and consequently bequeaths a smaller capital stock to the future generation. And, in fact, during World War II, we did limit the replacement and repair of a certain portion of our capital stock in order to achieve a maximum war effort.

To what degree debt financing was responsible for this postponement of burdens is, however, a different question. Even had the war been financed completely by current taxes, the same problem would have occurred, and it is doubtful that the solution would have been different in any fundamental way. Furthermore, it is possible to argue that an expansion of the national debt may in many circumstances effectively *increase* the capital stock available to a future generation. If an expansion of the debt is part of a successful fiscal policy that brings the economy closer to its full employment potential, then it has stimulated greater production today, part of which will go into

greater consumption today, but *part* of which will also probably go into greater investment today and hence a greater capital stock tomorrow.

This is not to say that the debt may not have an unfavorable effect on investment or that it may not involve postponement to later generations. For example, insofar as the government, faced with the need to market large quantities of bonds, comes into competition with private investors for sources of financial capital, it may contribute to "tighter" money, and hence to some lowering of private investment.[5] What it does mean, however, is that the picture is quite mixed. Some effects of the debt may be in the direction of increasing future burdens, while others—as in the case of a successful fiscal policy—may actually benefit our children's children.

National Debt in Relation to Government Activities

Taxes are considered politically unpopular. If the government does not have to balance the budget, it may, some people fear, engage in "reckless" spending projects, thus spurring inflation, increasing the sphere of government in our mixed economy, and appropriating resources that might be more effectively used in the private sector. This notion was apparent in President Nixon's defense of the principle of a full-employment balanced budget which "limits the inevitable tendency to waste and inflationary action."

One's judgment on the importance of this point depends upon one's

5. It is also possible to argue that the debt involves some redistribution of income between generations on the grounds that the "younger generation" of today has to work to pay the taxes to pay the interest payments to the bondholding "older generation." Actually, it is doubtful that this qualification is of much practical importance.

general opinion about the desirability or undesirability of governmental spending in the economy and also on the more specific question of the degree to which the pressure for balancing the budget is an effective means of limiting government spending. Insofar as one is committed to reducing government expenditures at all costs, it is probably true that by insisting on some form of a balanced budget, one is at least creating a further argument against additional public spending. The opposite point of view might be expressed as follows: (1) There are a great many public needs having to do with our cities, our environment, minorities, the aged, the poor, and the ill which must not be neglected because of an arbitrary budget-balancing principle; and (2) the question of balancing or not balancing the budget should be determined on the general grounds of its effect on employment and price stability in the economy as a whole.

Ultimately, this third feature of the debt comes down to the question of whether or not this country needs the kind of financial discipline which a balance-the-budget principle requires. This, in turn, is really a question not about the burden of the debt, but rather about the burden of "reckless" spending. It is undoubtedly true historically and even today that some governments need every possible constraint imaginable to keep them from spending themselves into financial insolvency. Whether this is true of the United States in the 1970s, however, is a very different question.[6]

In short, the picture with respect to this third point, as in the case of the other two points, is a mixed one. The truth lies somewhere between a total lack of

concern for the debt and raising it to the level of mortal sin. There should be ample room in this intermediate range for the application of a flexible fiscal policy in present-day America. Indeed, the main controversy among economists over fiscal policy in the early 1970s is not about the "burdens" of the debt, but about the mechanism by which this policy does (or does not) work. This brings us back to the subject of "monetarism" which we will take up in some detail next.

SUMMARY

The national debt has been a subject of controversy in this country for many years. Keynesian economists look upon the national debt as an instrument of a flexible fiscal policy; increases in the debt may sometimes be considered not only tolerable but desirable if the nation is suffering from serious unemployment and inadequate aggregate demand. On the other hand, there are many who espouse the principle of a balanced budget either in a rigid form (annual balance) or in a more flexible form (surpluses in inflationary periods to offset deficits during depressions or recessions). In 1971, President Nixon proposed a full-employment balanced budget as a guide to national policy. Such a principle modifies the strict balanced-budget approach, though it remains somewhat arbitrary as a criterion for fiscal policy.

Many of the arguments for a balanced budget are based on unduly alarmist fears of the supposed ill effects of a substantial national debt. The argument that the government is just like a private party and that private parties cannot keep going into debt is refuted by the facts that (1) the government is not identical to a private party in many instances, and (2)

6. On the specific question of the relationship of government spending to inflationary pressures, we must await an analysis of inflation in chapters 14 and 27.

individual and corporate debt in the United States has been growing more rapidly than the public debt in recent years. The argument that the federal debt is so "huge" that its repayment will cause the country to go bankrupt is refuted by the facts that (1) the national debt will almost certainly never be repaid in total and (2) as far as size is concerned, the federal debt has been declining as a percentage of GNP ever since World War II. Finally, the argument that the debt is a way of foisting our burdens upon our grandchildren is seen, in its simplistic form, to ignore the fundamental facts about the way resources are mobilized and used in an economy such as ours, as exemplified by our experience in World War II.

The actual costs and benefits of the public debt are much more subtle than these alarmists' arguments would imply. The costs of the debt include, among other things, substantial interest payments that are financed by taxation, possible diminution of business investment under certain circumstances, and a possible loss of financial discipline if "reckless" government spending is encouraged by the absence of a balance-the-budget constraint.

All these points have comebacks: e.g., interest charges have not risen as a percentage of GNP, investment may be increased if an increase in the debt results in higher general employment and output, government spending and deficits may be needed in many circumstances to promote the health of the economy.

Although no one would deny the importance of keeping an eye on the size of the national debt, it seems fairly safe to conclude that the burdens of the debt in the present circumstances of the United States do not in themselves constitute a major obstacle to the application of a flexible modern fiscal policy.

QUESTIONS FOR DISCUSSION

1. Comment on the theoretical and factual issues involved in the following statements:

(a) "The trouble with modern economics is that it does not play by its own rules. In theory, budget deficits in bad times should be balanced by budget surpluses in good times. But the proponents of deficit spending always seem to forget the latter. And this, of course, is the road to national bankruptcy."

(b) "When there is a balanced budget, the government is acting in a completely neutral way as far as the overall health of the economy is concerned."

(c) "When there is a full-employment balanced budget, the government is acting in a completely neutral way as far as the overall health of the economy is concerned."

(d) "A good general rule for modern fiscal policy is that the public debt should grow at the same overall rate as national income."

(e) "The government should follow the following maxims in regulating its tax and expenditure policies: (1) pay for all current expenditures out of taxation; (2) finance the construction of all capital assets (highways, school buildings, etc.) by bond issues."

2. Argue the pros and cons of having a specific, congressionally determined, limitation on the size of the federal debt.

3. Since private indebtedness has been growing more rapidly than public indebt-

edness in recent decades, should there be some attempt to limit the increase of private indebtedness in the economy? What might be some of the issues involved?

4. In the late 1930s and 1940s, a group of American economists called the "stagnationists" predicted that there would be a tendency for saving to outrun investment in the American economy and, consequently, that there would be increasing unemployment unless the government stepped up its intervention. Considering what has been said so far in this book about the performance of the American economy and the changing role of the government since World War II, do you feel that these predictions have been verified or refuted by our experience? Explain your answer.

SUGGESTED READING

Bowen, W. G.; Davis, R. G.; and Kopf, D. H. "The Public Debt." *American Economic Review* 50 (September 1960).

Buchanan, J. M. *Public Principles of Public Debt.* Homewood, Ill.: Richard D. Irwin, 1958.

Eckstein, Otto. *Public Finance.* 2nd ed. Englewood Cliffs, N.J.: Prentice-Hall, 1967, chap. 7.

Harris, Seymour E. *Economics of the Kennedy Years.* New York: Harper & Row, 1964, chap. 11.

Okun, Arthur M. *The Political Economy of Prosperity.* New York: W. W. Norton & Co., 1970, pp. 109–15.

Pechman, Joseph A. *Federal Tax Policy.* Rev. ed. New York: W. W. Norton & Co., 1971, chapter 2.

13
Controversies Over Money And Monetary Policy

In our discussion of the role of money in the economic system (chapter 11), we tried to avoid controversy so as to keep the overall theory of national income determination clearly in mind. This objective required us to go over certain aspects of the functioning of monetary mechanisms rather more quickly than we might have wanted. It also made us skim over the fact that there is disagreement not only on details, but also on the basic way in which money is related to our important macroeconomic variables—GNP, total employment and unemployment, and the price level.

This disagreement is centered on a debate over what is called *monetarism.* This debate has attracted the energies and abilities of some of the nation's leading economists. The father of monetarist thought in the United States is Milton Friedman, a University of Chicago economist whose incisive arguments and often provocatively conservative opinions have made him well known to the general public as well as to the economics profession.

One of Friedman's opponents has been Paul A. Samuelson of M.I.T., who probably vies with John Kenneth Galbraith for being the most famous economist in the world in recent decades. Samuelson, besides being active in public policy debates, is an outstanding economic theoretician who was the first American to be honored with a Nobel Prize in economics.

However, the debate is not between two men or even two groups of men. It concerns the correct analysis of the impact of money on a modern economy, and consequently the appropriate role of public policy, fiscal policy quite as much as monetary policy.

These questions are the subject of Great Debate Two: The Issue of Monetarism. In order to understand that debate, however, the reader must go somewhat more deeply into the complexities of money than we have done so far. This chapter can, therefore, be considered both a guide to Great Debate Two and an opportunity to deepen our comprehension of monetary phenomena.

Paul A. Samuelson. Samuelson is America's first Nobel laureate in economics. Although known to the general public for his widely read books and articles, he is best known to economists as a brilliant theoretician especially in mathematical economics.

Milton Friedman. By all odds the most articulate spokesman for the conservative point of view in economics, Professor Friedman has brought original thinking to many fundamental economic problems including particularly the role of money in the economic system.

INCOME ANALYSIS IN A SIMPLIFIED "REAL" WORLD

If we think back to Part Two A, when we were first discussing the theory of national income determination, we can recall that we did the original analysis in *real* terms. Not only was there no explicit discussion of money in the economy, but we dealt with national income as expressed in unchanging prices (constant dollars). In this world, Keynesian analysis told us that real national income would be determined by the sum of consumption, investment, and government spending, all expressed in given prices. Thus, in Figure 10-1 (p. 229), we used our 45-degree line diagram to determine real na-

tional income (and hence the level of employment) without mentioning money or possible changes in the levels of prices and money wages in our economy.

An interesting question arises: if these are the forces which determine where the level of real national income will be, what will determine where the level of *money* national income will be? To answer this, we would have to know how to determine the general price level (P) as well as the real level of GNP (let us call this Q, to signify that we are talking about real quantities). If consumption, investment and government spending determine real national income (Q), what determines money national income $(P \times Q)$?

Now a true Keynesian would have brought in the money-supply at an earlier stage of the analysis, but a more sloppy disciple might largely avoid it even now. He might say something like the following:

In order to determine prices, what we really have to know is the general level of money wages (W). *Let's suppose that these money wages have been set by union–management agreements throughout our fictitious economy. Basically, once this is done, P will be pretty well set, too. The reason for this is that once we have settled where real national income is, we have also settled where the level of employment is. This will roughly determine what labor's productivity is and this, in turn, will tell us what labor's real wage* (W/P) *will be. Knowing both the money wage and real wage, we more or less automatically know where the price level will be. Admittedly, the money supply has to be consistent with this overall solution, but this is not difficult, or particularly important to achieve.*[1]

In other words, this sloppy ultra-Keynesian might say that real national income (Q) is effectively determined by consumption, investment, and government spending, and that prices (P) for a given level of real national income are effectively determined by the level of money wages (W), and hence that P × Q can be determined with only the most minimal discussion of the money supply.

Now this kind of logic is associated with an extreme position which, in Great Debate Two, says: "money doesn't matter." No one, living or dead, has taken this position in quite such an uncompromising form, yet in the period just after World War II many economists left

money seriously underrepresented in their analyses. They would talk of W and P and Q and then, almost as an afterthought, they would say that, of course, the quantity of money (M) had to be mentioned as a factor, too. The truth is that many of these economists, unlike Keynes himself, felt that changes in the quantity of money had so little impact that, for practical purposes, they could be ignored.

QUANTITY THEORY OF MONEY

This emphasis on the real side of things contrasted in many (though not all) ways with the prevailing theory of the role of money prior to Keynesian analysis. In general, that previous theory, while it did not give money much of a role in affecting real national income or employment, nevertheless gave money an absolutely central role in determining the general price level. The basic hypothesis here is usually referred to as the *quantity theory of money*. The quantity theory of money can be expressed in terms of an equation such as the following:

$$M \times V = P \times Q$$

where M is the stock of money in the economy—for the moment, currency plus demand deposits—V is a term called the *income velocity of money*, P is the price level, and Q is the level of real national income.[2]

The key concept here is that of the income velocity of money. It is meant

---

1. This argument assumes, among other things, that labor will be paid according to its productivity. More specifically, it assumes that labor will be paid according to its *marginal productivity*. The reasoning behind this aspect of the argument is developed extensively in chapter 21, pp. 481–83.

2. This equation has many different forms, with approximately similar meanings. Thus, it is often written: $MV = PT$, where T stands for transactions, including, for example, purchases and sales of intermediate goods not included in national income. In this case, of course, we would have to speak of the transactions velocity of money, rather than its income velocity.

to measure the number of times the average dollar bill or demand deposit circulates through the economy in a given period in exchange for final output. In particular, it is defined as

$$V = \frac{P \times Q}{M}$$

or, in words, money national income in a given year divided by the total of currency and demand deposits available on the average during the course of that year.

This definition raises a possible source of confusion about our quantity theory equation: namely, that equation appears to be true by virtue of the meaning of income velocity. $MV = PQ$ becomes a truism that tells us nothing whatever about the real world. This is quite correct, and what it means is that in order to get a proper theory about the role of money in the economy from this equation we have to make some further statements about its terms. And this the quantity theorists did.

They said, first, that on the whole national income in real terms (Q) was determined by real factors—size of the labor force, amount of capital, technology, etc. These factors would alter over time, but very slowly, and in any event they would not be affected by the quantity of money in any serious or enduring way. This was full-employment economics in the tradition of Say's Law.[3]

Second, they argued that V was largely determined by institutional factors and could be regarded as also independent of changes in M. V would be influenced by such factors as the state of banking practice and the ways in which

wage payments and other disbursements of funds were made in the economy. Consider, for example, the differences in the velocity of money when a man gets his salary on a weekly basis and when he gets it on a monthly basis. If the man gets $250 a week by a weekly paycheck and spends it all each week, he will, at any given moment of time, be holding on the average $125 in money. (If all payments are by check, this will be his average bank balance.) If, however, he is paid by the month (something over $1,000 per month), his bank balance will on the average be over $500. The income velocity of money will be four or more times as great if his paychecks are on a weekly as opposed to a monthly basis.

What the quantity theorists said was that these and other such institutional factors largely determined V. At the same time, Q was largely determined by technology and the available quantities of factors of production. What then happened when you altered M? Clearly, the only variable left to be affected is P. And this was the main contention of the quantity theory; namely, that changes in the quantity of money produced roughly proportional changes in P (and presumably also in W) throughout the economy.

In a sense, this theory embodied a combination of two views of money: (1) "money doesn't matter" and (2) "money alone matters." In terms of real national income and employment, money mattered very little according to this theory. In terms of prices and wages, by contrast, the quantity of money more or less completely called the tune.

KEYNES WITH MONEY

Keynes was concerned about bridging the gap between real and mone-

3. Recall that we said earlier (p. 181) that the classical economists had regarded money as a "veil" as far as real phenomena were concerned. Another way of putting this is to say that changes in M have no effect on Q.

tary analysis. He did not deny that institutional factors could affect the velocity of money, nor even that, under certain special circumstances (particularly when full employment had been achieved), the quantity theory might be a fair approximation to reality. But he did deny that full-employment national income could be taken as the natural state of affairs, and he also stressed the effects of M on the interest rate (r).

As we have already indicated at the end of chapter 11, Keynes spoke of a transactions demand for money and also a liquidity demand for money. As far as the transactions demand for money is concerned, we are essentially in the world of the quantity theorists, i.e., given the prevailing institutional arrangements, the amount of money we will need to carry out our day-to-day transactions will depend on the size of money income in the economy ($P \times Q$). This is tantamount to saying that the V for transactions money is effectively given.

But in the liquidity sphere, this is not so. The amount of money people wish to hold for precautionary purposes was, we recall, dependent on the rate of interest. The higher r, the less money people would wish to hold for liquidity purposes, and vice versa. Translated into quantity theory terms, what this means is that the velocity of this liquidity money will depend on the rate of interest. At low rates of interest, people will be willing to hold large amounts of currency and deposit balances; at high interest rates, they will try to put this money to use in interest-bearing assets and they will be willing to hold only much smaller average bank balances. Thus, V, in terms of all kinds of money, will depend in the Keynesian theory on the interest rate—it is not simply given by institutional factors.

The problem that this kind of

analysis causes for the quantity theory can be shown with reference to what we earlier called the "liquidity trap" (p. 266). In a serious depression, it may happen that the interest rate is so low and expectations are so pessimistic that when the Fed keeps pumping M into the system everyone simply holds this money as money and does not try to invest it in bonds or other securities. Hence, there is no effect on the interest rate, investment, national income, or prices. In effect, an increase in M is being offset by a decrease in V with the consequence that $P \times Q$ is left unaffected.

But if the quantity theory is amended in this way—if, for example, the connection between M and P can be severed by the liquidity trap—then how exactly is P determined in the Keynesian system? If the quantity of money doesn't determine the level of prices and wages, what does?

This question is of some importance because a major objection to the Keynesian system (referred to by Friedman as the system's dependence on "rigidities or imperfections," pp. 307–08) has been that it works properly only if money wages are held up artificially, say by union-management wage contracts that prevent wages from falling. In the absence of such rigidities, it can be said, will not the existence of unemployment cause a progressive bidding down of money wages in the economy as the unemployed workers try to secure jobs? If wages and prices are falling, will this not lead to an increase in total employment and output? To put it in terms of the quantity theory equation: if P is falling, and if M and V remain constant, won't this mean a rise in Q?

Of course, the key phrase in that last question is "if M and V remain constant." In a sense that is the whole issue. To see why this is so, and to show how wages and prices fit into the Keynesian system, let us follow through on the suggestion that unemployed workers will bid down wages in order to get work. Let us imagine an economy with high unemployment, and wages flexible downward. W is going down and P along with it. What effects will this have, according to Keynes?

The interesting thing is that these declines in money wages and prices would theoretically have much the same net effect as an *increase* in the money supply:

As wages and prices fall, the value of money national income falls ($P \times Q$ falls). This means that, for a given quantity of money (M), less money is needed in the transactions sphere and more is available for the liquidity sphere. The effect of more money in the liquidity sphere, under favorable circumstances, will be a lower interest rate. This lower interest rate, according to our familiar chain of logic, should raise investment and, by the multiplier, national income (Q). Thus, the potentially favorable effects of a general fall in wages and prices on total output and employment will come through a similar route—via the interest rate—as the effects of an increase in the money supply.

And, by the same token, such favorable effects can be nullified by the liquidity trap (a falling V) in a seriously depressed economy. In other words, in the Keynesian theory, the route to full employment via either monetary policy *or* general wage cuts is a highly uncertain one.[4]

---

4. Another possible difficulty is that although *low* wages and prices might be favorable to higher employment (through these interest rate effects), *falling* wages and prices might be very discouraging to business investment. The reader should notice that there is a distinction between a *high* or *low* something and a *rising* or *falling* something. This distinction is frequently of considerable importance in this area of economics.

PIGOU EFFECT

There is, however, another effect of such wage–price cuts, often referred to as the *Pigou effect*.[5] It was, in part, this particular effect that led to the "rediscovery" of money and the spread of monetarism in the postwar period.

What Pigou said was that as wages and prices fell systematically throughout the economy, the *real* (as opposed to *nominal*) value of the money supply increases in the same proportion. Suppose we have an economy with unemployment (because of too low $C + I + G$) and a given stock of money, M. Wages and prices are completely flexible downward, we assume, and this means that unemployed workers will bid down wages and this will have the further consequence of lowering prices throughout our economy. Let us suppose that P falls to half its previous value. What Pigou said was that this means a doubling of the real value of the money wealth held in this economy. My individual share of the money supply (my average bank balance) is, say, $1,000. Before the fall in P this was equivalent to a certain amount of purchasing power. *After* the halving of P, this same $1,000 is equivalent to twice as much purchasing power—$2,000 at the original P. My *real wealth* has thus been increased by the fall in W and P and there is every likelihood that I will spend more. Thus, we would expect consumption to rise and this would have a favorable effect on the real national income and employment.

It might be objected that this increase in my real wealth from $1,000 to

---

5. After the British economist A. C. Pigou. Friedman notes that Haberler (Gottfried von Haberler, then of Harvard University) also made an important contribution on this matter.

effectively $2,000 is too small to have any major effect on my consumption, which would still depend mainly on my income. However, notice that, in our assumed economy, this process of raising the real value of M can go on indefinitely. If halving P isn't sufficient, then it can be lowered to a tenth or a thousandth of its original value. In this last case, my $1,000 becomes the equivalent of $1 million in terms of purchasing power at the original prices. Surely this will have substantial effects on my C.

Now the Pigou effects we have been discussing are not so easily applicable to the real world as it might seem from this discussion. In our modern economy, where the problem tends to be inflation even with considerable unemployment (see the next chapter), the notion of W and P falling to one-half their previous levels is rather fanciful. To expect them to fall to a tenth or a thousandth of their previous levels is simply delusionary. Furthermore, it is not so clear that the M in our equation would remain constant as this massive fall in W and P took place. To some extent, the supply of money in the economy depends, for any given level of bank reserves, on the demands for money in the system. Such a large contraction in the transactions demand for money might be expected to be accompanied by at least some contraction in M. And, finally, of course, the problem of *low* versus *falling* wages and prices arises again. The process of reducing W and P by half in the present-day American economy might be so fraught with hazard that it would nullify the goal for which the process was launched.

Nevertheless, the Pigou effect does suggest that money can enter into the macroeconomic picture in more ways than the original Keynesian model allowed for. Consideration of such effects had something to do with the desire of some economists to upgrade the role of money well beyond what the master himself had prescribed.

MONETARIST DOCTRINE

All that we have said so far represents a development and extension of the basic Keynesian or post-Keynesian position which, with innumerable variations, is accepted by most modern economists. But the monetarists go much further than this. As a guide to Great Debate Two, let us now summarize briefly the main doctrines, empirical issues, and policy questions raised by Professor Friedman and his monetarist colleagues.

Basically, monetarism involves a complicated restatement of the quantity theory of money and a return to the idea that "money matters much" or, as Professor Samuelson says critically, that "money alone matters." Once we know what M is in the monetarist world we can fairly well determine what money national income $(P \times Q)$ is. The whole income–expenditure approach to national income determination, including the basic macroeconomic role of fiscal policy, is abandoned in this doctrine.

This major difference is, in turn, premised on a variety of more specific differences. In an introductory essay to a book on the quantity theory,[6] Professor Friedman suggested three areas of difference between quantity theorists and Keynesians. The first concerns the "stability and importance of the demand for money." This has to do ultimately with the amount of variability of the velocity

---

6. Milton Friedman, ed., *Studies in the Quantity Theory of Money* (Chicago: University of Chicago Press, 1956).

of money, V. While Friedman does not argue that V is a numerical constant, nevertheless the monetarist position is dependent on reasonably modest fluctuations in V and on a limit to the number of variables that effect V. Second, the monetarist doctrine depends on the view that the demand and supply for money are to a large degree independent. If the banking system simply adjusts the supply of money to the demands for it, then changes in the quantity of money will be a reflection of, not a cause of, changes in economic conditions. Finally, a good quantity theorist will reject the notion that there is a "liquidity trap" and/or that the "only role of the stock of money and the demand for money is to determine the interest rate."

Given the monetarist approach to these issues—and especially the notion of a reasonably stable V—we can understand that M will largely determine $P \times Q$. But what will its specific effects on Q be? In the old-fashioned quantity theory, M merely affected P, while real national income remained happily pegged at something close to the full-employment level.

On this important point the monetarist position does not seem wholly clear. It is beyond doubt that the monetarists believe that changes in the money supply can have massive and disastrous effects on real national income and employment. Thus the depression of the 1930s (called the "Great Contraction" in Friedman's article) is attributed by monetarists largely to the fact that the Federal Reserve System followed a deflationary policy, reducing the amount of money in the economy by one-third. This implies an extremely potent role of money in its effects on real variables and, if the analysis is accepted, would indeed be "tragic testimony to the power of monetary policy."

On the other hand, as Friedman makes clear in his article on "The Role of Monetary Policy" (Great Debate Two), he does not feel that monetary policy can determine the long-run rate of employment in the economy. The role of M is to affect nominal quantities (like the price level) and not real quantities (like employment or real national income). This is because the initial effects of actions to alter M will be different from long-run effects. Thus, suppose the monetary authority increases the supply of money to raise the rate of employment above its "natural" level. *Initially* this will affect Q more than P, but in the long-run wages and prices will rise in money terms that—with a largely constant V—will mean a reverse in the increase of employment back to its original level.

Thus, the monetarist position would seem to be something like this: in the long run, real national output and employment are determined by real factors, not by M. However, M can substantially affect these factors in the short run and, indeed, when M gets out of whack, it can cause major dislocations in real, as well as money or nominal, values in the system.

EMPIRICAL ISSUES

At this point, the reader might wish to ask the simple question: well, which theory is right? The impulse behind this question is sound in that we are dealing with (or should be dealing with) questions of fact, not of ideology or normative values. However, as Great Debate Two makes clear (see especially James Tobin's article), there is very considerable disagreement on how to interpret the facts.

The difficulties here are characteristic of many economic problems and not just of the monetarist issue alone. They reflect the fact that the economic system is highly complex, that it is characterized by great interdependence among all the variables in the system, and that it is not subject—as, say, a chemistry problem might be—to carefully controlled experiments. In the particular case of monetarism these general difficulties are reflected in a number of problems.

What are the key variables we are talking about? Thus, for example, it is not perfectly clear what concept of money (M) the monetarists wish to emphasize. We have usually interpreted money in this book as currency plus demand deposits. Economists often use the term M_1 for this definition. Another definition (M_2) would include time and savings deposits as well. These deposits cannot be cashed by check on "demand" but they usually can be cashed within a reasonably short period of time. The difference between these two quantities is not small, since while M_1 currently runs at about $200 billion, M_2 is over $700 billion. Furthermore, it is not certain that it is either M_1 or M_2, but the *rates of change* of one or the other, that may be crucial. Thus, one of the differences between monetarists and their critics concerns the question of whether monetarists have played fair, or whether they change their key variables (and hence their theories) as the evidence alters.

What are the relevant leads and lags? Since economic effects are produced by causes that precede them in time, we might expect there to be various leads and lags when we come to examine the empirical relationships between variables. Thus, in the simplest case it might seem that if variable A is exerting a causal influence on variable B, this would be reflected in changes in A preceding changes in B by some fairly regular period of time. This

problem causes difficulties (1) because it is hard to determine what the appropriate "lead" or "lag" is, and (2) because economic systems are so complex that precedence in time may have no connection with causality at all. Thus, Tobin has constructed a theory in which the quantity of money has no influence on money income and yet in which it is regularly predicted to change in advance of changes in money income.[7]

How to distinguish cause and effect? The lag problem is one aspect of the more general problem of distinguishing cause and effect. How do we decide, when the money supply and money national income expand simultaneously, how much of this represents a response of the money supply to the expanded requirements of national income and how much represents the causal impact of an expanded money supply *on* national income? How do we decide whether money is an *exogenously* determined variable (determined by forces outside the system—e.g., by a policy decision of the Federal Reserve Board) or an *endogenously* determined variable (a function of other variables in the system)?

How to weigh "mountains" and/ or "hills" of evidence? Professor Friedman has done massive empirical research on the influences of money in the economy, as have a number of his colleagues. Because of the general difficulties we have cited, however, there is still more work to be done. Also, despite sophisticated modern statistical techniques, questions of judgment keep arising. Thus, the monetarist position heavily depends on some reasonable degree of stability in V. But how much? For example, income velocity of money (M_1) in the United States varied

7. In addition to Tobin's article in Great Debate Two, see James Tobin, "Money and Income: Post Hoc Ergo Propter Hoc?" *Quarterly Journal of Economics*, May 1970.

between 1.93 in the first quarter of 1946 to 3.87 in the fourth quarter of 1962—exactly doubling in this period. Furthermore, V went down in recessions and rose in prosperities during this period.[8] Should this be regarded as part of the "mountains of evidence" (to use Samuelson's terms) *for* Friedman's position or part of the "hills of evidence" Samuelson adduces *against* the Friedman position?

At the present sitting, the majority of economists believes that the verdict comes down slightly against the monetarists, but there are many exceptions in the universities, business, and government (the Federal Reserve Board of St. Louis is a notable example), and it is clear that the excavation of further mounds of evidence will be required.

THE POLICY ISSUES

It is also clearly of great importance that this further evidence be accumulated. The reason is that the monetarist versus Keynesian (or post-Keynesian) debate has enormous consequences for the policies that the government should follow in the whole area of macroeconomic stability.

We have already mentioned the increased potency attributed to monetary policy by the monetarists. Even more striking, however, is the *impotence* attributed by them to fiscal policy. This is the nub of the discussion between Friedman and Walter Heller. Heller's views on the impact of fiscal policy are in the Keynesian tradition as expressed in our own analysis (chapter 10). Friedman's position

is that fiscal policy influences the *division* of national income between the public and private sector but not the overall *level* of national income, employment, prices, etc. This is a direct consequence of the theory that M basically determines $P \times Q$. All that increasing government expenditures do is increase public Q as opposed to private Q. Being generally against increasing the public as opposed to the private sector, Professor Friedman is, of course, opposed to such a reallocation of resources.

This is a dramatic difference of opinion, and it is matched by another that is in some respects still more basic. This is the issue of whether or not the government should employ *any discretionary policy at all* in the area of macroeconomic stability. Friedman's general conclusion is that both logic and historical experience suggest that discretion produces far more errors (and serious errors) than it produces triumphs. Hence he favors the establishment of a fixed rule of conduct that the government should observe, increasing the money supply by a certain percentage every year—say, 3 to 5 percent a year—and then letting the market do the rest. This rule is perhaps even more restrictive in that it would focus the Federal Reserve Board's attention exclusively on a single monetary aggregate—the quantity of money—as opposed to interest rates, tightness of credit, general market conditions, and the like.

Thus the issues at stake are of great magnitude. Are the monetarists gaining ground or losing? In a paper presented to the annual meeting of the American Economic Association in December 1971, Andrew F. Brimmer, a member of the Board of Governors of the Federal Reserve System, spoke of the "highwater mark of monetarism in 1970," and concluded:

Continued on p. 334

---

8. Lawrence S. Ritter, "The Role of Money in Keynesian Theory," reprinted in *Readings in Macroeconomics*, ed. M. G. Mueller (New York: Holt, Rinehart & Winston, 1966), p. 171.

GREAT DEBATE TWO
THE ISSUE OF MONETARISM

F₄ 2

The following readings take up that large cluster of analytic and policy issues that center on the matter of monetarism. As the reader knows from chapter 13, this doctrine is one of the most hotly contested subjects in the whole area of macroeconomics.

The first reading is excerpted from the Presidential Address to the Eightieth Annual Meeting of the American Economic Association in 1967 by its (then) president, Milton Friedman. It is followed by an exchange between Friedman and Walter Heller, an outstanding neo-Keynesian economist and the chairman of the Council of Economic Advisers under President John F. Kennedy. This exchange has been excerpted from a discussion that took place between these two economists at the Graduate School of Business Administration of New York University in November 1968.

The final three readings are taken from another discussion about monetarism held under the auspices of the Federal Reserve Bank of Boston in 1969. The participants in this discussion, besides Paul Samuelson, are James Tobin, Sterling Professor of Economics at Yale University, and Allan H. Metzler, professor of Economics and Industrial Administration, Carnegie-Mellon University in Pittsburgh.

THE ROLE OF MONETARY POLICY

Milton Friedman

There is wide agreement about the major goals of economic policy: high employment, stable prices, and rapid growth. There is less agreement that these goals are mutually compatible or, among those who regard them as incompatible, about the terms at which they can and should be substituted for one another. There is least agreement about the role that various instruments of policy can and should play in achieving the several goals.

My topic for tonight is the role of one such instrument—monetary policy. What can it contribute? And how should it be conducted to contribute the most? Opinion on these questions has fluctuated widely. In the first flush

Excerpted from Milton Friedman, "The Role of Monetary Policy," *American Economic Review* 58, no. 1 (March 1968): 1–17. Reprinted by permission of the author and the publisher.

of enthusiasm about the newly created Federal Reserve System, many observers attributed the relative stability of the 1920s to the System's capacity for fine tuning—to apply an apt modern term. It came to be widely believed that a new era had arrived in which business cycles had been rendered obsolete by advances in monetary technology. This opinion was shared by economist and layman alike, though, of course, there were some dissonant voices. The Great Contraction destroyed this naive attitude. Opinion swung to the other extreme. Monetary policy was a string. You could pull on it to stop inflation but you could not push on it to halt recession. You could lead a horse to water but you could not make him drink. Such theory by aphorism was soon replaced by Keynes' rigorous and sophisticated analysis.

Keynes offered simultaneously an explanation for the presumed impotence of monetary policy to stem the depression, a nonmonetary interpretation of the depression, and an alternative to monetary policy for meeting the depression and his offering was avidly accepted. If liquidity preference is absolute or nearly so—as Keynes believed likely in times of heavy unemployment—interest rates cannot be lowered by monetary measures. If investment and consumption are little affected by interest rates—as Hansen and many of Keynes' other American disciples came to believe—lower interest rates, even if they could be achieved, would do little good. Monetary policy is twice damned. The contraction, set in train, on this view, by a collapse of investment or by a shortage of investment opportunities or by stubborn thriftiness, could not, it was argued, have been stopped by monetary measures. But there was available an alternative—fiscal policy. Government spending could make up for insufficient private investment. Tax reductions could undermine stubborn thriftiness.

The wide acceptance of these views in the economics profession meant that for some two decades monetary policy was believed by all but a few reactionary souls to have been rendered obsolete by new economic knowledge. Money did not matter. Its only role was the minor one of keeping interest rates low, in order to hold down interest payments in the government budget, contribute to the "euthanasia of the rentier," and maybe, stimulate investment a bit to assist government spending in maintaining a high level of aggregate demand.

These views produced a widespread adoption of cheap money policies after the war. And they received a rude shock when these policies failed in country after country, when central bank after central bank was forced to give up the pretense that it could indefinitely keep "the" rate of interest at a low level. In this country, the public denouement came with the Federal Reserve-Treasury Accord in 1951, although the policy of pegging government bond prices was not formally abandoned until 1953. Inflation, stimulated by cheap money policies, not the widely heralded postwar depression, turned out to be the order of the day. The result was the beginning of a revival of belief in the potency of monetary policy.

This revival was strongly fostered among economists by the theoretical developments initiated by Haberler but named for Pigou that pointed out a channel—namely, changes in wealth—whereby changes in the real quantity of money can affect aggregate demand even if they do not alter interest rates. These theoretical developments did not undermine Keynes' argument against the potency of orthodox monetary measures when liquidity preference is absolute since under such circumstances the usual monetary operations involve simply substituting money for other assets without changing total wealth. But they did show how changes in the quantity of money produced in other ways could affect total spending even under such circumstances. And, more fundamentally, they did undermine Keynes' key theoretical proposition, namely, that even in a world of flexible prices, a position of equilibrium at full employment might not exist. Henceforth, unemployment had again to be explained by rigidities or imperfections, not as the natural outcome of a fully operative market process.

The revival of belief in the potency of monetary policy was fostered also by a re-evaluation of the role money played from 1929 to 1933. Keynes and most other economists of the time believed that the Great Contraction in the United States occurred despite aggressive expansionary policies by the monetary authorities—that they did their best but their best was not good enough. Recent studies have demonstrated that the facts are precisely the reverse: the U.S. monetary authorities followed highly deflationary policies. The quantity of money in the United States fell by one-third in the course of the contraction. And it fell not because there were no willing borrowers—not because the horse would not drink. It fell because the Federal Reserve System forced or permitted a sharp reduction in the monetary base, because it failed to exercise the responsibilities assigned to it in the Federal Reserve Act to provide liquidity to the banking system. The Great Contraction is tragic testimony to the power of monetary policy—not, as Keynes and so many of his contemporaries believed, evidence of its impotence.

In the United States the revival of belief in the potency of monetary policy was strengthened also by increasing disillusionment with fiscal policy, not so much with its potential to affect aggregate demand as with the practical and political feasibility of so using it. Expenditures turned out to respond sluggishly and with long lags to attempts to adjust them to the course of economic activity, so emphasis shifted to taxes. But here political fac-

tors entered with a vengeance to prevent prompt adjustment to presumed need, as has been so graphically illustrated in the months since I wrote the first draft of this talk. "Fine tuning" is a marvelously evocative phrase in this electronic age, but it has little resemblance to what is possible in practice—not, I might add, an unmixed evil.

It is hard to realize how radical has been the change in professional opinion on the role of money. Hardly an economist today accepts views that were the common coin some two decades ago. The pendulum has swung far since then, if not all the way to the position of the late 1920s, at least much closer to that position than to the position of 1945. There are of course many differences between then and now, less in the potency attributed to monetary policy than in the roles assigned to it and the criteria by which the profession believes monetary policy should be guided. I stress nonetheless the similarity between the views that prevailed in the late twenties and those that prevail today because I fear that, now as then, the pendulum may well have swung too far, that, now as then, we are in danger of assigning to monetary policy a larger role than it can perform, in danger of asking it to accomplish tasks that it cannot achieve, and, as a result, in danger of preventing it from making the contribution that it is capable of making.

Unaccustomed as I am to denigrating the importance of money, I therefore shall, as my first task, stress what monetary policy cannot do. I shall then try to outline what it can do and how it can best make its contribution, in the present state of our knowledge—or ignorance.

I. What Monetary Policy Cannot Do

From the infinite world of negation, I have selected two limitations of monetary policy to discuss: (1) It cannot peg interest rates for more than very limited periods; (2) It cannot peg the rate of unemployment for more than very limited periods. I select these because the contrary has been or is widely believed, because they correspond to the two main unattainable tasks that are at all likely to be assigned to monetary policy, and because essentially the same theoretical analysis covers both.

Pegging of Interest Rates

History has already persuaded many of you about the first limitation. As noted earlier, the failure of cheap money policies was a major source of the reaction against simple-minded Keynesianism. In the United States, this reaction involved widespread recognition that the wartime and postwar pegging of bond prices was a mistake, that the abandonment of this policy was a desirable and inevitable step, and that it had none of the disturbing and disastrous consequences that were so freely predicted at the time.

The limitation derives from a much misunderstood feature of the relation between money and interest rates. Let the Fed set out to keep interest rates down. How will it try to do so? By buying securities. This raises their prices and lowers their yields. In the process, it also increases the quantity of reserves available to banks, hence the amount of bank credit, and, ultimately the total quantity of money. That is why central bankers in particular, and the financial community more broadly, generally believe that an increase in the quantity of money tends to lower interest rates. Academic economists accept the same conclusion, but for different reasons. They see, in their mind's eye, a negatively sloping liquidity preference schedule. How can people be induced to hold a larger quantity of money? Only by bidding down interest rates.

Both are right, up to a point. The *initial* impact of increasing the quantity of money at a faster rate than it has been increasing is to make interest rates lower for a time than they would otherwise have been. But this is only the beginning of the process not the end. The more rapid rate of monetary growth will stimulate spending, both through the impact on investment of lower market interest rates and through the impact on other spending and thereby relative prices of higher cash balances than are desired. But one man's spending is another man's income. Rising income will raise the liquidity preference schedule and the demand for loans; it may also raise prices, which would reduce the real quantity of money. These three effects will reverse the initial downward pressure on interest rates fairly promptly, say, in something less than a year. Together they will tend, after a somewhat longer interval, say, a year or two, to return interest rates to the level they would otherwise have had. Indeed, given the tendency for the economy to overreact, they are highly likely to raise interest rates temporarily beyond that level, setting in motion a cyclical adjustment process.

A fourth effect, when and if it becomes operative, will go even farther, and definitely mean that a higher rate of monetary expansion will correspond to a higher, not lower, level of interest rates than would otherwise have prevailed. Let the higher rate of monetary growth produce rising prices, and let the public come to expect that prices will continue to rise. Borrowers will then be willing to pay and lenders will then demand higher interest rates—as Irving Fisher pointed out decades ago. This price expectation effect is slow to develop and also slow to disappear. Fisher estimated that it took several decades for a full adjustment and more recent work is consistent with his estimates.

These subsequent effects explain why every attempt to keep interest rates at a low level has forced the monetary authority to engage in successively larger and larger open market purchases. They explain why, historically, high and rising nominal interest rates have been associated with rapid growth in the quantity of money, as in Brazil or Chile or in the United States in recent years, and why low and falling interest rates have been associated with slow growth in the quantity of money, as in Switzerland now or in the United States from 1929 to 1933. As an empirical matter, low interest rates are a sign that monetary policy *has been* tight—in the sense that the quantity of money has grown slowly; high interest rates are a sign that monetary policy *has been* easy —in the sense that the quantity of money has grown rapidly. The broadest facts of experience run in precisely the opposite direction from that which the financial community and academic economists have all generally taken for granted.

Paradoxically, the monetary authority could assure low nominal rates of interest—but to do so it would have to start out in what seems like the opposite direction, by engaging in a deflationary monetary policy. Similarly, it could assure high nominal interest rates by engaging in an inflationary policy and accepting a temporary movement in interest rates in the opposite direction.

These considerations not only explain why monetary policy cannot peg interest rates; they also explain why interest rates are such a misleading indicator of whether monetary policy is "tight" or "easy." For that, it is far better to look at the rate of change of the quantity of money.

Employment as a Criterion of Policy

The second limitation I wish to discuss goes more against the grain of current thinking. Monetary growth, it is widely held, will tend to stimulate employment; monetary contraction, to retard employment. Why, then, cannot the monetary authority adopt a target for employment or unemployment— say, 3 percent unemployment; be tight when unemployment is less than the target; be easy when unemployment is higher than the target; and in this way peg unemployment at, say, 3 percent? The reason it cannot is precisely the same as for interest rates—the difference between the immediate and the delayed consequences of such a policy.

At any moment of time, there is some level of unemployment which has the property that it is consistent with equilibrium in the structure of *real* wage rates. At that level of unemployment, real wage rates are tending on the average to rise at a "normal" secular rate, i.e., at a rate that can be indefinitely maintained so long as capital formation, technological improvements, etc., remain on their long-run trends. A lower level of unemployment is an indication that there is an excess demand for labor that will produce upward pressure on real wage rates. A higher level of unemployment is an indication that there is an excess supply of labor that will produce downward pressure on real wage rates.

Let us assume that the monetary authority tries to peg the "market" rate of unemployment at a level below the "natural" rate. For definiteness, suppose that it takes 3 percent as the target rate and that the "natural" rate is higher than 3 percent. Suppose also that we start out at a time when prices have been stable and when unemployment is higher than 3 percent. Accordingly, the authority increases the rate of monetary growth. This will be expansionary. By making nominal cash balances higher than people desire, it will tend initially to lower interest rates and in this and other ways to stimulate spending. Income and spending will start to rise.

To begin with, much or most of the rise in income will take the form of an increase in output and employment rather than in prices. People have been expecting prices to be stable, and prices and wages have been set for some time in the future on that basis. It takes time for people to adjust to a new state of demand. Producers will tend to react to the initial expansion in aggregate demand by increasing output, employees by working longer hours, and the unemployed by taking jobs now offered at former nominal wages. This much is pretty standard doctrine.

But it describes only the initial ef-

fects. Because selling prices of products typically respond to an unanticipated rise in nominal demand faster than prices of factors of production, real wages received have gone down—though real wages anticipated by employees went up, since employees implicitly evaluated the wages offered at the earlier price level. Indeed, the simultaneous fall ex post in real wages to employers and rise ex ante in real wages to employees is what enabled employment to increase. But the decline ex post in real wages will soon come to affect anticipations. Employees will start to reckon on rising prices of the things they buy and to demand higher nominal wages for the future. "Market" unemployment is below the "natural" level. There is an excess demand for labor so real wages will tend to rise toward their initial level.

Even though the higher rate of monetary growth continues, the rise in real wages will reverse the decline in unemployment, and then lead to a rise, which will tend to return unemployment to its former level. In order to keep unemployment at its target level of 3 percent, the monetary authority would have to raise monetary growth still more. As in the interest rate case, the "market" rate can be kept below the "natural" rate only by inflation. And, as in the interest rate case, too, only by accelerating inflation. Conversely, let the monetary authority choose a target rate of unemployment that is above the natural rate, and they will be led to produce a deflation, and an accelerating deflation at that.

To state the general conclusion still differently, the monetary authority controls nominal quantities—directly, the quantity of its own liabilities. In principle, it can use this control to peg a nominal quantity—an exchange rate, the price level, the nominal level of national income, the quantity of money by one or another definition—or to peg the rate of change in a nominal quantity—the rate of inflation or deflation, the rate of growth or decline in nominal national income, the rate of growth of the quantity of money. It cannot use its control over nominal quantities to peg a real quantity—the real rate of interest, the rate of unemployment, the level of real national income, the real quantity of money, the rate of growth of real national income, or the rate of growth of the real quantity of money.

II. What Monetary Policy Can Do

Monetary policy cannot peg these real magnitudes at predetermined levels. But monetary policy can and does have important effects on these real magnitudes. The one is in no way inconsistent with the other.

My own studies of monetary history have made me extremely sympathetic to the oft-quoted, much reviled, and as widely misunderstood, comment by John Stuart Mill. "There cannot . . . ," he wrote, "be intrinsically a more insignificant thing, in the economy of society, than money; except in the character of a contrivance for sparing time and labour. It is a machine for doing quickly and commodiously, what would be done, though less quickly and commodiously, without it: and like many other kinds of machinery, it only exerts a distinct and independent influence of its own when it gets out of order."*

*J. S. Mill, *Principles of Political Economy*, Bk. III, Ashley ed. New York, 1929, p. 488.

True, money is only a machine, but it is an extraordinarily efficient machine. Without it, we could not have begun to attain the astounding growth in output and level of living we have experienced in the past two centuries —any more than we could have done so without those other marvelous machines that dot our countryside and enable us, for the most part, simply to do more efficiently what could be done without them at much greater cost in labor.

But money has one feature that these other machines do not share. Because it is so pervasive, when it gets out of order, it throws a monkey wrench into the operation of all the other machines. The Great Contraction is the most dramatic example but not the only one. Every other major contraction in this country has been either produced by monetary disorder or greatly exacerbated by monetary disorder. Every major inflation has been produced by monetary expansion— mostly to meet the overriding demands of war which have forced the creation of money to supplement explicit taxation.

The first and most important lesson that history teaches about what monetary policy can do—and it is a lesson of the most profound importance—is that monetary policy can prevent money itself from being a major source of economic disturbance. This sounds like a negative proposition: avoid major mistakes. In part it is. The Great Contraction might not have occurred at all, and if it had, it would have been far less severe, if the monetary authority had avoided mistakes, or if the monetary arrangements had been those of an earlier time when there was no central authority with the power to make the kinds of mistakes that the Federal Reserve System made. The past few years, to come closer to home, would have been steadier and more productive of economic well-being if the Federal Reserve had avoided drastic and erratic changes of direction, first expanding the money supply at an unduly rapid pace, then, in early 1966, stepping on the brake too hard, then, at the end of 1966, reversing itself and resuming expansion until at least November, 1967, at a more rapid pace than can long be maintained without appreciable inflation.

Even if the proposition that monetary policy can prevent money itself from being a major source of economic disturbance were a wholly negative proposition, it would be none the less important for that. As it happens, however, it is not a wholly negative proposition. The monetary machine has gotten out of order even when there has been no central authority with anything like the power now possessed by the Fed. In the United States, the 1907 episode and earlier banking panics are examples of how the monetary machine can get out of order largely on its own. There is therefore a positive and important task for the monetary authority—to suggest improvements in the machine that will reduce the chances that it will get out of order, and to use its own powers so as to keep the machine in good working order.

A second thing monetary policy can do is provide a stable background for the economy—keep the machine well oiled, to continue Mill's analogy. Accomplishing the first task will contribute to this objective, but there is more to it than that. Our economic system

will work best when producers and consumers, employers and employees, can proceed with full confidence that the average level of prices will behave in a known way in the future—preferably that it will be highly stable. Under any conceivable institutional arrangements, and certainly under those that now prevail in the United States, there is only a limited amount of flexibility in prices and wages. We need to conserve this flexibility to achieve changes in relative prices and wages that are required to adjust to dynamic changes in tastes and technology. We should not dissipate it simply to achieve changes in the absolute level of prices that serve no economic function.

In today's world, if monetary policy is to provide a stable background for the economy it must do so by deliberately employing its powers to that end. I shall come later to how it can do so.

Finally, monetary policy can contribute to offsetting major disturbances in the economic system arising from other sources. If there is an independent secular exhilaration—as the postwar expansion was described by the proponents of secular stagnation—monetary policy can in principle help to hold it in check by a slower rate of monetary growth than would otherwise be desirable. If, as now, an explosive federal budget threatens unprecedented deficits, monetary policy can hold any inflationary dangers in check by a slower rate of monetary growth than would otherwise be desirable. This will temporarily mean higher interest rates than would otherwise prevail—to enable the government to borrow the sums needed to finance the deficit—but by preventing the speeding up of inflation, it may well mean both lower prices and lower nominal interest rates for the long pull. If the end of a substantial war offers the country an opportunity to shift resources from wartime to peacetime production, monetary policy can ease the transition by a higher rate of monetary growth than would otherwise be desirable—though experience is not very encouraging that it can do so without going too far.

I have put this point last, and stated it in qualified terms—as referring to major disturbances—because I believe that the potentiality of monetary policy in offsetting other forces making for instability is far more limited than is commonly believed. We simply do not know enough to be able to recognize minor disturbances when they occur or to be able to predict either what their effects will be with any precision or what monetary policy is required to offset their effects. We do not know enough to be able to achieve stated objectives by delicate, or even fairly coarse, changes in the mix of monetary and fiscal policy. In this area particularly the best is likely to be the enemy of the good. Experience suggests that the path of wisdom is to use monetary policy explicitly to offset other disturbances only when they offer a "clear and present danger."

III. How Should Monetary Policy Be Conducted?

How should monetary policy be conducted to make the contribution to our goals that it is capable of making? I shall restrict myself here to two major requirements for monetary policy that follow fairly directly from the preceding discussion.

The first requirement is that the monetary authority should guide itself by magnitudes that it can control, not by ones that it cannot control. If, as the authority has often done, it takes interest rates or the current unemployment percentage as the immediate criterion of policy, it will be like a space vehicle that has taken a fix on the wrong star. No matter how sensitive and sophisticated its guiding apparatus, the space vehicle will go astray. And so will the monetary authority. Of the various alternative magnitudes that it can control, the most appealing guides for policy are exchange rates, the price level as defined by some index, and the quantity of a monetary total—currency plus adjusted demand deposits, or this total plus commercial bank time deposits, or a still broader total.

For the United States in particular, exchange rates are an undesirable guide. It might be worth requiring the bulk of the economy to adjust to the tiny percentage consisting of foreign trade if that would guarantee freedom from monetary irresponsibility—as it might under a real gold standard. But it is hardly worth doing so simply to adapt to the average of whatever policies monetary authorities in the rest of the world adopt. Far better to let the market, through floating exchange rates, adjust to world conditions the 5 percent or so of our resources devoted to international trade while reserving monetary policy to promote the effective use of the 95 percent.

Of the three guides listed, the price level is clearly the most important in its own right. Other things the same, it would be much the best of the alternatives—as so many distinguished economists have urged in the past. But other things are not the same. The link between the policy actions of the monetary authority and the price level, while unquestionably present, is more indirect than the link between the policy actions of the authority and any of the several monetary totals. Moreover, monetary action takes a longer time to affect the price level than to affect the monetary totals and both the time lag and the magnitude of effect vary with circumstances. As a result, we cannot predict at all accurately just what effect a particular monetary action will have on the price level and, equally important, just when it will have that effect. Attempting to control directly the price level is therefore likely to make monetary policy itself a source of economic disturbance because of false stops and starts. Perhaps, as our understanding of monetary phenomena advances, the situation will change. But at the present stage of our understanding, the long way around seems the surer way to our objective. Accordingly, I believe that a monetary total is the best currently available immediate guide or criterion for monetary policy—and I believe that it matters much less which particular total is chosen than that one be chosen.

A second requirement for monetary policy is that the monetary authority avoid sharp swings in policy. In the past, monetary authorities have on occasion moved in the wrong direction—as in the episode of the Great Contraction that I have stressed. More frequently, they have moved in the right direction, albeit often too late, but have erred by moving too far. Too late and too much has been the general

practice. For example, in early 1966, it was the right policy for the Federal Reserve to move in a less expansionary direction—though it should have done so at least a year earlier. But when it moved, it went too far, producing the sharpest change in the rate of monetary growth of the postwar era. Again, having gone too far, it was the right policy for the Fed to reverse course at the end of 1966. But again it went too far, not only restoring but exceeding the earlier excessive rate of monetary growth. And this episode is no exception. Time and again this has been the course followed—as in 1919 and 1920, in 1937 and 1938, in 1953 and 1954, in 1959 and 1960.

The reason for the propensity to overreact seems clear: the failure of monetary authorities to allow for the delay between their actions and the subsequent effects on the economy. They tend to determine their actions by today's conditions—but their actions will affect the economy only six or nine or twelve or fifteen months later. Hence they feel impelled to step on the brake, or the accelerator, as the case may be, too hard.

My own prescription is still that the monetary authority go all the way in avoiding such swings by adopting publicly the policy of achieving a steady rate of growth in a specified monetary total. The precise rate of growth, like the precise monetary total, is less important than the adoption of some stated and known rate. I myself have argued for a rate that would on the average achieve rough stability in the level of prices of final products, which I have estimated would call for something like a 3 to 5 percent per year rate of growth in currency plus all commercial bank deposits or a slightly lower rate of growth in currency plus demand deposits only. But it would be better to have a fixed rate that would on the average produce moderate inflation or moderate deflation, provided it was steady, than to suffer the wide and erratic perturbations we have experienced.

Short of the adoption of such a publicly stated policy of a steady rate of monetary growth, it would constitute a major improvement if the monetary authority followed the self-denying ordinance of avoiding wide swings. It is a matter of record that periods of relative stability in the rate of monetary growth have also been periods of relative stability in economic activity, both in the United States and other countries. Periods of wide swings in the rate of monetary growth have also been periods of wide swings in economic activity.

By setting itself a steady course and keeping to it, the monetary authority could make a major contribution to promoting economic stability. By making that course one of steady but moderate growth in the quantity of money, it would make a major contribution to avoidance of either inflation or deflation of prices. Other forces would still affect the economy, require change and adjustment, and disturb the even tenor of our ways. But steady monetary growth would provide a monetary climate favorable to the effective operation of those basic forces of enterprise, ingenuity, invention, hard work, and thrift that are the true springs of economic growth. That is the most that we can ask from monetary policy at our present stage of knowledge. But that much—and it is a great deal—is clearly within our reach.

IS MONETARY POLICY BEING OVERSOLD?
Walter W. Heller

At the outset, let's clarify what is and what isn't at issue in today's discussion of fiscal-monetary policy. The issue is *not* whether money matters—we all grant that—but whether *only* money matters, as some Friedmanites, or perhaps I should say Friedmanics, would put it. Or really, whether only money matters *much*, which is what I understand Milton Friedman to say—he is more reasonable than many of the Friedmanites.

Again, in the fiscal field, the issue is not *whether* fiscal policy matters—even some monetarists, perhaps in unguarded moments, have urged budget cuts or tax changes for stabilization reasons. The issues are *how much* it matters, and how heavily we can lean on discretionary changes in taxes and budgets to maintain steady economic growth in a dynamic economy.

Summing up the key operational issues, they are: Should money be king? Is fiscal policy worth its salt? Should flexible man yield to rigid rules?

Let me review with you the factors that say "stop, look, and listen" before embracing the triple doctrine that only money matters much; that control of the money supply is the key to economic stability; and that a rigid fixed-throttle expansion of 4 or 5 percent

Reprinted from *Monetary vs. Fiscal Policy: A Dialogue* by Milton Friedman and Walter W. Heller. By permission of W. W. Norton & Company, Inc. Copyright © 1969 by the Graduate School of Business Administration, New York University. Excerpts from pp. 15–23, 25–28, 30–31.

a year is the only safe policy prescription in a world of alleged economic ignorance and human weakness and folly.

One should note in passing that Professor Friedman's findings and conclusions fit into a steady process of rescuing monetary policy from the limbo into which it was put by the interest-rate peg of World War II and the late 40s—a rescue effected by the Monetary Accord of 1951 and by the subsequent steady expansion of its scope. This has been a healthy renaissance. But having been resurrected from the debilitating rate peg of the 1940s, does monetary policy now face the threat of a new peg, Milton's money-supply peg, in the years ahead? Is it doomed to go from cradle to grave in twenty years?

I exaggerate, of course, for emphasis. President Nixon, for example, has been reported as saying that he doesn't buy the fixed-throttle formula. At the same time, he has reportedly suggested that he intends to put more emphasis on money supply. So this is a particularly apt juncture for a close look at the monetarists' doctrine.

Now, turning to doubts, unresolved questions, and unconvincing evidence, I group these into eight conditions that must be satisfied—if not completely, at least more convincingly than they have been to date—before we can even consider giving money supply sovereignty, or dominance, or greater prominence in economic policy.

The first condition is this: the monetarists must make up their minds which money-supply variable they want us to accept as our guiding star—M_1, the narrow money supply, just currency and bank deposits; M_2, adding time deposits; or perhaps some other measure

like the "monetary base?" And when will the monetarists decide? Perhaps Milton Friedman has decided; but if he has, his disciples do not seem to have gotten the word.

It doesn't seem too much to ask that this confusion be resolved in some satisfactory way before putting great faith in money supply as our key policy variable.

Second, I would feel more sympathetic to the money-supply doctrine if it were not so one-track-minded about money stock—measured any way you wish—as the *only* financial variable with any informational content for policy purposes.

As Gramley has noted, for example, if we look at money stock alone for 1948, it would indicate the tightest money in the post-war period.[*] Yet, the rate on Treasury bills was 1 percent, and on high-grade corporates 2¾ percent. (That *does* sound like ancient history.) But isn't it curious that we had tight money by the money-supply standard side by side with 1, 2, and 3 percent interest rates? We were swamped with liquidity—so interest rates do seem to have been telling us something very important.

Or, if we look at 1967 *only* in terms of the money stock, it would appear as the easiest-money year since World War II. M_1 was up 6 percent, M_2 was up 12 percent. Yet there was a very sharp rise in interest rates. Why? Probably because of a big shift in liquidity preference as corporations strove to build up their protective liquidity cushions after their harrowing experi-

---

[*]Lyle Gramley, "The Informational Content of Interest Rates as Indicators of Monetary Policy," in Proceedings: *1968 Money and Banking Workshop*, Federal Reserve Bank of Minneapolis (May 1968), p. 23.

ence the previous year—their monetary dehydration in the credit crunch of 1966. Again, the behavior of interest rates is vital to proper interpretation of monetary developments and guidance of monetary policy. Interest rates are endogenous variables and cannot be used alone—but neither can money stock. Either interest rates or money stock, used alone, could seriously mislead us.

I really don't understand how the scarcity of any commodity can be gauged without referring to its price—or, more specifically, how the scarcity of money can be gauged without referring to interest rates.

Third, given the fluctuations in money velocity, that supposedly inexorable link between money and economic activity has yet to be established. We should not forget this, however sweet the siren song of the monetarists may sound. Clearly, velocity has varied over time—some might say "greatly," others "moderately." Let me sidestep a bit and say, for purposes of this discussion, "significantly." For I would remind you that the income velocity of money rose roughly 28 percent during the 1960–68 period. Had velocity been the same in 1968 as it was in 1960, nominal GNP would have been not some $860 billion, but only $675 billion.

Fourth, it would help us if the monetarists could narrow the range on *when* money matters. How long *are* the lags that have to be taken into account in managing monetary policy?

Fifth, I'd be happier if only I knew which of the two Friedmans to believe. Should it be the Friedman we have had in focus here—the Friedman of the close causal relationship between money supply and income, who sees

changes in money balances worked off gradually, with long lags before interest rates, prices of financial and physical assets, and, eventually, investment and consumption spending are affected? Or should it be the Friedman of the "permanent-income hypothesis," who sees the demand for money as quite unresponsive to changes in current income (since current income has only a fractional weight in permanent income), with the implied result that the monetary multiplier is very large in the short run, that there is an immediate and strong response to a change in the money stock? As Tobin has noted, he can't have it both ways. But which is it to be?

Sixth, if Milton's policy prescription were made in a frictionless Friedman-esque world without price, wage, and exchange rigidities—a world of his own making—it would be more admissible. But in the imperfect world in which we actually operate, beset by all sorts of rigidities, the introduction of his fixed-throttle money-supply rule might, in fact, be destabilizing. Or it could condemn us to long periods of economic slack or inflation as the slow adjustment processes in wages and prices, given strong market power, delayed the economy's reaction to the monetary rule while policy makers stood helplessly by.

A seventh and closely related concern is that locking the money supply into a rigid rule would jeopardize the U.S. international position. It's quite clear that capital flows are interest-rate sensitive. Indeed, capital flows induced by interest-rate changes can increase alarmingly when speculators take over. Under the Friedman rule, market interest rates would be whatever they turned out to be. It would be beyond the pale for the Fed to adjust interest rates for balance-of-payments adjustment purposes. Nor is it clear that by operating in the market for forward exchange (which in any event Milton would presumably oppose) the system could altogether neutralize changes in domestic market rates.

Milton has heard all of this before, and he always has an answer—flexible exchange rates. Yet, suffice it to note that however vital they are to the workings of his money-supply peg, floating exchange rates are not just around the corner.

Eighth, and finally, if the monetarists showed some small willingness to recognize the impact of fiscal policy—which has played such a large role in the policy thinking and action underlying the great expansion of the 1960s—one might be a little more sympathetic to their views. This point is, I must admit, not so much a condition as a plea for symmetry. The "new economists," having already given important and increasing weight to monetary factors in their policy models, are still waiting for signs that the monetarists will admit fiscal factors to theirs.

The 1964 tax cut pointedly illustrates what I mean. While the "new economists" fully recognize the important role monetary policy played in facilitating the success of the tax cut, the monetarists go to elaborate lengths to "prove" that the tax cut—which came close to removing a $13 billion full-employment surplus that was overburdening and retarding the economy—had nothing to do with the 1964–65 expansion. Money-supply growth did it all. Apparently, we were just playing fiscal tiddlywinks in Washington.

It seems to me that the cause of balanced analysis and rational policy would be served by redirecting some of the brilliance of Friedman and his followers from (a) single-minded devotion to the money-supply thesis and unceasing efforts to discredit fiscal policy and indeed all discretionary policy to (b) joint efforts to develop a more complete and satisfactory model of how the real world works; ascertain why it is working far better today than it did before active and conscious fiscal-monetary policy came into play; and determine how such policy can be improved to make it work even better in the future.

In a related asymmetry, as I've already suggested in passing, some Friedmanites fail to recognize that if fiscal policy actions like the 1964 tax cut can do no good, then fiscal policy actions like the big budget increases and deficits associated with Vietnam can also do no harm. Again, they should recognize that they can't have it both ways.

Now, one could lengthen and elaborate this list. But enough—let's just round it off this way: if Milton Friedman were saying that (as part of an active discretionary policy) we had better keep a closer eye on that important variable, money supply, in one or more of its several incarnations—I would say well and good, by all means. If the manifold doubts can be reasonably resolved, let's remedy any neglect or underemphasis of money supply as a policy indicator relative to interest rates, free reserves, and the like. But let's not lock the steering gear into place, knowing full well of the twists and turns in the road ahead. That's an invitation to chaos.

Again, we need to stop, look, and

listen lest we let simplistic or captious criticism operate to deny us the benefits of past experience and thwart the promise of future discretionary action on the monetary and fiscal fronts.

What has been the course of the American economy during the postwar period of an increasingly active and self-conscious fiscal-monetary policy for economic stabilization? Or, for that matter, let's broaden it: what has been the course of the world's advanced industrial economies during this period? The correlation is unmistakable: the more active, informed, and self-conscious fiscal and monetary policies have become, by and large, the more fully employed and stable the affected economies have become. Casual empiricism? Perhaps—yet a powerful and persuasive observation.

Witness the conclusion of the two-and-a-half–year study for the OECD by a group of fiscal experts from eight industrial countries:

The postwar economic performance of most Western countries in respect of employment, production and growth has been vastly superior to that of the pre-war years. This, in our view, has not been accidental. Governments have increasingly accepted responsibility for the promotion and maintenance of high employment and steady economic growth. The more conscious use of economic policies has undoubtedly played a crucial role in the better performance achieved— an achievement which, from the point of view of the ultimate social objectives of policy, is of paramount importance.

Perhaps an even more telling testa-

ment to the effectiveness of active modern stabilization-policy is the change in private investment thinking and planning not only in the financial sense of sustained confidence in the future of corporate earnings and stock market values, even in the face of temporary slowdowns in the economy— but more important, in the physical sense of sustained high levels of plant and equipment investment which seem to be replacing the sickening swings that used to be the order of the day.

Why? In good part, I take it to be the result of a constantly deepening conviction in the business and financial community that alert and active fiscal-monetary policy will keep the economy operating at a higher proportion of its potential in the future than in the past; that beyond short and temporary slowdowns, or perhaps even a recession—that's not ruled out in this vast and dynamic economy of ours— lies the prospect of sustained growth in that narrow band around full employment.

REPLY
Milton Friedman

I want to comment on some of the points that Walter made initially and try to answer some of the questions he raised. I think that I might very well start with a point he made before and which he repeated now. He said that he would like us to stop being asym-

Reprinted from *Monetary vs. Fiscal Policy: A Dialogue* by Milton Friedman and Walter W. Heller. By permission of W. W. Norton & Company, Inc. Copyright © 1969 by the Graduate School of Business Administration, New York University. Excerpts from pp. 73–80.

metrical about tax increases or tax cuts on the one hand, and expenditure decreases on the other.

I want to make it clear that I have never favored expenditure decreases as a stabilization device. I agree with Walter that it would be inconsistent, completely inconsistent, for me to argue that tax increases and decreases are ineffective in stemming inflation or promoting expansion, but that spending decreases or increases are effective. That would be a silly position and, as far as I know, I have never taken it, though maybe I've been careless in what I have written and have given a misleading impression. I have been in favor of tax decreases and expenditure decreases in 1964, in 1966, and in 1968, but not for stabilization purposes. I am in favor of expenditure decreases from a long-range point of view because I think that the U.S. federal budget is too large compared to what we're getting for it. We're not getting our money's worth out of it. And, therefore, I would like to see government spending brought down. I have not argued—at least, if I have, I will immediately admit that I should not have and I don't know of any quotation in which I have (if Walter has any, I hope he will give them to me)— that expenditure decreases are a way to achieve stabilization at a time of inflationary pressure.

I have said something different. I have said that, from the point of view of the fiscalists, a tax increase or expenditure decrease are equivalent. And, therefore, I have often said that if you are going to adopt the policy of the fiscalist, I would rather see you adopt it through expenditure decreases than through tax increases. But I personally have never argued

that that is an effective stabilization device, and I don't believe that it is.

Let me turn to some of the specific issues that Walter raised in his first discussion and see if I can clarify a few points that came up.

First of all, the question is, Why do we look only at the money stock? Why don't we also look at interest rates? Don't you have to look at both quantity and price? The answer is yes, but the interest rate is not the price of money in the sense of the money stock. The interest rate is the price of credit. The price of money is how much goods and services you have to give up to get a dollar. You can have big changes in the quantity of money without any changes in credit. Consider for a moment the 1848–58 period in the United States. We had a big increase in the quantity of money because of the discovery of gold. This increase didn't, in the first instance, impinge on the credit markets at all.

You must sharply distinguish between money in the sense of the money or credit market, and money in the sense of the quantity of money. And the price of money in that second sense is the inverse of the price level—not the interest rate. The interest rate is the price of credit. As I mentioned earlier, the tax increase we had would tend to reduce the price of credit because it reduces the demand for credit, even though it didn't affect the money supply at all.

So I do think you have to look at both price and quantity. But the price you have to look at from this point of view is the price level, not the interest rate.

Next, he said that 1967 was the easiest money year since 1962. Yet there was a big rise in interest rates. In other connections, I have argued that our researches show that a rapid increase in the quantity of money tends to lower interest rates only for a brief period—about six months. After that, it tends to raise interest rates. Conversely, a slow rate of increase in the quantity of money tends to raise interest rates only for about six months, and after that, it tends to lower them.

If you ask where in the world interest rates are higher, the answer is in Brazil, Chile, places like that where the quantity of money has been going up like mad. Interest rates in the U.S. fell dramatically from 1929 to 1933. The quantity of money declined by a third. So it's not a surprise to us that you could have the quantity of money easy in the sense of quantity, and interest rates rise or fall or do almost anything else.

Next, he asks, "Which of the Friedmans do you believe—the one who stresses permanent-income relationships or the one who stresses the close causal connection?" Well, believe both of them if you take them at what they said. The permanent-income analysis has to do with the demand for real money balances, and it was an analysis that was based on annual data covering decades. There is no Friedman who has argued that there is an immediate, mechanical, causal connection between changes in the quantity of money and changes in income.

What I have always argued is that there is a connection which is, on the average, close but which may be quite variable in an individual episode. I have emphasized that the inability to pin down the lag means that there are lots of factors about which I'm ignorant. That doesn't mean that money doesn't have a systematic influence. But it

does mean that there is a good deal of variability in the influence.

The data support the view that a 1 percent change in the rate of expansion of the quantity of money tends to produce, on the average, a 2 percent change in the rate of growth of nominal income. There is a big multiplier, as the permanent income analysis would lead you to expect. And there is a cyclical relation. I'm sorry, but I really don't see any inconsistency between the position I've taken on these two points.

Next, Walter Heller asks, Which of the money supplies do you want? M_1 or M_2? Which quantity of money do you want to use? A perfectly reasonable and appropriate and proper question and I'm glad to answer it. In almost all cases, it makes no difference. The only time it makes a difference is when our silly Regulation Q gets in the way. We have a Regulation Q that pegs the maximum rate that commercial banks can pay on time deposits. Whenever you either hit that Regulation-Q limit or you come through from the other side, the two monetary totals diverge and tell you different stories, and you cannot trust either one.

At all other times, you will very seldom find that the message told to you by M_1 is much different than the message told to you by M_2.

Then there was all this talk about being locked into a rigid rule. You know, I have always found it a good rule of thumb that when somebody starts resorting to metaphors, there is something wrong with his argument.

When you start talking about cars driving along a road, and whether you want to lock the steering wheel, well that's a good image; the automatic pilot, I agree, is a good one. But metaphors or similes are to remind you of arguments; they are not a substitute for an argument.

The reason I believe that you would do better with a fixed rule, with a constant rate of increase in the quantity of money, is because I have examined U. S. experience with discretionary monetary policy. I have gone back and have asked, as I reexamine this period, "Would the U. S. have been better off or worse off if we had had a fixed rule?" I challenge anybody to go back over the monetary history of the United States, and come out with any other conclusion than that for the great bulk of the time, you would have been better off with the fixed rule. You would clearly have avoided all the major mistakes.

The reason why that doesn't rigidly lock you in, in the sense in which Walter was speaking, is that I don't believe that money is all that matters. The automatic pilot is the price system. It isn't perfectly flexible, it isn't perfectly free, but it has a good deal of capacity to adjust. If you look at what happened to this country when we adjusted to post–World War II, to the enormous decline in our expenditures, and the shift in the direction of resources, you have to say that we did an extraordinarily effective job of adjusting, and that this is because there is an automatic pilot.

But if an automatic pilot is going to work, if you're going to have the market system work, it has to have some basic, stable framework. It has to have something it can count on. And the virtue of a fixed rule, of a constant rate of increase in the quantity of money, is that it would provide such a stable monetary framework. I have discussed that many times in many different ways, and I really have nothing to add.

The final thing I want to talk about is the statement that Walter made at the end of his initial talk, when he said, Look at the world economy; hasn't it been far healthier during post–World War II than it was between the Wars? Of course. It certainly has been enormously healthier. Why? Well, again, I'm sorry to have to be consistent, but in 1953, I gave a talk in Stockholm, which is also reprinted in that collection of papers, under the title of "Why the American Economy is Depression Proof."

I think that I was right, that as of that time and as of today, the American economy is depression proof. The reasons I gave at that time did not include the fact that discretionary monetary and fiscal policy was going to keep things on an even keel. I believe that the reason why the world has done so much better, the reason why we haven't had any depressions in that period, is not because of the positive virtue of the fine tuning that has been followed, but because we have avoided the major mistakes of the interwar period. Those major mistakes were the occasionally severe deflations of the money stock.

We did learn something from the Great Depression. We learned that you do not have to cut the quantity of money by a third over three or four years. We learned that you ought to have numbers on the quantity of money. If the Federal Reserve System in 1929 to 1933 had been publishing statistics on the quantity of money, I don't believe that the Great Depression could have taken the course it did. There were no numbers. And we have not since then, and we will not in the foreseeable future, permit a monetary authority to make the kind of mistake that our monetary authorities made in the 30s.

That, in my opinion, is the major reason why we have had such a different experience in post–World War II.

THE ROLE OF MONEY IN NATIONAL ECONOMIC POLICY

PAUL SAMUELSON ● JAMES TOBIN ● ALLAN H. MELTZER

1
Paul Samuelson

The central issue that is debated these days in connection with macro-economics is the doctrine of monetarism.

Let me define monetarism. It's not my particular title. Monetarism is the belief that the primary determinant of the state of macro-economic aggregate demand—whether there will be unemployment, whether there will be inflation—is money, M_1 or M_2, and more specifically, perhaps, its various rates of change.

I'm going to borrow a method of exposition that I understand Jim Tobin used at an American Bankers' Association meeting some years ago, when *A Monetary History of the United States* of Mrs. Schwartz and Mr. Friedman was being discussed. I wasn't present, but I was told that Jim wrote three sentences on the blackboard: "Money doesn't matter," "Money matters," and "Money alone matters." And he then said that Professor Friedman,

Excerpted from Paul A. Samuelson, "The Role of Money in National Economic Policy," in Federal Reserve Bank of Boston, *Controlling Monetary Aggregates* (Boston: Federal Reserve Bank, 1969), pp. 7–13. Reprinted by permission of the publisher.

having established to everybody's satisfaction the untruth of the first statement, went on as if it were a *sequitur* to think that he had established the third statement.

Well now, I wasn't provided with a blackboard, and I can't lapse into my academic mannerisms, but I have written down a spectrum of remarks from "Money doesn't matter," to "Money matters," to "Money matters much," to "Money matters most," and to "Money alone matters." Now, monetarism is certainly at the right of this spectrum. There is nobody, I think, worth our notice on the American scene who is at the left end of that spectrum, although there still do exist in England men whose minds were formed in 1939, and who haven't changed a thought since that time, and who do belong at the left of that spectrum and say money doesn't matter. And so, monetarism, which is a correction to that extreme view—and, I think, an excess on the other side—is very much an item for export to the British Isles. For so many years they exported wisdom and knowledge to us, it's only proper that we requite that past with export. I would argue that the right view, the extreme view is not the most persuasive view, but monetarism is that.

Now, you may think that's a straw

man that I'm setting up—that there is nobody who believes in monetarism as I've defined it. But I believe that I'm correct in saying that there is at least one person in this country who does believe in it, and that is Dr. Friedman.

I've an advantage probably not vouchsafed to all of you. Once a week I am privileged for 28½ minutes to listen to the voice of Dr. Friedman—and his view, as expressed repeatedly in those tapes, is this: that as far as macro-economic aggregate state of demand is concerned, money alone matters. Now, this doesn't mean that money alone determines everything. It will not cure flat feet, or dandruff, or marital fidelity. It is not true, for example, that fiscal policy has no role: For example, how big the Galbraithian public sector is is very much determined by fiscal policy; and what the composition of any state of aggregate demand is, in terms of consumption goods and capital formation, does depend upon a fiscal policy. But as for the general issues—of whether you are going to have more inflation or deflation, or whether you are going to have unemployment—we know a very little bit about it. About something like half of the squared variation in the state of aggregate demand can be explained by the monetary factor; the rest is noise. There are no systematic predictable elements.

Now, I think that that is an extreme view, and it is not a persuasive view if you look at all of the evidence. There was a great debate at NYU between Professor Friedman and Walter Heller. I wasn't privileged to be there. I talked to various people in New York who were there and, generally speaking, those who were in favor of one view when they came in, went out thinking

that their man had won the debate. I talked to one Wall Street character who alleged to be neutral, and he said, "Well, Heller had the better wisecracks, but Friedman had mountains of evidence. He didn't have time to give those mountains of evidence there at that time, but, you can't laugh off the evidence."

I have reviewed these mountains of evidence, and I think that there is a great amount of evidence—much of it is due to the efforts of Professor Friedman at the National Bureau, much of it is due to workshop students working with him, and much of it to colleagues—but most of that evidence is not, in the sense of the statistician, a powerful test of monetarism as I've defined it.

Types of Evidence

Now, since other speakers have to speak, I can't review all these mountains of evidence, but let me just mention what some of the types of evidence are. First—and I've heard several tapes dealing with this—take particular incidents in American history. In 1919, for example, we came out of World War I; there was a much-underbalanced budget; the Federal Reserve was under the thumb of the Treasury; and then, on a certain day, it can be established, just as a diplomatic historian can establish facts, that the Federal Reserve was given its freedom from the Treasury. On that certain day, it took certain acts, so you have almost a controlled experiment in which something happened to the money supply and then—within six months or seven months or nine months, whatever the lag period is—something happened to the business conditions. Now, I think that is good evidence that money matters. That does not tell you what its role is with respect to the importance of fiscal policy or other matters. But we have a lot of evidence like that.

There is another kind of evidence. Namely, that people who use monetarism deliver the goods. Don't ask me why money matters; it's as if it matters, but we don't know what the exact connections are.

There's somebody in a Chicago bank who gets better forecasts using this method than anybody else in that part of the country; there's somebody in a New York bank which shall be nameless, who gets better estimates; and, in the academic community, there are a few people who are armed with this knowledge of monetarism and—why, we don't know—they deliver the goods.

We had a crucial experiment in 1966 in which the monetarists said certain things with which the other people—I'll call them neo-Keynesians or post-Keynesians, since nobody can quite stand to be called a Keynesian in this country—differed. There was a joust between these different forecasters, and who do you think won on that occasion? It was the monetarists.

The same thing happened again after the middle of last year.

Now, this is a very complicated story, but let me say that, if you are going to use that kind of evidence, you have to use all of it, and you have to be quantitative.

I keep a little black book, and I find there is a great overlap in estimates between different users, different methods, and at one time one of the groups seems, in its meaning, to differ from that of the other groups. Much of the time they, in fact, coincide . . . as, for example, I think right now the kind of forecasts I hear myself making on those tapes are not very different from that a monetarist makes. But occasionally you find a difference and, occasionally, the monetarist's view is the more accurate one. Occasionally the opposite happens.

Suffice it to say that since the middle of last year I have a collection of estimates from people of both schools that cross each other.

I have more pessimistic estimates for the first quarter of the year from monetarists, in some cases, than from the other method. In the middle of 1966, the monetarists tended to be right with respect to a slowing down ahead. By year's end they tended to be wrong in prophesying that recession of 1967.

Magic and Forecasting

And so I say, based upon this and much other evidence, that the people who call themselves monetarists do not have a magic way of making a better forecast. I simply assert that I have hills of evidence bearing upon that point. And I add something—namely, a man who believes he's a monetarist, who makes forecasts, does not himself know *what* his forecasts are based upon. Some of those whom I have observed most closely, who do make good forecasts, I find combine witchcraft and arsenic in killing their neighbors' sheep. If their flair for forecasting tells them *not* to follow monetarism to its logical conclusion, they don't; and they are amply rewarded.

I'm going to pass over the evidence

of timing and turning points, which is a very mixed kind of evidence, is consistent with many different theories, and also is not a powerful test of where you are on this spectrum that I spoke of . . . at the extreme right or something less than the extreme right.

It's important to decide whether monetarism is true, because whether, for example, the tax bill goes through and the surcharge is extended—which is now something that is in doubt—to a monetarist doesn't matter. It really doesn't matter; the Fed just does its business and keeps that money supply growing in the proper range at the proper rate. It couldn't matter less as far as aggregate demand is concerned. And that's point number one.

Another example. We had a big surprise. The SEC survey showed 14 percent intentions of increase in plant and equipment. What's the effect of that to a monetarist? Nothing. It's of absolutely no importance and—you might think I'm making this up, but I heard it right from the tape, itself—it's of absolutely no importance that investment is stronger than people had thought, because there is no systematic relationship. If there is no systematic relationship between government expenditures in the income accounts, and taxes in the income accounts, when you bracket this with autonomous changes in private investment, there is also no systematic thing.

Now, you might say it takes a stern man to follow his logic down to that extreme. Well, we've got a hero in this country who follows his logic all the way, and this is his assertion.

I think that's very unpersuasive in terms of all we know about economic history, and I think it's wrong.

Now, I want to conclude on a more academic note. What is it that makes one who doesn't even follow the year-to-year and month-to-month business cycle situation skeptical about monetarism in the extreme—and I think hard to defend—form that I have defined?

If you actually examine the logic of economics—and I now am going into the neo-classical economics on which I was brought up in the pre-Keynesian period—there is no reason in the world why, in an equation like $MV = PQ$, the V should be thought to be independent of the rate of interest. There is every plausible reason in terms of experience, in terms of rarified neo-classical theory, for the velocity of circulation to be a systematic and increasing function of the rate of interest; and the minute you believe that, you have moved from the right of the spectrum—that of monetarism—to that noble eclectic position which I hold, the post-Keynesian position.

Now, if you will, examine, for example, the new Encyclopedia of Social Sciences article by Professor Friedman on money—as I read that article which goes on for, I suppose, 100 paragraphs.

The first ninety-eight paragraphs of that, I could agree with completely. The demand for money is a complicated thing. It depends upon many things, including the rate of interest and all the plausible things, etc.

The last two paragraphs assert, quite strongly, the literary equivalent of the following equation: that the change in the level of money income with respect to government expenditures, or with respect to taxation, or with respect to the difference between them ($M = \bar{M}$, holding the supply of money constant) is zero. On the tapes,

I hear the exact equivalent of that. That is a *non sequitur.* It does not follow from the previous analysis.

Finally—and this, again, is the important thing that interests me as an academic—if you actually analyze different wealth assets in the differing degrees of liquidity, there is no reason in the world, that I can see, why an ordinary open market operation, in which you swap one kind of used asset for another kind of used asset, should be expected, when it gives rise to the increase in what the Federal Reserve Bank of St. Louis reports to me every-hour-on-the-hour as a change in the supply of money, to have the same effect and be in the same invariant relationship to a different kind of increase in money, let's say an increase in money due to gold mining, where income is created along the way, or an increase in money due to deficit financing.

So I've tried to make a thought experiment—to redo the period from February 1961, to, let's say early 1965, leaving out the war, and taking that wonderful Camelot period when the GNP grew mightily. Let us redo the experiment in which the money supply grows exactly as it did in that period but the budget is kept at a balance—at a low balance level—such as the outgoing Eisenhower Administration had promised and had looked to.

I think that what would have happened was that if you had to create the same amount of money by that method with an entirely different kind of fiscal policy, you would have had, in the short run, to have depressed interest rates.

I forget, for example, about the international exchange problem, because of course the exchange rate can

float; there is no restraint on domestic policy in a rational world. I don't, by the way, want to cast any scorn on that view. The biggest problem that we face in the world today is how to get from here to there. The "here" is rigid exchange rates and the "there" is exchange rates with some kind of flexibility.

But I think there is every theoretical reason for expecting there to have been a different effect and so, as I look over the evidence, I say, "Money, yes; but monetarism, no."

2
James Tobin

I will concentrate on the question of evidence, which is crucial to the great debate. One kind of evidence, which has been presented at some length, is timing evidence: namely, the leads of changes in stock of money, or of changes in the rate of change of the stock of money, or of other monetary aggregates over income, or over the rate of change of income or over other measures of economic activity. A large amount of the work of Friedman and Schwartz in their *Monetary History of the U.S. 1867–1960* and in their article, "Money and Business Cycles,"[*]

*Milton Friedman and Anna Jacobson Schwartz, *A Monetary History of the United States, 1867–1960* (Princeton, N.J.: Princeton University Press, 1963); Milton Friedman and Anna Jacobson Schwartz, "Money and Business Cycles," *Review of Economics and Statistics,* 65 (Supplement: February 1963), 32–78.

Excerpted from James Tobin, "The Role of Money in National Economic Policy," in Federal Reserve Bank of Boston, *Controlling Monetary Aggregates* (Boston: Federal Reserve Bank, 1969), pp. 21–24. Reprinted by permission of the publisher.

is concerned precisely with pinning down these timing patterns. Now I think it is clear that timing evidence—leads, lags and so on—is no evidence about causation whatsoever.

I have engaged in a little irreverent exercise which constructs two models: on the one hand, one of these British models that Paul Samuelson was referring to, an ultra-Keynesian model where money has no causal relationship to anything, and on the other hand, a Friedman-like model in which money is the driving force of the business cycle. I have then compared the timing patterns of money and the change in money relative to money income and the change in income implied by these two different worlds. As it turns out, the ultra-Keynesian world produces a pattern of leads and lags in business cycles that superficially looks much more like money causing income than the Friedman world in which money actually is causing income. Moreover, the ultra-Keynesian model produces patterns of leads and lags in business cycles which coincide precisely with the summary of empirical results about such timing that appears in the Friedman-Schwartz article, whereas the implications of Friedman's and Schwartz's own theory diverge considerably from their own empirical findings.

Milton Friedman has responded that he knows better than to think that timing evidence has anything to do with causation. If this is stipulated, we can regard as descriptive but irrelevant detail all those pages about timing that an unwary reader might think were there for the purpose of making some point about causation.

There is a related point about evidence, which has to do with the effects on the data of the sins of the Federal Reserve and other monetary authorities in the past. Now let me give you a ridiculous example to make the point. Don't take it too seriously. Suppose that some statistician observes that over a long period of time there is a high association, a very good fit, between gross national product and the sales of, let us say, shoes. And then suppose someone comes along and says, "That's a very good relationship. Therefore, if we want to control GNP, we ought to control production of shoes. So, henceforth, we'll make shoes grow in production precisely at 4 percent per year, and that will make GNP do the same." I don't think you would have much confidence in drawing this second conclusion and policy recommendations from the observed empirical association.

Over the years, according to the monetarists, the Federal Reserve has been acting like the producers and sellers of shoes. That is, the Fed has been supplying money on demand from the economy instead of using the money supply to control the economy. The Fed has looked at the wrong targets and the wrong indicators. As a result, the Fed has allowed the supply of money to creep up when the demand for money rose as a result of expansion in business activity, and to fall when business activity has slacked off. This criticism implies that the supply of money has, in fact, not been an exogenously controlled variable over the period of observation. It has been an endogenous variable, responding to changes in economic conditions and credit market indicators via whatever response mechanism was built into the men in this room and their predecessors.

The evidence of association between money and income reflects, to a very large degree, this response mechanism of the Federal Reserve and the monetary authorities. It cannot be used simultaneously to support the reverse conclusion: namely that what they have done is the *cause* of the changes in income and GNP. Perhaps the monetarists will be sufficiently persuasive of the Federal Reserve and of Congressional committees to bring about, in the future, a controlled experiment in which the stock of money is actually an exogenous variable.

Much evidence has been presented purporting to show the superior power of monetary variables over fiscal variables and private investment measures in explaining changes in GNP. This evidence comes in what I call pseudo-reduced-forms.

The meaning of the term *reduced-form* is this: If you think of the economy as really a complex set of equations—basic structural relationships describing business investment, demands for loans, demands for money, the consumption function and so on—conceivably you could solve such a system and relate the variables in which you are ultimately interested, such as GNP, to the truly exogenous variables including the instruments of the monetary and fiscal authorities. Such a solution of a big complicated model you would call a *reduced-form*. And then one possible way of estimating a model of the system would be not to estimate the structural equations, the building blocks of the system, but to estimate the condensed equations which relate the ultimate outputs like GNP to the ultimate causal factors. That would be reduced-form estimation.

There are a lot of difficulties in that procedure. Therefore, most builders of big and small models of the economy do not proceed in that way; but, instead, try to estimate the individual structural equations one by one. What I mean by a pseudo-reduced-form is an equation relating an ultimate variable of interest, like GNP, to the supposedly causal variables, but one which doesn't come out of any structure at all. Instead, the investigator just says, "Here are the effects and here are the causes, let's just throw them into an equation." The form and content of the equation—the list of variables and the lag structure—are not derived from any structural model. That is what we have had presented to us as the main evidence for the supposed superiority of monetary variables in explaining GNP.

When, in contrast, we try to take a *theory* of how money affects the economy, and test it in the form it is presented, we have to look at one of two things: either a demand for money equation, or some complicated set of linkage equations through which changes in the money stock affect investment demand, consumption demand, etc. As far as the demand for money equation is concerned, as Paul Samuelson mentioned, the crucial assumption of some monetarists is that interest rate variables are of no importance, so that there is a tight linkage between the stock of money and GNP. If real GNP and prices, current and lagged, are the only important factors in the demand for money balances, then we know that control of money stock is uniquely decisive, and we don't have to look elsewhere in the system. However, all the tests that I know in which interest rates are allowed to enter demand for money equations, indicate that interest rates have important explanatory power.

If we do not really know that the demand for money is exclusively determined by income, then things other than income may absorb changes in money supply. There is no short cut. We have to look for the effects of changes in the stock of money, and it is hard work. We have to look through the system of structural equations to see how money enters directly and indirectly into investment demand and consumption demand and so on. We have to examine long chains of causation. In those chains there could be many slips, and there could be many structural changes, innovations in markets and institutions. That is the purpose, I suppose, of the hard work involved in large econometric models, work which these other attempts to find evidence try to short-circuit completely.

3
Allan H. Meltzer

TWO OPPOSING VIEWS

An understanding of monetary policy, of the role of money as an indicator, and of the difference between the effects of changes in credit and money can be obtained by contrasting two frameworks. In one view, monetary and fiscal policies are seen as the means by which the public sector off-

Excerpted from Allan H. Meltzer, "The Role of Money in National Economic Policy," in Federal Reserve Bank of Boston, *Controlling Monetary Aggregates* (Boston: Federal Reserve Bank, 1969), pp. 27–29. Reprinted by permission of the publisher.

sets instability in the economy resulting from changes that occur in the private sector. Fluctuations in prices and output are seen as the result primarily of real forces and changes mainly in attitude or outlook that raise or lower investment, thereby raising or lowering the nominal value of income, market interest rates, and the demand for money. The task of monetary policy, in this framework, is to offset undesired changes in interest rates caused by the unforeseen changes in investment. The task of fiscal policy is to offset the unforeseen changes in the private expenditure and maintain expenditures at the full employment level. Monetary policy is called "restrictive" if market rates are permitted to rise; "permissive" if market rates are prevented from rising; and "coordinated" if the balance of payments is in deficit, and market rates are permitted to rise so as to attract an inflow of short-term capital from abroad. With this framework, it appears reasonable to accept interest rates as the main indicator of monetary policy. If the framework were correct, the decision might be more tenable—although still not correct.

The alternative view—at least my view—does not deny that changes in market interest rates are partly the result of changes in attitude or changes in technology that shift private expenditures. The difference—and it is an important difference—is a difference of emphasis and interpretation. Not only are changes in private expenditure assigned a smaller role, but many of these so-called autonomous changes are viewed as a delayed response to past monetary and fiscal policies.

The effect of a monetary or fiscal

policy is not limited to the initial change in interest rates. An expansive monetary policy raises the monetary base, stocks of money and bank credit, and initially lowers market interest rates. The expansion of money increases expenditure, increases the amount of borrowing, and reduces the amount of existing securities that individuals and bankers wish to hold at prevailing market interest rates. These changes in borrowing and in desired holdings of securities reverse the initial decline in interest rates; market rates rise until the stock of existing securities is reabsorbed into portfolios, and the banks offer the volume of loans that the public desires. If expansive operations continue, expenditures, borrowing, and interest rates rise to levels above those in the starting equilibrium. Later, prices rise under the impact of increases in the quantity of money, further reducing the desired holdings of bonds and other fixed coupon securities, and increasing desired borrowing. A rise in holdings of currency relative to demand deposits adds to the forces raising interest rates on the credit market.

In this interpretation, the effect of monetary (or fiscal policy) is not limited to the initial effect. The response to a maintained change in policy includes the effects on the credit market, the acceleration and deceleration of prices, and ultimately, if policy makers persist, the changes in attitudes and particularly in anticipations of inflation or deflation. These changes, however, are regarded as reliable consequences of maintaining an expansive or contractive monetary policy, just as much to be expected as the initial effect.

It is the temporary changes in the level of interest rates observed on the credit market that frequently mislead monetary policy makers into believing their policy is restrictive when it is expansive. Large changes in the growth rate of money become a main source of instability precisely because the credit market and price effects dominate the initial effect of monetary policy in an economy close to full employment. Misled by the change in market interest rates—or their interpretation of the change—the Federal Reserve permits or forces the stock of money to grow at too high or too low a rate for too long a time. Excessive expansion and contraction of money becomes the main cause of the fluctuations in output and of inflation or deflation. Inappropriate public policies, not changes in private expenditures, become the main cause of instability.

A portion of the second interpretation has now been accepted by the principal spokesman of the Federal Reserve System. In his March 25th statement to the Senate Banking Committee, Chairman Martin said:

I do not mean to argue that the interest rate developments in recent years have had no relation to monetary policy. We know that, in the short run, expansive monetary policies tend to reduce interest rates and restrictive monetary policy to raise them. But in the long run, in a full employment economy, expansive monetary policies foster greater inflation and encourage borrowers to make even larger demands on the credit markets. Over the long run, therefore, expansive monetary policies may not lower interest rates; in fact, they may raise them appreciably. This is the clear lesson of history that has been reconfirmed by the experience of the past several years.

With that statement, Chairman Martin abandoned the framework that has guided Federal Reserve policy through most of its history and has been responsible for major errors in policy. Recognition that interest rates generally rise fastest under the impact of monetary expansion—that the credit market effects dominate short-term changes in interest rates—is probably the single most important step toward an understanding of the role of money that has been taken in the entire history of the Federal Reserve System.

If we develop our analysis and concentrate on improving our understanding of money and of the differences between money and credit, rather than on the issue of whether Milton Friedman is wholly right or wholly wrong, we will have more progress to report next time we meet. Thank you.

Continued from p. 304

Taking the Federal Reserve as it is today, I would conclude that all elements in the system (with the exception of the Federal Reserve Bank of St. Louis) remain highly eclectic and pragmatic in their conception of the tasks of monetary management. They show no signs of being led astray by simple prescriptions offered by the monetarists as to how they should perform their jobs.[9]

Thus, the majority remains in the mainstream tradition, in government as well as in the academic world. However, almost everyone who has participated in this debate (including Brimmer) believes that the monetarists have both produced and stimulated important research that will definitely continue into the future.

SUMMARY

The debate over *monetarism* is a central issue in macroeconomics, both in terms of analysis and of public policy. In the Keynesian world, money fits into the analysis via a transactions demand (dependent on the level of money income) and a liquidity demand (dependent on the interest rate). Monetary policy may run into a liquidity trap when it tries to cure a depression and unemployment.

The monetarist position is a restatement of an older view known as the *quantity theory of money*. In this older theory, the tautology—$MV = PQ$—takes on meaning when it is hypothesized that Q is determined by technological and production factors and V is institutionally determined. In this case, changes in M are reflected in proportional changes in the price level.

The monetarists, under Professor Milton Friedman, have taken off from this starting point to develop an approach that differs from the Keynesian in terms of the analysis of monetary mechanisms, and also in terms of the appropriate range of governmental actions. Among the questions that are taken up in this chapter and Great Debate Two are: Does money matter—not at all, very much, or supremely? Does fiscal policy work or does M alone effectively determine long-run $P \times Q$? Should the government regulate its monetary policy in terms of the money supply alone, or in terms of interest rates and other credit conditions? Should the Fed use *any* discretion or should it bind itself to a fixed increase in the money supply rule?

The empirical issues are difficult to settle because of the interdependence of economic phenomena, the problems of sorting out leads and lags, and the difficulty of determining cause and effect. So far, most economists would give the edge to the eclectic post-Keynesians, although everyone gives credit to the monetarists both for their own intensive researches and for their stimulation of research by others.

QUESTIONS FOR DISCUSSION

1. Theories of the role of money in the economy have been ranked according to the following spectrum of possibilities:
   (*a*) Money doesn't matter.
   (*b*) Money matters.
   (*c*) Money matters much.
   (*d*) Money alone matters.

On this spectrum, rank the following

9. Andrew F. Brimmer, "The Political Economy of Money: Evolution and Impact of Monetarism in the Federal Reserve System," *The American Economic Review*, Papers and Proceedings, 62, no. 2 (May 1972): 351.

theories: quantity theory of money, Keynesian and post-Keynesian theories, and monetarism.

2. It has been claimed that Keynesian theory does not, contrary to common opinion, provide for the possibility of a genuine below-full-employment equilibrium, the reason being that unemployed workers will have a motive for bidding down the money wage, which, in turn, will bring a general fall in prices. To this the Keynesians have usually replied that although W and P might fall under these circumstances, their fall might have little or no effect on the rate of unemployment in the economy. Show how falling W and P could, in the Keynesian theory, affect the level of real national income and employment. What factors might keep this effect small? Why have we said that, in the Keynesian theory, a general fall in W and P is rather similar in effect to an increase in the money supply, M?

3. What is the Pigou effect? Would this effect apply to government bonds in the hands of the public? Discuss the issues involved.

4. When the government runs a budget deficit, it might sell its bonds to the public or to the Federal Reserve System. If it sells them to the Federal Reserve System, this will lead to a general increase in bank reserves and an expansion in M. (Remember our discussion of open-market operations in chapter 11.) With this in mind, explain why, according to the monetarists, an increase in government expenditures, G, unmatched by any change in taxes may have either (a) no effect or (b) a substantial effect on money national income, depending completely on how the deficit is financed.

5. Explain what you see as the advantages and disadvantages of an automatic versus discretionary monetary and fiscal policy.

SUGGESTED READING

Friedman, Milton. *Program for Monetary Stability.* New York: Fordham University, 1959.

_____. "Have Fiscal and/or Monetary Policies Failed?" *The American Economic Review* 62, no. 2 (May 1972).

Kaldor, Nicholas. "The New Monetarism," *Lloyds Bank Review*, July 1970.

Mueller, M. G. *Readings in Macroeconomics.* New York: Holt, Rinehart & Winston, 1966, chaps. 10–14; 24.

Samuelson, Paul A. "Monetarism Objectively Evaluated." In *Readings in Economics*, 6th ed., ed. Paul A. Samuelson. New York: McGraw-Hill, 1970.

Slesinger, Reuben E.; Perlman, Mark; and Isaacs, Asher. *Contemporary Economics.* 2nd ed. Boston: Allyn & Bacon, 1967, chaps. 43–45.

The Federal Reserve Bank of Boston. *Controlling Monetary Aggregates.* Boston: Proceedings of the Monetary Conference. Federal Reserve Bank of Boston, June 1969.

14
Inflation

Although we have made a number of references to the problem of inflation, particularly in our discussion of monetarism, we have spent most of Part Two discussing unemployment and below-capacity national income. This approach can be justified on several grounds: national income analysis was originally developed mainly as a theory of unemployment; many of the tools we have presented in connection with the analysis of depressions can readily be applied to the question of inflation; and the problem of unemployment has historically been a more serious one for the United States than that of inflation. It is seldom realized today (and therefore worth stressing) that prices in the United States during the nineteenth century were on the whole on a *downward* trend. At one point in our history, things actually cost *more* in "the good old days"!

But what was true of the last century has not been true of this one, and particularly not of the past ten or fifteen years. Prices in the United States have been rising ever since World War II and,

by 1970, the annual rate of increase had reached 6 percent. To make matters more complicated, substantial inflation and substantial unemployment were existing simultaneously. This has made even more difficult the application of those fiscal and monetary tools whose merits and demerits we have just been discussing.

Thus, we must now face the problem of inflation directly—in terms of effects, causes, and possible cures.

INFLATION
AND THE PUBLIC INTEREST

What exactly is inflation? And what is its impact on the public at large?

By *inflation*, we mean any general increase in the price level of the economy in the aggregate. This is a macroeconomic concept. While in microeconomics, one may be concerned with a rise in the price of one commodity relative to other commodities, inflation involves a rise in the prices of all commodities, or of most commodities, or, most commonly, of some *index* that measures the average of various prices taken together.

This definition, however, is still a bit general. For one thing, we might wish to know exactly *what* prices are being included in any particular index of inflation. In the United States, for example, there are three main indices of inflation in common use: (1) the Index of Consumer Prices, (2) the Wholesale Price Index, and (3) the GNP Price Deflator. The third index, which reflects the distinction between changes in *real* GNP and changes merely in money GNP, is the most general of these indices. For particular purposes, we may be more interested in one of the other two. As consumers, we may have a special concern about the consumer price index, since this attempts to estimate the cost of living as it affects the average American family.

Even more important, however, is the fact that this definition of inflation fails to distinguish between different *kinds* of inflation. In the very first chapter of this book, we mentioned the German hyperinflation of the 1920s when the price index soared into the trillions. Now this kind of runaway inflation, with its enormously destructive effects on the whole fabric of the society, has to be distinguished from the serious but very different kind of inflation that the United States suffered from, say, 1960 to 1970 when the cost-of-living index rose overall by perhaps 35 percent in the course of the decade.

Indeed, when we look at the world today, we find quite striking differences in the degree of inflationary pressures in different countries. In the less developed countries, and especially in certain Latin-American countries, rapid year-to-year (or even month-to-month) inflation is a fairly common occurrence. Between 1950 and 1965, it is estimated that prices in

Brazil were rising at a yearly rate of 31 percent; in Argentina, 25 percent; in Chile, 33 percent.[1] By contrast, the 6 percent increase in the cost-of-living index in the United States in 1970 and the 5 percent increase in 1971 seem quite modest.

The distinction between rapid or runaway inflation and this much more moderate general rise in prices is important when it comes to determining the impact of inflation on the well-being of the economy. Runaway inflation may have seriously destructive effects on a country's domestic economy and its economic relations with other nations. Moderate inflation—which will be our main concern here—is much more limited in its effects and, indeed, not all of these effects must be considered harmful. Most economists would consider stable prices to be ideal, but it is not unthinkable to take the position that a "little inflation" can be a "good thing." Take, for example, this well-known defense of moderate inflation written by the labor economist, Sumner Slichter, in the 1950s:

The obvious injustices of even a slow long-term rise in prices lead many people to insist that such a rise must be prevented—that nothing but a stable price level will be satisfactory. At the risk of being called an irresponsible and dangerous thinker, let me say that in the kind of economy possessed by the United States a slowly rising price level is actually preferable to a stable price level.

The reason for this conclusion is that the maintenance of a stable price level would conflict with other important interests of the country. For example, the maintenance of a stable price level in the long run would require that the country relax its efforts to keep business recessions as mild as possible.

1. Angus Maddison, *Economic Progress and Policy in Developing Countries* (New York: W. W. Norton & Co., 1970), p. 93.

Furthermore, the maintenance of a stable price level would require the acceptance of chronic unemployment or drastic intervention by the government in the relations between employers and employees. Finally, the policies necessary to keep prices stable would severely handicap the United States in its efforts to contain communism by building up the economies of the free world.[2]

The champions of a stable price level do not seem to be aware of the conflicts between the goal which they advocate and other desirable goals. Indeed, they are so impressed by the injustices caused by inflation that they fail to see that serious injustices would have to be imposed in order to keep the price level stable—injustices even greater than those which would accompany a slowly rising price level. . . .

The net advantage to the country of a slowly rising price level over a stable one is the greater amount of employment, and hence the greater amount of production and the higher standard of consumption, that are made possible by a slowly advancing price level.[3]

But if it is possible to argue that a moderate inflation is not all that bad, and perhaps even desirable, why has there been such an outcry in the United States on this subject in recent years? Why do some people seem to consider inflation an evil to be ranked with, if not worse than,

unemployment? Part of the answer, it seems, lies in a failure to look beyond immediate and apparent effects. Another part lies in the fact that inflation, even moderate inflation, does have certain clearly unfortunate consequences.

The misunderstanding stems from the fact that people often fail to connect the process that raises prices and the process that raises their earnings, with which they will meet these increased costs. They sometimes talk as if every rise in prices impoverishes them by exactly that amount, since they can buy that much less with a given income. Or they may speak disparagingly about how little a dollar is worth now, failing to ask at the same time how many more dollars per week or per year they and other people now earn. Such an approach is clearly inadequate. We know from our earlier discussion of the concept of gross national product that a rise in the money value of output will necessarily be a rise also in the money value of national income. They are two different ways of looking at the same thing. To speak of the harmful effects of a general rise in prices on the assumption that all money incomes in the society remain unchanged is very nearly a contradiction in terms. The interesting and much more relevant question is: What are the effects of inflation when prices and wages, salaries, and other incomes are all rising at the same time?

These effects might generally include the following:

(1) Changes in the distribution of income. Although all incomes may be rising to some degree in an inflation, some income-receivers will be gaining much more rapidly than others. The people who will be hurt will be those who are living on fixed pensions or on the interest from government or other bonds; or salaried

---

2. On this last point, Slichter's argument was that we could build up our allies economically only by accepting imports from them, and that American businessmen would be willing to do this (i.e., not press Congress for trade restrictions) only if there were also a rising demand for American products, reflected in a slow inflation of prices. In view of our present-day balance of payments difficulties (see the next chapter), it is doubtful that this specific defense of inflation is valid today. Slichter's other points, however, may be even *more* relevant today than they were when he wrote them in 1952.

3. Sumner H. Slichter, "How Bad is Inflation?" *Harper's*, August 1952, pp. 53–54; 57.

individuals employed by institutions, like churches, that may find it difficult to adjust their pay-scales to rapid increases in the cost of living. Although there are not many people in the economy whose incomes are strictly "fixed"—i.e., do not adjust at all to inflation—the rate of adjustment is different in different groups, and the ones who are left behind really will be "impoverished" by the rise in prices.

(2) Changes in the position of creditor, debtor, saver. Inflation undermines the value of past savings if these savings are held in a form that represents a fixed claim on money (i.e., savings accounts, government bonds, life insurance policies, etc.). More generally, it alters the creditor-debtor relationship. Creditors suffer because the real value of their credits falls while debtors benefit, since their debts are also falling in real value. Thus inflation involves not only a redistribution of income but also a redistribution of the stock of wealth in the community.

(3) Production and the use of resources. Inflation may cause productive resources to be devoted to speculative or other uneconomic uses. This problem is really serious only when the inflation is rapid, but it may exist to some degree even when prices are rising moderately. In general, inflation puts most business firms in a quite favorable profit position somewhat irrespective of their performance. It diminishes the penalties for mistakes and dulls the sharp incentive to maximum effort. Also, again especially if the inflation is fairly rapid, planning for the future may be more difficult if tomorrow's prices are substantially different from today's.

(4) Effects on the international balance of payments. Most countries, as we shall see in the next chapter, are concerned about preventing their imports from exceeding their exports. Inflation at home may generally go with high demand for imports from abroad. At the same time, our high domestic prices may discourage foreign countries from buying our exports. This can lead to difficult balance of payments problems. It should be noted, however, that this is not so much an argument against inflation, per se, as it is an argument against inflation that is more rapid than that of the countries with which one trades.

(5) Forced savings, investment, and growth. Under certain circumstances, inflation can lead to a redistribution of output at the expense of consumption and in favor of investment and future growth. This is one of the reasons inflation is sometimes favored in less-developed countries where the desire for growth is particularly intense. Suppose that all consumers are wage earners and that all wage earners wish to spend all their income on consumption. If it happens that prices rise more rapidly than wages, then the *real* incomes, and hence total consumption of the wage earners, will be less than they would have been under stable prices. The gain in a private economy will accrue to business firms that will have higher profits and will be able to invest more than they would be able to otherwise. The process is sometimes called *forced saving,* since the society as a whole is saving more, even though the wage earners themselves would have preferred to consume more.

It should be apparent from this list that inflation can and does have certain definitely harmful effects. The classic case of misfortune is represented by the widow or elderly couple living on a fixed pension with a small savings account and a few government bonds. This is no longer an exceptional case in our economy. Because of increasing life expectancies, the number of persons above the age of sixty-five in the American economy has increased from 4 percent in 1900 to 10 percent today. Furthermore, a fifth of these families have incomes below the poverty level. For such families, prolonged inflation even of the moderate sort means a continual reduction in the purchasing power of their already small incomes and the value of their past savings. For many elderly people, inflation can bring economic tragedy.

On the other hand, it is also apparent that some of the harmful effects of inflation really become serious only when the inflation is either very rapid or at least more rapid than that of other nations. Furthermore, it is apparent that there are some cases at least where a mild inflation may divert production away from consumption and into areas that are considered more important. This may be true in the case of investment and growth, especially in a less developed country.

In short, the picture is a mixed one. Stable prices remain the ideal. Yet it is also clear that people often overstate the dire consequences of moderate inflation.

CAUSES OF INFLATION

We have been speaking of effects; now let us turn to the question of causes. As we might expect, the monetarist controversy affects opinions about the causes of inflation as well as about other aspects of national income analysis. Let us begin, however, by considering inflation in terms of the basic theory of national income determination as presented in Part Two A. What we might call the "Keynesian" case is one where inflation is caused by an aggregate demand for goods and services that exceeds national income at the full-employment level.

Such a situation is depicted in Figure 14-1. This diagram is the same as those we have used before, except that the sum of consumption, investment, and government demand $(C + I + G)$ exceeds the level of national income at FE, or full employment. This means that we cannot follow our previous course, which has always been to say that the level of national income will be determined by the intersection of the $C + I + G$ curve with the 45° line. There is, of course, some flexibility in the concept of "full-employment national income." We can always work a little harder; more potential wage earners (e.g., housewives, young people) may enter the labor force; and so on. Still, there is some upper limit beyond which our total output cannot be increased in the short run. In Figure 14-1 we are assuming that the total demand of consumers, businessmen, and the government exceeds this upper limit. What happens in this case?

The answer is that something has to give. And what is likely to give is the general price level.

We cannot actually picture this process in the terms used in Figure 14-1, since this diagram depicts national income in *real* terms; i.e., as measured in "constant prices." We can easily imagine the inflationary process however. The situation at full employment is that not just one industry, but all industries in the economy, are faced with more demand for their products than they can supply.

When businessmen are confronted by a situation in which demand exceeds supply, we know from chapter 2 that there will be a rise in the prices of their products. This, however, is not the only effect. Businessmen in such circum-

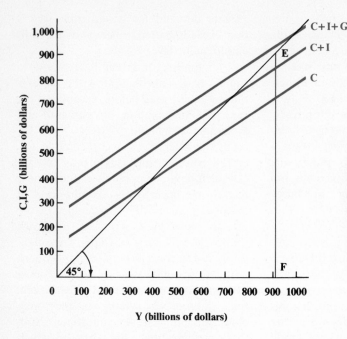

Figure 14-1. A "Classic" Demand-Pull Inflation.

When the sum of $C+I+G$ exceeds full employment income at FE, then there will be a natural tendency for prices to rise. Price rises, in turn, will be accompanied by wage increases, further price rises, further wage increases, and so on, in a continuing inflationary spiral.

stances will also be trying to expand production. To do this, they will try to hire more laborers. But the economy, as we know, is already at full employment. Consequently, the main effect of businesses bidding for laborers will be to raise the price of labor—i.e., the general level of wages throughout the economy. This rise in wages, however, will only *add fuel to the inflationary fire.* The rise in wages means that wage earners will have higher money incomes than before, and this will increase the money value of their demand for goods. This rise in demand will mean that aggregate demand still exceeds aggregate supply, even at the new and higher level of prices. Therefore, the whole process is likely to repeat itself. Businessmen will raise prices and attempt to expand production once again. Wages and consequently the money value of the wage earners' demand for goods and services will rise a second time. And again businessmen will find themselves with a situation in which the demand for their products exceeds the available supply. This will repeat for a third round, a fourth round, and so on. A continuing inflationary process is now under way.

We have here then the classic case of a Keynesian or what is often called a *demand-pull* inflation. We can relate it to our earlier discussion of national income analysis as follows: when the economy is suffering unemployment, increases in aggregate demand will ordinarily lead to increases in output and employment up to the point where full employment is reached. *After* this point, however, the effect of further increases in aggregate demand will be felt not in increased output, but inflation. Wages and prices will spiral upward in the fashion we have just described. The rapidity of the inflation will be determined in a very general way by how great the excess of aggregate demand is at the full-employment level.

A question arises immediately:

What could lead to such an excess of demand? It is here that one would seek for the causes of this kind of inflation.

The general answer to the question is, of course, that any factors which tend to bring consumption, business investment, or government spending to unusually high levels will be likely to result in an excess of $C + I + G$ at full employment. Historically, the major factor in our own experience has been wartime circumstances that have led to extraordinary expansions of G not fully balanced by taxes. However, excess demand can also originate in the private sector. Schumpeter, we recall, emphasized the role of innovation and private investment in causing swings of economic activity. Suppose there is some major technological breakthrough like the railroads in the mid-nineteenth century. The introduction of this new technology may require substantial investment, which may raise aggregate demand sufficiently to get the inflation started. But then the inflation itself may be a stimulus to further innovations. Prices are rising, profits are high; other innovators may come along wishing to invest in the railroads or in subsidiary industries or even in unrelated industries whose prospects have been improved by the generally buoyant state of demand in the economy as a whole. Sudden changes in private consumption demand could also in theory give rise to inflationary pressures, although this case is probably somewhat less common in actual fact.

In short, all those circumstances that may affect government, investment, and consumption demand—war, technology, new products, tastes, future expectations, the past and predicted behavior of prices—would be the elements we would want to study to explain a possible excess of aggregate demand at full employment as depicted in Figure 14-1.

FOOTNOTE ON MONETARISM

The above, however, is not the only possible analysis of inflation. (Nor is it the only kind of inflation that needs to be explained.) We need not dwell on this point, since we have explored the controversy over monetarism in detail in the last chapter and in Great Debate Two. Suffice it to say that, according to the monetarist doctrine, the basic cause of inflation would be a growth in the money supply that exceeded the growth of full employment national income. In its simplest terms, as expressed in the quantity theory of money, if the growth of real GNP (owing to capital accumulation, technological progress, etc.) is 3 percent per year and the growth of the money supply is 3 percent per year, we will have stable prices. If, however, the growth of the money supply exceeds 3 percent, we will have inflation roughly in proportion to the excess of the growth of the money supply above the rate of growth of real income. To evaluate this alternative explanation of inflation, the reader should consult the earlier discussion, especially where the assumptions of the monetarist and Keynesian positions are contrasted (pp. 298-304).

INFLATION *AND* UNEMPLOYMENT

There is another point regarding our discussion of inflation so far—it is not the only kind of inflation that needs to be explained. Most economists would agree that, on two related grounds, the kind of inflation analyzed above is inadequate as a rendering of present-day

American experience. First, it assumes that inflationary pressures arise completely from the demand side. Second, it describes inflation as occurring only when the economy is at full employment. But we know that there are forces on the "supply" side that can also lead to inflationary pressures, and we also know that prices in general often rise even when there is some unemployment in the economy.

Indeed, the characteristic situation in the 1970s in the United States is one in which inflation and unemployment exist simultaneously. We have said that consumer prices rose by perhaps a third during the decade 1960 to 1970; during this same period unemployment averaged nearly 5 percent of the labor force. It is widely believed that, had unemployment been less, inflation might have been at least somewhat higher: that is, that there is a "trade-off" between inflation and unemployment in a modern industrial economy.

The ultimate explanation of these facts lies in the structure of labor and business organization in the United States, which, as we know, is far from that implied by the theory of pure competition.[4] If labor unions throughout the economy or in certain major industries are particularly strong, they may be able to get wage increases that are excessive even when aggregate demand is not pressing against the full-employment barrier. By "excessive" here we do not mean *any* general rise in wages, for labor productivity is increasing annually, and the laborers would ordinarily expect to share in that productivity increase even in the most

4. Our case of classic inflation really assumes something like pure competition in the labor and product markets. Indeed, it is one of the limitations of Keynesian analysis in general that it tends to ignore market imperfections of various kinds. For our comments on the actual structure of American industrial and labor organization, see chapter 5 and chapters 24-26.

purely competitive economy. But suppose the wage increase exceeds the productivity increase. Laborers, say, are producing 3 percent more output this year because of technological progress, but they demand and receive a wage increase of, say, 10 percent. Such a wage increase is clearly inflationary. It will be sustainable by industry only if industry raises its prices. But a general rise in prices may stimulate further wage demands. The wage-price spiral is on. This upward movement of wages and prices would look very similar to that occurring in a demand-pull inflation (in fact, the two cases are not always easy to distinguish in practice), but it differs from it in that its origins have been inflationary wage increases, not the pressures of excess aggregate demand. And the main test of this fact is that such wage increases can and do take place when there is unemployment and other evidence of "slack" in the economy as a whole. This type of inflation is usually called *cost-push* inflation.

Such supply-originating inflations reflect the structure of American business as well as American labor. The ability of industry to absorb inflationary wage increases and to pass them on to the consumers through price increases is to some degree a testimony to the existence of substantial market power such as we would expect in oligopolistic industries. More generally, there is a considerable resistance to downward changes in prices in much of American business. This means that a fall in demand for an industry's products may be reflected in lowered output, employment, and excess capacity, rather than in lowered prices. An increase in demand, however, will ordinarily bring a rise in prices. When price changes take place only on a one-way street—rigid downward, but flexible upward—then inflationary situations can

arise even when there is no excess of aggregate demand in total. A shift in demand from one industry to another may
bring rising prices in one industry while
leaving prices in another unchanged. The
effect in total is inflationary although
there is no overall excess in demand.

Such institutional factors as these
help explain why inflation may arise in
a non-"classic" situation. They also help
explain why inflation may sometimes be
more difficult to cure than it would be
in a classic situation. For if inflation can
get started even when there is considerable slack in the economy, then it may
be impossible to control except at the expense of considerable unemployment.

The general relationship between
inflation and unemployment is sometimes
set out in terms of what is called a *Phillips
curve*, after the economist A. W. Phillips,
who originated it. The actual shape of this
curve for a given country at a given time
would have to be determined empirically,
but its typical shape would be like that
shown in Figure 14-2. The economy
shown in this figure would be able to get
stable prices (zero rate of price increase)
only if it was prepared to suffer 7 or 8
percent unemployment. At this level the
institutional and other factors exerting inflationary pressures on the supply-side are
exactly counterbalanced by the downward
pressures of inadequate aggregate demand. At lower levels of unemployment,
however, price rises begin to occur, even
though the economy is still short of full
employment.

Now the degree to which this conflict between full employment and price
stability is a problem will clearly depend
on the actual shape and position of this
curve. (For example, if the curve passed
through the point of zero price change at
a level of 2 percent unemployment, there
would be no great problem to worry

Figure 14-2. A Phillips Curve.

**This curve shows the relationship between
unemployment and inflation. At low levels
of unemployment, the hypothetical economy shown here would suffer substantial
inflation. The exact shape and position of
the Phillips curve must be determined empirically for any particular country at any
particular time.**

about.) Most economists believe that the
conflict does exist to a serious degree and
that it substantially complicates the measures one must take to remove or reduce
inflationary pressures.

POLICIES TO COMBAT INFLATION

We have spoken about effects
and causes. Now what about cures?

Insofar as there is a strong demand-pull element in any given inflation,
the obvious remedies consist of using fiscal policy or monetary policy or both to
restrain aggregate demand and hence to

reduce the inflationary pressures.[5]

In the case of fiscal policy, the measures to be taken would be some variant of increasing taxes or reducing government spending. An increase in taxes would lower the $C + I + G$ curve either by reducing personal consumption or, if the taxes were directed primarily at business corporations, by reducing business investment. A reduction of government spending would, of course, lower G directly. The choice between the reduced spending or the increased tax approach, and also the choice between different variants of these approaches, would reflect a number of other considerations. Are government spending programs essential or are they expendable? Is the allocation of output between consumption and investment too heavily weighted to the consumer or the investor? And so on.

In the case of monetary policy, the approach would be the reverse of that used in the case of a depression. The Federal Reserve system could increase reserve requirements, raise the discount rate, or engage in open-market sales of government securities. These open-market sales of securities would have the effect of lowering the reserves of the commercial member banks. If the banks in the system were fully "loaned up," there would be a curtailment of loans and investments to business. The money supply would fall, businesses would find it harder to obtain credit, the interest rate would rise. The effect would be to curtail areas of spending that are most sensitive to changes in the interest rate—certain kinds of business investment, construction, state and local government spending which is dependent on bond issues, and so on. This curtail-

ment, in turn, would mean a reduction of aggregate demand and of the inflationary pressures arising from the demand side.

In earlier chapters, we have noticed that monetary policy had certain weaknesses when it came to curing problems of depression and unemployment. Used to combat inflation, it is undoubtedly a somewhat stronger tool. Indeed, it is difficult to imagine an inflation of any substantial magnitude continuing very long unless there is an increase in the money supply to feed it. As the money value of national income rises, the amount of money necessary to support the transactions demand for money increases. If there is a continuing inflation and *no* increase in the money supply, there will be very little money left over for liquidity purposes. Ultimately this leads to such a "tight money" situation and to such a rise in interest rates that investment, and other interest-dependent spending, is almost certain to fall.

In ordinary circumstances, then, monetary policy is likely to be more effective in inflationary than in depressed situations. However, if monetary policy alone is used—i.e., without accompanying fiscal restraint—it may have to be applied so strenuously that it causes serious problems in certain areas of the economy. The United States faced a situation rather like this in 1966. The price level, which had been fairly stable up to this point, began rising more rapidly in 1966. Many voices were raised advocating fiscal restraint, and especially a rise in taxes, but on the whole these voices were not heeded; except for one or two measures, government spending and tax policies were unchanged. Thus, monetary policy was given the whole burden of restraining the inflationary pressures. It was applied quite vigorously. The money supply which had

---

5. Monetarists, of course, would place particular emphasis on using monetary policy as an anti-inflationary tool. In their view, we recall, fiscal policy has no long-run effect on aggregate demand.

heretofore been expanding with the general expansion of the economy at about 5 percent or 6 percent a year was actually reduced, falling, in the second half of 1966, from about $172 billion to $167 billion.[6]

And costs in terms of certain specific activities were quite high. Tight credit hurt local governments, which had to put off plans for needed schools, parks, and highways. The residential homebuyer was particularly hard hit. As mortgage rates climbed to 6 1/2 percent, housing starts fell to a postwar low, and the construction industry was in tight straits. The financial world went into something close to a psychological collapse. As the *New York Times* commented shortly afterward, the "credit markets were close to panic," and only timely fiscal action by the president, suspending the investment tax credit, helped save the day. The point is that the restrictive effects of monetary policy are felt keenly in certain particular areas of the economy; if general inflationary pressures are to be curbed by monetary measures alone, the result is likely to be very destructive to those specific areas.

Furthermore, monetary policy is unable to solve inflationary problems adequately when they originate from *cost-push* factors. This limitation applies also to fiscal policy and, indeed, to any set of measures that attempts to work through changes in the level of aggregate demand. For a given Phillips curve, these policies can be successful in curbing inflation only to the degree that they depress the economy sufficiently to create substantial unemployment.

---

6. Even a *constant* money supply would be considered something of a "restraint" in an economy that grows every year and consequently always needs more money for transactions purposes. An actual *reduction* of the money supply, therefore, is fairly strong medicine.

IMPROVING THE INFLATION-UNEMPLOYMENT TRADE-OFF

In the modern economy, therefore, even fiscal and monetary policy taken together will not usually be adequate to curb inflation, and direct attention may have to be given to altering the shape and position of the Phillips curve.

In the past ten or fifteen years, a number of different approaches have been used to this end. In the 1960s, a great deal of "moral suasion" or *jawboning* on the part of the federal government was common. Business and labor were urged and cajoled to keep wage and price increases down. In some cases, not very clearly disguised threats were used—the most notable example being the confrontation between the government and the steel industry in the Kennedy years. Because of the great impact of this episode, we present a reading on the Kennedy-steel confrontation in the appendix to this chapter.

In the 1960s, the federal government also attempted a somewhat more systematic effort to restrain inflation through the use of wage-price *guideposts*. These guideposts were indicated each year by the President's Council of Economic Advisers and were based on the principle that wage increases should be no greater in general than the nation's increase in productivity and that industry's prices, on the average, should be stable. (Industries where productivity increase was lower than the national average might raise prices under this policy, but this should be counterbalanced by reduced prices in industries with higher than average productivity increase.)

From 1968 to early 1971, President Nixon's Council of Economic Advisers shied away from guideposts and, instead, began issuing *inflation alerts*, which consisted of periodic reports designed to call attention to particularly disturbing features of inflationary price and wage behavior. The hope was that such reports would cause public opinion to focus on unacceptable business and labor settlements and that this public opinion might have some favorable effect on future settlements.

All the above approaches were basically voluntaristic (with occasional arm-twisting as in Kennedy vs. Big Steel), and on the whole they were disappointing in their effects. By 1970, inflation was more rapid than it had been before, and unemployment was still at an unacceptable level. This domestic situation (combined with a difficult international situation, which we shall consider in the next chapter) caused the president to strike a sharply different note. In a televised address on Sunday, August 15, 1971, President Nixon announced a "new economic policy" that included, besides its international provisions, a ninety-day *wage-price freeze*, and a package of measures designed to stimulate the domestic economy. The hope was that industry might be encouraged to expand and provide more jobs, while, at the same time, inflation would be handled by subjecting business and labor to stringent, direct controls. A cabinet-level Cost of Living Council was created, and the freeze was on.

Of course, this was only the beginning. After the ninety-day period, the administration decided that controls would have to be maintained on a mandatory basis in what was called *Phase II*. To this end, a seven-member Price Commission and a fifteen-member Pay Board (five business, five labor, and five public members) were established. These agen-cies promulgated a general approach suggesting that pay increases should not exceed 5 1/2 percent per year. Assuming a 3 percent annual increase in labor productivity, this would mean a 2 1/2 percent rate of inflation per year—clearly down from the much higher rate of 1970. Almost immediately, however, the Pay Board made certain exceptions to these guidelines; also the Board has been subjected to frequent attack from labor, including several of its labor members, who subsequently resigned from the Board.

We shall take up later some of the pros and cons of using wage-price controls to achieve price stability in a modern economy.[7] It seems clear in the first year of the new policy that its general effect has been to moderate the forces of inflation to some degree. It also seems clear that this approach to the problem is no panacea and that its ultimate success (if it indeed it is successful at all) will come only after long and arduous struggles.

Still there *are* things that can be done. Indeed, the administration and Congress might substantially aid the cause of Phase II policies if they turned their attention to certain other areas of government activity that influence the forces of inflation. There are many government programs that actually hold prices up. Certain farm programs, oil import quotas, fair trade laws, medical care payment systems, and other such programs are cases in point. These inflation-sustaining pieces of legislation could be altered as a start. More positively, the government could attempt through various manpower training programs to

---

7. See especially Great Debate Four: Wage-Price Controls (pp. 647–63). Our reason for postponing this discussion until later is that the issue of wage-price controls involves central problems of both *ma*cro- and *micro*economics. Thus, the debate can best be evaluated after the reader has completed both Parts Two and Three of this book.

reduce frictional unemployment and thus make possible a closer approach to full employment before serious upward pressure on prices was induced.

In general, a greater number of different and hopefully vigorous policies should be tried to lick this new version of the "macroeconomic problem." We do not face the disastrous form of that problem—mass unemployment—that we did in the 1930s. But we do face a particularly stubborn and persistent challenge in our efforts to move forward simultaneously towards two goals—price stability *and* full employment.

SUMMARY

Inflation is the economist's term for a general rise in prices, though there are many different kinds of inflation, some very rapid, others—like that of the United States in recent years—more moderate.

The harmful effects of a moderate inflation are sometimes overstated by those who fail to realize that rising prices and rising incomes (wages, salaries, profits, etc.) are not wholly separable phenomena. In general, a moderate inflation will have the following effects (some harmful, some less so) on an economy: (1) redistribution of income at the expense of groups whose incomes rise less rapidly than prices; (2) improvement in the position of debtors relative to creditors; (3) possible uneconomic use of resources; (4) harmful effects on the international balance of payments when inflation is more rapid than that of other countries; (5) possible forced saving as investment or government spending increases at the expense of consumption. In a society with certain vulnerable groups—for example, the elderly, who have become a substan-

tial portion of our population—the costs of inflation can be very real.

In the classic Keynesian case, inflation arises because of an excess of aggregate demand at the level of full-employment national income. However, inflation is not necessarily of the *demand-pull* type. It may result from structural features on the supply side, as in the case of *cost-push* inflation. Labor may succeed in reaching wage settlements that exceed the increase in labor productivity. Businesses may be resistant to downward adjustments of prices but may be able and willing to increase prices when there are shifts in demand or increases in wage costs. Because of these structural features, inflation may occur even when there is fairly substantial unemployment in the economy. The Phillips curve (to be derived empirically for any given country at any given time) shows the relationship between price changes and unemployment. Such a situation—where both inflation and unemployment coexist—is now characteristic of the American economy.

When inflation is of the demand-pull variety, fiscal and monetary policy can both be used to curtail aggregate demand. On the whole, monetary policy is probably better suited to "curing" inflation than it is to halting recessions; but if employed without fiscal restraint, it may lead to serious difficulties in certain areas of the economy. Both fiscal and monetary policy, moreover, are limited when the inflation originates in part from the supply side, because they may be able to halt the rise in prices only by lowering aggregate demand to the point where there is unemployment in the economy. The task of improving the inflation-unemployment trade-off is a central policy problem for today's industrial economy. In the past a variety of voluntary approaches such as wage-price *guide-*

posts and *inflation alerts* have been used, but without clear success. In 1971, President Nixon went to direct regulation with his ninety-day *wage-price freeze* followed by the mandatory controls of *Phase II.* The ultimate impact of this action will doubtless depend on what long-range steps the nation takes to mitigate the problem. Specific measures to reduce government legislation that supports higher prices and to improve the allocation of labor through manpower training programs are examples of tools that may have to be used if the nation is to achieve its goal of price stability and full employment at the same time.

QUESTIONS FOR DISCUSSION

1. Distinguish between the harmful effects of a runaway inflation and those of a moderate inflation. Can you see any way in which inflation might be cumulative, i.e., moderate price increases might lead to behavior on the part of businesses or individuals that would lead to more rapid price increases? Why is it said that a runaway inflation can never occur unless it is fed by a fairly substantial increase in the money supply?

2. "Inflation is an even worse threat to our economic well-being than depression: for whereas depression impoverishes only some of us, inflation impoverishes us all." Discuss.

3. Distinguish between *demand-pull* and *cost-push* inflation. Why might this distinction be difficult to ascertain in an actual empirical situation? What structural features of American business and labor markets might contribute to inflationary pressures from the supply side?

4. Draw two possible Phillips' curves, one showing a severe, the other a less severe, conflict between full employment and price stability. How would your recommendations for governmental policy be different depending upon which curve was descriptive of the situation the nation actually faced?

SUGGESTED READING

Bowen, William. *The Wage-Price Issue.* Princeton, N.J.: Princeton University Press, 1960.

Harlan, H. C., ed. *Readings in Economics and Politics.* New York: Oxford University Press, 1961, chap. VIII.

Heller; Johnson; Schnittker; and Wallich. "Current Economic Policies." *American Journal of Agricultural Economics* (May 1970).

Phelps, Edmund S., ed. *Problems of the Modern Economy.* New York: W. W. Norton & Co., 1966, pp. 63-105.

Samuelson, Paul A.; Coleman, John R.; Bishop, Robert L.; and Saunders, Phillip, eds. *Readings in Economics.* 4th ed. New York: McGraw-Hill, 1964, chaps. 14-16.

Schultze, Charles L. *National Income Analysis.* 2nd ed. Englewood Cliffs, N.J.: Prentice-Hall, 1967, chap. 5.

14
Appendix:
Kennedy and the
Steel Price Controversy

Few incidents in the war against inflation in the American economy have attracted as much attention as the famous confrontation between President Kennedy and the large steel companies in 1962. This incident is important not only as indicating the problems of controlling inflation, but also as confirming the complexities of the relationship between government and the private economy that we have stressed in earlier chapters on the "mixed" economy.

The background briefly was that a wage settlement in steel in 1959 had led to a rise in steel prices. As plans for the 1962 talks between labor and management were being made in 1961, speculations began to develop about the possibility of a rise in the price of steel by four to five dollars a ton. This led to a debate in Congress with liberal Democrats (like Senator Albert Gore of Tennessee) accusing the steel companies of "administering prices" above those dictated by the market, and conservative Republicans (like Senator Barry Goldwater of Arizona) rebutting these charges and accusing the Democrats of "laying the groundwork for controls." The following reading takes up the battle from the day of President Kennedy's first intervention.

The Steel Price Controversy

S. PRAKASH SETHI

THE PRESIDENT ACTS

On September 6, 1961, the day before the Republican rebuttal in the Senate, President Kennedy sent telegrams to the chief executive officers

Excerpted from S. Prakash Sethi, *Up Against the Corporate Wall: Modern Corporations and Social Issues of the Seventies,* pp. 364–78. © 1971. Reprinted by permission of Prentice-Hall, Inc., Englewood Cliffs, New Jersey.

of the twelve* largest steel companies, saying: "I am taking this means of communicating to you, and to the chief executive officers of eleven other steel companies, my concern for stability of steel prices. . . ."

Using 1947 as the base period he contended that between 1947 and 1958 steel prices rose by 120 percent—during the same period industrial prices as a whole

*Armco Steel Corporation, Bethlehem Steel Corporation, Colorado Fuel & Iron Corporation, Inland Steel Company, Jones & Laughlin Steel Corporation, Kaiser Steel Corporation, McLouth Steel Corporation, National Steel Corporation, Republic Steel Corporation, United States Steel Corporation, Wheeling Steel Corporation, and Youngstown Sheet & Tube Company.

rose by 30 percent, and employment costs in the steel industry rose by 85 percent—providing much of the inflationary impetus in the American economy and adversely affecting steel exports and United States balance of payments. He went on to say that although since 1958 the general price level and steel prices had stabilized, this was accomplished at the cost of persistent unemployment and underutilized productive capacity including that of the steel industry whose utilization rate during the preceding three years had averaged 65 percent. In consequence,

many persons have come to the conclusion that the United States can achieve price stability only by maintaining a

351

substantial margin of unemployment and excess capacity and by accepting a slow rate of economic growth. This is a counsel of despair which we cannot accept.

For the last three years, we have not had to face the test of price behavior in a high-employment economy. This is the test which now lies ahead.

The amount of the increase in employment cost per man-hour [on October 1] will be difficult to measure in advance with precision. But it appears almost certain to be outweighed by the advance in productivity resulting from a combination of two factors—the steady long-term growth of output per man-hour, and the increasing rate of operations foreseen for the steel industry in the months ahead.

The Council of Economic Advisors has supplied me with estimates of steel industry profits after October 1, . . . and the steel industry, in short, can look forward to good profits without an increase in prices.

The owners of the iron and steel companies have fared well in recent years.

A steel price increase in the months ahead could shatter the price stability which the country has now enjoyed for some time. In a letter to me on the impact of steel prices on defense costs, Secretary of Defense McNamara states: "A steel price increase of the order of $4 to $5 a ton, once its effects fanned out through the economy, would probably raise the military procurement costs by $500 million per year or more. . . ."

In emphasizing the vital importance of steel prices to the strength of our economy,

I do not wish to minimize the urgency of preventing inflationary movements in steel wages. I recognize, too, that the steel industry, by absorbing increases in employment costs since 1958, has demonstrated a will to halt the price-wage spiral in steel. If the industry were now to forego a price increase, it would enter collective bargaining negotiations next spring with a record of three and one-half years of price stability. The moral position of the steel industry next spring—and its claim to the support of public opinion—will be strengthened by the exercise of price restraint now.

I have written you at length because I believe that price stability in steel is essential if we are to maintain the economic vitality necessary to face confidently the trials and crises of our perilous world. Our economy has flourished in freedom; let us now demonstrate again that the responsible exercise of economic freedom serves the national welfare.

I am sure that the owners and managers of our nation's major steel companies share my conviction that the clear call of national interest must be heeded.

Sincerely,
John F. Kennedy

RESPONSE TO THE PRESIDENT'S LETTER

According to Iron Age, Kennedy's letter stunned the industry. The steel executives thought that by refraining from a price rise for three years, despite employment cost boosts, they were already acting in the national interest and being competi-

tive with foreign steel and domestic substitute materials.

Business Week said the response to the letter was "immediate anger and long-term alarm." The steel industry scorned Kennedy's reasoning, resented his motivation, and the list of United States presidents it did not trust now read: Harry Truman, Dwight Eisenhower, John Kennedy. Compounding the resentment was the widespread belief that Kennedy would not act against any excessive wage demands by the United Steelworkers. Where only selective price boosts were the most any "realist" could have expected from the industry, now even that was extremely unlikely. Where would the industry with such a rapidly advancing technology get the $1 billion a year needed to replace obsolete plants and implement new efficiencies?

The recipients of the president's letter—who were generally critical of the steel industry's being singled out while other causes of inflation were ignored—were largely noncommittal in regard to steel prices. The most publicized reply came from Roger Blough, chairman of U. S. Steel.

I am certain, Mr. President, that your concern regarding inflation is shared by every thinking American who has experienced its serious effects during the past twenty years. . . . First, let me assure you that if you seek the causes of inflation in the United States, present or future, you will not find them in the levels of steel prices or steel profits.

Blough then used 1940 as a base year and noted that

although steel prices had risen 174 percent since that time, employment costs had risen 322 percent. Wage-earner costs had increased and "far exceeded any productivity gains that could be achieved," despite new investment. Blough continued:

So far as profits are concerned, your advisers have chosen to measure them in terms of the return on reported net worth; and again I am afraid that this does more to confuse than' to clarify the issue in the light of the eroding effects of inflation on investments in steel-making facilities over the past twenty years. If we compare the 50-cent profit dollars of today to the 100-cent dollars that were invested in our business twenty years ago, the resulting profit ratio can hardly be said to have any validity. . . .

The most useful measurement of the profit trend in a single industry, over an inflationary period, is, of course, profit as a percentage of sales. On this basis . . . profits in the steel industry have only once in the past twenty years equaled the 8 percent level at which they stood in 1940, and have averaged only 6 1/2 percent in the past five years. . . . [Moreover] averages can be dangerously misleading. Some companies will earn more than the average, while some may be suffering losses which they cannot sustain indefinitely. So it was in 1960 that among the 30 largest steel companies the profit rate as a percentage of sales ranged from a plus 9.3 percent to a loss of 5.2 percent. Whatever figures your advisers may elect to use, however, the simple fact is that the profit left in any company,

WIDE WORLD PHOTO

A Presidential Press Conference. President Kennedy reacted strongly when, in 1962, the big steel companies announced plans to raise steel prices. As a result of intense pressure from the government, the companies involved rescinded the price increases.

after it pays all costs, is all that there is out of which to make up for the serious inadequacy in depreciation to repay borrowings, to pay dividends and to provide for added equipment. If the profit is not good enough to do these things, they cannot and will not be done; and that would not be in the national interest.

So reviewing the whole picture, I cannot quite see how steel profits could be responsible for inflation—especially when their portion of the sales dollar over the last twenty years has never exceeded 8 cents and is lower than that today.

As for the admittedly hazardous task which your economic advisers have undertaken in forecasting steel industry profits at varying rates of operation . . . it might reasonably appear to some—as frankly, it does to me—that they seem to be assuming the role of informal price-setters

for steel—psychological or otherwise. But if for steel, what then for automobiles, or rubber, or machinery or electric products, or food, or paper, or chemicals—or a thousand other products? Do we thus head into unworkable, stifling peacetime controls of prices? Do we do this when the causes of inflation—in a highly competitive economy with ample industrial capacity such as ours—are clearly associated with the fiscal, monetary, labor and other policies of Government?

Blough noted that steel prices were at a level "slightly lower" than two years previously and that competitive factors such as foreign steel and domestic substitute materials provided effective competition for steel. He argued that no company, industry, or for that matter, country could disregard the inexorable pressure of the market if it wanted to maintain its position in a competitive world. Furthermore, he contended that as far as inflation was concerned the price of steel was a symptom and not the major cause of the problem.

THE ADMINISTRATION AND THE STEEL TALKS

That steel prices were not raised in October was attributed to economic forces and not to the president's letter. Kennedy's letter was not the final involvement of the government in the industry's affairs, however, for—although the United Steelworkers' contract was to expire on July 1, 1962—in November 1961, Labor Secretary Arthur Goldberg pointed out that the administration was willing to use its good offices to achieve an early settlement not only to prevent steel users from stockpiling but also to achieve a modest contract and thus prevent another wage-price spiral.

In January several union and industry officials met at the White House to discuss with the president the importance of an early settlement. Goldberg later contacted both union and industry and they began negotiating in early February—the first time since World War II that the two parties had met so early in the year. By discussing the new contract at the time, the union was setting aside its strongest weapon—the threat of a strike at the last minute if its demands were not met. The union also limited its demands to a seventeen-cents-per-hour job security package, forgoing a wage increase. The four industry representatives to the talks said that while the demands "cannot be considered moderate in any sense," they were more moderate than previously and were appropriate considering the problems the country faced.

Apparently, after pressuring the industry, the administration was now pressuring the union (even on national television). Goldberg said that large-scale labor management conflicts were intolerable because of the Soviet threat and the competition from the European Common Market. (George Meany, head of the AFL-CIO, was reported to have exploded with anger at Goldberg's statements and said that he was "infringing on the rights of a free people and a free society.")

During the talks, in an interview in *U.S. News and World Report,* Blough said that steel employment costs had risen 12 percent in three years:

And you're asking me how long can that continue to increase and how long it can be borne without some kind of remedy. I would give you the answer that it's not reasonable to think of it as continuing. In other words, even now there should be a remedy. If any additional cost occurs, the necessity for the remedy becomes even greater.

Renewed negotiations fell flat on March 2, industry saying the benefit package cost was too high. Secretary Goldberg then talked to Roger Blough, who said that the union proposal was inflationary but agreed to resume talks if the union would lower its proposals. Upon Goldberg's intervention. David J. McDonald, president of the United Steelworkers Union, agreed to lower the demands.

Toward the end of March agreement was reached for a contract which would add ten to eleven cents an hour in a job security package. The contract, signed on April 6, was to be effective at least until April 1963. President Kennedy said the settlement was "obviously noninflationary and should provide a solid base for continued price stability."

Even the business community praised the contract. Roy Hoopes said: "Of course, the steel industry had given no commitment that it would hold the price line, but many people, including most businessmen, assumed that labor's restraint would be followed by no increase in the steel prices for at least six months to a year. Obviously the White House assumed this, and the settlement was considered not only a major victory for the Administration, but a long stride toward a historic transformation in labor-management relations."

THE SHATTERED MASTERPIECE*

With the strike threat averted most executives were optimistic about the near future. On April 9, 1962, the *Wall Street Journal* reported that most producers of steel doubted there would be a

_____

*All statements in the ensuing discussion not otherwise specifically documented can be found in Roy Hoopes, *The Steel Crisis* (New York: The John Day Company, 1963) (page references shown).

general rise in steel prices in 1962 (14). However on Friday, April 6, U.S. Steel's operations policy committee—the company's top ten executives—unanimously decided to raise base steel prices about 3.5 percent. On the following Tuesday the Executive Committee of the Board of Directors approved the decision. The Public Relations Department prepared a press release announcing the "catch-up" price as "adjustment."

The reason given for the price increase was the profit squeeze facing the company. The company had spent $1.2 billion for modernization and replacement of plant and equipment since 1958 of which the two sources of money for this investment— depreciation and reinvested profit—contributed only two-thirds. The rest of the money had to be borrowed and "must be repaid out of profits that have not yet been earned and will not be earned for some years to come." The release concluded that the new resources that would be generated by the price increase would improve the company's products and would be "vital not alone to the company and its employees, but to our international balance of payments, the value of our dollar, and to the strength and security of the nation as well" (293).

When the board meeting broke up at 3:00 P.M., Roger Blough phoned for an appointment with Kennedy and after flying to Washington was admitted to see the president at 5:45 P.M. on his as yet unannounced business (220). With a minimum of ameni-

ties, Blough handed Kennedy the company press release which was at that moment being sent to newspapers in Pittsburgh and New York, explaining that it was a matter of courtesy to inform the president personally. Kennedy is reported to have said, "I think you have made a terrible mistake." Forthwith he summoned Labor Secretary Arthur Goldberg who raced to the White House and angrily lectured Blough on the effect of the company's decision on the administration's economic policy, in which U.S. Steel also had an important stake, and the effect of the decision on Goldberg's, indeed the whole administration's, credibility in its pleas to unions to restrain their wage demands.

Blough quietly defended U.S. Steel's price increase and left the president's office in less than an hour. Neither Goldberg nor the president asked him to rescind the increase.

As soon as Blough left, Kennedy was reported to have "exploded" with anger and called together high level administration officials and the Council of Economic Advisers. During the meeting the president found that only a "gentlemen's agreement" and never a firm price commitment had been made during the negotiations. Indeed, a request for such a pledge might have violated antitrust laws. As the meeting progressed the president called his brother, Attorney General Robert F. Kennedy, who later released the announcement that "because of past price behavior in the steel industry, the Department of

Justice will take an immediate and close look at the current situation and any future developments." The president also called Senator Kefauver who agreed to issue a statement of "dismay" at U.S. Steel's action and to say that "I have ordered the staff of [my] subcommittee to begin an immediate inquiry into the matter" (22-26). Thus ended the opening moves of the war to hold steel prices. The *Wall Street Journal* said of the day's events, "Wage-price stability in steel was intended as the graven image of a total program of stability; the Kennedy sculptors unveiled it as a finished masterpiece—and then suddenly it was shattered" (53).

REACTION
TO THE PRICE HIKE

At the very least, U.S. Steel's timing was extremely poor and clearly embarrassed the White House for, as expected, the United Steel workers were later to say that they would have upped their demands if they had known prices would be raised. The business community was surprised at the move since the early settlement meant that steel users had not stock piled and that demand was expected to be low until fall. Even so, any price increases were expected to be selective—not across the board— and to occur *after* the union security package took effect on July 1.

The company's lack of understanding of the "gentlemen's agreement" angered administration officials because it had entered into labor management negotiations to keep the price of steel down. The *St. Louis Dispatch* was skeptical of U.S. Steel's motivations and said that "it looks very much as if the steel masters used the President and his Secretary of Labor, who happens to have been the steelworker's own agent in the 1960 settlement, for the purpose of beating down wage demands prior to a price decision they had in mind all along" (108).

The administration knew about Roger Blough's statement concerning the industry's poor profit situation but attributed it merely to the game of collective bargaining where each side attempts to justify its position. Regardless of Blough's actual reasons it appeared to the White House as either of two things: (1) a challenge to the administration on the broad issue of government intervention in labor-management disputes, or (2) a personal affront to Democratic President John F. Kennedy designed to demonstrate that American industry could be as tough as the much publicized toughness of the New Frontiersmen.

The president accepted the challenge. Rumors soon circulated in Washington that both the Justice Department and the FTC would be conducting antitrust investigations, that the Treasury Department would abandon plans to relax tax depreciation rules, and that the IRS was checking up on U.S. Steel's stock option plan.

In the Congress the Democrats attacked U.S. Steel's action and Speaker John McCormack called it "shocking, arrogant, irresponsible." Most Republicans were cautiously silent as the price hike had taken them by surprise. Senator Gore prepared legislation that would begin government regulation of the steel industry and would establish a cooling-off period before the new prices would be allowed to go into effect.

THE FIRST DAY OF BATTLE

On Wednesday morning, April 11, the president met with members of his administration at a regular pre-press-conference breakfast which was devoted entirely to what to do about steel. The decision was to concentrate on persuading a select group of the large steel companies to hold the price line. Industry sources friendly to the administration had told the White House that if companies producing 16 percent of the industry's output were to hold the line, they would soon capture 25 percent of the market. In a market as competitive as steel, this action would force the other companies to lower their prices. Everyone in the administration who knew anyone in the business world—especially in the steel industry—was urged to telephone him to explain the president's point of view. These calls were "an organized, strategic, integral part of the Administration's campaign." In none of the calls was there an attempt to coax or to threaten—the approach was to explain the government's position, nothing more. The callers discovered that important segments of the business community were far more opposed to the increase than they had been willing to admit publicly.

Inland Steel was deemed to be the key company in the dispute because of its close ties with the government through its board chairman, Joseph L. Block, and because it was probably the most profitable of the large steel companies. But Block was vacationing in Japan at the time.

The purpose of the calls was to get the industry to delay price increases long enough for the administration to launch a counterattack that would make other companies hesitate before raising their prices. The administration learned that if Inland or Armco Steel were to raise prices they would wait at least one or two days, but Bethlehem Steel did not wait. By noon Wednesday Bethlehem announced a raise of six dollars a ton, although less than a day before—at its annual meeting and before U.S. Steel raised its prices—its president had told reporters that Bethlehem would *not* increase prices.

According to *Business Week*, after Bethlehem's announcement, "it looked like a race against time for other producers to get themselves on record before Kennedy's press conference at 3:30 P.M. Most of them made it." These were Republic, Wheeling, Youngstown, and Jones & Laughlin—half of the twelve largest companies had announced higher prices. The president felt that the steel company actions had blatantly and openly challenged the antitrust laws in the noon to 3:30 P.M. rush. Of the six large companies that had not yet raised prices, five had not reached a decision. The combined volume of these five was 14 percent of the market—close to the 16 percent the administration thought necessary to hold the price line.

That afternoon as Kennedy rode to the State Department where he usually held his weekly press conferences, he put the finishing touches on his statement.

Good afternoon, I have several announcements to make.

The simultaneous and identical actions of United States Steel and other leading steel corporations increasing steel prices by some six dollars a ton constitute a wholly unjustifiable and irresponsible defiance of the public interest.

In this serious hour in our nation's history when we are confronted with grave crises in Berlin and Southeast Asia, when we are devoting our energies to economic recovery and stability, when we are asking reservists to leave their homes and families . . . to risk their lives—and four were killed in the last two days in Vietnam—and asking union members to hold down their wage requests . . . the American people will find it hard, as I do, to accept a situation in which a tiny handful of steel executives whose pursuit of private power and profit exceeds their sense of public responsibility, can show such utter contempt for the interest of one hundred and eighty-five million Americans . . .

In short, at a time when they could be exploring how more efficiency and better prices could be obtained, reducing prices in this industry in recognition of lower costs, their unusually good labor contract, their foreign competition and their increase in *production and profits which are coming this year, a few gigantic corporations have decided to increase prices in ruthless disregard of their public responsibility.*

Kennedy then praised the steel workers' union for abiding by its responsibilities; announced that the FTC would conduct an "informal inquiry" into the possibility that its 1951 consent order with the steel industry had been violated; hinted that the Department of Defense might shift its contracts for steel to price-line holding companies; and mentioned that proposed tax benefits to the steel industry through liberalized depreciation schedules were being reviewed (77–86).

In response to the president's accusation that U.S. Steel had not acted in the public interest, Roger Blough declared: "I feel that a lack of proper cost-price relationship is one of the most damaging things to the public interest." Blough announced that he would be giving his own news conference the next afternoon, Thursday, April 12.

THE SECOND DAY, APRIL 12

The Justice Department, considering a possible antitrust suit against various members of the steel industry, was much interested in the reported Tuesday afternoon statement by Bethlehem's President Martin that his company would not raise prices. But when U.S. Steel raised its prices, Bethlehem was the first to follow suit. There were antitrust implications here—U.S. Steel, because of its immense size, might exercise undue influence over other steel producers—so at 6:00 P.M. Wednesday, Attorney General Kennedy ordered his department to proceed with all possible speed in gathering necessary information. Apparently the FBI overreacted to this order, and between 3:00 A.M. and 4:00 A.M. Thursday phoned several reporters who had been present at Martin's press conference and announced their intention to come calling immediately.

On Thursday morning, Kennedy asked every cabinet member to hold press conferences in the next few days to outline the effect the price increase would have on each department and on every citizen of the land. The Justice Department, instead of the FTC, was given the principal responsibility for investigating the steel industry. The investigation was to include possible price collusion and the extent to which U.S. Steel had monopoly powers dangerous to the national interest.

Also on Thursday two more steel companies, one in the top twelve, announced price increases. On Wall Street the stock market dropped to a new low for 1962, with steel leading the retreat. On Thursday morning Blough himself called Treasury Secretary Douglas Dillon for his assessment of the situation. At the same time FBI agents showed up at eight steel companies with subpoenas requesting information and a look at their files—all but two of these (Inland and Armco) had already raised their prices. Talk from the Pentagon was that exceptions to the Buy

America Act might allow the Pentagon to increase its purchases of foreign steel. Secretary Luther H. Hodges gave a noon speech denouncing price fixing and other unethical business tactics (109–10).

THURSDAY AFTERNOON —BLOUGH'S PRESS CONFERENCE

On Thursday afternoon Blough held his news conference:

. . . We have no wish to add to acrimony or to misunderstanding. We do not question the sincerity of anyone who disagrees with the action we have taken. Neither do we believe that anyone can properly assume that we are less deeply concerned with the welfare, the strength, and the vitality of this nation than are those who have criticized our action. . . .

The President said, when questioned regarding any understanding not to increase prices, "We did not ask either side to give us any assurances, because there is a very proper limitation to the power of the Government in this free economy." Both aspects of this statement are quite right [118–120] . . .

Our problem in this country is not the problem with respect to prices; our problem is with respect to costs. If you can take care of the costs in this country, you will have no problem taking care of the prices. The prices will take care of themselves [133].

Blough also denied that U.S. Steel was in any way defying the president by its decision, which it had a right to make, and, on the White House role in labor negotiations said, "I have no criticism. I do believe that when the air clears a little bit, I think we will all realize that this type of, shall I say—assistance?—has some limitations."

Blough denied having an understanding with other companies about prices. That prices were raised in a Democratic administration but had been kept level during a Republican one was not significant: "You can readily see that I do not know anything about politics!" One reporter asked if the increase "coming as it did right on the heels of the labor pact—was timed to check expanded government influence in collective bargaining; in other words, that you acted politically as well as economically." Again Blough denied any political motivation. He did mention, though, that if other companies did not raise their prices, U.S. Steel would be obliged to reconsider. The administration interpreted this to mean that victory was possible and that U.S. Steel was seeking an escape route.

All in all, industry sources felt that Blough did not present the best possible case.

THE TURNING POINT

At seven o'clock Thursday evening Attorney General Kennedy announced that he had authorized the Grand Jury to investigate the steel price increases and to find out if U.S. Steel "so dominated the industry that it controls prices and should be broken up." At about the same time Walter Reuther, head of the United Auto Workers Union, proposed that a price board be created to hold hearings on important prices such as steel before they could be increased. Later in the evening Tyson (Chairman of the Finance Committee of U.S. Steel's board of directors) and several other U.S. Steel executives met in New York. According to Hoopes, "If there was any single turning point in the steel crisis, it probably came at this meeting." Previously the executives had thought all the uproar political in nature and probably short-lived but were now "convinced that the Administration men meant business." The executives had noticed that Inland had not gone along with the increase, and if it did not soon, Bethlehem would rescind its price and others would naturally follow (145).

THE THIRD DAY

Early in the morning of Friday the thirteenth, Kennedy talked to Roger Blough who suggested that communications should be maintained. Seeing this as a hopeful sign, Kennedy then moved to restrain members of his administration and to preserve a mood of conciliation. Also on Friday morning, Inland's late-Thursday decision not to raise prices was made public. The statement by Joseph Block was that although "profits are not adequate, we do not feel that an advance in steel prices at this time would be in the national interest." Attention now turned to Armco Steel, which had led off the price increase in 1958 when U.S. Steel refused and had a reputation for unpredictability. The real maverick of the industry, Kaiser Steel, had also

358

not yet raised its prices.

Meanwhile rumors circulated that Roger Blough would resign; Inland's stock prices rose; other steel stocks fell; Colorado Fuel and Iron intimated that any price increase would be selective; Youngstown and Reynolds Metals implied that they would wait and see before acting on price levels.

At 10:00 A.M. Defense Secretary Robert S. McNamara stated that "where possible, procurement of steel for defense production will be shifted to those companies which have not increased prices," but he put an end to speculation that the department might increase its purchases of foreign steel because of the resulting unemployment that it might cause in this country.

All during the battle between steel and the administration, public opinion was firmly behind the president as was shown by a number of newspaper polls and by telegrams received by the White House. According to Roy Hoopes, "the majority of the nation's most influential newspapers [were] critical of the steel companies' action, [and] the business community [was] only lukewarm in its support of the steel industry . . ."

THE FINAL BATTLE

The direct result of Blough's telephone conversation with Kennedy on Friday morning was a meeting the same afternoon of Clifford and Goldberg, and Blough, Tyson, and Worthington (president of U.S. Steel). According to reports, Clifford (a Washington attorney who was friendly to the Kennedy administration) explained that many continuing investigations of steel would be very uncomfortable, especially since Kennedy would be in office for a number of years and doing business in Washington might be difficult. Clifford and Goldberg also explored ways U.S. Steel could roll back its prices and still save face. During the meeting the various members were kept informed of events as they occurred outside: one in particular came at 3:25 P.M. announcing that Bethlehem had rescinded its price increase in order to remain competitive. This was the final blow to the company, and before the meeting was over, Blough and his fellow executives told Clifford and Goldberg that they too would later be announcing a rollback (164).

Within a few hours, in the words of *Time* magazine, there was a "precipitous rush to surrender" as the other steel producers rolled back their prices. The reason given for the rollbacks was "to remain competitive" in spite of poor profit conditions.

GRANT AT APPOMATTOX

Naturally the administration's plans for further attacks on the steel industry and proposed legislation were canceled or filed away and, for once, the administration was not crowing about its victory. As *Business Week* aptly said, "The President went out of his way to assure there will be no public recriminations now that the mistake has been retracted. Like Grant at Appomattox, he is letting the vanquished forces keep their horses and sidearms."

The relationship between the White House and U.S. Steel returned to normal, and Roger Blough agreed to stay on the president's business advisory committee. On other fronts, although the Grand Jury probe would continue, it was obvious that the administration would not press too hard for any indictments. (However, a New York Grand Jury did indict U.S. Steel, Bethlehem, Erie Forge and Steel, and Midvale-Heppenstall on price fixing charges from an investigation begun in March 1961.) The activities of the Justice Department and the FTC were effectively curtailed, and the House investigation of the steel industry was called off, but Kefauver's Senate subcommittee investigation did proceed as scheduled.

THE KENNEDY ANTIBUSINESS CRUSADE

Most of the steel companies held their annual meetings soon after the "price fiasco." All those that had originally raised prices and then backed down maintained that they were forced to do so because the competition did not follow. One element of agreement among all steel spokesmen was that the need for a price increase had not passed—even Joseph Block agreed on this point and said Inland had refused to raise its prices only as a concession to the national interest. One steel executive said, "No company or industry may now raise prices without harboring the fear, and justifiably so, that the Administration may decide to employ the crushing weapons so recently displayed." Despite the industry's unanimous cry for more profits, every company's profit picture for the first quarter of 1961 showed a substantial improvement over the recession-affected first quarter of 1962 (224–25).

Despite its campaign of conciliation, the administration persisted in its economic policies and announced that it might act to prevent a price hike in the aluminum industry. There then began to emerge a "growing hostility" by the business community toward Kennedy, and a stock market crash in the summer of 1962 was attributed by many businessmen to the "Kennedy crowd." According to Roy Hoopes, "By late June and early July, the 'hate Kennedy' mood in the business community had almost reached a state of hysteria" and even rated a cover story in *Newsweek*. Even the Kennedy jokes became bitter and personal.

The animosity collapsed, however, by mid-autumn, perhaps because the administration's attempts at dialogue eventually got through or because a number of business leaders (including Blough and Block) helped to restore the peace. During the summer the Congress passed an administration-backed investment tax credit law and the Treasury Department announced revised tax depreciation schedules.

KENNEDY'S LAST YEAR WITH STEEL

A year passed without steel's making any price increases, but in April 1963 Wheeling Steel Corporation, with less than 2 percent of the United States market, announced a selective price increase of $4.50–$10.00 per ton on six items. "It was as though an electric shock had hit the President and his aides. . . ."

The President's formal reply to the hike was a surprise:

I realize that price and wage controls in this one industry, while all others are unrestrained, would be unfair and inconsistent with our free competitive market . . . and that selective price adjustments up or down—as prompted by changes in supply and demand as opposed to across-the-board increases— are not incompatible within a framework of general stability and steel-price stability and are characteristic of any healthy economy.

In a free society both management and labor are free to do voluntarily what we are unwilling to enforce by law—and I urge the steel industry and the steel union to avoid any action which would lead to a general across-the-board increase.

Actually, throughout 1963 the government allowed increases on 75 percent of the industry's product mix—all without protest.

The sequel to the Kennedy-Steel experience involved further government-steel confrontations in the Johnson administration, though less dramatically than that described above. The steel companies raised their prices substantially in 1967, but in 1968 compromised a price increase under governmental pressure. In 1971 and 1972, of course, steel prices were subject to direct negotiation via the government's Cost of Living Council and Price Commission.

15

International Balance of Payments

No man is an island unto himself. Certainly no nation is. In this chapter we shall extend our macroeconomic analysis to the area of international trade, considering both the modifications of the theory of national income determination that are required for an "open" economy and also some of the urgent international problems facing the United States in the 1970s.

HISTORIC CONTROVERSIES

International trade is one of those areas of economics that has been of interest to economists since the dawning of the field. It has also been a particularly controversial subject, perhaps because it involves national self-interest—and nationalism, for good or ill, has been a major force shaping the modern world.

In the sixteenth and seventeenth centuries, much of the economic writing of Europe was dominated by the so-called mercantilists, who were passionately interested in trade, commerce, and other mercantile activities. These writers (who were a varied lot of public officials, merchants, and pamphleteers, and who gave only part of their time to economics) tended to see international trade as an instrument in the growing commercial and political rivalries among the then emerging nation-states. One of their characteristic doctrines was that each nation should strive to secure a *favorable balance of trade*—roughly an excess of exports over imports. This would bring precious metals into the country, providing revenues for the sovereign and also stimulating the domestic economy. They saw trade as competitive: my nation's gain is your nation's loss. And in this competition they wanted to see their own nation benefit at the expense of others.

The mercantilist view gathered strength in the seventeenth century, but in the eighteenth century it ran headlong into the "classical" economists. Adam Smith devoted a whole long section of *The Wealth of Nations* to an attack on the mercantile system. David Ricardo, and also a lesser known classical writer by the name of Robert Torrens, tried to show that trade was not necessarily a rivalry; i.e., that *all* countries could benefit from trade. The mercantilists had favored regulating trade, but the hallmark of classical thought was the cry for free trade, a battle climaxed by the repeal of the Corn Laws in 1846.[1]

Now many of these arguments about trade have to do with essentially microeconomic questions, and especially the problem of economic efficiency. These matters we shall take up in detail in Part Three and particularly in chapter 23. We shall be concerned there with the arguments for and against tariffs and other regulations of the flow of trade among nations.

A major part of the controversy about world trade does, however, have a macroeconomic focus, being concerned especially with what are called *balance of payments* problems. At no time has this been more true than in the United States in very recent years. In the immediate aftermath of World War II, everyone spoke of a dollar shortage in the world. Our European allies and former enemies were badly in need of our exports and yet lacked the productive capacity to send us their exports in sufficient quantity to pay for them. This dollar shortage produced the Marshall Plan and also a tendency for many Americans to assume that this country's balance of international payments was immune to any major difficulties. Thus it was with something of a shock

that economists and the general public awoke in the late 1950s and 1960s to realize that the United States was running a regular and substantial deficit in its balance of payments and, furthermore, that we were rapidly losing gold to other countries. Suddenly, old mercantilist fears began to arise again. We were losing gold. Would this bankrupt the nation? What would happen to our credit abroad? What would the effects on the domestic economy be?

BALANCE OF PAYMENTS ACCOUNTS

In order to answer such questions, our first task is to get a firm grasp on the concept of a balance of international payments. This is a fairly complicated subject, so let us begin by imagining the simplest possible situation.

Let us suppose that we have a hypothetical nation whose balance of payments can be represented by three items, as in Table 15-1: commodity exports, commodity imports, and gold exports or imports. Table 15-1 tells us that this nation has exported commodities to foreign countries to the value of $500 million, while importing $300 million worth of commodities from these countries. This leaves a $200 million excess of exports above imports. How are these paid for by the foreign countries? By shipping $200 million in gold to our hypothetical country. We have here then the simplest possible case of a nation with a favorable balance of trade *à la* the mercantilists. And the mercantilists would have been delighted with the country's position, since it is receiving "treasure" from abroad.

---

1. The Corn Laws involved duties on imported wheat. The issues at stake in the Corn Laws involved not only free versus regulated trade in general, but also a specific conflict between the interests of the English landowner (who wanted to keep food and raw materials out, so that there would be a great demand and high price for land) and the English manufacturer (who needed cheap food, to keep wages low, and cheap raw materials for his factories). The repeal of the Corn Laws thus became a kind of symbol of Britain's full emergence as an industrial—as opposed to agrarian—economy.

Table 15-1.   A SIMPLIFIED HYPOTHETICAL BALANCE OF PAYMENTS (in millions)

Debit	Credit
$300 Commodity imports	$500 Commodity exports
$200 Gold imports	

This hypothetical balance of payments table is simply a point of departure for studying trade problems. In reality, a country's balance of payments includes many different items. The classification of these items, however, is made easier if we remember the central principle that a *credit* item is any item that creates a demand for your currency, while a *debit* item is one that creates a supply of your currency demanding other currencies.

Now even this highly simplified situation can serve as a useful point of departure for understanding more complex matters. For one thing, we notice that we have listed two kinds of items—credits and debits. What makes one item a credit item and another a debit in international trade accounting?

Perhaps the best way to look at this matter is to recognize the fact that every transaction in international trade is essentially two-sided. Every good that we import from abroad must be paid for in one way or another. If we import an automobile from a European country we must pay for it either by exporting goods of equivalent value or by exporting gold abroad or by transferring dollars to a foreign account or by sending an IOU to the foreign country (in which case the foreign country is increasing its investment in the United States). Since every transaction is two-sided in this way, there is a certain accounting sense in which the balance of payments is always in "balance."

Now as far as the classification of items is concerned, the fundamental rule is that any transaction that creates a demand for your currency—say, dollars—is a credit item. By contrast, any transaction that creates a supply of your currency seeking other currencies—say,

dollars being offered in exchange for francs or pounds—is a debit item. Our commodity exports create a demand for dollars in terms of other currencies. The German who wants to buy an American good must ultimately pay the American producer in dollars. Hence he uses his marks to buy dollars to pay us for the export. This is a credit item in the U.S. balance of payments because it represents an increase in the demand for dollars. When Americans import commodities from abroad, however, they must pay the foreigner in *his* currency. In this case, we use the dollars we have to buy marks to pay for the import. The supply of dollars offered in exchange for other currencies has increased; consequently, our imports are a debit item. Gold imports are a bit more complicated to see, but, essentially, we can treat them as any other import. When a foreign country ships gold to us, it receives dollars in exchange, and thus the supply of dollars has been increased. (These dollars may then be used to pay for the extra exports the country has taken from us.) Thus gold imports are a debit item, and gold exports are a credit item.

Once these general principles are clear, it becomes possible to apply them to the many more complex items that make up a country's actual balance of payments; e.g., tourist expenditures of Americans abroad, our military expenditures abroad, interest and dividend payments to American owners of foreign securities, U.S. private business investment abroad, and so on. Take the last for example: a long-term investment by an American firm, say in a factory in France. Does this create a demand for dollars or a supply of dollars? The American puts up the dollars that are then exchanged for francs to pay workmen in France to build the factory. Hence, the answer is that the supply of dollars has been increased and that

---

Table 15-2.   U.S. BALANCE OF PAYMENTS, 1970
(Billions of dollars)*

Type of Transaction	Amount	Balances
Merchandise trade balance (net)	2.1	
Exports (+)†	42.0	
Imports (−)	−39.9	
Military transactions (net)	− 3.4	
Balance on investment income (net)	6.2	
U.S. investment abroad (+)	11.4	
Foreign investments in the U.S. (−)	− 5.2	
Balance on other services	− 1.4	
BALANCE ON GOODS AND SERVICES		3.6
Private remittances and government pensions	− 1.4	
Government grants (excluding military)	− 1.7	
BALANCE ON CURRENT ACCOUNT		0.4
Balance on direct private investments (net)	− 3.5	
U.S. direct investments abroad (−)	− 4.4	
Foreign direct investments in the United States (+)	1.0	
BALANCE ON CURRENT ACCOUNT AND LONG-TERM CAPITAL		−3.0
Errors and unrecorded transactions, etc.	− 0.7	
NET LIQUIDITY BALANCE		−3.8
Transactions in U.S. liquid short-term assets (net)	0.2	
Transactions in U.S. liquid liabilities to other than foreign official agencies (net)	− 6.2	
OFFICIAL RESERVE TRANSACTIONS BALANCE‡		−9.8

---

*Numbers are rounded and thus additions and subtractions are not always exact.

†A plus (+) represents a credit item; a minus (−), a debit item.

‡Official Reserve Transactions Balance financed by increase in dollar assets held by foreign official agencies (+7.6), export of U.S. official reserve assets, e.g., gold, convertible currencies (+2.5), and other (−0.3).

Source: Economic Report of the President, 1972, p. 150; adapted by the author.

U.S. investment abroad is to be treated as a debit item.

In Table 15-2, we present an actual (but still somewhat simplified) balance of payments table for the United States in 1970. From what we have just said, the classification of most of the items on this table should be quite clear. Thus, for example, U.S. private investment abroad is included as a debit item and, in 1970, was equal to $4.4 billion. Notice that income on previous U.S. investments

abroad is treated as a credit item and was equal, in 1970, to $11.4 billion. (Why a credit item? Because the income from an American investment in, say, a German factory creates a supply of marks that may be exchanged for U.S. dollars to pay the American investor.)

This table also helps us understand the concept, or various concepts, of *balance* in the balance of payments. In a certain accounting sense, as we have said, a country's balance of payments is always in balance. What then do we mean when we speak of a *surplus* or *deficit* is a country's balance of payments? Actually, there are many specific definitions involved, but a central characteristic is that the surplus or deficit is intended to measure pressure on the country's reserve assets. A deficit in the balance of payments means that the country in question is either losing gold (or other reserve assets, such as convertible foreign currencies) to other countries or that other countries are increasing their holdings of liquid claims against that country (claims that could ultimately be translated into a loss of gold or other reserve assets).

Now the different definitions of surpluses or deficits arise because there are many borderline cases to be classified. Thus, we have to decide whether our liquid liabilities abroad are to include only those held by official foreign agencies (e.g., central banks), or whether they also included dollar-holdings of private businesses and individuals. Similarly, we have to decide the difference between a capital transaction and a cash transaction. If a foreigner buys up an American firm, that is a capital transaction, listed under foreign direct investment in the United States. If he accumulates dollars, that is clearly a cash transaction. But suppose he holds his dollars in a short-term security—say, a three-month Treasury bill. Is that an investment (capital) or a cash transaction (he considers the bill equivalent to cash except that he earns some interest on it)? Usually, accountants include in the capital accounts only those claims having a maturity date of more than a year (or no maturity date). But this is fairly arbitrary and, in actual practice, the "correct" definition of surpluses or deficits will depend on the particular problem under consideration.

In Table 15-2, we might be inter-

ested to notice that the U.S. Balance on Current Account was favorable ($.4 billion) in 1970. This balance includes our basic exports and imports of goods and services, our government military and aid programs abroad, and our net income from business investments abroad. When we bring capital transactions into the picture, however, our balance turned negative. Since we invested $3.5 billion more abroad in 1970 than foreigners invested in the United States, our net Balance on Current and Capital Account was in deficit by about $3 billion. In addition, large short-term capital outflows and increases in private dollar holdings abroad left us with an Official Reserve Transactions Balance of −$9.8 billion. This deficit was financed by a combination of an increase in dollar reserve assets held by foreign official agencies, and a decrease in American holdings of official reserve assets (e.g., gold and convertible foreign currencies).

As we shall see in a moment, the U.S. balance of payments position worsened sharply in 1971. But first let us try to get a deeper sense of the economic principles underlying the accounts that we have been discussing.

CLASSICAL GOLD STANDARD

Going back to our very simple case again (Table 15-1), we now ask: what is the economic significance of the fact that this hypothetical country is running a surplus in its balance of payments? Suppose the figures were reversed and the country was exporting gold to the tune of $200 million a year. Would its basic economic position be any different? Why all the fuss about these matters?

In effect, this is what the British

classical economists said, in criticism of the mercantilists, about balance of payments problems. Say's law, you will recall, postulated that money didn't truly matter, that it was real phenomena (steel and potatoes) that counted. If a country is getting more potatoes (imports) for less steel (exports), then what difference does a little loss of "treasure" make? Perhaps a deficit should be a cause for rejoicing.

Of course, the classical economists were not so foolish as to offer such a naive argument, for it is clear on the face of the matter that, unless the country is a gold-producer (like Russia or South Africa), exports of gold cannot continue indefinitely. The country will run out, or run so low on gold that it will not have sufficient reserves to carry on trade on any substantial scale or without elaborate government currency restrictions.

To answer this problem, the classical economists, and especially the philosopher and friend of Adam Smith, David Hume (1711–1776), developed the notion of a self-correcting mechanism by which surpluses and deficits in international trade would automatically solve themselves. Let us imagine that the following conditions are fulfilled:

(1) The countries in question are on a pure *gold standard* under which the price of gold is fixed in terms of each of their currencies. This means that the exchange rates of the currencies are fixed, or, more accurately, fixed within the limits set by the cost of transferring gold from one country to another. If currency A became more expensive in terms of currency B, people would pay in gold rather than in currency A. In our simple case, let us assume that there is little or no cost of transferring gold; hence, currency exchange rates will be almost completely stable.

(2) A gold flow into (or out of)

a given country is matched by a roughly proportionate increase (or decrease) in the country's money supply (currency and demand deposits).

(3) The *quantity theory of money*[2] holds true. That is, an increase (or decrease) in the supply of money will lead to a roughly proportionate increase (or decrease) in a country's price level.

Given such assumptions, the *price-specie–flow* mechanism might work as follows:

Two countries, A and B, are trading together. Country A has a surplus with country B as in hypothetical Table 15-1. Country B has an equal and opposite deficit with Country A. Gold flows will now take place between the two countries, gold going from country B to country A. As a result of the gold flows, the money supply in country A will rise and the money supply in country B will fall. Because of the quantity theory of money, these changes in the money supplies will result in a rise in the price-level in country A and a fall in the price-level in country B. These changes in the price-levels, however, will lead to consequences for the trading positions of the two countries. Country A's exports are now more expensive, while exports from country B are less expensive. Citizens in country A will now want to purchase more goods from country B, while the citizens of country B are curtailing their purchases of the now more expensive goods from A. Under ideal circumstances, these changes will lead to (a) a correction of the original trade imbalance and (b) a cessation of the gold flow. The net result will be a redistribution of the world's gold supply between country A and country B.

Indeed, we can put the classical

2. For a discussion of the quantity theory, see above, pp. 297–98.

case quite simply by saying that the original problem between country A and country B was a maldistribution of gold stocks. Country A had too little gold (hence its prices were too low, and thus its exports were too high), while country B had too much (with consequent high prices and a poor export performance). The market mechanism, at one stroke, corrects the trade imbalance and the gold maldistribution, and brings overall equilibrium to both countries.

Any theory, unfortunately, is only as good as its assumptions.[3] In practice, few countries have been willing to stick with a pure gold standard (condition 1) when faced with massive gold losses. Furthermore, modern nations are seldom willing to allow their money supplies to be determined by gold flows (condition 2). In the United States, for example, the Federal Reserve Board *might* let an increase or decrease in the gold stock affect member bank reserves, or, on the other hand, it might *not*, i.e., it might "neutralize" the gold flows by open market operations. If gold were coming in, and the Fed feared an inflationary increase in the money supply, it might engage in open market sales of government securities, or other restrictive monetary actions, to offset the gold inflow. This happened in 1939–41, when the U.S. gold stock rose by over $5 billion and most of the increase was neutralized by open-market opera-

tions. The opposite happened in 1961–1963 when a loss of $4.4 billion in gold was completely offset by the Fed's actions.[4]

And, finally, of course, the quantity theory of money (condition 3) is not held in the uncritical classical form by any serious twentieth-century economist. Indeed, the overall weaknesses in the classical doctrine are so great that it should come as no surprise that the gold standard, in anything like a pure form, has long since disappeared from the modern world.

NATIONAL INCOME DETERMINATION IN AN OPEN ECONOMY

Still, we are left with the question of what effects a country's balance of payments actually does have on that country's domestic economy. What do we substitute for the unsatisfactory classical analysis?

Two main points should be made in this connection. The first concerns the monetary effects of a trade surplus or deficit such as we have been discussing. If a country's central bank is willing to allow a gold inflow or outflow to affect the nation's money supply, then we would analyze the monetary effects by the same kind of analysis we used in chapters 11 and 13. There is disagreement about this analysis, as we know, but mainstream economics would argue that effects would proceed from the money supply to the economy as a whole via the interest rate, according to our familiar chain of logic. The general effect of these changes would be in the *direction* of bringing equilibrium in international

3. The reader should notice that the classical mechanism requires even further assumptions than those we have mentioned. For example, we have tacitly assumed that export and import prices directly reflect changes in a country's overall price level. Also, we have assumed that when, say, a country's export prices fall, this will lead to an improvement in its balance of payments position (and vice versa for a rise in its export prices). But the effect of such changes will depend on various *elasticities.* If, for example, the increase in sales due to a fall in export prices is a smaller percentage than the fall in prices, then total receipts for the country will actually fall. Thus, the classical mechanism is even weaker than it might seem at first glance.

4. See Peter B. Kenen and Raymond Lubitz, *International Economics*, 3rd. ed. (Englewood Cliffs, N.J.: Prentice-Hall, 1971), pp. 63–72.

trade but (1) it is unlikely that the magnitudes of the effects would be sufficient to correct the payments imbalance, and (2) the mechanism would involve not only prices but also real phenomena, such as national income. In particular, a deficit country would suffer a fall in its money supply, which would lead to higher interest rates, which, in turn, would lead to some potential fall in national income (and hence to greater unemployment). The fall in national income would be in a corrective direction—that is to say, citizens of the country in question would have less income to purchase imports from abroad[5]—but the process is clearly more painful than when simple price decreases (without income and employment effects) are involved.

But this is not the only way in which trade affects national income. And here we come to our second main point, which concerns the direct influence of international trade on the level of aggregate demand in a given country.

Consider exports first. When we bring foreign nations into the picture, we have to recognize that the demand for the products of our country is no longer limited to domestic consumption, investment, and government expenditures. We also have a foreign demand for our products. When a foreign firm puts in an order for a certain number of our machines, its effects on production are the same as if it came from a business firm in the United States or from the U.S. government. Aggregate demand, therefore, must include an allowance for demand originating from abroad.

But there is also the import side to look at. As a consumer, say I have an income of $10,000 a year. I decide to save $1,000 of this, to buy $8,000 worth of American goods, and to buy $1,000 of goods imported from abroad. Now as far as *American* industry is concerned, it is not my total of $9,000 consumer demand that is relevant, but only the $8,000 that I shall be spending on American goods. The $1,000 I spend on goods abroad has no more direct effect on American industry than does the $1,000 I decided to put in my savings account. This is to say, then, that our import spending must be *subtracted* from our total spending to give us the aggregate demand that will be effective in creating jobs and income in this country.

If we use X to stand for exports, M for imports, and Y for national income, we can contrast the equilibrium situation in a "closed" and in an "open" economy as follows:

Closed Economy.

We have equilibrium when national income equals the sum of intended consumption, investment, and government spending:

$$Y = C + I + G$$

Open Economy.

We have equilibrium when national income equals the sum of intended consumption, investment, and government spending, *plus* exports *minus* imports:

$$Y = C + I + G + (X - M)$$

In the case of our particular hypothetical economy of Table 15-1, we could conclude that its balance of payments was

5. Also, higher interest rates would presumably attract some short-term capital from abroad.

definitely having an expansionary effect on the economy, since its net exports ($X - M$) was positive ($200 million).

This conclusion, incidentally, suggests why some modern writers have shown more tolerance for the mercantilist desire for a favorable balance of trade than did the classical economists. If a country's exports are buoyant and its imports are restrained, then the effect on a depressed economy will be just like a little dose of expansionary fiscal policy. The only problem with using the balance of payments as an instrument of domestic policy is that not every country can be doing it at once. If one country is exporting more than it imports, some other country will be importing more than it exports. A policy to curtail imports and expand exports is rather like trying to export one's depression abroad. And it is likely to be met by countervailing action by other countries, so that no one's position is improved (though all countries are likely to suffer the losses that occur when trade is subjected to detailed national regulation).

Even if trade policy is not to be used to correct domestic employment problems, however, the foregoing analysis suggests some rather deep flaws in a fixed exchange rate regime. If a country's balance of payments goes into deficit, the fall in aggregate demand would normally bring about a depressed domestic economy. Should a country allow this to happen? Should it permit the "international tail" to wag the "domestic dog"? Or should it try to find some way to insulate its domestic economy from these potentially harmful international effects?

Which brings us to the important possibility of allowing the main adjustments to be made not by the domestic economy, but by the exchange rates themselves.

FLEXIBLE INTERNATIONAL EXCHANGE RATES?

The extreme alternative to a completely fixed set of exchange rates among currencies (as implied by the pure gold standard) is a completely flexible set of exchange rates. The rate at which dollars could be exchanged for yen or marks or francs would be determined in the exchange markets of the world. One day the dollar might be up, another down, and this would also be true of pounds, pesos, and all other currencies.

The workings of flexible exchanges would depend on supply and demand. If there was a great demand for, say, Japanese products in Italy and there was little Japanese demand for Italian products, this would be reflected in a large supply of Italian lire being offered in exchange for a small supply of Japanese yen. Ignoring possible reserves of yen in Italy, this demand for yen would tend to raise the price of yen in terms of the lira. This rise in the price of yen would be equivalent to a rise in the prices of all Japanese exports in terms of lira; conversely, Italian exports to Japan would now fall in price. In its effects on importers and exporters in the two countries, the change in effective prices is similar to what might happen if the classical price-specie flow mechanism were functioning. The difference, of course, is that domestically, prices have remained unchanged. All the work is being done by the exchange rates.

Now the advantage of such a system is apparent from what we have already said. Instead of a painful adjustment of prices, wages, and very probably national income and employment to make our payments balance, the domestic economy is allowed to proceed along its own (presumably full-employment) course. Particularly in countries like our own, where trade is a fairly small proportion of national income, this seems a clearly correct ordering of priorities.

Convinced by this argument, most economists favor flexible exchanges to at least some degree. It should be said, however, that there are a number of counterarguments that suggest that perhaps the best international arrangement would be neither extreme of complete rigidity or complete flexibility, but something in between. The most important argument against total flexibility is that it would introduce great new uncertainties into the international trade picture. Although these uncertainties might be anticipated by speculators whose business it is to estimate future changes, they could not be removed altogether, with the consequence that domestic investors in this or that branch of industry might find themselves suddenly over- or under-invested depending upon changes in foreign exchange rates. If an unfavorable shift in exchanges subjected a branch of a nation's industry to sharp foreign competition, there would doubtless be a great demand for protection for that industry by the government. This protection could, in turn, provoke retaliation from other countries. The net result, according to Yale professor Henry Wallich, might be the "increasing disintegration" of the international economy. Wallich has contended that if nations were willing to cooperate enough to make flexible exchanges work, they could also make fixed exchanges work, so why not have the better system in the first place!

The difficulty of resolving such questions is increased, moreover, when we move from the abstract to the concrete. For real-life trade does not take place between country A and country B but between countries of vastly different eco-

nomic strength and impact, bound together in complicated political and economic arrangements, and on the basis of highly sophisticated balance of payments procedures. In this real-life trading world, the role of the United States has been a particularly special one. Indeed, this special role accounted for one of the most dramatic economic events of recent years—the Dollar Crisis of 1971.

THE DOLLAR CRISIS OF 1971

The Dollar Crisis of 1971 attracted such worldwide attention and involves so many important issues in international economics that it is worthwhile to use this episode to deepen our understanding of the trading relations among nations.

The Background. The basic facts are these: The United States had been running a deficit in its balance of payments since 1950. Figure 15-1 shows that, except for occasional years, the annual deficit (liquidity basis) had been quite substantial, averaging $2 to $3 billion a year. This deficit had generally been accompanied by a surplus of U.S. commodity exports over commodity imports. Our favorable balance on goods and services account averaged $6.5 billion a year in 1960–65 and, although it subsequently fell, it was, until 1971, definitely positive. This surplus item was offset by a number of debit items, including our foreign aid program, U.S. tourist expenditures in foreign countries, and U.S. private business investment abroad.[6]

6. For part of this period, we must also include the heavy balance of payments costs of the Vietnam war. In a careful study, it was estimated that, in the year 1967, the direct and indirect effects of the war were to contribute $4.0 billion to our payments deficit. See Leonard Dudley and Peter Passell, "The War in Vietnam and the United States Balance of Payments," *Review of Economics and Statistics* 50, no. 4 (November 1968).

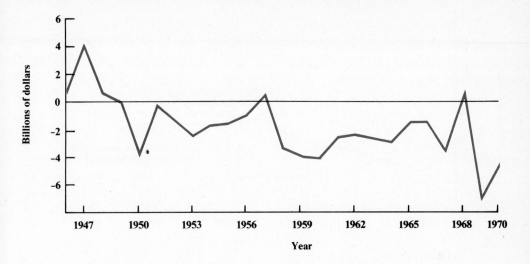

Figure 15-1. U.S. Balance of Payments, 1946-1970 (liquidity basis).
Source: Department of Commerce

How had this large and persistent deficit been financed? Partly, as we would expect, by the export of gold. The U.S. gold stock in 1949 was running in the neighborhood of $25 billion; by March 1971, it had fallen to less than $11 billion, about a 60 percent decline.

Our accumulated deficit, however, was much larger than the decline in our gold stock, and the fact is that by far the greater part of the deficit was financed by the export of dollars. During the past twenty-odd years, the dollar served along with gold as a generally acceptable medium of exchange for the purposes of international transactions. In fact, the matter in its most favorable light could be put this way: the United States' balance of payments deficit was a significant means of expanding the total supply of international "liquidity" during the past two decades. In the absence of vast new discoveries of gold, this expansion of dollars held by foreigners facilitated the enormous (and mutually beneficial) expansion of world trade that has been one of the most striking features of the postwar period.

The Crisis of 1971. But if this is so, what was the problem? How could it have come to pass that in May 1971, Americans in Europe suddenly found that they could not cash their travelers' cheques for foreign currencies? How could it have happened that by August 1971, President Nixon had fully severed the dollar from gold and allowed it to float freely in the world's currency markets?

There are many reasons why this state of affairs occurred, not least those suggested by Figure 15-2. As our deficit persisted, an increasing gap opened up between our liquid liabilities (dollars and dollar-convertible assets) held by foreigners and our reserves, especially our gold reserves, for meeting these liabilities. As long as the dollar is as good as gold, this gap need not be troublesome. But if it were widely believed that the dollar was *not* as good as gold—if, for example, it came to be believed that the dollar might be devalued in terms of gold (the dollar-

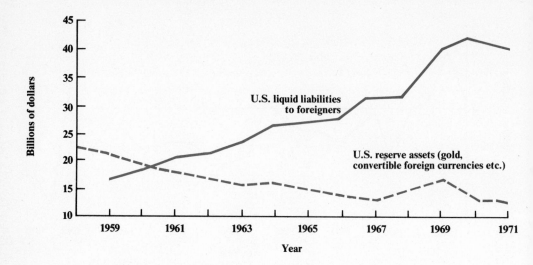

Figure 15-2. Foreign Claims in Relation to U.S. Reserves.

price of gold raised) or that the dollar might be altogether cut free from the price of gold—then it could be in the interest of foreign holders of dollars to convert them into gold. Clearly, this would be an impossible solution. In 1971, the central bank of Germany alone held enough U.S. dollars to exhaust our entire gold stock at $35 an ounce. Clearly, also, the existence of this gap between the enormous potential demand for, and the limited supply of, our reserves could become a major factor that might lessen confidence in the dollar.

Thus, the system was essentially poised on a knife-edge. Already, in March 1968, the U.S. government had divorced gold prices on the private market from the official parity price of $35 an ounce, leaving the private price to find its market level. The effect of this action, according to one leading monetary expert,[7] was to transform a "precarious 'gold-exchange' standard into an unbridled 'paper-dollar' standard."

Nor were our creditors exactly happy. They found themselves accepting vast quantities of dollars (it was estimated that there were $50 or $60 billion of Euro-dollars in existence in 1971) and thus financing the persistent U.S. balance of payments deficit. This was particularly galling when, as in the case of the Vietnam war, many of these countries disapproved of the nature of our overseas spending. Given this large supply of overseas dollars, moreover, these nations continually found themselves in the position of either buying these dollars with their own currencies, thus leading to domestic inflationary pressures, or revaluing upward their own currencies in terms of dollars. Revaluation is always a painful process, since it raises the costs of a country's exports in foreign markets and thus is likely to hurt those industries heavily engaged in export trade.

All these various elements began to come to a boil in early May, 1971, when there was a flood of dollars seeking to buy German marks in anticipation of a possible change in the exchange rate between the mark and the dollar. At first, West

---

7. Robert Triffin, "Europe's Dollar 'Tea Party,' " in the *New York Times*, May 14, 1971, p. 39.

Germany responded by a rapid increase in the supply of marks to meet the demand. Presently, however, the attempt to hold the dollar-mark exchange rate firm was abandoned; the mark was allowed to "float" upward to find a new and more viable exchange rate.

For a moment the crisis subsided, but only temporarily. The Netherlands had gone along with West Germany in allowing its currency to float upward, but the major U.S. creditor, Japan, had not. Moreover, evidence began coming in that the United States was facing its first deficit on its goods and services account since 1893. The stage was set for a dramatic development; and, on August 15, 1971, such a development did occur.

August 15–December 18, 1971. On the same August day he announced the wage-price freeze, President Nixon announced a package of international measures as part of his "new economic policy." These included a temporary 10 percent surtax on imports and, more sig-

nificantly, the removal of the last remaining tie between the dollar and gold. The United States would no longer buy gold even from the governments and central banks of foreign countries—the dollar would float and find its natural level in relation to other foreign currencies.

The upshot of this unilateral American decision was a period of intense international consultation and negotiation to establish a new and more viable pattern of exchange rates among the major currencies of the world. These efforts culminated in the Smithsonian agreement of December 18, 1971, in which the United States agreed to devalue the dollar in terms of gold (raising the price of gold from $35 to $38 an ounce), while our trading partners agreed to revalue their currencies upward in terms of the dollar. The main issues involved in these negotiations are brought out in the next reading, from the Annual Report of the President's Council of Economic Advisers, January 1972:

Developments after August 15

ECONOMIC REPORT OF THE PRESIDENT

Reactions abroad to the August 15 announcement were varied. The major European exchange markets closed during the week following the announcement. When the exchange markets were reopened, no country except France attempted to hold the exchange value of its currency against the dollar within the 1 percent upper limit of its parity rate. The exchange value of the dollar in these markets declined, and on average continued to decline during the succeeding months.

In France the exchange market was se-

Excerpted from "Developments after August 15," in Economic Report of the President (Washington, D.C.: U.S. Government Printing Office, 1972), pp. 155–61.

gregated. For dollars received as a result of transactions related to international trade, the French government continued to intervene in order to support the parity rate. All other dollars received were diverted to a "financial franc" market; here, severe restrictions were imposed on inflows of funds, but the rate was allowed to find its own level.

In Japan the exchange markets were not closed after the August 15 announcement, and the Japanese government continued to intervene by purchasing dollars at the official ceiling rate. During August alone the Japanese Central Bank took in $4.4 billion—an amount considerably larger than their $2.9 billion of *total* dollar holdings at the end of 1970. Official intervention to hold the dollar rate at its ceiling was then suspended, and limited intervention allowed the value of the yen to rise about 5 percent relative to the dollar. In subsequent months the government continued to intervene in order to dampen the pace at which the yen would appreciate relative to the dollar. In the process, dollar holdings by the Japanese Central Bank increased an additional $1.4 billion to $11.6 billion by the end of October.

ALTERNATIVE ROUTES
TO REALIGNMENT

Developments after August 15 made one fact clear: The immediate operational issue facing governments was a realignment of the pattern of exchange rates, especially a realignment of the U.S. dollar relative to the other major currencies.

Among the questions associated with this operation were these:

(1) How should the industrial nations arrive at a new set of equilibrium exchange rates? One route was to let all currencies float freely for a transitional period until a new set of equilibrium rates emerged. The other was to negotiate a multilateral shift to a new set of fixed rates.

(2) If the second route was to be used, should the United States "contribute" to the realignment by a formal devaluation of the dollar against gold? Or should negotiations concentrate on exchange rates among currencies, expressed in dollars, with the question of the gold price being left to subsequent negotiations on longer-range issues?

(3) How large was the readjustment required to restore the U.S. balance of payments to an equilibrium position? How large an average change in the dollar's exchange rate did this require? How should the effect of the proposed readjustment in the U.S. position be shared among other nations?

Mutually acceptable answers to all of these questions depended in part on related issues. The inclusion of trade practices and the question of mutual security costs as part of the overall negotiations involved other members of foreign governments besides financial officials. This affected the tempo and procedure as well as the substance of the negotiations.

REALIGNMENT THROUGH
FLOATING

One issue was whether market-determined exchange rates or negotiations provided the most efficient route to equilibrium.

In spite of intervention by central banks, at first to hold rates within limits set by parity values, and later to suppress the pace of the relative appreciation of the currencies, a significant pattern of exchange-rate realignment did take place in 1971, particularly after dollar convertibility was suspended. The general path of these upward movements relative to previous parities against the U.S. dollar is shown in Chart A.

The U.S. position on the issue was that a transitional period of free floating could lead the world swiftly and efficiently to a new pattern of equilibrium rates. This position was put forward by the Secretary of the Treasury on September 30, in his address to the Annual Meeting of the International Monetary Fund and World Bank, when he said:

. . . I believe we should welcome the help that the market itself can provide in reaching crucial decisions.

Many nations already are allowing their currencies temporarily to float, but they have done so with widely varying degrees of intervention and controls. As a result, some adjustments clearly needed are being delayed or thwarted, the process of multilateral decision-making impeded, and political questions multiplied. In this respect, our surcharge and restrictions on capital flows could, like those applied by other countries, themselves be a disturbing influence.

If other governments will make tangible progress toward dismantling specific barriers

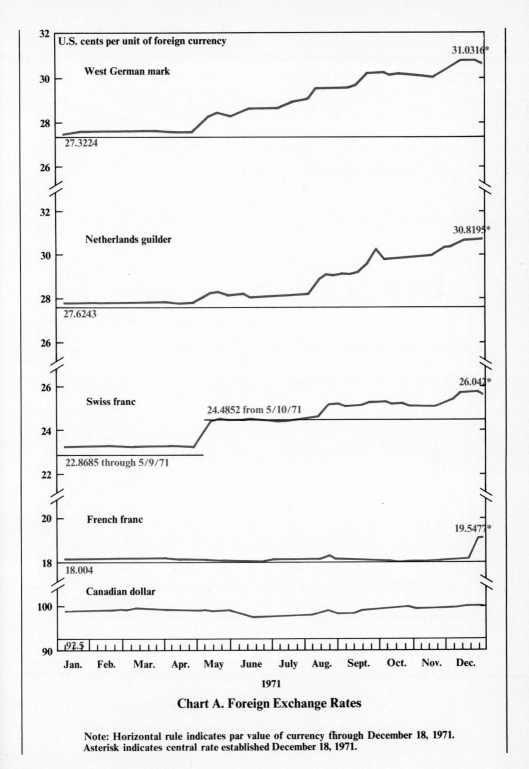

Chart A. Foreign Exchange Rates

Note: Horizontal rule indicates par value of currency through December 18, 1971.
Asterisk indicates central rate established December 18, 1971.

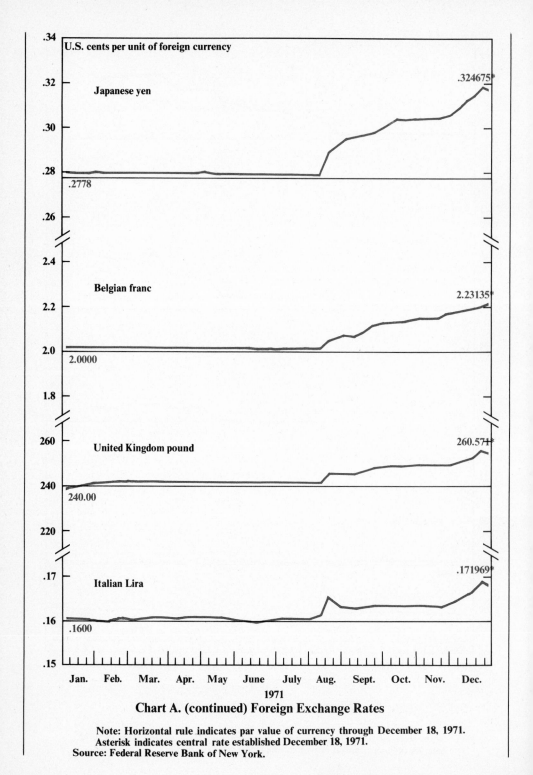

Chart A. (continued) Foreign Exchange Rates

Note: Horizontal rule indicates par value of currency through December 18, 1971.
Asterisk indicates central rate established December 18, 1971.
Source: Federal Reserve Bank of New York.

to trade over coming weeks and will be prepared to allow market realities freely to determine exchange rates for their currencies for a transitional period, we, for our part, would be prepared to remove the surcharge.

With few exceptions the suggestion of the United States was not accepted. In most countries market forces were suppressed by a variety of new measures, including regulation of inflows, exchange controls, and central bank intervention in the market. Eventually the question of realignment had to be settled through bilateral and multilateral negotiations.

The opposition to a policy of arriving at a new set of exchange rates via market-determined forces was motivated by a complex mixture of reasons.

RELUCTANCE TO REVALUE AGAINST THE DOLLAR

Many nations were reluctant to let their currencies appreciate too far against the dollar. This attitude was not, of course, an argument against floating as such; it applied equally well to revaluation via negotiation.

Raising the value of one's own currency (or permitting it to rise) reduces the price competitiveness of export industries. For many countries, expanding exports provided an impetus for overall economic expansion which these governments were reluctant to surrender. Even when governmental policies did not emphasize export expansion, the export industries were highly visible politically; governmental actions that might erode their prospects had to be taken with care. While revaluation also provided countervailing advantages to other segments of a revaluing economy— especially to consumers, importers, and tourists going abroad—these benefits tended to be spread more broadly and were therefore less visible. The reluctance of other countries to see their currencies appreciate relative to the dollar, regardless of how this was accomplished, was intensified in the second half of 1971 by the slowing of the boom conditions which had prevailed in many countries in prior years.

RELUCTANCE TO REVALUE AGAINST OTHER CURRENCIES

Reluctance to revalue against the dollar was one reason why many nations did not permit market pressures to express themselves freely. A collateral reason was the unwillingness to have the national currency revalued against other currencies whose values were being held down by intervention or controls. When one nation revalues relative to the dollar—which it may be willing to do in the interest of restoring equilibrium—it is thereby revalued relative to all other nations that do not revalue, and this it may not be willing to permit. Given the multilateral nature of the problem, the idea of floating toward a new equilibrium requires the cooperation of all nations. The abstention of even one important nation from the joint action may be enough to hold up the entire process. This is what happened in the autumn of 1971.

The French commercial franc was held to its previous parity value against the dollar (established in 1969). When the West German mark moved up to a range of from 10 to 12 percent above its parity with the dollar (also established in 1969), it moved up to the same extent against the French franc. Since France is West Germany's largest trading partner, both for exports and imports, this 10 to 12 percent increase in the mark's cross-rate against the franc was regarded as unacceptable by West Germany, especially since this cross-rate had already been increased by nearly 23 percent in the 1969 realignments.

Similarly the unwillingness of the Japanese authorities to let the value of the yen rise freely relative to the dollar was affected not only by a desire to limit the change in the yen-dollar rate; it was also affected by the rates between the yen on the one hand and European currencies on the other.

RELUCTANCE TO CORRECT
BY REVALUATION ALONE

There was a third set of motives for rejecting the floating route to realignment. This process of arriving at new rates would leave the dollar standing still in relation to gold while other currencies moved up by varying amounts. For one reason or another many nations were unwilling to accept such an outcome.

One of these reasons was that acceptance of the process would explicitly recognize the U.S. dollar as the benchmark against which all other national currencies set their values. There was a body of opinion in Europe that the benchmark should be an objective one, or at least a multinational one which did not bear the stamp of any single country. The existence of this body of opinion has important implications for the choice of a basic monetary unit of account in the international system of the future.

A second reason was that, if the United States devalued, other countries could reduce or avoid the political onus of revaluing. Thus it was easier for the United Kingdom, for example, to stand still for an 8 percent U.S. devaluation than to revalue by an equivalent amount with the United States standing still, even though the effect on exchange rates would be the same.

The third reason was that revaluation reduces the value, expressed in the domestic currency unit, of a nation's stock of foreign monetary assets. The value of its gold holdings measured in the national currency falls to the extent of revaluation, and so do its holdings of other reserve assets, notably the U.S. dollar. This balance-sheet loss for each revaluing nation, so far as the gold component is affected, could be reduced by requiring the United States itself to contribute to a realignment through an increase in the dollar price of gold.

The floating route was therefore rejected in favor of a negotiated pattern of change, in which the dollar itself made part of the adjustment by moving down relative to gold.

FINAL NEGOTIATIONS
ON EXCHANGE RATE
REALIGNMENT

By the end of November floating had moved exchange rates some distance from the old parities. The French commercial franc was the only major currency that was held to the upper limit of the narrow band around its parity value. Bilateral and multilateral negotiations between the United States and its principal trading partners on trade and mutual security costs had also commenced.

At the ministerial meetings of the Group of Ten nations held in Rome a hypothetical devaluation of the dollar against gold was discussed as one aspect of a possible overall package agreement (which included a pattern of currency revaluations by other nations and adjustments in existing impediments to trade). The United States offered to consider a new pattern of exchange rates involving an average adjustment that would not fully meet its objective of a turnaround of $13 billion.

The negotiations were completed on this basis at a later meeting of the ministers and governors of the Group of Ten nations held at the Smithsonian Institution in Washington on December 17–18. The key elements in the agreement were a new set of exchange rates and provisions for a wider band, within which market rates would be free to move up to 2.25 percent above or below the new "central rates." As part of the agreement the United States lifted the temporary surcharge on imports which it had imposed on August 15.

TOWARDS INTERNATIONAL MONETARY REFORM

Although the currency revaluations of the Smithsonian agreement should move in the direction of reducing the United States balance of payments deficits,[8] they will by no means cure all of the world's international economic ills. Indeed, if the U.S. balance of payments deficit is resolved, this may intensify what we mentioned earlier as another vital problem: the need for increased liquidity to finance a continuing expansion of world trade. Dollars, serving in the past as a reserve currency for other nations, helped to fulfill this function. If the flow of dollars is reduced (by reducing our payments deficit), and if the whole role of dollars as a reserve currency is questioned, then how is the growth of world trade to be sustained financially?

Of course, some steps to meet the need for increased international liquidity have already been taken. One of the most important of these was the creation of Special Drawing Rights (SDRs) in the International Monetary Fund beginning in 1969. Each member of the IMF received a certain quantity of SDRs proportionate to its original quota contribution to the fund, and these SDRs are meant to serve as additions to the country's reserve assets. Surplus countries are required to accept SDRs in settlement of payments claims (up to a limit of three times its own SDR allocation) and deficit countries are free to use these to meet payments deficits, subject to keeping a certain minimum balance of SDRs in their accounts. For most practical purposes, therefore, the SDRs can be used like gold or, in happier days, U.S. dollars. Furthermore, the potential for expansion of SDRs over time is very great. At the moment, however, the volume of SDRs is still small in com-

parison, for example, to the very large payments deficits run by the U.S. in some recent years.

Because of these larger world problems, the Smithsonian agreement and even the creation of SDRs appear not as the conclusion, but as the first steps in a general rearrangement of the international financial patterns that have been governing since the end of World War II. International monetary reform is very much in the air. What will the new system look like? What will be the role of the dollar? of gold? of SDRs?

With such questions in mind, we will end this chapter with a reading on monetary reform, excerpted from a speech to the American Bankers Association by Dr. Arthur F. Burns, chairman of the Federal Reserve Board, on May 12, 1972. The Burns speech was not applauded by all parties,[9] but it does lay out clearly a number of the important issues that will have to be resolved in the next several years.

---

8. The full impact of the Smithsonian exchange rate changes will be felt only over time. Figures for the first quarter of 1972 suggested an improvement in the U.S. balance of payments position. For example, the payments deficit on the Official Reserve Transactions basis was down from $6.3 billion in the fourth quarter of 1971 to $3.5 billion in the first quarter of 1972. The evidence, however, is still inconclusive.

9. Indeed, the newspapers reported that there was much unhappiness in the U.S. Treasury because of what some felt was too great an importance given to the role of gold in Burns' remarks. On the other hand, the speech could also be criticized for not coming down hard enough on the future use of the dollar as a reserve currency and for its even-handed treatment of the responsibilities of surplus and deficit nations. Around the same time Burns was speaking, a secret IMF proposal was made public in the *Wall Street Journal* (May 8, 1972), and this proposal came down very sternly on the use of dollars as a reserve currency in the future and placed major responsibility on deficit nations (notably the U.S.) to correct their payments problems. All this suggests that the road to world monetary reform, though the need for such reform is universally agreed, will be a long and rocky one.

Address on Monetary Reform

ARTHUR F. BURNS

On August 15 of last year, in the face of an unsatisfactory economic situation, the President of the United States acted decisively to alter the nation's economic course. The new policies, especially the decision to suspend convertibility of the dollar into gold or other reserve assets, were bound to have far-reaching consequences for international monetary arrangements. New choices were forced on all countries.

The next four months gave all of us a glimpse of one possible evolution of the international economy. Since exchange rates were no longer tied to the old par values, they were able to float—a prescription that many economists had favored. However, last fall's floating rates did not conform to the model usually sketched in academic writings. Most countries were reluctant to allow their exchange rates to move in response to market forces.

Instead, restrictions on financial transactions proliferated, special measures with regard to trade emerged here and there, new twists crept into the pattern of exchange rates, serious business uncertainty about government policies developed, fears of a recession in world economic activity grew, and signs of political friction among friendly nations multiplied.

HALTED BY AGREEMENT

Fortunately, this dangerous trend toward competitive and even antagonistic national economic policies was halted by the Smithsonian agreement. Despite recent developments in Vietnam, which may cause some uneasiness in financial markets for a time, the Smithsonian realignment of currencies is, in my judgment, solidly based. It was worked out with care by practical and well-informed men, and I am confident that the central banks and governments of all the major countries will continue to give it strong support.

PLAN FOR THE FUTURE

Developments in the American economy since last December have been encouraging. Aggregate activity in the United States has begun to show signs of vigorous resurgence. Price increases have moderated, and our rate of inflation has recently been below that of most other industrial countries. Moreover, the budget deficit of the Federal Government will be much smaller this fiscal year than seemed likely three or four months ago. These developments have strengthened the confidence with which businessmen and consumers assess the economic outlook. International confidence in turn is being bolstered by the passage of the Par Value Modification Act, by the convergence of short-term interest rates in the United States and abroad, and by some promising signs of improvement in the international financial accounts of the United States.

With the Smithsonian agreement and other indications of progress behind us, it is necessary now to move ahead and plan for the longer future. The Smithsonian meeting was preeminently concerned with realigning exchange rates. It did not attempt to deal with structural weaknesses in the old international monetary system. Yet they must eventually be remedied if we are to build a new and stronger international economic order.

We all have to ponder this basic question: given the constraints of past history, what evolution of the monetary system is desirable and at the same time practically attainable? For my part I should like to take advantage of this gathering to consider some of the elements that one might reasonably expect to find in a reformed monetary system.

First of all, a reformed monetary system will need to be characterized by a further strengthening of international consultation and cooperation among governments. Our national economies are linked by a complex web of international transactions. Problems and policies in one country inevitably affect other countries. This simple fact of interdependence gives rise to constraints on national policies. In a smoothly functioning system, no country can ignore the implications of its own actions for other countries or fail to cooperate in discussing and resolving problems of mutual concern. The task of statesmanship is to tap the great reservoir of international good will that now exists and to make sure that it remains undiminished in the future.

A SECOND REQUIREMENT

Sound domestic policies are a second requirement of a better world economic order. A well-constructed international monetary system should, it is true, be capable of absorbing the strains caused by occasional financial mismanagement in this or that country—such as are likely to follow from chronic budget deficits or from abnormally large and persistent additions to the money supply.

But I doubt if any international monetary system can long survive if the major industrial countries fail to follow sound financial practices. In view of the huge size of the American economy, I recognize that the economic policies of the United States will remain an especially important influence on the operation of any international monetary system.

Third, in the calculable future any international monetary system will have to respect the need for substantial autonomy of domestic economics policies. A reformed monetary system cannot be one that encourages national authorities to sacrifice either the objective of high employment or the objective of price stability in order to achieve balance-of-payments equilibrium.

More specifically, no country experiencing an external deficit should have to accept sizable increases in unemployment in order to reduce its deficit. Nor should a surplus country have to moderate its surplus by accepting high rates of inflation. Domestic policies of this type are poorly suited to the political mood of our times, and it would serve no good purpose to assume otherwise.

REALISTIC EXCHANGE RATES

I come now to a fourth element that should characterize a reformed monetary system. If I am right in thinking that the world needs realistic and reasonably stable exchange rates, rather than rigid exchange rates, ways must be found to insure that payments imbalances will be adjusted more smoothly and promptly than under the Brenton-Woods agreements.

The issues here are many and complex. There was a consensus at the Smithsonian meeting that wider margins around parities can help to correct payments imbalances, and should prove especially helpful in moderating short-term capital movements—thereby giving monetary authorities somewhat more scope to pursue different interest-rate policies.

Our experience has not yet been extensive enough to permit a confident appraisal of this innovation. It is clear, however, that no matter how much the present wider margins may contribute to facilitating the adjustment of exchange rates to changing conditions, the wider margins by themselves will prove inadequate for that purpose.

We may all hope that at least the major countries will pursue sound, noninflationary policies in the future. we should nevertheless recognize that national lapses from economic virtue will continue to occur. In such circumstances, changes in parities—however regrettable—may well become a practical necessity.

Moreover, even if every nation succeeded in achieving noninflationary growth, structural changes in consumption or production will often lead to shifts in national competitive positions over time. Such shifts will also modify the pattern of exchange rates that is appropriate for maintaining balance-of-payments equilibrium.

ONE OF CENTRAL ISSUES

In my judgment, therefore, more prompt adjustments of parities will be needed in a reformed monetary system. Rules of international conduct will have to be devised which, while recognizing rights of sovereignty, establish definite guidelines and consultative machinery for determining when parities need to be changed. This subject is likely to become one of the central issues, and also one of the most difficult, in the forthcoming negotiations.

Let me turn to a fifth element that should characterize a reformed monetary system. A major weakness of the old system was its failure to treat in a symmetrical manner the responsibilities of surplus and deficit countries for balance-of-payments adjustment. With deficits equated to sin and surpluses to virtue, moral as well as financial pressures were very much greater on deficit countries to reduce their deficits than on surplus countries to reduce surpluses. In actual practice, however, responsibility for payments imbalances can seldom be assigned unambiguously to individual countries.

And in any event, the adjustment process will work more efficiently if surplus countries participate actively in it. In my view all countries have an obligation to eliminate payments imbalances, and the rules of international conduct to which I referred earlier will therefore need to define acceptable behavior and provide for international monitoring of both surplus and deficit countries.

Sixth, granted improvements in the promptness with which payments imbalances are adjusted, reserve assets and official borrowing will still be needed to finance in an orderly manner the imbalances that continue to arise. Looking to the long future, it will therefore be important to develop plans so that world reserves and official credit arrangements exist in an appropriate form and can be adjusted to appropriate levels.

A SYMBOL OF SAFETY

This brings me to the seventh feature of a reformed international monetary system. It is sometimes argued that, as a part of reform, gold should be demonetized. As a practical matter, it seems doubtful to me that there is any broad support for eliminating the monetary role of gold in the near future. To many people, gold remains a great symbol of safety and security, and these attitudes about gold are not likely to change quickly. Nevertheless, I would expect the monetary role of gold to continue to diminish in the years ahead while the role of Special Drawing Rights increases.

The considerations which motivated the International Monetary Fund to establish the S.D.R. facility in 1969 should remain valid in a reformed system. However, revisions in the detailed arrangements governing the creation, allocation, and use of S.D.R.'s will probably be needed. In the future, as the S.D.R.'s assume increasing importance, they may ultimately become the major international reserve asset.

Next, as my eighth point, let me comment briefly on the future role of the dollar as a reserve currency. It has often been said that the United States had a privileged position in the old monetary system because it could settle payments deficits by adding to its liability instead of drawing down its reserve assets. Many also argue that this asymmetry should be excluded in a reformed system. There thus seems to be significant sentiment in favor of diminishing, or even phasing out, the role of the dollar as a reserve currency.

One conceivable way of accomplishing this objective would be to place restraints on the further accumulation of dollars in official reserves. If no further accumulation at all were allowed, the United States would be required to finance any deficit in its balance of payments entirely with reserve assets.

DISADVANTAGES AS WELL

I am not persuaded by this line of reasoning, for I see advantages both to the United States and to other countries from the use of the dollar as a reserve currency. But I recognize that there are some burdens or disadvantages as well. And in any event, this is an important issue on which national views may well diverge in the early stages of the forthcoming negotiations.

I come now to a ninth point concerning a new monetary system, namely, the issue of "convertibility" of the dollar. It seems unlikely to me that the nations of the world, taken as a whole and over the long run, will accept a system in which convertibility of the dollar into international reserve assets— S.D.R.'s and gold—is entirely absent. If we want to build a strengthened monetary system along one-world lines, as I certainly do, this issue will have to be resolved. I therefore anticipate, as part of a total package of long-term reforms, that some form of dollar convertibility can be re-established in the future.

I must note, however, that this issue of convertibility has received excessive emphasis in recent discussions. Convertibility is important, but no more so than the other issues on which I have touched. It is misleading, and may even prove mischievous, to stress one particular aspect of reform to the exclusion of others. Constructive negotiations will be possible only if there is a general disposition to treat the whole range of issues in balanced fashion.

IMPORTANT INTERDEPENDENCE

We need to guard against compartmentalizing concern with any of the issues, if only because the various elements of a new monetary system are bound to be interrelated. There is a particularly important interdependence, for example, between improvements in the exchange-rate regime and restoration of some form of convertibility of the dollar into gold or other reserve assets.

Without some assurance that exchange rates of both deficit and surplus countries will be altered over time so as to prevent international transactions from moving into serious imbalance, I would deem it impractical to attempt to restore convertibility of the dollar.

My tenth and last point involves the linkage between monetary and trading arrangements. We cannot afford to overlook the fact that trade practices are a major factor in determining the balance-of-payments position of individual nations. There is now a strong feeling in the United States that restrictive commercial policies of some countries have affected adversely the markets of American business firms.

In my judgment, therefore, the chance of success of the forthcoming monetary conversations will be greatly enhanced if parallel conversations get under way on trade problems, and if those conversations take realistic account of the current and prospective foreign trade position of the United States.

In the course of my remarks this morning I have touched on some of the more essential conditions and problems of international monetary reform. Let me conclude by restating the elements I would expect to find in a new monetary system that met the test of both practicality and viability:

First, a significant further strengthening of the processes of international consultation and cooperation;

Second, responsible domestic policies in all the major industrial countries;

Third, a substantial degree of autonomy for domestic policies, so that no country would feel compelled to sacrifice high employment or price stability in order to achieve balance-of-payments equilibrium;

Fourth, more prompt adjustments of payments imbalances, to be facilitated by definite guidelines and consultative machinery for determining when parities need to be changed;

Fifth, a symmetrical division of responsibilities among surplus and deficit countries or initiating and implementing adjustments of payments imbalances;

Sixth, systematic long-range plans for the evolution of world reserves and official credit arrangements;

Seventh, a continued but diminishing role for gold as a reserve asset, with a corresponding increase in the importance of SDRs;

Eighth, a better international consensus than exists at present about the proper role of reserve currencies in the new system;

Ninth, re-establishment of some form of dollar convertibility in the future;

And finally, tenth, a significant lessening of restrictive trading practices as the result of negotiations complementing the negotiations on monetary reform.

AN URGENT NECESSITY

I firmly believe that a new and stronger international monetary system can and must be built. Indeed, I feel it is an urgent necessity to start the rebuilding process quite promptly. It is not pleasant to contemplate the kind of world that may evolve if cooperative efforts to rebuild the monetary system are long postponed.

We might then find the world economy divided into restrictive and inward-looking blocs, with rules of international monetary conduct concerning exchange rates and monetary reserves altogether absent.

As we learned last fall, a world of financial manipulations, economic restrictions and political friction bears no promise for the future. It is the responsibility of financial leaders to 'make sure that such a world will never come to pass.

SUMMARY

This chapter has been concerned with the macroeconomic aspects of international trade, and especially with balance of payments problems. These are ancient problems: the mercantilist writers of the sixteenth and seventeenth centuries argued strongly for a favorable balance of trade; the classical writers of the eighteenth and nineteenth centuries called for laissez-faire in the international as well as in the domestic sphere.

Balance of payments accounting is complex because of the many different kinds of items that appear in international exchanges. Basically, credit items are those that create a demand for a country's currency, while debit items are those that create a supply of your currency seeking to purchase other currencies. An overall surplus or deficit in the balance of payments measures the pressure on the country's reserve assets. Thus, a deficit in the balance of payments means that a country is either losing reserve assets (gold, convertible currencies) or that other countries are increasing their liquid claims against this country's reserve assets. Depending on the question at hand, many different balances may be used, e.g., balance on goods and services account, liquidity balance, official reserve transactions balance, etc.

The classical economists (including the philosopher David Hume) argued that surpluses and deficits in the balance of payments would be self-correcting. According to the theory of the *price-specie-flow* mechanism, countries on the gold standard would lose gold if their balance of payments was in deficit and gain gold if it was in surplus. These gold flows would, on the quantity theory of money, bring rises in price-levels in surplus countries and declines in price-levels in deficit countries. These price changes, assuming that they were reflected in export and import prices as well, would correct the balance of payments disequilibria and also, in due course, terminate the gold flow.

This classical mechanism depends on many special assumptions, few of which are accepted uncritically today. Mainstream economics at the present time would analyze the monetary effects of gold flows via the money supply–interest rate–investment–GNP logic we have discussed before. Modern analysis would also link international trade to the more general theory of national income determination. Foreign demand for our exports is similar in effect to domestic consumption, investment, or government demand. Conversely, our demand for imports from abroad must be subtracted from overall demand for goods and services. The total aggregate demand for an economy therefore will be represented by domestic consumption, investment, and government spending, plus an item representing *net exports* $(X - M)$.

Because trade can affect national income and employment—an unfavorable balance, for example, could cause a recession, other things equal—many economists favor flexible exchange rates over the fixed exchange rates implied by a pure gold standard. Under a regime of flexible exchanges, favorable or unfavorable trade trends would be reflected in the supply-and-demand conditions relative to the country's currency, the price of that currency (its exchange rate) going up or down as the market determined. Although flexible exchanges do have many advantages, they also might increase the uncertainties of international trade, and could conceivably lead to widespread government intervention to protect domestic producers.

Turning to actual world trade problems, we discovered that the United States' balance of payments has been in substantial deficit for several years now. This deficit has caused a considerable outflow of monetary gold and a very large increase in the dollar holdings of foreigners. Although this increase in dollar holdings has helped finance the postwar expansion of world trade (dollars having been a reserve asset rather similar to gold), it also contributed directly to the Dollar Crisis of 1971.

Reactions to this Dollar Crisis have included the complete severing of the dollar from gold as part of the "new economic policy" of August 15, 1971, intense consultations leading to the revaluation of world currencies under the Smithsonian agreement of December 18, 1971, a new emphasis on alternatives to dollars as means of international payments—especially the Monetary Fund's new Special Drawing Rights (SDRs)—and, finally, an increased awareness of the need for a general reform of the international monetary system.

QUESTIONS
FOR DISCUSSION

1. Classify the following items as credits or debits in the United States balance of payments and explain your reasoning: export of computer hardware to Italy, German tourist expenditures in the United States, United States renting of the services of Norwegian ships, U.S. foreign aid grant to Thailand, import of Japanese automobiles, U.S. investment in a factory in Brazil, income for U.S. investors from a factory in France.

2. Until very recently, the United States enjoyed a favorable balance of merchandise exports over imports and yet still suffered from an overall deficit in its balance of payments. Explain how this was possible.

3. Imagine a country that has the following situation:
(a) a constant level of commodity exports;
(b) a level of commodity imports that increases with the level of national income;
(c) commodity exports exceed commodity imports at all levels of national income.

How would you display this general information in the familiar 45°-line diagrams we have used in the theory of national income determination?

4. Discuss the advantages of flexible exchanges over fixed exchanges in protecting a country's domestic economy. One of the disadvantages of flexible exchanges is said to be that they would encourage widespread inflation. Explain why this might be true in general, and why it might be particularly true of countries that depend heavily on trade for the basic necessities of life. (Hint: an exchange rate depreciation will raise the domestic cost of imported items.)

5. Write a critique of the Burns address on monetary reform from (a) the point of view of the United States' national interest; (b) the point of view of a major creditor nation, say West Germany or Japan.

SUGGESTED READING

Friedman, Milton. "The Advantages of Flexible Exchange-Rates," from U.S. Congress, Joint Economic Committee, *Hearings: The United States Balance of Payments,* 88th Cong., 1st sess., 1963.

Haberler, Gottfried. *A Survey of International Trade Theory.* Princeton: International Finance Section, 1961.

Kenen, Peter and Lubitz, Raymond. *International Economics.* 3rd. ed. Englewood Cliffs, N.J.: Prentice-Hall, 1971.

Mikesell, Raymond F. *Financing World Trade.* New York: Thomas Y. Crowell Co., 1969.

Wallich, Henry C. "A Defense of Fixed Exchange Rates," from U.S. Congress, Joint Economic Committee, *Hearings: The United States Balance of Payments,* 88th Cong., 1st sess., 1963.

16

The Problem of Economic Growth

In this chapter, we will complete our extensions and applications of macroeconomic analysis by introducing the problem of economic growth. Economic growth is such a large topic in our field that we shall be coming back to it many times again. In chapter 28, we shall consider growth in an international context. In chapter 30, we will be particularly concerned with the *costs* of economic growth. We have already talked about growth in the case of the underdeveloped nations (chapter 6), and we will return to this major twentieth-century problem in the final chapter of the book.

For the moment, we have two main objectives: (1) to indicate the extent and character of modern economic growth, and (2) to relate the problem of growth to the body of macroeconomic analysis we have been developing throughout Part Two.

SHORT- AND LONG-RUN MACROECONOMICS

Most of the analysis of Part Two to this point has been of a short-run na-

ture. We have assumed that the nation's basic productive capacity was given, and we have asked: where will a society's *actual* level of national income be in relation to this given productive *potential* in any particular period? In this analysis, we have put special emphasis on the factors that contribute to the aggregate demand for the nation's output—consumption, investment, government spending, and, in the last chapter, the net foreign demand for our exports.

Now when we shift our attention towards the long run, our emphasis has to change somewhat both in terms of analysis and in terms of policies. We can no longer take the productive capacity of the nation as given; its expansion over time is precisely what makes possible the growth phenomenon. And this fact is likely to influence the kind of policies we use to attack even our short-run problems. Thus, if we face a gap between actual and potential income and a substantial amount of unemployment, we may find that certain policies designed to correct this situation have an unfavorable effect on the expansion of productive capacity over time. Other policies may have a favorable effect. As in the case of balance of payments problems, the attempt to secure a higher rate of growth (if that is what the society wants) imposes certain restrictions on the kinds of policies we will want to employ.

These points can be made most clear by thinking of investment spending, a matter we have discussed frequently in the preceding chapters. In the *short run,* the main fact about investment spending is that it increases the level of aggregate demand and hence may help reduce the gap between potential and actual output. In the *long run,* however, the most significant fact about investment is that it means an increase in the society's stock of capital, or its productive capacity. A policy designed to reduce unemployment may work equally well in the short run whether it focuses on increasing consumer or investment spending; however, this question of focus may be a prime issue when we are concerned with long-run growth.

We shall return to these points again, but enough has been said in a preliminary way to indicate the relationship of the work we will take up now to the work completed in earlier chapters. Let us begin by getting some historical sense of what modern growth means.

BEGINNINGS OF MODERN GROWTH— THE INDUSTRIAL REVOLUTION

In discussing the emergence of the "market economy" (p. 26), we pointed out that this was a basically modern phenomenon, dating roughly from the eighteenth century. Very much the same thing can be said about modern economic growth.[1] The beginnings of the process are usually located in the English Industrial Revolution of the late eighteenth century. This dating is necessarily somewhat arbitrary. England had been making substantial economic progress for at least two centuries before the revolution occurred. Furthermore, even this earlier progress was dependent upon the general expansion of the European economy that had its roots back at least as far as the tenth or eleventh century. Historians, eager to prove the essential continuity of the British experience, are easily able to find antecedents for virtually every change that took place in the economic structure of late eighteenth-century England.

Still, the concept of a genuine revolution is not altogether arbitrary. For it was only in late eighteenth-century Britain that certain distinctive features of what we think of as "modern growth" appeared unequivocally on the scene. For the first time in the history of mankind, a nation began to produce an output of goods and services that was regularly expanding at a rate far in excess of its rate of population growth. We can put this even more strongly. The Industrial Revolution in England was accompanied by a marked acceleration in the rate of population growth. To have *matched* this growth of population with an equal growth of production would have been achievement enough by any previous historical standard. To have *exceeded* it so that output *per capita* was also growing rapidly was

---

1. Indeed, some commentators have felt that these two phenomena—the emergence of a market-oriented economy and the beginnings of rapid modern growth—were intrinsically related. Although there may be some historical truth in this for the case of England, it is not a point that can be pressed very far, for it has become abundantly clear in the twentieth century that highly controlled and centralized economies can also produce rapid growth. See chapter 28, pp. 672–89.

something basically new in historical experience.

And this is what we mean by "modern economic growth":

Modern economic growth is a sustained, relatively regular and rapid increase in a nation's GNP, and especially in its GNP per capita.

It is this kind of growth that was born in Britain in the late eighteenth century.

This birth process had many different aspects. Some of them were clearly favorable and were so regarded by the more perceptive observers of the time. This was particularly true of the rapid development of new technologies of production. Economically useful inventions were being developed and applied at what earlier would have been considered an astonishing rate. There were improvements in virtually all branches of industry—in cotton textile production, in iron and steel, in pottery making, even in agriculture. The greatest single invention of the period was probably James Watt's steam engine (1769). This invention came to affect many different branches of industry and was important in giving durability to the growth process as it continued on into the nineteenth century. It was not, however, the "cause" of the Industrial Revolution, since the process of technological change was general and pervasive, and the revolution was well under way before the steam engine made its impact felt.

Some other aspects of the birth process were clearly unfavorable. This period saw the development and spread of the factory system and, in consequence, a substantial dislocation of the traditional British way of life. It was a period that witnessed great distress among certain groups in society—children employed in the new cotton mills, craftsmen displaced by new techniques of production, rural villagers and squatters dispossessed of their lands. Indeed, these unpleasant features of the transformation of English society were so pronounced that the leading economists of the early nineteenth century (recall Thomas Robert Malthus) took a very pessimistic view of the future. They were convinced that society was heading towards a dismal "stationary state" in which the great mass of people would be buried in poverty.

As a great watershed in human history, the English Industrial Revolution has received many analyses, but none more penetrating than the classic work of the great French economic historian, Paul Mantoux. The following brief selection is the concluding summary of his masterpiece, *The Industrial Revolution in the Eighteenth Century*:

The Industrial Revolution in the Eighteenth Century

Paul Mantoux

CONCLUSION

In the first decade of the nineteenth century, which closes the period we set out to study, the industrial revolution was far from being completed. The use of machinery was still limited to certain industries, and in these industries to certain specialities or certain districts. Side by side with great metal works such as Soho and Coalbrookdale the small workshops of the Birmingham toyman and of the Sheffield cutlers continued to exist, and survived for many decades. Side by side with the Lancashire cotton mills and the West Riding woollen mills, thousands of weavers went on working

at home on their old hand looms. Steam, which was to multiply and generalize the results of all other mechanical inventions, had hardly begun its triumphant progress. Nevertheless the modern industrial system did already exist with all its essential features, and it is possible to detect in the developments which had taken place at that time the main characteristics of the great change.

From the technical point of view the industrial revolution consists in the invention and use of processes which made it possible to speed up and constantly to increase production: some are mechanical processes, as in the textile industries, others chemical as in the metal-working industries; they help either to prepare the raw material or to determine the form of the finished product, and the phrase machine industry is inadequate to the variety and to the possibilities offered by such developments. The invention of such processes (at least in the beginning) owed little to conclusions drawn from purely scientific discoveries. It is an established fact that most of the first inventors were anything but scientists. They were technical men who, being faced with a practical problem, used their natural faculties and their expert knowledge of the habits and needs of the industry to solve it. Highs, Crompton, Hargreaves, Dudley, Darby and Cort were men of this type. A few others, such as Wyatt and Cartwright, undertook their researches instinctively and out of pure curiosity, without either scientific or professional training. Under the pressure of necessity and on purely concrete data they set to work without a definite plan, and only reached their goal after much groping in the dark. They represent economic necessity, silently and powerfully moulding men to its will, overcoming obstacles and forging its own instruments. Science came later and brought its immense reserves of power to bear on the development which had already begun, thus giving at once to partial developments in different industries a common direction and a common speed. This is specially noticeable in the case of Watt

and the steam engine. Thus two streams from different sources met, and though it was to their combined power that the industrial revolution owed its actual size and strength, yet the change had already begun and its first results were conspicuous.

From the economic point of view the industrial revolution is characterized by the concentration of capital and the growth of large undertakings, the existence and working of which from being only exceptional came to be the normal conditions of industry. Though, not without reason, this concentration is often considered as the result of technical inventions, yet to a certain extent it preceded such inventions. It was essentially a commercial phenomenon and was connected with the gradual hold obtained by merchants over industry. Not only was it accompanied, but it was also prepared by the expansion of trade and credit. Its necessary conditions were internal security, the development of communications and of maritime trade. The historical transition between the master craftsman of the Middle Ages and the modern industrialist was provided by the merchant manufacturer. We find him at first, so to speak, on the margin of industry, with the sole function of linking up producers with markets which were becoming too large and too distant for them. Later on, as his capital grew and the manufacturer came to rely on him more and more, he became the master of production and finally the owner of all raw material, buildings and equipment, while independent workmen were degraded to the rank of mere wage-earners. This concentration of the means of production in the hands of capitalists who were more concerned with trade than with industry is a fact of paramount importance. No doubt 'manufacture', with the great number of men it employed, the highly specialized division of its labour and its many likenesses to the factory system, was a more striking fact, but it played a much smaller part in the evolution of industry. It marked a stage on the road, but a stage no sooner reached than passed. Economists, studying this evolution, have conceived and described it as a simple development, one phase following another like the different parts of a geometrical curve. But to the eyes of the historian a movement of such complexity is more like a river, which does not always flow at the same pace but sometimes slackens its course, sometimes rushes on, now running through narrow gorges and now spreading out over the plain, now breaking up into many divergent branches and now winding about, so that it seems to curve back on itself. Merely to enumerate the different points it passes by is not to describe it. To do this we must follow, step by step, its varied winding course, which in spite of its changes of direction remains continuous like the slope which bears it to its end.

From the social point of view the industrial revolution had such extensive and profound results that it would be presumptuous for us to attempt to summarize them in a short formula. Even though, unlike political revolutions, it did not actually alter the legal form of society, yet it modified its very substance. It gave birth to social classes whose progress and mutual opposition fill the history of our times. It would be easy, by quoting some of the facts mentioned in this very book, to try and show that in this respect there has been no revolution, that the same social classes were already in existence, that their opposition had begun long before, its nature and cause always remaining the same. One of the objects we have always kept in mind was precisely to show the continuity of the historical process underlying even the most rapid changes. None of these changes took place suddenly, as by a miracle, but each of them had been expected, prepared and outlined before it actually took place. It would be an equal error either to undervalue those preliminaries or to take them for what they only foreshadowed. We know that there were machines before the era of machinery, 'manufacture' before factories, combinations and strikes before the formation of industrial capitalism and of the 'factory proletariat'. But in the slow-moving mass of society a new element does not make itself felt immediately. And we have not only to note its presence but its relation to its environment and, as it were, the space it occupies in history. The industrial revolution is precisely the expansion of undeveloped forces, the sudden growth and blossoming of seeds which had for many years lain hidden or asleep.

After the beginning of the nineteenth century the growth of the factory system was visible to all. It was already influencing the distribution as well as the material condition of the population. To the factory system were due the importance and sudden prosperity of districts such as Lancashire, South Wales and part of the Lowlands of Scotland, which until then had been considered as being among the least prosperous parts of the country. It was the factory system which, following on the redistribution of landed property, quickened the migration of the rural population towards the factories. When the census of 1811 was taken, 60 to 70 percent of the inhabitants in the counties of Middlesex, Warwickshire, Yorkshire and Lancashire were employed in trade or industry, and at least 50 percent

THE BETTMANN ARCHIVE

Arkwright's spinning frame was one of many technological innovations in cotton textile production that ushered in the English Industrial Revolution.

of those of Cheshire, Leicestershire, Nottinghamshire and Staffordshire. In these new centres, full of such intense activity, with their constrasting extremes of wealth and poverty, the data of the social problem, much as we know them today, could already be descried. The moment was not far off when that problem was to be defined for the first time by Robert Owen in his *Letter to the Manufacturers of England* and his *Ob-*

servations on the Consequences of the Factory System. And he spoke not for England alone but for all the nations of the West, for while the factory system continued to develop in the country of its birth it had already begun to spread to other countries. It had made its appearance on the Continent, and from that time onward its history was no longer English but European—until it extended to the whole world.

Figure 16-1. The Spread of Modern Economic Growth

THE PROCESS SPREADS

By historical standards, the spread of the modern growth process of which Mantoux speaks was very rapid, although it is by no means universal even now. Figure 16-1 gives a rough sense of how the Industrial Revolution has reached across the map of the world. The United States was already very much embarked upon the growth race before the Civil War. Germany began making major strides in the second half of the nineteenth century. Russia was a very "backward" economy through most of the nineteenth century, but then, in the 1890s, she began to make her move. It is an interesting fact of history that the Russian Revolution of

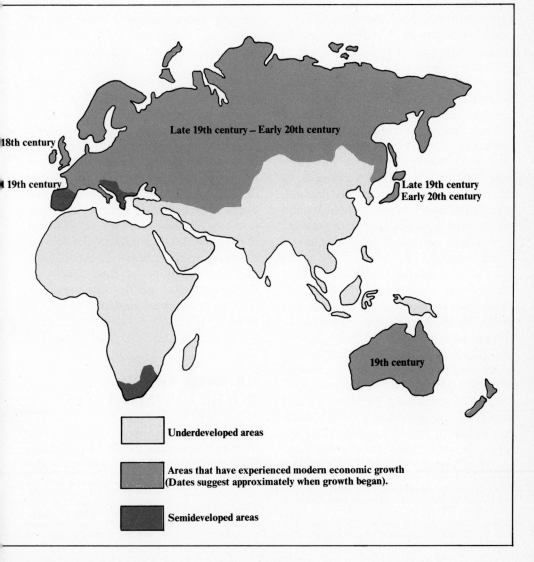

18th century

19th century

Late 19th century – Early 20th century

Late 19th century
Early 20th century

19th century

Underdeveloped areas

Areas that have experienced modern economic growth
(Dates suggest approximately when growth began).

Semideveloped areas

1917 came not when the Russian economy was deteriorating, but after two decades of quite substantial economic progress under the Czars.

The process went beyond the boundaries of Europe and the United States—to Canada, Australia, and, rather remarkably, to Japan. The astonishing rate of growth of the Japanese economy since World War II was made possible ultimately by the groundwork that Japan laid in the late nineteenth and early twentieth centuries. Indeed, this early achievement is really more astonishing than the later one. Japan had to face all kinds of obstacles—poor natural resources, heavy density of population, a culture largely isolated from the industrial world of Europe, relatively meager assistance through foreign investment—and yet she still managed to have an industrial revolution of her own beginning in the 1870s and 1880s. The Japanese experience, to this day, remains a particularly fascinating one for those who wish to understand the underlying causes of modern growth.[2]

The variety of conditions under which industrial revolutions have taken place make it difficult to generalize about the essential nature of this process. One well-known attempt to do so, however, was that of W. W. Rostow, who described the process with the phrase, "take-off into self-sustaining growth," and then attempted to apply this concept to the beginnings of modern growth in many different countries.[3] The underlying idea here is that growth begins only after a certain minimum speed of change has been achieved. Slow, marginal changes are insufficient; the country simply sinks back to its former

level of poverty. Only a spurt, a "big push" of some kind will do the trick.

Rostow then went on to analyze what he conceived to be the essential elements of this "take-off." Unfortunately, this proved to be an elusive goal. Some of the elements he described were too vague to be subjected to adequate historical tests. Other more specific elements—for example, the claim that a country engaged in take-off would experience a doubling of the percentage of its national income devoted to investment, from, say, 5 percent to 10 percent or more—have not convinced other economic historians.[4] What remains then is a sense that the beginnings of growth are in some sense "revolutionary." As to the specific form and content of the Revolution, detailed studies of each individual country seem required.

The process spread, but not everywhere. Large areas of the map—most of Asia, Africa, Latin America—are either blank or ambiguously shaded. But wherever the process did spread—Europe, North America, Australasia, Japan—the countries involved began to experience a dramatic expansion of their GNP and GNP per capita, and also rather extraordinary consequences for their general way of life.

GROWTH TRENDS IN THE UNITED STATES

In a later chapter (chapter 30), we shall examine some of the less fortunate consequences of this process. For the moment, let us simply sketch out a few of

2. See chapter 28, pp. 672–89, for a more extensive discussion of both the Japanese and Russian experiences.

3. For Rostow's analysis, see W. W. Rostow, *The Stages of Economic Growth* (London: Cambridge University Press, 1960).

4. For a major critique of Rostow's work, see Simon Kuznets, "Notes on the Take-off" (paper presented at the September 1960 meeting of the International Economic Association).

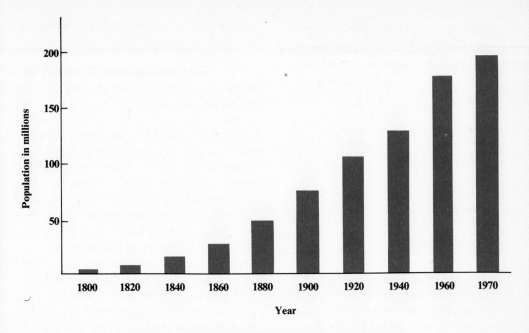

Figure 16-2. United States' Population 1800-1970
Source: Bureau of the Census, U.S. Dept. of Commerce

the statistical characteristics of this transformation, using the American economy as our example. The trends we will now describe, though differing in detail from one country to another, are fairly typical of the modern growth process in general.

(1) Population growth. Figure 16-2 shows the massive increase in American population over the past 170 years, from 5 million or 6 million to 205 million in 1970 and still growing. Population increase was more rapid in the United States than in most of the industrial nations during this period (because of special circumstances, including, of course, heavy immigration from Europe) but an increasing population is a characteristic feature of a growing economy, especially in the earlier stages of growth.

(2) Increase in life expectancy. One of the causes of our substantial population increase was a sharp increase in life expectancy during this period, as Table

16-1 shows. In the economically advanced countries, increases in life expectancies have been reflective of the overall growth process in the dual sense that growth

Table 16-1 INCREASING LIFE EXPECTANCY IN THE UNITED STATES	
Year	Average of male and female life expectancies at birth, years*
1850	39.4
1878-1882	42.6
1890	43.5
1900-1902	49.24
1909-1911	51.49
1919-1921	56.40
1929-1931	59.20
1939-1941	63.62
1949-1951	68.07
1954	69.6
1967	70.5

*For years 1850, 1878-1882, and 1890, life expectancies are for Massachusetts only. Source: Gilboy and Hoover, *Statistical Abstract of the U.S.*, 1970.

Table 16-2	URBANIZATION IN THE UNITED STATES

Year	Percentage of Population in Urban Areas
1800	6.7
1820	7.2
1840	10.8
1860	19.8
1880	28.2
1900	39.7
1920	51.2
1940	56.5
1950	64.0
1960	69.9

Source: U.S. Statistical Abstract, 1970.

brings higher standards of living and material comfort and that growth has also been accompanied by considerable improvement in our medical technology.

(3) **Urbanization.** The growth process has transformed the United States from a largely rural to a predominantly urban society. Increasing urbanization is a characteristic feature of modern economic growth.

(4) **Changing occupations.** At the beginning of the nineteenth century, the characteristic American worker was a farmer. Over the course of the century and a half since, the occupational structure of the American labor force has changed drastically. There has been an enormous decline in the number of farm families and farm workers. This has been accompanied by a substantial rise in the percentage of the labor force in manufacturing and construction and an even more dramatic increase in the percentage of the labor force in the professions, commerce and finance, government service, and other so-called service occupations. Within industry as a whole there has been a steady movement away from "blue-collar" to "white-collar" positions, as shown in Figure 16-3.

Table 16-3	PERCENTAGE DISTRIBUTION OF EMPLOYMENT OF THE U.S. LABOR FORCE*

Year	Agriculture, Fishing & Forestry	Mining	Manufacture, Construction †	Transport, Communications, Commerce & Finance	Professions, Government, Other Services‡
1820	72.0	—	—	—	—
1860	59.9	1.6	18.5	7.5	12.5
1870	50.8	1.6	23.5	11.5	12.8
1880	50.5	1.8	23.2	12.1	12.2
1890	43.1	2.0	26.3	14.9	13.5
1900	38.0	2.6	28.0	16.9	14.4
1910	32.0	2.9	29.2	19.6	16.3
1920	27.6	3.0	31.7	22.0	15.7
1930	22.6	2.3	29.5	25.9	19.5
1940	18.3	2.2	30.9	25.8	22.8
1950	11.6	1.7	35.7	27.0	23.8

*Excluding parts of the labor force whose industry is unknown.

†Includes also labor force in Electricity and Gas.

‡Covers the following categories: Professions and Entertainment; Forces; Other Government Services; Private Domestic Service; Other Services.

Source: Adapted from Colin Clark, *Conditions of Economic Progress*, 3rd ed. (London: Macmillan, 1957), pp. 519-20.

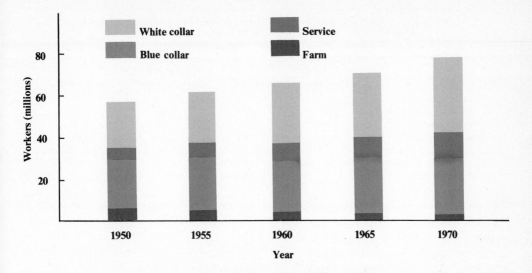

**Figure 16-3. Changing Composition of the
Labor Force, 1950-1970.**

Source: U.S. Statistical Abstract, 1970

(5) More leisure time. The standard workweek has been falling steadily over the past century. In the 1870s, the average was about sixty-seven hours per week. By 1920, it had fallen to forty-six hours; by 1970, to below forty hours. Individuals enter the work force later now and, with increasing life expectancies, they also have more leisure after retirement.

(6) Increasing education. Today the average American—man or woman—has far more formal education than he did in 1900. The number of years of schooling per member of the population over fourteen and per member of the labor force both increased by roughly 40 percent between 1900 and the present time. Around 1900, only about 7 percent of all children attended college. By the late 1940s the figure had already risen to approximately 20 percent, and it has more than doubled since. Table 16-4 shows how rapidly the percentages of young men and

women enrolled in school has increased in the past two decades.

(7) Growth in output per capita. Finally, we come to the trend in output per capita itself. Professor Raymond Goldsmith has estimated the growth of U.S. GNP and GNP per capita from 1839 to 1959 as measured in "constant 1929 prices." Table 16-5 tells us that while population was growing quite rapidly during this period (about 2 percent per year), GNP was growing so much more rapidly

Table 16-4   INCREASING EDUCATION IN THE UNITED STATES

Percentages of Age-Groups Enrolled in School

Age-Group	1950	1960	1969
16–17	71.3	82.5	89.7
18–19	29.4	38.4	50.2
20–24	9.0	13.1	23.0

Source: U.S. Statistical Abstract, 1970.

Table 16-5   INCREASE IN GROSS NATIONAL PRODUCT, POPULATION,
AND OUTPUT PER CAPITA, UNITED STATES, 1839-1959
(Percentage increase per year; constant 1929 prices)

	Entire Period 1839-1959	40-Year Sub-Periods		
		1839-1879	1879-1919	1919-1959
Gross national product	3.66	4.31	3.72	2.97
Population	1.97	2.71	1.91	1.30
Output per capita	1.64	1.55	1.76	1.64

Source: U.S. Congress, published in *Staff Report on Employment, Growth, and Price Levels*, 1959.

that output per capita was increasing by the healthy rate of 1.64 percent per year. Figure 16-4, based on Department of Commerce estimates, tells the same general story in terms of 1958 prices. From 1910 to 1970 per capita GNP in the United, States rose by 171 percent.

Are these rapid rates? By present-day American and European standards they are nothing very remarkable. By any past historical standard— that is, prior to the industrial revolution—they are, however, very extraordinary rates indeed. To see this, all one has to do is to get out a compound interest table and observe that a 1.64 percent an-

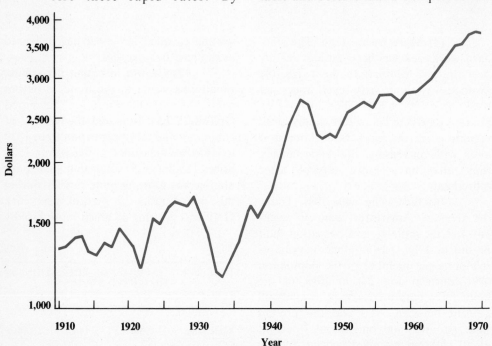

Figure 16-4. Growth in U.S. Per Capita GNP (in "constant" 1958 prices).

Over the past sixty years, per capita output in the United States has increased by over 170 percent.

Source: Department of Commerce

nual increase implies a fivefold increase every 100 years. The present level of family income in the United States is nearly $10,000 a year. If we actually succeed in continuing at a 1.64 percent annual expansion for the next century, then in the 2070s the average family income in the United States would be $50,000, and this in terms of *today's prices and purchasing power*. It is this extraordinary multiplicative power of apparently modest annual increases in output per capita that makes it clear that modern economic growth is a fairly recent historical phenomenon. Had it been going on long at these rates, we would be far richer than we are now.

This then is the story of modern growth as exemplified in the American experience. We live longer now, we are a much bigger nation, we live in cities instead of on the farm, we work at manufacturing and the professions rather than agriculture, we are much better educated, we enjoy an increased productive power that dwarfs anything in past history, and at the same time our leisure has been significantly increased. And all this is directly attributable to, or in large part a reflection of, the phenomenon of modern economic growth. This is not to say that we are happier now—the affluent society also has very deep problems—nor is it clear that this phenomenon can long continue, for the ecological costs of modern growth are high. But, without question, it does mean that our entire way of life has been transformed in what, historically speaking, is a very short period of time.

MAJOR FACTORS IN MODERN GROWTH

As we know, the growth process, technically speaking, involves a continual

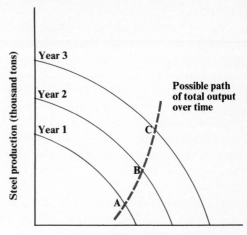

Figure 16-5.

Growth shifts the production-possibility curve outward. A society may follow the path indicated by line *ABC*. Food production is increasing absolutely, but steel production is increasing much more rapidly.

shifting outward of our production-possibility curve. In year one, we have to choose between various determinate amounts of, say, food and steel. In year two, we can have more of both commodities; in year three, still more. A possible path of choices is indicated in Figure 16-5, where our hypothetical society is seen to be choosing relatively more steel and relatively less food as it becomes richer. This reflects the relative shift toward industry and away from agriculture that we observe in all economically advancing societies.

But the matter is a bit more complicated than this, because some of the choices we make today may affect the rate at which the production-possibility curve shifts outward. If we consume all our income today in the form of luxuries and "riotous living," then we shall not be accumulating additional productive capacity for tomorrow. If instead of consuming champagne and caviar we use part of our output to build a factory, we shall have a higher potential output next year. If instead of spending our nights dancing, we study how to become engineers, we shall be more productive workers next year. As a consequence of such choices, our production-possibility curve will shift outward more rapidly, meaning that we may have more consumption (champagne and caviar) and more leisure (for dancing) in the future.

This brings us then to the question of the *causes* of modern economic growth. This question is a very large one, because growth is such a pervasive phenomenon that virtually no aspect of our social organization is irrelevant to it. For example, one can readily see that a society's political structure may have a decided impact on its rate of growth. We have already noted (chapter 3) that command-type or near-command economies might accumulate capital at a more rapid rate than a more consumer-oriented market economy. Even in a pure market economy there is an underlying assumption that the State is strong enough to guarantee the rights of property and the orderly administration of justice. In many societies, past and present, however, such an assumption is unjustified: property is destroyed, lawlessness is unchecked, civil strife is the order of the day. In such a society, it may be necessary to build up the political preconditions for stability before modern economic growth can even begin.

Faced with such a wide range of influences, economists tend to be selective. Roughly speaking, they try to analyze growth in terms of increases in factor inputs (notably, the labor force and the stock of capital) and increases in output per unit of input (especially technological change). Now the relationship of factor inputs to production will be a major con-

cern of Part Three of this book, and thus our fuller analysis of growth in later chapters must await the development of these theoretical tools. Even now, however, we can shed a good deal of light on the American growth record by making some comments about our specific historical experience in the areas of population growth, capital accumulation, and technological progress.[5]

ACCOUNTING FOR AMERICAN GROWTH

The American growth experience has been characterized by rapid increases both in factor inputs and in output per unit of input.

Population Growth

The main immediate cause of the growth of the American labor force, of course, has been our large growth in population as described in Figure 16-2. The deeper question might be put as follows: how did a country that experienced such a very rapid rate of population growth manage to escape the Malthusian fate, as described in chapter 6? Why didn't the famous law of diminishing returns keep output per capita and wage rates at or near the level of subsistence?

The answer, as might be imagined, has several parts. In the first place, it is clear that population growth did not take place in the context of anything like "fixed" natural resources as the British classical writers usually hypothesized. The century following the American Revolution saw a vast expansion of the United

---

5. The following account draws heavily on chapter 4 of my *Economic Development: Past and Present*, 2nd. ed. (Englewood Cliffs, N.J.: Prentice-Hall, 1967).

States territorial boundaries. The Louisiana Purchase in 1803 virtually doubled the country's land area—and at a cost of less than $12 million. Before the Civil War a further series of acquisitions, cessions, and purchases added well over a million square miles to the nation's land. Overall, between 1800 and 1860, the United States expanded more than three times geographically, with the consequence that, despite the rapid rate of population growth, the number of persons per square mile rose by the relatively slight margin of from 6.1 to 10.6 over a sixty-year span. Indeed, throughout the nineteenth century, we remained essentially a sparsely settled country.

Second, although our population growth was rapid, it by no means reached the rates that a thorough-going Malthusian would have anticipated. This was because, despite the fall in the death rate and substantial immigration, the birth rate in the United States did not react in Malthusian fashion. Very high in the early 1800s, the American birth rate was on the decline for the remainder of the century. Beginning long before the Civil War and continuing until the end of the nineteenth century, there was a trend in America both towards later marriages and smaller families.

Such a trend has in fact been characteristic of all the nations that have industrialized. Why would industrialization tend to lower a country's birth rate? Some of the reasons are: (1) urban living is less conducive to child-rearing than rural living; (2) industrial development means that women have job and career opportunities that they may prefer to their traditional roles as mothers and homemakers; (3) a rising standard of living may make parents want educational and other advantages for their children that can be better secured with smaller families; and (4) the fact that economic development tends to bring lower infant mortality rates means that parents need have fewer children to achieve a family of any given size.

Now the experience of the United States in this regard has not been absolutely uniform. We all know, for example, that there was a sharp *rise* in the American birthrate in the 1940s, producing the much publicized "baby boom" of the postwar period. However, birthrates in the late 1960s and early 1970s were falling again, and it seems reasonable to regard this phenomenon as a fairly predictable response to the growth process.[6] Thus, the United States was able to escape the effects of diminishing returns partly because of its large and increasing land resources and partly because of the less-than-maximum rate of population growth with which it had to cope.

This means that other favorable factors—those that would tend to *raise* the level of output per capita—had ample time to achieve their effects.

---

6. A general theory of the response of population growth to economic development has been put forward under the title: "the theory of demographic transition." This theory predicts first an increase and then a decrease in the rate of population growth as a country's standard of living improves. At the beginning, when the country is very poor, population growth is slow because, although the birthrate is high, so also is the death rate. When development begins, the first effect is to lower the death rate. (The birthrate, being more influenced by social and cultural factors, tends to change more slowly.) Thus, with a high birthrate and a falling death rate, population growth increases. At this point, however, the effects of industrialization and urbanization on the birthrate come into play. Birthrates begin to fall. This brings a slowing-down of the rate of population increase. Finally, we have both low birthrates and low death rates. Under these circumstances population growth will be fairly slow again.

Does such a theory hold out hopes for today's underdeveloped countries that hope to escape the population problem? Yes, some hope, but not too much. The reason is that population growth in many of these countries is rapid even *in advance of* any substantial economic development. It is extremely difficult to get the whole process off the ground (see pp. 158–62 and pp. 789–91).

Capital Accumulation

One of these factors, clearly, was capital accumulation. Since the early days of the republic, there have been vast additions to the American stock of capital. Raymond Goldsmith estimates that the stock of wealth as a whole rose from a little over $1 billion in 1805 to something over $400 billion in 1948.[7] This increase far exceeded the growth of American population and labor force. In the period from 1879 to 1944, for example, the capital-to-labor ratio in the United States nearly tripled.[8] The average American worker, whether in industry or on the farm, has continuously had more machinery, tools, equipment, buildings, and power to work with. At the same time, the housewife has come to be assisted by an impressive array of devices and mechanical appliances. Over this period, "produced means of production" have been systematically taking over and amplifying the labors of man.

The sources of the great expansion of the American stock of capital have been many. Some of it, particularly in the early stages, was foreign capital. In the 1860s and 1870s, probably half the capital invested in American railroads was foreign. Overall, the United States was an importer of capital throughout the nineteenth century.

Some of it was mobilized with the assistance of various agencies of the federal, state, and local governments. It was New York State that engineered the construction of the famous Erie Canal. The 9,000-mile southern railway network of 1860 cost $245 million to construct and, of this, over 60 percent of the financial capital was furnished by public authorities. In countless instances, the government has stepped in either directly or indirectly to provide the means whereby capital could be accumulated for important public needs.

Nevertheless, over this historical span as a whole, it is clear that the primary sources of American capital accumulation were found within the domestic economy and were in the hands of private individuals and institutions. Through direct investment, or through the complex mechanisms of securities markets, banks, and financial intermediaries, individual savings have found their way to private businesses that could use them to expand their physical plant and equipment. Moreover, businesses, farms, and corporations have regularly set aside part of their profits for reinvestment purposes. Such a pattern of "internal financing" has, indeed, increasingly become the dominant form of industrial and capital formation in the United States. In the modern American corporation, internal funds—retained profits and depreciation allowances—now provide well over half of corporate expenditures on gross investment.

These private, domestic sources of capital accumulation, in turn, can be looked on as largely a reflection of the growth of the American economy. Because this year's output has regularly been greater than last year's, it has been possible for Americans to increase their savings and investment without having thereby to cut into their previous levels of consumption. By the same token, businesses and corporations have found in their own expansion the source of surpluses that could be used for further expansion. Growing production, therefore, has made possible

7. Real reproducible wealth, including consumers durables and government wealth, but excluding military capital (in constant 1929 dollars). Raymond Goldsmith, "The Growth of Reproducible Wealth in the U.S.A. from 1805 to 1950," *Income and Wealth*, series II (Cambridge: Bowes and Bowes, 1952).

8. Simon Kuznets, "Long Term Changes in the National Product of the United States of America Since 1870," *Income and Wealth*, series II.

a growing absolute volume of investment over the course of American development.[9]

Technological Progress

Population growth and capital accumulation both involve increases in the supplies of our factors of production; by contrast, technological progress is concerned with the new and different ways in which we utilize our basic factors of production. Briefly,

We attribute to technological progress in the broadest sense those increases in output that cannot be accounted for by the increase in our inputs alone. Technological progress involves new knowledge and the application of this new knowledge to economically useful ends. It may occur through the development of new kinds of machinery, an increase in the skills of the labor force, a reorganization of the productive process, or through the development of new products hitherto unknown. In any case, the emphasis is on doing things in new and different ways as compared to times past.

Technological progress, in this broad sense, has been a characteristic feature of the growth process since the British Industrial Revolution. From the spinning jenny and steam engine of the eighteenth century to electricity, synthetics, atomic energy, and computer technology in our own, there has been a virtually unbroken line of major innovations in our methods of production.

In very recent years, economists have been attempting to separate out the effects of technological progress on growth from the effects due to the increases in factor inputs (labor and capital). In practice, this is very difficult to do. For one thing, new techniques of production may become effective only when they are embodied in new productive capacity. To develop the technology of the railroad is one thing; to make railroads economically effective is something else again, requiring large investments of capital. In general, the expansion of our capital stock and the expansion of our technological knowledge have gone hand in hand, and difficult interpretive problems arise when one tries to separate them. For another thing, there are some "investments" that are intended precisely to expand the technological know-how of the society and the ability of the society to absorb technological advance. Consider education, for example. If a person or firm devotes time and money to education or research, they are making an investment that may lead to the development of new technology or to an increased ability to operate the new technologies as they come into being. This process is very similar to ordinary capital accumulation, except that we are dealing not with physical capital but with what we might call "intangible" capital. We are saving and investing not in new machines, but in new knowledge. Again, the borderline between capital accumulation and technological progress may become blurred.

These points are well worth keeping in mind because they are important qualifications to a general conclusion of some significance that economists have developed in recent years. The conclusion is this: if we try to evaluate the effect of

---

9. The adjective "absolute" is necessary here because it does not seem to be the case that the *percentage* of national output saved and invested has been rising over the years. In the past half-century, at least, this percentage has remained constant or possibly declined. See, for example: L. R. Klein and R. F. Kosobud, "Some Econometrics of Growth: Great Ratios of Economics," *Quarterly Journal of Economics,* vol. 75, no. 2 (May 1961). In short, American *consumption* of goods and services has been rising as rapidly (and possibly even more rapidly) during this period as the level of national output itself.

technological progress as opposed to capital accumulation on the rise in output per capita in the American economy, we find (at least in our experience over the past fifty to seventy-five years) that technological progress is the more important factor. Some estimates are that technological progress may account for as much as 80 percent of our rise in output per capita, leaving only 20 percent or so to be explained by the fact that each worker has more capital to work with. This general conclusion has received some support from studies of various industrial economies in the post–World War II period. These studies suggest that even when we look at *total* output (as opposed to output per capita), the combined effects of capital accumulation and growth of the labor force together may account for little more than *half* of the growth of total output in these countries. The rest is attributable to a "residual" item that, in the very broad sense we are using the term, is closely related to technological progress.

Now this hypothesis—and it is no more than that because of the great difficulties of isolating and measuring "technological progress"—nevertheless has interesting implications. In particular, it suggests that the growth process is best understood as a continuing development into new areas rather than as a simple quantitative expansion of what we already have. And this makes sense intuitively. Consider the products we buy today. How many of them were in existence or even had equivalents one hundred years ago? The automobile, telephone, television, household appliances, electric lights, synthetics, plastics, and so on. And this is quite apart from the technological progress involved in finding new methods for producing "old" products. Think of the agricultural revolution in this country over the past century. Now 5 per-

cent of our population not only feeds us but sustains exports to the outside world. Growth, in other words, is not just more tools or more people to use the tools: it is new products, new methods, new approaches—nothing less than a continuing refashioning of our day-to-day lives.[10]

GROWTH AND AGGREGATE DEMAND

The bulk of the discussion in this chapter so far has been concerned with growth in terms of *potential* output. We have looked at population growth, capital accumulation, and technological change from, so to speak, the "supply" side. But Part Two has been especially concerned with the relationship of aggregate demand to our productive capacity. In growth terms, this question appears as follows: how can we be sure that aggregate demand will *grow* in such a way as to balance aggregate supply at something like a full employment level?

We have, in other words, certain factors making for a more or less rapid growth of potential output. How do we know whether aggregate demand will be able to keep pace with this growth on the supply side? Will we have approximately full employment over time, or occasional depressions, or—as Marx predicted—ever-worsening crises? These are very complicated questions and economists have often differed about the correct answers to them.

---

10. In this brief explanation of American growth, we have not mentioned one element that was probably quite important historically: *economies of scale.* The growth in size of the country and the development (especially with the aid of the railroads) of a large "national market" undoubtedly had favorable effects on per capita productivity, especially in the nineteenth century. We shall take up the concept of scale economies, pp. 417–18.

The Stagnationists

In the 1940s, for example, there developed a school of economists called the *stagnationists*. These economists, led by the distinguished Keynesian, Alvin Hansen, argued that there might be a persistent tendency for aggregate supply to outgrow aggregate demand over time. They argued that the nineteenth-century experience of the United States—during which time fairly full employment was not uncommon—was actually due to a set of special, favorable conditions. In particular, they noted that the expansion of the country, the rapid growth in population with its needs for more building and construction, the exploitation of the Western frontier, and the introduction of capital-intensive innovations like the railroads—all these factors had conspired to keep investment demand very high. Thus, more often than not, economic conditions were buoyant and employment reasonably good.

They then pointed out, however, that most of these conditions had ceased to exist in the twentieth century. The frontier had been exhausted, population growth was slowing down, new innovations were less capital-intensive than the railroads, and so on. They feared a persistent tendency of investment demand to fall short of savings and hence a tendency to deepening depressions, or economic "stagnation."

As it turned out, the post-war economy of the United States was far more buoyant than the stagnationists had anticipated, and it is reasonable to say that these theorists had been unduly influenced by the Great Depression of the 1930s. Still, their theory was important because it suggested that Keynesian-type problems might occur not only in the short run but as persistent difficulties in the growth of an economy over time. The gap between actual and potential output might not narrow in the long run; it might get increasingly larger and more difficult to handle.

Harrod-Domar Model

The problem of aggregate supply and demand in the long run is complicated by the dual role of investment that we have mentioned before. Investment is demand-creating—via the multiplier—but it is also supply creating—by adding to our productive capacity. How do we know which aspect will be more important over the long run?

This problem led, in the period after Keynes' *General Theory,* to a number of attempts to make that theory dynamic, i.e., to enable us to predict not only national income in a particular period, but its path of change over time. An example of this kind of approach is what is usually called the Harrod-Domar model. This theory, with somewhat different features, was developed independently by Sir Roy Harrod of England and Evsey Domar of Johns Hopkins and later M.I.T.[11] In its simplest form, the theory involves the careful examination of the following equation, where Y stands for annual national income (or output), ΔY stands for a year's increase in national income, I stands for annual investment, and S for annual savings:

$$\frac{\Delta Y}{Y} = \frac{\Delta Y}{I} \times \frac{S}{Y}$$

If we make certain assumptions, it is possible to use this equation to show some of the difficulties of keeping aggre-

11. See R. F. Harrod, *Towards a Dynamic Economics* (London: Macmillan & Co., 1949); and Evsey D. Domar, "A Theoretical Analysis of Economic Growth," in his *Essays in the Theory of Economic Growth* (New York: Oxford University Press, 1957).

gate supply and demand in proper balance in a growing economy. Taking the terms in reverse order, let us suppose that the fraction of income people wish to save is some fixed number, say, 1/10. This is not too unreasonable an assumption. Although in the short run, the marginal propensity to save might be expected to rise with income, this may not be the case at all in the long run as people have time to adjust their living standards to higher levels of income.

Let us further suppose that the amount of machinery and other capital goods used to produce a given level of output is more or less fixed. This is clearly a questionable assumption and is one of the reasons why the Harrod-Domar type models can be regarded only as a beginning in this difficult area. If, however, we do make this simplifying assumption, then we can argue that the term $\Delta Y / I$, which represents the *increase in income* in a year divided by the *increase in the stock of capital* (i.e., investment) in a year, will be some determinate number—say, 1/3. Or to put it another way: businessmen who expand their plant and equipment by $3 will have the capacity for producing $1 a year more output than before. Like our figure for savings, 1/3 is an "in the ball park figure" for this *output/capital ratio* in a modern economy.

Now from these first two ratios, we are able to determine a "rate of growth" for this economy. In equilibrium, the amount that households want to save will have to be equal to the amount that businessmen want to invest, or, $S = I$. Hence, it will be true that:

$$\frac{S}{Y} \cdot \frac{\Delta Y}{I} = \frac{\cancel{I}}{Y} \cdot \frac{\Delta Y}{\cancel{I}} = \frac{\Delta Y}{Y}$$

$\Delta Y / Y$, being the increase in output divided by the level of output, is the rate of growth of this economy. In particular, in our example, it will be equal to 1/30, or 3.3 percent:

$$\frac{\Delta Y}{Y} = \frac{\Delta Y}{I} \cdot \frac{S}{Y} = \left(\frac{1}{3}\right)\left(\frac{1}{10}\right) =$$
$$\left(\frac{1}{30}\right) = 3.3\%$$

But this seems rather strange. We have apparently determined a rate of growth for our economy—3.3 percent annually—but we have said nothing about major factors that might influence the growth of productive potential, e.g., population growth or technological progress. Suppose that these factors on the supply side can generate a growth of output of only 2 percent per year? Or suppose they can generate a very high rate of growth of 6 or 7 percent per year? How do *these* numbers relate to the 3.3 percent rate of growth that we have just determined?

And, indeed, it is this problem that the Harrod-Domar type of theories see as a major one for a growing economy. The growth rate that keeps investment and savings happily in balance (sometimes called the *equilibrium* or *warranted* rate of growth) may be quite different from the rate of growth that fundamental supply conditions permit (sometimes called the *natural* rate of growth). In this theory, there really is no guarantee at all that aggregate supply and aggregate demand will grow in harmony over time. On the contrary, the system is forever poised towards runaway inflations òr depressions.

GROWTH AND PUBLIC POLICY

The trouble with both the stagnationist theory and the Harrod-Domar type of theories is that they paint a rather worse picture of things than actual American experience would justify. We have had depressions, but these have not been getting worse as the stagnationists feared, nor is the system as wildly unstable as the Harrod-Domar theories might lead one to believe.

Consequently, economists have tried to develop somewhat more flexible theories than the examples we have cited.[12] And they have also inspected ways in which governmental fiscal, monetary, and other policies might profitably be adjusted when the growth of the economy is being taken explicitly into account. For the fact is that governmental policies—even those with short-run objectives—may have substantial effects on the growth rate of the economy. If a high rate of growth is a major goal of the economy (and it may *not* be—see pp. 719–21), then the following generalizations offer at least some guidance to the policy-maker:

(1) Full-employment policies will also usually be growth-promoting policies. Throughout Part Two, we have been discussing various ways in which the government can contribute to full employment in the economy. Insofar as these policies are successful in bringing the economy closer to its full-employment potential, they will have some favorable effect on growth. They will do this in the short run by speeding up the rate of growth as the economy moves from a below-full-employment to a near-full-employment level of output, and in the longer run by the presumably larger amount of investment that will occur at the higher levels of national output.

(2) Fiscal and monetary policies to secure full employment can also be specifically adapted to growth promotion. The point is that there is not simply one, but a variety of different fiscal and monetary policies to raise the level of aggregate demand and that, among these various alternatives, the nation can try to select measures that will be most favorable to future growth. Fundamentally, there are two approaches that may be used to achieve this end:

(a) *Follow a relatively expansionary monetary policy ("easy money"), to encourage as much business investment as possible, and if this threatens to create too much aggregate demand, follow a relatively contractionary fiscal policy,*

(b) *Select the instruments of fiscal policy so that the burdens fall more heavily on consumption while, simultaneously, attempts are being made to stimulate investment activity.*

In other words, keep interest rates low; and if it is necessary to increase taxes (to prevent inflation from developing), make sure that the tax burdens fall as much as possible on the consumer and as little as possible on investment.

Now the real problem with these policies is that they may conflict with other economic objectives. The greatest single conflict, as we know, is that between full employment and price stability. Although the policies we have just discussed may harmonize full-employment and growth objectives, they do nothing in themselves to reduce the full-employment–price–stability conflict.

But there are other possible conflicts, too. We have suggested selecting taxes that fall heavily on consumption and lightly on investment. But such taxes

---

12. See, for example, Robert M. Solow, "A Contribution to the Theory of Economic Growth," *Quarterly Journal of Economics*, 70 (February 1956).

are likely to increase rather than decrease the inequality of income distribution in our society. If growth and equality conflict, which will the average citizen choose? Who is to decide which is preferable?

Moreover, the balance of payments can be an added complication. Considering the extensive deficits in the U.S. balance of payments, policy-makers may prefer to have relatively high interest rates that will attract international capital to this country. A good balance-of-payments-plus-full-employment policy might consist of high interest rates with a relatively expansive fiscal policy to counteract the contractionary impact of tight money. But the growth-plus-full-employment policy we have just suggested is exactly the opposite: i.e., easy money and a contractionary fiscal policy.[13]

What this means is that there are limits to the degree that we can use full employment monetary and fiscal policies as a specific stimulant to economic growth. However, there is at least some flexibility in this area; and if a government continually has its eye on the goal of growth, in the long run it will doubtless produce a more rapidly growing economy than would otherwise be the case: This general conclusion is very much strengthened, moreover, when we come to our third point.

(3) Technological progress can be strengthened by giving greater emphasis to education and research. We know from our earlier discussion that technological change has been a major factor in American economic growth, especially in recent decades. We also know that such change involves new methods of production, new products, new skills in the labor force, new managerial talents, and so on. The most direct ways of encouraging this process are through increased basic and applied scientific research (the wellspring of technological progress) and through the increased education and training of our citizens (contributing both to the creation of new knowledge and to the introduction of new techniques into actual practice). That increased attention to education and allied fields is likely to promote a continuing high rate of growth (if that is our objective), there should be little doubt.

SUMMARY

In this chapter, we have presented our first extensive treatment of the subject of *modern economic growth.* We have given an historical and descriptive account of the growth process, and also shown how long-run and short-run macroeconomics are interrelated.

Modern economic growth can be said to have begun with the English Industrial Revolution of the late eighteenth century, the beginnings being characterized by rapid technological change, increased capital accumulation and the growth of the factory system, and profound consequences (by no means all favorable) on the status of different social and economic classes. The result was that output began to grow so rapidly that, even with an increased growth of population, output per capita in Britain began to rise significantly.

This growth process spread to many other countries in the following cen-

---

13. The effort to avoid this conflict in the 1960s gave rise to "Operation Twist." The Federal Reserve Board and the Treasury attempted to change the *structure* of interest rates, raising the short-term rate and lowering the long-term rate. The idea is that a high short-term rate will attract international capital, while a low long-term rate will make possible continued high levels of domestic investment. Such a policy may partially, but certainly not completely, remove the conflict we have been discussing.

tury and a half. In the case of the United States, as in most other countries, the process involved rapid population growth, increased life expectancies, urbanization, changing occupational structures, more leisure time, increased education for all classes of society, and, above all, rapid rates of growth of GNP and GNP per capita. (The environmental and other costs of this process will be discussed in chapter 30.)

Economists account for this growth in terms of increased factor inputs (especially labor and capital) and increased outut per unit of input (especially technological progress). In the case of the United States, although our population growth was rapid, it did not reach Malthusian proportions because of declining birthrates as industrialization proceeded. Also, abundant and increasing land enabled this country to escape the harsher effects of the law of diminishing returns. All of this meant that other factors that increased output per capita—massive capital accumulation and rapid technological change—had ample time to achieve their effects. In most studies, it appears that technological change was even more important than capital accumulation in accounting for the sustained increase in American output per capita, at least over the past fifty or seventy-five years.

The analysis of growth must include, beside these elements on the supply side, an indication of how aggregate demand can be expected to grow over time. It is here that the Keynesian-type analysis of the earlier chapters of Part Two has a bearing on economic growth. Will aggregate demand keep up with aggregate supply over time so that actual and potential output will be fairly close? Or will it grow too slowly or too rapidly?

Various theories have been presented to explain the growth of aggregate demand and supply over time, such as the *stagnationist* theory of the 1940s or the *Harrod-Domar* model. In this latter theory, we see some of the characteristic problems of relating long-run and short-run macroeconomics. Investment, in the short run, creates aggregate demand through the multiplier; in the long run, it adds to our productive capacity and hence to the growth of aggregate supply. Will the rate of growth that keeps investment and savings decisions in harmony also be the rate of growth that basic long-run factors such as population growth and technological change determine? Harrod and Domar were pessimistic on this point, though other models show somewhat more flexibility.

Also, of course, it is possible to influence the growth rate through governmental policies. If it is the objective of a government to increase the country's rate of growth, it will usually find (1) that full employment policies are also growth-promoting; (2) that, among the fiscal and monetary policies used to promote full employment, some will be more growth-promoting than others; and (3) that expenditures on education, training, and research are likely to yield important growth dividends.

QUESTIONS FOR DISCUSSION

1. Define *modern economic growth*. Indicate some of the changes in the structure of a society that usually accompany the growth process.

2. It has been said that since the English Industrial Revolution was largely self-generated, it was somewhat more gradual than similar industrial revolutions in other countries where many of the

changes were "imported" from abroad. Why might this be the case? What implications do you see in this for the modern underdeveloped country of today?

3. In the early twentieth century, the Austrian-American economist Joseph Schumpeter gave a central role to *innovation*—the introduction of new methods of production and new products into the economy—in the growth process. How has modern analysis tended to verify Schumpeter's basic intuition? Schumpeter also characterized the growth process as one of "creative destruction." Does this term seem apt to you?

4. "The problem with short-run national income analysis is that it focuses completely on the demand-creating side of investment and neglects the capacity-creating side." Discuss.

5. Suppose we are in an economy in which "natural" factors (e.g., population growth and technological progress) make for rather slow growth, but in which people want to save a very high proportion of their income. Why might this situation make for trouble in a Harrod-Domar type world? (Hint: Use the Harrod-Domar type equation,

$$\frac{\Delta Y}{Y} = \left(\frac{\Delta Y}{I}\right)\left(\frac{S}{Y}\right)$$

and show that if $\Delta Y/Y$ is low and S/Y is high, then businessmen will tend to find that they have more additional capital (I) than the extra output they are producing (ΔY) justifies. Explain why this might lead to a general contraction of output and employment.)

6. Show how a government that wished to promote economic growth might select certain policies above others when it was attempting to achieve short-run full employment.

SUGGESTED READING

Deane, Phyllis. *The First Industrial Revolution.* London: Cambridge University Press, 1965.

Denison, Edward F. *Sources of Economic Growth in the United States.* Committee for Economic Development, Supplementary Paper No. 13, January 1962.

Mansfield, Edwin. *Technological Change.* New York: W. W. Norton & Co., 1971.

North, Douglass C. *Growth and Welfare in the American Past: A New Economic History.* Englewood Cliffs, N.J.: Prentice-Hall, 1966.

Rostow, W. W. *The Stages of Economic Growth.* London: Cambridge University Press, 1960.

PART THREE
MICROECONOMICS: ANALYSIS AND PROBLEMS

In Part Three, we temporarily leave the world of macroeconomics and enter that of *microeconomics*—that part of economics concerned with the interrelationship of the individual business firms, industries, consumers, laborers, and other factors of production that make up a modern economy. (In our final section, Part Four, we shall be taking up a number of problems that feature significant macro- *and* micro- elements.)

Part Three A is mostly analytical. In particular it is a detailed analysis of the workings of a purely competitive economy (or what, in chapter 2, we sometimes called a pure market economy). In this economy, it is assumed that business firms, households, and the owners of factors of production are all price-takers. That is to say, each unit is too small to have any significant affect on the price of the product or service it buys or sells. This analysis will be designed to bring out certain overarching economic concepts, particularly *interdependence* and *efficiency*.

Part Three B will involve an application and modification of these tools for various real-life industrial situations, especially including a consideration of the problems—both in terms of analysis and public policy—involved when there are other than purely competitive structures in business and labor markets.

PART THREE A
ANALYSIS OF THE PURELY COMPETITIVE ECONOMY

17
Production and Competition: An Overview

Léon Walras, a great late nineteenth-century economic theorist, once wrote: "Pure economics is, in essence, the theory of the determination of prices under a hypothetical regime of perfectly free competition." This statement indicates the absolutely central place that the analysis of the purely competitive economy has held in the history of our subject.

For the modern student, however, some further justification is needed. Why give a special place to the analysis of pure competition when it is only one of a variety of possible market structures and, in the age of the great corporation and big labor union, not necessarily the most typical or influential?

We have given our answer before—that the tools we develop in this field can be applied to other market structures, that the analysis of pure competition allows us to show the overall coherence of an economic system and to bring out certain social welfare criteria—but seeing (not simply hearing about) is believing. In this chapter, therefore, we shall attempt to underline two of the central concepts that derive from the analysis of competitive markets: the notions of economic *interdependence* and economic *efficiency*. These concepts will be our guiding themes throughout Part Three A.

First, however, we must introduce a new and basic tool of economic analysis: the production function.

THE PRODUCTION FUNCTION

A *production function* for a commodity tells us all the different combinations of the factors of production that will enable us to produce different quantities of that commodity. To put it in other words, it shows the output of a commodity as a function of the factor inputs.

In Table 17-1 we have set out certain hypothetical data concerning the production of 1 million units of wheat. We are assuming for simplicity that wheat is produced by combinations of only two factors of production: labor and land. Table 17-1 gives us technological information concerning the ways in which labor may be substituted for land or land for labor in the production of wheat. Method

**Table 17-1   COMBINATIONS OF LABOR AND LAND TO PRODUCE
1 MILLION UNITS OF WHEAT**

Productive method	I	II	III	IV	V	VI	VII	VIII
Laborers (thousands)	138	90	64	48	35	27	22	19
Land (thousand acres)	50	75	100	125	150	175	200	225

I at one extreme is a highly labor-intensive method that one might find in a country like Japan, where every square foot of land is intensively cultivated. Method VIII at the other extreme is a land-intensive method such as one might find in land-rich countries like the United States or Canada. As we move from Method I to Method VIII we are using larger quantities of land and lesser quantities of labor to produce the same output.

   This same basic technological information can be displayed graphically, as in Figure 17-1. The only difference is that we have assumed that there are not just eight methods but an indefinite number of ways of combining labor and land to produce wheat, thus allowing us to draw the continuous curve *AB*. A curve such as *AB* is usually called an *isoquant* meaning "equal quantity"; e.g., 1 million units of wheat.

   If we had the necessary technological information, we could draw such isoquants for other quantities of wheat output: 2 million units, 3 million units, 4 million units, and so on. The production function would then appear graphically as in Figure 17-2. The spatially minded reader may want to think of this diagram as a shorthand version of a three-dimensional figure in which the output of wheat is measured along a third axis that extends perpendicular to the page of this book. What we are presenting here is a contour map exactly like the kind one would draw for terrain or for areas of equal pressure on a weather map. Each isoquant represents a level of production, just as each

line on a geographic contour map represents a level of elevation. The production function, seen three-dimensionally, would appear as a surface rising upward in space as we added more labor and land and thus were producing higher and higher levels of wheat output. An approximation of this view is presented in Figure 17-3. A more effective presentation can be made by taking a ruler or yardstick and holding it in a vertical position at the corner of a desk. On one side of the desk, we measure labor; on the other side, land; on the yardstick, quantity of wheat produced. Imagine the production surface as floating up from the base of the yardstick at the corner of the desk and rising higher and higher as you move along any diagonal from the corner of the desk (i.e., increasing land and labor inputs). Some such image of the production surface is useful, since we must now begin "cutting through" this surface to illustrate the basic characteristics of production.

BASIC CHARACTERISTICS OF PRODUCTION

   If we knew the exact shape of the production function for wheat—that is, if we really had all the data on the combinations of labor and land that could produce any conceivable output of wheat—then we could, of course, describe the characteristics of this function in great detail. Generally speaking, however, such data are lacking; consequently, economists have tried to develop certain broad gener-

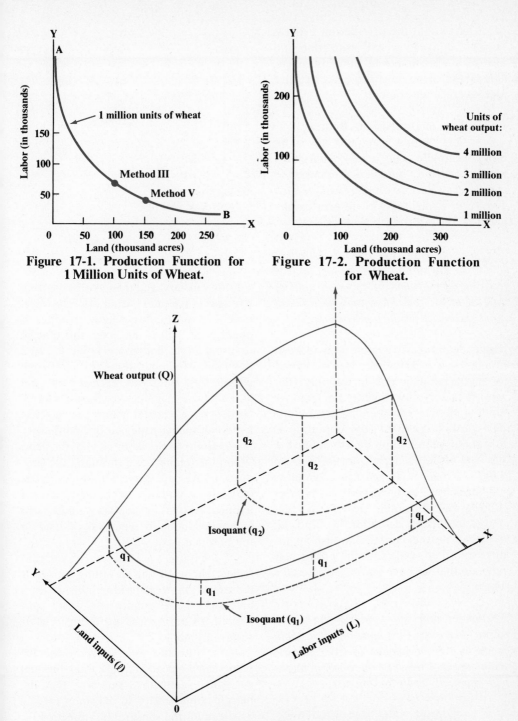

Figure 17-1. Production Function for 1 Million Units of Wheat.

Figure 17-2. Production Function for Wheat.

Figure 17-3. Representation of a Three-Dimensional Production Function with Two Inputs.

alizations about the production process that will apply to wheat production and also to a wide range of other products. The first of these generalizations we have met several times before.

1. The Law of Diminishing Returns

Let us now state this law a bit more accurately using a new "marginal" term (recall the "marginal propensity to consume" of Part Two): *marginal product.* This term is defined with respect to any given factor of production as follows:

The marginal product of a factor of production is the addition to total product derived from the employment of one more unit of that factor of production when we hold all other factors of production constant.

In this definition, it is important to keep in mind that marginal product is defined for an increase in one factor only (the *variable* factor) while holding the employment of all other factors (the *fixed* factors) at a constant level. It is also important to notice that marginal product is defined in physical or output terms, not in terms of value or money. Sometimes economists use the phrase *marginal physical product* to keep this point quite clear.

With this definition in mind, let us first state the law of diminishing returns and then relate it to the production function that we have just constructed for wheat.

The law of diminishing returns states that as we add more and more of a variable factor to a given quantity of fixed factors, the marginal product of the variable factor will eventually begin to diminish.

To display this law on our two-factor production function for wheat, we need to hold one factor fixed and allow

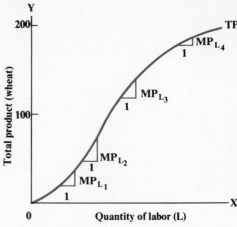

Figure 17-4. Total Product Curve.

the other to vary, and then to observe what happens to the total output of wheat. Suppose our particular wheat producer's quantity of land is ten acres and that he is hiring more and more labor to work this land. Move out along the land edge of your desk until you reach a point that hypothetically signifies ten acres of land. Now erect a vertical plane surface (use a piece of typing paper) at this point, running parallel to the labor edge of the desk. When this plane "cuts through" the production surface, a curve will be traced out in the plane, and this curve will show what happens to total product as we add more and more labor to ten acres of land in the production of wheat.

Figure 17-4 shows the characteristic shape of this resulting curve. It represents the total product (wheat) as a function of the quantity of labor employed, assuming a fixed quantity (ten acres) of land.

Now the marginal product of labor can be read off this total product curve in exactly the same way that the marginal propensity to consume (*MPC*) was read off the consumption function (p. 237). We again have our small triangles which (approximately) define the slope of the total product curve, and this slope, in turn, is the marginal product of labor. What the law of diminishing returns tells us is that while this slope may be increasing at the beginning ($MP_{L_2} > MP_{L_1}$), eventually it will begin to diminish ($MP_{L_4} < MP_{L_3} < MP_{L_2}$) as increasing quantities of labor are added to our fixed stock of machines.

In Figure 17-5, we have drawn the marginal product curve itself. We have increasing marginal product until point A, and then the law of diminishing returns begins to assert itself and the marginal product of labor falls.

2. Returns to Scale

The law of diminishing returns tells us what is likely to happen when we increase *one* factor of production and hold all others constant. But what happens to total output when we increase *all* factors simultaneously? Suppose our wheat producer doubles both the quantity of labor and the quantity of land employed. Will the output of wheat double? Less than double? More than double?

These questions refer to the overall size or *scale* of the production process. Economists use three categories to describe the possible responses of total output to changes in the scale of the production process:

(1) **Constant returns to scale.** When the employment of all factors of production is doubled, total output *doubles.*

(2) **Increasing returns to scale (*or economies of scale*).** When the employment of all factors of production is doubled, total output *more* than doubles.

(3) **Decreasing returns to scale (*or diseconomies of scale*).** When the employment of all factors of production is doubled, total output *less* than doubles.

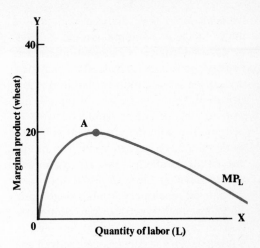

Figure 17-5. Marginal Product Curve.

The marginal product curve is essentially a curve representing the *slope* of the total product curve.

Of course, the employment of the factors could be tripled or quadrupled as well as doubled. The general form of the question is: given any proportionate increase in the employment of all factors, will total output increase in the same, a greater, or a lesser proportion? According to which answer is given, returns to scale will be constant, increasing, or decreasing.

Which of these three different returns to scale is most common? When addressing problems in the real world, economists often use production functions that exhibit constant returns to scale. In some ways, this seems the most natural assumption to make. After all, if 50 laborers and 10 acres of land can produce 1,000 units of wheat in a year, isn't it reasonable to expect that 100 laborers and 20 acres of land will be able to produce 2,000 units of wheat in the same period? But this is an assumption rather than an answer, and economists since the days of Adam Smith have recognized that sheer size may make a great difference. When we were discussing Smith in chapter 2, we mentioned that he considered the "division of labor" a major factor in economic growth. Indeed, he favored capital accumulation in part because he felt it would lead to increased division of labor. Smith argued that as the size of the productive operation was increased, the producer would be able to increase the skill and specialization of his workers, to save time in moving from one part of the productive process to another, and to develop more effective and more specialized machinery to increase output. The consequence according to Smith was that an increase from one to ten men in a given factory might increase output not tenfold but perhaps much more, perhaps even a hundredfold. In terms of modern analysis, he predicted very substantial *economies of scale.*

Experience since Adam Smith's time has, of course, only served to reinforce his prediction. By common consent, we live in the age of mass production and the age of specialization. All our major industrial producers use large-scale machinery that often simply cannot be replicated on a smaller scale; similarly, a small number of men, each a jack-of-many-trades, could not possibly hope to duplicate on a small scale what a highly trained and specialized labor force can achieve on a large scale. Many modern industries are virtually inconceivable except on a mass-production basis. Imagine trying to establish an automobile industry in Monaco or the Dominican Republic. Or imagine trying to produce steel with small "backyard blast furnaces." Actually, the Chinese *did* try to do this at the time of their "great leap forward" in the 1950s. The consequence: tremendous exertion, a great many melted-down pots and pans, and practically no usable steel.

Thus, while no broad generalization comparable to the law of diminishing returns is possible, present-day econo-

mists do recognize that in many modern industries, increasing returns to scale are highly significant over at least moderate ranges of production. If constant returns are often assumed in empirical analysis, it is only because of the great practical difficulty of determining the exact extent of the economies of scale that may exist. In this area of economics, the ultimate recourse must be to detailed studies of particular industries.

3. Convexity of the Isoquants

One final characteristic of our production function is that the isoquants are drawn convex to the origin. This is a slightly more complicated characteristic than the two just discussed. It reflects what is rather awkwardly called "the diminishing marginal rate of substitution of one factor of production for another as we increase the employment of that factor in the production of a given quantity of output."

Let's define these terms a bit. The marginal rate of substitution of one factor for another can be defined as the amount of one factor (say, land) that has to be added to replace a given amount of another factor (say, labor), while leaving production unchanged. Graphically, the marginal rate of factor substitution can be shown by the slope of the isoquant. In Figure 17-6, when we are using a great deal of land and little labor, we need a_1 units of land to replace b units of labor. Farther down on the curve, with more labor employed, we need add only a_2 units of land to replace the same amount of labor.

These little triangles can also be used to show the relationship of the marginal rate of factor substitution to the marginal products of the two factors, for the slope of the isoquant in Figure 17-6

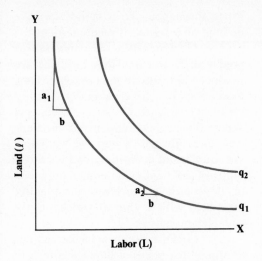

Figure 17-6. Convexity of Isoquants.

can be shown to be equal to the marginal product of labor divided by the marginal product of land. Or in general:

$$\frac{a}{b} = \frac{\text{marginal product of labor}}{\text{marginal product of land}}$$

This relationship can be readily understood if we remember that when we move from one point on an isoquant to a neighboring point, the *loss* of production caused by having less of one factor to work with is exactly counterbalanced by the *gain* in production caused by having more of the other factor to work with. (This is simply to say that all points on any isoquant represent the same level of output.) The loss of production when we give up b units of labor will be equal to $b \times MP_L$ (Figure 17-6.)[1] The gain in production when we add a units of land will be equal to $a \times MP_\ell$.

[1] MP_L tells us how much production we would lose if we gave up *one* unit of labor. If we give up b units, the loss will be equal to $b \times MP_L$. Of course, this will be true only when b is very small. All *marginal* changes in economics refer to such small changes only.

Since loss must equal gain, we have:

$$b \times MP_L = a \times MP_\ell$$

or

$$\frac{a}{b} = \frac{MP_L}{MP_\ell}$$

In other words, the slope of the isoquant is equal to the ratio of the marginal products of the factors.

Once we see this, we can understand quite easily why the isoquant normally has a convex shape. As we move down an isoquant in Figure 17-6, we are employing more and more labor and less and less land. This change in factor proportions should have the effect of reducing the marginal product of labor relative to the marginal product of land. But this is precisely what happens. The term MP_L/MP_ℓ is constantly declining. We know this because the slope of the isoquant is becoming less and less steep, and this slope is equal to the ratio of the marginal product of labor to that of land. Thus, the characteristic shape of each isoquant will be as we have drawn it.[2]

[2] Like all these "laws" of production, this is an empirical generalization, not a natural law. Indeed, there is an important exception to our rule when factors of production have to be used in *fixed proportions;* e.g., one man per machine. When proportions are fixed, the production function will appear as it does in the accompanying figure. Note that in this case, adding one more unit of one factor while holding the other constant will add nothing to production; i.e., the marginal product of that factor will be zero.

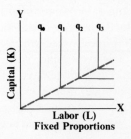

Fixed Proportions

This completes our brief survey of the basic characteristics of production and we are now ready to consider the principles of interdependence and efficiency that are so central to economic analysis and that can be brought out most clearly through the study of competitive markets.

THE PRINCIPLE OF INTERDEPENDENCE

We have really met the notion of *interdependence* in Parts One and Two through our use of the circular flow diagram. In a market economy, for example, we showed a flow of goods and services going to the product markets from private business firms, moving through the households to the factor markets, where, in the form of the services of factors of production, it returned to the private firms. In a general way, we might say that interdependence means that what happens in one of these markets (say, the product markets) will influence what happens in the other of these markets (say, the factor markets), and vice versa.

More specifically, we can say that the supply-and-demand mechanism, working through prices and markets, is expected—when all the dust is settled—to have answered four basic economic questions:

(1) **Relative values of commodities.** With the determination of the prices of all products, the society can answer the fundamental question of which products are more or less valuable (economically) than others. Does coffee have a higher or lower value (price) than tea? Is a vacuum cleaner worth one, two, or three carpet sweepers? When prices have been estab-

lished throughout the economy, we have definite answers to all such questions.

(2) **Quantities of commodities produced.** How many tons of coffee are produced annually in the economy? How many tons of tea? How many vacuum cleaners? How many carpet sweepers? When the supply-and-demand mechanism has completed its work, we will know the equilibrium quantities of all the thousands of different commodities produced in our economy. In each case, the quantity produced will be that at which supply equals demand.

(3) **Distribution of income.** By determining the prices of the factors of production in our economy, we are also determining the distribution of income in our economy. A high price for clerical workers' services means high *wages* for clerical workers; a low price, a low wage. Who gets more of the income of the society: the owner of land, the owner of capital, or the laborer? When supply-and-demand in the factor market has determined factor prices, all these questions about the distribution of income in the society can be answered.

(4) **Methods of production.** Should the businessman economize on the use of labor or machinery or land? Will he choose, say, a labor-intensive method of producing wheat or will he choose a highly mechanized method of farming? Once the prices of the factors of production have been determined, the businessman will know what method of production is most economical. In some economies, a given commodity will be produced with vast quantities of labor using the simplest tools; in other economies, highly mechanized, capital-intensive methods will be used. The "answer" will be determined by the factor prices that have been set through supply and demand.

The principle of interdependence

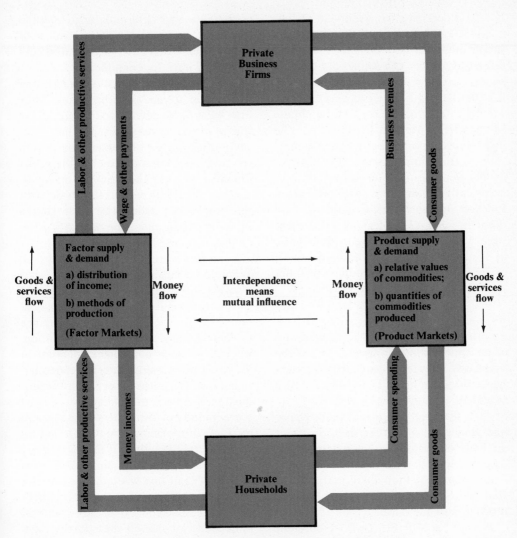

Figure 17-7. The Circular Flow of a Market Economy.

can now be expressed by saying that, in theory, the solution of each of these four basic questions is dependent upon the solutions of the others. Or, as suggested by Figure 17-7, there is mutual influence between product and factor markets. We determine, for example, what quantities of commodities are to be produced via supply and demand in the product market. *But* supply and demand in the product market will be influenced by factor prices

that, in turn, affect methods of production, the distribution of income, and so on.

Let us use our production function to illustrate this important principle in a specific case. In particular, let us show how the tastes and preferences of the households for different consumer goods might work through the entire economic system to influence the methods of production that businessmen will use in producing a given commodity—say, wheat.

421

Look back for a moment at Figure 17-1 and ask yourself the apparently simple question: How does the individual farmer (or society as a whole) decide what method to use to produce wheat? Suppose that the farmer is going to be producing 1 million units of wheat. Will he choose Method III or Method V? Where does he locate himself on this particular isoquant?

One thing is clear: the answer cannot be determined on physical or technological grounds alone. The production function precisely tells us that *all* these different methods are technologically feasible. What shall it be then, Method III or Method V? Or for that matter, I or IV or VIII or any of the hundreds of other methods that may be possible?

The moment one attempts to face this question squarely, one is forced back by a train of logic through the workings of the entire economic system. This is the essence of interdependence. How, roughly, would this train of logic go in the case of a market economy?

The first step would be to recognize, as we have, that the decision about methods of production cannot be made on technological grounds alone. In a market economy, the individual producer will want to know for any given output which method *costs* the least.

What will the costs of different methods depend on? Given the technological information contained in our production function, we shall find that the cost of any method will clearly depend on the *prices of the factors of production.* For example, if labor costs $100 a unit and land costs $50 a unit, we could, in fact, calculate whether Method III or Method V would be preferable. The answer would be Method V. Indeed, at these factor prices, Method V would be the least costly of all eight methods listed in Table 17-1. Demonstrate for yourself that this

is the case and determine what method would be preferable at a different set of factor prices—labor at $50 a unit and land at $100 a unit, for example.

But the prices of the factors of production are not given by nature. They also have to be determined by the workings of the economic system. We have simply pushed the problem back one step to the question: What determines the prices of land and labor? The answer to this question, as we might expect, has to do with the supply and demand of these factors or, as we might put it, the *relative scarcity* of these factors.

But scarcity in relation to what? What do we mean when we say that labor is scarce and land abundant, or vice versa? This, of course, is a complicated question, but a moment's reflection will convince us that in order to answer this question, we will at some point have to bring in the *tastes and preferences of the consumer.* In general, the prices of the factors of production will have to reflect in some part the demands of consumers for the commodities these factors produce. Is land a scarce factor? It will be, if the community is one where there is a limited physical supply of land *and* where consumers are very eager to buy agricultural products. Are cabinetmakers scarce? Are jewelers? It depends in part on the consumer demand for handmade cabinets and jewelry.

Our purpose has been to provide an example of interdependence by showing how consumer demands and tastes might influence the method of producing a given commodity, wheat. We are now in a position to see the rough outline of how this works. Let us suppose that there is a sudden change of consumer tastes (perhaps there has been a strong medical report on the virtues of dieting) that leads consumers in our economy to shift their purchases away from agricultural products and toward manufactured products. Let us suppose further that agricultural products on the whole tend to use more land and less labor in their production than do manufactured products. How will this shift in consumer tastes affect the method of producing wheat?

The shift in consumer demand will tend to lead to greater profits in manufactured goods production and lower profits in agricultural production. Businessmen will respond by trying to expand manufacturing industries as opposed to farming. But since manufacturing uses relatively more labor and relatively less land, the shift from agriculture to manufacturing will mean that the demand for labor will go up relatively, while the demand for land goes down relatively.

To put it another way, labor becomes more scarce and land more abundant, in relation to demand, than they were in the original situation. This change in relative scarcity will mean a tendency for the price of labor to rise relative to the price of land. Labor is getting more expensive; land less expensive. How will this affect the producers of wheat (and indeed of all other commodities)? Producers of wheat will now economize on the more expensive labor. If Method V was the least costly before, they may shift to Method VI, which uses more land and less labor, or perhaps even to Method VII. In short, a change in consumer tastes in one area of the economy has reached down through the whole system to affect the basic methods of production employed in that economy.

This illustration could easily be carried further. (For example, we could notice that the distribution of income in this economy has been altered: wages are now higher and land-rents lower.) But what we have done is sufficient to demonstrate the central point—the basic interdependence of the component parts of an economic system. It is all right for the layman to talk about changing this or that particular feature of an economy and neglecting the consequences. The student of economics will not do so, however; for he will realize that when one alters one component of the economy, one is characteristically altering the system as a whole. The understanding of these more remote consequences is not always easy; but for the economist, it is part of the appeal and challenge of the field.

WELFARE AND EFFICIENCY

An even greater challenge to the economist—and to the citizen—is to determine whether any particular set of economic arrangements is a "good" one, or at least a "satisfactory" one. This leads us to another question about the workings of a purely competitive economy: its relationship to social welfare and, more specifically, to what economists call efficiency.

First, let us indicate what the term *efficiency* means in the language of economics. And then let us relate this concept to the workings of a competitive price system.

A commonly accepted definition of this term would read as follows:

An economic system is operating efficiently when it is impossible to make any individual better off without making some other individual worse off in terms of their economic situations. Conversely, an economic system is operating inefficiently when it is possible to make one or more individuals better off economically without making anybody else worse off economically.

In other words, if we could improve the economic position of part of the society while not hurting the rest of society, it would be inefficient not to be doing so. An efficient economic system implies that there is no such room for maneuver—when we try to help someone it is at the expense of someone else.

As in the case of interdependence, the concept of efficiency can be made much clearer by means of an example. In particular, let us give an example of a society that could produce more of *all* commodities if it were organized more efficiently.

Figure 17-8 presents a production function for wheat again, but now we have also added another production function, this time for houses. Suppose that we have a rather curious economy that produces only these two commodities, wheat and houses, and that we are initially located at point W_1 on our wheat production function and at point H_1 on our house production function. Suppose further that in producing at these points we are using all the labor and land available to our economy (that is, it is not possible to get more wheat or houses simply by hiring previously unemployed resources).

Now it can be readily seen that this particular economy is behaving in an inefficient manner. The reason is that this society could have more of both wheat and houses (and hence more goods for everybody while depriving nobody of his present quantity of goods) without using any more labor and land than is presently employed. All that is needed is a reorganization of the factors of production, or as economists often describe it, a *reallocation of resources*. Land is being used inefficiently in house production, while labor

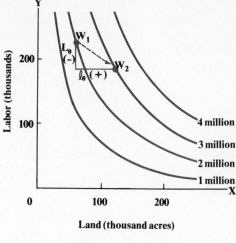

(a) Wheat production function

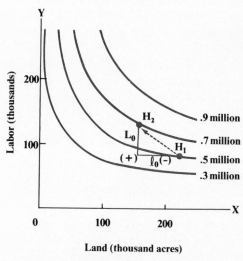

(b) House production function

Figure 17-8. Production Function for (a) Wheat, (b) Houses. Making Production More Efficient.

If an economy produces at W_1 (wheat) and H_1 (houses), it can get more of both wheat and houses (W_2 and H_2) by transferring l_0 land from house to wheat production, and L_0 labor from wheat to house production. By *reallocating resources*, the economy becomes more efficient (i.e., there are more goods for everybody from the same quantities of resources employed).

is being used inefficiently in wheat production. What is needed is a transfer of labor from wheat to house production and a transfer of land from house to wheat production.

This reallocation is accomplished at the new points of production, W_2 and H_2. We have transferred ℓ_0 land from house production to wheat production and L_0 labor from wheat production to house production. The total use of resources is unchanged, but the production of *both* products has increased: wheat from 2 million to 3 million units and houses from .5 million to .7 million units. Everyone in the society can have more goods without anyone being the worse for it. We have transformed an inefficient into a more efficient situation.

Now efficiency, as we have defined it, is not the *only* welfare objective of an economy, but it is an important goal, and the question arises: what is the relationship of economic efficiency to the workings of a competitive market economy?

The broad answer to this question is that under certain conditions and circumstances, a competitive market system guarantees an efficient allocation of resources in the economy as a whole. This is what Adam Smith, in more colorful language, was driving at when he spoke of the "invisible hand." This is why the study of the competitive economy remains important as providing a norm against which to measure other market structures and the activities of governmental agencies or, for that matter, socialist States.[3]

A caution: even if an economy were perfectly efficient, we might prefer another economy on other grounds—for example, on the grounds that it had a more equitable distribution of income.[4] Furthermore, as we shall be discussing frequently in later chapters, there are many ways in which inefficiencies can crop up even in a purely competitive economy. Air and water pollution afford characteristic modern examples.

Thus, the objective of the next few chapters is an important but still a limited one. In a world where scarcity exists, efficiency in the sense of getting the most out of our resources must be a central concern, and there is no doubt that in many cases competitive markets provide a quick route to that particular goal. But this is far, indeed, from saying that free and unfettered markets guarantee us a Panglossian "best of all possible worlds."

SUMMARY

The field of *microeconomics* is concerned with the ways in which the individual units that make up an economy—consumers, owners of the factors of production, businessmen—interact and, through their interaction, meet many of society's economic needs.

In a competitive market economy, this interaction is guided by the workings of the price system. This system gives determinate answers to four central questions: (1) relative values of commodities; (2) quantities of commodities produced; (3) the distribution of income; and

---

3. Recall the rediscovery of efficiency and markets in Russia and Eastern Europe in recent years (see pp. 82-3; 87.

4. There is nothing whatever about the "market solution" that suggests that the distribution of income will be fair. Who, for example, would argue that an orphaned child ought to starve because his low productivity would not bring in a living wage in a competitive economy? The question in this area is not really whether to let the purely competitive solution stand, but rather how much to alter it, and what the consequences of this alteration will be for other areas of the economy. See chapter 29.

(4) methods of production. It is worthy of careful study for two main reasons:

First, it illustrates the important economic principle of *interdependence.* In economic life, changes in one part of the system have complicated roundabout effects on the system as a whole. These effects may be demonstrated with the aid of what economists call a *production function,* a function that shows how a given commodity can be produced with a variety of different combinations of factors of production. In this chapter, we developed some characteristic features of the production function, including the law of diminishing returns, returns to scale, and the convexity of the isoquants.

The principle of interdependence tells us that the choice of factor combinations to use in any given situation will depend on everything else in the system. Thus, for example, a change in consumer tastes with respect to agricultural versus manufactured products may cause producers in the economy to shift from labor-intensive to land-intensive methods of production. The analysis of competitive markets brings home the principle of interdependence with great clarity.

Second, the workings of competitive markets give us an important guide to the implications of economic *efficiency.* An economy is said to be efficient when it is impossible to make one person better off without making someone else worse off. It would be *inefficient* if, for example, it had two commodities and could reallocate its resources to produce more of *both* commodities. Under certain circumstances, a competitive market economy will guarantee us an efficient allocation of resources simply through the play of private interest. Thus, such an economy provides a useful point of reference for considering the strengths and weaknesses of alternative real-life market structures.

For these reasons, Part Three A of this book will be devoted to a full analysis of the competitive price system. In careful steps, it will build an understanding of the principles of interdependence and efficiency. In doing this we recognize that efficiency is not the only desirable economic objective and that pure competition is not always the road to efficiency. In later chapters, we will fully consider these qualifications.

QUESTIONS FOR DISCUSSION

1. Define *microeconomics.* Since microeconomics is deeply concerned with prices, why do we say that inflation is a *macroeconomic* problem?

2. Does the law of diminishing returns refer only to labor, or could there be diminishing returns to land as well? How about capital (machinery, etc.)? Explain your answer.

3. The accompanying diagram gives a production function using two factors of production, labor and capital. The isoquant nearest the origin shows production

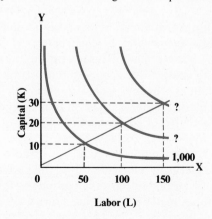

of 1000 units of the product. Suppose this production function displays constant returns to scale. What numbers would you put in for the other two isoquants? How would you change the numbers you have put in if the production function exhibited increasing returns to scale? Decreasing returns to scale?

4. We illustrated the principle of interdependence in this chapter by showing how a change in consumer demands might alter the methods of using land and labor in the production of wheat (and other commodities). Suppose that, instead, there is a sudden immigration of labor from abroad, increasing this economy's labor force by fifty percent. Trace the train of logic by which this change might affect the relative quantities of agricultural products and manufactured products consumers would purchase in this economy. (Remember that agricultural products are assumed to require relatively greater amounts of land, and manufactured products relatively greater amounts of labor, in their production.)

5. Suppose that you have ten pounds of meat and one pound of potatoes. Your friend has ten pounds of potatoes and one pound of meat. You might get together and trade some meat for potatoes, and both of you would be better off. If so, could we say that the trade is in some sense economically "efficient"?

6. As a consumer, do you ordinarily respond to market prices or do you have a significant influence on the prices of the goods you buy? How would you answer this question if you were a businessman or a laborer and the prices referred to were those of the goods or labor services you sold? What institutions in the present-day United States economy might you take into account in attempting to answer these questions?

18
Behind the Demand Curve

Our task in this and the next few chapters will be to go behind the supply-and-demand mechanism that determines product and factor prices in a competitive economy in order to relate that mechanism to the underlying data on which society's economic life is founded. These data concern (1) the basic technological facts of life (as expressed, for example, in the production functions of the last chapter) and (2) the basic psychology of the human beings whose wishes, motives, and actions give the economy its purpose and direction.

In this chapter, we will go behind the demand curve of the product market, relating this curve to underlying consumer preferences.

DEMAND AND SUPPLY— A REMINDER

In Part One, we showed how equilibrium price and quantity were determined by supply and demand for a particular commodity, apples. Figure 18-1 shows the same thing for tea. Let us recall the logic by which we concluded that the price at which supply equals demand (in this case, $1.50) would be the equilibrium price.

Essentially, our conclusion was based on the demonstration that neither higher nor lower prices could prove tenable in a competitive market. Suppose, for example, that the price was mistakenly established at $1.00. What would the consequences be? The main consequence would be excess demand in the amount *ab*. Consumers are ready and willing to buy over 200,000 pounds of tea at this price, while businessmen have brought forth only 100,000 pounds. What will happen? Will businessmen refuse to sell tea to consumers? Hardly, since it is precisely their business in life to sell tea to willing consumers. Each businessman will begin selling tea from his shelves, his back room, his storehouse; he will begin reducing his inventory. But still the consumer demand remains strong. Consumers now occasionally find stores that have run out of tea; they indicate a willingness to pay higher prices. Businessmen, sensing this willing-

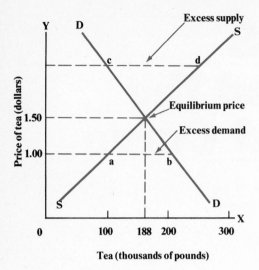

Figure 18-1. Price Determination by Supply and Demand.

Equilibrium price and quantity will be determined at the intersection of the demand and supply curves. At this equilibrium, quantity demanded and quantity supplied will be equal.

ness, begin both to raise prices on their remaining (now scarce) tea and also to increase their orders for tea from the wholesalers. We have begun a gradual process of rising prices and increasing production that must continue until the condition of excess demand is removed.

Essentially the same process happens in reverse when the price of tea is mistakenly established above its equilibrium level. Now we have, not excess demand, but excess supply. There is overproduction of tea in relation to demand, and this results in continuing, unwanted additions to the businessman's inventory of tea. He cannot sell each year's production; consequently, his tea supply begins to overflow his shelves, his back room, his storehouse. This time it is the producer who begins to make bargains with the consumer, offering lower prices while at

the same time cutting his orders from the wholesaler. Again, there is a process of price and quantity adjustment until the equilibrium price and quantity are reached.

Now to say that these higher or lower prices are untenable in a competitive market is not to say that such prices could never exist nor be maintained under other market structures or circumstances. Indeed, every modern nation has at one time or another practiced price control with the precise objective of keeping the price of some or all commodities below their supply-and-demand determined equilibrium values. Beginning in 1971, the United States, for example, entered upon a wage-price freeze and then a rather elaborate method of controlling wages and prices below the levels it was thought the market would establish. In terms of tea, this might be the equivalent of setting a price of $1.00 and legislating into existence excess demand of amount *ab*.

Can such legislation work? Some people think not.[1] Others would answer, "it depends." It depends on the particular crisis involved, the length of time the controls are in operation, and the general attitudes of the people towards governmental authority. In the United States during World War II, for a limited period and with a limited number of commodities, price controls in combination with a certain amount of direct rationing worked fairly well. Even under these conditions, the operation was imperfect—that is, illegal private or black markets developed. How the wage-price controls of 1971–72 will succeed in limited war conditions, for an unspecified length of time, and during a period when there is some skepticism about governmental authority in this country is much less clear. Certainly

1. See Great Debate Four: Wage-Price Controls.

it will be a substantial political and economic feat if they work successfully.

However, wage-price controls *could* succeed. That is to say, supply and demand *can* be interfered with—our earlier discussion of governmental agricultural programs showed this. At the same time, these curves do symbolize important forces. In a competitive economy, these forces will be strong enough to make violations of the "law" of supply and demand difficult to sustain, especially on any kind of permanent basis.

EARLY THEORIES OF VALUE

What are these "important forces"? Actually, for a long time economists could not really agree on what lay behind the supply and demand mechanism. In the late eighteenth and early nineteenth centuries this difference of opinion took the form of a disagreement about whether the value of tea, or any other commodity, should ultimately be related to the satisfaction or "utility" that the commodity brought to the consumers who used it or to the technological difficulty of procuring the commodity as reflected in its "cost of production."

In general, the British classical economists, including Adam Smith and his notable follower, David Ricardo (1792–1823), leaned toward a "cost of production" analysis. The main difficulties they found with "utility" were, first, the problem of measuring it (how could something as intangible as consumer satisfaction be given a numerical value that could then be related to the numerical price of a commodity?) and, second, the problem of divergences between "utility," however measured, and observed market prices. The second problem found expression in the famous *paradox of value* noted by both

Smith and Ricardo. By any conceivable standard, water gives greater satisfaction to consumers than gold or diamonds, but gold and diamonds have the higher prices. How then can the "utility" of a commodity help explain its price?

The general solution of the classical school was to state that utility was essential to the value of a commodity—useless products would command no price at all—but that the particular values of coffee and tea (or water, diamonds, and gold) were to be explained from the cost side. Since the concept of "cost" itself involves prices—the prices of raw materials used and the prices of labor and other factors of production employed—Ricardo went further and tried to analyze costs in terms of the quantities of physical labor involved in the production of a commodity. Why does coffee cost more per pound than tea? Ultimately, Ricardo said, because it takes more labor to produce a pound of coffee than it takes to produce a pound of tea. In this way, the relative prices of coffee and tea and all other commodities were grounded in the basic technological facts of production.

There were clearly deep problems involved in this approach, and Ricardo was aware of most of them. For example, what about the obvious problem of different *qualities* of labor? Why, if labor is the source of all value, do the products of one kind of labor (say, surgeons) command a much higher price than the products of other kinds of labor (say, unskilled factory hands)? There seemed, however, to be no satisfactory alternative to this approach. Economists who sought the answer on the utility side (like the French economists J. B. Say and the Abbé Condillac) were forced into unsatisfactory contortions by the paradox of value. Say was forced to conclude, for example, that air and water are so useful that their value is infinite and therefore we cannot buy them. Not a very convincing argument, especially to a rigorous mind like that of Ricardo. He (and Karl Marx, who was very much influenced by Ricardo in terms of technical economics) stayed with a labor-cost approach.

THE MARGINAL UTILITY REVOLUTION

All this changed around 1870 when a number of major economists in several different countries simultaneously brought forth a quite different approach to the value problem. The leaders were Carl Menger (1840–1921) from Austria, William Stanley Jevons (1835–1882) and Alfred Marshall (1842–1924) from England, and Léon Walras (1834–1910) from

HISTORICAL PICTURE SERVICES, CHICAGO

Alfred Marshall (1842-1924). Marshall was probably the most famous British economist in the late 19th and early 20th centuries. Although a marginal utility theorist, he stressed links with the earlier "cost of production" theorists, like Ricardo.

Switzerland. These economists, in turn, were following leads developed by a number of earlier writers: Jules Dupuit of France, Hermann Heinrich Gossen of Germany, and several others. Many of these economists were convinced that their new approach would "revolutionize" the whole field of economics.

As far as our problem is concerned, this group of economists made two significant contributions—one of which has proved durable, the other more transitional. The durable contribution was nothing less than the explicit recognition of the problem of interdependence. They showed the possibility of general equilibrium in all the markets of the economy simultaneously, a matter we shall return to later.

The more transitional but also

HISTORICAL PICTURE SERVICES, CHICAGO

William Stanley Jevons (1835-1882). An exponent of marginal utility and an enthusiast for mathematics in economics, Jevons is also remembered for his theory (not absurd in the case of an agricultural economy) that sunspots cause the business cycle.

highly significant contribution of this group was the development of a concept that permitted consumer satisfactions and preferences to be brought explicitly to bear on the analysis of price. This concept was *marginal utility*. These economists argued that the reason earlier writers had difficulty with the paradox of value was that they were always thinking in terms of total utility. Once one focuses on the correct concept—*marginal* utility—the paradox immediately dissolves. The definition is:

The marginal utility *of a commodity is the addition to the total utility (or satisfaction) we receive from having one additional unit of the commodity.*

Suppose, for the moment, that we do have some way of measuring utility. (This is a problem we shall consider presently.) Then what we ask about a given commodity is not how much total utility or satisfaction it affords us, but rather how much *additional* utility we get from one more unit of the commodity. We are consuming, say, 199 ounces of tea per year, and we add one more ounce, so that we are then consuming 200 ounces per year. How much has our total utility from tea consumption increased by virtue of having this one extra unit of tea? If we have a measuring unit for utility, say, "utils," then we can give a numerical answer to this question. If the total satisfaction of consuming 199 ounces of tea per year is 1,000 utils and the total satisfaction of consuming 200 ounces is 1,005 utils, then the marginal utility of tea, at the annual consumption rate of 200 ounces, is 5 utils. At some other annual rate of tea consumption (e.g., 100 ounces, a year), the marginal utility of tea to this particular consumer would be different (perhaps 12 utils). Given the possibility of making such measurements,

we could in principle determine the marginal utility of tea for each and every consumer at each and every rate of tea consumption.

Suppose that we have, in fact, made such a measurement for each different rate of tea consumption for an individual consumer. What would his *curve of marginal utility* from tea consumption look like? In answer to this question, these late nineteenth-century theorists brought forth a fundamental principle that they called the *law of diminishing marginal utility.* This laws states:

As a consumer increases his rate of consumption of a particular commodity (say, from 100 to 200 ounces of tea per year), its marginal utility for him will diminish.

Psychologically, this seems to make sense under ordinary circumstances. The first few units of tea presumably will satisfy our most deep-seated cravings for tea-drinking; by contrast, when we are having several cups a day, the addition of still another cup will add very little to our total satisfaction; at still higher rates of consumption, additional tea may bring no satisfaction whatever—indeed, you may have to pay the consumer to get him to take still another cup.

In Figure 18-2 we have plotted a hypothetical marginal utility curve for one consumer of tea. The particular shape is of no great importance to us, but we do notice that it slopes downward from left to right. In fact, we notice that it has very much the same general shape as the demand curve for tea described earlier in this chapter.

Are we to conclude then that Figure 18-2 is, in fact, the demand curve of a single consumer for tea? No, clearly not. In Figure 18-2 we are measuring *marginal utility* on the *y*-axis. In the case of a con-

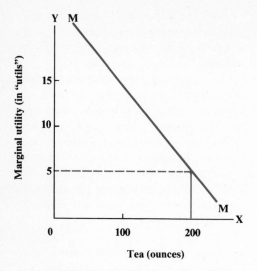

Figure 18-2. Marginal Utility Curve.

MM represents the marginal utility of tea to one consumer at different rates of tea consumption. The curve slopes downward from left to right because of the "law of diminishing marginal utility."

sumer demand curve for tea, we measure *price* on the *y*-axis. In order to relate these two quite different quantities, we must find some bridge between them.

The bridge can be found if we will now do two things. The first and most important is to make the assumption that the consumer will act in such a way that he will *maximize* his utility or satisfaction when he is making his purchases. How will a consumer act if he is interested in maximizing his satisfactions?

He will be maximizing his utility if he will spend his income on different commodities in such a way that the marginal utility he gets from spending a dollar on any one commodity will be equal to the marginal utility he gets from spending a dollar on any other commodity. Another way of putting this is to say that he will adjust his purchases of commodities so that the ratio

of their marginal utilities (for him) will be equal to the ratios of their prices. The consumer, purchasing n *commodities, then, will have achieved maximum satisfaction when he is obeying the following rule:*

$$\frac{P_1}{P_2} = \frac{MU_1}{MU_2} \; ; \; \frac{P_2}{P_3} = \frac{MU_2}{MU_3} \; ; \; \ldots ;$$

$$\frac{P_n - 1}{P_n} = \frac{MU_{n-1}}{MU_n} \; ; \; \ldots$$

where P_n *is the price of commodity n, and where* MU_n *is the marginal utility of commodity n.*

The common sense of this is not difficult to understand. If the last dollar I spend on tea consumption adds five utils to my total satisfaction, and if by spending an additional dollar on butter I can add *ten* utils to my total satisfaction, then I can improve my overall situation by shifting my purchases from tea to butter. A one-dollar shift will mean a loss of five utils and a gain of ten utils, or a *net* gain of five utils. If I am interested in maximizing my satisfactions, I will certainly make the shift. How long will such shifting continue? Not indefinitely, because of the law of diminishing marginal utility. As I continue making butter purchases, its marginal utility to me will fall; as I consume less and less tea, its marginal utility to me will rise. When I reach the following situation:

$$\frac{\text{Price of butter}}{\text{Price of tea}} = \frac{\text{M. U. of butter}}{\text{M. U. of tea}}$$

I will no longer be able to improve my position further; a condition of consumer equilibrium will have been achieved.

Now this principle—sometimes called the *equimarginal principle*—gives us an important link between marginal utility, on the one hand, and price, on the other. Indeed, in order to complete the connection between the marginal utility curve and the consumer demand curve, the late nineteenth-century theorists needed only one further assumption—that the commodity in question is sufficiently unimportant in the consumer's total budget, so that if he buys more or less of the commodity, he will not significantly affect the marginal utility of his income. This assumption (which we shall dispose of in a moment) means that for a consumer with a given income, the marginal utility of one dollar to him (to be spent on housing, clothes, automobiles, or any other commodity) will not be much affected, whether he buys 100 or 200 ounces of tea per year.[2]

The individual consumer's demand curve for tea can now be derived as follows: A consumer with a given income and a given marginal utility curve for tea (Figure 18-2) is asked, "How many ounces of tea will you be willing to buy at various prices per ounce?" Since tea is, by assumption, a relatively small item in this consumer's budget, we can say that the marginal utility of a dollar is constant for him—at, say, ten utils. Suppose the price of tea is set at 50¢ an ounce; how much will the consumer buy? By the equimarginal principle, we know that the consumer will be maximizing his satisfactions at this price if he buys tea to the point where its marginal utility per ounce is 5 utils. According to Figure 18-2, tea will have a marginal utility of 5 utils per ounce at the quantity 200 ounces. Consequently, the answer is that this consumer will buy 200 ounces of tea at 50¢ per ounce. This gives us one point on his demand curve. We could repeat the procedure for the prices 75¢, $1.00, $1.25, and so on. If we do this for all possible prices, we will in fact have constructed this individual consumer's demand curve for tea.

Thus, the "marginal utility revolution" has enabled us to go behind the demand curve for tea and to show how the consumer's behavior in the marketplace is related to his fundamental tastes and preferences.

But what of the paradox of value that stirred up so much trouble in the prerevolutionary era? Actually, this particular problem is now quite easily resolved. Water is admittedly more useful than diamonds in total, but it is available in such large quantities that its marginal utility is far below that of naturally (or artificially) scarce diamonds. Since it is *marginal* and not total utility that counts, water is therefore much cheaper than diamonds. Q.E.D.

MODERN INDIFFERENCE CURVE ANALYSIS

The marginal utility revolution in economic theory was a profound one, if for no other reason than that it caused economists throughout the field to begin focusing attention on *marginal changes.*[3]

2. If the commodity in question is very important in the consumer's budget, this assumption clearly will not hold. Suppose that I now spend twenty percent of my income on housing and decide to increase that to thirty percent. From a given income, this will mean that I will be able to buy decidedly less of other commodities in general. Consequently, these marginal utilities would rise, and the marginal utility of each dollar spent on those other commodities would also rise.

3. Much of economics, and especially microeconomics, is concerned with maximizing behavior of one sort or another. The consumer maximizes his satisfactions by purchasing this set of commodities instead of that. The businessman attempts to maximize profits for his firm. The laborer tries to find the maximally satisfying combination of work and leisure. Marginal analysis is well-suited to the logical (and also specifically mathematical) investigation of such problems. Many of the conclusions of the marginal analysts of the late nineteenth century can be accepted with little or no qualification even to this day.

Still, the revolution was not without its flaws. Indeed, the very central concept, the concept on which everything else seemed to hang—marginal utility—was suspect from the beginning. How *do* you measure marginal utility? The answer is that you don't. You can't. Or, at least, no one as yet has found any acceptable way of registering consumer satisfactions on a ruler or thermometer. An old-fashioned classical economist could have looked at the whole so-called revolution and dismissed it as scientifically unacceptable.

Oddly enough, this difficulty, though fundamental, did not pose as much of a problem in the area of price theory as might have been expected. Early in the twentieth century, certain economists— especially the Italian scientist, sociologist, and economist Vilfredo Pareto (1848– 1923)—discovered that you could develop much of the body of price theory without assuming a quantitatively measurable utility. If you could determine that a consumer "preferred" one set of goods to another or was "indifferent" as between them, you did not have to get him to specify that one set of goods gave him, say, 3.5 times as many utils as another set. Thus modern *indifference curve analysis* was born. In this section, we shall discuss what *indifference curves* are, and in the final section of this chapter we shall show how they may be related to consumer demand curves.

In constructing indifference curves for an individual consumer, we confront him with two different combinations or "baskets" of commodities, basket A and basket B, and ask him these basic questions: Would you prefer to have basket A instead of B? Would you prefer to have basket B instead of A? Or are you "indifferent" to which basket you have? Thus, basket A may contain five pounds of butter and three pounds of tea, while basket B may contain four pounds of butter and six pounds of tea. If the consumer is particularly fond of butter, he may prefer basket A; if he is an avid tea-drinker, basket B; if he is somewhere in between, he may just as soon have one basket as the other; i.e., he is "indifferent" about the two. When the consumer has answered these hypothetical questions for all possible combinations of butter and tea, then we can construct an indifference curve map for him with respect to these two commodities.

A somewhat more orderly way of doing this would be to start with one particular basket of tea and butter, basket A, which contains five pounds of butter and three pounds of tea; then we could try to locate all other combinations of butter and tea that are equally satisfactory to this consumer. In Table 18-1, we have set out the possible results of this investigation. What the table tells us is that this particular consumer would be equally satisfied with thirteen pounds of butter and one pound of tea or with one pound of butter and nine pounds of tea or with five pounds of butter and three pounds of tea or with any other combination listed. The consumer is "indifferent" about all the different choices represented on this table.

Table 18-1   A CONSUMER'S PREFERENCES

The following combinations of butter and tea are neither more nor less satisfactory to our consumer than the particular combination, five pounds of butter and three pounds of tea. That is, he is "indifferent" to which of the combinations we might offer him:

Combination	I	II	III	IV	V	VI
Butter (lb)	1	3.0	5	8	10.0	13
Tea (lb)	9	4.5	3	2	1.5	1

In Figure 18-3, we represent this information graphically, filling in the missing points to make a continuous curve. Such a curve is an *indifference curve*. Our

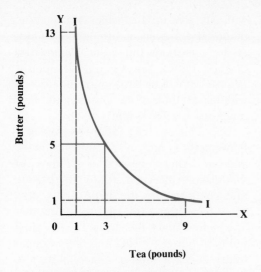

Figure 18-3. An Indifference Curve.

Curve *II* represents one indifference curve for an individual consumer of butter and tea. At any point on this curve, this consumer is equally well off.

consumer will be equally happy at any point on this curve, the loss in butter as he moves down the curve being exactly balanced (in terms of his satisfactions) by the gain in tea.

Having done this for one set of combinations of tea and butter, we can now repeat the process for other combinations. In Figure 18-4, we have added three more indifference curves for this particular consumer. In each case, we begin with a particular combination of butter and tea and then ask the consumer to list all other combinations of the commodities that are equally satisfactory to him. Each time we do this we get one more indifference curve; and, in principle, given a consumer of infinite patience, we could fill up the entire diagram with thousands of these indifference curves so derived.

Let us make a few comments now about what we have done. First of all, we should notice that the table we have set

out and the diagrams we have drawn are very similar to the production functions we described in chapter 17. Indeed, the question we asked the consumer ("What are all the possible combinations of butter and tea that will give you the same satisfaction?") is formally rather similar to the question we might ask a producer: "What are all the possible combinations of land and labor you might use to produce a given quantity of wheat?" Not only are the questions similar, but the general process by which the consumer economizes in his purchases of commodities is not very different from the process by which the producer economizes in his hirings of the different factors of production.

One rather strong difference exists, however, between the production

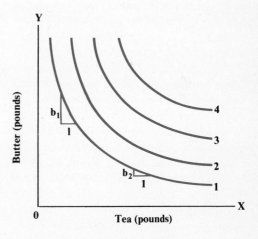

Figure 18-4. A Consumer's Indifference Map.

Each curve represents combinations that equally satisfy the consumer. He is "better off" on a higher curve, but we cannot say *how much* better. Diminishing marginal rate of substitution is shown in the diminishing amount of butter the consumer will give for 1 pound of tea as he accumulates more tea ($b_2 < b_1$).

function and the consumer's indifference map. In the case of an isoquant for wheat, we were able to specify the quantity of wheat produced: say, 1 million units. In the case of indifference curves, we have not specified a numerical quantity; we have simply labeled them curves 1, 2, 3, and so on. This difference reflects the fact that we are *not* attaching a specifically measurable utility to each curve. If utility were numerically measurable, we could say that curve 1 gave the consumer 1,000 utils of utility. But this is the kind of late nineteenth-century assumption that we are forbidding ourselves to use. What, then, *is* the significance of curve 1 as opposed to curve 2 as opposed to curve 3, and so on? In the modern analysis, the answer is that we assume that the consumer prefers more rather than less. We assume that he would be more satisfied to be on curve 3 than to be on curve 2 and more satisfied to be on curve 2 than curve 1. What we do not say is *how much* more satisfied he would be.[4]

Another point to notice about these indifference curves is that like the isoquants of the production function, they have been drawn convex to the origin. What does this particular shape mean in the case of consumer preferences? Essentially, it means that as we move down along the curve, giving up butter and gaining tea, it becomes harder and harder to substitute tea for butter and leave the consumer equally well off. At the beginning, the consumer has great quantities of butter and nothing to drink. He will

willingly give up a considerable quantity of butter for even a few ounces of tea. As he gets more and more tea and less and less butter, however, the situation is reversed. It will be hard to get him to part with his last units of butter, no matter how much tea is offered him.

One can see a family resemblance between the comments we have just made and our earlier discussion of the "law" of diminishing marginal utility. In the late nineteenth century, the shape of this curve could have been explained by saying that as we move down the curve, the marginal utility of butter is rising and the marginal utility of tea is falling; hence, more and more tea will have to be substituted for a given quantity of butter, to leave the consumer equally well off. Modern analysis cannot use this "law" because of its assumption of a quantitatively measurable utility, but what it can do is to make its own law: the *law of diminishing marginal rate of substitution in consumption.* This new "marginal" term is analogous to the similar term for production:

The marginal rate of substitution in consumption of commodity A for commodity B is the amount of commodity B the consumer will give up for one unit of commodity A while still remaining equally well off.

If we look at Figure 18-4 again, we can see that the marginal rate of substitution is measured by the slope of the indifference curve. The little triangle at the top of curve 1 tells us that the consumer will give up b_1 units of butter in exchange for 1 unit of tea, and he will remain equally well off. Lower on the curve, we see that the consumer will give up only b_2 units of butter for 1 unit of tea if he is to remain equally well off. The marginal rate of substitution of tea for butter in the first instance is b_1 and in the second instance,

---

4. In this connection, economists often distinguish between *cardinal* and *ordinal* measurement. In the late nineteenth century, utility was assumed to be *cardinally* measurable; i.e., 1,000 utils or 1,100 utils, etc. In the modern analysis, it is assumed simply that the consumer can order his choices. Given five different combinations of tea and butter, he can rank them by order of preference: first, second, third, fourth, and fifth. This is what is meant by *ordinal* measurement.

b_2. The law of diminishing marginal rate of substitution in consumption, then, says that in general b_1 will be greater than b_2.

Now this law is not irrevocable. Like the law of diminishing marginal utility, it is basically only an attempt at broad empirical generalization. It is a serviceable generalization, however, and it does avoid the specific fault of its predecessor in that it does not require us to measure that will-o'-the-wisp, utility.[5]

BEHIND THE DEMAND CURVE WITH INDIFFERENCE ANALYSIS

Our specific purpose in this chapter has been to root the consumer demand curve in the basic ground of consumer tastes and preferences. In this final section, let us indicate briefly how this may be done in terms of modern indifference analysis.

Essentially, what we must do is to take a consumer with a given income[6] and show what quantity of tea he will buy at a given price. Then we must show how his purchases of tea will change when the price of tea changes. This will give us the individual consumer's demand curve for tea.

To bring out the fundamental principle most clearly, let us assume that we are living in a world in which there are only two commodities: butter and tea.

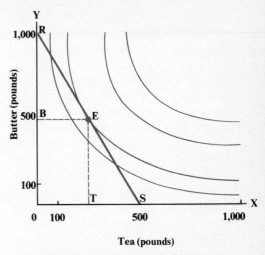

Figure 18-5. Consumer Equilibrium.

The consumer with a given income, facing given prices for tea and butter, achieves greatest satisfaction where his budget line is just tangent to one of his indifference curves (in this example, point *E*). At this point, the price of tea divided by the price of butter will equal the marginal rate of substitution of tea for butter.

The consumer has an income of $1,000. The price of butter is given at $1.00 per pound. Tea, *initially,* is $2.00 per pound. How much tea will the consumer purchase?

In order to describe these facts graphically, we have constructed (in Figure 18-5) an indifference map for this particular consumer, and on it we have drawn the straight line *RES*. This line, usually called a budget line, shows all the different combinations of butter and tea that a consumer can buy with $1,000 at the prices $1.00 per pound for butter and $2.00 per pound for tea. If he spends *all* his income on butter, he can buy *OR* or 1,000 pounds of butter. If he spends *all* his income on tea, he can buy *OS* or 500 pounds of tea. Any other point on this line shows him splitting his $1,000 in various ways between butter and tea purchases.

5. In this brief discussion, we are not able to set out all the characteristics of indifference curves and the assumptions on which they are based. There is one further point that should be mentioned, however—the assumption that the indifference curves of an individual consumer do not *cross* each other. The reader should draw two crossing indifference curves and analyze for himself what this assumption means.

6. More accurately, the consumer has a given income for a certain period of time; i.e., a month, or a year. Throughout this analysis we are dealing with rates of income, rates of tea purchases, etc., for some specified period of time.

Where, on this particular budget line, will the consumer choose to locate himself? The answer is obvious. He will locate himself at that combination of butter and tea purchases that brings him the greatest possible satisfaction. Graphically, this means that with his $1,000 income, he will locate himself on the highest achievable indifference curve. He will choose the point E, where his budget line just touches (is tangent to) one of his indifference curves. If he moves either up or down his budget line from point E, he will find himself on a lower indifference curve—i.e., worse off. The answer to our question then is: when tea is $2.00 per pound, this particular consumer will purchase OT quantity of tea, or about 240 pounds.

We can notice in passing that this equilibrium point of the consumer has a certain characteristic. Graphically, as we have said, it is located at the point where the budget line is just tangent to an indifference curve. This, in turn, means that the slopes of the budget line and of the indifference curves are exactly equal at this point. Now the slope of the indifference curve, as we already know, is the marginal rate of substitution of tea for butter. But what is the slope of the budget line? Actually a moment's reflection will show us that the slope of the budget line is the price of tea divided by the price of butter.[7] Thus, when we say that these two slopes are equal, we are saying that:

$$\frac{\text{Price of tea}}{\text{Price of butter}} = \frac{\text{The marginal}}{\text{rate of substitution}}$$
$$= \text{of tea for butter}$$

This is rather similar to the conclusion of marginal utility analysis that consumers will always regulate their purchases so that

---

$$\frac{P_1}{P_2} = \frac{MU_1}{MU_2}$$

---

for all commodities. The difference, of course, is that we are not positing a measurable "marginal utility." In the modern analysis, the conclusion becomes that in a competitive economy a consumer will be in equilibrium only when the ratio of the prices of all the commodities he buys is equal to the relevant marginal rates of substitution. Or, in symbols, for any commodities n and m:

$$\frac{P_n}{P_m} = MRS_{(n \text{ for } m)}$$

We shall consider this point again when we return to the study of the *efficiency* of the competitive economy.

We have now located one point on our consumer's demand curve for tea: when the price is $2.00, he will demand OT quantity of tea. In order to complete our task, we must now go through the same process with respect to other prices for tea. How much will the consumer demand at $1.00 per pound? How much at $3.00 per pound? And so on.

Graphically, a change in the price of tea (assuming a constant income of $1,000 and a constant price of butter at $1.00 per pound) involves rotating our budget line from the fixed point R. Thus,

---

7. This can be shown as follows: The slope of the line *RES* geometrically equals OR/OS. OR is the amount of butter that can be purchased for $1,000. Hence $OR = \$1,000/\text{price of butter}$. By the same logic, $OS = \$1,000/\text{price of tea}$. The slope of the budget line then is:

$$\frac{OR}{OS} = \frac{\dfrac{\$1,000}{P_B}}{\dfrac{\$1,000}{P_T}} = \frac{P_T}{P_B}$$

in the top half of Figure 18-6, *RS'* represents the $1,000 budget line when the price of tea is $1.00 per pound. (Notice that a lower price of tea moves the budget line farther out along the *x*-axis. This is because if the consumer spent his whole income on tea, he would be able to buy more tea at the lower price.) Conversely, *RS''* represents the budget line when the price of tea has increased to $3.00.

As before, the consumer will locate himself at the highest possible indifference curve: at *E'*, when the price is $1.00, and at *E''*, when the price is $3.00. These equilibrium points tell us how much tea the consumer will be demanding at these new prices: *OT'* at $1.00 and *OT''* at $3.00. If we now extend these quantities downward into the bottom half of Figure 18-6 and measure prices on the vertical axis, we will have three points on the consumer demand curve for tea in our hypothetical two-commodity world. Joining the points, we have a consumer demand curve of the familiar downward-sloping variety: the lower the price of tea, the greater the quantity that the consumer will demand.

Now this analysis has been simplified and is not quite complete. If we were going to derive the total consumer demand curve for tea, we would be required to do two further things: (1) expand the analysis so that we included not just butter but all other commodities in our economy,[8] and (2) add together the demand curves for tea of all individual consumers in our economy, so that we had the total consumer demand for tea.

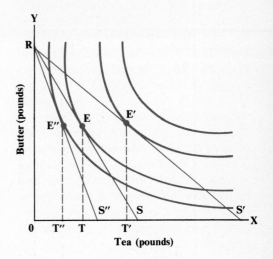

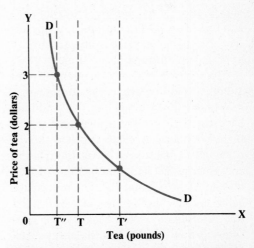

Figure 18-6. Derivation of a Consumer's Demand Curve from His Indifference Map.

What we have done, however, is quite sufficient to show the fundamental relationship between consumer preferences on the one hand and consumer demand on the other. This analysis also makes it possible for us to understand more clearly why it is that the consumer demand curve usually slopes downward from left to right. When the price of a commodity falls, two different things happen. First, the consumer is "richer" in gen-

---

8. The reader will see the general way of doing this if he will imagine that the other commodity in our diagram is not butter but "money" or "general purchasing power." In a multicommodity world, the consumer substitutes tea not just for butter, but for all other possible uses of money that his income allows.

eral, because with the same money income he can now buy more of all commodities; i.e., one price has fallen, and no others have risen. Thus, the "average" cost of living has fallen. Second, the commodity in question is now cheaper *relative* to other commodities. Now both of these effects will cause the consumer to buy more of the given commodity. That is, he will buy more of the given commodity because he is "richer" and thus will be buying more of *all* commodities including this one; and he will also buy more of this commodity because, since it is now *relatively* cheaper, he will be substituting it for other alternative commodities.

Economists usually divide these effects into (1) an *income effect* and (2) a *substitution effect*. Graphically, the effect of a change in price from equilibrium at *E* to equilibrium at *E′* (Figure 18-7) is decomposed into a movement first to a higher indifference curve and then a movement down along the new indifference curve to *E′*. The movement to the higher indifference curve is called the *income effect* because it is as though the consumer in fact had a budget line of *R′S′* instead of the original *RS*. The movement *along* the new indifference curve is called the *substitution effect* because the consumer is now substituting the cheaper tea for butter (or other commodities generally). Since both effects tend to increase the quantity demanded at the lower price, they give us an explanation of why the demand curve almost invariably slopes downward from left to right. This analysis also removes an important limitation on the old marginal utility analysis, for that earlier theory, as we recall, based its demand curve on the assumption that the marginal utility of the consumer's income was constant. This is tantamount to assuming that there is *no* income effect from a price change. With this more general

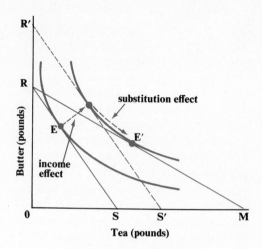

Figure 18-7. Income and Substitution Effects.

When the price of tea falls, the consumer will move from equilibrium at *E* to equilibrium at *E′*. This move can be decomposed into a move to a higher indifference curve equivalent to an increase in the consumer's income (income effect) and a movement down along the new indifference curve as the consumer substitutes tea for butter (the substitution effect).

analysis, we can now deal with all consumer goods and not simply those that are "unimportant" in the consumer's budget.

SUMMARY

In this chapter, we have begun the process of going behind the supply and demand curves for a commodity and rooting these curves in the basic psychological and technological data that are the underpinning of economic life.

In the early days of economics, the British classical economists, such as Smith and Ricardo, sought the key to economic values on the "cost" side. Although they recognized that consumer utility or satisfaction was a necessary element in the value of a commodity, they saw no way of measuring utility, nor could they reconcile a utility approach with the obvious fact that water is both more useful and less expensive than diamonds (the *paradox of value*).

In the latter part of the nineteenth century, one of these problems was solved by the *marginal utility* theory. A number of economists pointed out that the paradox of value could be resolved if we concentrated not on the *total* utility a commodity gave consumers but upon the *marginal* (additional) utility consumers derived from the last unit of the commodity they purchased. The total utility of water is greater than that of diamonds; but because of the great abundance of water, the last unit of water *adds* less to our total utility than an additional diamond.

The marginal utility theory also provided a way of relating a consumer's demand curve for a commodity to the consumer's psychological preferences. Each consumer would maximize his satisfactions by purchasing goods to the point where their price ratio P_1/P_2 was equal to the ratio of their marginal utilities MU_1/MU_2. By arguing that the marginal utility of a commodity for the consumer would diminish as he consumed more and more of it (a reasonable empirical generalization) and by assuming that the marginal utility of money was constant (or, effectively, that the particular commodity in question was unimportant in the consumer's total budget), the marginal utility theorists could construct a consumer demand curve.

This analysis, however, still contained the objectionable notion of a numerically measurable utility. Thus, in the late 1800s and early 1900s, economists turned to a different approach—*indifference curve* analysis—that requires simply that the consumer state whether he "prefers" one set of goods to another or is "indifferent" to a choice between them. In place of the law of diminishing marginal utility, the newer theory stated that there was a *diminishing marginal rate of substitution* as we increased the consumption of one commodity at the expense of the other. In place of the equality of price ratios and ratios of marginal utility, the newer theory said that the consumer would maximize his satisfactions when he obeyed the rule that:

$$\frac{P_n}{P_m} = MRS_{(n \text{ for } m)}$$

where n and m are any two commodities.

Furthermore, indifference curve analysis also permitted the grounding of the consumer demand curve in the basic data of consumer preferences, and this without a numerically measurable utility. It demonstrated that the consumer demand curve will ordinarily slope downward from left to right for two reasons: (1) the "income effect" (as the price of any commodity goes down the consumer will be "richer" and hence will buy more of all commodities in general, including this one); and (2) the "substitution effect" (as the price of the commodity goes down the consumer will substitute this commodity for other commodities along his indifference curve). This analysis, by bringing the income effect into play, also dispensed with the earlier assumption that the commodity in question had to be "unimportant" in the consumer's overall budget.

QUESTIONS FOR DISCUSSION

1. "There is no need to have a marginal utility theory to explain the paradox of

value. Water is less expensive than gold because water is cheaper to produce than gold and that is all that needs to be said about the matter." Discuss.

2. State the condition a consumer must fulfill in his purchases of commodities in order to achieve maximum satisfaction from a given income under (*a*) the marginal utility theory and (*b*) indifference curve analysis. How are these two conditions related?

3. Draw an indifference map for a consumer when the two "commodities" are $5 bills and $1 bills. These "commodities" are perfect substitutes for one another; but now suppose that we are dealing with goods that complement each other—say, flashlight bulbs and flashlight batteries. How might the indifference map look if we have such perfectly complementary goods?

4. Imagine a consumer with a given income buying two commodities, tea and butter. As the price of tea falls, the consumer will ordinarily purchase more tea. Will he also purchase more butter? Less butter? Can't say? Illustrate your answer diagrammatically and explain the logic behind it.

5. A criticism sometimes made of indifference curve analysis is that it presents the consumer's tastes and preferences as independent of the actions of other consumers in the economy. Explain why this criticism must be taken seriously. From your own experience, cite cases in which consumers' tastes have clearly been altered by the behavior of surrounding consumers.

6. Imagine that we have two consumers, A and B, and two commodities, food and books. Suppose the indifference maps are

given as in the diagram below:

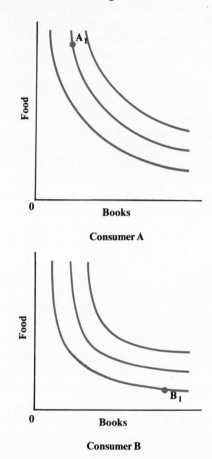

Consumer A

Consumer B

If consumer A is located at point A_1 and consumer B is located at B_1, do you think both could benefit by getting together and exchanging goods? If so, who would exchange what for what, and how long might the exchange continue? Why is it that the initial points A_1 and B_1 could not coexist in equilibrium if the market prices of both commodities were given and each consumer was trying to maximize his satisfactions? Does the reasoning you have followed in answering the above questions seem to you to have any implications concerning economic "efficiency"?

19
Supply and Cost

In the preceding chapter, we located the roots of the demand curve in the basic tastes and preferences of consumers. Now we must look behind the supply curve and perform a similar analysis. We shall do this in two stages. In this chapter, we shall try to show how supply curves in a competitive economy are related to the costs of production expressed in money terms. In the following chapter, we shall relate these money costs to the underlying theory of production. In both chapters, we shall focus special attention on the behavior of the business firm; for in a competitive economy, just as the behavior of the private consumer is central to the operation of demand, so the behavior of the small, private business firm is central to workings of the supply side.

TOTAL COST CURVE
OF THE FIRM

Let us suppose that we have a small business firm producing bicycles,

and that the businessman operating the firm is interested in maximizing profits.[1] He faces the consumer whose purchases of his products will provide him with his sales revenue, and on the other side he faces the costs of producing his particular commodity. The firm's total profits will be equal to the difference between its total revenues and its total costs. By hypothesis, the businessman will "supply" to the market that quantity of bicycles at which his total profit—excess of total revenues over total costs—is at a maximum.

What will his total costs include? Obviously, many different items. They will include the costs of the raw materials or the semifinished goods that he will be manufacturing into final products. They will include his payments to the laborers and professional workers who serve him in his factory. They will include the payments he must make for the rental of land or machinery that he is hiring from individuals or other firms. If the firm owns

1. Whether the managers of business firms in the real world are interested primarily or solely in "maximizing profits" is a question much debated by economists. See pp. 451–53.

its buildings, plant, and equipment, its costs will include the interest charges on the money tied up in the firm's physical capital (whether it was the owner's money or borrowed money makes no real difference). Also, in principle, it will include a payment for the services of the businessman himself. Such payments are sometimes called the *wages of management* or *normal profits,* although *normal profits* may be a misleading term, since these payments do not constitute part of the "pure" profits that the businessman is trying to maximize. If a businessman is to stay in a particular line of production, he must be paid the equivalent of what he could earn elsewhere, and this payment is properly considered a cost.[2] This point, incidentally, will help explain the possibility—which we shall come to in a moment—that competitive firms will continue to operate indefinitely even at *zero* (pure) *profits.*

The nature of the firm's costs will also be influenced by the length of time over which the businessman adjusts to changing conditions. For the moment, let us concentrate completely on the short run. By the term *short run* we mean, in this connection, a period sufficiently short that (*a*) the business firm has no time to alter its basic plant and equipment, its "capacity," and (*b*) there is insufficient time either for this firm to enter another industry or for firms in other industries to enter this one. Thus, we have firms with fixed plant capacity, and there is no exit

from, or entry into, the industry. In the short run, so defined, total costs may be conveniently grouped into two main categories:

(1) **Fixed costs.** These are costs that are incurred by the firm in the short run, *independent* of its level of output. They include, primarily, costs connected with the given "capacity" of the plant: rents paid for land, buildings, and equipment that are fixed by contract; depreciation of plant and machinery, which is independent of whether or not the equipment is being used; certain basic maintenance costs, and the like. Another commonly used term for such costs is *overhead costs.*

(2) **Variable costs.** These are costs that *vary* with the level of output produced. They include the costs of raw materials and semifinished goods and also most labor costs.

In the long run, of course, *all* costs are variable costs: contractual agreements run out; buildings and machinery can wear out, be replaced or expanded; basic plant "capacity" can be allowed to vary. In the short run (our present concern), however, each firm will find itself faced with certain unavoidable expenses even at zero output; after that, total costs will expand with output as variable costs are incurred.

These two categories of cost are displayed in Figure 19-1. The fixed costs of this particular firm in the bicycle industry are shown by a horizontal line that intercepts the y-axis at A. When the firm is producing zero output, its fixed costs will be OA, or $6,000; and, by definition, they remain OA at all levels of bicycle output. Variable costs, as we would expect, increase as the level of output increases. They are measured by the distance between the total cost curve and the

2. This kind of cost is sometimes called an *opportunity cost.* Similarly, if a businessman has invested his own money in his firm (instead of borrowing it), he must charge the firm interest on his money, as a cost (even though there is no actual outpayment of interest money), because opportunity cost is involved. Indeed, the concept of opportunity cost—meaning that the cost of anything is the alternative one must forego to secure it—is really applicable to economic phenomena in a quite general sense. For example, it underlies our whole concept of the production possibility curve (chapter 1, pp. 16-17).

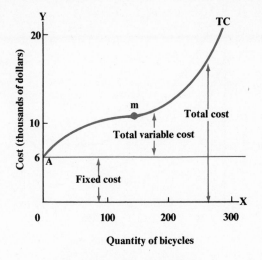

Figure 19-1. A Bicycle Firm's Total Cost Curve.

The firm producing bicycles or any other product is characteristically faced with a total cost curve like *TC*. It is composed of two main elements: (1) fixed costs and (2) total variable cost.

fixed cost line. At zero output, variable costs are zero (all costs are "fixed"); they rise to the northeast with increasing output.

We have drawn the total variable cost curve so that it rises in a rather special way—it increases at a diminishing rate until point *m* and then begins to increase at an increasing rate. This particular shape ultimately reflects the law of diminishing returns. At the beginning we are adding very small quantities of variable inputs— labor and raw materials—to our given set of buildings, machinery, and equipment; as we add more of these variable inputs, we begin to approach the natural capacity of our plant; as we add still more variable inputs, we begin to reach and go beyond the natural capacity of the plant, and it becomes more and more difficult to expand output. These facts are naturally reflected in our variable costs: they increase

less rapidly than output as we move toward the natural "capacity" of the plant and increase more rapidly thereafter.

With the total cost curve—and its components of fixed and variable cost— we have all the information on the cost side that we need to demonstrate the short run equilibrium of the purely competitive firm. However, it is convenient for some purposes to present this same data in an alternative form. The cost curves that we develop in the next section can all be derived from the total cost curve and its two components.[3]

AVERAGE AND MARGINAL COSTS

The new curves are those of *average total cost* (*AC*), *average variable cost* (*AVC*), and *marginal cost* (*MC*). Defining each of these concepts in words and symbols, we have:

(1) **Average total cost** at a particular level of output (*Q*) is equal to total cost divided by output, or:

$$AC = \frac{TC}{Q}$$

(2) **Average variable cost** at a particular level of output is equal to total variable cost divided by output, or:

$$AVC = \frac{TVC}{Q}$$

(3) **Marginal cost** is the *addition* to total cost occasioned by the production of one more unit of output.[4] We can use

3. See the appendix to this chapter for these derivations.
4. The reader should notice the similarity of this definition to that of the other "marginal" terms we have used, for example, *marginal utility* (p 433). In both cases, "marginal" refers to an addition to a total of something: previously "total utility," now "total cost."

the Greek symbol Δ, delta, to indicate a "small change" in any quantity. If a small increase in output (ΔQ) leads to a certain increase in total cost (ΔTC), then we can think of *marginal cost* as:

$$MC = \frac{\Delta TC}{\Delta Q}$$

Or, more specifically, where the small increase in output (ΔQ) is one unit:

$$MC = \frac{\Delta TC}{1}$$

Relationships among the Curves

In Figure 19-2, we have brought these three curves together in a single diagram. Let us look at the important characteristics and relationships of these cost curves and give a brief word of explanation about each.

(1) *Average cost, average variable cost, and marginal cost curves are all characteristically* U-*shaped—i.e., they are high at the beginning, fall to a minimum as output is increased, and then begin to rise again as output is increased still further.*

REASON: The basic *economic* reason is that, in the short run, with a fixed plant capacity, the cost per unit of output or the additional cost of units of output tend to be high at the beginning when we are underutilizing our plant, fall to a minimum as we approach the more effective utilization of our plant, and rise as we begin to press output beyond the normal plant capacity.

(2) *The average variable cost curve will always lie below the average total cost curve when there are any fixed costs.*

REASON: Average total cost at any output includes the average variable cost at that output *plus* average fixed cost.

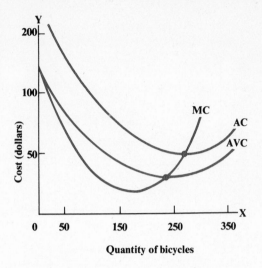

Figure 19-2. Average Total Cost, Average Variable Cost, and Marginal Cost Curves.

(3) *As output is increased, the average variable cost curve will approach closer and closer to the average total cost curve (though never reaching it, as explained in point 2).*

REASON: The difference between average total cost and average variable cost at any output, as just explained, is *average fixed cost.* Average fixed cost is defined as total fixed cost divided by the number of units of output. Total fixed cost is, by definition, a constant, independent of the number of units of output produced. As output increases, average fixed cost decreases. If the total fixed cost is $6,000, at 100 units of output the average fixed cost is $60; at 200 units of output, it is $30; at 1,000 units, it is $6. Since average fixed cost is declining as output increases, the difference between average total cost and average variable cost is diminishing.

(4) *Average variable cost reaches a minimum at a lower level of output than average total cost does.*

REASON: To say that average variable cost reaches a minimum before average total cost is to say, in effect, that when average variable cost is at a minimum, average total cost will *still be falling*. But this must be true, because the difference between these two curves is average fixed cost, and average fixed cost is *always* falling as output increases (point 3, above). It is only when average variable cost begins to rise, and when this rise just exactly counterbalances the fall in average fixed cost, that average total cost will be at a minimum. This, of course, will occur at a level of output higher than that of minimum *AVC*.

(5) *Marginal cost and average variable cost will be equal at the level of one unit of output.*

REASON: Marginal cost is the addition to total cost of producing one more unit of output. The addition to total cost of producing the *first* unit of output is the *total* variable cost, and the total variable cost of *one* unit of output is the same as the *average* variable cost. The economic importance of this point is that it brings home the significant fact that fixed costs have *nothing to do with marginal costs*. Fixed costs, so to speak, are already "there"; marginal cost is concerned with *additions* to total cost as we produce more output.

(6) *The marginal cost curve will lie* below *the average total cost curve when* AC *is falling and* above *it when* AC *is rising. It will* intersect *the* AC *curve at the minimum* point of AC. *The same can also be said of marginal cost in relation to average variable cost* (AVC).

REASON: This is a quite important point in terms of its economic conse-

quences, as we shall see presently. The logic involved applies to all *marginal* and *average* quantities and is essentially this: In order for an *additional* unit of anything to bring up an *average* it must itself be *above* average. Conversely, for an additional unit to *bring down* an average, it must be *below* average. Only when the additional unit is *equal* to the average will the average neither rise nor fall—i.e., be constant. Consider the following example: suppose an eleventh student walks into a class of ten students where the average I.Q. previously was 115. Suppose that with the eleventh student, the average I.Q. of the class now rises to 117. Is the I.Q. of the additional student above or below 115? Suppose the average I.Q. of the class falls to 112? Suppose it remains the same at exactly 115? An identical principle applies in the case of *marginal* (additional) cost and *average* (whether variable or total) cost. If average cost is rising, marginal cost must be above it to pull it up; if average cost is falling, marginal cost must be below it to pull it down; if average cost is neither rising nor falling (i.e., is exactly at its minimum), marginal cost must be equal to it.

Note carefully that what we have just said is *not* equivalent to the following statement: when marginal cost is *rising*, it must be above average cost. This is untrue. You should show that it is untrue in our diagram (Figure 19-2) and explain to yourself how this statement differs from our point 6.

REDEFINITION OF THE PURELY COMPETITIVE FIRM

To recapitulate our position: we are trying in this chapter to get behind the supply curve in a purely competitive market. We have focused on an individual business firm—a producer of bicycles—and we have said that this firm will operate on the principle of maximizing its profits. Profits were defined as the difference between the firm's total revenue and its total cost (including wages of management). We have now analyzed the different components and categories of cost, but we have so far said nothing about the revenue side.

In order to analyze the firm's revenue situation, we must now give a somewhat more formal definition of *pure competition* than we have used in the past. The basic idea of pure competition—the idea that is implicit in the very notion of a supply curve—is that the firm does not control prices or markets but essentially *responds to* price conditions as determined *by the market*. The supply curve, we recall, asks the individual producer not what price he will *set* for his product, but what quantity of the commodity he will offer for sale at various *given* prices.

We could phrase this idea by saying, as we have before, that this kind of business firm is a price-*taker* rather than a price-*setter*. The firm is so small in relation to the overall market (he may be one out of 30,000 bicycle producers) that he has no control whatsoever over the price of his product. He simply has to take whatever price is set in the market and make the best of it.[5]

Let us express this notion graphically and then relate it to the overall consumer demand for the commodity in question.

We define a *purely competitive* firm as follows:

Pure competition will exist in a given market when the individual firms that make up the market are so small that each faces a horizontal (perfectly elastic)[6] demand curve for its output. Such a demand curve (as shown in Figure 19-3) means that the individual firm cannot raise its price above the market level and still sell any output at all. It also means that the firm is so small that even if it doubled or tripled its output (or conversely dropped out of the market altogether) its individual impact on the industry-wide price of the commodity would be negligible. Another way of saying this is that the individual firm can sell all it reasonably can produce without causing any fall in the market price. Consequently, it has no motive to lower its price below the market level.

In short, the purely competitive firm simply takes the price as *given*. When he tries to maximize his profits, he does so solely by adjusting the quantity he produces in the light of a price over which he has no control.

But how is this perfectly horizontal demand curve for the individual bicycle producer to be related to the overall consumer demand curve for bicycles in the economy as a whole? After all, we spent considerable time in the last chapter showing why the consumer demand curve for a given product will be downward-sloping from left to right.

The answer that a wise man might give to this question is that, in truth, the demand curve facing the individual purely

---

5. Of course, it could not be true that the firm has literally *no* control over the price of his product: he could always *lower* the price beneath the market price if he so chose. What this analysis says really is: (*a*) that he cannot raise the price above the market price without losing all his customers; and (*b*) he has no motive to lower the price, since he can sell all he is capable of producing at the going market price.

6. Our definition of price elasticity of demand (p. 102) was percentage change in quantity demanded divided by the percentage change in price. As the demand curve gets flatter and flatter, elasticity gets larger and larger until, with a horizontal demand curve, it becomes *infinitely* (or *perfectly*) elastic.

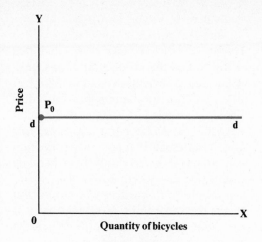

Figure 19-3.

In true pure competition, an individual producer has no control over the price of his product. This fact is expressed in the form of a horizontal (infinitely elastic) demand curve, which is the way the market appears to this small competitive firm.

competitive firm does slope downward, but so very slightly that, for practical purposes, the firm can and does ignore it. What we are, in effect, dealing with in the firm's demand curve is a tiny dot on the overall industry demand curve for bicycles. Our firm produces 300 bicycles. In the economy as a whole, 9 million bicycles are being produced. If this firm goes out of business (and produces zero bicycles) or if it trebles its output (to 900 bicycles), will it have any effect on the overall price of bicycles in the economy? Well, yes—a mini-minuscule effect. Will the owner calculate on that effect in making his decision as to whether to stop producing or to expand production threefold? Certainly not. The effect is so small that it would not be worth the time spent calculating it.

The preceding paragraph brings out what is in many ways the central paradox of the theory of pure competition. Individual firms believe and act as though they had no effect on prices; and yet when

all firms happen to act in a certain way, then the collective effect is to change and indeed to help determine what the price will be. Thus, the firms do affect prices but each feels that it is being governed by an external and impersonal market.

SHORT-RUN EQUILIBRIUM OF THE COMPETITIVE FIRM

We now need to take only one more step, and then we shall be in a position to show how an individual firm's supply curve in the short run is related to its costs. This step is to show how the firm determines the quantity of output at which its profits will be at a maximum. This is the problem of the short-run equilibrium of the competitive firm.

In Figure 19-4, we have brought together the whole of the analysis of this chapter, so far, in one diagram. We have set out our individual firm's average cost, average variable cost, and marginal cost curves. We have then superimposed on these cost curves the consumer demand curve for bicycles as it appears to this small firm; i.e., a horizontal line at the given price, P_0. The question is: at what output will this firm be maximizing its profits?

Let us give the answer first and then state the reasons behind it.

In pure competition, each individual firm will be maximizing its profits when it produces at that output where its marginal cost is equal to market price, or, in symbols, where $P = MC$.

In Figure 19-4, this particular bicycle producer will be maximizing profits when it is producing the output OQ_0.

Why? To understand this conclu-

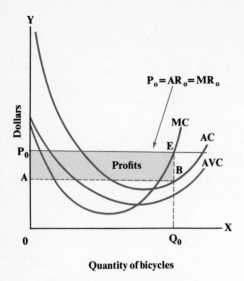

Quantity of bicycles

Figure 19-4. Short Run Profit Maximization for the Competitive Firm.

The competitive firm will maximize profits at that output where price = marginal cost. In pure competition, this follows from the fact that price is taken as given by the individual producer. This means, in turn, that price = marginal revenue. And the general condition for profit maximization is $MR = MC$.

sion, let us look at each term, MC and P, separately. MC, we know, measures the additional cost of producing one more unit of output. Now if the firm is interested in maximizing profits, it will have to make sure as it produces more and more units of output that each unit brings in at least as much additional revenue as it does additional cost. If a firm is producing 1,000 bicycles, should it produce 1,001 bicycles? If the additional revenue brought in by the 1,001st bicycle is greater than MC, then it will be profitable to do so. If, by contrast, the additional revenue of the 1,001st unit is below MC, then the added production will reduce profits, and the firm will not undertake it. To say that a firm is maximizing its profits, then, is

equivalent to saying that it will produce all units of output as long as the added revenue of each is above MC and that it will forego the production of any units if the added revenue is below MC.

What happens when the additional revenue is just *equal* to MC? Actually, this particular point is the dividing line. It represents that point where the firm can no longer *add* to profits by expanding production and where any further expansion of production will *reduce* profits. But this is the same thing as saying that it is the point of *maximum* profits. When the additional revenue is just equal to MC, the firm, under ordinary circumstances, will have squeezed out the last penny of profit possible.

The term economists use for this additional revenue is, as we might expect, *marginal revenue.*

Marginal revenue is the addition to total revenue the firm receives from selling one more unit of output.

Our conclusion about profit maximization, then, can be restated as follows:

The individual firm will be maximizing its profits when its marginal revenue is just equal to its marginal cost. Or, in symbols, when $MR = MC$.

Actually, this conclusion applies to imperfectly competitive as well as purely competitive firms, but our interest, for the time being, is solely with the latter.[7]

We now seem to have *two* conditions that our purely competitive firm

---

7. The condition $MR = MC$ is applied to the analysis of imperfectly competitive markets in chapter 24. It should be noted that this condition assures the firm maximum profits as long as MC is rising and MR is falling or constant as more units of output are produced. When MC is falling (as at the very beginning of the marginal cost curve), $MC = MR$ could actually mean *minimum* profits.

must fulfill in order to maximize profits: the first, that $P = MC$; the second, that $MR = MC$. When we look more closely at the term P, however, these two conditions turn out to be the same for the competitive firm. Price is related to revenue in a competitive market by the simple rule that the total revenue received by a firm is equal to the price of its product times the number of units of output it sells: $TR = P \times Q$. This is equivalent to saying that price is the same thing as *average revenue*, or

$$P = AR = \frac{TR}{Q}$$

But what about *marginal* revenue? Now here we come to a special feature of the purely competitive firm. Since its price is given (independent of the level of the firm's sales), its average revenue from sales is always equal to its marginal revenue, or $AR = MR$. This would not be the case if the price of the product fell as more units were sold, because then average revenue would be falling and marginal revenue would have to be below average revenue (remember point 6 from the previous section). But since in pure competition, price is taken by the firm as given, we have

$$P = \frac{TR}{Q} = AR = MR$$

Thus, in a purely competitive market, the condition that $MR = MC$ (the condition for maximizing profits) implies that $P = MC$. When the competitive firm produces up to the point where its marginal cost equals the given market price, it is, in fact, squeezing out the last penny of profit available to it.

To demonstrate to yourself that this conclusion applies in our diagram Figure 19-4, inspect what happens to the prof-

its of this particular bicycle producer when he deviates from the maximum profit output of OQ_0. Total profits in this diagram can be read off by means of rectangles such as the rectangle P_0EBA. That is: Total profits = Total revenue − Total costs = $(P \times Q) - (AC \times Q)$. If you will examine what happens to such a rectangle at higher and lower outputs, you will find that, in each case, it is smaller in size than the rectangle at output OQ_0.

One final caution: notice that the short-run profit maximization position of the firm is not necessarily (or characteristically) at the point where the difference between AR (or P) and AC (average total cost) is the greatest. This point defines the output where profit *per unit* is greatest. But what the firm is interested in is not per unit profits but *total* profits. In Figure 19-4, the firm will be producing at an output greater than that where per unit profits are highest, the reason being that the expansion of sales more than makes up for the slightly lower profit per unit at the higher quantity.

THE SHORT-RUN SUPPLY CURVE FOR THE FIRM

In analyzing the equilibrium of the competitive firm, we have really solved our problem of the firm's short-run supply curve. In the preceding section, we asked, in effect: what quantity of output will the competitive firm produce at a given price (P_0)? This is nothing but the standard question we ask any producer when we want to construct a supply curve for him. If we repeat the same question for all possible prices, we shall have that curve laid out before us.

In doing so, moreover, we will notice an interesting thing—that we do not need to draw any *new* curve at all; i.e., that the supply curve is already present in our diagram. The reason for this is quite simply that when we ask the firm what output it will produce at any price it will characteristically answer: the output where price equals marginal cost.[8] The firm's supply curve is thus *nothing but a segment of its* MC *curve.*

This statement needs slight amplification, because the individual firm, even in the short run, always has the option of producing no output at all. In Figure 19-5, the heavy line represents the firm's supply curve. We notice that the line travels up the *y*-axis until the price P_1 is reached; then it jumps over to the marginal cost curve and follows the MC curve upward indefinitely. The point is that when the market price is below P_1, the firm is better off producing no output at all. This is because at these very low prices, it is not covering its *variable* costs. When the price is below average variable cost (*AVC*), the firm does best simply to stand idle and suffer the losses due to fixed costs. If it produces any output, it will be losing money *additional* to its fixed costs. Once price rises above P_1 (is above average variable cost), however, the firm will do better to produce at the level where $P = MC$. Mind you, if the price is low—if it is above *AVC* but below *AC*—there will still be losses; however, since the price more than covers variable costs, losses will be smaller than if the firm stood idle. It will be making *something* toward covering its unavoidable (in the short run) fixed costs.

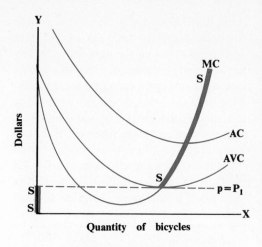

Figure 19-5. The Competitive Firm's Short-Run Supply Curve.

The competitive firm's short-run supply curve is nothing but a segment of its marginal cost curve (i.e., that segment lying above average variable costs). If the market-given price is below the minimum *AVC*, the firm will stop supplying output, even in the short run.

Summarizing, then,

In the short run, the supply curve of the purely competitive firm will be the segment of the firm's MC curve that lies above its AVC curve. At prices below AVC, the firm will supply zero output to the market.

When it is operating along such a supply curve, the competitive firm will be maximizing profits or (when price is below average total cost but above average variable cost), minimizing losses. In either case, the producer is doing the best he can, economically, in the situation he faces.

INDUSTRY SUPPLY AND THE LONG RUN

So far, we have been considering the supply curve of the individual firm

---

8. In real life, some business firms might object to this statement, saying, in effect, that they do not use the term "marginal cost" and would not recognize it if they saw it. However, such a comment cannot be taken at face value. If you ask a competitive firm whether it could alter its output and make more money, and if the firm said "no," then that firm is producing at $P = MC$, whether the manager has heard of marginal cost or not.

in the short run. But what happens when we consider the firm in the long run? And what are the consequences when we have not one firm, but a whole industry of firms expanding and contracting production simultaneously? We will complete the analysis of this chapter by considering these problems of industry supply in the long run.

Fundamentally, the shift from short run to long run and from firm to industry involves three major alterations in our analysis: (1) the firm has more flexibility in its productive operations, and therefore its cost curves are altered; (2) since firms have time enough to enter and leave different industries, no firms will be able to enjoy "abnormal profits" in the long run; and (3) the expansion and contraction of production in the industry as a whole will cause changes in the prices of the basic factors of production, leading to upward or downward shifts in the cost curves of each individual firm.

Let us comment briefly on each of these important points.

1. Costs in the Long Run

Earlier, we defined the *short run* as a period of time so short that each firm in the industry was saddled with a certain plant or productive capacity and that no firms could enter or leave the industry. Now when we move to the *long run,* one of the first things that changes is that the firm is no longer bound to any particular plant size. It can construct new factories, buy new machinery, enter into new contractual arrangements; or conversely, it can contract its operations, allow plant and machinery to depreciate without replacement, reduce its office staff, cut down on overhead, and so on. This added flexibility means that in the long run there is really no such thing as fixed costs. All costs are variable costs. It also means that there is

no reason for average costs or marginal costs to rise so steeply when the firm tries to expand its output. In the short run, such expansions of output are operating against the constraint of a given productive capacity. In the long run, the firm is free to adjust its capacity to the higher level of output.

In the next chapter, when we relate costs to the underlying productive apparatus, we can be somewhat more specific about the behavior of a firm's costs in the long run. However, the general relationship of long-run and short-run costs can be shown, as in Figure 19-6. The added flexibility of varying plant capacity means that the long-run average cost curve (LAC) is much flatter than the various short-run average cost curves (SAC_1, SAC_2, etc.), each of which represents a given plant capacity.

A similar alteration will affect the firm's MC curve. What this means is that the firm's supply curve in the long run will be more *elastic* than it is in the short run. Because firms can adjust their basic capacity, a change in market demand will produce a greater supply response in the long run than in the short run.

2. Entry of New Firms

Another important feature of the long run is the possibility that additional firms may enter (or leave) a particular industry. Free entry is an important component of the common-sense use of the term *competition,* and, indeed, it has a very significant long-run consequence.

If we look back at Figure 19-4, we can notice that we represented the firm as being in short-run equilibrium at OQ_0 and thus in a position to enjoy pure profits equal to the area of the shaded rectangle. These pure profits are *in addition to* what we earlier called *normal profits* or *wages of management* or essentially what the

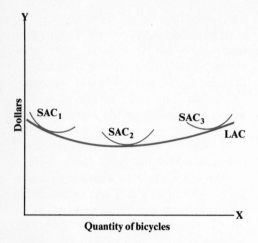

Figure 19-6. Relationship of Long-Run Average Cost (*LAC*) to Short-Run Average Cost Curves (*SAC*₁,*SAC*₂,etc.).

owners of this firm could have made in some alternative employment. Now the moment we move to the long run and allow free entry (and exit) of firms, such abnormal profits must disappear. For the existence of such pure profits is a beacon signaling producers in other industries to enter bicycle production and share the wealth. If the firm were burdened with losses, they would be a signal for firms to leave the industry.

The consequence of large numbers of new firms entering the bicycle industry will be a great expansion of bicycle output and, in turn, because of the downward-sloping consumer demand curve, a reduction in the price of bicycles. Thus, the short-run equilibrium position described in Figure 19-4 could not maintain itself in the long run. If all firms in the bicycle industry are making profits comparable to those shown in Figure 19-4, then firms from other industries will quickly be attracted into bicycle production. As bicycle production expands with this influx of firms, the market price will begin to fall below the original level P_0.

It will continue falling, indeed, until there are no longer abnormal profits in bicycle production, or to the point where price is equal to average total cost ($P = AC$).

This long-run equilibrium for the firm is shown in Figure 19-7. The price has been driven down by the entry of new firms until it is exactly equal to average total cost. The firm is enjoying normal profits but no pure profit. Long-run equilibrium price will be P_e and long-run equilibrium quantity will be OQ_e. At this output, $P = MC = AC$.

Now notice an interesting thing. The firm that in short-run equilibrium (Figure 19-4) was producing at rising average cost is now, in long-run equilibrium, producing at *minimum average cost*. It is operating at the very bottom of its U-shaped cost curve, and this will be true of all firms in the industry.

This is an important point, because *costs* in a market economy ultimately reflect the basic resources and factors of production required to produce the commodity. And what we have shown is that in pure competition, business firms will be producing at the lowest average cost—implicitly the least use of resources—per unit of the commodity in question. This is one of our first concrete examples of the meaning of *efficiency* in a competitive economy, and a rather striking illustration of what Adam Smith sensed intuitively when he spoke of the beneficent "invisible hand."

3. Industry Supply in the Long Run

With the foregoing consideration of the entry of new firms into an industry, we have entered the area of the supply curve for an industry as a whole. It is one thing for a particular firm to expand its output along its *MC* curve in response to different market prices. But what happens when all firms expand simulta-

sponse to any "pure" profits (i.e., profits above the "wages of management" included in the cost curves). What this means is that the individual firm will not be able to enjoy persistent "pure" profits in the long run in pure competition. The entry of other firms will drive the industry-wide price of the product down until a zero profit equilibrium has been achieved for each firm. Such an equilibrium in pure competition will be characterized by the fact that each firm will be producing where $P = MC = AC$. This will be at the minimum point of the AC curve. This conclusion suggests why pure competition is often described as an "efficient" market structure. Minimizing average costs per unit of output ultimately means (subject to later qualifications) minimizing the use of scarce resources to produce the commodity in question.

(3) The possibility of firms entering and leaving the industry in the long run means that the industry-wide supply curve will be more elastic than if there were a fixed number of firms in the industry. The question is then raised: Is there any reason why the long-run industry supply curve should have any upward slope at all? The answer (to be elaborated further in the next chapter) is that it may not do so—it could, for example, be perfectly horizontal—but that ordinarily it will have at least a gentle upward slope because the expansion of the industry will normally cause some rise in the average price of the factors of production employed in that industry.

QUESTIONS FOR DISCUSSION

1. "The theory of pure competition is completely bogus. It assumes that firms

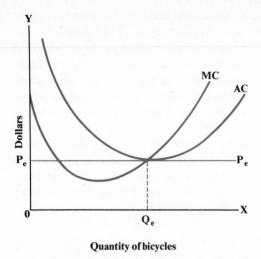

Figure 19-7. Long-Run Equilibrium of the Competitive Firm.

With free entry of other firms in the long run, abnormal profits disappear for the competitive firms, and long-run equilibrium is established where $P = AC (=MC)$. Note that AC is at a minimum at this equilibrium. This is one reason why economists speak of the *efficiency* of a purely competitive economy.

neously and when, moreover, new firms are free to enter the industry at the least sign of higher profits? This raises the question of the shape of the long-run supply curve for the bicycle industry as a whole.

The question may be put this way: is there really any reason to suppose that the long-run industry supply curve for bicycles will slope upward at all? May it not simply be a horizontal straight line? (Or, for that matter, may it not slope downward from left to right rather like a demand curve?)

These problems did not arise seriously in the short run because (*a*) the fixed plant and equipment of the firm guaranteed us a marginal cost curve that would rise as we pressed against capacity, and (*b*) we ruled out the possibility of other firms entering the industry. In the long

run, average and marginal costs as we have seen tend to become "flatter" (Figure 19-6). But even if they do ultimately curve upward,[9] we still have the problem of free entry. If additional firms are free to enter the industry and if their cost curves are identical, or very similar, to those of the firms already in the industry, then why should the long-run supply curve slope upward? The industry will expand its output not by each firm moving up its MC curve but rather by the addition of new firms to the industry, each of which will be producing at the same MC = minimum AC as the firms already there. The marginal cost of industry expansion will be constant.

Now the truth is that this may, in fact, happen. We have already said that the supply curve will be more *elastic* in the long run than in the short run. The possibility exists that it may be *infinitely elastic*—i.e., a horizontal straight line.

Although this is a *possible* case, it is not the characteristic case. The general reason for expecting the long-run supply curve of an industry to rise as output expands is that this expansion of the industry will generally cause a rise in the average price of the factors of production employed by that industry. The main reason for this rise in the prices of factors of production, in turn, is that the production of bicycles (or of any other commodity) does not use either the same kinds of factors of production or the same proportions of factors of production as do all other commodities. When production in the economy as a whole shifts from other com-

9. In the next chapter, we shall discuss the conditions under which they will or will not curve upward. It should be noted in advance that long-run average cost and marginal cost for a firm can, indeed, sometimes *not* curve upward—i.e., they may continue to fall as output increases. When this happens, we cannot have a purely competitive market; we have a *natural monopoly*. See p. 471.

modities in the direction of prod
more bicycles, this creates particula
mand pressure on the factors pecu
or heavily used in bicycle produ
Thus, the costs of producing bicycl
likely to go up.

Incidentally, we have really
this problem before in a less technica
in chapter 17, when we talked about
in demand from agricultural to mai
tured products. Further analysis
however, must await our analysis of
in relation to production, the subj
our next chapter.

SUMMARY

The main purpose of this cl
was to take the first major step in
"behind" the competitive supply cu
relating supply to cost in a money
In undertaking this task, we encou
the following cost and revenue co
for the individual firm:

Total cost	**Average cost**
Total fixed cost	**Average varial**
Total variable cost	**Marginal cost**

Total revenue
Average revenue
Marginal revenue

Be certain that you can define ea
these concepts exactly and that yo
derstand the various interrelation
among them.

Given these cost concepts,
cussed our attention first on the s
curve for an individual purely comp
firm in the short run. A *purely comp
firm* is defined as a firm so small i
tion to the overall market that it tak
price of the commodity as "give
other words, its own contribution t
industry production of the commo

much money for the firm as I can, but
I certainly don't make marginal revenue
equal marginal cost. In fact, I've never
even heard of those terms."

Discuss this hypothetical (but not uncommon) expression of sentiment about the
value of microeconomic theory.

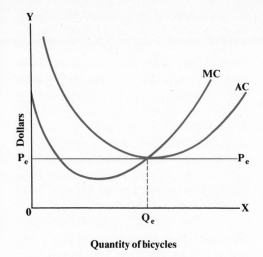

Figure 19-7. Long-Run Equilibrium of the Competitive Firm.

With free entry of other firms in the long run, abnormal profits disappear for the competitive firms, and long-run equilibrium is established where $P=AC\ (=MC)$. Note that AC is at a minimum at this equilibrium. This is one reason why economists speak of the *efficiency* of a purely competitive economy.

neously and when, moreover, new firms are free to enter the industry at the least sign of higher profits? This raises the question of the shape of the long-run supply curve for the bicycle industry as a whole.

The question may be put this way: is there really any reason to suppose that the long-run industry supply curve for bicycles will slope upward at all? May it not simply be a horizontal straight line? (Or, for that matter, may it not slope downward from left to right rather like a demand curve?)

These problems did not arise seriously in the short run because (*a*) the fixed plant and equipment of the firm guaranteed us a marginal cost curve that would rise as we pressed against capacity, and (*b*) we ruled out the possibility of other firms entering the industry. In the long

run, average and marginal costs as we have seen tend to become "flatter" (Figure 19-6). But even if they do ultimately curve upward,[9] we still have the problem of free entry. If additional firms are free to enter the industry and if their cost curves are identical, or very similar, to those of the firms already in the industry, then why should the long-run supply curve slope upward? The industry will expand its output not by each firm moving up its *MC* curve but rather by the addition of new firms to the industry, each of which will be producing at the same *MC* = minimum *AC* as the firms already there. The marginal cost of industry expansion will be constant.

Now the truth is that this may, in fact, happen. We have already said that the supply curve will be more *elastic* in the long run than in the short run. The possibility exists that it may be *infinitely elastic*—i.e., a horizontal straight line.

Although this is a *possible* case, it is not the characteristic case. The general reason for expecting the long-run supply curve of an industry to rise as output expands is that this expansion of the industry will generally cause a rise in the average price of the factors of production employed by that industry. The main reason for this rise in the prices of factors of production, in turn, is that the production of bicycles (or of any other commodity) does not use either the same kinds of factors of production or the same proportions of factors of production as do all other commodities. When production in the economy as a whole shifts from other com-

---

9. In the next chapter, we shall discuss the conditions under which they will or will not curve upward. It should be noted in advance that long-run average cost and marginal cost for a firm can, indeed, sometimes *not* curve upward—i.e., they may continue to fall as output increases. When this happens, we cannot have a purely competitive market; we have a *natural monopoly*. See p. 471.

modities in the direction of producing more bicycles, this creates particular demand pressure on the factors peculiarly or heavily used in bicycle production. Thus, the costs of producing bicycles are likely to go up.

Incidentally, we have really faced this problem before in a less technical way in chapter 17, when we talked about shifts in demand from agricultural to manufactured products. Further analysis now, however, must await our analysis of costs in relation to production, the subject of our next chapter.

SUMMARY

The main purpose of this chapter was to take the first major step in going "behind" the competitive supply curve by relating supply to cost in a money sense. In undertaking this task, we encountered the following cost and revenue concepts for the individual firm:

Total cost	Average cost
Total fixed cost	Average variable cost
Total variable cost	Marginal cost
	Total revenue
	Average revenue
	Marginal revenue

Be certain that you can define each of these concepts exactly and that you understand the various interrelationships among them.

Given these cost concepts, we focussed our attention first on the supply curve for an individual purely competitive firm in the short run. A *purely competitive firm* is defined as a firm so small in relation to the overall market that it takes the price of the commodity as "given." In other words, its own contribution to total industry production of the commodity is

so negligible that any conceivable expansion or contraction of its output would have a minimal effect on price, an effect the firm would be likely to ignore. Technically, this means that the purely competitive firm faces an infinitely (or perfectly) elastic demand curve for its product; i.e., a horizontal straight line at the going market price. *Short run* is defined as a period so short that there is no time (1) for the firm in question to alter its basic plant capacity nor (2) for firms to leave or enter the industry.

Our conclusion in this first case was that the purely competitive firm's supply curve in the short run would be a segment of its marginal cost curve; namely, that part of its marginal cost curve lying above its average variable cost curve (at lower prices, the firm "supplying" zero output). This conclusion followed from a previous conclusion that the purely competitive firm would ordinarily maximize its profits (or minimize its losses) by producing at an output where $P = MC$. This conclusion in turn derived from two considerations: (1) firms in general will maximize profits where $MR = MC$; and (2) in the specific case of pure competition, since $P (= AR)$ is given, it will be true that $MR = AR = P$.

We then turned to the questions of long run and industry supply. Three main points were established:

(1) In the long run, the individual firm will be able to adjust its plant capacity to different levels of output: there are no "fixed costs" in the long run. This means that the individual firm's cost curves (average and marginal) will be "flatter" in the long run than in the short run. Accordingly, the firm's supply curve will tend to be more elastic in the long run.

(2) In the long run, other firms will be free to enter the industry in re-

sponse to any "pure" profits (i.e., profits above the "wages of management" included in the cost curves). What this means is that the individual firm will not be able to enjoy persistent "pure" profits in the long run in pure competition. The entry of other firms will drive the industry-wide price of the product down until a zero profit equilibrium has been achieved for each firm. Such an equilibrium in pure competition will be characterized by the fact that each firm will be producing where $P = MC = AC$. This will be at the minimum point of the AC curve. This conclusion suggests why pure competition is often described as an "efficient" market structure. Minimizing average costs per unit of output ultimately means (subject to later qualifications) minimizing the use of scarce resources to produce the commodity in question.

(3) The possibility of firms entering and leaving the industry in the long run means that the industry-wide supply curve will be more elastic than if there were a fixed number of firms in the industry. The question is then raised: Is there any reason why the long-run industry supply curve should have any upward slope at all? The answer (to be elaborated further in the next chapter) is that it may not do so—it could, for example, be perfectly horizontal—but that ordinarily it will have at least a gentle upward slope because the expansion of the industry will normally cause some rise in the average price of the factors of production employed in that industry.

QUESTIONS FOR DISCUSSION

1. "The theory of pure competition is completely bogus. It assumes that firms

eager to maximize profits will cavalierly go about destroying each other's profits. Even worse, it ends up with a ridiculous equilibrium in which these profit maximizers are making no profits at all! Clearly, under these circumstances, any intelligent businessman would pull out of the industry altogether."

Give a critical analysis of the above statement.

2. Suppose that the cost curves of all firms in an industry and of all potential entrants into the industry are identical and that the prices of factors of production are unaffected by any expansion or contraction of this industry. Can you show why, under these circumstances, the long-run supply curve in this industry would be a horizontal straight line? Does it bother you that each firm in the industry also faces a horizontal demand curve? How would you determine where the price of the product and the quantity of the product supplied would settle in long-run equilibrium?

3. If there is a sudden increase in consumer demand for a product, it will usually be the case that the price of the product will rise higher and the quantity produced will increase less in the short run than in the long run. Explain the logic behind this statement and use diagrams to show how the process would work.

4. Now that you have a technical definition of pure competition, take a dozen or so consumer goods industries with which you are familiar in the real world and rank them according to the degree of closeness to the competitive model. What factors seem to you primarily responsible for the more extreme departures from the purely competitive market structure?

5. "I'm a businessman producing pencil sharpeners, and I do my best to make as

much money for the firm as I can, but I certainly don't make marginal revenue equal marginal cost. In fact, I've never even heard of those terms."

Discuss this hypothetical (but not uncommon) expression of sentiment about the value of microeconomic theory.

19

Appendix: Geometrical Derivation of Cost Curves

In this appendix for the geometrically minded, we shall derive average total cost, average variable cost, and marginal cost curves from a firm's total cost curves.

Average Total Cost

Average total cost is simply the total cost of a given quantity of output divided by that output; i.e., it is total cost *per unit* of output. Thus, at any level of output in Figure 1(*a*)—say, OQ_1—average total cost will be equal to total cost (TC_1) divided by that output. Or

$$AC_1 = \frac{TC_1}{OQ_1}$$

Similarly,

$$AC_2 = \frac{TC_2}{OQ_2} \, ;$$

$$AC_3 = \frac{TC_3}{OQ_3} \, ; \text{ and so on.}$$

Numerically, we have:

In Figure 1(*b*), we have plotted these points, using the *y*-axis to measure average total cost. If we had carried out the same operation for all possible levels of output, we would have the average cost curve as drawn in the lower half of the diagram.

It should be noticed that the slope of any line drawn from the origin to the total cost curve—say, line OR_1—will be equal to the total cost at that point divided by output; i.e., the slope of OR_1 is equal to $TC_1 \div OQ_1$. But since $TC_1 \div OQ_1$ is nothing but AC_1, we can see that the slope of any such line is exactly equal to average total cost. This is useful to know because it gives us a very simple way of determining whether average total cost is rising or falling. When the slope of this line is decreasing (as, for example, when we move from OR_1 to OR_2), then average cost will be falling. When the slope of the line is increasing (as when we move from OR_2 to OR_3) then the average total cost will be rising. This is shown by the relative positions of points *1*, *2*, and *3* on the average cost curve in Figure 1(*b*).

$$TC_1 = \$10,000; \; OQ_1 = 100 \text{ units; hence, } AC_1 = \$100.00$$
$$TC_2 = \$12,000; \; OQ_2 = 200 \text{ units; hence, } AC_2 = \$ \, 60.00$$
$$TC_3 = \$20,000; \; OQ_3 = 300 \text{ units; hence, } AC_3 = \$ \, 66.67$$

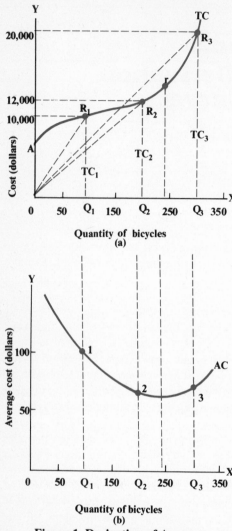

Quantity of bicycles
(a)

Quantity of bicycles
(b)

Figure 1. Derivation of Average Cost from Total Cost.

Average cost at a given output can be found geometrically as the slope of any line (such as OR_1) drawn from the origin to the total cost curve at that output.

To test your understanding of this matter, try now to show why point r on the total cost curve in Figure 1(a) represents that level of total cost and output where average total cost will be at a *minimum*.

Average Variable Cost

The geometrical procedure for deriving average variable cost from the total cost curve is exactly the same as that in the case of the average total cost curve except for *one* difference. This time, instead of drawing our lines from the origin, we draw them from point A on the y-axis. Average variable cost is equal to total *variable* cost divided by output. Hence, it is equal, at output OQ_1, to $TVC_1 \div OQ_1$ ($= AM_1$) in Figure 2(a). The expression $TVC_1 \div OQ_1$ ($= AM_1$) is equal to the slope of a line drawn from the point A to the total cost curve, i.e., the slope of line AR_1. Thus, to determine whether average variable cost is rising or falling, all we need do is to see whether these lines drawn from point A to the total cost curve are becoming steeper or flatter.

Since the procedure is the same as before, with this one difference, you can determine how the points *1*, *2*, and *3* on the average variable cost curve of Figure 2(b) are derived numerically from the total cost curve in Figure 2(a). To test your understanding still further, you should convince yourself that *minimum* average *variable* cost will always be at a lower output than *minimum* average *total* cost (i.e., to the left of point r).

Marginal Cost

The final member of our now rather extensive family of cost curves is the marginal cost curve. Marginal cost, as we recall, tells us the *addition* to total cost as we produce one more unit of output. We used the symbol Δ, delta, to signify a small change; and where the increase in output is one unit, marginal cost became

$$MC = \frac{\Delta TC}{1}$$

This can be shown graphically in relation

462

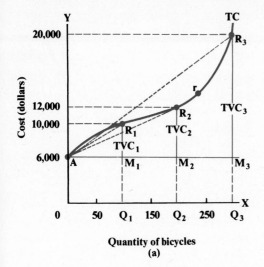

Quantity of bicycles

(a)

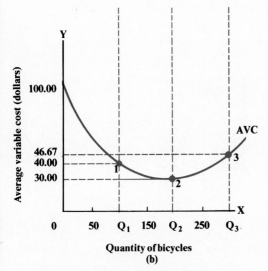

Quantity of bicycles

(b)

**Figure 2. Derivation of Average
Variable Cost from Total Cost Curve.**

**Average variable cost at output Q_1 (= 100)
is equal to TC at that output ($10,000)
minus fixed cost ($6,000) *divided* by that
output. Or,**

$$AVC_1 = \frac{\$10,000 - \$6,000}{100} = \$40.$$

Derive for yourself AVC_2 and AVC_3.

to the total cost curve by a series of small
triangles such as we have drawn in Figure
3(*a*). Actually, these triangles are blown
up slightly, since it would be physically
difficult to see any change in output as
small as one unit. The base of these triangles represents one unit of output (or
would do so, if they were drawn much
smaller), and the height of these triangles
represents the *addition* to total cost occasioned by producing that extra unit of
output. Thus, at output OQ_1, the addition
to total cost is ΔTC_1; at OQ_2, it is ΔTC_2;
and so on. At each level of output, the
additional cost of producing one more unit
of output changes; i.e., ΔTC_1 is greater
than ΔTC_2; ΔTC_2 is less than ΔTC_3, and
so on.

Now these little triangles can be
used (approximately) to measure the slope
of the total cost curve.[1] The slope of the
total cost curve at any output will be
roughly equal to the height of one of these
triangles divided by the base. For example, at output OQ_1, the slope of the total
cost curve will be roughly equal to

$$\frac{\Delta TC_1}{1}$$

Since, by our definition,

$$\text{marginal cost at output } OQ_1 = \frac{\Delta TC_1}{1}$$

this means that marginal cost is really the
same thing as the *slope of the total cost
curve.*

1. In exact terms, the slope of the total cost curve
at any point, p_0, will be equal to the slope of the
tangent to the curve at p_0. As these little triangles
get smaller and smaller, the hypotenuse more and
more closely approximates the tangent at any particular point on the curve. The reader familiar with
calculus will recognize that the exact definition of
marginal cost is $d(TC)/dq$. This point will help explain an earlier comment that marginal analysis in
general readily lends itself to mathematical expression.

Once this point has been demonstrated, we have a quite simple way of seeing from the total cost curve whether marginal cost is rising or falling. If the total cost curve is becoming flatter (the slope is decreasing), then marginal cost is falling. If, on the other hand, the total cost curve is becoming steeper (the slope is increasing), then marginal cost will be rising.

Because we have had to blow up the little triangles to make them visible, we cannot show numerically how one moves from Figure 3(*a*) to Figure 3(*b*). We can, however, show why the marginal cost curve in Figure 3(*b*) is higher at outputs OQ_1 and OQ_3 than it is at output OQ_2. The reason quite simply is that the total cost curve is steeper at both OQ_1 and OQ_3 than it is at OQ_2. When the total cost curve is steeper, marginal cost is higher.

Again, you should test your understanding of this matter. Explain to yourself why the marginal cost curve will be at a *minimum* when we are located at point *m* (the inflection point) on the total cost curve.

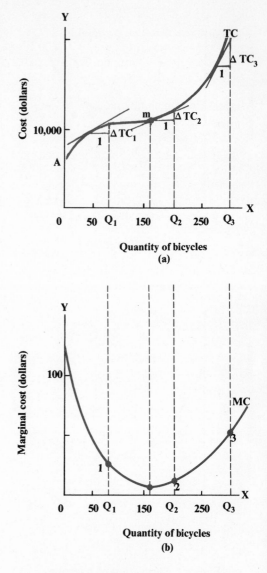

Figure 3.

Marginal cost is measured by the slope of the total cost curve.

EXERCISE

The following exercise will help deepen your understanding of concepts discussed in chapter 19 and the appendix.

(*a*) Draw a total cost curve of characteristic shape for an individual firm in the short run.

(*b*) In the same diagram, draw a total revenue curve for a purely competitive firm such that the firm will be making short-run "pure" profits.

(*c*) How would you measure the "pure" profits the firm is making at any given

level of output in this diagram?

(*d*) Describe how you would measure average revenue and marginal revenue from the total revenue curve you have drawn. Are they equal at every output?

(e) Determine in your diagram the output where the firm is equating marginal revenue and marginal cost. Is this the level of output where "pure" profits as measured in (c) above are at a maximum?

(f) Begin a new diagram by drawing the same short-run total cost curve you drew in (a) above. But now draw in a total cost curve for this firm in the *long run*. (Remember that there are no fixed costs in the long run. Assume, however, that average costs will still be U-shaped—though a somewhat flatter U—in the long run.)

(g) On the assumption that the firm has achieved a zero profit long-run equilibrium, draw in the firm's total revenue curve.

(h) Defining each of the following terms geometrically in your diagram, show that at this long-run equilibrium $P = AR = MR = MC = AC$.

20
Cost, Production, and Two Applications

Having shown the relationship between supply and cost, we must now try to root the concept of cost in the basic facts of production and technology in our economy, much as we rooted the demand curve in the basic preferences of consumers (chapter 18). Ultimately, the concept of "cost" involves not just the laws of production but everything else in the system (including consumer preferences). For the moment, however, we shall hold these more distant relationships in abeyance and concentrate on the analysis of cost as it would appear to a single small business firm. We shall complete the chapter with two applications of supply and demand analysis that will show the extent of the ground we have covered so far.

LAWS OF PRODUCTION— A REMINDER

We return in our analysis to the production function, which we introduced in chapter 17. In that presentation, we spoke of two factors of production, land and labor, cooperating in the production of the commodity wheat. Obviously a similar kind of production function could be devised for bicycles or any other commodity; also, we might be talking about different factors of production—capital, for example, instead of land or labor. Furthermore, since each of these factors of production is really a catch-all for a number of more specific factors (different kinds of labor, machinery, buildings, etc.), we would typically have more than two factors involved in any production process.

Thus, if we used "$f(\ )$" to mean "a function of," the production function might look mathematically like this:

$$q = f(f_1, f_2, f_3 \cdots f_n)$$

where q is the quantity of the commodity produced and f_n is the quantity of the nth factor of production used to produce that commodity. If we were speaking of a production process that used many factors like this, we would clearly have to present it in some form such as the above equa-

467

tion, since, graphically, we are limited to two-factor presentations. Even with two factors, as we know, we are already obliged to use contour lines (our isoquants).

The reader should remind himself of the basic characteristics of production described in that earlier chapter. We discussed: (1) the law of diminishing returns (or, as we rephrased it, the law of diminishing marginal productivity); (2) increasing, constant and decreasing returns to scale; and (3) the convexity of the isoquants. In this last connection, we established the fact that the slope of an individual isoquant would be equal to the ratio of the marginal products of the cooperating factors. We will now use these various pieces of analysis in showing the relationship between our cost curves and the theory of production.

EQUILIBRIUM OF THE COMPETITIVE FIRM

Our situation is this: we know from the last chapter that the supply curve of an individual firm will be a segment of its marginal cost curve. This follows from the fact that in pure competition the individual firm will be maximizing its profits when it produces that level of output where the price of the product (bicycles) is equal to the marginal cost of producing bicycles, $P = MC$. But bicycles can be produced in many different ways, as the production function tells us. Which way will the businessman choose? Only when we have answered this question will we be able to show how the marginal cost of bicycle production at any given output is related to the underlying productive process.

The answer to the question of methods of production can be summarily answered as follows:

The competitive businessman interested in maximizing his profits will always produce any output by the method that costs the least.

This is fine as far as it goes. But it fails to tell us exactly how the businessman can determine the least-cost method of producing any output. How might he go about finding this method?

The problem here is very similar to that faced by the consumer in deciding how to spend his money on consumer goods in a way that will maximize his satisfactions. Indeed, Figure 20-1 is reminiscent of Figure 18-5 in chapter 18. Let us assume that bicycles can be produced by two factors, labor and capital, and that the prices of labor and capital are given to the individual businessman by the market. The straight diagonal lines in Figure 20-1 represent the different combinations of labor and capital that can be bought for various amounts of money ($10,000, $20,000, and so on). The slope of each of these lines will be equal to the price of labor divided by the price of capital,[1] or P_L/P_K. These lines are usually called *equal-outlay* lines.

What methods of production will the businessman choose? Answer: those methods where the equal-outlay lines are just tangent to the isoquants. At these points, the businessman is getting the maximum output for his outlay of money; he is also producing any output at a minimum cost in terms of money. Thus, at a total cost of $20,000, the maximum output he can produce is 1,590 units, using the

---

1. The logic of this conclusion is exactly the same as that used to show that the slope of the consumer's "budget-line" would be equal to the price of one consumer good divided by the price of the other consumer good. The reader should try to work out the conclusion stated in the text above and then check his analysis with the identical argument presented for consumers, p. 425.

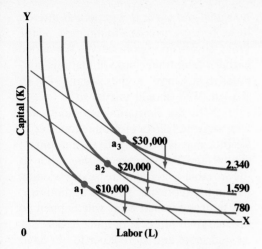

Y

Capital (K)

a_3 $30,000

a_2 $20,000   2,340

a_1 $10,000   1,590

780

0   Labor (L)   X

Figure 20-1. Least-Cost Combinations of Factors.

The businessman will be producing any output at least cost when the equal-outlay line is just tangent to the relevant isoquant (e.g., a_1, a_2, a_3, etc.) At these points, ratios of prices of the factors of production to their respective marginal products will be equal.

combination of factors represented by point a_2. Similarly, the reader can easily see that the minimum cost of producing 1,590 units of output is $20,000.

Thus, our summary answer to the effect that the businessman will produce any output by the method that costs least can be rephrased by saying that he will always produce at those points where his equal-outlay lines are just tangent to his isoquants. *This* statement, in turn, means that he will always produce where the slope of his equal-outlay line is exactly equal to the slope of his isoquant. The slope of the equal-outlay line, as we have just stated, is equal to P_L/P_K. We already know that the slope of the isoquant is equal to MP_L/MP_K. Hence, our summary statement can now be replaced by the

conclusion that the businessman will obey the following rule:

$$\frac{P_L}{P_K} = \frac{MP_L}{MP_K}$$

or equivalently:

$$\frac{P_L}{MP_L} = \frac{P_K}{MP_K}$$

The competitive businessman will be producing each output at minimum cost if he makes certain that the ratios of the prices of the factors of production to their respective marginal products are equal. We have shown this for labor and capital, but it applies to any number of factors of production. If we had n factors of production $(f_1, f_2, f_3 \cdots f_n)$, the rule for least-cost combinations of factors for the competitive firm would be:

$$\frac{P_{f_1}}{MP_{f_1}} = \frac{P_{f_2}}{MP_{f_2}} =$$

$$\frac{P_{f_3}}{MP_{f_3}} = \cdots = \frac{P_{f_n}}{MP_{f_n}} = \cdots$$

Indeed, as we shall show in chapter 22, failure to observe this rule can lead to economic *inefficiency*.

We have essentially answered our question about methods of production, and what remains now is to show the relationship of what we have just said to the concept of marginal cost. This relationship is not difficult to see if we concentrate our attention, as we should, on a very small increase in production. Suppose we add to our total productive capacity and labor force the services of one laborer for one week. Let us suppose that the week's services of the laborer cost us $100. Let us further suppose that the addition of this one week of labor results in an addition of two bicycles to our total productive output of bicycles during the year. What, then, is the marginal cost of producing bicycles? Roughly it is equal to $100 divided by two, or $50. In the language of the economist, it is equal to the price of the factor labor divided by the marginal product of labor (P_L/MP_L). Now it is true that if we were going to expand production, we might do so not just by adding more labor, but by adding the other cooperating factors as well. However, since our businessman is obeying the rule that the ratios of the prices of the factors of production to their marginal products are equal in all directions, we should get essentially the same result if we added more capital instead of labor or both capital and labor simultaneously. Thus, in the case of our specific example, we have:

$$MC = \$50 = \frac{\$100}{2} = \frac{P_L}{MP_L}$$

or more generally:

$$MC = \frac{P_{f_1}}{MP_{f_1}} = \frac{P_{f_2}}{MP_{f_2}} =$$

$$\frac{P_{f_3}}{MP_{f_3}} = \cdots = \frac{P_{f_n}}{MP_{f_n}} = \cdots$$

In competitive equilibrium, then, the marginal cost of producing any quantity of output will be equal to the price of each factor of production divided by its marginal product. In showing this, we have made possible a deeper understanding of the concept of cost in relation to the basic characteristics of production.

MARGINAL COST
IN THE SHORT RUN

Let us use this analysis to explain a matter we treated rather vaguely in the last chapter: the shape of an individual firm's cost curves.

The shape of the firm's short-run marginal cost curve is of particular interest to us because it is the foundation of the firm's short-run supply curve. We stated earlier, without much proof, that this marginal cost curve would usually be U-shaped. Why should this be so?

In the short run, we have fixed and variable factors of production. Let us assume that we have a fixed amount of capital and that we are adding labor as the variable factor to increase our production in the short run. The law of diminishing returns tells us what will happen to the marginal physical product of labor as we add more and more labor to our fixed quantity of capital. The marginal product of labor will at first rise; but presently, because of the changing proportions of labor to the fixed capital, it will begin to decline and will continue to decline as still more labor is added.

The marginal cost of producing bicycles will, in this case, be quite simply the price of labor divided by the marginal product of labor. Since we are dealing with an individual firm that has no possibility of influencing the price of labor in the economy, the businessman will take the price of labor as given. The behavior of marginal cost, therefore, will be determined by changes in the marginal product of labor according to the formula:

$$MC = \frac{P_L}{MP_L}$$

where P_L is the market-given wage.

At low levels of production, the marginal product of labor will be rising; hence, marginal cost will be falling. At higher levels of production (as diminishing returns take over) the marginal product of labor will be falling and marginal cost will be rising. Thus, marginal cost will first fall and then rise, or, as we have said, the curve will be U-shaped. Thus we have related the short-run marginal cost curve to the production process and thereby explained its shape.

COST CURVES
IN THE LONG RUN

In the long run, the individual firm does not face the constraint of a fixed plant capacity, and it can alter both capital and labor inputs as it chooses. What will the shape of its cost curves be under these more flexible long-run conditions? Three important cases need to be distinguished.

1. Natural Monopoly

Suppose a firm has a production function that exhibits increasing returns to scale (Figure 20-2) over the range of production relevant to the overall market for bicycles. As the individual firm increases its employment of both labor and capital, the production of bicycles will increase in a greater proportion—or, equivalently, the average amount of labor and capital per unit of output will decline. At given factor prices, this will mean a fall in the average cost of production as the firm's output increases. Since average cost is falling, marginal cost will be below average cost.

Now, in these circumstances, pure competition could not survive, nor would there be a firm or industry supply curve in the sense that we have described them. For the fact is that the bigger the firm, the lower its costs, and consequently the greater its ability to drive its competitors out of the market. In the long run, the bicycle industry in these circumstances would come to be dominated by a single producer. Hence, the term *natural monopoly* is used to categorize industries in which the individual firm enjoys ever-continuing economies of scale.

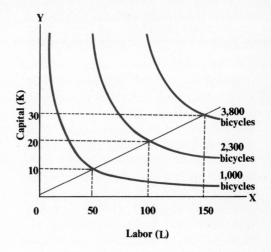

Figure 20-2. Increasing Returns to Scale.

Doubling inputs leads to more than doubled outputs in this production function. If this continued to occur for a firm over very large ranges of output, we would have a *natural monopoly*.

2. Competition and U-Shaped Average Cost

Pure competition can exist, then, only when economies of scale do not persist over such large ranges of output that "big"[2] firms are required for efficient production or where there is some *fixed* factor that causes diminishing returns even in the long run. The characteristic situation might be as follows: at very low levels of output, economies of scale predominate, and the firm will enjoy falling average costs. If these economies of scale are not too strong (i.e., if we are not dealing with an industry that is fundamentally of the mass-production kind), then presently they will be counterbalanced by the organizational problems of the larger firm. The "fixed" factor might, in many cases, be

2. "Big" in relation to the overall market for the particular commodity in question.

the decision-making authority of the firm. Even decision-making can, of course, be decentralized and specialized within a single firm. Nevertheless, there are some overall policy decisions that must be made at the center; and as the firm grows bigger and more complex, there will be increasing problems of organization, communication, and execution that will complicate this central function. If such problems do occur and if they are significant enough to outweigh any economies of scale that exist at higher levels of production, then the average cost curve will begin to rise. In this case, we will have a U-shaped average cost curve, though of course it will be a flatter curve than the short-run average cost curve. If, moreover, the minimum point of the average cost curve occurs at a level of output that is small relative to the market for bicycles in the economy as a whole, then the bicycle industry will be able to support a very large number of firms and the conditions of pure competition can be fulfilled.

3. Intermediate Cases

Between the extremes of natural monopoly and of efficient small-sized firms, there are, of course, many intermediate possibilities. In many real-world industries, productive conditions are such that the market can support more than one but not an indefinite number of firms. Economies of scale are strong but not so pervasive that they require a single giant firm. In such industries, it is typical to have a few large firms which engage in "competition" with each other but not in "pure" competition. Such firms have *some* control over the markets for their products but not monopoly control. These intermediate cases of *imperfect* or *monopolistic competition* will be our subject of interest frequently later in Part Three, and especially in chapter 24.

COMPETITIVE SUPPLY IN THE LONG RUN

Returning now to the competitive case, let us assume that productive conditions in our bicycle industry can support a large number of small firms. We now ask: what happens to "supply" in this industry when all firms together begin expanding or contracting production and when firms are free to enter the industry from the outside or to leave the industry?

Now when an industry as a whole expands or contracts, its effects on the economy may be far different from the scarcely noticeable results—if they exist at all—of the expansion or contraction of an individual firm. Some of these effects may not appear particularly significant to the industry or firms themselves, though they may have important effects generally on the economy. A case in point is air pollution. When a number of firms expand production in a particular area, they may discharge chemicals and other pollutants in the surrounding air, significantly affecting the lives and comforts of all those living in that area, but their expansion may have only negligible effects on productive costs within that industry. We shall call effects of this kind *external technological effects* and shall return to a consideration of them later on,[3] because they significantly alter the conclusion that pure competition is *efficient*. Where external technological effects are substantial, it will be found that some form of state intervention or regulation will be necessary to protect the interest of the community as a whole.

For the moment, however, let us concentrate on another kind of effect that is also external to the individual firm: the effect of the expansion of the industry as

---

3. See especially chapter 30.

a whole on the prices of the factors of production facing that firm.[4] As we noted in the preceding chapter, the main general reason for expecting the long-run supply curve of a competitive industry to rise upward (as opposed, say, to being perfectly horizontal) is that the expansion of the industry as a whole will cause a rise in the prices of the factors of production that are especially important in that industry. Suppose that bicycle production requires more capital and less labor (at the original factor prices) than the average industry in the rest of the economy. When bicycle production expands, what happens is that the economy as a whole is transferring resources from these other industries to bicycle production. These other industries, however, are releasing relatively too many units of labor and too few units of capital to meet the bicycle producers' demands at the going factor prices. The result will be an increase in the price of capital and a decrease in the price of labor. But this increase and decrease will not cancel out for the bicycle producers, because by hypothesis, they, more than other industries, are heavily dependent on (the now more expensive) capital. The net effect will be a general increase in the costs of producing bicycles—i.e., a shifting upward of the average and marginal cost curves of each bicycle producer.

An illustration of how such an effect might appear to the individual producer is shown in Figure 20-3. Let us suppose we are discussing an industry-wide expansion of bicycle output from, say, 9 million units to 18 million units. The possible effect of this expansion on factor prices

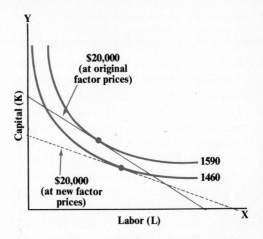

Figure 20-3(a). Industry Expansion and Changes in Factor Prices.

This diagram illustrates how an expansion of output in the bicycle industry as a whole might change relative prices of factors of production facing the individual firm.

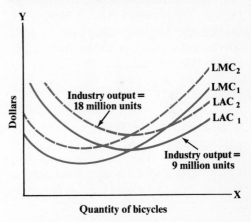

Figure 20-3(b). Industry Expansion and the Firm's Cost.

The result will be an upward *shift* of the firm's cost curves. Such shifts can explain why the long-run supply curve for the industry may be gently rising with increased output even in the very long run.

4. Such effects are sometimes called *external pecuniary effects*. A *pecuniary* effect will alter a firm's costs by altering the prices of its factors of production, but it will not affect the basic *technology* of production as expressed, for example, in the firm's production function.

is shown in Figure 20-3(*a*). Both equal-outlay lines represent expenditures of $20,000 by the firm. The solid equal-outlay line shows conditions before the expansion of industry demand. The broken equal-outlay line shows conditions when the industry as a whole has expanded and when, consequently, the price of labor has fallen and the price of capital has risen. But notice now what has happened to the cost situation of this bicycle producer. Earlier he could produce 1,590 bicycles for $20,000; now he can produce only 1,460 bicycles for the same amount. As a consequence, the total cost, average cost, and marginal cost curves of each individual bicycle producer will shift upward in the case described. This upward shift is illustrated for the firm's long-run average and marginal cost curves in Figure 20-3(b).

Of course, this is not the only possible case; there can be exceptions.[5] However, this is the general and most important case, and our analysis has now shown us how the long-run competitive supply curve can be related to the productive decisions that underlie it.

TWO APPLICATIONS OF SUPPLY AND DEMAND

Our discussion in the last section brought us to the edge of our next impor-

tant topic: the determination of the prices of the factors of production. Before turning to this subject in the next chapter, let us pause briefly to make two applications of our supply-and-demand analysis as developed thus far. These applications will bring into sharper focus a number of the relationships that we have been presenting in a step-at-a-time approach.

Application 1: Technological Change

Let us suppose that there is an invention that lowers the amount of capital and labor required to produce bicycles. What would be the general effect of this technological change on the price of bicycles and the quantity of bicycles produced?

The way in which the effects of such an invention would work themselves out is illustrated in the four diagrams of Figure 20-4. In Figure 20-4(a), we show the effects of this invention on the production function of a typical bicycle producer. These effects, of course, could be very different, depending upon the type of invention that occurred. (For example, it might be very labor-saving, or it might economize primarily on the use of machinery.) As we have drawn it, this particular invention has not much changed the shape of the individual isoquants, but it has brought about larger outputs for each different combination of labor and capital. Thus, for $20,000, we could earlier produce only 1,590 units of output; now we can produce 1,800.

Figure 20-4(b) shows the new total cost situation affecting our typical bicycle producer. The new curve has shifted to the right of the old one, signifying that at the same total money cost ($20,000) we can produce more output (1,800 as opposed to 1,590 bicycles) than we could before the invention.

Figure 20-4(c) shows the new

5. For example, it might happen that the bicycle industry and the economy as a whole used different factors of production in more or less the same proportions. In this case, the expansion of the bicycle industry might not affect factor prices or cause a shift upward in cost curves. Under such circumstances, the long-run supply curve would be horizontal (*perfectly elastic*).

The reader should note that, in this discussion, we are really taking up the same kind of issues that are involved in the production-possibility curve, which we introduced in Part One. Shifting resources from the production of other commodities to bicycles, or vice versa, is what is involved in moving from one position to another on the production-possibility (or transformation) curve. We shall develop the relationship of the theory of production to the transformation curve in the appendix to chapter 22 (p. 516).

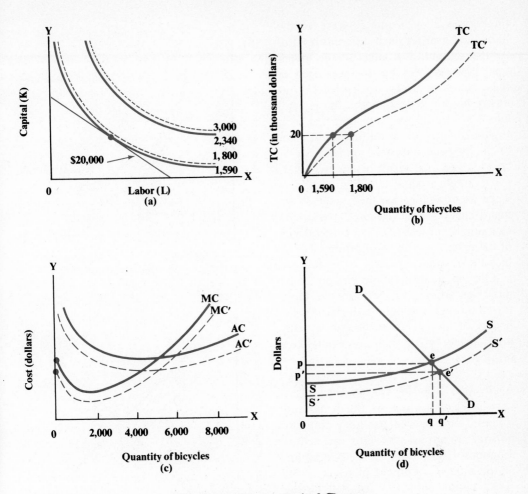

Figure 20-4. Technological Change.

A technological change makes it possible to produce more output for any given combination of factors. This leads to a downward shift in the total cost curve for each firm in the industry, which brings about a similar shift in each firm's average and marginal cost curves which brings about a shift in the industry-wide supply curve for bicycles. The ultimate effects are 1) an increased production of bicycles and 2) a lower price for bicycles.

average and marginal cost curves derived from the new total cost curve. Both curves have shifted downward, as we would expect, reflecting the rightward shift of the total cost curve.

  Finally, Figure 20-4(d) shows the effect of the shifting of the cost curves on the supply curve of the industry as a whole. This last step is a bit complicated because, as we know, when the industry as a whole expands, the prices of the factors of production facing each individual firm are likely to change. This means that to be completely accurate, we would have to draw different equal-outlay lines (in Figure 20-4(a)) and different cost curves (in Figures 20-4(b) and 20-4(c)) for the individual firm for each different level of *industry* output. The effect of the invention, however, will be to lower each of these new cost curves at *each* level of industry output; consequently, the general effect will be as we have depicted it in Figure 20-4(d)—i.e., a shifting to the right of the long-run industry supply curve.

The final result of our hypothetical example is shown in Figure 20-4(d) when we bring together the consumer demand curve for bicycles (DD) with the new supply curve (S'S'). As a consequence of the invention, the equilibrium price of bicycles has fallen from p to p' and the equilibrium quantity of bicycles produced has risen from q to q'. Thus, we have traced through a change in the basic technology of bicycle production to its ultimate effects on the consumer-purchaser of bicycles.

Application 2: A 10¢ Tax on Tea

Taxes on tea, as the American Colonists once proved, can have dramatic political repercussions. Our interest as economists is somewhat more pedestrian. Suppose the government places a tax of 10¢ a pound on tea. What will be the effects on the price of tea and the quantity of tea bought and sold in a competitive economy?

The answer to this question can be found by two different approaches, one centering on the consumer, the other on the producer. Let us approach it from the consumer's point of view first. In Figure 20-5(a) we present a typical consumer's indifference map for tea compared to all other commodities. Before taxation, the consumer would buy OT pounds of tea when the price was 40¢ per pound and OT' pounds of tea when the price was 50¢ per pound. Let us now impose the 10¢ per pound tax on tea. When the produc-

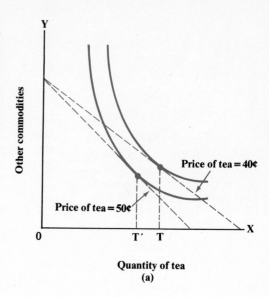

Quantity of tea
(a)

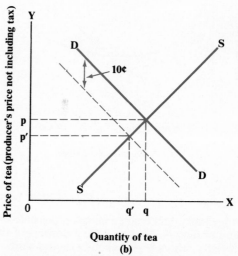

Quantity of tea
(b)

Figure 20-5. Analysis of a 10¢ Tax on Tea, from a Consumer's Point of View.

er's price[6] of tea is 40¢, the actual cost to the consumer is 50¢ per pound (producer's price + 10¢ tax). Hence when the producer's price is 40¢, the consumer will buy not OT but OT' pounds of tea.

---

6. By *producer's price*, we mean the revenue per unit of tea actually going to the producer. This is different, of course, from *market price* when the market price includes the tax.

When we perform this same operation for all consumers at all possible prices for tea, the net result will be a downward shift in the total demand curve for tea, as shown in Figure 20-5(*b*). On the vertical axis, we measure the producer's price of tea. The imposition of a 10¢ tax on tea results in a uniform downward shift of 10¢ in the consumer demand curve. The results of this shift in turn will be a reduction in the producer's price of tea from *p* to *p'*. The reader can see that the reduction in the producer's price is less than 10¢. Consequently, the tax-included price of tea will be higher now than before, but not by the full 10¢.

An equivalent analysis can be presented from the point of view of the *producer*. Assuming pure competition, we can say that each tea producer will produce tea to the point where $P = MC$. After the tax has been imposed, however, each time the producer sells one more unit of tea he must pay the government 10¢. Consequently, his marginal cost is now equal to the old marginal cost (*MC*) plus the tax: $MC' = MC + 10¢$. His new equilibrium position will be where the price (now *including* tax) is equal to MC'.

This analysis is illustrated in Figure 20-6(*a*) and (*b*), where we show first the shifting upward of the marginal cost curve for each individual firm and then the equivalent upward shift in the supply curve for the industry as a whole. The result, as in the earlier analysis, from the consumer's point of view, is a reduction in the quantity of tea produced from *q* to *q'*. The price result is slightly different in appearance, because we are now measuring the price of tea *inclusive* of tax on the vertical axis. The price of tea inclusive of tax rises from *p* to p_t'.

Incidentally, the reader will notice that the new equilibrium has resulted in a splitting of the 10¢ tax between the

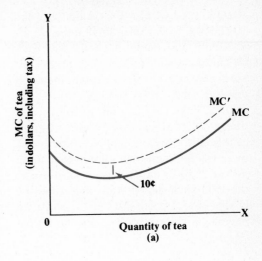

(a)

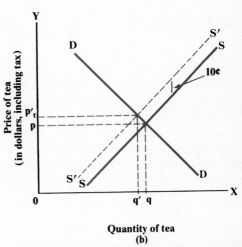

(b)

Figure 20-6. From a Producer's Point of View.
(a) Individual firm's marginal cost curve is shifted upward by the tax. (b) Industry shift in supply curve.

consumer and the producer. The consumer must pay more for tea now, but *not* the full 10¢ more. The producer receives (after tax) less per pound of tea now, but not the full 10¢ less. This question of who actually pays the tax is sometimes referred to as the problem of the *incidence of taxation.* You should demonstrate to yourself how the incidence of the 10¢ tax will vary, depending on the specific supply and demand curves involved. (What happens if the supply curve is almost perfectly horizontal? If the demand curve is nearly vertical?)

These applications of supply and demand analysis—to technological change and taxation—should indicate the wide range of problems for which these powerful tools can be used. Hopefully, they will also deepen your understanding of the various economic relationships we have been setting forth in the preceding chapters.

SUMMARY

In this chapter, we have attempted to relate a firm's cost curves (and thus its supply curve) to its underlying productive situation. The competitive firm will try to produce any given output at *least cost* by obeying the rule that the price of each factor will be in the same ratio to its marginal product as that of any other factor:

$$\frac{P_{f_1}}{MP_{f_1}} = \frac{P_{f_2}}{MP_{f_2}} = \cdots = \frac{P_{f_n}}{MP_{f_n}} = \cdots$$

Marginal cost for the firm at this given output will equal the price of any factor divided by its marginal product:

$$MC = \frac{P_{f_n}}{MP_{f_n}}$$

where *fn* is any factor of production.

Since the firm's short-run marginal cost curve is the basis of its short-run supply curve, we can now relate supply directly to productivity. Suppose we have a firm with one variable factor in the short run. The price of this factor is given by

the market. As we expand output by hiring more units of this factor, the marginal product of the factor will ordinarily rise and then (by the law of diminishing returns) fall. By the rule that

$$MC = \frac{P_{f_n}}{MP_{f_n}}$$

this means that marginal cost will first be falling and then rising; i.e., it will be U-shaped. The firm's short-run supply curve will be the segment of this *MC* curve above *AVC*.

In the long run, the cost curves of the firm will be affected by *scale* effects as all factors (except decision-making authority) can be expanded simultaneously. With persistent economies of scale, we have *natural monopoly. Pure competition* is possible only when economies of scale are not persistent over ranges of output that are large relative to the market for the commodity, or where the "fixed" decision-making authority causes the cost curves to rise while the firm is still very small in relation to the industry as a whole. Intermediate cases will lead to reasonably large firms (but not monopoly) and usually to some form of *imperfect competition*.

In the case of long-run competitive supply for the industry as a whole, expansions of output will involve the addition of more firms to the given industry. Even if these firms have exactly the same production functions as firms already in the industry, the supply curve will usually rise as industry output is increased. The reason: the prices of the factors most heavily used by this industry will tend to rise as new firms enter and industry output increases. These factor price changes will cause an upward shift in the average cost and marginal cost curves of all firms in the industry.

QUESTIONS FOR DISCUSSION

1. Suppose that a businessman consulted his engineers and found that the production function for his commodity did not display the usual convex isoquants but rather looked as follows:

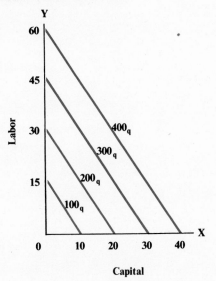

(a) What kind of returns to scale is exhibited by this production function?

(b) What can you say about the relationship of the marginal products of labor and capital in this case?

(c) Can you determine from this diagram how the businessman would choose to produce any given output (say, 200 units)? If not, what further information would you need?

(d) Derive four points on the total cost curve for this product, on the assumption that labor costs $6 a unit and capital costs $7 a unit. Do the same when labor costs $5 a unit and capital costs $8 a unit.

(e) How would the commodity be produced when labor costs $3.00 a unit and capital costs $4.50? Discuss.

2. The unlabeled diagram below could be either a consumer's indifference map or a producer's production function.

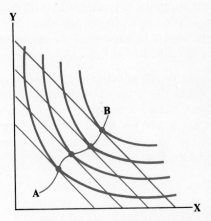

(a) Explain in detail the meaning of the diagram, first, on the assumption that it is a consumer indifference map and, second, on the assumption that it is a firm's production function.

(b) In the case of consumers, the line segment AB is sometimes called a *standard-of-life line;* in the case of producers, it is sometimes called a *scale line.* Explain why such terms might be used in each case.

(c) Write a brief essay comparing and contrasting the theory of production and the theory of consumer behavior in a competitive economy.

3. Suppose that a businessman is hiring a certain amount of capital and labor and producing a certain output so that he is maximizing profits. Suppose now that a technological change enables him, at this particular factor combination, to produce a higher output but also raises the marginal product of capital relative to that

of labor. Through the point of his original employment of capital and labor, draw a new isoquant reflecting this technological change. If the prices of capital and labor remain unchanged and if he were to produce at the level of output indicated by the new isoquant you have drawn, would he do so at the original combination of capital and labor? If not, why not? Why might such a technological change as we have described be called *labor saving*?

4. Analyze the effect of a tax on tea as we did in the example at the end of this chapter, but do it on the assumption that it is not a 10¢ tax but a *ten percent* tax added on to the price of each unit of tea purchased.

21
Demand and Supply of Factors of Production

In the last few chapters we have been slowly working our way around the circular flow (p. 421) of a competitive economy. We began with consumer households and the consumer preferences that lie behind the demand curves of the product markets. Then we looked behind the supply side of the product markets to the business firms whose decisions about output and factor combinations determine the quantities of commodities that will flow forth in response to consumer demands. But business decisions about hiring factors of production take us immediately to the factor markets. In these factor markets, business firms are the "demanders," and the owners of the factors of production (in our simple economy, private individuals) are the "suppliers." In taking up the demand and supply of factors of production in this chapter, therefore, we are essentially completing the circle. What will remain for the final chapter of Part Three A (chapter 22) will simply be to bring out the central features of what we have done, notably the concepts of interdependence and efficiency.

Now, however, let us focus directly on the problem of factor markets and how these markets function in a purely competitive economy.

DEMAND FOR THE FACTORS OF PRODUCTION

We have already laid the basic groundwork for our analysis of the *demand* side of a competitive factor market. In chapter 19, we said that the competitive firm would be maximizing its profits when it was producing at an output where $P = MC$. In chapter 20, we analyzed the concept of cost further and discovered that the competitive firm would be minimizing costs for any level of output when it was producing where

$$MC = \frac{P_L}{MP_L}$$

$$= \frac{P_K}{MP_K} = \cdots = \frac{P_{f_n}}{MP_{f_n}} = \cdots$$

When we put these two conditions together, we get

$$P = MC = \frac{P_{f_n}}{MP_{f_n}}$$

where P is the price of the product the firm is selling and P_{f_n} and MP_{f_n} are the price and marginal product of any factor of production employed by the firm in question. If we now drop out the term MC and rearrange this equation slightly, we get the following:

$$P_{f_n} = P \times MP_{f_n}$$

This equation says that a competitive firm will be in equilibrium only when it is hiring any factor of production to the point where the price of the factor of production is equal to the price of the product times the marginal product of that factor. The expression on the right—$P \times MP_{f_n}$—might be called the marginal product of the factor in money terms, or, more customarily, the *value of the marginal product* of the factor. Suppose that the particular factor of production is bicycle mechanics. Suppose further that adding one more bicycle mechanic to our staff results in an addition of forty bicycles produced per year, with bicycles selling at $100 each. The value of the marginal product in this case is $100 \times 40 = $4,000. And what our equation tells us is that the bicycle producer will be maximizing his profits only if this term is equal to the price (wage) of a bicycle mechanic. If the wage of bicycle mechanics happens to be $4,000, the businessman will be doing exactly what a profit maximizer should. If the wage is different—if it is $3,000 or

$6,000—then he will want to change his operations. In particular, he will want to hire either more or fewer bicycle mechanics.

What we have just stated is actually the crucial key to the understanding of a business firm's demand for a factor of production. To repeat:

In pure competition, a business firm will hire any factor of production up to the point where the value of its marginal product is equal to the price of the factor.

Why? What is the common sense of this statement? Why, for example, could a competitive firm not be in equilibrium when the value of the marginal product of bicycle mechanics was $6,000 and their wage $4,000? Wouldn't this, in fact, be a good thing for the businessman?

It might be a good thing, but the point is that he could do better—in particular, by hiring more bicycle mechanics. It is a simple matter of revenues and cost. Hiring another bicycle mechanic would bring $6,000 in additional revenue for the firm, and it would cost the firm only $4,000. This means $2,000 of additional "pure" profit. Any businessman in this position would therefore start hiring more bicycle mechanics. By similar logic, the reader can show that a value of marginal product *below* the given wage would cause the profit maximizing competitive businessman to lay off some of his bicycle mechanics.

The term *competitive* in the above sentence is essential, for the rule that a factor price must equal the value of its marginal product *holds true only under pure competition.* The rule is valid because the competitive firm has no control over the market price of its product or the market prices of the various factors of production. We shall consider in later chapters how the rule must be modified when these conditions are not fulfilled.[1]

How, then, can we generate a demand curve for a factor of production—bicycle mechanics—from this competitive rule that the value of the marginal product of bicycle mechanics must, in equilibrium, equal the wage of bicycle mechanics? We can best approach this problem in two steps: first, showing the demand curve of an individual bicycle producer for bicycle mechanics when this is the only variable factor of production; and second, showing how this analysis is altered when we allow other variable factors and also when we consider the demand for mechanics from the bicycle industry as a whole.

FACTOR DEMAND IN A SIMPLE CASE

We begin with the case in which bicycle mechanics are the only variable factor of production, because it is ex-

tremely easy in this case to relate the competitive rule—factor-price (P_F) equals value of marginal product (VMP)—to the individual firm's demand curve for bicycle mechanics.

We are dealing with a competitive firm that takes the price of bicycles as given by the market: $100. This firm also possesses, we assume, the technological information given in Figure 21-1(a); i.e., the marginal product curve for bicycle mechanics as we add more and more bicycle mechanics to a fixed stock of other factors (e.g., machinery). This curve, as we have drawn it, exemplifies the law of diminishing returns throughout. To translate this marginal physical product curve into the value-of-marginal-product curve in Figure 21-1(b), all we need do is multiply the MP for any quantity of labor employed by the price of bicycles, or $100. Thus, when the firm is employing 100 bicycle mechanics, the MP of bicycle mechanics is fifty and the VMP will be $50 \times \$100 = \$5,000$. By similar calculations, we can derive the VMP curve for all levels of employment of bicycle mechanics.

Now under our assumed conditions, this VMP curve *is* the firm's demand curve for bicycle mechanics. The competitive rule tells us that the firm will hire bicycle mechanics to the point where VMP equals their wage. Suppose the wage is set at w_0. How many bicycle mechanics will this firm be willing to hire? To get the answer, we simply keep adding bicycle mechanics until their $VMP = w_0$. This happens when the firm has hired q_0 bicycle mechanics. Thus, e_0 is one point on the firm's demand curve for bicycles. If we repeated the process for each and every possible wage, we would get the whole demand curve, and it would be identical with the VMP curve shown in Figure 21-1(b).

1. See especially pp. 613–14. In anticipation, we might give the following abbreviated explanation. The *general* rule is that a firm will hire a factor of production up to the point where the additional (marginal) revenue produced by one more unit of that factor is equal to the additional (marginal) cost of hiring one more unit of the factor. If, as in pure competition, the individual firm takes product and factor prices both as given by the market, then the value of the marginal product and the factor price will measure the additional revenue and additional cost of hiring that factor, respectively. Suppose, however, that the firm is aware that when it expands its output it will be able to market that larger output only at a lower price than previously obtained. In this case, the value of the marginal product of the factor will *overstate* its addition to total revenue. The reason is that as we hire more units of that factor and expand output, we are causing the price to fall on *all* units of output produced. Thus, to get the *net* addition to revenue, we must subtract from the value of the marginal product of the factor the loss of revenue per unit on all preceding units of output. Under these circumstances, the firm will generally hire fewer units of the factor (say, bicycle mechanics) than the competitive rule requires. For the moment, simply keep in mind that we are dealing with a special case, not a universal rule of business behavior.

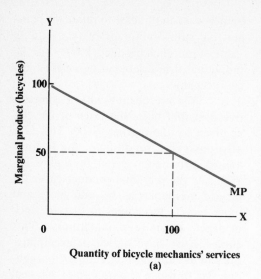

Quantity of bicycle mechanics' services

(a)

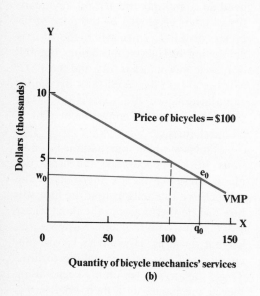

Quantity of bicycle mechanics' services

(b)

Figure 21-1. Relation Between
MP and VMP Curves.

The VMP curve will represent the firm's
demand curve for bicycle mechanics in the
simple case presented here.

OTHER VARIABLE FACTORS AND INDUSTRY-WIDE DEMAND

The factor demand curve we have just drawn is straightforward enough, but it does not take us as far as we need to go. For in the long run, bicycle producers can vary *all* factors of production, not just bicycle mechanics. Also, there is the problem that when all firms together expand or contract their employment of bicycle mechanics, this will alter the industrywide production and hence the *price* of bicycles. And in the final analysis, it is this industry-wide demand curve for bicycle mechanics that we are interested in.

1. Other Variable Factors

When all factors are allowed to vary—when the bicycle firm can hire more machinery as well as more bicycle mechanics—the firm's demand curve for a particular factor becomes somewhat more complicated. The reason is basically this: when the wage of bicycle mechanics goes down, the bicycle producer will now try to substitute bicycle mechanics for machinery. He will find it profitable to produce any level of output with machinery and mechanics in combinations different from those he used before. Consequently, we cannot draw the marginal product curve for bicycle mechanics on the assumption of a fixed stock of machinery, as we did in Figure 21-1(*a*).

This can be illustrated by our familiar "contour map" (Figure 21-2). We have drawn two equal-outlay lines, the solid one before a change in the price of mechanics, the dotted one after a fall in the price of mechanics. Imagine a series of these lines (representing different total outlays) super-

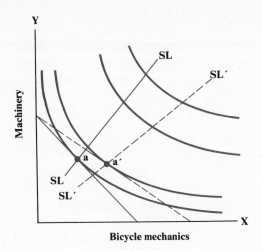

Figure 21-2.

imposed on the production function, and you will see that at the original factor prices, the least-cost combination factors will be located on SL (sometimes called the scale-line*); whereas after the fall in the wage of mechanics, the least-cost combinations will be located along line SL'. This means (as stated in the text) that, at the lower price of mechanics, the producer will find it profitable to produce any level of output with machinery and mechanics in combinations different from those he used before.*

Although this problem does complicate matters, it also brings out a principle of some importance. This principle is that the firm's demand for a particular factor of production will be influenced by the degree to which this factor is substitutable for other factors, and vice versa. If bicycle mechanics are easily substitutable for machinery, then even a slight fall in the wage of bicycle mechanics will cause a very substantial substitution of mechanics for machines. In this case, the demand curve for bicycle mechanics will tend to

be relatively *elastic*—i.e., a small percentage change in price will tend to lead to a large percentage change in quantity of bicycle mechanics demanded. On the other hand, suppose that there is very little flexibility in productive methods. It is almost a one-mechanic-to-one-machine production process. In this case, a fall in the price of bicycle mechanics will not permit any great substitution of mechanics for machines; hence, the factor demand will be relatively *inelastic.* In general:

The demand for a factor of production will be influenced by the ease with which other factors of production can be substituted for it in the production process. If there is high substitutability, then—other things equal—factor demand will tend to be elastic. *If there is little substitutability, other things equal, factor demand will tend to be* inelastic.

We have thus uncovered one of the important principles governing factor demand.

2. Industry-Wide Factor Demand

However, this is not the only principle involved. Indeed, there is a very important omission in our analysis so far. In chapter 17, when we were discussing the principle of interdependence, we noted that we could talk about the scarcity of factors of production only in relation to the demand for the products they produced—that is, consumer demands. Economists often talk about the demand for factors of production as *derived demand,* meaning precisely this point: business demand for factors is essentially "derived" from consumer demands for the products the businesses produce. But we have not yet brought the consumer into the picture at all. How, then, will the consumer demand for bicycles come to influence the producers' demand for bicycle mechanics?

In order to trace this particular influence, we must shift focus from the firm to the industry as a whole. The firm's factor demand curve (VMP curve) in Figure 21-1(b) was drawn on the assumption of a given price of bicycles ($100). This was appropriate because in pure competition the price of the product, as we know, is independent of the expansion or contraction of production of any individual firm's output. When *all* firms are expanding or contracting output and when new firms are entering or leaving the industry, however, this assumption no longer holds.

From this industry-wide point of view, let us follow through the consequences of a fall in the wage of bicycle mechanics.

The first consequence of a fall in the wage of bicycle mechanics (other things equal) will be a lowering of all the cost curves of firms in the bicycle industry. These new cost curves will be drawn substituting, wherever profitable, the now less expensive mechanics for machines at each level of output.

The next consequence will be that firms in the bicycle industry will find it profitable to begin hiring more factors of production and expanding output. Furthermore, new firms will begin to be attracted into the bicycle industry. The lowering of costs means that there are now abnormal profits in this particular industry. Hence, we will begin to get an expansion of output both by the expansion of existing firms and the entry of new firms.

The consequence of this expanding output, however, will be a *fall in the price of bicycles*. This is really the point where consumer demand enters crucially into the picture. The bicycle firms are hiring more bicycle mechanics both to substitute for machines and to expand output, but the consumers (having a downward sloping demand curve) will buy more bicycles only at a lower price.

What this means, in turn, is that, in the industry as a whole, the value of the marginal product of bicycle mechanics is falling not only because of diminishing marginal productivity but also because the price of the product is falling. (Remember: VMP = Price of the product $\times$ Marginal product.)

When final equilibrium is reached, there will be a greater bicycle output in the industry as a whole at a lower price. Bicycle mechanics will have been hired to the point where their marginal product valued at the new (and lower) price is equal to the new wage. $P_F = VMP$ still holds for each and every firm in the industry, but the V has changed as well as the MP.

By understanding the process just outlined, you will be able to see the essence of the notion of *derived demand*. Suppose, for example, that the consumer demand for bicycles is highly inelastic. Consumers will expand or contract their purchases of bicycles only slightly in response to considerable changes in bicycle prices. Now in this case it can be shown that a fall in the wage of bicycle mechanics will produce only a slight increase in the quantity of mechanics demanded; for as firms in the industry begin expanding bicycle production as outlined above, the price of bicycles will immediately turn sharply downward. This will very quickly lower the VMP of bicycle mechanics to the new, lower wage level. There will be little expansion of bicycle output and consequently relatively little increase in the employment of bicycle mechanics. An inelastic consumer demand curve, in other words, has led to a relatively inelastic factor demand curve. You must satisfy yourself that the opposite is also true—i.e., the more elastic the consumer demand curve,

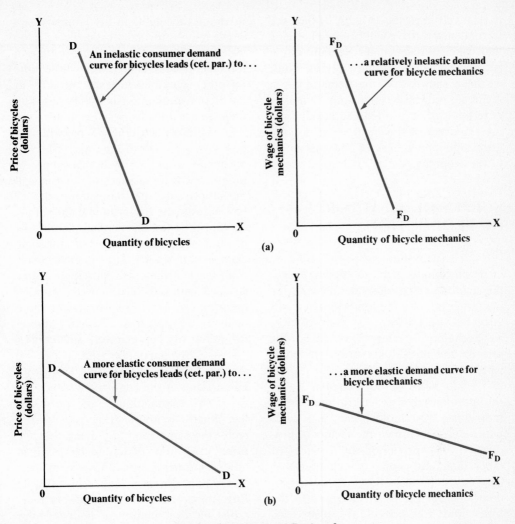

Figure 21-3. Derived Demand.

These diagrams point up the important fact that the demand for a factor of production is influenced by the consumer demand for that factor's products.

the more elastic the factor demand will tend to be. In general,

The elasticity of the demand for a factor of production, other things being equal, will depend upon the elasticity of consumer demand for the products which that factor helps to produce. If consumer purchases of the products of the factor are highly responsive to price changes, then the business

firms' demand for the factor will also be more responsive to changes in its price.

This important principle is illustrated in Figure 21-3. Given the necessary technological information, we could derive the industry-wide demand curve for bicycle mechanics from the consumer demand curve for bicycles. The point to note here is that when that consumer demand curve is relatively inelastic (Figure 21-3*a*), the factor demand curve will be more inelastic than when the consumer demand curve is relatively elastic (Figure 21-3*b*). Thus, we have shown that the demand for a factor of production is not simply a matter of technology; it also reflects, through the intermediary of the business firms, the tastes and preferences of the consumers of the economy.

SUPPLY OF A FACTOR OF PRODUCTION

To determine the price of a factor of production, we need to know not only the conditions that affect the demand for the factor, but also the conditions that will affect its supply. How many hours of bicycle mechanics' services will be offered for sale on the market at various different wages for those services?

In terms of our "circular flow," this question takes us back to the private individuals (households) who, in a competitive economy, own the factors of production. The prices of the services of labor, land, and capital, which appear as *costs* to the business firms, appear as incomes—*wages, rent,* or *interest*—to the households who provide those services. What circumstances will influence these factor supplies?

As we might expect, one important consideration will be the *time period* in view. As in the case of the supply curves for commodities, the supply curves for factors of production will generally tend to be more elastic in the long run than in the short run. This will not always be the case, but it is a good general rule that we can illustrate by our hypothetical example of bicycle mechanics.

In the very short run—a few weeks perhaps—the quantity of bicycle

mechanics available in the economy as a whole may be virtually fixed. There is too little time for bicycle mechanics to retrain for other trades, and equally little time for other workmen to learn the skills of the bicycle mechanic. In the very short run then, we are drawing from an almost fixed pool of bicycle mechanics. What will happen in this case when the wage of bicycle mechanics goes up? Will the supply of their services be unaffected? That is, will the supply curve be completely inelastic? Not necessarily. It is true that the supply curve will be less elastic than it would be in the longer run, but there is still some element of flexibility. This element derives from the fact that each bicycle mechanic is faced with a choice between working more or fewer hours per week, or more or fewer days per year. He has a choice, in other words, between work and leisure.[2]

This particular choice can be thought of in much the same way as we might think of the consumer's choice between two commodities—say, tea or coffee. When the hourly wage rises, this is really the same thing as saying that the price of an hour of leisure has risen in terms of other commodities. With each leisure hour now more expensive than before, the worker will presumably rearrange his combination of hours-of-work versus leisure, so that he has maximum satisfaction. Thus, even in the very short run, there is likely to be some variation in hours of work offered and, hence, *some*

2. In real life, such a choice may be considerably modified by the fact that the number of hours per week and the amount of vacation time per year may be institutionally fixed for any given job. When this occurs, the worker faces on all-or-nothing proposition; and unless he has a private income, he will customarily choose "all" rather than "nothing." However, even where hours of work are institutionally set, there is usually some flexibility, either in terms of overtime work or, in many cases, taking additional part-time work elsewhere (moonlighting). The many modifications that collective bargaining and unionization make in these and other matters in the labor market are discussed in chapter 26.

elasticity of supply in response to factor price changes.[3]

As we move into the longer run, of course, this elasticity greatly increases. Consider, for example, a period of one or two years. During a period of this length, bicycle mechanics will be able to shift into related trades (e.g., auto mechanics), and workers in related trades will be able to learn the skills of the bicycle mechanic. If the price of bicycle mechanics rises above that of other mechanics generally, then there will be a substantial shifting of workers from these related fields into the bicycle field. Supply elasticity will be much increased.

In the very long run—say, a generation of thirty years—the elasticity of supply will increase even further. For now it will be possible for the entire supply of mechanics in the economy generally to expand. Young men who might have become welders or bricklayers or plumbers

may now decide to train themselves for the more lucrative field of the mechanic (including the bicycle mechanic). In the very long run indeed—assuming, of course, a purely competitive economy— the wage of bicycle mechanics could not long sustain itself above the wage of any other employment of comparable skill and attraction. This is to say that the supply of bicycle mechanics will be more or less perfectly elastic at the going wage for comparable trades.

In Figure 21-4 we have drawn a possible supply curve for bicycle mechanics in the intermediate run. It is neither perfectly elastic nor perfectly inelastic. It tells us that as the wage of bicycle mechanics goes up, this will draw workers from related fields into this particular trade. On the other hand, the period is not so long that it makes possible the redirection of a whole new generation of workers. Consequently, there is some limit

---

3. How would a worker's supply curve reflect his changing evaluation of work and leisure? The interesting thing is that it might *bend backward* if the wage rate rose high enough. Such a backward-bending supply curve is shown in the accompanying figure. This curve tells us that a worker will at first respond to higher wages by offering more of his services but that as the wage rate rises still higher, he will begin to curtail his labor and work less.

To understand why such a shape is possible, we must remember what we said in chapter 18 when we were discussing substitution effects and income effects in connection with the consumer demand curve. When the laborer's wage per hour goes up, this is the same thing as a rise in the price of leisure and a fall in the price of all other commodities. On this account, the laborer will want to substitute other commodities for leisure—i.e., he will work more hours. This effect is dominant as the wage rate rises from a fairly low level, and it explains the northeasterly slope of the bottom half of the supply curve. Higher wage rates, however, also have an *income effect*—the wage earner is richer in general as wages go up—and this income effect is likely to make him want to buy more of all commodities, including the commodity leisure. If it happens that as he gets richer and richer, the income effect (causing him to want more leisure—i.e., to work less) becomes dominant over the substitution effect (which would lead him to work more at higher wages), then we will have a backward-bending supply curve of the type shown.

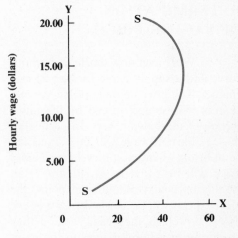

Backward-Bending Supply Curve.

This supply curve for the services of an individual laborer might bend backward at high hourly wages. At the higher income level, he might wish to purchase more leisure.

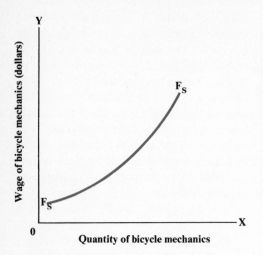

Figure 21-4. A Factor Supply Curve.

Curve F_S represents a reasonable shape for the supply curve of a factor (bicycle mechanics' services) in the intermediate run.

to the increased supply of bicycle mechanics as the wage rises.

DETERMINATION OF FACTOR PRICE

We have now both a demand curve and a supply curve for bicycle mechanics. The price or wage of bicycle mechanics will be determined by the intersection of these two curves. In particular, the equilibrium wage will be w_0 and the equilibrium quantity of bicycle mechanics hired will be equal to q_0 (Figure 21-5). At this particular equilibrium point, the bicycle firms will be satisfied that they are doing as well as they can, because they are hiring bicycle mechanics to the point where their $VMP = w_0$. At the same time, the supply curve assures us that the workers are also doing as well as they can under the circumstances, for the supply curve includes within it the adjustments that individual workmen have made between work and leisure at the various pos-

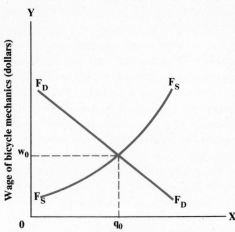

Figure 21-5. Supply and Demand in the Factor Market.

If F_D is the factor demand curve and F_S is the factor supply curve, equilibrium wage will be w_0, and equilibrium quantity of bicycle mechanics hired will be q_0.

sible wage rates and also the shifting of labor in and out of the bicycle mechanic field in the intermediate run. Taking all these elements into consideration, the workers at w_0 will offer q_0 units of bicycle mechanics' services for hire, and this is precisely the quantity that is being hired at the equilibrium point.

To test your understanding of this matter, explain to yourself why a wage higher than w_0 would leave labor unsatisfied (leading them to bid the wage down) and why a lower wage would leave the bicycle producers unsatisfied (leading them to bid the wage up).

THE TRIAD OF LAND, LABOR, AND CAPITAL

In our analysis so far, we have considered a rather specific factor of production: bicycle mechanics. In the course of this discussion, however, we found that the supply of bicycle mechanics would be influenced by what was happening in the rest of the labor force. Thus, in the very long run, a high wage for bicycle mechanics would lead to a redirection of the training of considerable segments of the labor force. In long-run equilibrium, then, the wage of bicycle mechanics would have to be more or less the same as the going wage for all other trades of comparable difficulty and attractiveness. But what will determine this "going wage"?

Actually, we have already discussed *one* theory about the determination of the overall wage level—the Malthusian theory, which we mentioned In Part One (pp. 153-59). According to this theory, population growth is very rapid whenever the wage gets above some very low "subsistence level." We could now rephrase this by saying that the long run supply of labor is assumed to be perfectly (or infinitely) elastic at the subsistence wage. Thus, in this theory, even though technological change may occasionally push out the demand for labor curve (by pushing out labor's marginal productivity curve), the "going wage" will forever tend to the subsistence level. The reader should go back to Figure 6-3 on p. 158 and make sure he understands what that diagram means in terms of our now more advanced level of analysis.

The point we are making now, however, is that as the economist starts from a particular factor of production—bicycle mechanics—he finds himself moving inevitably into a consideration of wider and wider categories of factors of production. The long-run supply of bicycle mechanics will be influenced by the supply of mechanics generally, which will be influenced by the supply of skilled workingmen, which will be influenced by the size of the labor force as a whole, and so on.

To meet this kind of problem, economists have traditionally grouped together the various specific factors of production—like bicycle mechanics or wheat-producing land or blast furnaces—into certain broad categories. The traditional categories are *labor,* including professional and white-collar as well as blue-collar workers; *land,* including all kinds of natural resources as well as land in the customary sense; and *capital,* including machinery, buildings, tools, and in general, all *produced* means of production. It is argued that each of these categories has certain broadly defining characteristics and that by grouping the more specific factors together under these heads, a number of useful generalizations can be developed.

Since we have already made some comments about labor markets, and since we will return to them again in Part Three, let us confine ourselves now to the other two factors—land and capital. For the remainder of this chapter we shall say a few words about land and rent, capital and interest, and then add a very brief note about "profits."

LAND AND RENT

In the early nineteenth century, David Ricardo defined *land* as meaning "the original and indestructible" powers of the soil. The implied generalization was that land and natural resources are given to the economy once and for all, or in more technical terms, that the supply of land for the economy as a whole is perfectly inelastic even in the long run. (Indeed, land was treated by classical authors as more or less the economic opposite of labor, which, as we have just mentioned, was assumed to be in perfectly *elastic* supply.)

Now this generalization about the fixity of land is obviously not completely accurate: land and natural resources can be depleted by excessive or improper usage; mineral deposits can be exhausted; *new* land can be created by drainage, irrigation of desert areas, and so on. But on the whole, our natural resource base does tend to change relatively slowly compared with the other factors of production. Consequently, we might represent the supply curve for land as we do in Figure 21-6—a vertical straight line. No matter what the price of land is, the supply of land will be roughly the same.

The British classical economists called the payment to land *rent*. Even today the term *economic rent* is used to describe the payment to any factor that is offered in completely inelastic supply.[4] Such rent payments have two rather special and interesting characteristics.

The first is that, given the fixed supply of the factor, it is the demand for the factor that determines the price (rent). Thus, in Figure 21-6, any shift in the demand curve of the factor (from F_D to F'_D) will completely determine the change in rent going to the factor (from r to r'). Supply is given; demand does all the work. In cases like this we can see with special clarity why factor prices and consequently "costs" in a society cannot be determined without reference to consumer preferences. The demand curve for

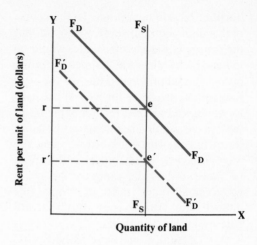

Figure 21-6. Land and Rent.

This diagram could be applied to land or to any other factor in completely inelastic supply.

land will (as all factor demand curves do) reflect consumer demands for the products of land. If the consumers suddenly conceive a dislike of products with a high land factor component, their distaste will bring down the demand curve, bring down the rent of land, and change the "costs" facing each firm that uses land in its production process.

The other rather special characteristic of rent is that it is in some senses a surplus or unnecessary payment. By this we mean that although most economic payments serve as inducements to secure more work from the factors of production, rents do not function in this way. By definition, *economic rents* refer to payments made to a factor in inelastic supply—the amount of factor services offered in the market is the same, no matter what you pay for them. This has led many economists—especially the nineteenth century "single-tax" economist Henry George—to advocate concentrating taxation on land rent. In terms of our diagram, we can see that if the government took away from

---

4. Economists today, however, recognize more clearly than their predecessors that other kinds of factors of production besides land may be in inelastic supply. Opera singers and professional football quarterbacks are cases in point. As you might say, there was only one Caruso—had the price of tenors increased, there still would have been only one. It is therefore perfectly proper and logical to say that opera singers and other inelastically supplied factors earn a "rent" in basically the same way that land earns rent.

the landowner an amount equal to the rectangle *rr'e'e*, the supply of land offered on the market would be unaffected. (In theory, of course, the same principle could be applied to other inelastically supplied factors. You could heavily tax opera singers, and they would doubtless still continue to sing.) While this feature of rent taxation is a clear advantage, it does not necessarily mean that such taxes are best, for a *major* consideration in taxation must be its effects on *income distribution*. Do you want landowners (or opera singers for that matter) to be taxed much more heavily than factory owners, business managers, or government officials? Rent taxation does avoid some of the incentive distortions of other taxes, but it must also be evaluated in terms of its effects on the distribution of income in the society as a whole. We shall return to this large question of income distribution in chapter 29.

CAPITAL AND INTEREST

The other big category of factors of production, beside labor and land, is *capital.* It includes machinery, tools, plant, equipment, buildings, inventories, and all those means of production that are themselves a product of the economic system. If land is a gift of nature, capital is clearly one factor of production whose creation and continuing supply is determined by the workings of the economy as a whole. For capital, as we have said before, is a *produced* factor of production, and the motives governing its production are almost wholly economic in nature.

Actually, this distinction between capital and land is more significant in the long run than in the short run. At any given moment of time, it makes little difference to a producer whether the factor of production he is using to make bicycles was wholly or partially "produced" by man. It is very doubtful that he could (or would want to) separate out the "natural" from the "man-made" component of a steel wrench or a hammer. At any given moment of time, we have a stock of goods that can be used in production; these goods are the cooperative product of man and nature in times past, and they can be substituted for each other more or less easily as the particular production functions permit. Indeed, in the short run, it can be said that man-made machines earn a payment that is very much like land-rent. If the demand for the products of machinery increases, then the prices of those machines will go up. Since, in the short run, it is impossible to increase the stock of machines substantially, they tend to be in rather inelastic supply and to earn what the great British economist, Alfred Marshall, called a *quasi-rent.*

In the longer run, however, quasi-rents will disappear because capital can be accumulated. In many societies, indeed, the rapid accumulation of capital is a major objective of national policy.

We have already discussed capital accumulation in two contexts. The first was in the analysis of economic growth and development (chapters 6 and 16) where we emphasized the role of capital in expanding production over time. The second was in Part Two A, where we were discussing the macroeconomic effects of investment. We noted the differences between saving and investment decisions and how these differences could lead to excessive or inadequate aggregate demand—inflation or below-full-employment national income.

In microeconomics it is customary not to forget, but to abstract from these macro-effects. Let us suppose we are operating in an economy in which there are no complications of a monetary nature that stand in the way of full employment. Given our stocks of factors of production—labor, land, capital—we can then determine what our full employment income will be. Having settled all this, we then ask: what will the process of capital accumulation look like in this society? What forces will determine how much income people in this society will set aside for capital accumulation—investment—as opposed to consumption?

One might think of the basic process this way: the economy has a choice between consuming all the goods it produces in a given year or *saving* some of its income and *investing* this income in new machines, tools, and other capital goods. We have produced a national income of $100 billion. Shall we consume all the $100 billion or shall we consume $80 billion and realize the remaining $20 billion in the form of machinery, plant, and equipment? The primary reason for a society's saving and investing $20 billion in this way is that with more capital, it will be able to produce a higher income in the future. The choice is between greater satisfaction *now* (consuming the whole $100 billion) and greater satisfaction *later* (saving and investing $20 billion and thus having the tools to produce a greater income in future years).

Now in a society free from short-run fluctuations of income and other macroeconomic problems, we can see that a rather key element in the supply and demand for capital will be the *rate of interest*. Look at it first from the consumer's point of view: shall he consume all his income today or shall he save some of it for tomorrow? On the whole, he will be willing to save some of his income (say, $1,000) only if he can expect to get something rather larger tomorrow (say, $1,050). The rate of interest tells the consumer how

much future income he may expect to get from a sacrifice of some of today's income. Thus, on the saving side, within limits, a higher rate of interest may induce people to save more.[5]

From the producer's side, the interest rate represents the price he must pay for his capital. If a machine costs $1,000 and the interest rate is 6 percent a year, then, assuming no depreciation, the effective cost of that machine to that businessman is $60 per year. When the businessman hires a unit of capital, he must make sure that its net rate of return (the marginal productivity of capital) is above or equal to the interest rate. The businessman will add units of capital to his firm until, at the margin, the net productivity of capital is just equal to the interest rate. What

---

5. We have to say "within limits" because the effect of the interest rate on savings is a bit complex. Essentially, the problem comes from our familiar friends, the *income* and *substitution effects* (see p. 489, where we discuss these effects in relation to labor supply). We can imagine the savings process in terms of a consumer buying some income for tomorrow with some of today's income. For $100 saved today, I can get $110 tomorrow (or more accurately, a year from today) if the rate of interest is ten percent. Now suppose the rate of interest increases to, say, fifteen percent. This is the equivalent to a *fall in the price of tomorrow's income.* I used to have to pay $100 to get $110 tomorrow. Now I can get $110 tomorrow for about $95.65 (i.e., $110 ÷ 1.15).

Now, according to the *substitution effect*, when the price of a commodity goes down, the consumer will substitute it for other more expensive commodities. This effect would tend to *increase* saving when the interest rate rose. Tomorrow's income is cheaper; hence, I will substitute more of tomorrow's income for today's—i.e., I will save more.

But the *income effect* works differently. When the interest rate goes up, I am richer in general since I can have more income tomorrow and no less today. But when I am richer in general, I want to buy more of all commodities in general. In particular I want to have more consumption today. But this would mean *less* saving today.

The net result of an increase in the interest rate on savings, therefore, is hard to gauge, since it will be the resolution of these two quite different effects.

This, of course, also abstracts from the *further* complications raised by money, liquidity preference, etc., which we discussed in Part Two.

this means is that the higher the interest rate, the lower will be the quantity of additional capital demanded.

Thus we have the two sides of our capital market. At very high interest rates, the consumers' desire to save will exceed the willingness of businessmen to invest; at very low interest rates, businessmen will want to accumulate more capital than consumers wish to save. Equilibrium will be achieved at that level of the interest rate where savings decisions are equated to investment decisions. What this means at a deeper level is that the consumer's evaluation of present income in relation to future income (sometimes called *consumer time-preference*) will have been equated to the technological possibilities of turning present into future income via the accumulation of capital (reflecting the marginal productivity of capital). At this deeper level, we can understand that a *higher* interest rate (i.e., above the equilibrium level) would, in effect, be an unkeepable promise to consumers to bring them future income at a rate beyond that which is technologically feasible. Conversely, a *lower* rate would represent a failure of the society to recognize and exploit the full possibilities of translating present into future income by a more capital-using technology.

In the real world, as we know, these issues are much complicated by the role of uncertainty, by the operation of "money," and by the complex financial, credit, and other institutions that influence the capital market. These complications, however, should not be allowed to obscure the element of fundamental truth in what we have just been saying. Societies *do* have basic choices to make between present and future, and what we have just indicated is that the most important way such choices are made economically is through the mechanism of capital accumulation.

A NOTE ON PROFITS

In discussing the basic factors of production—land, labor, and capital—we have also described three categories of payment: rent, wages, and interest. What we have said, in effect, is that in determining the prices of the factors of production, we are determining the distribution of income in the society. Very roughly, the owners of land will get rent, laborers will get wages, and the owners of capital will get interest. This is "very roughly" the case because, as we have noticed, these categories are broad and sometimes overlapping. (Thus, if opera singers are in inelastic supply, they may earn a rent; moreover, machinery and buildings may be in inelastic supply in the short run, and they then earn a *quasi-rent*; and so on.)

There is, however, one omission that is a bit more worrisome: the category of *profits*. For as any national income accountant will tell you, the total income of our society includes rents, wages, interest, *and profits*. Indeed, in some sense, the pursuit of profits is what a private, competitive economy is supposed to be all about, so let us make a few brief comments about this problem of profits.

(1) Our rent, wages, and interest payments include *part* of what people often call profits. You will recall that our cost curves always include normal profits or what we have sometimes called *wages of management*.

(2) We know that in long-run equilibrium in a purely competitive economy, no "pure" profits would exist. Whenever pure or abnormal profits exist in any particular industry, firms will quickly enter in and compete them down to the normal wages-of-management level.

Be sure to note that there is nothing contradictory in saying that (*a*) profits are the motive spur of the entire system and (*b*) in long-run equilibrium, no pure profits will exist. For it is precisely the attempt by firms to maximize profits that drives them in and out of various industries and leads to the elimination of abnormal profits where they exist. This may be a paradox, but it is not a contradiction; indeed, this paradox lies at the very core of a private market economy.

(3) The real world is, in fact, more complex than our purely competitive world. Some element of what are called profits represents the exercise of market control by individual firms in an *imperfectly* competitive way. This monopoly element in profits has no place in the present chapter but will be discussed in Part Three B.

(4) We should remember that in this analysis of pure competition we have largely skirted important questions having to do with uncertainty and change. One of the great sources of turbulence in our economic life is the fact that the products we consume and their methods of production are both *constantly being revolutionized.* There is, as the great Austro-American economist Joseph A. Schumpeter (1883–1950) used to say, a constant process of *innovation* in the modern economy. Schumpeter said that beside the laborer, landowner, and capitalist, there is another figure in modern industrial life that must be reckoned with: the *entrepreneur.* The precise role of the entrepreneur is to innovate, to introduce new products and new methods of production, to discover new markets and new sources of new materials, and so on. He is regarded as the agent of change, and his reward, according to Schumpeter, is *profits.* The process works as follows: The economy is in equilibrium with no abnormal profits for anyone. The entrepreneur bursts in with his new innovation. (Think of computers, imagine automation, plastics, other synthetic materials.) The first men in the field enjoy tremendous advantages over their competitors. Presently, the competition sees what the situation is; hosts of firms swarm into the new field; the temporary advantages are lost. In the interim, however, there has been a once-over accrual of profits to the original entrepreneurs. Moreover, since there is always some innovation going on *somewhere* in the economy, there will always be someone earning profits at any given moment in time. Profits due to innovation are temporary in any one field; but in an economy where innovation is quite general, they become a permanent category of income.

Thus, the closer we approach real-world conditions, the more important it becomes for us to recognize that in addition to the standard factor payments—wages, rent, and interest—there exists a fourth category of income—profits—which is closely linked with the uncertainty, change, and imperfection of the modern industrial economy.

SUMMARY

Like product prices, factor prices in a competitive economy are also determined by supply and demand. The demanders, however, are now business firms and the suppliers are factor owners.

Under pure competition, each firm will hire a factor to the point where its price (or wage) is equal to the value of its marginal product, or $P_f = P \times MP_f$. This follows from the two conditions, developed in earlier chapters, that the firm will be producing where $P = MC$, and where $MC = P_f/MP_f$.

This rule enables us to determine a *demand curve for a factor* quite directly in a simple case. If we have an individual firm hiring one variable factor in the short run, then its demand curve for the factor will simply be the marginal product curve of that factor multiplied at each *MP* by *P*, or the value-of-the-marginal-product curve.

When several variable factors are taken into account, the demand for any factor will depend in part on the ease with which this factor can be substituted for other factors and vice versa. The easier it is to make these substitutions, the more *elastic* will be the factor demand.

When we move from the individual firm to the industry as a whole, we must now take into account the fact that as all firms expand hirings of a factor and increase the output of the commodity in question, the price of the commodity will fall. In general, the more elastic the consumer demand for the product the factor produces, the more elastic the factor demand will be. Because of this relationship between consumer demand and factor demand, the latter is often spoken of as a *derived demand*. In an ultimate sense, producers demand the services of factors only because consumers are demanding the products that those factors help produce.

The *supply curve of a factor* will depend on the nature of the particular factor involved and also, quite generally, on time. For the most part, the longer the period allowed for, the more *elastic* the factor supply.

Given both factor demand and factor supply curves, the price of any factor will be determined by the intersection of these curves. At this factor price, quantity supplied and quantity demand will be equated.

Factors of production are sometimes divided into broad categories and, in particular, into *labor, land,* and *capital.* Having discussed labor markets already, and planning to return to them in chapter 26, we confined ourselves to a few comments on land and capital.

Land. This factor includes all natural resources as well as land in the ordinary sense. In the past, it was considered that the distinguishing feature of land was that it was in completely inelastic supply: the "original and indestructible" powers of the soil. Although this characterization is not accurate, nevertheless it is true that natural resource supplies tend to change relatively slowly in comparison to the other two factors of production—labor and capital. The payment to land is often called *rent* although the modern economist also uses *rent* to mean the payment to other factors besides land that may be in inelastic supply (e.g., opera singers). Rent payments have the characteristic that they are a taxable surplus in the sense that, by definition, factor supply (being perfectly inelastic) will not be affected by a reduction in the payment to the factor in question.

Capital. Capital consists of produced means of production, and its accumulation will be much influenced by economic motives. In a simplified full-employment economy, we may imagine capital accumulation involving a choice between present and future consumption. In this simple world, the *rate of interest* will be such that supply and demand in the capital market are equated. A high interest rate, within limits, may encourage consumers to save more in order to enjoy greater income in the future. A high interest rate, by contrast, will discourage producers from investing in more capital, since they will undertake projects only to the point where the marginal productivity of capital is equal to the interest rate. Equilibrium will be achieved when the interest rate is such that the consumers' desires to save (reflecting their feelings about present versus future income) are equated to the businessmen's desires to invest (reflecting their judgments about the marginal productivity of capital). In the real world, uncertainty, "money," and a host of other factors tend to complicate this process.

Finally, besides rents, interest, and wages, there is a fourth category of income: *profits. Pure* profits do not exist in equilibrium under pure competition. However, *normal profits, or wages of management*, are included in the competitive cost curves. Also, profits may arise in the real world because of monopoly elements in the economy and because of uncertainty, change, and innovation.

QUESTIONS
FOR DISCUSSION

1. Suppose that we have a marginal product curve for bicycle mechanics as drawn in Figure 21-1(a). Suppose further that bicycle mechanics are necessary to producing bicycles in the sense that when no mechanics are employed, bicycle output will be zero.

(a) Define the term *average product* of bicycle mechanics.

(b) Draw in an approximate *average product curve* for bicycle mechanics, to go with your marginal product curve.

(c) Comment on the following statement: "It is unfair to pay labor its marginal product only; what labor should get is what it actually produces; namely, its average product."

2. Suppose that the consumer demand curve for a particular product were completely inelastic (consumers will buy the same amount of the product, no matter what the price). Do you think that this would lead to a completely inelastic demand for a factor of production engaged in producing that product? Explain your answer fully.

3. Another element affecting the elasticity of demand for a factor of production, besides those mentioned in this chapter, is the importance of the factor in relation to the total costs of the firms hiring the factor. It is claimed that if the factor is relatively *un*important, the demand for that factor will tend to be relatively more *in*elastic. Explain the reasoning that might produce this conclusion. Can you see any argument here that might lead a labor organizer to advocate a union with membership based on a particular craft rather than on the industry-wide labor force as a whole?

4. What would a modern ecologist be likely to say about the view that land (natural resources) is "original and indestructible"?

5. Suppose that you are a consumer who is asked to describe his indifference map not between two commodities today (say, tea and butter) but between consumption this year and consumption next year. Thus, in the diagram below, you might be asked about point *A* (100 units of consumption this year and 100 units of consumption next year) and point *B* (75 units of consumption this year and 210 units of consumption next year). Would you prefer *A* to *B*, *B* to *A*, or be "indifferent" between them?

(a) Draw three or four indifference curves in this diagram that describe how you yourself feel about present versus future consumption.

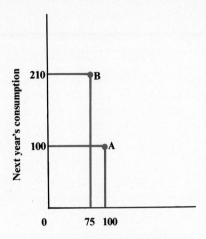

This year's consumption

(*b*) Does the diagram you have drawn suggest that you would be relatively sensitive to the level of the interest rate in deciding whether to save your money now in order to buy more things later?

(*c*) Why would any intelligent businessman ever be willing to pay more than $1 next year for the dollar you lent him this year?

6. Write an essay on the possible effects of capital accumulation and technological progress on the real wages of labor in a competitive economy.

22
Interdependence and Efficiency

With the work of chapter 21, we have completed our analysis of the basic relationships that link together the determination of prices and quantities in a purely competitive economy. At the very beginning of this analysis, we said that its purpose was twofold. In the first place, the study of the purely competitive economy allows us to demonstrate the fundamental *interdependence* of the elements of an economic system. This principle of interdependence applies to all kinds of economic systems, but the variety and complexity of the real world often modify and obscure the principle to the point where it is almost impossible to discern. What the analysis of pure competition gives us is a useful starting point for making our way through this real-world maze. The general tendencies we have been describing *are* meaningful, although they may not fit without qualification in any particular case.

In the second place, we said that pure competition gives us a standard by which to judge the *efficiency* of an economic system. Adam Smith's invisible hand referred to a union of private and social interest. The analysis of pure competition enables us to indicate under what circumstances this is true and under what circumstances it is not true. By comparing the functioning of other systems, including socialist systems, with the purely competitive model, we are able to gain important clues for economic *policy*. Should the government intervene? If so, how? What are the consequences? Efficiency, as we shall stress, is not the only significant economic objective, but it is an important one that no citizen or State would wish to ignore for long.

In this final chapter on the competitive system, we shall pull together various strands from earlier discussions and attempt to demonstrate the meaning of *interdependence* and *efficiency* from an overall point of view.

FOUR INTERDEPENDENT QUESTIONS

Why does coffee cost more per pound than tea? In the early days of economics, writers (like Ricardo or Marx) tried to detach this question from the overall workings of the economic system, and they argued that the answer depended on the quantity of labor embodied in each commodity. Modern economics, by contrast, recognizes that this question is simply one of a series of interdependent questions and that, in principle, one can answer it only by addressing all these other questions simultaneously.

Ultimately, there are four basic sets of questions involved in the kind of economy we are dealing with. Two of these sets of questions deal with *prices*; the other two deal with *quantities*. The reader should be able to recognize the four sets of problems described below as simply rephrasings of the questions we raised in chapter 17.

(1) **Prices of all commodities.** Our economic system must find some way of giving a determinate value to the prices of coffee, tea, bicycles, vacuum cleaners, and all other commodities.[1]

(2) **Quantities of commodities produced.** How many units of tea, coffee, bicycles, vacuum cleaners, and all other commodities will be produced by our economy in equilibrium?

(3) **Prices of the factors of production.** We must determine the prices of land, labor, and capital as their services are employed in the productive process. Since these factor payments are the incomes of the factors (rent, wages, and interest), we earlier referred to this question as that of the "distribution of income" in our economy.

(4) **Quantities of the factors of production employed in producing each commodity.** We have to determine what quantities of different kinds of labor, land, and capital will be used in the production of each commodity. This involves knowing how much labor, land, and capital will be supplied to the economy as a whole and how these supplies are divided up among all the different producers of commodities. The answer to this question will tell us the methods of production in use in our economy in equilibrium.

These, then, are the basic questions that, when the economy is in overall or *general equilibrium*, must all be answered.

Now if these questions were *not* interdependent, we could separate questions 1 and 2 in one group and questions 3 and 4 in another group. Questions 1 and 2 refer to the market for commodities, or the *product markets*. If we have a consumer demand curve for each and every product and an industry supply curve for each and every product, then we could simultaneously determine: (1) the prices of all commodities and (2) the quantities of all commodities produced. The intersection of each supply and demand curve, as we recall, determines both equilibrium price and equilibrium quantity produced.

Similarly, we can recognize that questions 3 and 4 refer to the markets for the services of the factors of production, or, briefly, the *factor markets*. If we had a business demand curve and a factor supply curve for each factor of production, we could determine the price of the factor of production and the quantity of that factor of production that would be employed in the economy as a whole. We would also have the information needed to show what quantity of that (and every other) factor of production would be used by each industry and business firm in the

---

1. In chapter 17, we called this the question of the "relative values of commodities." In a more advanced treatment, it would be shown that one commodity (tea, if you will) is used as a measuring rod for the prices of other commodities. That is, price of tea = 1. Other prices are then determined *in relation to* the price of tea.

economy. As in the case of products, supply and demand would enable us to determine both (1) factor prices and (2) factor quantities.

Now what the principle of interdependence tells us is that these two markets are in fact *interrelated*. The results in one market will influence the results in the other market, and vice versa. Thus, in the final analysis, *both* markets must reach equilibrium simultaneously. To prove this point, let us show (*a*) how the results in the factor market can influence the product market and (*b*) how the results in the product market can influence the factor market.

Factor Market Influences
Product Market

Suppose that there is some new invention that greatly economizes on labor and greatly increases the productivity of land. This invention is likely to cause an upward shift in the business demand curve for land. Suppose now that the supply and demand process has worked itself out and, in particular, that new factor prices have been determined in the factor market. Will these new prices of the factors influence consumer demands for commodities in the product market? The answer, in general, is yes.

Factor prices, in our example, have been altered in such a way that the price of land has risen in relation to the price of labor. This is the same thing as saying that there has been a redistribution of income in favor of the landowner compared to the laborer. How will this affect consumer demand? Suppose landowners as a group are richer than laborers (i.e., per individual). An increase in landowners' income relative to laborers' income should then have the effect of increasing consumer demand for "luxury" goods (yachts, trips to the Riviera) as

opposed to "necessaries" (meat and potatoes). The new total equilibrium situation therefore may be characterized by a relative increase in the quantity and price of "luxuries" compared to the quantity and price of "necessaries."

In short, a change in factor prices has altered consumer incomes, and these incomes influence the patterns of consumer purchases in the product market.

Product Market Influences
Factor Market

The influence of the product market on the factor market has been noted in earlier chapters, particularly in our consideration of derived demand. Suppose that there is a sudden shift in demand by consumers, away from handicraft products (mainly produced by labor) and toward various kinds of mechanical household appliances (produced, let us say, by highly capital-intensive methods). Now the final result in the product market of this shift in demand will be an increase in both the price and quantity of household appliances and a decrease in the price and quantity of handicraft products. Will this change in the product market influence the determination of prices and quantities in the factor market? Again, the general answer is yes.

The initial effect of the shift in consumer demand will be to raise the value of the marginal product of those factors (mainly certain kinds of capital) employed in the household appliance industries and to lower the value of the marginal product of those factors (mainly certain kinds of labor) employed in the handicraft industries. If these factors were specific to these industries and were in completely inelastic supply, the end result would be simply a shift upward in the demand curve and an increase in the

CHARLES PHELPS CUSHING

Léon Walras (1834-1910). A French-Swiss economist, Walras is known for his theory of general equilibrium and, in terms of economic methodology, his strong preference for the use of mathematics in economics.

price of the appliance-capital factors and a shift downward in the demand curve and the price of the handicraft-labor factors. This would be a direct impact of the shift in consumer demand on the factor market.

In the long run, however, it is more likely that labor and capital can be shifted between the two industries. As handicraft production falls, it will release labor and capital for the appliance industry. But it will release very little capital and a great deal of labor. Thus the supply of labor will exceed the demand for it in the appliance industry, whereas the supply of capital will be inadequate. The total long-run effect, then, will be: a rise in the price of capital, compared to the original situation; a fall in the price of labor; and depending upon the ease of factor substitution, a general tendency to use a higher proportion of the now cheaper labor in the production of both handicraft goods and household appli-

ances. Thus price-and-quantity determination in the factor market has been altered by the changed circumstances of the product market.

In sum, the principle of interdependence tells us that our four questions must all be solved at the same time. Prices and quantities in the factor market and prices and quantities in the product market are all component parts of one overarching, indivisible system of economic relationships.

INTERDEPENDENCE AND THE CIRCULAR FLOW

The discovery of the full implications of interdependence is usually credited to Léon Walras, the late nineteenth-century economist whom we have mentioned before, although many other economists, including England's Alfred Marshall, should be acknowledged as well. It is no accident that Walras' work—unlike that of the classical school of Smith, Ricardo, and Malthus—was presented in mathematical form. For what we have been describing reduces essentially to a set of simultaneous equations. Since Walras' day, economic theory at advanced levels has increasingly been formulated in mathematical terms, and we can now begin to appreciate the reasons why.

For our purposes, however, the essence of the relationships we have been describing can be set forth in our familiar circular flow diagram. Since this diagram (Figure 22-1) has now been expanded to include much of what we have been saying in the preceding chapters, it is necessarily a bit complex and requires some study and comment.

We start out by taking certain

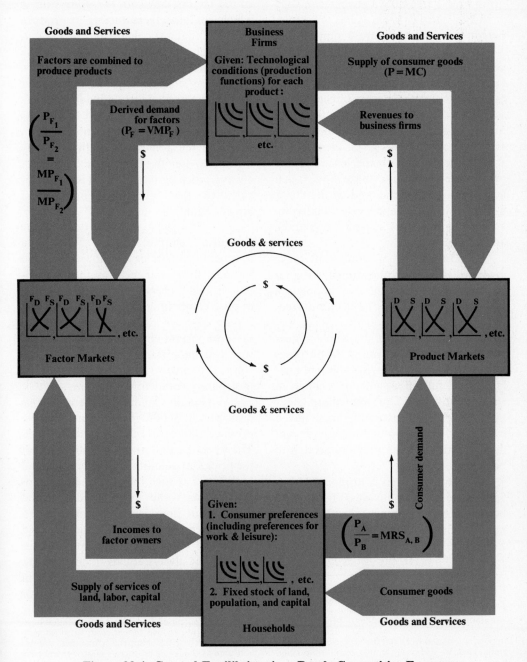

Figure 22-1. General Equilibrium in a Purely Competitive Economy.

things as *given*. In the case of the business firms, we are assuming a given technology or *technological horizon*, as it is sometimes put. In particular, we are assuming that we have the necessary production functions for each product in our economy. On the household side, we are given the basic tastes and preferences of consumers, as reflected in their various indifference maps. As part of these tastes and preferences, we also take as given their preferences as between work and leisure. These preferences will determine how much labor supply will be offered on the factor market at various wage levels. Finally, we assume that the stock of land, population, and capital is given.

Over time, of course, all these *givens* will change. Innovations will alter business production functions, population will grow, capital will be accumulated, even consumer tastes will alter. When any of these changes occur, the whole system will be altered. Indeed, one of the purposes of this analysis is to provide a way of analyzing the full effects of any change in basic conditions.[2] Our immediate question, however, is: assuming these given conditions, how are our four interdependent questions of the previous section to be solved?

The next step is to represent our two basic units—business firms and households—as coming together in two markets: the product market and the factor market. As described previously, we have two flows. In the *goods-and-services*

flow, the households dispatch the services of the factors they own to business firms, which combine these factors to produce products that they then can sell back to the households as consumer goods.[3] In the case of the *money* ($) flow: the households, demanding consumer goods, spend their money incomes, which provide business firms with the revenues to hire the factors of production whose payments, in turn, return to the households as their money incomes. After the fact, these flows must always match perfectly since it is tautologically true that "quantity bought" must always equal "quantity sold."

Now what we have done in the preceding chapters is to spell out a number of conditions that households and business firms will meet as they participate in this process under the assumption of pure competition. Within the arrows of Figure 22-1 we have indicated some of these important conditions. Make certain that you understand what each of these conditions means and why it holds true in a purely competitive economy.

Finally, guided by these various principles of action, the flows meet in the product market and in the factor market. The overall equilibrium condition is that the price and quantity of each product and each factor is such that the quantity supplied equals the quantity demanded throughout the entire economy. When this happens, not only will the money and goods-and-services flows be equal (quantity bought always equals quantity sold), but more significantly, no participant in the economy—whether business firm or

---

2. The analysis of the effects of changing conditions in this manner is sometimes called *comparative statics*. We start with a set of *givens* and work out the equilibrium prices and quantities. Then we change the *givens* (introducing, say, a 20 percent increase in population) and work out the new overall equilibrium. Then we compare the two equilibrium situations to see what the total effect of the change has been. A somewhat different approach to the treatment of economic change concerns itself with the *path of change over time*. This is usually called *economic dynamics*.

3. We have purposely neglected the fact that business firms also produce *capital goods* for *investment* purposes. When this happens, consumers cannot consume all the goods the factors of production have produced: some of these goods are added to the society's capital stock or equivalently, society is *saving* part of its income for future production. For the introduction of saving and investment into the circular flow, see Part Two, p. 203.

householder—will be able to improve his position by any indicated change in his actions. Overall equilibrium will have been achieved.

COMPETITIVE EQUILIBRIUM AND EFFICIENCY

But is it a good thing? The general equilibrium we have just described proves the interdependence of a competitive economy, but does it prove its efficiency? We turn now to our second main question, that of the relationship between a market economy and economic welfare.

The general proposition we wish to demonstrate is the following:

Under certain circumstances, a purely competitive economy will achieve a general equilibrium of prices and quantities such that we cannot improve the position of any participant in the economy without diminishing someone else's satisfactions. Under these circumstances, we say that the purely competitive economy has achieved an efficient *allocation of resources.*

We shall be qualifying this statement many times in later chapters; for the moment, let us concentrate on its positive aspects.[4]

---

4. Even while concentrating on the positive aspects, however, we must keep reminding ourselves that there are many objectives besides "efficiency" for which an economy will ordinarily strive; for example, a better distribution of income or a high rate of growth. In general, when we try to decide which objectives should have the highest priorities, we cannot escape making value judgments. Value judgments are ascientific in the sense that each person must ultimately make up his mind about what he considers desirable or undesirable. It is impossible to make statements about the goals or the welfare of an economy without making such personal value judgments. This is one reason why economists who share the same analytic framework can nevertheless differ sharply on many economic policy questions.

We have already given a number of illustrations of how pure competition may be efficient in this sense. In chapter 19 we noted that under pure competition, the business firm would be in long-run equilibrium only when it was producing at the minimum of its average cost curve —or at a minimum average cost per unit of the product. Since costs reflect the underlying scarcity of resources in the economy, we could see that purely competitive firms would be using the least possible quantities of scarce resources to produce their products. This is *efficient*, since if firms were using more than the minimally required resources to produce their outputs, it would generally be possible to produce more of all commodities (and hence make everyone better off) simply by reallocating resources throughout the economy.

We can now generalize from such examples by looking first at the problem of production, second at the problem of consumption, and third at the relationship between production and consumption.

1. Efficiency in Production.

We will have efficiency in production when it is impossible to shift our factors of production from one product to another in order to increase the production of both products (or to increase one without decreasing the other). This condition will be fulfilled when the ratio of the marginal products of the factors (say, labor and land) is the same in the production of all commodities. Or to put it in symbolic terms: if we represent the marginal product of labor in the production of commodity A as MP_{L_A}, the marginal product of labor in the production of commodity B as MP_{L_B}, the marginal product of land in the production of commodity A as MP_{ℓ_A}, and the marginal product of land in production of commodity B as MP_{ℓ_B}, then the condition for efficiency in production is

$$\frac{MP_{L_A}}{MP_{\ell_A}} = \frac{MP_{L_B}}{MP_{\ell_B}}$$

To see why this is so, imagine that these ratios differed. Suppose (to take the simplest possible numbers) that

$$MP_{\ell_A} = 1; MP_{L_A} = 1;$$
$$MP_{\ell_B} = 1; \text{ but } MP_{L_B} = 2$$

This would mean that the ratio of the marginal product of labor to land in the production of commodity A was 1, while for commodity B, the ratio was 2. It can now be shown this would be inefficient. Why? Because we can increase total production by transferring factors from one commodity to the other. In particular, let us transfer one unit of labor from commodity A to commodity B and one unit of land from commodity B to commodity A. Now notice what the consequence is. Production of commodity A is unchanged. Since the marginal products of labor and land in the production of A are both equal to one unit, the substitution of a unit of land for a unit of labor makes no difference at the margin. But notice that the production of commodity B has increased! B producers lost one unit of output when they gave up a unit of land, but they have gained *two* units of output when they added a unit of labor. This is because $MP_{L_B} = 2$. The reallocation of resources has thus increased commodity B production by one unit and left commodity A unchanged. If the ratios of the marginal products had been the same, no such overall improvement would have been possible—i.e., we would have had efficient production.

Now the significance of this point for the market economy is that when pure competition prevails, the condition of equal ratios of the marginal products of all factors in the production of all commodities will be guaranteed by the workings of the marketplace. In our general equilibrium diagram (Figure 22-1), we indicated in the upper left-hand corner that the ratio of the marginal products of the factors in producing any one commodity would have to be equal to the ratio of the factor prices. Assuming that the price of each factor is uniform throughout the economy, this condition will guarantee us that the ratios of the marginal products of the factors in all their uses will also be equal. In other words, pure competition working through decentralized markets will make certain that efficiency in production is achieved.

2. Efficiency in Consumption

In the case of the consuming households, we have a quite analogous problem. We will have efficiency in consumption when it is impossible to transfer commodities between any two consumers in such a way that we make both consumers better off (or make one better off without making the other worse off). This condition will be fulfilled when any two consumers are purchasing commodities A and B in such a way that the marginal rate of substitution (*MRS*) of A for B is the same for both consumers.

Again, a moment's reflection will show us why this is so. Suppose, for example, that I am purchasing bananas and apples and that, at the margin, one banana is worth four apples as far as my satisfaction is concerned. Suppose that you are also purchasing these two commodities but that at *your* margin, one banana brings you the same additional satisfaction as one apple. Bring us together and what will happen? Clearly, we can perform an exchange and *both* of us will be better off.

For example, suppose I offer to give you four apples for two bananas. Will you accept the exchange? Yes, because apples and bananas are equally satisfying to you at the margin, and you get four of one in exchange for only two of the other. But my position is improved too! Two bananas are actually worth eight apples to me, but I had to give up only four apples to get them. If, on the other hand, our marginal rates of substitution had been equal to begin with, no such mutually profitable exchange would have been possible—i.e., there would have been efficiency in consumption.

As in the case of production, the interesting thing here is that pure competition will bring about the desired result without any conscious effort to promote this kind of efficiency. In the lower right-hand corner of our general equilibrium diagram, we notice that each consumer will purchase commodities to the point where their price ratios are equal to their marginal rates of substitution. That is, for any given consumer,

$$\frac{P_A}{P_B} = MRS_{A,B}$$

Since all consumers face the same market prices, we can conclude that $MRS_{A,B}$ for consumer 1 will be equal to the $MRS_{A,B}$ of consumer 2, and so on for all consumers in the economy. The competitive market has given us efficiency in consumption as well as efficiency in production.

3. Relationship of Consumption and Production

If we now bring these two sides together—production and consumption—we can perceive what efficiency means in terms of a competitive economy in full general equilibrium. In the upper right-hand corner of our general equilibrium diagram, we state the familiar condition that under pure competition, the price of any commodity will be equal to its marginal cost. Stated in terms of two commodities, this means

$$\frac{P_A}{P_B} = \frac{MC_A}{MC_B}$$

Now what this condition tells us is that given efficiency in both production and consumption, there is no way in which production can be altered to increase the satisfactions of any consumer without hurting some other consumer. We already know that consumers will so adjust their purchases of the two commodities that the ratio

$$\frac{P_A}{P_B}$$

will be equal to the marginal rate of substitution of A for B for each and every consumer. This new condition now tells us that this marginal rate of consumer substitution will be equal to the ratio of the marginal costs of producing the two commodities.

Think of it this way: the consumers in our economy substitute apples for bananas according to their preferences. The producers in our economy also perform such a substitution, in the sense that they can shift factors of production from banana to apple production. Now the MRS for consumers for apples in terms of bananas tells us under what terms consumers desire to make this first substitution. Similarly, the ratio of the marginal costs of the two commodities tells us under what conditions the producers can make this second substitution. If the marginal cost of apples is twice that of bananas, then producers will be able to "transform" one unit of apples into two units of bananas through shifting of factors.

The equality of price ratios and marginal costs, then, signifies the following:

When $P = MC$ throughout the economy, the marginal rate of consumer substitution of one commodity for another will be equal to the marginal rate of producer substitution of that commodity for the other. If we think of the producers as "transforming" one commodity into another by shifting factors of production, we can say that the $P = MC$ condition means that the marginal rate of substitution (MRS) of consumers will be equal to the marginal rate of transformation (MRT) of producers. Or, simply, MRS = MRT for the economy as a whole.

The analysis here may seem complicated, but the common sense of this conclusion can be made clear. What we are saying broadly is that the economy will be "efficient" overall only if the consumer valuation of different products at the margin corresponds to their relative difficulties of production. Suppose that we have ended up in a curious kind of position in which all consumers consider apples to be twice as valuable as bananas at the margin. Suppose, however, it is equally easy (in terms of marginal cost) for the society to produce apples or bananas. Could this be a satisfactory position? Clearly not. We would want a system that would produce more apples and fewer bananas. And we know in principle that we could get this result, since we know that producers are economically able to transform a unit of bananas into a unit of apples simply by shifting the factors of production.

In short, for the economy to be efficient overall, we need not only efficiency in consumption and efficiency in production, but also the assurance that the marginal rates of consumer substitu-

tion for all commodities are everywhere equal to the marginal rates of producer transformation. When these conditions are fulfilled—and pure competition will (subject to later qualifications) fulfill them—then we will have achieved a truly "efficient" economy.[5]

A FOOTNOTE ON SOCIALISM

Is this analysis of the "efficiency" of pure competition really relevant? Interestingly, one of the strongest affirmative answers, historically, has been given not by the defenders of free enterprise but by the theoreticians of socialism!

In chapter 3, when we were discussing the Lange-variety of market socialism, we suggested that the plant managers in such an economy would have to obey certain "rules"—in effect, they would be required to *pretend* that they were in a market economy. What we have just provided in this chapter is the basic structure of those rules. As a plant manager, I shall be required by law to combine factors of production so that their price ratios are equal to the ratios of their marginal products and to produce output up to the point where $P = MC$. A socialist society (like a free enterprise society) may not get the prices exactly right the first time—i.e., there is a certain amount of trial-and-error involved in any real-life economic operation — but the criteria for the price system will be strongly influenced by the example of pure competition.

Thus, far from being a defense of the *status quo*, the arguments in this

5. For a graphical development of some of the themes presented in the above section, including the derivation of a production-possibility (or transformation) curve, see the appendix at the end of this chapter.

chapter have sometimes been used to call for a socialist revolution. *Only* under socialism, it has been claimed, can we really get pure competition functioning properly. What Adam Smith would have made of this particular argument, we do not venture to guess.

SUMMARY

Two central questions about any economic system are those of *interdependence* and *efficiency*. In this chapter, the workings of a competitive economy are examined from these two points of view.

The four questions that the competitive price system must solve are: (1) prices of commodities; (2) quantities of commodities produced; (3) prices of the factors of production; and (4) quantities of the factors of production employed in producing each commodity. The first two questions refer to the product market; the second two—which we might alternatively call the questions of income distribution and methods of production—refer to the factor market.

The principle of *interdependence*, as exemplified in a competitive economy, shows that these two markets are interrelated. The operation of the factor market will influence the workings of the product market, since factor prices are the incomes of the factor owners and these incomes will influence the consumer demands for goods in the product market. Similarly, the operation of the product market will influence the workings of the factor market, since consumer demands will influence the demands for factors of production and, hence, factor prices, income distribution, and methods of production.

The final general equilibrium solutions to all these questions must, therefore, be reached simultaneously. The resulting situation can be conveyed in a circular flow diagram in which supply will be equal to demand for every product and every factor, and each participant in the economy will be maximizing his satisfactions subject to the conditions facing him.

This competitive general equilibrium also has (subject to later qualifications) certain *efficiency* attributes. Efficiency in production normally requires that the ratios of the MP's of all factors be the same in the production of all commodities. Since every purely competitive firm will hire factors so that the ratios of their MP's are equal to the ratios of their P_f's (and assuming that the price of every factor is uniform throughout the economy), this condition will be met. Efficiency in consumption normally requires that the MRS's of all commodities be the same for all consumers throughout the economy. In pure competition, each consumer will equate his MRS for any two commodities to their price ratios; hence, the MRS's for all consumers will be equal. Finally, efficiency ordinarily requires that the MRS of consumers for any two goods be equal to the MRT (marginal rate of transformation) for the firms producing those goods. This condition means roughly that the relative satisfactions consumers derive from different goods at the margin should be equated to the relative difficulties of producing those goods in terms of the use of society's scarce resources. This requirement is met when the production of all firms is such that $P = MC$, and this is nothing but the condition for maximizing profits in pure competition.

There are all kinds of modifications and developments that must be made to render this analysis applicable to the real world. But a certain *fundamental* relevance is suggested by its use as a model by socialist thinkers and planners.

QUESTIONS FOR DISCUSSION

1. Return to the general equilibrium diagram (Figure 22-1) and explain carefully why each of the equations in the various arrows holds true under pure competition. In each case, try to imagine circumstances in which, competition not being "pure," the equation might not hold. (For example, suppose firms charged different prices to different consumers for the same services—say, doctors charging different prices to different patients. Would it then be true that the MRS's for any two goods would be the same for all consumers?)

2. "The beauty of pure competition is that every individual is able to maximize his own satisfactions. This means that—subject to the overall limitations of resources in the economy—every individual is as well off as he could possibly be."

Set the author of this declaration straight by a careful critical analysis of his statement.

3. Using your full knowledge of the workings of a competitive economy as developed in Part Three A, but employing as little technical vocabulary as possible, explain to someone who knows no economics why a typewriter costs on the average five times as much as a pair of shoes.

4. Suppose that you have a purely competitive economy in which there is only one factor of production: labor of a standard, homogeneous quality. Would the labor theory of value (prices of goods are proportional to the quantities of labor employed in their production) hold true in this case? Explain your answer.

5. Would you like to live in a perfectly "efficient" society? For what economic objectives might you be willing to sacrifice some economic efficiency? For what non-economic objectives?

22
Appendix:
A Diagrammatic Treatment
of Production Efficiency

Let us relate the analysis of this chapter to some of our earlier diagrams. To do this, let us return to a problem we mentioned in the first chapter of Part Three A. Read page 417 again. In Figure 17-8 we described a situation in which an economy was producing two commodities—wheat and houses—in an *in*efficient way. We were able to prove this inefficiency by showing that a reallocation of land and labor could permit us to produce *both* more wheat and more houses without using additional resources.

This reallocation was possible because the original situation did not fulfill what we have described on p. 424 as *efficiency in production.* It did not meet the condition that the ratio of the marginal products of labor and land in wheat production was equal to the ratio of the marginal products of labor and land in house production.

In order to show graphically what the fulfillment of this condition means, let us draw a new diagram that, in effect, puts together Figure 17-8(*a*) and Figure 17-8(*b*). This has been done in Figure 1 in what is usually called a box diagram.

To construct this diagram, let us imagine that we have a given amount of labor and land in our economy. We measure labor vertically (the height of the box is the amount of labor available to the economy) and land horizontally (the

length of the box is the amount of land available to the economy). Imagine that we start in the lower left-hand corner: the wheat origin. We can now draw isoquants for wheat production (the solid isoquants) showing how we can produce different quantities of wheat as we use different quantities of land and labor for wheat production. Starting from the wheat origin, our diagram is constructed exactly as we constructed Figure 17-8(*a*). (The only difference is that we have boxed in the isoquants to indicate a given amount of land and labor available to the economy.)

The next step is a bit more complicated to visualize. Essentially, what we now do is to repeat the same procedure for houses—i.e., Figure 17-8(*b*)—but this time we start off in the upper right-hand or northeast corner. Turn the page upside down and imagine drawing isoquants for house production (the broken-line isoquants), showing how house production will alter as we use different quantities of labor and land to construct houses.

The virtue of putting both these diagrams in one picture is that we can show by any point in the diagram the following *six* quantities: (1) the amount of wheat produced, (2) the number of houses produced, (3) the amount of labor used in wheat production, (4) the amount of land used in wheat production, (5) the amount of labor used in house production, and (6) the amount of land used in house production. Take points A and B and show how these six quantities can be determined for either of these points. (To do this numerically, we really need numbers on our isoquants and, in the case of point B, we must draw in additional isoquants. Test your understanding of the diagram by supplying the necessary hypothetical data.)

With the box diagram before us, we can now show very readily what efficiency in production involves. In the first place, we can see that this economy will be efficient only if it is producing at points where the isoquants of wheat and houses are just tangent to each other; i.e., at points on the line from O_w to O_h through A. To prove this, let us compare point A with

a point off the line, point B. It can be easily seen that when we move from point B to point A, we are increasing wheat production; but it can just as easily be seen (turning the page upside down) that when we move from B to A, we are also increasing house production. In general, when we are off this "efficiency-line," it can be shown that we can make a move toward the line in such a way that we increase the production of both commodities. Hence, we can conclude that the economy will be efficient in production only if it is producing at a point where the isoquant of wheat production is just tangent to an isoquant for house production.

But what does it mean to say that these isoquants are tangent? Mathematically, it means that at these points the

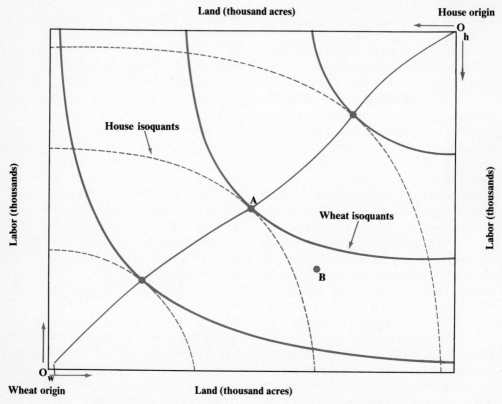

Figure 1. Box Diagram Showing Efficiency in Production.

slopes of the two isoquants are equal. We have already learned (chapter 17, p. 418–19) what the slope of an isoquant is. It is equal to the ratio of the marginal products of the factors of production; in this case, the ratio of the marginal product of land to the marginal product of labor. To say that slopes of the isoquants of wheat and house production are equal, therefore, is to say *that the ratios of the marginal products of land to labor are the same for both commodities.* The analysis is therefore complete.

RELATION TO PRODUCTION-POSSIBILITY OR TRANSFORMATION CURVE

We can also use this diagram to explain a familiar tool we have been using throughout this book: the production-possibility or transformation curve. Having derived the efficiency line (often called the *contract line*) in Figure 1, we could use the information indicated by that line in a diagram in which we measured house production on one axis and wheat production on the other. If we had numbers on the isoquants in Figure 1, we could say that point *A* represented so many houses and so many units of wheat. Point *A* would then appear as a point on a new curve as in Figure 2. If we proceeded to do this for all points on the efficiency or contract line, we would then have derived our old friend, the transformation curve.

What about point *B*? Essentially, it lies *inside* the transformation curve. In this form, the meaning of production efficiency may be more easily seen than in the somewhat more complicated-appearing box diagram. For it is quite clear that, other things equal, most societies would prefer to be at point *A* than at point *B*.

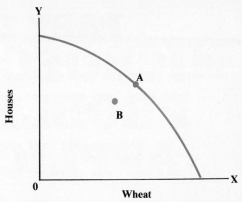

Figure 2. The Transformation Curve.

We can have more of *both* houses and wheat at *A*, and without additional resource costs.

EXERCISE

Construct a box diagram for two consumers and two commodities, similar to that constructed for producers on p. 514. Draw in the *contract line*. Why is any point on this line *efficient*? Draw in a point *P,* somewhere in the middle of the diagram but not on the contract line. Decide whether each of the following statements about point *P* is true or false:

(*a*) It is better to be at *P* than at any point on the contract line.

(*b*) It is better to be at any point on the contract line than at point *P*.

(*c*) There are always some points on the contract line better than *P*.

(*d*) It is always better to be at *P* than at some points on the contract line.

(*e*) It may be better to be at *P* than at some points on the contract line.

(Think carefully before you answer each of these questions. Decide, among other things, the meaning you wish to give the word *better* in the above statements.)

PART THREE B
MICROECONOMICS: PROBLEMS AND APPLICATIONS

23
Efficiency and International Trade

It is highly appropriate to begin our applications of the tools of microeconomics with the field of international trade since it was in this field, historically, that some of the most significant advances in microeconomic analysis first took place. We shall say a word about these early steps and then bring the theory of the benefits of trade up to date. In the second half of the chapter, we shall take up some of the varied arguments that have been used to support restrictions on trade, featuring in particular two readings on the subject of oil import quotas.

RICARDO—
ENGLAND AND PORTUGAL, CLOTH AND WINE

The question of efficiency in international trade is very much like the question of efficiency with respect to the domestic economy. Essentially, that question is: can we reallocate our resources so as to make everybody better off, or at

least somebody better off and nobody worse off?

A difference in the case of international trade, of course, may be political. We may not *want* to make everybody better off, or they us. In the extreme case of a war, a country may go to great lengths (including blockades in some cases) to prevent another nation from becoming "better off" even though this effort is at great cost to the originating country. We shall return to some of the political aspects of trade in a moment. Let us begin, however, with the assumption that the countries involved are concerned with economic efficiency only—i.e., that they wish to continue to trade as long as it can be shown that there are *mutual benefits* to be achieved that way.

Now it was one of the great triumphs of the British classical economists of the late eighteenth and early nineteenth centuries to have demonstrated that "efficient" trade (though they did not use that term) could best be secured by *free trade.* In earlier mercantilist thought, the tendency had been to regard international trade as a case of my (or your) gains versus your (or my) losses. "Whatsoever is somewhere gained is elsewhere lost" is a characteristic statement of mercantilist philosophy. The general question of economic efficiency, as we have been discussing it in the past few chapters, however, is precisely concerned with situations where *all* parties can gain. And this was precisely what the later British classical economists showed for international trade: remove tariffs, quotas, and restrictions, they said, and *all nations will benefit*.

Since the classical argument is largely convincing even to this day, let us quote directly from one of its first proponents, David Ricardo:

CULVER PICTURES

David Ricardo (1782-1823). David Ricardo was a businessman before he became an economist, but his economic writings are very lean and abstract. Besides his contribution to international trade theory, he expounded Malthusian ideas on population, developed a version of the labor theory of value (which greatly influenced Karl Marx), and set an example of rigor in economics which influenced generations of economists who followed. Keynes said that Ricardo conquered England the way the "Holy Inquisition conquered Spain."

ON FOREIGN TRADE

DAVID RICARDO

Under a system of perfectly free commerce, each country naturally devotes its capital and labour to such employments as are most beneficial to each. This pursuit of individual advantage is admirably connected with the universal good of the whole. By stimulating industry, by rewarding ingenuity, and by using most efficaciously the peculiar powers bestowed by nature, it distributes labour most effectively and most economically: while, by increasing the general mass of productions, it diffuses general benefit, and binds together by one common tie of interest and intercourse, the universal society of nations throughout the civilized world. It is this principle which determines that wine shall be made in France and Portugal, that corn shall be grown in America and Poland, and that hardware and other goods shall be manufactured in England.

If Portugal had no commercial connexion with other countries, instead of employing a great part of her capital and industry in the production of wines, with which she purchases for her own use the cloth and hardware of other countries, she would be obliged to devote a part of that capital to the manufacture of those commodities, which she would thus obtain probably inferior in quality as well as quantity.

The quantity of wine which she shall give in exchange for the cloth

Excerpted from David Ricardo, "On Foreign Trade," in **On the Principles of Political Economy and Taxation** (New York: Cambridge University Press, 1951), pp. 133-35. Reprinted by permission of the publisher.

of England, is not determined by the respective quantities of labour devoted to the production of each, as it would be, if both commodities were manufactured in England, or both in Portugal.

England may be so circumstanced, that to produce the cloth may require the labour of 100 men for one year; and if she attempted to make the wine, it might require the labour of 120 men for the same time. England would therefore find it her interest to import wine, and to purchase it by the exportation of cloth.

To produce the wine in Portugal, might require only the labour of 80 men for one year, and to produce the cloth in the same country, might require the labour of 90 men for the same time. It would therefore be advantageous for her to export wine in exchange for cloth. This exchange might even take place, notwithstanding that the commodity imported by Portugal could be produced there with less labour than in England. Though she could make the cloth with the labour of 90 men, she would import it from a country where it required the labour of 100 men to produce it, because it would be advantageous to her rather to employ her capital in the production of wine, for which she would obtain more cloth from England, than she could produce by diverting a portion of her capital from the cultivation of vines to the manufacture of cloth.

This rather sparse prose in presenting a major argument is typical of Ricardo, who was, in his way, one of the most rigorous economists of all time. Let us rephrase his argument, using tools we have developed earlier in this book.

What we really have here are two production-possibility curves—one for

England and one for Portugal—each for the two products, wine and cloth. They are rather special production-possibility curves, however, in that they are not bowed out (see our earlier discussion on pp. 16–17), but are straight lines. The basic reason for this is that Ricardo is talking about one factor of production only—labor. In his example, the amount of labor it takes to produce either commodity in either country does not *vary* as the production of that commodity increases or decreases. Since this is the hypothetical situation, England (or Portugal) could expand cloth production at the expense of wine production without running into the problem of increasing costs.[1]

Two such production-possibility curves are shown in Figure 23-1. Notice, first, that each country's curve has a constant slope—meaning, as we have just said, that we can add more of one commodity at an unchanged cost in terms of the other commodity no matter what the level of production is. Also notice, however, that this constant slope is a *different* slope from one country to the other. In particular, England's slope is steeper.

Why? The answer is in the Ricardo reading. England uses relatively less labor to produce cloth, relatively more to produce wine; in Portugal, it is the reverse. With all her labor devoted to wine production, England would produce only 5/6 as many units of wine as she would produce units of cloth if all her labor were devoted to cloth production. In the case of Portugal, the comparable number would be 1 1/8. The reader should make sure he understands these two numbers and can relate them to the slopes of lines

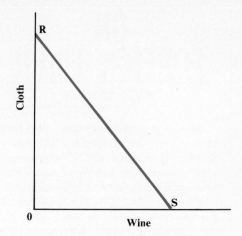

England's production-possibility curve.
(a)

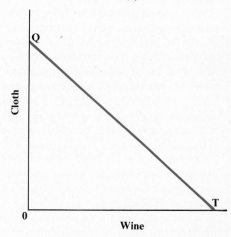

Portugal's production-possibility curve.
(b)

Figure 23-1. Production-Possibilities in the Ricardian Example.

RS and *QT* in Figures 23-1(a) and (b).[2]

Now to show how both countries can benefit from trade, we bring these two

---

1. By "increasing costs" here, we would mean precisely that as cloth production expanded along a given production-possibility curve, it would take increasingly larger quantities of wine production foregone to add a unit of cloth. We shall take up this case (p. 522).

2. What we have said in the text will explain the fact that these two production-possibility curves have (a) a constant slope and (b) a different slope. What we have not explained is the position of these two lines—i.e., how far out from the origin. This position, of course, would basically reflect the size of the two countries. In our hypothetical case, for convenience, we have made the countries about the same size.

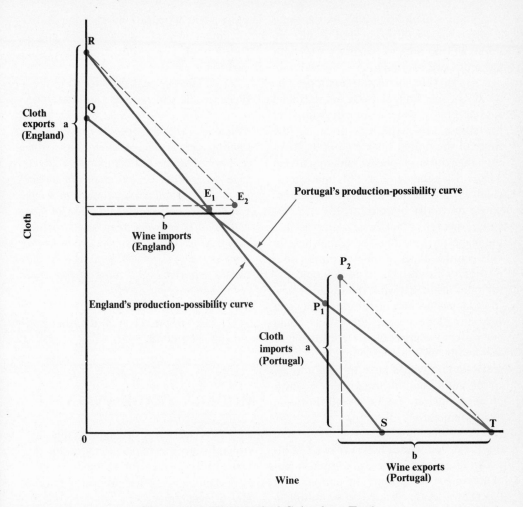

Figure 23-2. Hypothetical Gains from Trade.

Suppose hypothetically, that England and Portugal, without trade, are located at points E_1 and P_1, respectively. Ricardo showed that, (*with* trade, both countries could be better off (e.g., moving to points E_2 and P_2, respectively). In this example, both countries specialize completely.

production-possibility curves into one dia-gram, as in Figure 23-2. Ignoring the little triangles for a moment, let us suppose that England, initially, is at some point, E_1, on its production-possibility curve, and that Portugal, initially, is at P_1. How then can we show that trade can be mutually bene-ficial?

Ricardo says that England should specialize in cloth and import its wine; Portugal, the reverse. After this specializa-tion has taken place, England's produc-tion position will be at R (producing OR units of cloth), but, by trading a units of cloth for b units of Portuguese wine, she will end up at E_2, having more of *both* commodities than originally. By the same logic Portugal will produce at T, but, by trade, will be able to reach P_2, *also* with more of both commodities.

In the Ricardian example, he speaks of one unit of cloth being traded for one unit of wine. In our drawing, this exchange ratio would be given by the slope of the dotted lines RE_2 or P_2T. An exchange ratio of one would mean that $a/b = 1$, or that $a = b$. This specific exchange ratio is not required to demonstrate mutually beneficial trade in this case, however. What *is* necessary is that the slope of these lines be somewhere in between the slopes of the two production-possibility curves. The reader should figure out for himself what the range of possible slopes would be in this case and why any slope *outside* the range would not work. Of course, the determination of the finally effective exchange rate in a real situation would have to take into account additional information, e.g., how much people in England and Portugal liked wine, etc.

Without going any further into the Ricardian world, however, we can already note the impressive accomplishment of this piece of analysis. In particular, it has shown us that trade can be mutually beneficial between two countries even when one country—in this case, Portugal—has an absolute advantage in the production of *both* commodities. Portugal requires less labor to produce wine *and* cloth than England, in Ricardo's examples. The key is relative cost, or what economists call *comparative advantage*. Portugal has an absolute advantage in both wine and cloth, but England has a *comparative* advantage in cloth because she has to give up fewer units of wine to produce a unit of cloth than does Portugal. This is shown by the greater steepness of her production-possibility curve. By the same logic, Portugal has a comparative advantage in wine—shown by the greater flatness of *her* production-possibility curve.

The classical theory and philosophy of trade can now be summed up:

Countries can gain benefits from trade in almost every conceivable circumstance since it is not absolute *but* comparative *advantage that counts. Countries should specialize in those commodities in which they have comparative advantages and trade for those commodities in which they have disadvantages. Since restrictions on trade simply limit the degree to which mutual benefits can be enjoyed by all nations, free trade is the best way for everyone!*

A simple, clear and rather convincing statement!

MODERN TRADE ANALYSIS

As it basically remains to this day. Probably more economists agree on the desirability of free (or at least "freer") trade than on any other proposition in the field of economics.

Still, the case as presented so far is clearly based on rather special assumptions, and also there are a few plausible arguments against free trade that should be noted. Let us first modernize the Ricardian argument and then take up some of the reasons that are urged for placing tariffs or other restrictions on international trade.

The main limitations of the Ricardian argument derive from the fact that it uses only one factor of production, labor, and that it presents a final equilibrium in which one country produces all of one commodity and the other all of the other commodity. In real life, several factors of production cooperate in the production of any given commodity. Furthermore, the characteristic trading situation is for a country to produce part of the supply of a commodity domestically and to import the rest. It would be very rare for a country to import all its machinery, or all its food, or even all its wine.

We can avoid these limitations by presenting the analysis in terms of production-possibility curves of the same shapes as those developed earlier in this book. Two such curves are drawn in Figure 23-3, one for England and one for Portugal. The curves are bowed out this time, because we are using more than one factor of production to produce these commodities. As either country tries to produce more of one commodity, she must pay a higher cost in terms of the other commodity (opportunity cost) because the factors of production suited to one commodity are not ideally suited to the production of the other and these commodities ordinarily use different factors in different proportions. This point has been discussed before. The difference between England and Portugal that makes trade desirable in this case is that the two countries have different factor availabilities, or *factor endowments*, as it is sometimes called. England has large quantities of textile machinery, Portugal abundant vineyard land. Without trade, the two countries might be located at points E_1 and P_1 respectively. Notice that at these two points, England has a comparative advantage in cloth production and Portugal has a comparative advantage in wine production. How do we know this? Because the slope of England's production-possibility curve is steeper at E_1, than Portugal's at P_1. The spirit of the Ricardian argument now tells us that England will tend to specialize in cloth production and Portugal in wine pro-

This is correct, but the specialization will no longer be complete. That is to say, both countries in this example will end up producing both commodities. In each case, trade will have the effect of increasing the country's production of the commodity in which she has a compara-

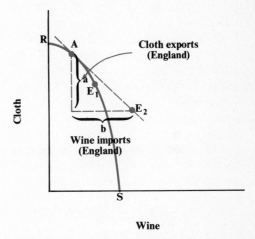

England's production-possibility curve (England has lots of textile machinery).
(a)

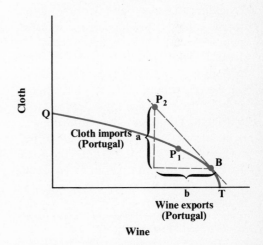

Portugal's production-possibility curve (Portugal has abundant vineyard land).
(b)

Figure 23-3. Trade Between England and Portugal.

tive advantage.

A possible equilibrium situation is shown by the triangles in Figures 23-3 (a) and (b). Portugal is now producing at point B (as opposed to P_1) and is consuming wine and cloth at P_2. This involves her exchanging b wine exports for a cloth imports from Britain. The fact that she is better off is indicated by her ability to move out beyond her original production-possibility curve. Trade in this sense is very much like an outward shift of the production-possibility curve such as we associate with economic growth.

The same sort of thing has happened to England, although she has moved from E_1 to A in terms of production (*increasing* cloth and *decreasing* wine production) and ends up consuming at point E_2.

The reader will notice that we have drawn the dotted lines AE_2 and P_2B as tangent to the two production-possibility curves at points A and B respectively. What does this signify? Mathematically, it signifies that the slope of these dotted lines is equal to the slope of the transformation curves at these points. What is the slope of AE_2?[3] It is a/b, or the quantity of cloth England must export in order to get the quantity of wine she has imported—i.e., the exchange ratio between wine and cloth. Or to put the same thing in terms of prices: in order for trade to balance, the price of cloth (P_c) times the quantity of cloth exported (a) must equal the price of wine (P_w) times the quantity of wine imported (b), or:

$$P_c \times a = P_w \times b,$$

or

$$\frac{a}{b} = \frac{P_w}{P_c}.$$

Knowing this, we can now understand the significance of the tangency of these dotted lines to the production-possibility curves. It signifies that the price ratios of the two commodities will be qual to the ratios of their marginal costs (see p. 462). Assuming that we are dealing with competitive economies, this must be so or else we would not be in equilibrium. If the price ratio differed from the marginal cost ratio in either country, then producers in that country would have a motive to shift production away from the relatively high to the relatively low marginal cost product. It is only when these price and marginal cost ratios are equal, and when, of course, the values of exports and imports are equal,[4] that the countries will reach a possible equilibrium situation.

This analysis enables us to show in a more complicated case how trade benefits both parties, and it also gives us some insight into the underlying economic reasons that make this possible. Essentially, what our example tells us is that trade is a way of getting around shortages of various factors of production. Portugal is short of textile machinery, but she can so to speak "ease" this factor scarcity by letting British machinery produce some of her cloth for her. The same thing happens in reverse for the British who, being short of vineyards, can happily enjoy Portugal's abundance of the same.[5] Thus, this mod-

3. Or, equivalently, what is the slope of P_2B? These slopes are equal, being in each case equal to a/b.

4. In this hypothetical commodity world, balance of payments surpluses or deficits have no role. But see chapter 15.

5. In advanced theoretical treatments of trade, it is sometimes pointed out that not only will commodity prices be equalized between the countries trading, but also that there will be a tendency towards the *equalization of factor prices.* We cannot develop this point here, but the reader can already see some of the basic logic involved. Before trade, textile machinery would tend to be relatively scarce (and expensive) in Portugal and vineyard land relatively scarce (and expensive) in Britain. Since the effect of trade is to "ease" these scarcities in each country, it will tend to bring the factor prices closer together.

ern analysis, far from contradicting the essential message of the classical economists, tends to strengthen and expand upon those early insights. It leaves the case for free trade largely intact.

SOME ARGUMENTS FOR RESTRICTING TRADE

Still, there is a bit more to the story than this. For although economists as a group are fairly unanimous about the wisdom of freer trade, the fact is that tariffs, quotas, and other trade restrictions have been a central fact in the economic history of every modern nation, the United States very much included. Before Ricardo ever wrote his analysis, Alexander Hamilton was defending protection for infant industries in his famous *Report on Manufactures.* In the period between the War of 1812 and the Civil War there was great strife between the North and the South on the tariff question. When the so-called Tariff of Abominations was passed in 1828, South Carolina responded by proclaiming the doctrine of "nullification."

Actually, the tariff history of the United States is one of great upswings and downswings in tariff rates as one or the other side of the controversy has held the upper hand. After World War I, there was a sharp rise in tariffs around the world, including the United States, but since the mid-1930s, the trend has been downward. Thus, while in 1930–31, duties collected on dutiable imports into the United States averaged over half the value of the imports, by 1970 the percentage had fallen below 10 percent. In the early 1970s, however, the United States began hearing renewed murmurings in favor of increased protection.

Clearly, statesmen and governments from time to time have felt compelling reasons for restricting trade. What are some of these reasons? And how do they stand up to modern analysis?

The truth is that some of them don't stand up very well at all. Many of them involve arguments that are incomplete. For example, it is often stated that United States' industries need protection against low-wage foreign industries. This argument is incomplete because it does not take into account the fact that wage rates in different countries will reflect to a significant degree the productivity of labor in those countries. The incompleteness of the argument can be seen by noting how easily the whole thing can be reversed. That is, low-wage foreign industries often demand protection on the grounds that their laborers, unskilled and without much machinery, cannot compete with the well-trained American labor force with its complement of high-speed computers and assembly-line techniques.

There are, however, some arguments for tariffs and other trade restrictions that cut a bit deeper than this. In most cases, these arguments involve a weighing of one objective against another. In particular, free trade is usually agreed to be the most "efficient" arrangement at any given moment of time; but it is then argued that other objectives can outweigh economic efficiency and that quotas or tariffs will help achieve these other objectives. Let us mention a few of these arguments:

1. Short-Run Macroeconomic Objectives

We know from chapter 15 that international trade can have significant effects on macroeconomic objectives, such as achieving full employment. Since imports are like savings in having a direct negative impact on aggregate demand, it has been argued that a country, suffering unemployment, should restrict trade through tariffs or import quotas (or conversely stimulate exports by various kinds of subsidies). These actions would increase aggregate demand for domestic products and cause a general expansion of employment in the country. Tariffs can also be used in a general macroeconomic way to "protect" the country's balance of payments. This was the stated purpose behind President Nixon's 10 percent import surcharge of August 15, 1971.[6]

Since we have discussed these macroeconomic problems before, let us simply note here that there are two main disadvantages of using tariff or other trade restrictions as a way of solving these problems. The first is the general point that these restrictions always impose *some* cost in terms of efficiency. The second is that retaliation is so easy. In our interdependent modern world, if one nation is suffering from severe unemployment problems it is not unlikely that others will face similar difficulties. The effort to improve one's own position by tariffs is essentially an effort to impose one's own problems on other nations. (After all, if it is good for us to cut imports, it is very likely to be harmful for them to have their exports reduced.) If retaliation does take place, then the nations involved may have achieved the worst of all possible worlds—trade has been inefficiently reduced, while no one's employment position has improved.

2. National Security

Tariffs, quotas, and other restrictions are sometimes justified as a necessary cost that must be paid by the nation for overall security reasons. Usually this involves some strategic goods, or, in the case of exports, certain classified processes. One is not allowed to export the plans and materials for building a hydrogen bomb factory! Where trade in strategic goods is limited, there are two possible arguments involved. One is that we should try to conserve our domestic supplies of the good; this would lead in theory to high imports of the good and restrictions on export of the good. The second line of argument is the reverse, namely, that we should keep our domestic producers vigorous by protecting them from foreign competition; this would lead to the imposition of tariffs or quotas on the import of the product from abroad. We simply mention this difficulty so the reader will have it in mind when we take up the specific question of oil import quotas on p. 528.

3. Terms of Trade Arguments

If a country holds a significant position in trading relations with other countries, it may try to exert monopoly power through the use of trade restrictions in order to improve what economists call its *terms of trade*. There are various technical definitions of this phrase, but its simplest meaning is the ratio of the prices a country receives for its exports to the prices it pays out for its imports. Suppose that a country is aware that the price of a particular import will rise as it imports more of that commodity from abroad. It may be in the country's interest to restrict imports of that particular commodity so as to keep its price lower. Although the advocates of free trade are correct in saying that, under ordinary conditions, departures from free trade cannot benefit *both* parties, nevertheless it may be true that departures from free trade can benefit one party *at the expense of* the other. This "beggar-my-neighbor" policy is like the similar policy of improving a country's domestic employment situation by exporting its depression abroad. In both cases,

---

6. However, this action was also clearly used as a bargaining weapon in the effort to get certain other countries, like Japan, to revalue their currencies. See p. 363

the policy invites retaliation. Thus, a country seeking to improve its terms of trade by worsening the terms of trade of its neighbor runs the risk of gaining only a short-term advantage until the exploited country or countries retaliate, and then all parties together lose because of the inefficiency of heavily regulated trade.

4. Infant Industries and Development

Another category of arguments for protection has to do with young or "infant" industries that, if unprotected, might fall victim to disastrous competition from abroad. These arguments clearly have most relevance to underdeveloped countries where the necessary capital and skills have not yet been accumulated to make competitively viable modern industries possible. However, they could also be applied to particular industries in more developed countries where the country happens to take up this industry at a later date than a few leading countries and, in particular, where substantial economies of scale exist. In the long run, free trade is the natural ally of industries with large economies of scale, since it offers the largest possible market for the product, i.e., the world market. However, in the short run, it may take time before an industry can reach the stage where it is large enough to enjoy the potential economies of scale involved; in this interim, protection could be justified to keep the industry's head above water.

These arguments have wide appeal today in many of the less developed countries of the world, particularly among those who feel that they are suffering worsening terms of trade at the hands of the industrialized nations.[7] However, these

arguments run some danger of being overused. It is certainly not clear in efficiency terms (though it may be defended on national security or other grounds) that every nation should have every large-scale modern industry represented within its borders. Nor is it clear that when infant industries "grow up" the clamor for their continued protection will cease. There *are* some valid cases for infant industry protection, but most economists suspect that they are rather fewer in number than their proponents might suggest.

5. Protection for Particular Industries

Finally, there are a number of arguments for trade restrictions that have to do with the well-being of particular sectors of the economy. These arguments are perhaps the ones most frequently heard when it comes, say, to removing any particular tariff or other trade barrier; indeed, some cynics believe that such arguments underlie most, if not all, of the other "defenses" of protection.

Occasionally, protection for particular industries is supported on a merely transitional basis. It may be agreed, for example, that X-industry is less efficient than its foreign competitors, but it may be felt that it would be too harsh on both the employers who have sunk their capital in this industry and the workers whose livelihoods depend on this industry to subject them to the full force of foreign competition. This is, so to speak, the infant industry argument in reverse—protect a decaying industry so that it can decay with less hardship to the people currently working in that industry. This argument sometimes gains added force if a whole region is heavily dependent upon the particular industry, and, therefore, the problems of shifting capital and labor to other industries are more difficult.

One of the troubles here is that

---

7. The thesis that poor countries will face deterioration in their terms of trade over time (a generalization with many critics) is sometimes called the *Prebisch Thesis*, after Dr. Raoul Prebisch, a Latin American economist who argued that this would be the case.

decaying industries, like infant industries, may stay that way for a very long time. When this happens, what we have is the pure form of the question—namely, do we want to use tariffs, quotas, and other trade restrictions as a way of redistributing income in our society? There are really two subquestions to this larger question: (1) does this kind of trade legislation usually benefit those people in society who are most needy; and (2) is this the most efficient way of benefitting those people?

In general, most economists would be inclined to answer no to both questions. It seems highly unlikely that the very crude instruments of tariff or quota legislation would be able to single out exactly those people in society who are most deserving of aid on welfare grounds. Nor is there any evidence that the comparative neediness of the recipients has, historically, been a determining factor in judging who is to be so helped. Furthermore, the efficiency argument applies here as elsewhere. Tariffs and quotas lead to departures from the norm of efficiency that we have developed in earlier chapters, and, although all attempts to redistribute income are likely to have some adverse effects on efficiency, those that operate directly on the prices and quantities of commodities bought and sold are likely to have the most serious effects. Thus, the majority of economists tend to prefer to let the price system work as well as it can, and then to redistribute income through taxes and direct subsidies that have as few disincentive effects as possible. At a minimum, such programs make it perfectly clear what is being done by way of income distribution, and do not hide it in the enormous complexities of international trade transactions.

In short, the above qualifications suggest that while the case for free trade is by no means crystal clear, it is still no bad place to start in formulating actual government policies.

A CASE STUDY— OIL IMPORT QUOTAS

We end this chapter with two readings presenting the pros and cons of a particular piece of U.S. government trade policy: quotas on the imports of oil. The reader will notice a heavy reliance on the national security argument by Senator Long, and a denial of the view that the oil industry is being specially favored by this action. Professor Fisher, by contrast, questions the national security argument and raises several economist-type questions about efficiency and income distribution.

Legislative Quota on Imports of Oil

SENATOR RUSSELL LONG

Mr. President, I have today introduced a bill which would establish a legislative quota on imports of oil.

Mr. President, many nations of the free world, particularly those of Western Europe and Japan, today face a threatening and costly situation because their traditional oil supplies from the Middle East and Africa have been disrupted. The director of the Office of Oil and Gas, Department of the Interior, recently stated that a study of the implications of the Middle East crisis showed that "Japan and the nations of Western Europe stood to lose upward of 80 percent of their oil supply. By contrast, less than 3 percent of our own supply would be affected." That is not the full story, be-

Excerpted from Senator Russell Long, "Legislative Quota on Imports of Oil," *Congressional Record*, Senate, August 23, 1967. pp. 23777–80.

BLACK STAR

Oil import quotas. Of the many issues involving oil in a modern industrial society (oil-spills, pollution, exhaustibility of reserves, depletion allowances, etc.) U.S. oil import quotas rank high in promoting controversial opinions. They are also a case-study in free vs. regulated trade.

cause when the dictators of the Middle East cut off their oil from the consuming countries, the United States was fortunate enough to have a shut-in capacity available for such an emergency. Not only was this reserve sufficient to replace the 3 percent of our requirements previously supplied by the Middle East, but in addition it has been called upon to supply substantial quantities to our friends of the free world who were heavily dependent on the Middle East.

In brief, this very recent experience presents the reasons and justification and need for the bill I have introduced, much more forcefully than any words could possibly portray.

We can take great pride in the fact that our Nation, through the years, has encouraged the development within our own borders of a strong domestic petroleum industry. Credit for this fortunate situation must be shared by Congress, the executive branch of the Federal Government, and the governments of the several oil-producing States which have all contributed in providing policies enabling and encouraging the development of a domestic industry which is the envy of the world. Whatever problems we have had in assisting friendly nations in meeting their petroleum needs as a result of the current Middle East crisis, it takes little imagination to visualize how much more acute those problems would be if the United States were dependent on Middle

East or African oil to fuel our industrial machines, our automobiles and trucks, our trains, to heat our homes, and to supply our military forces, including the troops in Vietnam. In the absence of a domestic petroleum industry able to rise to the emergency, we would be in a desperate crisis. As in World War I, World War II, the Korean war, and the 1956 Suez crisis, the current Middle East episode persuasively demonstrates that the United States cannot afford to become dependent upon foreign sources for our oil supplies. This vital lesson has been repeatedly impressed upon us: that America's economic strength, its military supremacy, its freedom, its influence in the world, all depend heavily upon the health of the domestic oil-producing industry and its capability of meeting our growing petroleum needs.

The demand for oil in the United States currently is in the order of 12 million barrels daily. Prior to the current Middle East crisis, total imports of oil were averaging about 2,500,000 barrels daily. Of this total amount of imports, about 1 million barrels daily is residual fuel oil. This is a heavy fuel oil which is used by industry and large commercial users. Under the present mandatory oil import program, there are two separate programs, one for residual fuel oil and the other for crude oil and light petroleum products. The bill I have introduced does not cover residual fuel oil. The present administrative program covering residual fuel oil would continue unchanged. The bill would apply only to imports of crude oil and light products which have been averaging in the order of 1,500,000 barrels daily. My bill basically is designed to write the present mandatory oil import program for crude oil and light products into law. It would not require any major overhaul or alteration in the present program. What it would do is establish a few principal legislative guidelines, leaving the administrators of the program with broad discretionary authority in the administration of the program within these legislative guidelines.

EXPLANATION OF BILL

Under the mandatory oil import program, which has been in effect since 1959, the United States is divided into two areas: First, district I-IV which includes the District of Columbia and all the States of the United States except those States in district V; and, second, district V which includes the States of Arizona, Nevada, California, Oregon, Washington, Alaska, and Hawaii. Under the program, these two geographical areas are treated separately and differently; and the bill I have introduced would continue this treatment.

Paragraph (e)* of the bill would establish a legislative limit on imports into the United States east of the Rockies, that is district I-IV, of 12.2 percent of oil production in that area. The 12.2 percent limitation is the same that is presently in effect under the mandatory oil import program. This limitation has been in effect since the latter part of 1962. This is the key provision of the import program. If the program is to be meaningful and effective, if it is to have stability and if the industry is to have confidence in the program, this limitation on imports into district I-IV must be firmly established. Unfortunately, during the past

year, administrative actions have been taken which very seriously threaten the stability and integrity of the 12.2 limitation.

An example which clearly shows the need for firmly establishing the 12.2 limit by law involves imports from Canada. Under the Presidential proclamation establishing the mandatory oil import program, imports from Canada are within the 12.2 limit. In carrying out this mandate, imports from Canada each year are estimated and included within the 12.2 limit, the balance of permissible imports then being allocated for import from all other source countries. This method is fine in theory; but unfortunately, Canadian imports have consistently exceeded the estimate. Last year, imports from Canada exceeded the estimate by about 50,000 barrels daily. This is a large loophole in the program and it threatens to grow larger. If the mandatory oil import program is to be meaningful and effective, this Canadian loophole and the other loopholes and threats to the program which I have mentioned must be closed.

Paragraph (f)† of the bill applies to the Western States which are included in district V. Under the present program, district V is accorded separate and different treatment because within that area there is an inadequate local production as compared with consumption. In contrast, in the Eastern States, that is districts I-IV, we have historically had a substantial excess producing capacity. That is the basic reason these two areas under the present program have been treated differently. It is important that the program in district V be designed to encourage the development of

*"(e) Imports of petroleum into Districts I-IV shall not exceed 12.2 per centum of production of crude petroleum and natural gas liquids in those Districts during the most recent appropriate period for which U.S. Bureau of Mines statistics are available."

†"(f) Imports of petroleum into District V shall be limited so as to encourage development of District V production and use of domestic supplies in that District, but in no event shall the maximum level of overseas imports which shall be subject to allocation, be greater than the amount necessary, when added to domestic supply available to the District and to the volume of overland imports into the District which shall be exempt from allocation, to approximate total District V demand. Determination of supply-demand relationships in the District shall be made by the U.S. Bureau of Mines for appropriate periods."

production within that area and for the fullest use economically feasible of oil from States located east of the Rocky Mountains. To date the program in district V has generally served this purpose and for this reason I believe the present program for their area should be continued without basic change.

THE NEED FOR CONGRESSIONAL ACTION

Mr. President, the petroleum industry in the United States today fortunately is strong and capable of meeting our current requirements. But, unfortunately, there is pursuasive evidence that, during recent years, in fact, for the past ten years, the industry has suffered persistent deterioration and there is real danger that it may not remain strong enough in the years ahead to meet our ever-increasing requirements. For ten years the drilling of wells, both exploratory and development and other activities which constitute the major indicators of the industry's health and vigor have declined. These trends may be summarized as follows:

1966 DECREASE BELOW BASE PERIOD, 1957-59

[percent]	
Geophysical activity	—38.7
Active rotary rigs	—40.5
Exploratory wells	—24.7
Total wells	—27.5
Employment	—15.3
Crude oil price	— 4.0

These trends for the past ten years show that there has not been adequate incentive for the exploration and development of new reserves of petroleum in the United States. This is reflected in the facts which show that during the past ten years we have found and developed new reserves barely equal to our consumption. Prior to the past decade, we found 1 1/2 or 2 times current requirements. If we are to meet the increasing needs of the future, the current drilling and finding rate must be increased—as it certainly can be—otherwise, at some period in

the near future, we may not be able to meet our requirements. If such should ever be the case, a Middle East crisis such as we now have would be disastrous. For this reason, we must not permit these declining trends in the domestic petroleum industry to continue. We must not sit idly by. It is clear that action is needed, and I believe the primary responsibility lies with Congress.

The bill I have introduced may not be the full answer to this problem. No one can be sure that firmly limiting imports to the 12.2 ratio will provide adequate incentive to the domestic petroleum industry so as to enable it to reverse the deteriorating trends of the past ten years. But it is obvious that the present situation cannot be permitted to continue. It is obvious that positive and affirmative action is required in order to assure our future energy needs. It is obvious that the present mandatory oil import program has been weakened by the creation of loopholes in the program and is seriously threatened by additional ones. As a result, the industry is losing confidence in the program. Its stability and effectiveness has been impaired. The program no longer provides the assurance that is necessary if the domestic industry is to have the incentive to plan long-range programs in the development of new reserves of petroleum. This failure of the program is causing serious threats to our domestic economy throughout the oil producing States; but far more important is that our security position is weakened. We cannot as a nation permit this to continue.

Mr. President, the Congress has the responsibility to firm up the mandatory oil import program and make it more effective so as to provide the consuming public of the United States with insurance against some future Middle East crisis.

The nations in Western Europe and Japan are paying dearly for the disruption of their traditional oil supplies from the Middle East and Africa. The oil formerly shipped through the Suez Canal must now be hauled around the continent of Africa to reach its European destinations. Tanker rates have soared and prices to consumers have reflected these increased costs. However, shipments of Middle East and North African oil to Great Britain and the United States is not available at any price. These Arab nations have declared a boycott on oil shipments to us and our British friends and several of them have also included West Germany among the boycotted nations. So currently Middle East and North African oil laid down in the principal consuming nations is very expensive indeed, rather than cheap, and in certain instances is not available at any price.

Therefore, Mr. President, I submit that the present mandatory import program the objective of which is the maintenance of a healthy petroleum industry in the United States capable of meeting our needs in peace and in war must be firmed up in order

to insure this Nation against becoming overly dependent on overseas supplies of oil which are beyond our control. This insurance policy would be reflected in adequate supplies for our needs and substantial emergency reserves available to alleviate the needs of free world nations which have become dependent on Middle East oil.

Mr. President, I know there are those who contend that the limitation of oil imports means that the consuming public will have to pay ever-increasing and unreasonably high prices for oil. The record completely disproves this contention. The mandatory oil import program has been in effect since 1959 and during the intervening years oil prices compare most favorably with prices for other commodities. The following two tables compare oil prices with other commodity prices:

RETAIL PRICE TRENDS FOR OIL AND ALL COMMODITIES
[1957-59 = 100]

	Retail price index, regular grade gasoline		Consumers' price index, all commodities
	Tax excluded	Tax included	
1957	102.4	101.2	98.5
1962	94.3	100.1	103.2
1966	99.9	104.8	102.2
June 1967	103.7	107.1	110.5

WHOLESALE PRICE TRENDS FOR OIL AND ALL COMMODITIES
[1957-59 = 100]

	Crude oil price index	Wholesale price index, principal oil products (gasoline, kerosene, distillate and residual fuel oil)	Wholesale price index, all commodities
1957	102.9	106.0	99.0
1962	96.8	95.8	100.6
1966	96.0	96.0	105.9
June 1967	96.7	98.8	105.8

The price record speaks for itself.

The oil industry can point with pride at their record of prices. Far from contributing to the inflation record, the facts show that crude oil prices and the refinery prices of the principal oil products have assisted in alleviating the inflationary push as reflected in the prices for all commodities.

The reasonableness of oil prices can also be demonstrated in other ways. For example, an hour's wage, based on the average for all manufacturing industries now buys 8.5 gallons of gasoline which is one-third more than ten years ago and 10 percent more than five years ago. Additionally, today's gasoline is a far superior product to that used ten or even five years ago.

The facts on oil prices show that the import program has not resulted in higher prices but that prices to the producer and to the refiner have actually declined. The import program has been an insurance policy for assuring adequate domestic supply in normal times and in emergencies such as the current Middle East debacle without causing unreasonable prices. Actually the insurance policy has cost nothing while providing a domestic industry that can supply our needs so that we need be beholden to no foreign government for our energy supplies.

Mr. President, there are also those who contend that a limitation on oil imports leads to unreasonable and unjustified profits by the oil industry. An analysis of profits and the earnings record of the petroleum industry shows this argument to be false. A comparison of the rate of return after taxes for all manufacturing corporations, except newspapers as reported by the FTC-SEC when compared with the rate of return on stockholders' equity for the domestic petroleum industry show that the domestic petroleum industry's rate of return has consistently lagged behind that for all manufacturing corporations.

Mr. President, by any test an effective mandatory oil import program is cheap insurance for the American consuming public.

SUMMARY OF STATEMENT BEFORE THE COMMITTEE ON FINANCE

FRANKLIN M. FISHER

The argument that quotas on petroleum imports enhance the security of the United States is a false one. To ensure the preservation of domestic oil supplies in the event of a petroleum crisis, the United States should import freely and reduce consumption of domestically produced oil. While it is true that this would sharply curtail petroleum exploration, it is not true that petroleum discoveries would be so greatly affected as to make

Franklin M. Fisher, "Summary," Statement, Hearing of the Committee on Finance, 90th Congress, 1st sess., 1967, pp. 1–5.

domestic reserves decrease substantially if at all. If it is desirable for strategic purposes to ensure that some oil reserves are kept in a readily producible state, this should be done by stockpiling reserves in the ground analogous to the treatment of other strategic materials. It should not be done by keeping gasoline and other oil prices high at the expense of American consumers.

In fact, the main effect of oil import quotas is the maintenance of high prices and the subsidization of various relatively inefficient domestic producers at the expense of the American motorist. Quotas should be discontinued, not written into law.

I. OIL IMPORT QUOTAS AND NATIONAL SECURITY

The basic argument put forward in favor of oil import quotas is one of national security. It is argued that free imports of oil make us reliant on foreign sources which may be (and have been) cut off or diminished in the event of an emergency. By limiting imports, we free ourselves from international political blackmail (principally by the

Arabs). I believe this argument to be false. The imposition of oil import quotas does not advance the security of the United States and it unduly penalizes the American motorists.

It is obvious that for the national security argument for oil import quotas to be right, it must be so for somewhat subtle reasons. If free imports lead to heavy use of imported oil and a cutback in domestic production displaced by imports, the natural conclusion is that domestic oil will not be used up so fast and there will be more of it around in the event of an emergency than would be the case if imports were limited and domestic production expanded. If one wants to have strategic material on hand for crises, a reasonable way to behave is to stockpile it and use foreign sources in non-crisis situations, not to use up domestic supplies faster. This is United States government policy with respect to most other strategic materials.

This argument is realized by quota proponents. They claim that the true situation is as follows:

(A) Domestic supplies of crude oil in the ground change when oil is produced (a subtraction) and when new oil is discovered (an addition).

(B) Free imports will reduce domestic production and thus indeed reduce the rate at which we subtract from known oil reserves.

(C) However, free oil imports will also reduce the price of crude oil. This will reduce the incentive to exploration for and discovery of oil. Exploration is very sensitive to such incentives and will fall off drastically.

(D) This will greatly reduce additions to oil reserves through new discoveries and

(E) The net result of the two effects will be a reduction in oil reserves.

This fairly complicated argument is not ridiculous, but it is almost certainly completely false. A good deal of recent quantitative research (mine and others) has shown that while oil exploration is indeed rather sensitive to price, the *discovery* of new crude oil supplies is not so sensitive as exploration. The principal reason for this is that higher prices lead prospectors to drill many fields that would be too small to be worth drilling at lower prices. Indeed, diminishing returns to oil exploration induced by higher prices tend to set in rather quickly. The best estimate of the effects of a price increase[1] seems to be that a 10 percent price increase (other things equal) leads to about a 16 percent increase in the number of wild cat wells but only about a 9 percent increase in discoveries. Whether this means that discoveries are sufficiently sensitive to prices to make the pro-quota argument true is not clear. What is clear is that such sensitivity is not so obviously high as to make that argument highly persuasive. (In this connection, it is worth noting that the supposed high sensitivity of oil

---

1. This estimate is taken from Edward W. Erickson, "Economic Incentives, Industrial Structure and the Supply of Crude Oil Discoveries in the U.S., 1946–58/59," paper delivered at the Toronto Meetings of the Econometric Society, August, 1967.

discoveries to economic incentives is used to buttress any special treatment for crude oil producers, principally the percentage depletion provisions of the tax laws. It is not a strong buttress.)

Moreover, whatever the effects of free imports on oil discoveries, and even, if new oil discoveries were to cease altogether on the abandonment of quotas, the United States is in no danger whatever of running out of oil. This is so for three reasons:

(A) Proved reserves of crude oil are sufficient for about ten to twelve years production at current rates. (This figure has been roughly constant for a long time.)

(B) Proved reserves are a deliberately conservative estimate of the amount of oil in known oil fields and pools. They measure oil in place in such fields close to existing wells and available pretty much without further exploration. The total amount of recoverable oil in already discovered deposits is at least 1.3 times proved reserves (thirteen years supply, and I am being conservative here).

(C) Production of crude oil from oil shale is technologically feasible. There is at least forty years supply of such oil in known deposits (but it would be somewhat more expensive to produce than domestic crude out of the ground).

(D) And, of course, in the event of a prolonged oil crisis, exploration would rise sharply. A good argument as to national security is that whatever the long-run supplies of oil, an emergency requires that oil be readily available (although the nature of crises since World War II may suggest that the ability to produce more oil *in a great hurry* is not of primary importance). This makes points B–D irrelevant in the short run. Further, the possible need to keep oil supplies readily available may require that the industry not shut in known fields, but keep them in a state ready to produce as well as keeping in being the capacity to produce already proved known reserves in a hurry. To the extent that such very short-run considerations are indeed important, however, it is obviously efficient and appropriate for the government to stockpile producible oil in known fields by buying up fields or developing fields on federal lands (these are quite substantial) or to directly subsidize such stockpiling. (One way to do this is by paying producers in fields closed down as a result of import competition to maintain those fields and their equipment in a state of readiness.) It is both inefficient and inequitable to subsidize the entire domestic industry by keeping gasoline prices high. For no other strategic material do we engage in such inefficient action in place of direct stockpiling.

The question should be consciously studied (or existing studies used) and direct action taken to stockpile readily producible oil in the ground if this turns out to be necessary. There is no reason to do this at the expense of every motorist by limiting imports of efficiently produced cheap petroleum (largely produced by American firms, by the way).

II. THE REAL EFFECTS OF QUOTAS

The national security argument for quotas is thus respectable and bogus. The real effects of quotas are the maintenance of high domestic prices and the protection of relatively inefficient domestic oil producers. The system works as follows.

For reasons of conservation, crude oil production is exempted from the effects of the anti-trust laws and interstate shipment of crude oil produced outside of state conservation limitations is prohibited. In practice, when the market for petroleum weakens, state conservation authorities (principally the Texas Railroad Commission) limit production far below the levels which would be dictated by conservation considerations. However such limitations are rationalized, their effect is the adjustment of production to demand and the maintenance of relatively high prices for crude petroleum and petroleum products. In particular, state production restrictions limit production from efficient low-cost high-production wells very severely. This keeps prices artificially high and inefficient high-cost producers in business. In recent years, there has been an abundance of

domestic oil and production has been kept far below capacity.

Obviously, this system could not work if low-cost foreign oil were freely imported. It is thus greatly in the interest of the domestic oil producers to limit such imports. It is not in the interest of the United States as a whole, nor is it in the interest of most of its citizens.

III. CONCLUSIONS

(A) Import quotas on petroleum should be abandoned, not written into law. They do not advance the security of the United States and they penalize the American motorist for the benefit of domestic oil producers.

(B) A study of the advisability of stockpiling readily producible oil in the ground should be undertaken and such stockpiling done by direct action in the cheapest possible manner.

(C) The present practice of maintaining oil prices at an artificially high level under the guise of conservation should be abandoned. Although free imports should go a long way toward accomplishing this, Congress should consider whether direct legislation toward this end would be appropriate.

SUMMARY

In this chapter, we have applied our microeconomic tools to the field of international trade, investigating especially the relationship of trade to economic efficiency.

The general result of this analysis is to suggest that free trade tends to produce the most efficient overall result. This was shown in the early nineteenth century by economists like Ricardo, who used a model in which labor is the only factor of production and in which the quantities of labor used to produce wine and cloth are constant no matter what the levels of production of either commodity. In this case, the two countries involved will each specialize completely in the commodity in which they have a *comparative advantage*. A country has a comparative advantage in the production of a particular commodity when the relative cost (in terms of other commodities) of producing a unit of that commodity is less than in the other country. According to Ricardo, this specialization will result in mutual benefits for both countries, i.e., everybody is better off with free trade.

Modern analysis generally confirms this point. Using a production-possibility curve where more than one factor of production is employed, we get increasing costs as we expand one commodity as compared to the other. In this world, countries will again specialize in the commodities in which they have a comparative advantage, but not fully. In the final equilibrium situation, both countries will characteristically be producing both commodities at a common international price ratio, and this price ratio will be equal to the ratio of marginal costs in each country. Again, free trade will bring increased benefits to *both* countries.

Although these general points enjoy wide acceptance, there are a number of specific arguments for restricting trade that help explain why countries throughout history have used tariffs, quotas, and other protective devices to at least some degree. These arguments generally involve weighing other objectives against the claims of economic efficiency. These other objectives may include short-run macroeconomic objectives (such as increasing domestic employment), national security (see Senator Long's argument on oil import quotas), improving the terms of trade ("beggar-my-neighbor" policy), protection of infant industries (mostly relevant to underdeveloped countries), and

protecting particular domestic industries (see Professor Fisher on oil import quotas). In almost every case, these arguments are subject to the criticism that they would involve the nation in certain efficiency losses; in many cases, also, they lead to policies that invite retaliation.

QUESTIONS FOR DISCUSSION

1. Suppose that we have country A and country B each capable of producing commodity X and commodity Y according to the following table:

Country	X	Y
	Man-hours required to produce 1 unit	
A	5	50
B	12	40

(*a*) Which country has a comparative advantage in producing commodity X? Commodity Y?

What is the range of possible exchange rates of X for Y under which mutually beneficial trade between A and B could take place?

(*b*) Fill in the blank in the following table so that neither country has a comparative advantage in either commodity:

Country	X	Y
	Man-hours required to produce 1 unit	
A	5	50
B	12	?

2. "The fairest tariff policy is that which puts our domestic producers on equal terms with their foreign competitors." Discuss.

3. Take two countries with ordinary (bowed-out) production-possibility curves. Show how the price ratios of the two commodities might be different in the two countries if there were no trade between them. Show how trade might bring an equalization of these price ratios.

4. "Tariffs and trade restrictions are an expression of national interest; free trade is an expression of world interest." Discuss critically.

5. Write an essay giving your own views on the subject of oil import quotas for the United States in the 1970s.

SUGGESTED READING

Haberler, Gottfried. *A Survey of International Trade Theory.* Princeton: International Finance Section, 1961.

Kenen, Peter B., and Lubitz, Raymond. *International Economics.* 3rd ed. Englewood Cliffs, N.J.: Prentice-Hall, 1971.

Meier, Gerald M. *International Trade and Development.* New York: Harper & Row, 1963.

Miller, Roger LeRoy, and Williams, Raburn M. *The New Economics of Richard Nixon: Freezes, Floats & Fiscal Policy.* San Francisco: Canfield Press, 1972, chap. 10.

Ricardo, David. *Principles of Political Economy and Taxation.* Edited by P. Sraffa. Cambridge: Cambridge University Press, 1951, chaps. VII, XXII.

Slesinger, Reuben E.; Perlman, Mark; and Isaacs, Asher. *Contemporary Economics.* 2nd ed. Boston: Allyn and Bacon, 1967, pp. 511–39.

24
Monopoly and Imperfect Competition

In this chapter and the next, we shall take up a number of issues that arise because industrial markets in the real world are at best "imperfectly competitive." Pure competition, as we know, is efficient under certain circumstances: it leads producers in the society to produce the goods that consumers want at the least possible cost. It takes us out to the edge of our production-possibility curve and then locates us on that curve in accord with consumer preferences as expressed through their money demands.

But if competition is *not* pure, what then? Will the consumer get what he wants, or will he get a shoddy deal instead? Will large firms engage in "workable competition," or will they have to be regulated by governmental controls or prosecuted for antitrust violations? In this chapter, we shall present an analysis of the different kinds of market structure in a modern industrial economy, and in the following chapter we shall take up some of the public policy issues raised by our analysis.

AN UNRESOLVED ISSUE

First, however, we have to recognize the fact that economists differ in a very basic way about how these issues should be handled. In the social sciences, no theory is ever sufficiently precise to account for all the known facts. Political, economic, and social life is simply too complex for that. What this means is that it is possible for social observers to look at roughly the same collection of facts and to differ fundamentally about the best way to treat them.

Something like this is happening today in the area of industrial organization. There is a more or less traditional approach that begins, as we have, with the theory of purely competitive markets and then uses tools developed in that analysis to help explain imperfectly competitive market structures. Another approach is more drastic. Its most striking advocate is John Kenneth Galbraith, who, in a number of books (but most especially in his *The New Industrial State*), has argued that the traditional approach misses not only some of the facts but the *essence* of modern industrial life.

No one can deny the importance of the questions Galbraith raises. Is the modern industrial firm best viewed as responding to a market or largely controlling it? If the firm is no longer controlled by the market, why do we imagine that it must continue to strive for maximum profits? Indeed, with managers (not owners) in control, must we not rethink altogether the goals of business enterprise in a modern industrial society? Incidentally, what happens to consumers' sovereignty in this society? Are not the goals of the "technostructure" largely producer-oriented, and is it not the case that consumers (through advertising and other

John Kenneth Galbraith. Perhaps the most famous of all contemporary economists, Galbraith has sought an audience in the public at large as well as among his fellow economists. His views—whether about the structure of modern industry or the perils of "affluence"—are invariably highly stimulating. BLACK STAR

persuasions) are simply made to agree to what is being done to them?

There are obviously important truths implicit in each of these questions, and the reader is urged to study Great Debate Three: Galbraith and the New Industrial State (pp. 545–73) with some care. That we are presenting a somewhat more traditional approach in the text proper indicates no lack of concern for these important truths. On the contrary, the author's belief is that when these points can be incorporated into systematic economic theory, that theory will be immensely more valuable. It is also the author's belief, however, that *until* this happens, these particular insights will have little real impact on the way we handle basic economic problems in our society.[1] Ultimately, this is the problem of interdependence again. Since everything in economic life interacts with everything else, nothing short of a fully systematic analysis will really do. Professor Galbraith has argued that he has provided such an analysis; the author does not feel that this is yet the case, although he strongly urges readers of this book to study the Galbraithian literature (*The Affluent Society* and *American Capitalism*, as well as *The New Industrial State*) and to savor to the full the perceptions (and witticisms) of this very original thinker.

THE "REVOLUTION" IN TRADITIONAL ECONOMICS

Nor should we give the impression that traditional economics has been static in its theoretical treatment of industrial organization. In the 1930s and 1940s, somewhat overshadowed by the Keynesian Revolution but not unimportant in itself, there was another "revolution" in economic analysis, specifically concerned with imperfectly or "monopolistically" competitive markets.

One of the leaders of this intellectual break-through was the late Edward H. Chamberlin,[2] who not only stressed the complexity of modern industrial life but, at least in one important case, showed how the theory of pure competition would have to be modified to make it applicable to real-world conditions. Chamberlin's book was called *The Theory of Monopolistic Competition*, and the title itself is intriguing. We think of competition as involving very large numbers of small firms. Monopoly, on the other hand, means a *single* seller. How can such polar opposites be combined, as by implication they are, in the phrase "monopolistic competition"?

Actually, the difficulty quickly disappears if we think of products with brand names. The makers of Ivory Soap have an absolute monopoly on the specific product "Ivory Soap," but not on soap products generally. The soap "monopolist" is, in fact, engaged in competition with other similar soap "monopolists," each of whom has his own particular variety of the product with its own particular brand name. The brand name problem, in turn, is simply one example of a general phenomenon that Chamberlin called *product differentiation*. The following reading is from his classic treatment of this subject.

---

1. Malthus, for example, had important insights about the causes of depressions (or "universal gluts"), but it wasn't until a century later, when Keynes took similar insights *and incorporated them into standard economic theory*, that the thinking of men and nations was truly affected. Incidentally, Keynes developed his theory on the assumption of *purely competitive* business firms. In this way, it may be said that he missed the "whole of the truth," but he was able to develop the full implications of that part of the truth with which he was concerned.

2. Another very important contributor to this field was Joan Robinson, whose *The Economics of Imperfect Competition* was published a few months after Chamberlin's book in 1933. For Mrs. Robinson's views on Marx, see pp. 61–64.

HARVARD NEWS BUREAU

Edward H. Chamberlin (1899–1967). Chamberlin helped bring an increasing realism to microeconomics by his study of monopolistic competition and other imperfectly competitive market structures.

THE DIFFERENTIATION OF THE PRODUCT

EDWARD H. CHAMBERLIN

***

A general class of product is differentiated if any significant basis exists for distinguishing the goods (or services) of one seller from those of another. . . .

Differentiation may be based upon certain characteristics of the product itself, such as exclusive patented features; trade-marks; trade names; peculiarities of the package or container, if any; or singularity in quality, design, color, or style. It may also exist with respect to the conditions surrounding its sale. In retail trade, to take only one instance, these conditions include such factors as the convenience of

the seller's location, the general tone or character of his establishment, his way of doing business, his reputation for fair dealing, courtesy, efficiency, and all the personal links which attach his customers either to himself or to those employed by him. In so far as these and other intangible factors vary from seller to seller, the "product" in each case is different, for buyers take them into account, more or less, and may be regarded as purchasing them along with the commodity itself. When these two aspects of differentiation are held in mind, it is evident that virtually all products are differentiated, at least slightly, and that over a wide range of economic activity differentiation is of considerable importance.

In explanation of the adjustment of economic forces over this field, economic theory has offered (a) a theory of competition, and (b) a theory of monopoly. If the product is fairly individual, as the services of an electric street railway, or if it has the legal stamp of a patent or a copyright, it is usually regarded as a monopoly. On the other hand, if it stands out less clearly from other "products" in a general class, it is grouped with them and regarded as part of an industry or field of economic activity which is essentially competitive.

***

Monopoly and competition are very generally regarded, not simply as antithetical, but as mutually exclusive. To demonstrate competition is to prove the absence of monopoly, and vice versa. Indeed, to many the very phrase "monopolistic competition" will seem self-contradictory—a juggling of words. This conception is most unfortunate. Neither force excludes the other, and more often than not both are requisite to an intelligible account of prices.

***

Monopolistic competition is evidently a different thing from either *pure* monopoly or *pure* competition. As for monopoly, *as ordinarily conceived and defined*, monopolistic competition embraces it and takes it as a starting point.

The theory of monopoly, although the opening wedge, is very soon discovered to

Chapter 24 / Monopoly and Imperfect Competition

be inadequate. The reason is that it deals with the isolated monopolist, the demand curve for whose product is given. Although such a theory may be useful in cases where substitutes are fairly remote, in general the competitive interrelationships of groups of sellers preclude taking the demand schedule for the product of any one of them as given. It depends upon the nature and prices of the substitutes with which it is in close competition. Within any group of closely related products (such as that ordinarily included in one imperfectly competitive market) the demand and cost conditions (and hence the price) of any one are defined only if the demand and cost conditions with respect to the others are taken as given. Partial solutions of this sort, yielded by the theory of monopoly, contribute nothing towards a solution of the whole problem, for each rests upon assumptions with respect to the others. Monopolistic competition, then, concerns itself not only with the problem of an *individual* equilibrium (the ordinary theory of monopoly), but also with that of a *group* equilibrium (the adjustment of economic forces within a group of competing monopolists, ordinarily regarded merely as a group of competitors). In this it differs both from the theory of competition and from the theory of monopoly.

The matter may be put in another way. It has already been observed that, when products are differentiated, buyers are given a basis for preference, and will therefore be paired with sellers, not in random fashion (as under pure competition), but according to these preferences. Under pure competition, the market of each seller is perfectly merged with those of his rivals; now it is to be recognized that each is in some measure isolated, so that the whole is not a single large market of many sellers, but a network of related markets, one for each seller. The theory brings into the foreground the monopoly elements arising from ubiquitous partial independence. These elements have received but fragmentary recognition in economic literature, and never have they been allowed as a part of the general explanation of prices, except under the heading of "imperfections" in a theory which specifically excludes them. It is now proposed to give due weight to whatever degree of isolation exists by focusing attention on the market of the individual seller. A study of "competition" from this point of view gives results which are out of harmony with accepted competitive theory.

CLASSIFICATION OF MARKET STRUCTURES

Differentiation of the product is certainly one feature of modern industrial life that must cause us to modify the theory of pure competition developed in Part Three A. Perhaps an even more important modification is caused by the *size* of firms. In chapter 5, we spent some time describing the large modern corporation and its influence on certain sectors of the economy. This influence varies greatly from sector to sector of the economy. Large firms still have very little impact in construction, agriculture, forestry, certain types of mining, the service trades, and in much of wholesale and retail trading. But in public utilities, transportation, manufacturing, and in other branches of mining, they are very significant and, in many cases, dominating.

This variety makes it necessary for us to expand our analysis of pure competition by adding not just one "real-world" market structure, but a range of such structures. A useful and common classification is as follows:

(1) Pure competition. We have already discussed this market structure at length. It involves large numbers of small firms, each producing a homogeneous product and each responding to impersonally given market prices. In the American economy, the most important industry approximating pure competition is agriculture. There are over 2 million farming units in the United States; and, although they are expanding somewhat in the 1970s, very large corporations are still of negligible importance in this sector. Although agriculture has a basically competitive structure, it must be remembered, of course, that government intervention in this sector has been frequent and significant for many decades. Other industries that approximate purely competitive conditions are lumbering and some forms of mining, notably bituminous coal mining.

(2) Pure monopoly. We have "pure monopoly" where there is a single seller of a particular product for which no close substitutes are available. Since all products in an economy are to *some* degree substitutes for one another, even the pure monopolist is subject to a degree of competitive influence. However, where the substitutes are not close, the monopolist will have considerable freedom to vary the price of his product to achieve maximum profits. Pure monopoly, in an unregulated state, does not exist in the United States, being expressly forbidden by our antitrust laws. In a regulated state, it does exist in a number of important industries, notably in transportation and public utilities, especially at the local level.

(3) Monopolistic competition. As we have suggested above, monopolistic competition involves a combination of elements from pure monopoly and pure competition. It is characterized by large numbers of sellers who sell not a homogeneous but a "differentiated" product. Many of the products we buy, from soap to automobiles, are surrounded by clusters of similar products—other brands of soap or makes of automobile—which, though distinguishable in the minds of

consumers, nevertheless clearly belong to the same product classification. Products within the same industry can be differentiated on many different grounds: design, style, special features, attractive packaging, brand-name advertising, convenience of location of the retail outlet, even the manner of their sale (e.g., "service with a smile"). A hardheaded consumer might classify some product differentiation as "real" (one product actually gives better service than another) and some as "irrelevant" ("A rose is a rose is a rose."), but if these "irrelevant" differences actually influence consumer behavior in the sense that housewives will pay a higher price for one product than another, then they are important data for economists to analyze.

The element of "monopoly" in monopolistic competition derives from the fact that once products are "differentiated," each particular firm has an absolute monopoly on its own special brand. Only the Lorillard Corporation can produce Kent cigarettes. There is thus literally a single seller of Kents. The element of "competition" arises because other firms can produce very close substitutes (Camel Filters, etc.). If there are a great number of firms producing close substitutes, then we have the market structure of monopolistic competition.[3] In the American economy, the best examples of this structure are to be found in the retail and service trades. There are thousands upon thousands of grocery stores, barber shops, beauty parlors, stationery stores, shoe-repair shops, etc., in which product differentiation is based on small differences in the products or, very often, on the loca-

Continued on p. 574

---

3. This structure is sometimes specifically called "Chamberlinian monopolistic competition," since this was the case that the late Professor Chamberlin did so much to analyze. See the reading on p. 542.

GREAT DEBATE THREE
GALBRAITH AND THE NEW INDUSTRIAL STATE

No economics book has attracted more public attention in the last decade than John Kenneth Galbraith's *The New Industrial State*. It stimulated, among other discussions, a sharp debate in the pages of the journal, *The Public Interest*, in 1967 and 1968. Besides Galbraith, the participants in the debate were the British economist Robin Marris, on whose work on corporate behavior Galbraith based some of his conclusions, and the highly respected M.I.T. economist, Robert M. Solow. To make the debate more comprehensible, we have introduced first a few pages from *The New Industrial State* in which some of Galbraith's basic contentions are presented. Although these pages will help make the debate clearer, the reader should not expect to reach any very simple or dogmatic conclusion after going through the warmly argued points of view presented here. What he should gain from these arguments is a sense of some of the "frontier" issues in the economic analysis of the modern corporation. The issues are very fundamental, having to do with whether the producer or the consumer is "sovereign" and what basic goals motivate modern business behavior. It is safe to predict that these will be important issues in the field for many years to come.

The New Industrial State
JOHN KENNETH GALBRAITH

The market has only one message for the business firm. That is the promise of more money. If the firm has no influence on its prices, as the Wisconsin dairy farm has no influence on the price of milk, it has no options as to the goals that it pursues. It must try to make money and, as a practical matter, it must try to make as much as possible. Others do. To fail to conform is to invite loss, failure and extrusion. Certainly a decision to subordinate interest in earnings to an interest in a more contented life for workers, cows or consumers would, in the absence of exceptional supplementary income, mean financial disaster. Given this need to maximize revenue, the firm is thus fully subject to the authority of the market.

When the firm has influence on market prices—when it has the power commonly associated with monopoly—it has also long been assumed that it will seek as large a profit as possible. It could settle for less than the maximum but it is assumed that it seeks monopoly power in order to be free of the limitations set by competition on its return. Why should it seek monopoly power and then settle for less than its full advantages? When demand is strong, the monopolistic firm can extract more revenue from the market; when demand slackens, it can get less. But so long as it tries to get as much as possible it will still be subject to control by the market and ultimately, as sustained by the compulsions of avarice, by the preferences of consumers, as expressed by their purchases. Were the monopolist regularly to settle for something less than a maximum return, the causes of this restraint would have to be explained by forces apart from the market. Along with the state of demand these forces would be a factor determining prices, production and profit. Belief in the market as the transcendent regulator of economic behavior requires, therefore, a parallel belief that participating firms will always seek to maximize their earnings. If this is assumed there is, by exclusion, no need to search for other motives.

When planning replaces the market this admirably simple explanation of economic behavior collapses. Technology and the companion commitments of capital and time have forced the firm to emancipate itself from the uncertainties of the market. And specialized technology has rendered the market increasingly unreliable. So the firm controls the prices at which it buys materials, components and talent and takes steps to insure the necessary supply at these prices. And it controls the prices at which it sells and takes steps to insure that the public, other producers or the state take the planned quantities at these prices. So far from being controlled by the market, the firm, to the best of its ability, has made the market subordinate to the goals of its planning. Prices, costs, production and resulting revenues are established not by the market but, within broad limits later to be examined, by the planning decisions of the firm.

The goal of these planning decisions could still be the greatest possible profit. We have already seen that a high and reliable flow of earnings is important for the success of the technostructure. But the market is no longer specifying and enforcing that goal. Accordingly profit maximization—the only goal that is consistent with the rule of the market—is no longer necessary. The competitive firm had no choice of goals. The monopoly could take less than the maximum; but this would be inconsistent with its purpose in being a monopoly. But planning is the result not of the desire to exploit market opportunity but the result, among other factors, of the unreliability of markets. Subordination to the market, and to the

instruction that it conveys, has disappeared. So there is no longer, *a priori*, reason to believe that profit maximization will be the goal of the technostructure. It could be, but this must be shown. And it will be difficult to show if other things are more important than profit for the success of the technostructure. It will also be difficult to show if the technostructure does not get the profit.

It is agreed that the modern large corporation is, quite typically, controlled by its management. The managerial revolution as distinct from that of the technostructure is accepted. So long as earnings are above a certain minimum it would also be widely agreed that the management has little to fear from the stockholders. Yet it is for these stockholders, remote, powerless and unknown, that management seeks to maximize profits. Management does not go out ruthlessly to reward itself—a sound management is expected to exercise restraint. Already at this stage, in the accepted view of the corporation, profit maximization involves a substantial contradiction. Those in charge forgo personal reward to enhance it for others.

The contradiction becomes much sharper as one recognizes the role of the technostructure. If power is regarded as resting with a few senior officers, then their pecuniary interest could be imagined at least to be parallel to that of the owners. The higher the earnings the higher the salaries they can justify, the greater the return on any stock they may themselves hold, and the better the prospect for any stock options they may have issued to themselves. Even these contentions stand only limited examination. There are few corporations in which it would be suggested that executive salaries are at a maximum. As a not uncritical observer has recently observed, ". . . [the] average level of salaries of managers even in leading corporations is not exceptionally high."* Astronomical figures, though not exceptional, are usually confined to the very top. Stock holdings by management are small and often non-existent. Stock options, the right to buy stock at predetermined prices if it goes up in value, though common, are by no means universal and are more widely valued as a tax dodge than as an incentive. So even the case for maximization of personal return by a top management is not strong.

But with the rise of the technostructure, the notion, however tenuous, that a few managers might maximize their own return by maximizing that of the stockholders, dissolves entirely. Power passes down into the organization. Even the small stock interest of the top officers is no longer the rule. Salaries, whether modest or generous, are according to scale; they do not vary with profits. And with the power of decision goes opportunity for making money which all good employees are expected to eschew. Members of the technostructure have advance knowledge of products and processes, price changes, impending government contracts and, in the fashionable jargon of our time, technical breakthroughs. Advantage could be taken of this information. Were everyone to seek to do so—by operations in the stock of the company, or in that of suppliers, in commodity markets, by taking themselves and their knowledge into the employ of another firm for a price—the corporation would be a chaos of competitive avarice. But these are not the sort of thing that a good company man does; a remarkably effective code bans such behavior. Group decision-making insures, moreover, that almost everyone's actions and even thoughts are known to others. This acts

*Wilbert E. Moore, *The Conduct of the Corporation* (New York: Random House, Inc., 1962), p. 13.

to enforce the code and, more than incidentally, a high standard of personal honesty as well. The technostructure does not permit of the privacy that misfeasance and malfeasance require.

So the technostructure, as a matter of necessity, bans personal profit-making. And, as a practical matter, what is banned for the ordinary scientist, engineer, contract negotiator or sales executive must also be banned for senior officers. Resistance to pecuniary temptation cannot be enforced at the lower levels if it is known that the opportunity to turn a personal penny remains the prerogative of the high brass.

The members of the technostructure do not get the profits that they maximize. They must eschew personal profit-making. Accordingly, if the traditional commitment to profit maximization is to be upheld, they must be willing to do for others, specifically the stockholders, what they are forbidden to do for themselves. It is on such grounds that the doctrine of maximization in the mature corporation now rests. It holds that the will to make profits is, like the will to sexual expression, a fundamental urge. But it holds that this urge operates not in the first person but the third. It is detached from self and manifested on behalf of unknown, anonymous and powerless persons who do not have the slightest notion of whether their profits are, in fact, being maximized. In further analogy to sex, one must imagine that a man of vigorous, lusty and reassuringly heterosexual inclination eschews the lovely, available and even naked women by whom he is intimately surrounded in order to maximize the opportunities of other men whose existence he knows of only by hearsay. Such are the foundations of the maximization doctrine when there is full separation of power from reward.

The mature corporation, as we have seen, is not compelled to maximize its profits and does not do so. This allows it to pursue other goals and this accords similar alternatives to the members of the technostructure. The need for consistency, nonetheless, still holds. The goals of the corporation, though so freed, must be consistent with those of the society and consistent, in turn, with those of the individuals who comprise it. So also must be the motivations.

More specifically, the goals of the mature corporation will be a reflection of the goals of the members of the technostructure. And the goals of the society will tend to be those of the corporation. If, as we have seen to be the case, the members of the technostructure set high store by autonomy, and the assured minimum level of earnings by which this is secured, this will be a prime objective of the corporation. The need for such autonomy and the income that sustains it will be conceded or stressed by the society.

So with other goals, and so matters work also in reverse. If the society sets high store by technological virtuosity and measures its success by its capacity for rapid technical advance, this will become a goal of the corporation and therewith of those who comprise it. It may, of course, be subordinate, as a goal, to the need to maintain a minimum level of income—the fact that the goals of the mature corporation are plural rather than singular does not mean that all have the same priority. Rather, a hierarchy of goals is quite plausible. And given the requisite consistency between social, corporate and individual goals there is no *a priori* reason for assuming that the priorities will be exactly the same for any two corporations.

The same consistency characterizes motivation—the stimuli that set individuals and organizations in pursuit of goals. Pecuniary compensation is an extremely important stimulus to individual members of the technostructure up to a point. If they are not paid this acceptable and expected salary, they will not work. But once this requirement is met, the offer of more money to an engineer, scientist or executive brings little or no more effort. Other motivation takes over. Similarly, until the minimum requirements of the corporation for earnings are reached, pecuniary motivation will be strong. For it too, above a certain level, additional income brings little or no additional effort. Other goals become more important.

Consistency is equally necessary in the case of identification. The individual will identify himself with the goals of the corporation only if the corporation is identified with, as the individual sees it, some significant social goal. The corporation that is engaged in developing a line of life-preserving drugs wins loyalty and effort from the social purpose its products serve or are presumed to serve. Those engaged in the design or manufacture of a space vehicle identify themselves with the goals of their organization because it, in turn, is identified with the scientific task of exploring space or the high political purpose of outdistancing the Russians. The manufacturer of an exotic missile fuel, or a better trigger for a nuclear warhead, attracts the loyalty of its members because their organization is seen to be serving importantly the cause of freedom. It is felt no doubt that human beings, whose elimination these weapons promise, have an inherent tendency to abuse freedom.

There is no similar identification if the firm is simply engaged in making money for an entrepreneur and has no other claimed social purpose. It is noteworthy that when a corporation is having its assets looted by those in control it simultaneously suffers a very sharp reduction in executive and employee morale. All concerned recognize that the corporation is no longer serving any social purpose of any kind.

Consistency in the identification of individuals and organizations with social goals is possible because, running as a parallel thread from individual through organization to social attitudes, is the presence of adaptation as a motivating force. The individual serves organization, we have seen, because of the possibility of accommodating its goals more closely to his own. If his goals reflect a particular social attitude or vision, he will seek to have the corporation serve that attitude or vision. More important, he will normally think that the goals he seeks have social purpose. (Individuals have a well-remarked capacity to attach high social purpose to whatever—more scientific research, better zoning laws, manufacture of the lethal weapons just mentioned—serves their personal interest.) If he succeeds, the corporation in turn will advance or defend these goals as socially important. The corporation becomes, thus, an instrument for attributing social purpose to the goals of those who comprise it. Social purpose becomes by this process of adaptation what serves the goals of members of the technostructure.

This process is highly successful in our time. Much of what is believed to be socially important is, in fact, the adaptation of social attitudes to the goal system of the technostructure. What counts here is what is believed. These social goals, though in fact derived from the goals of the technostructure, are believed to have original social purpose. Accordingly, members of the corporation in general, and of the technostructure in particular, are able to identify themselves with the corporation on the assumption that it is serving social goals when, in fact, it is serving their own. Even the most acute social conscience is no inconvenience if it origi-nates in one's own.

The process by which social goals become adapted to the goals of the corporation and ultimately the technostructure is not analytical or cerebral. Rather it reflects a triumph of unexamined but constantly reiterated assumption over exact thought. The technostructure is principally concerned with the manufacture of goods and with the companion management and development of the demand for these goods. It is obviously important that this be accorded high social purpose and that the greater the production of goods, the greater be the purpose served. This allows the largest possible number of people to identify themselves with social function.

From a detached point of view, expansion in the output of many goods is not easily accorded a social purpose. More cigarettes cause more cancer. More alcohol causes more cirrhosis. More automobiles cause more accidents, maiming and death; also more preemption of space for highways and parking; also more pollution of the air and the countryside. What is called a high standard of living consists, in considerable measure, in arrangements for avoiding muscular energy, increasing sensual pleasure and for enhancing caloric intake above any conceivable nutritional requirement. Nonetheless, the belief that increased production is a worthy social goal is very nearly absolute. It is imposed by assumption, and this assumption the ordinary individual encounters, in the ordinary course of business, a thousand times a year. Things are better because production is up. There is exceptional improvement because it is up more than ever before. That social progress is identical with a rising standard of living has the aspect of a faith. No society has ever before provided such a high standard of living as ours, hence none is as good. The occasional query, however logically grounded, is unheard.

There are other examples. Successful planning in areas of expensive and sophisticated technology requires that the state underwrite costs, including the costs of research and development, and that it insure a market for the resulting products. It is important to the technostructure, therefore, that technological change of whatever kind be accorded a high social value. This too is agreed. In consequence, the underwriting of sophisticated technology by the state has become an approved social function. Few question the merit of state intervention for such social purpose as supersonic travel or improved applications of nuclear power. Even fewer protest when these are for military purposes. Social purpose is again the result of adaptation. This is a matter of obvious importance and one to which I will return.

None of this is to suggest that all social attitudes originate with the technostructure and its needs. Society also has goals, stemming from the needs which are unassociated with its major productive mechanism, and which it imposes on the mature corporation. As elsewhere I argue only for a two-way process. The mature corporation imposes social attitudes as it also responds to social attitudes. Truth is never strengthened by exaggeration. Nor is it less the truth by being more complex than the established propositions that assert the simple eminence of pecuniary goals and pecuniary motivation.

The New Industrial State
or
SON OF AFFLUENCE

ROBERT M. SOLOW

More than once in the course of his new book Professor Galbraith takes the trouble to explain to the reader why its message will not be enthusiastically received by other economists. Sloth, stupidity, and vested interest in ancient ideas all play a part, perhaps also a wish—natural even in tourist-class passengers—not to rock the boat. Professor Galbraith is too modest to mention yet another reason, a sort of jealousy, but I think it is a real factor. Galbraith is, after all, something special. His books are not only widely read, but actually enjoyed. He is a public figure of some significance; he shares with William McChesney Martin the power to shake stock prices by simply uttering nonsense. He is known and attended to all over the world. He mingles with the Beautiful People; for all I know, he may actually be a Beautiful Person himself. It is no wonder that the pedestrian economist feels for him an uneasy mixture of envy and disdain.

There is also an outside possibility that the profession will ignore *The New Industrial State* (Houghton, Mifflin) because it finds the ideas more or less unhelpful. The world can be divided into big-thinkers and little-thinkers. The difference is illustrated by the old story of the couple who had achieved an agreeable division of labor. She made the unimportant decisions: what job he should take, where they should live, how

From Robert M. Solow, "The New Industrial State or Son of Affluence," *The Public Interest* no. 9, Fall 1967, pp. 100-108. Copyright © National Affairs, Inc., 1967. Reprinted by permission of the publisher and the author.

to bring up the children. He made the important decisions: what to do about Jerusalem, whether China should be admitted to the United Nations, how to deal with crime in the streets. Economists are determined little-thinkers. They want to know what will happen to the production of houses and automobiles in 1968 if Congress votes a 10 percent surcharge on personal and corporate tax bills, and what will happen if Congress does not. They would like to be able to predict the course of the Wholesale Price Index and its components, and the total of corporate profits by industry. They are not likely to be much helped or hindered in these activities by Professor Galbraith's view of Whither We Are Trending.

Professor Galbraith makes an eloquent case for big-thinking, and he has a point. Little-thinking can easily degenerate into mini-thinking or even into hardly thinking at all. Even if it does not, too single-minded a focus on how the parts of the machine work may lead to a careful failure ever to ask whether the machine itself is pointed in the right direction. On the other side, Professor Galbraith gingerly pays tribute to the little-thinkers whose work he has used, but it is evident that he has been exposed only very selectively to the relevant literature. There is no point squabbling over this: big-think and little-think are different styles, and the difference between them explains why this book will have more currency outside the economics profession than in it. It is a book for the dinner table not for the desk.

I shall try to summarize the main steps in Galbraith's argument, and shall then return to discuss them, one by one.

(1) The characteristic form of organization in any modern industrial society is not the petty firm but the giant corporation, usually producing many different things, and dominating the market for most of them. Nor is this mere accident. The complicated nature of modern technology and the accompanying need for the commitment of huge sums of capital practically demand that industry be organized in large firms.

(2) With few exceptions, the giant corporation is in no sense run by its owners, the common stockholders. The important decisions are made—have to be made—by a bureaucracy, organized in a series of overlapping and interlocking committees. The board of directors is only the tip of an iceberg that extends down as far as technicians and department managers. The members of the bureaucracy are all experts in something, possibly in management itself. Galbraith calls them the "technostructure," but that awkward word is probably a loser.

(3) It is the nature of the highly-capitalized bureaucratically controlled corporation to avoid risk. The modern business firm is simply not willing to throw itself on the mercy of the market. Instead, it achieves certainty and continuity in the supply of materials by integrating backward to produce its own, in the supply of capital by financing itself out of retained earnings, in the supply of labor by bringing the unions into the act. It eliminates uncertainty on the selling side by managing the consumer, by inducing him, through advertising and more subtle methods of salesmanship, to buy what the corporation wants to sell at the price it wants to charge. The major risk of general economic fluctuations is averted by encouraging the government in programs of economic stabilization.

(4) It would be asking much too much of human nature to expect that the bureaucracy should manage the firm simply in the interests of the stockholders. There is, therefore, no presumption that the modern firm seeks

the largest possible profit. Nor does it. The firm's overriding goal is its own survival and autonomy; for security it requires a certain minimum of profit and this it will try to achieve. Security thus assured, the firm's next most urgent goal is the fastest possible growth of sales. (Since firms grow by reinvesting their earnings, this goal is not independent of profits; nevertheless, once the minimum target in profits is achieved, the modern firm will expand its sales even at the expense of its profits.) There are two lesser goals: a rising dividend rate, presumably to keep the animals from getting restless, and the exercise of technological virtuosity.

(5) Modern industry produces mainly things, and it wishes to grow. Everyone will be happier if everyone believes that a growing production of things is the main object of the national life. People will be happier because that is what they in fact get, and the bureaucracy will be happier because they can feel that they serve the national purpose. This belief has been widely inculcated, but it takes effort really to believe it, because American society already has more things than it knows what to do with.

(6) The key resource in the modern industrial state is organized intelligence, especially scientific and managerial intelligence. One of the important things the government does to support the system is the extension of education to provide a supply of recruits for the bureaucracy, and the subsidization of scientific and technological research to provide something interesting for them to do. What Galbraith calls the "scientific and educational estate" therefore acquires a certain moral authority and even mundane power in the society. This is an important circumstance, because the scientific and educational estate—at least its youngest members— can see through the cult of the GNP

and observe that it slights the claims of leisure, art, culture, architectural design, and even the innocent enjoyment of nature. Here is the most promising source of social change and of a rather more attractive national style of life.

There is a lot more in the book, much of it full of insight and merriment, but the main logic of the argument seems to be roughly as I have stated it.

It may be unjust and pointless to consider the degree of literal truth of each of the assertions that make up this argument. One would hardly discuss *Gulliver's Travels* by debating whether there really are any little people, or criticize the *Grande Jatte* because objects aren't made up of tiny dots. Nevertheless, it may help to judge the truth of Galbraith's big picture if one has some idea about the accuracy of the details. So, at the risk of judging big-think by the standards of little-think, I proceed.

(1) Professor Galbraith is right that modern economics has not really come to terms with the large corporation. Specialists in industrial organization do measure and describe and ponder the operations of the very large firm. Occasionally some of these specialists propound theories of their financial or investment or pricing behavior. It cannot be said that any of these theories has yet been so successful as to command widespread assent. Perhaps for that reason, much economic analysis, when it is not directly concerned with the behavior of the individual firm, proceeds as if the old model of the centralized profit-maximizing firm were a good enough approximation to the truth to serve as a description of behavior in the large. But this is not always done naively or cynically. Professor Galbraith is not the first person to have discovered General Motors. Most close students of industrial investment or pricing do make room in their statistical behavior equations for behavior that is neither

perfectly competitive nor simply monopolistic. (The long debate over the incidence of the corporate profits tax hardly suggests universal reliance on any simple model.)

There is, after all, a moderate amount of economic activity that is not carried on by General Motors, or by the 100 largest or 500 largest corporations. In fact, only about 55 percent of the Gross National Product originates in nonfinancial corporations at all. Not nearly all of that is generated by the giant corporations (of course, some financial corporations are among the giants). Nor is it entirely clear which way the wind is blowing. The giant corporation is preeminently a phenomenon of manufacturing industry and public utilities; it plays a much less important role in trade and services. If, as seems to be in the cards, the trade and service sectors grow relative to the total, the scope of the large corporation may be limited. Alternatively, big firms may come to play a larger role in industries that have so far been carried on at small scale.

Enough has been said to suggest that it is unlikely that the economic system can usefully be described either as General Motors writ larger or as the family farm writ everywhere. This offers at least a hint that it will behave like neither extreme. In any case, counting noses or assets and recounting anecdotes are not to the point. What is to the point is a "model"—a simplified description—of the economy that will yield valid predictions about behavior.

(2) The "separation of ownership from control" of the modern corporation is not a brand new idea. It is to be found in Veblen's writings and again, of course, in Berle and Means' *The Modern Corporation and Private Property*. Recent investigation shows that the process has continued; only a handful of the largest American corporations can be said to be managed by a coherent group with a major ownership interest. (The non-negligible rest of the economy is a different story.) I do not think the simple facts have ever been a matter for dispute. What is in dispute is their implications. It is possible to argue—and many economists probably would argue—that many management-controlled firms are constrained by market forces to behave in much the same way that an owner-controlled firm would behave, and many others acquire owners who like the policy followed by the management. I think it may be a fair complaint that this proposition has not received all the research attention it deserves. It is an error to suppose it has received none at all. Such evidence as there is does not give a very clear-cut answer, but it does not suggest that the orthodox presupposition is terribly wrong. Galbraith does not present any convincing evidence the other way, as I think he is aware. The game of shifting the burden of proof that he plays at the very end of this book is a child's game. Economics is supposed to be a search for verifiable truths, not a high-school debate.

(3) The modern corporation—and not only the modern corporation—is averse to risk. Many economic institutions and practices are understandable only as devices for shifting or spreading risk. But Galbraith's story that the industrial firm has "planned" itself into complete insulation from the vagaries of the market is an exaggeration, so much an exaggeration that it smacks of the put-on.

Galbraith makes the point that the planning of industrial firms need not always be perfect, that a new product or branch plant may occasionally go sour. By itself, therefore, the Edsel is not a sufficient argument against his position. His is a valid defense—but it is not one he can afford to make very often. No doubt the Mets "plan" to win every ballgame.

Consider the supply of capital. There is a lot of internal financing of corporations; it might perhaps be better if companies were forced more often into the capital markets. But external finance is hardly trivial. In 1966 the total flow of funds to nonfarm nonfinancial corporate business was about $96 billion. Internal sources accounted for $59 billion and external sources for the remaining $37 billion. Besides, depreciation allowances amounted to $38 billion of the internal funds generated by business, and much of this sum is not a source of net finance for growth. External sources provided about one-half of net new funds. In 1966, bond issues and bank loans alone added up to about two-thirds of undistributed profits. Trade credit is another important source of external funds, but it is complicated because industrial corporations are both lenders and borrowers in this market. I don't know how the proportions of external and internal finance differ between larger and smaller corporations, but the usual complaint is that the large firm has easier access to the capital market. I do not want to make too much of this, because self-finance is, after all, an important aspect of modern industrial life. But there is, I trust, some point in getting the orders of magnitude right. There might also be some point in wondering if the favored tax treatment of capital gains has something to do with the propensity to retain earnings.

Consider the consumer. In the folklore, he (she?) is sovereign; the economic machinery holds its breath while the consumer decides, in view of market prices, how much bread to buy, and how many apples. In Galbraith's counterfable, no top-heavy modern corporation can afford to let success or failure depend on the uninstructed whim of a

woman with incipient migraine. So the consumer is managed by Madison Avenue into buying what the system requires him to buy. Now I, too, don't like billboards or toothpaste advertising or lottery tickets of unknown—but probably negligible—actuarial value with my gasoline. (Though I put it to Professor Galbraith that, in his town and mine, the Narragansett beer commercial may be the best thing going on TV.) But that is not the issue; the issue is whether the art of salesmanship has succeeded in freeing the large corporation from the need to meet a market test, giving it "decisive influence over the revenue it receives."

That is not an easy question to answer, at least not if you insist on evidence. Professor Galbraith offers none; perhaps that is why he states his conclusion so confidently and so often. I have no great confidence in my own casual observations either. But I should think a case could be made that much advertising serves only to cancel other advertising, and is therefore merely wasteful.

If Hertz and Avis were each to reduce their advertising expenditures by half, I suppose they would continue to divide the total car rental business in roughly the same proportion that they do now. (Why do they not do so? Presumably because each would then have a motive to get the jump on the other with a surprise advertising campaign.) What would happen to the total car rental business? Galbraith presumably believes it would shrink. People would walk more, sweat more, and spend their money instead on the still-advertised deodorants. But suppose those advertising expenditures were reduced too, suppose that all advertising were reduced near the minimum necessary to inform consumers of the commodities available and their elementary objective properties? Galbraith believes that in absence of persuasion, reduced to their already satiated biological needs for guidance, consumers would be at a loss; total consumer spending would fall and savings would simply pile up by default.

Is there anything to this? I know it is not true of me, and I do not fancy myself any cleverer than the next man in this regard. No research that I know of has detected a wrinkle in aggregate consumer spending behavior that can be traced to the beginning of television. Perhaps no one has tried. Pending some evidence, I am not inclined to take this popular doctrine very seriously. (It is perhaps worth adding that a substantial proportion of all the sales that are made in the economy are made not to consumers but to industrial buyers. These are often experts and presumably not long to be diverted from considerations of price and quality by the provision of animated cartoons or even real girls.)

Consider the attitude of the large corporation to the economic stabilization activities of the Federal Government. It is surely true that big business has an important stake in the maintenance of general prosperity. How, then, to account for the hostility of big business to discretionary fiscal policy, a hostility only lately ended, if indeed traces do not still persist? Here I think Professor Galbraith is carried away by his own virtuosity; he proposes to convince the reader that the hostility has not come from the big business bureaucracy but from the old-style entrepreneurial remnants of small and medium-sized firms. Their fortunes are not so dependent on general prosperity, so they can afford the old-time religion. Professor Galbraith is probably wrong about that last point; large firms are better able than small ones to withstand a recession. He is right that the more Paleolithic among the opponents of stabilization policy have come from smaller and middle-sized business.

But up until very recently, the big corporation has also been in opposition. Even in 1961 there was considerable hostility to the investment tax credit, mainly because it involved the government too directly and obviously in the management of the flow of expenditures in the economy at large. It was only after further acquaintance with the proposal excited their cupidity that representatives of the large corporation came around. More recently still, they have generally opposed the temporary suspension of the credit as a counter-inflationary stabilization device, and welcomed its resumption. (This warm attachment to after-tax profits does not accord well with the Galbraith thesis.) There is a much simpler explanation for the earlier, now dwindling, hostility that would do no harm to the argument of the book: mere obtuseness.

(4) Does the modern industrial corporation maximize profits? Probably not rigorously and singlemindedly, and for much the same reason that Dr. Johnson did not become a philosopher—because cheerfulness keeps breaking in. Most large corporations are free enough from competitive pressure to afford a donation to the Community Chest or a fancy office building without a close calculation of its incremental contribution to profit. But that is not a fundamental objection to the received doctrine, which can survive if businesses merely *almost* maximize profits. The real question is whether there is some other goal that businesses pursue systematically at the expense of profits.

The notion of some minimum required yield on capital is an attractive one. It can be built into nearly any model of the behavior of the corporation. I suppose the most commonly held view among economists goes something like this (I am oversimplifying): for any given amount of invested capital, a corporation will seek the largest possible profits in some appropriately long-run sense, and with due allowance for cheerfulness. If the return on capital thus achieved exceeds the minimum required yield or target rate of return, the corporation will expand by adding to its capital, whether from internal or external sources. If the return on equity actually achieved (after corporation tax) is any guide, the target rate of return is not trivial. The main influence on profits in manufacturing is obviously the business cycle; for fairly good years one would have to name a figure like 12 percent, slightly higher in the durable-goods industries, slightly lower in nondurables. In recession years like 1954, 1958, 1961, the figure is more like 9 percent.

Alternatives to this view have been proposed. Professor Galbraith mentions William Baumol and Robin Marris as predecessors. Baumol has argued that the corporation seeks to maximize its sales revenue, provided that it earns at least a certain required rate of return on capital. This is rather different from Galbraith's proposal that corporations seek growth rather than size. These are intrinsically difficult theories to test against observation. Some attempts have been made to test the Baumol model; the results are not terribly decisive, but for what they are worth they tend to conclude against it. Marris's theory is very much like Galbraith's, only much more closely reasoned. He does propose that corporate management seeks growth, subject to a minimum requirement for profit. But Marris is more careful, and comes closer to the conventional view, because he is fully aware, as Galbraith apparently is not, of an important discipline in the capital market. The management that too freely sacrifices profit for growth will find that the stock market puts a relatively low valuation on its assets. This may offer an aggressive management else-where a tempting opportunity to acquire assets cheap, and the result may be a merger offer or a takeover bid, a definite threat to the autonomy of the management taken over. Naturally, the very largest corporations are not subject to this threat, but quite good-sized ones are.

Professor Galbraith offers the following argument against the conventional hypothesis. A profit-maximizing firm will have no incentive to pass along a wage increase in the form of higher prices, because it has already, so to speak, selected the profit-maximizing price. Since the modern industrial corporation transparently does pass on wage increases, it can not have been maximizing profits in the first place. But this argument is a sophomore error; the ideal textbook firm will indeed pass along a wage increase, to a calculable extent.

There is, on the other hand, a certain amount of positive evidence that supports the hypothesis of rough profit-maximization. It has been found, for instance, that industries which are difficult for outsiders to enter are more profitable than those which are easily entered and therefore, presumably, more competitive. It has been found, also, that there is a detectable tendency for capital to flow where profits are highest. Serious attempts to account for industrial investment and prices find that the profit-supply-demand mechanism provides a substantial part of the explanation, though there is room for less classical factors, and for quite a lot of "noise" besides.

(5) Professor Galbraith does not have a high opinion of the private consumption of goods and services. "What is called a high standard of living consists, in considerable measure, in arrangements for avoiding muscular energy, increasing sensual pleasure and for enhancing caloric intake above any

conceivable nutritional requirement. . . . No society has ever before provided such a high standard of living as ours, hence none is as good. The occasional query, however logically grounded, is unheard." One wonders if that paragraph were written in Gstaad where, we are told, Professor Galbraith occasionally entertains his muse.

It is hard to disagree without appearing boorish. Nevertheless, it is worth remembering that in 1965 the median family income in the United States was just under $7000. One of the more persistent statistical properties of the median income is that half the families must have less. It does not seem like an excessive sum to spend. No doubt one could name an excessive sum, but in any case the reduction of inequality and the alleviation of poverty play negligible roles in Galbraith's system of thought. His attitude toward ordinary consumption reminds one of the Duchess who, upon acquiring a full appreciation of sex, asked the Duke if it were not perhaps too good for the common people.

(6) I have no particular comment on Professor Galbraith's view of the role of the scientific and educational estate as an agent of social and cultural improvement. But this is perhaps a convenient place for me to state what I take to be the role of this book. Professor Galbraith is fundamentally a moralist. His aim is to criticize seriously what he believes to be flaws in American social and economic arrangements, and to make fun of the ideological myths that are erected to veil the flaws. More often than not, in such expeditions, his targets are well chosen and he is on the side of the angels—that is to say, I am on his side. I trust that readers of his work will acquire some resistance to the notion that any interference by the government in a corporation's use of its capital is morally equivalent to interfer-

ence in the citizen's use of his toothbrush. I share his belief that American society is under-provided with public services and over-provided with hair oil. I agree with him that men ought to be more free to choose their hours of work, and that this freedom is worth some loss of productivity.

But Professor Galbraith is not content to persuade people that his values ought to be their values. I don't blame him; it's slow work. He would like an elaborate theory to show that his values are, so to speak, objective, and opposition to them merely ideological. He would like to do, in a way, for the scientific and educational estate what Marx and "scientific socialism" tried to do for the proletariat. The ultimate point of the basic argument is that the economy does not efficiently serve consumer preferences—first because industrial corporations evade the discipline of the market by not seeking profit anyway, and second because the preferences are not really the consumer's own.

As theory this simply does not stand up, a few grains of truth and the occasional well-placed needle notwithstanding. There are, however, other powerful arguments against *laissez-faire:* the existence of monopoly power, inadequate information and other imperfections of the market, the presence of wide divergences between private and social benefits and costs, and a morally unattractive distribution of income. These need to be argued and documented from case to case. It is a kind of joke, but if Professor Galbraith would like to see more and better public services, he may just have to get out and sell them.

A Review of a Review

JOHN KENNETH GALBRAITH

Professor Robert Solow is one of the most distinguished and prestigious economists of our time. He is a calm and confident scholar with rare mastery of the technical tools of economic and quantitative analysis. To the extent that economics qualifies as a science, it is men like Professor Solow who have earned it the reputation. The rather subjective standards of the social sciences in general and of economic theory in particular allow men a certain liberty in defining their own competence. A scholar is often what he claims to be. But Professor Solow's superior mastery of his discipline is acknowledged and admired I think by all.

It is because Professor Solow is so intimately associated with the scientific claims of our profession that I find myself writing this comment. It is not to dispute his view of *The New Industrial State*; this naturally differs from mine, and did I agree with it I would hardly have been justified in publishing the book. But the book is in the public domain and to a degree surpassing my far from modest expectations. Reviews of books that are technical or otherwise obscure are of no slight importance. Others depend on them as do theatre goers to whom first night admission is denied. But human vanity what it is, the person who has seen for himself will reach his own conclusions. So it is here, and this is the principal reason, as I have often said, why I years ago determined to seek a substantial audience. One is not at the risk of those who react adversely to that with which they disagree or find otherwise distasteful.

From John Kenneth Galbraith, "A Review of a Review," *The Public Interest* no. 9, Fall 1967, pp. 109-18. Reprinted by permission of the author.

However, Professor Solow's review seems to merit a word on its own account. It exemplifies a tendency of social scientists, unconscious but not above reproach, to divest themselves of the rules of scientific discourse when they encounter something they do not like. Carelessness also no doubt plays a part. This tendency acquires its special poignancy when, as in the case of Professor Solow, the writer is, and with reason, conscious of his scientific prestige. He is held to even higher standards than the rest of us. The phenomenon is worth explicit examination, and I trust that Professor Solow will not be perturbed by my using him, in effect, as a case study. Thus this review of his review.

2

Although the rules of scientific discourse have never been fully codified, a number enjoy wide acceptance in the common law. They can all best be stated in negative form. One should avoid comment *ad hominem*—that is to say, one should not attack a position by slighting or adverse comment on the personality or behavior of the person who defends it. One should be accurate. One should avoid *obiter dicta*; that is to say, nothing should be allowed to rest on the unsupported word of the speaker, however great his prestige. Both over- and understatement should be avoided—matters where I long ago learned to confess guilt. It is possible that another rule might be added although this may be a counsel of perfection. The scientist should be aware of, and disclose, personal interest. It is this, more than incidentally, that may cause him to violate the other rules. In the review in question Professor Solow is in more or less serious violation of the first three canons. There is at least a possibility that he violates the last. Even for a scholar with no special scientific pretensions this is a poor score. Let me specify.

He begins his review with a number of *ad hominem* observations—the alleged social life of the author and his association with what he calls the Beautiful People, the power that "he shares with William McChesney Martin . . . to shake stock prices by simply uttering nonsense," and this form of comment recurs when he takes exception to my suggestion that higher living standards are not a primary measure of social excellence. "One wonders if that paragraph were written in Gstaad where, we are told, Professor Galbraith occasionally entertains the muse."

Were this all and true, one would doubtless dismiss it as harmless needling, not damaging to careful discourse. I wouldn't, in reply, comment on Professor Solow's social preoccupations or choice of recreation or residence, but these are matters on which there is room for many levels of taste. But the reader will observe, I think, that these observations are in keeping with, and in some small measure serve, the larger design of his article. They suggest a certain frivolity of purpose. (One notices the use of the word nonsense.) Clearly, the deeply serious scholar should not be detained. It would surely be better scientific method though rather more demanding work simply to argue the case. More significant, perhaps, none of it is true. I regard most social activities, fashionable or otherwise, as a bore, and since I have been an ambassador there is even documentary evidence in the archives. In March of 1955 I gave testimony before the Senate Banking and Currency Committee, carefully prepared and not before described as nonsense, on the nature of the speculative fever in 1929 and the measures that might prevent a recurrence. I had just finished a book on the subject. While I testified the market dropped very sharply. On *no other* occasion have I ever seen it suggested that a remark of mine has affected the market. As opportunity allows, I certainly do go to Switzerland (as did Alfred Marshall), but in recent years it has been because I can work there free of both interruption and a disagreeable respiratory ailment. So even Professor Solow's personal comments, it will be evident, establish a rather disconcerting pattern of unreliability. Presumably, even *ad hominem* argument should be accurate. And his reliability does not become greater when he comes to substantial matters, and we measure his essay against the scientific canon that requires accurate meaning accurately conveyed. Let me offer what can only be a partial list.

3

The *New Industrial State* draws rather extensively from the empirical work of other economists. That, presumably, is one thing such empirical work is for. Professor Solow states that the author "gingerly pays tribute to the little-thinkers [his term and assuredly not mine] whose work he has used. ..." That most readers will take to mean that I was miserly in my credit to others. Here, that the reader may judge, is what I said:

This book has not, it will be agreed, been confined to narrow points. But I have singularly little quarrel with those who so restrict themselves. I have drawn on their work, quantitative and qualitative, at every stage; I could not have written without their prior efforts. So I have nothing but admiration and gratitude for the patient and skeptical men who get deeply into questions, and I am available to support their application to the Ford Foundation however minute the matter to be explored. I expect them to judge sternly the way their material has been used in this book.*

In commenting on my contention that the large corporation is a highly important, strongly characteristic feature of the American economy Professor Solow says that "Professor Galbraith is not the first person to have discovered General Motors" and that "There is, after all, a moderate amount of activity that is not carried on by General Motors, or by the 100 largest or 500 largest corporations." Most readers would conclude from Professor Solow that I somehow claim originality as the discoverer of the great corporation and that I equate all economic activity with the large firms. There are no such suggestions in the book. I do say that the great firm has not made its way in modern economic theory. This Professor Solow concedes. I am careful to point out that the world of the large corporations, what I call the Industrial System, is not the whole of the economy. The remaining "part of the economic system is not insignificant. It is not, however, the part of the economy with which this book . . . [is] concerned."

I might add that Professor Solow then concludes this part of his discussion by saying that "enough has been said to suggest that it is unlikely that the economic system can usefully be described either as General Motors writ larger or the family farm writ everywhere." His logic here will surely seem casual. He is saying, in effect, that one cannot (as I do) describe a part of the economy, even a highly important part. One must do nothing unless he has a model that will cover all. This, I am sure, he does not intend.

Professor Solow says that "The 'separation of ownership from control' in the modern corporation is not a brand

*The New Industrial State. John Kenneth Galbraith (Boston: Houghton Mifflin Co., 1967), p. 402.

new idea," adding that it is to be found in Veblen's writings as well as in Adolph A. Berle, Jr. and G. C. Means.* Again the reader will suppose that Professor Solow is correcting, perhaps mildly rebuking, a spurious claim to novelty. None was made. Veblen's great point was, in fact, a different one. The engineers and the technicians he believed to be held in check by the greater power of the controlling pecuniary interest. The owners were unduly in control. Relying on his admitted competence on these matters, rather than more meticulous scholarship, Professor Solow uses error to rebuke precision. And my acknowledgement of the work of Adolf Berle, R. A. Gordon as well as of such later writers as Edward Mason, Carl Kaysen and Robin Marris on the separation of ownership from control could hardly be more complete or heartfelt.[†] But there is no need to argue a point that can otherwise be decided. Let Professor Berle, the scholar mentioned by Professor Solow as somehow slighted, say whether or not, both here and over the years, I have done less than justice to his work.

The reader will see what Professor Solow, however innocently, has sought to suggest. Here speaks the superior scholar. I must warn you against something that is not quite careful. I do not protest Professor Solow's superior view

*The Modern Corporation and Private Property (New York: Macmillan, 1934). When this book first appeared economists and statisticians of high technical reputation, the men of the professional establishment, led in this instance by Professor W. L. Crum of Harvard, attacked it vigorously. They pointed to shortcomings in its measures of concentration and in its concept of control. These being present, it was held, in effect, that the book should be ignored.

†One name, to my embarrassment, is missing, that of James Burnham. Scholars, perhaps put off by his subsequent extreme views on foreign policy, have not given sufficient credit to the ideas he offered in The Managerial Revolution. Their importance is at least suggested by the phrase he added to the language and which I do, of course, acknowledge.

of his competence; it has much to commend it, and we are all allowed the enjoyment of our vanity. He has, however, gravely underestimated his task. An author will usually be more knowledgeable about his work than any critic. Accordingly, the latter has only slight leeway for error. And it will be evident that Professor Solow, so far from being careful, has been very careless. One final small example will show what he has let himself in for. In noting the importance that I attach to growth as a goal of the corporation he observes that Mr. Robin Marris, the distinguished British economist, has reached the same general conclusion, only his effort is "much more closely reasoned." Again the warning flag. But I do not disagree. Marris' reasoning occupies an entire book as compared with a chapter in my case. And as I told in the book, and most explicitly in the Reith lectures which have also been published, I made great use of Mr. Marris' argument. I did not duplicate it. In large measure I followed it. Professor Solow is in the odd position of finding something less well done that wasn't attempted.

In arguing against growth and in favor of profit maximization as a primary goal of the corporation, Professor Solow comes out on the side of the latter. That, of course, is his privilege; it is the received view and one that is vital if the omnipotence of the market is to be assumed. But it is hardly proper that Professor Solow should ignore what, from his viewpoint, is the most difficult point. If the technostructure—the autonomous and collegial guiding authority of the corporation—maximizes profits, it maximizes them, in the first instance at least for others, for the owners. If it maximizes growth, it maximizes opportunity for, among other things, advancement, promotion and pecuniary return for itself. That people should so pursue their own interest is

not implausible. Professor Solow, as he elsewhere makes clear, does not think it so.

In attacking the importance that I attach to the control by the large corporation of its own capital supply—an importance that Professor Solow also concedes—he compares for 1966 the total flow of funds from within nonfarm, nonfinancial corporation to that coming from outside. More came from outside. Professor Solow then observes: "I don't know how the proportion of external and internal finance differs between large and smaller corporations although the usual complaint is that the larger firm has easier access to the capital market." It is hard to explain this by carelessness. For Professor Solow knows that construction and trade (the latter with its need to finance inventories and sales) rely heavily on borrowed funds. Firms here tend also to be relatively small—as he agrees elsewhere in the case of trade. It is from such firms as he also knows that complaints come when money is tight. And his reference to the easier access to the capital market of the larger firm is surely disingenuous. He knows that the security that is associated with an ample flow of funds from internal sources will favor the firm so blessed when it goes into the capital markets for additional supplies. Such "ease of access" proves nothing as regards reliance on outside funds.

When there is an industrywide wage increase a normal expectation is of a compensatory price increase with, perhaps, something more. I note that if an industry is able to so increase revenues the day after a wage increase, it could have done so the day before, always assuming that it could find some substitute for the wage increase as a signal for action. It follows that before the wage increase it was not maximizing its revenues; it had some unliquidated margin of monopoly gain. The conclusion is based, Professor Solow states, in language that many will think a trifle lofty if not otherwise unsuited to scholarly discourse, on "sophomore error." The textbook firm, already maximizing its profits, would also raise its prices "to a calculable extent." Alas, the error is again Professor Solow's—though I naturally forego any pejorative adjectives. He omitted to notice that the two responses—my full and immediate compensation for the wage increase and an unspecified response to a cost change—are not the same. The first would not generally be possible were profit already at a maximum. And he did not notice that I carefully allowed for the second.*

One will sense that Professor Solow's desire to attribute error has undermined his instinct to precision. This is most disturbingly evident in the last example I will cite. He suggests that I ignore the danger of a "takeover bid" for the firm that sacrifices earnings for growth and thus abnormally depresses the value of its securities thereby making them open to acquisition. Thus I am indifferent to the disciplines of the capital market. But then he concedes that the takeover is not a threat to the very large firms with which I am concerned. (It arises only farther down the size scale.) And he has elsewhere himself suggested that I write of an economy in which General Motors is writ large. The reader at this point will surely have

begun to wonder. I am accused of being indifferent to dangers that by his admission do not exist for the large firms with which I am excessively concerned. In point of fact I considered this problem at length. The danger of involuntary takeover is negligible in the management calculations of the large firm and diminishes with growth and dispersal of stock ownership.

The list of the points on which Professor Solow has left himself vulnerable could be extended. I have not said, as he states, that the "industrial firm has 'planned' itself into complete insulation from the vagaries of the market." To have to make a point vulnerable by exaggeration is again to suggest a determination to find error so compulsive as to allow it to be invented. On the defense of consumer sovereignty, a vital matter as I will suggest presently, there is already something approaching an agreed line. To this Professor Solow adheres. I have not shown that demand can be managed fully and for all. So the effort can be safely dismissed. (Much or most advertising Professor Solow ventures "serves only to cancel other advertising and is therefore merely wasteful." He suspects that I am influenced by a dislike for billboards and singing commercials.) I argue only for a partial management of consumer choice. But it will hardly be suggested that what is imperfect or incomplete can, as a matter of sound scientific method, be ignored. Professor Solow to the contrary, I do deal with the stabilization of markets for nonconsumer's goods, and I treat at length of the influence of producers on public procurement including, in particular, weaponry. Enough has been said, I think, to indicate a fairly serious default in the canon of scientific discourse that requires careful attention to subject and statement. Let me now advert more briefly to the use of *obiter dicta*— to reliance not on evidence but on the

---

*I fear that I, in some sense, tricked Professor Solow into this error. In an article in *The Review of Economics and Statistics* in 1957 I explored this problem in detail. I did not refer to it in *The New Industrial State*—I sought to ration footnotes beginning with those to my own work. Had Professor Solow been reminded of this earlier work he would not have fallen into the error of assuming a more simplistic rather than a more comprehensive view than his own. But it could be also argued that scholars should check the literature before reacting so strongly.

undoubted scientific reputation of the speaker.

4

There are two of these which troubled me and which may well have troubled readers who have approached these matters with more care than Professor Solow. One is his concluding statement, which I confess I came upon with surprise, that "the reduction of inequality and the alleviation of poverty play negligible roles in Galbraith's system of thought." Rightly or wrongly the treatment of poverty in *The Affluent Society* has been widely cited as helping pave the way for the modern belief that, in the forms therein described, it would survive a steady increase in aggregate income. (The observations of Michael Harrington are perhaps relevant in this regard.) The same book had at least something to do with drawing attention to deficiencies in the public sector— shortcomings in education, the squalor of the cities—as sources of residual poverty and the anger we now experience in the ghettoes.* A paper I presented before a special group working on the problem of "pockets of poverty" in the autumn of 1963 was at least well-timed in relation to the legislation establishing the Office of Economic Opportunity the following year.† I participated actively in drafting that leg-

---

*The very first title of this book was *Why People are Poor*, and it was under this cachet that I negotiated a small grant for research from the Carnegie Corporation of New York in the early fifties. Later titles, *The Opulent Society* and then *The Affluent Society*, reflected my more mature view of the problem. That was less why people are poor than why residual poverty persists and other problems remain unsolved under conditions of generally high and rising income. I think it possible that Professor Solow might wish to plead that he has not read *The Affluent Society*. This is a wholly ligitimate defense, one that would be offered by many other intelligent people, but it does, I would judge, deny him the right to pass on my preoccupations.

†"Let Us Begin" published in Harper's Magazine in the spring of 1964.

islation and served on the statutory advisory board to the Office until new legislation, plus possibly my views on Vietnam, brought my involuntary severance. I also served, though not with any great usefulness, on Mayor Lindsay's task force on this problem. None of this is final proof of a preoccupation with poverty and inequality, and in the nature of the case my own assessment is hardly to be trusted. But most fairminded readers will agree, I believe, that it is sufficient to place a certain burden of proof on Professor Solow. He could conceivably be suggesting, though the words do not imply it, that *The New Industrial State* is not directly concerned with poverty and inequality. But one does not cover all subjects in one book, and I was additionally careful to say:

There are many poor people left in the industrial countries, and notably in the United States. The fact that they are not the central theme of this treatise should not be taken as proof either of ignorance of their existence or indifference to their fate. But the poor, by any applicable tests, are outside the industrial system. They are those who have not been drawn into its service or who cannot qualify. And not only has the industrial system—its boundaries as here defined are to be kept in mind— eliminated poverty for those who have been drawn into its embrace but it has also greatly reduced the burden of manual toil. Only those who have never experienced hard and tedious labor, one imagines, can be wholly indifferent to its elimination.*

With equal absence of proof Professor Solow suggests that I have exposed myself only "very selectively" to the vast empirical literature relevant to the

---

*The New Industrial State, op. cit., p. 318.

facets of the system I establish. Here again one is a poor witness for himself. I am naturally impressed by the time I have spent in the last ten years in tracking down and assimilating the distressingly vast material within the ambit of this volume—the case material on the management of the corporation, monographs on organization theory and practice, on the nature of scientific and technical development, trade union development and attitudes, socialist and Soviet planning including one substantial and one lesser journey for work on the ground, literature on political change and business ideology and the newer materials on the much more limited range of matters on which I consider myself a specialist and much, much more. (I need scarcely add that to my distress I keep on encountering materials that I should have seen.) Professor Solow as a teacher and scholar and distinguished public servant has, most plausibly, covered even more completely this same range of literature. Only as a result of having done so could he claim to pass on the adequacy or inadequacy of anyone else's coverage. But again the reader can rightly ask for at least some argument on behalf of his own greater and more systematic diligence. To let it stand on his own unsupported assertion is surely to trade unduly on scholarly reputation.

5

I come now to the point of it all. And here I am on less certain ground. Professor Solow's error and his use of *obiter dicta* are objective. They are visible to all. To ascribe reasons other than the obvious one of carelessness in the case of so distinguished a scholar involves elements of subjectivity. One could easily find himself in scientific default. Moreover, I am not wholly critical of Professor Solow for failing to disclose the interest which forces him

into so unappealing a posture and performance. He may not be fully aware of it.

The issue concerns the future of economics in general and of the highly prestigious work with which Professor Solow is associated in particular. That work is within a highly specific frame. Within that frame it is the best of its kind. But it is only good if the frame is reasonably intact. When the frame goes so do the scholars it sustains.

What is the frame? It is that the best society is the one that best serves the economic needs of the individual. Wants are original with the individual; the more of these that are supplied the greater the general good. Generally speaking the wants to be supplied are effectively translated by the market to firms maximizing profits therein. If firms maximize profits they respond to the market and ultimately to the sovereign choices of the consumer. Such is the frame and given its acceptance a myriad of scholarly activities can go on within. Any number of blocks can be designed and fitted together in the knowledge that they are appropriate to—that they fit somewhere in—the larger structure. There can be differences of opinion as to what best serves the purposes of the larger structure. Mathematical theorists and model builders can squabble with those who insist on empirical measurement. But this is a quarrel between friends.

Should it happen, however, that the individual ceases to be sovereign —should he become, however subtly, the instrument or vessel of those who supply him, the frame no longer serves. Even to accommodate the possibility that humans are better served by collective than by individual consumption requires the framework to be badly warped. Should the society no longer accord priority to economic goals— should it accord priority to aesthetic accomplishment or mere idleness—it would not serve. And no one quite knows the effect of such change. One can only be certain that, for a long time, economics, like the lesser social sciences, will be struggling with new scaffolding. And the work of economists will be far less precise, far less elegant, seemingly far less scientific than those who are fitting pieces into a structure the nature of which is known and approved and accepted. And if social priority lies elsewhere, it will be less prestigious.

The threat to economics is a serious one; it could become like sociology and partly a branch of political theory. And there are even more pointed aspects. Students are attracted to economics partly by the fascination of working with men of precise and well articulated mind like Professor Solow. But they must be assured, also, that their work is within a framework of sound social purpose. (There remains considerable attraction, though not sufficient attraction, in being a member of a small band of technical initiates. It is somewhat like being a member of a fraternity, a lodge or a chess club.) To enhance the well-being of the individual has, in the past, seemed a sound social purpose. To assist the individual in his subordination to General Motors will not be so regarded. The sanctity of economic purpose will also be questioned if well-being as conventionally measured continues to improve and leaves unsolved the problems associated with collective need—those of the cities and their ghettoes and the by-passed rural areas—or if this progress involves an unacceptable commitment to the technology of war. And the doubts so engendered will be especially acute if concentration on narrow economic priority appears to be a cause of other social shortcomings. The fate of the business schools is a warning of what happens when scholars lose their reputation for association with social purpose. The better students desert in droves and what is a scholar without a school?

I have been looking, however inadequately, at the frame. This, it is plain from the response, does not seem an unreasonable exercise to those outside the profession. Nor to those within who do not feel endangered—whose temperament allows them to watch and philosophically adjust. But it is a threat to those whose prestige and academic position is profoundly associated with the existing structure. It is perhaps not too surprising that it should inspire a counter-offensive. It is less agreeable that it should be compulsively negligent of the scientific mood which, given the old frame, could be so proudly avowed.

A Rejoinder

ROBERT M. SOLOW

I have always laughed at Professor Galbraith's jokes, even when they have been directed at me or my friends. So it is naturally a little disappointing that he should come on so solemn when I tease him a little.

There are one or two places where Professor Galbraith, and therefore possibly other readers, may have misunderstood me. I mentioned that the existence of very large corporations, and the separation of ownership from control within them, had been observed before now. My intention was not at all to hint that Professor Galbraith has tried to palm these off as brand new observations of his own. He has not. My purpose was to suggest to the reader that ideas so long in circulation must

From Robert M. Solow, "A Rejoinder," *The Public Interest* no. 9, Fall 1967, pp. 118–19. Copyright © National Affairs, Inc., 1967. Reprinted by permission of the publisher and the author.

have evoked some response, one way or the other, from economists. I agreed that the response had not been wholly satisfactory from an analytical point of view, but I did not think Professor Galbraith had done it justice. The facts about the size and organization of industrial firms matter to the workaday economist mainly as they affect the substance of pricing, production, and investment decisions. There is, in fact, a large body of empirical work on pricing, production and investment behavior in manufacturing industry. Much of it explains the data moderately well while staying loosely within the framework of supply-demand theory. The facts of large size and diffused stock-ownership do not seem to change that very much.

By the way, it was this range of material that I had in mind when I observed that Professor Galbraith seemed to have missed some of the relevant literature.

I wrote that the reduction of inequality and the alleviation of poverty play negligible roles in Galbraith's system of thought. Professor Galbraith interprets me to be accusing him of indifference to the plight of the poor. But the context of my remarks was a discussion of the low valuation Professor Galbraith puts on the growth of private consumption and real output generally. My point was not that Professor Galbraith is hard-hearted, but that it is difficult to accommodate drastic reduction of the extent of poverty in a system of thought based on the unimportance of increased real output, except perhaps by sharply redistributive taxation. But the mean income is not so high as all that, and anyway Professor Galbraith does not talk much about redistribution.

Professor Galbraith is wrong to ascribe to me a belief in wants that are "original with the individual" and in "the omnipotence of the market." As to the first, it is hardly a deep thought that

nearly all consumer wants beyond the most elementary physiological ones are socially or culturally determined. Indeed, that is precisely why I fear the whole issue is rather tricky. It is a very fine line between analytical statements about the creation of wants by advertising and elaborate indications that one believes one's own tastes to be superior to those of the middle classes.

As to the second, it is only to Professor Galbraith that I seem to believe in the omnipotence of the market. To people who really believe in it, I suppose I seem like Professor Galbraith. I do believe that market forces operate over a large part of the modern economy, sometimes loosely, sometimes tightly. That does not mean that whatever the market turns up is good, or immune from tinkering on the part of the political authority. It does suggest that it will often be efficient to accomplish the social good by *using* the market.

Finally, Professor Galbraith suggests that I disbelieve his argument not because it is unconvincing or unhelpful, but because I have a personal interest to protect. His doctrine is so subversive of conventional economics that if it were to be widely accepted my sort of work would fall in the academic pecking order, my students would diminish in number and quality, and economics would take a tack uncongenial to my sort of mind. About my motives, he may of course be right. Who knows what evil lurks in the hearts of men, as Lamont Cranston used to say. As for the rest, he may equally be right. I shall try to roll gracefully with the punch, and if I cannot, well, then *Après moi, la sociologie.*

Galbraith, Solow, and the truth about corporations

ROBIN MARRIS

I have volunteered to intervene in the Solow-Galbraith controversy, which began in the Fall issue of this journal, because I have some doubts whether, at the end of the day, the lay reader was left clear about the basic issues.

THE REAL WORLD OF THE FIRM

When we reach the core of the debate—i.e., the economic theory of corporate behavior—the truth is that Solow was disingenuous, but that Galbraith had left out vital elements and laid himself open to legitimate attack. What Solow omitted to tell was that my theory implies that *in spite* of the existence of "an important discipline in the capital market," the real-world system almost certainly behaves very differently from the way implied in the conventional theory: the conventional theory would imply that corporations would choose to grow considerably more slowly and reward stockholders significantly better. Galbraith, however, in failing to meet the argument that profits are needed for growth, failed to explain how this divergence can occur. In offering to put the record straight, I am motivated not only by vanity, but also by the conviction that an accurate theory about corporate growth is essential for a correct understanding of a wide range of contemporary problems of economic and social policy. The theory cannot be made simple, but can be summarized as follows.

A growing corporation faces two problems: the problem of creating a growing demand for its products, and the problem of financing the necessary growth of capacity. The corporation may strive to be as efficient as possible, in the sense of squeezing the maximum profit from its existing markets; but the search for (or creation of) *new* markets inevitably costs money (in research, marketing, and losses from failures), and so, as the growth process is accelerated, the average return realized on the *total* assets of the corporation must be adversely affected (even if the development expenditure is deployed as efficiently as possible). In theoretical language, we say there is consequently a "functional relationship" between the rate of return and the rate of growth of saleable output, which varies from corporation to corporation (in the sense that some can get a better return with a given growth rate than others) and from time to time, but that at a given phase in a particular corporation's history, when all the facts are known, the relationship is unique. At the same time, any given growth rate of sales must be supported by a corresponding growth rate of production capacity and hence requires an adequate supply of financial capital. If the main source of finance is internal, the existing level of profits is obviously a major factor governing the sums available, so we get a "feed-back" loop in which the rate of growth both influences and is influenced by the rate of profit. In fact, it is not difficult to see that if retained earnings were the only source of finance, and if the *proportion* retained were arbitrarily fixed by law or convention, we would already have what is called a "closed model": given the relationships described, for each individual corporation there would be only one rate of growth which could satisfy both conditions simultaneously (the unique value would, however, vary *between* cor-

Excerpted from Robin Marris, "Galbraith, Solow, and the Truth about Corporations," in *The Public Interest* 11 (Spring 1968): 37, 41–45. Copyright ⓒ National Affairs, Inc., 1968. Reprinted by permission of the publisher and the author.

porations). This would be an "equilibrium" relationship between growth rate and profit rate, in the sense that the profit rate was at the same time just *low* enough to be consistent with the growth rate of sales and just *high* enough to provide adequate finance. This is about the simplest and neatest "theory of the growth of the corporation" one can conceive. To the best of my knowledge it was invented by Carl Kaysen, now Director of the Institute for Advanced Studies at Princeton, New Jersey, in an unpublished seminar paper given in England about ten years ago. It is not difficult to make the theory more realistic by allowing for flexibility in the retention/pay-out decisions and by bringing in outside finance. In my earlier work I put considerable emphasis on the role of internal finance, and more particularly on the balance between internal and external finance in "closing" a more realistic model. More recently, I have become increasingly impressed by the theoretical work of other economists which suggests that the basic implications are much the same whether one assumes finance to be all internal, all external, or a mixture of the two. In other words, I now think it may not matter too much whether Galbraith or Solow was most right in their confrontation on this point. But to explain the next step in the argument most easily (and for that reason only), it is convenient to write as if all finance were internal.

If we accept that, within very wide limits, the retention ratio is effectively decided by the management, the basic structure of the theory remains unchanged—but it is turned around. If the management chooses to go for a certain growth rate, this will determine the profit rate, so there is now only one value of the retention ratio which will provide the continuous finance required. Once the management has decided its target growth rate, it *must* adopt a corresponding retention ratio; if not, the corporation will either (1) run out of money or (2) fail to achieve its target. Of course, Boards of Directors do not see their problems in these precise terms; but there is considerable evidence that they feel and understand the essential structure of the problem in this way.

PROFITS AND/OR GROWTH

If the process of growth were steady and continuous, and if the numerical values of the relations involved remained unchanged (neither conditions, of course, being satisfied in real life), a decision by the management to grow at a certain rate, and to choose the consistent retention ratio, must also evidently imply a unique level and expected rate of growth of the dividend; and so, in a rational stock market, the decision must imply a unique current price and prospective capital gain in the corporation's stock. Up to a point, actual or potential stockholders may be content to see increased growth creating prospects of future gain at the expense of current dividends; beyond this point, any further increase in the growth rate chosen by the management must have a depressing effect on the stock price. There is no reason to suppose that a growth-oriented management will always refrain from accelerating beyond this point; and if they go too far they will undoubtedly lay themselves open to a variety of dangers (e.g., a take-over raid). I suggested in my theory that we might describe a typical "managerial" objective as maximum growth subject to a *minimum* on the stock price.

Solow said that my theory, in recognizing the minimum stock-price constraint, "came closer to the conventional view." On the contrary, in the conventional view management exists only to serve stockholders, and the essential technical problem is to find decision rules that would establish the policy which will, in fact, *maximize* the price of the stock. The two theories become "similar" only in the special conditions where the minimum and maximum position lie close together. These conditions are most improbable; in other words, the traditional theory is literally a "special case."

Because large-scale, professional management, not personally owning large supplies of finance, has such predominant technical advantages in the modern economy; because, although it may *use* stockmarket investors and bankers, it no longer *depends* on them; because the (not insubstantial) true capitalists who remain in our system avoid speculating in large manufacturing businesses unless these are going very cheap (they prefer real estate); because the other potential take-over raiders are typically themselves management-controlled—because of all this and much more, it is inevitable that the safe minimum level of the price of a corporation's stock will be significantly lower, and the safe maximum growth rate correspondingly higher, than the values which would be chosen by a management that really did care only for the welfare of the stockholders. Numerical calculations based on statistical observation suggest that a rather growth-conscious management could typically grow almost twice as fast, setting the stock market value at all times about one-third lower, as compared to the values which would be obtained in an otherwise comparable corporation dominated by stockholders who knew all the facts. Furthermore, the growth-oriented management could safely continue the policy indefinitely, even if there were quite a number of others who chose to behave otherwise. Since the growth-oriented managements will by definition be located in the faster growing corporations, this type of behavior must in time drive out other types—a process which, I suggest, has been going on for some time. The further the process goes, the weaker is the power of the stock market to resist. Since the growth-oriented firms are technically efficient, they display not unattractive levels and growth rates of dividends, the incentive to resistance is dampened, and the latent preference for slower growth and higher current dividends remains unrecognized.

Furthermore, because managements, in fostering growth, also create technical progress, new wants, new goods, and a generally different dynamic environment, the implications of the two types of theory cannot easily be compared. We cannot possibly assert that it would necessarily be in the public interest to compel managements to conform to the traditional norm; we might very likely make many people worse off and few better off. Galbraith, however, imposed the value judgment (the "affluent-society" thesis) that the higher rate of consumer innovation resulting from "managerial" behavior by the corporations is undesirable, because it is biased against the expression of leisure preferences and against the development of "public" goods. He does not, however (as maybe does Solow in saying "it might perhaps be better if companies were forced more often into the capital market"), suggest that the remedies lie in the direction of the traditional model.

The conclusion I draw (and it is an implication which I suspect to be one of the causes of the considerable ideological drive of "neoclassical" economics in the United States) would probably be disliked by both parties: namely, that once the classical idealization of capitalism is thus destroyed, there is no *economic* case for its superiority over socialism. Consequently, the attempt to impose capitalism all around the world, in some cases virtually by force, can only be justified on political grounds. The latter, however, seem to get thinner every day. In the miserable developing countries of the "free" world, where we cheerfully give aid to almost any form of dictatorship provided no industries are nationalized (the case of Tito being a historical freak, much disliked by the Congress, I understand), there is no dearth of greedy *profit* maximizers, many living in considerable luxury. What the nonaffluent majority of the world's population so badly needs is a much greater number of *growth* maximizers.

The truth further refined:
A COMMENT ON MARRIS

ROBERT M. SOLOW

I want to welcome Robin Marris to this performance of Our Gang. . . .

ON CORPORATE BEHAVIOR

Marris has summarized, with quite wonderful economy, his own theory of corporate behavior. It is a self-contained determinate theory, with implications that are testable at least in principle. Like any theory, this one raises two questions. Does it tell a true story? And, if it does, what are its larger implications about economic life?

As I mentioned in my review of Galbraith, it is not easy to invent a clearcut statistical test of the Marris theory of corporate growth against the more standard model of long-run profit maximization anchored by a target rate of return. I suggested that this is because the two theories do not have drastically different implications. Marris objects; like any student of advertising, he would like to stress the differences between his

Excerpted from Robert M. Solow, "The Truth Further Refined: A Comment on Marris," *The Public Interest* no. 11, Spring 1968, pp. 47, 49–52. Copyright © National Affairs, Inc., 1968. Reprinted by permission of the publisher and the author.

own product and Brand X. I should have been more precise. The two theories need not have very different implications, but they may. Whether they do depends on the height of the minimum acceptable-rate-of-return (or stock price) in Marris' model. The higher it is, or the closer to the target rate of return, the more similar a Marris economy will be to mine. I am uncertain about the source of Marris' conviction that the differences are in fact large, since so far as I know his theory has not yet been given a large-scale run against the facts. One would like to know, for example, how well it does as a predictor of plant and equipment spending.

In the meanwhile, we are reduced to casual empiricism about the assumptions and implications of the Marris theory. This is hardly the place to discuss the matter in detail. I will simply say that the theory, interesting and attractive as it is, seems to me to rest on two fairly weak assumptions. The first is that for a given corporation in a given environment there must be a well-defined relation between its rate of growth (of output) and its rate of return on capital, independent of the absolute size of the corporation. It is not enough for the theory that, with everything else momentarily given, a corporation's profitability should depend on how rapidly it is trying to expand its sales and its capacity. What is required is that this relation hold for long intervals of time during which the corporation is actually growing. Both at the beginning of the period, when the company is small, and at the end, when it is large, it has to be true that to a particular, more or less steady rate of growth of x percent a year corresponds the same more or less steady rate of profit of y percent a year. This is not outlandish, but I think the assumption rests on too simple a view of the business of sales promotion, and on insufficient attention to the production-cost side of the problem.

The second dubious assumption is the one that names growth of sales as the prime object of the corporation. Marris does not simply assert this; he argues it with care and sociological circumstance in his book. He gives two versions: a management may "choose to go for a certain growth rate," or else it may seek "maximum growth subject to a minimum on the stock price." In a more technical statement of the theory he can allow profits and growth to be two separate objectives which have to be weighed against each other. The more weight a corporation attaches to profits and the less to growth, the more nearly it will behave according to the conventional theory.

There is certainly a lot of talk in the business press about growth and expansion. But this, by itself, is hardly support for the Marris-Galbraith doctrine. In the first place, the alternative theory— that corporations maximize long-run profits more or less, and expand whenever they earn more than a target rate of return—also entails that successful companies will be growing most of the time, and will no doubt be talking about it. In the second place, one must keep in mind that the federal government taxes long-term capital gains only half as heavily as dividends, and under some circumstances considerably less than that. Retention and reinvestment of earnings—i.e., internally financed growth—is the obvious way for a corporation to convert dividends into capital gains for its shareholders, including its officers. So devotion to growth is quite consistent with profit-maximization if profit is interpreted as the after-tax return to the stockholder.

Theories that emphasize the separation of ownership and control tend to ignore the fact that, if the common stockholder cannot control the policy of the corporation he owns, he can arrange to own a different corporation by merely telephoning his broker. He can even buy shares in a mutual fund that will tailor a portfolio to his expressed preferences between current dividends and capital gains. Indeed, such theories generally tend to ignore the large-scale institutional investors, whose presence on the other side of the market makes the balance of power between management and owner look a little different.

This would seem to be important, even within the framework of Marris' theory. He admits that some corporations can be more growth-oriented and less profit-oriented than others. If any substantial number of stockholders strongly favors immediate profits over growth, their demands can be mobilized by institutional investors. Corporate managements are sure to be found or created who will be prepared to get their kicks by catering to these demands.

I realize that these casual remarks about the plausibility of assumptions can never be decisive. For that we will have to wait for serious empirical testing. And if I am right that the two theories could turn out to have similar implications, we may have to wait even longer—but of course it will matter less.

ON IDEOLOGY

Marris considers his theory to be subversive of the existing order. Since the consumer is presumably manipulated and the stockholder presumably ignored, no intellectual case remains for capitalism as an efficient economic system. Even leaving aside the question whether this argument applies to the regulated mixed economy of today, it is the damnedest argument for socialism I ever heard. Who would storm the Winter Palace so that units of production could be "endowed with the social norm of growth maximization (subject to financial constraints)" even if "manipulation of the financial rules to offset various kinds of built-in bias . . . would be much easier"?

Marris also suspects that only an ideological drive can explain the persistence with which economists in the United States cling to some (incomplete) confidence in market mechanisms. I would not deny that some academic disputes have a genuine ideological content. But I would also assert that there is far less ideology wrapped up in academic economics in the United States than a man from Cambridge, England, can possibly realize. In fact, I don't think that my argument with Galbraith and Marris is really ideological in character. My own view is that any economic system can be made to work, if you go at it cleverly. But to do that, you have to get the analysis right. If Marris' theory of the firm turns out to work better, which is conceivable, I will buy it cheerfully.

Continued from p. 544
tion, attractiveness, and general atmosphere of the place of sale.

(4) Oligopoly. Oligopoly means "few sellers." Since, as we have seen, large corporations play a dominant role in many industries in the manufacturing sector, much of that sector can be classified as oligopolistic. This classification is in many ways less precise and covers more ground than the others on our list. For one thing, an industry dominated by a few sellers may produce either a homogeneous or a differentiated product. Automobile production in the United States is highly oligopolistic (largely dominated by three firms), and the products are significantly differentiated. By contrast, copper production is relatively undifferentiated, though there is very high concentration of sellers of newly-mined copper.

Another problem is that "few sellers" may mean anything from more than one or two[4] to less than the vast numbers required for strict pure or monopolistic competition. There is no reason to expect the same behavior patterns in an industry like automobile manufacturing, where one firm (General Motors) produces roughly half the national output and the top three firms 90 percent of output, and an industry like meat-packing, where the top three firms (Swift, Armour, Wilson) control only one-third of the market, and the rest is serviced by over two thousand other firms. A final problem with oligopoly—though not so much with the classification as with the difficulty of analyzing this market structure—is that it is likely to be characterized by mutually recognized interdependence among the larger firms in the

industry. Where a few firms dominate a particular market, each is likely to realize that *its* actions will produce reactions from the other firms involved, and the whole strategy of decision making is made much more complex by that fact.

The above classification of market structures is only one of several that could be—and have been—made. It is useful, however, in bringing out two of the important dimensions along which the structures of different industries may vary. One dimension is that of numbers. Pure competition and monopolistic competition are alike in requiring very large numbers of small firms; monopoly involves one firm; oligopoly an intermediate number though, in reality, there are often a few rather large firms that play a significant role in a particular industry. The second dimension concerns degrees of product differentiation. Purely competitive, monopolistic, and some oligopolistic firms sell homogeneous products; monopolistically competitive and other oligopolistic firms sell differentiated products.

A summary of these structures arranged along these two dimensions is presented in Table 24-1. This summary also brings out two other features of market structures that are of interest. One is the role of advertising in different market structures. There is no need for advertising in pure competition (the firm can sell all it can produce at the going price) and little need in pure monopoly or undifferentiated oligopoly. Advertising is mainly significant, therefore, in monopolistic competition and in differentiated oligopoly.

The other important aspect of market structures suggested by the table has to do with the question of the recognition of interdependence among business firms. The taking into account of the reactions of other firms to *its* action is characteristically significant only for the oligopo-

---

4. Economists have a specific name for a market in which there are precisely two sellers: *duopoly*. We shall not consider this particular structure in the analysis that follows.

Table 24-1   A CLASSIFICATION OF MARKET STRUCTURES

Number of Firms in the Industry

		Many Small Firms	A "Few" Large Firms	A Single Firm
Degree of **Product** **Differentiation** **in the** **Industry**	*Homogeneous Product*	**Pure Competition** (many small firms; no product differentiation; no advertising; price is taken as *given*; U.S. agriculture closest approximation)	**Undifferentiated Oligopoly** (a few usually dominating firms; not much advertising; more or less identical products; firms' decisions tend to be interdependent)	**Monopoly** (a single seller of a product without close substitutes; "public interest" advertising; is rare in the U.S.; usually governmentally regulated as in public utilities)
	Differentiated Product	**Monopolistic Competition** (many small firms with slightly different products; local advertising; fairly common in retail markets)	**Differentiated Oligopoly** (a few big firms with much competition through product differentiation and advertising; interdependent decisions; *both* forms of oligopoly common throughout U.S. industry)	

listic firm. The absence of direct rivals in monopoly and the inability of a very small firm to *have* a significant effect on its rivals in pure and monopolistic competition mean that recognition of mutual interdependence is of little importance in these market structures.

These varying characteristics result in firm and industry behavior different from what might be expected if, as in Part Three A, we were dealing with a wholly competitive economy. Using this earlier analysis as our framework, let us now analyze briefly how these other market structures cause departures from the conclusions derived in the case of pure competition.

ANALYSIS OF MONOPOLY IN THE PRODUCT MARKET

Monopolies may be either "natural"—as, for example, when economies of scale produce a continuously falling average cost curve and thus make it inefficient to maintain more than one firm in a particular industry—or "contrived"—as, for example, when firms with rising average cost curves merge simply to enjoy the increased profits possible through the exploitation of monopoly. In most industrial nations, the growth of large firms has resulted at one time or another from either

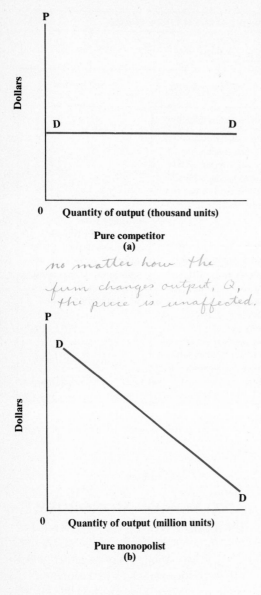

no matter how the firm changes output, Q, the price is unaffected.

Figure 24-1. Firm Demand Curves for Pure Competitor and Pure Monopolist.

In pure monopoly, the firm has the industry-wide consumer demand curve for its firm demand curve. Notice the different units of measurement on the quantity axes in the two diagrams.

or both of these circumstances; where "natural" monopoly was unavoidable (as in telephone or postal service), governments have either regulated or, more usually, nationalized the services.

Whatever the original source of the monopoly, the main effect in the product market is that the individual firm (monopolist) will have as *its* demand curve the industry-wide consumer demand curve for the product in question. The contrast with pure competition is shown in Figure 24-1. In pure competition, the individual firm faces a horizontal (perfectly elastic) demand curve, signifying that its share of total industry output is so small that the overall price of the product will be virtually unaffected by any conceivable contraction or expansion of output by that firm. This horizontal demand curve represents little more than a dot on the industry-wide consumer demand curve (see our earlier discussion, p. 450). The monopolist, by contrast, faces the downward-sloping demand curve of the industry as a whole He is, therefore, confronted by a set of decisions unknown to the pure competitor. He can *set* the price of his product as he chooses. Of course, he is not without constraints in doing this. If he sets a higher price, consumers will buy less; if he sets a lower price, they will buy more. However, the questions facing the pure competitor and the monopolist are different. The pure competitor must determine how he will maximize profits at the *given* price. The monopolist must determine how he should *set* the price, to maximize profits.

In one sense, since both firms are attempting to maximize profits, the answers given to these different questions will be the same. We learned in chapter 19 that the purely competitive firm will maximize profits by producing where its marginal revenue equals its marginal cost

$(MR = MC)$. The same logic applies to a profit-maximizing monopolist—he, too, will continue to expand output until that point where the additional cost of a unit of output is equated to the additional revenue from that unit of output. To produce at a lower output would mean foregone additional profits; to produce at a higher output would mean a diminution of profits, since added revenues are now below added costs.

The difference arises when we come to the further conclusion about the purely competitive firm: that it will produce at an output where price equals marginal cost. In the case of pure competition, where P ($=$ Average Revenue) is given, MR is always equal to P. Hence the condition $MR = MC$ also implies the condition that $P = MC$. But this is not true of the monopolist. In his case, $P(= AR)$ is falling as he produces more and more output for sale on the market. When an "average" of anything is falling, the "marginal" of that thing must be below it.[5] Since P ($= AR$) is falling for the monopolist as sales expand along the industry-wide consumer demand curve, MR must be below AR. When the monopolist produces at an output where $MR = MC$, therefore, he is producing at an output where P is greater than MC.

The equilibrium of the monopolist is shown in Figure 24-2. The MR curve starts at the intersection of the demand curve (DD) with the vertical axis $(MR = AR$ at one unit of output) and then falls more sharply down to the right as the "marginal" brings the "average" down. The monopolist will maximize profits by producing the output OQ_0 and setting a price of OP_0. Explain to yourself why the amount of "pure" profits in this case will

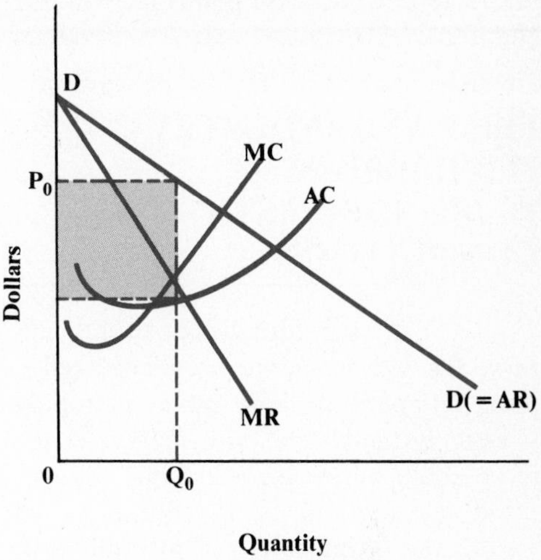

Figure 24-2. Equilibrium of the Pure Monopolist.

The monopolist, like the pure competitor, will maximize profits where $MR = MC$; but unlike the purely competitive case, this will *not* mean $P = MC$. In monopoly, equilibrium P will be greater than MC, and "pure" profits (equal to shaded rectangle) may persist over time.

be equal to the area of the shaded rectangle.

Two points should be noticed about this equilibrium position. The first is that, as we have said, the monopolist's equilibrium price will not be equal to marginal cost; it will always be above it. The second point to stress is that unlike the case of pure competition where abnormal profits are always temporary (being competed away as other firms enter the industry), the profit rectangle in Figure 24-2 can persist indefinitely. By hypothesis, there are no close competitors. Unless there is some change in fundamental conditions (in the real world an antitrust suit or government regulation would be a strong possibility), abnormal profits may persist as a condition of *long*-run equilibrium in the case of a monopolist. We shall

---

5. Cf. analysis of "average" and "marginal" cost, pp. 447-49.

return to both of these points later in this chapter.

FIRM AND INDUSTRY EQUILIBRIUM IN MONOPOLISTIC COMPETITION

Until the third decade of this century, the two cases we have analyzed—pure competition and pure monopoly—were virtually the only market structures about which the economic theorist could say anything very definite. As we know, this situation was altered with Chamberlin's analysis of markets where there are large numbers of small firms competing with differentiated products.

One of the interesting aspects of Chamberlin's work was that it showed the possibility (though not the necessity) of a zero-profit equilibrium under monopolistic competition. We remember that in this particular market structure, each firm does have a "monopoly" of its own individual product, which may be *Movie Stars,* a picture magazine about Hollywood. At a given moment in time, there may be a number of other roughly similar magazines in the field, including such hypothetical competitors as *Flickland* and *Reel Romances.* Since *Movie Stars* is a differentiated product, it will be able to raise its subscription price within limits above those of the others in the field and still retain some subscribers; by lowering its price, it may hope to increase the volume of its sales. In short, it has a downward sloping demand curve as shown in Figure 24-3(a). Because it has a number of fairly close competitors, its demand curve may be relatively more elastic than that of a "pure" monopolist, and its profits may not be quite so high. However, in other respects, the firm's equilibrium is rather

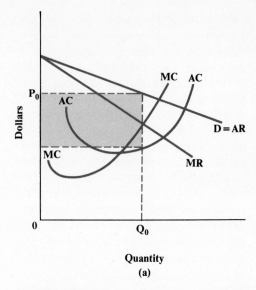

(a) Monopolistic competitor in the short run (profits are shaded area).

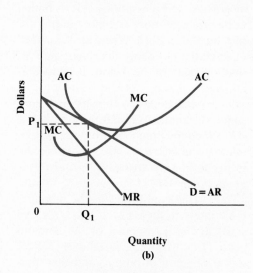

Figure 24-3. Equilibrium under Monopolistic Competition.

(b) In the long run, other monopolistic competitors might enter in with new (but similar) products. In this case, pure profits will disappear; but unlike the pure competitor, this firm produces with (1) $P > MC$ and (2) "excess capacity."

similar to that of the monopolist in that
it will achieve maximum profits at a point
where $MC = MR$; P will be above MC;
and, for the moment at least, the firm will
be making abnormal profits.

Now the position described in
Figure 24-3(a) may be where the matter
ends. Unlike pure competition, where the
product is homogeneous and any competent businessman can presumably produce
it, there is no certainty that the abnormal
profits earned by *Movie Stars* (and the
similar profits, let us assume, earned by
its competitors) will give some businessmen the idea for still further differentiation in the movie magazine field. However, it *may* do so. *If* it does so, we can
imagine the demand curve for *Movie Stars*
(and that of each of the other magazines
in the field) being pushed to the left until
it reaches the position shown in Figure
24-3(b). What has happened is that a
number of new competitors—*Stardust,
Falling Stars,* and *Startled!,* among
others—have been attracted by the profits
in this field and have, so to speak, crowded
into the not unlimited economic space of
consumer demand for movie magazines.

Notice that in this new equilibrium position, *Movie Stars* is not making
profits beyond the normal profits included
in the cost curve itself. In this respect,
monopolistic competition can lead to a
long-run, zero-profit equilibrium similar
to that of pure competition. Even in this
case, however, the equilibrium position is
different from that of pure competition in
that (1) P is still above MC, and (2) the
firm is not producing at the minimum
point of its average cost curve. Because
the firm's demand curve is downward-
sloping, such a zero-profit condition,
where the demand curve is tangent to the
average cost curve, will always be to the
left of the point of minimum average cost.
As it is sometimes put, each firm will be

operating under conditions of "excess capacity."

Two further departures of monopolistic competition from pure competition should be noticed. The first is that
the possibility of advertising now makes
a significant appearance on the economic
scene. In pure competition, advertising
does not occur, since the individual firm
is able to sell all that it can reasonably
produce at the going price and (unless it
joins in the activities of a noncompetitive
trade association) it is too small by its own
actions to affect the industry-wide demand
for its product. Advertising could in theory
occur under pure monopoly, since the firm
might hope to alter favorably the overall
consumer demand for its product. Still, its
prospects would be somewhat limited by
the fact that since the firm has no close
rivals, their share of the market cannot
be captured by advertising. When product
differentiation occurs, however, advertising becomes a significant means for creating special preferences and attachments
among consumers for one's own particular
version of the product in question. Advertising expenditures, moreover, tend to be
highest where product differentiation is
relatively slight and where, therefore, the
creation of buyer preferences rests most
heavily on various kinds of promotional
campaigns.[6]

The other departure from pure
competition lies in the fact that the firm
must decide not only what output of its
product to produce, but the nature of the
product itself. Product differentiation is
not a once-for-all phenomenon, but
occurs continuously over time. *Movie
Stars* may change its format, its mix of
articles and photography, the slant of its
stories. Television watchers have all ob-

6. See Richard Caves, *American Industry: Structure,
Conduct, Performance,* 2nd ed. (Englewood Cliffs,
N.J.: Prentice-Hall, Inc., 1967), pp. 46–47.

served the virtues of a new brand-name detergent being touted at the expense of the old version of the same brand. Changes of style, design, chemical formula, color, shape, and gadgetry (some doubtless improvements; others less clearly so) in the product itself become an important form of *nonprice* competition in all industries where product differentiation has taken hold.

PATTERNS OF BEHAVIOR IN OLIGOPOLISTIC MARKETS

Many of the comments we have just made about nonprice competition under monopolistic competition could also be widely applied to oligopolistic firms. For constant changes in the style, design, and technical gadgetry of its products, no industry is a better exemplar than the American passenger car industry, which, as we know, is highly concentrated. Advertising may also be a significant factor in oligopolistic industries. Three American industries noted for their very high advertising expenditures are the makers of soap, cigarettes, and liquor, each of which spends over 10 percent of its revenues (excluding excise taxes) on advertising. All three are clearly oligopolistic industries. In soap, 80 percent of the market is held by the "Big Three": Procter & Gamble, Colgate, and Lever Brothers; in cigarettes, the top three firms account for over 70 percent, and the top six nearly 100 percent, of the national market; in liquor, the largest eight firms account for about three-quarters of the American market.

The special feature of oligopoly—whether the product is differentiated or not—is, as we have said, the problem of mutually recognized interdependence among the larger producers of the industry in question. When there are large numbers of competitors ("pure" or otherwise) in an industry or where there is only one (monopoly), the problem of estimating the actions and reactions of one's rivals is of relatively little significance. When there are a few, often mammoth firms in the industry, this problem is of the essence.

One important consequence of the problem is that the characteristic oligopoly firm does not have a firm-demand curve in the same sense in which we have drawn such curves for other market structures. Let us suppose that we have a fairly well-defined, industry-wide consumer demand curve for the product in question and that there are four firms in the industry producing slightly differentiated products, each with a roughly equal share of the market and a price more or less in line with the others. For any one of the firms (say, Firm A) we would appear to have one point on its demand curve defined by its price and quantity of sales. However, the firm-demand curve should tell the businessman what will happen to his quantity of sales when he *alters* his price over a wide range of alternatives. But this we cannot do for Firm A, at least not in any simple sense. If Firm A were to cut its price by 10 percent *and* if there were no reaction from Firms B, C, and D, then the firm might be able to determine how its quantity of sales would increase. But the essence of the problem is that, in general, the other firms *will* react and, further, that Firm A is *aware* of that fact. In order to determine the impact on his sales of a given change in price, therefore, the businessman must know in advance exactly how the other firms will react, and whether their reaction will cause a further reaction on his part, and whether in that event there will be still further reactions from his rivals—matters that, in the absence of some form of collusion, are likely to be obscure.

One partial way of getting around this problem is to try to make certain generalizations about the *kind* of assumptions an oligopolistic firm will make about his rivals' reactions. Suppose we make the not unreasonable assumption that oligopolistic firms like to undersell their rivals but dislike being undersold. If a firm's price is just slightly below its rivals, it may gain appreciably at their expense in increasing its overall share of the market in question but without much sacrifice in revenue per unit. Even more specifically, the owner of Firm A may conclude that if he raises his price, his rivals, now put in the preferred position of underselling him, will hold theirs constant; whereas if he lowers his price, his rivals, not wishing to be undersold, will lower their prices along with him.

Given these assumptions and Firm A's initial price and output position, we can now draw a form of demand curve—usually called a *kinked demand curve*—for Firm A, as shown in Figure 24-4. Firm A is originally located at point B, producing OQ_0 output and selling it at the price OP_0. If the businessman raises his price, other firms are assumed to hold theirs constant, meaning that he is now being undersold and that he can expect a sharp reduction in his sales. Thus the segment of the demand curve *AB* is quite elastic—a large percentage decrease in quantity following upon a small percentage increase in price. If he lowers price, the hypothesis states that other firms will lower with him to avoid being undersold. This means that he will make little or no gains with respect to his competitors, and the increase in quantity sold will reflect only consumer willingness to buy more of the commodity from all producers at the now lower industry-wide price. Hence, the segment of the demand curve *BD* is much

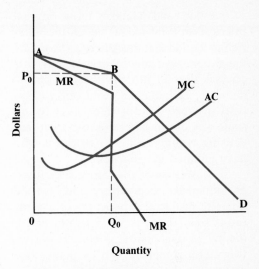

Figure 24-4. Kinked Demand Curve under Oligopoly.

If an oligopolist assumes that his rivals will react to an "I lower, they all lower; I raise, I raise alone" philosophy, then he will have a *kinked demand curve*. Explain why this might lead to rigid prices.

less elastic—a given percentage decrease in price bringing only a small percentage increase in quantity. The *MR* curve, in this case, will have the rather peculiar shape shown in Figure 24-4, sloping gently downward at first and then breaking vertically downward when the "kink" in the demand curve occurs. It should be apparent that it will be in the interest of Firm A to maintain the original price and quantity even if there should be quite substantial shifts in its cost curves, since *MC* will equal *MR* at a different output only with a radical increase (or decrease) in costs.

The kinked demand curve is useful in explaining an element of rigidity in oligopolistic pricing and also the preference many of these firms seem to show for nonprice competition—advertising and product differentiation—as discussed earlier. However, it does not explain the setting of the original prices for the firms in question, and it makes those original prices seem a bit *too* stable. In the inflationary period that the American economy has experienced since World War II, it is obvious that all firms in the economy—definitely including those in oligopolistically organized industries—have found some way or other to raise prices without causing traumatic losses to those who have initiated the changes.

Because of the intricacies caused by mutual interdependence and also the different historical experiences of various industries, there is no airtight "pure theory" of oligopolistic pricing. However, two useful comments can be made. The first is that there may be certain patterns or formulas for setting prices in a particular industry. When Firm A finds that conditions make it desirable to raise its price, such formulas can give it reasonable assurance that the other firms will come to similar conclusions. Firm A will not be left out on a limb. A fairly common method of setting prices in oligopolistic industries is to add a certain percentage markup above average or, usually, average variable costs. At a certain level of output, this markup will cover fixed costs, and the firm will have hit its break-even point; further increases in output will lead to positive net profits. If firms in a particular industry behave in this way and there is a sudden change in cost conditions that affect all firms in the industry—perhaps a new higher-wage labor contract is negotiated in the industry—then each firm will be able to raise its prices with some confidence that its rivals will do the same. Each firm has acted independently, yet the net effect is as if they had acted in concert.

Such common formulas do not usually cover all relevant changes in conditions, however, and oligopolistic industries will often develop other means for initiating orderly price changes. This leads to our second comment, which is that a quite common mechanism for meeting this problem is *price leadership*. One of the firms in the industry—always a large firm but not necessarily the largest—undertakes to make an assessment of the relevant conditions in the market and to initiate a price change that, if the pattern is functioning effectively, other firms will follow. Of course, the price leader must be sure that its actions take into account the interests of other firms in the industry, as well as its own interest; also, it must be aware of the possibility of potential new entrants into the field who may threaten the profits of all existing firms including itself. If these factors are taken into account—if, in effect, the problem of mutual interdependence is wisely handled by the price leader—then this pattern of behavior can lead to orderly changes in prices with only tacit (and not illegally collusive) cooperation among the firms in the industry.

Even then, of course, formulas and patterns can always break down. And the history of American industry is filled with challenges for the role of price leadership (the struggle over price leadership in the tobacco industry in the 1930s is a good example) and defections by follower firms who feel that their interests are not being adequately served. It is also filled with numerous cases in which covert but explicit, direct agreements among oligopolistic firms have been made for setting prices. The complications and uncertainties of mutual interdependence make such agreements perhaps understandable, though it is also perhaps understandable that when they are detected, the Justice Department takes a dim view of them.

One final question about oligopolistic firms we have raised before: are these firms truly interested in the maximization of profits in the first place? This is a very basic question since it is an underlying presumption of a market economy that individuals are expected to pursue their own private interests and that businessmen's private interest can be equated to profits. The motives of individuals, however, are usually more complicated than this—prestige, respectability, and standing in the community will ordinarily count for something with even the most hardheaded businessman—and for giant corporations that dominate many industries in the American manufacturing sector, there is the divorce of ownership and control to complicate matters further.

Where such a divorce of ownership and control occurs, the private interest of the stockholder in higher profits (and higher dividends) need not in theory correspond with the private interest of the management of the firm. To take a crass case, management might like higher managerial salaries and more time on the golf course in preference to maximum profits for the owner-stockholders. More generally, as some economists have argued, management may be primarily interested in the prestige, influence (and often higher salaries) associated with big firms, and managers may therefore make decisions conducive to the growth of the firm even when these decisions conflict with strict profit-maximization objectives.

In an even more philosophic vein, Professor Galbraith has suggested that the goals of management may be a reflection of the goals of the members of what he calls the "technostructure." Thus, for example, achieving rapid technological change may become an important management objective that is independent of the traditional pursuit of profits.[7]

Although these qualifications are important to keep in mind, it is not abso-

7. See Great Debate Three, pp. 548–49.

lutely clear that they require us to abandon the profit-maximization hypothesis *in toto*. Profit-maximization may be a necessary condition for the achievement of other possible corporate objectives such as the growth of the firm over time. Also, what appears to be a failure to maximize profits in the short run may often be the result of trying to maximize them in the longer run. Thus, although some businessmen would doubtless be annoyed at being referred to as crude profit-maximizers, they might be equally annoyed if different language were used and they were charged with having failed to cut costs or having missed some opportunity to increase revenues. And that, of course, is what profit maximization is all about.

IMPERFECT COMPETITION AND EFFICIENCY

Having analyzed the behavior of variously imperfectly competitive markets, let us conclude this chapter by briefly considering the significance of these departures from pure competition in relationship to economic efficiency. In the following chapter, we shall comment on some of the public policy issues these departures raise.

A layman's indictment of monopolies or monopolistic elements in an economy might go as follows:

Monopolistic power is bad, economically, for three reasons: (1) monopolists are rich and make high profits at the expense of laborers whom they exploit and of poor people in general; (2) monopolistic power enables firms to overcharge consumers —i.e., to set higher prices than the goods are "worth"; and (3) monopolistic power allows firms to "hold back" on production and thus to provide the economy with fewer of the monopolized goods than it would have had under pure competition.

To this, he might add the essentially political criticism that the concentration of economic power in the hands of very large firms may lead to the concentration of political power in a way that is inimical to the processes of a democratic society. We recall that President Eisenhower's concern about the military-industrial complex in the United States was focussed on the potential effects of the concentration of economic power (in this case a linking of governmental and private power) on political decisions. (See chapter 4, pp. 102-07.) The political question is important, as is the sociological question of the effects of working for large, impersonal, corporate bureaucracies—though, of course, the economist has no special qualifications to render final judgments on these matters.

Even the more narrowly "economic" points in the indictment are rather complicated. The first point has to do with the evils of monopoly profits. We have shown in the preceding analysis that many forms of imperfect competition can lead to persistent "pure" profits. We have also shown, however, that there can be monopoly elements without pure profits, as in the zero-profit case of monopolistic competition; nor is the characteristic monopolistic competitor—say, the corner grocery store—necessarily a very rich firm. If large firms do make substantial profits, it is in theory possible to tax the profits of these firms without affecting their immediate price and output decisions. If Firm X is maximizing profits at a certain level of price and output, it will still be maximizing profits at that price and output if the government taxes away a given percentage of those profits.

Whether it is desirable to have such taxes—and how large they should be—is likely to be determined by the effects of such action on growth (a large part of investment in the United States is financed by the reinvestment of retained earnings) and on income distribution (what *is* an equitable income distribution?). We shall return to the growth question in the next chapter and to the problem of income distribution in chapter 29.

The second and third points of the layman's indictment of monopoly power center on what we have come to call the problem of economic *efficiency*. Monopoly power, it is asserted, allows firms to charge too much and to produce too little. The implicit judgment is that there are "better" levels of price and output—i.e., those that will lead to a more efficient allocation of resources in the economy as a whole.

This implicit argument can easily be made explicit on the basis of our analysis of efficiency in chapter 22. Let us suppose that we have a very simple economy producing two goods, Good A and Good B, and that Good A is produced by a pure monopolist and Good B is produced by a large number of purely competitive firms. The price of Good A will be above its marginal cost, since it is produced by a monopolist. When the economy is in general equilibrium, let us suppose that $P_A = \$10$ and that $MC_A = \$5$. The price of competitive Good B, by contrast, will be equal to its marginal cost. For simplicity, let us suppose that both goods have the same marginal cost. Hence, $MC_B = \$5$ and also $P_B = \$5$. Why is this inefficient?

The answer is that this economy does not fulfill the condition that the rate of consumer substitution between these two goods be equal to the rate of producer transformation of these same goods. In equilibrium, *consumers are paying twice as much for a unit of Good A ($10) as they are for a unit of Good B ($5). This means that the rate of substitution of Good A for Good B is 1/2. Give any consumer 1/2 unit of A and he will be willing to give up 1 unit of B and still remain equally well off. The rate of producer transformation between A and B, however, is not 1/2 but 1. If we transfer $5 of resources from the production of B to the production of A, we lose 1 unit of B and gain 1 unit of A. Since this is the case, it should be clear that the economy as a whole can gain from a reallocation of resources, specifically a transfer of resources from the production of Good B to Good A. Each time $5 of resources is so transferred, consumers lose 1 B and gain 1 A, but 1 A is worth twice as much to consumers as 1 B, and hence there is a net gain from the reallocation.*

A few comments should be made about this simple analysis. The first is that as the process of reallocation goes on, the rates of substitution and transformation will, of course, change. As the consumers get more and more of Good A relative to Good B, the marginal rate of substitution of A for B will rise (i.e., it will take more than 1/2 unit of A to compensate the consumer for the loss of 1 unit of B). Similarly, as resources are transferred from the production of B to the production of A, the ratio of the marginal costs is likely to alter; the marginal cost of A will rise relative to that of B. The final "efficient" equilibrium (occurring if industry A is reorganized along purely competitive lines) will ordinarily involve a price ratio between the two goods intermediate between the original price ratio (2:1) and the original ratio of marginal costs (1:1).

A second point is that this example should make clear what is meant by

a monopolist's charging "too much" and producing "too little." Our reorganization of this economy toward greater efficiency has involved a relative lowering of the price of Good A and a greater production of Good A relative to Good B in the economy as a whole.

A final point about this analysis is that, although we have used a "pure monopolist" in our example, the same general kinds of conclusions could be reached for oligopoly and monopolistic competition as long as the firms involved charged a price that was above marginal cost. This is the case even when we are dealing with the zero-profit monopolistic competitor. For we recall that even in that case, the tangency of the firm's demand curve to its average cost curve will involve charging a price above marginal cost and producing under conditions of "excess capacity."

The conclusion of the above analysis seems—and is—a strong economic argument against monopoly elements in the private sector of the economy. Before we jump to the brave judgment that the American government should immediately start breaking up all large firms and instituting pure competition throughout our economy, however, we had best be aware that the making of public policy is always a very complicated matter, and perhaps particularly so in this area of industrial structure.

We will turn to these complications and to the fascinating general problem of devising a public policy towards business in our next chapter.

SUMMARY

The private sector of a modern industrial economy is far more complex than the theory of pure competition suggests. Industries in the present-day American economy vary along a number of different dimensions. In some industries, there are many firms, in others only a few. In some industries, there is vigorous product differentiation; in others, very little. Advertising is very intense in some industries; almost absent in others. In some markets, firms largely ignore their rivals; in others, they are intensely aware of every move (or potential move) the other firms make.

Such facts suggest the need for a fairly elaborate classification of market structures. One such classification is:

Pure competition: large numbers of small firms selling a homogeneous product.

Pure monopoly: a single seller of a product without close substitutes.

Monopolistic competition: large numbers of small firms selling differentiated products.

Oligopoly: a "few" firms selling either a homogeneous or a differentiated product.

Each of these imperfectly competitive market structures will lead to market behavior and conduct different from that predicted for pure competition.

Monopoly. The firm's demand curve will now be identical with the industry-wide consumer demand curve for its particular product. The firm will maximize profits where $MR = MC$; but since it has a downward sloping demand curve, MR will be below price, and hence, $P > MC$. In the absence of competitors producing close substitutes, the monopolist will be able to enjoy persistent "pure" profits, although he is also likely to enjoy some form of government regulation.

Monopolistic competition. (This was the case particularly stressed by Edward H. Chamberlin in the 1930s.) A mo-

nopolistic competitor will also face at least a slightly downward-sloping demand curve, since it has a "monopoly" of its own particular brand or other variant of the product in question. It will maximize profits where $MR = MC$, and it may enjoy persistent "pure" profits. However, since other monopolistic competitors can enter the field with their own version of the product, competition may reduce the monopolistic competitor to a zero-profit equilibrium. The absence of "pure" profits makes this equilibrium position similar to that of pure competition, but it differs from the latter in that $P > MC$, and the firm will be producing under conditions of "excess capacity." Other contrasts with pure competition are (1) the importance of advertising and (2) the continuing further differentiation of the product in a monopolistically competitive industry.

Oligopoly. Oligopoly, in one form or another, is particularly important in the American manufacturing industry. Oligopolists, with some product differentiation, are likely to engage in advertising and other nonprice competition, as do monopolistic competitors. The special feature of oligopoly is the recognition of mutual interdependence by the large firms in the industry. Such interdependence may lead to price rigidity (as explained by the *kinked demand curve*), to the adoption of commonly accepted procedures for setting prices, to a pattern of price leadership, or in extreme cases, to illegally collusive activity. In large oligopolistic firms, the divorce of ownership and control raises thorny questions for the theory of profit maximization. Perhaps management will pursue other objectives than profits—prestige, expansion of the size of the firm, rapid technological advance under the influence of Professor Galbraith's "technostructure." However, many observers believe that, in the long run at least, even oligopolistic firms are likely to give substantial attention to the profit-maximizing objective (but see Great Debate Three).

These different patterns of behavior raise important questions about the performance of imperfectly competitive firms in relation to significant economic objectives. Apart from possible political and social arguments, one of the main economic arguments against monopolistic elements in the economy is that they lead to "too high" profits and prices and to "too low" outputs. The question of prices and outputs is essentially one of economic efficiency. It is possible to show in a simple world, where one part of the economy is "monopolized" and the other is purely competitive, that resources will be misallocated. An efficient reallocation would require a lower price and a greater output for the previously monopolized product.

Although this argument is an important one, it is not sufficient to serve as an unqualified basis for public policy decisions in this complex area—as we shall show in chapter 25.

QUESTIONS
FOR DISCUSSION

1. Give specific examples, from your own experience or observation, of business firms that seem to you to fall approximately within the categories of pure competition, pure monopoly, monopolistic competition, and oligopoly. Explain in each case why you think the industries in question developed along the particular lines they did.

2. We mentioned in this chapter that it might be possible to tax the profits of a monopolist without altering the immedi-

ate price and output decisions of the firm. Suppose we have a monopolist whose before-tax equilibrium may be described as follows:

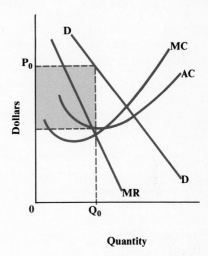

Analyze the effects, if any, that the following taxes would have on price and output:

(a) a lump-sum tax of $1 million on this firm (assume that the profit rectangle is larger than $1 million)

(b) a 50 percent corporate profits tax

(c) a tax of $X on each unit of the product sold

(d) a tax of y percent of the price of each unit of the product sold

3. Write an essay on the following topic:

"In the real world, as opposed to the theoretical world of pure competition, consumer preferences are not a datum but are a creation of industrial producers who must find markets for their products."

4. In the case of oligopoly, the problem of price setting is seriously complicated by the problem of mutually recognized interdependence. Might this problem also apply to nonprice competition? Discuss.

5. State the economist's case against monopoly elements in the economy on "efficiency" grounds. Might these arguments hold even in an industry where "competition" was quite fierce?

6. "For all its faults, advertising *does* increase the competitiveness of the economy." Discuss critically.

SUGGESTED READING

Baumol, William. "The Revenue Maximization Hypothesis." In *Economic Analysis and Policy: Background Readings for Current Issues*, 3rd ed., edited by Myron L. Joseph, Norton C. Seeber, and George Leland Bach. Englewood Cliffs, N.J.: Prentice-Hall, 1971.

Galbraith, John Kenneth. "Economics in the Industrial State: Science and Sedative." *American Economic Review*, May 1970.

Kahn, Alfred. "The Structure and Functioning of the U.S. Petroleum Industry." In *Microeconomics: Selected Readings,* edited by Edwin Mansfield. New York: W.W. Norton & Co., 1971.

"A Symposium":

Peterson, Shorey. "Corporate Control and Capitalism."

Berle, Adolf A. "The Impact of the Corporation on Classical Economic Theory."

Kaysen, Carl. "Another View of Corporate Capitalism."

(The above three articles are in the *Quarterly Journal of Economics,* 79, No. 1, February 1965).

25
Public Policy Towards Business

This chapter is basically a continuation of chapter 24, but with the focus now on the public policy issues that are raised by imperfectly competitive markets. If pure competition is often "efficient," does that mean that the United States government should immediately break up all but the very smallest of firms? Or should it regulate the behavior of these firms? Or is there some standard of workably competitive markets that would enable the beneficial effects of competition to be felt without a new set of inefficiencies (or worse) caused by the daily intervention of the State? These are the questions to which we now address ourselves.

WHY THE SIMPLE SOLUTION ISN'T SIMPLE

In the last chapter, we made the important theoretical point that, in a simple case, pure competition could be shown to be more efficient than monopoly. In an economy where there were two products, one produced by a purely competitive industry and the other by a monopoly, we proved that, under certain circumstances, the monopolist's output would be too low and his price too high to achieve an efficient outcome. We could apparently make everybody better off by making both industries purely competitive.

This raises the obvious question: why not do it? Why not dismantle all large firms and insist that their successors be reduced to a size where they would have little or no control over the markets they serve?

If the question is obvious, there is also an obvious response: can one seriously propose to institute in the industrial sector of the American economy the very kind of market which, in the agricultural sector, has led to overproduction, low prices, low incomes and persistent government intervention for several decades? The response is not quite so shattering as it might seem, since it can be argued that although American agriculture *approximates* pure competition, it does not completely fulfill its conditions, and that this is the main source of the so-called "farm problem."[1] Still, our common sense tells that, even apart from the nightmarish *administrative* task that dismantling all these firms would involve, there is something over-simple about this pat solution. Three major difficulties should be noted:

(1) **Economies of scale.** One clear difficulty is that a regime of very small firms will *not* be efficient if there are significant economies of scale. These economies of scale need not be so extensive that they create a condition of "natural monopoly"[2]—a single firm industry. Production techniques may be such that an industry can support a number of firms, but not the number necessary to make pure competition effective. This is one of the reasons why we always have to qualify our statements about the efficiency of pure competition with phrases like "under certain circumstances." Insofar as important economies of scale exist, the dismemberment of large firms might lead not towards but *away from* productive efficiency.

2. **The problem of growth.** In addition to the question of productive efficiency, there is the question of growth over time. The late Joseph A. Schumpeter argued that whereas small-firm competition might lead to efficiency at a particular moment of time, it was large-scale industry that promoted growth. He visualized modern capitalism as involving a constant competition not between producers of the same product but between producers of new and producers of old products. The true competition for a stagecoach producer comes not from another stagecoach producer but from the new railroad entrepreneurs. They, in turn, find their competition not from other railroads but from the new aviation industry. And so on. In such a world, a case for the large firm with some fairly strong monopoly powers can be made along the following lines: (*a*) *negatively:* the consumer cannot be hurt too much by monopoly at any moment of time because it is transitory and subject to the constant competition of new products; (*b*) *positively:* monopoly profits are necessary in an uncertain, fluctuating state of affairs, to provide businessmen with incentives and to give them some minimum of security against the threat of change; (*c*) as progress becomes more and more a regular feature of economic enterprise, it will require expensive research and development operations that only larger firms can afford. To which can be added the point that profits are a very important source of investment or capital accumulation in the economy as a whole and, therefore, that monopoly profits may contribute to a strong overall growth performance.

Now none of these pro-large-firm arguments is decisive. In fact, they often rest upon highly controversial readings of the historical record. The advocate of pure competition can point to numerous large firms that have decentralized their productive operations, thus suggesting that economies of scale were not all-important, or to smaller firms that have engaged in more active research and produced proportionately more innovations than larger firms produced. However, these points about scale economies and growth do suggest caution in any draconic scheme of dismantling our larger firms, and this caution is reinforced by our third point.

---

1. Thus, it can be said that agriculture does not fulfill one of the assumptions upon which pure competition is based—the free and full mobility of labor among the various sectors of the economy. *If* this condition were fulfilled, it can be argued, there would be no problem of "low incomes" on the farms, since the wage earners would all move to the "higher income" jobs in the city.

2. See page 471.

(3) **The problem of "second best."** Our analysis in the last chapter described a simple world in which there was monopoly in one industry and pure competition in the other. In the real world, as we know, the more accurate description is that of monopoly elements *pervading* the economy, though in varying degrees. What this fact means is that instituting pure competition in one or few selected industries may not be an "efficient" thing to do. This is sometimes referred to as the problem of *second best*. What the theory of second best[3] tells us is that if anywhere in the economy there are departures from the efficiency conditions (say, the rule that price should equal marginal cost) then the fulfillment of those conditions in a particular sector (say, making marginal price equal marginal cost in the steel industry) will not necessarily lead to an optimal resource allocation for the economy. In general, some solution where price deviates from marginal cost in the steel industry will be more efficient. Now this approach does not refute any of the arguments about efficiency made in the last chapter or anywhere in this book; it is concerned, as the name of the theory suggests, with second-best situations—i.e., with situations where complete efficiency is impossible to achieve. Nevertheless, the second-best logic has great practical bearing on an economy where monopoly elements are rather pervasive, for it casts doubt on the wisdom of any selective or piecemeal approach to increasing the "competitiveness" of the economy. Since a total reconstruction of any modern economy along purely competitive lines is difficult to conceive (there are certainly *some* important economies of scale around and

Schumpeter's arguments cannot be completely dismissed), and since even state ownership and market socialism will not totally avoid the monopoly problem (remember Yugoslavia!), it should be clear that second-best considerations really do complicate the role of the public policy maker in this area. In practical situations, it is difficult to know not only exactly what to do but even in what direction to move.

THE RISE OF CONSUMERISM

Still, the opposite approach of leaving the business sector pretty much to its own devices is definitely unsatisfactory too. This point needs no stressing in the 1970s, since we are witnessing a great ground swell of discontent about business malpractice in almost every sector of the economy. The general name for this new popular movement is *consumerism*, and it owes its origins and much of its continuing strength to the remarkable Ralph Nader. Through his personal leadership and with vigorous teams of Nader's Raiders operating out of the newly-established Center for Responsive Law, a constant flow of comments, complaints, documents, reports and books have brought to the attention of the American people areas in which the business sector has not provided consumers with the goods and services that they seek (or that they thought they were getting!).

The example of Ralph Nader proves that the modern world of communications makes possible not only the rise of the large corporation, but also the rise of the large individual. His work has stimulated a critical approach to the claims of business advertising and public relations campaigns, but it has also point-

3. For a rather technical discussion of this problem, see R. G. Lipsey and Kevin Lancaster, "The General Theory of Second Best," *Review of Economic Studies*, no. 63 (1956–1957).

ed up the difficulties of correcting business behavior. For Nader-sponsored research has shown that the consumer is threatened not only by the concentration of economic power in small numbers of firms, but also by the failure in many cases of the so-called regulatory commissions to do anything to improve the situation. Who regulates the regulators? If—as we noted earlier in discussing the military-industrial complex—the business and public sectors tend to merge together in a union of common goals, then there is obviously great danger in relying upon an agency of the government to curb the possible abuses of power by vested industrial interests.

The following brief reading was written by Ralph Nader as a "foreword" to a book that developed out of a report of a Ralph Nader Summer Study Group researching the food industry. It conveys the flavor of consumerism and also points out the difficulties of relying on regulatory agencies in consumer matters.

"Foreword" to The Chemical Feast

RALPH NADER

Food is the most intimate consumer product. Back many decades, public concern over contaminates and adulterates led to early regulation by the states. The failure of such regulation to insure safe, pure, and nutritious food in the world's largest breadbasket has been in step with each new ingenious technique for manipulating the content of food products as dictated by corporate greed and irresponsibility.

Making food appear what it is not is an integral part of the $125 billion food industry. The deception ranges from the surface packaging to the integrity of the food products' quality to the very shaping of food tastes. The industry's catering is calculated to sharpen and meet superficially consumer tastes at the cost of other critical consumer needs. These tastes include palatability, tenderness, visual presentability, and convenience. They are met by a versatile misuse of modern chemistry, packaging, and merchandising techniques. But meeting these tastes does not lead, unfortunately, to fulfilling the requisites of purity, wholesomeness, safety, and nutrition. In fact, very often the degradation of these standards proceeds from the cosmetic treatment of food or is its direct cost by-product. For example, the nutritional deception about "enriched white flour" covers up the permanent stripping in the processing stages of most nutrients. Coloring additives, preservatives, seasonings, and tenderizers camouflage the rapid increase of fat content in frankfurters (33 per cent [1969] of weight on the average), their decrease in meat protein, and the substandard quality of the meat. The hazards of hundreds of untested or inadequately tested food additives are about to be given some of the governmental attention that they have so long deserved.

Further, the heavy promotional emphasis on "unfoods" such as near-zero-nutrition "snacks," chemically doused bakery goods, and soft drinks have a serious distorting effect on young people's food habits and concepts of nutrition. Millions of youngsters are growing up watching the television ads and believing their messages that Pepsi-Cola and Coca-Cola provide health and vigor. Small wonder then that the United States Department of Agriculture shows a decline in nutritional adequacy of American family diets. Food tastes and habits are largely the product of cultural determination, and in the United States this means largely the policy of the food industry and its determined effort to shape those tastes that maximize its immediate projects and sales. What Frenchman, for instance, would think of going down to the marketplace to buy a Wonder bread? His concept of bread differs from that which has prevailed in this country since the mid-twenties, when spongy-baked bread began its road to commercial devitalization.

For too long there has been an overwhelmingly dominant channel of distorted information from the food industry to the consumer. There has been almost no authoritative and countervailing force for information as to what is happening to the quality of food and why the Food and Drug Administration has so shirked its duties. This may not be surprising when it is remembered that the country just "discovered" mass malnutrition in its midst in 1967-1968 while the economy was booming. That countervailing force for standards and detailed information was to have been in large part the Food and Drug Administration and the United States Department of Agriculture. As Mr. Turner and his assistants show in this report, the Food and Drug Administration, for a variety of reasons within its reasonable control and for the lack of a public constituency, failed to close out the options for corporate cost reduction and camouflage which the industry developed via additives, adulterants, and numerous deceptive practices. Company economy very often was the consumer's cost and hazard. As a result, competition became a way of beating one's competitor by racing for the lowest permissible common denominator. In

allowing the proliferation of these abuses and in declining to develop sound, competitively uplifting food standards, the Food and Drug Administration also did a serious disservice to any scrupulous food processors who might have viewed competition as a drive for quality and nutrition rather than the opposite situation which has prevailed.

In sum, the Food and Drug Administration has acted as an official sponsor of processing and marketing practices that have transformed the defrauding of consumers into a competitive advantage—a kind of reverse competition (deceptive packaging alone costs consumers billions yearly).

Predictably, such a pattern has helped the concentration of this giant industry into fewer and fewer corporate hands. The competition, such as it is, has focused heavily on massive promotional expenditures (between 16 and 18 per cent of gross revenues) on brand-name identification, wasteful nonprice competition, and other marketing expenses that do not provide added value for the consumer but simply increase food prices. In addition, the food companies have one of the tiniest research budgets (for nutrition and food quality) of any United States industry.

The quantity of food pouring from our farms and ranches must never be confused with its quality by the time it reaches the consumers' dinner table or whether it adequately reaches many poor consumers at all. For years the Food Group, as the food lobby is known in Washington, has nearly determined the limits of public dialogue and public policy about food quality. It is time for consumers to have information that will provide them with an effective understanding of the secrecy-clouded situation. This report proposes to contribute toward

| that objective as well as to spur the additional disclosure of facts and materials. |

PUBLIC POLICIES TOWARDS MONOPOLY AND COMPETITION IN THE UNITED STATES

The eternal vigilance towards corporate abuses that is the hallmark of consumerism will doubtless continue to play an important role in rendering American business more responsive to public needs. However, it is also clear that such vigilance is not enough; one also needs systematic policies that set the basic structure within which business activities take place. One needs alert referees, but one also needs a clear book of rules.

As we might expect, partly because of the complexity of the problem, partly because of the pressures and counterpressures of the political process, public policy towards business in this country sometimes seems a maze of conflicting principles. There is not one book of rules but several; not one game, but many different games are being played.

In one area of the economy, for example, bigness is taken as an accepted fact and government policy is exercised via various regulatory commissions at the state and federal levels. This is true in the general areas of transportation, utilities, and communications. In these sectors, the main federal agencies are the Interstate Commerce Commission, the Civil Aeronautics Board, the Federal Power Commission, and the Federal Communications Commission. In each of these cases, the consumerist question (How can we insure vigorous and effective protection for the consumer in the face of a general tendency for regulators and regulated to see problems from a common point of view?) is very much to the point. However, the main premise of the regulatory approach—namely, the acceptance of large, noncompeting firms, whose behavior is then controlled by public commissions—makes sense to the economist in an area where "natural monopoly," at least in a local sense, is characteristic.

Much less sensible from the economist's point of view are those governmental interventions that seem designed to restrict or eliminate competitive behavior. In agriculture, our price-support programs are clearly designed to modify the ordinary workings of supply and demand. In the retail trades, the Robinson-Patman Act of 1936 and various state "fair trade" laws have restricted competition in retail pricing. Our patent system is a publicly protected means of granting monopolies to individual inventors. In each of these and other cases, there are specific justifications for the programs involved—low farm incomes, protecting small retail outlets against the chain stores, encouraging and rewarding inventors, and so on—but in each case this form of state intervention has at least some negative effect on economic efficiency. Economists generally would prefer other forms of intervention than those that limit competition—say, direct subsidies to individuals or families injured by competition—precisely because of these efficiency considerations.

In any event, the forms of state intervention that limit competition, like those that permit (but regulate) natural monopolies, clearly operate from rule books quite different from what many observers consider the *basic* American policy. This policy roughly consists of these elements: (1) let the private sector do the job if possible; (2) keep the private sector, if not purely, at least "workably," competitive; and (3) where private forces do not produce such workably competitive results, let the state intervene to make the market more effective. After what we have said above, no one will be inclined to think that this is our only national policy (or that that policy is in any way consistent); still, the notion that private competition is desirable and that at least some minimal government intervention may be necessary to secure it runs deep in our national history[4] and deserves special comment.

Let us now say a few words about the main form that this governmental intervention has taken—the American antitrust laws—and then take up a specific current problem to show some of the complications of applying these laws.

ANTITRUST LEGISLATION

The two main antitrust laws in this country are the Sherman Act of 1890 and the Clayton Act of 1914. The Sher-

4. European countries and Japan have on the whole taken a rather more relaxed view about promoting competition and restricting monopoly or "cartel-like" arrangements in their business sectors than we have. Indeed, in the 1970s, as trading relations between the U.S. and its industrial competitors have become more intense, it has been suggested that we might have to ease off on our antitrust laws if we are to survive internationally. Peter G. Peterson, President Nixon's assistant for international economic affairs, is quoted in the *Wall Street Journal* (January 5, 1972) as follows: "Mr. Peterson also elaborated on his previous references to a possible need to revamp the U.S. antitrust laws so that American businesses can compete on a more equal basis with foreign rivals. The 'basic premise' of American law 'has to be looked at very seriously,' he declared. Other nations generally apply looser standards to the overseas operations of their corporations than to their domestic operations, he said. But the U.S. policy, he noted, is to apply equally strict standards to domestic and foreign operations of American corporations. This, he has indicated previously, generally prevents smaller U.S. companies from banding together as their foreign rivals do in a 'trading company' that concentrates on exports."

man Act prohibits "every contract, combination in the form of trust or otherwise, or conspiracy, in restraint of trade or commerce" and prescribes punishments for "every person who shall monopolize, or attempt to monopolize, or combine or conspire with any other person or persons, to monopolize any part of trade or commerce among the several States, or with foreign nations." The Clayton Act adds to this a number of prohibited business policies, such as price discrimination against different buyers, and, in Section 7, forbids mergers that might "substantially lessen competition or tend to create a monopoly." The anti-merger provisions of Section 7 of the Clayton Act were greatly strengthened by the passage of the anti-merger Celler-Kefauver Act of 1950.

The meaning and impact of these laws has, of course, depended very much upon the vigor with which cases under them have been initiated and by the interpretations given them by the courts. The prosecution of antitrust suits by the Justice Department has followed a somewhat erratic course since the passage of the Sherman Act in 1890. There have been periods of relative inactivity, as in the decade after the Sherman Act was passed or in the period from World War I to the Depression of the 1930s, and periods of vigorous prosecution, as in the early 1900s and especially beginning in the late 1930s under the then Assistant Attorney General Thurman Arnold.

Similarly, court interpretations of the laws have altered considerably over time. For example, in two famous cases in 1911 (Standard Oil and American Tobacco), the Supreme Court enunciated a "rule of reason" in interpreting the phrase "restraint of trade" in the Sherman Act. Firms were to be condemned not merely for size, nor merely for restraint of trade, but only when they did so "unreasonably."

In 1945, however, in the landmark *Alcoa* case, the Court ruled that mere size *could* constitute a violation of the antitrust laws. *How big* was big enough to constitute a monopoly was left somewhat vague, but clearly the Court felt that Alcoa's control of 90 percent of U.S. aluminum production was too big even in the absence of any unreasonable or predatory practices.

Underlying the shifting fortunes of antitrust activity in this country have been certain questions about the *criteria* to be used in deciding whether particular industries should be subject to legal action. In a sense, it seems that the key criterion should be *market performance*. By *market performance* we mean how a firm, industry, and ultimately the economy as a whole fulfill certain roughly agreed upon economic objectives. These would include efficiency in the use and allocation of resources, the "progressiveness" of the firms and industries in the economy, and perhaps also some approximate standard of a desired distribution of income. If these various performance goals could be achieved, we should all probably agree that public policy had been successful in this area.

The problem of using performance as a criterion for governmental intervention (in addition to the very considerable problems of actually *measuring* performance) is that it would be likely to involve the government in a constant, direct, and intimate regulation of the affairs of all the firms and industries in the economy. The key feature of a private economy is that the market bears the main responsibility for assuring satisfactory performance in the economy as a whole. If we believed that the market would fail completely in this task, we might want to go to some scheme whereby the government directly regulates profits,

input combinations, output levels, prices, advertising expenditures, etc., and thus controls the performance of firms and industries by explicit directive. (To some degree, the battle against inflation and the initiation of price and wage controls in the early 1970s moved us in precisely this direction.) The more common approach in the United States, however, has been to continue central reliance on the market for assuring satisfactory performance and to limit governmental intervention to making sure that the market is given a chance to work as it should.

This more limited approach, however, is still rather vague about how and when the government should intervene. In particular, two basic strands of thought have been evident in the history of antitrust policy in the United States. One strand emphasizes governmental regulation of the *market conduct* of firms. This approach tends to emphasize predatory practices, collusion between rivals, and direct agreements that have the effect of undermining competition and enhancing the monopoly powers that firms in an industry may collectively possess. Even Adam Smith, in the early days of capitalism, was well aware of such dangers. "People of the same trade," he wrote, "seldom meet together, even for merriment or diversion, but the conversation ends in a conspiracy against the public, or in some contrivance to raise prices."[5] Such activities illustrate bad market conduct. The "rule of reason" is another example of the market conduct approach—judging firms in violation of the antitrust laws when they misbehave, possibly lowering their prices beneath costs in certain localities, to drive out potential competitors. The 1961 case against several major compa-

5. Adam Smith, *Wealth of Nations* (New York: Modern Library, 1937), p. 250.

nies in the electrical industry is a similar illustration of legal action based on unacceptable market conduct. The companies were found guilty of holding secret meetings to fix prices and divide up the market (some executives were actually imprisoned).

The second strand of thought emphasizes not conduct but *market structure.* The *Alcoa* case (1945) is a good example of this approach, since the Court did not allege misconduct on Alcoa's part but simply that the firm, by virtue of its dominant size in the industry, constituted an illegal monopoly. On the structural approach, the fact that a firm had substantial monopoly power (how much is *substantial* is a difficult question) would make it subject to the antitrust laws even if its conduct were impeccable and even if its efficiency, progressiveness, and other performance attributes were wholly satisfactory.

In theory, these various concepts are not unrelated. The last chapter (24), was largely devoted to showing how different market structures (monopoly, oligopoly, etc.) lead to different kinds of conduct (determination of prices, differentiation of products, etc.) that, in turn, lead to different kinds of performance (i.e., in terms of efficiency, and so on). In practice, however, the approaches tend to differ rather significantly. On the conduct approach, even relatively small firms will be forbidden to engage in collusive agreements that limit competition, while a much bigger firm, already in existence, may be allowed to stand even though it is capable of exercising far more monopoly power than the smaller conspirators. One of the interesting features of American antitrust policy is that it is relatively tough on mergers within an industry, though it may not touch existing corpora-

tions larger than the merged firms in the same industry.

There is also an underlying philosophic difference that may separate these approaches. Some observers feel that in addition to the ordinary economic performance goals, there is an independently valuable goal of limiting the concentration of economic power in the nation. These observers are likely to be thinking of the potential political and social effects of huge agglomerations of economic wealth, a point we mentioned earlier. If such limitation of power is an important goal in and of itself, then the way in which that power is exercised either in terms of conduct *or* performance is not of the essence; a structural criterion will be preferred.

Finally, we should note that the application of *either* of these criteria in a consistent way is made very difficult because financial and industrial developments are constantly posing new sets of problems, many of them largely unforeseen, and some of which contradict older categories of thought. A challenging (and, to some, upsetting) development of this nature began taking place in the late 1960s with the rise of the *conglomerate merger* movement in American industry. As a way to increase our understanding of public policy towards business in actual practice, therefore, let us present some readings on this current phenomenon.

A CASE STUDY— CONGLOMERATE MERGERS

The first of the two readings below ("Take-Overs Shake Business," by John J. Abele) describes the extent of the conglomerate merger movement at the end of the 1960s. This article needs no comment or explanation. The second reading ("Policy Towards Conglomerate Mergers," by F. M. Scherer) takes up some of the economic and legal complications of conglomerates that continue to concern us in the 1970s. Let us try to put these complications in context.

The central feature of a *conglomerate merger* is that it involves firms operating in different markets. As Professor Scherer points out in his article, these markets may simply be geographically separated; however, the *pure* form of conglomerate involves firms producing quite distinct and unrelated products. One firm produces toothpaste, another textbooks: their merger would give us a pure conglomerate.

Now the significance of such mergers from the point of view of our analysis in this and the preceding chapter is that they tend to break the linkages we developed between firm size, market structure, market conduct, and performance—or certainly to alter these relationships. With a conglomerate merger, we may have a huge firm that has only a small share of the sales in any particular market. If we look at firm size alone, we are likely to come to a different conclusion than if we look at market structure as measured, say, by our "concentration ratios" of chapter 5. But the link between market structure, so conceived, and conduct and performance is also likely to be affected. For surely it is not irrelevant that a firm, though small in a particular market, has tremendous overall financial assets behind it. Clearly such a firm would be *capable* of misconduct in that industry in a way that a firm of equal size in that industry, but without other industrial connections, would not. The latter could hardly sustain a long predatory price war; the former clearly could.

And market performance is also at stake. Are there economies of scale that occur when firms in different industries merge? What kind of economies are they and how, if at all, should they be taken into account?

Professor Scherer's reading touches on all these matters and suggests how truly complex the courts' tasks are in deciding how to apply our antitrust laws to these new corporate giants. He suggests that four main grounds have been used for prohibiting or restricting conglomerates:

(1) Reduction of potential competition. This has been applied even when neither of the firms was in the industry in question but each had been considering going into that industry; the conglomerate is prevented on the grounds that it reduces the number of potential entrants into the industry and hence the competitiveness of the industry.

(2) Potential for predatory pricing. That is to say, potential market misconduct; this applies to the firm that, though small in the particular industry, has great resources behind it. Scherer finds this "one of the shakiest pillars of existing anti-merger law."

(3) Reciprocal purchasing leverage. Firm A acquires Firm B and then tells Firm C that, if it doesn't buy from Firm B, it will lose its sales to Firm A; the Supreme Court rules these out if Firm A is sufficiently large to be able to exert this kind of leverage on Firm C.

(4) Efficiency advantages of merged firm. A performance criterion almost in reverse; it is not clear whether this criterion will be sustained by the courts, but certain decisions by the Federal Trade Commission argue that, if smaller firms are hurt, the merger should not be allowed to stand even if the problem is the superior efficiency of the conglomerate.

The case of the conglomerates should provide the reader a good opportunity to exercise his economic judgment and to see the difficulty of translating that judgment into clear and effective laws.

NEW YORK TIMES

Take-Overs Shake Business

JOHN J. ABELE

In the world of business, as in other areas of American life, the Establishment is under fire.

The flood tide of corporate mergers that has swept over the business world in recent years has begun to lap against some members of the industrial elite once considered impervious to outside bids for control.

It also has begun to affect leading companies in the fields of insurance, banking and finance.

The situation has reached the point where some financial observers have begun to pose the possibility that not even the nation's largest corporations — General Motors and United States Steel among them—are immune from take-over bids.

W. T. Grimm & Co., a Chicago consulting firm that specializes in mergers and acquisitions, has estimated that

Excerpted from John J. Abele, "Take-Overs Shake Business," *New York Times* March 9, 1969. Copyright © 1969 by The New York Times Company. Reprinted by permission.

some 4,400 merger proposals were made last year.

That was an increase of 50 percent over the 1967 figure, which, in turn, was 25 percent higher than in 1966. Grimm expects merger proposals in 1969 to top 5,400.

REACTIONS ARE SHARP

The lightning pace of mergers has begun to produce thunderclaps of reaction in Washington and Wall Street:

Representative Wilbur D. Mills, the powerful chairman of the tax-writing House Ways and Means Committee, has introduced a bill that would sharply limit the tax advantages of debt securities issued in mergers.

Richard W. McLaren, the new head of the Justice Department's Antitrust Division, has served notice that he plans to move "promptly" against some conglomerate mergers—those involving unions of companies in different fields.

Robert W. Haack, president of the New York Stock Exchange, has warned that the dubious quality of some debt securities issued in mergers makes them unfit for listing on the exchange and could impair the common-stock listings of the issuers.

Other aspects of mergers are now under study by a variety of Government investigators, including the Federal Trade Commission, the Securities and Exchange Commission and committees of the House and Senate.

The proliferation of merger activity has affected the lives of millions of Americans who work for, do business with and invest in the securities of companies involved in mergers.

For some, it has meant lost jobs. For others, it has provided new opportunities for success. Long-standing relationships between suppliers and customers have been disrupted by changes in control of once independent companies. The business lives of scores of communities throughout the nation have been drastically affected by mergers.

AN ILLUSTRATION

The problems that can arise from the merger boom are amply illustrated by the Allis-Chalmers Manufacturing Company, a large but ailing producer of farm, construction and electrical machinery that has alternately embraced and rebuffed a half-dozen corporate suitors in the last two years.

In a last-ditch effort to revamp its operations so that it would be more resistant to take-over attempts, Allis-Chalmers last year brought in a new president, fifty-two-year-old David C. Scott, who began a program of "major surgery" to build a "new" company.

Last week, in a progress report of sorts, Mr. Scott gave the results to date of his "Operation Turnaround":

Allis-Chalmers had a net loss of $54 million in 1968, including special charges of $33 million related to plant closings and other major changes.

The company reduced its corporate staff from 1,510 persons to 132 in six months. By the end of 1969, it expects to "release" 5,000 nonproduction workers.

Twenty-two changes were made in the company's top management. Among the executives who left the company were its chairman and its chief financial officer.

Despite all these changes, Allis-Chalmers still faces a take-over bid by White Consolidated Industries, a one-time sewing machine manufacturer that now is a highly diversified conglomerate.

Allis-Chalmers hopes to deflect the White bid on antitrust grounds, contending that the two companies are in similar lines of business.

The applicability of antitrust laws to the welter of corporate consolidations is a growing source of controversy in the business world.

To some observers, the merger boom is seen as an increase in economic concentration and a threat to competition. To others, it is instilling new vitality into companies who have lagged competitively because their managements have failed to utilize fully their resources of production, financing and people.

Many recent mergers and acquisitions do not fit into traditional antitrust concepts. A large number, for example, have been carried out by conglomerate companies expanding into fields in which they have not been represented previously.

The conglomerates have adopted the use of mergers and acquisitions as a principal mode of producing rapid growth that gives them massive manufacturing and financial resources.

They have been highly successful. More than a dozen companies generally recognized as conglomerates now rank among the largest industrial corporations in the nation with sales and revenues of more than $1 billion a year.

The merger boom is rapidly changing the face of American industry. About 80 companies that were in Fortune magazine's 1962 listing of the nation's 500 largest industrial companies are now part of, or controlled by, other corporations.

A SCORE OF OTHERS

A score of additional companies in the fields of finance, transportation and merchandising also have been absorbed by other companies.

More than thirty of the companies in Fortune's 1968 listing of largest companies will not appear on next year's list because they will have been merged into companies. A dozen more are currently involved in merger discussions or contests.

B. F. Goodrich, one of the nation's largest rubber companies, currently is waging a major battle to prevent a

take-over by Northwest Industries, a holding company that controls the Chicago & North Western Railway.

The General Host Corporation, a tourist services and food company, has won control of a majority of the stock of Armour & Co., one of the largest meat packers. The Youngstown Sheet and Tube Company, a major steel producer, has agreed to a merger with the Lykes Corporation, a shipping company that had been rebuffed by Youngstown in two earlier bids.

The ranks of independent sales finance companies, among the most asset-rich corporations in the country, have been decimated by the acquisitions of the Commercial Credit Corporation, the Associates Investment Company and the Seaboard Finance Company.

In the field of insurance, the Home Insurance Company, the Reliance Insurance Company and the Hartford Fire Insurance Company have been, or are about to be taken over.

On Wall Street, the merger boom has produced a land-office business for the investment bankers, commercial bankers and lawyers who help arrange mergers or conduct the proxy and tender fights that accompany contested merger bids.

And stocks of merger prospects have been a fruitful source of business for the financial community.

Although many stock market analysts look askance at the feverish trading in merger stocks, stockbrokers and investors have greeted the deluge of merger announcements with wild abandon, gleefully bidding upward the stocks of the companies involved.

Among the eager participants in this bidding spree have been many institutional investors, a category that includes mutual funds, pension funds, insurance companies and banks.

Investment institutions of this type used to buy and hold stocks for the long term. But the increasing emphasis on stock market "performance" in recent years has made many of these institutions as eager to cash in on a quick profit as the most speculation-minded brokerage-house board-room trader.

FEVER SPREADS

The merger fever also has spread to many of the nation's 26 million stockholders.

In addition to trading profits, merger situations have given stockholders a new source of power at the expense of a corporation's management and directors.

Long relegated to the role of interested but quiet bystanders in the affairs of major corporations, stockholders now have come to represent the balance of power when a company is fighting a take-over bid.

By their decision to accept or reject the blandishments of a premium price for their shares from a company bent on a take-over, the stockholders can decide whether the company in which they have invested will continue on its own way or be merged into another company.

The merger boom has produced substantial profits for many investors. It also has

produced risks and losses for many others.

DODGING A TAKE-OVER

Shares of the United Fruit Company, for example, soared from a price of $52 a share early last fall to a high of $88 under the impact of a series of competing bids that ended with the AMK Corporation's acquiring more than 80 percent of the stock of the company once considered a prime example of "Yankee Imperialism" in Latin America.

Shares of the Sinclair Oil Corporation soared from $76 a share to $138 as the company, eager to turn back a bid for control by Gulf and Western Industries, quickly arranged a merger with the Atlantic Richfield Company, another major oil concern.

Sinclair stock plunged $17 a share, to $94, on February 18 after a Federal judge temporarily blocked the merger, then rebounded to $127

when the merger finally took place.

Last September, shares of the C.I.T. Financial Corporation zoomed from $46 a share to $60 on news of a proposed merger with the Xerox Corporation. They fell back to $46 in November, when the agreement was canceled as abruptly as it had been made.

Before making its bid for Sinclair, Gulf and Western had accumulated a large block of the oil company's stock. It later agreed to sell the stock to Atlantic Richfield at a price that reportedly gave Gulf and Western a pre-tax profit of some $50 million, almost as much as Gulf and Western earned from its own operations in 1968.

These and similar situations have prompted some financial observers to suggest some supposedly merger-minded companies appeared to be more interested in stock market profits than in run-

.. .vos). .. gh Low Close Chg.					(in twos) High Low Close			
..co pf2.20	3	37¼	37¼	37¼	Penn Fruit	6	9	9	9
..aseway .44	34	50	49⅝	49⅝ — ⅛	Penney 1.04	16	82	82	82 —
..eedsN .50	21	30½	30¼	30½ + ⅛	PaPwLt 1.68	5	24⅝	24⅝	24⅝ ..
..eesona .40	1	13¾	13¾	13¾	Pa PwLt pf 8	z340	102½	101¼	102 —
..hPCem .60	4	17	17	17 + ⅛	Pennwlt 1.20	10	28⅞	28½	28½ —
..hVal Ind	18	2⅜	2¼	2¼ — ⅛	Penwlt pf1.60	1	25¾	25¾	25¾ —
..nmn 1.11e	16	17½	17¼	17½ + ¼	Pennzoil .80	151	24½	23½	23¾ —
..nnar Corp	5	22¼	22½	22¼ + ¼	Pennz pf1.33	8	34	34	34 —
..enox Inc .50	1	41	41	41 — ¼	PeopGas 2.16	21	35⅞	35⅝	35⅝ —
..everFd Cap	1	12⅝	12⅝	12⅝	PepsiCo 1	18	86⅛	85½	85½ —
..eviStrau .40	24	46¼	45⅝	45¾ — ⅜	PerkElmr .21	14	36	35¾	35¾ —
..evitz Furn	78	40⅝	39¾	39¾ — ⅜	Pet Inc 1.35	6	41⅝	41	41 ..
..ibbOFd 2.20	24	38¾	38¼	38⅝ + ⅛	PetePaul 1.20	1	26½	26½	26½ —
..ib OF pf4.75	2	78¼	78¼	78¼ + ⅛	Petrie Str .40	250	63	63	63 ..
..ibbMcNL	3	5⅝	5⅝	5⅝	Petrolan .34	3	31½	31⅜	31½ +
..ibrtyCp .20a	11	20	20	20	Petrlm 1.86e	10	21¾	21¾	21¾ ..
..ibertyLn .50	19	10¾	10½	10⅝ + ⅛	Pfizer .64	91	42	41½	41⅝ —
..igg't My 2.50	14	42½	42	42¼ — ¼	Phelps D 2.10	12	39¾	39⅝	39¾ ..
..ily Eli .73	43	74⅜	74¼	74⅜ + ¼	Phila El 1.64	56	22	21⅞	22 +
..inc Nat 1.04	13	39	38¾	39 + ⅛	Phil El pf7.80	1	103½	103½	103½ ...
..ncNt pf 3	4	80⅜	80⅛	80⅜ + ¼	Phil El pf7.75	z50	102	102	102 ...
..onel Corp	2	6½	6⅜	6½ + ⅛	PhilMorr 1.27	62	106¼	105½	105½ —
..tton Ind .69f	139	11⅝	11½	11½	Philip Ind .20	9	15¼	15	15¼ +
..tton ptc pf	5	13⅝	13½	13½ — ⅛	Phill Pet 1.30	184	35¾	35½	35⅝ +
..'ton cv pf 3	4	39¼	38½	38½ —1½	Pickwick Int	2	44¾	44¾	44¾ —
..ckheed Air	30	10⅝	10½	10⅝ + ⅛	PiedNGs 1.24	2	17⅛	17	17½ +
..ews Cp 1.04	34	48¾	48⅝	48⅝ + ¼	Pillsbury 1.44	4	42¼	42¼	42¼ — ⅜
..masFin .32	14	23	22¾	23	PionNGas .84	12	16¾	16½	16½ —
..m Mt 3.30e	17	42¼	42	42 + ½	PitneyB .68	65	20⅝	20⅜	20⅜ — ¼
..ndontwn	4	10⅛	10⅛	10⅛	Pittston .60b	58	29¼	29	29¼ ...
..neStarin 1	.. 5	26	26	26 +	Plan Resrch	10	10¾	10⅝	10⅝

Conglomerate mergers in the late 1960s brought many sharp ups and downs of stock prices. They also raised difficult issues for antitrust policy.

ning their own businesses.

Critics also have charged that, knowing of the tendency of investors to bid upward the prices of stocks involved in possible merger situations, some companies have used merger proposals to stimulate stock price increases that bring substantial profits on stock they purchased before disclosing their interest in another company.

Some observers even suggest that some companies appear to be acting in collusion in concocting merger proposals that have little chance of actually being successful. The proposals, however, do bring immediate publicity to the offer maker and frequently result in large price increases for its stock.

Policy Toward Conglomerate Mergers

F. M. SCHERER

Conglomerate mergers—mergers between companies operating in separate and distinct markets—pose especially knotty antitrust policy problems. Diversification into numerous fields or markets might conceivably alter behavior in a variety of subtle ways. Conglomerates may be more inclined to wage predatory price warfare against specialist firms; or they may refrain from competing vigorously with fellow conglomerates, entering into tacit or explicit agreements to respect each others' spheres of influence; or they may promote the sale of their products by offering reciprocally to purchase potential customers' products. Of these three alleged abuses, predatory pricing and reciprocal dealing have been successfully attacked in actual merger cases.

Conglomerate mergers take many shapes and forms. It is customary to distinguish three main varieties: market extension mergers, in which the partners sell the same products in spatially isolated markets; product line extension mergers, which add to the acquiring firm's product list new items related in some way to existing production processes or marketing channels; and 'pure' conglomerate merg-

Excerpted from F. M. Scherer, "Policy Toward Conglomerate Mergers," in *Industrial Market Structure and Economic Performance*, pp. 482–87. Copyright © 1970 by Rand McNally & Company, Chicago. Reprinted by permission of the publisher.

ers, which have no discernible functional link with prior operations. All three types have now been challenged under the Celler-Kefauver Act.

One of the most important weapons for attacking conglomerate mergers of all types is the doctrine that such mergers violate new Section 7 if they reduce *potential* competition. This precedent was established firmly in a case involving acquisition of the Pacific Northwest Pipeline Corporation, a concern tapping extensive natural gas reserves in New Mexico and Western Canada, by the El Paso Natural Gas Co., which supplied natural gas to California users. Pacific Northwest had no pipeline into California and had never sold its gas in that state, but the trial record showed that it had repeatedly considered entering the California market and had in fact bid unsuccessfully to supply California electrical utilities. The Supreme Court ordered the merger dissolved because it eliminated a substantial potential competitor, noting that "We would have to wear blinders not to see that the mere efforts of Pacific Northwest to get into the California market, though unsuccessful, had a powerful influence on El Paso's business attitudes within the state." The potential competition doctrine has since been applied in numerous cases. Typical examples during the mid-1960s involved some nationwide dairy products chain or retail supermarket chain moving into a new territory by acquiring a local firm, where there was evidence that the chain had shown sufficient interest in that market to be considered a serious candidate for entry by building its own facilities.

The only defeat suffered up to 1968 by the antitrust enforcement agencies in appealing adverse Celler-Kefauver Act decisions to the Supreme Court on substantive grounds came in an attempt to extend the potential competition doctrine to cover situations in which neither of the parties served the market in question before their fusion. It concerned a joint venture, the Penn-Olin Chemical Co., formed by the Pennsalt Chemicals Corporation and the Olin Mathieson Corp. to produce sodium chlorate, a paper pulp bleaching agent, in southeastern United States. Pennsalt had built its own sodium chlorate plant in Oregon. Olin Mathieson operated related chemical processes and used sodium chlorate purchased from others as an intermediate product. Each of the parties had seriously considered entering the rapidly growing southeastern market independently during the 1950s, but they rejected the idea or deferred it because of disappointing profitability calculations. In 1960 they formed Penn-Olin to enter jointly, building a plant with 28 percent of all southeastern U.S. sodium chlorate production capacity as of 1961. The Justice Department brought suit to dissolve the consortium, but a district court dismissed the complaint, concluding that competition was not substantially lessened because it was extremely unlikely that *both* firms would have entered the market independently. On appeal, the Supreme Court in 1964 vacated this judgment, ruling that the relevant question was whether one of the two firms would have entered, with the other remaining "at the edge of the market, continually threatening to enter," and hence keeping pressure on the oligopolists actually operating sodium chlorate plants. Reconsidering the facts under these new instructions, the district court decided that independent entry by either of the two firms was improbable. After a second appeal, the Supreme Court divided four-to-four on overturning the lower court's decision, so the joint venture was allowed to stand. Despite losing this battle on specific questions of fact and probability, the Justice Department won its war, since the Supreme Court's 1964 *Penn-Olin* opinion provides a strong precedent for preventing mergers and joint ventures consummated by potential entrants into oligopolistic markets.

In March of 1969 the Justice Department sought to extend the potential com-petition doctrine still further to cover the pure conglomerate acquisition of the Jones & Laughlin Steel Corporation by Ling-Temco-Vought. It charged *inter alia* that any such merger between two very large corporations reduces the number of firms capable of entering concentrated markets more or less loosely related to those already supplied by the partners. Also, such mergers were said to reduce the number of independent companies with the capability and incentive for competitive innovation. This approach stretches Clayton Act Section 7 well beyond previous precedents, and the LTV–Jones & Laughlin case or some similar action will undoubtedly go to the Supreme Court for final resolution.

Another argument advanced against conglomerate mergers, especially in Federal Trade Commission actions, is that the intrusion of conglomerate power into a market previously occupied by small independent sellers increases the likelihood of predatory pricing, which in turn could drive small firms out of business or make them more docile because they fear punishment. This was a major point in an appellate court opinion affirming the Federal Trade Commission's order that Reynolds Metals Co., the nation's leading producer of aluminum foil, dissolve its merger with a small firm specializing in florists' foil (a decorative wrapping for flowers):

> The power of the "deep pocket" or "rich parent" for one of the . . . suppliers in a competitive group where previously no company was very large and all were relatively small opened the possibility and power to sell at prices approximating cost or below and thus to undercut and ravage the less affluent competition.[1]

Similarly, the Commission found in a decision establishing guidelines for dairy products industry mergers that:

> A firm strongly entrenched in a number

---

1. *Reynolds Metals Co. v. Federal Trade Commission,* 309 F. 2d 223, 229 (1962), affirming 56 F.T.C. 743 (1960). The opinion was delivered by Judge (and later Supreme Court Chief Justice) Warren Burger.

of markets may thereby be able to engage in deep, sustained, and discriminatory price cutting in selected markets to the detriment of weaker competitors.[2]

While such conduct is forbidden by the price discrimination laws, the Commission continued, a conglomerate could legally meet the equally low price of a rival, and . . .

In the hands of a powerful firm, able to sustain selective price cuts for so long as may be necessary to ensure against a loss of trade, such price cutting may be a potent weapon for repulsing new competition and preventing entry into concentrated markets.[3]

This view was reiterated in a Supreme Court decision concerning Procter & Gamble's acquisition of the Clorox Co. "There is every reason to assume," the Court said, "that the smaller firms would become more cautious in competing due to their fear of retaliation by Procter.[4]

Whether conglomerate enterprises actually engage in predatory pricing more frequently than others, as implied in these judgments, is debatable. Distinguishing price cutting with predatory intent from price cutting in good faith to meet tough local competition is singularly difficult. In the cases cited here, the evidence was insufficient to support such a distinction. It is fair to say that the predatory pricing doctrine is one of the shakiest pillars of existing antimerger law. Its absence would not be mourned by lovers of competition and/or logic.

A few conglomerate mergers have been challenged successfully, and with more compelling factual support, because they led to the creation and exercise of reciprocal purchasing leverage. The leading case

concerns the acquisition of Gentry, Inc., a specialist in the manufacture of dehydrated onion and garlic, by the Consolidated Foods Corporation, which had far-flung interests in food products wholesaling, manufacturing, and retailing. The record shows that Consolidated brought reciprocal buying pressure to bear on some of its suppliers, especially those making soups and related products on which Consolidated affixed its own brand labels for retail distribution, to use Gentry onion and garlic. Although the Gentry products were qualitatively inferior to those of a leading competitor, the reciprocal buying campaign had modest success, and Gentry's average share of the combined onion and garlic market rose from 32 to 35 percent in the ten years following the merger, increasing in onions while falling in garlic. Climaxing eight years of litigation, the Supreme Court rejected the decision of an appellate court that the reciprocity program had no substantial effect on competition, and it ordered that Consolidated divest itself of Gentry. It went on to assert that it was neither necessary nor desirable to wait many years until evidence on the actual effects of a merger become available before rendering judgment; rather, mergers should be judged by their *probable* effects. Framing a general rule for reciprocal buying cases, the Court stated that not all mergers offering reciprocity opportunities should be prohibited, but where "the acquisition is of a company that commands a substantial share of a market, a finding of probability of reciprocal buying . . . should be honored, if there is substantial evidence to support it."

We have noted earlier that the courts have been unwilling to absolve mergers with probable anti-competitive effects merely because economies would be achieved. This is not an ideal policy, but it may be the best one can do in a world of imperfect knowledge and cumbersome procedures. In a few conglomerate merger cases, however, the courts *have* taken prospective cost savings into account, adopting the view that merger-related economies might actually *harm* competition.

This was one of the central issues in the *Procter & Gamble–Clorox* case, resolved by the Supreme Court in 1967. Procter &

2. *In re Beatrice Foods Co.*, CCH Trade Regulation Reporter, Federal Trade Commission Complaints and Orders, Para. 17, 224, p. 22,334 (1965).
3. *Loc. cit.*
4. *Federal Trade Commission v. Procter & Gamble Co. et al.*, 87 S. Ct. 1224, 1230 (1967).

Gamble was the nation's largest producer of soaps, detergents, dentifrices, and related products, with sales of $1.1 billion in 1957, when it consummated a product line extension merger with the Clorox Company. Clorox was by comparision a midget, with sales of $40 million, but it dominated the household liquid bleach (sodium hypochlorite) field, its specialty, with a 49 percent market share. One feature which drew antitrust attention to the bleach industry was its high concentration. The leading six firms accounted for 80 percent of total sales in 1957, despite the fact that 200 more firms operated on the industry's fringe. Another was the success some producers experienced building up cumulative brand preferences for their products through advertising and related promotional efforts. Clorox often commands a 10 to 20 percent price premium over lesser-known rival products, even though the active ingredients are chemically identical. As a result of the merger, Clorox bleach could be put on supermarket shelves through Procter & Gamble's farflung merchandising channels, with undoubted cost savings. More important, Clorox would be able to take advantage of the alleged advertising discounts received by Procter & Gamble by virtue of its $80 million annual expenditures. This combination of Clorox's market power with Procter & Gamble's marketing power led the Federal Trade Commission to question the merger.

In its decision opposing the acquisition, the FTC conceded that advertising and sales promotion economies might in some cases be as beneficial as economies in production and physical distribution. It went on, however, to state:

. . . [T]here does reach a point "at which product differentiation ceases to promote welfare and becomes wasteful, or mass advertising loses its informative aspect and merely entrenches market leaders." We think that point has been reached in the household liquid bleach industry. . . . Price competition, beneficial to the consumer, has given way to brand competition in a form beneficial only to the seller. . . . [C]ost advantages that enable still more intensive advertising only impair

price competition further; they do not benefit the consumer.[5]

Procter & Gamble appealed, and an appellate court reversed the FTC's decision, arguing that:

The Supreme Court has not ruled that bigness is unlawful, or that a large company may not merge with a smaller one in a different market field. Yet the size of Procter and its legitimate, successful operations in related fields pervades the entire opinion of the Commission, and seems to be the motivating factor which influenced the Commission to rule that the acquisition was illegal.[6]

The Federal Trade Commission thereupon appealed to the Supreme Court, which reversed the lower court's decision and ordered the merger dissolved. Its opinion stressed three grounds for holding the merger illegal: the fact that Procter & Gamble had considered entering the liquid bleach market independently, and hence was a potential competitor; the possibility of predatory pricing supported by Procter & Gamble's enormous financial resources, making smaller producers more timid in their competition; and the tendency of the merger to raise entry barriers by bolstering Clorox's advertising power.

In its brief substantive analysis the Supreme Court dealt with the Clorox problem as a special case, offering no general guidelines for determining when economies realized through merger might be harmful to competition. Certain decisions of the Federal Trade Commission go much further, suggesting that *any* economies realized through merger in an industry har-

---

5. *In re Procter & Gamble Co.*, CCH Trade Regulation Reporter, Federal Trade Commission Complaints and Orders. Para. 16,673, p. 21,586 (1963). The internal quotation is from Joel B. Dirlam, "The Celler-Kefauver Act. A Review of Enforcement Policy," in U.S. Senate, Committee on the Judiciary. Subcommittee on Antitrust and Monopoly, *Administered Prices: A Compendium on Public Policy* (Washington 1963). p. 103.

6. *Procter & Gamble v. Federal Trade Commission.* 358 F.2d 74. 84 (1966).

boring small, vulnerable firms should be regarded unfavorably. This attitude emerges most clearly in a dairy products chain merger decision which was not appealed to the Supreme Court:

. . . the necessary proof of violation of [Section 7] consists of . . . evidence showing that the acquiring firm possesses significant power in some markets *or* that its over-all organization gives it a decisive advantage in efficiency over its smaller rivals.[7]

This, as former Assistant Attorney General Turner has said, is not only bad economics but bad law. It interprets the purpose of the Celler-Kefauver Act as that of protecting existing *competitors*, especially small ones, rather than protecting *competition*. Whether it will be supported in Supreme Court pronouncements, with a consequent bias against mergers which do no more than increase efficiency, remains to be seen.

In general, the law on conglomerate mergers is much less settled than the law concerning horizontal and vertical mergers.* As of 1969 there were several precedents under which market extension and product line extension mergers had been successfully challenged, but all required more conclusive evidence of tangible or probable injury to competition (or to competitors) than the typical horizontal merger case. Under this approach, which amounted to a weak rule of reason, the vast majority of all conglomerate mergers escaped censure.

Whether or not this is a desirable policy has been the subject of vigorous debate. Resolution is difficult in part because there is so little hard evidence on the economic consequences of conglomerate mergers and partly because one's choice may turn on a basic value judgment regarding the social and political acceptability of bigness untainted by more familiar manifestations of monopoly power. Up to 1968 even the enforcement agencies had divided views, with the Justice Department seeing little harm in relatively pure conglomerate mergers while the Federal Trade Commission sought new precedents to combat them.

However, the enormous surge of conglomerate acquisitions during 1968 and the early months of 1969—many carried out largely for empire-building or speculative reasons—shocked a new Justice Department administration into adopting a tougher policy line. A test suit stretching the potential competition and reciprocal buying doctrines was initiated to block Ling-Temco-Vought's acquisition of Jones & Laughlin Steel. More such test cases were expected to follow. Indeed, Attorney General John N. Mitchell announced in June of 1969 that any merger between two companies large enough to be included among the 200 largest industrial corporations would probably be challenged, as would mergers between one of the 200 largest and another smaller enterprise among the sales leaders in some concentrated industry. The Federal Trade Commission concurrently announced a program requiring corporations with assets of $250 million or more to notify the Commission in advance and submit a detailed report on any planned acquisitions of companies with assets exceeding $10 million. Similar reports were required for any merger creating a firm with consolidated assets exceeding $250 million. These steps, which signify movement toward a policy actively discouraging all sizeable conglomerate acquisitions by large corporations, will undoubtedly be tested before the Supreme Court. The outcome is difficult to predict, since the Court's membership will have changed substantially as a result of new Nixon administration appointments. Should the Court find that the Celler-Kefauver Act's language cannot be construed to strike down significant but relatively pure conglomerate mergers, it seems likely that a hue and cry for new and stronger legislation will be heard.

---

7. *In the matter of Foremost Dairies, Inc.,* 60 F.T.C. 944, 1084 (1962) (emphasis added).

*[*Horizontal* mergers involve firms in the same stage of production in a given industry; vertical mergers involve firms merging with firms at different stages of production, e.g., their suppliers.]

SUMMARY

Despite the efficiency advantages of pure competition under certain circumstances, few economists would advocate a wholesale dismemberment of large firms in the American economy. Besides the administrative problems involved, realistic policy would have to take into account possible economies of scale, the growth-advantages of large firms in some industries, and the general complications raised by the problem of *second best*. On the other hand, a do-nothing attitude to industry is unsatisfactory, too. *Consumerism* shows popular discontent with many of the practices of modern business and the need for more adequate consumer protection.

In actual fact, public policy towards business in the United States is something of a mixed bag, involving the recognition of "natural monopolies" in certain areas such as transportation, utilities, and communications, the *limitation* of competition in other areas such as agriculture, retail trade, and patents, and—what many would consider the *main* theme of U.S. policy—the encouragement of "workable" competition and the restriction of excessive monopoly through the antitrust laws.

The ultimate goal of such laws as the Sherman Act of 1890, the Clayton Act of 1914, and the Celler-Kefauver Act of 1950 has been to secure a satisfactory *market performance* by American firms and industries in terms of efficiency and other economic objectives. Rather than regulate this performance directly, however, the government has sought to make the market a more effective regulator. In doing this, two approaches have been used at various times: (1) a *market conduct* approach, stressing the prosecution of collusive and other predatory practices that undermine competition (e.g., the 1911 "rule of reason") and (2) a *market structure* approach, stressing the size and market power of a firm even if that power is impeccably exercised (e.g., the 1945 *Alcoa* case).

One of the problems of applying any criterion consistently is that changing circumstances are continually throwing up new challenges to antitrust concepts. The conglomerate merger movement of the late 1960s is a case in point. When firms become large through the merger of smaller firms in unrelated industries, the traditional links between firm size, market structure, market conduct, and economic performance are likely to be broken or at least altered. The courts are now struggling with this latest major development on the antitrust scene.

QUESTIONS FOR DISCUSSION

1. It has been said of certain U.S. policies towards business that they protect not competition but *competitors*. How would you interpret such a statement? Give examples of policies that might fit this description.

2. If you were engaged in the regulation of a "natural monopoly" in, say, the utility field, do you think that the analysis of competitive efficiency would have any effect on the policies—say, pricing policies—you might determine for this firm? Discuss.

3. "The main problem with American business is not how the game is played, but the nature of the game itself." Discuss

this statement, relating it to such topics as consumerism, and the debate between market conduct and market structure in antitrust policy.

4. This chapter has emphasized efficiency as a "performance" goal, though noting that there are other equally (or more) important goals that also must be taken into account. State some of these other goals. Would taking them into account make you more, less, or sometimes-more-and-sometimes-less sympathetic to monopoly elements in the economy than when you consider efficiency alone?

5. Show how conglomerate mergers complicate the traditional analysis of linkages between firm size, market structure, market conduct, and market performance.

SUGGESTED READING

Kaysen, Carl, and Turner, Donald F. *Antitrust Policy*. Cambridge, Mass.: Harvard University Press, 1959.

Letwin, William, ed. *American Economic Policy Since 1789*. Garden City, N.Y.: Doubleday & Co., Anchor Books, 1961, pp. 199–246.

Scherer, F. M. *Industrial Market Structure and Economic Performance*. Chicago: Rand McNally & Co., 1970.

Sethi, S. Prakash. *Up Against the Corporate Wall*. Englewood Cliffs, N.J.: Prentice-Hall, 1971.

26
Labor and Collective Bargaining

Not only product markets, but also factor markets show significant departures from pure competition in a modern industrial economy. In this chapter, we shall consider these "imperfections" in a general sense and then develop some points about the American labor market and the important process of *collective bargaining*.

IMPERFECT COMPETITION IN THE FACTOR MARKET

In chapter 5 of Part One, we gave a first approximation view of imperfectly competitive factor markets when we discussed a labor union bargaining for, and getting, a wage above the supply-and-demand determined level (Figure 5-5, p. 141). The analysis at that time was incomplete because we had not yet derived the demand curve for labor (electricians, in that particular case); nor had we specified anything about the process that would determine how high the wage demand might be. If the wage could be set at 10 percent above the supply-and-demand determined level, why not 15 percent—or 80 percent! In short, what we did was to illustrate a departure from the competitive market result without explaining the forces that might determine the nature and extent of the departure.

Let us now go into that explanation, analyzing first the demand side, then the supply side, and then bringing the two together. This theoretical analysis will give us a framework for seeing how the process of collective bargaining fits into the modern industrial scene.

DEMAND FOR FACTORS

In a private economy, the "demanders" of factors of production are business firms. When these firms are not purely but imperfectly competitive, this will have effects on their demand for the several factors.

Recall first the purely competitive situation: under pure competition, business firms will find it profitable to hire any factor to the point where its price equals the value of its marginal product $(P_f = VMP_f)$. For the individual firm hiring a single variable factor in the short run, its demand curve for the factor will be the marginal product curve of that factor multiplied at each point by the going market price of the product. In the longer run and for the industry as a whole, the demand for the factor will be influenced by the ease of substituting that factor for other factors and also by the nature of the consumer demand for the product. The demand curve for the factor will slope downward to the southeast, partly because the marginal product of the factor is falling as more units are hired but also because the price of the product will be falling as there is industry-wide expansion in its production.

When business firms are no longer "pure" but "imperfect" competitors, the above analysis must be modified. One important reason is that when there are monopoly elements present, each business firm will be aware that it can sell additional output only at a lower price. When it hires more of a factor and expands output, therefore, it must take into account not only the new revenue added but also *the loss in revenue on each previous unit of product sold because of the fall in the price of the product.* The relevant concept here, as the reader may have guessed, is marginal revenue. The competitive rule for factor hirings that $P_f = VMP_f$ (where $VMP_f = P \times MP_f$) is now replaced by the rule that $P_f = MRP_f$ (where $MRP_f = MR \times MP_f$). The term

MRP_f is usually called the *marginal revenue product* of the factor. Hence, where business firms have some element of monopoly power in the product market, we can state that they will hire any factor of production to the point where the price of the factor equals its *marginal revenue product.*

To make this logic clear, the reader should microscopically examine the behavior of one firm in its decision about hiring the services of one more factor—an additional acre of land. Suppose the businessman knows that the addition of this one acre of land will increase production of his product by 10 units. Suppose he also knows the shape of the demand curve for his product and estimates that when he increases his production by 10 units—from 500 units to 510 units—the price of his product will fall from $100 per unit to $99 per unit. Now to estimate the net addition *to total revenue from hiring this factor, we must subtract from the gross revenue added by the factor the loss in revenue on each preceding unit of sales. The gross additional revenue is equal to the marginal product of the factor times the new price, or 10 × $99 (= $990). The loss in revenue on preceding units of output is 500 × $1 ($1 being the estimated fall in price). Hence the* net addition *to revenue, or marginal revenue product, is $990 minus $500, or $490. If the price of an acre of land is below $490, the businessman will buy it; if above, he will not. By contrast, in pure competition, where the firm assumes that the price of the product ($100) is independent of his output, the businessman would be prepared to hire land to the point where its price was $1,000 per acre ($100 × 10 units of product).*

Since marginal revenue is below price in imperfect competition, this general conclusion means that, other things equal, the business firm will hire fewer units of a factor of production and pay them a lower price than under pure competition.

This analysis applies when there are monopoly elements in the *product* markets of firms hiring factors of production. But there could also be monopoly *buying* power on the part of the firm when it hires its factors. This will also affect the firm's demand for the factor.

To illustrate monopoly *buying* power, we must imagine some very large firm that is the only industry in a particular locality. It is in a monopoly position with respect to the hiring of the services of labor and land in that immediate vicinity. Such monopoly buying power we have earlier called *monopsony* (meaning "single buyer"). Now the monopsonistic firm must take into account a still further element in its hirings of factors of production. When it tries to hire more laborers, for example, by offering them higher wages, it will also have to pay higher wages to all the laborers currently employed.[1] Thus, the *cost* of hiring one more laborer is not simply the wage of that laborer but also the *increase in wages going to all previously employed laborers*. The net effect of monopsony elements, where they exist, will also be to reduce hirings and wages as compared to the purely competitive case. In this case, moreover, the firm will not have any simple demand curve for labor, since the price of labor (or land or any other factor in the locality) will not be taken as a given by the firm but will be *set* by the firm in order to maximize its profits.

---

1. We are tacitly assuming here that whatever the wage, it has to be uniform for all laborers of a given quality in the market. Throughout our analysis we are ignoring the possible complications that would arise if *price discrimination* were employed— i.e., paying different wages to different laborers for the same work, or in the product market, charging different consumers different prices for the same product.

SUPPLY OF FACTORS

Throughout the above analysis of demand for factors, we have assumed that there was pure competition in terms of the supply of factors. Now let us exactly reverse course and imagine that we are dealing with competitive business firms (with neither monopolistic nor monopsonistic power to any degree) but that we have monopoly elements on the part of *factor owners*. To be specific, let us imagine that we are talking about labor and that the "monopoly" elements are institutionalized through a union of workers in some particular craft.

If this union were a "pure monopolist"—that is, if the entire supply of labor hours in this particular craft were subject to a collective decision by the union—then the analysis of its effects would be closely analogous to that of the effects of a "pure monopolist" in the product market. In the case of a monopolistic firm in the product market, the businessman faces, on the revenue side, the consumer demand curve for his product. On the cost side, he has his marginal cost curve representing the costs of producing additional units of output. He will maximize profits by producing where $MR = MC$. This will be at a higher price and lower quantity of output than under pure competition.

Compare this now to the situation of our "pure monopolist" union. On the revenue side, the union faces the demand curve for *its* product—i.e., the business demand curve for hours of labor of this particular craft. This demand curve (since the firms are assumed to be purely competitive) will be the VMP_f curve of the firms hiring this factor.

What about the "cost" side? If the union has a fixed number of craft laborers under its control, then the cost to each laborer of supplying additional hours of work is the cost of foregoing additional leisure.[2] The union leadership might find out these costs by asking its membership: How many hours would you be willing to work at a wage of $3.00 an hour? At $3.50? At $3.62? And so on. Each worker would attempt to answer this question in such a way that the cost to him of the last hour of work supplied (the marginal cost of work in terms of leisure foregone) was equal to the wage in question, say, $3.00

But this is not the end of the matter. In our simple case, the union is acting as a pure monopolist, and hence it does not take the wage as given—it *sets* the wage. Under what principle will it do this? As in the case of the product monopolist, the union will set the wage where $MR = MC$, where MR now stands for the marginal revenue (addition to total income) coming to the workers for the last hour of labor sold, and MC stands for the marginal cost in terms of leisure foregone for the last hour of labor supplied. To offer *more* labor than this would mean incurring *additional* costs above the *additional* revenues received or, in other words, that the added income for the workers gave them less additional satisfaction than they would have obtained from the added leisure.

The contrast between this "monopoly" equilibrium and the competitive equilibrium is shown in Figure 26-1. $F_D F_D$

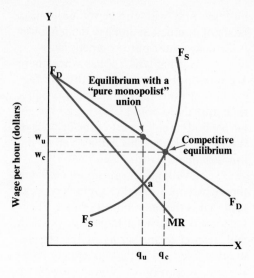

Quantity of labor hours

Figure 26-1. Effect of Pure Monopoly of Factor Supply.

When we have pure competition on both sides of the factor market, we get the competitive equilibrium where the factor demand and supply curves intersect. We have drawn the factor supply curve in a "backward-bending" fashion. Why? (See pp. 488–89.) If the firms continue to be purely competitive, but there is a "pure monopolist" union, then the union will equate the additional income from the sale of one more labor hour (this will be given by the MR curve drawn from the $F_D F_D$ curve) to the additional cost in terms of leisure foregone by selling one more labor hour (this will be given by the $F_S F_S$ curve, which is the MC curve of providing more labor hours). Result: higher wages and fewer hours of work than under pure competition.

is the ordinary factor demand curve for this particular kind of labor. $F_S F_S$ is the supply curve of this factor on the assumption that the laborers act individually and take the wage as independent of their individual actions—i.e., the competitive supply curve. The equilibrium wage and quantity of labor hours under pure competition are w_c and q_c respectively.

2. Of course, the assumption of a constant number of laborers in the union is a simplification. In a more realistic analysis, we would want to recognize that one of the important questions facing the union leadership would be how much or how rapidly to expand union membership. More members might strengthen the bargaining power of the union, but it might also mean loss of some income to the current membership. Also, we would want to recognize that laborers are not forever bound to any particular union or particular craft. In deciding how much of his labor to offer, the worker will consider alternative employments as well as the possibility of enjoying more or less leisure.

To get the "monopoly" solution, the union must first determine the MR curve from the business demand curve. Then it must determine the marginal cost of offering additional hours of labor. But this is what the competitive supply curve F_sF_s tells it. Under pure competition, each worker will offer hours of labor until the point where the wage per hour is equal to the marginal cost in terms of foregone leisure. Thus, F_sF_s is the relevant marginal cost curve.

Finally, MR and MC are equated at point a, and the equilibrium wage and quantity of labor employed under this form of "union monopoly" are equal to w_u and q_u respectively. As simplified as this analysis is, it does bring home the important point that monopoly elements on the factor-supply side tend to lead to a higher factor price and lower employment of the factor than would be the case under pure competition. This particular union has succeeded in raising hourly wages and lowering hours of work in this particular industry. And, of course, even in the complicated real world, these are two highly important objectives of union activity.

IMPERFECT COMPETITION ON BOTH SIDES OF THE MARKET

But the real world *is* complicated, and by looking at each side of the market separately, we run the risk of creating a misleading general impression. Although there may exist a few cases where imperfect competition exists only on one side of the factor market, the characteristic situation is to have monopoly (or monopsony) elements on both sides simultaneously, and in varying degrees. We

have already mentioned (p. 132) that John Kenneth Galbraith developed the concept of "countervailing powers" to explain this phenomenon. According to Galbraith, economic units in a modern industrial economy are subject to restraints not so much from competitors on the same side of the market (e.g., other firms producing the same or similar products) as from countervailing forces on the *opposite* side of the market (in this case, big business facing big labor on opposite sides of the factor market). Thus, while monopoly (or monopsony) elements on the demand side for labor would ordinarily produce a lower wage than would obtain under pure competition, monopoly elements on the supply side of labor would ordinarily produce a wage higher than the purely competitive. Where the actual wage will be will depend on the relative strengths of the countervailing forces involved.

One of the complications that arises when we have imperfect competition on both sides of the factor market is that the equilibrium factor price may be indeterminate, at least in terms of the ordinary assumptions of economic theory. This is not difficult to see if we imagine the extreme case where we have one huge firm facing one large union in a particular labor market. The firm, making an assessment of the individual laborers' willingness to work rather than be idle (or having to move or train for a new occupation), determines that it will maximize profits at a certain wage: $2.00 an hour. The union, making its assessment of the firm's ability and willingness to pay for labor services, determines that the welfare of the union members will be maximized at a different wage: $3.30 an hour. Now either wage is a *possible* wage in the sense that if the government stepped in and fixed either wage by law (and if there were no possibility of a union strike or a business lockout), then it would be in the private interest of the firm to hire labor even at the higher wage, and it would be in the private interest of labor to work even at the lower wage. But if no outside agency steps in, where will the actual wage be?

The point is that it is impossible to say. Or rather, that it is impossible to say without specifying a host of factors that might affect the relevant bargaining strengths of the two parties. What is the state of the firm's profits? What is the anticipated state of demand for its product? Is the union treasury large enough to sustain a strike? How strong is the allegiance of union members in view of the personal costs of a strike? What is the state of unemployment in that industry or in the economy as a whole? How likely *is* it that the government may step in if a work stoppage affects the public interest? And so on.

In short, when there is strong imperfection on both sides of the factor market, we enter a new world of *bargaining,* where the private interest of one party or group may be opposed to the private interest of another,[3] and where the outcome may be significantly affected by historical and institutional circumstances, and even by the personal characteristics of the participants in the bargaining process. In particular, it is at this point that *collective bargaining* has such a significant role to play in the modern American economy.

---

3. The reader should notice that when we were discussing "efficiency," we were generally dealing with situations in which we could improve the private position of one (or all) parties without harming the position of anyone else. Thus, when production is "inefficient" we can produce more of some goods without cutting the production of others—i.e., there are more goods for everybody. But "bargaining" situations often involve the problem that one person's gain is another person's loss—the question is one of distributing income as between the parties involved. Income distribution is a large subject that we shall touch on at the end of this chapter, and in more detail in chapter 29.

COLLECTIVE BARGAINING IN THE LABOR MARKET

That collective bargaining is terribly important in the United States in the 1970s everyone is agreed. *Defining* the process, however, is a rather different matter. Witness the comment of a seasoned observer:

I am a great believer in collective bargaining; the only trouble is that after thirty years of watching it at close range in dozens of industries, large and small, I am not sure I know what it is.[4]

The problem derives from the many different institutions, methods, and goals involved in union-management bargaining.

For one thing, firms and unions differ greatly in their structures and in their influence over their respective markets. We have already discussed the variety of market structures in industry. In the case of unions, an important distinction is between those organized on a *craft* basis (a single craft cutting across industries) and those on an *industrial* basis (a single industry cutting across crafts). This distinction was a heated matter in the 1930s and was an important factor in causing the Congress of Industrial Organizations to splinter off from the craft-oriented American Federation of Labor. (They merged, however, in 1955, to form the combined AFL-CIO.) In practice, collective bargaining may involve management in negotiations not with one but with a whole variety of different unions.

Also, there are the legal aspects of unionization and collective bargain-

---

4. A. H. Raskin. "Two Views of Collective Bargaining." in *Challenges to Collective Bargaining,* ed. L. Ulman for the American Assembly (Englewood Cliffs. N.J.: Prentice-Hall. 1967), p. 155.

ing. Since the 1930s, and especially since the Wagner Act of 1935, the people and government of the United States have expressed a commitment to the right of workers to organize and to engage in collective bargaining with management. However, as in the case of antitrust legislation, the interpretation of the laws is not always clear-cut, nor do the laws themselves always express a consistent position. Thus, a commitment to unions might mean a commitment to permitting a *closed shop* (only union members may be hired), a *union shop* (nonunion members may be hired but must join the union after a specified period of time), or an *open shop* (unions are permitted, but employees may or may not be union members and, if nonmembers, may remain so). Now the Taft-Hartley Act of 1947 permits the establishment of union-shop agreements, but it also provides that the states may prohibit such agreements under certain circumstances. This has caused many labor leaders to attack the law as, in effect, an encouragement to states to pass "right to work" legislation that, in their view, completely undermines the effectiveness of union activity.

Finally, there is the major complication that collective bargaining does not have just one goal—the setting of a particular money-wage for a particular group of workers—but a variety of different objectives. Indeed, one of the major defenses of collective bargaining (including the right to strike, if bargaining breaks down) is that it resolves a great many issues that arise in industrial situations that might otherwise have to be resolved by complex bureaucratic procedures.[5] The following reading by two outstanding labor experts—John Dunlop, an econo-

mist, and Derek Bok, a lawyer and now president of Harvard University—will give the reader an appreciation of the varied tasks that collective bargaining is called upon to perform in this country.

LABOR AND THE AMERICAN COMMUNITY

DEREK C. BOK AND JOHN T. DUNLOP

THE SOCIAL AND ECONOMIC FUNCTIONS OF COLLECTIVE BARGAINING

If society is to evaluate the institution of collective bargaining and compare it with alternative procedures, its social and economic functions must be clearly perceived. Five functions seem particularly important.

Establishing the Rules of the Workplace

Collective bargaining is a mechanism for enabling workers and their representatives to participate in establishing and administering the rules of the workplace.* Bargaining has

*Some writers have contended that collective bargaining is a process of joint decision making or joint management. It is true that many rules are agreed to by the parties and written into the collective agreement. But many other functions are left exclusively to management. Moreover, labor agreements typically specify areas within which management takes the initiative, with unions being left to file grievances if they feel that management has violated the contract. Although management may consider it wise to consult with the union before taking certain types of action, it is normally not obligated to seek advance consent from the union. It is misleading to equate collective bargaining with joint management by unions and employers.

Excerpted from Derek C. Bok and John T. Dunlop, **Labor and the American Community** (New York: Simon and Schuster, 1970), pp. 222-28. Copyright © 1970 by the Rockefeller Brothers Fund, Inc. Reprinted by permission of Simon and Schuster.

5. On the possible bureaucratic costs of alternative procedures, see the article by Thomas Kennedy, pp. 134-40.

resulted in the development of arbitration and other safeguards to protect the employee against inequitable treatment and unfair disciplinary action. More important still, the sense of participation through bargaining serves to mitigate the fear of exploitation on the part of the workers. Whether or not wages would be lower in the absence of bargaining, many employees would doubtless feel that their interests would be compromised without the presence of a union or the power to elect a bargaining representative. In view of these sentiments, collective bargaining may well serve as a substitute for sweeping government controls over wages as a device for insuring adequate, visible safeguards to protect the interests of employees.

Choosing the Form of Compensation

Collective bargaining provides a procedure through which employees as a group may affect the distribution of compensation and the choices between money and hours of work. One of the most significant consequences of collective bargaining over the past two decades has been the growth of fringe benefits, such as pensions, paid holidays, health and welfare, and vacations with pay. If unions had not existed, it is unlikely that individual workers would have spent added income in exactly the same way; indeed, it is doubtful whether, in the absence of collective bargaining, health and pension plans at present prices would have grown widespread. Moreover, though speculations of this kind are treacherous, the history of social-insurance legislation in the United States suggests that, under a system where the government was responsible for setting wages and terms of employment, fringe benefits would not have grown to the extent they have.

These fringe benefits have had a significant impact upon the whole economy. There can be little question that collective bargaining played a major role in focusing priorities and attention upon medical care in the past decade. With the growth of health and welfare plans, information about medical care has been widely disseminated and developed; a body of experts in business and labor have arisen, and the pressures for public programs in the medical field have been accelerated. In much the same way, the extent of expansion in vacation-oriented industries—motels, resorts, transportation, boating, and leisure goods—must be partly attributed to the emphasis in collective bargaining on greater vacation benefits for employees.

Standardization of Compensation

Collective bargaining tends to establish a standard rate and standard benefits for enterprises in the same product market, be it local or national. Labor contracts in the ladies' garment industry seek to establish uniform piece rates (and labor costs) for all companies that produce the same item within the same general price brackets; all the firms in the basic steel industry confront virtually the same hourly wage schedule for all production and maintenance occupations; and all construction firms bidding on contracts in a locality confront known and uniform wage schedules.

Such uniformity is naturally sought by unions. As political institutions, they desire "equal pay for equal work" in order to avoid the sense of grievance that results when one group of members discovers that another group is performing the same job in another plant at a higher wage. Thus, unless there are strong economic reasons for maintaining wage differentials, unions will normally push hard for standardization.

From the standpoint of employers, it should be observed that uniform wage rates do not necessarily imply uniform labor costs. Firms paying the same hourly rates may have varying wage costs as a result of differences in equipment and managerial efficiency. But competition tends to remove these differences and promote more uniform labor costs among close rivals. In highly competitive industries, employers often have a keen regard for such standardization; it protects the enterprises from uncertain wage rate competition, at least among firms subject to the collective agreement.

From the standpoint of the economy as a whole, the effects of standardization are mixed. In some instances, wage uniformity may be broadened artificially beyond a product market area, as when the wage rates in a tire company are extended to apply to its rubber-shoe work. The effect is to produce a less efficient use of economic resources. The resulting premium over the wages paid in other rubber-shoe plants eventually will compel the tire companies to give up doing business in the rubber-shoe field. In a more important sense, however, the effect of uniformity has been positive in that it has favored the expansion of more profitable, more efficient firms. In a country like France, on the other hand, bargaining establishes only minimum rates, so that backward companies can often survive by paying lower wages than their competitors if they can somehow manage to retain the necessary work force.

Determining Priorities on Each Side

A major function of collective bargaining is to induce the parties to determine priorities and resolve dif-

ferences within their respective organizations. In the clash and controversy between the two sides, it is easy to assume a homogeneous union struggling with a homogeneous management or association of employers. This view is erroneous and mischievous. In an important sense, collective bargaining consists of no less than three separate bargains—the agreement by different groups within the union to abandon certain claims and assign priorities to others; an analogous process of assessing priorities and trade-offs within a single company or association; and the eventual agreement that is made across the bargaining table.

A labor organization is composed of members with a conglomeration of conflicting and common interests. The skilled and the unskilled, the long-service and the junior employees, the pieceworkers and the day-rated workers, and those in expanding and contracting jobs often do not have the same preferences. A gain to one of these groups often will involve a loss to another. Thus, in George W. Taylor's words, "To an increasing extent, the union function involves a mediation between the conflicting interests of its own membership."

Similarly, corporate officials may have differing views about the negotiations, even in a single company. The production department and the sales staff may assess differently the consequences of a strike. The financial officers may see an issue differently from the industrial-relations specialists. These divergences are compounded where an association of companies bargains with a union, for there are often vast differences among the member firms in their financial capacity, vulnerability to a strike, concern over specific issues, and philosophy toward the union.

One of the major reasons that initial demands of both parties often diverge so far from final settlements is that neither side may have yet established its own priorities or preferences, or assessed the priorities of the other side. In many cases, these relative priorities are established and articulated only during the actual bargaining process. (This view of the bargaining process helps to explain the sense of comradeship that labor and management negotiators often develop through the common task of dealing with their respective committees and constituents.)

This process of accommodation within labor and management is central to collective bargaining. It should not be disparaged as merely a matter of internal politics on either side. In working out these internal adjustments in a viable way, collective bargaining serves a social purpose of enormous significance. The effective resolution of these problems is essential to the strength of leadership and to the continued vitality of both the company and the union.

Redesigning the Machinery of Bargaining

A most significant function of collective bargaining in this country is the continuing design and redesign of the institution itself. While it is true that the national labor policy—as reflected in legislation, administrative rulings, and court decisions—has a bearing on some features of collective bargaining, the nature of the institution is chiefly shaped by the parties themselves. As previously noted, the collective-bargaining process largely determines the respective roles of individual bargaining and union-management negotiations. It defines the subjects to be settled by collective bargaining. It determines the structure of bargaining relationships. It establishes the grievance procedures and prescribes the uses of arbitration and economic power in the administration of an agreement. It decides the degree of centralization and decentralization of decision making. It influences the ratification procedures of the parties. The results are seldom fixed. The bargaining parties must reshape their bargaining arrangements from time to time in response to experience and emerging new problems. Thus, the design of collective bargaining and its adaptation to new challenges and opportunities have much to do with its capacity to fulfill its social functions effectively and without undue cost to the public.

FIVE MAJOR ISSUES

In certain respects, collective bargaining is being subjected to a closer scrutiny than in the past, because of the special circumstances in which the country now finds itself. On the one hand, it is plain that society is becoming more critical of its institutions and more demanding in the performance it expects of them. Collective bargaining must now be judged in the light of the American position in the world, which has created new demands for economic progress and monetary stability. The consequences of labor negotiations must be viewed in the light of more insistent demands for full employment. And though labor and management have grown more professional in their dealings with each other and more successful in avoiding strikes, Secretary of Labor Willard Wirtz could still observe that "... neither the traditional collective-bargaining procedures nor the present labor-dispute laws are working to the public's satisfaction, at least as far as major labor controversies are concerned."

At the same time, the climate in which collective bargaining must operate has also become more trying. In recent years, bargaining has been spreading rapidly into the field of public employment, where the parties are often inexperienced in labor relations and the problems involved are in many respects more difficult than in the private sector. Full employment has also placed new strains upon the bargaining process. With jobs so plentiful employees are less amenable to discipline and control. Their demands have grown larger, particularly in an economy where the cost of living has been creeping upward. Labor shortages have likewise created difficulties by forcing managers to hire less-experienced and less-qualified employees.

From these pressures have emerged five groups of questions that have been debated increasingly in recent years.

(1) Economic strife and dispute settlement. What can be done to protect the public interest when the parties to collective bargaining engage in economic warfare? Is the exertion of economic and political pressure an appropriate way to resolve bargaining disputes? Would not compulsory arbitration be a superior procedure, substituting facts and reason for power? What can the parties themselves and the government do to improve the performance of collective bargaining?

(2) Efficiency and productivity. What is the impact of collective bargaining upon management efficiency? How extensive and serious are restrictive work practices, and what can be done about them? Does the rule-making character of collective bargaining necessarily stifle management in its quest for reductions in labor costs? When is a rule of collective bargaining an appropriate protection of the health, safety, or convenience of a worker, and when is it an undue limitation of efficiency? How can uneconomic work practices be eliminated in the future?

(3) Inflation. What are the consequences of collective bargaining for inflation? The experience of many Western countries since World War II, including our own, raises the question whether free collective bargaining, continuing high employment, and price stability are compatible. What can be done to make collective bargaining less conducive to inflation or to reduce its inflationary bias at high levels of employment?

(4) Public employees. In recent years, the process of negotiations has been spreading rapidly to many sectors of public employment. Are the procedures of private bargaining appropriate to public employment? Is the strike a suitable means to induce agreement in the public sector? What is the proper relation between negotiations in the public sector and legislative bodies and civil service? What machinery is appropriate to resolve disputes in public employment?

(5) New opportunities for bargaining. What are likely to be the new subjects of collective bargaining in the private sector in the years ahead? What are the new needs and opportunities to which collective bargaining procedures can fruitfully be applied?

DO UNIONS HAVE A FUTURE?

The above reading ended with a series of questions, some of which we have touched on before (for example, the problem of economic strife in chapter 5), and some of which we will raise in detail presently (for example, the inflation issue in chapter 27 and Great Debate Four on wage-price controls). Taken together, these questions really pose the more general query: What is the future of unions and the collective bargaining process in this country?

Despite the obvious values of collective bargaining in many connections, we know that total labor union membership in the United States has been relatively stagnant over the past fifteen or more years (pp. 132–33). Furthermore, we know that there are changes in the American labor force that might militate against unionization on a long-term basis. These changes include the decline in the number of blue-collar, as opposed to white-collar, workers, the increasing employment in sectors such as the government and service industries that, historically, have been nonunion sectors, and, in general, the increasing professionalization of the American economy.

These various points add special importance to question (4) at the end of the Bok-Dunlop reading. Will unions come to embrace rapidly growing sectors of the American labor force (such as public employees) and hence have an ever larger impact on the economic scene? Or will they simply decline in relative importance as changes in the character of employment in this country render historical union methods inappropriate?

Actually, there is already some evidence to suggest that the positive response is the more likely. This is especially true of public sector unionization, which increased from 5 percent of total union membership in 1956 to 9 percent a decade later. Had this not been the case, total union membership during this period would have declined sharply as a percentage of the American labor force. There is also evidence that unionization is beginning to enter certain professions that, even a few years ago, might have scorned the collective bargaining process. The two readings that follow suggest changes in the making that may have an enduring impact on the American labor movement.

Trade unionism goes public

EVERETT M. KASSALOW

THE RESPECTABILITY OF UNIONS

Large-scale unionization of government workers is a relatively new phenomenon in this country, although it has been common in almost all other democratic industrial countries of the world. That large-scale public-employee unionism was also inevitable in the United States at some time is clear. But why now? What new forces account for the current upsurge of public unionism?

The first of these forces has been the institutionalization of trade unionism in American life. Unions date back more than 150 years in the United States. But large-scale unionism dates only from the late 1930s, and it has only been in the past decade or so that collective bargaining has become widely accepted as the appropriate way to settle wages and working issues. During this decade unionists have become respectable. Union leaders have been named to innumerable presidential commissions dealing with every conceivable problem area of the country's foreign and domestic business.

It is not surprising thus that, despite the revelations in the Senate investigations of the malfeasance of Jimmy Hoffa and a few other union leaders, public opinion surveys show that union officers have registered a significant gain in occupational prestige between 1947 and 1963. This gain is clearly attributable to the widespread acceptance of the basic value of unionism in society, and this legitimacy is being transferred to public employees as well. For this reason, unionism among government workers has begun to advance rapidly, and there is every prospect it will continue to grow.

There is a second, more specific reason for the recent growth of government unionism, and this is Executive Order 10988 issued by President John F. Kennedy in January 1962, which encouraged unionism in the federal service. In its support of public unionism, this order was as clear and unequivocal as the Wagner Act of 1936 had been in its support for unions and collective bargaining in the private sector.

Excerpted from Everett M. Kassalow, "Trade Unionism Goes Public," *The Public Interest* 14 (Winter 1969): 118–20, 125–30. Copyright © National Affairs, Inc., 1969. Reprinted by permission of the publisher and the author.

THE NEW YORK TIMES

The 1968 New York City teachers' strike raised with particular force, the issues of unionization and strike action in the public sector.

It declared that "the efficient administration of the government and the well-being of employees require that orderly and constructive relationships be maintained between employee organizations and management."

In New York City, earlier orders issued by Mayor Robert Wagner resulted in the "breakthrough" of unionism in 1961 among 44,000 teachers. Kennedy's order has a spillover effect in legitimating unionism in states and local public service. Further, the reapportionment of state legislatures seems to have had a generally liberalizing effect, and a flow of new legislation in a dozen states has expedited public employee bargaining.

The enormous growth in public employment has also acted to transform the status of the government worker. Between 1947 and 1967, the number of public employees increased over 110 percent. (During the same period, private nonagricultural employment increased only 42 percent.) Clearly, the day has passed when being a civil servant is a prestigious matter. At a time when unions and bargaining have become increasingly accepted elsewhere in the society, this expansion of public employment, with its consequent bureaucratization and depersonalization of relationships, has undoubtedly encouraged unionization in the public sector.

STRIKES IN THE PUBLIC SERVICE

No subject in recent years has provoked as much heat as the matter of strikes among public employees. It is probably the most difficult problem in the public employee field. Even expert arbitrators and mediators, men of hardheaded, pragmatic experience, have taken surprisingly rigid, ideological positions on this matter.

Because there are inherent difficulties in the adjustment to new bargaining public officials need to approach these difficulties with caution, rather than be obsessed with strikes and punishment for strikes. Admittedly, in today's transition period, most cities or states are not likely to concede the right to strike to public employees. However, rather than setting forth elaborate punishment systems for strikes which may occur, officials should take positive steps, wherever possible to improve relations.

The operation of the so-called Taylor Law in New York State illustrates the problem with punitive legislation. Despite provisions banning public employee strikes, with penalties such as dismissal or the withdrawal of recognition or check-off rights from the unions, etc., the law did not head off the New York City teachers' strike or the sanitation strike. If anything the withdrawal of the teachers' union check-off of dues and the eventual imprisonment of the local union's president Albert Shanker for fifteen days, in the wake of the 1967 New York City strike, seems to have kept union militancy at a high pitch long after the strike was over.

Theodore Kheel, an experienced mediator of New York City public employee disputes, has attacked the Taylor Law on the ground that "by prohibiting strikes of public employees, the law eliminates collective bargaining. . . ." It also creates a bad atmosphere for bargaining, Kheel contends, by compelling unions to exert pressure through threats to violate the law. Kheel's critique of the Taylor Law and its pat formula is quite cogent. But in his refusal to make any distinction between public and private collective bargaining, so far as the right to strike is concerned (though he does not rule out strikes by policemen and firemen as "unthinkable") he does go too far. One should not anticipate that in all states, or in the federal government, collective bargaining must necessarily take on all the features of private bargaining including the right to strike for most employees.

It does not seem that the strike issue will be important in *federal* labor-management relationships. A liberal managerial policy, including important wage and benefit improvements in the past decade, has set a good framework. In his recent appearance before a special government committee reviewing experience to date under Federal Executive Order 10988, AFL-CIO President George Meany concluded that the order "has brought significant improvements in labor relations within the federal government." Although Meany recommended a number of changes in the workings of the new system, he did not question the legislative ban on strikes in the federal service. Nor did

the AFL-CIO December 1967 convention resolution on federal employee bargaining say anything about the existing legal prohibition on strikes by federal government employees. Most of the unions which deal with federal employees have a voluntary strike ban provision in their constitutions.

At the state and local level, where organizing has met with more resistance, the strike issue remains more troublesome. Even here, in the words of AFSCME* President Wurf, whose own union jealously defends the right to strike, at least

The debate [now] seems to center around the right to strike, rather than the right to organize and bargain. . . . It seems only yesterday . . . that the right to bargain was at stake. . . . Now the right to strike is what is being discussed. . . . As painful as the situation is at times, it is an important step forward.

From what has already been suggested, bargaining in the public sector has to be viewed as an evolving process. What might seem to be best today, is likely to be obsolete tomorrow. The first written agreement between General Motors Corporation and the United Automobile Workers Union signed some thirty years ago was a one-page memorandum. Twenty-five years later it was a printed contract running over 200 printed pages.

At present, general wage and hour conditions are not subject to negotiations in most public employee bargaining relationships. Both in the case of classified federal civil servants and a large proportion of state and local employees, these matters are reserved to the legislators. It seems difficult to believe that public employees, once their unions are established, will be content with a situation in which bargaining over the most basic issues is outside their purview. The general management attitude that, "We can talk about individual workers' problems, or the lights or noise in this room, but general wages and hours are out— left solely to the legislature," won't go down

*[American Federation of State, County, and Municipal Employees.]

well. Here again the United States can look to the experience of other countries. The typical European nation entered the modern era with civil servants regarded as part of "His Majesty's Service." The private, let alone the public lives of these servants was subject to close and highly arbitrary scrutiny by the government. Personal oaths to king or emperor were given as a condition of employment. The Europeans have passed from these quaint and paternalistic times to a situation where full bargaining rights are now accorded to public employee unions. Their activities and rights now run to bargaining power over general wage and hour changes, holidays, vacations, and most of the economic benefits that one associates with a private sector collective agreement in the United States.

PUBLIC EMPLOYEE BARGAINING AND JOINT MANAGEMENT

The bitter struggles by management against union organization which were part of the beginnings of unionism almost everywhere in the private sector, have little counterpart in the upsurge of public unionism today. (Some Southern states and a few Northern cities where very difficult urban-racial factors severely complicate labor relations are exceptions. New York City's 1968 teachers' strike, for example, was more a product of racial tensions than a traditional labor relations problem.) From this new start a potentially far more cooperative relationship is possible.

Public employees in their capacities as citizens often feel they "own" the government service. Indeed, one of the most interesting aspects of the public employee unionism is that union officials frequently criticize public agencies as much in their capacities as citizens as union members. This has certainly been the case with hospital unions in New York City, nurses in public hospitals in many states, and, of course, unionized teachers everywhere. Public administrators, for their part, have generally been fearful of union interests and positions that go beyond wages and working conditions and raise questions about the very nature of the organizations and policies of the agencies themselves. New York City teacher union of-

ficials have bitterly remarked that the Board of Education has taken the position that all that really concerns the teachers are money and money related matters, whereas the teachers have had community problems in mind.

In the present era there is probably an unparalleled opportunity to make public employee union-management relationships something new and unique in American labor history. In the United States there has been an important scaling upward of educational attainments in the past twenty years. As a result of this and other factors, one finds, especially among many white collar employees, a growing desire for wider participation in the decision making processes. If public managers turn their thoughts on how to *widen*, rather than limit, the scope of management-union relationships, to embrace serious consultation with their employees on policy matters and the organization of their agencies, all sorts of new possibilities may be opened. The public sector may provide a useful training ground for what in other countries has been variously termed co-determination, joint-consultation or workers' participation in management. Obviously these possibilities vary from agency to agency and from union to union, and there may be greater possibilities in state and local service than at the federal level. But the potentialities for new types of relationships based as much, and possibly more, on cooperative rather than conflicting bonds are formidable in the public service. As yet, however, the public managers have been more fearful than expansive in their reactions to the "new unionism."

The demands of many professional employees, most notably teachers and nurses, have from the very beginning gone far beyond wages and hours. Their very professionalism turns them to the substantive policy questions affecting the agencies that employ them. Curriculum content, the size of classes, the organization of the educational system—these and other matters run to the heart of a teacher's interests, and one can list similar professional areas for nurses.

In the long run, indeed, if public managers are to carry forward the process of enlarging the scope of union-management relationships, the unions might find it difficult to depend upon *traditional-union* member loyalty patterns and appeals. The increasing professionalization of society may be the beginning of a new kind of role for organized labor, not the guild socialism once proposed by G. D. H. Cole, but some new form of participation in authority. That is one of the aspects of what Daniel Bell has called the "post-industrial" society, the coming of a new society in which professionalization becomes the commonplace mark of skilled employment. A large-scale society of professionals inevitably means a reduction of that status. But it also means the upgrading of an older worker status, and this adds to the importance of the sweeping new public employee unionism in the United States.

Professors' Unions Are Growing

M. A. FARBER

The unionization of professors, a movement that is beginning to realign economic, political and academic power on many campuses, has emerged as a leading and contentious issue in higher education.

Collective bargaining agents for professors have been recognized at 133 of the country's 2,500 colleges and universities in the last several years. Hundreds of other campuses have adopted looser arrangements for negotiation.

Ten to 15 percent of the half-million teaching faculty in the nation are subject to collective agreements beyond their individual contracts, or will soon be, and expansion is in prospect.

Major drives to win the allegiance of professors and obtain exclusive bargaining rights are being waged by three rival organizations—the National Education Association, the Ameri-

Excerpted from M. A. Farber, "Professors' Unions Are Growing," *The New York Times*, November 14, 1971. Copyright 1971 by The New York Times Company. Reprinted by permission.

can Federation of Teachers, A.F.L.-C.I.O., and the American Association of University Professors.

Officials of the N.E.A., which previously shunned unionization as "unprofessional," trek from campus to campus, their suitcases laden with pamphlets that say unionization spells "dignity" as well as "security" for professors.

In a campaign at Fordham University, the A.A.U.P. invoked the encyclicals of three Popes on the right of labor to organize; and on another campus, it challenged the very existence of a competing local organization.

Yet the A.A.U.P., despite a commitment by its national council last month to step up bargaining efforts, remains deeply divided over unionization and the association's involvement in it.

PROS AND CONS WEIGHED

The quandary of the A.A.U.P. — will the advantages of bargaining outweigh the drawbacks—is not unlike the predicament of many professors who never expected to see campus unionization.

Some faculty members, especially in the senior ranks, argue that bargaining is incompatible with the cooperative traditions of a profession that they believe is largely self-regulated. They caution that it will erode the "diverse" character of colleges and universities and result in a "leveling" of quality and a turn away from rewarding merit.

Other professors, equally adamant in their regard for educational quality, assert that the real power on campus has been usurped by administrators and public budget officials. They hold that the right and needs of professors can only be met through collective action supported by more muscle than that vested in the typical faculty senate.

The appeal of unions has been heightened by what Dr. Joseph W. Garbarino of the University of California calls "the end of affluence" in higher education.

Salaries are not rising as fast as in the mid-1960s; research and teaching posts are being cut back and promotions curtailed; and relatively few posts are opening to a crush of new applicants.

A mood of acrimony prevails in many faculty clubs

and lounges as legislatures demand that professors spend more time in the classroom with larger numbers of students. Students themselves seek influence over faculty appointments, and critics charge that tenure does more harm than good by protecting "dead wood."

PROFOUND EFFECT EXPECTED

Since only a handful of contracts are more than a year old, unionization had had less of an impact on campus conditions than on attitudes. Yet many educators are convinced that bargaining will ultimately have a profound effect on expenditures and programs.

"Make no mistake about it, the advent of bargaining will result in radical changes in the nature of colleges and universities in the next decade," said Dr. David Newton, vice chancellor for faculty and staff relations at the City University.

Current negotiations cover virtually every faculty concern: book space and secretarial help in offices, sabbaticals and funeral leaves, the privacy of personnel files, salaries, work loads and schedules, class sizes, curricular policies, standards of academic freedom and rules governing tenure.

"We'd gladly bargain on everything that takes place in the university, including the improvement of instruction," said Jim Williams, a top organizer for the N.E.A.

The most significant gains for faculties, so far, according to negotiators on both sides of the table, are broad grievance clauses that provide for

review and, sometimes, arbitration of a variety of administrative decisions, especially regarding employment.

FORCE FOR GREATER 'PARITY'

On the whole, unionization has not produced dramatic salary increases; it has been a force for greater "parity" in pay among professors.

A number of contracts contain provisions that have not been fully implemented. For example, the contracts signed by the City University in 1969—City was the first major university to engage in bargaining—stipulate that every faculty member would have a minimum of 120 square feet of private office space. Many professors still have closer to three square feet.

The "paradox of faculty unionism" to date is that the greatest gains have accrued to faculty on the margin of institutions—lecturers and part-time instructors; nonteaching professionals such as librarians and counselors; and professors at the "lower-level" campuses of university systems, Dr. Garbarino said.

Dr. Garbarino, who is preparing a study on "creeping unionism and the faculty labor market" for the Carnegie Commission on Higher Education, said that regular, full-time faculty "have shored up some of their benefits from possible attack but otherwise have gained the least from bargaining." For them, he said, unionization has been "essentially defensive in character."

The growth of bargaining in the public sector has been

facilitated by the passage of public employee relations laws or similar measures in nineteen states. Many other states are expected to follow suit in the near future.

The prospects for unionization at private institutions, which employ 30 percent of all faculty, were much enhanced in 1970 when the National Labor Relations Board assumed jurisdiction at private colleges and universities with gross incomes of more than $1 million.

Two months ago the labor board denied a challenge by Fordham University to its jurisdiction saying that faculty members at private institutions are "entitled to all the benefits of collective bargaining if they so desire."

The A.A.U.P. has moved to obtain bargaining rights at Fordham and New York University, and is considering an attempt at Columbia University as well.

A representation election is generally held when an organization secures petitions from 30 percent of the unit for which it wants to bargain. In a few elections, such as at Pace College two weeks ago, faculty have rejected bargaining.

RANGE OF PROBLEMS

Many administrators, caught off guard by unionization, are only now starting to assess it. Some maintain that the costs of financing contracts will be prohibitive; others—like some members of the A.A.U.P.—stress that the faculty are managers as well as employes of an academic institution and could lose more in tradeoffs at the bargaining table than they stand to gain.

"I don't have the same bugaboos about bargaining that some of my colleagues have," said Robben W. Fleming, president of the University of Michigan. "But the next five or ten years will be very much of an experi-mental period in this area. It will be a real shakeout."

COLLECTIVE BARGAINING AND FACTOR SHARES

We have left to the last what might seem to be one of the most important, if not *the* most important, questions about imperfect competition in factor markets: What is the effect of this imperfection on the prices (i.e., the incomes) going to the several factors of production? In the specific case of labor, what has been the effect of unions and collective bargaining on wage rates?

Unfortunately, although numerous studies of income distribution have been made in the United States,[6] we do not really have data on factor payments in any pure sense. Ideally, we should like to have separate figures for wages, rents, interest, and profits, each defined in the economist's terms. However, national income accounts are not drawn up in this precise way, a particular problem being the income of unincorporated enterprises in which interest, rents, profits, and the wages of the proprietor are effectively thrown together.

In very broad terms, however, certain estimates of relative factor shares can be made. In Table 26-1, income from unincorporated enterprises is listed as *entrepreneurial income;* interest, rent, and corporate profit are grouped together under one heading. This table reveals a perceptible growth in employee compensation (wages and salaries) over the past half-century; a small relative decline in interest, rent, and corporate profit; and a sharp relative decline in entrepreneurial income. This last reflects a strong move out of self-employment into regular wage and salary employment over the past fifty-odd years.

We could, if we wished, try to separate entrepreneurial income into wages, on the one hand, and all other income on the other, and thus divide total national income into a "labor share" and a "property share." Professor Bernard F. Haley of Stanford University has drawn together various different estimates of such a division, and on each estimate he finds that the "labor share" has risen and the "property share" declined since 1900.

Such data are useful—they enable us to dispose of any oversimplified Marxian theory of "exploitation" or "immiserization" of the working classes—but they are not sufficiently sharply defined to allow us to comment much about the effect of market structure on factor shares. Much the same must be said about the more specific question: the effect of unions on wage rates. When attempting to determine whether unions have raised wages above what they would have been in the absence of union activity, we run into two major problems. One is the effect of union activity on the wages of *non*union workers. Unions will often claim, with some justice, that when they succeed in raising wages for their members they also indirectly force employers to raise wages for nonunion members. The other problem is that the composition of the unionized and nonunionized labor force is different— unions are strong in manufacturing and among blue-collar workers, less strong in

6. See chapter 29, pp. 699–700.

Table 26-1   U.S. NATIONAL INCOME BY PERCENTAGE "FACTOR"
SHARES 1900-1963

| | Distributive shares (percent) | | |
Period	Employee compensation	Entrepreneurial income	Interest, rent, and corporate profit
1900–09	55.0	23.6	21.4
1905–14	55.2	22.9	21.8
1910–19	53.2	24.2	22.6
1915–24	57.2	21.0	21.8
1920–29	60.5	17.6	22.0
1925–34	63.0	15.8	21.1
1930–39	66.8	15.0	18.1
1934–43	65.1	16.5	18.4
1939–48	64.6	17.2	18.3
1944–53	65.6	16.4	18.1
1949–58	67.4	13.6	19.0
1954–63	69.9	11.8	18.3

Source: Adapted from Bernard F. Haley, "Changes in the Distribution of Income in the United States," in *The Distribution of National Income* ed. Jean Marchal and Bernard Ducros (New York: St. Martin's Press, 1968). Table 9, p. 24.

agriculture or in white-collar and professional work. Since supply and demand conditions may affect these different components of the labor force differently, it is difficult to single out the specific impact of unionization and collective bargaining.

Labor professor Albert Rees notes that there are some periods, as in the time of strong unionization in the mid-1930s, when unions undoubtedly contributed to a rise in real wages for union members; and other periods, as in 1939–1948, when unionized labor was actually losing ground relative to unorganized labor. Since the late 1940s, unions may have contributed to a relative rise in the real wages of organized labor in manufacturing, but he points out that "real wages in manufacturing were rising long before unions were important" and that much of the increase in real wages must be due to "technological progress, to the growing supply of capital per worker, and

to the rising skill and education of the work force."[7] These factors, of course, would operate to raise wages even in an economy in which factor markets were operated on wholly competitive lines.

The difficulty of making generalizations about the impact of union activity on the economy *as a whole* is an important one to note, because it takes us to the borderline where microeconomic analysis must essentially merge into *macro*economics. We know from Table 26-1 that employee compensation (wages and salaries) comprises some 70 percent of national income. When we begin to talk, therefore, about *general* increases in money wages in the economy, we are talking about a change that will deeply affect consumer incomes and hence the demand curves for

7. Albert Rees, "Patterns of Wages, Prices and Productivity," in *Wages, Prices and Productivity,* The American Assembly (New York: Columbia University Press, 1959), p. 33.

the products of all the business firms in the economy. These changed business demand curves, in turn, will, of course, affect the demand curves for the factors of production, including labor.

This, then, is a good point at which to conclude our analysis of microeconomic problems in isolation and to move on to Part Four, where almost all the issues under discussion will involve both microeconomic *and* macroeconomic dimensions.

SUMMARY

In applying theories of factor incomes to the modern American economy, we are forced to recognize certain departures from the competitive model. On the *demand* side, the theory of pure competition states that firms will hire a factor according to the rule that the price of the factor equals the value of its marginal product ($P_f = VMP_f$). When the hiring firms enjoy some degree of monopoly in the product market, however, they will hire factors according to the rule that the price of the factor equals its *marginal revenue product* ($P_f = MRP_f$). Also, the firms may possess some *monopsony* buying power. When such power exists, they will take into account the increase in wages they have to pay previously employed laborers when they add additional laborers at a higher wage. Both these factors on the demand side will tend to lower the wage and reduce the amount of labor (or any other factor) employed as compared to a purely competitive situation.

On the *supply* side, there also may be monopoly elements as illustrated by our example of a purely monopolist craft union. If we assume competitive factor demand, then the intrusion of monopoly on the supply side will bring about a higher wage and a lower quantity of labor employed than would obtain under pure competition. In our simple case, the monopoly union will maximize benefits for its members by setting labor supply so that the marginal revenue of the last hour of labor supplied is equated to the marginal cost in terms of leisure foregone by offering that last hour.

Even these modifications of competitive theory are insufficient to describe real-world factor markets, however, since the characteristic industrial situation involves *imperfect competition* on *both* sides of the factor market, simultaneously. In such circumstances, actual wage determination often becomes theoretically indeterminate; or rather, it will depend upon the specific characteristics of the *bargaining* situation involved.

In the labor market in the United States, participation of unions and management in *collective bargaining* is an important method for setting wages and other conditions of work. The collective bargaining process is not easy to define, because of the variety of its objectives and methods. Legally, collective bargaining has been upheld by numerous pieces of legislation since the Wagner Act of 1935, although labor leaders claim that some postwar legislation has been unfriendly to union activities. In the future, the unionization of public employees and of professional workers is likely to have an important effect on wage-setting in this country, creating important new avenues for the collective bargaining process.

As far as their effects on income distribution are concerned, it is unclear statistically whether, or how much, American labor unions have raised the real wages of their members. The difficulties are that union activity may have favorable effects on the wages of nonunion members and also that the types of labor that are unionized or nonunionized are characteristically different. Although one might assume from *micro*analysis that union activity must have produced some relative rise in real wages, the problem is complicated by the *macro*economic effects of any general round of wage increases through the economy as a whole.

QUESTIONS FOR DISCUSSION

1. Suppose someone made the following argument:

In the case of pure competition, business firms will hire factors of production to the point where $P_f = P \times MP_f$ (or the value of the marginal product). But we also know that in pure competition it will be true for the firm that $P = MR$. Therefore, we can rephrase the rule to read that in pure competition, the firm will hire the factor to the point where $P_f = MR \times MP_f$ (or the marginal revenue product). Now this is exactly the same rule that the firm with monopoly power in the product market will observe. Therefore, there is no difference as far as factor demand is concerned whether the demanders are purely competitive firms or pure monopolists in the product market.

Analyze this statement carefully, indicating precisely where you may agree or may disagree with the analysis.

2. Why do we say that a firm enjoying monopsony buying power does not have a standard demand curve for the factor it is hiring? Explain.

3. Suppose that our "monopoly union" convinced management to set the wage, w_u (Figure 26-1, p. 612) but neglected to

make provision for setting the number of labor hours to be employed. Instead, the union simply allowed its members to apply for as many hours work as each wanted at the wage w_u. Can you see a possible problem here? (Hint: The supply curve, $F_s F_s$ tells us how many labor hours the union members would in total be willing to work at any given wage.)

4. Do you think there should be compulsory arbitration of all labor disputes? Some? None? Describe the advantages and disadvantages of the proposal you have offered.

5. Professor Kassalow points out that collective bargaining among public employees need not have exactly the same features as collective bargaining in the private sector (p. 623). What important differences do you see between these two sectors as far as union-management issues are concerned?

6. Using the academic world as your example, describe the potential gains and losses of unionization in the professions.

7. "Since it cannot be shown that labor unions actually raise the real wages of union members, it cannot be shown that such unions are necessary—or even desirable—for the modern worker." Discuss.

SUGGESTED READING

The American Assembly. *Challenges to Collective Bargaining.* Englewood Cliffs, N.J.: Prentice-Hall, 1967.

Bowen, William G., ed. *Labor and the National Economy.* New York: W. W. Norton & Co., 1965.

Bok, Derek C., and Dunlop, John T. *Labor and the American Community.* New York: Simon & Schuster, 1970.

Garbarino, Joseph W. "Precarious Professors: New Patterns of Representation." *Industrial Relations* X, No. 1, February 1971.

Taft, Philip. *Organized Labor in American History.* New York: Harper & Row, 1964.

PART FOUR
CONTEMPORARY
ECONOMIC
PROBLEMS

27
Some Dilemmas Of Modern Economic Policy

In Parts Two and Three of this book, we focussed attention on macroeconomic and microeconomic problems respectively. In this final part, we shall be delineating some further outstanding economic issues that confront modern society. These further issues characteristically involve both macro- and microeconomic dimensions and, indeed, they often involve conflicts among different worthwhile objectives. Another characteristic of these issues is that they require us to make decisions—usually collective or public decisions—about the directions in which we wish our society to go. We sometimes forget the point, but in today's world even a decision for a do-nothing, laissez-faire policy would still be a decision.[1] Finally, these issues have been chosen because they have, or seem to the author to have, considerable urgency in the 1970s.

DILEMMAS FACING THE POLICY-MAKER

Since the problems we shall be discussing in the ensuing chapters all raise

---

1. In fact, it would be a huge decision. Just imagine the political and economic changes that would be required in our very "mixed" economy if the State were literally to institute a hands-off policy. In some ways, this would be the most radical decision of all!

633

important public policy issues, it seems worthwhile to enumerate some of the difficulties that face policy-makers in the actual carrying out of their work. Whether the decisions in question are being made by the president, or Congress, or the Federal Reserve Board, or—in 1972—by the Price Commission or the Pay Board, the responsible parties face certain typical problems that make economic policy rather different from its ordinary textbook presentation. Here is a brief listing and commentary on some of these practical difficulties:

1. Different Analyses of the Problem To Be Solved.

A major difficulty for the policy-maker is that there is seldom perfect agreement among the "experts" on the actual causes of any given economic problem. In some cases, the differences of opinion are extreme. This is certainly so in the case of monetarism, for example. Consider a politician who must make up his mind about how to fight inflation. One expert says: "Inflation can be generated only by the government"; the only way to control it "is to control the rate of growth in the stock of money and credit."[2] Another expert says: "The battle against inflation today is primarily an attack on inflation psychology." The only way to control it is "to create a climate where future inflation is not universally expected."[3] Still other experts might refer to labor union power, or oligopolistic industries, or what have you. Each analysis

would suggest a different cure. The policy-maker, sometimes without special expertise of his own in the particular area in question, must make choices on the basis of conflicting testimony. While it is not true, as the joke goes, that ten economists in a room will give you eleven different opinions, they will seldom be able to narrow things down to a single clear-cut answer either.

2. Conflicts Among Objectives.

Even if there were perfect agreement about the causes of economic problems, the policy-maker will normally find it very difficult to decide what his ultimate goals are. An important reason for this is that economic objectives often conflict. The issue of wage-price controls (See Great Debate Four, pp. 647–63) is an example of the difficulties of conflicting objectives. In the first place, controls have been instituted because of the apparent conflict between the objectives of maintaining full employment and achieving reasonable price stability. Now the institution of wage-price controls might conceivably resolve *this* conflict—that is, if the controls can hold wages and prices down, then the government might be able to use the full arsenal of fiscal and monetary weapons to bring about full employment. However, the controls might at the same time bring about a new conflict among objectives, this time between full employment with stable prices, on the one hand, as against such objectives as efficiency in the allocation of resources, or freedom of individuals or groups to make their own decisions, etc. We shall return to this general problem again, but for the moment we should note that the conflict of objectives will cause policy-makers to seek solutions that minimize the conflict and, where this is impossible, to find some basis for determining priorities among ob-

---

2. W. Allen Wallis, "Wage-Price Controls Won't Work," *Wall Street Journal*, December 22, 1971. Dr. Wallis is chancellor of the University of Rochester and a noted monetarist.

3. Sidney Homer, "Phase Three: Triumph or Defeat," *New York Times*, November 14, 1971. Mr. Homer is a limited partner in the brokerage house, Salomon Brothers.

jectives. Neither of these tasks is easy in practice.

3. Problems of Timing.

By the time the analysis of a given problem has been decided upon and the conflicts among objectives resolved—in other words, by the time the policy-maker is ready to act—the problem may have changed. This question also came up in the debate over monetarism (p. 315), in terms of the issue of using discretionary monetary policy versus a fixed-increase-in-the-money-supply rule, but it is really quite a general problem. By the time a society understands what its social and economic needs are, and has geared itself up to action, the basic problems are likely to have altered substantially. It is probably true, for example, that by the time economists understood the Great Depression of the 1930s, we were out of it for other reasons (largely World War II) and our approach to the problems of an expanding economy (with inflationary tendencies) in the postwar period was to some degree distorted by this lag.

4. Problem of Factors Outside the Control of the Policy-Maker.

This is the problem of what economists call *exogenous* (operating from "outside the system") forces. The previously cited problems, especially the problem of timing, are all intensified by such forces. The most notable exogenous factor in modern times has been war. Historically, weather was an extremely important exogenous factor for agrarian societies (and still is, in some of the less developed countries). In the sixteenth century, the Spanish discovery of gold and silver in the New World was an exogenous factor that may have had important effects on the subsequent commercialization of the Western European economy. In the twentieth century, wars, both major and minor, have had a tendency to surprise economic policy-makers, making irrelevant or even counter-productive their solutions of a few months earlier.

5. Problems of the Political Process.

Societies differ greatly in their political systems, but it will seldom be the case that any economic policy-maker can take a perfectly dispassionate and Olympian view of the problems to be solved. He will be subjected to other pressures that may affect his prestige, his standing with the "Central Committee," his ability to win reelection, his effectiveness with Congress, Parliament, or whatever. One of the basic contentions of the "consumerist" movement in this country is that special interests are too highly represented and the consumer's interest too little represented in the thinking of politicians. Political opportunism is not always a bad thing. Sometimes in seeking to gain reelection or curry favor with the populace, leaders adopt better policies than they would if they had functioned in isolation. Indeed, one of the cornerstones of democratic theory is that responsiveness to such political pressures will produce better results than if (as under a dictatorship or hereditary monarchy) popular opinion could be largely ignored. But it is equally true that the sum of a group of special interests is not necessarily the public interest.

What is one to conclude from this list? Are economic policies merely imperfect, or are they hopeless? Before looking into the future, let us assess the record of the past. The following reading by Otto Eckstein, professor of economics at Harvard, and a former member of the Council of Economic Advisers, represents an informed account of economic policy-making in the 1960s.

ECONOMIC POLICY IN THE SIXTIES

THE ECONOMICS OF THE 1960s— A Backward Look

OTTO ECKSTEIN

The 1960s are behind us. What have we learned? And what should we forget? Regretfully, there still is little study of the history of economic policy. Historians record the minutiae of foreign affairs and domestic politics, but the successes and failures of the economic policy, which affect the lives of the people more directly than the struggles of personalities for power, are still not the subject of serious study. The books by Arthur Schlesinger and Eric Goldman on the Kennedy and Johnson administrations give short shrift to economic management.

This essay cannot fill that void. It presents only the reflections of a brief participant in the economic policies of the 1960s, and a partial assessment of that decade in the area of domestic policy.

CONCERNS OF THE LATE 1950s

In 1959 the Joint Economic Commit-

From Otto Eckstein, "Economics of the 1960s—A Backward Look," The Public Interest Spring 1970, pp. 86–97. Copyright © 1970 by National Affairs Inc. Reprinted by permission of the publisher and the author. Footnotes have been omitted.

tee studies on Employment Growth, and Price Levels expressed concern about the slow growth of the economy in the 1950s, the rising unemployment, and the increasing frequency of recessions. All these were blamed on the restrictive policies in the management of aggregate demand, a low rate of increase in the money supply of only 1.9 percent for 1953–1959, and a destabilizing fiscal policy because of the gyrations of the defense budget. The Committee issued reports about the dimensions of poverty and the inadequacy of health care, but it implicitly argued that if the economic growth rate was increased, poverty would be reduced and the resources would be created to help solve all our problems. Economic growth, then, was the major issue as we entered the 1960s.

The critics of the 1950s maintained that the "natural" growth of the American economy was substantially higher than the performance. By "natural" growth they meant the performance that is possible, given advancing technology, the institutional arrangements (e.g., sector distributions) of the economy, and full utilization of this potential. Leon Keyserling, who made economic growth a major issue, argued that the economy was capable of growing at a full 5 percent a year. James Knowles, in his pioneer aggregate production function study for Employment, Growth, and Price Levels, produced a medium estimate 3.9 percent, with a half percent on either side for low or high growth policies. In reply to these voices, Edward F. Denison, in his famous study Sources of Economic Growth, concluded that the natural rate of growth was only 3 percent, implying that the policy of the 1950s was not in error, and that even major changes in investment in physical and human capital would accelerate the rate of growth by only a few small decimals. If 1 percent sounds like a quibble, we should realize that an additional 1 percent of economic growth during the decade is $85 billion of extra output by 1969.

NO EXTRA JOBS

Actually, the economy grew at an annual average rate of 4.6 percent during the decade 1959–1969. To obtain the natural rate of growth one must correct for the gap of 4 percent between actual and potential GNP in 1959 and for an overfull employment of 2 percent of potential in 1969. Thus, the apparent growth of potential GNP was 4 percent for the decade; James Knowles was right.

Where did Denison go wrong? The depression of the 1930s did more harm to the economy than the Denison analysis indicated. The loss in capital formation, and perhaps the lost technology and innovations as well, were not fully made up when World War II brought full employment. High employment has raised potential growth above prewar standards.

How was the high growth rate achieved in the 1960s? Economic measures enacted in 1962 stimulated the rate of growth of the economy's potential through the investment credit and more liberal depreciation allowances. The neoclassical school of investment analysts, led by Dale Jorgenson, assigns great weight to this stimulus, though other equations can probably explain the historical record as well. Without doubt, these measures helped accelerate capital goods spending by mid-1963. They led to certain abuses, including an excessive growth of leasing. But the investment credit idea has not obtained a firm place in our institutional structure and is about to disappear.

The government also launched manpower programs designed to reduce structural unemployment. These programs are generally judged to be a mixed success. Some disadvantaged workers and youth were helped, but the distribution of unemployment was little changed. The supply of highly skilled labor was not augmented significantly. Indeed, this supply, particularly in the construction trades, appears to have worsened during the decade. The bulge at the bottom of unskilled, poorly educated, and youth remains.

The government also invested heavily in health. During the 1960s, Medicare and Medicaid financed major outlays for the aged and the poor. Although desirable from a human point of view, there is little immediate impact on economic growth from such spending, though Medicaid will improve the health care of children and will ultimately help growth.

Federal outlays on education rose rapidly, though again there was little direct impact on output from these expenditures. The Elementary and Secondary Education Act is a strategic human investment that should yield handsome returns if administered properly. Government support of science and technology continued to grow in the 1960s, though mainly as a by-product of other goals; the defense and space programs paid for over half of all physical research, though toward the close of the decade the cost of the Vietnam war had begun to squeeze the vast outlays for research.

Policies to stimulate area and regional growth loomed large in the early agenda of 1960. The Area Development Act, the Appalachia programs, and their successors reflected this impulse. But it was prosperity that solved most of this problem, as the number of major labor market areas with substantial unemployment fell from twenty-five to just three (two of them in Puerto Rico). In most instances programs succumbed to politics; they provided federal public works money with above-normal generosity, but this was spread thin over too many areas. The regional development focus has now shifted to the ghettos. It remains to be seen whether the money will be spent more wisely.

In sum, the policies to stimulate growth were substantial and had some success. But the high growth performance of the decade was mainly the result of the normal, rapid technological advance which has characterized the American economy for a century (except for the depression) and the resumption of a normal rate of national investment. But all this was possible as a result of the success of the administration's "new economics" fiscal policies which created the environment in which natural growth forces could flourish.

THE ACHIEVEMENT OF FISCAL POLICY

The central feature of economics in the 1960s was the triumph of modern fiscal policy. It was a victory slow in coming. Six years passed from the time in 1958 when many economists, Arthur Burns as well as the Keynesians, saw the need for a tax cut until the needed policy prevailed. Why did it take so long to take the common-sense step of reducing an excessive burden of taxation, so obviously in the interest of politicians and their constituencies? It is a dramatic example of the power of established prejudices over self-interest, even of ideas that were quite wrong.

First, even Keynesian economists forgot the lesson of their master, that an economy could remain at under-employment equilibrium. Public and scientific opinion had come to accept the necessity of government deficits when the economy was sliding into recession. But the classical view of the natural tendency to return to full employment remained deeply ingrained. At the bottom of the 1958 recession, the leading indicators established that the lower turning point had been reached and tax reduction was ruled out. The Samuelson task force to president-elect Kennedy concluded that the economy was in an upswing, and therefore did not endorse immediate tax reduction. Even this sophisticated group fell into the classical trap. (Or was it political realism?) Recovery proceeded, and by 1962 unemployment had fallen to 5.5 percent. But then the economy stalled. Months dragged by as a good set of figures would raise hopes of renewed advance and the next month would dash them. Only gradually was it recognized that the tax burden was excessive and that the economy was going nowhere. In this respect, the Council of Economic Advisers understood the issue long before its academic allies.

Second, the concept of the annually balanced budget and the fear of debt still held many persons in its grip. Few outside the government believed that a tax cut would pay for itself—as it did—and so it appeared that the initial impact of tax reduction would be an enlargement of the budget deficit.

Third, the structuralists, with a following both in the Federal Reserve Board and the Department of Labor, argued that the high unemployment was the outcome of an imbalance between the new, technologically advanced jobs and the supply of unskilled, disadvantaged workers. The structuralists had a legitimate point in advocating an upgrading of a portion of the labor force. But in overstating their case they were obstructionists to modern fiscal policy. When the economy finally approached full employment after 1964, the job gains of the unskilled and of the disadvantaged greatly exceeded the gains of the more skilled; we discovered the social power of a tight labor market.

Fourth, Professor Galbraith's voice, carrying from Delhi to Washington, argued that tax reduction would permanently lower the government's ability to command resources. He favored the traditional Keynesian route of stimulating the economy through expenditures. Whatever the merits of greater public spending, the simple fact was that the Congress of the early 1960s would not go that route.

Fifth, advocates of tax reform felt that tax reduction offered them the only opportunity to put together a political package which would make the Congress accept the closing of loopholes. The theory was that Congress would give the President some tax reform in exchange for the privilege of cutting taxes. Actually it was the President and his advisors who wanted tax reduction, while tax reform was a millstone around fiscal policy. Ironically, tax reform has finally been enacted by an eager Congress, forcing a mildly enthusiastic administration to accept reform in exchange for a brief extension of the tax surcharge.

Sixth, the monetary school of economists argued that tax reduction was a minor element in economic policy, and that what was really needed to stimulate the economy was a more suitable increase in the money supply. At the time of the great fiscal debate, however, the monetary school had little influence and cannot be said to have been a significant factor in the delay.

After six years the taxes were cut. By July 1965, before defense contracts began to rise, unemployment was down to 4.5 percent and falling rapidly, the economy was growing at over 5 percent a year, and wholesale prices were still stable and no higher than five years earlier. The economy had shown, at least for eighteen happy months, that it could prosper without war with sensible, modern economic management; doubts about fiscal policy were wiped out, and for a year or two economists rode high indeed.

Then came the Vietnam war and the end, for a period at least, of modern fiscal policy. The budget underestimated defense spending by $10 billion for fiscal 1967 and $5 billion for fiscal 1968. The impact on the economy was underestimated by larger amounts because of the greater jumps in defense contracts. If the economic impact of the war had been known, the excise taxes would not have been cut in the summer of 1965. In early 1966 there should have been a broad across-the-board tax increase. But taxes were not increased because the President could not get the American people to pay for the war. In the end, the war paralyzed the political process, producing the surrealistic debate over the tax surcharge from mid-1967 to mid-1968. International financial crises followed one on another. Demand became excessive. The tax surcharge of mid-1968, which Congress voted, finally restored some fiscal order.

The impact of the federal budget on the economy in the 1960s can be measured crudely by the high employment budget surplus—an estimate of the surplus that the budget would produce if the economy were at full employment and producing revenues accordingly. The excessively restrictive policies of the 1950s had raised the full employment budget surplus to about $13 billion in 1960. Increased expenditures to fight recession, the military buildup over the Berlin crisis, and the investment credit and depreciation reform lowered the surplus to about $6½ billion in 1962. Delay in tax reduction and a slowdown in expenditure increases raised the surplus once more, reaching an $11 billion peak at the end of 1963.

The tax cuts, and the increases in spending, caused an enormous swing in the federal budget. By the beginning of 1967, the full employment budget showed a deficit of $12 billion —a welcome stimulus during the slowdown; but its deepening to $15 billion by mid-1968 was a disaster. Once the tax surcharge was passed and expenditure restraint became effective, the swing in the opposite direction was equally massive. By the second quarter of 1969 the high employment surplus approached $10 billion again. No wonder that the economy got rather out of hand, and now faces a period of slow growth.

What judgment can be passed about discretionary policy in the light of this record?

First, while the necessary alternative model simulations have not been done, and so answers must remain qualitative at best, the record of the 1960s seems to repeat the verdict of the 1950s. Discretionary policy did harm as well as good. The policy proposed by the Committee for Economic Development in 1947, if it had been followed, would have done better. The CED recommended that the government maintain a small full employment surplus in its budget, and normally eschew the attempt to pursue a more ambitious, discretionary stabilization policy. The CED policy would have avoided the excessive full employment surpluses in the late 1950s and the early 1960s, the swings which led to the re-emergence of a very large surplus in 1963, and it would have forced the financing of the Viet-

nam war by current taxes. The Great Society programs still could have been financed out of the increase in full employment revenues during a period of rapid growth.

Second, it is evident that the major movements in the full employment surplus were not the result of deliberate stabilization policy. The big swings were due to exogenous events: i.e., the Vietnam war and the inability of the political process to make revenues respond to swings in expenditures. Even if the government had abandoned discretionary policy altogether, and sought to maintain a steady full employment balance of small surplus, the same political difficulties would have gotten in the way. Taxes would have had to be raised. It is likely that the political process would have failed to execute the CED policy, just as it failed to carry out a rational discretionary policy.

THE PRIVATE-PUBLIC MIX

In the 1960s, expenditures by government rose at a substantially higher rate than the gross national product. The total outlays (on national income account) of all levels of government were 27.1 percent on the GNP in 1960; by 1969, the figure rose to 31.4 percent. The outlays of states and localities rose from 9.9 percent to 13.1 percent of GNP; federal outlays rose from 18.5 to 20.5 percent.

This increase in part represents the Vietnam war, which absorbed about 3 percent of GNP, some of it at the expense of other defense outlays. Most of the remainder was due to the growth of public activities in response to a rising population and to slow productivity growth of government service activities. But a major reason for the rise of government spending was the Great Society programs enacted from 1964 to 1966.

It is important to understand how this change in the public-private mix came about. So long as the issue was posed in Galbraithian terms—public versus private spending—the Congress did not respond. The Great Society programs were made possible by the large spurt in the growth rate from 1964 to 1966. Public spending came out of economic growth, not out of private spending.

These are the summary figures: in 1964, before the Great Society programs, the federal government collected $113 billion and spent $119 billion, producing a $6 billion deficit. By 1968, following the substantial tax reductions, revenues were up to $154 billion, a rise of $41 billion, expenditures were up to $179 billion, a rise of $60 billion. As a result, the $6 billion budget deficit rose to $25 billion. What happened is clear enough: military spending, mainly for Vietnam, rose by $27 billion. Spending on education at the federal level rose from $2 to $7 billion; on health, from $2 to $10 billion; and the total of all other fields, including Social Security, agriculture, urban affairs, and the old-line programs, went up from $61 to $81 billion.

Thus, during the period of the Great Society legislation, there was plenty of spending for old and new programs, civilian and military. Economic growth produced the revenues, though in the end we did stumble into an enormous deficit.

MONETARY POLICY IN THE 1960s

Because human beings are fallible and policymakers all over Washington are subject to common tides of opinion and politics, the record of

monetary policy has similarities to fiscal policy. Until 1965, monetary policy accommodated the gradual recovery to full employment, while interest rates remained fairly stable. One might argue that interest rates should have risen as the economy moved toward full employment, but one should also remember that interest rates were already high at the beginning of the decade because of the excessively restrictive monetary policies of 1959.

The monetary school of economists, led by Milton Friedman, claims that the recovery to full employment was really due to a good expansion of the money supply, perhaps prompted by the need to finance the budget deficits. The theoretical debate about the relative importance of fiscal and monetary policy is not likely to be settled here; but one can observe a striking contrast for the period under review. The rhythm of the economy seemed to respond to changes in fiscal policy. Unemployment stayed high so long as the budget aimed for large high employment surpluses. It fell after the tax cut of 1964. The increase in the broad money supply was fairly steady, both in the period of high level stagnation and during full recovery. If easy money alone sufficed, full employment should have come more quickly.

From 1965 on, the Federal Reserve Board no longer fully accommodated the economic growth, and interest rates began to rise. With the benefit of hindsight about the war, the federal deficit, the capital goods boom, and the inflation, it is now evident that monetary policy should have become tougher earlier. Further monetary policy was too aggressive during the 1967 slowdown, and if ever there was a case of overkill, the antirecession fiscal and monetary policies of 1967 were an example. In the summer of

1968, monetary policy eased too quickly after the passage of the tax surcharge, and the authorities have been struggling ever since to bring the banking system and inflation under control.

The monetary theorists sing a siren song which says that if money supply is expanded at a constant rate, we would free ourselves of the fallibility of human judgment about the timing of restricting or loosening the amount of money in response to the economic cycle. There is little doubt that we have overmanaged money, perhaps never more so than during the extreme restraint of 1969–70. But there are hurdles on the way to a more stable policy: if it really is the money supply that is to be regulated, there had better be agreement on the figures. The record of the money supply for the first half of 1969 has been rewritten, as it was for several other crucial periods. Who would rest a policy on so weak a statistical reed? Further, it is difficult to define a "neutral" policy. Structural changes in the financial system give different growth trends to the various monetary magnitudes.

There has been little study of the quantitative relationships between the various monetary measures, explaining the differences in the growth of such variables as unborrowed reserves, the narrow money supply, the broad money supply, the monetary base, total bank credit, bank loans, total credit in the economy, etc. Until this work is done, adoption of any rule applicable to one concept will simply convert the present disputes into a quarrel about the selection and care of statistics.

The level of interest rates is also an indicator of monetary policy, and to me still the most unambiguous. But it is evident from experience that a stable interest rate is not a neutral policy. Interest rates should rise and fall with the business cycle. Indeed, a stable interest rate policy is probably significantly destabilizing for the economy. Thus, while interest movements are a useful gauge, they do not provide a simple rule which policy can follow.

THE GUIDEPOST EPISODE

By the end of the 1950s the need to reconcile full employment and price stability was widely recognized. The new administration, building on earlier Economic Reports, established "Guideposts for Wage-Price Stability." At first the guideposts only asserted some rather bland principles about price and wage behavior which a competitive economy would achieve on its own. It reminded labor that wage increases beyond productivity served mainly to raise prices; it reminded business that price increases beyond trend costs raised profits only temporarily. But until January 1966, when the guideposts were breached by the New York subway settlement, the administration had pursued an active policy of seeking to hold settlements close to the productivity rate.

The guidepost policies must be understood in the context of their day. The economy was moving toward full employment; industrial operating rates were rising. Productivity was advancing rapidly and wage demands were predicated on stable consumer prices. The longer the stable costs and prices could be preserved, the closer the economy could come to full employment without stumbling into the inflationary difficulties which had haunted us in the mid–1950s.

In their heyday, in 1964–66, the

guideposts were a major element of government policy. Government spending programs, fair labor standards proposals, minerals stockpile policy, civil service pay, agricultural policy, and protective measures for specific industries both internal and at the frontier, were examined, at the President's direction, for their effect on cost-price stability. This probably was the first time in history that an administration examined its policy proposals fully from the objective of price stability.

In addition, the guideposts partially reoriented the usual government interventions in collective bargaining. Settlement of industrial conflicts was not an objective by itself but was coordinate with cost stability. For some time, at least, a Democratic government modified its traditional role of urging management to settle for large increases in order to restore industrial harmony. On the price side, presidential intervention slowed down the increases of some highly visible basic materials and a few final products.

Did these policies have any effect? Wage equations which explain other years of the postwar period fail during the guidepost years. To be sure, other explanations have been found for the extraordinarily low wage increases of 1963–66, but they are not totally convincing. Without claiming statistical proof, I would evaluate the episode as prolonging the virtuous circle of high productivity growth, stable costs, and stable price expectations by some months, and slowing the pickup of the price-wage spiral.

The guidepost policies were politically very difficult. Every time the president reduced a government program, intervened in a labor dispute, rolled back a price, let goods in from abroad, or made a release from the stockpile, he trod on sensitive toes. In due time, the affected industries sought retribution through the political process. Only a president elected by an enormous majority and commanding firm control over the Congress could withstand the politicking of industries, which President Johnson did.

As the Vietnam war escalated and the president's popularity began to fade, the authority of the guidepost policies shrank. When the president lost his command over the Congress in the 1966 elections, the most active phase of guidepost policies drew to a close, though there were some successful interventions as late as the summer of 1968.

There has been criticism of the guideposts as violating the principles of a free market economy. These criticisms are misplaced. The markets in our economy are relatively free compared to other economies; but many industries benefit from government programs, from government purchases, government-enforced production controls, import restrictions and tariff, artificial reductions of supply through stockpile policies, and so on. Similarly, the strength of labor unions is immensely aided not only by the basic laws which redress the balance between employer and worker, but also by the Davis-Bacon Act which strengthens the grip of the construction unions, Walsh-Healey, and so on. We saw in the opening months of 1969 that the government cannot shelve all its powers to influence wage and price decisions. The absence of guidepost policies does not make the government neutral.

The guideposts were swept away in a wave of excess demand. The present administration is wise to seek to attempt to limit the growth of demand through restrictive monetary and fiscal policies. At this stage of inflation there is no other way to bring prices back under control. The present vigorous policies of anti-trust and the reorganization of human investment programs will ultimately yield rewards in price stability as well. The job of resisting textile quotas, of easing oil import quotas, and of making sure that the government promotes rather than hurts price stability in its detailed decisions, still needs doing, however. There is no point in confusing these matters with vague talk of market ideology.

The guidepost episode and the recent inflationary explosion leave a nagging question: is the inflationary bias of the economy excessive at a 4 percent unemployment rate, and does the rate of inflation inevitably worsen at full employment? The United States has never had uninterrupted prosperity before. Now that we have unlocked the secret, are we unable to use it because we do not know how to live with full employment?

SOME LESSONS FOR THE 1970s

What should we have learned? What mistakes have we no right to repeat? And where is the new ground that should be broken? A review of the predictions made at the beginning of this decade indicates that one cannot anticipate what will be the dominant problems. In 1960 no one thought about the Vietnam war or appreciated that the inequality of economic opportunity and disparities between black and white would become the central social problem. The impact of an advancing economy on the physical environment was not totally a surprise, but was far down the agenda of the decade. Even such traditional items as the deterioration of the cities, the improvement of health and education, housing, and rural opportunity had little specificity ten years ago. So

don't expect much help here in pinpointing the major problems of the 1970s even within the area of economic performance.

Nonetheless we owe it to ourselves to attempt to distill a few points from the review of the past period.

(1) The natural rate of growth of the economy for the 1970s exceeds 4 percent and we should judge economic performance accordingly. The growth of the labor force accelerated in the mid-1960s and will remain at a high rate. The advance of technology gives every sign of remaining very rapid. The current high rate of growth of the capital stock indicates the prospect of a natural rate of growth at least as great as in the 1960s.

We will begin the decade with a very slow growth year. The overfull employment of recent months will be converted into a small gap between actual and potential output in 1970. If we focus economic policy exclusively on fighting inflation, and if the fight on inflation is confined to the strictly classical medicine, we condemn ourselves to several years of slow growth and the development of a considerable gap between actual and potential output.

(2) The economy still seems unable to reconcile full employment with price stability. The need for structural changes to improve the competitiveness and flexibility of markets and to minimize the harm of government protectionist policies remains as strong as ever. Government machinery could be strengthened for these pursuits.

(3) The trend cycle in the private economy will be in an upswing phase at the beginning of the decade. While government policy may temporarily slow the conversion of fundamental strength into economic activity, rapid family formation with the resultant need for housing and durables will

keep the underlying tone of the private economy strong. This is in sharp contrast to the beginnings of the 1960s.

(4) Fiscal and monetary policies should avoid the extreme swings which have characterized them in the last twenty years. Very full employment surpluses and deficits have been mistakes without exception. Periods of extreme advance or no advance in the money supply have been mistakes without exception.

(5) The informed public finally understands the question of priorities of resource use. The searching examination of our military budget and the attempt to determine the economic costs of our foreign policy commitments contain the promise of a more rational approach to resource allocation in the public sector.

(6) Economic performance is increasingly judged by its ability to meet the social and environmental goals of the society. The 1960s have shown that good macro-performance is a necessary but not a sufficient condition for adequate social progress. The realization that the resources are available may well have heightened the impatience of the black and the young with our halting efforts. The systematic changes in the private and public sector necessary to assure adequate social progress and halt deterioration of the environment appear to be the main challenges to economic policy for the 1970s. But then again, the main tasks may prove to be something else; by 1980 we will know.

POTENTIAL CONFLICTS IN THE SEVENTIES

In the remainder of Part Four, we shall be examining some of the economic problems that seem likely to face public policy-makers with particular force in the 1970s. As Professor Eckstein recognizes in his article, these are not likely to be exactly the same problems that occupied us in the 1960s. One can go further and suggest that perhaps a special characteristic of the economic issues of the seventies will be the degree to which conflicts of objectives are involved. In anticipation, let us suggest three ways in which these conflicts may appear.

1. Wage-Price Policies:

In a sense, we are dealing here with a carry-over from the 1960s for, as Eckstein remarks, the economy ended that decade still "unable to reconcile full employment with price stability." However, the issue in the 1970s is further intensified by the worsening of our balance of payments position in 1970 and 1971, meaning that any attempt to achieve full employment in the economy might lead to highly undesirable international effects that we can no longer sustain. Thus, the achievement of full employment faces now not a single but a twin obstacle—the dangers of inflation and the perils of a balance of payments heavily in deficit.

President Nixon's approach to this matter—the "new economic policy," with its wage-price controls and international aspects (cutting the dollar off from gold, etc.)—reflects the increased intensity of the conflict among these several objectives. Nixon's new approach, however, although it may lessen the inflation-balance of payments-employment conflict, does run the risk of new conflicts, as stated earlier. Since these matters are taken up directly or indirectly in Great Debate Four, we need not develop them further here.

2. The New and Complicated Role of Economic Growth.

Economic growth is still an important issue in the 1970s but its role seems much more ambiguous than it did a decade ago. There is an increased awareness now of the things that growth cannot accomplish by itself. One of these—and a very important one—is a more equitable distribution of income between rich and poor in the society. Another is the removal of technological or structural unemployment. Although it is not clear that technological advance, even in the form of computer technology and automation, need reduce the number of jobs available in the economy as a whole, it *is* clear that the kinds of labor and management skills required in a growing economy need not correspond exactly to those abundant in the labor force. Rapid growth and pockets of heavy unemployment can occur simultaneously.[4]

Perhaps even more significant is the increased belief that growth actually contributes to rather than helps solve our problems. This is a clear example of the kind of conflict among economic objectives that seems increasingly characteristic of the present decade. For one thing, rapid growth could easily intensify our balance of payments difficulties. Growth in national income could mean a growth in imports, which could further increase our payments deficit. Also, as we have mentioned earlier, growth-stimulating and payments-deficit-reducing policies can be in conflict (p. 396).

The most important example of conflict, however, is concerned with the environmental and ecological costs of economic growth. It is widely believed that unfettered economic expansion at the rates common during the past century or two in the industrial societies could lead to societies so congested, polluted, and dehumanized that they would suffocate, or perhaps revert to a state of irrational primitivism.

This conflict is further intensified in the 1970s as development efforts begin to mount in the poorer and still relatively unindustrialized areas of the world. Can the world stand growth on the North American-European-Japanese scale in India, China, Africa, Latin America? The conflicts of objectives (not to mention the possible conflicts among nations) inherent in this new view of growth are manifold.

3. Public and Private Sectors.

Whereas in the 1960s, the increase in the role of government in the American economy came (as Eckstein notes) "out of growth," the situation may be substantially different in the 1970s. A study published by the Brookings Institution in 1972 under the direction of Charles L. Schultze, former Budget Director (*Setting National Priorities: The 1973 Budget*), suggests that we may be entering a new phase in which any further expansions of the public sector will have to be financed by new taxes, i.e., public expenditures will become fully competitive with private expenditures. There are several reasons for this change, including the fact that there have been tax cuts in 1964, 1965, 1969, and 1971, meaning that tax revenues have not risen as rapidly as they might have with the growth of GNP during this period. Even more significant, however, is the fact that the growth of federal programs in the area of domestic welfare has been very substantial during the past decade and that many of these programs have built-in expansionary features of their own.

Thus, comparing the federal budget in terms of expenditures between fis-

---

4. For a good discussion of the issues involved in technological change in relationship to employment, see Robert M. Solow, "Technology and Unemployment," *The Public Interest*, Fall 1965.

Continued on p. 664

GREAT DEBATE FOUR

WAGE PRICE CONTROLS

One of the most difficult conflicts among economic objectives in the last decade for most industrial countries has been that between full employment and price stability. Since most observers feel that a high rate of unemployment is too great a price to pay for stable prices, the natural question has been: why not pursue vigorous fiscal and monetary policies to achieve full employment and then—to prevent inflation—control prices and wages directly?

In the United States, the advocacy of wage-price controls has usually been associated with the liberal range of the liberal-conservative political spectrum. And until recently, it was fairly standard for Republican congressmen to criticize Democratic administrations for interfering too greatly in the market mechanism via wage-price guideposts or executive pressures (see p. 341). This past history made the occasion all the more dramatic, on August 15, 1971, when President Richard Nixon announced a series of startling economic measures, including a ninety-day freeze on all wages and prices in the nation.

PRESIDENT NIXON ANNOUNCES THE WAGE-PRICE FREEZE

RICHARD M. NIXON

One of the cruellest legacies of the artificial prosperity produced by war is inflation. Inflation robs every American. The 20 million who are retired and living on fixed incomes are particularly hard hit. Homemakers find it harder than ever to balance the family budget. And 80 million wage-earners have been on a treadmill. In the four war years between 1965 and 1969 your wage increases were completely eaten up by price increases. Your paychecks were higher, but you were no better off.

We have made progress against the rise in the cost of living. From the high-point of 6 percent a year in 1969, the rise in consumer prices has been cut to 4 percent in the first half of 1971. But just as is the case in our fight against unemployment, we can and must do better than that.

The time has come for decisive action—action that will break the vicious circle of spiralling prices and costs. I am today ordering a freeze on all prices and wages throughout the United States for a period of ninety days. In addition, I call upon corporations to extend the wage-price freeze to all dividends.

Let me emphasize two characteristics of this action: First, it is temporary. To put the strong, vigorous American economy into a permanent straitjacket would lock in unfairness; it would stifle the expansion of our free enterprise system. And second, while the wage-price freeze will be backed by Government sanctions, if necessary, it will not be accompanied by the establishment of a huge price control bureaucracy. I am relying on the voluntary cooperation of all Americans—each one of you—workers, employers, consumers—to make this freeze work.

Working together, we will break the back of inflation, and we will do it without the mandatory wage and price controls that crush economic and personal freedom.

Excerpted from Richard M. Nixon, Economic Report of the President and television address of August 15, 1972.

Two months later, the president revealed the next stage in his plan to stem the tide of inflation, widely known as Phase II. Under Phase II (as operating in 1971–72), a Cost of Living Council was authorized to set broad goals for the economy, the main objective being to reduce the rate of inflation to 2 or 3 percent per year by the end of 1972. Under this Cost of Living Council, a Price Commission and Pay Board were established to make actual decisions on changes in wages and prices. A number of other, largely advisory, boards were also created (Figure 1).

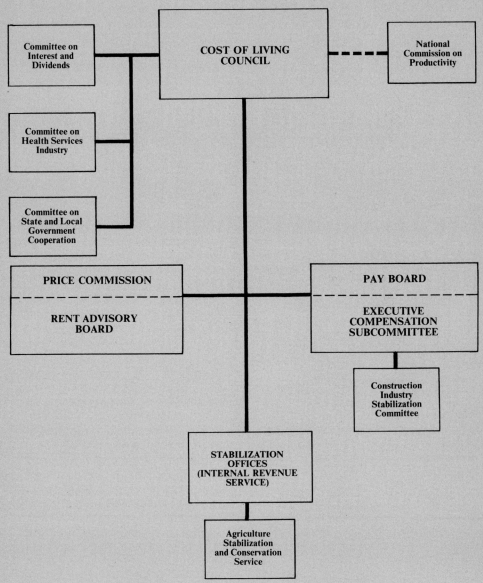

Figure 1. Post-Freeze Organization (Phase II)
Source: Economic Report of the President, 1972

Table 1   REQUIRED REPORTING OF PRICE AND WAGE INCREASES IN PHASE II

Tier	Action required	Price increases (size of firm)	Wage increases (number of workers)
I . . .	(a) Prenotification of Price Commission or Pay Board (increase to be effective with approval of Commission or Board). (b) Tier I firms to submit quarterly price, cost, and profits reports to Price Commission.	Sales of $100 million and over (1500 firms with 45 percent of all sales).	Affecting 5,000 or more workers (10 percent of all employees).
II . . .	(a) Report to Price Commission or Pay Board. (b) Tier II firms to submit quarterly price, cost, and profits report to Price Commission.	Sales of $50 million to $100 million (1,000 firms with 5 percent of all sales).	Affecting 1,000 to 5,000 workers (7 percent of all employees).
III. . .	No reports (but increases to be made only in accordance with Price Commission and Pay Board regulations and to be subject to monitoring and spot checks).	Sales of less than $50 million (10 million enterprises with 50 percent of all sales).	Affecting less than 1,000 workers (83 percent of all employees).

Source: Cost of Living Council.

Phase II differed from the freeze period in that there was to be some upward flexibility allowed in both wages and prices, the aim being not to stop inflation completely at one stroke but to slow it down. Also, Phase II involved the government in differential treatment of various "tiers" of the economy. In the areas of the economy where large oligopolistic firms and/or large labor unions were in operation, the governmental participation in wage-price setting was to be direct and unequivocal; in the case of small businesses and local wage settlements, the intervention of the government was to be limited and indirect (Table 1). Substantial areas of the economy were exempted from direct controls altogether, notably raw agricultural products. Indeed, the rise in meat prices in the early months of 1972 caused a substantial outcry from consumers and labor unions.

Although the long-run effects of the freeze and of Phase II could not immediately be known, these actions did prompt considerable discussion among economists as to the merits of price-wage controls both in a general sense and as applied to the specific circumstances of the American economy in the 1970s. One of the more interesting of these discussions took place under the auspices of the Brookings Institution in Washington, D.C., in the period immediately following the announcement of the wage-price freeze. The authors are William Poole, of the Special Studies Section, Division of Research and Statistics, Board of Governors of the Federal Reserve System, and George L. Perry, an economist with the Brookings Institution and an editor of the *Brookings Papers on Economic Activity*, from which these articles have been excerpted. The papers represent, of course, the personal opinions of the authors, and not of the institutions with which they are associated. They are followed by brief comments from James Tobin, James Duesenberry, Arthur Okun, and Franco Modigliani, outstanding economists all.

THOUGHTS ON THE WAGE-PRICE FREEZE

WILLIAM POOLE

After racing small sailboats for twenty years I have learned that when one is behind in an early race of a series, it rarely pays to split with the lead boats in the vague hope of finding a favorable wind shift. One is better off sailing the most favorable course, which usually involves simply following the lead boats, and capitalizing on any opportunity that arises, meanwhile consolidating position on the boats be-

Excerpted from William Poole, "Thoughts on the Wage-Price Freeze" in *Brookings Papers on Economic Activity* 2 (1971): 429–43, edited by Arthur Okun and George L. Perry. ©1971 by The Brookings Institution, Washington, D. C. Reprinted by permission of the publisher.

hind. A middle-of-the-fleet finish is not dramatic, but it preserves the chances of finishing well in the series as a whole, while a different course may involve poor winds and adverse currents that risk the near-last-place finish. A different course is best only when it is clearly the better course, and then it would have been the right one, whether one was ahead or behind.

In reading the newspapers since August 15, I have been impressed with the frequency of the arguments that "something" had to be done about the economy and the paucity of the arguments that the program announced by the President will actually accomplish the desired objectives at an acceptable cost. There is no assurance that the new course is better, only that it is different. This paper concentrates on the wage-price controls part of the program which, in my view, raises the most serious issues.

A major difficulty in discussing controls is the absence of a generally accepted vocabulary, which means that those on opposite sides of the issue are not always talking about the same concepts. In an attempt to improve communication, I would like to propose the following, necessarily imprecise, definitions. The term "comprehensive controls" may be defined by reference to the wage and price controls of the Second World War. The term "mild controls" means a set of mandatory controls over major firms and unions, perhaps involving the 500 largest firms, which could take the form of detailed wage and price ceilings, or of a board with authority to roll back any wage or price changes found to be excessive. By "guidelines" I mean the type of guidepost program followed under the Kennedy and Johnson administrations, which involves both behind-the-scenes and public pressures but not legal enforcement powers.

It is also useful in avoiding misunderstanding to specify rather precisely the predicted effect of controls. It may be argued, for example, that mild controls will reduce the inflation rate by a specified number of percentage points on a particular price index. Even so, this approach encounters difficulty since the meaning of the price index will change if previously hidden discounts disappear or product quality deteriorates.

Finally, it is important to be precise about time periods. In the last week of the ninety-day freeze, the price level will surely be below what it otherwise would have been. The issue is whether the price level will be below what it otherwise would have been two years, and even five years, from now. Little is to be gained from trading less inflation now for more inflation later.

The economists who favor controls generally do so with the idea that they are a lesser evil than inflation accompanied by unemployment. The controls issue is more one of differing empirical judgments about benefits and costs than of differing doctrinal viewpoints. While economists give different weights to various aspects of their ideals of "the good life," most cherish the maximum possible freedom for economic decisions, a reduction of which is one of the costs of controls. But individual decisions, of course, ought to be taken within the context of the full employment economy necessary to provide genuine choices among job opportunities and among investment opportunities, as well as the stable incomes and goods required for a widely shared prosperity.

THE COSTS OF WAGE-PRICE CONTROLS

Controls incur three different types of costs. The first is the loss of individual freedom resulting from central control over individual wage and price decisions. The second is the misallocation of resources resulting from controls. And the third is the administrative cost. All these costs are interrelated. For example, if administrative cost is kept low, enforcement of the controls will be weak and will have relatively little effect after a time. Also, it is obvious that the costs of controls are a function of their duration.

The resource allocation and administrative costs of controls are not likely to prove great if the controls last for at most several years, especially if they are of the mild variety and really "buy" lower unemployment and greater price stability. In any event, a rich society can bear these costs. The important issue concerns the costs in individual freedom and the way in which they affect the nature of controls that are politically acceptable. The question is whether temporary mild controls will make any lasting contribution to the goals of full employment and price stability.

Considerable governmental power was applied when the wage-price freeze was put into effect. All contracts voluntarily reached by individuals and firms, with each other and with governmental units, have been suspended insofar as they provide for increases in wages and prices. But the central question about the efficacy of temporary controls is precisely whether they will have any lasting effect if existing contracts are permitted to resume force once the freeze ends. The cost of controls will be high if existing contracts must be rewritten following the freeze. This issue will be examined in the next section.

Several examples may serve to amplify the hitherto vague references to "individual freedom." These examples should not be taken to concern "mere details," for one of the major arguments against controls is that there is no satisfactory way of handling these details. To consider the problems of enforcing wage controls, suppose that a firm wants to increase the pay of an employee to a level above the controlled level, perhaps because he is threatening to take a job with a competitor. An obvious technique is to promote him—indeed, so obvious that one of the first clarifications issued during the current freeze was that wages could be increased only in the event of a "bona fide" promotion.

What is a "bona fide" promotion? One approach is not to allow promotions into newly created positions. A firm is not permitted to create new vice presidents, or new foremen, or new senior accountants just to have more higher paying slots to put employees in. But clearly this approach to wage control cannot last very long since many firms have valid reasons for creating new positions.

What criteria can the controllers then use to distinguish between bona fide and control-avoidance promotions? Beyond the cases where the issues are clear-cut, many problems will arise, for example, in connection with corporate mergers and reorganizations. To offer another example, how does a government official know how many foremen are needed in a new plant producing a new product?

Comprehensive wage control is no easy matter. Many arbitrary decisions must be made. Wage control will be relatively easy and most complete over standardized types of jobs, including most blue collar and clerical jobs. Managerial and professional jobs, on the other hand, are more varied and more subject to change. The inequities will multiply, and so will the pressure for a more and more elaborate control machinery to limit the inequities by adjusting wages and salaries.

To obtain wage increases some individuals will be forced to change jobs because one firm, though willing, is not permitted to grant an increase in pay, while another obtains permission for a new position, or has a vacancy in an existing position. Excessive job changing is not only inefficient but also tends to break down wage control. To combat this tendency, controls may be imposed on job moves, or directly on the pay of individuals rather than of jobs.

Price control presents problems that are just as serious. How is the price on a new product to be determined? To set the price on the basis of the firm's costs requires the perhaps expensive attempt to understand its cost accounting methods. To set it equal to that of the closest competitive product is unsatisfactory if the new product costs more to produce but has superior characteristics that are not permitted to bring a higher price, or if it has roughly the same performance characteristics but costs less to produce. In the latter case the cost savings are not passed on to the purchasers of the new product.

Another problem arises when firms face cost increases, some of which in practice will prove unavoidable. Is a firm to be permitted to pass these increases on in the form of higher prices? If not, what happens if the firm simply stops production of an unprofitable item? Will a firm be forced to continue production of an item "vital to the national interest"? If cost increases on "vital" products, however defined, are considered a valid reason for price increases, how many officials will be required to administer the price controls?

Product specifications are constantly changing, sometimes reflecting improvement, sometimes deterioration. In comprehensive price control firms have an obvious incentive to reduce the quality of their goods and services. If the inflationary pressures to be suppressed by controls are powerful, control over product specifications will be required.

Although economists disagree as to the severity of these problems, they acknowledge their existence and believe that they will become more apparent with time. As problems appear, some economists will call for an escalation of controls, while others, like me, will argue that there is no natural end to the escalation of controls. How can these administrative problems be handled without a large bureaucracy? Only administrative guidelines that permit individuals, firms, and control administrators to know what changes in wages and prices, and in job and product specifications, are and are not permitted could make a small bureaucracy feasible. I do not believe such guidelines can be constructed, and, if these matters must be handled on a case-by-case basis, will not the sheer volume of cases overwhelm the control bureaucracy? Will the decisions by controllers be subject to legal appeal, and if so what is the case load likely to be?

Whether controls can work without a large bureaucracy is an empirical question. In my view the issue involved is whether the inflation problem arises primarily from relatively few sources of market power, both on the labor side and the product side, that can be effectively controlled without an elaborate control machinery.

I believe that the economy is far more competitive than surface appearances would indicate. Suppose that, following the freeze, mandatory controls were placed on the wages and prices of the 200 or the 500 largest corporations in the nation. Furthermore, suppose that prices were not permitted to increase at all, and wage increases were limited to the 3.2 percent productivity guideline. Assume, too, that the controls were really strict and all the problems of evasion were handled successfully. How would the experiment work out?

Those who favor this approach would predict that the rate of increase of prices and wages in the whole economy would be drastically slowed. Firms with controlled prices would take business away from those that raised prices and thereby effectively control all prices. Since the prices of uncontrolled firms would in fact be effectively controlled, they would be forced to limit their wage increases. Furthermore, wage demands made to the uncontrolled firms would moderate because the big, visible unions would not be obtaining big wage increases for others to emulate.

Those predicting failure for this approach expect, of course, that some evasion of the controls would take place. To the extent that it is stemmed, the controlled firms would lose their operating flexibility. Their key employees would be bid away, and in some product lines they would find themselves unable to meet the market demand at the prices allowed. Customers, therefore, would turn to uncontrolled firms. Furthermore, the controls and the uncertainty of their application would limit the incentive for large firms to invest in expanded facilities, further eroding their positions.

Some find it hard to believe that in a situation of deficient aggregate demand such as now characterizes the U.S. economy there can be a significant number of cases in which controlled firms would be unable to meet market demand. This view underestimates the normal amount of dispersion in price changes, much of which is caused by differences in demand pressures in different industries. For example, from June 1970 to June 1971 the wholesale price index rose by 3.6 percent. But of the ninety-eight detailed product categories in the index, nineteen had price increases of over 7 percent, and of these thirteen had increases of over 10 percent. Also, seventeen of the categories had actual price declines, and of these six had declines of more than 3 percent. Of the thirty-six changes that were either increases greater than 7 percent or declines, twenty-four involved industrial commodities and twelve involved farm products and processed foods and feeds. There are, of course, many individual products within the ninety-eight categories and further disaggregation surely would show more variability.

I do not believe that the controllers will be able to rely on a few judicious exceptions to solve the problem of excess demand for some products and labor skills. To make many exceptions will risk pressures for still more. Furthermore, prices that would have declined without controls will tend to stay up because firms will fear difficulties in raising them in the future if conditions change. I expect that fewer price declines will occur under a system of controls than occurred in the period preceding the freeze.

I predict that in a relatively short space of time competitive forces would be operating so powerfully that the control experiment described above would be dropped or altered to meet the competitive situation. If the controls were altered, the uncontrolled sectors would determine the level of the wage and price controls in the controlled sectors, rather than the controls affecting the level of wages and prices.

These predictions are straightforward, but the experiment is unlikely to be undertaken. It simply is not politically possible to place strict controls on the largest firms. The reason lies beyond the political power they and unions hold and people's strongly held beliefs about equity. Rather, the reason is primarily the severity of the economic dislocations that would ensue from controls. To counter that it is "unrealistic" to set a 3.2 percent limit on wage increases when wages have been rising at two or three times that rate is not sufficient. If wage increases cannot be set at 3.2 percent, the economic realities control the controllers,

rather than the other way around.

If mandatory controls on the largest firms and unions won't work, there is, of course, little hope for a voluntary guidelines approach. Voluntary compliance is possible only when the guidelines are very close to what would have happened anyway.

THE DURATION OF CONTROLS

From the first days of the wage-price freeze there has been discussion of "Phase II," or of what happens when the freeze expires. It has been widely recognized from the first, on the one hand, that a simple freeze, fully enforced, produces economic and political strains in a relatively short space of time, and, on the other, that if the freeze is unenforced, voluntary compliance will fade away. A rigid freeze by itself cannot last long enough to have any lasting benefits and so a Phase II program is required. Without it, the freeze has no point.

Aside from the issue of enforcement, the basic problem with controls is that the adjustment to inflation by the private economy has proceeded so far that innumerable contracts already incorporate inflationary anticipations. Recent wage contracts have provided for large increases, especially in their first year. The price increases required by these wage increases have not all been put into effect at this time. If they are entirely suppressed, either through economic depression or through controls, many firms will find themselves in difficult financial positions. The upshot of this analysis is that without the renegotiation of existing wage contracts dramatic progress in reducing the rate of inflation will not be possible.

To a much smaller degree, a similar problem exists with the costs of corporate capital. The cost pressures, as seen by the individual firm, are not as obvious for debt costs as for labor costs because debt contracts provide for a constant interest rate whereas labor contracts provide for rising wage rates. For example, per $1,000 of debt, an extra 3 percent interest costs the firm $30 per year, or $90 over three years. The same figure of $90 over three years could have come about had the debt contract called for 1 percent extra interest the first year, 3 percent extra the second year, and 5 percent extra the third year. With the steady 3 percent extra the firm expects to have a lower profit rate the first year and a higher profit rate the third year as prices rise but interest costs stay the same. But the expectation of higher prices and therefore higher profit the third year is necessary to balance the lower profit the first year in order to justify borrowing at the higher interest rate. Except for the difference in the time when the extra costs are increased, the debt case is identical to the wage case.

During the past five years, corporations have undertaken a rapid expansion of their capital investment, financing much of it with high-interest debt. If substantially less inflation occurs than corporations expected, the ex post real rate of interest will prove to be higher than expected. Corporate profits, accordingly, will be lower than anticipated. Indeed, they have been below normal for some time.* If the economy is sufficiently depressed that corporations are unable to increase prices very much, the high debt service many of them face will force dividend cuts and perhaps in some cases, bankruptcy. If the economy is strong, firms surely will try to raise prices to cover these high fixed costs.

The nature of the dilemma is clear. Individuals and firms have gone a long way in adjusting to inflation. Wage and debt contracts have been written under the assumption that inflation over the next several years will average, say, 4 percent per annum. Even if temporary controls are successful in damping inflationary expectations and affecting the new contracts signed as the old ones expire, once the freeze is lifted the old contracts not yet expired will resume force. And these contracts—both wage and debt contracts—are not consistent in my view with a quick reduction of inflation to around, say, 2 percent per annum (GNP deflator) *and* the maintenance of a vigorous business recovery. The existing wage contracts can be ignored only if it is assumed that all price increases prompted by the wage increases have already occurred.

Given this analysis, existing wage contracts cannot be permitted to resume force in Phase II if a dramatic and sustained reduction is to occur in the inflation rate. Ideally, interest costs on outstanding debt issued in the period since 1965 should also be scaled down, but this problem is not serious since interest is a far smaller fraction of firms' costs than wages and salaries. However, an issue of equity may be raised since creditors receiving interest at the old rate will have a higher real yield than anticipated if inflation is in fact suppressed. The issue here is no different from that which surrounds wage earners who happened to get large increases just before the freeze, or happened to have signed contracts before the freeze that provide for second- and third-year wage increases above the overall wage ceiling adopted for Phase II. Equity, and probably proper resource allocation as well, will require that *relative* wages and real interest rates be restored to "normal" levels. In the case of wages this restoration will require either that wage increases just prior to the freeze be rolled back, or that frozen wages be permitted to catch up.

---

*See Arthur M. Okun and George L. Perry, "Notes and Numbers on the Profits Squeeze," *Brookings Papers on Economic Activity 3* (1970):466–72.

Personally, I believe it will not be possible either to roll back wages that were substantially increased just prior to the freeze or to scale down the interest rate on outstanding bonds issued since 1965. The most that can be done, it seems to me, is not to permit existing wage contracts to resume force to the extent that they provide for future wage increases above the Phase II ceiling.

If mild controls take the form of a wage-price board with power to roll back wage and price increases deemed excessive, some of the problems connected with determining formal ceilings will be avoided. However, if too strict a definition of "excessive" is imposed, the number of cases that will come to appeal may make the procedure unworkable, while a definition that is too lenient will rob mild controls of all effect.

On balance, I expect the politically possible controls that will emerge will ensure a price performance not much different from what would have occurred in their absence.

THE RISKS OF CONTROLS

Some of those who favor temporary controls share my misgivings but nevertheless are eager to make the experiment. Even if the control effort collapses, something may have been gained and little will have been lost. Of course, if a thoroughgoing experiment works as poorly as I predict, it should at least end for some time the political pressures for controls. On the other hand, if the Phase II controls are not strict, failure of controls to work may only produce pressures for more stringent enforcement. Since the public has been promised more than mild controls can deliver, if they fail the danger is that semipermanent comprehensive controls will be invoked. Enforcement of controls of any variety is unlikely to be easy. Definition of "goods" and "services," and the large number of individual cases, will require many arbitrary decisions. The difficulties and dangers of bringing individual wage and price determinations into the political process on top of the many economic and other issues already there should not be ignored.

In my view, however, the major damage likely to result from controls is a postponement of the achievement of a stable full employment economy with a reasonably stable price level. I believe that there is no feasible method, including controls of the severity acceptable in our society, that would permit a quick return to both full employment and price stability. Controls may have the effect of hiding the genuine short-run conflict between full employment and price stability and lead to monetary and fiscal policies that are more expansionary than is consistent with progress toward the objective of sustainable economic stability.

AN ALTERNATIVE PROGRAM

As in the sailing analogy, "doing something" is not always better than "doing nothing." I am prepared to defend the basic prefreeze monetary and fiscal policies as superior to those now being followed. But this is not to say that the prefreeze policies were the best of all possible policies.

The basic aim of economic policy at this time should be to maintain a steady but moderate expansion. The immediate objective should be to push unemployment down to 4½ to 5 percent by the end of 1972. It seems likely that if unemployment is pushed much below 4½ percent no forces will operate to depress the rate of inflation.

However, further action could certainly have been taken. A strong case can be made for attacking some of the structural causes of high prices and excessive unemployment. It should be emphasized that the word used here is "high" and not "rising." Structural deficiencies in the economy raise the level of unemployment consistent with stability in the rate of inflation, but do not by themselves cause the inflation. But while structural reforms were being put into effect the result would be downward pressure on some wages and prices. This transitional effect would be most welcome, given the present public concern over inflation, and would help to generate support for the reforms.

Steps could have been taken—through executive action where possible and submission of new legislation where necessary—in at least the following areas: (1) modification or elimination of minimum wage laws; (2) modification of the tax laws to provide for the inclusion of all corporate profits rather than dividends alone in the definition of personal taxable income of common stock shareholders, in order to encourage increased dividend payouts and discourage corporate agglomerations; (3) antitrust action leading to dissolution of large firms in excessively concentrated industries; (4) elimination of farm price supports to reduce the cost of food; (5) elimination of regulation of transportation fares and rates; (6) elimination of tariffs and quotas on imported goods and services; (7) strengthening of retraining programs and employment services, perhaps including subsidies to encourage migration out of labor surplus areas. This list could no doubt be extended, but it is long enough to give the flavor of the reforms I would favor.

At the same time, to ease the burdens of unemployment, unemployment benefits should be extended and the welfare reform program enacted. In addition, temporary adjustment assistance should be provided to cushion the impact on individuals and firms unduly affected by the structural reforms proposed above.

The program outlined here has at least as good a chance of reducing inflationary expectations as does a temporary freeze followed by either mild controls or guidelines. The program is designed to go to the heart of the structural problems, providing extra stimulus now while minimizing the probability of overshooting the full employment mark. If overshooting can be avoided, a real possibility exists of achieving a gradual decline in the rate of inflation at the same time that unemployment is falling.

SOME CONCLUDING COMMENTS

The structural reforms discussed above would generate much political opposition. For this reason many will dismiss them as the equivalent of a "do nothing" program on the grounds that they could never be enacted. I am not optimistic about the chances for large-scale structural reforms, but I believe that some of them might be enacted, given the mood of the nation.

It is a mistake, I believe, to think that controls will be politically viable for very long. The fine reception the freeze received in its first days resulted largely from the failure to comprehend what controls involve. Most people seem to believe that the controls will be more effective on what they buy than on what they sell. My prediction is that the problems with controls will become more and more apparent as time goes on, that mild controls will prove ineffective, and that comprehensive controls will have less long-run political viability than structural reform.

I do not believe, however, that an alternative course of action exists that would ensure a prompt return to both full employment and price stability. It took five years—from 1964 to 1969—for inflation, as measured by the GNP deflator, to climb from 1.5 percent to 5.8 percent at annual rates. I am not optimistic that inflation can be reduced to the 1964 rate in the same length of time while, simultaneously, full employment is maintained.

Following 1964 the inflation rate rose relatively slowly in the face of an overheated economy, because the economy had been well adjusted to a low inflation rate. Now the economy is adjusted to a higher inflation rate, perhaps around 4 percent. This adjustment is not simply a matter of inflationary expectations. It includes countless private contracts and established methods of operation.

Now that controls have been imposed, for better or for worse, it is important that the nation learn what it can from the experiment. This process will be furthered if economists will state what they expect to occur. I have tried to make such predictions throughout this paper about administrative and political difficulties, changes in job and product specifications, and the likely outcome in terms of the GNP deflator. If in three years, say, my predictions can be shown to have been false, I will change my attitude toward controls.

Advocates of controls ought to be willing to think along the same lines. In particular, they ought to decide what type of observations in the months ahead would lead them to decide that the controls are not working and ought to be abandoned. Given the dangers that temporary controls will prove to be semipermanent, and that mild controls will escalate into a comprehensive system, the control effort must be continuously monitored.

Since the economy is so well adjusted to an inflationary environment, the cost of continued inflation at a 3 to 5 percent rate is relatively small. While it is not zero, it is low enough to be much below the cost of attempting to suppress inflation through tighter controls or a prolonged period of high unemployment. I believe that the costs of mild controls or guidelines are greater than their likely contribution, and that the controls should be phased out as soon as possible regardless of whether the inflation rate has declined. The least costly policy, I believe, is to accept the fact that inflation—very moderate inflation by world standards—is here to stay for a while. In terms of the analogy in the opening paragraph of this paper, we are sailing along in the middle of the racing fleet, not up with the lead where we belong, but not down in last place either. A conservative policy is in order. If we do not push too hard and if we avoid another inflationary boom caused by overshooting full employment, there is an excellent chance that unemployment and inflation will both decline in the years ahead.

AFTER THE FREEZE
GEORGE L. PERRY

William Poole has offered a model of incomes policy that is like balancing an egg. The policy can be far too oppressive—the egg falls left; or it can be totally ineffectual—the egg falls right. Finding a middle approach for policy that works is like trying to stand the egg on its head: It's clearly unstable and can't be done.

I don't think anyone in the administration is contemplating a permanent, comprehensive set of controls. And it is certainly not the program that I am prepared to defend or that most economists who favor an incomes policy of

From George L. Perry, "After the Freeze," in *Brookings Papers on Economic Activity* 2 (1971): 445–49, edited by Arthur Okun and George L. Perry. © 1971 by The Brookings Institution, Washington, D. C. Reprinted by permission of the publisher.

some sort have in mind. What is relevant is a middle-of-the-road program that can be adopted after the ninety-day freeze. Whether the middle road on incomes policy can work depends on the environment it has to work in. My view of the environment is different from Poole's. In the sand, the egg stands on its head very easily.

Recently I wrote about structural changes that have led to a deterioration of the tradeoff between inflation and unemployment.* There I developed measures of labor market tightness that took account of these changes and showed that labor markets had been extremely tight during the 1966–69 period. An inflation model based on these measures explained the rapid increase of wages and prices over this interval and through the first half of 1970. But even the structural changes identified there do not account for the rate of inflation the United States has been suffering recently. Labor markets are not tighter now than they were in 1965, even by my measures. Operating rates are not higher now than in the early 1960s. There is no way today's inflation can be seen as a result of tight labor markets or excess demand in product markets; those conditions exist in only a few isolated sectors of the economy. Nor can today's inflation be explained by the weight in the wage index of long-term wage settlements that are still catching up for past inflation, although these headline makers may have important indirect, demonstration effects.

Although the concept lacks theoretical elegance, I am persuaded that inflation is now perpetuated to an important degree because of high "habitual" rates of wage and price increase. Although we conceal a lot of our ignorance about the inflation process when

*George L. Perry, "Changing Labor Markets and Inflation," *Brookings Papers on Economic Activity* 3 (1970): 411–41.

we employ past changes in wages or prices to help explain the present, we have to attribute a large impact to recent experience in order to explain today's situation. But the present rapid wage increases need not imply that shifts have occurred in some well-defined labor supply curve that would lead to a model of accelerating inflation. I see no evidence for this interpretation and choose the description "habitual" to emphasize this. If this habitual situation in wage setting is interrupted, there need be no consequences for real output and employment. I am offering a treadmill explanation of the present situation. A middle-road incomes policy is designed to get us off the treadmill, down to a lower habitual average rate of wage and price increase.

In this environment, I cannot share Poole's misgiving about a middle-road incomes policy. He fears that a policy that is enforceable only against large firms and unions would find controlled firms unable to meet the demand for some of its products. In this situation, he sees customers forced to switch their purchases to uncontrolled firms, and this development leading either to broader controls or to their complete abandonment. In today's economy, would this really be a problem? Not only are markets not tight enough, but controls need not be so rigid.

I am not dissuaded by Poole's finding that, for nineteen out of ninety-eight product categories, wholesale prices rose more than 7 percent during the past year while average wholesale prices rose only 3.6 percent. Some of the nineteen were agricultural products, raw materials whose prices are set in world markets, or products fabricated from them. Some may have been industrial products whose price increases resulted from increased labor costs. We do know that the first-year cost of many wage increases was more than 3.4 percent above the average rate of wage increase. And we know that long-run productivity experience varies substantially among individual industries, so that any given change in hourly wage costs is translated into widely differing changes in standard unit labor costs. Thus Poole's reported dispersion in price behavior makes a good case for flexible controls and intelligent price guidelines. But it does not persuade me that suppressed excess demand would be a problem. We could, of course, create that problem for ourselves—say, by trying to hold the price of lumber in the midst of the current housing boom. But that straw man should not be the subject of discussion.

If the nation can emerge from the ninety-day freeze with a deescalation policy aimed at wages and prices broadly but, in practice, enforceable only in labor and product markets where market power is considerable, I would expect favorable results and only small costs. To opt for this kind of program is not to imply that oligopolistic industries and powerful unions are the main cause of the inflation. But they are a good place to concentrate an incomes policy for several reasons.

If we are to slow down the treadmill, highly visible price and wage situations are the one place in which the government can call attention to the new rules and show it means business. This kind of demonstration should help reduce the present "habitual" rate of price and wage increases in other sectors as well. I would expect weak markets over a long enough period to do it too. But that seems to be a long and costly process.

Furthermore, while these concentrated sectors did not give birth to the inflation, they have been an important factor in keeping it so healthy. Having been late to get started and having finally caught up, they are unlikely, of their own accord, to lead the way down toward price stability. That is not what union members pay their dues for. I find it somewhat contradictory that the same observers who doubt that such a limited incomes policy could work frequently stress structural changes to diminish market power among concentrated industries and unions as a longer-run inflation cure.

Finally I want limited and flexible controls because I do not want more. A price-wage board can hope to exercise control in these visible sectors and do so in a fairly flexible way. They can consider ten appeals a month with some care. They cannot sensibly monitor prices and wages everywhere. I am against comprehensive controls just as Poole is and for the same reasons. The initial ninety-day freeze is short enough—and voluntary enough—to no serious problems of efficiency. It may have been the best way to start off. But I want to emerge from it with a limited and flexible system.

The circumstances behind the present inflation make this a particularly favorable time for such a limited program. With excess demands virtually absent, it is hard to visualize significant misallocations arising from a wage standard that deescalated average wage increases to, say, a 5 percent annual rate. Why should we expect to see the steel companies, who are under scrutiny, lose workers to small, competitive firms who are not? Firms have been granting large wage increases because they have become the general pattern. If the treadmill slows, so does the wage increase that an individual firm must grant to meet its labor requirements. To raise wages faster than this, firms would have to behave irrationally just because they are not under the scrutiny of controls.

Of course, there will be some reallocations through changing relative wages, but they do not require today's average inflation rate. Resources were reallocated in the early 1960s with no loss of efficiency and with a stable price level. Nor need the resource transfer be a flow governed by wage movements in the uncontrolled sector alone. A flexible control system would permit promotions, competition for particular skills in short supply, and similar departures from any general rule.

Under a new incomes policy, I expect prices generally to be governed by costs and so to present no special problem. For the areas where market power is great, a price-wage board would monitor price movements. While excessive price increases in oligopolistic sectors are not the main cause of the recent inflation, there are reasons to guard against them: First, it is important to demonstrate an even-handed treatment of wages and prices under the incomes policy; second, we want to ensure a prompt pass-through of cost moderation into prices; third, we want to avoid the occasional instance in which administered pricing might contribute independently to inflation. The biggest problems would come from a few sectors in which classical market power is not the issue but in which prices have been rising inordinately for special reasons. If allowed to continue, these increases would make cooperation under the incomes policy in other sectors more difficult. For example, medical costs have been rising rapidly. Here the government could slow price increases by using its control over the medicare and medicaid programs.

A more difficult problem for incomes policies arises when the economy expands more and markets begin to tighten. Even here, an incomes policy should be helpful, just as I believe the guideposts were helpful in their day despite their almost totally voluntary nature. What we see as a fairly gradual tradeoff curve between inflation and aggregate market tightness arises, I believe, as an increasing fraction of only loosely connected individual markets grows tighter. Adjustments among the markets takes place continuously through changing relative wages and prices. As the fraction of tight markets grows, the price changes average out to be more inflationary. On this highly simplified view, an incomes policy that modified the absolute price increases in the tighter sectors could still permit the needed adjustments, but with less net price increase than now occurs. An incomes policy need not break down until a substantial part of the economy experienced excess demand and certainly not before markets grew much tighter than they are today.

If over the next year the price deflator for the private sector could be slowed to a 2½ percent rate of increase while real output grew at a rate that noticeably reduced unemployment, the policy would have been a clear success. Before the new initiatives, there was virtually no sign of slowdown in the inflation rate, and policy makers seemed inhibited from stimulating the economy to speed up real growth by the fear of worsening the inflation. Over the last four quarters, real gross national product grew only 2.2 percent. Even a doubling of that rate of expansion would merely have held unemployment rates near recent levels, and there was little sign that the expansion would be faster than that.

An incomes policy imposes some costs, so if inflation is really costless, we should not have one. But I take it for granted that policy will fight against a rate of inflation like the current one. This means the choice we face is between an incomes policy and letting our concern over inflation take the unemployment rate where it will. Poole's optimism that a "do nothing" policy will achieve a good result is hard to accept, not only because the result is not assured, but because the price of waiting for something good to happen is so high. I am not a sailor, and Poole is an expert, so it might be wiser to forgo his sailing analogy. Nevertheless, I always thought that on a serious voyage, sailors carried a small motor on board precisely so that they would not be at the mercy of the winds. The economic winds have not been blowing favorably, and a firm incomes policy seems a good way to stop our drifting for now.

DISCUSSION: THE POOLE AND PERRY REPORTS

BROOKINGS PAPERS

James Tobin noted that an equitable price guideline would imply price declines in industries in which productivity growth was particularly rapid. He felt that, in practice, some of these industries would pose especially difficult problems for a wage-price policy. George Perry observed that this problem would be minimized if the target of policy were a modest rate of inflation, such as 2½ percent, rather than complete price stability.

James Duesenberry thought that existing labor contracts calling for substantial wage increases, about which Poole expressed concern, were a valid problem for a new policy. Arthur Okun agreed that this was a problem in some individual contracts. But most three-year contracts were front-loaded, with large increases in the first year and moderate ones—6 percent or so—in the second and third years. In this case, the post-freeze policy could accept the wage increases provided for in existing contracts.

From "Discussion: The Poole and Perry Reports" in Brookings Papers on Economic Activity 2 (1971): 450–51, edited by Arthur Okun and George L. Perry. ©1971 by The Brookings Institution, Washington, D. C. Reprinted by permission of the publisher.

Franco Modigliani said that until just recently he had been thinking in terms of a model in which the recent wage increases were fundamentally big-union increases. In the late 1960s, the relative wages of the high-wage unions had decreased compared with those in the rest of the economy, and this was followed by some catching up. But recent events suggested to him that the pressure may be coming equally from the nonunionized sector, which nobody plans to control directly.

In reply, Duesenberry agreed with Perry's paper, noting that the rise in nonunion wages did not reflect labor shortages. It occurs because, with prices rising rapidly and big increases in the visible settlements, employers believe that the wages they pay must keep pace if they are to maintain their positions as good employers. He called attention to the system of wage surveys used to establish nonunion wages. Banks, insurance companies, department stores, and even the federal government are granting wage increases on the basis of comparability, as determined by wage surveys. These wage increases would not have accelerated without tight labor markets. But after the market pressure evaporated, there was nothing to stop the process from continuing. In this situation, a standard for the visible, well-organized sector would result in a wage slow-down elsewhere in the economy as well.

Continued from p. 646
cal year 1963 and fiscal year 1973, the study finds that there have been these increases in domestic programs: older income maintenance programs, from $28.4 to $74.9 billion; major Great Society Programs, from $1.7 to $35.7 billion; commerce, transportation, natural resources, from $7.6 to $16.5 billion; and total federal domestic expenditures (i.e., total federal expenditures minus defense, space, and foreign affairs), from $52.6 to $158.3 billion. Although GNP has been growing through this period, the percentage of GNP devoted to federal domestic expenditures has risen from 8.7 percent in fiscal 1963 to an estimated 13.4 percent in fiscal 1973. Furthermore, many of these programs may still be due for large expansions. One of the conclusions of the study is that a major increase in Social Security benefits, currently under congressional consideration, could exhaust the regular growth of federal revenues through fiscal year 1977.

The main impact of this point is the same as that of the two preceding points: namely, that the current decade is likely to see a greater conflict among objectives than in the recent past. Instead of simply *adding* things on, we may have to *subtract* as well. The diminished enthusiasm for growth (because of its conflicts with other objectives) will only heighten the conflict between public and private sector expenditures. In a word, things are "tightening up" a bit.[5]

5. Of course, all this could be altered substantially if there were a favorable "exogenous" change on the Cold War front. The end of the Vietnam War would ease the U.S. balance of payments problem and the scaling down of defense expenditures would make more resources available for civilian needs. These points, indeed, suggest that there is no economic need to fear the transition from War to Peace that our economy may some day (hopefully) make. This transition problem is discussed more fully in chapter 31, pp. 764–68.

THE ECONOMIST AND PUBLIC POLICY

We shall be taking all these matters up in more detail in the following chapters, but we should notice here that these conflicts of economic objectives do have a bearing on the role of economic analysis in public policy-making. Certain conclusions are fairly obvious. For one thing, it seems clear that, when objectives are in conflict, great attention should be given to the search for those policies that reduce, or at least do not increase, the range of conflict. Example: that full-employment policies do not hurt but assist low income groups, and thus promote a better income distribution, is a good further argument for adopting such policies. "Two (or more) birds with one stone" policies must be sought out as enthusiastically as possible.

For another thing, the great number of different and conflicting objectives should suggest skepticism about the use of single policy tools to the exclusion of all others. A range of approaches will usually be required. Decision-making theorists sometimes put this in terms of a distinction between *objectives* and *instruments*. The former concern what we are trying to achieve (full employment, stable prices, equitable income distribution, a certain rate of growth, etc.) while the latter concern the tools we may use to achieve these goals (money supply, taxes, wage-price controls, investment incentives, etc.). Under certain technically specifiable conditions, decision theory tells us that, for the model to work, the number of effective instruments used must be equal to the number of objectives. In general, the more objectives we have, the greater the number of instruments we shall have to use.[6]

Perhaps most important of all is the fact that conflicting objectives involve us in what is, after all, the heartland of economics, and especially microeconomics: the theory of choice. Indeed, we can readily see analogies between a society's choices between food and steel (competitive production possibilities) and between, say, higher levels of employment and reducing a balance of payments deficit (possibly conflicting economic objectives). Along these lines, we could represent the possible combinations of two economic objectives in a curve analogous to our production-possibility or transformation curve, as in Figure 27-1. This diagram also suggests that, as we increase the number of policy instruments utilized, we may be able to do better on both employment and balance of payments fronts simultaneously, i.e., to move out from curve I to curve II.

If we now knew how society valued these conflicting objectives, we could carry this analysis further. Suppose that we had not only the possibility curves as between these objectives, but also society's preferences as between these objectives shown via collective indifference curves, *ii* and *i'i'* in Figure 27-2. These curves are drawn convex to the origin, suggesting that as we achieve more and more of one objective it becomes increasingly important to us at the margin to achieve more of the other objective. Along the path *OM* in this diagram, the marginal rate of preference substitution between these objectives is equal to the marginal rate of possibility substitution or

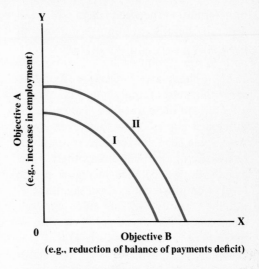

Figure 27-1. Objectives and Instruments.

By using a greater number of policy instruments (say manpower training as well as fiscal and monetary policy), we may be able to achieve more of both of two conflicting objectives, i.e., to move out from curve I to curve II.

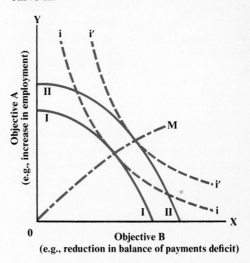

Figure 27-2. Choosing Between Objectives.

If we had collective indifference curves like *ii* and *i'i'*, then the desirable balance between Objective A and Objective B would lie somewhere on path, *OM*.

6. A pioneer in this area of work is the Nobel Prize-winning Dutch economist, Jan Tinbergen; e.g., *On the Theory of Economic Policy* (Amsterdam, 1952); and *Economic Policy: Principles and Design* (Amsterdam, 1956). We consider some of Tinbergen's thinking in another connection, pp. 769-76.

transformation between them. We will generally be able to improve our overall position by moving from a point off this path to some point on it.[7]

There are dangers in trying to carry this kind of analysis too far. What, after all, are these so-called "collective indifference curves"? Do they even exist? Also, some economic objectives are much less easily quantifiable than others. How exactly do we balance increases in the level of employment against, say, increasing the "beauty" of our cities and our countryside? The basic point we wish to make here is valid, however, This is that economic analysis lends itself very naturally to the subject of choice among alternatives, even when these choices are as complex as those facing a public policy-maker. In later chapters, whether the question is how to limit air pollution, or how to evaluate government expenditures, we shall find that economic analysis, while seldom giving us the complete answer, usually has something interesting and useful to say in public policy decisions.

SUMMARY

This chapter was concerned with some of the problems facing public policy-makers in the area of economic policy, and with the help that economic analysis might provide in the decision process.

Economic policy-making in practice is hampered by a number of difficulties: (1) expert advice on the causes of economic problems is seldom completely consistent; (2) there are frequently con-

flicts among several economic objectives that have to be resolved; (3) by the time policies are formulated and implemented, the problems may have altered; (4) exogenous factors, like war, may upset all predictions; and (5) the political process may cause conflicts between special interests and the public interest.

A survey (by Otto Eckstein) of American economic policy in the 1960s reveals some triumphs and defeats. A key triumph was that of "modern fiscal policy." On the other hand, war, political pressures, and "extreme swings" in fiscal and monetary policies prevented the decade from being an unqualified success.

In the decade of the 1970s, evidence so far indicates the likelihood of increasing conflict among economic objectives. This can be seen on the wage-price, employment, balance of payments front. Wage-price controls in the "new economic policy" of the early 1970s may lead to still further conflicts of objectives (Great Debate Four). Also, there are potential conflicts between the goal of growth and the goal of preserving the environment, and between public and private sector expenditures that may be more competitive in the 1970s than they were in the 1960s.

The existence of conflicting economic objectives suggests an important role for economic analysis. This analysis can tell us something about minimizing conflicts among objectives, about the selection of instruments to meet more than one objective, and, in general, about the theory of policy-making choice. Although the analogy cannot be carried too far, the balancing of different objectives has many of the same characteristics as economic choice between, say, food and steel. Microeconomic analysis will thus provide a useful guide (though no simple answers) to the public policy-maker.

---

7. A lengthy discussion of economic policy along the lines of the foregoing paragraphs is contained in E. S. Kirschen and Associates, *Economic Policy in Our Time,* vol. I (Amsterdam: North Holland Publishing Co., 1964), especially chap. IX.

QUESTIONS
FOR DISCUSSION

1. Sometimes economic goals are complementary—e.g., if we decrease the rate of unemployment, we will usually increase the short-run rate of economic growth—but often they are conflicting. Try to imagine circumstances in which we might have conflict between each member of the following pairs of economic objectives: (a) price stability/full employment; (b) price stability/balance of payments equilibrium; (c) full employment/balance of payments equilibrium; (d) higher rate of growth/balance of payments equilibrium; (e) higher rate of growth/ecological balance; (f) higher rate of growth/full employment; (g) price stability/efficiency; (h) efficiency/more equitable distribution of income; (i) more equitable distribution of income/higher rate of growth.

Can you imagine any further possible areas of conflict beyond those mentioned above?

2. Political pressures may affect economic policy in both a democratic and a more centralized or authoritarian political system. Discuss what some of these pressures might be under both kinds of system.

3. Using Professor Eckstein's account of the 1960s as a basis, evaluate the degree to which United States economic policy during this period was influenced by rational economic analysis as opposed to other factors (e.g., exogenous forces, political pressures, etc.).

4. On the basis of the record of prices and wages in the 1960s, would you argue for or against wage-price controls in the 1970s?

5. Explain why economic policy in the 1970s may be particularly concerned with conflicts of objectives and how economic analysis may help us sort through these conflicts.

SUGGESTED READING

Eckstein, Otto. *Public Finance.* 2nd ed. Englewood Cliffs, N.J.: Prentice-Hall, 1967.

Kirschen, E. S. and Associates. *Economic Policy in Our Time.* 3 vols. Amsterdam: North Holland Publishing Co., 1964.

Okun, Arthur M. *The Political Economy of Prosperity.* New York: W. W. Norton & Co., 1970.

Slesinger, Reuben E.; Perlman, Mark; and Isaacs, Asher, *Contemporary Economics.* 2nd ed. Boston: Allyn & Bacon, 1967, section IV.

28

International Growthmanship

In the 1950s and early 1960s, there was little doubt about what seemed the main economic issue facing the United States. It was concern about the growth performance of this country in relation to that of the other industrialized nations—especially Russia, but also Japan and the countries of the European Common Market. In the early 1970s, our concerns altered somewhat. We became more domestically oriented, and problems of income distribution and poverty within our borders took on new urgency (chapter 29). Also, we became far more worried about pollution and the other environmental costs of growth than we were a decade before (chapter 30).

Still, "international growthmanship" has by no means disappeared as a major issue of our times. If we take more than a very short-run view, there is little in our lives that will not be affected by the pattern of growth performance in the next quarter-century. In the year 2000, will the United States still be the major producer among the nations of the world, or will it be only one among many equals,

or will it (like Britain, the "workshop of the world" in the nineteenth century) have fallen to the status of a second-rank economic power? Which outcome should we prefer? What might the political and social consequences of these various outcomes be?

These questions make it clear that the problem of growth is still very much with us. In this chapter, we shall discuss economic growth in an international context, focusing especially on the growth experiences of the Soviet Union, Japan, and the Common Market countries.

MACROECONOMIC AND MICROECONOMIC ASPECTS OF GROWTH

First, however, let us try to single out some of the key issues in the discussion to follow. As in the case of wage-price controls discussed in the last chapter, economic growth ultimately involves a combination of macroeconomic and microeconomic factors. Indeed, the borderline between the two fields becomes rather vague. Capital formation, for example, is clearly an important factor in growth and yet we treat it both as a macroeconomic subject (focusing on investment demand) and a microeconomic subject (discussing such topics as the marginal productivity of capital and consumer time-preference with respect to present versus future income).

Generally speaking, any improvement either in the macroeconomic or microeconomic functioning of the economy will contribute positively to a nation's rate of economic growth. Take for example the problem of reducing unemployment, a central concern of Part Two of this book. If a country is able to use effective fiscal and monetary policies to reduce its rate of unemployment over time, it may achieve as high a rate of growth as another country with higher growth potential but with increasing unemployment (Figure 28-1).[1]

The same thing can be said about making improvements in the *efficiency* of an economy—a central concept of microeconomics in Part Three. An inefficient economy can achieve some degree of growth by moving closer to its production-possibility curve, even though that curve may not be shifting outward very rapidly. Figure 28-2 shows examples of two different patterns of growth. Both hypothetical countries have grown by the

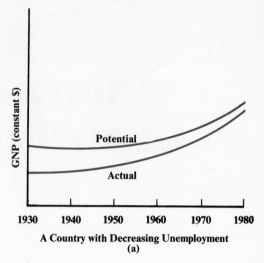

A Country with Decreasing Unemployment
(a)

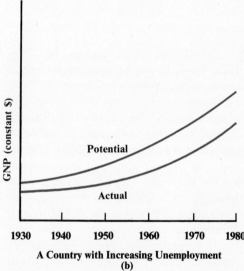

A Country with Increasing Unemployment
(b)

Figure 28-1.

The actual rates of growth of these hypothetical countries are identical although (b) has much greater growth potential. Reason: country (a) is doing a much better job of reducing unemployment.

1. The country in Figure 28-1 (b) shows the kind of pattern of growth that was predicted for the United States by the *stagnationists* (See chapter 16, p. 405). These economists felt not so much that growth opportunities would be absent as that increasing unemployment would prevent our seizing these opportunities. Or, more accurately, that if we wanted to seize them we would require a much more active monetary and fiscal policy along Keynesian lines. A latter day stagnationist could claim even today that we escaped a dismal future primarily because of the increased role of government in the past thirty years.

same amount between 1930 and 1980. The country in (a) has achieved this in no small part by reallocating its resources in a more efficient way; the country in (b), by contrast, has become increasingly *in*efficient but, either through great expansion of factor inputs or technological progress, has experienced a marked outward shift of its production-possibilities. We can now understand a comment we made in chapter 3 when we noted that the Soviet economy had exhibited both numerous inefficiencies and rapid growth. Clearly, something like the pattern of Figure 28-2 (b) was involved.

Indeed, we can go a step further, and notice that the effects of macro- and microeconomic factors on growth may be quite similar. Thus, Figure 28-1, which describes the effects of falling or increasing unemployment, is actually interchangeable with Figure 28-2, which shows the effects of increasing or decreasing allocative efficiency. Among other things, mass unemployment is clearly "inefficient" in the technical sense of that term.

What all this means is that the number of influences that conspire to affect a country's growth rate is very great indeed. In our earlier discussion of growth in chapter 16, we spoke of growth as being a result of increases in factor inputs (capital and labor force) and increases in output per unit of input (especially technological progress). Now we would want to know not only how great the increases in capital and labor force are, but also whether the capital and labor are being allocated in efficient ways, and to what degree they are being fully employed. We might get a certain rate of growth in total output because our labor force had increased, or it might come about, with a given labor force, because we had more efficiently transferred labor from low to high productivity occupations.

The situation is similar with respect to increased output per unit of input. This might come about because of the application of new technologies, or it might

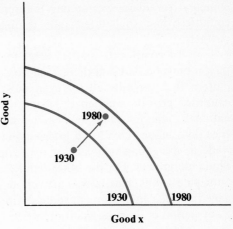

Growth with Increasing Efficiency
(a)

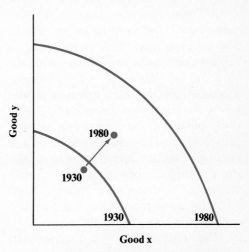

Growth Despite Increasing Inefficiency
(b)

Figure 28-2.

These two countries have grown identically between 1930 and 1980, but in quite different ways. Country (a) has made up in increasing efficiency what it lacks in expanded production possibilities.

come about because a reorganization of industry had permitted economies of scale to be exploited, or it might occur because (à la the theory of international trade) comparative advantages among different countries had benefitted all trading partners.

To complicate matters a bit further, it must be said that there is no single pattern that explains all (or even most) countries' growth experience. Take international trade, for example. Many countries (like Japan) have used international trade as a significant means of fostering economic growth. On the other hand (to anticipate a bit), Russia was actively engaged in *reducing* its foreign trade during a key period of its industrialization effort.

Many students of growth have thus come to speak of certain patterns of growth or "models," such as the "English model," the "American model," the "Soviet model," and the "Japanese model." The notion is that different countries, in different circumstances, may combine the elements of growth in very dissimilar ways, but also that each different pattern has to have a certain internal logic of its own—otherwise there wouldn't be any growth at all. The following sections and readings in this chapter attempt to suggest some of the constituents of such "growth models" in countries other than the United States. After reading the remainder of this chapter, the reader should go back to chapter 16, where we discussed the growth record of the United States, and see what contrasts and parallels he can draw.

THE SOVIET GROWTH MODEL

When he was locating the *take-off* periods[2] for various nations emerging onto the path of modern growth, W. W.

Rostow selected the years 1890–1914 for Russia. The particular years are of no special significance, but the fact that Russia's industrial revolution is often placed before the Communist revolution of 1917 is obviously of some importance. If, as many observers believe, getting started on the path of modern growth is the hardest part of the battle, and if Russia had succeeded in accomplishing this task before the radical transformation of her economic system, then our evaluation of the successes and failures of the Soviet command economy must be significantly affected.

Unfortunately, the matter is not quite so clear-cut as this. On certain points, almost everyone would be agreed: first, that Russia was an economically backward nation (as compared, say, to most Western European countries) during the nineteenth century. England, for example, had seen the end of serfdom for all practical purposes by the middle of the sixteenth century. In Russia, two centuries later, roughly 15 million out of the country's 19 million people were serfs. It was not until 1861, almost a century after the beginning of the British Industrial Revolution, that the Russian serfs were finally emancipated.

It would also be agreed that Russia had made serious efforts both before and during the nineteenth century to "catch up" with the more economically advanced nations. Peter the Great (1682–1725) launched such an effort with the particular purpose of strengthening the army and navy. His visits to England and Western Europe and his hiring of foreign technicians are well known; and he also used his state treasury directly to initiate the building of factories and new industries. In the late nineteenth century, the Czarist government financed extensive railroad construction; the state bank lent assistance to private enterprises; the

2. See pp. 380–81.

government continued to press for the entry of technicians and technology from abroad; and government tariffs were used to protect new industries. Thus, in the period of which Rostow speaks, there was without doubt very substantial economic progress in Russia: it would have seemed, indeed, that she was moving through her industrial revolution, with somewhat more active State participation, but nevertheless in a manner roughly comparable to what had happened in Europe proper.

What makes all this difficult to evaluate, however, is the succession of cataclysmic events that followed. The toll of war and revolution in Russia was enormous. It has been estimated that between 1913 and 1921, Russian agricultural output fell by 50 percent, industrial output by 80 percent, and total national income by over 60 percent. An interruption of this magnitude makes any projection of past trends a questionable procedure. What we can say is that, when Russia did resume her forward progress in the late 1920s, it was on the basis of a substantially altered political and economic system. State intervention had been significant in the past, but now it was totally dominant, and this domination was being exercised economically for the almost exclusive purpose of achieving the most rapid possible rate of economic growth.

We have spoken earlier of the problems of administering the Soviet system (pp. 77–83); now we direct our attention to the growth performance in particular. The central fact here is that, despite evidences of certain inefficiencies, the Soviet Union has shown persistently high rates of growth ever since the beginning of the first Five-Year Plan in 1928. The best Western estimates[3] are that Russian

industrial output grew between ten and eleven times from 1928 to 1961. This is a rate of growth of over 7 percent per year for thirty-three years. Agricultural production grew less rapidly during this period, but it did show at least some increase and, consequently, the overall growth rate of total national income was substantial.

Table 28-1 shows a recent comparison between U.S. and U.S.S.R. growth rates from 1913 to 1965. Comparisons of rates of growth of GNP are always extremely difficult to evaluate. In this particular case, moreover, the significance of the figures would have to be modified by our knowledge: (1) that the U.S.S.R. began at a much lower level and thus had all the advantages of coming up from behind; (2) that the periods include both World Wars I and II when Russia suffered terrible economic and other losses; and (3) that there is evidence that in the late 1960s the Soviet rate of growth was beginning to slow down substantially.[4] Some of these points cut one way, some the other. Still, the overall conclusion is clear:

The Soviet Union has clearly achieved very rapid growth over a substantial period of

Table 28-1 COMPARATIVE GROWTH RATES OF TOTAL OUTPUT (GNP) U.S.A. AND U.S.S.R., 1913-1965

Annual Average Compound Growth Rate		
	U.S.A.	U.S.S.R.
1913–38	2.0	2.8
1938–53	5.1	3.4
1953–65	3.3	6.1

These very rough estimates of growth show that the Soviet Union, beginning at a much lower starting level, has generally grown more rapidly than the United States during recent decades.

Source: Angus Maddison, *Economic Growth in Japan and the U.S.S.R.*, (New York: W. W. Norton and Co., 1969), pp. 36, 47, 51.

3. See Robert W. Campbell, *Soviet Economic Power*, 2nd ed. (Boston: Houghton Mifflin Company, 1966), pp. 124–25.

4. See Martin L. Weitzman, "Soviet Postwar Economic Growth and Capital-Labor Substitution," *American Economic Review*, September, 1970, p. 677.

time and under a very highly directed and controlled economy.

But directed and controlled in what way? *How* was this growth achieved? Or, to put it in terms of our earlier discussion, what can we say about the "Soviet model" of economic growth?

The following reading by Charles Wilber, excerpted from a longer chapter, is a systematic attempt to account for the particular aspects of Soviet growth strategy that differentiate it from our own experience, or, indeed, from that of most Western nations. Although there are always some differences of opinion, Wilber's basic points would be widely accepted by most Western experts on the Soviet economy:

THE SOVIET STRATEGY OF DEVELOPMENT

CHARLES K. WILBER

Strategies are ways of using resources in order to attain a given long-run objective. In the Soviet Union the overriding objective has been rapid economic development. As in market economies in wartime, all resources were mobilized and allocated to activities that furthered the attainment of the primary objective. Activities that detracted from that objective were suppressed or neglected.

The atmosphere and terminology during the 1930s was that of a wartime economy—bottlenecks, campaigns, assaults, and victories. As in wartime, mistakes were made and there was a great deal of waste. Economic criteria were often ignored and entire sectors of the economy, mainly the consumer sectors, were neglected. Yet, despite the lack of balance and other shortcomings in Soviet development, significant progress in the transformation of the Soviet economy to a modern economy was made in a very brief period of time.

Excerpted from Charles K. Wilber, "The Soviet Strategy of Development" from The Soviet Model and Underdeveloped Countries (Chapel Hill: University of North Carolina Press, 1969), 76–78, 83–92, 94–99, 101–4, 106–8. Reprinted by permission of the publisher.

The main features that distinguished Soviet industrial development strategy may be summarized as follows:

(1) Industry was treated as the leading sector in the development program and investment in agriculture held to the minimum necessary to allow agriculture to provide industry with a growing marketed surplus of agricultural products and an expanding source of labor supply.

(2) A very high investment (and savings) rate was maintained, because of the planners' propensity to discount the future at a low rate.

(3) An unbalanced growth pattern was adopted of allocating a very large share of industrial investment to heavy industry.

(4) In choosing among alternative productive techniques, the most advanced technology was utilized, while at the same time, the scarcest inputs—capital and skilled labor—were economized.

(a) A mixed or dual technology was adopted. Advanced Western technology with a high capital-labor ratio was favored in the basic production processes while old-fashioned methods and techniques with a low capital-labor ratio were favored in auxiliary and subsidiary processes.

(b) They utilized multiple shift operation and plants and equipment were typically kept in operation long after they would have been retired in the more advanced countries of the West.

(c) Strong preference was shown for the construction of integrated, large-scale plants, specialized with respect to product and having a high fixed cost to variable cost ratio.

(5) During the industrialization drive heavy emphasis was placed upon vocational and technical training to build up the stock of human capital and the factory itself was used as a major training device.

(6) An import-substitution policy of international trade was adopted.

INDUSTRY AS THE LEADING SECTOR IN THE SOVIET DEVELOPMENT PROGRAM

In the Soviet Union, industry has been treated as the leading sector in the development program. Consequently, investment in agriculture has been held to the minimum necessary to allow agriculture to provide industry with food, raw materials, and labor. Gross investment in agriculture accounted for 16.1 percent of total gross investment during the period 1928–32, 12.6 percent during 1933–37, 11.4 percent during 1938–41, 12.8 percent during 1946–50, 15.5 percent during 1951–55, 17.6 percent in 1956, 16.3 percent in 1957, 15.8 percent in 1958, and 15.8 percent during the period 1959–64. In 1928, at the beginning of industrialization, 49.2 percent of the net national product originated in agriculture, forestry, and fisheries. By 1958, the share of agriculture in net national product had declined to 22.1 percent. Agriculture has continuously received, therefore, a smaller share of gross investment than its share of net national product. In addition, agricul-

American Stock Photo

Novolipetsk Iron and Metal Works. Russian industrialization from the early days on emphasized iron and steel, capital goods, and other heavy industry.

ture's share in net investment has been much lower. Naum Jasny estimates that up to 1938 net investment was zero, because of the vast decline in livestock, and that half of the prewar investment in agriculture was lost during World War II.

Soviet investment in agriculture was sufficient to generate enough agricultural output to feed the growing industrial work force, to provide the required raw materials for industry, to provide for export needs, and to release the labor necessary to fill the new jobs. This enabled the modern industrial sector to be constructed. However, the Soviets probably went too far in emphasizing industry and minimizing investment in agriculture. That is, more investment in agriculture would probably have increased the growth rate of national income. At the same time, however, it should be remembered that the agricultural investment picture would look much better if the blunders of livestock collectivization and World War II had not occurred.

THE CHOICE OF AN INVESTMENT RATE

Once having made the decision to embark upon a development program, the choice of an appropriate investment rate assumes prime importance.

In the Soviet Union, the rate of gross investment increased from 12.5 percent of gross national product in 1928 to 25.9 percent in 1937 and 28.1 percent in 1955. Over fairly long periods in the past in Argentina, Canada, Germany, Norway, the United States, and the Union of South Africa, the gross investment rate exceeded 20 percent. What is distinctive about the Soviet experience is the speed at which the rate was increased. Furthermore, in comparison with underdeveloped countries generally, investment rates over 20 percent are very high.

The reason that a high investment rate is desirable, of course, is because it rapidly increases the stock of capital in the economy. The size of the stock in any period, in turn, is a main determinant of total output in that period. If the capital-output ratio does not significantly increase, higher rates of investment will yield higher growth rates of total output.* In the Soviet Union, incremental capital-output ratios only increased, on a gross basis, from 3.53 in 1928–40 to 3.69 in 1950–58, and actually declined

on a net basis from 2.76 to 2.60. No capitalist economy has combined over long periods relatively low incremental capital-output ratios with high investment rates. Kuznets has pointed out that "... the distinctive feature of the USSR record is that so much capital formation was possible without an increase in the capital-output ratio to uneconomically high levels."

What was the optimum rate of investment for the Soviet Union in the 1930s? There is no uniquely determinate economic solution to this question. Increasing the rate of investment today means lowering the share of consumption in gross national product (though not necessarily the absolute amount) in the present in exchange for a larger income and consumption in the future. A lower rate of investment will yield greater consumption in the present, but lower amounts in the future, than would higher rates of investment. The key to the solution, therefore, is the trade-off between present and future consumption contained in a community's social time preference function.

A central planning board cannot simply imitate the rate of investment that would emerge from individual time preferences. The social perspective of the future and the time horizon of a community differ significantly from those of an individual. More importantly, the choice of investment rate cannot be determined independently of the choice of investment projects and technique. The decision on the investment rate, is dependent on the allocation of investment and vice versa. In the Soviet Union particularly, the decision on allocation greatly affected the final determination of the rate of savings and investment. This problem of allocation between sectors and projects is the next aspect of the Soviet experience to be considered.

*[We have met the concept of the capital-output ratio earlier—in the form of its reciprocal, the output-capital ratio (pp. 394). If K is capital, Y is income (or output) and I is investment, the capital-output ratio is K/Y. The "incremental" (or marginal) capital-output ratio is $\Delta K/\Delta Y$ or $I/\Delta Y$. It was the reciprocal of this last term, which we discussed in chapter 16.]

THE ALLOCATION OF INVESTMENT AND UNBALANCED GROWTH

Exponents of unbalanced growth have stressed that if a country decides to industrialize, the correct development strategy is not to seek an optimal allocation of resources at any given time nor to dissipate scarce resources by attempting to advance on all fronts simultaneously but, rather, to concentrate on a few major objectives most conducive to transforming the economy to a higher stage. Efficiency is attained in the dynamic sense of finding the most effective sequences for converting a stagnant, backward economy into one which is dynamic and modern. In other words, to be breathlessly climbing a peak in a mountain range is considered more important than standing poised on the crest of a ridge in the foothills.

There is not an infinite number of alternative investment allocation patterns. Because of complementarities and indivisibilities each individual investment project cannot be evaluated in isolation. The construction of a steel industry requires increased coal mining and investment in steel using industries.

"... problems of economic planning seem to acquire a resemblance to the problems of military strategy, where in practice the choice lies between a relatively small number of plans, which have in the main to be treated and chosen between as organic wholes, and which for a variety of reasons do not easily permit of intermediate combinations. The situation will demand a concentration of forces round a few main objectives, and not a dispersion of resources over a very wide range."[†]

The Soviet Union pursued a "shock" strategy of bottlenecks successively created and resolved. Thus, Soviet planning concentrated on certain key branches in each plan to overcome particular bottlenecks. Scarce capital and managerial talent were then concentrated on these key targets. This gave Soviet planning its peculiar nature of planning by "campaigning." During the first Five-Year Plan the main target was heavy industry with particular emphasis on machine building. During the second and third Five-Year Plans the target was again heavy industry with metallurgy, machine building, fuel, energetics, and chemicals singled out for emphasis. This emphasis on key branches yielded high growth rates. The average annual rates of growth in Soviet heavy industry between 1928/29 and 1937 were 18.9 percent for machinery, 18.5 percent for iron and steel, 14.6 percent for coal, 11.7 percent for petroleum products, 22.8 percent for electric power, and 17.8 percent for all heavy industry. Sectors which did not contribute directly to further growth (consumption) were neglected while sectors which enhanced growth (capital goods) were emphasized.

Growth tempos such as these caused acute shortages and strains. The industrial bottlenecks which appeared then became the new targets. This is unbalanced growth with a vengeance. However, economic planning of the type used by the Soviet Union during the industrialization period, and by extension in less developed countries today, is a relatively crude affair. "Campaigns,"

[†]Maurice Dobb, *Soviet Economic Development Since 1917* (London: Routledge & Kegan Paul, 1960), p. 6.

with their ensuing bottlenecks, substitute for the profit motive in keeping the planning bureaucracy on its toes.

"... the entire **rationale** of the Soviet 'campaign' approach to economic planning rests upon ... the need to stimulate not only the executants but also the controllers ... Campaigns are among other things, a means of goading the goaders, of mobilizing the controllers, of providing success indicators for officials at all levels.
"... Hence the vital role of campaigns as controller mobilizers. Hence the value of bottlenecks as stimulators to effort."‡

This does not imply that the Soviets deliberately created bottlenecks or that they understood the meaning of unbalanced growth. Rather, the bottlenecks and unbalanced growth were necessary by-products of the high growth tempos that the planners adopted.

As an economy becomes more sophisticated, "campaign" planning becomes less appropriate. The number of products multiply and "balance" becomes more important. Since structural change is slower, and firms and industries are operating closer to equilibrium, marginal calculations become more feasible. This seems to be the present situation of the economy of the Soviet Union. Failure to pull up lagging sectors, particularly agriculture, and to develop more sophisticated planning methods is causing

‡Alec Nove, *The Soviet Economy* (New York: Frederick A. Praeger, 1961), p. 292. Also, see Gregory Grossman, "Soviet Growth: Routine, Inertia and Pressure," *American Economic Review* 50 (May 1960): 62–72. Preplanned co-ordination of investment projects through central planning does not conflict with unbalanced growth and "campaigns." Unbalanced growth is a strategy designed to obtain a dynamic equilibrium through time, and "campaigns" are a means of implementing the plan.

the Soviets severe problems and slowing their growth tempo.

CHOICE OF TECHNOLOGY AND SOVIET DEVELOPMENT STRATEGY

Another feature of Soviet industrial strategy involves choice of technology in production. In Soviet literature this problem resolved into a question of whether capital should be devoted to large-scale units using advanced and expensive technology or to smaller-scale enterprises using simple tools and employing relatively more workers. It is often argued in Western economic writings that since, practically by definition, there is a shortage of capital and a surplus of labor in less developed countries, labor-intensive techniques should be used wherever possible so as to conserve on capital and provide as much employment as possible.

Dual Technology

Soviet development policy has been aware of this conflict between requirements of progress and factor endowment and has dealt with it by adopting the strategy of a "dual technology." On the one hand, in the key industries, they utilized to the maximum the advantage of borrowing the most advanced technologies developed in economies with very different factor endowments. On the other hand, they allowed for these differences by utilizing manual labor in auxiliary operations and by aiming at high performance rates per unit of capital instead of per man. In this fashion they obtained the best of two worlds and achieved the overall effect of saving capital.

In many Soviet plants it is common to find the most advanced capital equipment in the basic processes and, at the same time, the most primitive labor-intensive methods in maintenance, intra-plant transport, and materials handling. In such enterprises as the Gorky Automotive Plant, which was a direct copy of the Ford River-Rouge plant, they allowed for their lower level of labor skills by redesigning job descriptions so that each worker performed fewer and simpler tasks. Thus, the Soviets obtained the advantages of advanced technology, conserved scarce capital in auxiliary operations that did not limit output, and utilized their relatively abundant unskilled labor.

Multi-shift Operation

Another way capital was used intensively was by multi-shift operation of plants. In both the prewar and postwar periods, many Soviet industrial plants operated on a two-shift basis. Three-shift operation, although introduced in manufacturing plants in the early 1930s, has been discarded except in those industries where the technology demands it. It was soon discovered that the third shift was needed for repairs, clean up, and the production of deficit parts. Multi-shift operation reached a peak in the Soviet Union in 1932 when the shift coefficient (the ratio of total man-days worked to those in the main shift) reached 1.73. It declined slightly in the mid-1930s. When figures were next published in 1959 the coefficient for all industry had declined to 1.55. These figures may be compared with figures for United States manufacturing in 1959–60 of 1.30. In England and leading European industrial countries the ratio is even lower. It is clear that Soviet practice regarding multi-shift operation of her plants deviated from the pattern in the United States and other advanced Western countries.

The difference in multi-shift operations stems partly from the relative scarcity of capital in the Soviet Union and the concern of Soviet planners to minimize the use of capital. With labor and output measured as flows and capital as a stock, two-shift operation, for example, reduces the capital-labor ratio by one-half. If capital is also measured as a flow of services to take account of more rapid physical wear and tear under multi-shift operation the reduction would be somewhat less. As a consequence of multi-shift operation the Soviets have been able to adapt a more advanced technology with a higher capital-labor ratio than would have been possible with single shift operations. Thus, the benefits of modern technology were reaped while at the same time minimizing the demand for capital, which is the scarce factor.

The Soviets have also used another means to obtain this result. While progressively adding the newest capital equipment they have continued to operate obsolescent plants far beyond the time possible in a competitive market system. Here again, within limits, the factor endowment of the Soviet Union was taken into consideration.

Plant Scale and Design

Another consideration regarding Soviet choice of technique concerns the scale and design of fixed plants. The Soviets exhibited a strong preference for large-scale, integrated plants with high fixed-to-variable cost ratios and specialized with respect to product. This emphasis upon size has often been pointed to by Western economists as an apt illustration of the irrationality of Soviet planning. In a number of instances this was undoubtedly the case. Indeed, the Soviet leadership itself became concerned with wastes involved and roundly condemned the "gigantomania" of the early 1930s.

In addition to building large plants, the Soviets tended to build highly integrated plants. During the early stages of the Soviet industrialization drive in the late 1920s and early 1930s, the Soviet economy lacked the well developed system of separate supplier plants necessary to support a complex, highly specialized industrial economy. The transport system was overloaded, as well, and the delivery of parts or materials from other plants could not be relied upon. Under such circumstances new plants, if they were to operate successfully, had to be constructed along highly integrated, less specialized lines than was originally intended by Soviet planners. In the automotive industry, for example, the major plants included every process from the pouring of metal to shipping the finished product. They also manufactured repair parts for machine tools and even made their own special tools and equipment in the absence of other suppliers.

THE ROLE OF VOCATIONAL AND TECHNICAL TRAINING IN THE FORMATION OF HUMAN CAPITAL

A basic feature of Soviet development strategy is the stress upon vocational and technical training and the use of the factory itself in the educational process. From the outset of the industrialization drive the Soviets have indicated a profound appreciation of the importance of human capital in the development process and have shown a willingness to commit substantial sums and effort to build up not only a skilled labor force but also professionals able to lead and direct the industrial effort.

Most of the training was on-the-job in character, but numerous schools known as F.Z.U. (factory and work apprentices' schools) were opened at the factories to train apprentices for skilled trades. During the first Five-Year Plan the F.Z.U. schools trained over 450 thousand skilled workers. Each year since the first Five-Year Plan about 100 thousand skilled workers have been trained through these factory apprentice schools. In addition, an annual average of 2.5 million workers and employees between 1940 and 1959 were taught new trades and specialities on the job, and an additional 5.0 million were trained to improve their skills each year. Also, many workers learned their "three R's" in factory-run evening schools.

In the Soviet Union, formal education has been devoted principally to those subjects most amenable to classroom methods of instruction and which are considered to be especially important for economic development. The natural sciences and engineering have been particularly emphasized. Night schools for adults have been extensively used to train technicians. Table A summarizes the Soviet emphasis on development oriented subjects at the higher educational level.

THE ROLE OF INTERNATIONAL TRADE

The final question that arises in a discussion of development strategy is the role of international trade in the Soviet model. Foreign trade in the Soviet Union has always been subordinated to the requirements of economic development and central planning. It is seen as a means to an end— the end being the attainment of needed imports.

Table A.   U.S.S.R., 1928–1959, AND U.S.A., 1926–1958: NUMBER
OF GRADUATES OF HIGHER EDUCATIONAL ESTABLISHMENTS

Field	U.S.S.R.	U.S.A.	U.S.S.R. as percent of U.S.A.
Engineers	1,117,800	620,300	180.0
Science majors	430,000	704,400	61.0
Medical doctors	420,000	181,700	231.2
Agricultural specialists	389,200	166,400	233.9
Sum of above fields	2,357,000	1,672,800	140.9
Humanities, social sciences, etc.	1,772,300	5,198,600	34.1
All fields	4,129,300	6,871,400	60.1

Source: Warren W. Eason, "Labor Force," in *Economic Trends in' the Soviet Union*, eds. Abram Bergson and Simon Kuznets (Cambridge: Harvard University Press, 1963), p. 63.

Both political and economic considerations shaped Soviet trade policy. The Soviet Union undoubtedly would have preferred to increase its imports through long-term credits but in the world situation of the 1930s was unable to do so. A high degree of self-sufficiency was deliberately pursued because of fear (rightly or wrongly) of further foreign attack.

Viewed from static equilibrium analysis the Soviet strategy of import substitution—substituting higher cost domestic production for imports—led to a misallocation of resources and a reduction in real national income. However, if the Soviet policy of allocating investment to import-replacing industries instead of to export-oriented industries is viewed dynamically, it is possible that this policy increased the rate of growth enough to cover any static allocation losses. In the case of the Soviet Union, the import-replacing industries were the heavy capital-goods industries and the export-oriented industries were in nondurable consumer goods, wood products, and agriculture.

During the first Five-Year Plan the Soviet Union exported relatively large quantities of agricultural products, consumer goods, and wood products in return for capital goods that enabled them to expand their import-replacing industries. While the Soviet Union probably pushed its import-substitution policy too far, there is no reason why other countries must pursue the strategy to the same degree. International trade can certainly alleviate some of the difficulties of economic development. Trade is particularly important for smaller countries because it can enable them to develop without establishing the entire range of modern industry. But, at a minimum, industrialization in those areas of potential comparative advantage seems necessary. Comparative advantage shifts over time with changes in relative development patterns between countries. This makes static equilibrium analysis inapplicable in the context of economic development.

It is necessary in ending this chapter on Soviet development strategy to emphasize again that the policies comprising this strategy have application mainly to a backward economy trying to achieve the one overriding goal of economic development. The methods are basically those of a war economy. As such, when the economy has reached some level of sophistication, the time for war economy methods has passed. The required economic strategy then changes from one of maximum concentration of available resources on a few main goals towards successively greater dispersion.

THE JAPANESE ECONOMIC "MIRACLE"

In the period after the end of the Marshall Plan in the early 1950s, it became common to discuss various economic "miracles" in Western Europe: the very rapid growth of West Germany, then of Italy, then of France. The persistent rapid growth of the Soviet Union, which we have just discussed, was also very much noted. It was actually only a bit later that economists began to notice that the real economic "miracle" hadn't taken place in Europe at all, but in Asia. From 1950 to 1960, Japan had the highest rate of growth of any major industrial nation in the world. Not only did she outmatch the Soviet Union, but her growth was substantially higher even than that of the "miracle" countries of Western Europe: twice that of France, 40 percent higher than that of Italy, and 25 percent higher than that of West Germany. Indeed, by the 1970s Japan had become the third-ranking industrial producer in the world.

This phenomenal rate of growth —often averaging around 10 percent per year in *real* GNP—clearly could not have taken place without preparation. Since the reading below focuses primarily on Japan's postwar experience, let us say just a few words about the earlier Japanese development that laid the groundwork for what followed.

The key dates in this earlier history are probably 1853 and 1868: the former representing the arrival of Commodore Perry and the opening of Japan to Western culture and influence; the latter representing the political revolution that led to the restoration of the emperor (Emperor Meiji) and to the installation of a number of vigorous samurai-bureaucrats in government who began promoting modern-style Western growth. As in the case of the British Industrial Revolution (pp. (376–81), one cannot stress discontinuities too much—there is increasing evidence of economic progress in the pre-Meiji (Tokugawa) period, nor was Japan totally closed off from Western ideas before Perry's visit. Still, the last half, and especially the last quarter of the nineteenth century, does seem a particularly decisive period in Japan's development. Something very much like a take-off seems to have occurred at this time.

Now the Japanese model necessarily shows some resemblances to the Soviet model that we have been analyzing, if only because of the similar objective of increasing the growth rate. Thus, both countries had to find some way to raise the rate of investment so as to accelerate capital formation. Both countries had to introduce new technologies and, since both countries were economically backward during the nineteenth century, they were each heavily reliant on foreign technological inventions and innovations. Furthermore, since not everything could be done at once, both countries exhibited dualistic economies—i.e., the existence of both modern capital-intensive methods and traditional labor-intensive methods side by side over long periods of time.

Still, the Japanese experience was affected by the fact that her fundamental conditions were in many ways quite different from those of Russia. She was very densely populated even in the nineteenth century; unlike Russia, she was highly deficient in natural resources, including many resources necessary for modern industrial growth; and, finally, her political "revolution" was not so drastic as that of the Russians in 1917. These differences probably account for the following aspects of the Japanese model that differentiate it from that of the Soviet Union:

Agriculture

Although the Japanese relied, as did the Russians, for agriculture to provide support for the industrial sector, there was no vast institutional reorganization of agriculture in Japan comparable to collectivization in the late 1920s and 1930s in the Soviet Union. The Russian picture is one of a heavy reorganization of agriculture, tremendous exactions from the agricultural sector to support industrial development, and stagnant agricultural productivity until fairly recent years. Japan, by contrast, appears to have secured at least moderate increases in agricultural output throughout the key period of the last quarter of the nineteenth century. Some commentators believe that it was such progress in the traditional sectors of the Japanese economy that made possible the "initial establishment and subsequent development of the modern economy."[5] Given her heavy population density, it is doubtful whether Japan could have subjected agriculture to quite such abusive treatment as did the Russians in the late 1920s and 1930s and still achieved general economic development.

International Trade

If Japan was somewhat more dependent on the traditional sector than the Russians, she was certainly substantially more dependent on international trade. While the Russian experience in the 1930s involved increasing isolation from the rest of the world, the Japanese experience involved an "invasion" of foreign markets

to secure the exports necessary to pay for the vital raw material and industrial imports without which modern growth could not take place. Even with her extraordinary export efforts, Japan's history in the nineteenth and twentieth centuries was dotted with balance of payments' crises because of her exceptional need for foreign imports (reflecting, in part, the deficiencies in her natural resource endowment mentioned earlier). Her initiative in seeking foreign markets, for silk and textiles in the nineteenth century, and for every conceivable product in recent times, has undoubtedly been a highly significant feature of the Japanese achievement.

Role of the State

Finally, we must mention the quite different political situation, affecting virtually every aspect of the development process. While the Soviet picture is one of almost total State domination of the earlier phases of industrialization, the Japanese picture is quite mixed. The Japanese state did, of course, stimulate capital formation, but there was also substantial private saving and investment, encouraged in the nineteenth century by an extremely unequal distribution of income, and also by historically low consumption patterns. More generally, the relationship of the Japanese State and private business, and especially the large, oligopolistic *Zaibatsu*—huge firms like Mitsubishi, Mitsui, and Sumitomo, with interests in a great variety of financial and industrial enterprises—has been very involved and complex. In some cases, in the early Japanese industrialization effort, the government would act as innovator in a particular industry, establishing new enterprises that were then subsequently turned over to large private capitalistic firms. In sum, as compared to the Soviet picture of opposition between private and public insti-

---

5. Kazuschi Ohkawa and Henry Rosovsky, "A Century of Japanese Economic Growth," in *The State and Economic Enterprise in Japan,* ed. William W. Lockwood, (Princeton, N.J.: Princeton University Press, 1965), p. 68. It should be noted, however, that the *degree* of Japan's progress in agriculture in this period is still a subject for debate among historians.

tutions, the Japanese model has involved more of a cooperative or partnership arrangement.

With these background comments in mind, let us turn to Japan's exceptional achievements in the postwar period.

JAPAN:
Achievements and Prospects

G. C. ALLEN

Japan, having successfully overcome the difficulties caused by her immense material losses and the post-war disorganization of her economy, came within a few years to rank with the leading industrial countries of the world. Her 'recovery' may be said to have been accomplished by the middle 1950s. By then she had restored financial stability, rebuilt in large part her industrial and commercial organization, increased manufacturing output to twice that of the middle 1930s, and raised income a head above the pre-war level. An achievement of this magnitude was remarkable when viewed against the adversities with which the post-war world had afflicted her. Her traditionally intimate economic relations with North East Asia had been destroyed by territorial changes and political upheaval. Her former specialization in textiles proved to be ill suited to the demands of post-war markets. Her technology had been cut off from the sources of invention just when they were gushing copiously in the outside world. Meanwhile, her old centres of initiative had been dissolved, and resources for re-equipment were scarcer than ever at a mo-

Adapted from pp. 247–62 in *Japan's Economic Expansion* by G. C. Allen, published by Oxford University Press under the auspices of the Royal Institute of International Affairs. Reprinted by permission of the publisher.

ment when they were most urgently required.

There can be little wonder that the outlook was considered bleak. The rehabilitation of the economy called for qualities of resilience and energy which the Japanese, in their exhaustion and despair at the end of the war, seemed unlikely to command. Foreign opinion about Japan's capacity to find a successful issue from her troubles was for some years deeply pessimistic, largely because attention in the outside world was focused on the persistent weakness of the export trade. Up to 1955 the Japanese themselves shared this opinion. At that time they still spoke of themselves as 'marginal suppliers' of manufactures for international trade, and they feared that such recovery as had occurred was insecurely based on American 'special procurement' and on temporary shortages of capacity in competitor-countries.

The contrast in temper between that period and the early 1960s is striking. Pessimism and diffidence have given place to an easy self-confidence, The present mood can find ample justification. Since 1950 Japan has achieved a rate of growth which is the marvel and envy of the rest of the world. She cannot claim to have enjoyed 'stable growth', but a least she has been skilful in coping with the recurrent balance-of-payments crises which her rapid development has provoked, and she has so far avoided serious inflation.

In manufacturing industry, where her major successes have been won, she has found a new dimension. Her accomplishment is demonstrated not merely by the growth of industrial output as a whole but also in the wide extension of her range of products. Trades that went unremarked during the pre-war decade now rank among her largest industries, and several entirely new branches of manufacture have grown to great size. Many of her leading industries still rest on her resources of skilled and assiduous labour, but the most notable developments of the last seven or eight years have occurred in industries that depend on advanced technology. The result is that her industrial activities are now centred upon the production of metal, engineering, and chemical goods, including the latest innovations among them, and Japan has joined the company of the half a dozen countries which are responsible for the bulk of these products. Among the leaders her position has constantly improved. For instance, in the non-Communist world she has lately come to occupy the second place in steel production; she is the largest producer of ships and of some kinds of electrical apparatus; she is second only to the United States as a manufacturer of synthetic fibres. In the generation of electric power and the production of finished textiles, machinery (including machine tools), motor vehicles, plastics, and certain kinds of chemicals, she holds rank with the four or five largest producing countries. . . .

The factors mainly responsible are:

(1) The closing of the technical gap by the import of new technology.

(2) An exceptionally high rate of investment buttressed by a very high rate of saving, both institutional and personal.

(3) The direction of investment into uses which yielded quick returns and the absence of wasteful investment in armaments.

(4) The large reserve army of workers at the beginning of the period of growth and the successful transference of huge numbers from low-productivity to high-productivity occupations.

(5) The reconstruction of the *Zaibatsu* and the creation of other business groups capable of organizing development.

(6) A monetary system and policy which were successful both in providing industries with the finance needed for expansion and also in cutting back credit quickly whenever the economy became 'overheated'.

(7) A taxation system which kept clear of measures likely to curb industrial investment and damage personal incentives.

(8) The effective use of official controls over foreign trade and payments. . . .

Some other comments on Japan's economic experience are necessary. First, it should be emphasized that Japan today possesses one of the most highly competitive economies in the world. This characteristic is revealed most obviously by the conduct of small and medium-sized firms in manufacturing industry and distribution, but it is also present among large-scale enterprises. Indeed, the fierce rivalry among oligopolists has undoubtedly been responsible for much of the breathless innovation and lavish investment in new equipment during the last few years. The progress of Japan, the flexibility of her costs and prices, and her quick adaptation to economic change owe much to these conditions. Yet keen competition and the boisterous struggles of free enterprise are not there associated with *laissez-faire.* On the contrary the government in regulating, guiding, and directing the economy, during the post-war period as in the past, has made an essential contribution to the achievement. The public sector itself is small by modern standards. Many industries which in the majority of Western countries are under State ownership, in Japan are in private hands. Nevertheless, the government has made constant use of a number of powerful instruments in shaping the economy, e.g., the official banks which direct capital resources into the preferred fields, fiscal devices, foreign trade controls, and 'indicative planning'.*

This combination of free enterprise and government control imposed at key points in the economy has been a familiar feature of Japan since early Meiji. Throughout the modern era up to the Second World War responsibility for development and innovation had been shared between the State and the *Zaibatsu.* During the war economic authority became more highly centralized in the government, and the eclipse of the Zaibatsu after 1945 and the circumstances of the Occupation confirmed this concentration. For a time private entrepreneurial initiative seemed to have lost direction and purpose. After 1952, however, the broad pattern of leadership in industry and commerce was redrawn. While the government, aided by a highly competent bureaucracy, steadily gained assurance and skill in its administration of economic policy, some of the economic empires of the past were reorganized and other powerful centres of initiative arose. In this way the forms of economic direction were restored and its efficiency augmented.

Responsibility for reconstruction was,

---

*[For the meaning of *indicative planning*, see pp. 690–91.]

of course, shared with the Americans. For over six years after the end of the war the Occupation authorities were in control of policy, and even after 1952 the United States government exerted a powerful influence upon it. In certain respects, the effect of the intervention, at any rate in the early post-war period, may have been to retard recovery; but on balance there can be no doubt that the American association with Japan's affairs during the Occupation period conferred signal benefits upon her. Without the aid so abundantly provided between 1945 and 1951, Japan would almost certainly have sunk deeper into economic chaos. The same conclusion applies to the subsequent period when, although her trading enterprise was handicapped by limitations imposed by the United States on her dealings with China, she enjoyed the advantage of a vast dollar expenditure at a critical stage of her reconstruction. Then in 1960 the flow of private American capital began, with great benefit to the balance of payments. . . .

The Occupation period during which the foundations of future growth were laid can now be viewed in perspective. Even the most censorious foreign commentator must pay tribute to the generosity of the Americans in providing resources for rebuilding Japan's economy, and to their enthusiasm, if not their tact, in reshaping her institutions. And when Americans themselves are reflecting glumly on the great stream of dollar aid which maladministration or corruption, in one recipient country after another, has allowed to run to waste, they can perhaps find some solace in recalling one Asian protégé who has used their benefactions to good effect. For their part in these transactions the Japanese also deserve credit. They showed a sure political instinct in their readiness to co-operate in the institutional innovations imposed by the victors. A people less opportunist in temper and less adroitly governed might well have rejected the chance of testing the merits of what the Americans have devised for them. Since on balance the innovations were instrumental in promoting both economic and social progress, the

LOS ANGELES TIMES PHOTO

An Assembly Line at Nissan Motor Co., Oppama, Japan. The ability of the Japanese to capture a significant share of world export markets has been a major factor in postwar Japanese growth.

Japanese were rewarded for their inspired empiricism.

No one acquainted with their history is likely to be surprised at their acquiescence on this occasion. The Japanese have never hesitated to use foreign models when they have been devising institutional constructions apt for some new national purpose. They have always welcomed novelties and have then proceeded to adapt them to their needs.

Up to the middle 1950s Japan inhabited two worlds. To the Asian she appeared as a modern state masquerading as undeveloped; to the Westerner, and to many Japanese themselves, it was the vestigial remains of a pre-industrial society that were most prominent. Peasant agriculture, though far more efficient than elsewhere in Asia and yielding higher financial returns than before the war, was still overstocked with labour. The same was true of the great mass of very small units in manufacturing industry and the service trades where (though by no means universally) productivity, incomes, and conditions of work compared unfavourably with those of large modern establishments. In manufacturing industry these contrasts are fast disappearing. In other sectors also the dichotomy is becoming less and less obvious. It was once usual to contrast the efficient and up-to-date railway and shipping services with the ill-developed system of motor transport, handicapped as it was (and still is) by the primitive roads. The proposed heavy investment in both urban and trunk roads may well remove this contrast by the end of the present decade. In distribution the most casual observer was impressed by the coexistence in the great cities of the huge departmental stores and the multitude of family shops with a minute turnover. The distributive trade as a whole is now on the eve of a transformation brought about by the introduction of supermarkets, and many of the small shops are likely to disappear in the years ahead. Again, the premises occupied by large industrial, financial, and commercial concerns are indistinguishable from their counterparts in the West, and the most recently built are impressively well-equipped. Yet throughout the country the standard of housing accommodation remains exceedingly low.[†] This contrast may persist for many years, but the present Income Doubling Plan, which looks forward to a substantial increase in housing investment, should gradually make it less glaring. Thus throughout all branches of the economy there is a trend towards uniformity.

In the past Japanese economists were much preoccupied with the problem of 'disguised unemployment' or 'underemployment' in the small-scale sectors of industry, agriculture, and the service trades. This condition had been associated with the insufficiency and biased distribution of capital in a society in which the labour supply was rapidly increasing. Throughout the modern era a high proportion of new fixed investment was directed into a narrow range of industries, mainly those concerned with capital and intermediate goods, where for technical reasons factor-proportions were rigid. The result was that agriculture and most of the consumption-goods industries and service trades, where factor proportions were elastic, attracted comparatively little investment, and they were left to absorb, in low-productivity occupations, a large share of the increasing labour supply. Such a distribution of capital was probably justified in a period when rapid development depended on the establishment of basic industries, especially those concerned with power and transport. It has been argued, however, that in the early 1950s an excessively high proportion of the new investment was directed by the government and its financial agencies towards a few large-scale undertakings. The productivity of Japanese industry as a whole might have benefited if the smaller establishments had been able to obtain improved equipment and to gain readier access to new techniques. However this may be, it is evident that as soon as the demands by large-scale industry for labour became of such a magnitude as to absorb the bulk of the recruits to the labour market and also to draw off the surplus workers from agriculture, the problem of underemployment was on the way

---

[†]The Japanese point out that people who are comfortable at work but uncomfortable at home have every inclination to 'keep at it'!

to solution. Once the small firms were forced to pay rates of wages as high as those in the large firms, they could survive only by modernizing their methods and so raising their productivity. The same forces at work in agriculture have led to a substitution of capital for labour to an extent unimaginable only a few years ago. It is true that Japan by the standards of industrial Western countries still retains a high proportion of its occupied population in the primary industries and in small-scale industry and trade. For some years to come she will have reserves to draw upon (more particularly, reserves of female labour), and they will help to sustain her rate of growth. But the time when massive and apparently inexhaustible reserves were available has gone.

It is clear that in many respects Japan has entered upon a new phase in her economic development. . . . The time is in sight when some of the most familiar contrasts between Japan and the West will have faded . . . and Japan is likely to meet with difficulties of choice in the field of social as well as of economic policy similar to those that have long perplexed Western countries.

Neither her recent successes nor her capacity for dealing with the problems that lie ahead can be assessed solely in economic terms. The proximate forces responsible for the high felicity of her economic achievement are not difficult to identify and to analyse. But observers of the process of development are tempted to extend their curiosity towards the deeper springs of this unique accomplishment. It may perhaps be rewarding to refer briefly to the social and political conditions that made possible the emergence of Japan as a modern State in early Meiji, and underlay her subsequent achievement, and then to consider how far those conditions have persisted into the present era. The causes of the early development may be summarized as, first, a political and social system that presented opportunities for the exercise of leadership to persons (private individuals or bureaucrats) whose interests lay in promoting economic change; secondly, an inheritance of organizing capacity and skill; and finally, institutional arrangements conducive to the

rapid accumulation of capital. The society that satisfied these conditions was hierarchical, drawing its leaders mainly from a privileged class constantly invigorated by the entry of men of talent from outside its ranks. When, by a conjunction of political and social changes, the leaders were enlisted on the side of modernization and economic development, they found in the mass of the people long trained in obedience to authority, a ready instrument to their hand. There was a fine legacy of skill in textiles and metal manufactures, and certain family businesses had a long experience of large-scale organization. The capital accumulation required for development was a function of the unequal distribution of income characteristic of that type of society and of the propensity of the wealthy to apply their savings to industrial and commercial development. The taxation system which succeeded the old feudal arrangements was very regressive, pressing lightly on high personal and corporate incomes and harshly on the peasants. These conditions persisted with comparatively little modification up to the Second World War.

The war, the inflation, and the post-war reforms destroyed powerful sections of the oligarchy, chiefly the military cliques and the rural landlords. These formed, however, the most conservative or reactionary element in society, elements which in Japanese opinion were largely responsible for the catastrophe of 1945. The dismissal of the chief 'architects of ruin' still left power highly concentrated and, in spite of the growth of parliamentary institutions, the leadership of the official and business oligarchies has not yet been seriously disturbed. Labour organizations have arisen and their economic foundations, once weak, have been strengthened by the changes in the labour market. But the political side of the movement has not yet acquired the power that it has long enjoyed in Britain and other European countries. On the other hand the mood of the people has changed. They now breathe the air of freedom. They are less pliable than in the past and more concerned with enjoying the amenities of life which prosperity has presented to them. The release of energy by the social and political reforms immediately after the Second World War probably deserves a high place among the causes of growth.

It will be generally conceded that the progress that began in the Meiji era cannot be explained solely in terms of economic calculation. As in all great movements in human affairs, in the material no less than in other aspects of national life, an element of grandeur was present, a touch of the idealism which, as Alfred Marshall said, 'can generally be detected at the root of any great outburst of practical energy'. In Japan it was patriotic fervour that supplied the impulse to achievement and at the same time made it possible for her to undergo massive material changes without the disruption of social unity. In the end this sentiment was polluted and drove the country to a disastrous indulgence in military aggression. Present-day Japanese have been deeply affected by this experience and have displayed new powers of self-criticism. Yet self-criticism is more likely to chill the ardour of ambition than to inspire practical endeavour. It cannot furnish a clue to the enterprise and self-confident leadership of recent years. Where, then, is an explanation to be found? Japanese writers, teachers, and politicians lament that their country has failed to discover a new source of inspiration or a strong unifying purpose. One may suggest to them that a certain ideological scepticism is to be expected of the victims of an age of faith, and it may be that material progress itself has proved to be a sufficiently absorbing pursuit. Perhaps the explanation is that the challenge presented to Japan after her defeat was of a kind that called forth the full energies of her people and concentrated them on economic achievement. The disaster that had overtaken her former policy was so complete that she was impelled to set out on a new course undistracted by regrets for past ambitions. . . .

Japan today moves with assurance among the most progressive nations of the world. But the problems which are now emerging out of the revolutionary economic changes of the last decade are different in kind from those which have previously confronted her. Their solution will make heavy demands on her resources of administrative ingenuity, political wisdom, and social tact. The problems, economic and political, are for the most part those with which advanced industrial societies have long been familiar. Japan has taken her place with them and now shares their perplexities. It is yet another question to ask how far the transformation in her economic life will permit the survival of the more graceful qualities of the old Japan—the fine manners, the etiquette that relieves the acerbities of personal relations in a materialistic society, the aesthetic traditions, the strong sense of reciprocal obligation among individuals that corresponds to the recognition of public duty in the West. To such a question, which is similar to that posed in all countries during periods of rapid economic progress, no easy answer can be found. There are Japanese who turn a cold eye on the past and view ancestral institutions and conventions with indifference or distaste. But others have been able to combine a liberal and modern outlook with respect for aesthetic and social traditions. One can at least hope that their influence will prevail.

THE UNITED STATES AND WESTERN EUROPE

While the twentieth century growth of Russia and Japan are clearly massively important developments on the international scene, the traditional home of modern industrial growth—Western Europe—should not be overlooked either. Indeed, with the entry of the United Kingdom and a number of smaller countries into the continental Common Market in the early 1970s, this organization came to possess a political and economic potential that could conceivably make it more than a match for Russia, Japan, *or* the United States.

While it would be too long an assignment for us to discuss the enormous variety of European experience during the past few decades, it is nevertheless of interest to ask whether the growth records of these countries are, in general, different from or roughly the same as that of the United States since the end of World War II. An approximate answer to this question is given in Table 28-2. It is clear from this table that, whether the measure be total national income, national income per person employed, or per capita national income, European countries did substantially better than the United States between 1950 and 1964. In the particular case of national income per capita, European rates of growth averaged more than twice our own during this period.

The significance of such comparisons is something else again. Roughly speaking, there are two explanations of

this phenomenon. The first argues that European countries (with some notable exceptions, like Britain, which on the whole did *less* well than the United States) managed their economies more effectively than we did in the postwar period. It may be claimed, for example, that our tax, expenditure, and monetary policies have inhibited growth. In a widely discussed book, *Modern Capitalism: The Changing Balance of Public and Private Power,* a British observer, Andrew Shonfield, pointed out that this country was suffering particularly deep recessions as compared to most European countries:

Plainly the special difficulties of the United States in recessions are bound up with its relatively slow secular rate of economic growth. But it may also be that the slow rate of growth is itself largely caused by the incompetent handling of business cycles. If the bungling of the recovery following the 1958 slump is regarded as normal, and it turns out that any *vigorous economic expansion is habitually aborted in the womb, then the feebleness of the American average performance during the second half of the 1950s and the early 1960s would be readily explicable.*[6]

Neither Shonfield, nor anyone else, would regard business cycle policy as the whole explanation. Nevertheless, a number of observers in the late 1960s came to wonder if our overall governmental policies, or perhaps our seeming lack of overall policies, might not account for the growth differential. There was increasing interest in such approaches as the French use of *indicative planning*. This system involves a particular blend of governmental and private action in which the govern-

Table 28-2   GROWTH RATES OF REAL NATIONAL INCOME (TOTAL, PER PERSON EMPLOYED, AND PER CAPITA), 1950-64
(In percentages)

Area	National income		National income per person employed		National income per capita	
	1950-64	1955-64	1950-64	1955-64	1950-64	1955-64
U.S.	3.5	3.1	2.2	2.0	1.8	1.4
N.W. Europe	4.8	4.4	3.9	3.6	3.9	3.3
Belgium	3.4	3.5	2.8	3.0	2.8	2.9
Denmark	3.6	4.8	2.7	3.5	2.9	4.1
France	4.9	5.0	4.7	4.7	3.8	3.7
Germany	7.1	5.6	5.3	4.3	5.9	4.3
Netherlands	4.9	4.3	3.7	3.1	3.5	2.9
Norway	3.8	3.9	3.6	3.7	2.9	3.0
U.K.	2.6	2.8	2.0	2.3	2.2	2.1
Italy	5.6	5.4	5.2	5.4	4.9	4.7

Source: Edward F. Denison, assisted by Jean-Pierre Poullier. *Why Growth Rates Differ: Postwar Experience in Nine Western Countries* (Washington, D.C., Brookings Institution, 1967), p. 18.

6. Andrew Shonfield, *Modern Capitalism: The Changing Balance of Public and Private Power* (London: Oxford University Press, 1965), p. 16.

ment draws up a plan that "indicates" (but does not "command") certain patterns of business activity that, in total, will meet national goals in a coherent way. If there is a reasonable nucleus of significant business firms who will be responsive to such state initiatives, then *indicative planning* might achieve some of the happier effects of a centralized system without the compulsion that is required in a rigid command economy.

In short, one type of explanation of the differential in growth rates is that our public policies affecting the growth of the economy were relatively deficient. Usually, a more vigorous, directional role for the State was prescribed.

The second—and quite different—line of explanation is more fatalistic. It is based on the general hypothesis that, excluding the special difficulties of the take-off period, the countries with lower levels of per capita income who are "catching up" will grow faster than the front-runners. In a very rough and ready way, this hypothesis would cover the basic facts we have been discussing—i.e., that Japan has been growing faster than Russia, which has been growing faster than Western Europe, which has been growing faster than the United States. The obvious fact is that the "catching-up" countries have a vast reservoir of modern technology to draw on, and that, even if scientific advance and innovation on the frontiers of knowledge stopped altogether, they would still have the possibility of several decades of economic advance.

This second explanation is both generally plausible, and supported by more specific evidence. The following reading is from a 1967 study of comparative growth rates, directed by an outstanding expert on the causes of economic growth, Edward F. Denison. It gives some backing to the thesis that our relatively

unfavorable growth performance in the 1950s and 1960s was due more to the fact that we were already operating from very high levels of per capita income, than from any overall failures of economic policy.

Contrast Between Europe and the United States
Edward F. Denison

In the first of the television debates between John F. Kennedy and Richard M. Nixon that were held during the Presidential election campaign of 1960, then-candidate Kennedy stated that he was not satisfied with the lowest rate of growth among all industrialized nations, that it was time to get America moving again. This theme recurred throughout his campaign.

If comparisons are made over a period long enough to iron out fluctuations in the business cycle, but not extending back beyond the postwar period, Kennedy's original statement that United States growth was the lowest among industrialized countries needs little amendment. Among countries covered in this study, only the United Kingdom and perhaps Belgium are exceptions (the position of Belgium depends on the exact period compared). In the period ahead, comparisons will be influenced by the accident that age distributions will yield a much larger employment increase in the United States than in Europe, but the United States can match European growth rates of income *per person employed* over an ex-

tended period only if Europe fails dismally to grasp its opportunities.

The analysis of this book indicates that the low past and prospective standing of the United States in the "International Growth Rate League" is not an indication of poor economic performance. Rather, it has come about because the same sort of changes produce larger percentage increases in national income in Europe than they do in the United States and, in addition, there are opportunities to increase efficiency in European countries that do not exist to the same degree in the United States.

The European countries have higher growth rates but they have not, on balance, done more in any relevant sense to obtain growth. It is worth recapitulating some of the data that support this conclusion.

Consider labor, which represents 75 or 80 percent of total input. From 1950 to 1962 the United States increased employment more than any other country except Germany. Insofar as changes in employment simply reflect changing numbers in the working ages, this is, to be sure, hardly germane. But the employment increase in the United States was so big only because large numbers of women and children and young people who were also attending school entered the labor force. Given the demographic factors, the American people were doing more to add to the numbers at work than the people of any other country.

Hours of work and education are key determinants of the quality of a year's work and both can be altered by individual and social decisions. Only France did not reduce the hours of full-time workers appreciably more than the United States. No European country matched the increase in the education of the labor force that was achieved by the United States. For all the Northwest European countries this is shown by any measure I can devise, and Italy is an exception only if comparisons are based on the percentage change in years of education, a very poor measure. It is possible that the gap between the pace of work on the continent and that in the United

States has been reduced by increased fluidity and improved motivation on the continent; but even if this speculation is correct, it indicates only that the continental countries were eliminating a deficiency in comparison with the United States.

Consider capital, which represents 15 or 20 percent of total input. Here, the situation was mixed. Percentage increases in the stock of nonresidential structures and equipment and inventories were generally larger in the European countries than in the United States and Europe obtained more growth from this source. The difference was accentuated by particularly low capital formation in the United States during the period of deficient demand from 1958 to 1962—a deficiency subsequently remedied—but it would probably have been present in any case. One cannot easily judge the extent to which larger percentage increases in the stock of this type of capital in Europe stem from the difference between European and American conditions. The much lower capital-labor ratio in Europe is perhaps relevant, and in earlier chapters the complications introduced by differences in the absolute level of the stock and by differences in relative prices were discussed. By any simple test, however, the United States has done less than Europe to stimulate growth by investment in nonresidential structures and equipment and inventories. This appears to be the only important field in which the United States was doing less.

The United States had exceptionally large increases in the stock of dwellings and in international assets, and obtained more growth than any of the European countries from these sources. Over the 1950–62 period these sources almost entirely offset the bigger contribution from domestic business capital obtained by Northwest Europe as a whole, and the offset was more than half in all the individual countries except Germany and the Netherlands. Investment in dwellings contributed less to growth, as measured, than an equal amount of investment in enterprise capital might have but it is not clear that it contributed less to welfare. The contribution made by international investment should not be overlooked. If, in the future, American investment in Europe is impeded by restrictions imposed in response to the American balance of payments problem, or by European opposition, it will be unfortunate for growth in both areas.

The total percentage of national income saved in the form of physical capital was higher in Europe (especially Germany, the Netherlands, and Norway) than in the United States when percentages for each country are based on output valued in its own prices, though generally not when output in all countries is valued in the same prices. The former is the more appropriate measure of effort, the latter is more pertinent to raising the national income.

Consider resource allocation. The United States has been as successful as any European country and more successful than most in reducing misallocation associated with agriculture and nonfarm self-employment of a fringe character. It has not made comparable changes in barriers to international trade but the potential gains available, especially from any action the United States could take without European reduction of barriers to United States exports, were slight.

Finally, consider advances in knowledge. The United States has devoted far more of its resources to technical research and development than any of the European countries. It also seems clear that it has devoted more attention both within business and in schools of business administration to advances in business organization and management practices. In this area the European effort has concentrated upon learning what the United States is already doing and upon adapting and stimulating the adoption of American practices.

The conclusion, I believe, is clear. Although most of the European countries have achieved higher growth rates than the United States, this was not because they were doing more to obtain growth. They were able to secure higher growth rates only because they were operating in a different environment. Conditions were very different with respect to factor proportions; to misallocation of resources; to the existing level of technology, management, and general efficiency in the use of resources; and to economies of scale. Some have supposed that the United States could have matched the growth rates of European countries if only Americans had done as the Europeans did. I conclude that this is simply not so.

Comparisons with the postwar growth rates of European countries, therefore, do not provide grounds for dissatisfaction with the American growth record. The point needs stressing because the conditions that enabled Europe to obtain higher growth rates are not exhausted. Aside from short-term aberrations Europe should be able to report higher growth rates, at least in national income per person employed, for a long time. Americans should expect this and not be disturbed by it. Nothing in this analysis suggests that the conditions making for higher European growth would continue to operate if the European countries were to reach American levels of national income per person employed.

A comparison provided earlier should be recalled for perspective. In 1960, national income per person employed was 69 percent larger in the United States than in Northwest Europe and 150 percent larger than in Italy. This is the comparison most favorable to Europe, obtained when the output of all countries is measured in United States prices. If, with equal validity, the prices of European countries are used in the comparisons, United States national income per person employed was 117 percent larger than that of Northwest Europe and 317 percent larger than that of Italy. Thus, the level of output per person employed in the United States is still far above levels in Europe. In percentage terms these differentials have been narrowing. But from 1950 to 1964 none of the eight European countries narrowed the absolute gap when output is uniformly measured in United States prices. This means, of course, that from 1950 to 1964 none achieved a larger absolute increase than the United States in national income per person employed. This situation cannot be expected to continue indefinitely and, indeed, the comparisons showed larger increases after 1955 in France and Norway than in the United States. But it will be a long time before American levels will be approached.

The performance of the American economy is not, of course, all that it might be. I doubt that inability to produce and distribute a large and rising total of goods and services—the aspect of economic life with which this book is concerned—should be listed among its defects. But an appropriate evaluation would have to be based on a comparison of United States achievements with United States possibilities. It cannot be based on casual comparisons of the United States growth rate with the rates of countries having quite different opportunities for growth.

SUMMARY

The full study of economic growth involves an interweaving of macroeconomic and microeconomic elements. In general, a country's growth rate will depend upon the increases in its factor inputs, labor and capital, its technological progress, changes in the degree of employment of the factors and in the efficiency of their allocation among different employments. Different countries have combined the elements of growth in different ways, leading many economists to speak of different *models* of growth, as, for example, the "Soviet model" or the "Japanese model."

Economic growth under the Soviet Five-Year Plans followed upon earlier Russian economic progress in the late nineteenth and early twentieth centuries, but also took place after massive disruptions in the economy due to the revolution and World War I. Soviet growth was characterized by heavy emphasis on industry above agriculture, very high investment rates, emphasis within industry on heavy industry, dualistic technology, vocational and technical training, and an import-substitution international trade policy. This model involved State domination of the economy through industrial planning and, in agriculture, forced collectivization of farming.

The Japanese model of growth involved many of the same elements as the Russian model, since Japan in the nineteenth century as also an economically "backward" nation and since she was also striving to "catch up" with the West. However, a number of differences did exist because Japan, as compared to the Soviet Union, faced a different population problem (more densely settled), a different resource situation (fewer resources), and a different political situation (the Meiji Restoration was not as violent or as total a reconstruction of society as the Russian revolution was). In general, these differences are reflected in the fact that there was a greater increase in agricultural productivity, a much heavier reliance on international trade, and a more mixed pattern of State intervention and private initiatives in Japan during her take-off than was the case in Russia. Japanese growth since World War II has been phenomenal, exceeding even that of the Soviet Union.

A comparison of growth rates among nations in the Western world shows that the United States has ranked fairly low in "international growthmanship" during the past two decades. Some commentators explain this in terms of deficient American growth policies, although a more reasonable explanation (which can also be applied to the Russian and Japanese experience) is that, once a country gets on the track of modern growth, it is those countries furthest behind that tend to grow most rapidly.

QUESTIONS
FOR DISCUSSION

1. In the light of this chapter's discussion of economic growth in an international context, what features of U.S. growth (see chapter 16) seem to you to be (a) fairly universal or (b) rather specific to the particular conditions of the American economy?

2. Explain why it is true that, if the capital-output ratio is constant, a high rate of investment will yield a high rate of economic growth. What factor's might alter the value of an economy's capital-output ratio? From the point of view of growth, would a society prefer a high or a low capital-output ratio?

3. "When a country is 'catching up,' its growth pattern is necessarily different from that of a country, like Britain or the United States, that was one of the 'early developers.'" Discuss with reference to (a) capital formation, (b) technological change, and (c) economic efficiency.

How might attitudes to (a), (b), and (c) above change as the "catching up" economy became more "mature"?

4. "Although many of the world's underdeveloped nations have flirted with the 'Soviet model' of growth, the true and natural 'model' for these countries is that of Japan." Discuss, paying special attention to such problems as population, agriculture and trade.

5. Do you think that the joining together of the major West European economies in the Common Market will tend to increase the rates of growth of these countries? Explain what growth factors might have this effect.

6. If you had the choice, would you prefer a society that took its potential growth in the form of increased goods or increased leisure? Does society have this choice? Do you personally have this choice?

SUGGESTED READING

Bergson, Abram. *Planning and Productivity Under Soviet Socialism.* New York: Columbia University Press, 1968.

Broadbridge, Seymour. *Industrial Dualism in Japan.* Chicago: Aldine Publishing Co., 1966.

Campbell, Robert W. *Soviet Economic Power.* 2nd ed. Boston: Houghton Mifflin, 1966.

Lockwood, William W., ed. *The State and Economic Enterprise in Japan.* Princeton: Princeton University Press, 1965.

Shonfield, Andrew. *Modern Capitalism: The Changing Balance of Public and Private Power.* London: Oxford University Press, 1965.

Supple, Barry, ed. *The Experience of Economic Growth.* New York: Random House, 1963.

29
Income Distribution And Poverty

It was common in the 1950s and early 1960s when economic growth, as discussed in the last chapter, was a prime subject of interest among statesmen and economists, to argue that growth had deprived the issue of *income distribution* of most of its bite. The problem of income distribution—who gets how much?—had, of course, been a very important one in the history of economics. Even those economists who had been most impressed by the "efficiency" of a private enterprise system had usually admitted that it might not do very well in terms of income distribution. The British classical economist David Ricardo, for example, was generally for laissez-faire in economic matters but he was also aware that landowners under such a regime might reap increasingly large incomes over time—incomes that

they had done nothing in particular to deserve. Henry George, the American economist, used Ricardian logic to argue for heavy taxes on rents in his famous "single tax" scheme. Karl Marx, who was actually very much in debt to Ricardo in terms of economic theory, made bourgeois income distribution (especially as between capitalists and the proletariat) a central objection to capitalism.

But economic growth seemed to have solved, or at least to have taken most of the sting out of this issue. If the pie was constantly getting bigger, who cared whether one's particular share of the pie was growing or diminishing relative to someone else's? When everyone could count on getting more, how the extra income was distributed seemed a relatively minor matter.

In the 1970s, however, this view of the question of income distribution seems wholly unsatisfactory. Seldom in the history of our nation has the striving for greater equality—and not in economic matters alone—been more to the forefront than now. Why is this so? Especially why is this so after the great economic advances of the post-Depression–World War II period?

Observers will naturally differ on the explanation, but the author's view is that two main elements have been involved. The first is that there are aspects of economic growth that not only do not moderate but actually *intensify* the concern over income distribution. When the poor are very poor—like the poor, say, in an underdeveloped country where survival is often literally at stake—then economic growth, by raising living standards to some minimum level of comfort, may satisfy the primary aspirations of the lower economic classes, even though the society's income distribution is grossly unequal. As the society, including the poor, gets increasingly better off, absolute gains in income may be less important than *relative* gains. If I don't have enough to eat, my main concern is more food. If I do have enough to eat, my main concern may be my position relative to my neighbor's position. In a rich society, inequality can be more galling than in a poor society.

The other element in the picture is that in those cases where something close to "absolute poverty" exists, the situation seems particularly disgraceful when the surrounding society is so comfortable. Poverty in the affluent society is hard to forgive because it is, in principle, easily correctable.

These two considerations have done much to make the subject of income distribution one of the most heatedly discussed economic topics in America in the early 1970s.

INCOME DISTRIBUTION IN GENERAL

There are many different ways of analyzing a society's income distribution. In Part Three, when we were concerned with the microeconomics of the price system, we discussed income distribution in terms of factor prices and factor "shares."[1] In this kind of analysis one begins with the competitive case in which factors of production are paid the values of their marginal products and then takes up the deviations from such payments caused by various forms of market imperfection and by economic uncertainty and change.

From the point of view of social welfare, however, the more interesting view of income distribution has to do with the sizes of the incomes going to different groups in the society. This concern, in turn, may be about *absolute* incomes or about *relative* incomes.

In some ways, the question of the absolute levels of income seems the most important. Do the poor in a given society have enough food to eat, clothing to wear, shelter from the elements? This is obviously a basic concern for any society.

Still, as we have said, the question of relative income distribution can, in an affluent society, be felt almost as keenly. What proportion of the income of the society goes to the top 5 percent of rich families; the top 10 percent? How much is left over for the bottom quarter or half? What are the trends in this relative distribution of income over time?

---

1. See especially chapters 21 and 26.

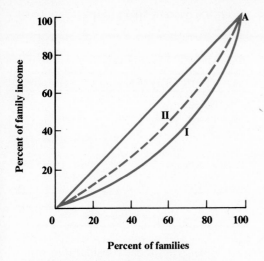

Figure 29-1. Income Distribution as represented by Lorenz Curves.

Curves I and II each show an income distribution that departs from complete equality. Many people feel that in view of the problem of relative poverty, our society should attempt to move toward a more equal income distribution; e.g., from a distribution like that of Curve I to a distribution like that of Curve II.

The general pattern of a society's income distribution in this relative sense can be illustrated as in Figure 29-1 by what is called a Lorenz curve. If there were a perfectly equal distribution of income in the society, then income distribution could be prepresented by the straight line, *OA*. Twenty percent of the households have 20 percent of the income; 60 percent of the households have 60 percent of the income, and so on. The degree of *in*equality of the income distribution can then be measured by the extent to which the curve departs from the straight line. Curve I represents a greater, and curve II a lesser, inequality of income distribution.

There is some slight evidence to suggest that, in the very long run, economic growth tends to move a society in

the direction of a somewhat greater equality of income distribution (i.e., moves the economy from curve I towards curve II).[2] However, this process is uncertain and slow, and it also varies greatly from country to country.

INCOME DISTRIBUTION IN THE UNITED STATES

What of the income distribution in the United States? Does poverty exist in the affluent society? What trends can we observe?

In the mid-1960s, using an income of $3,000 or below as the standard of being "poor," the President's Council of Economic Advisers drew this picture:

One-fifth of our families and nearly one-fifth of our total population are poor.

Of the poor, 22 percent are nonwhite; and nearly one-half of all nonwhites live in poverty.

The heads of over 60 percent of all poor families have only grade-school educations.

Even for those denied opportunity by discrimination, education significantly raises the chance to escape from poverty.

But education does not remove the effects of discrimination: when nonwhites are compared with whites at the same level of education, the nonwhites are poor about twice as often.

One-third of all poor families are headed by a person over sixty-five, and almost one-half of families headed by such a person are poor.

Of the poor, 54 percent live in cit-

2. See Simon Kuznets, *Six Lectures on Economic Growth* (New York: The Free Press, 1959).

ies, 16 percent on farms, 30 percent as rural nonfarm residents.

Over 40 percent of all farm families are poor. More than 80 percent of nonwhite farmers live in poverty.

Less than half of the poor are in the South; yet a southerner's chance of being poor is roughly twice that of a person living in the rest of the country.

One-quarter of poor families are headed by a woman; but nearly one-half of all families headed by a woman are poor.

When a family and its head have several characteristics frequently associated with poverty, the chances of being poor are particularly high: a family headed by a young woman who is nonwhite and has less than an eighth-grade education is poor in 94 out of 100 cases. Even if she is white, the chances are 85 out of 100 that she and her children will be poor.

This description emphasizes both the extent of poverty in the United States and how it falls with a particularly cruel burden on certain groups in American society—the blacks, the relatively uneducated, the elderly, the poor southern farmer, the fatherless household, and so on.

A second description, consistent with the first, but giving a sharper sense of the rate of progress toward solving the poverty problem is suggested by Table 29-1. In the decade 1959–68, the number of persons below the "poverty level" in the United States fell from 39.5 million to 25.4 million and the percentage of such persons from 22.4 to 12.8. Furthermore, if we went back some years earlier, we should find that there was a fairly considerable reduction of income inequality in the United States between the early 1930s and the end of World War II. Over the past forty years the percentage of Americans with incomes of less than $3,000 (in constant dollars) has probably fallen from

60 or 65 percent to perhaps 10 percent in the early 1970s.

Table 29-1				
POVERTY IN THE UNITED STATES (1959–1968)				
Persons Below Poverty Level			Year	
	1959	1963	1966	1968
Number (millions)	39.5	36.4	28.5	25.4
Percent (%)	22.4	19.5	14.7	12.8

Source: Statistical Abstract of the United States, 1970.

Clearly, then, considerable progress has been made if we are thinking in terms of *absolute* poverty. But what of *relative* poverty? And also what can we say about the effect of various governmental policies—tax policies and also transfer payments—on the trend of income distribution?

The following reading gives an authoritative presentation of where matters stand in the United States, and includes some suggestions for possible tax reform:

The Rich, The Poor, and The Taxes They Pay

Joseph A. Pechman

I. THE DISTRIBUTION OF INCOME

Despite the proliferation of sophisticated economic data in this country, the United States government does

Excerpted from Joseph A. Pechman, "The Rich, the Poor, and the Taxes They Pay," The Public Interest No. 17 (Fall 1969), pp. 20–25, 32–34, 41. Copyright © National Affairs, Inc. 1969. Reprinted by permission of the publisher and the author.

not publish official estimates of the distribution of income. Such estimates were prepared by the Office of Business Economics for a period of years in the 1950s and early 1960s, but were discontinued because the sources on which they were based were acknowledged to be inadequate. We have data from annual field surveys of some 30,000 households conducted by the Bureau of the Census, as well as from the annual Statistics of Income prepared by the Internal Revenue Service from federal individual income tax returns. But both sources have their weaknesses: the Census Bureau surveys systematically understate income, particularly in the top brackets; tax returns, on the other hand, understate the share received by low income recipients who are not required to file. Nevertheless, if used with care, the two sources provide some interesting insights.

Before turning to the most recent period, it should be pointed out that a significant change in the distribution of pre-tax income occurred during the Great Depression and World War II. All experts who have examined the data agree that the distribution became more equal as a result of (a) the tremendous reductions in business and property incomes during the depression and (b) the narrowing of earnings differentials between low-paid workers and higher-paid skilled workers and salaried employees when full employment was reestablished during the war. The most authoritative estimates, prepared by the late Selma Goldsmith and her associates, suggest that the share of personal income received by the top 5 percent of the nation's consumer units (including families and unrelated individuals) declined from 30 percent in 1929 to 26.5 percent in 1935–36; the share of the top 20 percent declined from 54.4 percent to 51.7 percent in

the same period. The movement toward greater equality appears to have continued during the war up to about 1944. By that year, the share of the top 5 percent had dropped another notch to 20.7 percent, and of the top 20 percent to 45.8 percent.

The income concept used by these researchers did not include undistributed corporate profits, which are a source of future dividends or of capital gains for shareholders; if they had been included, the movement of the income distribution toward equality from 1929 to 1944 would have been substantially moderated, but by no means eliminated.*

The movement toward equality seems to have ended during World War II, at least on the basis of the available statistics. In 1952, for example, the share of the top 5 percent was 20.5 percent and of the top 20 percent, 44.7 percent. (The differences from the 1944 figures are well within the margin of error of these data, and can hardly be called significant.)

To trace what happened since 1952, we shift to the census data that provide the longest continuous and comparable income distribution series available to us. The best way to appreciate the trend is to look at the figures for income shares at five-year intervals.

The figures indicate that the share of the top 5 percent declined slightly between 1952 and 1957, and has remained virtually unchanged since 1957; the share of the top 20 percent changed very little. Correspondingly, the shares of the groups at the bottom of the income scale (not shown in

---

*The year 1929 must have been the high point of inequality during the 1920s, so that the distribution of income in the more recent period may not have been very different from what it was in the early 1920s if account is taken of undistributed profits. Unfortunately, the available data for those years are simply not good enough to say much more.

Table A.   BEFORE-TAX INCOME
SHARES, CENSUS DATA
(percent)

Year	Top 5 Percent of Families	Top 20 Percent of Families
1952	18	42
1957	16	40
1962	16	42
1967	15	41

Source: Bureau of the Census. Income includes transfer payments (e.g., social security benefits, unemployment compensation, welfare payments, etc.), but excludes capital gains.

the table) also changed very little throughout the period.

Tax data are needed to push the analysis further. These data are better than the census data for our purposes, because they show the amount of realized capital gains and also permit us to calculate income shares after the federal income tax. But the great disadvantage of the tax data is that the bottom part of the income distribution is underrepresented because of an unknown number of nonfilers. Furthermore, the taxpayer unit is not exactly a family unit, because children and other members of the family file their own income tax returns if they have income, and a few married couples continue to file separate returns despite the privilege of income splitting, which removed the advantage of separate returns with rare exceptions.

There is really no way to get around these problems, but the tax data are too interesting to be abandoned because of these technicalities. So, we make an assumption that permits us to use at least the upper tail of the income distribution. The assumption is that the top 10 or 15 percent of the nation's tax units are for the most part similar to the census family units and the cases that differ represent roughly the same percentage of the total number of units each year. Because we have official Department of Commerce estimates of income (as defined in the tax code) for the country as a whole, the assumption enables us to compute income shares before and after tax for the top 1, 2, 5, 10, and 15 percent of units annually for the entire postwar period.

The tax series confirms much of what we learned from the census series, and adds a few additional bits of information besides. Here are the data for selected years chosen to represent the three sets of federal income tax rates levied, beginning with the Korean War:

Table B.   BEFORE-TAX INCOME SHARES, TAX DATA
(percent)

Year	Top 1 Percent of Tax Units	Top 2 Percent of Tax Units	Top 5 Percent of Tax Units	Top 10 Percent of Tax Units	Top 15 Percent of Tax Units
1952	9	12	19	27	33
1963	8	12	19	28	35
1967	9	13	20	29	36

Source: *Statistics of Income.* Income excludes transfer payments, but includes realized capital gains in full.

According to tax returns, the share of total income, including all realized capital gains, going to the top 1 percent of the tax units was about the same for the entire period from 1952 through 1967. But the shares of the top 2, 5, 10, and 15 percent—which, of course, include the top 1 percent—all rose somewhat. These trends differ from the census figures which show that the entire income distribution was stable. By contrast, the tax data show that the 14 percent of income recipients just below the top 1 percent—this group reported incomes between $12,000 and $43,000 in 1967—increased their share of total income from 24 percent to 27 percent.

If the figures are anywhere near being right, they suggest two significant conclusions:

First, in recent years the very rich in our society have not enjoyed larger increases in incomes, as defined in the tax code, than the average income recipient. Although realized capital gains are included in our figures, they do not include nonreported sources, such as tax-exempt interest and excess depletion; correction for these omissions would probably not alter the results very much, because the amounts involved are small relative to the total of reported incomes. Even a correction for the undistributed profits of corporations wouldn't change the result very much because undistributed gross corporation profits have remained between 10 and 13 percent of total reported income since 1950.

Second, a change in the income distribution may have occurred in what are sometimes called the "middle income" classes. These classes consist of most of the professional people in this country (doctors, lawyers, engineers, accountants, college professors, etc.) as well as the highest paid members of the skilled labor force and white collar workers. The increase in their share of total income from 24 percent to 27 percent, if it actually occurred, represents a not insignificant improvement in their relative income status.

Clearly, this improvement in the income shares of the middle classes could come only at the expense of the lower 85 percent of the income distribution. But this is not the whole story. These figures contain only incomes that are generated in the private economy; they do not include transfer payments (e.g., social security benefits, unemployment compensation, welfare payments, etc.) which are, of course, concentrated in the lower income classes. Correction of the figures for transfer payments might be just enough to offset the increased share of the middle income classes. If this is the case, the constancy of the shares of pre-tax income shown by the census data is fully consistent with the growth in shares of the middle incomes shown by the tax data. And, if this is the explanation of the constancy of the income shares in the census distribution, it means that the lower classes have not been able to hold their own in the private economy; large increases in government transfer payments were needed to prevent a gradual erosion of their income shares.

II. THE EFFECT OF TAXES

Since one of the major objectives of taxation is to moderate income inequality, it is appropriate to ask how the tax system actually affects the distribution of income and whether it has become more or less equalizing.

It is not easy to arrive at an accurate estimate of the impact of the whole tax system at various income levels. Taxes are reported to different federal, state, and local government agencies. No single agency has the responsibility to compel reporting of taxes on a meaningful and consistent basis. A number of isolated attempts have been made by students of public finance to piece together from the inadequate data estimates of the distribution of all taxes by income classes. These studies were for different years, make different assumptions for the incidence of the various taxes, and use different statistical sources and methodologies to correct for the inconsistencies in the data. Nevertheless, they all arrive at similar conclusions regarding the relative tax loads at different income levels.

The most recent estimates were prepared by the Council of Economic Advisers for the year 1965. They show the distribution of taxes by the income classes of families and unattached individuals, income being defined exclusive of transfer payments. The estimates for taxes and transfers separately, and in combination, are summarized in Table C.

The following are the major conclusions that can be drawn from these and previously published estimates:

(1) Since at least the mid-1930s, the federal tax system has been roughly proportional in the lower and middle income classes, and clearly progressive for the highest classes. Federal income tax data suggest that the preferential rate on capital gains, and the exclusion of interest on state and local bonds and other items from the tax base, have produced some regressivity for the very small group at the top of the income pyramid, say, beginning with incomes of $100,000 or more.

(2) State and local taxes are regressive throughout the income scale.

(3) The combined federal, state, and local tax burden is heaviest in the very bottom and top brackets, and lowest in the middle brackets. This statement is, of course, based on averages for each group and there are wide variations around these averages for specific individuals, depending on the sources of their incomes, the kind of property they own, and where they live.

(4) The poor receive numerous transfer payments (e.g., social security, unemployment compensation, public assistance, etc.) that are financed by this tax system. The net effect of transfers as against taxes is distinctly progressive, because transfer payments make up such a large proportion of total income at the bottom of the income distribution—56 percent for those with incomes of less than $2,000 in 1965. (To some extent, this progressivity is overstated because the transfers do not always go to the same people who pay taxes, the best example being social security retirement benefits that are received only by retirees—many of whom are not poor—while $1.5 billion of the payroll tax levied to pay for these benefits are paid by the poor.) There is no reason in the abstract, why a nation should not levy taxes on and pay transfers to the same groups; but while the nation wages a war on poverty, it is surely appropriate to consider the possibility of providing additional financial assistance to the poor by tax reduction as well as through transfer payments.

Table C.   TAXES AND TRANSFERS AS PERCENT OF INCOME, 1965

Income Classes	Federal	Taxes		Transfer Payments	Taxes Less Transfers
		State and Local	Total		
Under $2,000	19	25	44	126	−83*
$ 2,000- 4,000	16	11	27	11	16
4,000- 6,000	17	10	27	5	21
6,000- 8,000	17	9	26	3	23
8,000-10,000	18	9	27	2	25
10,000-15,000	19	9	27	2	25
15,000 and over	32	7	38	1	37
Total	22	9	31	14	24

Source: *Economic Report of the President*, 1969. Income excludes transfer payments, but includes realized capital gains in full and undistributed corporate profits.
*The minus sign indicates that the families and individuals in this class received more from federal, state, and local governments than they, as a group, paid to these governments in taxes.

III. REFORMING THE NATIONAL TAX SYSTEM

The preceding discussion indicates that the agenda for reforming this country's tax system to correct its regressive features is lengthy and complicated. It involves reconstruction of the tax systems at all levels of government, and the development of new forms of intergovernmental fiscal relations. State and local governments need to rely more heavily on income taxes, relieve the poor of paying sales taxes, and deemphasize the property tax. At the federal level, the most important items on the agenda are to alleviate the payroll tax on the poor, to deliver—at last—on promises made by both political parties to close loopholes in the income taxes, and make the estate and gift taxes more effective.

The classic objection against an attack on tax regressivity has been that there is simply not enough income in the higher classes to do the job. Would a substantial reduction in regressivity require confiscatory rates? To appreciate one of the significant magnitudes involved, suppose the federal government decided to refund all general sales, payroll, and property taxes on housing paid by those who are officially classified as poor. (The remaining taxes are selective excise taxes levied for sumptuary purposes or in lieu of user charges, which could not be refunded in any practical way. After this year, the poor will not pay any federal income taxes.) These refunds would amount to about $4 billion—perhaps three-quarters of the total tax burden of the poor and one-sixth of the burden of those with incomes below $4,000—less than what this year's tax reform bill may give away in higher standard deductions and rate reductions.

It might be thought that such a proposal—to lift three-quarters of the tax burden of the poor—is too timid. Why not go further? That indeed could be done, but only as part of a larger redistribution of the tax burden. After all, it is both inequitable and politically impossible to create a noticeable "tax divide" between the poor (a fluid concept, in any case) and the rest of society. To make the tax system progressive, it would not be enough drastically to reduce the tax burden of the poor; the burdens of the near poor and others at the lower end of the income scale would have to be cut simultaneously. Indeed—again on principles of equity and political feasibility—the relief should be diffused upwards until it benefits, say, the lower half of the income distribution (or, more technically, those receiving less than the median income, which is now in excess of $9,000).

There are a number of ways of modifying the tax system to redistribute the tax burden in this way. The most straightforward—and perhaps even the most practical, given the federal system of government in this country—would be to give taxpayers credits against the federal income tax for a declining percentage of the major taxes they now pay to federal, state, and local governments, except for income taxes. Suppose we make refunds to the poor for the general sales, payroll, and property taxes they pay and permit others to claim credits against their federal income taxes for 75 percent of these same taxes if they are in the $2,000–4,000 class, 50 percent in the $4,000–6,000 class, and 25 percent in the $6,000–8,000 class. (Obviously, refunds would be paid to those with credits larger than their federal income taxes.)

Let us further assume that the taxes paid by those with incomes between $8,000 and $10,000 remain the same, and that the revenues needed to pay for the relief below $8,000 would come from those with incomes above $10,000 in proportion to the taxes they now pay. Again, we need not be concerned with the details of how this can be done. It would certainly be more equitable to close the major federal income tax loopholes first and then raise whatever additional revenue is needed by an increase in the rates above $10,000. Either way, the ratio of total taxes to income for any specific income class could be set at the same figure, although the burden within each class would be distributed much more equitably if the loopholes were closed first.

It turns out that, in 1965, the credits (and refunds) would have reduced taxes for those with incomes of less than $8,000 by $19 billion, and this would have required an increase in the taxes paid by those in the $10,000–15,000 class from an average of 27 percent to 32 percent and by those above $15,000 from 38 percent to 46 percent, or an average tax increase of about a fifth. The resulting effective rates of tax in this system compare with the rates as they were in 1965 as shown in Table D.

Table D.   TAXES AS PERCENT OF INCOME, 1965

Income Classes	Present Tax System	Alternative Tax System
Under $2,000	44	13
$ 2,000– 4,000	27	14
4,000– 6,000	27	19
6,000– 8,000	26	23
8,000–10,000	27	27
10,000–15,000	27	32
15,000 and over	38	46
Total	31	31

Income includes capital gains, but excludes transfer payments.

A glance should convince anyone that this tax system would by no means eradicate taxes at the lower end of the income scale. Most people would regard tax burdens of as much as 13–14 percent for those with incomes below $4,000 and 23 percent for those between $6,000 and $8,000 as much too high. Yet, the idea of relieving tax burdens for the lower half of the income distribution even in this relatively modest way is clearly impractical; Congress would face a revolt if it tried to raise taxes on incomes above $10,000 by an average of 20 percent.

Perhaps we exaggerate the difficulties by using 1965 figures? Incomes have risen substantially so that there is much more income to be taxed above $15,000. But state and local taxes have also risen and the degree of regressivity in the tax system has been aggravated. On balance, the rise in incomes has probably been more powerful, but not enough to alter very much the general conclusions that we have reached from the 1965 data.

The prospects for making the tax system progressive are more discouraging when one notes the way Congress usually behaves when it reduces taxes. On the basis of past performance, one can predict with certainty that Congress will not limit income tax reduction to the lowest income classes. In 1964, when federal income taxes were reduced by an average of 20 percent, incomes above $15,000 were given a tax cut of 14 percent. This year, much more than the revenue to be gained from closing the loopholes and repealing the investment credit may be given away in tax rate reductions. Of course, these actions reflect the pressures on the Congressmen. The influence of the groups arrayed against a significant redistribution of the tax burden is enormous,

and there is no effective lobby for the poor and the near poor.

It may be that, at some distant future date, the well-to-do and the rich will have enough income to satisfy not only their own needs, but also to help relieve the tax burdens of those who are less fortunate. In the meantime, the tax system will continue to disgrace the most affluent nation in the world.

POVERTY AND THE GHETTO

Our discussion so far has been largely in terms of overall income distribution. We have noticed in passing, however, that poverty in the United States is characteristically felt much more deeply by particular groups in the society. Take, for example, the elderly. In 1968, while only 11.5 percent of households with heads under sixty-five were "poor," 30.6 percent of households with heads sixty-five or older were below the poverty line—nearly three times as high a percentage. One of the main arguments against inflation, indeed, is precisely that it is so damaging to the increasing number of elderly in our society.

In the last few years, however, special attention has centered on our minority populations, and the problems of the blacks and the inner city ghettos in particular—and for good reason. Table 29-1 showed us that the percent of persons below the poverty level in the United States had declined from 22.4 to 12.8 percent in 1959–1968. But a breakdown of the 1968 figures reveals that while white poverty was only 10.0 percent, Negro and other nonwhite poverty was 33.5 percent.

This represents improvement—in 1959, well over half the black population of the country lived in poverty—but it still leaves *one-third* of all Negro and nonwhite persons in the United States below the poverty level.

The data on unemployment are equally striking. A rather dramatic way of putting the problem is to draw two Phillips curves, one for total unemployment and one for nonwhite unemployment. Figure 29-2 shows that even when there is price inflation of 4 percent a year, nonwhite unemployment is around 8 percent. At 1 percent inflation, nonwhite unemployment is around 13 percent—a level literally reminiscent of the Great Depression of the 1930s.[3]

Not only is income lower and unemployment higher among blacks, but their opportunities to spend their incomes may be restricted by discrimination. Discrimination in housing is especially important and, indeed, it has been cited by Professor John Kain as the "Big Cities' Big Problem."[4] Because this problem involves not only income distribution but also our urban crisis and questions of economic "efficiency," it is worth saying a word about.

It is well known that one of the causes of the economic crisis in our cities has been the movement of jobs, stores, industry, and also middle and upper income families from the central city to the

---

3. This suggests that the interests of the black minority and of the elderly minority may sometimes conflict. The former might benefit more from policies that increase employment even at the expense of higher inflation, while the latter might benefit more from a stricter anti-inflation policy even at the expense of heavier unemployment. Not all conflicts about income distribution need be between rich and poor; they can also involve different groups within any given income class.

4. John F. Kain, "The Big Cities' Big Problem," *Challenge* 15, no. 1 (September–October, 1966).

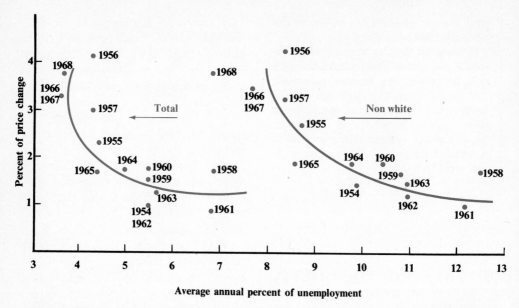

Figure 29-2. Phillips' Curves for Total and Non-white Unemployment, 1954-1968.

Source: Economic Report of the President, January 1969 (Washington, D.C.; U.S. Government Printing Office), p. 95, Chart 8, and p. 255, Table B-24. Taken from Carolyn Shaw Bell, *The Economics of the Ghetto* (New York: Pegasus, 1970), p. 106.

surrounding suburbs.[5] In a certain sense, this phenomenon represents a move toward a more decentralized form of economic life made possible by improved transportation and communications and changes in the methods of production and distribution of goods and services. To this extent, the problems of the cities may represent transitional difficulties such as one might expect in any society moving toward a preferred form of economic organization.

Such "market forces" as have been operating, however, have been

greatly distorted by various kinds of discrimination against minority groups. Discrimination against blacks in housing —involving greatly diminished access to housing in the suburban areas and substantial segregation in ghettos within the central cities—has had especially important effects. The change in the composition of population in our central cities is well known. In the New York City area, for example, between 1950 and 1960, the white population of the central city declined by nearly half a million persons, while the black population increased by a quarter of a million. At the same time, the suburban ring outside the central city showed an increase in white population of nearly 2 million, while the increase in black population was about 67,000. That this shift in balance does not indicate simply an income-class phenomenon—i.e., more whites are well-to-do, and more well-to-do people move to the suburbs—is

5. For a more detailed presentation of the following analysis, see John F. Kain and Joseph J. Persky, "The Ghetto, the Metropolis and the Nation," Program on Regional and Urban Economics, Discussion Paper no. 30 (March, 1968). Also see Kain, "The Big Cities' Big Problem," and John F. Kain, "The Distribution and Movement of Jobs and Industry," in *The Metropolitan Enigma*, ed. James Q. Wilson (Washington, D.C.: Chamber of Commerce of the United States, 1967), p. 81.

shown by the fact that in all our cities, low-income whites move out to the suburbs in much larger numbers than blacks in the same income class. The percentage of low-income white families in urban areas living in the suburbs ranges from twice to nearly twenty times the percentage of Negro families of the same income class.

What are the economic consequences of housing segregation? Kain's analysis suggests that, in addition to income distribution, it affects jobs, efficiency, transportation, and indeed, the whole fabric of city life.

When jobs are moving out of the central city to the suburbs, the black worker, largely segregated in the ghetto, will be unaware of opportunities available to him and will find it difficult and costly to live in the central city if he does take a job in the suburbs. The cost to the society of black unemployment is high. (Kain estimates that, in 1956, because of residential segregation, 30,000 jobs were lost to blacks in the Chicago urban area.) The transportation problem also becomes a serious one. If the black worker, forced by discrimination to live in the ghetto, takes a job in the suburbs, he will face a difficult transportation problem. But the white family living in the suburbs faces a difficult transportation problem as well, since many whites still hold jobs in the central city. The expansion of the ghetto within the central city is likely to intensify this problem as more and more whites with central city jobs find life in the city unacceptable and move out on this account. The prospect is raised of the city inefficiently shipping blacks back and forth to jobs on the outskirts and shipping whites back and forth to jobs in the central city. Since many whites are more well-to-do than blacks, moreover, this residential pattern is likely to cause a crisis

in the city's finances. As income levels and property values fall and as the city accumulates a larger number of low-income families dependent on welfare and other social services, the city's ability to sustain the financial burden of its public responsibilities may prove—as, indeed, it is proving—wholly inadequate.

In sum, discrimination in housing (in addition, of course, to discrimination in employment and even in the prices charged for ordinary goods and services) has warped the operation of market forces to the point where they produce something approaching a major social catastrophe. The net effects are to intensify the crisis of the cities, to produce an "inefficient" allocation of resources, and, not least, to deepen the poverty of a group in society that has few resources for defending itself.

It is no wonder that when reformers criticize the unequal distribution of American income today they often have the ghetto population foremost in mind.

POLICIES TO ALTER INCOME DISTRIBUTION

Although many observers would agree that the extremes of income inequality in the United States ought to be corrected, the manner in which this is to be accomplished is subject to deep controversy. Questions of income distribution almost invariably involve some social conflict, since any redistribution of income is precisely that—taking away one person's income and giving it to another. The one who receives is likely to feel that this is only proper; the one who loses may take a different view. There are, however, some ways in which poverty can be ameliorated without incurring heavy costs to others.

In the first place, any move towards the solution to the great macroeconomic problems of full employment and price stability is likely to have at least some favorable effects on the distribution of income. To put it negatively, the burdens of unemployment and price inflation are likely to fall with particular severity on the nation's poor, and, consequently to worsen the poverty problem both in a relative and absolute sense. This is perhaps especially true of unemployment with respect to the nation's blacks, though we have also noted the harmful effects of inflation on the nation's elderly. In other words, if we succeeded in solving our great macroeconomic problems (or coming closer to solving them), then we would with one stroke (1) benefit society as a whole by providing a greater social product and (2) benefit those groups who suffer particularly when the economy in the aggregate is unstable.

Much the same thing can be said about the great microeconomic issue of an efficient allocation of resources. Namely, there are many measures designed either to make the market work better (as in removing various forms of discrimination) or to improve the health, education, training, and skills of the underprivileged, wherein there is a net gain in social product for all to share. Insofar as poverty represents an inefficient use of society's resources, it will be possible in theory to reduce poverty and increase society's overall income at the same time. To that degree, an improved income distribution need not come at the expense of the incomes of the nation's well-to-do.

The above represents the bright side of the picture. Conflict emerges when we go a step further, however. Thus, many critics of society feel that improving the macro- and microeconomic functioning of

the economy would barely scratch the surface of the distribution problem. They argue that any society in which the top 5 percent of income recipients receive perhaps four times as much income as the bottom 20 percent (or, in other words, where average income in these classes varies by a factor of *twenty*!) needs a thorough and fundamental overhauling. In the early 1970s much of the interest in restructuring American "capitalism" undoubtedly stems from this concern about income inequality.

Even those who would work in more modest ways to limit the extremes of affluence and poverty are likely to run into serious social conflicts. Take the problem of housing discrimination, for example. Since the workings of the marketplace are unlikely to solve this problem, public intervention will almost certainly be necessary to improve matters. This intervention will be costly for the taxpayer. Public monies may have to be spent in increasing the flow of employment information to the isolated ghetto dweller, in improving mass transport from the ghetto to the suburbs, in providing rent subsidies for poorer families. Further, Professor Kain suggests that the government may have to step in to provide low-income, nondiscriminatory housing, not in the cities but in the suburbs. In the early 1970s, the New York City newspapers were filled with the objections of local residents to various "scatter-site" housing projects within the city. Imagine the social conflict that would develop if large-scale housing projects of this nature were imposed upon the plush suburbs surrounding our major cities. Direct attacks on the roots of poverty in this country are unlikely to escape debate and disagreement. The test of the strength of our society will be whether it can encompass such disagreements and work out solutions that, though perfectly

710

satisfactory to no one, will be at least grudgingly accepted by all.

While these long-range approaches are being developed, there is in the meantime the obvious fact that many people in our society are extremely poor and must be taken care of in one way or another. This raises the question of various *income-maintenance* programs or, in everyday language, *welfare* programs. Welfare, we know, is here to stay and it is a big operation (we recall that state and local expenditures on welfare have increased sixfold in the past twenty years). No real possibility of dismantling this operation exists, but there are many important decisions to be made about what kind of operation it should be. These include questions about:

The *scale* of welfare programs. Have these programs grown out of hand and do they require important cutbacks? Or are they still insufficient to remove even the grossest forms of poverty that stain the conscience of a rich society?

The *administration* and *funding* of these programs. Whose responsibility is it to see that the incomes of the poor are maintained at a decent level? The city? county? state? federal government? This raises the issue of revenue-sharing[6] and also the question of centralizing versus decentralizing the administering of the funds, however they may have been provided.

The *form* of the program. In some ways the most difficult of the problems concern the system by which incomes are to be maintained. Should there be a means' test and if so, how should it be administered? Should welfare recipients be required to work (say, on public projects) in order to receive welfare? What relationship in general should there be between employment opportunities and welfare payments? Do present schemes negatively affect the incentive to work? Do they tend to drive families apart (say, if the wife loses her welfare payment if the husband and father comes home to live)? Is there any agreement about the best form in general that income-maintenance programs should take?

To go into all these issues would take up far more space and time than are at our disposal here. However, we can sharpen the debate considerably by looking at one specific income-maintenance program that has attracted great attention from economists in the past few years. This is the program (which has been advanced by both "liberal" and "conservative" economists) of a *negative income tax.*

THE NEGATIVE INCOME TAX

The basic idea of the negative income tax is simple. Under the present federal personal income tax system, there is (say, for a family of four) a certain level of income at which taxes are zero. Below this level, taxes remain zero. What is proposed is that, for very low incomes, taxes become *negative*—result in payments from the government to the taxpayer—rather than remain at zero, and that these payments *to the citizen* be handled in exactly the same systematic way that taxpayers' payments *to the government* are handled for higher income levels.

Even this brief description should make it clear that we are dealing with not a single program but a family of possible programs, some of which would involve very heavy, and some relatively small, government expenditures. Decisions that would have to be made for any single plan would include these matters: (1) determining the level of incomes at which taxes

---

6. See chapter 4, pp. 107–12.

would become negative; (2) determining the percentage of income that would come back to the poor family and whether or not that percentage would increase as the family's income was lower; and (3) establishing a method for allowing for the number of children and other dependents. Generous decisions on these questions could lead to a program that would cost many times what more niggardly decisions would entail. This may help explain why neither liberals nor conservatives as a group oppose the negative income tax idea.

The advantages that supporters of this idea see are several. For one thing, such a program would place on the federal government some of the welfare responsibilities that are now burdening lower levels of government. Many people feel that welfare is simply too big a job for cities and states to handle financially, particularly when the federal government has substantially (though, of course, not completely) taken over the personal income tax as a source of revenue. Building welfare schemes into the federal tax system seems a fairly obvious response to this difficulty.

For another thing, there are many flaws in present-day welfare schemes that would be avoided by the negative income tax proposals. These flaws include everything from what many consider a degrading "means' test" (as compared to the negative income tax plan where the poor would do no more nor less than the rich—i.e., fill out an income tax form) to the effect on family life of welfare plans that reduce welfare payments by the amount of the husband's income and thus make it advisable for him to live away from home. More generally, as Professor James Tobin of Yale has noted, our welfare programs often involve a "marginal tax rate" of "100 percent" for poor

families. This happens when welfare payments plus family income are adjusted to meet some minimum level. Suppose the level is $2500 and that if family income is zero, the state provides $2500; if family income is $1000, the state provides $1500; and so on. In effect, each dollar earned (up to $2500) is completely "taxed" away. The effect of such schemes on incentives to work can hardly be favorable.

Finally, many supporters like the idea that the negative income tax implies governmental support of the poor as a matter of governmental obligation and private right. They see this relationship as analogous to that of the taxpayer who is obliged to pay taxes as a matter of the government's right. The relationship is thus seen as symmetrical and fitting, not a question of charity or "the dole."

All of these arguments, of course, have responses. Thus, opponents of the negative income tax are worried by the very notion of a "right to income" that supporters of the plan usually praise. Representative Thomas B. Curtis of Missouri has written:

Can a right to income without work be adopted without creating deep cleavages and conflicts in our society? Is it possible to have a dual set of values and norms; one predicated on income for work and one on income without work? Isn't it possible that the existing gulf between the middle-class culture and the subculture of poverty will be deepened and problems of national cohesiveness and accommodation be aggravated? In fact, another serious rift may develop within the lower economic class: between the approximately one-third of all American families that earn income above the poverty line but below the national median and those families receiving government subsidies. At a time when many analysts discern a growing alienation of the poor from the mainstream of American society, the divisive tendencies fostered by income guarantees are clearly anathema.[7]

Furthermore, just as both conservatives and liberals can find reasons to support the negative income tax idea, so can both groups find reasons to oppose it. Opponents can argue that it will cost too much, *or* that it will not cost enough—i.e., that it will be used as a substitute for other important welfare programs that aid the poor directly in terms of health, housing, education, training, and so on. In the following reading, the pros and cons of a specific negative income tax scheme[8] are discussed by one of the long-term advocates of such a program, Milton Friedman.

7. Thomas B. Curtis, "Income Maintenance Guarantees," U.S. Congress, Joint Economic Committee, *Hearings Before the Subcommittee on Fiscal Policy,* 90th Cong., 2nd sess.; quoted in Myron L. Joseph, Norton C. Seeber, and George Leland Bach, eds., *Economic Analysis and Policy,* 3rd ed., (Englewood Cliffs, N.J.: Prentice-Hall, 1971), p. 451.

8. For a summary of other possible variants of the negative income tax program, see Martin Schnitzer, "The Negative Income Tax," in Neil W. Chamberlain, ed., *Business and the Cities* (New York: Basic Books, 1970), pp. 213–219.

Negative Income Tax

Milton Friedman

I

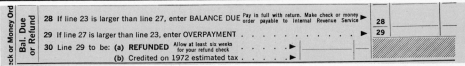

The 1040 A Tax Form. The negative income tax could be administered in the same way that tax payments or refunds are handled today.

The negative income tax, as Paul Samuelson remarked in one of his recent columns, is a striking example of an idea whose time has come. First suggested decades ago, it has attracted widespread interest only in the past few years as the defects of present methods of assisting the poor have become more obvious and more flagrant.

The widespread interest is remarkable. But the appearance of growing agreement—of support for a negative income tax by the right and the left, by businessmen and professors, by Republicans and Democrats—is highly misleading. In large part, it reflects the use of the same term to describe very different plans. For example, some months ago, more than 1,200 economists from 150 different colleges and universities signed a petition favoring a negative income tax. Despite my longtime advocacy of a negative income tax, I found it impossible to join in sponsoring the petition or even to sign it because I did not agree with the plan it advocated or the arguments it presented.

A SPECIFIC PLAN

The basic idea of a negative income tax

is to use the mechanism by which we now collect tax revenue from people with incomes above some minimum level to provide financial assistance to people with incomes below that level.

Under present law, a family of four (husband, wife and two dependents) is entitled to personal exemptions and minimum deductions totaling $3,000 ($2,400 personal exemptions, $600 deductions).

If such a family has an income of $3,000, its exemptions and deductions just offset its income. It has a *zero taxable* income and pays no tax.

If it has an income of $4,000, it has a *positive taxable income* of $1,000. Under current law, it is required to *pay* a tax of 15.4 percent, or $154. Hence it ends up with an income after tax of $3,846.

If it has an income of $2,000, it has a *negative taxable income* of −$1,000 ($2,000 minus exemptions and deductions of $3,000 equals −$1,000). This negative taxable income is currently disregarded. Under a negative income tax, the family would be entitled to *receive a fraction* of this sum. If the negative tax rate were 50 percent, it would be entitled to receive $500, leaving it with an income after tax of $2,500.

If such a family had no private income, it would have a negative taxable income of −$3,000, which would entitle it to receive $1,500. This is the minimum income guaranteed by this plan for a family of four.

Let me stress the difference between the *break-even income* of $3,000 at which the family neither pays taxes nor receives a subsidy and the *minimum guaranteed income* of $1,500. It is essential to retain a difference between these two in order to preserve an incentive for low-income families to earn additional income.

Let me stress also that these numbers are all for a family of four. Both the break-even income and the minimum guaranteed income would be higher for larger families and lower for smaller families. In this way, a negative income tax automatically allows for differences in need because of differences in family size—just as it does for differences in need because of differences in income.

This plan is intended to replace completely our present programs of direct relief—aid to dependent children, public assistance, and so on. For the first year or two, it might cost slightly more than these programs—because it is so much more comprehensive in coverage. But, as the incentive effects of the plan started to work, it would begin to cost far less than the present exploding direct-assistance programs that are creating a permanent class of people on welfare.

ALTERNATIVE PLANS

By varying the break-even income and the negative tax rate, by adding the negative income tax to present programs rather than substituting it for them, it is possible to go all the way from the rather modest and, I believe, eminently desirable plan just outlined to irresponsible and undesirable plans that would involve enormous redistribution of income and a drastic reduction in the incentive for people to work. That is why it is possible for persons with so wide a range of political views to support one form or another of a negative income tax.

The proposal to supplement the incomes of the poor by paying them a *fraction* of their unused income-tax exemptions and deductions, which I termed a *negative income tax* years ago, has many advantages over present welfare programs:

(1) It would help the poor in the most direct way possible.

(2) It would treat them as responsible

individuals, not as incompetent wards of the state.

(3) It would give them an incentive to help themselves.

(4) It would cost less than present programs yet help the poor more.

(5) It would eliminate almost entirely the cumbrous welfare bureaucracy running the present programs.

(6) It could not be used as a political slush fund, as so many current programs —notably in the "war on poverty"—can be and have been used.

In the course of advocating a negative income tax like the one outlined above, I have repeatedly encountered the same objections time and again. Let me try to answer a few of them.

(1) *By removing a means test, the negative income tax establishes a new principle in the relation between citizens and the government.*
This is simply a misunderstanding. The negative income tax retains a means test— the straightforward numerical test of income rather than the present complex and demeaning test. It uses the same means test to decide who shall receive assistance from the government as the one we now use to decide who shall pay the expenses of government.

True, it guarantees a minimum income to all. But that is not a new principle. Present welfare arrangements guarantee a minimum income in practice, and in some states, even in law. The trouble is that these present welfare programs are a mess.

(2) *The minimum levels of income proposed are too low.* We are talking about a Federal program and a *nationwide* minimum. The levels of assistance are decidedly higher than current levels in most states. They are decidedly lower than current levels in states like New York, Illinois, California. It would be absurd to enact such high levels as national standards. But there is every reason to encourage the more afflu-

ent states to supplement the Federal negative income tax out of state funds—preferably by enacting a supplementary state negative income tax.

(3) *The poor need regular assistance. They cannot wait until the end of the year.* Of course. The negative income tax, like the positive income tax, would be put on an advance basis. Employed persons entitled to negative income tax would have supplements added to their paychecks, just as most of us now have positive taxes withheld. Persons without wages would file advance estimates and receive estimated amounts due to them weekly or monthly. Once a year, all would file a return that would adjust for under- or over-payments.

(4) *The negative income tax destroys incentives to work.* Under present programs, persons on welfare who obey the law generally lose a dollar in relief for every additional dollar earned. Hence, they have no incentive whatsoever to earn the dollar. Under the negative income tax plan that I propose, such a person would keep fifty cents out of every additional dollar earned. That would give him a far greater incentive than he now has.

One additional point. A welfare recipient now hesitates to take a job even if it pays more than he gets on welfare because, if he loses the job, it may take him (or her) many months to get back on relief. There is no such disincentive under a negative income tax.

(5) *The negative income tax will foster political irresponsibility.* If we adopt an open and aboveboard program for supplementing the incomes of people below some specified level, will there not be continued political pressure for higher and higher break-even incomes, for higher and higher rates on negative income? Will the demagogues not have a field day appealing to have-nots to legislate taxes on haves for transfer to them?

These dangers clearly exist. But they must be evaluated in terms of the world as it is, not in terms of a dream world in which there are no governmental welfare measures. These dangers are all present now—and have clearly been effective. The crucial question is, how do we get out of the mess into which these pressures have driven us? The negative income tax offers a gradual and responsible way to work ourselves out of this mess. No other way of doing so has as yet been suggested.

SUMMARY

Income distribution has become one of the most heated topics of discussion in the United States in the early 1970s. Income distribution may be viewed in many ways: in terms of factor prices (as in Part Three), or in terms of income size in either an absolute or a relative sense. Relative income distribution is often characterized by means of the Lorenz curve.

Income distribution in the United States shows considerable inequality. In absolute terms, the rising living standard of the nation has resulted in a steady reduction of the percent of families with below poverty-level incomes. In relative terms, however, although there was some movement towards greater equality from the 1930s to the end of World War II, there appears to have been little change in the degree of equality since that time. At the present time the top 5 percent of income receivers may get about one-fifth of total personal income. Although the federal tax system is progressive over a certain range, state and local taxes tend to be regressive and thus the considerable inequality of American income distribution survives the impact of taxes.

(Transfer payments to the poor, however, are clearly progressive in their impact.)

Poverty in this country is concentrated heavily in certain groups, such as the elderly, and especially the blacks, and other minorities. In terms of income, unemployment, housing, and other measures, the special difficulties of the ghetto population become apparent. Racial discrimination, besides worsening the inequality of income distribution, also helps produce inefficient patterns of residence and production and contributes substantially to the crisis of our metropolitan areas.

Eliminating the worst extremes of high-income and (especially) low-income categories need not always involve conflicts of interest. Improving the economy in its macroeconomic performance with respect to unemployment and inflation would do much to help the poor. Similarly, eliminating discrimination and other artificial barriers may improve income distribution and efficiency simultaneously. Nevertheless, important conflicts will often arise when society attempts to redistribute income from one group to another. There are notable divisions in American society in the early 1970s about welfare programs—their desirable scale, administration, and structure.

One attempt to eliminate serious poverty is the plan for a *negative income tax*. Advanced by both conservative and liberal economists, this plan involves extending the federal income tax negatively (that is, in terms of payments *to* the taxpayer) for low levels of income. It has been criticized for involving too heavy (or too little) government expenditure in this area, but the plan appeals to many because of its simplicity and because it avoids many of the disincentive and other harmful effects of current welfare programs.

QUESTIONS
FOR DISCUSSION

1. "Economic efficiency is a concept applicable to situations where all parties can benefit from reallocations of economic resources; in the case of income distribution, however, it is always a case of one person's gain against another person's loss." Discuss critically.

2. The following table represents income distribution in three hypothetical countries (A, B, and C) for the year 1975:

DISTRIBUTION OF FAMILY PERSONAL INCOME IN THREE HYPOTHETICAL COUNTRIES IN 1975

Quintiles	Percent Distribution Country		
	A	B	C
Lowest	5	5	20
Second	7	11	20
Third	9	16	20
Fourth	11	23	20
Highest	68	45	20

Show how these patterns of income distribution could be displayed in terms of Lorenz curves. Incidentally, which of these income distributions comes closest to approximating that of the United States in the early 1970s?

3. If you were a citizen of one of the hypothetical countries in question 2, and if you had reason to believe that the pattern of income distribution would not affect other economic objectives (growth, efficiency, etc.), would you prefer the pattern of country C to that of the other countries? If you would permit any inequalities, on what basis would you do so?

4. The preceding question assumed no conflicts among economic objectives, but a characteristic problem is that objectives often do conflict. A highly progressive income tax, for example, may be strongly advocated on income-distribution grounds, yet may be criticized on efficiency grounds because it involves a high *marginal* rate of taxation (you pay more on additional dollars earned) and therefore may undermine incentives to work. Similarly, high taxes on profits may be preferred on income-distribution grounds but opposed on the grounds that they may limit investment and hence the expansion of employment and production.
(*a*) Explain how conflicts of objectives may arise in the case of the two tax programs mentioned above.
(*b*) Give examples of other public programs in which you can see potential conflicts between income distribution and other economic objectives.

5. In chapter 6, we spoke of the possibility of a kind of "vicious circle of poverty" in the less developed countries of Asia, Africa, and Latin America. Might such a concept be applicable to the ghetto populations of our inner cities? Discuss.

6. Write an essay either for or against the negative income tax, including a consideration of the main arguments of the opposing position, and also a statement of how your particular plan might differ from that of Professor Friedman as outlined in his *Newsweek* articles (pp. 713–16).

SUGGESTED READING

Beer, Samuel H., and Barringer, Richard E., eds. *The State and the Poor.* Cambridge, Mass.: Winthrop Publishers, 1970.

Bell, Carolyn Shaw. *The Economics of the Ghetto*. New York: Pegasus, 1970.

Budd, Edward C., ed. *Inequality and Poverty*. New York: W. W. Norton & Co., 1967.

Lampman, Robert J. "Nixon's Choices on Cash for the Poor." Institute for Poverty Research, University of Wisconsin, May 1969.

Marchal, Jean, and Ducros, Bernard, eds. *The Distribution of National Income*. London: Macmillan & Co., 1968.

Meade, J. E. *Efficiency, Equality and the Ownership of Property*. Cambridge: Harvard University Press, 1965.

Schnitzer, Martin. *Guaranteed Minimum Income Programs Used by Governments of Selected Countries* (Joint Economic Committee of Congress, 1968).

30

External Effects, Pollution, And Public Policy

We noted in the last chapter that economic growth by no means automatically "solves" the problem of income distribution. In this chapter, we take up a number of problems that arise at least in part *as a consequence* of economic growth. Many of these problems, moreover, are not likely to be handled satisfactorily by the private marketplace, since they involve certain effects which are "external" to the ordinary supply-and-demand mechanism. Adam Smith's "invisible hand" fails us here, and public intervention of one sort or another is almost certain to be necessary.

THE COSTS OF ECONOMIC GROWTH

In the early 1970s, citizens and scholars have raised a fundamental question: is economic growth desirable? Or to put it only slightly less grandly: when a society has reached a stage of wealth where all the necessities of life and a high (by historical standards) degree of comfort have been assured to the overwhelming number of its citizens, does it thereby reach a stage when the costs of growth begin to exceed its benefits, when its energies should properly be turned in other directions?

This is not an altogether new question. Even in the nineteenth century, the great philosopher-economist John Stuart Mill yearned for the day when mankind would look for "better things" than a continuation of the constant "struggle for riches." Mill wrote:

I confess I am not charmed with an ideal of life held out by those who think that the normal state of human beings is that of struggling to get on; that the trampling, crushing, elbowing, and treading on each other's heels, which form the existing type of social life, are the most desirable lot of human kind, or anything but the disagreeable symptoms of one of the phases of industrial progress.

719

John Stuart Mill (1806–1873): Mill was a logician and political philosopher as well as an economist. Raised in the British Classical tradition, he had David Ricardo for an economics tutor.

Mill actually looked forward to the coming of a "stationary state," providing, of course, that the population problem (which had worried his predecessors, Malthus and Ricardo) could be handled and a decent standard of life could be guaranteed to the working classes.

In the United States in the eighth decade of the twentieth century, we have achieved a standard of life for the average man that far exceeds anything that Mill had hoped for. In consequence, there are those who argue that the time has now come to reconsider the pivotal role of economic growth in our social life. The argument has many variants, but it is built around two fundamental themes.

The first theme stresses the *declining benefits* of modern growth in the affluent society. Why do we want more goods, the critics ask. Certainly not out of economic necessity. Not even for added material comfort; historically, men have been content with far less abundance than we now enjoy. Essentially, they answer, we want more goods because a growing society creates the very wants that it in turn supplies. These wants may be created by other consumers in the manner of "keeping up with the Joneses": my neighbor has a new and fancy automobile and thus I, too, must have a new and fancy automobile. Or they may be created by the industrial producers through advertising and other means of public persuasion—if you do not buy such-and-such a product, your personal and social life will be jeopardized if not ruined. In either case, a kind of self-cancelling process of want-creation and want-satisfaction is established. If I buy more because my neighbor buys more, and if he buys more because I buy more, then we can both keep on accumulating purchases indefinitely without either being any better off than if we had remained content with less in the beginning. Similarly, in the case of producer-induced demand: business firms advertise to convince the consumer that they need the goods that they would not have missed had the advertising and the additional production never occurred.

Few critics would claim that these are the *only* motives that make consumers wish additional goods—one may want to buy more records or books, for example, simply because one likes to listen to music or to read—but such motives clearly do enter into many of our purchases and, to this degree, the benefits that accrue from still additional economic growth are far less than they appear in the statistics. As the society becomes ever more affluent, these benefits can be expected continually to decline.

The second theme of this argument, and increasingly the more important theme, has to do with the *costs* of economic growth. Growth has always had associated costs. At the time of the English Industrial Revolution, there was the tremendous dislocation in the traditional pattern of life that the birth of the industrial system involved. Indeed, even the *measurement* of growth is made difficult by the fact that many of the products that we include in our GNP may actually be nothing but costs of an industrial-urban society. Suppose we lay tracks and set up a commuter train service from the suburbs to the city. Should we consider this act of production an addition to GNP, or should we argue that commuter services are simply a required cost of having an industrial-urban society and would have no value were our society organized differently?[1] Within the category of costs of growth, critics can point to a number of effects that amount to a catalog of the weaknesses of our industrial-urban society. Our air is becoming befouled with chemicals and smog. Our streams and rivers are being polluted with industrial wastes and detergents. We are despoiling our natural resource base. Our fields, meadows, and forests are being defaced by highways and billboards. The story is nearly endless and, in the 1970s, very familiar.

The critics of growth emphasize these and other deficiencies arising from the growth process while at the same time pointing to the declining benefits (at least for the rich countries) that this process brings. They ask: is it not a paradox that the affluent society should be creating not great works of art, beauty, and culture, but the megalopolis, the freeway, and the slum?

1. See chapter 8, pp. 194–95, and also the appendix to chapter 8.

SPACESHIP EARTH

For some observers, the questions raised in the above paragraphs suggest that a total reconstruction of our social purposes and patterns is now required. Indeed, many in this group believe that the alternative is social and economic disaster. These dramatic issues are taken up in Great Debate Five: Ecology and Economic Growth. The reader of this debate will notice that scientists are by no means agreed on the degree of ecological dangers that are involved in a perpetuation of our present industrial system. It is also probably true that economists (with exceptions, of course) are slightly skeptical of the doomsayers, partly because they have heard a very similar story before (from Malthus, in particular), but mainly because they have studied the way in which societies, through technological change, have been able to adjust to developing scarcities and shortages. They see economic growth as a main source of society's increasing capacity to cope with problems of pollution, waste, and so on. If growth imposes costs, they say, it also confers the ability to mitigate or remove those costs.

Still, the sharp current interest in ecology is a major fact of our times and, even for the most cautious observer, it raises questions about the basic way in which we view our economic system. One of the more interesting of the new views of the economy has been put forward by Kenneth Boulding, a philosophically minded economist who has served as president of the American Economic Association. He suggests that what we are required to do now is to move from a *throughput economy* to the concept of *spaceship earth.* It is fundamental, Boulding writes, that:

all of economics . . . assumes that economic activity is a throughput, a linear process from the mine to the garbage dump. The ultimate physical product of economic life is garbage. The system takes ores and fossil fuels (and in a boom the unemployed) out of the earth, chews them up in the process of production, and eventually spews them out into sewers and garbage dumps. . . .

The throughput is going to come to an end. . . . Up to now, man has psychologically lived on a flat earth—a great plain, in fact a "darkling plain" where "ignorant armies clash by night," as Matthew Arnold says. Man has always had somewhere to go. . . .

The photographs of the earth by astronauts in lunar orbit symbolize the end of this era. Clearly the earth is a beautiful little spaceship, all blue and green and white, with baroque cloud patterns on it, and its destination is unknown. It is getting pretty crowded and its resources rather limited.

The problem of the present age is that of the transition from the Great Plains into the spaceship or into what Barbara Ward and I have been calling spaceship earth. We do not have any mines and we do not have any sewers in a spaceship. The water has to go through the algae to the kidneys to the algae to the kidneys, and so on, and around and around and around. If the earth is to become a spaceship, we must develop a cyclical economy within which man can maintain an agreeable state.[2]

2. Kenneth E. Boulding, "Fun and Games with the Gross National Product," in *The Environmental Crisis*, ed. Harold W. Helfrich, Jr. (New Haven: Yale University Press, 1970), pp. 162–63. For further discussion of the concepts of a throughput or spaceship economy, see Edwin G. Dolan, *TANSTAAFL** (**There ain't no such thing as a free lunch*) (New York: Holt, Rinehart & Winston, 1971), chapter 1.

What is new about this concept of a spaceship? After all, haven't economists long presented the workings of the economic system as cyclical via the image of the *circular flow*? The contrast between the spaceship view and the old view is suggested by Figures 30-1 and 30-2.

In Figure 30-1, we present the traditional circular flow representation of economic life, but now amended so that its character as a *throughput* system is made clear. In this economy natural resources are pumped into the system either as household-owned factors (private property) or "free" resources (air, water, sunlight, etc.); the circular flow combines these with labor and other factors to produce goods that go to consumers; in the course of this production, industrial wastes are produced and, later, the acts of household consumption create further wastes. In a throughput economy, this is the end of the process. The wastes go into dumps and sewers. The total amount of wastes accumulated tends ever to increase (suggested by the dotted line); simultaneously, the quantity of available natural resources tends ever to decrease (shown, similarly, by the dotted line in the natural resource container). In the long run, such a process cannot keep going on because natural resources will run out. This is alleged to be a major flaw in a throughput economic system.

The specific picture we have drawn in Figure 30-1 must be considered only a point of departure. In two major ways, it tends to *understate* the problem. In the first place, it does not explicitly represent the costs of *pollution*. To do this, we would have to acknowledge that, as the wastes accumulate on the right side of the diagram, there will be negative consequences on the natural resource picture on the left side of the diagram. It is not only that we are using up our supplies of, say, petroleum, but that, in so doing, we are also diminishing our supplies of pure air, water, and so on.

The second major understatement in Figure 30-1 derives from the fact that the circular flow is presented as unchanging in dimension, whereas the characteristic form of modern industrial life, as we know, involves rapid economic growth. To represent the consequences of growth, we would have to show the circular flow in the top half of the diagram increasing in size over time. As it increased in size it would make increased demands on our natural resources and also would accelerate the rate at which

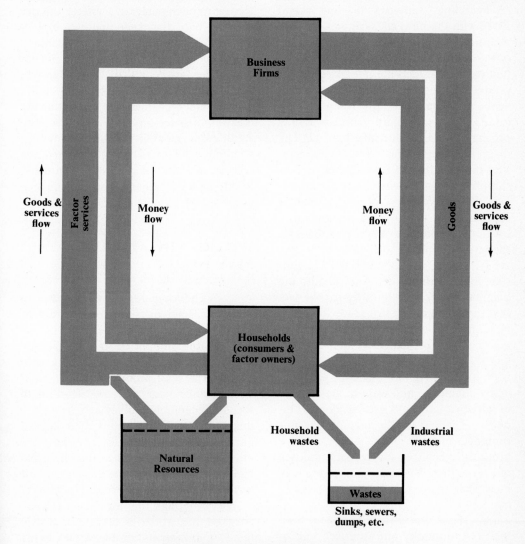

Figure 30-1. A Throughput Economy.

In this diagram, the economic flow is fuelled by natural resources that come from outside the system. These resources are, in effect, converted into garbage by the system.

wastes (and hence pollution) are being accumulated.

On the other hand, the diagram can also be faulted for *overstating* certain aspects of the problem. Those who take a more optimistic view of our ecological situation might criticize the diagram on at least three grounds: (1) It ignores natural recycling. Although no one would agree with the pure classical view of land as the "original and indestructible" powers of the soil,[3] nevertheless it is clear that many resources are not "used up" in production, but can be used over and over again. If the total natural resource base is fairly large, these natural processes may protect us for a considerable time. (2) The diagram suggests the erroneous conclusion that production leads either to consumption or waste, whereas a very important product of our economic system is capital. That is to say, we translate iron ore in the ground into a much more useful shape—a hammer, a steel girder, a bridge, etc.—many of which products have considerable durability. (3) And, finally, the diagram makes no allowance for the fact that the economic system tends to economize on scarce resources—the scarcer they become, the more expensive they become, and the more we try to find ways to do without them. Human ingenuity will generally attempt to find ways of making use of what we have and getting along without what we no longer have (or are fast running short of). These attempts have historically been very successful, though, of course, there is no way of knowing how long that pattern of success can be maintained.

Thus, the picture is mixed. Still, the need to modify our approach to economic life in the direction of spaceship-thinking is widely acknowledged.

This new approach is suggested by Figure 30-2, in which a vital link has been added between the waste container and the resource container. What this diagram suggests is that our economic survival and/or comfort in the long run may depend significantly on our ability to recycle our waste products in such a way that, far from producing negative effects on our resource base, they keep that base replenished. Whether such a cyclical economy could sustain growth over time is not clear—the advocates of Zero Growth would doubtless say no. It seems fairly certain, however, that at a minimum the creation of spaceship earth would require a different mentality from that which stimulated the Industrial Revolution of the eighteenth and nineteenth centuries. Maintenance, rather than expansion, might easily become the key word.

WHERE THE MARKET MAY FAIL

The foregoing discussion raises a very important question for the student of economics. In Part Three, we spent a considerable amount of time developing the point that a market economy produces, or at least produces under certain circumstances, an "efficient" solution to society's economic problems. Now we are talking about the possibility of ecological and environmental disaster. What, we must ask, has happened to the "invisible hand"? Has Adam Smith's metaphor turned out to be nothing but a cruel hoax?

Although this conclusion is a bit hard on the workings of a market system—environmental problems may easily be as serious in the command economy of the Soviet Union as in our mixed market economy—nevertheless, it is true that the qualifications to the invisible hand

---

3. See chapter 21, p. 491.

doctrine seem to loom particularly large in an advanced industrial economy. Let us list some of the areas in which, even in pure theory, the market economy may be deemed to give an unsatisfactory social outcome; then let us show how this analysis applies in the specific case of air pollution.

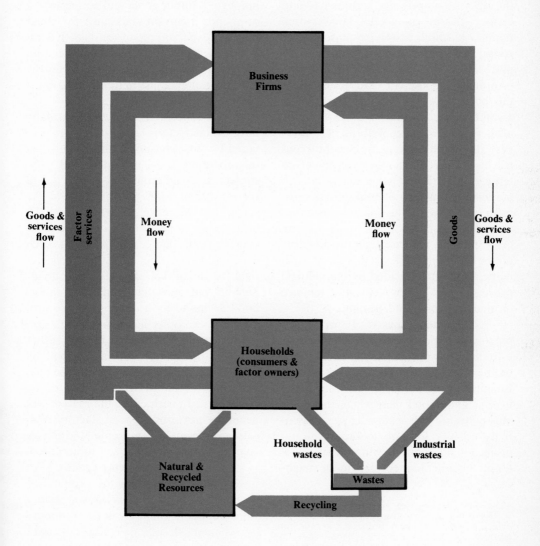

Figure 30-2. Spaceship Earth.

In this economy, wastes are recycled to keep the total of resources constant. There is a similarity between this kind of economy and life aboard a spaceship.

First, our brief list:[4]

(1) Unacceptable consumer wants. Consumer sovereignty is highly prized in a market-oriented society, but not invariably. Certain classes of consumers—infants, the insane, imprisoned criminals—and certain classes of goods—tanks, atom bombs, harmful drugs or poisons—are considered to have a status in the marketplace different from ordinary consumers or ordinary goods. We shall not dwell on this point since, for the most part, we do assume that consumers are the ultimate arbiters of economic performance; however, it is notable that many currently controversial questions about government intervention in the economy touch on such matters. Examples: Should the government forbid the production and consumption of marijuana? Should it pass a gun law? Should it regulate cigarette advertising or "immoral" television shows? Such matters are often decided by the political process rather than by any simple reliance on market supply and demand.

(2) Public goods. It would be practically impossible to sell certain goods to individual consumers; the goods must be provided collectively or not at all. Imagine an individual homeowner living in a neighborhood near which there is a mosquito-infested swamp. There is essentially no way for him to buy mosquito protection for himself without buying it for all the other homeowners in the neigh-borhood. Unless there is some collective agreement to control insect life in the swamp as a whole, there may be no mosquito protection for anyone.

National defense is the classic example of a public good, and an important one, since it currently accounts for about half the expenditures of the U.S. federal government. Other important examples are police protection and provision for the administration of justice through the court system.

Public goods and services usually have the characteristic that if they are provided to some consumers there is no cost in providing them to additional consumers. If a lighthouse is set up, it will service 100 or 1,000 passing ships at the same cost. Moreover, it will usually be difficult or impossible to exclude consumers from the consumption of such goods and services even if they have not paid for any of their costs. If fifty individuals in our mosquito-ridden neighborhood decide to set up a mosquito control program, the other homeowners will also be protected, even though they have not paid for the service. (In fact, it will be in their purely *private* interest not to pay, but to accept the protection provided by the others.) In such cases, the market will generally not provide a satisfactory allocation of resources, and some kind of collective political decision will be required.

(3) Decreasing-cost goods. We have already mentioned the problem of decreasing-cost industries in connection with monopoly elements in the economy (see chapter 24, p. 575). We raise it again here only to point up a special feature of the problem—namely, that simple government regulation of such industries may not be enough to bring economic efficiency. More active intervention, including subsidies or outright public ownership, may be required.

---

4. This is not an exhaustive list of all the possible defects of a market system. It does not include, for example, the fact that a market economy does not necessarily (or ordinarily) produce a socially desirable distribution of income (see chapter 29) or the whole range of issues involved in the fiscal and monetary policies required to maintain full employment (Part Two). This list is focused primarily on those areas where the market fails to bring us "efficiency" and where public intervention of one sort or another will ordinarily be required. The reader should also supplement the list by recalling our discussion of market imperfections—especially in chapters 24–26.

Take the case of a public utility or a mass transport system. We may have a situation in which two conditions are fulfilled: (*a*) it is socially desirable that this particular service be provided; and (*b*) if the government requires a private monopolist to price the service in an economically "efficient" way, the monopolist would have to go out of business. The problem is that in a decreasing-cost industry, the average cost of the firm is falling as output increases and, hence, marginal cost is below it. To secure efficiency, the government may regulate the industry so that $P = MC$. (If $P > MC$, output would be too low, since consumers could get greater satisfaction out of additional units of the service than the additional [marginal] cost to society of providing those services.) But as Figure 30-3 shows,

such a price would involve the firm in perpetual losses, as indicated by the shaded rectangle.

Of course, not *all* such industries should exist at all. It is also necessary that the first condition be fulfilled—i.e., the total benefits that consumers receive from having this particular industry must exceed the total costs of providing those services.[5] However, it is not difficult to think of cases in which this holds true. We might imagine a highway that is expensive to construct, but the cost of driving additional cars on it is very low. Bridges are often cited as examples. In such cases, private ownership with government regulation may not be adequate to guarantee efficiency; public ownership, or other complicated forms of public subsidy, may be required.

(4) External economies and diseconomies. In addition to *internal* economies of scale (the decreasing-cost industries just discussed), production in our economy may involve certain *external* effects. Indeed, such "externalities" may occur with respect to consumption as well as production.

An external economy *occurs when the activity of an economic unit confers a real benefit upon other producers or consumers in the economy, beyond the benefits for*

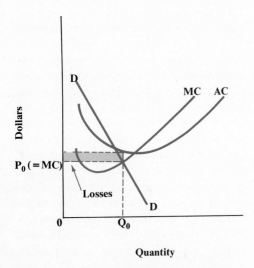

Figure 30-3. Decreasing-Cost Industry.

If the government requires a private monopolist to price his product efficiently ($P=MC$) when decreasing costs prevail, the firm will make losses (as shown by the shaded rectangle). If the industry is to continue, therefore, the government may have to subsidize it or engage in public ownership.

5. The examination of this issue is technically complicated, involving concepts such as *consumer's surplus,* which we have not developed in this book. The basic idea can be understood, however, if we reflect that consumers generally get greater satisfactions from the consumption of the first units of a commodity than from subsequent units. Since the price of the good reflects satisfaction at the margin—i.e., of the last units purchased—consumers derive a kind of "surplus" satisfaction on all the previous units consumed. Thus, if the choice were between paying more for the good or doing without it *in total,* consumers would undoubtedly be willing to pay more than they do at the margin. Such "surpluses" have to be taken into account in deciding whether any good is worth producing in terms of total net benefits.

which the individual unit is paid. An external diseconomy *occurs when this unit confers real costs upon other producers or consumers, for which it is not charged.*

Although the concept may seem complicated, such external effects are among the everyday experience of anyone living in a modern economy. Take the area of education, for example. A person benefits from an education because it provides direct satisfactions and enhances his earning power. But it is also a benefit to society at large to have widespread education for political, social, and cultural purposes. *I* benefit because *you* are educated, and vice versa. My benefit is an external economy of your education, for which you are not recompensed. External *dis*economies are also easy to find, especially in modern urban life. Many of the costs of economic growth that we discussed earlier in this chapter involve external diseconomies. Pollution is a notable example, which we shall consider in a moment.

The significance of external economies and diseconomies is that they create a gap between *private* benefits and costs (measured through prices in the marketplace) and *social* benefits and costs. It may be socially undesirable to have a boiler factory in a residential neighborhood; but if the businessman is not charged for the mental anguish of the neighbors caused by the constant noise, it may be in his private interest to build the factory anyway. Consider why school education is generally publicly financed in the United States.

If education were left purely in private hands, each person would theoretically purchase it to the point where the additional private gains from one more unit (say, another year of schooling) were equal to the additional cost of that unit. But from society's point of view, this will

be too little education, since the additional *social* benefit (private benefit plus external effects) is greater than the marginal cost of having this person take another year of schooling. Where such external effects are important, a strong case can be made for public intervention, ranging all the way from regulation to subsidies and taxes and, as in the case of public education, direct provision of the goods and services by the State.[6]

(5) Inadequate access to product and factor markets. A final category of problems that may lead the market to produce unsatisfactory social results is the differential access of various individuals *to* the markets of the economy. Generally, in our analysis of market economies, we assumed that individuals in the economy were aware of the available alternatives in purchasing goods or seeking employment and that they were able to act effectively on this knowledge. But in any society there will always be groups for which this assumption is not true. Sometimes the problem may be informational and geographical. Appalachia has sometimes been cited as a particular area of the economy where workers and their families, being poor, isolated, and little educated, lack any real knowledge of market alternatives; nor do they have the physical and cultural mobility necessary to take advantage of them if known. But access to the market can also be artificially contrived, as in the important case of racial discrimination. Racial discrimination can be

Continued on p. 752

---

6. The case for public intervention does not apply to all external effects of any kind. When more firms enter an industry, they may cause a rise in the factor prices and hence costs to other firms in the industry, but these higher factor prices *do* reflect the increased scarcity—and hence social cost—of using these factors. Such external effects, where there is no divergence between private and social benefits and costs, are sometimes called *pecuniary external economies* (or *diseconomies*), as noted on p. 473n.

GREAT DEBATE FIVE
ECOLOGY AND ECONOMICGROWTH

In the early 1970s, a number of documents were published purporting to show that economic growth in the industrialized world was not only of questionable benefit, but harmful, and in the not so very distant future, potentially disastrous. These works included Jay Forrester's *World Dynamics* (Wright-Allen Press, 1971), the Club of Rome's *Limits To Growth* (New York: Universe Books, 1972) and the British "A Blueprint for Survival," excerpts from which are included below.

These works made front-page news in the *New York Times* and countless other newspapers and have been discussed at length in articles and editorials in this country and abroad. The reader who wishes to pursue the matter further after studying the Great Debate that follows should consult the above-mentioned works directly and also some of the criticisms that have been levied at the methods employed and conclusions reached in those works. Such criticisms appear in the works of a Columbia University economist, Peter Passell, and a Columbia University lawyer, Leonard Ross, such as "Don't Knock the $2-Trillion Economy," in *The New York Times Magazine* (March 5, 1972) and in their book, *The Retreat from Riches: The Gross National Product and Its Enemies* (New York: Viking Press, 1972).

In view of the passionate nature of the concern shown in the following readings, it is unnecessary to stress that the issues involved are clearly of monumental importance to modern man.

A BLUEPRINT FOR SURVIVAL[*]

The Ecologist

I. INTRODUCTION: THE NEED FOR CHANGE

The principal defect of the industrial way of life with its ethos of expansion is that it is not sustainable. Its termination within the lifetime of someone born today is inevitable—unless it continues to be sustained for a while longer by an entrenched minority at the cost of imposing great suffering on the rest of mankind. We can be certain, however, that sooner or later it will end (only the precise time and circumstances are in doubt), and that it will do so in one of two ways: either against our will, in a succession of famines, epidemics, social crises and wars; or because we want it to—because we wish to create a society which will not impose hardship and cruelty upon our children—in a succession of thoughtful, humane and measured changes.

Radical change is both necessary and inevitable because the present increases in human numbers and *per capita* consumption, by disrupting ecosystems and depleting resources, are undermining the very foundations of survival. At present the world population of 3,600 million is increasing by 2 percent per year (72 million), but this overall figure conceals crucially important differences between countries. The industrialised countries with one-third of the world population have annual growth rates of between 0.5 and 1.0 percent; the undeveloped countries on the other hand, with two-thirds of the world population, have annual growth rates of between 2 and 3 percent, and from 40 to 45 percent of their population is under fifteen. It is commonly overlooked that in countries with an unbalanced age structure

*This document has been drawn up by a small team of people involved in the study of global environmental problems.

of this kind the population will continue to increase for many years even after fertility has fallen to the replacement level. As the Population Council has pointed out: "If replacement is achieved in the developed world by 2000 and in the developing world by 2040, then the world's population will stabilise at nearly 15.5 billion (15,500 million) about a century hence, or well over four times the present size."

The *per capita* use of energy and raw materials also shows a sharp division between the developed and the undeveloped parts of the world. Both are increasing their use of these commodities, but consumption in the developed countries is so much higher that, even with their smaller share of the population, their consumption may well represent over 80 percent of the world total. For the same reason, similar percentage increases are far more significant in the developed countries; to take one example, between 1957 and 1967 *per capita* steel consumption rose by 12 percent in the U.S. and by 41 percent in India, but the actual increases (in kg per year) were from 568 to 634 and from 9.2 to 13 respectively. Nor is there any sign that an eventual end to economic growth is envisaged, and indeed industrial economies appear to break down if growth ceases or even slows, however high the absolute level of consumption. Even the U.S. still aims at an annual growth of GNP of 4 percent or more. Within this overall figure much higher growth rates occur for the use of particular resources, such as oil.

The combination of human numbers and *per capita* consumption has a considerable impact on the environment, in terms of both the resources we take from it and the pollutants we impose on it. A distinguished group of scientists, who came together for a "Study of Critical Environmental Problems" (SCEP) under the auspices of the Massachusetts Institute of Technology,

state in their report the clear need for a means of measuring this impact, and have coined the term "ecological demand," which they define as "a summation of all man's demands on the environment, such as the extraction of resources and the return of wastes." Gross Domestic Product (GDP), which is population multiplied by material standard of living appears to provide the most convenient measure of ecological demand, and according to the UN *Statistical Yearbook* this is increasing annually by 5 to 6 percent, or doubling every 13.5 years. If this trend should continue, then in the time taken for world population to double (which is estimated to be by just after the year 2000), total ecological demand will have increased by a factor of six. SCEP estimate that "such demand-producing activities as agriculture, mining and industry have global annual rates of increase of 3.5 percent and 7 percent respectively. An integrated rate of increase is estimated to be between 5 and 6 percent per year, in comparison with an annual rate of population increase of only 2 percent."

It should go without saying that the world cannot accommodate this continued increase in ecological demand. *Indefinite* growth of whatever type cannot be sustained by *finite* resources. This is the nub of the environmental predicament. It is still less possible to maintain indefinite *exponential* growth—and unfortunately the growth of ecological demand is proceeding exponentially (i.e., it is increasing geometrically, by compound interest).

The implications of exponential growth are not generally appreciated and are well worth considering. As Professor Forrester explains it, ". . . pure exponential growth possesses the characteristic of behaving according to a 'doubling time.' Each fixed time interval shows a doubling of the relevant system variable. Exponential growth is treacherous and misleading. A system variable can continue through many doubling intervals without seeming to reach significant size. But then in one or two more doubling periods, still following the same law of exponential growth, it suddenly seems to become overwhelming."

Thus, supposing world petroleum reserves stood at 2,100 billion barrels, and supposing our rate of consumption was increasing by 6.9 percent per year, then as can be seen from Figure 1, demand will exceed supply by the end of the century. What is significant, however, is not the speed at which such vast reserves can be depleted, but that as late as 1975 there will appear to be reserves fully ample enough to last for considerably longer. Such a situation can easily lull one into a false sense of security and the belief that a given growth rate can be sustained, if not indefinitely, at least for a good deal longer than is actu-

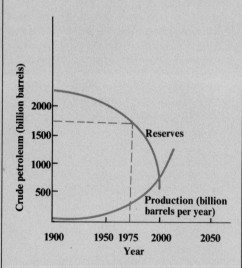

Figure 1. World Reserves of Crude Petroleum at Exponential Rate of Consumption.

Note that in 1975, with no more than fifteen years left before demand exceeds supply, the total global reserve has been depleted by only 12½ percent.

ally the case. The same basic logic applies to the availability of any resource including land, and it is largely because of this particular dynamic of exponential growth that the environmental predicament has come upon us so suddenly, and why its solution requires urgent and radical measures, many of which run counter to values which, in our industrial society we have been taught to regard as fundamental.

If we allow the present growth rate to persist, total ecological demand will increase by a factor of thirty-two over the next sixty-six years—and there can be no serious person today willing to concede the possibility, or indeed the desirability, of our accommodating the pressures arising from such growth. For this can be done only at the cost of disrupting ecosystems and exhausting resources, which must lead to the failure of food supplies and the collapse of society. It is worth briefly considering each in turn.

Disruption of Ecosystems

We depend for our survival on the predictability of ecological processes. If they were at all arbitrary, we would not know when to reap or sow, and we would be at the mercy of environmental whim. We could learn nothing about the rest of nature, advance no hypotheses, suggest no "laws." Fortunately, ecological processes *are* predictable, and although theirs is a relatively young discipline, ecologists have been able to formulate a number of important "laws," one of which in particular relates to environmental predictability: namely, that all ecosystems tend towards stability, and further that the more diverse and complex the ecosystem the more stable it is; that is, the more species there are, and the more they interrelate, the more stable is their environment. By stability is meant the ability to return to the original position after any change, instead of being forced into a totally different pattern—and hence predictability.

Unfortunately, we behave as if we knew nothing of the environment and had no conception of its predictability, treating it instead with scant and brutal regard as if it were an idiosyncratic and extremely stupid slave. We seem never to have reflected on the fact that a tropical rain forest supports innumerable insect species and yet is never devastated by them; that its rampant luxuriance is not contingent on our overflying it once a month and bombarding it with insecticides, herbicides, fungicides, and what-have-you. And yet we tremble over our wheatfields and cabbage patches with a desperate battery of synthetic chemicals, in an absurd attempt to to impede the operation of the immutable "law" we have just mentioned—that all ecosystems tend towards stability, therefore diversity and complexity, therefore a growing number of different plant and animal species until a climax or optimal condition is achieved. If we were clever, we would recognise that successful long-term agriculture demands the achievement of an artificial climax, an imitation of the pre-existing ecosystem, so that the level of unwanted species could be controlled by those that did no harm to the crop-plants.

Instead we have put our money on pesticides, which although they have been effective, have been so only to a limited and now diminishing extent: according to SCEP, the 34 percent increase in world food production from 1951 to 1966 required increased investments in nitrogenous fertilisers of 146 percent and in pesticides of 300 percent. At the same time they have created a number of serious problems, notably resistance—some 250 pest species are resistant to one group of pesticides or another, while many others require increased applications to keep their populations within manageable proportions—and the promotion of formerly innocuous species to pest proportions, because the predators that formerly kept them down have been destroyed. The spread of DDT and other organochlorines in the environment has resulted in alarming population declines among woodcock, grebes, various birds of prey and seabirds, and in a number of fish species, principally the sea trout. SCEP comments: "the oceans are an ultimate accumulation site of DDT and its residues. As much as 25 percent of the DDT compounds produced to date may have been transferred to the sea. The amount in the marine biota is estimated to be in the order of less than 0.1 percent of total production and has already produced a demonstrable impact upon the marine environment. . . . The decline in productivity of marine food fish and the accumulation of levels of DDT in their tissues which are unacceptable to man can only be accelerated by DDT's continued release to the environment. . . ."

There are half a million man-made chemicals in use today, yet we cannot predict the behaviour or properties of the greater part of them (either singly or in combination) once they are released into the environment. We know, however, that the combined effects of pollution and habitat destruction menace the survival of no less than 280 mammal, 350 bird, and 20,000 plant species. To those who regret these losses but greet them with the comment that the survival of *Homo sapiens* is surely more important than that of an eagle or a primrose, we repeat that *Homo sapiens* himself depends on the continued resilience of those ecological networks of which eagles and primroses are integral parts. We do not need to utterly destroy the ecosphere to bring catastrophe upon ourselves: all we have to do is to carry on as we are, clearing forests, "reclaiming" wetlands, and imposing sufficient quantities of pesticides, radioactive materials, plastics, sewage, and industrial wastes upon our air, water and land systems to make them inhospitable to the species on which their continued stability and integrity depend. Industrial man in the world today is like a bull in a china shop, with the single difference that a bull with half the information about the properties of china as we have about those of ecosystems would probably try and adapt its behaviour to its environment rather than the reverse. By contrast, *Homo sapiens industrialis* is determined that the china shop should adapt to him, and has therefore set himself the goal of reducing it to rubble in the shortest possible time.

Failure of Food Supplies

Increases in food production in the undeveloped world have barely kept abreast of population growth. Such increases as there have been are due not to higher productivity but to the opening up of new land for cultivation. Unfortunately this will not be possible for much longer: all the good land in the world is now being farmed, and according to the FAO, at present rates of expansion none of the marginal land that is left will be unfarmed by 1985—indeed some of the land now under cultivation has been so exhausted that it will have to be returned to permanent pasture.

For this reason, FAO's programme to feed the world depends on a programme of intensification, at the heart of which are the new high-yield varieties of wheat and rice. These are highly responsive to inorganic fertilisers and quick-maturing, so that up to ten times present yields can be obtained from them. Unfortunately, they are highly vulnerable to disease, and therefore require increased protection by pesticides, and of course they demand massive inputs of fertilisers (up to 27 times present ones). Not only will these disrupt local ecosystems, thereby jeopardising long-term

productivity, but they force hardpressed undeveloped nations to rely on the agro-chemical industries of the developed world.

Whatever their virtues and faults, the new genetic hybrids are not intended to solve the world food problem, but only to give us time to devise more permanent and realistic solutions. It is our view, however, that these hybrids are not the best means of doing this, since their use is likely to bring about a reduction in overall diversity, when the clear need is to develop an agriculture diverse enough to have long-term potential. We must beware of those "experts" who appear to advocate the transformation of the ecosphere into nothing more than a food-factory for man. The concept of a world consisting solely of man and a few favoured food plants is so ludicrously impracticable as to be seriously contemplated only by those who find solace in their own wilful ignorance of the real world of biological diversity.

We in Britain must bear in mind that we depend on imports for half our food, and that we are unlikely to improve on this situation. The 150,000 acres which are lost from agriculture each year are about 70 percent more productive than the average for all enclosed land, while we are already beginning to experience diminishing returns from the use of inorganic fertilisers. In the period 1964-9, applications of phosphates have gone up by 2 percent, potash by 7 percent, and nitrogen by 40 percent, yet yields per acre of wheat, barley, lucerne and temporary grass have levelled off and are beginning to decline, while that of permanent grass has risen only slightly and may be levelling off. As *per capita* food availability declines throughout the rest of the world, and it appears inevitable it will, we will find it progressively more difficult and expensive to meet our food requirements from abroad. The prospect of severe food shortages within the next thirty years is not so much a fantasy as that of the continued abundance promised us by so many of our politicians.

Exhaustion of Resources

As we have seen, continued exponential growth of consumption of materials and energy is impossible. Present reserves of all but a few metals will be exhausted within fifty years, if consumption rates continue to grow as they are. Obviously there will be new discoveries and advances in mining technology, but these are likely to provide us with only a limited stay of execution. Synthetics and substitutes are likely to be of little help, since they must be made from materials which themselves are in short supply; while the hoped-for availability of unlimited energy would not be the answer, since the problem is the ratio of useful metal to waste matter (which would have to be disposed of without disrupting ecosystems), not the need for cheap power. Indeed, the availability of unlimited power holds more of a threat than a promise, since energy use is inevitably polluting, and in addition we would ultimately have to face the problem of disposing of an intractable amount of waste heat.

Collapse of Society

The developed nations consume such disproportionate amounts of protein, raw materials and fuels that unless they considerably reduce their consumption there is no hope of the undeveloped nations markedly improving their standards of living. This vast differential is a cause of much and growing discontent, made worse by our attempts at cultural uniformity on behalf of an expanding market economy. In the end, we are altering people's aspirations without providing the means for them to be satisfied. In the rush to industrialise we break up communities, so that the controls which formerly regulated behaviour are destroyed before alternatives can be provided. Urban drift is one result of this process, with a consequent rise in anti-social practices, crime, delinquency, and so on, which are so costly for society in terms both of money and of well-being.

At the same time, we are sowing the seeds of massive unemployment by increasing the ratio of capital to labour so that the provision of each job becomes ever more expensive. In a world of fast diminishing resources, we shall quickly come to the point when very great numbers of people will be thrown out of work, when the material compensations of urban life are either no longer available or prohibitively expensive, and consequently when whole sections of society will find good cause to express their considerable discontent in ways likely to be anything but pleasant for their fellows.

It is worth bearing in mind that the barriers between us and epidemics are not so strong as is commonly supposed. Not only is it increasingly difficult to control the vectors of disease, but it is more than probable that urban populations are being insidiously weakened by overall pollution levels, even when they are not high enough to be incriminated in any one illness. At the same time international mobility speeds the spread of disease. With this background, and at a time of widespread public demoralisation, the collapse of vital social services such as power and sanitation, could easily provoke a series of epidemics—and we cannot say with confidence that we would be able to cope with them.

At times of great distress and social chaos, it is more than probable that governments will fall into the hands of reckless and unscrupulous elements, who will not hesitate to threaten neighbouring governments with attack, if they feel that they can wrest from them a larger share of the world's vanishing resources. Since a growing number of countries (an estimated thirty-six by 1980) will have nuclear power stations, and therefore sources of plutonium for nuclear warheads, the likelihood of a whole series of local (if not global) nuclear engagements is greatly increased.

By now it should be clear that the main problems of the environment do not arise from temporary and accidental malfunctions of existing economic and social systems. On the contrary, they are the warning signs of a profound incompatibility between deeply rooted beliefs in continuous growth and the dawning recognition of the earth as a space ship,* limited in its resources and vulnerable to thoughtless mishandling. The nature of our response to these symptoms is crucial. If we refuse to recognise the cause of our trouble the result can only be increasing disillusion and growing strain upon the fragile institutions that maintain external peace and internal social cohesion. If, on the other hand, we can respond to this unprecedented challenge with informed and constructive action, the rewards will be as great as the penalties for failure.

Our task is to create a society which is sustainable and which will give the fullest possible satisfaction to its members. Such a society by definition would depend not on expansion but on stability. This does not mean to say that it would be stagnant—indeed it could well afford more variety than does the state of uniformity at present being imposed by the pursuit of technological efficiency. We believe that the stable society, as well as removing the sword of Damocles which hangs over the heads of future generations, is much more likely than the present one to

*[See discussion of this concept, pp. 721-24.]

bring the peace and fulfilment which hitherto have been regarded, sadly, as utopian.

II. TOWARDS THE STABLE SOCIETY

Introduction

The principal conditions of a stable society—one that to all intents and purposes can be sustained indefinitely while giving optimum satisfaction to its members—are: (1) minimum disruption of ecological processes; (2) maximum conservation of materials and energy— or an economy of stock rather than flow; (3) a population in which recruitment equals loss; and (4) a social system in which the individual can enjoy, rather than feel restricted by, the first three conditions.

The achievement of these four conditions will require controlled and well-orchestrated change on numerous fronts and this change will probably occur through seven operations: (1) a control operation whereby environmental disruption is reduced as much as possible by technical means; (2) a freeze operation, in which present trends are halted; (3) asystemic substitution, by which the most dangerous components of these trends are replaced by technological substitutes, whose effect is less deleterious in the short-term, but over the long-term will be increasingly ineffective; (4) systemic substitution, by which these technological substitutes are replaced by "natural" or self-regulating ones, i.e., those which either replicate or employ without undue disturbance the normal processes of the ecosphere, and are therefore likely to be sustainable over very long periods of time; (5) the invention, promotion and application of alternative technologies which are energy and materials conservative, and which because they are designed for relatively "closed" economic communities are likely to disrupt ecological processes only minimally (e.g. intermediate technology); (6) decentralisation of polity and economy at all levels, and the formation of communities small enough to be reasonably self-regulating and self-supporting; and (7) education for such communities.

In putting forward these proposals we are aware that hasty or disordered change is highly disruptive and ultimately self-defeating; but we are also mindful of how the time-scale imposed on any proposal for a remedial course of action has been much-abbreviated by the dynamic of exponential growth (of population, resource depletion and pollution) and by the scarcely perceived scale and intensity of our disruption of the ecological processes on which we and all other life-forms depend. Within these limitations, therefore, we have taken care to devise and synchronise our programme so as to minimise both un-unemployment and capital outlay. We believe it possible to change from an expansionist society to a stable society without loss of jobs or an increase in real expenditure. Inevitably, however, there will be considerable changes, both of geography and function, in job availability and the requirements for capital inputs—and these may set up immense counter-productive social pressures. Yet given the careful and sensitive conception and implementation of a totally integrated programme these should be minimised, and an open style of government should inspire the trust and co-operation of the general public so essential for the success of this enterprise.

Minimizing the Disruption of Ecological Processes

Ecological processes can be disrupted by introducing into them either substances that are foreign to them or the correct ones in the wrong quantities. It follows therefore that the most common method of pollution "control," namely dispersal, is not control at all, but a more or less useful way of playing for time. Refuse disposal by dumping solves the immediate problem of the householder, but as dumping sites are used up it creates progressively less soluble problems for society at large; smokeless fuels are invaluable signs of progress for the citizens of London or Sheffield, but the air pollution from their manufacture brings misery and ill-health to the people near the plants where they are produced; in many cases the dispersal of pollutants through tall chimneys merely alters the proportion of pollution, so that instead of a few receiving much, many receive some; and lastly, in estuarine and coastal waters—crucial areas for fisheries—nutrients from sewage and agricultural run-off in modest quantities probably increase productivity, but in excess are as harmful as organochlorines and heavy metals.

Thus dispersal can be only a temporary expedient. Pollution control proper must consist of the recycling of materials, or the introduction of practices which are so akin to natural processes as not to be harmful. The long-term object of these pollution control procedures is to minimise our dependence on technology as a regulator of the ecological cycles on which we depend, and to return as much as possible to the natural mechanisms of the ecosphere, since in all but the short-term they are much more efficient and reliable.

Conversion to an Economy of Stock

The transfer from flow to stock economics can be considered under two headings: resource management and social accounting.

Resource management. It is essential that the throughput of raw materials be minimised both to conserve non-renewable resources and to cut down pollution. Since industry must have an economic incentive to be conservative of materials and energy and to recycle as much as possible, we propose a number of fiscal measures to these ends: (*a*) A raw materials tax. This would be proportionate to the availability of the raw material in question, and would be designed to enable our reserves to last over an arbitrary period of time, the longer the better, on the principle that during this time our dependence on this raw material would be reduced. This tax would penalise resource-intensive industries and favour employment-intensive ones. Like (*b*) below it would also penalise short-lived products.

(*b*) An amortisation tax. This would be proportionate to the estimated life of the product, e.g., it would be 100 percent for products designed to last no more than a year, and would then be progressively reduced to zero percent for those designed to last 100+ years. Obviously this would penalise short-lived products, especially disposable ones, thereby reducing resource utilisation and pollution, particularly the solid-waste problem. Plastics, for example, which are so remarkable for their durability, would be used only in products where this quality is valued, and not for single trip purposes. This tax would also encourage craftmanship and employment-intensive industry.

Social accounting. By the introduction of monetary incentives and disincentives it is possible to put a premium on durability and a penalty on disposability, thereby reducing the throughput of materials and energy so that resources are conserved and pollution reduced. But another important way of reducing pollution and enhancing amenity is by the provision of a more equitable social accounting system, reinforced by anti-disamenity legislation. Social account-

ing procedures must be used not just to weigh up the merits of alternative development proposals, but also to determine whether or not society actually wants such development. Naturally, present procedures require improvement: for example, in calculating "revealed preference" (the values of individuals and communities as "revealed" to economists by the amount people are willing and/or can afford to pay for or against a given development), imagination, sensitivity and commonsense are required in order to avoid the imposition on poor neighbourhoods or sparsely inhabited countryside of nuclear power stations, reservoirs, motorways, airports, and the like; and in calculating the "social time preference rate" (an indication of society's regard for the future) for a given project, a very low discount should be given, since it is easier to do than undo, and we must assume that unless we botch things completely many more generations will follow us who will not thank us for exhausting resources or blighting the landscape.

The social costs of any given development should be paid by those who propose or perpetrate it—"the polluter must pay" is a principle that must guide our costing procedures. Furthermore, accounting decisions should be made in the light of stock economics: in other words, we must judge the health of our economy not by flow or throughput, since this inevitably leads to waste, resource depletion and environmental disruption, but by the distribution, quality and variety of the stock. At the moment, as Kenneth Boulding has pointed out, "the success of the economy is measured by the amount of throughput derived in part from reservoirs of raw materials, processed by 'factors of production,' and passed on in part as output to the sink of pollution reservoirs. The Gross National Product (GNP) roughly measures this throughput." Yet, both the reservoirs of raw materials and the reservoirs for pollution are limited and finite, so that ultimately the throughput from the one to the other must be detrimental to our well-being and must therefore not only be minimised but be regarded as a cost rather than a benefit. For this reason Boulding has suggested that GNP be considered a measure of gross national cost, and that we devote ourselves to its minimisation, maximising instead the quality of our stock. "When we have developed the economy of the spaceship earth," he writes, "in which man will persist in equilibrium with his environment, the notion of the GNP will simply disintegrate. We will be less concerned with income-flow concepts and more with capital-stock concepts. Then technological changes that result in the maintenance of the total stock with *less* throughput (less production and consumption) will be a clear gain." We must come to assess our standard of living not by calculating the value of all the air-conditioners we have made and sold, but by the freshness of the air; not by the value of the antibiotics, hormones, feedstuff and broiler-houses, and the cost of disposing of their wastes, all of which put so heavy a price on poultry production today, but by the flavour and nutritional quality of the chickens themselves; and so on. In other words, accepted value must reflect real value, just as accepted cost must reflect real cost.

Stabilising the Population

We have seen already that however slight the growth rate, a population cannot grow indefinitely. It follows, therefore, that at some point it must stabilise of its own volition, or else be cut down by some "natural" mechanism—famine, epidemic, war, or whatever. Since no sane society would choose the latter course, it must choose to stabilise.

Our task is to end population growth by lowering the rate of recruitment so that it equals the rate of loss. A few countries will then be able to stabilise, to maintain that ratio; most others, however, will have to slowly *reduce* their populations to a level at which it is sensible to stabilise. Stated baldly, the task seems impossible; but if we start now, and the exercise is spread over a sufficiently long period of time, then we believe that it is within our capabilities. The difficulties are enormous, but they are surmountable.

First, governments must acknowledge the problem and declare their commitment to ending population growth; this commitment should also include an end to immigration. Secondly, they must set up national population services with a fourfold brief:

(1) to publicise as widely and vigorously as possible the relationship between population, food supply, quality of life, resource depletion, etc., and the great need for couples to have no more than two children. The finest talents in advertising should be recruited for this, and the broad aim should be to inculcate a socially more responsible attitude to child-rearing. For example, the notion (derived largely from the popular women's magazines) that childless couples should be objects of pity rather than esteem should be sharply challenged; and of course there are many similar notions to be disputed.

(2) to provide at local and national levels free contraception advice and information on other services such as abortion and sterilisation;

(3) to provide a comprehensive domiciliary service, and to provide contraceptives free of charge, free sterilisation, and abortion on demand;

(4) to commission, finance, and coordinate research not only on demographic techniques and contraceptive technology, but also on the subtle cultural controls necessary for the harmonious maintenance of stability. We know so

little about the dynamics of human populations that we cannot say whether the first three measures would be sufficient. It is self-evident that if couples still wanted families larger than the replacement-size no amount of free contraception would make any difference. However, because we know so little about population control, it would be difficult for us to devise any of the socio-economic restraints which on the face of it are likely to be more effective, but which many people fear might be unduly repressive. For this reason, we would be wise to rely on the first three measures for the next twenty years or so. We then may find they are enough—but if they aren't, we must hope that intensive research during this period will be rewarded with a set of socio-economic restraints that are both *effective* and *humane.* These will then constitute the third stage, and should also provide the tools for the fourth stage—that of persuading the public to have average family sizes of slightly *less* than replacement size, so that total population can be greatly reduced. If we achieve a decline rate of 0.5 percent per year, the same as Britain's rate of growth today, there should be no imbalance of population structure, as the dependency ratio would be exactly the same as that of contemporary Britain. Only the make-up of dependency would be different: instead of there being more children than old people, it would be the other way round. The time-scale for such an operation is long of course.

Creating a New Social System

Possibly the most radical change we propose in the creation of a new social system is decentralisation. We do so not because we are sunk in nostalgia for a mythical little England of fetes, olde worlde pubs, and perpetual conversations over garden fences, but for four much more fundamental reasons:

(*a*) While there is good evidence that human societies can happily remain stable for long periods, there is no doubt that the long transitional stage that we and our children must go through will impose a heavy burden on our moral courage and will require great restraint. Legislation and the operations of police forces and the courts will be necessary to reinforce this restraint, but we believe that such external controls can never be so subtle nor so effective as internal controls. It would therefore be sensible to promote the social conditions in which public opinion and full public participation in decision-making become as far as possible the means whereby communities are ordered. The larger a community the less likely this can be: in a heterogeneous, centralised society such as ours, the restraints of the stable society if they were to be effective would appear as so much outside coercion; but in communities small enough for the general will to be worked out and expressed by individuals confident of themselves and their fellows as individuals, "us and them" situations are less likely to occur—people having learned the limits of a stable society would be free to order their own lives within them as they wished, and would therefore accept the restraints of the stable society as necessary and desirable and not as some arbitrary restriction imposed by a remote and unsympathetic government.

(*b*) As agriculture depends more and more on integrated control and becomes more diversified, there will no longer be any scope for prairie-type crop-growing or factory-type livestock-rearing. Small farms run by teams with specialised knowledge of ecology, entomology, botany, etc., will then be the rule, and indeed individual small-holdings could become extremely productive suppliers of eggs, fruit, and vegetables to neighbourhoods. Thus a much more diversified urban-rural mix will be not only possible, but because of the need to reduce the transportation costs of returning domestic sewage to the land, desirable. In industry, as with agriculture, it will be important to maintain a vigorous feedback between supply and demand in order to avoid waste, overproduction, or production of goods which the community does not really want, thereby eliminating the needless expense of time, energy and money in attempts to persuade it that it does. If an industry is an integral part of a community, it is much more likely to encourage product innovation because people clearly want qualitative improvements in a given field, rather than because expansion is necessary for that industry's survival or because there is otherwise insufficient work for its research and development section. Today, men, women and children are merely consumer markets, and industries as they centralise become national rather than local and supranational rather than national, so that while entire communities may come to depend on them for the jobs they supply, they are in no sense integral parts of those communities. To a considerable extent the "jobs or beauty" dichotomy has been made possible because of this deficiency. Yet plainly people want jobs *and* beauty, they should not in a just and humane society be forced to choose between the two, and in a decentralised society of small communities where industries are small enough to be responsive to each community's needs, there will be no reason for them to do so.

(*c*) The small community is not only the organisational structure in which internal or systemic controls are most likely to operate effectively, but its dynamic is an essential source of stimulation and pleasure for the individual. Indeed it is probable that only in the small community can a man or woman be an individual. In today's large agglomerations he is merely an isolate—and it is significant that the decreasing autonomy of communities and local regions and the increasing centralisation of decision-making and authority in the cumbersome bureaucracies of the state, have been accompanied by the rise of self-conscious individualism, an individualism which feels threatened unless it is harped upon.

(*d*) The fourth reason for decentralisation is that to deploy a population in small towns and villages is to reduce to the minimum its impact on the environment. This is because the actual urban superstructure required per inhabitant goes up radically as the size of the town increases beyond a certain point. For example, the *per capita* cost of high rise flats is much greater than that of ordinary houses; and the cost of roads and other transportation routes increases with the number of commuters carried. Similarly, the *per capita* expenditure on other facilities such as those for distributing food and removing wastes is much higher in cities than in small towns and villages. Thus, if everybody lived in villages the need for sewage treatment plants would be somewhat reduced, while in an entirely urban society they are essential, and the cost of treatment is high. Broadly speaking, it is only by decentralisation that we can increase self-sufficiency—and self-sufficiency is vital if we are to minimise the burden of social systems on the ecosystems that support them.

Although we believe that the small community should be the basic unit of society and that each community should be as self-sufficient and self-regulating as possible, we would like to stress that we are not proposing that they be inward-looking, self-obsessed or in any way closed to the rest of the world. Basic precepts of ecology, such as the interrelatedness of all things and the far-reaching effects of ecological processes and their disruption, should influence community decision-making, and therefore there must be an efficient and sensitive communications network between all communities. There must be procedures whereby community actions that affect regions can be discussed at regional level and regional actions with extra-regional effects can be discussed at global level. We have no hard and fast views on the size of the proposed communities, but for the moment we suggest neighbourhoods of 500, represented in communities of 5,000, in regions of 500,000, represented nationally, which in turn as today should be represented globally. We emphasise that our goal should be to create *community feeling* and *global awareness*, rather than that dangerous and sterile compromise which is nationalism.

III. THE GOAL

There is every reason to suppose that the stable society would provide us with satisfactions that would more than compensate for those which, with the passing of the industrial state, it will become increasingly necessary to forgo.

We have seen that man in our present society has been deprived of a satisfactory social environment. A society made up of decentralised, self-sufficient communities, in which people work near their homes, have the responsibility of governing themselves, of running their schools, hospitals, and welfare services, in fact of constituting real communities, should, we feel, be a much happier place.

Its members, in these conditions, would be likely to develop an identity of their own, which many of us have lost in the mass society we live in. They would tend, once more, to find an aim in life, develop a set of values, and take pride in their achievements as well as in those of their community.

It is the absence of just these things

that is rendering our mass society ever less tolerable to us and in particular to our youth, and to which can be attributed the present rise in drug addiction, alcoholism and delinquency, all of which are symptomatic of a social disease in which a society fails to furnish its members with their basic psychological requirements.

Real Costs

We might regard with apprehension a situation in which we shall have to make do without many of the devices such as motor-cars, and various domestic appliances which, to an ever greater extent are shaping our everyday lives.

These devices may indeed provide us with much leisure and satisfaction, but few have considered at what cost. For instance, how many of us take into account the dull and tedious work that has to be done to manufacture them, or for that matter to earn the money required for their acquisition? It has been calculated that the energy used by the machines that provide the average American housewife with her high standard of living is the equivalent of that provided by five hundred slaves.

In this respect, it is difficult to avoid drawing a comparison between ourselves and the Spartans, who in order to avoid the toil involved in tilling the fields and building and maintaining their homes employed a veritable army of helots. The Spartan's life, as everybody knows, was a misery. From early childhood, boys were made to live in barracks, were fed the most frugal and austere diet and spent most of their adult life in military training so as to be able to keep down a vast subject population, always ready to seize an opportunity to rise up against its masters. It never occurred to them that they would have been far better off without their slaves, fulfilling themselves the far less exacting task of tilling their own fields and building and maintaining their own homes.

In fact "economic cost," as we have seen, simply does not correspond to "real cost." Within a stable society this gap must be bridged as much as possible.

This means that we should be encouraged to buy things whose production involves the minimum environmental disruption and which will not give rise to all sorts of unexpected costs that would outweigh the benefits that their possession might provide.

Real Value

It is also true, as we have seen, that "economic value" as at present calculated does not correspond to real value any more than "economic cost" corresponds to real cost.

In a stable society, everything would be done to reduce the discrepancy between economic value and real value, and if we could repair some of the damage we have done to our physical and social environment, and live a more natural life, there would be less need for the consumer products that we spend so much money on. Instead we could spend it on things that truly enrich and embellish our lives.

In manufacturing processes, the accent would be on quality rather than quantity, which means that skill and craftsmanship, which we have for so long systematically discouraged, would once more play a part in our lives. For example, the art of cooking would come back into its own, no longer regarded as a form of drudgery, but correctly valued as an art worthy of occupying our time, energy and imagination. Food would become more varied and interesting and its consumption would become more of a ritual and less a utilitarian function.

The arts would flourish: literature, music, painting, sculpture and architecture would play an ever greater part in our lives, while achievements in these fields would earn both money and prestige.

A society devoted to achievements of this sort would be an infinitely more agreeable place than is our present one, geared as it is to the mass production of shoddy utilitarian consumer goods in ever greater quantities. Surprising as it may seem to one reared on today's economic doctrines, it would also be the one most likely to satisfy our basic biological requirements for food, air and water, and even more surprisingly, provide us with the jobs that in our unstable industrial society are constantly being menaced.

There must be a fusion between our religion and the rest of our culture, since there is no valid distinction between the laws of God and Nature, and Man must live by them no less than any other creature. Such a belief must be central to the philosophy of the stable society, and must permeate all our thinking. Indeed it is the only one which is properly scientific, and science must address itself much more vigorously to the problems of co-operating with the rest of Nature, rather than seeking to control it.

This does not mean that science must in any way be discouraged. On the contrary, within a stable society, there would be considerable scope for the energies and talents of scientist and technologist.

Basic scientific research, plus a good deal of multidisciplinary synthesis, would be required to understand the complex mechanisms of our ecosphere with which we must learn to co-operate.

There would be a great demand for scientists and technologists capable of devising the technological infrastructure of a decentralised society. Indeed, with the application of a new set of criteria for judging the economic viability of technological devices, there must open a whole new field of research and development.

The recycling industry which must expand very considerably would offer innumerable opportunities, while in agriculture there would be an even greater demand for ecologists, botanists, entomologists, mycologists, etc., who would be called upon to devise ever subtler methods for ensuring the fertility of the soil and for controlling "pest" populations.

Thus in many ways, the stable society, with its diversity of physical and social environments, would provide considerable scope for human skill and ingenuity.

Indeed, if we are capable of ensuring a relatively smooth transition to it, we can be optimistic about providing our children with a way of life psychologically, intellectually and aesthetically more satisfying than the present one. And we can be confident that it will be sustainable as ours cannot be, so that the legacy of despair we are about to leave them may at the last minute be changed to one of hope.

A RESPONSE TO THE BLUEPRINT

Nature

I. THE CASE AGAINST HYSTERIA

Britain is being assaulted by the environmentalists. This weekend, Dr. Paul Ehrlich, president of Zero Population Growth Inc., and a professor of biology at Stanford University, is to recite for the Conservation Society his now familiar dirge that the world is about to

"A Response to the Blueprint," excerpted from editorials in *Nature*, January 14, 1972 and January 28, 1972. Reprinted by permission of the publisher.

breed itself to death. Last week, a distinguished group of doctors, many of whom should have known better, published in *The Lancet* and the *British Medical Journal* a declaration that Britain is so overcrowded that there is "a direct threat to the mental and physical well-being of our patients" and a plea that doctors should unite "to combat the British disease of over-population." At the same time, the new magazine *The Ecologist* published what it called "A Blueprint for Survival" which reflects and sometimes amplifies a good many of the half-baked anxieties about what is called the environmental crisis. On this occasion, the doctrine that dog should not eat dog notwithstanding, the magazine deserves to be taken to task if only for having recruited a "statement of support" from thirty-three distinguished people, many of them scientists, at least half of whom should have known better. Nobody pretends that there are no serious problems to be worried about but the time seems fast approaching when the cry of disaster round the corner will have to be promoted to the top of the list of causes for public concern.

That professional people should lend their names to attempts like these to fan public anxiety about problems which have either been exaggerated or which are nonexistent is reprehensible. It is especially regrettable that declarations like these should myopically draw attention to the supposed difficulties of moderating population growth in Britain when there is no evidence worth speaking of to suggest that Britain is overpopulated (which is not, of course, the same thing as to say that the country is properly managed). The doctors who signed the round robin to the medical weeklies say that the problems of the developing countries "are formidable and may defy any rational solution," but that they are also "gravely concerned" at the pace of growth of the British population, which exceeds 55 million, and which is expected to increase to 66.5 million by the end of the century.

In reality, the doctors seem to have added an extra 500,000 to the latest estimates of the population of the United Kingdom in the year 2000, for the Government Actuary's latest calculation, published three months ago, gives an even 66 million for that date. It is, however, much more relevant that the forward projections of the British population have been declining steadily over the past decade, as the statisticians have been persuaded by experience that the trend of fertility in Britain, like that in much of the rest of Western Europe, is downward. The doctors also choose, by design or ignorance, to overlook the plain truth that only a quarter of such increase of the British population as there may be between now and the end of the century can be attributed to what they call "the present reproductive bonanza." The rest is simply a consequence of their own craft, which has now made it possible for people to live longer and to survive a good many of the previously fatal hazards of middle life. So is it to be expected that the same people will band together in public to wring their hands about the once and for all increase of the British population which is likely to come about when, at some time in the next two decades, ways are found of treating or even preventing some forms of cancer?

The same unreflectiveness appears to have marred *The Ecologist's* "Blueprint for Survival." Those who have compiled it say that "the relevant information available has impressed upon us the extreme gravity of the global situation today." They foresee "the collapse of society" and consider that if present trends persist, "life support systems on this planet" will be irreversibly disrupted if not by the end of the century then "within the lifetime of our children." Governments, they say, are either refus-

ing to face facts or are "briefing their scientists in such a way that their seriousness is played down." So, the argument goes, there must be a redefinition of the philosophy of civilized life and a restructuring of society as a whole.

The errors in this simplistic view of the present stage in the history of the human race are by now familiar. Much turns on the way in which industrialized societies are at present consuming raw materials at a substantial rate, and it is true that it seems increasingly unlikely that petroleum companies will be able indefinitely to discover new reserves at such a pace that future supplies are always ensured. Oil, indeed, may be the most vulnerable of the resources at present used, just as in Europe 2000 years ago native stands of timber proved not to be inexhaustible. But does it follow from this simpleminded calculation that there will come a time when, to everybody's surprise, petroleum deposits are worked out and industry is forced to grind to a halt? Is it not much more likely, about a century from now, that prices for petroleum will be found to be so high that even the least successful nuclear power companies will find themselves able to sell reactors more easily?

In the same way, is it not likely that the apparently impending scarcity of copper (belied for the time being by the obstinately low price at which the metal is at present marketed) will encourage the use of aluminum as a conductor of electricity? To be sure, as the developing countries gather economic momentum, they will begin to make larger demands on raw materials such as these, yet it does not follow that they will have to repeat in every detail the industrial history of the countries now industrialized, and it remains a comforting truth that the raw materials on which the products of modern industry are based loom less large in economic terms than the products of the Industrial Revolution. Computers, after all, need very little copper for their manufacture. In general, the problem of raw materials is not a problem of the exploitation of a finite resource, however much it might be made to seem as such, but is a problem in economics—how best to regulate the prices of raw materials so as to balance the present demand against the probable demand in the future, how best to encourage what kinds of substitutions, how best to bring into production new reserves (not the least of which are the oceans of the world). Nobody should think that there is nothing to worry about. Good planetary housekeeping, as *The Ecologist* would no doubt describe it, should be an important objective of public policy. But it is a public disservice to describe such intricate and interesting problems in such simple and scarifying terms.

Similar fallacies attend *The Ecologist's* analysis of the supply of food. The document says that food production in the developing world has "barely kept abreast of population growth" and that such increases as there have been are a consequence of the "opening up of new land for cultivation." It goes on to say that this will not be possible for much longer, for "all the good land in the world is now being farmed." Factually, these statements are incorrect. In many parts of South-East Asia, the past few years have seen dramatic improvements in agricultural productivity, acre for acre. In any case, it remains a fact and even something about which agronomists should hang their heads that tropical regions are still comparatively unproductive of food. But the chief complaint of this declaration is that the "FAO programme to feed the world" depends on an intensification of agriculture and that the strains of wheat and rice likely to be the work horses of Asian agriculture are more vulnerable to disease and more demanding of fertilizer.

So what? must surely be the moderate reply. In North America and Western Europe, after all, agriculture is much more intensive than most agricultural practices likely to be common in Asia in the next few years. And the benefits of intensive agriculture are not merely that a given acre of land can produce more food each year but that it can be made to do so at a lower labour cost. Indeed, it might well be calculated that until the populations of the developing world are able to feed themselves without employing more than half of their labour force on the land, they will not be free to develop either along the lines of Western industrialization or along some other route that they might prefer. The fact that intensive agriculture entails crops which are highly specialized and therefore vulnerable to epidemic diseases of one kind or another is no more relevant in Asia than in, for example, North America.

The abiding fault in these discussions is their naivety, and nowhere is this more true than in speculations about the social consequences of the phenomena over which *The Ecologist* wrings its hands. Starting with the assertion that the developed nations have already collared the raw materials with which developing nations might seek to improve their standards of living, the journal goes on to say that "we are altering people's aspirations without providing the means for them to be satisfied. In the rush to industrialize, we break up communities, so that the controls which formerly regulated behaviour are destroyed. Urban drift is one result of this process, with a consequent rise in antisocial practices, crime, delinquency and so on. . . ." This is an echo of the distinguished doctors' declaration about the consequences of crowding, but is it fair to describe this, as *The Ecologist* does, as a portent of the collapse of society? Is it reasonable to say that in such circumstances, "it is more than probable that governments will fall into the hands of reckless and unscrupulous elements, who will not hesitate to threaten neighbouring governments with attack if they feel they can wrest from them a larger share of the world's vanishing resources"? The truth is, of course, that this is mere speculation. All the attempts which there have been in the past few years to discover correlations between such factors as population density and prosperity per head of population with the tendency to violence, either civil or international, have been fruitless. Who will say that the crowded Netherlands are more violent than the uncrowded United States? And who will say that the forces which have in the past 2000 years helped to make civilized communities more humane can now be dismissed from the calculation simply because a new generation of seers sees catastrophe in the tea leaves?

II. CATASTROPHE
OR CHANGE?

Predictably, anxiety about environmental catastrophe has spread to Britain, and it is hard not to remember Professor D. J. Bogue's description of the same phenomenon in the United States as the "nonsense explosion." Many readers of *Nature* appear to have been surprised that a journal which counts Sir Julian Huxley's grandfather as one of its sponsors should have taken such a fierce line on the warnings of environmental catastrophe now commonly to be heard. The truth is that public confusion which has been created in the past few years by warnings of catastrophe is a serious impediment to the rational conduct of society. A part of the difficulty is technical, for whether the prophets are complaining of the hazards of DDT, carbon dioxide in the environment, the threatened exhaustion of natural resources or the growth of population, a proper understanding of what happens and is likely to happen is fraught with uncertainty, complexity and error. Understandably, people at large are puzzled to know what weight to give to warnings of catastrophe around the corner and to assurances that the problems are not nearly as alarming as they are said to be.

The question whether the years immediately ahead will bring catastrophe is not so much technical as philosophical. The document published two weeks ago by *The Ecologist* says that "the principal defect of the industrial way of life . . . is that it is not sustainable. Its termination within the lifetime of somebody born today is inevitable—unless it continues to be sustained for a while longer by an entrenched minority at the cost of imposing great suffering on the rest of mankind." The calculations supposedly implicit in statements like this are that particular resources, petroleum for example, may be seriously depleted on time scales of the order of a century, or that, after a century of unrestricted growth, the population of the world may have grown to such a point that life is intolerable or even insupportable. As yardsticks which show what kinds of problems may in future be important, pieces of arithmetic like this are no doubt of some value. The error in supposing that they constitute a proof of imminent calamity is the assumption that administrative and social mechanisms which exist already or which are in the course of being developed will do nothing to fend them off, but this is to ignore the beneficent tendencies already apparent—the rapid decline of fertility in the past decade in South-East Asia and the Caribbean and the working of the classical economic laws of scarcity, originally described by the great Victorians, to strike a balance between exploitation and conservation and the way in which governments in

North America and Western Europe have succeeded in improving the quality of urban air and water by laying out money on pollution control. In short, those who prophesy disaster a century or more from now and ask for apocalyptic remedies overlook the way in which important social changes have historically been effected by the accumulation of more modest humane innovations.

In the circumstances, it is not surprising that the remedies suggested for the avoidance of catastrophe are often unpleasantly unrealistic. *The Ecologist*'s manifesto may be controversial because of its over-sharp definition of the supposed threat, but it shares with other declarations of this kind the advocacy of thoroughly pernicious changes in the structure of society. It is tempting to ask how many of those who gave their names to the document solemnly consider that industrialized societies such as Britain will be better off if they are organized in small communities in which social mobility is deliberately restricted and in which agriculture is central to everybody's life. Are these not potentially illiberal arrangements? Is there not a serious danger that to strive for them will weaken the will of civilized communities, developed and developing, to work towards humane goals—the removal of poverty and the liberty of the subject?

TO GROW AND TO DIE

Anthony Lewis

I

Our diverse worlds—developed, underdeveloped, East, West—have at least one article of faith in common:

Excerpted from Anthony Lewis "To Grow and To Die," in *The New York Times* January 29, January 31, February 5, 1972. © 1972 by The New York Times Company. Reprinted by permission.

economic growth. For individuals, for economic enterprises and for nations, growth is happiness, the specific for ills and the foundation of hope. Next year our family will be richer, our company bigger, our country more productive.

Now the ecologists have begun to tell us that growth is self-defeating, that the planet cannot long sustain it, that it will lead inevitably to social and biological collapse. That was the central thesis of the recent "Blueprint for Survival" published in Britain, and it is a theme increasingly found in analytical studies of the earthly future.

The proposition is so shocking that the natural reaction is to wish it away. Some economists, the apostles of growth, do just that. There was an especially acute example of wishfulness in a Newsweek column by Henry C. Wallich, Yale professor and former U.S. economic adviser, condemning the opposition to growth as dangerous heresy.

"It is an alarming commentary on the intellectual instability of our times," Professor Wallich said, "that today mileage can be made with the proposal to stop America dead in her tracks. Don't we know which way is forward?"

As long as there is growth, he said, "everybody will be happier." By "allowing everybody to have more" and refusing to "limit resources available for consumption," we shall also have "more resources" to clean up the environment.

If Professor Wallich's opinion is representative of the American intellectual community, it is an alarming comment on our awareness of the most important facts of life today. For he is evidently in a state of ecological illiteracy.

There are no such things as endless growth and unlimited resources for everyone and everything. We live in a finite world, and we are approaching the limits. Discussion of growth as an environmental factor has to begin with some understanding of such considerations.

The crucial fact is that growth tends to be exponential. That is, it multiplies. Instead of adding a given amount every so often, say 1,000 tons or dollars a year, the factors double at fixed intervals. That tends to be true of population, of industrial production, of pollution and of demand on natural resources—some of the main strains of planetary life.

The rate of increase determines the doubling time. If something grows 7 percent a year, it will double in ten years. Right now world population is growing 2.1 percent a year; at that rate it doubles in thirty-three years. And with each doubling, the base is of course larger for the next increase. The world had about 3.5 billion people in it in 1970. At the present rate of increase, it will have seven billion in 2003.

Exponential growth is a tricky affair. It gives us the illusion for a long time that things are going slowly; then suddenly it speeds up. Suppose the demand for some raw material is two tons this year and doubles every year. Over the next fifteen years it will rise to only 32,768 tons, but just five years later it will be 1,048,576 tons.

That phenomenon is what makes it so hard for people to understand how rapidly we may be approaching the limits of growth. For as population and per capita consumption both grow, the curves of demand suddenly zoom upward.

Consider the case of aluminum as a sample of resource demand and supply. The known reserves of aluminum are enough to supply the current demand for 100 years. But the use is increasing exponentially, and at the rate of increase the supply will be enough for only 31 years. Moreover, the multiplying demand is a much larger factor, mathematically, than any likely discovery of new sources of supply. If reserves were multiplied by five, the same growth of demand would still exhaust them in 55 years.

The example of aluminum is not especially chosen to disturb, for there are others that even more dramatically indicate the way exponential growth can run up to projected limits. One is simply arable land. At the present rate of world population growth, the supply of land necessary for food production will run out by the year 2000. If agricultural productivity were doubled, the limit would be pushed back thirty years.

II

A hundred years ago John Stuart Mill urged human society to limit its population and wealth and seek "the stationary state." He had a vision of a cramped and depleted earth. he sincerely hoped, he said, that men "will be content to be stationary long before necessity compels them to it."

Mill's was a premature vision, and for a long time hardly anyone shared it. Now, suddenly, impressive scientific evidence is being put to us that necessity compels an early end to the dominant earthly ambition of economic growth. For the exponential growth of population and production is putting strains on our environment that cannot be sustained.

To talk about limiting growth as a philosophical matter is easy enough. But when one begins to consider the specific changes of course that would be required of mankind, the difficulties are soon seen to be enormous. The economic habits of a millennium, the motivations, the very conception of a good society would be affected.

The whole question of equality as a social goal, for example, would be transformed. In most societies, East and West, there are gross inequalities of wealth today. They are made politically tolerable in good part by the notion of the whole economic pie growing constantly larger so that everyone can have a bigger slice. That is why politicians from Brezhnev to Edward Heath promise their constituents faster economic growth.

But what happens if everyone in a society knows that there can be no increase in the total volume of material goods? Is it still bearable that one man has three cars in his garage and another not enough to eat?

Similar considerations affect our traditional view of competition as a motivating economic force. Leading ecologists say we must adopt a policy of no net increase in capital investment from now on—only enough to match depreciation of capital.

But if the United States had such a policy, how could manufacturers compete in the traditional way of more productive machinery? Would it not follow that new forms of social control would have to be imposed on production, on marketing, on advertising? And how would they be squared with our ideas of freedom?

Equality is an issue not only within but between societies. If the ecologists are right, then it is foolish and dangerous for developing countries to dream of having industrial economies and a standard of material wealth like the developed world's.

But how can the rich few advise the poor many that they will be better off forsaking the old material goals? And does not that again imply a change in one's whole view of social organization, toward a less material society on the Chinese model, with enough for everyone to eat but little competition for goods or ease? Does it not follow in international as in national life that an end to growth must not be an imposition by the rich on the poor and hence requires a fresh commitment to a decent level of equality?

Merely to state such problems is to make one thing evident: the complete irrelevance of most of today's political concerns to the most important problem facing the world in the long run. And not very long at that.

A WORLD WITHOUT GROWTH?

Henry C. Wallich

Anthony Lewis, in two recent issues of The New York Times, warns us of the deadly consequences of growth. Running out of resources, running into total pollution, running to the point of total exhaustion and collapse—those are the ultimate rewards of growth. We must stop growth, not just of population, but of production and income.

The group of ecologists who generated this well meaning scare are members of an old club. Its founder, the Rev. Thomas Malthus, issued dire warnings of inevitable starvation in 1798. This having proved a poor bet, the emphasis today shifts to a dearth of all natural resources and mounting pollution.

It does not take an ecologist to explain that if the world's population doubles every so many years, after a while there will be Standing Room Only, at least on the surface of this planet. Likewise, it is fairly obvious that if we deplete existing resources without discovering new sources, developing methods of recycling, and inventing substitutes, we shall some day run out. But perhaps an economist can be helpful in clarifying why these problems are not top priority today.

In the first place, the economy will simply substitute things that are plentiful for things that become scarce. If

From Henry C. Wallich "A World Without Growth?" in The New York Times February 12, 1972. © 1972 by The New York Times Company. Reprinted by permission.

we run out of aluminum, the price of aluminum will go up. That will encourage manufacturers to use something else, and will stimulate research and development to produce substitutes.

Some scientists believe that matter and energy are fundamentally interchangeable in many forms, but as a layman, I would not bet on any near-term miracles. The simple processes of economics will keep us going. If they don't, the ecologists' advice to slow down will not be worth much—it would only postpone the day of disaster without avoiding it.

In the course of centuries, more basic adjustments will probably be needed. Population may stop growing, production may stop growing. The chances are that the world will adapt to the changing environment gradually. Lack of space will cause families to shrink, if families then still exist. Great per capita income will reduce interest in producing and consuming more. We do not need to rely on "misery," as the Rev. Malthus thought, to bring about the adjustment.

The real question is at what time this transition will have to be faced. New York restaurants carry signs to the effect that occupancy by more than some maximum number is unlawful. If half a dozen persons were to gather in an otherwise empty restaurant with such a sign and discuss heatedly the urgency of keeping newcomers out, they would be in something like the position of Americans debating the zero growth notion. To stop growing now, generations before the real problems of growth arise if ever, would be to commit suicide for fear of remote death.

The ecologists do not seem to be aware of what it would mean to freeze total income anywhere near today's level. Do they mean that the present income distribution is to be preserved, with the poor frozen into their inadequacies? Would that go for the underdeveloped countries too? Or do they have in mind an equalization of incomes? It will take pretty drastic cuts in upper income bracket standards to bring them down to the average American family income of about $10,000, to say nothing of a cut to average world income. We can and perhaps should approach this condition over generations. Trying to do it quickly would create completely needless problems.

The ecologists also do not seem to be aware of what their prescriptions, contrary to their wishes, might do to the environment. If growth came to a halt, it is obvious that every last penny of public and private income would be drawn upon to provide minimal consumer satisfactions. There would be very little left for the cleaning-up job that needs to be done. Growth is the main source from which that job must be financed.

I would like to end with a quote from my Newsweek column on which Mr. Lewis commented. "A world without growth, that is, without change, is as hard for us to imagine as a world of everlasting growth and change. Somewhere in the dim future, if humanity does not blow itself up, there may lie a world in which physical change will be minimal . . . hopefully a much more humane and less materialistic world. We shall not live to see it."

Continued from p. 728
thought of in economic terms as a special form of market imperfection, though it is different from other such imperfections in its historical and social roots, and it may not depend on the overt existence of monopoly power in the rest of the economy.

Where access to markets is denied either by lack of information, by cultural disadvantages, or discrimination, the market will not give an efficient allocation of resources as indicated in purely competitive theory. Society as a whole loses when productive individuals are either unemployed, partly unemployed, or employed in lower productivity positions than their abilities warrant. In such cases, society may decide that collective action to increase information and mobility and to lower or remove artificial barriers is required.[7]

URBAN AIR POLLUTION

The above discussion of market failure is somewhat abstract. It is easy, however, to make it quite concrete, and also to show its bearing on some of the "costs" of modern industrial society. There is probably no better nor more important example than that of urban air pollution.

This problem is by no means confined to the United States, but may be found in any industrial society with large numbers of people and machines crowded into a limited space. It affects virtually all European countries at the present time, and is very intense in Japan, where people sometimes go out into the streets with gas masks because of traffic-polluted air. Nor is it a phenomenon of the last few years only.

One of the most dramatic examples of the harmful effects of urban air pollution occurred in London in 1952. Because of certain atmospheric conditions, the London fog suddenly turned black, and this black fog lasted a week. During that period, it is estimated that the normal death toll increased by 4,000. The basic cause: polluted air.[8]

The effects of air pollution are not always so dramatic as this, but they are evident in hundreds of ways in most of our major cities. Polluted air can damage eyes, lungs, crops, animals, building materials, metals. It can create an atmosphere of dirt and grime and destroy the pleasure ordinary citizens take in breathing pure air. If pollution continues to mount, it may even be sufficient to affect the earth's weather and temperature. No one can live in a major urban area today without at times feeling depressed if not outraged that man seems to be systematically destroying one of the most precious, indispensable features of his natural environment.

Polluters are both consumers and producers. The automobile is the prime single offender; transportation in general accounts for about 60 percent of total air pollution in American cities. Other major sources are industry, electric power generation, space heating, and refuse incineration.

From the point of view of the economic analyst, urban air pollution is a dramatic case of the operation of external diseconomies. Pollution almost invariably represents an external cost that the individual or private business firm places

---

7. See discussion of ghetto economics, pp. 707–9.

8. See Roger Revelle, "Pollution and Cities," *The Metropolitan Enigma*, ed. James Q. Wilson (Washington, D.C.: Chamber of Commerce of the United States, 1967), p. 81.

upon society without charge to himself. When such externalities exist, a divergence between private and social interest will arise and some form of collective intervention will be required if the problem is to be solved.

This is shown by the need, for example, to have a legal requirement that automobiles be equipped with anti-pollution devices. The cost of such devices may not be exorbitant—let us suppose they are $50 per car on the average. However, the *private* benefit to any individual from installing such a device will be negligible, i.e., the effect of his own contribution to total pollution on himself is practically nil. Hence, unless he is required to do so, or unless he is operating in the spirit of public-mindedness rather than of private interest, he will not install such a device. In short, there is nothing in the workings of the market that will encourage either the private motorist or the automotive manufacturer to correct the situation.

If this is true of devices that can be installed on private cars, it is even more true of other solutions of a more public nature. One expert, Professor Roger Revelle, has suggested that it may be necessary to reconstruct our cities in two layers, "one for automobiles and one for people":

All vehicle traffic would be in tunnels and other enclosed spaces from which air could be rapidly pumped and treated to remove noxious substances. Alternatively one might conceive of a system for penetrating the atmospheric inversion layers and replacing the polluted air with fresh air sucked from aloft. The construction of many very high stacks equipped with enormous pumps has sometimes been discussed by engineers for the Los Angeles area, but the costs and amount of energy required,

not to mention the hazards to air traffic, seem prohibitive.[9]

Such a reconstruction of our cities would clearly fall in the category of a public rather than a private project. Similarly, the provision of more effective mass transit systems—a favorite recommendation for reducing urban air pollution—would require government intervention in one form or another.

Indeed, the problems facing mass transit systems illustrate vividly how the "invisible hand" may fail us in this important area. The ideal situation for a private individual may be to have a mass transit system that everyone else uses while *he* enjoys the convenience (particularly with the uncrowded streets that would occur) of his own automobile. Since all individuals would tend to look at the matter in the same way, the potential subversion of the socially preferable solution is easily understood.

If, then, the market fails in this area, what is to be done about the pollution problem? Clearly, public programs will have to be introduced, and these may be costly. Revelle, for example, estimates that if we wished to control *all* pollution in the United States—air, water, and land pollution—it might cost in the vicinity of 3 percent of national income over the next fifteen years. In a trillion dollar economy, this would be upwards of $30 billion per year (which works out to about $600 a year, on the average, for a family of four). The difficulty of evaluating governmental expenditures to make sure that these monies are spent wisely will be taken up in the next section.

Another possible approach—and one favored by many economists—is to try, by appropriate tax and subsidy policy, to make private and social interest coin-

9. Ibid., p. 88.

cide. Under this approach, one would try to *use* market forces so as to make them produce a better solution rather than replacing them completely with public ownership or yes-or-no controls. In the case of pollution, which involves external diseconomies, this would mean taxing the polluter—say, the private motorist—according to the amount of pollution for which he was responsible.

The logic of this approach derives from our considerations of efficiency in chapter 22. At that time we discussed the virtues of having $P = MC$ under ordinary circumstances.[10] These circumstances are not fulfilled when there are external diseconomies, since MC does not cover the true cost to society of the good in question. To discover that cost, we must also add the external pollution cost. What is proposed, then, is that a tax be added to the use of automobiles in such a way that MC *plus* the tax will reflect the true cost of the automobile to society.

In the following reading, such a proposal is briefly outlined and defended.

10. See pp. 509–10.

How to Make Pollution Go Away

Edwin G. Dolan

If pollution is such an undisputably bad thing, the reader may say, not only unpleasant and aesthetically offensive but inefficient and harmful to polluter and victim alike, then let's just get rid of it! Let's get the government to ban leaded gasoline, outlaw DDT, regulate the type of fuel used

Excerpted from "How to Make Pollution Go Away," in TANSTAAFL* (*There Ain't No Such Thing As A Free Lunch), *The Economic Strategy for Environmental Crisis*, pp. 32–36, by Edwin G. Dolan. Copyright © Holt, Rinehart and Winston, Inc., Reprinted by permission of Holt, Rinehart and Winston, Inc.

by Con Ed, require secondary treatment for all sewage, impose standards on atomic power stations, insist on chemical toilets on all pleasure boats, punish people who litter the highways, and control the phosphate content of detergents! After all, isn't that what the government is for—to ban, outlaw, regulate, require, impose, insist, punish, and control?

This seems to be the instinctive reaction of a great many Americans upset about the pollution problem. The politicians whom they send to our legislatures at regularly appointed intervals are only too happy to oblige—if this new public concern will give them a chance to control something which they do not yet control, or set up a bureau or regulatory commission where one does not yet exist, what intelligent politician would pass up the opportunity?

To succumb to the urge to control pollution via the imposition of direct controls out of the belief that these are quick, expedient, or effective ways of getting the job done, would, I believe, be a grave mistake. Instead, I would like to offer some guidelines for a more efficient, equitable, and effective pollution abatement policy.

The first guideline which I propose is to make minimum use of direct controls in fighting pollution, and maximum use of market mechanisms and the price system. To illustrate how this guideline might be applied in a specific case let us take the very important example of automobile exhaust pollution. This is, incidentally, an area in which direct controls are already being used in the form of requiring certain emisson control devices on all cars produced in and imported into the United States. Other direct controls are pending, including regulation of permissible types of fuels, still more effective emission control devices, and the outright banning of automobile traffic from certain urban areas.

As an alternative to such proposals, I would argue in favor of controlling auto exhaust pollution by putting a price tag on the privilege to pollute. In our Capitalist economy you can impose upon me the inconvenience of work or the inconvenience of using my lawn as a parking lot only by paying a price, and if I do not judge the price to be high enough I am free to decline your offer. Why, then, should you be able to impose upon me the inconvenience of breathing the noxious gases emitted from your exhaust pipe without paying a price, when, because of the simple physics of the situation, I don't even have the opportunity to refuse your offer to have me breathe them?

The idea of putting a price on exhaust emission at first may bring to mind the image of a little gadget like a water meter which would be clamped on the tailpipe of a car to be read once a month and a bill sent out, so much per cubic foot. If the construction of such a meter were practical, it would be an ideal method to use. As far as I know, this meter has not yet been developed, but a somewhat more primitive approach using existing institutions and technology could accomplish much the same purpose. For example, in a state like Vermont, which already requires a semiannual trip to the inspection station, the pollution charge could be combined with regular inspection. When a car was taken in, it would be rated according to an established scale of points. Starting with a basic score scaled to the engine displacement and mileage since the last inspection, so many points could be deducted for a P.C.V. system, and so many points for fuel injection, a catalytic muffler, and so on and so forth. At the end, a fee would be paid in proportion to the points remaining, which might range, let us imagine, from $100 for a massive Chrysler with no technical refinements down to $2.00 for a Volkswagen converted to run on natural gas.

Compared to the current system of direct controls, the price system would offer distinct advantages with respect to efficiency, equity, and incentives. Let us look at these advantages one by one.

The price system would be more efficient because it would observe the equimarginal principle. If you are going to use up resources in a variety of related but not identical activities, you will get the greatest yield per unit expenditure by dividing your resources among the different activities in such a way that the benefit of spending an additional penny at the margin is the same for each activity.

LOS ANGELES TIMES PHOTO

Smog Contributors. Cars on the Pomona Freeway near Los Angeles city limits add to air pollution as the sun, looking more like the moon, tries to penetrate the eye-watering smog.

This principle applies also to the control of automobile exhaust. The total amount of pollution control expenditure should be divided among individual cars in such a way that the marginal yield, measured in terms, say, of cubic feet of carbon monoxide reduction per dollar spent, would be the same for all cars.

Now, direct controls clearly violate this principle. The current law requires that some fixed sum—let us say about $10.00—be spent on every car for positive crankcase ventilation. In the case of a big car which is driven a lot that $10.00 does a great deal of good. In the case of a little car, or a little used one, it does less good. Clearly, it would be more efficient to spend some of the money used on the little cars for still better control devices on big cars.

Under the price system this would be done. A Buick-owning traveling salesman would probably get almost every device in the book before he got to the point where another dollar spent on technical refinements would not pay off in terms of reduced inspection tax, while the proverbial little old lady who drives her Renault once a week to church might find that even the most basic devices weren't worth putting on.

The second point of superiority of the price system lies in its equity. This has already been hinted at in our previous example—it is clearly equitable that the salesman pay more pollution tax than the little old lady. In addition to this aspect of equity, which makes people pay in proportion to the cost which they impose on others by pollution, there is another, almost reverse aspect. It is also equitable to allow people to pollute more in proportion to the benefit which they gain from pollution! Compare two car owners, one of whom views his car just as a means of getting from place to place and the other for whom his car is his principal hobby and driving his chief source of amusement. The first man will be little inconvenienced by the slight reduction in performance which is produced by the mandatory P.C.V. system. The second man, however, will be grievously annoyed when he finds that his zero to sixty acceleration time has risen from 9.6 seconds to 9.7. Would it not be more equitable to allow this second man to take his P.C.V. valve off, as long as he is willing to pay the increased inspection tax which will result and as long as that tax realistically reflects the cost which he imposes upon others by so doing?

Finally, the price system for exhaust emission control would be superior to the direct control system with respect to its incentive value. This must already be clear in general terms, but let us add a few specifics. It must be pointed out that under the current system there is no incentive whatsoever for the car owner to *maintain* pollution control devices installed by law on his car. Here we are not just worried about the hot rodder who purposely takes the thing off to get that extra edge of performance. More significantly, how many

car owners even *know* that the Rochester valve of the P.C.V. system must be replaced every 10,000 miles or the system is rendered useless? And of those who do know this, how many are tempted to save the dollar or two a year involved by just letting the matter slide?

Furthermore, in the matter of incentives it is not so much the car owner as the car manufacturer who counts. The present system by insisting that every car maker, domestic and foreign, be treated exactly equally guarantees that no manufacturer can get a competitive advantage by producing a more pollution-free car. In fact, the situation is if anything the exact opposite. If the manufacturer is going to act rationally in his own self-interest to maximize his profits, it will pay him to spend millions not in the research laboratories but in the lobbies of Congress fighting pollution control legislation tooth and nail! There is much talk about a "conspiracy" of the big three to suppress technical developments which could reduce pollution. Maybe there is a conspiracy and maybe there isn't, but how long do you think one could last against the competition of Volkswagen, Fiat, and Toyota if the annual pollution charge paid by the owner for an American car was triple that for their foreign competitors? Let's take the profit out of pollution and put it into pollution *control,* then we'll get a real look at the Capitalist economy in action.

There are a few signs on the horizon that the price system for pollution control may be gaining favor. For automobiles, President Nixon's tax on the lead additive in gasoline appears to be a small step in the right general direction. The system has been widely suggested for control of water pollution also, where the metering of wastes is more practical. A similar system is already in use in the Ruhr Valley in Germany, and pilot programs are underway in this country. The possibilities have still not been fully explored. How about, for example, a differential charge for garbage collection in the city according to whether noisy metal cans or quiet plastic ones are used? How about a differential liquor tax on beer according to whether the product is sold in indestructible aluminum cans or biodegradable plastic containers?

EVALUATING GOVERNMENT EXPENDITURES

In discussing approaches to the pollution problem, we have more or less automatically argued for an increased government intervention in the economy—whether by taxing the polluter, subsidizing a mass transit system, direct controls, or whatever. Such arguments apply to virtually all the categories in the economy presented on our brief list of "where the market may fail."

In solving one set of issues, however, we raise another set—the question of the efficacy of governmental action. For if real-world markets may "fail," so also may real-world governments. An omniscient and omnibenevolent government might solve a great many problems in our society; but, like completely "pure" competition, such governments have never existed. How, then, can we be sure that public intervention will not do more harm than good?

The answer is that we cannot be certain. History has shown us countless examples where governments have acted inefficiently or counter to the wishes of the consuming public. As we know, Adam Smith was aware of the antisocial propensities of some businessmen, but he also considered that the British government of his day was wasteful, extravagant, and unproductive. The Soviet government in the 1930s did not hesitate to place cruel and extraordinary hardships upon the backs of the Russian peasantry. In fact, when it comes to the problem of pollution, what are we to make of the fact that even State ownership of industry is no necessary protection, as seen in the pollution of Lake Baikal in present-day Russia?

The fact is that governments everywhere are plagued by problems of bureaucracy and inefficient management. In our own particular form of democracy, governmental action often seems at the mercy of various groups and counter-groups who exert pressures for ends that seem more serving of self than of society as a whole. Furthermore, just as we might worry about the agglomerations of power in the hands of giant private corporations, so will many citizens be concerned about the concentration of power in the hands of the most giant of all our corporations, the federal government. The federal government, for example, has become increasingly involved in the financing of higher education in this country. There may be good and compelling reasons for a still further increase in federal involvement in our colleges and universities, but is this a desirable thing? For many, the answer will depend not simply on considerations of efficiency and the like, but also on judgments about the long-run political and cultural consequences of increasing the scope of governmental responsibility.

In short, it is not sufficient to say that the market departs from our ideal and hence that public intervention is required. We must also make a judgment as to whether, in total, the less than ideal form of public intervention we are likely to get will bring us closer to, or perhaps lead us even further away from, the desired outcome. Such judgments will generally require the skills of the political scientist and sociologist as well as the economist and, indeed, a great deal of informed intelligence and common sense.

Even when such judgments have been made—and in some cases, as, for example, urban air pollution, it is difficult to see how public intervention can be avoided—we have the further difficult task of assuring efficiency in the operation of the public sector.

Economists in recent years have spent much time in extending their traditional techniques so that they might be helpful in evaluating governmental expenditures. Perhaps the best known example is *benefit-cost analysis*. The government may be faced with a number of possible projects, and it may wish to determine criteria for selecting some projects and rejecting others. Or with a given project, the government may wish to determine a criterion for judging what the scale of output should be. Benefit-cost analysis provides a systematic way of approaching these public resource allocation problems.

In one sense, benefit-cost analysis is exactly analogous to the analysis of private decision-making. Suppose the government is constructing an urban transport system and wishes to determine the appropriate level of output of public transport services. Benefit-cost analysis will indicate that the government should produce at the point where the marginal cost of the project equals the marginal gains or benefits derived from it. This is very much like the private businessman determining his output where $MC = MR$. However, the governmental decision is complicated by the fact that public outputs are often not directly sold in the market (e.g., we do not buy national defense on the market, but rather collectively through public taxation). Also, even if the public services are sold to consumers (as might be the case with public transport), the market test may not cover the many externalities that the government will wish to take into account.

Hence, the relevant sense of costs and benefits is in terms of *social costs* and *social benefits*.[11] In Figure 30-4, we have

<hr>

11. This, of course, is basically the same principle by which taxing polluting motorists is defended in the previous section. The tax is meant to bring private and social marginal cost in line together.

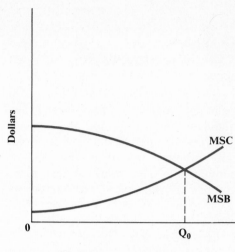

Figure 30-4. Benefit-Cost Analysis.

The government will ideally guide its expenditure decisions on the principle that *marginal social benefits* should equal *marginal social cost*. These terms are not easy to measure, however, either in theory or in practice.

drawn hypothetical curves of marginal social cost and marginal social benefit for the output of public urban transport services. By the principle of benefit-cost analysis, the government should determine its output at OQ_0 where marginal social benefit and marginal social cost are equal. At any lower output, society will be losing potential benefits, since additional dollars spent on the project will bring further net gains to society. At any higher output, additional dollars spent on the project will cost more, in terms of alternative uses of that money either in the private or the public sector, than the additional benefits accruing.

Although it is easy enough to draw hypothetical curves such as those in Figure 30-4, the matter is understandably much more complicated in reality. In measuring benefits in this social sense, for example, the government faces the problem that external effects, even when they are theoretically measurable, will by definition not be reflected in the market in any simply observable way. Moreover, many of these external effects may be essentially intangible. How do we evaluate numerically the effect of the new urban transport system on the beauty of the city? If we are talking about education, how do we measure the political and cultural importance of having an alert, well-informed citizenry? The problem of external effects and intangibles has raised the criticism that benefit-cost analysis, in a search for false precision, may concentrate too heavily on those aspects of a problem that are measurable and hence lead to socially undersirable results.

There are other problems. One of the more difficult is the fact that most government projects will involve expenditures and benefits running over considerable periods of time. This implies that the government must use some form of interest rate to discount future costs as well as benefits. But what interest rate to choose? This raises certain practical problems, but it also may raise difficult theoretical issues since it is not clear that collective decisions about the accumulation of capital and private decisions as reflected in market interest rates will necessarily be the same.[12]

Furthermore, the benefits accruing from any public project will often involve different objectives. One project may contribute important efficiency benefits but may do little to improve the distribution of income. One project may accelerate growth but may actually cause sacrifices in terms of efficiency or income-distribution benefits. In such cases, the government may be faced with the complicated task of trading off one kind of benefit against another.

Despite these difficulties, however, benefit-cost analysis can be an important technique for encouraging the systematic exploration of the issues that must be answered whenever the government undertakes an expenditure program. It is a clear improvement over commonly used alternative approaches that do not relate benefits to costs at all, simply saying either "We must do this" (no matter what the costs) or "We can only afford that" (no matter what the benefits). Former Budget Director Charles Schultze believes that benefit-cost analysis can help to improve the public decision making process by:

Uncovering the irrelevant issues
Identifying the specific assumptions and factual bases upon which alternative recommendations rest, and,
Tracing out the knowable consequences and costs of each alternative[13]

In this way, economic analysis has decid-

---

12. See, for example, Stephen A. Marglin, "The Social Rate of Discount and the Optimal Rate of Investment," *Quarterly Journal of Economics* 77, no. 1 (February 1963). By "discounting" in this connection, we refer to the process by which future dollars are translated into the equivalent of present dollars. How many dollars today are $110, a year from today, worth to me? If the rate of interest is 10 percent, the answer will be $110/1.10, or $100. The general formula for deriving the "present value" of a stream of future dollars is:

$$P.V.(\$) = \$a_0 + \frac{\$a_1}{(1+i)} + \frac{\$a_2}{(1+i)^2} + \dots \frac{\$a_n}{(1+i)^n} + \dots$$

where P.V. ($) is present value of the income stream,

$\$a_n$ is the number of dollars received in year n, and i is the interest rate. In benefit-cost analysis, it will generally be necessary to discount both benefits *and* costs, since the expenditures on a project as well as its benefits will usually take place over long periods of time.

13. Charles L. Schultze, "Why Benefit-Cost Analysis?" in *Program Budgeting and Benefit-Cost Analysis* (Pacific Palisades, Calif.: Goodyear Publishing Co., 1969), p. 6.

ed relevance for some of the hard practical issues of public policy in the modern American economy.

SUMMARY

Industrial societies have come under increasing criticism in the past few years because of the costs they impose on the environment. Many critics believe that the benefits of further economic growth are now outweighed by the costs in terms of pollution, tension, and the destruction of natural resources. Some, indeed, believe that the process cannot go on much longer without destroying our natural environment (see Great Debate Five: Ecology and Economic Growth).

One suggestion is that we move from a *throughput* to a *spaceship* economic system. In the former, we use up natural resources and turn them into garbage that is deposited in dumps and sewers, causing pollution that, in turn, further diminishes our natural resource base. In the spaceship concept, wastes are recycled so that the natural resource base is maintained and the accumulation of pollutants is limited.

The worries about ecological disaster raise an important question for the student of economics: Why has the "invisible hand" of the market apparently failed in this area of economic life?

The answer is that there are important problems where, even in pure theory, the invisible hand of the market will not ordinarily give us a socially desirable result. A partial list of these problems includes: (1) unacceptable consumer wants; (2) public goods; (3) decreasing-cost goods; (4) external economies and diseconomies; and (5) inadequate access to product and factor markets.

External effects are particularly

important in explaining one of the most urgent of modern problems: air pollution. Pollution represents an external cost that the individual or business firm places upon society without charge to himself. This causes a gap between private and social marginal cost and is likely to require State intervention, either through direct controls, the provision of mass transit systems, or various schemes of taxation that attempt to use market forces while modifying them so as to bring private and social costs and benefits into line.

Although government intervention is to be expected in most of these areas where the market "fails," it is no panacea (witness the pollution problem in the State-run Soviet economy). Also, care must be taken that government intervention is as socially efficient as possible. Economists can help here through the techniques of *benefit-cost analysis*. These techniques apply tools used in the theory of the private economy to evaluating government expenditures in terms of marginal social costs and benefits. Although this analysis has its weaknesses, it can be used effectively to outline some of the issues involved in alternative solutions to public problems.

QUESTIONS FOR DISCUSSION

1. "The critics who complain so loudly about the dangers of modern growth are simply rehashing old Malthusian arguments. And, in point of fact, they are just as wrong today as he was then." Discuss.

2. One of the ways in which an economy would protect itself, at least partially, against running out of natural resources

would be to economize on the use of those resources that had become particularly scarce. Show how a price system in general equilibrium (see chapter 22) would react to a shortage of, say, iron ore, by altering (*a*) methods of production and (*b*) quantities of different goods produced.

3. Show that a private price system will tend to overproduce goods that have external diseconomies and to underproduce goods that enjoy external economies. Give examples of each from present-day economic life. Show the arguments for imposing taxes in some cases and giving public subsidies in others.

4. Selling hand guns on a simple supply-and-demand basis has been attacked by some as involving a serious divergence between private and social interest. It can be argued that this is an area involving unacceptable consumer wants (use of guns for robberies, etc.), public goods (the security of the community), and external effects (your possession of a gun affects my well-being). Write an essay on the economics of regulating the sale of hand guns to private individuals.

5. Do we as a society seek *no* pollution or merely *less* pollution? Discuss.

6. What is the difference between *private marginal cost* and *social marginal cost*? Between *private marginal benefit* and *social marginal benefit*? Why would we want to use the "social" concepts when evaluating a proposed public project? What difficulties could you envisage in making such evaluations for a project that, say, involved forbidding all vehicular traffic from the center of a large city and creating a large park and pedestrian mall there?

SUGGESTED READING

Eckstein, Otto. *Water Resource Development.* Cambridge, Mass.: Harvard University Press, 1958, pp. 1–70.

Hinrichs, Harley H., and Taylor, Graeme M., eds. *Program Budgeting and Benefit-Cost Analysis.* Pacific Palisades, Calif.: Goodyear Publishing Company, 1969.

North, Douglass C., and Miller, Roger LeRoy. *The Economics of Public Issues.* New York: Harper & Row, 1971.

Phelps, Edmund S., ed. *Private Wants and Public Needs.* rev. ed. New York: W. W. Norton & Co., 1965.

Smerk, George M. *Urban Transportation.* Bloomington, Ind.: Indiana University Press, 1965.

Turvey, R., ed. *Public Enterprise.* Baltimore, Md.: Penguin Books, 1968.

31
The Industrial Society: An Uncertain Future

Ever since the day in October 1929, when Professor Irving Fisher of Yale (a distinguished economic theorist) said that the stock market had reached a permanently high plateau, economists have been cautious about predicting the future. The Eternal Optimists have often been wrong, but so have the Eternal Pessimists. If we look at the actual predictions made by Malthus, Marx, the "stagnationists" of the Great Depression period, and other prophets of doom, we will find that they have not done much better on the average. In the intellectual world, one tends to get a certain number of academic credits for being grim about future prospects—but this does not necessarily mean that one has a better percentage as a prognosticator.

Despite the dangers of looking into the future, the task seems peculiarly necessary as the industrial nations of the world march towards the last quarter of the twentieth century. The reason lies basically in the vast technological revolution that gained strength in the eighteenth and nineteenth centuries and that continues on at the present time. Besides creating the possibilities of global destruction and ecological disaster, this continuing revolution also holds out the promise of extraordinary abundance. Indeed, it may be that our central problem is precisely the enormous range of these possible outcomes. In olden times, the future seemed to grow out of the present as the present had grown out of the past almost automatically—sometimes with changes barely perceptible. Now change is evident everywhere. And this creates an obligation upon us, not always a pleasant one either, to mold our future, to choose among these outcomes. The following pages contain not so much predictions as the discussion of a few interesting possibilities.

THE FEASIBILITY OF PEACE

One rather dramatic possibility is that peace might break out. The likelihood of this prospect is a matter for the historian (or better, the prophet) to judge. But the economist is useful in answering the question: is peace really possible? There is a widely held, Marx-derived view that the only way in which capitalistic countries have been able to avoid massive depressions and crises has been through the employment of vast quantities of men and resources in armies, navies, air forces, and, above all, defense-related industries. In support of this view, it has been argued that, even with over $4\frac{1}{2}$ million persons either in the armed forces or directly employed by the Department of Defense and with an equal number employed as a direct or indirect result of defense contracts in private industry—perhaps as many as 10 million jobs overall!—the United States still has not achieved what could be properly called "full employment." If the half of the federal budget now devoted to war-related expenditures were removed, it is claimed, the country would sink into a collapse that would make the Great Depression of the thirties look like a mild setback!

Whether cold war tensions—or worse—are intrinsic to our economic system clearly depends on a judgment on this matter. Could we demobilize without disaster? Is the military-industrial complex (see pp. 102-7) an avoidable cost or a necessary crutch for the American economy?

In point of fact, there is a strong prima facie case for believing that the Marxian argument is erroneous. It derives from the fact that we did perform an extraordinary demobilization after World War II and without major untoward consequences. At the height of World War II, we had three times as many men in the armed forces as today (out of a smaller labor force) and we were devoting something like half our GNP to the war effort. We reduced these numbers and percentages drastically in the late 1940s, and although defense activities have grown since, they have never come close (in relation to the size of the economy) to matching those earlier figures. Despite this very considerable reduction, and despite obvious deficiencies in some areas of the economy, the fact is that the more than a quarter-century since World War II has been one of the most prosperous periods in American history.

A convincing answer, however, must rest not on one period alone, but rather on a general analysis of the economics of demobilization. This analysis involves both a macroeconomic and a microeconomic dimension.

The *macroeconomic* aspect involves our basic $C + I + G$ analysis from Part Two. Essentially what is involved in "peace" is large-scale reduction of that part of G which goes into defense or defense-related expenditures. If uncompensated by any other change, this reduction would mean a multiplied fall in national income according to our familiar analysis. The question, then, is whether it is possible to compensate for the fall in G by other measures. These measures could involve either reducing taxes, or increasing other components of G, or some combination of both.[1]

Although in principle it would be possible to match the fall in G by tax re-

---

1. For this basic analysis, see Part Two A, especially pp. 233-36.

ductions that would then stimulate private consumption and investment demand, exclusive reliance on this alternative would be objected to by many on the grounds that the tax reduction would have to be larger than the reduction of expenditures (recall that the tax multiplier is generally less than the expenditure multiplier), that such a program would consequently mean increases in the federal debt, that even with tax relief private consumption may not expand sufficiently, and/or that what we really need is not more private consumption but more public consumption—clean air, urban mass transit systems, hospitals, etc.

Consequently, the argument about compensating for the fall in defense expenditures that peace would entail often comes down to the question of whether there really are a sufficient number of useful projects of a public nature that our society should undertake. Can we, in other words, effectively match a fall in one part of G with an expansion of the remainder?

After what we have said in the last chapter about the costs of reducing pollution alone, it might seem that the answer to this question was obvious. And, indeed, it is the author's opinion that we should have no difficulty for the foreseeable future in finding useful public projects on the scale required. In the late 1960s, the President's Cabinet Coordinating Committee on Economic Planning for the End of the Vietnam Hostilities did a study on the economic implications of "a full withdrawal of troops from Vietnam with accompanying cutbacks in other outlays."[2] In the course of this study they prepared an estimate of new or expanded federal programs that might be launched

in 1972 as recommended by various specific task forces. As Table 31-1 indicates, they were able to expand G by about $40 billion, and this without by any means exhausting possibilities in urban, environmental, transportation, and other areas.

Indeed, the main macroeconomic question in this matter is not *whether* demobilization could be compensated but what the *implications* of this compensation might be. In particular, the shifting of part of G from defense (a traditional function of government dating back to Adam Smith and long before) to social and environmental problems (a more recent function) would probably mean an attitudinal shift of some magnitude away from the older concept of private enterprise towards newer concepts of the "welfare state" and (in the eyes of some) socialism. Those opposed to such a shift would very probably prefer to compensate for reducing G as much as possible by reducing T and hence increasing private expenditures. Others would welcome the modification of our already mixed system in the direction of taking further collective responsibilities for the quality of our environment both natural and manmade; they would also see, in this modification, additional evidence of the *convergence* of economic systems that we shall discuss in a moment. In either event, it does not seem likely that the purely macroeconomic problem of sustaining aggregate demand (and this was the main point of the Marxist critics) should rule out "peace" for a mixed capitalistic economy.

Nor do the *microeconomic* aspects of large-scale demobilization pose insuperable obstacles—though they would require considerable attention. These microeconomic problems derive from the fact that our defense program has an uneven impact on the economy, being particularly heavy in certain geographical re-

---

2. *Economic Report of the President* (Washington, D.C.: Government Printing Office, 1969), p. 191.

Table 31-1   HYPOTHETICAL PEACE EXPENDITURES

Illustrative new programs or major expansions of existing Federal civilian programs, fiscal year 1972 (derived from proposals of task forces and study groups).

Program	Hypothetical expenditures (billions of dollars)	
Total expenditures		39.7
Education	7.0	
Preschool		1.0
Elementary and secondary		2.5
Higher		3.0
Vocational		.5
Health	3.8	
Kiddie-care		.5
Medicare for disabled		1.8
Comprehensive health centers		1.0
Hospital construction and modernization		.5
Nutrition	1.0	
Community service programs	.8	
Jobs and manpower	2.5	
Public jobs		1.8
Manpower Development Training Act		.5
Employment service		.2
Social security and income support	9.5	
Unemployment insurance		2.0
Public assistance		4.0
Social security improvements		3.5
Veterans	.3	
Economic, area, and other special development programs	2.2	
Entrepreneurial aid		.5
Area redevelopment		.5
Rural development		1.0
Indian assistance		.2
Crime, delinquency, and riots	1.0	
Violence and riot prevention		.1
Safe streets programs		.3
Rehabilitation of offenders and delinquents		.3
Prevention of delinquency and crime by special measures for delinquency-prone youth		.3

Quality of environment	**1.7**
Air pollution prevention and control	.1
Public water supply construction programs	.3
Water pollution control and sewage treatment	1.0
Solid waste disposal	.1
Natural beautification, environmental protection, and recreational development	.2
Natural resource development and utilization	**1.4**
Land and forest conservation	.2
Water resources and related programs	.5
Mineral and energy (excluding hydroelectric) development	.2
Natural environmental development	.5
Urban development	**5.5**
New cities	.5
Land acquisition and financial planning (surburban)	.5
Urban mass transportation	.5
Model cities	2.0
Other urban facilities and renewal	2.0
Transportation	**1.0**
Airway and airport modernization	.4
Rapid interurban ground transit	.1
Modernization of merchant marine	.2
Motor vehicle and transportation safety research and safety grants	.3
Science and space exploration	**1.0**
Post-Apollo space program	.5
Scientific research in oceanography, communications, social and behavioral sciences, and natural sciences	.5
Foreign economic aid	**1.0**

Source: *Economic Report of the President* (1969), p. 204.

gions, particular industries and occupations, and also involving certain attitudes that are not easily transferable to civilian production.[3] Thus, seven states—California, Connecticut, Massachusetts, New Jersey, New York, Texas, and Washington—account for over half our military production. In the small (population) state of Alaska, nearly a third of the total work force was employed in defense and space work in 1968. Defense contracts account for three-quarters of aircraft production, a third of electronic components, over a quarter of transportation equipment and machine shop products. The heavy reliance of these industries on certain occupations—engineers, draftsmen, metalworkers, scientifically trained personnel—became all too apparent in the early 1970s when cutbacks in certain programs led to great unemployment among qualified scientists and engineers along the

3. For more detailed discussion of these matters, see Seymour Melman, ed., *The War Economy of the United States* (New York: St. Martin's Press, 1971), pp. 201–44.

well-known Route 128 in the Boston-Cambridge area.

The microeconomic problem of demobilization is essentially that we could not expect the new civilian industries that will take over from the defense program to display the same configuration of geography, products, and personnel as those they are replacing. Furthermore, insofar as these new industries are in the purely private sector, they may require attitudes rather different from those that have grown up in the competition-sheltered defense area.

Now this kind of problem is not insuperable. In fact, it is precisely the kind of problem that the price system is designed to solve. That system is, so to speak, "expert" at reallocating resources, which is what is at stake here. Given the size of the change, and the great difficulty of relocating either physically or professionally at certain stages of life, however, it seems obvious that the humane thing would be for the government to help ease this transition as much as possible. Numerous programs can and have been imagined: expanded manpower training, relocation assistance, veterans' employment consultation services, homeowner assistance, a strengthened federal-state employment service. A G.I. Bill applying to veterans of military industry (as well as military service) has been suggested. Walter Reuther once proposed that a quarter of all profits of defense contractors should be given over to preparing the way for a conversion from war to peace.

The conclusion: the microeconomic aspect (like the macroeconomic aspect) of the problem will require attention, but it *can* be handled. Peace is not an economic threat. Indeed, by freeing resources for civilian activities in which productivity is almost certainly much higher, the coming of peace should be an economic—as well as a human—blessing.

CAPITALISM, COMMUNISM, OR CONVERGENCE?

In discussing the possibilities for peace, one inevitably comes to wonder about the future of the great rival economic systems of East and West. Some years ago, Joseph Schumpeter posed the question, Can capitalism survive? Schumpeter was himself a rather conservative economist, but he answered the question in the negative, indicating that this was his prediction but not necessarily his preference.

Schumpeter's prediction was based on his own particular analysis of capitalism, which we have touched on before (p. 215). He saw the central feature of capitalism as growth and the central initiator of growth in the figure of the innovator or *entrepreneur*. According to Schumpeter, capitalism ultimately destroys itself by its own success. As growth becomes routinized, there is no longer any need for the robber baron entrepreneur of an earlier era—a bureaucracy (whether of General Motors or of a socialist state planning commission) will do just as well. Also, capitalism by its achievements spawns a large educated class; the intellectuals become very critical of the flaws of capitalism, and also of the business entrepreneurs who are increasingly on the defensive as time goes on. In due course, and largely because of its historic triumphs, capitalism becomes weaker and weaker, and socialism is the "heir apparent."[4]

On the other hand, a fair-minded observer might also come up with a nega-

4. Schumpeter's fascinating analysis is contained in his *Capitalism, Socialism and Democracy,* 3d ed. (New York: Harper & Row, 1950), part II.

tive answer to the question, Can communism survive? Our discussion of the stirrings within Eastern European countries and even within the Soviet Union herself (chapter 3) suggested that a move towards greater decentralization of decision-making was evident throughout the Communist world. Also, it seems at least probable that this decentralization might take the form of a greater use of a price system and even of such concepts as "profits." One could go further and argue that communism will very probably be undone by *its* success. Thus, one could say that a key goal of the Communist system has been to forge the rapid industrialization of relatively backward countries by ensuring an emphasis on investment above consumption, industry above agriculture, heavy industry above light industry, and so on. This goal has been largely achieved in countries like the Soviet Union. Now—the argument would go—communism is likely to become eroded for two reasons: (1) there is no longer a need for a command economy to produce forced-draft industrialization; and (2) in the more mature stage of society, the task of getting the consumers the goods they want in a reasonably efficient way is much better handled by decentralization.

But if we seem to be a step or two on the road to socialism and if they are a step or two on the road to capitalism, may we not, in fact, meet? And here we come upon one of the more interesting speculations of the postwar period—the doctrine of *convergence*. This doctrine, in its broadest form, derives from the view that there are basic similarities in the running of all modern industrial systems (that is, once the initial hurdles of getting on the path have been overcome). Thus, we should expect that the common problems in ours and the Soviet experience would

prove in the long run more significant than our different starting-points. In due course, the systems should converge in some kind of "mixed economy," not very far apart in practice— though, of course, the rhetoric of the two systems might still be quite different.

This doctrine is a rather tricky one, for it is by no means demonstrable that the converging of the two rival economic systems would diminish that rivalry in a political sense. Sometimes, one's deepest quarrels are with those who are closest to one in spirit. Nevertheless, the convergence hypothesis is highly interesting in its own right. It is explored in the following reading by the Nobel Prize-winning economist from the Netherlands, Jan Tinbergen.

Do Communist and Free Economies Show a Converging Pattern?

Jan Tinbergen

(1) We are witnessing today the co-existence of two radically different economic systems, the "communist" and the "free" economies (according to western terminology) or the "socialist" and "capitalist" systems (according to the eastern vocabulary). The various names given to them are far from precise. Perhaps the most imprecise thing about them is the suggestion that each of these systems represents something well-defined and hence invariant. Reality shows

From Jan Tinbergen, "Do Communist and Free Economies Show a Converging Pattern?" in Soviet Studies 12, no. 4 (April 1961): 331–41. Reprinted by permission of Basil Blackwell & Mott Ltd. and the author.

Jan Tinbergen. An outstanding Dutch economist, Tinbergen is noted for his work in econometrics (mathematical economics applied to real-world quantitative data) and the theory and practice of economic planning.

both to be in permanent change. Analysis of the nature of this change can prove quite fascinating. This essay proposes to show that the changes are in many respects converging movements. As will be seen, our essay is a very brief sketch only, trying to indicate a few main tendencies and not going into any detail, or, for that matter, into differences between the communist countries.

The main forces behind the changes may be brought under two broad headings. On the one hand each system is learning from experience and trying to overcome some of its own weaknesses. On the other hand the systems begin to influence each other

more and more. While in the beginning the communist system was not taken seriously by the free system this has changed to a considerable extent. The communist system has been interested in some "capitalist" achievements from its very start. Now it is not so much imitating some of the western methods as learning economics from its own experience.

(2) Some of the major changes which have occurred in the communist system since the Russian revolution will very briefly be summarized in this section:

(i) For a short while it was thought that specialized management was superfluous and that "the workers" could take care of this activity. It was soon learned that specialization is more efficient with regard to management. In fact, the traditional principle of resistance to specialization in all forms is becoming increasingly less prevalent.

(ii) For a short while an attempt was made to equalize incomes in a drastic way. The well-known consequences of such equalization by decree forced the regime to introduce a wage system which makes wages largely dependent on productivity. Strangely enough, this was then labelled "socialist wage policy."

(iii) For some time planning was done in terms of physical quantities and not in terms of money values. Gradually the use of money as a common denominator penetrated into the planning system and the significance of prices and costs was more and more recognized.

(iv) For a long time interest was considered an unnecessary concept as a consequence of the elimination of private ownership of capital goods. Gradually it was discovered that the elimination of interest as a form of private income does not mean that it should also be disregarded as a cost element.

(v) Rationing was abolished a few years after the Second World War and free consumer choice accepted as a proper institution. Gradually some more emphasis was given to consumption as the purpose of production.

(vi) Mathematical methods of planning, considered as "capitalist" for a long period, were recently recognized to be objective and helpful and are now widely discussed and applied.

(vii) A profound change is under way in the concepts of international trade, not only between communist countries but also between communist and free economies. The idea that each country should have its own heavy industry is no longer adhered to.

(3) The so-called free economies have also undergone thorough changes, which will now be summed up.

(i) The public sector nowadays is considerably larger than it was in the nineteenth century. Especially in western Europe public utilities are publicly owned; railways and tramways, coal mines, steel works, insurance companies and banks are often in the public sector.

(ii) The amount of taxes levied in western economies, often in the neighborhood of one quarter of national income, means that taxes are among the important regulators of economic activity. In addition a considerable portion of the nation's savings is made in the public sector.

(iii) Free competition has been limited in many ways as a natural consequence of some technical forces (high fixed costs of production). It has also been voluntarily restricted by such movements as the drive for standardization.

(iv) Partly as a consequence of (iii) governments have limited the freedom of entrepreneurs by anti-trust laws.

(v) Access to education has been given gradually to an increasing portion of the population, often by providing education without charge. Moreover, education has been made compulsory up to a certain age.

(vi) Market forces have been eliminated or modified in some particularly unstable markets, especially in agriculture and in some cases even international commodity agreements have been concluded.

(vii) Planning has gradually been given an increasingly important role, both in big private enterprises and in the design of national economic policy.

(viii) Deliberate development policies have been in existence for a long time. In the nineteenth century already, transportation facilities were often created with public help. At present a whole range of measures, from tax facilities to government investments in infrastructure as well as in manufacturing industry proper, are applied to further the development of remote areas or poor regions.

(ix) Some forms of price and wage control as a direct means to prevent inflation have been used recently in a few "free" economies.

(4) Several of the changes recorded above are in fact bringing the communist and the free economies closer together. This cannot be said, however, to mean that the differences are already small. There are very large differences still. But the process has not stopped. Both types of economies are facing many problems. They will have to move further. In this section we try to give a picture of the most striking differences still in existence and in the subsequent sections of the most important problems to be solved in both types of economies.

(i) The most striking difference is, of course, the size of the public sector. It should not be forgotten, however, that the power of the private sector in western countries is not commensurate with its formal size. In many indirect ways western societies have reduced this power. For example, taxes take away almost half of the profits. Of the remainder, a large part is invested and only a small part paid out as dividends. Western as well as communist economies are to a large extent dominated by managers. In the west, shareholders are no longer powerful. Social legislation in many respects also restricts the freedom of action of private entrepreneurs. So do a number of regulations with regard to quality control, pollution of water and air, building activity, town and country planning and so on.

(ii) Another important difference is the degree of freedom in production decisions. Factory managers in the west have much more freedom in this respect than managers in communist countries where a still very large number of items is planned centrally.

(iii) Accordingly, there is a considerable difference in the degree of detail in which the future course of the economy is planned in communist countries and in "free" economies. This refers to production as well as, e.g., to foreign trade.

(iv) Prices are controlled centrally in the communist countries to a much higher degree than in western countries, where, as a rule, only a few agricultural prices are under direct control. Here again, however, western countries use more indirect means of influencing prices. Among these, competition is the main institutional means, but import duties and monetary policies and (in Holland) wage control and price control of some other items are supplementary instruments.

(v) Industrial democracy is very different in the two types of countries. In the west only some beginnings have been made with co-determination of workers or their organizations in some social issues. In the communist world workers are given opportunities to participate in the discussions about the economic plans of the enterprise and about the use of a portion of the enterprise surplus.

(vi) Education constitutes another subject in which there is still considerable difference. In the "free" countries a certain portion of the potential students of secondary and university training cannot receive the education they need for lack of financial means. The portion is declining, however, as a consequence of several types of financial help, which in some countries enable as much as half of the student body to carry on their studies.

(vii) The differences in the level of savings are recently less striking between such countries as the continental European countries and the communist countries than they were before. Savings of about 20 percent of national income are now no exception in these western countries; Japan is saving

nearly 30 percent. The United States and the United Kingdom, however, save considerably less.

(viii) Regarding the principles of the international division of labour and priorities of investment projects the differences between east and west are rapidly disappearing.

(5) Corresponding to these problems the communist countries may have to face the following issues:

(i) A major problem seems to be the question of whether or not a gain in efficiency will result from making a large number of small enterprises in essence "private" enterprises by some sort of lease or concession system. If one tries to imagine the volume of administration now usual, say, in shops, it must be a burden on general efficiency.

(ii) A second major problem seems to be whether or not more freedom in production decisions can be given to managers. With rising real incomes citizens of the communist countries will require a finer pattern of qualities and assortment which it is hardly possible to plan centrally. Those closest to the market can probably best judge the needs. There does not seem to be any danger of the central authorities losing control over general economic development as a consequence of granting this type of freedom for the individual manager.

(iii) One also wonders whether or not the number of items planned centrally should be diminished in order to relieve the central planning agencies of a heavy burden which appears to have relatively unimportant qualifications in terms of increments in national well-being produced. The same may well apply to international trade planning.

(iv) The next question communist countries might put to themselves relates to price fixing. What harm is there in permitting prices to move as a consequence of relative shortages or abundances and letting them contribute to restore equilibrium? Is not such a method in fact quicker than a mere adaptation in production programs or stocks? Prices will have to move anyhow as a consequence of technical progress and changes in crops. It remains an open question whether the changes should be permitted to individual sellers or only to central authorities. In other words, there seems to be a choice here where the answer is not so clear beforehand and where there is an element of discretion.

(v) A very fundamental question, going far beyond economic institutions is of course the one about a possible widening of democracy in our sense. It is not within the scope of this essay to make any speculations on this important subject.

(6) Certainly the "free" economies also have to face questions.

(i) Has the public sector the correct size? In the United States important commentators have made the point that it is too small in that country and that recently some public tasks have been neglected.

Even if in European countries the question does not seem to be a controversial issue, the related question of how further to restrict the privileges of some forms of private income or capital still is one under discussion. There is an interesting argument about the possibility of restricting consumption financed out of capital gains, introduced by Nicholas Kaldor's book on "An Expenditure Tax." Possible restrictions on the income paid to directors are discussed and the case for higher inheritance taxes has not been decided upon. The impression of a certain stagnation in the reforms in this field is due not so much to general satisfaction about the present state of affairs as it is to the fact that progressive political parties are re-thinking their programs.

(ii) There is not much debate in western countries about restricting the freedom of decisions of managers about their production programs. Rather there is an increasing interest on the side of management for general economic forecasts and market analysis to help them in their decisions.

(iii) Accordingly the case for some more planning is a living issue in the west. One government after the other feels it has to do something in this field. The most recent example is Belgium, with a possibility for Germany to follow. In Asian countries planning is generally accepted; only the methods differ. The borderline European and Asian country, Turkey, has just established a planning agency. Latin American countries are one after the other engaging in some planning. There is a wide variation in the degree of detail planned and the time has come to discuss in a more precise way which degree of detail is the most appropriate. The outcome of such a discussion may also have its value for the communist countries.

(iv) Price formation is an issue of discussion in the west mainly when the general price level is at stake: should not governments have more instruments to counteract inflationary price rises, especially of the cost-push type? The existing situation is unsatisfactory. The use of only monetary and financial means contains the danger of creating unemployment before the price level goes down. Wage control as an indirect means of controlling prices is not accepted. International integration in order to strengthen competition may give some help in small countries, but does not solve the problem for larger countries. It may therefore be that after all some new form of price setting is necessary.

(v) There is a continued pressure in western countries to facilitate the access to education for larger groups of the population. Some of the proposals are going into the direction of the communist solution, namely to pay a wage to the student. Other proposals are more traditional.

(vi) Industrial democracy is an unsolved question too. The attempts so far made in Western Europe differ from country to country. None is very satisfactory.

(7) The picture given shows that communist as well as "free" countries have to solve some problems and that there may be further tendencies to a converging movement. This is true particularly for the main question about the degree of decentralization in production decisions and planning. It is to some extent also true for the process of price formation. It is less clear with regard to the formal side of property, but a distinction between formal property and the real situation

must be made. As already observed, both the income from property and the freedom of decision with regard to its use have been strongly reduced in the west and the process may continue.

It is interesting to add a more theoretical analysis to the factual description already attempted. What does economic science have to tell us about the probability of a further convergency of the organization patterns? It is evident that economic science can only tell us something about the subject in so far as economic forces will determine the movements. Clearly in the past other than economic forces have been at work. Nevertheless, would it be denied that economic considerations are important both to communists and, let us say, to Americans?

The chapter of economic science we may first consult is welfare economics. In principle, it tells us about the conditions which the optimum pattern of organization of society has to fulfil. Its contents have long been considered a defense of the free enterprise system, but wrongly so. It is true that welfare economics show that uniform prices (i.e., absence of price discrimination) are among the conditions for maximum welfare. But these can be established just as well by a system of government-controlled pricing as by competitive markets.

Another proposition of welfare economics is that prices should be equal to marginal costs. This statement implies that for the activities characterized by high fixed costs and technical surplus capacity private enterprise cannot be the system leading to maximum welfare.* Socialization may be the best solution therefore for all the activities concerned.

Similar remarks are valid with regard to activities showing external effects. It can be shown, at the basis of welfare economics, that activities of this kind should be carried out by integrated units; integrated, that is, with the producers or consumers whose well-being is affected by the external effects. Socialization may again be a solution.

In concrete terms, the most important activities falling under these two categories are about the same as those already socialized in Western European countries, namely public utilities, rail and air transportation, highway construction and education. Possibly also steel and coal should be added and perhaps other types of transportation.

A further subject relevant to welfare economics is taxes. Two principles are important: first, that there must be some form of income redistribution and second, that income tax is not the optimal way of doing so. The redistribution taxes should approach as much as possible the lump-sum type, i.e., the type not taxing marginal income. Wealth taxes are perhaps the nearest example we know today.

All this points to the desirability of some sort of a mixed system, as far as property is concerned, and to a tax system which may hit personal wealth more than it now does in the west. It also points in the direction of admitting more decentralization with regard to the activities showing constant or increasing costs, i.e. generally for industries where small units are justified as the communist countries may discover in the future.

(8) Reference to another chapter (or chapters) of economics may be needed, in order to answer the following questions. What element of truth is there in the contention sometimes made that there is no optimum in the middle, but rather a tendency for optima to be at the extremes?

---

*[This is a reference to what we called falling (average) cost industries, pp. 471.]

This opinion is sometimes illustrated by the argument that "once you start to deviate from market price formation you have to regulate more and more until the whole economy is regulated." Is this illustration relevant to our subject and would it, in a general way, disprove the assumption of an optimum somewhere halfway? The alleged tendency to divergency rather than convergency can no doubt be observed in some cases of war economy regulations. If you start rationing and price control in some markets you will soon find it necessary to regulate other markets too. The argument does not necessarily apply to other types of intervention, however. An interesting example to the contrary can be found in business cycle policy. Here it is generally accepted that if you regulate the total flow of demand by appropriate instruments—e.g., financial and monetary policy—you may then leave most markets to themselves. You can, in addition, select a few markets showing characteristics of instability, which may be controlled without the necessity for controlling other markets. Those to be controlled are the ones showing long production lags or a long life of the products.

In the same manner the ownership of the means of production is not characterized as such by a tendency to spread. In Western Europe there exists a public sector of a certain size which has maintained itself for years without making it necessary to expand it rapidly in order to preserve some equilibrium. If in the USSR private business has virtually vanished it is because it was discriminated against on ideological grounds and, in the initial period, for reasons of political power.

In the case of planning a similar position can be maintained. Planning the main elements of the economy does not necessarily imply the need for detailed planning.

It cannot be argued therefore that there is an inherent tendency for economic regimes to move to the extremes. Our theoretical reconnaissance therefore, seems to support rather than to undermine the views derived from observation. No doubt the optimum organization of the economy will differ from country to country and from period to period. It is also hardly conceivable that we will soon be able to indicate precisely where the optimum lies, or even to say whether "east and west" will actually "meet" in their attempts to find the "welfare summit."

(9) This essay may be concluded with a few remarks about the "non-committed" countries, that is non-committed to one of the two economic systems at the extremes. Being underdeveloped countries at the same time, they still have a significant number of feudal elements. They are less subject to preconceived ideas about the economic system. If the state sector plays an important role in some of them it is because the necessary initiative was first taken in this rather than in the private sector (Turkey, India).

This group of countries is now facing some very urgent economic needs, partly as a consequence of increasing contacts with the outside world, partly because they have only recently become independent states. The most pressing need is the one for a higher level of production. Another need is to live under a system of stabler prices. Several secondary aims of policy can be derived from these primary ones, such as the full use of resources, an increase in investment levels and a diversification of their production pattern.

Because of the presence, in today's world, of the two major systems the underdeveloped countries are looking to both in order to learn from them. They are above all interested in rapid growth and less in such issues as parliamentary democracy, since they have hardly ever had it. The communist example impresses them greatly. Planning is in high esteem. State initiative does take up part of the tasks neglected by private initiative. The willingness to interfere with price formation is understandable since they are often depending on typically unstable markets. Conditions seem favorable in these countries to try to combine the best elements from communism and free enterprise. These countries therefore may become the experimental ground for economic regimes.

They may, as they sometimes do in technical matters, skip one phase in their development and at once aim at the best solution. They should try to. And we may follow with particular interest the pattern of society that is emerging.

THE POSSIBILITIES OF AFFLUENCE

Tinbergen's essay (above) ends with a reference to the underdeveloped countries, a subject we shall return to in our final chapter. For the moment, however, our interest is in the future of the industrial societies. Many feel (presuming, of course, that we pay sufficient attention to the problems of war, pollution and ecology) that that future holds out the promise of unparalleled affluence.

The Affluent Society is, of course, the title of Professor Galbraith's famous book. The argument of that book does not ignore the economic deficiencies of our society—income distribution, poverty,

pollution, the need for more public services, etc.—but it does suggest that fundamentally we have reached a new state of affairs, where abundance rather than scarcity has become the major problem. Galbraith writes:

The greatest prospect that we face—indeed what must now be counted one of the central economic goals of our society—is to eliminate toil as a required economic institution. This is not a utopian vision. We are already well on the way. Only an extraordinarily elaborate exercise in social camouflage has kept us from seeing what has been happening.[5]

In this stage of society, the central social goal (apart from securing peaceful survival) is to expand what Galbraith calls the "New Class." This New Class is that group of individuals in modern life whose work is interesting and rewarding in itself. He divides work into two major categories (with all kinds of possible overlapping): (1) work whose only reward is the pay, and (2) work that is basically an end in itself. Members of the New Class may not in the least object to high pay, but they would be offended by the notion that pay was what really motivated them. The key thing is to find work that is personally satisfying, and members of the New Class also pass on this attitude to their children.

Historically speaking, there has always been a leisure class (whose members, incidentally, may have worked very hard at their hobbies, whether archeology, social intrigue, or simply "putting on the dog"), and also there have been artists and members of the various professions who have taken it for granted that their work would be interesting and valuable even in the absence of monetary

5. John Kenneth Galbraith, *The Affluent Society* (Boston: Houghton Mifflin Company, 1958), p. 340.

recognition. However, the great mass of mankind has faced work as a necessary, but disagreeable, monotonous and toilsome duty, required by the basic fact of scarcity. The novel feature of the age to come is that it may prove possible to expand the New Class so that it includes not simply a handful, but the great majority of citizens.

The reader will recognize in the above an anticipation and somewhat more formal statement of the arguments, current in the 1960s and early 1970s, that everyone should "do his own thing." We should look not for jobs but for self-fulfillment and self-realization. Some would argue that this slogan, and Galbraith's case, are a bit premature, but it is interesting that somewhat similar ideas were put forward by John Maynard Keynes over forty years ago. What is even more remarkable is that, when Keynes was writing about the prospects of leisure and abundance, there was a massive worldwide depression going on.

Both as an indication of Keynes' extraordinary sense of perspective and as a still highly relevant statement about the possibilities (and problems) of affluence, we reproduce his brief essay in its entirety.

Economic Possibilities For Our Grandchildren

JOHN MAYNARD KEYNES

I

We are suffering just now from a bad attack of economic pessimism. It is common to hear people say that the epoch of enor-

From "Economic Possibilities for Our Grandchildren" from pp. 358–73 *Essays in Persuasion* by John Maynard Keynes. Included in the *Collected Writings of John Maynard Keynes*, vol. 9, *Essays in Persuasion* published by Macmillan London and Basingstoke and St. Martin's Press, Inc. New York. Reprinted by permission of the publisher.

mous economic progress which characterised the nineteenth century is over; that the rapid improvement in the standard of life is now going to slow down—at any rate in Great Britain; that a decline in prosperity is more likely than an improvement in the decade which lies ahead of us.

I believe that this is a wildly mistaken interpretation of what is happening to us. We are suffering, not from the rheumatics of old age, but from the growing-pains of over-rapid changes, from the painfulness of readjustment between one economic period and another. The increase of technical efficiency has been taking place faster than we can deal with the problem of labour absorption; the improvement in the standard of life has been a little too quick, the banking and monetary system of the world has been preventing the rate of interest from falling as fast as equilibrium requires. And even so, the waste and confusion which ensue relate to not more than 7½ percent of the national income; we are muddling away one and sixpence in the £, and have only 18s. 6d., when we might, if we were more sensible, have £1; yet, nevertheless, the 18s. 6d. mounts up to as much as the £1 would have been five or six years ago. We forget that in 1929 the physical output of the industry of Great Britain was greater than ever before, and that the net surplus of our foreign balance available for new foreign investment, after paying for all our imports, was greater last year than that of any other country, being indeed 50 percent greater than the corresponding surplus of the United States. Or again—if it is to be a matter of comparisons—suppose that we were to reduce our wages by a half, repudiate four-fifths of the national debt, and hoard our surplus wealth in barren gold instead of lending it at 6 percent or more, we should resemble the now much-envied France. But would it be an improvement?

The prevailing world depression, the enormous anomaly of unemployment in a world full of wants, the disastrous mistakes we have made, blind us to what is going on under the surface—to the true interpretation of the trend of things. For I predict that both of the two opposed errors of pessimism which now make so much noise in the world will be proved wrong in our own time—the pessimism of the revolutionaries who think that things are so bad that nothing can save us but violent change, and the pessimism of the reactionaries who consider the balance of our economic and social life so precarious that we must risk no experiments.

My purpose in this essay, however, is not to examine the present or the near future, but to disembarrass myself of short views and take wings into the future. What can we reasonably expect the level of our economic life to be a hundred years hence? What are the economic possibilities for our grandchildren?

From the earliest times of which we have record—back, say, to two thousand years before Christ—down to the beginning of the eighteenth century, there was no very great change in the standard of life of the average man living in the civilised centres of the earth. Ups and downs certainly. Visitations of plague, famine, and war. Golden intervals. But no progressive, violent change. Some periods perhaps 50 percent better than others—at the utmost 100 percent better—in the four thousand years which ended (say) in A.D. 1700.

This slow rate of progress, or lack of progress, was due to two reasons—to the remarkable absence of important technical improvements and to the failure of capital to accumulate.

The absence of important technical inventions between the prehistoric age and comparatively modern times is truly remarkable. Almost everything which really matters and which the world possessed at the commencement of the modern age was already known to man at the dawn of history. Language, fire, the same domestic animals which we have today, wheat, barley, the vine and the olive, the plough, the wheel, the oar, the sail, leather, linen and cloth, bricks and pots, gold and silver, copper, tin, and lead—and iron was added to the list before 1000 B.C.—banking, statecraft, mathematics, astronomy, and religion. There is no record of when we first possessed these things.

At some epoch before the dawn of history—perhaps even in one of the comfortable intervals before the last ice age—there must have been an era of progress and invention comparable to that in which we live to-day. But through the greater part of recorded history there was nothing of the kind.

The modern age opened, I think, with the accumulation of capital which began in the sixteenth century. I believe—for reasons with which I must not encumber the present argument—that this was initially due to the rise of prices, and the profits to which that led, which resulted from the treasure of gold and silver which Spain brought from the New World into the Old. From that time until to-day the power of accumulation by compound interest, which seems to have been sleeping for many generations, was re-born and renewed its strength. And the power of compound interest over two hundred years is such as to stagger the imagination.

Let me give in illustration of this a sum which I have worked out. The value of Great Britain's foreign investments to-day is estimated at about £4,000,000,000. This yields us an income at the rate of about 6½ percent. Half of this we bring home and enjoy; the other half, namely, 3¼ percent, we leave to accumulate abroad at compound interest. Something of this sort has now been going on for about 250 years.

For I trace the beginnings of British foreign investment to the treasure which Drake stole from Spain in 1580. In that year he returned to England bringing with him the prodigious spoils of the *Golden Hind*. Queen Elizabeth was a considerable shareholder in the syndicate which had financed the expedition. Out of her share she paid off the whole of England's foreign debt, balanced her Budget, and found herself with about £40,000 in hand. This she invested in the Levant company—which prospered.

Out of the profits of the Levant Company, the East India Company was founded; and the profits of this great enterprise were the foundation of England's subsequent foreign investment. Now it happens that £40,000 accumulating at 3¼ percent compound interest approximately corresponds to the actual volume of England's foreign investments at various dates, and would actually amount to-day to the total of £4,000,000,000 which I have already quoted as being what our foreign investments now are. Thus, every £1 which Drake brought home in 1580 has now become £100,000. Such is the power of compound interest!

From the sixteenth century, with a cumulative crescendo after the eighteenth, the great age of science and technical inventions began, which since the beginning of the nineteenth century has been in full flood—coal, steam, electricity, petrol, steel, rubber, cotton, the chemical industries, automatic machinery and the methods of mass production, wireless, printing, Newton, Darwin, and Einstein, and thousands of other things and men too famous and familiar to catalogue.

What is the result? In spite of an enormous growth in the population of the world, which it has been necessary to equip with houses and machines, the average standard of life in Europe and the United States has been raised, I think, about fourfold. The growth of capital has been on a scale which is far beyond a hundredfold of what any previous age had known. And from now on we need not expect so great an increase of population.

If capital increases, say, 2 percent per annum, the capital equipment of the world will have increased by a half in twenty years, and seven and a half times in a hundred years. Think of this in terms of material things—houses, transport, and the like.

At the same time technical improvements in manufacture and transport have been proceeding at a greater rate in the last ten years than ever before in history. In the United States factory output per head was 40 percent greater in 1925 than in 1919. In Europe we are held back by temporary obstacles, but even so it is safe to say that technical efficiency is increasing by more than 1 percent per annum compound. There is evidence that the revolutionary technical changes, which have so far chiefly affected industry, may soon be attacking agriculture. We may be on the eve of improvements in the efficiency of food production as great as those which have already taken place in mining, manufacture, and transport. In quite a few years—in our own lifetimes I mean—we may be able to perform all the operations of agriculture, mining, and manufacture with a quarter of the human effort to which we have been accustomed.

For the moment the very rapidity of these changes is hurting us and bringing difficult problems to solve. Those countries are suffering relatively which are not in the vanguard of progress. We are being afflicted with a new disease of which some readers may not yet have heard the name, but of which they will hear a great deal in the years to come—namely, *technological unemployment*. This means unemployment due to our discovery of means of economising the use of labour outrunning the pace at which we can find new uses for labour.

But this is only a temporary phase of maladjustment. All this means in the long run *that mankind is solving its economic problem*. I would predict that the standard of life in progressive countries one hundred years hence will be between four and eight times as high as it is to-day. There would be nothing surprising in this even in the light of our present knowledge. It would not be foolish to contemplate the possibility of a far greater progress still.

II

Let us, for the sake of argument, suppose that a hundred years hence we are all of us, on the average, eight times better off in the economic sense than we are to-day.

Assuredly there need be nothing here to surprise us.

Now it is true that the needs of human beings may seem to be insatiable. But they fall into two classes—those needs which are absolute in the sense that we feel them whatever the situation of our fellow human beings may be, and those which are relative in the sense that we feel them only if their satisfaction lifts us above, makes us feel superior to, our fellows. Needs of the second class, those which satisfy the desire for superiority, may indeed be insatiable; for the higher the general level, the higher still are they. But this is not so true of the absolute needs—a point may soon be reached, much sooner perhaps than we are all of us aware of, when these needs are satisfied in the sense that we prefer to devote our further energies to non-economic purposes.

Now, for my conclusion, which you will find, I think, to become more and more startling to the imagination the longer you think about it.

I draw the conclusion that, assuming no important wars and no important increase in population, the *economic problem* may be solved, or be at least within sight of solution, within a hundred years. This means that the economic problem is not—if we look into the future—*the permanent problem of the human race.*

Why, you may ask, is this so startling? It is startling because—if, instead of looking into the future, we look into the past—we find that the economic problem, the struggle for subsistence, always has been hitherto the primary, most pressing problem of the human race—not only of the human race, but of the whole of the biological kingdom from the beginnings of life in its most primitive forms.

Thus we have been expressly evolved by nature—with all our impulses and deepest instincts—for the purpose of solving the economic problem. If the economic problem is solved, mankind will be deprived of its traditional purpose.

Will this be a benefit? If one believes at all in the real values of life, the prospect at least opens up the possibility of benefit. Yet I think with dread of the readjustment of the habits and instincts of the ordinary man, bred into him for countless generations, which he may be asked to discard within a few decades.

To use the language of to-day—must we not expect a general "nervous breakdown"? We already have a little experience of what I mean—a nervous breakdown of the sort which is already common enough in England and the United States amongst the wives of the well-to-do classes, unfortunate women, many of them, who have been deprived by their wealth of their traditional tasks and occupations—who cannot find it sufficiently amusing, when deprived of the spur of economic necessity, to cook and clean and mend, yet are quite unable to find anything more amusing.

To those who sweat for their daily bread leisure is a longed-for sweet—until they get it.

There is the traditional epitaph written for herself by the old charwoman:

Don't mourn for me, friends, don't weep for me never,
For I'm going to do nothing for ever and ever.

This was her heaven. Like others who look forward to leisure, she conceived how nice it would be to spend her time listening-in—for there was another couplet which occurred in her poem:

With psalms and sweet music the heavens'll be ringing,
But I shall have nothing to do with the singing.

Yet it will only be for those who have to do with the singing that life will be tolerable—and how few of us can sing!

Thus for the first time since his creation man will be faced with his real, his permanent problem—how to use his freedom from pressing economic cares, how to occupy the leisure, which science and compound interest will have won for him, to live wisely and agreeably and well.

The strenuous purposeful money-makers may carry all of us along with them into the lap of economic abundance. But it will be those peoples, who can keep alive, and cultivate into a fuller perfection, the art of life itself and do not sell themselves for the means of life, who will be able to enjoy the abundance when it comes.

Yet there is no country and no people, I think, who can look forward to the age of leisure and of abundance without a dread. For we have been trained too long to strive and not to enjoy. It is a fearful problem for the ordinary person, with no special talents, to occupy himself, especially if he no longer has roots in the soil or in custom or in the beloved conventions of a traditional society. To judge from the behaviour and the achievements of the wealthy classes to-day in any quarter of the world, the outlook is very depressing! For these are, so to speak, our advance guard—those who are spying out the promised land for the rest of us and pitching their camp there. For they have most of them failed disastrously, so it seems to me—those who have an independent income but no associations or duties or ties—to solve the problem which has been set them.

I feel sure that with a little more experience we shall use the new-found bounty of nature quite differently from the way in which the rich use it to-day, and will map out for ourselves a plan of life quite otherwise than theirs.

For many ages to come the old Adam will be so strong in us that everybody will need to do *some* work if he is to be contented. We shall do more things for ourselves than is usual with the rich to-day, only too glad to have small duties and tasks and routines. But beyond this, we shall endeavour to spread the bread thin on the butter—to make what work there is still to be done to be as widely shared as possible. Three-hour shifts or a fifteen-hour week may put off the problem for a great while. For three

hours a day is quite enough to satisfy the old Adam in most of us!

There are changes in other spheres too which we must expect to come. When the accumulation of wealth is no longer of high social importance, there will be great changes in the code of morals. We shall be able to rid ourselves of many of the pseudo-moral principles which have hag-ridden us for 200 years, by which we have exalted some of the most distasteful of human qualities into the position of the highest virtues. We shall be able to afford to dare to assess the money-motive at its true value. The love of money as a possession—as distinguished from the love of money as a means to the enjoyments and realities of life—will be recognised for what it is, a somewhat disgusting morbidity, one of those semi-criminal, semi-pathological propensities which one hands over with a shudder to the specialists in mental disease. All kinds of social customs and economic practices, affecting the distribution of wealth and of economic rewards and penalties, which we now maintain at all costs, however distasteful and unjust they may be in themselves, because they are tremendously useful in promoting the accumulation of capital, we shall then be free, at last, to discard.

Of course there will still be many people with intense, unsatisfied purposiveness who will blindly pursue wealth—unless they can find some plausible substitute. But the rest of us will no longer be under any obligation to applaud and encourage them. For we shall inquire more curiously than is safe to-day into the true character of this "purposiveness" with which in varying degrees Nature has endowed almost all of us. For purposiveness means that we are more concerned with the remote future results of our actions than with their own quality or their immediate effects on our own environment. The "purposive" man is always trying to secure a spurious and delusive immortality for his acts by pushing his interest in them forward into time. He does not love his cat, but his cat's kittens; nor, in truth, the kittens, but only the kittens' kittens, and so on forward for ever to the end of cat-dom. For him jam is not jam unless it is a case of jam to-morrow and never jam to-day. Thus by pushing his jam always forward into the future, he strives to secure for his act of boiling it an immortality.

Let me remind you of the Professor in *Sylvie and Bruno:*

"Only the tailor, sir, with your little bill," said a meek voice outside the door.

"Ah, well, I can soon settle his business," the Professor said to the children, *"if you'll just wait a minute. How much is it, this year, my man?"* The tailor had come in while he was speaking.

"Well, it's been a-doubling so many years, you see," the tailor replied, a little gruffly, *"and I think I'd like the money now. It's two thousand pound, it is!"*

"Oh, that's nothing!" the Professor carelessly remarked, feeling in his pocket, as if he always carried at least that amount about with him. *"But wouldn't you like to wait just another year and make it* four *thousand? Just think how rich you'd be! Why, you might be a king, if you liked!"*

"I don't know as I'd care about being a king," the man said thoughtfully. *"But it dew sound a powerful sight o' money! Well, I think I'll wait—"*

"Of course you will!" said the Professor. *"There's good sense in* you, *I see. Good-day to you, my man!"*

"Will you ever have to pay him that four thousand pounds?" Sylvie asked as the door closed on the departing creditor.

"Never, my child!" the Professor replied emphatically. *"He'll go on doubling it till he dies. You see, it's always* worth while waiting *another year to get twice as much money!"*

Perhaps it is not an accident that the race which did most to bring the promise of immortality into the heart and essence of our religions has also done most for the principle of compound interest and particularly loves this most purposive of human institutions.

I see us free, therefore, to return to some of the most sure and certain principles of religion and traditional virtue—that avarice is a vice, that the exaction of usury is a misdemeanour, and the love of money is detestable, that those walk most truly in the paths of virtue and sane wisdom who take least thought for the morrow. We shall once more value ends above means and prefer the good to the useful. We shall honour those who can teach us how to pluck the hour and the day virtuously and well, the delightful people who are capable of taking direct enjoyment in things, the lilies of the field who toil not, neither do they spin.

But beware! The time for all this is not yet. For at least another hundred years we must pretend to ourselves and to every one that fair is foul and foul is fair; for foul is useful and fair is not. Avarice and usury and precaution must be our gods for a little longer still. For only they can lead us out of the tunnel of economic necessity into daylight.

I look forward, therefore, in days not so very remote, to the greatest change which has ever occurred in the material environment of life for human beings in the aggregate. But, of course, it will all happen gradually, not as a catastrophe. Indeed, it has already begun. The course of affairs will simply be that there will be ever larger and larger classes and groups of people from whom problems of economic necessity have been practically removed. The critical difference will be realised when this condition has become so general that the nature of one's duty to one's neighbour is changed. For it will remain reasonable to be economically purposive for others after it has ceased to be reasonable for oneself.

The *pace* at which we can reach our destination of economic bliss will be governed by four things—our power to control population, our determination to avoid wars and civil dissensions, our willingness to entrust to science the direction of those matters which are properly the concern of science, and the rate of accumulation as fixed by the margin between our production and our consumption; of which the last will easily look after itself, given the first three.

Meanwhile there will be no harm in making mild preparations for our destiny, in encouraging, and experimenting in, the arts of life as well as the activities of purpose.

But, chiefly, do not let us overestimate the importance of the economic problem, or sacrifice to its supposed necessities other matters of greater and more permanent significance. It should be a matter for specialists—like dentistry. If economists could manage to get themselves thought of as humble, competent people, on a level with dentists, that would be splendid!

WHAT ARE OUR GOALS?

In the title of this chapter, we included the phrase, "an uncertain future." Considering that observers have seen as a logical projection of the trends of our industrial society either (1) everybody on the average being "eight times better off" (Keynes), or (2) "a succession of famines, epidemics, social crises and wars" (Great Debate Five, p. 729), it is clear that "uncertain" is a rather mild adjective for what we face.

Interestingly enough, however, even in these rather widely separated views we can find a certain common theme. This theme may be said to involve the erosion of the *idea of progress.* In terms of the future-abundance school of thought, the necessity for further material advance will decline as we become richer and richer. What we must look forward to is a society in which, far from building for the tomorrow, we must develop the capacities for enjoying today. Yesterday's virtues—saving, thrift, abstinence—will have no relevance in a society ripe with riches.

But a similar basic theme is also present in the ecological-cataclysm school.

The outlook is pessimistic—they would say that what we have called economic "progress" has been deeply delusive—but their conclusion is much the same. We must move from an expanding, spreading, aggressive society to a much more stable, non-exploitive society. This may be Boulding's spaceship earth, or John Stuart Mill's "stationary state." In any event, instead of always moving forward, we must learn to become content with a society whose basic dimensions remain unchanged over time.

Now this decline in the notion of progress is a development of extraordinary importance, the full consequences of which have not yet been analyzed. In the 1930s, in an introduction to J. B. Bury's classic work, *The Idea of Progress,* the historian Charles Beard wrote: "Now among the ideas which have held sway in public and private affairs for the last two hundred years, none is more significant or likely to exert more influence in the future than the concept of progress."[6] J. B. Bury himself argued that, by the end of the nineteenth century, the idea of progress was becoming a "general article of faith." In many ways, it was a this-worldly equivalent to the concept of immortality and an afterlife of the great religions that had so dominated thought in earlier periods. Through progress, the individual could find redemption for himself, not in the thought of heavenly rewards, but in the imagination of the better world that would come in the future. Mankind was seen as moving forward and upward—whether inevitably or as a result of one's hard efforts was never fully resolved—but the movement was definitely in a positive

6. Charles A. Beard, "Introduction," in *The Idea of Progress,* J. B. Bury (New York: Dover Publications, Inc., 1955), p. xi. Beard's introduction was written in 1931; Bury's original book was published in 1920.

direction, and this provided both a discipline and a sense of purpose in life.

The idea of progress is clearly not an economic phenomenon only. It was rooted in the philosophic thought of the Enlightenment of the eighteenth century (before the Industrial Revolution had struck with full force); it was given practical reality and much wider appeal by the great strides in science, technology, and material standards of living from the late eighteenth century on; and it was also given an enormous boost by the mid-nineteenth century development of the theory of evolution. Man was not only progressing in historic time, but also in biological time. The French philosopher, Henri Bergson, expressed this in his notion of "creative evolution." It is not too much to say that Western man—the peoples living in the economically advanced, industrial world—entered the twentieth century with the concept of progress in economics, science, art, biology, democracy, all phases of human life writ large on the banners of his beliefs.

It is this idea—basically a religious idea—that is coming under fire. It raises the embarrassingly direct but extremely difficult question: if we are not living for the good of posterity, exactly what are we living for?

Now in the economic sphere in particular this painful question may be avoided for a time, perhaps for a very long time. The essential reason is that economic inequalities of major dimension exist in the modern world—within the affluent societies, but even more as contrasted with the poor societies of the world. It may be possible that the new interest in equality (see chapter 29) is, in part, an attempt to avoid the still deeper question of long-run purposes. There is something close to a contradiction in arguing (1) that the rich are corrupted by their wealth and

(2) that we should all have the same as they have.

Perform the mental experiment: We all have equal goods and enough. We are recycling as a matter of course. The future will be no worse than today, but also no better. We will not achieve salvation through our children, nor they through theirs. We will live securely, painlessly, without toil, for today.

In such a world, the phrase from Keynes' essay might haunt us bitterly. How few of us can sing!

Still, this world is not yet. And economics, born in the Enlightenment, nourished by the industrial revolution and the advance of material well-being, fresh from the conquest of Great (if not smaller) Depressions, is not yet ready to close its books. Thus, we end this text not with this chapter about the future of the wealthy of the world, but with a further chapter on that large part of mankind still buried in ancient poverty.

SUMMARY

In this chapter, we have discussed a few of the many possibilities that may lie ahead for the industrialized world in the future.

One such possibility is peace and general disarmament. Economics does not enable us to predict the likelihood of such a development but it does allow us to analyze the consequences demobilization would have on our mixed capitalistic economy. In macroeconomic terms, the reduction of defense expenditures would have to be compensated by a reduction of taxes, an increase in other components of G, or a combination of both. In an age when the demand for various civilian public services is very high, the macroeconomic problem is by no means insurmountable. Nor is the microeconomic aspect of disarmament impossible to solve, though careful attention would have to be paid to easing particular burdens that derive from the present unequal impact of defense expenditures in geographical, industrial, and occupational terms.

Another question for the future is, what will happen to the great rival economic systems of East and West? A case can be made that neither capitalism nor communism can survive. Indeed in both cases, following Schumpeter's example, it can be argued that both will be undone by their own respective "successes." But if both systems seem to be on their way to modification, what is the possibility that they may converge? The doctrine of *convergence* is discussed in the reading by Jan Tinbergen, who considers a move in this direction a reasonable possibility.

Another question, frequently discussed in recent years, concerns the implications of growing affluence in the industrial world. An affluent future is not certain because of the dangers of global war and ecological disaster, but it is a possibility that, in view of our past history, cannot be overlooked. Galbraith has seen in affluence a challenge to rid ourselves of "toil" and to expand the New Class of those whose work is rewarding and self-satisfying in its own terms. Lord Keynes, in an early essay, considers some of the opportunities but also problems that living for today may bring to mankind.

There is a common bond between the affluence-school and the ecological-disaster school—namely, a downgrading of the *idea of progress* which, in the nineteenth century at least, was one of the most important guiding concepts of Western man. Since this idea was basically a spiritual idea (though nourished, of course, by material advancement), its ero-

sion poses the very deepest kind of problem in terms of the psychological goals and purposes of modern society.

QUESTIONS FOR DISCUSSION

1. When speaking of public projects that would be made possible by peace and the reduction of defense expenditures, economists sometimes refer to a "wish-list"—a list of projects that one would like to see undertaken if, somehow, the funds became available. Construct a rough wish-list of your own for the United States in the 1970s. Compare your list with the priorities suggested in Table 31-1 (p. 766-67).

2. Schumpeter considered that society's intellectuals, whose education and elevation were essentially a product of the capitalistic system, would be in the forefront in undermining that system. Do you consider this analysis accurate? If it were accurate, would there be anything improper in intellectuals behaving in this way?

3. "The convergence of economic systems has nothing to do with world peace. The greatest wars in modern history have been fought between nations with closely parallel economic systems." Beginning with the Napoleonic Wars, discuss this statement with reference to the major wars of the nineteenth and twentieth centuries.

4. In the discussion of affluent societies, the distinction between work that is satisfying in itself and work that is done merely for the pay is often made. Consider the difficulties involved in making such a distinction with respect to the academic work a student does in college. Sometimes people do similar work but for very different motives—the farmer plants vegetables to sell, the retired businessman plants a gar-

den for his own pleasure. Is the real distinction not in the kind of work but in the fact that one has chosen it oneself? If expanded choice is involved, do you feel that it is the case that people in the 1970s want more choices? Or are they anxious and bewildered because of the array of choices they already face? Do you yourself feel that you have too few or too many choices to make in shaping your future life?

5. What are the implications of Keynes' statement that in an ideal future society economists would be in the same category as dentists? (Hint: the correct answer is *not* that economists would then get better pay.)

6. "Living in a society without progress would be like living in a room with walls and no windows. Only a spiritual monk could accomplish it." Discuss.

Toffler, Alvin. *Future Shock.* New York: Bantam Books, 1971.

SUGGESTED READING

Boulding, Kenneth E. "Is Scarcity Dead?" In *Is Economics Relevant?* ed. Robert L. Heilbroner and Arthur M. Ford. Pacific Palisades, Calif.: Goodyear Publishing Company, 1971, pp. 177–91.

Bury, J. B. *The Idea of Progress.* New York: Dover Publications, 1955.

Galbraith, John Kenneth. *The Affluent Society.* Boston: Houghton Mifflin Co., 1958.

Carson, Robert B., ed. "What if Peace Breaks Out?" In *The American Economy in Conflict.* Boston: D. C. Heath and Co., 1971, pp. 238–53.

Schumpeter, Joseph A. *Capitalism, Socialism and Democracy.* New York: Harper & Row, 1950.

32
The Underdeveloped World: A Present Crisis

If the industrial nations are preoccupied with an uncertain future, the poor countries of the world are very much in the thick of a critical present. Poverty is an existing reality for many of these countries: the question is, what to do about it now?

We have described these conditions earlier (chapter 6), and here, in the concluding chapter of this book, we want to consider various policies that might help promote development in these nations. Our interest now is in what has been and what can be done to help.

LESSONS FROM ECONOMICS

The first point to make is that, although political and social systems are highly important for development (see Great Debate Six: Economic Develop-

ment Versus Democracy?), no underdeveloped country can afford to ignore underlying economic phenomena, as these have been analyzed by economists and scholars over the past century.

More specifically, the policymakers in such countries must have a thorough grasp of the main topics covered in a text such as this one. They must be concerned to preserve overall macroeconomic stability (Part Two), since an economy with rampant unemployment or inflation is unlikely to be a successful developer. They must be concerned with microeconomic interdependence and efficiency (Part Three), since they are too near the edge of survival to waste resources by allocating them unwisely and without concern for their alternative uses. And, of course, they must acquaint themselves with the factors that make for economic growth (chapter 6, 16, 28, and 30) since growth is their immediate need and objective.

Nothing that we have studied is irrelevant to their needs—international trade, for example, is obviously a crucial subject for many poor countries, but so also are income distribution, economic controls, pollution, and, really, everything we have discussed. At the same time, however, we must add that nothing that we have learned can be applied to these countries without adaptation and qualification. Indeed, to fail to be aware of this latter point could be almost as costly as ignoring the former.

Let's take a specific case. We have mentioned that many poor countries are suffering from massive unemployment. Often this is covert or disguised unemployment (people appear to be working but a reorganization of production would show them to be redundant). In Taiwan, for example, in 1965 unemployment was estimated at 11.5 percent. This is about twice the rate that, in the United States, led to great complaints about unemployment in the 1970s. Actually, many countries are doing far less well than Taiwan on this front; rates of 20 or even 30 percent effectively unemployed may not be unrealistic.

A student, fresh from mastering the theory of national income determination, might easily say: the problem is clearly one of inadequate aggregate demand. Through modern fiscal and monetary policies, we must raise $C + I + G$ to the point where full employment is achieved or, more realistically, where employment is so high that we begin running into serious inflationary problems.

But this would be dangerous advice and would be very likely to lead to high inflation without any commensurate effect on employment. The reason is that the student has failed to study sufficiently the specific causes of unemployment in an underdeveloped country. One of the major causes is likely to be the relative lack of factors of production complementary to labor—in agriculture, land; and in industry, capital. If the land is overcrowded and if industry is plagued by factor proportions inherited to some degree from the advanced industrial nations (i.e., relatively high capital-intensity), then merely demanding more products is not going to generate a demand for more laborers to produce them. The bottlenecks are elsewhere, and so also must be the solutions. The real solutions to this kind of unemployment thus would not involve Keynesian style fiscal-monetary policies as much as policies to reduce the increase in the labor supply (population policy), to develop more labor-intensive techniques of production (technology), and to increase the supply of the complementary factors (capital accumulation).

In short, we must apply what we have learned *but* we must apply it to actual, not general or hypothetical, problems. With this in mind, let us now consider approaches to some of the difficulties we have earlier singled out as being particularly acute for today's underdeveloped countries.

POPULATION POLICY

While population growth did not pose a serious obstacle to economic development in the West, it clearly does for today's underdeveloped countries, particularly those that are already heavily overpopulated.

Fundamentally, there are two ways of approaching the problem of population growth. The first is to take the rate of population growth as given and to try to cope with its effects. The other is to try to alter the rate of increase itself.

Coping with Effects

The first approach—dealing with effects only—may seem a mere palliative, but it is important not to neglect this aspect of the phenomenon. For no matter how successful attempts at population control are, there is no doubt that rates of growth will remain quite high for many years and, unless this fact is understood, much human misery could result. Perhaps the most harmful effect of population growth is the painful unemployment that will result unless countermeasures are taken. As we have said above, this unemployment arises as a consequence of the fact that the industrial capital stock is not growing rapidly enough to employ massive increases in the labor force, while the land—in the more populated underdeveloped countries—offers few further effective opportunities for employment on the required scale.

Under these circumstances, *employment-creation* becomes an independent goal of national policy. The mobilization of the rural unemployed in community development projects where village authorities cooperate with the government in undertaking public-works programs becomes a task of high priority. The country, furthermore, may attempt to emphasize high-labor/low-capital industries. Thus, a handicraft industry may be preferred to its factory equivalent, not on the grounds of efficiency, but because it provides more jobs for those who would otherwise go idle. The difficulty here, of course, is that the goals of employment-creation and economic growth do not necessarily coincide. Should a country use its scarce capital where it will provide the most jobs or where it will provide the greatest increase in output?

In the early postwar period, some economists felt that a way could be found around this dilemma by using the unemployed and/or the disguised unemployed to create capital.[1] Similar logic seems to have been applied in China during the Great Leap Forward period when there was considerable emphasis on establishing communes that would mobilize the rural labor force to produce not only agricultural improvements but also industrial products, like the famous "backyard blast furnaces" for increasing iron and steel production.

The theory of this approach is unassailable—a country has surplus labor and little capital: why not use the former to increase the latter? In practice, however, the problems of organizing a largely unskilled labor force, plus the drain on the very scarce factor of production, managerial capacity, have made it doubtful that the hoped-for wonders can be achieved by this approach. Even China had to abandon many of the Great Leap Forward concepts; as someone has said, the main result of the backyard blast furnaces was to produce a lot of unusable steel at the cost of a great many melted down pots and pans. In sum, a poor country is well-advised (1) to pay serious attention to its unemployment problem and (2) not to hope for miracles in this area. In the long run, control of the rate of population growth itself is indispensable.

Altering the Rate of Population Growth

We come then to the second aspect of population policy—that having to do with causes. The main cause, as we know, is the continuation of high birthrates in countries where medical and public health advances have brought sizeable reductions in the deathrates. The

---

1. This was one of the themes of the classic work of Ragnar Nurkse, *Problems of Capital Formation in Underdeveloped Areas* (New York: Oxford University Press, 1953). This was a seminal work in the development field and is still worth reading today.

basic cure is to foster means that will bring the birthrates down (as they are already down in the industrialized countries) as rapidly as possible.

The major poor countries of the world are agreed on this objective. In India, for example, economic planners in the early 1960s were given a great shock when they realized, as the preliminary results of the 1961 census became available, that they had badly underestimated the nation's population growth. Expenditures on family planning programs have increased rapidly since that time and ten million Indian men and women have undergone voluntary sterilization. China also now supports population control measures, though in the early period after the civil war, Chinese leaders were rather ambiguous on this point.[2] A Chinese official was quoted in October, 1971:

Family planning is fundamental for the economic planning of the country. It involves an ideological revolution to change basic concepts and traditional ways. Furthermore, family planning represents the demands of the masses, especially of the many women who want to be free of the burden of excessive children in order to be able to contribute to the reconstruction of the country.[3]

Reports are that contraceptive devices and abortion are readily available in

China and that official policy now encourages small families and later marriages.

There is also evidence that, in a few countries at least, birthrates are now beginning to fall. Taiwan is often cited as such an example. Between 1951 and 1966, the number of registered births per 1000 women (aged fifteen–forty-nine) fell from 211 to 149; during the same period the birthrate declined from 50 to 32 per thousand of population. However, the case of Taiwan brings out some of the difficulties of judging the potential success of birth control and other similar family planning programs. For the fact is that this decline was mainly accomplished before the family planning campaign in Taiwan began (1963). The population expert, Kingsley Davis, attributes most of Taiwan's success to the fact that it "is sufficiently developed to be placed in the urban-industrial class of nations."[4] Already in 1950, over half of Taiwan's population was urban and her rate of economic development during the past twenty years has been among the most rapid in the underdeveloped world. This, plus the fact that she is very densely populated, undoubtedly created pressures for reducing births even in the absence of a family planning program. Undoubtedly, too, these factors created a favorable environment for such a program to be effective.

These comments about Taiwan bring out what is essentially the most difficult issue in this whole field: Will family planning programs be able to have any major effect on birthrates in the absence of the other accoutrements of development—urbanization, rising standards of living, increased levels of education, and so on? In the West, we know, birthrates

2. The problem was at least in part ideological. Karl Marx had argued that Malthusianism was a "libel on the human race," because it suggested that natural causes were at the root of human misery, rather than flaws in the capitalistic system. We also, of course, have an ideological issue in the West, in terms of the attitude of Catholicism towards family planning. It is notable, however, that European Catholic countries have been among the lowest in rates of population increase.

3. Quoted by Jaime Zipper, M.D., in the *New York Times*, April 30, 1972, section 12 (Supplement sponsored by the Population Crisis Committee in association with the Planned Parenthood Federation of America), p. 21.

4. Kingsley Davis, "Population Policy: Will Current Programs Succeed?" *Science*, 158, reprinted in Garrett Hardin, ed., *Population, Evolution and Birth Control* (San Francisco: W. H. Freeman and Co., 1969), p. 352.

did fall (and in the absence of such population control programs) as development proceeded. Can the poor countries reverse the order of this process, bringing down birthrates in order to help *produce* development?

Although optimism is hardly justified yet, there is no reason to be unduly pessimistic on this point. We have, first of all, the dramatic increase in awareness of the problem throughout the world. (India's expenditures on family planning, for example, rose by over tenfold just between her Second Five Year Plan [1956–61] and her Third Five Year Plan [1961–66]). We have, second, the fact that the technology of birth control has improved dramatically over the last several years and will undoubtedly show similar advances in the future. Hopes can be dashed here—the "loop," for example, has not proved to be quite the panacea that it was once proclaimed—but the efforts to improve this area of technology are now going forward rapidly. Third, and strengthening the above, economists have shown that in many cases investment in family planning programs can yield much higher economic results than similar amounts of money invested in factories or machinery.[5] If great steel mills were the early signs of development efforts, increasingly the proffered evidence is the family planning clinic or research institute.

In short, although population growth continues to be a major hazard for the underdeveloped world, there is at least some evidence that mankind is using its capacity for creative adaptation to respond to this new challenge.

5. See especially the work of Stephen Enke, such as "Population and Development: A General Model," *Quarterly Journal of Economics,* February 1963; or *Economics for Development* (Englewood Cliffs, N.J.: Prentice-Hall, 1963).

TECHNOLOGICAL ADVANCE

One of the most important means of creative adaptation is the development of new technology. In the case of birth control for the poor countries, such new technology would ideally involve devices that are highly effective, very cheap (where average per capita income may be $100–200 per year, cost is clearly a decisive factor), easily applied under circumstances where literacy is low and knowledge of personal hygiene may be rudimentary, and acceptable to prevailing attitudes and customs. Because of the basically different economic circumstances, the technological approach best suited to a poor country might not be the same as that which would be most effective in a highly developed country.

What is true in the specific case of birth control technology is true of advanced technology in general. As we know, the great single advantage that today's poor country has over the developers of the past is the tremendous accumulation in the storehouse of Western technology. The great *dis*advantage of using that technology is that it is ill-suited to the economic and/or geographic conditions in most poor countries. The major problem in this area, therefore, is to develop a new technology that is basically an adaptation of Western scientific know-how to the specific circumstances of today's underdeveloped country.

As in the case of the population problem, there was some pessimism on this point in the 1950s and early 1960s. It seemed that some poor countries, in their desire to achieve "showcase" development, had overemphasized industrial development and especially the big, modern project at the expense of slow, steady, fundamental improvements, particularly in the agricultural sector. The fear was that this would lead to a worsening unemployment picture (because the big, modern projects seldom require much unskilled labor), to unbalanced growth (with a lagging agricultural sector)[6] to balance of payments problems (agricultural imports being required, along with Western machinery for the big industrial projects), and *enclave* development (the relative overdevelopment of certain urban sectors of the economy while the rural hinterland is allowed to remain wholly stagnant). These fears were heightened by the fact that, in the crucial agricultural sector, Western technology had been developed for the soils and climate characteristic of the temperate zone, while most of today's poorer countries lie in whole or in part in the tropics.

Indeed, the problem of introducing new technology seemed to be virtually centered in the agricultural sector. Industry might be expected to make fairly rapid strides. But what about the dominant (often 70 or 80 percent of the population) rural sector with its remote, tradition-bound, poverty-stricken ways?

These early fears make what has happened since all the more remarkable. Although (as we shall see presently) all the returns are not yet in, the early 1970s have witnessed a substantial change in outlook about the future prospects of the agricultural sectors of the less developed countries. The basis for a sudden up-

swing of hope is what is called the *Green Revolution.*

The Green Revolution involves the development of certain new seeds, particularly for wheat and rice, that produce very large increases in crop yields under certain circumstances. Most relevant for our purposes is the fact that these new seeds have been developed with particular reference to conditions in the less developed countries, i.e., to tropical and subtropical weather and especially to the great availability of solar energy in areas near the equator.

Figure 32-1 shows the dramatic gains in yield per acre that have been made possible by the new seeds, particularly in Mexico and Taiwan where this research was originally launched. Even more dramatic in some ways is what has been happening in India in the early

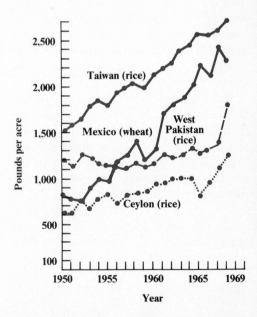

Figure 32-1. Rice and Wheat Yields Per Acre in Mexico, West Pakistan, Ceylon and Taiwan.
Source: Brown, *Seeds of Change*, pp. 37, 39.

---

6. However, it should be said that some economists feel that unbalanced growth—certain key sectors of the economy shooting ahead of other sectors—is actually a desirable strategy for a poor country. The main reason is that these "unbalances" create pressures on the lagging sectors to catch up, and general development may result. For a good account of the unbalanced growth arguments, see Albert O. Hirschman, *The Strategy of Economic Development* (New Haven: Yale University Press, 1965).

1970s. In 1971, India produced a record grain output of 108 million tons. In 1972, it was estimated that grain output would be up at least another 5 million tons and that, indeed, India would now have to look for foreign markets to export an expected surplus of some 8 million tons.[7] Considering the pessimistic predictions that have been made about India's prospects in the past,[8] this achievement is clearly one of substantial importance.

Despite these gains, the Green Revolution is controversial. The new seeds generally require changes in fertilizer and irrigation practice. There is the danger of rusts and blights developing in response to the new varieties. (This has already happened in the case of new corn in certain areas of the United States.) Without continuing agricultural research efforts, the advantages of the new seeds may be temporary and the ecological vulnerability of the less developed countries may actually grow worse. Also, if mishandled, the new technology might lead to further displacement of labor from the land, increasing both rural and urban unemployment and unrest.

Because of the importance of these issues, and because they so well illustrate the specific problem of adaptive technological research, the following two brief readings on the Green Revolution present some leading (and opposing) points of view.

---

7. Kasturi Rangan, "Surplus of Grain Reported in India," *New York Times*, April 30, 1972, p. 4.

8. See Paul R. Ehrlich's comments about India, pp. 793–95. It should be said that, as one swallow does not make a summer, so one or two good crop years do not prove the viability of the Green Revolution. Ehrlich's more general comments still have to be taken seriously.

Green Revolution: Con

PAUL R. EHRLICH

All of the technological panaceas for increasing food production are either impractical, impossible, ludicrous, or worse. One that is highly touted by our Department of Agrobusiness in Washington is known in the trade as the "Green Revolution." I believe the "Revolution" is to be created in the bankrolls of certain businesses in the United States, because it certainly is not being created anywhere else. The reversal of stories from the U.S. Department of Agriculture is something magnificent to behold. In the 1965–66 "bad weather" time, everybody was filled with pessimism. Then, in 1967, the weather improved in India and the other key regions. All of a sudden agriculture was doing a great job; all the high-yield wheat, sorghum, and rice varieties were going to save the world. This is still the current story.

If we are going to increase food production, the most intelligent way is to get higher yields from land already in cultivation. There is nothing wrong with that idea if it is done with great care for the ecological consequences —which, of course, it is not. But there are all kinds of problems in the new high-yield grains; they are high-yield only with proper cultivation, including a great input of fertilizer, and in most of the areas where they are being planted, there are serious problems of fertilizer distribution.

Excerpted from "Famine 1975: Fact or Fallacy?" by Paul R. Ehrlich in Harold W. Helfrich, Jr., ed. The Environmental Crisis (New Haven: Yale University Press, 1970), pp. 58–61. Reprinted by permission of the publisher.

Raymond H. Ewell at the State University of New York (Buffalo) has been India's chief fertilizer consultant for the last dozen years; he says quite frankly that he does not think that India has a hope of producing enough. It is certainly impossible for the United States to produce enough fertilizer for India, in addition to meeting our domestic needs, to get the maximum yield out of these grains; it also seems unlikely that the world will donate enough fertilizer to India. So there is a very big fertilizer problem. You have to grow crops exactly right to get successful harvests. From what other people and I have seen personally in India, the chance of their doing things exactly right seems to be about zero. An even more serious problem arises in planting grains which have been inadequately field tested against pest and blight resistance because this project is rush-rush. Already IR-8 rices have had a lot of trouble from this problem (recently "miracle rats" have invaded "miracle rice" fields in the Philippines), but even bigger monocultures are being created. A complete switch to the new high-yield grain varieties would leave India with only about half of the possible diversity of wheat strains. This means that, instead of a Bihar or a Pakistan famine, when a virus gets in and wipes out the crops, it will cover a much larger area. These are dangers of increased monoculture.

Another problem which seems to be endemic to agriculturists is that almost all of their projections are based on optimism—that good years are normal years. When I visited Australia, that country was having a colossal drought, and the agriculturists were saying in the press: "This is once in a million years; we have got to build, we have got to get relief; everything is going to be all right when the rains come." However, Australian weather records indicate that similar droughts occur with monotonous regularity every ten years or so. It is the same story in India, the same in China. They have deforested most of their land; among other things, this helps to create unstable weather. We know very well that you cannot expect long stretches of good years. There are good years interspersed with doses of bad years. For instance, last July the Indian government—which was churning out all kinds of propaganda about how it is going to become self-sufficient in agriculture by 1971—was so pleased with the year's crops that it created a special commemorative postage stamp about the great agricultural breakthrough. If India, which now can feed adequately only 10 million out of 530 million inhabitants, is to gain self-sufficiency in food by 1971, it will mean feeding 530 million people—plus an increment of 50 to 60 million. I have yet to meet any person who has been there who thinks that India could possibly be close to self-sufficiency in food by 1971. Indeed, I am willing to predict that India will never be self-sufficient in food unless it succeeds in cutting its population far back.

The headlines of the "Green Revolution" have been seen all over India. The Indian government is afraid that we will not send them any more food if it does not make progress in agriculture, so it makes unwarranted claims. However, if you look in the New York Times, you will find the following pieces of information: on September 24, 1968, six of seventeen Indian states were drought-stricken, with uncertain crop outlooks; the Indian government was looking around for additional food; on October 13, a cholera epidemic hit other states of India which were flooded.

American Stock Photo   American Stock Photo

The Green Revolution has led to some remarkable increases in crop yield (see corn on the left above), but some commentators worry that the new miracle crops may be vulnerable to blight and pest (picture on the right), and that they may increase the ecological instability of agriculture in the underdeveloped countries.

Still, agriculturists have a general feeling that somehow these new crops will solve the world's food problem. This feeling resulted primarily from a square yard of corn planted in Iowa. Five agronomists crouched over it constantly, gave it absolutely perfect everything, and got a yield from it. Then they ran inside, took out an atlas, and figured how many square yards there are in the Amazon basin. By multiplication they determined the amount of food that could be provided in the Amazon basin—and everything is going to be all right.

Unfortunately, that just is not the way the game is played. We do not know how to farm the tropics. We do know that most tropical soils are abysmal. We are not really making substantial progress with farming anywhere in the tropics, and it seems highly unlikely that we are going to. In other words, we will score some little gains with these high-yield crops, but they will be made at great ecological risk.

Green Revolution: Pro

JAMES G. HORSFALL

What about a Green Revolution in the hungry nations?

It has been written that in the tropics the stork has passed the plow. The question is: Can we put wings on the plow so it can fly faster than the stork? Paul Ehrlich, speaking in this series, has suggested clipping the wings of the stork. I do not quarrel with that. This is another device, and we will probably have to use both of them. As a biologist concerned with the food supply, I make it my busi-

Excerpted from James G. Horsfall, "The Green Revolution: Agriculture in the Face of the Population Explosion" in The Environmental Crisis, ed. Harold W. Helfrich Jr., pp. 93–98. Reprinted by permission of Yale University Press. Copyright © 1970 by Yale University.

ness to put wings on the plow so that it can fly at least as fast as the stork. To do this we must engineer a Green Revolution in the tropics through education and applied science.

The hungry nations are at the crossroads where the United States stood a century ago. They have their universities as we did at that time, but the teaching of agriculture has a pretty low priority in those universities—as it had here 100 years ago. Commissioners of Agriculture throughout the tropics are not agriculturally educated. That is tantamount to having a farmer for the Surgeon-General. Who would think of putting the Ministry of Medicine in the hands of a lawyer? Yet the Ministers of Agriculture in the hungry nations are most often lawyers or nonagriculturists. Training of agricultural specialists in the universities of the tropics is almost nonexistent. Universities have traditionally served the elite; they will have to educate the common man if they hope to engineer a Green Revolution similar to ours.

Ever since World War II, the United States has been promising to raise the hungry nations out of their predicament by industrialization. We enunciated that policy in the Department of State right after the war. But that puts the cart before the horse. Nobody can industrialize a nation with 85 to 90 percent of the people on the land any more than we could have done so 100 years ago. It has been a terrific waste of our strength; we poured money into industrializing India, and food production declined through the entire period.

Then we adopted a second procedure: the exportation of American knowhow. We would send retired county agents into the hungry nations. We would export our American agricultural technology. Those farmers in Iowa know how to grow good food,

we said; now why don't you foreign farmers do it the same way? This operation sadly failed, too. Congress did not learn about it very fast; in fact, it recently passed another edition of the Food for Freedom business and created a section called Farmer to Farmer. It decided to send farmers to carry the knowhow, since the county agents had failed. That program, too fell by the wayside. This is what I call the knowhow, showhow fallacy.

Why didn't the program work? We can send Jeeps that can negotiate the roads in underdeveloped countries. Why can't we send hybrid corn to help solve their food supply problems? Biologically, the answer is not very complicated to understand. If we put fertilizer—our classical method for increasing yields—on most of the crops of the tropics, we get less yield than if none was applied. This is not always the case, but it is true often enough. For thousands of years the plants growing in the tropics have had no appreciable applications of fertilizer. If a plant had a high-yielding gene, it almost certainly would have been lethal because it would overgrow the rest of its environment. If we come along and put fertilizer on a plant that has lost its high-yielding genes by natural selection, we will damage the plant more than help it. The result: if you tell an Indian farmer to put on fertilizer and he gets less yield than he had before, you lose your lofty position on your self-erected pedestal.

I was in India about ten years ago, when our national efforts were at their nadir. There were no agricultural universities in the sense of our land-grant colleges and, therefore, very weak training of agricultural experts in India. The country had its Oxfords and Cambridges (somebody called them "Oxbridge" schools) in which were educated the future lawyers and doctors and clergymen, but few in the practical world of agriculture. Only the Brahmans—the top caste—were educated in India in those days. The Brahmans were supposed to become educated, but not to soil their hands. They could not very well improve the agriculture because that involved working in the soil. And so India remains today a vast nation with a relatively few rich and educated people on top and the multitude of poor farmers with no means of education and a dismal food supply at the bottom. It is now in the process of establishing agricultural universities.

The Rockefeller Foundation has already engineered quite a respectable revolution by using precisely the same technique which we used in this country: education plus adaptive research. It encouraged the establishment of a sophisticated College of Agriculture in Mexico in 1943.

The Foundation's efforts began in that year when George Harrar went to Mexico. He quickly discovered the knowhow, showhow fallacy. He learned that we cannot go down there and transfer American knowhow directly, that we have to develop the technology on the specific site. This principle has since been called adaptive research; it involves "on location" plant breeding, genetics, soils work, and plant protection.

Of course, Harrar's staff started out by trying fertilizers, and they quickly learned that this remedy—so successful in the United States—tended to reduce the wheat and corn yields of Mexico. Then they imported some high-yielding varieties of corn and wheat that grow so well in Nebraska, Minnesota, and Iowa. Again, failure; these varieties achieved less yield than the Mexicans got with their own corn, and put on practically no ears at all. They later found out that the diurnal length was wrong. U.S. corn

and wheat grow in long days, and the days are relatively short in Mexico's lower latitudes. Besides, the high-yield varieties wound up with all kinds of diseases that they never suffered up in Iowa.

So the Rockefeller Foundation researchers had to work with the measly corn and wheat that they found in Mexico because those varieties were adapted to the day length, the high temperatures, low rainfall, high elevation, and all the rest of the ecological factors involved. They introduced high-yielding genes from Iowa and Minnesota into the local varieties, and then selected the hybrids with both high-yielding genes and local adaptation. It was simple plant breeding, but it had to be done right there in Mexico; it could not be done in Iowa or in Connecticut.

When the genes of the local varieties were sufficiently upgraded, then fertilizer worked wonders as it does in the United States. The Connecticut Agricultural Experiment Station is proud of discovering the principle of hybrid corn, but hybrid corn which will flourish in Mexico had to be developed in Mexico. We cannot successfully transfer the Connecticut strains to Mexico.

Adaptive research is the principle discovered by the Rockefeller Foundation in its work in Mexico. Using this principle, it developed some strains that just about doubled the yield of Mexican wheat. The success in Mexico led the Foundation to decide about 1957 to set up, in cooperation with the Ford Foundation, a similar place—the International Rice Research Institute—in the Philippines.

What did the researchers do when they got to the Philippines? They tried fertilizer. Even after the work in Mexico, they tried fertilizer first. The Foundation had new researchers in the Philippines, fresh out of agricultural

America. They put fertilizer on the rice, and grew less rice than they harvested without any fertilizer. They had to learn the hard way. They acquired rice with high-yielding genes from Taiwan and Japan, and crossed them with the locally adapted plants that did not have high-yielding genes. When they put fertilizer on the resultant strains they tripled the yield.

Somebody once said farmers may be ignorant but they are not stupid. All the researchers had to do was put IR-8 rice, this elegant new variety, in a Filipino's field beside the old indica rice, pile on fertilizer, and wait for results. The farmer wound up with three times as much rice from the new variety. He did not have just 10 percent more rice; you need a computer to tell the difference with such a small increase. A farmer is not interested in computers; he is interested in crops. When he gets 300 percent more yield, he does not need a college degree to see it. He is no fool; he wants that new rice as fast as he can get it. As a result, a vast black market has developed all over the tropics for IR-8 rice.

The same thing has happened with wheat. India's Punjab wheat area is at just about the same latitude as Mexico's. It too is on a higher elevation, and the daylight hours are approximately equal in both regions. Wheat can be transported across the lines of longitude because day length is the same. Thus, Mexican wheat will do as well in India as in Mexico. The yields in the Punjab went up two and three times, and the farmers started a sprawling black market in wheat. When such a black market develops, we know we have hit on something pretty good.

At last we fairly well understand the methodology for improving agriculture in the hungry countries of the world: research must be done locally.

The tropics, for all their lush beauty, desperately need a Green Revolution in agriculture. Easing the hunger of those nations will depend on a huge number of factors. A few bright spots have become visible. For the first time, the Philippines are exporting rice instead of importing it at almost unbearable cost—thanks to IR-8. The yields of wheat have doubled in Mexico, in the Punjab, and in Pakistan.

We dare not forget, however, that the population also is rapidly increasing. Food is life, but if we would bequeath to our descendants their full measure of that life, we should remember John Muir's words: "Everybody needs beauty as well as bread, places to play and pray in which nature may heal and cheer and give strength to body and soul alike."

CAPITAL AND FOREIGN AID

We come finally to the third main element in growth—capital accumulation. For observers from the industrial world, this third element also raises the large question of foreign aid. If capital accumulation is difficult for a poor country to sustain from its own resources, can the problem be mitigated by an inflow of resources from abroad?

That a purely domestic solution to the capital accumulation problem will involve great hardship for an underdeveloped country we have mentioned before. The difficulties derive from the intense poverty of many of these countries, from their consequent desire for rapid growth, from the capital-using bias of much Western technology, and, in the early stages, from the inability of many

Continued on p. 826

GREAT DEBATE SIX
ECONOMIC DEVELOPMENT VS. DEMOCRACY ?

Ever since the "discovery" of the underdeveloped countries after the Second World War, an important debate has been waged about the political and social auspices under which their economic development might take place. We have pointed out earlier in this book (chapter 6, p. 145) that the development problem facing today's poor countries is in many respects different from (and in some respects, more difficult than) that which faced Britain, the United States, and even Russia and Japan when these countries forged their industrial revolutions. Since the problem is different, the solution may also be different. Perhaps the political and cultural forms that promote growth today are quite unlike those that promoted growth in the past.

To some, this has meant that communism, or something like communism, will guide the destinies of tomorrow's successful developers. The issue is quite complicated because the Russian experience is hardly parallel to that of the great overpopulated regions of the modern world. Japan's experience is closer, but even her case does not provide an exact model. Furthermore, the recent experiences of the underdeveloped countries themselves do not help us too much. Their development efforts have been too short-lived and too variable to give us decisive evidence one way or another.

In sum, the issue is not yet resolved, though its importance is clearly substantial. In the following debate, Robert L. Heilbroner, economist, social commentator, author of The Worldly Philosophers, The Great Ascent, and many other books and articles, takes the view that political and social revolutions, presumably Communist in nature, will be the probable path for the successful developing countries. His opponent is Dennis H. Wrong, a Canadian-born sociologist who is professor at New York University and is the author of numerous works, including Population and Society. He suggests that totalitarian revolutionary regimes may face quite as many difficulties in promoting development as democratic regimes. In assessing these points of view, the reader might want to apply the various arguments to the issues of development raised in chapter 32—population policy, technological change, and capital accumulation. For it is on these bedrock economic issues that the long-run future of the developing countries is likely to be determined.

COUNTERREVOLUTIONARY AMERICA

ROBERT L. HEILBRONER

Is the United States fundamentally opposed to economic development? The question is outrageous. Did we not coin the phrase, "the revolution of rising expectations"? Have we not supported the cause of development more generously than any nation on earth, spent our intellectual energy on the problems of development, offered our expertise freely to the backward nations of the world? How can it possibly be suggested that the United States might be opposed to economic development?

The answer is that we are not at all opposed to what we conceive economic development to be. The process depicted by the "revolution of rising expectations" is a deeply attractive one. It conjures up the image of a peasant in some primitive land, leaning on his crude plow and looking to the horizon, where he sees dimly, but for the *first time* (and that is what is so revolu-

Excerpted from Robert L. Heilbroner "Counterrevolutionary America," from Commentary April 1967, pp. 31–38. Reprinted from Commentary by permission; copyright © 1967 by the American Jewish Committee.

tionary about it), the vision of a better life. From this electrifying vision comes the necessary catalysis to change an old and stagnant way of life. The pace of work quickens. Innovations, formerly feared and resisted, are now eagerly accepted. The obstacles are admittedly very great—whence the need for foreign assistance—but under the impetus of new hopes the economic mechanism begins to turn faster, to gain traction against the environment. Slowly, but surely, the Great Ascent begins.

There is much that is admirable about this well-intentioned popular view of "the revolution of rising expectations." Unfortunately, there is more that is delusive about it. For the buoyant appeal of its rhetoric conceals or passes in silence over by far the larger part of the spectrum of realities of the development process. One of these is the certainty that the revolutionary aspect of development will not be limited to the realm of ideas, but will vent its fury on institutions, social classes, and innocent men and women. Another is the great likelihood that the ideas needed to guide the revolution will not only be affirmative and reasonable, but also destructive and fanatic. A third is the realization that revolutionary efforts cannot be made, and certainly cannot be sustained, by voluntary effort alone, but require an iron hand, in the spheres both of economic direction and political control. And the fourth and most difficult of these realities to face is the probability that the political force most likely to succeed in carrying through the gigantic historical transformation of development is some form of extreme national collectivism or Communism.

In a word, what our rhetoric fails to bring to our attention is the likelihood that development will require policies and programs repugnant to our "way of life," that it will bring to the fore governments hostile to our interna-

tional objectives, and that its regnant ideology will bitterly oppose capitalism as a system of world economic power. If that is the case, we would have to think twice before denying that the United States was fundamentally opposed to economic development.

But is it the case? Must development lead in directions that go counter to the present American political philosophy? Let me try to indicate, albeit much too briefly and summarily, the reasons that lead me to answer that question as I do.

I begin with the cardinal point, often noted but still insufficiently appreciated, that the process called "economic development" is not primarily economic at all. We think of development as a campaign of production to be fought with budgets and monetary policies and measured with indices of output and income. But the development process is much wider and deeper than can be indicated by such statistics. To be sure, in the end what is hoped for is a tremendous rise in output. But this will not come to pass until a series of tasks, at once cruder and more delicate, simpler and infinitely more difficult, has been commenced and carried along a certain distance.

In most of the new nations of Africa, these tasks consist in establishing the very underpinnings of nationhood itself—in determining national borders, establishing national languages, arousing a basic national (as distinguished from tribal) self-consciousness. Before these steps have been taken, the African states will remain no more than names insecurely affixed to the map, not social entities capable of undertaking an enormous collective venture in economic change. In Asia, nationhood is generally much further advanced than in Africa, but here the main impediment to development is the miasma of apathy and fatalism, superstition and distrust that vitiates every attempt to improve hopelessly inefficient modes of work and patterns of resource use: while India starves, a quarter of the world's cow population devours Indian crops, exempt either from effective employment or slaughter because of sacred taboos. In still other areas, mainly Latin America, the principal handicap to development is not an absence of national identity or the presence of suffocating cultures (although the latter certainly plays its part), but the cramping and crippling inhibitions of obsolete social institutions and reactionary social classes. Where land-holding rather than industrial activity is still the basis for social and economic power, and where land is held essentially in fiefdoms rather than as productive real estate, it is not surprising that so much of society retains a medieval cast.

Thus, development is much more than a matter of encouraging economic growth within a given social structure. It is rather the *modernization* of that structure, a process of ideational, social, economic, and political change that requires the remaking of society in its most intimate as well as its most public attributes.* When we speak of the revolutionary nature of economic development, it is this kind of deeply penetrative change that we mean—change that reorganizes "normal" ways of thought, established patterns of family life, and structures of village authority as well as class and caste privilege.

What is so egregiously lacking in the great majority of the societies that are now attempting to make the Great Ascent is precisely this pervasive modernization. The trouble with India and Pakistan, with Brazil and Ecuador, with the Philippines and Ethiopia, is not merely that economic growth lags, or proceeds at some pitiable pace. This is only a symptom of deeper-lying ills.

---

*See C. E. Black, *The Dynamics of Modernization.*

The trouble is that the social physiology of these nations remains so depressingly unchanged despite the flurry of economic planning on top. The all-encompassing ignorance and poverty of the rural regions, the unbridgeable gulf between the peasant and the urban elites, the resistive conservatism of the village elders, the unyielding traditionalism of family life —all these remain obdurately, maddeningly, disastrously unchanged. In the cities, a few modern buildings, sometimes brilliantly executed, give a deceptive patina of modernity, but once one journeys into the immense countryside, the terrible stasis overwhelms all.

To this vast landscape of apathy and ignorance one must now make an exception of the very greatest importance. It is the fact that a very few nations, all of them Communist, have succeeded in reaching into the lives and stirring the minds of precisely that body of the peasantry which constitutes the insuperable problem elsewhere. In our concentration on the politics, the betrayals, the successes and failures of the Russian, Chinese, and Cuban revolutions, we forget that their central motivation has been just such a war *à l'outrance* against the archenemy of backwardness—not alone the backwardness of outmoded social superstructures but even more critically that of private inertia and traditionalism.

That the present is irreversibly and unqualifiedly freed from the dead hand of the past is, I think, beyond argument in the case of Russia. By this I do not only mean that Russia has made enormous economic strides. I refer rather to the gradual emancipation of its people from the "idiocy of rural life," their gradual entrance upon the stage of contemporary existence. This is not to hide in the smallest degree the continuing backwardness of the Russian countryside where now almost 50—*and formerly perhaps* 80—percent of the population lives. But even at its worst I do not think that life could now be described in the despairing terms that run through the Russian literature of our grandfathers' time. Here is Chekhov:

During the summer and the winter there had been hours and days when it seemed as if these people [the peasants] lived worse than cattle, and it was terrible to be with them. They were coarse, dishonest, dirty, and drunken; they did not live at peace with one another but quarreled continually, because they feared, suspected, and despised one another. . . . Crushing labor that made the whole body ache at night, cruel winters, scanty crops, overcrowding, and no help, and nowhere to look for help.

It is less certain that the vise of the past has been loosened in China or Cuba. It may well be that Cuba has suffered a considerable economic decline, in part due to absurd planning, in part to our refusal to buy her main crop. The economic record of China is nearly as inscrutable as its political turmoil, and we may not know for many years whether the Chinese peasant is today better or worse off than before the revolution. Yet what strikes me as significant in both countries is something else. In Cuba it is the educational effort that, according to the New York *Times*, has constituted a major effort of the Castro regime. In China it is the unmistakable evidence—and here I lean not alone on the sympathetic account of Edgar Snow but on the most horrified descriptions of the rampages of the Red Guards—that the younger generation is no longer fettered by the traditional view of things. The very fact that the Red Guards now revile their elders, an unthinkable defiance of age-old Chinese custom, is testimony of how deeply change has penetrat-

ed into the texture of Chinese life.

It is this herculean effort to reach and rally the great anonymous mass of the population that is *the* great accomplishment of Communism—even though it is an accomplishment that is still only partially accomplished. For if the areas of the world afflicted with the self-perpetuating disease of backwardness are ever to rid themselves of its debilitating effects, I think it is likely to be not merely because antiquated social structures have been dismantled (although this is an essential precondition), but because some shock treatment like that of Communism has been administered to them.

By way of contrast to this all-out effort, however short it may have fallen of its goal, we must place the timidity of the effort to bring modernization to the peoples of the non-Communist world. Here again I do not merely speak of lagging rates of growth. I refer to the fact that illiteracy in the non-Communist countries of Asia and Central America is increasing (by some 200 million in the last decade) because it has been "impossible" to mount an educational effort that will keep pace with population growth. I refer to the absence of substantial land reform in Latin America, despite how many years of promises. I refer to the indifference or incompetence or corruption of governing elites: the incredible sheiks with their oildoms; the vague, well-meaning leaders of India unable to break the caste system, kill the cows, control the birthrate, reach the villages, house or employ the labor rotting on the streets; the cynical governments of South America, not one of which, according to Lleras Camargo, former president of Colombia, has ever prosecuted a single politician or industrialist for evasion of taxes. And not least, I refer to the fact that every movement that arises to correct these conditions is instantly identified as "Communist" and put down with every means at hand, while the United States clucks or nods approval.

To be sure, even in the most petrified societies, the modernization process is at work. If there were time, the solvent acids of the twentieth century would work their way on the ideas and institutions of the most inert or resistant countries. But what lacks in the twentieth century is time. The multitudes of the underdeveloped world have only in the past two decades been summoned to their reveille. The one thing that is certain about the revolution of rising expectations is that it is only in its inception, and that its pressures for justice and action will steadily mount as the voice of the twentieth century penetrates to villages and slums where it is still almost inaudible. It is not surprising that Princeton historian C. E. Black, surveying this labile world, estimates that we must anticipate "ten to fifteen revolutions a year for the foreseeable future in the less developed societies."

In itself, this prospect of mounting political restiveness enjoins the speediest possible time schedule for development. But this political urgency is many times compounded by that of the population problem. Like an immense river in flood, the number of human beings rises each year to wash away the levees of the preceding year's labors and to pose future requirements of monstrous proportions. To provide shelter for the three billion human beings who will arrive on earth in the next forty years will require as many dwellings as have been constructed since recorded history began. To feed them will take double the world's present output of food. To cope with the mass exodus from the overcrowded countryside will necessitate cities of grotesque size—Calcutta, now a cesspool of three to five millions, threatens us by the year 2000 with a prospective population of from thirty to sixty millions.

These horrific figures spell one importunate message: haste. That is the *mene mene, tekel upharsin* written on the walls of government planning offices around the world. Even if the miracle of the loop is realized—the new contraceptive device that promises the first real breakthrough in population control—we must set ourselves for at least another generation of rampant increase.

But how to achieve haste? How to convince the silent and disbelieving men, how to break through the distrustful glances of women in black shawls, how to overcome the overt hostility of landlords, the opposition of the Church, the petty bickerings of military cliques, the black-marketeering of commercial dealers? I suspect there is only one way. The conditions of backwardness must be attacked with the passion, the ruthlessness, and the messianic fury of a jehad, a Holy War. Only a campaign of an intensity and single-mindedness that must approach the ludicrous and the unbearable offers the chance to ride roughshod over the resistance of the rich and the poor alike and to open the way for the forcible implantation of those modern attitudes and techniques without which there will be no escape from the misery of underdevelopment.

I need hardly add that the cost of this modernization process has been and will be horrendous. If Communism is the great modernizer, it is certainly not a benign agent of change. Stalin may well have exceeded Hitler as a mass executioner. Free inquiry in China has been supplanted by dogma and catechism; even in Russia nothing like freedom of criticism or of personal expression is allowed. Furthermore, the economic cost of industrialization in both countries has been at least as severe as that imposed by primitive capitalism.

Yet one must count the gains as well as the losses. Hundreds of millions who would have been confined to the narrow cells of changeless lives have been liberated from prisons they did not even know existed. Class structures that elevated the flighty or irresponsible have been supplanted by others that have promoted the ambitious and the dedicated. Economic systems that gave rise to luxury and poverty have given way to systems that provide a rough distributional justice. Above all, the prospect of a new future has been opened. It is this that lifts the current ordeal in China above the level of pure horror. The number of human beings in that country who have perished over the past centuries from hunger or neglect, is beyond computation. The present revolution may add its dreadful increment to this number. But it also holds out the hope that China may finally have been galvanized into social, political, and economic attitudes that for the first time make its modernization a possibility.

Two questions must be answered when we dare to risk so favorable a verdict on Communism as a modernizing agency. The first is whether the result is worth the cost, whether the possible—by no means assured—escape from underdevelopment is worth the lives that will be squandered to achieve it.

I do not know how one measures the moral price of historical victories or how one can ever decide that a diffuse gain is worth a sharp and particular loss. I only know that the way in which we ordinarily keep the books of history is wrong. No one is now toting up the balance of the wretches who starve in India, or the peasants of Northeastern Brazil who live in the swamps on crabs, or the undernourished and permanently stunted children of Hong Kong or Honduras. Their sufferings go unrecorded, and are not present to counterbalance the scales when the furies of revolution strike down their victims. Barrington Moore has made a nice cal-

culation that bears on this problem. Taking as the weight in one pan the 35,000 to 40,000 persons who lost their lives—mainly for no fault of theirs—as a result of the Terror during the French Revolution, he asks what would have been the death rate from preventable starvation and injustice under the *ancien regime* to balance the scales. "Offhand," he writes, "it seems unlikely that this would be very much below the proportion of .0010 which [the] figure of 40,000 yields when set against an estimated population of 24 million."[*]

Is it unjust to charge the *ancien regime* in Russia with ten million preventable deaths? I think it not unreasonable. To charge the authorities in pre-revolutionary China with equally vast and preventable degradations? Theodore White, writing in 1946, had this to say: . . . "some scholars think that China is perhaps the only country in the world where the people eat less, live more bitterly, and are clothed worse than they were five hundred years ago."[†]

I do not recommend such a calculus of corpses—indeed, I am aware of the license it gives to the unscrupulous—but I raise it to show the onesidedness of our protestations against the brutality and violence of revolutions. In this regard, it is chastening to recall the multitudes who have been killed or mutilated by the Church which is now the first to protest against the excesses of Communism.

But there is an even more terrible second question to be asked. It is clear beyond doubt, however awkward it may be for our moralizing propensities, that historians excuse horror that succeeds; and that we write our comfortable books of moral philosophy, seated atop a mound of victims—

---

[*]*Social Origins of Dictatorship and Democracy*, p. 104.

[†]*Thunder Out of China*, p. 32.

slaves, serfs, laboring men and women, heretics, dissenters—who were crushed in the course of preparing the way for our triumphal entry into existence. But at least we are here to vindicate the carnage. What if we were not? What if the revolutions grind flesh and blood and produce nothing, if the end of the convulsion is not exhilaration but exhaustion, not triumph but defeat?

Before this possibility—which has been realized more than once in history—one stands mute. Mute, but not paralyzed. For there is the necessity of calculating what is likely to happen in the absence of the revolution whose prospective excesses hold us back. Here one must weigh what has been done to remedy underdevelopment —and what has not been done—in the past twenty years; how much time there remains before the population flood enforces its own ultimate solution; what is the likelihood of bringing modernization without the frenzied assault that Communism seems most capable of mounting. As I make this mental calculation I arrive at an answer which is even more painful than that of revolution. I see the alternative as the continuation, without substantial relief—and indeed with a substantial chance of deterioration—of the misery and meanness of life as it is now lived in the sinkhole of the world's backward regions.

I have put the case for the necessity of revolution as strongly as possible, but I must now widen the options beyond the stark alternatives I have posed. To begin with, there are areas of the world where the immediate tasks are so far-reaching that little more can be expected for some decades than the primary missions of national identification and unification. Most of the new African states fall into this category. These states may suffer capitalist, Communist, Fascist, or other kinds of regimes during the re-mainder of this century, but whatever the nominal ideology in the saddle, the job at hand will be that of military and political nation-making.

There is another group of nations, less easy to identify, but much more important in the scale of events, where my analysis also does not apply. These are countries where the pressures of population growth seem sufficiently mild, or the existing political and social framework sufficiently adaptable, to allow for the hope of considerable progress without resort to violence. Greece, Turkey, Chile, Argentina, Mexico may be representatives of nations in this precarious but enviable situation. Some of them, incidentally, have already had revolutions of modernizing intent—fortunately for them in a day when the United States was not so frightened or so powerful as to be able to repress them.

In other words, the great arena of desperation to which the revolutionizing impetus of Communism seems most applicable is primarily the crowded land masses and archipelagoes of Southeast Asia and the impoverished areas of Central and South America. But even here, there is the possibility that the task of modernization may be undertaken by non-Communist elites. There is always the example of indigenous, independent leaders who rise up out of nowhere to overturn the established framework and to galvanize the masses—a Gandhi, a Marti, a pre-1958 Castro. Or there is that fertile ground for the breeding of national leaders—the army, as witness Ataturk or Nasser, among many.*

---

* What are the chances for modernizing revolutions of the Right, such as those of the Meiji Restoration or of Germany under Bismarck? I think they are small. The changes to be wrought in the areas of greatest backwardness are much more socially subversive than those of the nineteenth century, and the timespan allotted to the revolutionists is much smaller. Bourgeois revolutions are not apt to go far enough, particularly in changing property ownership. Still, one could

Thus there is certainly no inherent necessity that the revolutions of modernization be led by Communists. But it is well to bear two thoughts in mind when we consider the likely course of non-Communist revolutionary sweeps. The first is the nature of the mobilizing appeal of any successful revolutionary elite. Is it the austere banner of saving and investment that waves over the heads of the shouting marchers in Jakarta and Bombay, Cairo and Havana? It most certainly is not. The banner of economic development is that of nationalism, with its promise of personal immortality and collective majesty. It seems beyond question that a feverish nationalism will charge the atmosphere of any nation, Communist or not, that tries to make the Great Ascent—and as a result we must expect the symptoms of nationalism along with the disease: exaggerated xenophobia, a thin-skinned national sensitivity, a search for enemies as well as a glorification of the state.

These symptoms, which we have already seen in every quarter of the globe, make it impossible to expect easy and amicable relations between the developing states and the colossi of the developed world. No conceivable response on the part of America or Europe or, for that matter, Russia, will be able to play up to the vanities or salve the irritations of the emerging nations, much less satisfy their demands for help. Thus, we must anticipate an anti-American, or anti-Western, possibly even anti-white animus from any nation in the throes of modernization, even if it is not parroting Communist dogma.

Then there is a second caution as to the prospects for non-Communist revolutions. This is the question of what ideas and policies will guide their revolutionary efforts. Revolutions, especially if their whole orientation is to the future, require philosophy equally as much as force. It is here, of course, that Communism finds its special strength. The vocabulary in which it speaks—a vocabulary of class domination, of domestic and international exploitation—is rich in meaning to the backward nations. The view of history it espouses provides the support of historical inevitability to the fallible efforts of struggling leaders. Not least, the very dogmatic certitude and ritualistic repetition that stick in the craw of the Western observer offer the psychological assurances on which an unquestioning faith can be maintained.

If a non-Communist elite is to persevere in tasks that will prove Sisyphean in difficulty, it will also have to offer a philosophical interpretation of its role as convincing and elevating, and a diagnosis of social and economic requirements as sharp and simplistic, as that of Communism. Further, its will to succeed at whatever cost must be as firm as that of the Marxists. It is not impossible that such a philosophy can be developed, more or less independent of formal Marxian conceptions. It is likely, however, to resemble the creed of Communism far more than that of the West. Political liberty, economic freedom, and constitutional law may be the great achievements and the great issues of the most advanced nations, but to the least developed lands they are only dim abstractions, or worse, rationalizations behind which the great powers play their imperialist tricks or protect the privileges of their monied classes.

Thus, even if for many reasons we should prefer the advent of non-Communist modernizing elites, we must realize that they too will present the United States with programs and policies antipathetic to much that America "believes in" and hostile to America as a world power. The leadership need-

imagine such revolutions with armed support and no doubt Fascistic ideologies. I doubt that they would be any less of a threat than revolutions of the Left.

DOES THE CHINESE REVOLUTION POINT THE WAY?

Robert Heilbroner argues that Communist revolutions may be necessary for economic development because of their ability to "reach and rally the great anonymous mass of the population." The Chinese spokesman, quoted below, believes that it will be the Chinese model that will inspire the peoples of the underdeveloped world.

SIGNIFICANCE OF CHINESE REVOLUTION

PEKING REVIEW

Among the changes which have taken place in Asia since World War II, the victory of the Chinese people in their democratic revolution and the start of the socialist era in Chinese history are historical events of the first magnitude. They have not only influenced Asia but have deeply influenced the whole world. The Chinese revolution has, in the first place, fundamentally changed the world's balance of forces between revolution and counter-revolution, between the socialist camp and the imperialist camp. The victory of the Chinese revolution delivered a crushing blow to imperialist domination. Yesterday's great rear of imperialism has been turned into a base area, into a forefront of the anti-imperialist struggle. Everything is turning into its opposite. China's area is approximately the same as that of Europe. China's population is larger than that of Europe. The forces of the world's revolutionary camp obviously exceed those of the world's counter-revolutionary camp.

In the second place, the victory of the Chinese democratic revolution and the advent of socialism in Chinese history have set a brilliant example for the colonial and semi-colonial countries of the world. The victory of the Chinese people over imperialism and its lackeys and the founding of the People's Republic of China have greatly inspired the people of many colonial and semi-colonial countries in their struggle for national independence and the complete victory of their people's democratic revolution. The Russian October Socialist Revolution served as an example for revolution in the oppressor nations, that is, for revolution in the imperialist countries; while the Chinese revolution set an example for revolution in the oppressed nations, that is, the colonial or semi-colonial countries. In studying the changes in Asian history since World War II, we need to make an adequate appraisal of the path as well as the influence of the Chinese revolution. For it is of significance for the whole world far beyond the East or Asia.

The modern history of Asia today appears at once more complicated and simpler than ever before. On the one hand, it has witnessed the impact of the two great historical currents of the national democratic revolutionary movement and the international socialist revolutionary movement; on the other, it is seeing the death-bed struggles and desperate attacks put up by U.S. imperialism and all the old and new colonialists. . . .

"Significance of Chinese Revolution," excerpted from Lu Ta-nien, "How to Appraise the History of Asia?" *Peking Review,* 5 November 1965, quoted in Harry G. Shaffer and Jan S. Prybyla, eds., *From Underdevelopment to Affluence* (New York: Appleton-Century-Crofts, 1968), pp. 197–98. Reprinted by permission of the publisher.

ed to mount a jehad against backwardness—and it is my main premise that only a Holy War will begin modernization in our time—will be forced to expound a philosophy that approves authoritarian and collectivist measures at home and that utilizes as the target for its national resentment abroad the towering villains of the world, of which the United States is now Number One.

All this confronts American policymakers and public opinion with a dilemma of a totally unforeseen kind. On the one hand we are eager to assist in the rescue of the great majority of mankind from conditions that we recognize as dreadful and ultimately dangerous. On the other hand, we seem to be committed, especially in the underdeveloped areas, to a policy of defeating Communism wherever it is within our military capacity to do so, and of repressing movements that might become Communist if they were allowed to follow their internal dynamics. Thus, we have on the one side the record of Point Four, the Peace Corps, and foreign aid generally; and on the other, Guatemala, Cuba, the Dominican Republic, and now Vietnam.

That these two policies might be in any way mutually incompatible, that economic development might contain revolutionary implications infinitely more far-reaching than those we have so blandly endorsed in the name of rising expectations, that Communism or a radical national collectivism might be the only vehicles for modernization in many key areas of the world—these are dilemmas we have never faced. Now I suggest that we do face them, and that we begin to examine in a serious way ideas that have hitherto been considered blasphemous, if not near-traitorous.

Suppose that most of Southeast Asia and much of Latin America were to go Communist, or to become controlled by revolutionary governments that espoused collectivist ideologies and vented extreme anti-American sentiments. Would this constitute a mortal threat to the United States?

I think it fair to claim that the purely *military* danger posed by such an eventuality would be slight. Given the present and prospective capabilities of the backward world, the addition of hundreds of millions of citizens to the potential armies of Communism would mean nothing when there was no way of deploying them against us. Even the total communization of the backward world would not effectively alter the present balance of military strength in the world.

However small the military threat, it is undeniably true that a Communist or radical collectivist engulfment of these countries would cost us the loss of billions of dollars of capital invested there. Of our roughly $50 billions in overseas investment, some $10 billions are in mining, oil, utility, and manufacturing facilities in Latin America, some $4 billions in Asia including the Near East, and about $2 billions in Africa. To lose these assets would deal a heavy blow to a number of large corporations, particularly in oil, and would cost the nation as a whole the loss of some $3 to $4 billions a year in earnings from those areas.

A Marxist might conclude that the economic interests of a capitalist nation would find such a prospective loss insupportable, and that it would be "forced" to go to war. I do not think this is a warranted assumption, although it is undoubtedly a risk. Against a Gross National Product that is approaching three-fourths of a trillion dollars and with total corporate assets over $1.3 trillions, the loss of even the whole $16 billions in the vulnerable areas should be manageable economically.

By these remarks I do not wish airily to dismiss the dangers of a Communist avalanche in the backward nations. There would be dangers, not least those of an American hysteria. Rather, I want only to assert that the threats of a military or economic kind would not be insuperable, as they might well be if Europe were to succumb to a hostile regime.

But is that not the very point?, it will be asked. Would not a Communist success in a few backward nations lead to successes in others, and thus by degrees engulf the entire world, until the United States and perhaps Europe were fortresses besieged on a hostile planet?

I think the answer to this fear is two-fold. First, as many besides myself have argued, it is now clear that Communism, far from constituting a single unified movement with a common aim and dovetailing interests, is a movement in which similarities of economic and political structure and ideology are more than outweighed by divergencies of national interest and character. Two bloody wars have demonstrated that in the case of capitalism, structural similarities between nations do not prevent mortal combat. As with capitalism, so with Communism. Russian Communists have already been engaged in skirmishes with Polish and Hungarian Communists, have nearly come to blows with Yugoslavia, and now stand poised at the threshold of open fighting with China.

Second, it seems essential to distinguish among the causes of dangerous national and international behavior those that can be traced to the tenets of Communism and those that must be located elsewhere. "Do not talk to me about Communism and capitalism," said a Hungarian economist with whom I had lunch this winter. "Talk to me about rich nations and poor ones."

I think it *is* wealth and poverty, and not Communism or capitalism, that establishes much of the tone and tension of international relations. For that reason I would expect Communism in the backward nations (or national collectivism, if that emerges in the place of Communism) to be strident, belligerent, and insecure. If these regimes fail —as they may—their rhetoric may become hysterical and their behavior uncontrolled, although of small consequence. But if they succeed, which I believe they can, many of these traits should recede. Russia, Yugoslavia, or Poland are simply not to be compared, either by way of internal pronouncement or external behavior, with China, or, on a smaller scale, Cuba. Modernization brings, among other things, a waning of the stereotypes, commandments, and flagellations so characteristic of (and so necessary to) a nation engaged in the effort to alter itself from top to bottom.

Nevertheless, there *is* a threat in the specter of a Communist or near-Communist supremacy in the underdeveloped world. It is that the rise of Communism would signal the end of capitalism as the dominant world order, and would force the acknowledgement that America no longer constituted the model on which the future of world civilization would be mainly based. In this way, as I have written before, the existence of Communism frightens American capitalism as the rise of Protestantism frightened the Catholic Church, or the French Revolution the English aristocracy.

It is, I think, the fear of losing our place in the sun, of finding ourselves at bay, that motivates a great deal of the anti-Communism on which so much of American foreign policy seems to be founded. In this regard I note that the nations of Europe, most of them profoundly more conservative than America in their social and economic dispositions, have made their peace with Communism far more intelligently and easily than we, and I conclude that this is in no small part due to their admission that they are no longer the leaders of the world.

The great question in our own nation is whether we can accept a similar scaling-down of our position in history. This would entail many profound changes in outlook and policy. It would mean the recognition that Communism, which may indeed represent a retrogressive movement in the West, where it should continue to be resisted with full energies, may nonetheless represent a progressive movement in the backward areas, where its advent may be the only chance these areas have of escaping misery. Collaterally, it means the recognition that "our side" has neither the political will, nor the ideological wish, nor the stomach for directing those changes that the backward world must make if it is ever to cease being backward. It would undoubtedly entail a more isolationist policy for the United States vis-à-vis the developing continents, and a greater willingness to permit revolutions there to work their way without our interference. It would mean in our daily political life the admission that the ideological battle of capitalism and Communism had passed its point of usefulness or relevance, and that religious diatribe must give way to the pragmatic dialogue of the age of science and technology.

ECONOMIC DEVELOPMENT AND DEMOCRACY

Dennis H. Wrong

I

Robert Heilbroner's essay, "Counterrevolutionary America," is the most intelligent and forceful statement of a point of view that is widely held by writers on economic development in the Third World. Although Heilbroner

From Dennis H. Wrong "Economic Development and Democracy: A Debate on Some Problems of the Third World" in Dissent, November–December 1967, pp. 723–33. Reprinted by permission of the publisher. Not all footnotes appear.

is an economist, his conclusions rest only to a minor degree on economic expertise. Both in the article and in his earlier book-length essay, The Great Ascent, he fully recognizes that economic development necessarily involves massive social and political changes in addition to the changes in the techniques and the organization of production that the term connotes in its narrow sense. Heilbroner's argument, anticipated in his earlier book but stated far more strongly and without qualification in the more recent article, is that the obstacles posed to rapid economic development by traditional values and old established ruling elites are so great that a revolution bringing to power a Communist-type totalitarian dictatorship can alone be expected to overcome them and proceed with the urgent task of modernizing backward societies.

It is worth reviewing step by step the reasoning by which Heilbroner reaches this conclusion. The essentials of his position are shared by many other writers—indeed, some of them have become virtual commonplaces in discussions of economic development. By summarizing the argument as schematically as possible, shorn of Heilbroner's considerable eloquence and richness of allusion, it should be possible to see its main structure and to separate the truths from the assumptions and hypotheses contained in it.

Only the starting point of the argument involves an economic proposition: namely, that the task of initial capital accumulation in underdeveloped countries requires the holding down for a time of the living standards of the peasants, who constitute the mass of the population; not until the "infra-structure" of a modern economy has been built will it be possible for the resulting gains in productivity to be widely distributed.

But strictly economic considerations

are transcended as soon as we ask what groups and agencies in contemporary underdeveloped countries are capable of organizing and directing the economic task of drawing a portion of the peasantry off the land to build capital, and of collecting part of the agricultural produce of the remaining peasants to feed this new nonagricultural labor force. The absence of rising commercial and entrepreneurial classes resembling the European *bourgeoisie*, or of any group imbued with an ethos favoring, like the Protestant ethic, hard work and the sacrifice of present material gains for the future, means that the state alone can play the necessary role in today's backward countries. Most experts on economic development concede (in the large at least) that the state must assume the entrepreneurial function in the majority of the nations of the Third World and that these nations are therefore likely to adopt some form of collectivism or "state socialism." Only a handful of neoclassical economists disagree. The state must be a strong state if it is to initiate successful programs of economic development. That is, it must, in the first instance, possess the power and the will to coerce or buy off traditional elites that resist modernizing measures. But, more important, it must command the allegiance of a significant portion of the population.

II

There is little in this analysis so far that is likely to arouse much disagreement. The next step in Heilbroner's argument, however, goes beyond the limits of general consensus. In order to win the support of the masses, the argument runs, the state must promote a new ideological creed that will penetrate their minds and hearts, win them away from traditional habits, beliefs and loyalties—"reach and rally

them," as he puts it—and induce them to acquiesce in the sacrifices and rigors of the period of capital accumulation. Such a creed is bound to be intolerant of all dissent and is likely to contain a strong negative component, branding foreigners, in particular the West, as carriers of evil and as actual or potential supporters of oppositionists at home. Clearly, this description is matched most closely by a revolutionary regime which has seized power after mobilizing a sizable segment of the population against the old order or foreign imperialists, or, most probably, a combination of both. Only a militant revolutionary state can make the sharp break with the past and impose the strict totalitarian discipline on a sprawling agrarian society that are needed to begin "the Great Ascent" to the heights of modernization.

Heilbroner's rejection of the belief or hope that democratic, constitutional governments, preserving and fostering the political liberties of the individual citizen, are capable of achieving economic development is presented in less detail than his reasons for thinking that some form of totalitarian collectivism can do the job. But his case against democratic government is implicit in much of his argument and has been more fully stated by other writers who share his general outlook. I shall draw on some of them to flesh out his thesis.*

Most of the states in the Third World are far from being genuine nations. Democratic institutions and practices, it is held, can only delay the task of nation-building by encouraging all the diverse ethnic, religious, tribal, and linguistic groups that make up the populations of the new states to articulate

*For a critique resembling in some respects the present one of prevalent assumptions about modernization in the Third World, see Charles C. Moskos, Jr., and Wendell Bell, "Emerging Nations and Ideologies of American Social Scientists," *American Sociologist* 2 (May 1967): 67–72.

their distinctive values and interests. The new states must create an overriding sense of national purpose and identity transcending parochial group loyalties if they are to carry out effective economic development programs. A democratic multiparty system will perpetuate and even accentuate the fragmentation of their populations. This argument has been applied most widely in defense of one-party dictatorships in Africa. It makes a specifically *political* case against democracy in the Third World, seeing nation-building as the prime requisite for the strong state that is in turn a prime requisite for economic development.

Unlike Africa, most Asian and Latin-American nations do not confront the immediate necessity of welding together collections of tribal peoples who have often been traditional enemies and have never acknowledged any central political authority. The case against democracy in Asia and Latin America rests less on the alleged requirements of nation-building than on the contention that democratic governments cannot succeed in breaking the resistance to far-reaching social reform offered by old classes and elites—parasitic landlords, village moneylenders, *compradore* merchants, corrupt military and bureaucratic cliques, hoary priestly oligarchies. Democracy is likely to be no more than a facade behind which these groups retain full power, occasionally lulling the masses with token reforms.

A more general argument against democracy in the Third World, one that is more closely linked to the initial prerequisites for economic development, holds that the masses are likely to vote themselves welfare state benefits, opting for immediate improvements in their standard of living rather than for capital investment and thus defeating long-range development programs. Argentina under Peron, and particularly the persistence of Peronist sympathies among the industrial workers long after the dictator's fall from power, are frequently cited as the standard horrible example. There is an obvious contradiction between the assertion that democracy in the Third World is doomed to be a mere facade manipulated by the traditional ruling classes and the expressed fear that it will result in the mass electorate voting for immediate, "uneconomic" gains in income; but we shall let this pass for the moment.

Such in broad outline is Heilbroner's thesis, omitting only his observations on the probable attitude of the United States to revolutionary regimes in the Third World, which I shall discuss very briefly later. The thesis, both in Heilbroner's and other versions, has evoked vigorous objections from liberals and democrats unwilling to accept the necessity and inevitability of the totalitarian trend it postulates. Their reactions, however, have usually failed to go beyond ringing reaffirmations of democratic and humanitarian values, and expressions of moral outrage at the apparent readiness of so many Western writers to regard violence and repressive government as the unavoidable price of modernization. Heilbroner is entitled to reply to such protests—indeed, he has already so replied (see the correspondence columns of the July 1967 *Commentary*)—"don't blame me for being the bearer of bad news. To refute me you must first show that the news is not as bad as I've reported, that my analysis is mistaken, and this you have failed to do."

III

The Heilbroner thesis outlines certain social prerequisites for economic development and maintains that democratic institutions are bound to present obstacles to fulfilling them. Since democracy runs the risk of promoting anarchic factionalism, permitting privileged classes to retain covert control over the government, and encouraging all groups to seek to use the state to advance their material interests, the thesis possesses an immediate plausibility. This plausibility carries over to the next step in the argument, where it is asserted that a government lacking democratic features will be able to avoid the problems of democracy and meet the requirements of modernization. But what if we start by asking what are the difficulties that a totalitarian revolutionary regime is likely to face in carrying out development programs? These difficulties are conceded in passing by Heilbroner, but they fail to receive the attention they deserve because of the initial critical focus on the difficulties apt to be encountered by "mild," democratic governments.

To begin with, the inflammatory nationalism, the xenophobia, and the exaltation of the state—which are, according to Heilbroner, invariable ingredients of the "mobilizing appeal" of revolutionary elites—lead to the investment of considerable resources in armaments and the maintenance of large standing armies. Such expenditures are, of course, an utter waste from the standpoint of economic development. If demonstration steel mills and airlines are to be regarded as economically irrational national status symbols, how much more so are jet planes, tanks, and well-drilled armies? True, the desire for national strength and military glory may powerfully motivate a nation to modernize its capital equipment and thus lay the foundation for eventual increases in productivity that will wipe out mass poverty and improve every citizen's material lot. A nation that can send sputniks into outer space is presumably capable of mass-producing shoes and automobiles, although the Soviet Union has yet to confirm this. However, underdeveloped nations are more likely to purchase the sinews of war from the advanced nations by intensifying their production of staple raw materials—the very syndrome that is part of the whole syndrome of their economic backwardness. Moreover, the trouble with large defense expenditures is that they tend to become self-perpetuating, not merely because they create vested interests, but because they persuade insecure neighbors to arm themselves and thus make the claim that a large military establishment is necessary for national security. Surely, those nations that have followed most closely Heilbroner's prescription—Russia, China, Egypt, Sukarno's Indonesia—have diverted enormous human and material resources from peaceful economic development to military uses.

In addition, the enhanced importance of the army makes a military take-over more probable should the revolutionary regime falter. If any "wave of the future" is discernible in the Third World at the present moment, it is in the direction of military dictatorships rather than Communist revolutions. Since 1960 revolutionary national socialist or left-nationalist reformist regimes have been overthrown in Argentina, Brazil, Bolivia, Algeria, Ghana, and Indonesia, and have been discredited—to put it mildly—in Egypt and Syria. It is still altogether possible that in China, Mao's "cultural revolution" will be terminated by an army take-over. Military dictatorships have also replaced shaky democratic civilian governments in Nigeria, the Congo, Greece, and a number of smaller African nations. A few of these new regimes are national socialist and even pro-Communist in ideological orientation (e.g. Algeria); a larger number are right-wing, strongly anti-Communist or even proto-fascist (e.g. Argentina, Brazil, Greece, Indonesia).

Finally, aggressive nationalism and militarism may induce nations to seek

DID CUBA TAKE THE WRONG WAY?

Dennis Wrong argues that Communist Revolutions are by no means always productive of economic development—witness Cuba, which may be "undergoing actual economic decline." The complications of maintaining a true revolutionary spirit to foster economic growth are suggested below.

PROBLEMS CAN OCCUR AFTER THE REVOLUTION
GEORGE VOLSKY

"It is more difficult to govern than to wage guerrilla warfare," Premier Fidel Castro of Cuba remarked last month.

The remark pointed up the extent to which the former guerrilla leader is bedeviled by the task of governing, which in Communist Cuba means directing the country's economy.

The 1971 performance of the sugar-dominated economy of the island must have been disappointing to Mr. Castro, who recently suggested that prospects for an economic improvement this year were not very bright.

As a result, Cuba's dependence on Soviet aid—estimated at $750 million a year, or more than $2 million a day—became greater than ever.

"Without [Soviet] fuel, raw materials, equipment, machinery and factories Cuba could not function," the Economics Minister, Carlos Rafael Rodriguez, said last April.

Last year, Cuba registered some gains in the industrial sector and in fishing, and continued to invest heavily in expanding output.

But agricultural production declined. Intensive efforts to revitalize the sagging production of rice, coffee, tobacco, cattle and fruit proved unrewarding. Strict rationing of food and consumer goods continued, and on a few items it had to be tightened.

More important, the 1971 sugar output of 5.9 million tons was a million tons below the target, and Mr. Castro predicted that 1972 production would be even lower.

Western experts believe that Cuba will produce 5 millions tons of sugar this year. A recent Soviet purchase of 200,000 tons of Brazilian sugar was regarded as an indication of Moscow's concern that Havana might find it difficult to fulfill its sugar export commitments.

In all, Cuba is believed to owe the Soviet Union $4 billion, a debt that Moscow cannot realistically hope to collect.

While a shortage of trained personnel along with governmental inefficiency has adversely affected production, the main economic problem seems to be the apparent apathy of Cuban workers and peasants, who do not respond with the required enthusiasm to constant governmental exhortations for harder work.

Last year, which Mr. Castro called "the year of productivity," a campaign was ordered against what he described as "laziness, loafing, disloyalty, parasitism, selfishness and bourgeois mentality."

At the year's end, a Cuban radio commentator reported that despite the shortage of manpower "loafers are on the rise."

Excerpted from George Volsky, "Problems Can Occur After the Revolution," in The New York Times, January 28, 1972, p. 60. © 1972 The New York Times Company. Reprinted by permission.

territorial expansion, causing wars that risk spreading to engulf entire subcontinents, if not the world. Barrington Moore, Jr., observes that military defeat in World War II was part of the price paid by Japan for following a conservative-fascist path to modernization.* In other words, the dead of Hiroshima and Nagasaki, the Tokyo fire-bomb raids, and the Pacific islands campaigns must be cast into the balance against the "preventable deaths" from starvation and injustice under the old regime in toting up the costs of Japanese modernization. Should not the Soviet Union's enormous losses in World War II be assessed, along with the victims of Stalin's purges and enforced collectivizations, as part of the price of totalitarian Communist modernization? Stalin's army purges, his opportunistic foreign policy toward Germany, and his unpopularity with the peasants who first hailed the Nazi invaders as liberators, stemmed from his totalitarian rule and contributed to Russian military defeats in the early stages of the war.

Some Western nations also went through a military-expansionist phase in the course of their modernization. But in the present century technology has made even "conventional" warfare far more destructive than in the past. If, as Heilbroner argues, greater population growth and density make economic development more urgent in the Third World today than in the West in the last century, then the changed scale of warfare and a more unstable international environment should also be taken into account if militaristic regimes are to be recommended as arch modernizers.

What countries have achieved economic development to date as a result of nationalist-communist revolutions? Let us concede the case of the Soviet

Union, although the entire issue of whether the Bolshevik October revolution as distinct from the February revolution, let alone Stalin's totalitarian rule, was necessary for Russian economic development remains highly debatable among economists and historians. Heilbroner tells us that for himself he would rather be "an anonymous peasant" in China or Cuba than in India, Peru, or Ecuador. But by his own admission "it may well be that Cuba has suffered a considerable economic decline" since Castro took power, and "we may not know for many years whether the Chinese peasant is better or worse off than before the revolution." He praises Cuba for its educational effort, and China for having freed its youth from the bondage of the traditional family system. However, these achievements—assuming their reality—at most facilitate economic development rather than constituting development itself. Heilbroner might also reflect that the peasants of India and Peru evidently do not share his view of their prospects, having rejected in large numbers the opportunity to vote for Communist parties in free elections. In short, with the ambiguous exception of the Soviet Union, the Communist promise of rapid industrialization remains no more than a promise.

IV

Heilbroner's case for the necessity of totalitarian ruthlessness to achieve modernization rests ultimately on his conviction of the enormous urgency of the problems of the backward countries. They cannot proceed according to the more leisurely timetable of past Western industrialization; they must take a giant step forward within the next three or four decades or mass famine and internal chaos are sure to be their fate. Essentially, Heilbroner

*Barrington Moore, Jr., *The Social Origins of Dictatorship and Democracy* (Boston: Beacon Press, 1966), p. 271.

sees the continuing population explosion as imposing the need for an all-out attack on backwardness which must have priority over other values and objectives. Not the entire Third World, but "primarily the crowded land masses and archipelagos of Southeast Asia and the impoverished areas of Central and South America" must look to revolutions led by modernizing elites to rescue them from deepening poverty. The extent to which Heilbroner's argument rests on the population explosion is striking, considering that, though there are many exceptions, economists as a rule are more optimistic than demographers in their estimates of the prospects for economic development in backward countries. Economists perceive the economic job to be done and are impressed by the ample technical resources—including their own counsel—available to do it, while demographers, horrified by the floods of additional people indicated by extrapolated population growth rates, insist that without birth control any development program is doomed to founder.

But are Communist countries likely to check population growth? Heilbroner refers patronizingly to India's failure to control the birth rate, but there is not the slightest evidence that China has had any greater success. Indeed, China's leaders lag behind India's in their awareness of the need for an anti-natalist population policy. The relatively sparsely-settled Soviet Union never faced a population explosion comparable to that of Southeast Asia —a further reason, incidentally, for questioning the necessity of totalitarianism for Russian economic development. The doctrinal anti-Malthusianism of Communist ideology imposes a special handicap on Communist countries with regard to birth control. Nor do non-Communist revolutionary elites imbued with aggressive nationalism and anti-Western fervor seem promising candidates to assign high priority to diffusing family planning over building steel mills and armies.

But what if birth rates should turn downwards *before* the "take-off" point in economic development has been reached? In a recent article in *Public Interest*,* Donald Bogue, the University of Chicago demographer, departed from the conventional pessimism of his colleagues, to predict the imminent end of the population explosion in the Third World. There is good reason to believe, he insists, that by the end of the present decade the efforts of government and private agencies promoting family planning will at last pay off and birth rates in India and several other Asian countries will begin unmistakably to decline. Bogue is unable to present decisive evidence supporting his forecast—he claims that the "catching on" of new birth control methods in peasant populations is still too recent to have been statistically recorded. His main tangible evidence is based on studies in several countries, the most impressive of which was conducted in South Korea, showing that peasant women have in surprising numbers adopted in an exceedingly short space of time such recently developed contraceptive methods as intra-uterine devices and even pills. Maybe Bogue will turn out to be a false prophet, but it is worth recalling that sharp reversals of demographic trends have happened simultaneously before in a number of quite different countries, so there is no reason why sudden mass adoption of family planning resulting in lower birth rate might not occur in large areas of the Third World. Writing about Latin America, another demographer, J. Mayone Stycos of Cornell, also expresses cautious optimism in a recent book reporting his research in Peru and several

*Donald Bogue, "The End of the Population Explosion," *Public Interest* 2 (Spring 1967): 11–20.

Caribbean nations.†

V

I have argued that, though the difficulties faced by democratic governments in carrying out economic development are real ones, totalitarian revolutionary regimes also face difficulties peculiar to them that Heilbroner and others tend to slight. Military dictatorships, a third and at present the most common type of regime in the Third World, have not been notoriously successful modernizers either. One might conclude in an even more pessimistic vein than Heilbroner that neither democracy, revolutionary collectivism, nor military rule are capable of achieving modernization and that it is therefore unlikely to take place at all. Yet such a conclusion would clearly be unjustified. In the past there have been a variety of paths to modernization: it has been achieved by essentially conservative regimes in Germany and Japan, by postrevolutionary bourgeois democracies in England and France, under a pure bourgeois democracy in the United States, and by Communist dictatorship in Russia; even a few military regimes have made considerable progress as in Turkey and Mexico. There is apparently no intrinsic connection at all between economic progress and formal political institutions. The pace of economic development has also varied greatly, particularly among smaller nations free from the tensions of international rivalry.

Democratic institutions such as parliamentary government, elementary civil liberties and the rule of law, though not—except in the United States—universal suffrage, preceded economic development in the Western bourgeois democracies. Why should it be so widely assumed that democracy can only emerge in the Third World after modernization has been carried out by authoritarian governments? Those who argue this confuse the *strong* state that is indeed required for economic development with a monolithic, authoritarian state. The sceptics about democracy, with all their talk of avoiding ethnocentric evaluations of the institutions of non-Western people, often project the experience of Western democracies into the different social context of backward societies when they contend that Asian and African electorates will use the ballot to advance their short-term interests like voters in the West accustomed to government whose rationalized welfare and service functions have succeeded, as Michael Walzer has argued, in demystifying the very idea of the state itself. Actually, the demands of the masses in underdeveloped areas are likely to be too modest rather than excessive from the standpoint of stimulating development. Democracy, moreover, may take many different forms: ancient village communal bodies like the old Russian *mir* and the Indian *panchayats* can serve as two-way communication channels between modernizing elites and the base of the social structure, giving rise to a kind of "democratic centralism" that is a reality rather than a facade for unilateral dictation by the leadership. Also, even after universal suffrage was in effect in the Western democracies, the political organization and mobilization of the lower classes was a long, slow process. The masses in the Third World are not going to leap at once into the political arena to make short-sighted and selfish immediate group demands. There is no reason why they cannot be trusted to accept the guidance of enlightened modernizing elites that truly consult them and give them a

---

†J. Mayone Stycos, *Population Control in Latin America* (Ithaca, New York: Cornell University Press, 1967).

sense of participation in the process. It is precisely such a sense of participation that Heilbroner sees as the *forte* of Communist revolutionaries, but there is no inherent reason why they alone should be capable of instilling it.

What about American policy toward the Third World? Although a secondary issue, this was ostensibly the main subject of Heilbroner's essay. Heilbroner's denial notwithstanding, the United States has not been consistently anti-revolutionary nor indeed consistently anything except opposed to states that have directly aligned themselves politically and militarily with the Soviet Union or China. The United States has given aid to Communist Yugoslavia; to nationalist, pro-Communist and anti-American states such as Ghana under Nkrumah, Algeria, and Egypt; as well as to non-Communist revolutionary regimes such as Bolivia in the 1950s. Admittedly, the bulk of American aid has gone to such "client states" ruled by conservative dictatorships as South Korea, Taiwan, and South Vietnam. But American policy has on the whole been shortsightedly opportunistic rather than ideologically consistent, willing to support almost any government, Left or Right, that is not a direct dependency of Russia or China. When Heilbroner suggests that the United States is unlikely to allow any nations in the Third World to remain neutral in the Cold War, he seems to be taking seriously Dulles's rhetoric of a decade ago—even then the rhetoric did not correspond to American practice. More probably, he has in mind the war in Vietnam, but the flimsy American justification for the war rests on the assumption that China is the "real" enemy, not the Viet Cong or Hanoi. The United States accepted, after all, a neutral government in Laos.

Latin America, however, is obviously the area where Heilbroner's label "Counterrevolutionary America" is most applicable. Not only do the pocketbook interests of American businessmen have a greater influence on government policy there than elsewhere in the world, but the fall-out in domestic politics of victories by Communist or proto-Communist revolutionaries is bound to be far greater. The Dominican tragedy reveals the panic which may strike an American Administration if it persuades itself that there is even the slightest possibility of a repetition of the Cuban experience. It is indeed hard to imagine the United States passively tolerating *any* anti-American, revolutionary government in this hemisphere.

Finally, let us suppose that American policy-makers accept Heilbroner's analysis and become convinced that modernization of the Third World is possible only under Communist or authoritarian left-nationalist auspices. The results may be curious indeed. *The New Republic* of July 8, 1967, reports that a privately distributed newsletter subscribed to by Wall Street insiders suggests that it may very well be in the American national interest to allow the Third World to go Communist. The United States will save money in economic aid as the new Communist regimes seek development by sweating their own peasantries whose labor will have to carry the whole burden of capital accumulation. If they fail, the United States cannot be blamed. If they succeed, they will in a decade or two become moderate and "bourgeois" in spirit like the Russians and not only can we live in peace with them but we can engage them in mutually profitable trade. Such a view may very well spread among those whom C. Wright Mills once called "sophisticated conservatives," and it may become more influential than the anger and frustration at the failure of American capitalism to convert the world that Heilbroner imputes to our leaders. And, as is so often the case in politics, the diagnosis may become self-confirming if America reduces instead of expands its aid to the Third World in expectation of a wave of totalitarian revolutions. The Heilbroner thesis might thus ironically help bring about the conditions it claims to deplore in counseling us to resign ourselves to their inevitability.

REPLY TO "ECONOMIC DEVELOPMENT AND DEMOCRACY"

ROBERT L. HEILBRONER

I am grateful to Dennis Wrong for his thoughtful and carefully argued reply to my article in *Commentary* and to *The Great Ascent.* Here and there I disagree with him on small points, most of which will emerge in the paragraphs below. But in the main I feel that somehow even Wrong, who so scrupulously avoids the rhetoric of outrage, has failed to come squarely to grips with the contentions on which my own point of view is based. Let me therefore attempt to answer him by restating my position and emphasizing where I think the issue lies between us.

I

The essential starting point must be whether or not one believes that modernization will take place under the aegis of *present* governments in most of Latin America, Southeast Asia, and the Near East. I have made it clear that I do not think it will. What is more,

From Robert L. Heilbroner, "Robert L. Heilbroner Replies," "Economic Development and Democracy," *Dissent,* November–December 1967, pp. 734–41. Reprinted by permission of the publisher. Footnotes have been omitted.

I rather doubt that Wrong would disagree with this pessimistic appraisal, although he would no doubt wish to see it qualified. If this is so, then economic development will have to wait until the regimes that now seem incapable of mounting a successful modernization program are replaced by other regimes. The question is, what kinds will they be?

II

Are the chances propitious for the emergence of democratic governments as the modernizing forces in these areas? I do not think so for the following reasons, some mentioned by Wrong and some not:

(1) In many states only a revolutionary party will be able to oust the incumbent regimes.
(2) In most nations the tradition of democratic opposition is unknown or thinly held, and the tradition of "strong man" government very widely accepted.
(3) The changes needed to bring modernization are not only political, but economic, social, intellectual, and even religious. Such deep-seated changes are extraordinarily difficult to achieve under the best of circumstances. I suspect that only authoritarian regimes can impose them.

Against these doubts Wrong suggests some counterarguments. One of these is that "democracy" is capable of many guises. This is certainly true and some measure of "democracy" in a *consultative* sense (e.g., the Russian soviets, at least in theory) may exist even under dictatorships. What cannot, I think, be tolerated is a recognized and potentially powerful *opposition party.*
A second counterargument of Wrong's is that the Western nations

have climbed to modernity under various sorts of governments, including a number of democratic (although not always very consultative) ones. This is of course so. The question then arises as to the relevance of Western (or Japanese post-Meiji) experience to the critical areas of the underdeveloped world. I think the relevance is slight for the following reasons:

(1) The population crisis enjoins a much greater degree of haste for the contemporary backward world.
(2) There has been no period of preparation comparable to the three centuries of European commercialization.
(3) The backward world is handicapped by the deformations of imperialism.

Thus I hesitate to apply the lessons of the West to the East and South. However, if Wrong is merely arguing that the developing elites need not display the worst forms of totalitarianism; that a degree of tolerance is compatible with a strong modernization movement; and that a measure of freedom may be functional rather than otherwise, I would not disagree. Much depends on the personalities of the development leader and his opposition, on the tradition and circumstances of the country, etc. Nonetheless, I would argue (and again I doubt that Wrong would disagree) that strong tendencies must exist for extending and deepening the control of leadership, not only over political and economic life but into social and intellectual life as well. Perhaps I should point out, although Wrong has been good enough to do so for me, that in making this prediction I am not saying what I wish to have happen, but only what I think will happen, whether I wish it or not.

III

Taking off from these premises, I go on to state that left-authoritarian regimes, very likely, although not necessarily Communist, probably offer the best chance for a breakthrough in the backward areas. Here several points are to be examined:

1. Is such a breakthrough needed? Will not a slower process of change suffice? As Wrong points out, my prognosis rests heavily on the urgency of the population program. It is this above all that sets the timetable. If Bogue is right, the timetable may be much extended and the necessity for rapid and radical action accordingly reduced. But is Bogue right? I am certainly far from convinced, and evidently neither is Wrong. Moreover, even if population growth *slows down*, will the deceleration come in time to avert economic and social crisis? Do not forget that populations will double in the most impoverished areas by the year 2000.

2. Will a revolutionary regime succeed in "breaking through"? One cannot be sure. As Wrong points out, a Communist government may be ideologically unable to institute birth control. Or its ideological fervor, etc., may fall on deaf ears. Or it may just make terrible mistakes. In that case, I should think the probable outcome would be that mentioned at the end of his piece—there will be *no* modernization, and the future will be one of gradual deterioration, starvation, etc. I consider this an entirely possible state of affairs for the next generation. Yet one must ask, what is the chance for modernization if there is not an all-out revolutionary effort? This brings us back to my initial two premises.

3. Is there any evidence that the

Communists can mount a successful development effort? Wrong states that the Communists have so far delivered no more than promises. I would reply that promises are better than nothing. But are they only promises? Russia, to be sure, is a great mystery—is her development due to Communism or to pre-1913 industrialization? I would suggest that without Communism Russia would today be a kind of Brazil, with the extremes of Sao Paolo and the San Francisco Valley. But that is only a guess. The evidence as to Cuba buttresses my feeling that Castro has instituted a genuine and deeply-rooted change. Reston's *New York Times* articles (written after my *Commentary* piece) provide grist for my mill. As for China, who knows? What matters is the outcome after the present power struggle is resolved. I am impressed by Edgar Snow's observation in *The Other Side of the River* that whatever one may think of the Communist effort, there is no doubt that China has been profoundly and irreversibly changed. It is this kind of change that I believe to be an absolutely necessary condition for development; and at the base of my argument is my belief that among the existing political forces in the world only Communism is likely to be able to administer such a change. What other force does anyone suggest?

IV

Wrong emphasizes the destructive side of authoritarianism and its penchant for war. There is something to be said for this, although I fear that democracy provides no guarantee of peace. (Do I dare mention India and Goa; England and Suez; France and Algeria; and the U.S. and its military adventures?)

But once again I am forced back to choosing between ugly alternatives.

Revolutionary regimes bring a ruthless will and a desire to change everything; nonrevolutionary regimes seem unable to change even the few things that cry out for it. *If* we could have the best of both worlds—the enthusiasm, the dedication, the clear-cut program of the revolutionary, and the tolerance, open-mindedness, and decency of the gradualist—who would not welcome it? But I fear that in the existing condition of things we will have to make a far less palatable choice. If so, I opt for the party of "total" change. I repeat that if I had to take my chances here and now as an anonymous particle of humanity in China or India or in Cuba or Brazil, I would unhesitatingly choose the Communist side. Furthermore, I suspect Wrong would too. (To be sure, if I could choose to be an intellectual in both nations I would opt for the other side. But only a tiny few of the particles of humanity are intellectuals.)

V

Last, I am not much alarmed over the possibility of my counsel becoming a self-fulfilling prophecy. Even if it were, I would prefer the difficulties of living in a world that was largely Communist in the backward areas and isolationist here in the U.S., to one that threatens to go Communist and that evokes from us the military response of a Vietnam. But in the end I am interested in making a historical forecast, not in preparing a blueprint for action. My forecast is that if modernization takes place in the backward world (and again I caution that it may not), it will be because of the efforts of revolutionary, and very likely Communist, regimes. I forecast as well that the successes of milder, democratic government in bringing modernization to the peoples of Latin America, Southeast Asia, and the Middle East will be small, if any. Let us wait ten or twenty years and see which of us is right.

"ECONOMIC DEVELOPMENT AND DEMOCRACY": A REBUTTAL

DENNIS H. WRONG

I am glad Robert Heilbroner finds that I have correctly understood and presented his views. He has done as well with mine. Hopefully, the absence of rhetoric and polemical flourishes in our exchange will clarify the issues between us.

Heilbroner reiterates his conviction that left-authoritarian or communist movements "offer the best chance for a breakthrough in the backward areas." Whether he is right or wrong in this belief, he fails fully to confront the prior question of how likely in the near future such movements are to come to power at all and win the chance to show what they can do. Far from foreseeing any upsurge of democratic modernizing forces in the Third World, I argued that the present trend was toward the overthrow of *both* democratic governments and left-authoritarian regimes by the armed forces. Heilbroner is more hopeful—given his assumptions—than I am that there will be successful Communist revolutions; I am more hopeful than he that some modernization will take place under a variety of political regimes. He apparently regards such recent events as China's declining prestige in the Third World, the turmoil inside China, the overthrow of left-nationalist "strong men" in Indonesia, Algeria, and Ghana, the misadventures

Excerpted from Dennis H. Wrong, "A Rebuttal by Dennis H. Wrong," in "Economic Development and Democracy" *Dissent*, November–December 1967. Reprinted by permission of the publisher.

of "Arab socialism," and the repeated failures and defeats of Cuban-sponsored guerrillas in Latin America, as mere eddies in a broad historical current favoring revolutionary authoritarian regimes and movements. I, on the contrary, think that the Viet Cong may be the leaders of the last Communist-directed "war of national liberation" rather than the forerunners of a new revolutionary wave.

But if Heilbroner is right and Communist revolutions do take place in much of the Third World, can they achieve modernization? Communists have won power primarily by their own efforts in only five countries: Russia, Yugoslavia, China, North Vietnam, and Cuba. None of the three conditions Heilbroner adduces for doubting relevance of past Western experience to the contemporary underdeveloped world was fully present in Russia or Yugoslavia, so their record is scarcely more pertinent to the argument than the successful modernization achieved under democratic auspices by England and the United States. As to China, I agree with Heilbroner—who knows? China may indeed have been "profoundly and irreversibly changed," but such change may or may not in the end facilitate the particular kind of "profound and irreversible change" we call modernization. In its exaltation of an ascetic, chiliastic revolutionary brotherhood, Mao's "cultural revolution" appears to be directed *against* assigning high priority to economic development and the materialism it inevitably brings rather than the reverse. North Vietnam has been involved in wars for over a decade. Cuba, a partially modernized country before Castro, has at most established some of the prerequisites for balanced modernization (e.g., mass literacy) while undergoing actual economic decline. I agree that promises are better than nothing, but Communists are not the only people in the Third World promising modernization.

The very polycentrism of the Communist world that makes nonsense out of the anti-Communist slogans invoked by Washington to justify the Vietnam war reduces the likelihood that future national Communist regimes will be the ruthless modernizers Heilbroner expects them to be. Would Egyptian national communism differ in any important way from Nasser's regime? Would an Algerian revolution create a state markedly different from the Ben Bella and Boumedienne dictatorships? Revolutions led by hard-bitten, Moscow-trained Stalinist orgmen might have a chance of successfully using totalitarian methods to impose the drastic surgery of modernization on a recalcitrant peasantry. So might revolutions led by men like Mao's original cadres. So might revolutions led by orthodox Marxist-Leninists like most of the national Communists of Eastern Europe. But post-Stalinist Moscow no longer tightly controls the Communist parties in the Third World (or, indeed, anywhere), and Maoism today has little in common with traditional Marxist-Leninist doctrine. Revolutionary movements in the Third World are likely to be shaped to a greater extent by national character traits than was the case in past Communist revolutions and such traits have usually been an obstacle—though by no means the only one—to modernization. The degree to which Communist parties in the Third World base themselves on dissatisfied ethnic, religious, and caste minority groups in their struggle against existing governments has been documented by Donald Zagoria. Can we really expect such parties, should they win power, to be as relentlessly future-minded as the puritanical, iron-willed Bolsheviks who are the prototypes for our model of totalitarian modernization?

If Heilbroner is right that Communist revolutions offer the only hope for modernization and I am right in doubting that there will be many successful revolutions in the near future, then the obvious conclusion is that there may be little or no modernization and that economic deterioration and political fragmentation are likely results. I agree that this is an entirely possible outcome for the next generation. It seems to me much more probable that disciplined, authoritarian revolutionaries will be able to seize power under conditions of mass famine and chaos than that they will succeed in overthrowing present governments which are maintaining some degree of order and economic progress, painfully slow though the latter may be. After all, in four of the five countries where indigenous communist movements have triumphed (Cuba is the one exception), the Communist seizure of power occurred during or immediately after devastating wars and foreign invasions that had disrupted agricultural life and destroyed the control of the previous governments over much of their territories. In such circumstances, determined revolutionary movements have their best chance of succeeding. But this possibility is not what Heilbroner has in mind: he sees Communist revolutions as a way of *averting* political and economic collapse rather than as an eventual consequence of collapse.

The issue of the timetable for modernization is really the crucial one. I agree that none of the existing regimes in the Third World, neither the formal democracies, the collectivist one-party states, nor the military dictatorships, have achieved full modernization. But "when we look at the positive side of our ledger sheet, we perceive an astonishing fact. Against all the obstacles to development that we have described, economic progress has in fact been taking place, and at a pace which by comparison with the past amazes us with its rapidity." So writes

Robert Heilbroner on page 89 of his book *The Great Ascent*. He immediately observes that both the gains already achieved as well as future gains risk "being washed out by population growth."

Now I am indeed not fully convinced that Donald Bogue is right in predicting the imminent end of the population explosion. Who can have complete confidence in any forecast of something that has never happened before, like the mass adoption of birth control by peasant populations within a decade or two? But the probability of this happening seems to me somewhat greater than the probability of a wave of Communist revolutions in the Third World followed by the rapid achievement of modernization by the revolutionary regimes. The populations of the advanced countries, including Japan, have altered their childbearing habits in very short periods of time and without having been exposed to large-scale, state-directed campaigns urging them to do so. Since I wrote my original article, another leading American demographer, Frank Notestein, president of the Population Council, has expressed in the October *Foreign Affairs* qualified optimism over the prospect of new birth control methods spreading in the underdeveloped world and reducing current rates of population growth before the end of the century. If this should happen it will not remove entirely the urgency of the need for rapid modernization in the larger, more densely-populated areas, for even a rate of growth that is half the present one (and this Notestein considers possible) will still be an economic burden. But slower population growth will certainly make it easier for any regime committed to modernization to make some progress and will allow a wider margin for retrievable error.

I am aware that Heilbroner is making a forecast rather than advocating a course of action. But forecasts can become self-fulfilling if those who possess power are persuaded by and act on them. I too would prefer a Communist Third World and an isolationist United States to a succession of Vietnams; but is Heilbroner really prepared to give up all hope that the United States and the West in general can have any constructive influence on the economic development of the backward areas? Did the author of *The Future as History* mean by that phrase that it is as futile in the end to reflect on what still might be as it is to mourn over what might have been?

Continued from p. 798
of these countries to produce certain types of equipment and machinery—thus requiring imports from abroad.

Whether the domestic efforts of a poor country to increase its rate of saving and investment are largely private or wholly governmental in origin, the effect must be a restraining of private consumption for a substantial period of time. If capital formation is undertaken under something like Western-style business auspices, then this restraint will be reflected in a substantially unequal income distribution with low wages, high profits, and a high reinvestment of profits into business capital expansion. If the bulk of investment is undertaken under State auspices, the process will still involve low wages, but now the surplus for investment will be reflected in high tax revenues and government expeditures, or, alternatively, high "profits" to State-run enterprises. In any given society, the choice of which method is preferable may depend in part on where the Schumpeterian "entrepreneurs" are mostly located. High profits do not guarantee capital accumulation if the rich are interested in luxury and ostentation (or, as Adam Smith would have put it, in the employment of "unproductive labourers"); on the other hand, high taxes and government expenditures may lead to corruption, favoritism, and even greater personal aggrandizement. In one southeast Asian country, for example, the accumulated fortune of a now deceased ruler represented a substantial fraction of the country's entire national income!

In either case, the process of capital accumulation is bound to be difficult and this brings us to our special interest in this matter as citizens of the affluent world. What about foreign aid? Can it really help?

As we all know, for the past two and a half decades, the United States has been engaged in one form of foreign aid program or another. At the start of this period, our foreign aid was heavily focused on European reconstruction through the Marshall Plan. Beginning in 1949 with President Truman's Point Four program of technical assistance and continuing on to the present time, however, the United States has been giving regular and substantial economic assistance to the less developed countries of the world. We are currently giving such assistance both unilaterally and multilaterally, as in our contributions to the World Bank. Although cold war motives and strategic considerations have played a part in these programs, simple humanitarianism has never been completely absent, either.

Still, foreign aid is controversial, and it has become increasingly so in the early 1970s. Why?

Some of the criticism of aid derives primarily from noneconomic considerations. There is, for example, the sometimes expressed view that by aiding foreign countries we are likely to find ourselves entering into military commitments that may in turn lead us into ever more costly wars. The economist alone cannot judge this kind of criticism, since it is basically a political or foreign policy criticism. Still, one may wonder in passing whether it is foreign aid that is leading us into these further commitments or whether it is simply that these commitments provide part of the motive for the foreign aid. If the latter is the case, we should ask if there are other grounds that justify aid even if further commitments are not to be entered into.

There are, however, at least two criticisms of foreign aid that deal fairly directly with economic questions. The first has to do with the *cost* of the aid program to this country and whether or not it is sustainable over time. Foreign aid clearly does cost this country something, both directly and in terms of the balance of payments problem we discussed in chapter 15. Without belittling these costs, it is only accurate to state the following facts: (1) our economic assistance to underdeveloped countries constitutes a very small percentage of the expenditures of the federal government and a minuscule percentage (under 1/2 of 1 percent) of our gross national product; (2) the percentage of our national income going into foreign aid has been declining in recent years and, indeed, is very substantially below the percentage of national income we devoted to the economic assistance of Europe under the Marshall Plan; (3) the practice of tying aid expenditures to purchases of American goods has drastically curtailed the net cost to the American balance of payments of aid expenditures. Some cost is clearly there, but it is not so heavy as the critics would suggest, and furthermore it has been declining over time.

The other central criticism from an economic point of view has to do with the effect of aid on the prospects of the recipient countries. Does aid really help? Or does it simply encourage dependence on the United States, with the consequence that the aid program may go on forever?

These questions are very difficult to answer, the main reason being that time is still too short to tell. Some Americans have been disappointed because the aid program has not brought quick results.[9] Such expectations were encouraged perhaps by the outstanding success of the Marshall Plan in Europe. Some of it may have been due to the overzealous advo-

cacy of aid by its supporters in the early days. In any event, in the early 1970s it does begin to seem to many citizens that the aid program is going on forever, and they begin to wonder if it is really having any useful effect at all.

Economic analysis helps put this problem in some perspective. For one thing, it makes it clear why the analogy with the Marshall Plan is virtually irrelevant. There we were dealing with countries that had already mastered the tricks of modern technology and growth, had a literate, technically skilled labor force and abundant managerial talent, and needed only a modest infusion of resources to put them on the path again. In the case of the underdeveloped countries, however, the problems they face are extremely difficult and their poverty is so acute that, even under the best of circumstances, the achievement of a decent living standard will be accomplished only by the end of the century. To demand quick results under these circumstances is simply to misconceive the nature of the problem.

Economic analysis can also help us in understanding more specifically the potential impact of aid on an underdeveloped country. Some economists have described these countries as facing two fundamental *gaps* as they try to make their way to self-sustaining growth.[10] The first is a gap between domestic savings and the rate of investment required for a desired rate of growth—the *investment gap*. The second is the gap between the country's exports and the imports required for a desired rate of growth—the *trade gap*. The investment gap arises, as we have seen, because the need for capital is so great and the ability of the poor

9. In the case of the Green Revolution, of course, quick results have been forthcoming in some countries. This particular example of aid mainly involved the inflow of new technology, rather than massive infusions of capital.

10. See, for example, Hollis Chenery and A. M. Strout, "Foreign Assistance and Economic Development," *American Economic Review* 56, no. 4, part 1 (September 1966).

country to provide the capital is so limited. The trade gap arises because the export capabilities of the poor country may be limited, and yet it may require imports to provide the capital and other industrial goods needed for growth.

Now the fundamental *economic* case for foreign aid (assuming, of course, that it is our goal to assist these countries develop) rests on three propositions.

(1) If these various gaps are not filled, the countries involved will not be able to achieve modern development, or at least not in an acceptable length of time.

(2) Foreign aid is an effective means for filling these gaps.

(3) There is reason to believe that these gaps will diminish and ultimately disappear as development proceeds over time.

This third proposition is particularly relevant for those who ask whether foreign aid must go on forever. It is based on the belief that as a country develops, various forces will emerge that will reduce its dependence on foreign assistance. In the ideal case, this will happen because: (1) development will raise total output and output per capita, and it will be possible to channel a large fraction of these increases in output into added saving and investment; (2) development will provide the country with a greater export capacity and, at the same time, with a greater ability to produce domestically the capital and other industrial goods needed for further development; (3) development will bring improvements in the agricultural sphere and hopefully, an improved environment for solving the population problem. If such trends occur, then aid still may be required for a substantial length of time, but an eventual end will be in sight.

Now these propositions cannot guarantee us that aid will do the job. (Guarantees are seldom to be found in

any area dealing with complex economic, social, and political problems.) Nor can they tell us that foreign aid is the only route to these ends. China is receiving no foreign assistance at the present time; she is attempting to fill her gaps by an extraordinary reorganization of her national life. Perhaps the most that can be said is that foreign aid seems to be one possibly effective alternative to other alternatives, and these other alternatives are likely to be very harsh on the people of the countries involved, and they may have disruptive international consequences.

Nothing is certain. There is no ironclad case for foreign aid. But there is *a* case for it, and the reader himself will have to decide whether it is strong enough to merit the sustainable but nevertheless real costs aid involves.

EAST MEETS WEST

Despite the numerous obstacles we have mentioned, the period since World War II has seen substantial economic advance in many of the less developed countries of the world. It has been estimated, for example, that between 1950 and 1967, total output in the underdeveloped countries grew at an annual average rate of 4.8 percent and that this so far exceeded the (rapid) rates of population growth that output *per capita* increased at an annual average rate of 2.2 percent during this period. This rate, although slow by some expectations, is in fact higher than the historic rate of growth of the United States.

The more development in the poor countries succeeds, however, the more intense become those global problems that the industrial countries are already beginning to face. In particular: how much growth and development can this planet earth sustain? If China or India or Pakistan in fact had anything like the standard of living of the United States or Western Europe, the potential drain on the world's resources and the potential sources of industrial pollution would, of course, be greatly magnified.

The issue thus becomes whether man can adapt creatively to this global problem, or whether the forces unleashed are simply too strong to be coped with. Is new and better technology the answer, or should we seek the simple and the primitive? Should we move forward, or should we stand still? As a matter of fact, which way *is* forward?

For the moment, these development issues tend to divide the world rather than unite it. For whatever consolation it is, however, the long-run outlook is rather different. In that more distant future, mankind, East and West, for better or for worse, is likely to share a common problem and a common destiny.

SUMMARY

The economic outlook for the underdeveloped countries will depend largely on how they handle the basic problems of population growth, technological change, and capital formation.

In the short run, rapid population growth requires poor countries to pay serious attention to employment-creation as well as economic growth. In the longer run, however, the key objective must be to lower the birthrate and the key question is, can this be done in the absence of prior urban and industrial development? Experience so far is somewhat limited (Taiwan's success in lowering the birthrate, for example, may be due more to her general economic growth than to her family-planning program), but there is hope in that most countries now give

a high priority to family planning, that birth control technology is steadily developing, and that economists have shown that investments in population control can be among the most economically productive a poor country can undertake.

The advantage to an underdeveloped country from using the storehouse of Western technology is considerably qualified by the fact that this technology is seldom exactly appropriate to the economic or climactic conditions prevailing in that country. That creative adaptation of Western technology can take place, and even within what had been thought to be the relatively stagnant agricultural sector, is shown by the recent Green Revolution. Although there are dangers in this Revolution—without continuing research, the new crops might actually increase the economic vulnerability of a poor country—there is strong evidence that the new technology can increase crop yields many times and thus give the less developed countries an opportunity to gain a stride or two in the race with population growth.

Capital formation is likely to cause many sacrifices in a poor country (consumption must be held down whether investment is being undertaken by the State or by private capitalists), and the question arises: can we in the West help through foreign aid? The political outlook for foreign aid is very clouded in the early 1970s, partly perhaps because of its association with military involvements abroad. Nor is it clear that *over*dependence on foreign aid necessarily helps a poor country (China, for example, is doing without any aid at all). Still, an economic case can be made for foreign aid as helping to fill two important development gaps—the investment and the trade gaps.

Despite obstacles, economic development in the poor countries has shown some modicum of progress in the last two decades. In the long run, their "present crisis" may fade into the same problem of an "uncertain future" that perplexes the affluent nations of the West.

QUESTIONS
FOR DISCUSSION

1. In chapter 29, we indicated that there was still considerable inequality in the income distribution within the United States. This inequality is much greater, however, if we consider disparities among nations (see the illustrative Figure A). Should the United States take the same attitude towards income equality across its borders as within its borders? Make a rough calculation (see Table 6-1, p. 147) of what an equalization of average income between, say, the United States and India would mean in terms of per capita income in both countries. What economic arguments would you use to support or oppose such an equalization program?

2. "Ghandi was not only not foolish in supporting handicraft industry in India, he was being very wise considering what we know about factor proportions in factory industry and about population growth." Discuss.

3. What are the possible obstacles and advantages to the poor countries of the world if the developed nations follow a policy of "trade not aid" (e.g., lowering tariff barriers to imports rather than sending gifts of foreign resources through an aid program)?

4. Are you convinced by Robert Heilbroner's arguments or Dennis Wrong's arguments (Great Debate Six) on the matter of revolution and development? Write an essay stating your criticisms of each of these writers.

5. "The full economic development of the poor countries of the world will be the greatest economic (blessing) (disaster) planet earth has ever seen." Choose and discuss.

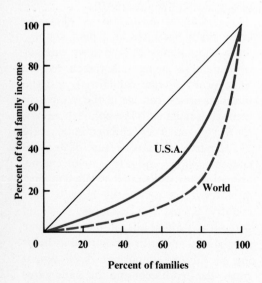

Figure A. Income Distribution in U.S.A. and the World (approximate).

SUGGESTED READING

Brown, Lester B. *Seeds of Change*. New York: Frederick A. Praeger, 1970.

Goulet, Denis. *The Cruel Choice: A New Concept in the Theory of Development*. New York: Atheneum, 1971.

Higgins, Benjamin. *Economic Development*. Rev. ed. New York: W. W. Norton & Co., 1968).

Lewis, W. Arthur. *Development Planning*. New York: Harper & Row, 1966.

Maddison, Angus. *Economic Progress and Policy in Developing Countries*. New York: W. W. Norton & Co., 1970.

List of Readings

Index

A

Adelman, M. A., 127
Advertising
  demand stimulation and, 71-72, 550, 555-56,
    574, 579, 720
  food industry and, 593
  Galbraith on, 563-64
  as nonprice competition, 586, 593
  Solow on, 555-56
Affluence, possibilities of, 776-83, 785
  Galbraith on, 776, 785
  Keynes on, 777-83
Affluent Society, The (Galbraith), 541, 564, 776
AFL-CIO, 133, 139, 354, 614, 621-22, 624
Agricultural revolution in United States, 404.
    See also Green Revolution
Agriculture
  government intervention in, 99-104, 594
  Green Revolution in, 165-66, 792-98
  limited competition in, 594, 607
  as pure competition, 543-44, 589-90, 590fn
Air pollution, 199, 472, 550, 721, 752-54, 757.
    See also Ecology; Growth, economic,
    costs of; and Pollution
Alcoa case (1945), 596, 597
American Association of University Professors
  (A.A.U.P.), 624-25
American Capitalism (Galbraith), 541
American Federation of Labor (AFL), 133, 614
American Federation of Teachers, 624
American Motors sales (1970), 126fn
American Telephone & Telegraph assets (1970),
  121
Antitrust legislation, 595-97, 607
Appalachia, 10, 728
Automatic stabilizers, 239
Average total cost (AC), 447-49, 461-62
Average variable cost (AVC), 447-49, 462

B

"Baby boom," 401. *See also* Population growth
Balance of payments, international, 361-84, 645,
  666
  accounts, 362-65, 383
  classical view of, 361-62, 366, 383-84
  economic growth and, 408

foreign aid and, 827
inflation and, 340
mercantilist view of, 361
surplus (or deficit), 364, 383
trade restrictions and, 526
U.S. (1970), 364
Balanced budget, 237fn, 291
  Byrd's insistence on, 279-81
  financial discipline implied by, 291
  with full-employment (Nixon), 282-83, 290,
    291
Balanced budget multiplier, 237fn
Baumol, William, 557
Beard, Charles A., 783
"Beggar-my-neighbor" policy, 526, 536
Benefit-cost analysis, 758-59, 760
Benefits
  fringe, 616
  private, 728
  social, 728, 758
  standardization of, 616-17
Bergson, Henri, 784
Birthrate. *See* Population growth
Black markets (during World War II), 430
Boulding, Kenneth, 721
  on spaceship earth versus throughput
    economy, 721-24, 725
Bourgeoisie, Marx's view of, 57-61
Bureaucracy, 128-32, 552
Burns, Arthur F., 379
Bury, J. B., 783
Business, public policy toward, 589-607
Business enterprises, legal forms of, 120, 142
Business expectations, investment demand and,
  218

C

Capital
  as factor of production, 491, 497, 498
  interest and, 493-95
Capital (Marx), 50, 72
Capital accumulation, 150-52, 171, 493-94, 497
  economic growth and, 402-3
  foreign aid and, 798, 826-28
  Smith on, 33
  technological change versus, 404
  in underdeveloped countries, 798, 826-28

PART ONE
BASIC ECONOMIC SYSTEMS

Scarcity,
Choice, Prices,
Market Economy,
Socialism, Communism,
Mixed Public and Private
Sectors, The Underdeveloped
Economy

PART TWO
MACROECONOMICS

Economic Aggregates—
GNP, Employment, Price Level,
Consumption, Investment

Keynesian
Economics

Money
and Banks

Multiplier,
Fiscal and Monetary
Policies,
Balance of Payments,
Growth

PART THREE
MICROECONOMICS

Individual Units—Consumers,
Business Firms,
Factors of
Production

Competition,
Oligopoly,
Monopoly,
Labor Unions

Consumerism,
Anti-Trust,
Collective Bargaining

Efficiency,
Interdependence,
Allocation of Resources,
Comparative
Advantage

PART FOUR
CONTEMPORARY ECONOMIC PROBLEMS

Policy Dilemmas,
Unemployment and Inflation,
New Economic Policy,

Soviet Growth Rate,
Japanese 'Miracle',

Income Distribution,
The Ghetto,
Negative Income Tax,

External Effects,
Pollution,
Costs and Benefits,

Transition from War to
Peace,

Burdens of Affluence,

Crisis in The Third World,
Population Explosion,
Capital, Technology, Foreign Aid